The SAGE Handbook of
Qualitative Data Collection

International Advisory Editorial Board

Rosaline S. Barbour, Emerita Professor at the Open University, United Kingdom
Marie Buscatto, Professor of Sociology, University of Paris 1 Pantheon Sorbonne, France
Kerry Chamberlain, Professor at Massey University, Albany, New Zealand
Jan K. Coetzee, Senior Professor of Sociology, University of the Free State, Bloemfontein, South Africa
Amanda Coffey, Professor at Cardiff School of Social Sciences, Cardiff, United Kingdom
Norman Denzin, Professor of Sociology at University of Illinois, Urbana-Champaign, United States
Nigel G. Fielding, Professor of Sociology, University of Surrey, United Kingdom
Jay Gubrium, Professor of Sociology, University of Missouri, United States
Karen Henwood, Professor of Social Sciences, Cardiff University, United Kingdom
Sonia Livingstone, Professor of Media Research, LSE, London, United Kingdom
Annette N. Markham, Professor at Loyola University, United States, and Aarhus University, Denmark
Joseph A. Maxwell, Professor Emeritus in the Graduate School of Education, George Mason University, United States
Donna M. Mertens, Professor Emeritus in the Department of Education, Gallaudet University, Washington, United States
Michael Murray, Professor of Psychology, Keele University, United Kingdom
Hiroshi Oda, Associate Professor Graduate School of Letters, Hokkaido University, Sapporo, Japan
Jin Sun, Professor at the Institute for International & Comparative Education, Beijing Normal University, China
Wivian Weller, Professor at Faculdade de Educação Universidade de Brasília, Brasilia, Brazil

The SAGE Handbook of Qualitative Data Collection

Edited by
Uwe Flick

SAGE reference
Los Angeles | London | New Delhi | Singapore | Washington DC | Melbourne

SAGE

Los Angeles | London | New Delhi
Singapore | Washington DC | Melbourne

SAGE Publications Ltd
1 Oliver's Yard
55 City Road
London EC1Y 1SP

SAGE Publications Inc.
2455 Teller Road
Thousand Oaks, California 91320

SAGE Publications India Pvt Ltd
B 1/I 1 Mohan Cooperative Industrial Area
Mathura Road
New Delhi 110 044

SAGE Publications Asia-Pacific Pte Ltd
3 Church Street
#10-04 Samsung Hub
Singapore 049483

Editor: Mila Steele
Editorial Assistant: Serena Ugolini
Production Editor: Sushant Nailwal
Copyeditor: Sunrise Setting
Proofreader: Jill Birch
Indexer: Sunrise Setting
Marketing Manager: Susheel Gokarakonda
Cover Design: Wendy Scott
Typeset by Cenveo Publisher Services
Printed in the UK

At SAGE we take sustainability seriously. Most of our products are printed in the UK using FSC papers and boards. When we print overseas we ensure sustainable papers are used as measured by the PREPS grading system. We undertake an annual audit to monitor our sustainability.

Introduction and editorial arrangement © Uwe Flick, 2018

Introduction to Part I © Uwe Flick, 2018
Chapter 1 © Uwe Flick, 2018
Introduction to Part II © Uwe Flick, 2018
Chapter 2 © Joseph A. Maxwell, 2018
Chapter 3 © Donna M. Mertens, 2018
Chapter 4 © Brianna L. Kennedy and Robert Thornberg, 2018
Chapter 5 © Giampietro Gobo, 2018
Chapter 6 © Margrit Schreier, 2018
Chapter 7 © Andrew Bengry, 2018
Chapter 8 © Christopher Joseph Jenks, 2018
Chapter 9 © Katharina Resch and Edith Enzenhofer, 2018
Chapter 10 © Estrid Sørensen, Alison Marlin and Jörg Niewöhner, 2018
Chapter 11 © Louise Corti, 2018
Chapter 12 © Jonathan Potter and Chloe Shaw, 2018
Chapter 13 © Norman K. Denzin, 2018
Chapter 14 © Rosaline S. Barbour, 2018
Introduction to Part III © Uwe Flick, 2018
Chapter 15 © Kathryn Roulston and Myungweon Choi, 2018
Chapter 16 © David L. Morgan and Kim Hoffman, 2018
Chapter 17 © Michael Murray, 2018
Chapter 18 © Clare Jackson, 2018
Chapter 19 © Asta Rau, Florian Elliker and Jan K. Coetzee, 2018
Chapter 20 © David Wästerfors, 2018
Chapter 21 © Marie Buscatto, 2018
Chapter 22 © Margarethe Kusenbach, 2018
Chapter 23 © Hubert Knoblauch, Bernt Schnettler and René Tuma, 2018
Chapter 24 © Tim Rapley and Gethin Rees, 2018
Chapter 25 © Thomas S. Eberle, 2018
Chapter 26 © Lothar Mikos, 2018
Chapter 27 © Michael Bull, 2018
Introduction to Part IV © Uwe Flick, 2018
Chapter 28 © Simon Lindgren, 2018
Chapter 29 © Annette N. Markham and Ane Kathrine Gammelby, 2018
Chapter 30 © Katrin Tiidenberg, 2018
Chapter 31 © Wivian Weller, Lucélia de Moraes Braga Bassalo, and Nicolle Pfaff, 2018
Chapter 32 © Hannah Ditchfield and Joanne Meredith, 2018
Chapter 33 © Annette N. Markham, 2018
Introduction to Part V © Uwe Flick, 2018
Chapter 34 © Uwe Flick, 2018
Chapter 35 © Sharlene Hesse-Biber, 2018
Chapter 36 © Janice M. Morse, Julianne Cheek, and Lauren Clark, 2018
Chapter 37 © Nigel G. Fielding, 2018
Chapter 38 © Karen Henwood, Fiona Shirani, and Christopher Groves, 2018
Introduction to Part VI © Uwe Flick, 2018
Chapter 39 © Colin MacDougall and Philip Darbyshire, 2018
Chapter 40 © Christine Stephens, Vanessa Burholt, Norah Keating, 2018
Chapter 41 © Alexander Bogner, Beate Littig and Wolfgang Menz, 2018
Chapter 42 © Kerry Chamberlain and Darrin Hodgetts, 2018

Apart from any fair dealing for the purposes of research or private study, or criticism or review, as permitted under the Copyright, Designs and Patents Act, 1988, this publication may be reproduced, stored or transmitted in any form, or by any means, only with the prior permission in writing of the publishers, or in the case of reprographic reproduction, in accordance with the terms of licences issued by the Copyright Licensing Agency. Enquiries concerning reproduction outside those terms should be sent to the publishers.

Library of Congress Control Number: 2017961304

British Library Cataloguing in Publication data

A catalogue record for this book is available from the British Library

ISBN 978-1-4739-5213-3

Contents

List of Figures   ix
List of Tables   x
Notes on the Editor and Contributors   xi
Acknowledgements   xxvii

PART I   CHARTING THE ROUTES   1

1. Doing Qualitative Data Collection – Charting the Routes   3
   Uwe Flick

PART II   CONCEPTS, CONTEXTS, BASICS   17

2. Collecting Qualitative Data: A Realist Approach   19
   Joseph A. Maxwell

3. Ethics of Qualitative Data Collection   33
   Donna M. Mertens

4. Deduction, Induction, and Abduction   49
   Brianna L. Kennedy and Robert Thornberg

5. Upside Down – Reinventing Research Design   65
   Giampietro Gobo

6. Sampling and Generalization   84
   Margrit Schreier

7. Accessing the Research Field   99
   Andrew Bengry

8. Recording and Transcribing Social Interaction   118
   Christopher Joseph Jenks

9. Collecting Data in Other Languages – Strategies for Cross-Language Research in Multilingual Societies   131
   Katharina Resch and Edith Enzenhofer

10. From Scholastic to Emic Comparison: Generating Comparability and Handling Difference in Ethnographic Research   148
    Estrid Sørensen, Alison Marlin and Jörg Niewöhner

11	Data Collection in Secondary Analysis *Louise Corti*	164
12	The Virtues of Naturalistic Data *Jonathan Potter and Chloe Shaw*	182
13	Performance, Hermeneutics, Interpretation *Norman K. Denzin*	200
14	Quality of Data Collection *Rosaline S. Barbour*	217

PART III TYPES OF DATA AND HOW TO COLLECT THEM   231

15	Qualitative Interviews *Kathryn Roulston and Myungweon Choi*	233
16	Focus Groups *David L. Morgan and Kim Hoffman*	250
17	Narrative Data *Michael Murray*	264
18	Data Collection in Conversation Analysis *Clare Jackson*	280
19	Collecting Data for Analyzing Discourses *Asta Rau, Florian Elliker, and Jan K. Coetzee*	297
20	Observations *David Wästerfors*	314
21	Doing Ethnography: Ways and Reasons *Marie Buscatto*	327
22	Go-Alongs *Margarethe Kusenbach*	344
23	Videography *Hubert Knoblauch, Bernt Schnettler and René Tuma*	362
24	Collecting Documents as Data *Tim Rapley and Gethin Rees*	378
25	Collecting Images as Data *Thomas S. Eberle*	392

26	Collecting Media Data: TV and Film Studies *Lothar Mikos*	412
27	Sounds as Data *Michael Bull*	426

PART IV DIGITAL AND INTERNET DATA — 439

28	The Concept of 'Data' in Digital Research *Simon Lindgren*	441
29	Moving Through Digital Flows: An Epistemological and Practical Approach *Annette N. Markham and Ane Kathrine Gammelby*	451
30	Ethics in Digital Research *Katrin Tiidenberg*	466
31	Collecting Data for Analyzing Blogs *Wivian Weller, Lucélia de Moraes Braga Bassalo and Nicolle Pfaff*	482
32	Collecting Qualitative Data from Facebook: Approaches and Methods *Hannah Ditchfield and Joanne Meredith*	496
33	Troubling the Concept of Data in Qualitative Digital Research *Annette N. Markham*	511

PART V TRIANGULATION AND MIXED METHODS — 525

34	Triangulation in Data Collection *Uwe Flick*	527
35	Toward an Understanding of a Qualitatively Driven Mixed Methods Data Collection and Analysis: Moving Toward a Theoretically Centered Mixed Methods Praxis *Sharlene Hesse-Biber*	545
36	Data-Related Issues in Qualitatively Driven Mixed-Method Designs: Sampling, Pacing, and Reflexivity *Janice M. Morse, Julianne Cheek, and Lauren Clark*	564
37	Combining Digital and Physical Data *Nigel G. Fielding*	584
38	Using Photographs in Interviews: When We Lack the Words to Say What Practice Means *Karen Henwood, Fiona Shirani and Christopher Groves*	599

PART VI COLLECTING DATA IN SPECIFIC POPULATIONS 615

39 Collecting Qualitative Data with Children 617
    Colin MacDougall and Philip Darbyshire

40 Collecting Qualitative Data with Older People 632
    Christine Stephens, Vanessa Burholt, and Norah Keating

41 Generating Qualitative Data with Experts and Elites 652
    Alexander Bogner, Beate Littig and Wolfgang Menz

42 Collecting Qualitative Data with Hard-to-Reach Groups 668
    Kerry Chamberlain and Darrin Hodgetts

Author Index 686
Subject Index 695

List of Figures

4.1	Interview protocol	56
4.2	First visual representation of theory	59
4.3	Visual representation of final theory	60
5.1	The research topic and its attributes (A)	69
5.2	The (spiral-shaped) model of ethnographic research	76
5.3	Models from Atlas.ti 7 (left) and NVivo 10 (right)	78
11.1	European qualitative archives, date started collecting data and data volume	168
11.2	Datalist for an archived study at the UK Data Service	174
11.3	Cited extract from qualitative text in the UK QualiBank	176
11.4	Header information for a qualitative interview text in the UK QualiBank	177
23.1	Comparison of 'conventional' and 'focused' ethnography (based on Knoblauch, 2005)	364
23.2	Sketch of experimental setup/positioning the camera for a long shot of the room	369
23.3	Street market interaction	370
23.4	Shots from two camera angles (left: speaker, right: audience)	371
23.5	Navigation experiment recorded with eyetracking camera and follower	372
23.6	The research process (from Knoblauch et al., 2015)	376
30.1	Tumblr study, research context	474
30.2	Instagram study, research context	475
34.1	Within-method triangulation	533
34.2	Areas of everyday knowledge in the episodic interview	535
34.3	Between-methods triangulation	536
34.4	Levels of triangulation in data collection	538
35.1	A theoretically-driven mixed methods process	550
35.2	Sequential exploratory mixed methods design	556
35.3	Vikström's (2003, 2010) Concurrent mixed methods design	558
36.1	Sampling plan for two individual samples, pooled data for two data sets	572
36.2	One sample, one data set, and two data types	575
36.3	Schematic representation of a complex, qualitatively-driven mixed-method study featuring integration of a core qualitative and three supplemental quantitative components	579
38.1	Laura's bike seats	605
38.2	Peter's gas canister	606
38.3	Christine's greenhouse	607
38.4	Jeremy's greenhouse	608
38.5	Suzanna's Barbie	609
41.1	Experts and elites	656

List of Tables

4.1	Sample codes	58
5.1	The link between category, properties, and dimensional range	74
5.2	Some differences between qualitative and quantitative research	75
5.3	Main methodologies and techniques in qualitative research	81
6.1	Sampling guide for stratified purposive sampling of patients	92
8.1	Representational decisions	126
9.1	Strategies in cross-language data collection	137
11.1	Key questions to ask of existing data and useful sources of evidence for appraisal	172
15.1	Challenges encountered in interviewing, and potential strategies that researchers use to address these	241
30.1	Comparing risk and privacy for the Tumblr study and the Instagram study	476
34.1	Comprehensive triangulation	531
36.1	Mixed-method design: two samples, two data types, two data sets	573
36.2	Mixed-method design: single core sample, two linked data sets, two data types	575
36.3	Mixed-method design: single sample, single set of data transformed	576
36.4	Mixed-method design: delineated group, multiple samples and data sets	577
41.1	Forms of expert and elite interviews in relation to their function in the research design and epistemological background	660

Notes on the Editor and Contributors

THE EDITOR

Uwe Flick is Professor of Qualitative Research in Social Science and Education at the Freie Universität of Berlin, Germany since 2013. He trained as a psychologist and sociologist and received his PhD from the Freie Universität of Berlin in 1988 and his Habilitation from the Technical University of Berlin in 1994. He has been Professor of Qualitative Research at Alice Salomon University of Applied Sciences in Berlin, Germany and at the University of Vienna, Austria, where he has continued to work as a Guest Professor. Previously, he was Adjunct Professor at the Memorial University of Newfoundland at St. John's, Canada and has been a Lecturer at the Freie Universität of Berlin in Research Methodology, a Reader and Assistant Professor at the Technical University of Berlin in Qualitative Methods and Evaluation, and Associate Professor and Head of the Department of Medical Sociology at the Hannover Medical School. He has held visiting appointments at the London School of Economics, l'Ecole des Hautes Etudes en Sciences Sociales in Paris, at Cambridge University (UK), Memorial University of St. John's (Canada), University of Lisbon (Portugal), University of Vienna, in Italy and Sweden, and at the School of Psychology at Massey University, Auckland (NZ). His main research interests are qualitative methods, social representations in the fields of individual and public health, homelessness and health, health and ageing, migration and health, unemployment, and technological change in everyday life. He is author of *Introducing Research Methodology – A Beginners' Guide to Doing A Research Project*, 2nd edition (Sage, 2015), *An Introduction to Qualitative Research*, 5th edition (Sage, 2014), *Designing Qualitative Research*, 2nd edition (Sage, 2018), *Managing Quality in Qualitative Research*, 2nd edition (Sage, 2018), *Doing Triangulation and Mixed Methods* (Sage, 2018), and *Doing Grounded Theory* (Sage, 2018). He is editor of *The SAGE Handbook of Qualitative Data Analysis* (Sage, 2014), *The SAGE Qualitative Research Kit*, 2nd edition (Sage, 2018 – 10 Volumes), *The Psychology of the Social* (Cambridge University Press, 1998), and *La perception quotidienne de la Santé et la Maladie: Théories subjectives et Représentations sociales* (L'Harmattan, 1993) as well as co-editor of *A Companion to Qualitative Research* (Sage, 2004), *Quality of Life and Health: Concepts, Methods and Applications* (Blackwell Science, 1995) and *Handbuch Qualitative Sozialforschung*, 3rd edition (PVU, 2012). Most of his books have been translated in several languages throughout Asia, Latin America and Europe.

THE CONTRIBUTORS

Rosaline (Rose) S. Barbour is Emerita Professor at the Open University, UK. Throughout her career in medical sociology she has carried out research into a variety of topics, including reproductive and maternal health, HIV/AIDS, obesity and cancer. What all these projects have in common is their location at the intersection of the social and the clinical, thus affording a vantage point for developing and interrogating disciplinary and theoretical frameworks. She has specialized and published widely on qualitative research, particularly expertise in relation to focus groups and the issue of rigor. Her most recent publications include *Introducing Qualitative Research: A Student's Guide*, 2nd edition (Sage, 2014); *Doing Focus Groups*, 2nd edition (Sage, 2017) and *A New Era of Focus Group Research: Challenges, Innovation and Practice* (co-edited with David L. Morgan) (Palgrave, 2017).

Lucélia de Moraes Braga Bassalo is Professor of Sociology of Education and Qualitative Research Methods at the State University of Pará – UEPA (Brazil). Her main research interests include youth cultures, feminism, gender and education as well as the study of educational trajectories and academic projects of college students of the Amazon Region in Brazil. Major publications are *Fotografie als Gegenstand qualitativer Sozialforschung* (ZQF – Zeitschrift für Qualitative Forschung, 2015 – with Wivian Weller), *Jovem e Mulher: um estudo sobre os posicionamentos de internautas feministas* (Liber Livro, 2015 – with Wivian Weller), *Origem familiar, percursos acadêmicos e projetos de estudantes universitários brasileiros e chineses* (Ipea, 2016 – with Chen Weidong and Wivian Weller).

Andrew Bengry is a Senior Lecturer in Psychology at Bath Spa University, UK. He has been a qualitative researcher for over 15 years, worked in higher education for over 10 years and has held positions at the Bath Spa University, University of Bath, University of Southampton and University of Birmingham. His interests are in youth and identity, and how culture shapes social identification and identity construction processes. He is also interested in methodological and ethical issues in qualitative research design and implementation. He is currently researching how students from different socio-economic backgrounds experience higher education and constitute their future graduate identities and progression strategies. He has co-developed the NERUPI framework for evaluating the impact of Widening Participation Outreach activities, which is currently being piloted by a number of higher education institutions in the UK. He has also conducted research on youth consumption and identity practices, focusing specifically on music festivals and free party networks (illegal raves), alcohol consumption and young men's appropriation of motorcars in identity practices. He has published in journals including the *International Journal of Social Research Methodology*, *Qualitative Research*, *Journal of Youth Studies*, *Sex Education*, *Sociology* and has co-authored a number of chapters in edited volumes. Key publications are Griffin, Bengry-Howell, Morey, Szmigin and Riley (in press) '"We Achieve the Impossible": Discourses of Freedom and Escape at Music Festivals and Free Parties', *Journal of Consumer Culture*; Hayton and Bengry-Howell (2016) 'Theory, Evaluation and Practice in Widening Participation: A Framework Approach to Assessing Impact', *London Review of Education*, 14(3): 41–53; Wiles, Bengry-Howell, Crow and Nind (2013) 'But is it Innovation? The Development of Novel Methodological Approaches in Qualitative Research', *Methodological Innovations Online*, 8(1): 18–33.

Alexander Bogner is a sociologist and senior researcher at the Institute of Technology Assessment of the Austrian Academy of Sciences in Vienna, Austria. His research interests include science and technology studies, social theory and qualitative research methods. Current publications are 'Different Ways of Problematising Biotechnology – and What it Means for Technology Governance', in *Public Understanding of Science*, 24(5): 516–32, in 2015 with Helge Torgersen; 'Decision-making under the Condition of Uncertainty and Non-knowledge: The Deliberative Turn in Genetic Counselling', in Matthias Groß and Linsey McGoey (eds.), *Routledge International Handbook of Ignorance Studies* (Routledge, 2015), 199–205.

Michael Bull is Professor of Sound Studies at the University of Sussex. He is the author of two monographs based upon the use of sonic ethnographies – *Sounding out the City: Personal Stereos and the Management of Everyday Life* (Berg, 2000) and *Sound Moves: iPod Culture and Urban Experience* (Routledge, 2007). He is the co-founder of the journals *Senses and Society* and *Sound Studies*, both published by Routledge. He has co-edited *The Auditory Culture Reader* (Bloomsbury, 2003, 2016) and edited a four-volume work on Sound Studies (Routledge, 2014). He is currently editing *The Routledge Companion to Sound Studies* and completing a monograph on 'Sirens' for Bloomsbury.

Vanessa Burholt (BSc, PhD, FAcSS) is Professor of Gerontology and Director of the pan-Wales Centre for Ageing and Dementia Research (CADR), and the Centre for Innovative Ageing (CIA) at Swansea University, both world-class research centres addressing key questions in ageing and dementia. CADR integrates multi-disciplinary activity and develops areas of expertise from biological, through psychosocial and environmental, to social policy in ageing and dementia. Vanessa's research focuses on older people's attachment to people and places and she has published over 50 papers and book chapters on rurality, loneliness, support networks, intergenerational relationships, ethnicity, and migration. She co-edited (with Profs Catherine Hennessey and Robin Means) *Countryside Connections: Older People, Community and Place in Rural Britain* (Policy Press, 2014). She was Principal Investigator for the South Wales arm of *Cognitive Function and Ageing Study (Wales)* and has recently completed work on *Dementia and Imagination: Connecting Communities and Developing Well-being Through Socially Engaged Visual Arts Practice*.

Marie Buscatto is Professor of Sociology at the University of Paris 1 Panthéon Sorbonne, France. She is a sociologist of work, of gender and of arts. She also develops epistemological reflections related to the uses of ethnography and qualitative methods. Her publications in English include the special edition of *Qualitative Sociology Review*, III (3), *Ethnographies of Artistic Work*, co-edited with Howard S. Becker in 2007, and the chapters Artistic Practices as Gendered Practices: Ways and Reasons, in Tasos Zembylas (ed.), *Artistic Practices* (Routledge, 2014), 44–55; and 'Practising Reflexivity in Ethnography', in David Silverman (ed.), *Qualitative Research: Issues of Theory, Method and Practice*, 4th edition (Sage, 2016), 137–51.

Kerry Chamberlain is Professor of Social and Health Psychology at Massey University, Auckland, New Zealand. His research interests are in health and the everyday, with a specific focus on inequality and disadvantage, medications, media, materiality, mundane ailments, food, and in innovative qualitative research methodology. He is co-editor (with Antonia Lyons) of the book series *Critical Approaches to Health* (Routledge), co-author (with Antonia Lyons) of *Health Psychology: A Critical Introduction* (Cambridge, 2006), and co-editor (with Michael Murray) of *Qualitative Health Psychology: Theories and Methods* (Sage, 1999).

Julianne Cheek is currently a professor at Østfold University College, Norway. She is an Associate Editor of *Qualitative Health Research* as well as being an editorial board member of a number of journals related to qualitative inquiry. Her publications, which include three books and over 100 journal articles and book chapters, reflect her ongoing interest in qualitative inquiry and the politics of that inquiry as it relates to the world of health and social care. In addition, she has a long interest in the mentoring and development of qualitative inquirers. She has developed post-doctoral programs in this regard, as well as having responsibility for the development of PhD and Master's by research programs. In 2010–2012 she had the honor of serving as the Vice President of the International Association of Qualitative Inquiry and currently serves on the External Advisory Board of the International Congress of Qualitative Inquiry held annually at the University of Illinois.

Myungweon Choi is an Associate Professor in the Department of Business Administration at Ajou University, South Korea. Her research interests include employee training, mentoring and coaching, and career development. Her research has appeared in *Human Resource Management*, *International Journal of Human Resource Management*, *Human Resource Development Quarterly*, and *Asia Pacific Journal of Human Resources*.

Lauren Clark, PhD is a Professor, College of Nursing, University of Utah. As a public health nurse by clinical background, she has worked with diverse communities in the USA, including Native American communities in the Arizona and Montana and Mexican American communities in Arizona, Colorado, and Utah. With post-doctoral training in cultural anthropology methods and a certificate in medical anthropology, she uses photography, comparative ethnography, and grounded theory qualitative methods. The US National Institutes of Health funds her research on health disparities and the experiences of people with chronic and disabling conditions and their families. She serves on the editorial boards of *Qualitative Health Research* and *Global Qualitative Nursing Research*.

Jan K. Coetzee is Senior Professor in the Department of Sociology at the University of the Free State, South Africa. He is program director for *The Narrative Study of Lives*, supervising and researching projects within interpretive and qualitative designs. His recent publications include 12 articles with postgraduate students and research fellows in *Qualitative Sociology Review* XIII (1), 2017, covering a range of aspects of the lifeworlds of South Africans living in the central part of the country. He is a practicing visual artist and his latest work focuses on books as documents of lives, using old texts juxtaposed with found and sculpted objects to draw attention to the book as symbolic knowledge object and potential source of criticality.

Louise Corti is Associate Director at the UK Data Archive and currently leads the UK Data Service's Collections Development team and Data Publishing teams. She works closely with data producers from all sectors to ensure that high quality data are created and acquired. Louise actively researches and publishes regularly in books and journals on key aspects of data management, sharing and reuse of social science data, and has directed research awards in this area. She was instrumental in helping operationalize the ESRC's Research Data Policy from 1995 and extending this to accommodate qualitative data. She acts as a consultant for qualitative data archives setting up around the world, and is currently working on helping to enable the UKDS to scale-up for managing big data.

Philip Darbyshire has been a children's nurse, educator, writer, researcher and educator for over 40 years, working across many clinical, education, research leadership, and consulting areas. He is internationally recognized as a leader in nursing and health care research promotion and service development. For 13 years he led one of Australia's most successful practice-based research departments at Women's & Children's Hospital in Adelaide, described by the Australian Council on Healthcare Standards as, 'an example of excellence in research leadership'. He is a part-time Professor of Nursing at Monash University and a proud AWCH (Association for the Wellbeing of Children in Healthcare) ambassador. His book 'Living with a sick child in hospital' (https://goo.gl/0f9HLA) helped change children's nursing care in hospitals and his most cited and influential work is 'Multiple methods in qualitative research with children: More insight or just more?' (https://goo.gl/p6lxGn) with MacDougall and Schiller, *Qualitative Research* 5(4): 417–36, November, 2005.

Norman K. Denzin is Distinguished Professor of Communications, College of Communications Scholar, and Research Professor of Communications, Sociology, and Humanities at the University of Illinois, Urbana-Champaign, is the author or editor of more than two dozen books, including *The Qualitative Manifesto* (Routledge, 2010); *Qualitative Inquiry Under Fire* (Routledge, 2009); *Reading Race* (Sage, 2002); *Interpretive Autoethnography* (Sage, 2014); *The Cinematic Society: The Voyeur's Gaze* (Sage, 1995); and four books on the American West. He is past editor of *The Sociological Quarterly*, co-editor (with Yvonna S. Lincoln) of five editions of the *SAGE Handbook of Qualitative Research*, co-editor (with Lincoln) of the methods journal *Qualitative Inquiry*, founding editor of *Cultural Studies ↔ Critical Methodologies* and *International Review of Qualitative Research*, and founding director of the International Congress of Qualitative Inquiry.

Hannah Ditchfield is a Media and Communication PhD candidate and Graduate Teaching Assistant at the University of Leicester (UK). Her PhD research focuses on how individuals manage and utilize the affordances of social media technologies within their interactions. She is particularly interested in how users edit their interactions 'pre-post' as well as how users multi-communicate on the social networking site, *Facebook*. Her research uses analytical approaches such as discursive psychology and conversation analysis and collects Facebook interactions via screen capture software.

Thomas S. Eberle is Professor Emeritus of Sociology at the University of St. Gallen, Switzerland, where he was co-director of the Research Institute of Sociology (1988–2015). He served as president of the Swiss Sociological Association (1998–2005) and as vice-president of the European Sociological Association (2007–2011). His major research areas are sociology of culture and of communication, of knowledge and of organization, as well as interpretive sociology, methodology, phenomenological sociology, and qualitative methods. Publications include 'Photographing as Creative and Communicative Action', in *Culture, Communication, and Creativity Reframing the Relations of Media, Knowledge, and Innovation in Society* (Peter Lang, 2014); 'Phenomenology as a Research Method', in *The Sage Handbook of Qualitative Data Analysis* (Sage, 2014); 'Qualitative Cultural Sociology', in *The Sage Handbook of Cultural Sociology* (Sage, 2016) and *Photography and Society* (in German, transcript Verlag, 2017).

Florian Elliker is Senior Lecturer in Sociology at the University of St. Gallen (Switzerland) and Research Fellow at the Department of Sociology, University of the Free State (South Africa). His publications deal with right-wing populism, experiences of social decline and precarity in ethnically diverse societies, a phenomenological sociology of knowledge approach to discourse and ethnography, and qualitative methods and methodology. Publications are

Democracy within Boundaries: On the Discursive Structure of Social Belonging (2013, Springer VS, German title *Demokratie in Grenzen*); *Populism as Radicalized Conservative Discourse* (2015, Swiss Journal of Sociology, German title *Populismus als radikalisierter konservativer Diskurs*); *The Art of Becoming a Minority* (with Yehonatan Alsheh, 2015, African Studies). He is currently co-editing a thematic issue of the *Journal for Discourse Studies* on 'discourse ethnography'.

Edith Enzenhofer, Social Researcher with focus on migration studies (dynamics and patterns of social belonging in diverse societies, social construction of 'security' from the perspective of people with migrant background) as well as qualitative and quantitative methodology. She is the author of several publications on quality standards in multi-lingual research designs. Currently she holds the position of Coordinator for a public educational program in Vienna (Austria) focusing on socially excluded children and she is active in human rights education. Relevant publication is with Katharina Resch (2011), 'Übersetzungsprozesse und deren Qualitätssicherung in der qualitativen Sozialforschung', *Forum Qualitative Sozialforschung/ Forum: Qualitative Social Research*, 12(2), retrieved via http://www.qualitative-research.net/index.php/fqs/rt/printerFriendly/1652/3176.

Nigel G. Fielding is Professor of Sociology at the University of Surrey and a Fellow of the Academy of Social Sciences. His research interests are in new technologies for social research, qualitative research methods, and mixed methods research design. He has authored or edited 20 books, over 70 journal articles and over 200 other publications. In research methodology his books include a study of methodological integration (*Linking Data*, Sage, 1986, with Jane Fielding), an influential book on qualitative software (*Using Computers in Qualitative Research*, Sage, 1991, editor, with Ray Lee), a study of the role of computer technology in qualitative research (*Computer Analysis and Qualitative Research*, Sage, 1998, with Ray Lee), two sets on interview methods (*Interviewing*, Sage, 2002; *Interviewing II*, Sage, 2009) and the SAGE Handbook of Online Research Methods (co-editor, Sage, 2017, second edition). He is presently researching 'merged methods'.

Ane Kathrine Gammelby is a PhD Fellow in Media Studies at Aarhus University, Denmark. Her research focuses on how lay people with health-related issues use online peer-networks (e.g. Facebook groups) to discuss their health. Through her work she inquires how people in the digital age make sense of their bodily sensations by consulting various sources of expertise. Her research is grounded in symbolic interactionism, and her approach is ethnographic. Main research interests comprise the methodological implications and ethical dilemmas when researching digital culture and digitally saturated lived experience, not least how such experience can(not) be captured and represented as 'data' in digital research. Key concepts of interest are social construction of knowledge, digital intimacies, empowerment and digital saturation of everyday life.

Giampietro Gobo, PhD, is Professor of Methodology of Social Research and Evaluation Methods, at the University of Milan. Former Director of the center ICONA (Innovation and Organizational Change in the Public Administration), he was the first chair of the 'Qualitative Methods' Research Network of ESA (European Sociological Association). Consulting Editor of the *International Journal of Qualitative Research in Work and Organizations*, he has published over fifty articles in the areas of qualitative and quantitative methods. His books include *Doing Ethnography*, 2nd edition (Sage, 2017, with Andrea Molle), *Qualitative Research*

Practice (Sage, 2004, co-edited with Seale, Gubrium and Silverman) and *Collecting Survey Data. An Interactional Approach* (Sage, 2014, with Sergio Mauceri). His interests concern the decolonization of methodology, the reduction of inequality in women's scientific careers, and the relationship between quantum physics and social sciences. He is currently undertaking projects in the area of coordination and workplace studies.

Christopher Groves is a Research Fellow in the Cardiff University School of Social Sciences, and is currently working on the FLEXIS project. His research interests focus on how people and institutions negotiate and deal with an intrinsically uncertain future. Relevant publications include Groves, Henwood, Shirani, Parkhill, Butler and Pidgeon (2016) 'The Grit in the Oyster: Questioning Socio-Technical Imaginaries Through Biographical Narratives of Engagement with Energy', *Journal of Responsible Innovation* 3(1): 4–25, and Groves, Henwood, Shirani, Parkhill, Butler, and Pidgeon (2016) 'Invested in Unsustainability? On the Psychosocial Patterning of Engagement in Practices', *Environmental Values* 25(3): 309–28.

Karen Henwood is a Professor in the Cardiff School of Social Sciences. Her empirical work involves in-depth longitudinal and community case studies, and uses interpretive, qualitative research methods to engage with local communities on issues of risk, environmental controversy and identity. Her UK Research Council-funded projects include: *Energy Biographies: Exploring the Dynamics of Energy Use for Demand Reduction* (Economic and Social Research Council, 2011–2016), and *Homing in: Sensing, Sense-making and Sustainable Place-making* (Arts and Humanities Research Council, 2013–2014). Currently (2016–2021), and as part of her work with Cardiff University's Understanding Risk Group, she is investigating how the UK can make the transition to a flexible, integrated energy system. This is new work involving a social sciences–engineering consortium with support from European Structural Funds to Wales (WEFO, the Flexis project). This work continues to reflect her wider interests in methodological innovation and development, and investigating the challenges posed by environmental and sociocultural risks and uncertainties in changing times.

Sharlene Hesse-Biber is professor of sociology and the director of the Women's and Gender Studies Program at Boston College in Chestnut Hill, Massachusetts. She publishes widely in the field of qualitative and mixed methods research methodology. She is author of *The Practice of Qualitative Research*, 3rd edition (Sage, 2017) and *Mixed Methods Research: Merging Theory with Practice* (Guilford, 2010). She is co-editor (with R. Burke Johnson) of *The Oxford Handbook of Multimethod and Mixed Methods Research Inquiry* (Oxford, 2015). She published an award-winning monograph, *Waiting for Cancer to Come: Genetic Testing and Women's Medical Decision-Making for Breast and Ovarian Cancer* (University of Michigan Press, 2014). She is co-developer of the software program *HyperRESEARCH*, a computer-assisted program for analyzing qualitative and mixed methods data, and a transcription tool, *HyperTRANSCRIBE*. A fully functional free demo of these programs is available at www.researchware.com.

Darrin Hodgetts is Professor of Societal Psychology at Massey University Albany. Prior to taking up his current post he held positions in Community Medicine at Memorial University (Canada), psychology and media at the London School of Economics and Political Sciences (UK), and community psychology at the University of Waikato (New Zealand). Darrin's research focuses on urban poverty, homelessness, the precariat, and health inequalities. Darrin is currently co-editing the *Sage Handbook of Applied Social Psychology* and his other publications include: Hodgetts, Drew, Stoltie, Sonn, Nikora and Curtis, *Social Psychology and Everyday Life* (Palgrave/Macmillan, 2010); Hodgetts and Stolte (2016) 'Homeless People's Leisure Practices Within and Beyond Urban Socio-scapes', *Urban Studies*, 53(5): 899–914; Hodgetts and Stolte, *Urban Poverty, Penal Welfare and Health Inequalities* (Routledge, 2017).

Kim Hoffman is a Senior Researcher with the Oregon Health and Science University in Portland, Oregon. She received her PhD in Urban Studies from Portland State University. Topics of study include organizational improvement, capacity development, health and health services, and community-based programs. Her expertise includes short-term or large-scale/multi-year studies using quantitative, qualitative, and mixed methods. She is the coordinator for the US National Institute on Drug Abuse Clinical Trials Network Peru Node and has received funding from the US National Institute of Health, the Robert Wood Johnson Foundation, and the Faster Forward Foundation as a Principal Investigator. Dr Hoffman currently leads and has led numerous international program evaluation projects including the 21-country United Nations Office on Drugs and Crime Treatnet project.

Clare Jackson is a lecturer in sociology at the University of York, UK. She uses conversation analysis to study both ordinary and institutional interactions. She has particular interests in the ways that gender is made relevant and oriented to in ordinary talk, and in how decision-making occurs in interaction in healthcare contexts. Her interests in gender and healthcare are currently combined in a project examining how decisions are made in the interactions that occur between midwives and women during labor. Illustrative publications are 'The Gendered "I"', in S. A. Speer and E. Stokoe (eds.), *Gender and Conversation* (Cambridge University Press, 2011); in 2016, 'I sort of did stuff to him', *Narrative Inquiry*, 26(1): 150–70; in 2017, Jackson, Land and Holmes, 'Healthcare Professionals' Assertions and Women's Responses During Labor: A Conversation Analytic Study of Data from One Born Every Minute', *Patient Education and Counseling*, 100(3): 465–72.

Christopher Joseph Jenks is Associate Professor of English at the Hong Kong Polytechnic University. He has also taught at the University of South Dakota, City University of Hong Kong, Newcastle University, and Konkuk University. He specializes in the political and cultural implications of the global spread of English. His research interests also include multiculturalism, critical race theory, national identities, and discourse analysis. Christopher's eight books cover a range of topics, including chat room interaction, intercultural communication, and second language acquisition. His 2010 co-edited collection on second language acquisition was runner-up for the 2011 British Association for Applied Linguistics (BAAL) Book Award. He is currently working on a project that examines how roadside billboards of the Midwest represent discursive spaces for national identity construction.

Norah Keating is Professor of Rural Ageing, Swansea University; Co-Director of Research on Aging, Policies and Practice at the University of Alberta; and Extraordinary Professor, North-West University, South Africa. As part of her international research and capacity-building activities, she directs the International Association on Gerontology and Geriatrics' (IAGG) Global Social Issues in Ageing. She has served as President of the Alberta Association on Gerontology and the Canadian Association on Gerontology; and as Chair of the North American Region, International Association on Gerontology and Geriatrics. Professor Keating is a social gerontologist whose professional life has been devoted to enhancing the quality of life of older adults. She has an international reputation for her work in families, livable communities, and care. Her recent work includes editorship of special issues on 'Families and Aging in Global Context' (*Canadian Journal on Aging*, 2015); and on 'Ageing and Community' (*Journal of Community and Social Psychology*, 2014). Her work on social isolation includes a book *From Exclusion to Inclusion in Old Age: A Global Challenge* (Policy Press, 2012, with Professor T. Scharf) and articles on loneliness of older Canadians. Recent publications on ageing and community include a meta-synthesis on community characteristics and wellness of older rural adults (*Journal of Rural Studies*, 2016); and on age-friendly environments and their roles in healthy ageing (*Oxford Textbook of Geriatric Medicine*, 2017).

Brianna L. Kennedy, is Universitair Docent in the Faculty of Social and Behavioral Sciences at Utrecht University. Her research centers on under-served K-12 students who do not demonstrate traditionally defined academic and social success. Adopting methodological plurality, she tends to address research questions that require the use of traditional, emergent, and bricolaged qualitative research methodologies. She has published numerous articles addressing the racial discipline gap in the United States and is currently developing projects regarding social justice issues in schools in the Global North. Before pursuing a PhD in Urban Education at the University of Southern California, Dr Kennedy taught early adolescents in the Los Angeles Unified School District.

Hubert Knoblauch is Professor of General Sociology at the Technical University of Berlin. His areas of research are Sociological Theory, Sociology of Knowledge, Religion and Communication, Qualitative Methods, particularly Videography and Ethnography. Recent book publications in English include *Videography: Introduction to Interpretive Videoanalysis of Social Situations* (with René Tuma and Bernt Schnettler: Peter Lang, 2014); *Culture, Communication, and Creativity: Reframing the Relations of Media, Knowledge, and Innovation in Society* (edited with Mark Jacobs and René Tuma; Peter Lang, 2014) and *Powerpoint, Communication, and the Knowledge Society* (Cambridge University Press, 2013).

Margarethe Kusenbach is Associate Professor in the Department of Sociology at the University of South Florida, Tampa. Besides qualitative research methods, her interests include cities and communities, emotions and identity, sustainability and disasters. Her current work investigates issues of home and belonging among migrants and other marginal social groups. She has published numerous articles and book chapters in the United States and in Europe. In 2013, she edited a book titled *Home: International Perspectives on Culture, Identity, and Belonging* (Peter Lang, 2013, with Krista E. Paulsen). The chapter in this *Handbook* is based on her 2003 article 'Street Phenomenology: The Go-Along as Ethnographic Research Tool', in the journal *Ethnography*, which has been widely cited and reprinted several times.

Simon Lindgren is Professor of Sociology and director of the Digital Social Research Unit (DIGSUM) at Umeå University, Sweden. His research is about social interaction, participation, power, and self-organization in networked online media. He also works with developing methodological tools and strategies for analyzing discursive and social network aspects of the evolving digital media landscape. He is the author of *New Noise: A Cultural Sociology of Digital Disruption* (2013, Peter Lang), *Digital Media and Society* (2017, Sage), and the editor of *Hybrid Media Culture: Sensing Place in a World of Flows* (2014, Routledge).

Beate Littig is a sociologist and senior researcher at the Institute for Advanced Studies in Vienna. In addition she is a permanent lecturer at the University of Vienna and teaches at international summer schools and workshops. Her research interests are the future of work, social sustainability, practices of change, gender studies, and qualitative research methods. Publications include Bogner, Littig and Menz (eds.) *Interviewing Experts* (Palgrave Macmillan, 2009); Jonas, Littig and Wroblewski (eds.) *Methodological Reflections on Practice Oriented Theories* (Springer, 2017); 'Good "Green Jobs" for Whom? A Feminist Critique of the "Green Economy"', in MacGregor, Sherilyn (ed.) *International Handbook on Gender and Environment* (Routledge, 2017).

Colin MacDougall is Professor of Public Health at Flinders University, Honorary Principal Fellow at University of Melbourne and visiting professor at Pokhara University in Nepal, whose overarching research interest is equity and social justice. He has experience with children as a psychologist, community health service manager and policymaker, and in academia. Colin uses rights-based qualitative methods to explore how children experience and act on their worlds, including an international perspective on children's rights and disasters in the context of climate change. He has taught and researched at universities in the UK, France, Germany, New Zealand, and Nepal. He is co-editor, with Helen Keleher of the fourth edition of the textbook *Understanding Health* (Oxford University Press, 2016). A highly cited research glossary is Baum, MacDougall and Smith (2006) 'Participatory Action Research Glossary', *Journal of Epidemiology and Community Health*, 60: 854–7. A discussion of children's rights and disasters is in Gibbs, Mutch, O'Connor and MacDougall (2013) 'Research with, by, for, and about children: Lessons from disaster contexts', *Global Studies of Childhood*. 3. 2. http://dx.doi.org/10.2304/gsch.2013.3.2.129.

Annette N. Markham is Professor MSO of Information Studies at Aarhus University, Denmark and Affiliate Professor of Digital Ethics in the School of Communication at Loyola University, Chicago. Annette is internationally recognized for developing epistemological frameworks for rethinking ethics and qualitative methods for digitally saturated social contexts. A long-time member of the internet research community, Annette conducts sociological and ethnographic studies of how identity, relationships, and cultural formations are constructed in and influenced by digitally saturated socio-technical contexts. Her pioneering work in this area is well represented in her first book *Life Online: Researching Real Experience in Virtual Space* (Altamira, 1998). Annette Markham (PhD Purdue University in Organizational Communication, 1997) brings a multidisciplinary approach to her work, with training in rhetorical theory and criticism, Frankfurt School critical approaches, organizational theory, ethnography, and interpretive research methods. More information can be found on http://annettemarkham.com

Alison Marlin is a Visiting Researcher at the Center for Science and Technology Studies, UC Davis. She recently received her PhD from the University of Melbourne, using interviews and observation to investigate family intimacies that involve technologies such as Skype, Facebook, email, and mobile phones. She is interested in how methodologies and theoretical approaches from Sociology, Anthropology and Science and Technology Studies can be brought together to more fruitfully study humans and technology.

Joseph A. Maxwell is a Professor (Emeritus) in the Research Methods program in the College of Education and Human Development at George Mason University. His doctoral degree is in anthropology, but his research and teaching have mainly been in education, with a focus on methodology. He is the author of *Qualitative Research Design: An Interactive Approach*, 3rd edition (Thousand Oaks, SAGE: 2013) and *A Realist Approach for Qualitative Research*

(Thousand Oaks, SAGE: 2012), as well as many papers on qualitative and mixed methods research. His current research deals with using qualitative methods for causal explanation, validity in qualitative and quantitative research, the history and breadth of mixed methods research, the value of philosophic realism for research, and the importance of diversity and dialogue across research paradigms and methods.

Wolfgang Menz is Professor of Sociology, in particular Work, Organization and Innovation, at University of Hamburg. His research interests include the sociology of work and organizations and science and innovation studies. Publications include Bogner, Littig and Menz (eds.), *Interviewing Experts* (Palgrave Macmillan, 2009); Birken, Menz and Kratzer 'Management by Customers and Customer Control: (Im-)Balances of Power in Interactive Service Work', in Dunkel and Kleemann (eds.), *Customers at Work: New Perspectives on Interactive Service Work* (Palgrave Macmillan, 2013), S. 76–99.

Joanne Meredith is a Lecturer in Psychology at the University of Salford, Manchester (UK). She specializes in using interactional methods, including conversation analysis and discursive psychology, for online communication. Her research has focused predominantly on studies of instant messaging communication, and comparing these interactions to other forms of interaction. She is also interested in developing new and innovative methods for collecting qualitative data from online sources. She has contributed a chapter on analyzing online interaction using conversation analysis and discursive psychology to the fourth edition of David Silverman's edited collection *Qualitative Research* (Sage, 2016). She has also recently published an article in *Journal of Pragmatics* on how to analyze the technological affordances of online interaction using conversation analysis.

Donna M. Mertens, PhD, is Professor Emeritus who served in the Department of Education at Gallaudet University for over 30 years; she also served as the editor of the *Journal for Mixed Methods Research*. The primary focus of her work is transformative mixed-methods inquiry in diverse communities, which prioritizes ethical implications of research in support of human rights and social justice. Her recent books include *Mixed Methods Design in Evaluation* (2018, Sage), *Program Evaluation Theory and Practice: A Comprehensive Guide* (2012, Guilford, authored with Amy Wilson), *Transformative Research and Evaluation* (2009, Guilford Press), *Research and Evaluation in Education, Psychology: Integrating Diversity with Quantitative, Qualitative, and Mixed Methods* (2015, Sage, 4th edition), and *Indigenous Pathways into Social Research* (2013, Left Coast Press, co-edited with Fiona Cram and Bagele Chilisa).

Lothar Mikos is Professor of Television Studies in the Department of Media Studies at the Filmuniversity Babelsberg in Potsdam, Germany. His main areas of work are Economy of the International TV Format Trade, Television Series Worldwide, Digital Distribution, (De-)Convergence Culture, Popular Television Genres and Formats, Qualitative Audience Studies. His latest publications in English: 'From the Office to Stromberg: Adaptation Strategies on German Television', in *Continuum – Journal of Media and Cultural Studies*, 29, 5, 2015; 'Television Drama Series and Transmedia Storytelling in an Era of Convergence', in *Northern Lights: Film & Media Studies Yearbook*, 14, 1, 2016; 'Digital Media Platforms and the Use of TV Content: Binge Watching and Video-on-Demand in Germany', in *Media and Communication*, 4, 3, 2016; 'Germany as TV Show Import Market', in Larson Powell/Robert Shandley (eds.), *German Television: Historical and Theoretical Perspectives* (Berghahn Books, 2016).

David L. Morgan is a Professor Emeritus in the Department of Sociology at Portland State University. He is a sociological social psychologist, who is widely known for his work on focus groups, including his book, *Focus Groups as Qualitative Research* (Sage, 1996), and as co-author of *The Focus Group Kit* (with Richard Krueger; Sage, 1997). In addition, he has worked extensively on mixed methods, including a book for Sage, *Integrating Qualitative and Quantitative Methods* (2014). Most recently, he has published *Essentials of Dyadic Interviewing* for Routledge (2015), and *A New Era in Focus Group Research*, co-edited, with Rosaline Barbour, for Palgrave-Macmillan, 2017.

Janice M. Morse, PhD (Nurs), PhD (Anthro) is a Professor and Barnes Presidential Chair, College of Nursing, University of Utah, and Professor Emeritus, University of Alberta, Canada. Her research contributions are developing the *Praxis theory of suffering and comforting, fall prevention* (the Morse Fall Scale is used internationally), and advancing qualitative and mixed-methods research. She has edited *Qualitative Health Research* (*QHR*), and *Global Qualitative Nursing Research*, and was founding editor of the *International Journal of Qualitative Methods* (*IJQM*). Her publications include *Principles of Mixed-Method Designs* (Left Coast Press/Routledge), *Qualitatively-driven Mixed-method Designs* (Routledge), *Preventing Patient Falls* (Springer) and several qualitative methods texts. In 1997, she founded the International Institute for Qualitative Methodology (IIQM), directing a network of 8 international hubs and 115 universities, supporting training for QHR and mentoring qualitative researchers globally. She was the recipient of the 5th Sigma Theta Tau Episteme Award, and Hall of Fame, and has honorary doctorates from Australia and Canada.

Michael Murray is Professor of Social and Health Psychology and Head of the School of Psychology at Keele University, UK. He has published journal articles and chapters and (co-) authored and edited several books and collections on critical and qualitative approaches to health psychology including *Qualitative Health Psychology: Theories and Methods* (Sage, 1999, with Chamberlain), *Critical Health Psychology* (Palgrave, 2014) and *Health Psychology: Theory, Research & Practice* (Sage, 2018, with Marks and Estacio). He is the Associate Editor of *Psychology & Health*, and sits on the editorial boards of several other journals including *Health, Psychology & Medicine*, *Health Psychology Review*, and *Arts & Health*. His current research interests include the use of participatory and arts-based methods to engage older people and the development of narrative research methods.

Jörg Niewöhner is Professor of European Ethnology and Human–Environment Relations at the Institute of European Ethnology, Humboldt-Universität zu Berlin, and the Deputy Director of the Integrative Research Institute Transformations of Human -Environment Systems (www.iri-thesys.org). His research develops a relational anthropology in the fields of global environmental change and the life sciences, particularly psychiatry and molecular biology. He is a member of the Laboratory: Social Anthropology of Science and Technology (hu-berlin.de/sts). Recent publications deal with questions of infrastructure, scale, comparison, and co-laboration in ethnographic research.

Nicolle Pfaff is Professor of Inequality and Migration Research at the University of Duisburg-Essen (Germany). Her main research interests lie in the field of educational inequality and social segregation, youth (culture) research, youth activism and civic education. Relevant publications include: *Handbuch der Peerforschung* (Barbara Budrich Publishers, 2016, with Sina-Mareen Köhler and Heinz-Hermann Krüger); *Kritische Bildungsforschung* (Barbara Budrich

Publishers, 2016, with Anne Schippling and Cathleen Grunert); *Qualitative Analysis and Documentary Method in International Educational Research* (Barbara Budrich Publishers, 2010 – with Ralf Bohnsack and Wivian Weller); *Metodologias da Pesquisa Qualitativa em Educação*, 3rd edition (Vozes, 2013, with Wivian Weller).

Jonathan Potter is Distinguished Professor, and Dean of the School of Communication and Information at Rutgers University, New Brunswick. He has worked on basic theoretical and analytic issues in social psychology for more than 30 years. This is seen in his engagement with, and development of, post-structuralism (in *Social Texts and Contexts*, with Margaret Wetherell and Peter Stringer), discourse analysis (in *Discourse and Social Psychology*, with Margaret Wetherell), discursive psychology (in *Discursive Psychology*, with Derek Edwards) and constructionism (in *Representing Reality*). He is currently interested in the way basic psychological notions such as 'socialization' can be reconfigured as an object in and for interaction. Working with naturalistic materials has provided a way of unlocking fundamental and subtle issues about the nature of 'cognition' (in *Conversation and Cognition*, with Hedwig te Molder). This sits alongside a long-term critical and applied interest in topics such as racism (in *Mapping the Language of Racism*, with Margaret Wetherell) and, more recently, morality, asymmetry, and emotion in family-mealtime and child-protection settings (with Alexa Hepburn).

Tim Rapley is a Senior Lecturer in the Institute of Health & Society at Newcastle University, UK. His current research interests are in detailed empirical studies of medical work, knowledge and practice, and social studies of research. He is author of *Doing Conversation, Discourse and Document Analysis* (Sage, 2018) and recently re-wrote a chapter he is (still) quite proud of, 'Some Pragmatics of Data Analysis', for the fourth edition of David Silverman's edited collection *Qualitative Research* (Sage, 2016).

Asta Rau is Director of the Centre for Health Systems Research & Development at the University of the Free State, South Africa. Her key expertise is in conceptualizing, theorizing, and designing research, and operationalizing designs into a range of methodologies: qualitative, quantitative, and mixed-methods. She has completed 30 research projects focused on social aspects of HIV, and on health communication. She co-edited the 2017 Special Edition (XIII, 1) of *Qualitative Sociology Review*, where her work in narrative methodology appears. An example of her quantitative research on HIV-TB stigma among healthcare workers appears in *Clinical Infectious Diseases*, 2016, 15 (62 Suppl 3). Threading throughout her research career is a strong interest in the functioning of power – an interest underlying Chapter 19 in this Handbook.

Gethin Rees is Lecturer in Sociology at Newcastle University. His research involves understanding the intersection of the institutions of medicine and law as embodied in the forensic professional. He has investigated the ways that doctors and nurses perform forensic examinations of rape victims, the work of sleep experts in assessing the veracity of a sleepwalking defense, and is about to commence a Wellcome Trust-funded study of nurses working within police stations in England. Notable publications include 'Making the Colposcope "Forensic": The Medico-Legal Management of a Controversial Visualization Device'; '"Morphology is a Witness Which Doesn't Lie": Diagnosis by Similarity Relation and Analogical Inference in Forensic Medicine'; and '"It Is Not For Me To Say Whether Consent Was Given Or Not": Forensic Medical Examiners' Justifications for "Neutral Reports" in rape cases'.

Katharina Resch is Sociologist and Interpreter, working for the University of Vienna (Austria). Her fields of research include the sociology of health and illness, cross-language research, educational sociology, and research in the fields of careers and counseling. She is the author of several publications in these fields, including 'Übersetzungsprozesse und deren Qualitätssicherung in der qualitativen Sozialforschung', *Forum Qualitative Sozialforschung/ Forum: Qualitative Social Research*, 12(2), retrieved via http://www.qualitative-research.net/index.php/fqs/rt/printerFriendly/1652/3176 (2011, with Edith Enzenhofer).

Kathryn Roulston is Professor in the Qualitative Research Program in the College of Education at the University of Georgia in Athens, Georgia, where she teaches qualitative research methods. She has a PhD in Education from the University of Queensland. Her research interests include qualitative research methods, qualitative interviewing, and analyses of talk-in-interaction. She is author of *Reflective Interviewing: A Guide to Theory and Practice* (Sage, 2010), and has contributed chapters to *The SAGE Handbook of Interview Research: The Complexity of the Craft*, 2nd edition (2012) and *The SAGE Handbook of Qualitative Data Analysis*, as well as contributing articles to *Qualitative Research*, *Qualitative Inquiry*, *International Journal of Research and Method in Education*, and *International Journal of Music Education*.

Bernt Schnettler is Professor of Sociology at the University of Bayreuth. His research is based on the New Sociology of Knowledge. Figuring among his recent publications is his book, *Videography: Introduction to Interpretive Video Analysis of Social Situations*, co-authored with Hubert Knoblauch, and René Tuma (Peter Lang, 2015).

Margrit Schreier is Professor of Empirical Research Methods at Jacobs University Bremen. Her research interests include qualitative research methods and methodology, mixed methods, media psychology, empirical study of literature, and health research. She has been a principal investigator in several third party funded research projects on these topics, and she has authored and co-authored more than 90 book chapters and articles. She is co-editor of the issue 'Qualitative and Quantitative Research: Conjunctions and Divergences' of *Forum: Qualitative Social Research* (2001, with Nigel G. Fielding), co-author of *Forschungsmethoden in Psychologie und Sozialwissenschaften für Bachelor* (with Walter Hussy and Gerald Echterhoff), and author of *Qualitative Content Analysis in Practice* (Sage, 2012).

Chloe Shaw is a Research Fellow at the Global Institute of Psychosocial, Palliative, and End-of-Life Care (GIPPEC), at the Princess Margaret Cancer Centre, Toronto. She resides in the UK, with an honorary research associate position within the Institute for Women's Health, University College London. She first used the method of conversation analysis (CA) to study advice-giving between mothers and daughters in telephone conversations, and now uses CA to study naturalistic talk in health care settings. This began with the Parents and Neonatal Decision Study, examining end-of-life decision-making for critically ill babies in the neonatal unit. Chloe is currently using the method of conversation analysis to study the process of CALM (Managing Cancer and Living Meaningfully) therapy with advanced cancer patients. Her research interests include communication in end-of-life care, therapy interactions, examining the process of mentalization from a CA perspective, the social organization of decision-making and advice-giving, and the social organization and management of emotion in interaction.

Fiona Shirani is a Research Associate in the Cardiff School of Social Sciences. She is currently working on the FLEXIS project; which integrates social science and technical research to address issues concerning the energy system of the future. Her research interests encompass qualitative longitudinal methods, family lifecourse transitions and imagined futures. Relevant publications include: Shirani, Parkhill, Butler, Groves, Pidgeon and Henwood (2016) 'Asking about the Future: Insights from Energy Biographies', *International Journal of Social Research Methodology*, 19(4): 429–44; and Shirani, Butler, Henwood, Parkhill and Pidgeon (2015) '"I'm not a Tree Hugger, I'm Just Like You": Changing Perceptions of Sustainable Lifestyles', *Environmental Politics*, 24(1): 57–74.

Estrid Sørensen is a Professor of Cultural Psychology and Anthropology of Knowledge at the Department for Social Science at the Ruhr-University Bochum in Germany, and a Co-Director of the Centre for Anthropological Knowledge in Scientific and Technological Cultures, CAST. Her research addresses knowledge practices in a technologized and globalized world, across standardization and contextualizations. She is the author of *The Materiality of Learning* (Cambridge, 2009) and has additionally published on technology and knowledge production in social psychology and in practices of computer game play.

Christine Stephens co-leads the cross-disciplinary Health and Ageing Research Team at Massey University where she is a Professor of Social Science Research. The focus of the team's activity is a longitudinal study of quality of life in ageing (Health, Work and Retirement study) and in-depth qualitative studies on topics such as family relationships and housing needs. Christine's research is located at the intersection of health psychology and gerontology. She has authored or co-authored papers in these areas for *Health Psychology*, *Psychology and Health*, *The Journal of Health Psychology*, *Health and Ageing*, *Journal of Ageing and Health*, *Ageing and Society*, *International Psychogeriatrics*, *Critical Public Health*, and *The Journals of Gerontology*. She has also contributed to *Health Psychology Review* and *Qualitative Research in Psychology* on qualitative approaches. Her book *Health Promotion: A Psychosocial Approach* (Open University Press, 2008) argues for the importance of the broader social and structural foundations of health. She is currently co-authoring a book for Routledge about critical approaches to research on ageing.

Robert Thornberg, is Professor of Education in the Department of Behavioural Sciences and Learning at Linköping University. He is also the Secretary of the Board for the Nordic Educational Research Association (NERA). His current research is on school bullying, especially with a focus on social and moral processes involved in bullying, bystander rationales, reactions and actions, and students' perspectives and explanations. His second line of research is on values education including morals, norms, and student participation in everyday school life. A third line of research is on teacher education, especially student teachers' motives to become a teacher and their experiences of distressed situations during teacher training. Professor Thornberg uses a range of research methods such as qualitative interviewing, focus groups, questionnaires, and ethnographic fieldwork but has a particular expertise in grounded theory. He has published numerous articles in a range of peer-reviewed journals and written and co-authored book chapters on grounded theory in various method books.

Katrin Tiidenberg is a Postdoctoral Researcher at Aarhus University, Denmark, and Associate Professor of Social Media and Visual Culture at the Baltic Film, Media, Arts and Communication School of Tallinn University, Estonia. She is currently publishing on selfie culture and visual research methods. Her research interests include ethics, sexuality, gender, and normative ideologies as mediated through social media practices and visual culture.

René Tuma is working at the Technische Universität Berlin on a Postdoc position. He is interested in, and working on, the Sociology of Knowledge, Sociological Theory, Interpretive Methods, and Sociology of Technology. One of his main foci is the use of visual data in the social sciences and the reflexive study of methodology. In his PhD he scrutinized the vernacular use of video analysis in professional fields such as police work, sports training, and market research. Recent work: *Videoprofis im Alltag – Die kommunikative Vielfalt der Videoanalyse* (Springer VS, 2017); *Videography: Introduction to Interpretive Videoanalysis of Social Situations* (Peter Lang, 2014, with Hubert Knoblauch and Bernt Schnettler).

David Wästerfors is Associate Professor at Lund University in Sweden. His publications include 'Playfights as Trouble and Respite' in *Journal of Contemporary Ethnography*; Safety Work with an Ethnic Slant (with Veronika Burcar) in *Social Inclusion*; 'Businessmen as Folk Ethnographers' in *Ethnography*; and 'Taking Ownership of Gaming and Disability' (with Kristofer Hansson) in *Journal of Youth Studies*. Apart from his interest in institutional youth care (especially school work), he has been engaged in studies of corruption, disabilities, and masculinities from interactionist, ethnomethodological, and narrative viewpoints. Currently he is studying violence in youth care institutions.

Wivian Weller is Associate Professor of Sociology of Education and Qualitative Research Methods at the University of Brasilia – UnB (Brazil) and research fellow from the National Council for Scientific and Technological Development – CNPq. Her main research focuses on youth (culture) research, educational inequality as well as the effects of large-scale achievement testing in access to higher education. Major publications: *HipHop in São Paulo und Berlin – Ästhetische Praxis und Ausgrenzungserfahrungen junger Schwarzer und Migranten* (Springer VS, 2003); *Bian ge shi jie zhong de da xue sheng – zhong guo, ba xi bi jiao yan jiu* (Social Sciences Academic Press China, 2016 – with Tom Dwyer, Eduardo Zen, Jiu Shuguang and Guo Kaiyuan); *Qualitative Analysis and Documentary Method in International Educational Research* (Barbara Budrich Publishers, 2010 – with Ralf Bohnsack and Nicolle Pfaff); *Metodologias da Pesquisa Qualitativa em Educação*, 3rd edition (Vozes, 2013, with Nicolle Pfaff).

Acknowledgements

The idea for this *Handbook* goes back to some conversation with Mila Steele at SAGE. We had both the impression, that despite the central role of data and their collection in qualitative research, this step was not sufficiently covered in the existing literature. The idea for such a handbook is also a consequence of the publication of the earlier *SAGE Handbook of Qualitative Data Analysis*, that I edited in 2014 (Flick, 2014). Mila Steele was very stimulating in the planning phase of the *Handbook* in many respects and supported the process of making the plan happen and of making a book out of a concept. Thank you very much for this help and to everybody else involved in this process at SAGE!

A major role in supporting the development of the book from proposal to manuscript was played by the members of the International Advisory Editorial Board. They also were important for extending the vision on qualitative data collection with an international perspective covering not only Europe and the United States, but also African, Asian, and Latin American backgrounds. The Board members were also very helpful in reviewing the chapters of the book in the writing process. A big 'thank you' to all of them!

The most important role in such a handbook in the end is that of the authors. Without their readiness to write their chapters, to deliver them on time, and to format and revise them after the reviews, the book would not have come to look as it does now. The authors, also, were ready to engage in the peer-reviewing process for the other chapters. Both the writing of their own and their reviews of other chapters are most appreciated!

Uwe Flick

PART I
Charting the Routes

Part I is a *general introduction* to the *Handbook* and its contents. It aims to give a brief and concise overview of the state of the art of qualitative research, with a particular focus on data collection, and to orient the reader through the *Handbook* and its chapters, making the background, structure and the rationale of the book explicit.

Doing Qualitative Data Collection – Charting the Routes

Uwe Flick

INTRODUCTION

Collecting qualitative data has become a hot topic in qualitative research on various levels. Qualitative data analysis is less contested as a basis for doing qualitative research, although a wide range of approaches and procedures for analyzing qualitative data has been developed that exist side by side and in competition (see Flick, 2014a). But also in that context the relevant question is what counts as data to analyze and what is the best way to analyze social phenomena etc. In the context of collecting qualitative data, such discussions are much more intense and fundamental. Here, the three terms are discussed, rejected and defended: What means *data* for qualitative analysis? Should we *collect* data or focus on phenomena that occur in natural contexts? And does *qualitative* (research, analysis, data collection) still have the same meaning and relevance as it had given the interest that mixed methods have found. Discussions, as the contributions to this *Handbook* will show, address several levels of doing qualitative data collection. That we need data for doing any kind of qualitative research is quite unproblematic for most of those who do qualitative research. However, the concept of 'data' is something that has become ambivalent in several respects, not necessarily or immediately linked to doing qualitative research. First, there is a growing concern about big companies using 'my' data, when I use a credit card, buy in online shops and on websites, go on Facebook and the like. Second, the issue of 'big data' produces fears and irritations as well, that the traces left in such contexts are connected and produce an image of the individual or collectivities that is much more comprehensive than people can imagine and would (or should) accept. In this context, data are understood as the traces people, activities, or technologies leave behind, that can be used or misused for various purposes. When we start using such traces (or something else) as data for (qualitative or quantitative) research, the meaning of data is a different one. As the discussion about 'raw data' (as an oxymoron – see Gitelman, 2013) highlights, researchers never find data *per se*, but construct or interpret phenomena in specific ways so that they can be used (as data) in social research (see also Lindgren, Chapter 28, this volume and Markham, Chapter 33, this volume). That this distinction is not just relevant for computer scientists and digital researchers but also for qualitative researchers in general can be demonstrated with two examples.

On the one hand, we find the heated discussion about elicited versus naturally occurring data (see Potter and Shaw, Chapter 12, this volume). It is driven by the idea that researchers should take an interest in the world as it occurs, without the researchers and independent of their practices, constructions and methods. Research should be restricted to (simply) recording events, interactions and activities and then analyzing the materials resulting from such recording. This is opposed to research that uses methods such as interviews (see Roulston and Choi, Chapter 15, this volume) or observation and participation (see Buscatto, Chapter 21, this volume, and Wästerfors, Chapter 20, this volume) for producing materials that can be analyzed. The question in the background is, whether the world captured in such data is the same, as it would be, without the researchers' activities? But then the next question is to what extent is recording and registration not also based on decisions by the researchers – what to select for recording, when to record, how to record, when to begin and when to stop, how to elaborate and further process these data and the like? Thus the problematic of data is nearly the same in both cases – we cannot work with 'raw' data, but we decide to turn something into data, document it in a specific way, and work with it in our analysis. And then the crucial point is, *how* we turn something into data – which steps and decisions about sampling (see Schreier, Chapter 6, this volume), about recording and transcribing (see Jenks, Chapter 8, this volume) or about comparison (see Sørensen et al., Chapter 10, this volume) are framing the production of data. Thus, the core argument of the new materialism against the concept of data – that things, words, events etc. 'become data only when theory acknowledges them as data' (St. Pierre, 2011, p. 621; see also Denzin, Chapter 13, this volume) – is also relevant for naturally occurring data.

On the other hand we find a similar reservation against the use of methods for turning issues into data in one of the more traditional approaches in qualitative research. This is documented in the debates between Glaser and other protagonists in grounded theory research. Glaser (e.g. 1992) argues that 'all is data' and that researchers should not obstruct the immediacy of their analysis by using more formalized methods of data collection but 'just do it' (the analysis leading to discovering theories from the data). Charmaz (2014) or Clarke (2005) are much more sensitive to the notion that data are collected; that theories are not simply discovered in phenomena but are constructed by the researchers; and that their decisions have a strong impact on what becomes data, category and theory in the end (see Flick, 2018b), and thus, that the field on which qualitative research 'happens' – qualitative data analysis – is much less controversial than how the materials to analyze should have become visible. Therefore, the major task in the earlier *Handbook of Qualitative Data Analysis* (Flick, 2014a) and the introductory chapter to it (Flick, 2014b) was to 'map the field' (as the title of that introduction conveyed). For the area of data collection, it is more the task to outline, discuss and juxtapose the ways of doing this step and thus to 'chart the routes' that can be taken to data, material and to the field on which analysis happens in the end. That there are many roads that lead to Rome, and that some are straighter whereas others are (seen as) more meandering, has its reason in the ongoing diversification of qualitative research, of what is seen as data, and of what is seen as an adequate way to produce them.

DOING QUALITATIVE RESEARCH – SOME CORE ASSUMPTIONS

Before looking at this diversification in more detail in the chapters of this volume, it may be helpful to consider what can be seen as the core of qualitative research, going beyond just simply saying it is '*not* quantitative research'. Such a definition could demonstrate that qualitative research has developed an identity (or maybe multiple identities) of its own. However, is there an identity of qualitative research, which is accepted in the multiplicity of approaches to qualitative research, reaching from more traditional concepts of (post-positivist) research with qualitative methods to the 'new materialism' talking about post-qualitative research (e.g. St. Pierre, 2011)?

We can identify some common features of qualitative research despite the multiplicity of approaches to qualitative research. First of all, qualitative research is approaching the world(s) 'out there' (instead of doing studies in specialized research settings such as laboratories). It intends to understand, describe, and sometimes explain social phenomena 'from the inside' in a number of different ways: First, experiences of individuals or groups are analyzed. Experiences can be related to biographical life histories or to (everyday or professional) practices; they may be addressed by analyzing everyday knowledge, accounts, and stories. Second, interactions and communications are analyzed in the making. This can be based on observing or recording practices of interacting and communicating and analyzing this material. Third, documents (texts, images, film, or sounds, and more and more digital documents) or similar traces of experiences or interactions are analyzed.

Common to such approaches is that they seek to understand how people construct the world around them, what they are doing, how they are doing it or what is happening to them in terms that are meaningful and that offer rich insights. Interactions and documents are ways of constituting social processes and artifacts collaboratively (or conflictingly). All of these approaches represent ways of meaning-making, which can be reconstructed and analyzed with various qualitative methods that allow the researchers to develop (more or less generalizable) models, typologies and theories as ways of describing and explaining social (or psychological) issues. Given these aims of qualitative research, what characterizes the research practice in which they are pursued in rather general terms again? Is it possible to identify common ways of doing qualitative research if we take into account that there are different theoretical, epistemological, and methodological approaches to qualitative research and that the issues that are studied are also very diverse? At least some common features of how qualitative research is done can be mentioned (see Flick, 2018c, p. x): Qualitative researchers are interested in accessing experiences, interactions and documents in their natural context and in a way that gives room to the particularities of them and the materials in which they are studied. This means for data collection that qualitative researchers travel into the worlds they want to study and do not transfer these worlds into their scientific environments, such as laboratories. Qualitative researchers refrain from setting up a theoretically well-defined concept of what they study and from formulating hypotheses in the beginning in order to test them. Rather, they develop and refine concepts (or hypotheses, if they are used) in the process of research and of collecting data. Qualitative researchers start from the idea that their methods and theories should be appropriate to what they study. If the existing methods do not fit to a concrete issue or field, they are adapted or new methods or approaches are developed. Researchers themselves are an important part of the research process, either in terms of their own personal presence as researchers, or in terms of their experiences in the field and with the reflexivity they bring to the role – as are members of the field under study. Qualitative researchers take context and cases seriously for understanding an issue under study. A bigger part of the current qualitative research is based on case studies or a series of case studies, and often the case (its history and complexity) is an important context for understanding the issue that is studied. A major part of qualitative research is based on text and writing – from field notes and transcripts to descriptions and interpretations and finally to the presentation of the findings and of the research as a whole. Therefore, issues of transforming complex social situations (or other materials such as images) into texts – issues of transcribing and writing in general – are major concerns of qualitative research. If methods are supposed to be adequate to what is under study, approaches to defining and assessing the quality of qualitative research (still) have to be discussed in specific ways (see Barbour, Chapter 14, this volume) that are appropriate for qualitative research and even for specific approaches in qualitative research.

Outlines of common aspects of qualitative research start from the practice of doing qualitative research. But a common understanding of what qualitative research is, and is about, goes beyond describing practices. A suggestion for such a concept can be found in Denzin and Lincoln's (2011a) *Handbook*, where the editors offer an 'initial, generic definition':

> Qualitative research is a situated activity that locates the observer in the world. It consists of a set of interpretive, material practices that make the world visible. These practices transform the world. They turn the world into a series of representations, including field notes, interviews, conversations, photographs, recordings, and memos to the self. At this level, qualitative research involves an interpretive, naturalistic approach to the world. This means that qualitative researchers study things in their natural settings, attempting to make sense of, or interpret, phenomena in terms of the meanings people bring to them. (2011b, p. 3)

Such a definition is also strongly linked to doing qualitative research and it tackles most of the issues mentioned above – such as natural contexts, turning issues into representations, interpretation and sense-making. However, in the newer edition of the same *Handbook* (Denzin and Lincoln, 2018a) this definition has not been taken up, but it is stated that the 'separate and multiple uses and meanings of the methods of qualitative research make it difficult to agree on any essential definition of the field, for it is never just one thing … qualitative research is a set of complex interpretive practices' (2018b, p. 13). In attempts to define, or to avoid defining, qualitative research in a comprehensive way, the terms of data and of the methods for collecting/producing/documenting them are not really mentioned as a central feature of the practices. In order to fill this (definitional) gap a bit more, we will now look at what qualitative data collection means in the context of this *Handbook* and of its chapters, although not necessarily all authors will, or have to, agree to this outline.

WHAT IS QUALITATIVE DATA COLLECTION?

The main focus of this book is the variety and diversity of the ways of doing qualitative data collection. Therefore it might be helpful to first outline the common core of qualitative data collection by (1) giving a working definition, followed by (2) discussing the aims of qualitative data collection and finally by (3) looking at theoretical backgrounds and basic methodological approaches.

Definition

In Box 1.1, a rather general definition of qualitative data collection is outlined, which emphasizes the moves toward data for catching meanings or representations.

> **Box 1.1 What is Qualitative Data Collection?**
>
> Qualitative data collection is the selection and production of linguistic (or visual) material for analyzing and understanding phenomena, social fields, subjective and collective experiences and the related meaning-making processes. Meaning-making can refer to subjective or social meanings. Qualitative data collection also is applied to discover and describe issues in the field or structures and processes in routines and practices. Collection can refer to naturally occurring or elicited data. It can be based on talking, listening, observing, analyzing materials as sounds, images or digital phenomena. Data collection can include single or multiple methods. The aim is often to arrive at materials that allow for producing generalizable statements by analyzing and comparing various exemplars, phenomena or cases.

In this definition, several aims of qualitative data collection are already mentioned, which we will address now in a little more detail.

Aims of Qualitative Data Collection

The major aim of collecting qualitative data is to provide materials for an empirical analysis of a phenomenon that a study is about. This has less to do with finding phenomena in the field than with deciding to turn phenomena into something that we can analyze. This 'turning' is based on a number of decisions taken by the researchers. First of all, to decide on something that is relevant and interesting for a study – for example, a problem or process that is not adequately understood yet and is worth being analyzed, described, compared, or explained. Second, to decide about which aspect of this problem or process shall be the focus – some people's experiences with the phenomenon, the unfolding practice related to it, the public perceptions linked to it and the like. This means taking a perspective on the phenomenon and formulating a research question to answer. This has also the consequence that the phenomenon is formatted in a particular way to highlight some aspects, yet putting aside other aspects that are characteristic for it. Third, to take a methodological perspective on the phenomenon and to decide which methodological approach should be taken – such as asking people about their experiences, observing practices and analyzing interactions or materials such as documents, images, sounds or traces of social communication related to the phenomenon. This process should lead to defining a methodological approach for collecting the data that is adequate for understanding the interesting phenomenon, problem, or process. Thus we are not working with 'raw' data but data that are selected, formatted, conceived, and processed on the basis of our research interests and approaches.

A second level of aims of qualitative data collection refers to how to do the collection. What this means in concrete terms and detail, of course, depends on the methodological approach that is taken (see the chapters in this volume). However, for qualitative research, we can formulate some overarching aims for data collection (see Flick, 2014c). The guiding idea here is the appropriateness of methods, theories and approaches as a principle for selecting methods of data collection and for how they are applied. Appropriateness can refer to giving room for the experiences and perspectives of the participants (e.g. in the way we ask them or conceive our observations). But it can also refer to conceiving and adapting our methodological strategies to what we want to study. Thus we will more and more turn to studying materials and objects for covering the development of social phenomena – such as photos (see Eberle, Chapter 25, this volume), sounds (see Bull, Chapter 27, this volume), but also Facebook (see Ditchfield and Meredith, Chapter 32, this volume) or blogs (see Weller et al., Chapter 31, this volume). We will increasingly need to adapt and extend our familiar approaches such as ethnography (see Buscatto, Chapter 21, this volume) to walking with participants through their lifeworlds (for go-alongs, see Kusenbach, Chapter 22, this volume) or videographing the settings and processes we are interested in (see Knoblauch et al., Chapter 23, this volume). Another consequence is that we need to combine multiple methods (several qualitative or qualitative and quantitative methods – see the chapters in Part V, this volume) for understanding a complex phenomenon. And finally it may mean that we turn to existing data (see Corti, Chapter 11, this volume) or to doing our interviews in other languages than our own (see Resch and Enzenhofer, Chapter 9, this volume).

Theoretical Backgrounds and Basic Methodological Approaches

As mentioned earlier, we can identify mainly three basic approaches to collecting data on the methodological level, which are materialized in the traditional forms of data in qualitative research. 1) We can start from individuals' (or group members') knowledge and experiences about an issue and the world surrounding them and collect our data by *talking to people*. Then the participants' reflexivity and ability to report and relate what they experience and know is the researchers' starting point for analyzing social phenomena. 2) We can start from the common, shared or conflicting practices linked to a phenomenon or process and collect our data by *walking to people* and observe what they do and what the context of this doing is like. Then the participants' activities and abilities to do meaningful things in everyday or professional practices are the researchers' starting points for analyzing social phenomena. 3) We can start from *the traces left behind* by people, their practices or social processes, and analyze these traces. Then the traces left behind by people consciously or without being aware of this are the researchers' starting point for analyzing social phenomena, and subjects are not necessarily involved as participants in the research. The traditional forms of data collection for these basic approaches were talking to people in interviews, walking to people in ethnographies, and tracing people's lives by analyzing documents. These traditional forms of data collection have led to more and more proliferating forms of data in qualitative research. Talking to people and interviewing have been extended to semi-structured (see Roulston and Choi, Chapter 15, this volume), narrative (see Murray, Chapter 17, this volume), or episodic (see Flick, Chapter 34, this volume), and expert interviews (see Bogner et al., Chapter 41, this volume), and focus groups (see Morgan and Hofman, Chapter 16, this volume). Walking to people and ethnography have proliferated to observations (see Wästerfors, Chapter 20, this volume), multi-sited ethnographies (see Buscatto, Chapter 21, this volume), visual sociologies (see Eberle, Chapter 25, this volume, and Knoblauch et al., Chapter 23, this volume) and mobile methods (see Kusenbach, Chapter 22, this volume). Tracing people's lives has diversified into analyzing documents (see Rapley and Rees, Chapter 24, this volume), images (see Eberle, Chapter 25, this volume, and Henwood et al., Chapter 38, this volume), media such as films and TV (see Mikos, Chapter 26, this volume), internet documents (see the chapters in Part IV), and finally existing data and archives (see Corti, Chapter 11, this volume). But in the end, researchers are still traveling on the three basic routes to their data – using people's reflexivities and accounts; analyzing their practices; and looking at what is left behind by them and behind their backs in documents of all sorts.

DIVERSIFICATION OF QUALITATIVE RESEARCH

As should have become evident already, qualitative research is in a permanent process of proliferation (see also Flick, 2014b, 2014c, 2018a) and diversification. We now have a growing number of research approaches, which are applied in parallel and exist in competition. First of all, there are different research programs in qualitative research, which have different issues of research, specific methods, and theoretical backgrounds. Examples of these may include more traditional approaches such as grounded theory research (see Kennedy and Thornberg, Chapter 4, this volume), conversation analysis (see Jackson, Chapter 18, this volume), or discourse analysis (see Rau et al., Chapter 19, this volume). These approaches are linked to different interests and methodological principles, but are prominent in both the qualitative research that is done in various fields in research projects and in qualification works such as PhDs or Master's theses. Second, we can see differences in what is understood as qualitative research in the US, in the UK, or for example in Germany (see Flick et al., 2004 and Flick, 2014a for overviews and Knoblauch et al., 2005 for a comparative view on qualitative research in different countries). The first diversification, of course, is also relevant inside each of these national traditions. Third, we find different discourses about qualitative research in different disciplines. Qualitative researchers in psychology have specific interests and problems, as do their colleagues in sociology, for example, but both are not necessarily the same. Fourth, we find a strong development toward qualitative online or digital research (see the chapters in Part IV of this volume). Established methods are transferred and adapted (e.g. online interviewing, see Roulston and Choi, Chapter 15, this volume) and new approaches such as digital ethnography (see Buscatto, Chapter 21, this volume) are developed for analyzing internet-related issues and phenomena. Fifth, a specific understanding of qualitative research as part of a broader enterprise has developed. Qualitative research, then, is either seen as a part of mixed methods research and not necessarily as the junior partner of quantitative research (see Hesse-Biber, Chapter 35, this volume and Morse et al., Chapter 36, this volume), or the awareness that complex social phenomena over-challenge single methods approaches, which leads to combining multiple qualitative methods (see Flick, Chapter 34, this volume; Fielding, Chapter 37, this volume; and Henwood et al., Chapter 38, this volume). Sixth, we see a growing diversity of area-specific discourses about qualitative research. Examples are contracted qualitative research in health sciences, or in management or evaluation. These areas have their special needs and limitations, which are different from, for example, university research in the context of master's or doctoral theses or in the context of 'basic' research (for examples of specific fields of applying qualitative research with specific populations see the chapters in Part VI of this volume).

GLOBALIZATION AS A CHALLENGE FOR QUALITATIVE DATA ANALYSIS

A specific form of diversification still comes as more of a challenge than an established trend. The globalization in general, and of qualitative research in particular, raises issues linked to using qualitative methods for analyzing experiences and issues in the context of migration and in working with refugees. We have addressed this topic in a special issue in *Qualitative Inquiry* (Flick, 2014d). In the contributions, it became evident, that language is a major issue here, in particular if we work with interviews (see Resch and Enzenhofer, Chapter 9, this volume). However, it is also the wider distinctions rooted in cultural diversities that play a role in planning qualitative research, and data collection in particular, in this realm.

If we extend our research in this direction, we face challenges on various levels (see Flick and Röhnsch, 2014, p. 1105). Our concepts of research (e.g. non-directive interviews and ethnography) may not always be compatible with what our participants with a migration or different cultural background expect from social scientists, based on what they have experienced as researchers in their countries of origin. Several authors have discussed how our understanding of using interviews is in conflict with what people with a Russian background, for example, see as research – they expect clear question–answer schemes instead of open-ended questions (see, for example, Fröhlich, 2012; Weaver, 2011). Gobo (2012) has highlighted the implicit assumptions the use of interviews is based on and how these are rooted in a Western, democratic concept of society. A second challenge is to find access to such a hard-to-reach group (see Bengry, Chapter 7, this volume, and Chamberlain and Hodgetts, Chapter 42, this volume) and to overcome language barriers (see Resch and Enzenhofer, Chapter 9, this volume) here. Working with native-speaking researchers may help to bridge the language gap. In some of our own studies, however, Russian-speaking researchers, for example, produced some mistrust in potential participants with a Russian background, based on their associations with interrogations in their countries of origin (Flick and Röhnsch, 2014). In interviews and ethnography, it becomes necessary for qualitative researchers to work with translators and interpreters (Littig and Pöchhacker, 2014). Then we have to take into account the influence of these additional agents on the interview situation and on what is said. Alternatives for dealing with their roles are (1) to try to minimize the translators' influences or (2) to try to make them an explicit part of the research situation (see Resch and Enzenhofer, Chapter 9, this volume). When we want to understand the specific problems and experiences of a migrant group (e.g. Russian-speaking migrants) in the German health and addiction care system, we need to reflect on how to take culture, and cultures, into account when analyzing the data, without neglecting it, but also without overemphasizing it (see Sørensen et al., Chapter 10, this volume). Not to use available support can also be observed in drug users coming from Germany, but the aim of our research is to identify the culture-specific barriers and obstacles. A particular challenge is then to reveal the cultural concepts of addiction behind our interviewees' statements and the differences to our (and the service system's) concepts (see also Flick, 2015).

TRENDS AND CHALLENGES FOR QUALITATIVE DATA COLLECTION

Challenge I: Trends to Clusters, 'Big Data', and 'Big Research'

Novotny (2014) highlighted several trends on the level of the research politics and funding of the European Union. These trends in funding led to advancing 'big research', big data, interdisciplinary research (of social sciences with natural sciences), and the integration of research funding into bigger programs of political program development. For German contexts, we can currently state a trend of research funding toward financing big clusters (of many projects coming from several disciplines). This funding is intended not only to finance the study and answer research questions and social problems, but also (or even more so) to build up and change the structure of universities by establishing clusters of excellence. In Germany, the Research Council had already spent more than half of its budget on such clusters in 2009 (Meier and Schimank, 2014). This trend has been growing at the mercy of the numbers of smaller, projects with less amounts of funding, which had been funded by this source before. In these developments, the chances for obtaining funding for studies like the above example of studying migrants' problems with addiction and with finding access to therapeutical support (Flick and Röhnsch, 2014), become less and less likely.

Challenge II: Ethical Issues and Serendipity in Qualitative Data Collection

Research ethics, informed consent, and a review by an ethics committee are important contributions to making research better and improving researchers' responsibility toward their participants. Following the issues just discussed, a number of practical, and at the same time more general problems, become relevant: If we start interviews, for example, by asking participants for their (informed) consent – are such permissions for doing research, or the informed consents obtained, valid for the reuse of data for all purposes and for every other researcher? What does this mean for clearances by ethics committees? We should reflect how far, in every case, a general permit for collecting data and using them in the current project, and using them in any kind of later project, is desirable. This means the trend to making qualitative data widely available and also independent from the context for which they are originally collected, produces a number of ethical issues and consequences. This can make the actual research much more complicated and questionable.

Working in fields like those in the above example from our research has raised another question: What does it mean if we have obtained beforehand the ethical permissions for interviewing specific people (e.g. drug users or patients) and subsequently find, in running our study that we need other interviewees (e.g. their relatives) or other methods (e.g. for analyzing their interaction with therapists) to answer our research questions?

Such extensions and shifts are not uncommon in a flexible research strategy, such as ethnography or exploratory research projects. As expressed by Robert Merton, this approach to research can also be labeled as 'serendipity' (Merton and Barber, 2004). How far does the (necessary) ethical grounding of our research delimit the flexibility of our research practice in this sense – as an essential of qualitative data collection, different from standardized quantitative research – in an inappropriate way? How do we deal with this?

Challenge III: Reanalysis and Meta-analysis of Qualitative Data

This challenge is based on the expectation that qualitative data should no longer be produced exclusively for the concrete research project for which they are created. Rather, they should be made available for a wider public of researchers or other audiences. In Germany again, we find pressure on funding institutions and research politicians and managers, to build up 'research infrastructures'. Several expectations are linked to developing such infrastructures consisting of archives for qualitative data: First, the expectation that research infrastructures are a precondition for societal relevance of social and qualitative research is mentioned. A second argument refers to the quality of research, seen as depending on the establishment of archiving and the availability of qualitative data, the coding instruments, or the intermediary findings of other researchers.

Archiving Qualitative Data as a New Standard?

The idea of developing such infrastructures is often linked to the idea of building up archives where data are stored, available, and accessible for other researchers and studies. Archiving is linked to a number of questions about qualitative data collection. The first set of these questions refers to the role of context in qualitative data and just how far archiving bears the danger of decontextualizing data and research: Can we use and reuse qualitative data in a meaningful way without really knowing the context of data collection and the methodological particularities and without taking them into account? To analyze qualitative data without being involved in the context of the study, without referring to the original research questions pursued or for which they were produced may lead to rather bloodless and abstract findings. To produce such decontextualized data is not really what qualitative research is about. The aim and claim of archiving data to become a standard procedure in qualitative research and of establishing infrastructures for qualitative research that make data available for reuse by other researchers, means to allow other researchers to take the data out of their original context and to assess and reuse them widely, and may have some appeal. But the challenge is how to really take into account the contexts present in the data, which are an essential part of the narrative interview, for example, in further or reuse of data in secondary analyses? In particular, when data (e.g. statements) are embedded in a more extensive structure such as a narrative or ethnography, it will be difficult to reuse them without seeing this context as essential. This leads to the *major question* here: Which kinds of data, of research, of approaches/schools of research fit into archives and the expectations linked to them?

This trend is not only embedded in making qualitative data available for other researchers but also to make them available for other kinds of research, such as meta-analysis. The second trend here is to reuse and reanalyze qualitative data and to expect that qualitative research will be able to support this, which refers to trends in data *analysis*. Several strategies for qualitative meta-analysis have been discussed now for some time (see Timulak, 2014), such as meta-study and meta-summary.

To go into detail about how the concrete approaches work is beyond this chapter. But two more general remarks seem necessary. First, our discussion does not mean to suggest that it is a bad idea to import the approach of meta-analysis into the realm of qualitative research, *per se*. The more that results can unfold a bigger contribution to answering relevant questions in this way, the better it is. However, again, if such an approach becomes a *general* trend or even a general expectation – in that qualitative data have to be ready for reanalysis – the danger is that a lot of the variety of doing qualitative data collection and of the data we produce will not fit into such reanalysis schemes. For example, statements from interviews will fit into such schemes much more easily than descriptions coming from observation protocols in ethnography. If availability and readiness for reanalysis become pre-conditions for funding or for integrating approaches in teaching, the danger again is that we lose parts of the variety and the openness of qualitative research. The challenges here lead to questions such as, how far does the trend to meta-analysis, meta-synthesis etc. lead to new implicit or explicit standards for qualitative data? And will this reduce the openness and variety in qualitative data collection?

THE ROLE OF DATA IN THE RESEARCH PROCESS

This brief attempt to chart the routes to collecting qualitative data can be summarized by way of some considerations about the role of data in the qualitative research process. If we take up the question of what data are, we should keep in mind, first, that data result from communication with and in the field, when people talk to researchers. Data also result from researchers observing participants' activities and from writing notes about what participants do. Data result from what researchers select as parts of the processes they document. Second, data are researchers' ways of communicating with the field, and with the 'world out there' about the field, and the insights that were available or produced in it. Thus, data are a means of communication between researchers and institutions and audiences. Researchers argue, using the information that people talked to them about. They illustrate this by watching what participants do and then writing about it. Researchers demonstrate how processes worked and went wrong with what was documented as data. And data (and the analysis thereof) provide researchers' with ways of communicating their contribution to understanding and changing routines and social problems in the field.

QUALITATIVE DATA BETWEEN PHENOMENA AND ANALYSIS – OVERVIEW OF THE *HANDBOOK*

The issues mentioned in this brief chart of the routes to collecting qualitative data will be addressed in the major parts and single chapters of the *Handbook* in more detail.

Part II takes a perspective on issues prior to the work of collecting qualitative data and addresses the *concepts*, *contexts*, and *basics* of qualitative data collection. It begins with an outline of a theoretical position on collecting qualitative data against a realist background (see Maxwell, Chapter 2, this volume). The ethical issues of qualitative research that are often strongly linked to collecting qualitative data are discussed in the next chapter (see Mertens, Chapter 3, this volume). A third, rather general issue for qualitative data collection is the approach to inference behind the concrete procedure – inductive, deductive, or abductive reasoning, which are compared in the following chapter (see Kennedy and Thornberg, Chapter 4, this volume). After this block of chapters that deal with more fundamental background concepts, some more practical issues are next at stake. The idea of designing qualitative research is discussed critically and outlined in its practical implication (see Gobo, Chapter 5, this volume), before issues of sampling (see Schreier, Chapter 6, this volume) and field access (see Bengry, Chapter 7, this volume) are treated in detail as major steps on the way to collecting data. This is rounded up with issues of recording and transcribing social interaction (see Jenks, Chapter 8, this volume). This, more practically oriented, block of chapters is followed by articles addressing contextual issues of data collection. It is becoming more and more apparent that qualitative research is increasingly facing the problem of working with participants in multilingual societies and collecting data in other languages (see Resch and Enzenhofer, Chapter 9, this volume). This is not only a technical issue but also linked to more general challenges, such as what comparison means, both in this context (see Sørensen et al., Chapter 10, this volume) and in general. A specific extension of the classic setting of data collection is the secondary analysis of already existing or archived data, which raises questions of what it means to do data collection in this approach (see Corti, Chapter 11, this volume). The next two chapters question classical concepts of data collection from two angles. First, the discussion about using naturalistic data instead of eliciting them with specific methods is discussed, because also naturalistic data have to be collected to turn phenomena into data (see Potter and Shaw, Chapter 12, this volume). The skepticism against the concept of data in general is unfolded in the next chapter with a stronger emphasis of performance and interpretation (see Denzin, Chapter 13, this volume). This part is rounded up with considerations about the quality of data collection in qualitative research (see Barbour, Chapter 14, this volume).

Part III takes a stronger focus on the practicalities of data collection and on various types of qualitative data and the methods that are available for collecting them.

It comprises three basic groups of qualitative data – verbal, ethnographic, and material data. The first block focuses five chapters on collecting *verbal data* and the methods used for collecting them. In the first chapter, ways of doing qualitative interviews are presented (see Roulston and Choi, Chapter 15, this volume) before focus groups are discussed as an alternative (see Morgan and Hoffman, Chapter 16, this volume). Narrative data can go beyond narrative interviews, but are a form of putting experiences, processes and developments into words (see Murray, Chapter 17, this volume). Conversation analysis (see Jackson, Chapter 18, this volume) takes a different, more formal stance to verbal data and to data collection, with its emphasis on naturally occurring data, but is confronted with the issues of the preceding chapters in Part II as well. Discourse analysis brings the formal aspect (how people, media etc. communicate about something) and the content aspect (what is mentioned in a discourse and what is not) back together again (see Rau et al., Chapter 19, this volume). In the second block of four chapters, the focus shifts to collecting data for *observation* and *ethnography*. The various forms of using observational data with and without participation are the first issue here (see Wästerfors, Chapter 20, this volume) before ways and reasons for doing ethnography are discussed (see Buscatto, Chapter 21, this volume). The remaining two chapters in this block extend the perspective in different ways by adding a mobile component to the classical ethnographic attitude of 'being there' (for go-alongs, see Kusenbach, Chapter 22, this volume) and integrating the use of video in this context (see Knoblauch et al., Chapter 23, this volume). The third block of four chapters extends the perspective beyond the rather classical verbal and observational data to *material data*. Here again, the use of documents, a type of data with a long history of being used in qualitative research is addressed (see Rapley and Rees, Chapter 24, this volume). More specific is the focus on the chapters addressing images (see Eberle, Chapter 25, this volume), media, film, and TV studies (see Mikos, Chapter 26, this volume), or sounds (see Bull, Chapter 27, this volume) as qualitative data.

In recent years, a specific kind of data has become more and more important as an extension of what has been used as qualitative data over the years, which is addressed in Part IV – *digital* and *internet data*. As a first step, the concept of data in digital research is discussed for its particular characteristics (see Lindgren, Chapter 28, this volume). Flow as an epistemological and practical approach is outlined next (see Markham and Gammelby, Chapter 29, this volume), before the specific challenges of ethics in digital research are discussed (see Tiidenberg, Chapter 30, this volume). More specific forms of digital qualitative data are the subjects of the next two chapters, which address blogs (see Weller et al., Chapter 31, this volume) and Facebook (see Ditchfield and Meredith, Chapter 32, this volume) as sources for qualitative studies. In the final chapter in this part, a critical reflection about the concept of data in digital research is to be found (see Markham, Chapter 33, this volume).

A different kind of extension of the traditional use of one kind of qualitative data is the subject of Part V, which focuses on *triangulation* and *mixed methods*. In the first chapter in this part, the triangulation of multiple qualitative methods and the use of various types of qualitative data are unfolded in more detail (see Flick, Chapter 34, this volume). The next two chapters address the use of qualitative data in a mixed methods context and in particular in a qualitatively driven mixed methods approach (see Hesse-Biber, Chapter 35, this volume, and Morse et al., Chapter 36, this volume). More specific combinations are the topics of the next two chapters – the combination of digital and physical data (see Fielding, Chapter 37, this volume) and of photographs and interviews (see Henwood et al., Chapter 38, this volume).

The last part (Part VI) of the *Handbook* addresses *collecting data in specific populations*. Here a large variety of populations could be used as examples, but the ones represented here approach the field on two dimensions from extreme points: (1) Children (see MacDougall and Darbyshire, Chapter 39, this volume) and older people (see Stephens et al., Chapter 40, this volume) mark the dimension of age; and (2) Experts and elites (see Bogner et al., Chapter 41, this volume) and hard-to-reach groups (see Chamberlain and Hodgetts, Chapter 42, this volume) mark the dimension of establishment and positionality.

CONCLUSION

All in all, this *Handbook* is designed to provide those who are involved in collecting qualitative data with an awareness of many of the contemporary debates in the field. It is less designed to provide definitive answers to what is the best approach to collecting data but, rather, to introduce the variety of ways scholars are addressing qualitative data collection from different disciplinary, conceptual, epistemological, and methodological standpoints. It will provide practical tips on using the methods outlined in detail as well as conceptual discussion of the major intellectual challenges of each method. It is designed to increase the sensitivity of the strengths and limits of the various methodological alternatives and also for the specific challenges coming from various – traditional and new – phenomena and the types of data for analysing these phenomena.

FURTHER READING

Denzin, Norman K., and Lincoln, Yvonna S. (eds.) (2018a) *The SAGE Handbook of Qualitative Research* (5th edn). London and Thousand Oaks, CA: Sage.
Flick, Uwe (ed.) (2014a) *The SAGE Handbook of Qualitative Data Analysis*. London and Thousand Oaks, CA: Sage.
Flick, Uwe (2014c) *An Introduction to Qualitative Research* (5th edn). London and Thousand Oaks, CA: Sage.
Flick, Uwe (ed.) (2018a) *The SAGE Qualitative Research Kit* (2nd edn). London and Thousand Oaks, CA: Sage.

REFERENCES

Charmaz, Kathy (2014) *Constructing Grounded Theory: A Practical Guide Through Qualitative Analysis* (2nd edn). London: Sage.
Clarke, Adele (2005) *Situational Analysis. Grounded Theory after the Postmodern Turn*. Thousand Oaks, CA: Sage.
Denzin, Norman K., and Lincoln, Yvonna S. (eds.) (2011a) *The SAGE Handbook of Qualitative Research* (4th edn). London and Thousand Oaks, CA: Sage.
Denzin, Norman K., and Lincoln, Yvonna S. (2011b) 'Introduction: The discipline and practice of qualitative research', in Norman K. Denzin and Yvonna S. Lincoln (eds.), *The SAGE Handbook of Qualitative Research* (4th edn). Thousand Oaks, CA: Sage, pp. 1–20.
Denzin, Norman K., and Lincoln, Yvonna S. (eds.) (2018a) *The SAGE Handbook of Qualitative Research* (5th edn). London and Thousand Oaks, CA: Sage.
Denzin, Norman K., and Lincoln, Yvonna S. (2018b) 'Introduction: The discipline and practice of qualitative research', in Norman K. Denzin and Yvonna S. Lincoln (eds.), *The SAGE Handbook of Qualitative Research* (5th edn). Thousand Oaks, CA: Sage, pp. 1–26.
Flick, Uwe (ed.) (2014a) *The SAGE Handbook of Qualitative Data Analysis*. London and Thousand Oaks, CA: Sage.
Flick, Uwe (2014b) 'Mapping the field', in Uwe Flick (ed.), *The SAGE Handbook of Qualitative Data Analysis*. London and Thousand Oaks, CA: Sage, pp. 3–18.
Flick, Uwe (2014c) *An Introduction to Qualitative Research* (5th edn). London and Thousand Oaks, CA: Sage.
Flick, Uwe (ed.) (2014d) 'Special issue "Qualitative research as global endeavour"', *Qualitative Inquiry, 20* (9): 1059–127.
Flick, Uwe (2015) 'Qualitative inquiry – 2.0 at 20?: Developments, trends, and challenges

for the politics of research', *Qualitative Inquiry,* 21 (7): 599–608.

Flick, Uwe (ed.) (2018a) *The SAGE Qualitative Research Kit* (2nd edn). London and Thousand Oaks, CA: Sage.

Flick, Uwe (2018b) *Doing Grounded Theory* (Book 8 of the *SAGE Qualitative Research Kit*, 2nd edn). London, Thousand Oaks, CA, Delhi: Sage.

Flick, Uwe (2018c) *Designing Qualitative Research* (Book 1 of the *SAGE Qualitative Research Kit*, 2nd edn). London, Thousand Oaks, CA, Delhi: Sage.

Flick, Uwe, and Röhnsch, Gundula. (2014) 'Migrating diseases: Triangulating approaches – Applying qualitative inquiry as a global endeavor', *Qualitative Inquiry,* 20, (10): 1096–109.

Flick, Uwe, Kardorff, Ernst von, and Steinke, Ines (eds.) (2004) *A Companion to Qualitative Research.* London, Thousand Oaks, CA, New Delhi: Sage.

Fröhlich, Christian. (2012) 'Interviewforschung im russisch-sprachigen Raum – ein Balanceakt zwischen methodologischen und feldspezifischen Ansprüchen [Interview research in the Russian-speaking area – An act balancing between methodological and field specific demands]', in Jan Kruse, Stephanie Bethmann, Debora Niemann, and Christian Schmieder (eds.), *Qualitative Interviewforschung in und mit fremden Sprachen.* Weinheim, Germany: Beltz Juventa, pp. 186–202.

Gitelman, Lisa (ed.) (2013) *Raw Data is an Oxymoron.* Boston, MA: MIT Press.

Glaser, Barney G. (1992) *Basics of Grounded Theory Analysis: Emergence vs. Forcing.* Mill Valley, CA: Sociology Press.

Gobo, Giampietro (2012) 'Glocalizing methodology? The encounter between local methodologies', *International Journal of Social Research Methodology,* 14 (6): 417–37.

Knoblauch, Hubert, Flick, Uwe, and Maeder, Christof (eds.) (2005) 'Special issue "The state of the art of qualitative research in Europe"', *Forum Qualitative Social Research,* 6 (3): September, available at http://www.qualitative-research.net/fqs/fqs-e/inhalt3-05-e.htm.

Littig, Beate, and Pöchhacker, Franz (2014) 'Socio-translational collaboration in qualitative inquiry: The case of expert interviews', *Qualitative Inquiry,* 20 (9): 1085–95.

Meier, Frank and Schimank, Uwe (2014) 'Cluster-building and the transformation of the university', *Soziologie,* 43 (2): 139–66.

Merton, Robert K., and Barber, Elinor (2004) *The Travels and Adventures of Serendipity: A Study in Sociological Semantics and the Sociology of Science.* Princeton, NJ: Princeton University Press.

Novotny, Helga (2014) Ein gemeinnütziges Labor für die Gesellschaft. In Institut für Höhere Studien (ed.), *50 Jahre Institut für Höhere Studien – Festschrift.* Vienna: Institut für Höhere Studien, pp. 16–21.

St. Pierre, Elizabeth Adams (2011) 'Post qualitative research: The critique and the coming after', in Norman K. Denzin and Yvonna S. Lincoln (eds.), *Handbook of Qualitative Research* (4th edn). Thousand Oaks, CA: Sage, pp. 611–26.

Timulak, Ladislav (2014) 'Qualitative meta-analysis', in Uwe Flick (ed.), *The SAGE Handbook of Qualitative Data Analysis.* London: Sage, pp. 481–95.

Weaver, Dorothy (2011) 'Neither too scientific nor a spy: Negotiating the ethnographic interview in Russia', *Comparative Sociology,* 10: 145–57.

PART II
Concepts, Contexts, Basics

Part II outlines *concepts*, *contexts* and *basics* of qualitative data collection in thirteen chapters. *Concepts* discussed include: what are the implications of specific topics and frameworks, like theory (see Maxwell, Chapter 2, this volume) and ethics (see Mertens, Chapter 3, this volume) for collecting qualitative data? And how are issues of inference (deduction, induction, and abduction – see Kennedy and Thornberg, Chapter 4, this volume) currently reflected, discussed and solved in qualitative data collection?

Contexts to be discussed here are questions of sampling material that become relevant for data collection (see Schreier, Chapter 6, this volume) or finding access to the research field (see Bengry, Chapter 7, this volume). Technical aspects such as recording and transcription (see Jenks, Chapter 8, this volume), working with secondary data (see Corti, Chapter 11, this volume) and comparison (see Sørenson et al., Chapter 10, this volume) are complemented by more general issues like working with naturalistic data (see Potter and Shaw, Chapter 12, this volume) and questions about the role of data as a concept (see Denzin, Chapter 13, this volume).

Basics to be discussed here include research designs (see Gobo, Chapter 5, this volume), working with data in other languages (see Resch and Enzenhofer, Chapter 9, this volume) and the quality of qualitative data collection (see Barbour, Chapter 14, this volume).

Guideline questions as an orientation for writing chapters were the following: how has this issue become relevant for the collection of qualitative data? What are basic assumptions of this concept? What are differing ways to deal with this issue in collecting qualitative data? What is the impact of these alternatives on the collection of data? What are new developments and perspectives in this context? What is the contribution of the concept/discussion to the collection of qualitative data and critical reflection of it?

Reading the chapters in Part II should help to answer questions like the following ones for a study and its method(s): what is the impact on producing qualitative data from context matters like theory, research ethics or selecting materials? How do we refer to subjective experience and culture in qualitative data collection? How do we develop insights in qualitative data collection? How do aims and strategies of comparison influence the process of qualitative data collection?

In answering questions like the ones just mentioned, the chapters in this part are meant to contribute to the contextualization of specific approaches to collecting qualitative data and highlight the impact of the ways in which the data are produced and made up for their analysis.

Collecting Qualitative Data: A Realist Approach

Joseph A. Maxwell

INTRODUCTION

This chapter considers qualitative data collection from the perspective of realism, a philosophical position that has gained significant attention in discussions of research and evaluation methods (e.g. Clark, 2008; Hammersley, 1992, 1998, 2008, 2009; Maxwell, 1990a, 1990b, 1992, 2012a, 2012b; Madill, 2008; Pawson, 2006; Pawson and Tilley, 1997; Sayer, 1992). I argue that this position has important implications for qualitative research, including qualitative data collection. In this chapter, I provide a brief introduction to realism, and then discuss how this approach can inform the theory and practice of qualitative data collection.

WHAT IS REALISM?

There are many varieties of realism across the philosophical landscape. In this chapter, I focus on what is often called 'critical realism,' a term that is usually associated (at least in the UK) with the work of the philosopher Roy Bhaskar (1975, 1978, 1989, 2011; Archer et al., 1998)[1]. However, this term was used even earlier (apparently independently of Bhaskar's work) by the American social researcher and methodologist Donald Campbell (1974, p. 432; Cook and Campbell, 1979, pp. 28–30). For both Bhaskar and Campbell, a key feature of critical realism is the combination of ontological realism (the belief that there is a real world that exists independently of our perceptions and constructions) with epistemological constructivism (our *understanding* of the world is inevitably our own construction; there can be no perception or understanding of reality that is not mediated by our conceptual 'lens') (Bhaskar, 1989, pp. 12–25; Campbell, 1988, p. 447).

Many other philosophers and methodologists, including some well-known qualitative researchers (Hammersley, 1992, 1998;

Huberman and Miles, 1985), have taken similar positions, but used a variety of different terms for these, obscuring the widespread acceptance of this stance (Madill, 2008). One prominent advocate of realism in social research has explicitly aligned himself with Campbell's critical realism, rather than Bhaskar's more recent advocacy of what he called 'dialectical critical realism' (Pawson, 2006, p. 20). For this reason, I will use the term 'critical realism' broadly, to include a range of positions that explicitly combine ontological realism with epistemological constructivism. (For a more detailed discussion of these issues, and their implications for qualitative research, see Maxwell, 2012b.)

Following Kuhn's and others' demonstrations that all observation is 'theory-laden', and that our understanding of the world is inherently shaped by our prior ideas and assumptions about the world, a constructivist epistemology has been widely, although often implicitly, accepted by researchers. For example, Shadish et al., in their influential work on experimental and quasi-experimental designs, stated that 'all scientists are epistemological constructivists and relativists' (2002, p. 29); there is no possibility of purely 'objective' or 'theory-neutral' description independent of some particular perspective and theoretical stance. This is consistent with our common-sense belief that our everyday perceptions and interpretations may be mistaken.

Similarly, most of us accept a realist ontology in our everyday lives. When our cars break down, we believe that there is a real problem that a mechanic can identify and repair. Most of us also believe that global warming is a real phenomenon that is occurring independently of our beliefs about this. Thomas Schwandt, in his *Dictionary of Qualitative Research*, argued that

> On a daily basis, most of us probably behave as garden-variety empirical realists – that is, we act as if the objects in the world (things, events, structures, people, meanings, etc.) exist as independent in some way from our experience with them. We also regard society, institutions, feelings, intelligence, poverty, disability, and so on as being just as real as the toes on our feet and the sun in the sky. (2015, p. 264)

Although realism is often (incorrectly) associated with quantitative rather than qualitative approaches, a realist ontology 'is compatible with many qualitative methods and is the position of choice of many qualitative researchers' (Madill, 2008, p. 731).

However, a substantial number of qualitative researchers have adopted, at least in their espoused philosophical views, a thoroughgoing constructivism that denies the existence of any reality external to our constructions, a position most systematically developed by Guba and Lincoln (1989; Lincoln and Guba, 2013). A key argument for this view has been that a constructivist stance on epistemology makes a realist ontology irrelevant, since we have no way to access this 'reality' that avoids the constraints of a constructivist epistemology (Smith, 2008; Smith and Deemer, 2000). Lincoln similarly argued that 'the naturalistic/constructivist paradigm effectively brought about the irrelevance of the distinction between ontology and epistemology' (1995, p. 286), leading to what Lincoln and Guba called the 'ontological/epistemological collapse' (2000, pp. 175–6).

Certainly, a constructivist epistemology rules out the possibility of any direct or 'objective' perception of reality. However, Lincoln's and Smith's arguments ignore the possibility of *testing* our theories about reality, seeking evidence that allows us to assess the plausibility of these theories (Campbell, 1984; Maxwell, 2012b, chapter 8). While this strategy can never lead to a complete or certain understanding, it does enable us to *improve* the ability of our theories and interpretations to capture something about the phenomena we study, and thus to increase our ability to deal with these phenomena.

A classic statement of this position was by Herbert Blumer, the main architect of the approach termed 'symbolic interactionism', an important influence on the development of qualitative research (Williams, 2008). Blumer argued that

> I shall begin with the redundant assertion that an empirical science presupposes the existence of an empirical world. Such an empirical world exists as something available for observation, study, and analysis. It *stands over against* the scientific observer, with a character that has to be dug out and established through observation, study, and analysis ... 'Reality' for empirical science exists only in the empirical world. (1969, pp. 21–2)

However, Blumer joined this ontological realism with epistemological constructivism (although, since this term was not available to him, he referred to this position as 'idealism'). He asserted that

> the empirical necessarily exists always in the form of human pictures and conceptions of it. However, this does not shift 'reality', as so many conclude, from the empirical world to the realm of imagery and conception ... [This] position is untenable because the empirical world can 'talk back' to our pictures of it or assertions about it – talk back in the sense of challenging and resisting, or not bending to, our images or conceptions of it. (1969, p. 22)

The combination of a realist ontology and a constructivist epistemology is not only an important (if often implicit) stance in qualitative research, but is a prominent feature of our everyday strategies for dealing with the world. The philosopher Hilary Putnam stated that

> The notion that our words and life are constrained by a reality not of our own invention plays a deep role in our lives and is to be respected. The source of the puzzlement lies in the common philosophical error of supposing that the term 'reality' must refer to a single superthing instead of looking at the ways in which we endlessly renegotiate – and are *forced* to renegotiate – our notion of reality as our language and our life develop. (1999, p. 9)

Ontological realism is also shared by many versions of pragmatism (Maxcy, 2003, p. 56; Biesta, 2010, p. 111); Putnam said he should have called his version of realism 'pragmatic realism' (Kuenne, 2002, pp. 149–50). Buchler (1940) said of Charles Peirce, the founder of American pragmatism, that

> Underlying every phase of Peirce's thought is his realism. The supposition that there are real things – the real is 'that whose characters are independent of what anybody may think them to be' – he regards as the 'fundamental hypothesis' of science, for it alone explains the manner in which minds are compelled to agreement. (p. xiv)

There are a number of positions typically incorporated in critical realism that are particularly compatible with qualitative research. First, most critical realists hold that *meaning* (including concepts, beliefs, intentions, values, and other 'mental' phenomena) is just as real as physical phenomena (as implied in the Schwandt quote above); we simply don't have access to the kinds of evidence about these that we have for many physical entities. This acceptance of the reality of mental phenomena is a major difference between critical realism and logical positivism. The latter was fundamentally anti-realist in rejecting any reference to 'unobservable' entities unless they could be 'operationally defined' in terms of the methods and data we use to gain an understanding of these; positivists typically denied that theoretical terms were more than 'convenient fictions' that were useful in prediction, but had no claim to any 'reality'.

However, the actual nature of mental phenomena, and their relationship to physical phenomena, is currently a contested issue in philosophy. The most credible theory, in my view, is that of the philosopher Hilary Putnam (1999), who argued for the legitimacy of both 'mental' and 'physical' ways of making sense of the world, and for a distinction between mental and physical *perspectives* or languages, both referring to reality, but from different conceptual standpoints. This is a rejection of both reductionist physicalism (mental phenomena will ultimately be reducible to physical, e.g. neurological, phenomena) and dualism (mind and matter are separate, independent, and irreducible entities with nothing in common). The 'mental' framework pertains to phenomena that might, in principle, also be conceptualized in physical terms, but it provides an essential perspective on these phenomena that physical theories currently lack, and for which the latter may never be able to substitute (Maxwell, 2012b, chapter 2).

Thus, for critical realists in the social sciences, the meanings, beliefs, and values held by individuals are *part of* the reality that we seek to understand, although an epistemologically distinct part from observable physical objects and behavior. From this perspective, qualitative data and interpretations are data about real phenomena, including behavior, meanings, and the processes that connect these.

Second, critical realists assert the reality of *causation*, a concept that has been rejected by many qualitative researchers for some of the same reasons that they rejected ontological realism (Maxwell, 2012a, 2012b, chapter 3). Accepting the 'reality' of causation seemed to acknowledge the existence of objective causal 'laws' that were independent of particular situations and the beliefs of participants; Guba and Lincoln (1989) asserted that 'there exist multiple, socially constructed realities ungoverned by natural laws, causal or otherwise' (p. 86) and that '"causes" and "effects" do not exist except by imputation' (p. 44). This assumption was based on a largely accurate perception of the positivist 'covering law' view of causation, which accepted Hume's argument that all we could know of causation was the observable regularities in associations of events, and which rejected any reference to unobservable entities and mechanisms. This view inherently privileges quantitative research, with randomized experiments as the 'gold standard' for causal investigation (Maxwell, 2004).

Unfortunately, qualitative researchers' rejection of causation failed to recognize that an alternative, realist view of causation was being developed at about the same time, following the demise of logical positivism. In this view, causation inherently refers to the actual (even if unobservable) mechanisms and processes that result in particular outcomes (e.g. Salmon, 1989, 1998). In this view, 'explanatory knowledge opens up the black boxes of nature to reveal their inner workings. It exhibits the ways in which the things we want to explain come about' (Salmon, 1989, p. 182). This alternative understanding of causation is particularly compatible with qualitative research, with its emphasis on the processes taking place in specific settings (Maxwell, 2012a). In a report on a realist qualitative study, Fletcher (2016) stated, 'I identify two key causal mechanisms shaping the lives of farm women and suggest a future direction for feminist political economy theory to more effectively analyze women's work in agricultural contexts' (p. 1).

This stance also permits combining mental and physical perspectives in a single theory, and accepts that mental phenomena are causally connected to physical ones. As the critical realist Bhaskar stated,

> Two crude philosophical distinctions, between mind and body and reasons and causes, have done untold damage here ... reasons, and social forms generally, must be causes (as well as effects) ... we have to see the natural and social dimensions of existence as in continuous dynamic causal interaction. (1989, p. 6)

Finally, critical realism emphasizes the importance of *context*. The positivist approach to causation focused on *general* causal laws, and ignored (or treated simply as 'error') the influence of contexts on outcomes. In contrast, the mechanisms postulated in a realist causal theory are seen not as general laws, or as having invariant outcomes, but as situationally contingent; their actual context is inextricably part of the causal process (Cartwright, 1999: 73; Little, 1998, 197 ff.; Pawson and Tilley, 1997). The focus of qualitative research on particular contexts and processes, mental and social as well as physical, provides a powerful tool for understanding the actual causal interactions that led to a specific outcome in that situation.

A realist ontology has many broader implications for qualitative research – for example, questioning the ontological status of the 'preconceptualized experience' postulated by some phenomenological approaches. However, the remainder of this chapter focuses on the collection of qualitative data, through interviewing, observation, and other means, and how a realist perspective can suggest ways to make these more productive. The primary emphasis is on seeing qualitative data, not simply as texts to be interpreted, or as the constructions of participants (although they obviously may be these), but as *evidence* about the real phenomena (physical, behavioral, and mental) that the researcher wants to understand (Maxwell, 2012b, chapter 8). This inherently involves issues of validity, but the focus will be on theories of, and procedures for, data collection.

It is also useful to view research designs as real entities – not simply a plan *for* the research, but also the actual conceptualizations and practices employed in the study, which may be different from the intended or stated design (Maxwell, 2013). Kaplan (1964, p. 8) described this as the difference between the 'reconstructed logic' and the 'logic-in-use' of a study. The 'reconstructed design' includes what may be presented in a proposal or research publication, or even what the researcher *believes* about the study; the 'design-in-use' is the design as realized 'on the ground', in the actual conduct of the research. A planned 'unobtrusive' observation, or an 'open-ended' interview, may be reactive or leading in ways that the researcher isn't aware of, and researchers may have goals, assumptions, and questions that they haven't consciously recognized. Thus, a realist stance implies a reflective and critical attitude toward one's own beliefs, plans, and actions.

There are several implications of critical realism that apply generally to all strategies for qualitative data collection. The first is that, because context matters, the results of any qualitative study are *local* results, with no inherent generalizability or transferability. Systematic attention to sampling issues can support the *internal* generalizability of the results to the particular setting, case, or population studied, but generalization or transferability beyond these depends on different sorts of arguments and evidence (Maxwell and Chmiel, 2014). In addition, the transferability of conclusions about the *processes* occurring in a particular case or population doesn't imply that the *outcomes* will necessarily be the same in other contexts (Becker, 1991; Cartwright and Hardie, 2012).

Similarly, data collection (and analysis) strategies need to be appropriate to the context in which they are used; there are no generic strategies that can automatically be applied in any situation to provide valid results. There is general agreement, across measurement, quantitative, and qualitative approaches, that *no* method or design guarantees the validity of the inferences or conclusions (Brinberg and McGrath, 1985; Maxwell, 2017; Messick, 1995, 1998; Phillips, 1987, p. 121; Shadish et al., 2002). Certainly methods matter, but they can never be assumed to generate valid data or conclusion without consideration of contextual issues, as well as of the purposes and questions the data are intended to address.

Finally, a realist focus on local and context-specific phenomena needs to recognize that individuals and situations are diverse, and thus that qualitative researchers need to use methods that respect and clarify that diversity. Both quantitative and qualitative methods contain biases that, intentionally or inadvertently, tend to conceal the existence of diversity and make it more difficult to understand its nature and influence (Maxwell, 2012b, chapter 4). In quantitative research, data on a diverse set of individuals or settings are typically reduced to a mean value (Rose, 2016), and diversity itself is summarized as the 'standard deviation' of that data from the mean, ignoring the complex reality of that diversity.

However, qualitative research, which accepts the particularity of its subject and is aimed at developing in-depth understandings of single cases or small samples, also has methodological biases toward uniformity. The sample size and sampling strategies used in qualitative studies are often inadequate to identify and characterize the actual diversity that exists in the setting or population studied. In addition, qualitative researchers often use data collection and analysis methods that emphasize uniformity, such as relying on key informants and focusing on shared themes and concepts. An important step toward avoiding these errors is to recognize both the reality of diversity and the potential for uniformist biases in interpreting this.

RESEARCHER SUBJECTIVITY AND RESEARCH RELATIONSHIPS

In order to obtain data about the settings or participants that qualitative researchers select, they need to establish *relationships*, both with potential participants, and with gatekeepers or other influential persons who may control or facilitate access to these settings or participants. With few exceptions, researchers need to actually interact (including electronic interaction) with participants and other people in the settings they study. Hammersley and Atkinson (2007, pp. 16–22) referred to this interaction as 'reflexivity': 'the fact that we are part of the social world we study' (p. 21) and must therefore understand how we influence, and are influenced by, this world. This mutual influence is both a necessary aspect and facilitator of data collection, and a potential validity threat to your conclusions.

The personal characteristics that you bring to the research play a major role in this interaction. There is a saying that in quantitative research, the researcher *has* instruments, but in qualitative research, the researcher *is* the instrument (Brodsky, 2008). These two components of methods, the researcher's identity and perspective, and the research relationships that these influence, are part of the actual methods used in the research. Here, I use 'methods' in a broad sense that includes all of the things that the researcher actually does to acquire and make sense of the data collected. By calling this a 'realist' model, I mean that I see these components (as well as others not discussed here) not simply as theoretical abstractions or methodological principles, but as real phenomena, things that have an influence on the research, the data collected, and the conclusions.

Researcher Subjectivity

The traditional view of 'subjectivity', derived from logical positivism, treats this as 'bias', something to be eliminated, or at least controlled, in the interest of 'objectivity'. The collapse of positivism implies that no such 'immaculate perception' exists, and that the standpoint of the researcher is inevitably involved in, and interacts with, the data that are collected; this is a major reason for the 'epistemological constructivism' of critical realism. This perspective requires the researcher to take account of the actual beliefs, values, and dispositions that she brings to the study, which can serve as valuable resources, as well as possible sources of distortion or lack of comprehension.

The grain of truth in the traditional view of subjectivity as bias (with which critical realists would agree) is that researchers' personal (and often unexamined) motives, beliefs, and theories have important consequences for the validity of their conclusions. If your research decisions and data analyses are based on personal desires or theoretical commitments *without* a careful assessment of the implications of these for your methods and conclusions, you are in danger of creating a flawed study or reaching incorrect conclusions.

However, rather than treating subjectivity as a variable to be controlled and ideally reduced to zero, critical realists see it as a component of the actual process of understanding, one that can have a variety of consequences, both good and bad. Even researchers who take an interpretive or constructivist stance toward qualitative research often approach this process in ways that are quite consistent with a critical realist understanding. For example, Tappan states,

> the interpreter's perspective and understanding initially shapes his interpretation of a given phenomenon, but that interpretation is open to revision and elaboration as it interacts with the phenomenon in question, and as the perspective and understanding of the interpreter, including his biases and blind spots, are revealed and evaluated. (2001, p. 50)

The main issue for data collection is *how*, specifically, one becomes aware of this subjectivity and its consequences, and how one uses this subjectivity productively in the research. One strategy for understanding the influence of these beliefs and prior experiences on your research is reflective analysis and writing, or what qualitative researchers often call 'memos'.[2] Peshkin, in order to better understand his own subjectivity during his study of a multiethnic school and community (1991), 'looked for the warm and the cool spots, the emergence of positive and negative feelings, the experiences I wanted to have more of or to avoid' (p. 287), and recorded these on 5 × 8-inch cards. (A diary or field journal, or a computer file of memos, would also work, but index cards allow more immediacy of recording.) In analyzing these cards, he identified six 'I's' – aspects of his identity that influenced his research – and was able to better understand both the benefits and the risks of these identities.

Another strategy is an exercise that I call a 'researcher identity memo'. The purpose of this memo is to help students examine their background, purposes, assumptions, feelings, and values as they relate to their research, and to discover what resources and potential concerns their identity and experience may create. Preissle (2008) refers to such memos, which may be published as well as used for personal reflection, as 'subjectivity statements'. For more discussion, and examples of such memos, see Maxwell (2013, chapter 3).

Research Relationships

The second component of the researcher's role is the researcher's relationships with those studied. This relationship is usually addressed in qualitative methods books and research reports, but it has often been reduced to narrow and oversimplified concepts such as 'entry', 'access', or 'rapport', something to be 'attained' at some point. These concepts obscure the complexity of research relationships, which are real, evolving phenomena that shape the context within which the research is conducted, and have a profound influence on the research and its results. Thus, their actual nature and operation need to be understood in order to use them productively. As stated earlier, these relationships are an essential part of the 'design-in-use' of a study; they form one component of the methods that the researcher uses to collect data, as well as influencing the analysis of these data. Hammersley and Atkinson argued:

> Once we abandon the idea that the social character of research can be standardized out or avoided by becoming a 'fly on the wall' or a 'full participant', the role of the researcher as active participant in the research process becomes clear. (2007, p. 17)

There are several potential pitfalls in developing relationships with participants. Seidman (1998, pp. 80–2) argued that it is possible to have too much rapport, as well as too little, but the *nature* of the relationship, and its consequences, and not simply the *amount* of rapport, is critical. 'Rapport' may be an exploitative or oppressive imposition on a participant; Burman (2001, p. 263) criticized the concept of rapport as a commodification of relationship into manipulative strategies to promote disclosure. Lawrence-Lightfoot and Hoffman Davis (1997, p. 135) also criticized the tendency to treat relationship as a tool or strategy for gaining access to data, rather than as a connection. They argued that 'relationships that are complex, fluid, symmetric, and reciprocal – that are shaped by both researchers and actors – reflect a more responsible ethical stance *and* are likely to yield deeper data and better social science' (1997, pp. 137–8), and emphasized the continual creation and renegotiation of trust, intimacy, and reciprocity. From a realist perspective, this involves seeing research relationships neither as variables to be controlled or manipulated, nor simply as 'constructions' created by the researcher and/or participants, but instead as real, complex processes that have profound, and often unanticipated, consequences for the research. Glesne (2011, pp. 141–50), Tolman and Brydon-Miller (2001), and McGinn (2008) provide detailed discussions of the different aspects of field relations that need to be considered in planning and conducting a qualitative study.

However, there is often an unstated assumption that difference *per se* is an inherent problem for relationship and dialog, one that must be overcome by recognizing or creating commonalities. This is a belief with deep roots in Western social thought (Maxwell, 2012a, chapter 4), one that has been challenged by postmodernism. Critical realism is consistent with the postmodern view that diversity is real and fundamental; researchers need to guard against romantic and illusory assumptions of equality and intimacy that distort the actual relationships they engage in, and they need to develop strategies that enable them to understand the actual nature, amount, and consequences of diversity in their relationships, as discussed above.

DATA COLLECTION METHODS

The main implication of realism for qualitative data collection is that data are usefully seen, not simply as 'texts' to be interpreted, or as the 'constructions' of participants (although some of them are these), but as *evidence* for real phenomena and processes (including mental phenomena and processes). These data can be used to make *inferences* about these phenomena, which can then be tested against additional data. This follows directly from the basic premises of critical realism: that there is a real world that we seek to understand, but that our understandings of this world are inevitably incomplete and fallible, and unavoidably shaped by the particular assumptions and perspective that we bring to the research – the 'lens' through which we view the world.

A key implication of this view for data collection is the importance, in planning and conducting data collection, to consider how the data that you collect can enable you to develop and test your emerging understandings of the phenomena you are studying. Both the use of data to develop theory and the 'verification of statements against data' (Strauss and Corbin, 1990, p. 108) are key aspects of the 'grounded theory' approach to qualitative research, but the latter use of data, to explicitly test your ideas, is less commonly addressed in the qualitative literature. This is sometimes equated with the 'hypothesis testing' of quantitative research, and seen as inappropriate for qualitative research.

However, thinking about the data that you could collect in terms of how these could expand, support, or test your current understandings is not the same as the statistical testing of prior, theoretically derived hypotheses, which in any case is now highly problematic in quantitative research (Cohen, 1994; Gigerenzer, 2004; Nuzzo, 2014; Trafimow and Marks, 2015). It simply requires constantly being aware of how your views might be wrong or inadequately developed, and planning your data collection explicitly to address these issues, rather than simply proceeding along a predesigned path and accumulating data with no clear sense of how to use your data to support *and* test your preliminary conclusions.

Two key issues in selecting and using data collection methods are the relationship between your research questions and data collection methods, and the joint use of different methods, often termed 'triangulation'.

The Relationship Between Research Questions and Data Collection Methods

The methods used to collect data (including interview questions) don't necessarily resemble, or follow by logical deduction from, the research questions; the two are both real parts of the design, but distinct and separate parts. This can be a source of confusion, because researchers often talk about 'operationalizing' their research questions, or of 'translating' the research questions into interview questions (see Roulston and Choi, Chapter 15, this volume). Such language is a vestige of logical positivist views of the relationship between theory and methods. From a realist perspective, although research questions necessarily *inform* data collection methods, there is no way to mechanically 'convert' research questions into methods. Your methods are the *means* to answering your research questions, not a logical transformation of the latter, and depend fundamentally on the actual context of the research and the researcher's relationships with participants. Research questions formulate what you want to understand; your *interview* questions are what you ask people in order to gain that understanding. The development of good interview questions (and observational strategies) requires creativity and insight, rather than a simple translation of the research questions into an interview guide or observation schedule, and depends fundamentally on how the interview questions and observational strategies will actually work in practice in that context.

There are two important implications that the lack of a direct logical connection between research questions and interview questions has for your research. First, you need to anticipate, as best you can, how particular questions will actually work in practice – how people will understand them, and how they are likely to respond in the actual context of the interview. Try to put yourself in your interviewee's place and imagine how you would react to these questions (this is another use of 'thought experiments'), and get feedback from others on how they think the questions (and the interview guide as a whole) will work. Second, if at all possible, you should *pilot-test* your interview guide with people who are as much like your planned interviewees as possible, to determine if the questions work as intended, and what revisions you may need to make.

This lack of a deductive relationship between questions and methods also holds, more obviously, for observation and other data collection methods. As with interviews, you need to anticipate what information you will actually be able to collect, in the setting studied, using particular observational or other methods, and how this information will contribute to your understanding of the issues you are studying, as discussed above. If possible, you should pretest these methods to determine if they will actually provide this information. Your data collection strategies will probably go through a period of focusing and revision, even in a carefully designed study, to enable them to better provide the data that you need to answer your research questions and to address any plausible validity threats to these answers.

The Uses of Multiple Qualitative Methods

Collecting information using a variety of sources and methods reduces the risk that your conclusions will reflect only the systematic biases or limitations of a specific source or method, and allows you to gain a broader and more secure understanding of the issues you are investigating. This strategy is usually called 'triangulation' (see Flick, Chapter 34, this volume), but the term has been used in both a broad and a narrow sense. The former refers to any use of multiple methods; the latter refers specifically to using a second method as a *check* on the results of another method, to confirm or challenge these results (Rothbauer, 2008). The narrow definition has been widely used, but Greene (2007, pp. 98–104) has argued that this purpose (corroboration or convergence on a single conclusion) is often less valuable than using multiple methods for complementarity (revealing *different* aspects of a single complex phenomenon), expansion (investigating different *phenomena* that interact and need to be understood jointly), or initiation (to generate divergent or contradictory interpretations and fresh insights, or to force the researcher to seek a deeper and more complex understanding).

One belief that inhibits triangulation is the widespread (though often implicit) assumption that observation is mainly useful for describing behavior and events, while interviewing is mainly useful for obtaining the perspectives of participants. It is true that the *immediate* result of observation is description, but this is equally true of interviewing: the latter gives you a description of what the informant *said*, not a direct understanding of their perspective. Generating an interpretation of someone's perspective is inherently a matter of inference from descriptions of their behavior (including verbal behavior), regardless of whether the data are derived from observations, interviews, or some other source such as written documents (Maxwell, 1992).

While interviewing is often an efficient and valid way of understanding someone's perspective (see Roulston and Choi, Chapter 15, this volume), observation (see Wästerfors, Chapter 20, this volume) can enable you to draw inferences about this perspective that you couldn't obtain by relying exclusively on interview data. This is particularly important for getting at tacit understandings and 'theory-in-use', as well as aspects of the participants' perspective that they are reluctant to directly state in interviews. For example, watching how a teacher responds to boys' and girls' questions in a science class (e.g. Sadker and Sadker, 1994) may provide a much better understanding of the teacher's actual views about gender and science than what the teacher says in an interview.

Conversely, although observation often provides a direct and powerful way of learning about peoples' behavior and the contexts in which this occurs, interviewing can also be a valuable way of gaining a description of actions and events–often the *only* way, for events that took place in the past or to which the researcher can't gain observational access. Interviews can also provide additional information that was missed in observation, and can be used to check the accuracy of the observations.

However, in order for interviewing to be most useful for this purpose, interview questions need to ask about *specific* times and events, tapping into what has been termed 'episodic memory', an important and distinct neurocognitive memory system (Dere et al., 2008; Tulving, 1983; Tulving and Craik, 2000). In this system, information is organized by temporal sequencing and spatial connection, rather than abstractly in terms of semantic relationships.

Tulving argued that this memory system makes possible mental 'time travel', uniquely enabling interviewees to retrieve their own previous experiences, and Flick (2000) applied this concept to qualitative interviewing, developing a specific procedure for accessing episodic memory that he called episodic interviewing. Similarly, Weiss (1994, pp. 72–6) stated that asking a question in present tense (e.g. 'What happens while you're waiting to be called [in a court case]?') elicits a generalized account, and that when respondents provide such an account, 'their description expresses a kind of theory about what is most typical or most nearly essential' (1994, pp. 72–3) in such situations, rather than a concrete description of what actually happened. The latter is better obtained by using past tense ('What *happened* while you were waiting to be called?') to refer to a particular occasion, or by questions such as 'Can you walk me through that incident?'

Weiss (1994) also argued, however, that generalized accounts permit respondents to minimize information about which they feel diffident, and to avoid potentially embarrassing details; these are more difficult to do in recounting an actual experience. For this reason, a researcher should be reasonably sure that her relationship with the participant will support asking for a description of a particular event, and should have thought about how to respond if the participant seems uncomfortable. In this situation, the joint use of both generalized, present tense and specific, past-tense questions, as with the joint use of observations and interviews, can address the same issues and research questions, but from different perspectives. In both of these situations, use of multiple methods can provide a more complete and accurate account than either of them could alone.

CONCLUSION

In summary, I have tried to indicate some ways in which a realist perspective can usefully inform qualitative data collection. The common-sense, though usually implicit, ontological realism of many qualitative researchers is already well incorporated into much qualitative research practice – for example, in the attention given to the actual perceptions of participants, the context within which the research takes place, and the ways in which these influence, and are influenced by, the methods used and the results of these. However, explicitly seeing the goal of qualitative research as gaining a better understanding of real phenomena, mental and physical, as well as seeing the processes and practice of qualitative research as conducted in a real context, which the researcher must interact with and adequately understand, can help researchers to better address all of these aspects of collecting qualitative data.

Notes

1 Bhaskar originally used the terms 'transcendental realism' (1975) and 'critical naturalism' (1978) for his views, and only later combined these as 'critical realism', http://en.wikipedia.org/wiki/Roy_Bhaskar.
2 Although 'memo' is used in the grounded theory tradition specifically for theoretical reflections written during data analysis, I am using the term more broadly for *any* reflective writing done during, or in preparation for, research (Bazeley, 2013, p. 103; Schwandt, 2015, pp. 196–7).

FURTHER READING

Hammersley, Martyn (1992) 'Ethnography and realism', in Martyn Hammersley, *What's Wrong with Ethnography? Methodological Explorations*. London: Routledge, pp. 43–56.
Maxwell, Joseph A. (2012b) *A Realist Approach for Qualitative Research*. Thousand Oaks, CA: Sage.
Pawson, Ray, and Tilley, Nick (1997) *Realistic Evaluation*. London: Sage.

REFERENCES

Archer, Margaret, Bhaskar, Roy, Collier, Andrew, Lawson, Tony, and Norrie, Alan (Eds.) (1998) *Critical Realism: Essential Readings*. London: Routledge.
Bazeley, Pat (2013) *Qualitative Data Analysis: Practical Strategies*. Thousand Oaks, CA: Sage.
Becker, Howard S. (1991) 'Generalizing from case studies', in E. W. Eisner and Alan Peshkin (Eds.), *Qualitative Inquiry in*

Education: The Continuing Debate. New York: Teachers College Press, pp. 233–42.

Bhaskar, Roy (1975) *A Realist Theory of Science*. London: Verso.

Bhaskar, Roy (1978) *The Possibility of Naturalism*. Brighton: Harvester Press.

Bhaskar, Roy (1989) *Reclaiming Reality: A Critical Introduction to Contemporary Philosophy*. London, England: Verso.

Bhaskar, Roy (2011) *Critical Realism: A Brief Introduction*. London: Routledge.

Biesta, Gert (2010) 'Pragmatism and the philosophical foundations of mixed methods research', in Abbas Tashakkori and Charles Teddlie (Eds.), *The SAGE Handbook of Mixed Methods in Social and Behavioral Research* (2nd edn). Thousand Oaks, CA: Sage, pp. 95–118.

Blumer, Herbert (1969) 'The methodological position of symbolic interactionism', in Herbert Blumer (ed.), *Symbolic Interactionism: Perspective and Method*. Berkeley, CA: University of California Press, pp. 1–60.

Brinberg, David, and McGrath, Joseph Edward (1985) *Validity and the Research Process*. Newbury Park, CA: Sage.

Brodsky, Anne (2008) 'Researcher as instrument', in Lisa Given (Ed.), *The SAGE Encyclopedia of Qualitative Research Methods*. Thousand Oaks, CA: Sage, pp. 766–7.

Burman, Erica (2001) 'Minding the gap: Positivism, psychology, and the politics of qualitative methods', in Deborah L. Tolman and Mary Brydon-Miller (Eds.), *From Subjects to Subjectivities: A Handbook of Interpretive and Participatory Methods*. New York: New York University Press, pp. 259–75.

Campbell, Donald T. (1974) 'Evolutionary epistemology', in Paul Arthur Schilpp (Ed.), *The Philosophy of Karl Popper*, pp. 413–63. Reprinted in Donald T. Campbell, (1988). *Methodology and Epistemology for Social Science: Selected Papers* (S. Overman, Ed.) Chicago, IL: University of Chicago Press, pp. 393–434.

Campbell, Donald T. (1984) 'Can we be scientific in applied social science?' in Ross F. Conner, David G. Altman, and Christine Jackson (Eds.), *Evaluation Studies Review Annual*, vol. 9, pp. 26–48. Reprinted in Donald T. Campbell (1988) *Methodology and Epistemology for Social Science: Selected Papers* (S. Overman, Ed.) Chicago, IL: University of Chicago Press, pp. 393–434.

Campbell, Donald T. (1988). *Methodology and Epistemology for Social Science: Selected Papers* (S. Overman, Ed.) Chicago, IL: University of Chicago Press.

Cartwright, Nancy (1999) *The Dappled World: A Study of the Boundaries of Science*. Cambridge: Cambridge University Press.

Cartwright, Nancy, and Hardie, Jeremy (2012) *Evidence-based Policy: A Practical Guide to Doing it Better*. Oxford: Oxford University Press.

Clark, Alexander M. (2008) 'Critical realism', in L. Given (Ed.), *The SAGE Encyclopedia of Qualitative Research Methods*. Thousand Oaks, CA: Sage, pp. 167–70.

Cohen, J. (1994) The Earth is round (p<.05). *American Psychologist*, 49(12), 997–1003.

Cook, Thomas D., and Campbell, Donald T. (1979) *Quasi-experimentation: Design and Analysis Issues for Field Settings*. Boston, MA: Houghton Mifflin.

Dere, Ekrem, Easton, Alexander, Nadel, Lynn, and Huston, Joe P. (Eds.) (2008) *Handbook of Episodic Memory*. Amsterdam: Elsevier.

Fletcher, A. J. (2016) 'Applying critical realism in qualitative research: Methodology meets method', *International Journal of Social Research Methodology*, 20(2), 181–94.

Flick, Uwe (2000) 'Episodic interviewing', in Martin W. Bauer and George Gaskell (Eds.), *Qualitative Researching with Text, Image and Sound*. London: Sage, pp. 75–92.

Gigerenzer, G. (2004) 'Mindless statistics', *Journal of Socio-Economics*, 33(5), 587–606.

Glesne, Corinne (2011) *Becoming Qualitative Researchers: An Introduction* (4th edn). Boston, MA: Pearson.

Guba, Egon G., and Lincoln, Yvonna S. (1989) *Fourth Generation Evaluation*. Thousand Oaks, CA: Sage.

Hammersley, Martyn (1992) 'Ethnography and realism', in Martyn Hammersley (Ed.), *What's Wrong with Ethnography? Methodological Explorations*. London: Routledge, pp. 43–56.

Hammersley, Martyn (1998) 'Get real! A defence of realism', in P. Hodkinson (Ed.), *The Nature of Educational Research: Realism, Relativism, or Postmodernism*. Crewe, England: Crewe School of Education, Manchester Metropolitan University.

Reprinted in Heather Piper and Ian Stronach (Eds.) (2004) *Educational Research: Difference and Diversity*. Aldershot: Ashgate, pp. 59–78.

Hammersley, Martyn (2008) *Questioning Qualitative Inquiry: Critical Essays*. Thousand Oaks, CA: Sage.

Hammersley, Martyn (2009) 'Why critical realism fails to justify critical social research', *Methodological Innovations Online*, *4*(2), 1–11.

Hammersley, Martyn, and Atkinson, Paul (2007). *Ethnography: Principles in Practice* (3rd edn). London: Routledge.

Huberman, A. Michael, and Miles, Matthew B. (1985) 'Assessing local causality in qualitative research', in David N. Berg and Kenwyn K. Smith (Eds.), *Exploring Clinical Methods for Social Research*. Beverly Hills, CA: Sage, pp. 351–82.

Kaplan, Abraham (1964) *The Conduct of Inquiry: Methodology for Behavioral Science*. San Francisco, CA: Chandler.

Lawrence-Lightfoot, Sara, and Hoffman Davis, Jessica (1997) *The Art and Science of Portraiture*. San Francisco, CA: Jossey-Bass.

Lincoln, Y. S. (1995). 'Emerging criteria for quality in qualitative and interpretive research', *Qualitative Inquiry*, *1*(3), 275–89.

Lincoln, Yvonna S., and Guba, Egon G. (1985) *Naturalistic Inquiry*. Thousand Oaks, CA: Sage.

Lincoln, Yvonna S., and Guba, Egon (2000) 'Paradigmatic controversies, contradictions, and emerging confluences', in N. K. Denzin and Y. S. Lincoln (Eds.), *Handbook of Qualitative Research* (2nd edn). Thousand Oaks, CA: Sage, pp. 163–88.

Lincoln, Yvonna S., and Guba, Egon E. G. (2013) *The Constructivist Credo*. New York: Routledge.

Little, Daniel (1998) *Microfoundations, Method, and Causation*. New Brunswick, NJ: Transaction.

Madill, Anna (2008) 'Realism', in Lisa Given (Ed.), *The SAGE Encyclopedia of Qualitative Research Methods*. Thousand Oaks, CA: Sage, pp. 731–5.

Maxcy, Spencer J. (2003) 'Pragmatic threads in mixed methods research in the social sciences: The search for multiple modes of inquiry and the end of the philosophy of formalism', in Abbas Tashakkori and Charles Teddlie (Eds.), *Handbook of Mixed Methods in Social & Behavioral Research*. Thousand Oaks, CA: Sage, pp. 51–90.

Maxwell, J. A. (1990a) 'Up from positivism (essay review of DT Campbell, *Methodology and epistemology for social science*), *Harvard Educational Review*, *60*(4), 497–501.

Maxwell, J. A. (1990b) 'Response to "Campbell's retrospective and a constructivist's perspective"', *Harvard Educational Review*, *60*(4), 504–8.

Maxwell, J. A. (1992) 'Understanding and validity in qualitative research', *Harvard Educational Review*, *62*(3), 279–300.

Maxwell, J. A. (2012a) 'The importance of qualitative research for causal explanation in education', *Qualitative Inquiry*, *18*(8), 655–61.

Maxwell, Joseph A. (2012b) *A Realist Approach for Qualitative Research*. Thousand Oaks, CA: Sage.

Maxwell, Joseph A. (2013) *Qualitative Research Design, An Interactive Approach* (3rd edn). Thousand Oaks, CA: Sage.

Maxwell, Joseph A. (2017) 'The validity and reliability of research: A realist perspective', in D. Wyse, L. E. Suter, E. Smith, and N. Selwyn (Eds.), *The BERA/SAGE Handbook of Educational Research*. London: Sage. pp. 116–40.

Maxwell, Joseph A., and Chmiel, Margaret (2014) 'Generalization in and from qualitative analysis', in Uwe Flick (Ed.), *SAGE Handbook of Qualitative Data Analysis*. London: Sage, pp. 540–53.

McGinn, Michelle K. (2008) 'Researcher–participant relationships', in Lisa Given (Ed.), *The SAGE Encyclopedia of Qualitative Research Methods*. Thousand Oaks, CA: Sage, pp. 767–71.

Messick, S. (1995) 'Validity of psychological assessment', *American Psychologist*, *5*(9), 741–9.

Messick, S. (1998) 'Test validity: A matter of consequence', *Social Indicators Research*, *45*, 35–44.

Nuzzo, R. (2014). Statistical errors. *Nature, 506* (13 February 2014), 150–52.

Pawson, Ray (2006) *Evidence-based Policy: A Realist Perspective*. London: Sage.

Pawson, Ray, and Tilley, Nick (1997) *Realistic Evaluation*. London: Sage.

Peshkin, Alan (1991) *The Color of Strangers, the Color of Friends: The Play of Ethnicity in School and Community*. Chicago, IL: University of Chicago Press.

Phillips, Denis Charles (1987) *Philosophy, Science, and Social Inquiry: Contemporary Methodological Controversies in Social Science and Related Applied Fields of Research*. Oxford: Pergamon Press.

Preissle, Judith (2008) 'Subjectivity statements', in Lisa Given (Ed.), *The SAGE Encyclopedia of Qualitative Research Methods*. Thousand Oaks, CA: Sage, p. 844.

Putnam, Hilary (1999) *The Threefold Cord: Mind, Body, and World*. New York: Columbia University Press.

Rothbauer, Paulette (2008) 'Triangulation', in Lisa Given (Ed.), *The SAGE Encyclopedia of Qualitative Research Methods*. Thousand Oaks, CA: Sage, pp. 892–4.

Sadker, Myra, and Sadker, David (1994) *Failing at Fairness: How Our Schools Cheat Girls*. New York: Simon and Schuster.

Salmon, Wesley C. (1989) 'Four decades of scientific explanation', in P. Kitcher and Wesley C. Salmon (Eds.), *Scientific Explanation*. Minneapolis: University of Minnesota Press, pp. 3–219.

Salmon, Wesley C. (1998) *Causality and Explanation*. New York: Oxford University Press.

Sayer, Andrew (1992) *Method in Social Science: A Realist Approach* (2nd edn). London: Routledge.

Schwandt, Thomas A. (2015) *The SAGE Dictionary of Qualitative Inquiry* (4th edn). Thousand Oaks, CA: Sage.

Seidman, Irving E. (1998) *Interviewing as Qualitative Research: A Guide for Researchers in Education and the Social Sciences* (2nd edn). New York: Teachers College Press.

Shadish, William R., Cook, Thomas D., and Campbell, Donald T. (2002) *Experimental and Quasi-experimental Designs for Generalized Causal Inference*. Boston, MA: Houghton Mifflin.

Smith, John K. (2008) 'Relativism', in Lisa Given (Ed.), *The SAGE Encyclopedia of Qualitative Research Methods*. Thousand Oaks, CA: Sage, pp. 749–53.

Smith, John K., and Deemer, Deborah K. (2000) 'The problem of criteria in the age of relativism', in Norman K. Denzin and Yvonna S. Lincoln (Eds.), *Handbook of Qualitative Research* (2nd edn). Thousand Oaks, CA: Sage, pp. 877–96.

Strauss, Anselm, and Corbin, Juliet (1990) *Basics of Qualitative Research*. Thousand Oaks, CA: Sage.

Tappan, Mark (2001) 'Interpretive psychology: Stories, circles, and lived experience', in Deborah L. Tolman and Mary Brydon-Miller (Eds.), *From Subjects to Subjectivities: A Handbook of Interpretive and Participatory Methods*. New York: New York University Press, pp. 45–56.

Tolman, Deborah, and Brydon-Miller, Mary (2001) *From Subjects to Subjectivities: A Handbook of Interpretive and Participatory Methods*. New York: New York University Press.

Trafimow, D., and Marks, M. (2015) 'Editorial', *Basic and Applied Social Psychology*, 37(1), 1–2.

Tulving, Endel (1983) *Elements of Episodic Memory*. Oxford: Oxford University Press.

Tulving, Endel, and Craik, Fergus I. M. (Eds.) (2000) *The Oxford Handbook of Memory*. Oxford: Oxford University Press.

Weiss, Robert S. (1994) *Learning from Strangers: The Art and Method of Qualitative Interviewing*. New York: The Free Press.

Williams, J. Patrick (2008) 'Symbolic interactionism', in Lisa Given (Ed.), *The SAGE Encyclopedia of Qualitative Research Methods*. Thousand Oaks, CA: Sage, pp. 848–53.

Ethics of Qualitative Data Collection

Donna M. Mertens

Qualitative data collection brings complex ethical issues to the surface because of the personal nature of this activity when qualitative methods are used. As we have all heard many times, 'the researcher is the instrument', thus qualitative research includes an integral aspect of the need to be responsive to interpersonal relations that may not be as salient in quantitative research. While ethical review boards have criteria for defining ethical research, the approval process for research through this process is sometimes interpreted to be a hurdle that has to be jumped over and then the study can begin. In qualitative research, it is critically important that researchers are aware of how they are conducting themselves in an ethical manner throughout the course of the research, especially during the data collection. Qualitative data collection involves working closely with participants and this brings with it the complexities associated with cultural norms, beliefs, values, and behaviors. This complexity is of special import when collecting qualitative data in populations that are unaccustomed to participating in research, unaware that they are participating in research, or not part of the research power structure, so that the rights of such individuals are respected. In this chapter, I examine the ethics of qualitative data collection from multiple perspectives: philosophical, institutional, and methodological. I explore tensions that arise in the territory that covers responsiveness to ethical regulations and the practical challenges that arise in the field, as well as issues related to the purpose of the qualitative research as an ethical consideration.

ETHICAL THEORIES AND PHILOSOPHICAL FRAMING FOR RESEARCH

Three branches of normative ethics provide a historical framing for research ethics: virtue ethics (or aretaic ethics), consequentialism (teleological), and deontological ethics. This section provides a brief overview of these theories, notes their responsiveness to the philosophical foundations of qualitative research, and continues with further explanation of theories of ethics that are commensurate with these foundations. This is followed by a discussion of philosophical assumptions associated with the ethics of qualitative research.

Virtue theory, as espoused by Aristotle, defines ethical behavior as having good character and acting in accord with virtues such as wisdom, honesty, courage, and bravery (Kitchener and Kitchener, 2009). According to this theory, people who were raised in a proper social setting were assumed to be capable of acting in a trustworthy and ethical manner. Certainly, one could argue that researchers should be of good character and demonstrate these virtues in their work. Unfortunately, historical evidence in the form of scientific studies that caused great harm (e.g. biomedical experiments on pain and disease progression on death camp inmates in Nazi Germany and experiments in the United States that allowed syphilis to remain untreated in African-American men) lead to the conclusion that researchers cannot rely solely on a virtue theory of ethics.

A second normative branch of ethics, the theory of consequential ethics, as explained in Mill's *Utilitarianism* (1861/1957) and *A System of Logic* (1843/1893), holds that the correct course of action is the one that maximizes human happiness (Christians, 2011). The definition of what is good in terms of consequences to the largest number of people means that researchers could insure the ethics of their work by maintaining a value neutral position, allowing empirical data to demonstrate that the greatest good had or had not been achieved by a selected course of action. However, the focus on one moral imperative, that is, to produce the most good, results in utilitarianism being inadequate to the task for guiding researchers' thinking about ethical issues in which there are conflicting moral principles, such as equal distribution, honesty, non-violence, or prevention of injury.

As Lincoln (2009) and Christians (2011) point out, a teleological, consequential, utilitarian theory of ethics leaves out the voices of members of marginalized groups by virtue of defining what is good in terms of the majority. Thus, such a stance is incompatible with the fundamental philosophical assumptions associated with constructivist, qualitative research.

A third normative ethical theory, deontological ethics, as explained by Kant (1781/1964) in *Categorical Imperative*, holds that ethics is defined in terms of two principles. First, 'the morally correct behavior is that which a person would will the maxim of one's action to become a universal law of human conduct' (Kitchener and Kitchener, 2009, p. 17). Second, 'one should never exploit people, but treat them as intrinsically valuable' (2009, p. 18). The first principle is not in keeping with constructivist philosophical assumptions about the nature of reality because it assumes that it is possible to have a universal law for human conduct. However, the second principle is in keeping with appropriate ethical practice in the realm of qualitative research and opens the door to consideration of social justice theories of ethics.

Social justice theories of ethics provide a platform for the discussion of issues of diversity, politics and power structures, and oppression as elements integral to the conduct of ethical research. Rawls (2001) explicitly raised the issue of the need for ethical theory to be inclusive of social justice when he asserted that 'every person has an equal right to personal liberty and that social and economic equality demands that the needs of the least advantaged be given priority and the principle of equal opportunity be applied to all available positions' (cited in Mertens et al., 2009, p. 88). Simons (2006) described rights-based and social justice theories of ethics as follows:

> Rights-based theories justify their actions on the basis that every person must be treated with dignity and respect and that avoidance of harm must be the primary principle. The social justice theory of ethics takes the rights-based theory to a group or societal level (House, 1993), leading to an

awareness of the need to redress inequalities by giving precedence or at least equal weight, to the voices of the least advantaged groups in society. (cited in Mertens et al., 2009, p. 89)

These ethical theories are commensurate with the stance taken by such thought leaders in the qualitative research community as Denzin's (1997, 2009) and Christians' (2011) feminist communitarian ethics, Brydon-Miller's (2009) covenantal ethics, and Chilisa's (2012) and Cram's (2009) Indigenous relational ethics. Feminist communitarian ethics holds that the conduct of ethical research is dependent upon the inclusion of the voice of participants in decisions about what is to be researched and how it will be done (Christians, 2011). Ethical research is that which is designed to support community transformation. This theory of ethics aligns well with covenantal ethics, described by Brydon-Miller (2009) as emphasizing the goal of positive social change by means of forming 'relationships among the research participants and the deep and sustained commitment to working together to address important problems' (2009, p. 246). This relational concept of ethics is also reflected in the writings of Indigenous scholars. For example, Chilisa (2012) describes relational ethics in Indigenous research as work 'guided by the principles of accountable responsibility, respectful representation, reciprocal appropriation, and rights and regulations' (2012, p. 117). The Bantu's concept of *ubuntu* illustrates this idea; it includes three principles: '(1) I am we, I am because we are; (2) relations of people with the living and the nonliving; and (3) spirituality, love, harmony, and community building' (2012, pp. 117–18).

PHILOSOPHICAL FRAMING FOR ETHICAL QUALITATIVE DATA COLLECTION: PARADIGMS

Theories of ethics are useful from historical and practical perspectives and for guiding thinking about the interrelationships of constructs. However, theories are more limited than paradigms because paradigms serve as meta-physical umbrellas for sets of philosophical assumptions that frame the overall approach to research. Lincoln and Guba (in their writings between 1994 and 2009) borrowed the concept of paradigm from Kuhn (1996) and adapted and expanded it to elucidate the assumptions that are dominant in the social research world. Their conceptualization of paradigms are philosophical frameworks that include four sets of assumptions: (1) axiology – the nature of values and ethics; (2) ontology – the nature of reality; (3) epistemology – the nature of knowledge and the relation between the researcher and the participants; and (4) methodology – the nature of systematic inquiry. In this section, I explore the axiological assumptions and methodological implications of three paradigmatic positions that have relevance for qualitative researchers: constructivist, transformative and indigenous.

Christians (2011) and Lincoln (2009) provide critical insights into the axiological assumptions of qualitative researchers who situate themselves in the constructivist paradigm. Ethical theories commensurate with the constructivist paradigm were discussed in the previous section. Early on, Guba and Lincoln (1989) identified criteria for the ethical conduct of qualitative research that are linked to increased research quality (see Barbour, Chapter 14, this volume); these include the following:

- Credibility: Confidence in the accuracy of the findings
- Transferability: Provision of sufficient detail to allow readers to judge the applicability of findings to other contexts
- Dependability: Provision of access to data that demonstrates the emergence of hypothesis and changes in understandings
- Confirmability: Ability to provide a chain of evidence between data and conclusions that are reached
- Authenticity: Provision of a balanced and fair view of multiple perspectives (Adapted from Mertens, 2015)

Lincoln (2009) expanded the criteria of authenticity to include fairness and balance, ontological authenticity (improved understandings of participants in terms of their constructions of reality and associated feelings, attitudes, beliefs, and values), educative authenticity (making others aware of diverse constructions of reality), catalytic authenticity (construction of findings in ways that support community action), and tactical authenticity (supporting training for participants to make use of the data in ways that challenge an oppressive status quo). Clearly these thought leaders support ethical principles that include social justice; however, this is not an assumption that is held by all qualitative researchers (Hammersley, 2008). Most qualitative researchers adhere to the ethical principle that they must accurately represent diverse constructions of reality; however, not all agree that pursuit of social justice is a defining ethical principle. Yet, with each edition of *The Sage Handbook of Qualitative Research* (Denzin and Lincoln, 2011), the volume authors have increased their advocacy for social justice and human rights.

Mertens (2009, 2015; Mertens and Wilson, 2012) conceptualized transformative axiological assumptions that are commensurate with those that are evolving from constructivist worldviews and extend that concept by framing ethical research as research that explicitly prioritizes the conduct of research for the purpose of social transformation. 'This paradigm emerged in response to the everyday realities, needs and aspirations of those marginalized within societies to broader concerns about human rights and equity that speak to providing avenues for transformative change' (Cram and Mertens, 2015, p. 93); 'Transformative axiological assumptions speak to the need for a research ethic that is cognizant of and responsive to history, culture (in)equity, and the importance of relationships and reciprocity' (2015, p. 95).

Within this framework, researchers believe that there are different opinions about reality, but that some of those versions of reality constitute barriers to the furtherance of social justice and human rights. This leads to the need to use culturally responsive methods of research that take into account the lived experiences of those who face discrimination and oppression. Culturally responsive research is characterized by awareness of power differentials both between the researchers and the participants and within communities. The transformative researcher focuses on establishing relationships with participants that allow for voices of all relevant constituencies to be heard, especially those associated with positions of least privilege (Mertens, 2012a, p. 22).

These two worldviews, constructivist and transformative, are associated with the use of either qualitative methods or mixed methods (in other words, the combination of quantitative and qualitative methods in one study or a program of study) (Mertens, 2018). Researchers who focus on collecting quantitative data sometimes claim that their research is objective because their personal opinions are not involved in the collection and analysis of the data and thus do not influence the results of the study. However, constructivists object to the reduction of human experience to a single number and raise questions about whose judgment was used to decide what data to collect, how to analyze those data, and how to interpret them. Constructivists openly acknowledge that researchers need to do a careful critical analysis of themselves and be sensitive to how their values and biases influence the research situation. Transformative researchers agree on the importance of self-awareness, but they also emphasize awareness of the differences in power relations in the research situation and how their research can be used to address issues of social justice. Additional ethical issues arise in constructivist and transformative research because of closer involvement with researched communities and increased emphasis on the use of research findings for social transformation (Mertens, 2012a, p. 23).

Indigenous scholars (Chilisa, 2012; Cram, 2009; Smith, 2012) have increasingly brought their voices into the conversations about ethics in research and the philosophical framing for ethical research. At surface level, commonalities in the social justice orientation emerging in the constructivist paradigm and prioritized in the transformative paradigm would seem to fit rather nicely with Indigenous assumptions about ethical conduct of research. Some Indigenous scholars use the term 'paradigm' to describe the framing for their research (Chilisa, 2012; Cram and Phillips, 2012; Wilson, 2008). Others describe their approach as a methodology, theoretical lens, or perspective (Smith, 2012). Whichever terminology is used, when constructivist, transformative, and Indigenous researchers are brought together, philosophical tensions arise by virtue of the history of colonization and lack of self-determination experienced by Indigenous communities. These factors are at the base of understanding the meaning of ethical research in Indigenous communities and this is a perspective that is not present in the other paradigms. For Indigenous peoples, the concepts of social justice and transformation need to be stretched to include issues of sovereignty, land, resources, and the freedom to live as Indigenous peoples (Cram and Mertens, 2015). These three paradigms also offer differences in perspectives about appropriate review strategies to insure ethical qualitative research is conducted, as is explained in the next section.

INSTITUTIONAL ETHICAL STANDARDS AND QUALITATIVE DATA COLLECTION PRINCIPLES

Institutional ethical standards come in the form of professional association guidelines, organizational policies, and government imposed standards of review. Professional associations across the world provide guidance to their members on the ethical conduct of research, and qualitative researchers certainly benefit by having an awareness of these ethical guidelines (Lincoln, 2009). Institutional ethical standards emerged from the consideration of ways to prevent the atrocities mentioned earlier in this chapter that were uncovered during the Nuremberg Trials in Nazi Germany and at later times in the United States and elsewhere in the world. In response to these tragedies, the National Commission for the Protection of Human Subjects of Biomedical and Behavioral Research (1978) in the United States produced the *Belmont Report* to guide ethical review and the conduct of research.

One critically important outcome of the *Belmont Report* is the requirement for ethical review that is mandated by many funding agencies. In the United States, federal law requires that any institution that receives federal funding has an Institutional Review Board (IRB) (Mertens, 2015). All researchers that meet the criteria specified in federal legislation are required to go through a review process with their institution's IRB, no matter what the methodological orientation of the researchers. When IRBs work well, they 'serve as a watchdog community to ensure that fundamental ethical considerations – those outlined in federal law and regulations – are weighed carefully and that adequate provisions are in place to meet or exceed the requirement of legal protections' (Lincoln, 2009, p. 158).

Tensions arise for qualitative researchers in their interactions with ethical review boards for several reasons. The origins of ethical review boards are linked to biomedical experimentation history, thus many times the requirements seem to be a better fit for that approach to research than for qualitative researchers (Kitchener and Kitchener, 2009). When qualitative researchers propose data collection strategies that are appropriately flexible and responsive to the ideas that emerge from early data collection results, this is not in keeping with the demand that everything about data collection be detailed in advance of the study in order to obtain approval from the ethics review board. Also, qualitative researchers

> appear to be having more difficulty recently with IRBs, and it is likely that this new circumstance has arisen because of the likelihood that IRBs are experiencing a new and different sense of the 'accountability culture' arising as a result of a larger politically conservative pendulum swing around research design and what constitutes evidence more broadly. (Lincoln, 2009, p. 158)

In addition, regulatory aspects of ethics are intertwined with the role of review boards which have, in turn, been criticized as being less concerned about protecting research participants and more concerned with protecting the research institution (Speiglman and Spear, 2009).

In order to obtain approval for research studies of a more emergent nature, qualitative researchers need to educate their institution's IRB members about ethical principles and methodologies associated with qualitative approaches. The differences that arise are not simply a matter of knowledge gaps; it also involves the differences in philosophical assumptions that were discussed in earlier sections of this chapter. Although outside the purview of qualitative data collection, the qualitative research community has also undertaken political activism in the interest of furthering understandings of the meaning of the ethical conduct of research (Denzin and Giardina, 2008).

Indigenous communities and other community/cultural groups have established or recommended processes for ethical data collection outside of the institutional regulatory review process. Indigenous groups in different countries have developed unique review processes; however, they share the principle that members of the Indigenous communities should have the final word on what is considered to be ethical for themselves. For example, LaFrance and Crazy Bull (2009) describe the ethical regulations and processes that have emerged from American Indian communities in the United States, and First Nations and Aboriginal Peoples in Canada. In the United States, a few tribes have developed their own ethical review processes and all health-related research conducted on tribal land is subject to tribal review through the Indian Health Service, or in some cases, through tribal colleges. In Canada, researchers must submit their work to research ethics boards that follow the Tri-Council Policy Statement. This statement was developed by the Canadian Institute of Health Research (2005) and acknowledges the unique perspectives of First Nations and Aboriginal people and their right to be part of the review process for research conducted with their communities. In New Zealand, the Maori community developed guidelines for the conduct of research in their communities (Hudson et al., 2010). Cram (2012) describes the processes involved in planning and conducting research in the Maori community in terms of principles of relationship – researchers need to conduct themselves in ways that are respectful of the Maori culture and that follow appropriate protocols in terms of introductions and sharing of personal information.

ETHICAL PRINCIPLES ASSOCIATED WITH INSTITUTIONAL REVIEWS: QUALITATIVE PERSPECTIVES

As guidance for ethical reviews, the *Belmont Report* identified three ethical principles that researchers should follow: beneficence, respect, and justice. It also identified six research norms: use of a valid research design, researcher competency, identification of research consequences, appropriateness of sample selection, voluntary informed consent, and compensation for harm (Mertens, 2015). When these principles are brought into the overlapping territory, encompassed by constructivist, transformative, and Indigenous research, additional insights can be gained as to the ethical practice of qualitative data collection. For example, the *Belmont Report*

(National Commission, 1979) defines beneficence as maximizing the good that comes from research for science and humanity and minimizing harm to individuals. Researchers who work for social transformation redefine the principle of beneficence to support the use of the research process and findings to support transformative change that is viewed as beneficial by members of marginalized communities. Researchers from the disability community ask questions about the intrusiveness of the research and the potential for reciprocity (Sullivan, 2009); similar questions are asked by members of Indigenous groups such as Maori researchers in New Zealand (Cram, 2009) and American Indians in the United States and First Nations people in Canada (Battiste, 2000; LaFrance and Crazy Bull, 2009). This perspective on beneficence implies that qualitative researchers need to start data collection by gathering information about the community and its views of benefits and potential harms of research. Such an ethical perspective might be reflected in a question such as: Should beneficence be operationalized as avoiding harm and perhaps giving tangible items such as money to a community, or if the real root of the problem is systemic oppressive power and discriminatory practices, should beneficence be redefined in terms of supporting systemic change through political activism?

The second ethical principle, respect, is enmeshed with the way beneficence is conceptualized within particular communities. The *Belmont Report* (National Commission, 1979) defines respect in terms of treating people with respect, particularly in populations that might not have full autonomy, such as elderly people, people with disabilities, and prisoners. Qualitative researchers have raised questions about the meaning of respect based on their immersion in diverse cultural contexts. From the Indigenous community, Maori (Cram, 2009) and American Indian (LaFrance and Crazy Bull, 2009) groups have developed terms of reference for the conduct of ethical research, which require the researcher to show up prior to beginning the research project and have a face-to-face meeting with community members to explain what the researcher will get out of the research (e.g. money, fame, publications) and what the community will get (e.g. opportunities to improve services, change laws), as well as any potential risks (making their community look bad). Members of the American Sign Language-using community also developed terms of reference for the conduct of ethical research in their community that explicitly acknowledges the need to address hearing and spoken language privilege in planning and conducting the research (Mertens et al., 2009). These issues have relevance for collection of qualitative data in ethical ways, whether or not the researcher is a member of the community. Qualitative researchers should give consideration to the need to review data collection strategies through a community review process to insure that the work is viewed as being ethical by the larger community – not only by the home institution of the researcher.

The third ethical principle in the *Belmont Report* (National Commission, 1979), justice, 'refers to the fair selection of research participants and ideal distribution of risks and benefits. This is commonly known as *distributive justice*' (Cross et al., 2015, p. 1015). This has been interpreted to mean that the people who participate in the research should be the ones who will benefit from the findings (or other members of their community, if not them individually). This principle was included in order to avoid the collection of data from captive audiences (e.g. prisoners) who would not potentially benefit from the results. 'The second component of justice, known as *procedural justice*, is concerned with fairness in the processes for resolving disputes, making decisions, and allocating rewards' (Cross, et al., 2015, p. 1015). When the principle of justice is reframed using a constructivist, transformative, or Indigenous lens, 'researchers are reminded of the diverse nature of groups, some characteristics of which can be used as a basis for excluding members of marginalized communities from participating in and benefiting from research' (Mertens, 2012a, p. 27). In terms of data collection, qualitative researchers need to be aware of characteristics that might result in the exclusion of members of hard to reach groups, such as those who do not use the dominant language or who have disabilities that require accommodations. Qualitative data collection also needs to be conducted with an awareness of the consequences of including members of groups who may not want their marginalizing characteristic to be revealed, such as members of the LGBTQ community, users of illegal drugs, or women who experience intimate partner violence. The issues that arise from the philosophical framing of qualitative research have methodological implications that are explored in the next section.

METHODOLOGICAL ETHICAL ISSUES

Neale (2013) provides a segue between ethical principles and frameworks and ethical practice in qualitative data collection:

> There is ongoing debate about the relative weight to be accorded to principles and 'situated' or 'emergent' ethical practices. Ethical guidelines or frameworks that researchers can draw on as the starting point for their research are crucial. They can be adapted for specific research designs, and used as a benchmark against which to address specific issues and dilemmas as they arise ... Situated ethics ... emphasizes the particularities of ethical questions and practice; these are context specific and require a sensitive appraisal of local circumstances and situated knowledge (Edwards and Mauthner, 2002, p. 27). Such an approach typically calls for researcher reflexivity and negotiation in resolving ethical questions, rather than relying on the application of general rules (Mauthner and Edwards, 2010). Emergent ethics has particular relevance for longitudinal enquiry, where there is increased likelihood of unanticipated ethical dilemmas emerging over time. (2013, p. 2)

Methodologically, qualitative researchers face numerous ethical challenges when designing and conducting their data collection strategies, and when obtaining informed consent from participants as part of the data collection process. Topics related to the ethics of particular data collection approaches and strategies such as ethnography, digital data, mixed methods, field access, research design, and transcription are addressed in other chapters in this volume and thus will not be discussed further here. In this section, I address issues related to ethics and the accuracy of data collected, the amount of time spent in data collection, the criteria for rigor, informed consent, and the implications of the size of the community in which the research takes place. Qualitative data collection is fraught with ethical issues that arise throughout the process. King and Stahl (2015, p. 185) give some insight into these ethical challenges in their questions: 'When does an experience become a study? Does the data collected before informed consent was obtained qualify as data? Do the students we teach have the right to refuse their involvement?'

Accurate Representation and Time Spent Collecting Data

How can the researcher insure that the data collection will be conducted in ways that will accurately reflect the experiences of the participants? Partial answers to this question have been presented by qualitative research scholars for decades. Criteria for addressing this particular issue include having sustained involvement in the community, engaging in peer debriefing, conducting member checks, monitoring self-perceptions and values, and using multiple data sources (Lincoln, 2009; Mertens, 2015; see Barbour, Chapter 14, this volume). Yet, scratching beneath the surface of these useful practices reveals more complex ethical dilemmas. Arguments about how long to collect data in the field, and from how many participants, are common in the literature. Yet, many variables influence how long a researcher can stay and the quality of the time spent in the field. If logistical factors such as limited time and funding, a restricted grant timeframe, or a need for information for rapid decision-making in situations such as natural disasters, limit data collection time in the field, should researchers abandon their planned qualitative data collection activities for ethical reasons?

What are the ethical implications when the tables are turned and the researcher is conducting a longitudinal qualitative study? How does prolonged engagement for an extended period of time influence the ethics of qualitative data collection strategies? Neale (2013) raises these questions and identifies ethical issues that arise, such as the need to obtain ongoing informed consent and considerations of violations of promises of confidentiality that might become more probable in a sustained relationship. However, the paramount ethical issue in longitudinal qualitative data collection is the quality of the relationship. The dynamics of a long-term relationship need to be critically examined in terms of reciprocity for time spent by participants and the dangers of dependence or coercion. It also raises questions about boundaries in the research relationship – what are the ethics of the researcher helping out with tasks (e.g. picking up groceries, washing up dishes) around the participants' house? What if the participant is poor and does not have adequate resources to pay for healthy food or transportation? Is it ethical for the researcher to take on roles such as this? What if the need is greater, such as a character reference for a job or watching the participants' children? Is this a manifestation of ethical reciprocity and respect, or does it cross the boundary of an appropriate researcher/participant relationship?

Longitudinal Data Collection and Data Archiving and Additional Uses

Longitudinal qualitative studies also provide more opportunities for archiving data and providing it for additional uses. This secondary use of qualitative data raises ethical issues that are addressed more fully in another chapter in this *Handbook*. Ethical storing of qualitative data requires obtaining consent from the participants for the archiving and future use of the data (Neale, 2013; see Corti, Chapter 11, this volume). Ethical concerns also include how to control the use of the data by researchers who were not involved in its collection and who might be using the data to answer questions that were not part of the original research purposes. Some recommended solutions include restricting access to the archived data set to those who have been given permission by the primary research team and have been trained in how to use the data set. This does not resolve issues for the ethical interpretation of the data, viewed by some to be the responsibility of the individual researchers and by others as needing to be responsive to the perspectives of community members whose data are included in the data set (Mertens, 2014).

Longitudinal collection of qualitative data also brings with it the possibility that ethical issues might arise that could not have been anticipated when the data collection was first conceived. Neale (2013) recommends having a strategy in place to reactively address and respond to such dilemmas as and when they arise. Several models have been formulated (reported in Wiles, 2013). A 'belt and braces' model (based on Israel and Hay, 2006), would include: clear identification of the problem and the stakeholders involved; assessing the context for decision-making, including the longer-term implications and consequences of alternative courses of action for all; considering this situated knowledge against a backdrop of ethical principles; consulting with researchers or research networks; implementing a course of action; and reflecting on the issue and the outcome and what may be learned from it. Documenting these processes for sharing with others is also useful; the Timescapes Knowledge Bank for Research Ethics (www.timescapes.leeds. ac.uk) is designed to facilitate this process.

Ethical issues related to methods of data collection also arise with regard to the methods utilized for involving members of communities in decisions about data collection strategies and the accuracy of the data collected, and the extent to which these methods are employed. Member checks are associated with the concept that the researcher should consult the people who provide the data in order to insure the accuracy and completeness of the data. They can also be used to clarify and extend ideas or to permit the participant to withdraw their data (or portions of their data) as is their right under the ethical principles discussed later in this chapter. What are the ethical implications when participants review a transcript and then claim that they did not say what is in the transcript, especially when the researcher recorded the interview? Under ethical regulations, the researcher is obligated to delete data that the participant chooses to withdraw.

Purpose of the Research

The purpose of the research has important implications for the consideration of ethical data collection practices. For example, in community-based participatory research (CBPR), ethical challenges arise that are distinct from biomedical research that has the purpose of creating new knowledge (Cross et al., 2015). The purpose of CBPR research is 'to work for the benefit of community participants, to create social change, to improve social justice, and/or to encourage social action' (2015, p. 1009). To this end, ethical issues arise that involve engagement with communities in terms of who is tapped to be part of the process, who is excluded from the process, the role played by community members in terms of determination of research questions and methods of data collection, and the maintenance of long-term relationships. Cross et al. (2015, p. 1012) explain that the purpose of CBPR leads to 'discussion and negotiation of ethics in research [that] is integrated into each stage of research and the community interacts with researchers throughout, rather than only during recruitment and participation in the study'. This requirement is in conflict with an ethical review board requirement that participant and data collection methods and instruments (e.g. interview guides) be developed and approved before the researcher enters the field. The act of educating ethical review boards about the ethical principles involved in CBPR is once again in evidence if qualitative researchers are to collect data ethically when working with this approach.

Qualitative researchers who accept that their work needs to address issues of social justice and human rights need to design their data collection in ways that reflect how they can contribute to the transformative change needed to decrease discrimination and oppression and move communities toward greater equity. Issues that contribute to capturing more accurate pictures of the experiences of members of marginalized communities are important, with special emphasis on going beyond descriptive research. Members of marginalized communities are tired of being told that they have 'problems' without the opportunity to use research as a pathway toward solutions that they view as necessary and appropriate. How can qualitative researchers design their data collection to enhance their ability to ethically contribute to needed transformative change?

When the purpose of research involves conscious engagement with communities, then member checks are useful because community members are aware that they are participants in a research study. But what are the ethical implications when the participant is unaware that they are part of a research study, as in Ellis's (2009) research on people who live in a mountain community where she spends her summers. She gathers data through informal observation and conversation and then writes about issues such as racism, homophobia, and sexism that are entrenched in the regional culture. She knows that if the people who live there were to read what she is writing about them that it would hurt them and damage her relationship with them. Yet she feels an ethical obligation to continue to collect data in order to write about critical issues as she witnesses them. How do qualitative researchers deal with such complex ethical issues in their data collection (Mertens, 2014)?

In cases such as Ellis's work and other researchers who use covert approaches, a different kind of ethical issue arises in qualitative data collection. Generally speaking, covert methodologies are frowned upon and are viewed as a method of last resort (Calvey, 2008). The Economic and Social Research Council (2012) includes the following warnings about the use of covert methods in research:

> The broad principle should be that covert or deceptive research should not be undertaken lightly or routinely. It is only justified if important issues are being addressed and if matters of social and/or scientific significance are likely to be discovered which cannot be uncovered in other ways. Social scientists should, wherever possible, ensure that research participants are aware of and consent to arrangements made with regard to the management and security of data, the preservation of anonymity, and any risk that may arise during or beyond the project itself, and how these might be minimised or avoided. (Web based document, no page number)

Calvey (2008) argues that this 'second class citizen' view of ethics and informed consent results in a certain hesitancy on the part of qualitative researchers to collect data on important topics such as illegal behaviors, violence, discriminatory practices, and research that might be viewed as a threat to the powerful. Calvey described his reliance on situated ethics as a means for maneuvering through a covert research study: 'Hence, I abstained from value judgments about the participants or, put another way, was indifferent to them. The management of situated ethics is not only about adopting a theoretically reflexive attitude but also about a whole series of practical manoeuvres and tactics' (2008, p. 912). This is quite a different ethical stance toward data collection and interaction with participants than is associated with community-based research. In this context, Calvey was able to collect data that included information about drug-taking, violence, withholding information from police, and taking cuts of money from the intended beneficiaries. He writes that his covert stance allowed for the exploration of sensitive topics in a non-reactive way that would not have been possible otherwise:

> Covert research is part of a somewhat submerged tradition that needs to be recovered for future usage in its own right rather than being treated correctively as teaching material for cases of 'failed or bad ethics'. In many cases, covert research is an informed choice of research style rather than an enforced one. Moreover, research in this mold is a tradition that has significantly shaped, often in controversial ways, debates about the research relationship. (2008, p. 914)

Population Size and Ethical Implications

What are the ethical implications for data collection when the community from which the data are collected is very small, e.g. Black Deaf administrators (Moore and Mertens, 2015) or Deaf Blind leaders of educational organizations (Shariff, 2014)? I became acutely aware of this problem when I was collecting data in a project in marine biology for gifted deaf adolescents. Many of the problems in the program's first year were the result of poor planning and decision-making by the project director. As I collected data, I became aware of the animosity that was growing among the staff at all levels toward the director. I reported interim results to the project director in hopes that modifications could be made early that would save the project. However, the project director greeted each statement that came out of my mouth, with 'I know who said that. I can tell who said that.' This was not a comfortable position for me and I seriously worried about the ramifications for the staff members who had trusted me with their thoughts and feelings.

Damianakis and Woodford (2012) describe ethical concerns that arise when qualitative researchers conduct studies with small, connected communities in which relationships exist among community members. They note that: 'When engaging such communities, researchers might face ethical issues in upholding confidentiality standards while they work to achieve their dual mandate. Qualitative scholars have paid little attention to the ethical challenges that might arise in this context' (2012, p. 708). One of the primary concerns when researching in a small community is the increased probability that the identity of participants will be revealed unintentionally. If the qualitative researcher has responded to the criteria of thick description that is put forth as desirable in qualitative studies, then this might come in conflict with the promise of confidentiality. Solutions might include not reporting any personally identifying information, not identifying the specific community, or giving the participants the choice of being identified in the study or not. These suggested solutions are clearly not panaceas and will not be appropriate in all contexts. Qualitative researchers need to be continually reflexive as they collect data and, when possible, share these concerns with community members in order to develop acceptable strategies for dealing with them.

NEW DEVELOPMENTS AND PERSPECTIVES

Philosophical frameworks and ethical theories might not appear to have a place in the discussion of new developments and perspectives, but they do indeed need to be kept in the discussion. Critical examination of the philosophical assumptions that are in the scholarly literature for qualitative researchers has led to improved understandings of the ethical issues that arise in qualitative data collection for the purpose of uncovering inequities, redressing the impact of discrimination and oppression, and supporting the action needed for transformative change. Engagement with communities, whose views were not included in scholarly literature until more recently, have led to increased understandings of the meaning of ethics in marginalized communities. Critical examination of ethical theories has led to insights into their limitations within a qualitative data collection context. The juxtaposition of philosophical frameworks, ethical theories with methodological challenges, bring up concerns about how to prepare qualitative researchers for the ethical collection of data.

This chapter opened with reference to the qualitative researcher's mantra: the researcher is the instrument. What competencies are needed for qualitative researchers to conduct ethical data collection and how can those competencies be nurtured? If the researcher is the instrument, then how does the professional community support the preparation of qualitative researchers who can demonstrate competency in representation of self in data collection contexts (Mertens, 2012a, p. 31)?

King and Stahl (2015) point out the complex notion of forming relationships in order to do ethical qualitative data collection. At first glance, there is a simplicity in the concept of 'who am I?' and presenting myself as the researcher. However, preparing researchers to act in ethically defensible ways is not a matter of conveying knowledge about the issue. Rather:

> Relationships within our research are framed by these inherent biases, or personal inclinations toward the research. We all know that how we start a study, the 'who' we are when we commence inquiry, can have ripple effects on the whole study. In our presentation of self, we can imagine our potential participants in the early stages of an unfolding study of classroom literacy

practices asking 'Who are you, and what do you want?' if only to themselves. Yet, the effects of their inquiry about our intended inquiry have a wave impact on subsequent research interactions, the resulting data, and the results. 'Who are you, and what do you want?' are, in fact, ethically legitimate questions. (2015, p. 186)

Because of the fluid nature of ethical challenges in qualitative data collection, Hsiung (2016) recommended that teaching of qualitative research be conceptualized as involving a set of transgressive practices that sustain and realize critical perspectives and practices. Von Unger (2016) operationalized this approach using a teaching strategy of learning by doing. Sociology students conducted a research project that explored the meaning of a trial against a neo-Nazi group in Munich, Germany. In teams, the students conducted qualitative interviews on how members of local communities viewed the trial. During the course, the students engaged in discussions about their responsibilities as researchers to address current social problems such as right-wing extremism. They questioned the ethics of informed consent when interviewing people from a right-wing extremist group in fear that the participant would not be willing to provide data in an honest way or might not be willing to take part at all. The students came to appreciate the complexity of ethical issues in data collection by virtue of their own experiences of collecting data, conferring with their fellow students, engaging in dialog with ethical experts, and reviewing the literature on ethics in qualitative data collection. It is useful to have examples of effective teaching of ethics in research, but many complexities remain to challenge the novice researcher, as well as the experienced researcher, in their data collection.

CONCLUSION

One of the critical issues that has emerged from this chapter on ethics of qualitative data collection is just what do we consider to be data (see Flick, Chapter 1, this volume)? How do we define the dividing line in terms of data collected for research and data collected that is later understood to be relevant to a research interest? This is a dilemma faced by practitioners in schools, clinics, and other organizations, who want to be critically reflective in their practices and to share their learning through a systematic process. What is considered data, especially considering the almost infinite amount of data to which we have access through our daily observations and through online resources?

How do we reconcile the place of ethics in qualitative data collection between the need to be respectful of our participants and the awareness that revealing our role as researcher and our desire for social change can impact the willingness to participate or the type of information that is revealed? King and Stahl (2015) suggest a possible radical reversal: 'Perhaps it would be more ethical to make sure that everyone has access to all of the data and the writing products and processes' (2015, p. 188). Would this be more ethical or would this lead to more harm than good? Would this destroy the ability of researchers to collect data on sensitive topics, especially when it means an indictment of people in powerful positions? There are many ethical questions that have been raised in this chapter. Von Unger (2016) provides us with this list of questions for critical reflection:

a. How do we as researchers see our roles and responsibilities?
b. How do we position ourselves in the field including vis-à-vis powerful actors?
c. What is the purpose of our research? If we aim for critical, participatory, and transgressive forms of qualitative research, what are the ethical implications and how do we manage the pressures from mainstream academia?
d. In what way and to whom do we identify ourselves as researchers in the field – what information do we reveal about ourselves and our intent?

e. What if we study a situation in which people are suffering great need – may we help? Are we even obligated to help or should we avoid doing so?
f. What if participants tell us 'secrets', are we to use them in our analysis? How do we avoid harming the participants?
g. What if the participants do not want to be anonymized and want to claim their 'voice' in the publications? (2016, p. 89)

Ethical theories and philosophical frameworks help guide thinking about these questions. The professional community is in a good position to continue these debates in public ways with the goal of increasing the ethical nature of qualitative data collection by this process.

FURTHER READING

Chilisa, Bagele (2012) *Indigenous Research Methodologies*. Thousand Oaks, CA: Sage.
Christians, Clifford G. (2011) 'Ethics and politics in qualitative research', in Norman K. Denzin and Yvonna S. Lincoln (eds.), *The Sage Handbook of Qualitative Research* (4th edn). Thousand Oaks, CA: Sage, pp. 61–80.
Mertens, Donna M. (2012b) 'Ethics and social justice in ethnocultural qualitative research', in Donna K. Nagata, Laura Ed Kohn-Wood and Lisa A. Suzuki (eds.), *Qualitative Strategies for Ethnocultural Research*. Washington, DC: American Psychological Association, pp. 61–84.

REFERENCES

Battiste, M. (2000). *Reclaiming Indigenous Voice and Vision*. Vancourver, CA: UBC Press.
Brydon-Miller, Mary (2009) 'Covenantal ethics and action research: Exploring a common foundation for social research', in Donna M. Mertens and Pauline Ginsberg (eds.), *Handbook of Social Research Ethics*. Thousand Oaks, CA: Sage, pp. 243–58.
Calvey, D. (2008) 'The art and politics of covert research', *Sociology*, 42(5): 905–18.
Canadian Institute of Health Research. (2005) Tri-Council policy statement: Ethical conduct for research involving humans. Ottawa: Author.
Chilisa, Bagele (2009) 'Indigenous African-centered ethics: Contesting and complementing dominant models', in Donna M. Mertens and Pauline Ginsberg (eds.), *Handbook of Social Research Ethics*. Thousand Oaks, CA: Sage, pp. 407–25.
Chilisa, Bagele (2012) *Indigenous Research Methodologies*. Thousand Oaks, CA: Sage.
Christians, Clifford G. (2011) 'Ethics and politics in qualitative research', in Norman K. Denzin and Yvonna S. Lincoln (eds.), *The Sage Handbook of Qualitative Research* (4th edn). Thousand Oaks, CA: Sage, pp. 61–80.
Cram, Fiona (2009) 'Maintaining indigenous voices', in Donna M. Mertens and Pauline Ginsberg (eds.), *Handbook of Social Research Ethics*. Thousand Oaks, CA: Sage, pp. 308–22.
Cram, Fiona (2012) *Safety of Subsequent Children. Māori children and whānau – A review of selected literature*. Research Report 2/12 for the Families Commission – Kōmihana ā Whānau, January 2012.
Cram, Fiona, and Mertens, Donna M. (2015) 'Transformative and indigenous frameworks for multimethod and mixed methods', in Sharlene Nagy Hesse-Biber and Burke Johnson (eds.), *The Oxford Handbook of Multimethod and Mixed Methods Research Inquiry*. Oxford: Oxford University Press, pp. 91–109.
Cram, F., and Phillips, H. (2012) 'Claiming interstitial space for multicultural, transdisciplinary research through community-up values', *International Journal of Critical Indigenous Studies*, 5(2), 36–49.
Cross, J. E., Pickering, K., and Hickey, M. (2015) 'Community-based participatory research, ethics, and institutional review boards: Untying a Gordian knot', *Critical Sociology*, 41(7–8): 1007–26.
Damianakis, T., and Woodford, M.R. (2012) 'Qualitative research with small connected communities: Generating new knowledge while upholding research ethics', *Qualitative Health Research*, 22(5): 708–18.
Denzin, Norman K. (1997) *Interpretive Ethnography: Ethnographic Practices for the 21st Century*. Thousand Oaks, CA: Sage.

Denzin, Norman K. (2009) *Qualitative Inquiry under Fire: Toward a New Paradigm Dialogue*. Walnut Creek, CA: Left Coast Press.

Denzin, Norman K., and Giardina, Michael D. (eds.) (2008) *Qualitative Inquiry and the Politics of Evidence*. Walnut Creek, CA: Left Coast Press.

Denzin, Norman K., and Lincoln, Yvonna S. (eds.) (2011) *The Sage Handbook of Qualitative Research* (4th edn). Thousand Oaks, CA: Sage.

Economic and Social Research Council (ESRC) (2010; revised September 2012) Framework for Research Ethics (FRE), available at http://www.esrc.ac.uk/about-esrc/information/research-ethics.aspx.

Edwards, Rosalind, and Mauthner, Melanie (2002) 'Ethics and feminist research: Theory and practice', in Melanie Mauthner, Maxine Birch, Julie Jessop and Tina Miller (eds.), *Ethics in Qualitative Research*. London: Sage, pp. 14–31.

Ellis, C. (2009) 'Telling tales on neighbors: Ethics in two voices', *International Review of Qualitative Research*, 2(1): 3–38.

Guba, Egon, and Lincoln, Yvonna S. (1989) *Fourth Generation Evaluation*. Newbury Park CA: Sage.

Hammersley, Martyn (2008) *Questioning Qualitative Inquiry: Critical Essays*. London: Sage.

House, Ernest R. (1993) *Professional Evaluation: Social Impact and Political Consequences*. Newbury Park, CA: Sage.

Hsiung, P.C. (2016) 'Teaching qualitative research as transgressive practices', *Qualitative Inquiry*, 22(2): 59–71.

Hudson, Maui, Milne, Moe, Reynolds, Paul, Russell, Khyla, and Smith, Barry (2012) *Te Ara Tika Guidelines for Maori Research Ethics: A Framework for Researchers and Ethics Committee Members*. Auckland, NZ: National Ethics Advisory Committee.

Israel, Mark, and Hay, Iain M. (2006) *Research Ethics for Social Scientists: Between Ethical Conduct and Regulatory Compliance*. London: Sage.

Kant, I. (1781/1964) *Critique of Pure Reason*. London: St. Martin's Press.

King, J.R., and Stahl, N. (2015) 'Revisiting ethics: Updating earlier beliefs with a queer exemplar', *Qualitative Inquiry*, 21(2): 184–93.

Kitchener, Karen Strohm, and Kitchener, Richard F. (2009) 'Social science research ethics: Historical and philosophical issues', in Donna M. Mertens and Pauline Ginsberg (eds.), *Handbook of Social Research Ethics*. Thousand Oaks, CA: Sage, pp. 5–22.

Kuhn (1996) *The Structure of Scientific Revolutions*. Chicago, IL: University of Chicago Press.

LaFrance, J., and Crazy Bull (2009) Researching ourselves back to life: Taking control of the research agenda in Indian country', in Donna M. Mertens and Pauline Ginsburg (eds.), *Handbook of Social Research Ethics*. Thousand Oaks, CA: Sage, pp. 135–49.

Lincoln, Yvonna S. (2009) 'Ethical practices in qualitative research', in Donna M. Mertens and Pauline Ginsberg (eds.), *Handbook of Social Research Ethics*. Thousand Oaks, CA: Sage, pp. 150–69.

Mauthner, N., and Edwards, R. (2010) 'Feminist research management in higher education in Britain: Possibilities and practices', *Gender, Work and Organization*, 17(5): 481–502.

Mertens, Donna M. (2009) *Transformative Research and Evaluation*. New York: Guilford.

Mertens, Donna M. (2012a) 'Ethics in qualitative research in education and the social sciences', in Stephen D. Lapan, MaryLynn T. Quartaroli and Frances J. Riemer (eds.), *Qualitative Research*. Hoboken, NJ: Jossey-Bass, pp. 19–40.

Mertens, Donna M. (2012b) 'Ethics and social justice in ethnocultural qualitative research', in Donna K. Nagata, Laura Ed Kohn-Wood and Lisa A. Suzuki (eds.), *Qualitative Strategies for Ethnocultural Research*. Washington, DC: American Psychological Association, pp. 61–84.

Mertens, Donna M. (2014) 'Ethical use of qualitative data and findings', in Uwe Flick (ed.), *The Sage Handbook of Qualitative Data Analysis*. Thousand Oaks, CA: Sage, pp. 510–23.

Mertens, Donna M. (2015) *Research and Evaluation in Education and Psychology* (4th edn). Thousand Oaks, CA: Sage.

Mertens, Donna M. (2018) *Mixed Methods Design in Evaluation*. Thousand Oaks, CA: Sage.

Mertens, Donna M., and Wilson, A.T. (2012) *Program Evaluation Theory and Practice: A Comprehensive Guide*. New York: Guilford.

Mertens, Donna M., Holmes, Heidi M., and Harris, Raychelle L. (2009) 'Transformative research and ethics', in Donna M. Mertens and Pauline Ginsberg (eds.), *Handbook of Social Research Ethics*. Thousand Oaks, CA: Sage, pp. 85–102.

Mill, John Stuart (1893) *A System of Logic, Ratiocinative and Inductive, Being a Connected View of the Principles of Evidence and the Methods of Scientific Investigation* (8th edn). New York: Harper and Brothers. (Original work published in 1843.)

Mill, John Stuart (1957) *Utilitarianism*. Indianapolis: Bobbs-Merrill. (Original work published in 1861.)

Moore, Elizabeth A., and Mertens, Donna M. (2015) 'Deaf culture and youth resilience in diverse American communities', in Linda C. Theoron, Linda Liebenberg and Michael Ungar (eds.), *Youth Resilience and Culture*. London: Springer, pp. 143–55.

National Commission for the Protection of Human Subjects of Biomedical and Behavioral Research (1979) *The Belmont Report*. Washington DC: Department of Health, Education and Welfare.

Neale, B. (2013) 'Adding time into the mix: Stakeholder ethics in qualitative longitudinal tesearch', *Methodological Innovations Online*, 8(2): 6–20.

Rawls, John (2001) *Justice as Fairness: A Restatement*. Cambridge, MA: Belknap Press of Harvard University Press.

Shariff, Risa A. (2014) 'Leaders Who Are Deaf-blind: A Phenomenological Study of Educational Experiences', PhD dissertation, Gallaudet University, Washington DC.

Simons, Helen (2006) 'Ethics in evaluation', in Ian Shaw, Jennifer Greene and Melvin M. Mark (eds.), *The Sage Handbook of Evaluation*. London: Sage, pp. 243–65.

Smith, Linda Tuhiwai (2012) *Decolonizing Methodologies: Research and Indigenous Peoples*. London: Zed Books Ltd.

Spieglman, Richard, and Spear, Patricia (2009) 'The role of institutional review boards: Ethics: now you see them, now you don't', in Donna M. Mertens and Pauline Ginsberg (eds.), *Handbook of Social Research Ethics*. Thousand Oaks, CA: Sage, pp.121–34.

Sullivan, Martin (2009) 'Philosophy, ethics, and the disability community research', in Donna M. Mertens and Pauline Ginsberg (eds.), *Handbook of Social Research Ethics*. Thousand Oaks, CA: Sage, pp. 69–84.

Von Unger, H. (2016) 'Reflexivity beyond regulations: Teaching research ethics and qualitative methods in Germany', *Qualitative Inquiry*, 22(2): 87–98.

Wiles, R. (2013) *What are Qualitative Research Ethics?* London: Bloomsbury Academic.

Wilson, Shawn (2008) *Research Is Ceremony: Indigenous Research Methods*. Black Point, Nova Scotia: Fernwood.

Deduction, Induction, and Abduction

Brianna L. Kennedy and Robert Thornberg

When conducting qualitative research, scholars should consider the relation between data collection and analysis as well as between theory and data. There are at least two ways to relate data collection to analysis in the research process. In a *linear-sequential approach*, researchers first collect all data and then start to analyze. This is common in quantitative research but could also be applied in qualitative research, for instance when doing content, thematic, discursive, conversational, or phenomenological analysis after collecting all data. In contrast, an *iterative approach* refers to an interplay between data collection and analysis. Researchers move back and forth between data collection and analysis during this research process. The ongoing data analysis guides researchers to change or add a new data gathering method, to decide which data to collect next and where to find them. The iterative approach is essential, for example, in ethnography and grounded theory, but could be adopted in a range of qualitative research approaches. The two approaches of how to relate data collection and analysis to each other should be understood as ideal types or the opposite ends of a continuum, in which researchers could be more or less close to one of the ends.

Concerning the relation between theory and data, researchers might either use theoretical knowledge to interpret and analyze their data or else try to ignore previous theoretical knowledge to be open to discover patterns, themes, concepts, or theory from data. Once again, these two approaches should be considered as located on a continuum. When it comes to this complex and even contested relation between theory and data, Kelle (2014) argues that qualitative researchers have to deal with two conflicting challenges: (a) 'the general accepted epistemological tenet that empirical research must always refer to previous insights and already existing knowledge' (2014, pp. 554–5); and (b) that social life and its meanings, actions and structures are constantly changed and reinvented, and therefore, the researchers have to be open to explore the unknown and unpredictable at the same time as being aware that such 'an openness may be hampered by theoretical preconceptions researchers carry with them' (2014, p. 555). The relation between data collection and analysis and between theory and data can be discussed in terms of deduction, induction, and abduction, which is the aim of the current chapter. Because deduction and induction have often been discussed in the social research literature, we focus in particular on abductive reasoning and its potential role in the relation between data collection and analysis and between theory and data in qualitative research.

DEDUCTION AND INDUCTION

Deduction begins with a specific theory or rule and examines how the raw data support the rule (Reichertz, 2007). It can substantiate or disconfirm existing understandings. To illustrate deduction, induction, and abduction, the American pragmatist philosopher Charles S. Peirce (1960) gave examples of how to reason and make inferences using beans. Here is his example of deduction: If the general rule is that all the beans from a certain bag are white, and the beans in a certain case are from this particular bag, we can from the rule draw the conclusion that the beans in the case are white. In quantitative research, a hypothesis could be deduced from theory and then empirically tested in order to confirm or falsify the hypothesis, and thus the theory. In qualitative research, deduction often means that data are analyzed according to an existing theoretical framework. The aim is usually not to 'test' the theory but to adopt the theory as an analytical tool or lens when collecting and analyzing data. However, the write-up of such a procedure might give the impression that the theory is 'true' or has been 'proven' or 'supported' by the data.

One advantage of deducing from theory in qualitative research is that the theory helps researchers attend to details and nuances in the data that otherwise might be overlooked. However, one possible drawback is that researchers only attend to aspects of the data prescribed by the theory while overlooking other aspects of the data that are outside the scope of the theory. There is also a risk of over-interpreting data. Thus, the theoretical framework might force data into pre-existing concepts that distort, or do not fit with, the data or have little, or poor, relevance to the studied field or phenomenon (cf. Glaser, 1998, 2005). For instance, Dressman (2007) conducted a systematic review of 69 studies in literacy research (61 qualitative studies and 8 quantitative studies) and found that in 60 of these 69 studies, researchers rarely challenged any precepts of the social theories (e.g. discursive theories, social constructivism, structuralism/poststructuralism, and gender theories) adopted in their studies. Later, Dressman concluded:

> As a consequence, many areas of social theory within educational research, such as social constructivism and Bakhtinian theories of language, get taken up and are uncritically applied to an ever expanding range of settings, but the validity of the theories is never examined, nor are theories ever expanded upon or reshaped through their engagement with empirical evidence. (2008, p. 92)

In these uses of theory, the research contributes to the stagnation and misapplication of theory and results in blindness toward, or disregard for, data that do not support the theory.

If researchers are not open to being surprised by the data – to the possibility that the reality might 'talk back' (Blumer, 1969) and that the theoretical framework is fallible – but instead take for granted in a rather uncritical manner that the theory is true, right, or superior, they will end up in circular reasoning, and the study will act as a self-fulfilling prophecy. In such cases, the researchers 'are so wedded to a conceptual framework that all they do is repeat or add a minor nuance to their preferred theory' (Tavory and Timmermans, 2014, pp. 1–2). A critical colleague might ask, 'Why bother with gathering data when you already know *a priori* what results you will come up with?' Thus, the risk with deduction is that researchers become less sensitive to participants, the field under study, and the collected data, since the main concern simply is to 'prove' or 'demonstrate' the theory and assert their *a priori* arguments.

In *induction* researchers use a series of empirical cases to identify a pattern from which to make a general statement. Inductive logic consists of inferring categories or conclusions based upon data (Thornberg and Charmaz, 2014). Induction sticks closely to the data and can reveal new understandings of existing knowledge and conclusions (Reichertz, 2007). Continuing the bean example above (cf. Peirce, 1960), we can think about a sealed bag with a small tear on the top. Each time we take out a couple of beans, we find that the beans in our hand are white. After repeating this ten times with the same outcome, we conclude that it is plausible to assume that all the beans in the bag are white, a general statement based on the pattern found in the data. In qualitative research, induction means that patterns, concepts and theories emerge from data through the researchers' interactions with the data without pre-supposing such outcomes *a priori*. However, inductive conclusions are always hypothetical and fallible. Although it seems to be the case that the sealed bag contains only white beans according to our empirical observations, one or more red beans might be inside the bag even though we have not observed them yet.

Philosophers of science have also criticized the assumptions that support 'pure' induction, namely that researchers can collect and analyze theory-free data without any prior theoretical knowledge (e.g. Chalmers, 1999; Hanson, 1965). Such naïve inductivism (Chalmers, 1999) fails to recognize that researchers are situated within a historical, ideological, and socio-cultural context. As Kelle (1995) states, 'Researchers who investigate a different form of life always bring with them their own lenses and conceptual networks' (1995, p. 38). Data can never be free of theoretical influence because observing and collecting data are already 'theory-laden' undertakings (see Maxwell, Chapter 2, this volume). Prior knowledge of a phenomenon inevitably shapes researchers' observations (Alvesson and Kärreman, 2011; Hanson, 1965; Kelle, 1995). Even though early positivists made the claim that 'it's all there in the data' (Kelle, 2014), which is the basic claim in pure induction, we can no longer retreat behind it (Bryant, 2009).

Nevertheless, researchers can still construct meaningful explanations of the data. As Hammersley and Atkinson explain:

> [To] say that our findings, and even our data, are *constructed* does not automatically imply that they do not or cannot represent social phenomena. To believe that this is implied is to assume that the only true form of representation would involve the world imprinting its characteristics on our senses without any activity in our part, a highly implausible account even of the process of perception. (2007, p. 16)

Thus, when induction is adopted in an interpretive or constructivist qualitative research tradition, the empirical cases are always considered as *interpreted data* rather than raw data. In line with their underlying epistemology, researchers therefore do not claim to offer an exact picture but rather an interpretive portrayal of the phenomenon studied (Charmaz, 2014).

ABDUCTION

Peirce (1960/1979) developed *abduction* as a third mode of reasoning or inference, using different terms when writing about abduction (i.e. abduction, retroduction, presumption, and hypothesis) and developing the meaning of abduction over time. Later scholars have also debated various definitions of abduction (e.g. Anderson, 1986, 1987; De Waal, 2013; El Khachab, 2013; McKaughan, 2008; Paavola, 2004; Reichertz, 2007; Schurz, 2008; Tavory and Timmermans, 2014). In this chapter, we understand abduction as selecting or inventing a provisional hypothesis to explain a particular empirical case or data set better than any other candidate hypotheses, and pursuing this hypothesis through further investigation (Charmaz et al., 2018; Douven, 2011). Abduction is about discovering new concepts, ideas and explanations by finding surprising phenomena, data, or events that cannot be explained by pre-existing knowledge. Inspired by Pierce's (1960) illustrative examples of making inference using beans, Thornberg and Charmaz (2014) illustrated abductive reasoning by describing a situation in which we enter a backyard with beans and bags (see Box 4.1).

In abduction, qualitative researchers use a selective and creative process to examine how the data support existing theories or hypotheses as well as how the data may call for modifications in existing understandings (Thornberg, 2012). They go beyond the data and pre-existing theoretical knowledge by modifying, elaborating upon, or rejecting theory if needed, or putting old ideas together in new ways to examine, understand, and explain the data. Like the fictional detective Sherlock Holmes, they constantly move back and forth between data and theories, and make comparisons and interpretations in searching for patterns and the best possible explanations (Bryant, 2009; Carson, 2009; Eco, 1981; Thornberg, 2012; Truzzi, 1976). These researchers strive to be open and sensitive to the data while also allowing for the use of pre-existing theories, not to mechanically derive a hypothesis to test (as in deduction), but as a source of inspiration, and identification and interpretation of patterns (Alvesson and Sköldberg, 2008). Thus, abduction requires an iterative interplay

---

Box 4.1

Here we find five bags in a line next to a wall. Bag A only contains white beans; Bag B only contains green beans; Bag C only contains red beans; Bag D only contains brown beans; and Bag E only contains black beans. Four meters in front of the line of bags, we discover three white beans on the ground. Based on these data and our accessible knowledge of Bag A, Bag B, Bag C, Bag D, and Bag E, we infer at once as a probability, or as a fair guess, that the three beans on the ground come from Bag A. On further investigation we discover footsteps on the ground parallel to the lines of bags but four meters in front them. The three white beans are just a few centimeters next to one of these footsteps. In addition, from our further investigations we see that there are no footsteps near the bags, and all the five bags are sealed. Thus, we come up with a new, more plausible hypothesis: the three white beans come from a person who has passed by and accidently or deliberately dropped the three beans. Fortunately, we know that there are three people in the neighborhood who happen to love white beans, usually have some in their pocket and eat them like candy. Two of them are children – an 8-year-old girl and a 10-year-old boy. The third is a very old man, and he happens to have the very same shoe size that you have. We therefore investigate the shoeprints closer, and you put your foot next to one of the shoeprints. It is the same size! We therefore dismiss the two children and choose the very old man as a reasonable hypothesis: as he was passing by, three white beans happened to fall out of his pocket when he pulled his hand from his pocket during his bean snack. But then we detected a 'surprising fact'. There are no imprints from a stick at the side of the footsteps. This is very puzzling because we know that the old man has a severe knee injury on the left side and always walks with a stick. In light of this new surprising data, we no longer hold the old-man-who-loves-white-beans hypothesis as plausible (well, that is if we do not consider the possibility that he recently had undergone a new miracle treatment with an extremely fast-healing process). It is more reasonable that another person (perhaps someone we do not know) passed by and dropped the three white beans. We decide to follow the footsteps in a search for more data.

(From Thornberg and Charmaz, 2014, pp. 161–2)

between (a) data collection and analysis, in which the ongoing analysis of data suggests plausible hypotheses to investigate further; and (b) data and theory, in which researchers have to draw implicitly or explicitly on previous theoretical knowledge (Kelle, 2014) but also re-think, revise, or challenge established theoretical assumptions to resolve surprising or puzzling data (Alvesson and Kärreman, 2011).

Abductive inference usually begins when researchers recognize an anomaly or surprising data, and therefore take 'an interest in the problematization and re-thinking of dominating ideas and theory, [since] empirical impressions encourage such a need for novel thinking' (Alvesson and Kärreman, 2011, p. 58). Even non-surprising data can be approached as surprising, such as when educational ethnographers who conduct fieldwork in familiar settings use a lens that exposes taken-for-granted assumptions (Delamont and Atkinson, 1995; Delamont et al., 2010); or when these ethnographers focus on unusual situations or events, or on neglected, taken-for-granted features of the field under study (Delamont, 2002). Alvesson and Kärreman describe these acts as *defamiliarization*, or 'trying to refrain from using familiar concepts and frameworks and instead opening up the studied reality as an unknown and unfamiliar place' (2011, p. 41). Researchers can also produce abductive insights by genuinely asking questions like, 'What is actually happening in the data?' and 'What is this data a study of?' (Glaser, 1978, p. 57), as in grounded theory methodology.

One criticism of abduction is that it appears to permit inferences of all sorts of wild hypotheses (see Paavola, 2004). If a hypothesis has been selected among infinite possibilities that can be imagined as an explanation, why should we bet on the chosen hypothesis? Or, as stated by Lipscomb, 'surmising that something "may be so" is not the same as demonstrating that it is so (or is likely to be so)' (2012, p. 254). To address this problem, Paavola (2004) emphasizes the importance of adopting strategic rules in abduction. When searching for a plausible hypothesis for a certain empirical case, researchers have to strive for constraining and guiding their search by requiring that the hypothesis explain, or at least be consistent with, most other clues, constraints, and information that are available concerning the empirical case. Therefore, 'wild' hypotheses are not reasonable if they do not fit well with other relevant information. Paavola explains:

> Strategically, it would be bad reasoning to suggest such implausible hypotheses, if there were no good reasons or backing for these ... [I]n strategies, the reasoner tries to anticipate the counterarguments, and to take into account all the relevant information, and this rules out very 'wild' hypotheses, except when there is no other available, or alternatively, when these are presented simply as 'wild guesses'. (2004, p. 271)

These wild guesses have to be further examined. Thus, the analysis in the interplay between theory and data has to be both creative and critical.

Another related problem with abduction regards multiple legitimate explanations, that is, that there might exist more than one strongly plausible explanation or hypothesis, leading to a situation in which researchers face difficulties in choosing between these (Lipscomb, 2012). Once again, researchers have to constantly compare the candidate hypotheses with the particular empirical case and with other available information to further examine the plausibility of each hypothesis (cf. Paavola, 2004). Contrasting theories or hypotheses have to be seriously considered, compared, and examined, and thus rejected on good grounds. However, 'while all observation is theory laden, even hypotheses grounded upon uncontested factual claims are in the social/human world frequently unavailable for "testing"' (Lipscomb, 2012, p. 249). The generally accepted epistemological position that states that data are inevitably shaped by prior knowledge and thus theory-laden (Hanson,

1965; Kelle, 1995) does not only challenge induction but also abduction. If we assume that evidence or data cannot be identified outside of theory, multiple plausible theories or hypotheses are always available to shape evidence (Lipscomb, 2012). This is not at all controversial. Even postpositivists recognize that data are theory-laden and that theory is underdetermined by evidence (Phillips and Burbules, 2000). The latter means that 'we cannot claim that observational or other evidence unequivocally supports a particular theory or fully warrants the claim that is true because there are many other (indeed, a potentially infinite number of other) theories that also are compatible with this same body of evidence (and can thereby claim to be warranted by it)' (Phillips and Burbules, 2000, p. 17). As with deduction, we might therefore run into circular reasoning, particularly if we are very attached to a favorite theory – or early in the research process develop a preference for a certain hypothesis – and thus turn away from abduction to engage in a data-insensitive quasi-deduction that focuses only on data that support the theory or hypothesis.

Nevertheless, a range of strategies could be considered to help researchers avoid circular reasoning. These include: (a) *theoretical agnosticism*, that is, always treating theories, concepts and hypotheses as provisional, fallible, disputable and modifiable conceptual proposals (Thornberg, 2012; also see Charmaz, 2014; McCallin, 2006); (b) *theoretical pluralism*, that is, insisting on the need for a conversation between different perspectives/theories/hypotheses based on the understanding that knowing is social, situated, and continually in need of re/adjustment, correction, and re/construction (Thayer-Bacon, 2003; Thornberg, 2012; also see Alvesson and Kärreman, 2011; Tavory and Timmermans, 2014); and (c) *theoretical playfulness*, that is, playing with theories in innovative and unorthodox ways (Thornberg, 2012; also see Charmaz, 2014). Kelle (1995) emphasizes that the capacity to draw good abductive inferences is dependent upon researchers' prior knowledge, rejection of dogmatic beliefs, and development of open-mindedness.

AN EXAMPLE OF USING DEDUCTIVE, INDUCTIVE, AND ABDUCTIVE LOGICS IN ITERATIVE DATA COLLECTION AND ANALYSIS

Contemporary grounded theory methodology perhaps best illustrates the uses of all three logics in the research process (Charmaz, 2011). Whereas the original grounded theory (Glaser and Strauss, 1967) and the further developed Glaserian grounded theory (e.g. Glaser, 1978, 1998) advocated researcher objectivity without preconception in the use of inductive logics, constructivist grounded theory positions itself within a constructionist epistemology and embraces the researcher's active involvement in the deduction, induction, and abduction that drive iterative data collection, analysis, and theorizing (Reichertz, 2007; Thornberg and Charmaz, 2014). For instance, a researcher might first rely upon inductive reasoning to create categories to represent the data, test those categories against additional data in an iterative cycle of data collection and analysis, use abduction to generate a theory to explain relationships between categories, and then return to deduction to test that theory.

Grounded theory relies upon cycles of data collection and analysis that require the researcher to use each round of analysis to drive the subsequent round of data collection (Glaser and Strauss, 1967). Consequently, it is necessary not only to focus on the data collection process, but also to describe data collection and analysis in relation to each other and to show how each of the three types of logic contributes to this methodological approach. Next, we give an example from the work of Kennedy et al. (2017) to illustrate how the three logics of inference – deduction, induction and abduction – can drive iterative data collection and analysis.

Overview of the Study

In this grounded theory study, Kennedy et al. (2017) sought to describe how school administrators made decisions regarding student discipline. Situated in the field of school discipline studies and responding to educators' disproportionate use of punitive discipline with students of color and those from low-income backgrounds in US schools (Losen and Gillespie, 2012), this study examined administrators' perceptions of how they respond to students who commit behavioral infractions. Based on literature establishing the importance of educators' beliefs and sense-making to their implementation of discipline (for example, see Lorie and Lee, 2007; Mukuria, 2002), the study focused on how administrators described assigning disciplinary consequences such as in-school suspension, out-of-school suspension, corporal punishment, and expulsion.

Setting and Initial Participants

This study focused on middle level schools in the state of Florida that served a high percentage of students living in poverty. Kennedy et al. (2017) were interested in how school administrators chose among the options available to them as they disciplined students, and particularly focused on how they described the choice between corporal punishment (legal in 19 of the United States) and suspension. Nineteen of the 28 Florida districts that allowed corporal punishment agreed to participate. The research team recruited 27 administrators in 25 schools, with at least one school participating in each of the districts where consent was received. After generating an initial theory utilizing this sample, Kennedy et al. recruited an additional theoretical sample as discussed below.

Using Logics in Initial Data Collection and Open Coding

The research team used a deductive process based on their professional experiences and knowledge of the literature to develop an interview protocol that would address the research questions (see Figure 4.1).

They did not do this in a mechanical way but as a starting point (Charmaz, 2014) in which professional experiences and research literature made them aware of previous patterns, helped them formulate relevant research questions (Thornberg, 2012), and pointed to aspects in need of further examination and development (Corbin and Strauss, 2015). We could say that the researchers deductively began with a sort of hypothesis about what would be important to ask in order to understand administrators' disciplinary decision-making, and then they created interview questions based on that understanding. For instance, their review of the literature pointed them toward the importance of administrators' beliefs and dispositions in choosing disciplinary consequences, so they asked administrators to discuss their beliefs and how they came to have those beliefs. At the same time, the majority of the interview questions were open-ended questions that allowed the research team to collect and analyze the interview data using inductive logic.

After conducting one interview using this protocol, each member of the research team conducted open coding on that transcript. Coding that assigns emergent codes to data slices requires inductive logic because the analyst begins with the data and groups similar data slices together under common codes. The team created code maps that spatially grouped similar codes together and positioned groups in relation to each other where they had begun to postulate connections between groups. Each of their lists of codes and spatial code maps were distinct, and the maps helped to guide their conversations about which could compose the strongest list of codes that they would use to proceed

1. What are your beliefs about how children should behave in school?
    a. What factors in your life have shaped those beliefs? Could you give me an example?
    b. Why do you think some children do not behave in those ways sometimes? Example?
    c. What factors need to be in place in order for children to meet the school's behavioral expectations? Example?

2. What is this school's approach to preventing challenging behavior?
    a. Do you think that most of the educators here use the same prevention strategies? Example?
    b. ~~To what degree do the prevention strategies used here match your personal beliefs about how to prevent challenging behavior?~~
    c. Do you think different children require different approaches? Explain.
        i. Is it more important to be consistent or to address the individual situation?
        ii. How do you balance consistency with handling discipline on a case-to-case basis?
        iii. What role does understanding the causes for challenging behaviors play in assigning consequences?
    d. Do you use PBIS? How exactly do you use it? What is the relationship between PBIS and discipline consequences?
    e. *What impacts have you seen as a result of your prevention strategies?*

3. What happens at this school when children do not meet the schools' behavioral expectations? ~~At the classroom level? At the administrative level?~~
    a. *In your opinion, which behaviors should be handled in the classroom and which should be handled by you?*
    b. *When is it appropriate for teachers to write office referrals?*
    c. *To what degree do the teachers at your school use them effectively?*
    d. *How do you deal with teachers who give the most referrals? Are there things that you emphasize and require school-wide?*
    e. *What happens when a child receives a referral? Could you walk me through a recent example?*
    f. *How do referrals get coded and how do those codes shape the consequences you choose?*
    g. *What impacts do referrals have on children's educational futures? [How] does knowing that shape the way your school deals with giving referrals?*

4. ~~What sorts of behavioral issues do you have to deal with as an administrator at this school?~~
    a. ~~How is your role similar to and different from that of other administrators?~~
    ~~**b. Referrals: What role do referrals play? Walk us through what happens when you get a referral.**~~
    b. What options are available to you in responding to misbehavior? (What are the roles of in-school suspension, out-of-school suspension [and corporal punishment] in your practice?
        i. What are your thoughts and feelings about each of these strategies? Which is most effective? Least effective? Examples?
        ii. How do you decide which approach to use with which students? Example?
        iii. Do your feelings come into play when you discipline students?
        iv. How do students typically respond to these different approaches? How do you feel about that?
        v. Are there other approaches you wish you could use? Explain.
    c. *Can you describe how discipline practices at this school have been different under different leadership and/or with different faculty? [If not applicable, ask about another school where participant has worked.]*

5. To what degree do you believe that the school's responses to challenging behaviors are effective?
    a. Could you describe your experiences with a student with whom you felt your behavioral approach was especially effective?
        i. ~~What was that student like? How often did you interact? Under what circumstances?~~
        ii. ~~Why do you think your approach worked?~~

Figure 4.1 Interview protocol[*1]

~~iii. Was that student ever [suspended in school; suspended out of school; corporally punished]? How many times? (for each method)~~
~~iv. Tell me about how these different forms of discipline impact the child. What happened after each consequence? Please describe one specific example.~~
v. What was the most important factor in your success with that child? Explain.

b. Could you describe your experiences with a student with whom you felt your behavioral approach was ineffective?
~~i. What was that student like? How often did you interact? Under what circumstances?~~
~~ii. Why do you think your approach did not work?~~
~~iii. Was that student ever [suspended in school; suspended out of school; corporally punished]? How many times? (for each method)~~
~~iv. Tell me about how these different forms of discipline impact the child. What happened after each consequence? Please describe one specific example.~~
v. What do you believe would have been necessary for you to succeed with that child? Explain.

6. Is there anything that would help you and/or your school improve your approaches to challenging behavior as well as the outcomes of those approaches?

~~7. If you could tell policymakers anything about school discipline, what would it be?~~

~~8. Any other thoughts?~~

Figure 4.1 *(Continued)*

*Note: Regular font indicates original protocol. Bold font indicates questions added after approximately one-third of the interviews were completed and open coding was conducted. Italic font indicates questions that were added to target selective coding and theme development. Strike through font indicates questions that were not asked during this final stage of data collection.

with coding. This further act of synthesis also required inductive logic, and by continuing with this process through three separate interview transcripts, the team arrived at a set of open codes that they then defined in a code book and used to code the first third of the interviews once they were completed (see Table 4.1).

The research team moved between deduction, induction, and abduction here; they were constantly open to revising their initial hypothesis and to considering other hypotheses in the iterative comparison between data and theory if their inductive open coding generated patterns that challenged or did not fit with the initial deduced hypothesis.

This next act of coding consisted primarily of deductive logic as the team compared data to the code book. However, the team also relied upon induction in identifying data slices that did not fit with the code book, and they used memos written during this phase to revise their codes once they had coded one-third of the interviews (see Table 4.1). For instance, participants' descriptions of how they would build relationships with students as part of their administrative roles surprised the research team because the participants made distinctions between building relationships with students as a preventative measure before students broke rules and then also during the discipline event itself. The team used abductive logic to revise their code book and interview protocol (see Figure 4.1), choosing a more plausible hypothesis regarding the nature and importance of relationship-building based on the data.

Table 4.1 Sample codes*

Code List		
Alternative School	Expectations for Behavior	Student Development
~~Behavior_Reasons~~ Choose between Outside Factors and Getting the Whole Story	Factors Outside of School That Impact School Discipline (Outside_Factors)	Student Responses to Punishment
~~Black_White_and Gray Areas~~ Choose between Beliefs About Rules, Getting the Whole Story, or Choosing Punishment	Family Background_Administrators	Teacher Responsibilities
Choosing Corporal Punishment	~~Focus on Relationships~~ Change to Focus on Relationships_Prevention and Focus on Relationships_During Discipline	**Beliefs About Rules**
Choosing ISS	Local Strategies_Consequences	**Focus on Relationships_ Prevention**
Choosing OSS	Local Strategies_Prevention	**Focus on Relationships_ During Discipline**
Choosing Punishment	~~Middle School_Development~~ Code as Student Development	**Getting the Whole Story**
~~Classroom Procedures~~ Code as Local Strategies or Teacher Responsibilities	~~OSS_Student Responses~~ Code as Student Responses to Punishment	Referrals
~~Communication with Parents~~ Code as Role of Family	~~Peers~~ Code as Middle School Development, Student Development, or something else.	School Culture
~~CP_Student Responses~~ Code as Student Responses to Punishment	Personal Opinions and Feelings	*Administrator Definitions of Their Roles*
Detention	Role of Family (Replace Family Background_Students)	*Emotional Work*
Discipline as Deterrence	Role of Infrastructure	*Uneasy Compromise*
Discipline as Opportunity	~~Rules_In Vivo~~ Change to Beliefs About Rules	
Discipline Procedures	Severity of Punishment	

*Codes deleted after the first round of coding are struck through once. Codes deleted later in the analysis are struck through twice. Codes added after open coding are listed in bold. Codes added during selective coding are listed in bold italics. Notes about code changes are made in plain italics.

Abduction and Further Iterations of Data Collection, Analysis, and Theory-Building

Kennedy et al. (2017) continued to collect data with their revised interview protocol and to code the interviews using their code book. They also made detailed memos about their understandings of each code as well as relationships between codes, also called theoretical coding (Glaser, 1978, 1998, 2005; Thornberg and Charmaz, 2014). During this phase, the research team relied upon abductive logic as they hypothesized about the relationships between codes and incorporated their new insights. To push their thinking, they created diagrams that helped them to explore the dimensions and ranges of meanings within different codes and related codes to each other (cf. Corbin and Strauss, 2015; see Kennedy-Lewis, 2014). Such diagrams helped the team make

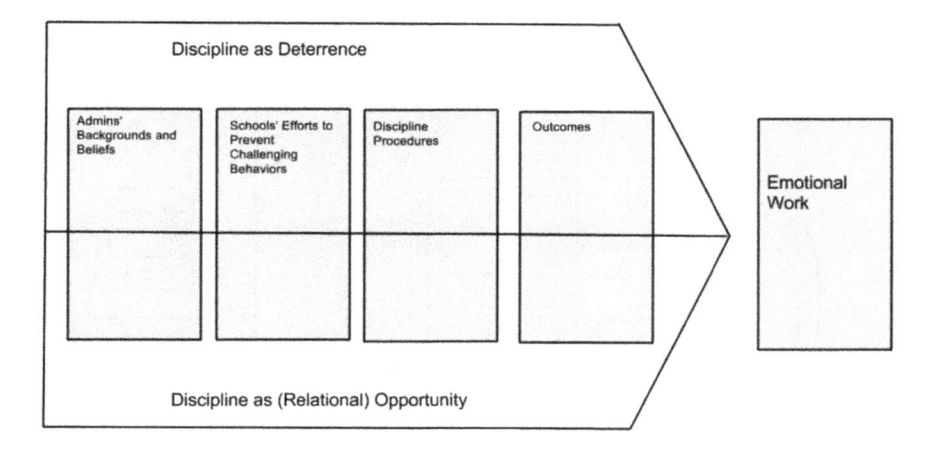

Figure 4.2 First visual representation of theory[2]

sense of a variety of seemingly contradictory perspectives. They used abductive reasoning to construct or select as provisional candidates for further investigation the hypotheses that seemed to explain the data better than the other candidate hypotheses. They also kept a table documenting the development of every code they were using and the relationships they saw developing between codes. These connections remained important as they began to understand how administrators considered and reconciled various factors in their day-to-day decision-making.

The team's decisions about when to create diagrams, which concepts required further thinking and investigation, and how big ideas related to each other reflect abductive logic; the defining of the categories required induction; and the assignment of data slices to check the defined categories as well as hypothetical relationships between categories required deduction. Moving among these logics and employing them in the analysis enabled the researchers to produce a first draft of a theory that answered their research question after the second third of the initial interviews had been completed and analyzed (see Figure 4.2).

This version of the theory reflects how the research team interpreted the tensions administrators described as being present in each part of their decision-making process. One example of something the team continued to be curious about was how administrators defined their own roles in school discipline since the researchers saw a connection between administrators' beliefs about their roles and the purposes they identified for disciplinary consequences. The research team's abductive thinking, in which they compared a range of possible hypotheses with their data and codes, led them to make these connections and consequently to add specific questions to the interview protocol (see Figure 4.1) and codes to the code book (see Table 4.1). The research team used these revisions for the third and final iteration of data collection and analysis.

Using Deduction, Induction, and Abduction to Finalize the Theory

During this final iteration of data collection and analysis, Kennedy et al. (2017) moved away from the codes, interview questions,

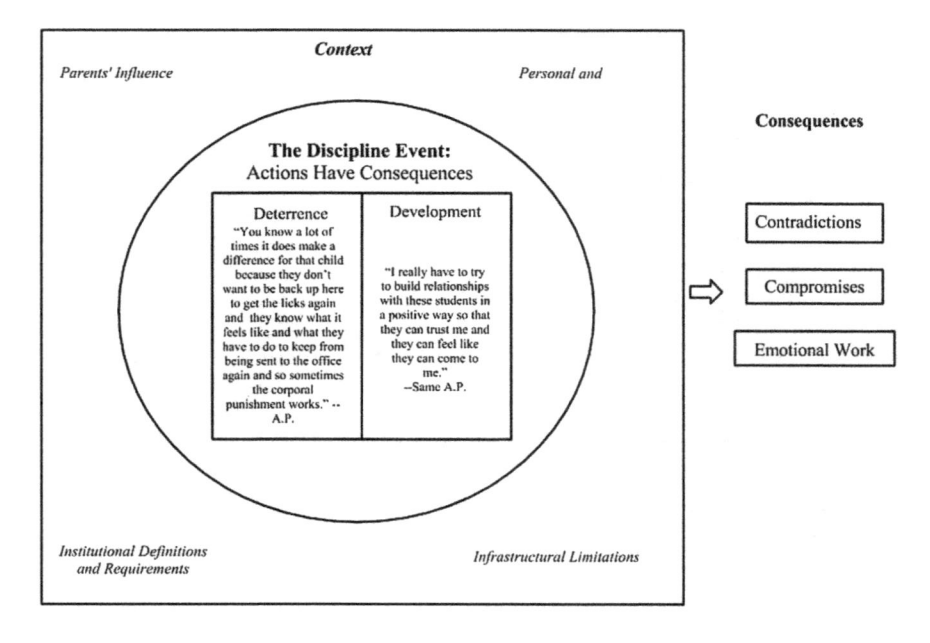

Figure 4.3 Visual representation of final theory[3]

Diagram shows a rectangular "Context" frame with corner labels: *Parents' Influence* (top-left), *Personal and* (top-right), *Institutional Definitions and Requirements* (bottom-left), *Infrastructural Limitations* (bottom-right). Inside is a circle titled "The Discipline Event: Actions Have Consequences" divided into two columns:

- **Deterrence**: "You know a lot of times it does make a difference for that child because they don't want to be back up here to get the licks again and they know what it feels like and what they have to do to keep from being sent to the office again and so sometimes the corporal punishment works." – A.P.
- **Development**: "I really have to try to build relationships with these students in a positive way so that they can trust me and they can feel like they can come to me." – Same A.P.

An arrow points from the circle to **Consequences**: Contradictions, Compromises, Emotional Work.

and concepts that were not continuing to arise in the data, and they honed their focus on vital elements of the theory that continued to puzzle them. For instance, they did not understand how the same administrators could discuss their desires to build relationships with students while also wanting to instill fear in the children. The research team also still lacked information about exactly how administrators chose which consequence and wanted more information about the referral and discipline processes. They knew that administrators talked about the role of emotion in their work, which was unexpected and which the research team included as an outcome in the first draft of their theory, but they needed to ask the administrators more directly about the roles their feelings played in their work. Continuing to use abductive logic to collect data to develop a better fitting theory, the researchers added the interview questions in italics in Figure 4.1 and continued coding using the added codes in bold in Table 4.1. They proceeded with data collection and analysis to address the conceptual gaps in their theory.

The biggest shift in their thinking occurred when they realized that their initial theory could not account for conflicting philosophies that were simultaneously held by the same individuals. In an act of abduction, the research team followed an informed 'hunch' that they later tested deductively using additional data (Atkinson and Delamont, 2005; Charmaz, 2014; Thornberg and Charmaz, 2014). That hunch was that the overarching goal of participants was to teach students that actions have consequences, and administrators often took a pragmatic approach to doing whatever they deemed necessary to teach students this important lesson, regardless of whether their actions were consistent with their prior decisions or with school discipline policies.

Kennedy et al. (2017) reconfigured their theory based on their evolving understanding and abductive conclusions (see Figure 4.3).

They then engaged in a deductive process composed of two stages to test their theory. First, they re-read transcripts from all 27 of the participants, specifically examining the 'fit' between the data and the theory and making sure that their abductive leaps accounted for the data. They remained open-minded and considered other possible hypotheses in an iterative process between deduction, induction, and abduction, and thus between data and theory. Second, they recruited an additional sample from which to collect new data to test their theory, again illustrating the interplay between the three logics of inference driving the iterative process between data collection and analysis. To see how well the theory fit the experiences of administrators in different districts that had similar challenges with student behavior, the research team identified the school districts in Florida that did not allow the use of corporal punishment and that had the lowest documented uses of exclusionary discipline. They recruited nine participants from seven schools across two out of the three qualifying districts and conducted a final round of data collection and analysis. They approached the analysis of these interview transcripts primarily with a deductive eye toward testing their existing theory. The team found that the new data supported the theory, meaning that the administrators in this additional sample in very different contexts also described their roles and disciplinary decision-making in similar ways as the original sample, giving the researchers confidence in the theory.

CONCLUSION

As we see in this example, grounded theory methodology particularly lends itself to the use of deductive, inductive, and abductive logics in data collection and analysis (Thornberg and Charmaz, 2014). Deduction allows the analyst to test conclusions at different stages of the research process. Induction assists in the creation of codes, categories, themes, and theoretical constructs and relationships that explain the data. Abduction produces a plausible explanation of the data that accounts for surprises that arise during data collection and analysis. Specifically, using these logics in a complementary fashion allows for targeted data collection techniques that strengthen research findings.

Although some researchers gravitate toward grounded theory for its step-by-step approach to data analysis, the interplay between inductive, deductive, and abductive logics is anything but prescriptive. As mentioned above, the movement among logics requires flexible applications of both creativity and critique, which position the researchers' judgments as critical to data collection and analysis. The researchers' involvement can yield novel and important findings as well as raise questions regarding the trustworthiness of the process. As an interpretive research process, the application of inductive, deductive, and abductive logics can be subjected to the same standards of trustworthiness used with other interpretive qualitative research. Researchers should adequately describe methodology and methods and give sufficient details about their decision-making so that readers can determine the trustworthiness of the results as well as the applicability of the results to other contexts (Stake, 1995). Ultimately, the validity of the research can be judged according to whether it provides new lenses with which to view social problems, new insights into possible solutions, practical wisdom to guide action, and/or empathic experiences to motivate advocacy (Lincoln et al., 2011; Schwandt, 1996).

Although the research example described in this chapter focused on grounded theory methodology, the data collection method of interview can serve many methodological orientations and the use of deductive, inductive, and abductive logics can be applied to a variety of data collection methods and research methodologies. Interplay between induction (in which the researchers are never tabula rasa), deduction (in which the researchers are always open to re-think, modify, challenge, and reject the theory or hypothesis in their interaction with data), and abduction (in which the researchers always consider their conclusions as fallible and provisional) creates powerful iterative processes between data collection and analysis, and between data and theory. In these iterative processes, qualitative researchers will not only situate their studies and their findings in the current knowledge base of the field but also contribute to it by extending, challenging, refining, or revising it.

Notes

1 Thornberg, Robert, and Charmaz, Kathy (2014) 'Grounded theory and theoretical coding', in Uwe Flick (ed.), *The SAGE Handbook of Qualitative Data Analysis*. London: SAGE. pp. 153–69. Reprinted with permission.
2 Kennedy-Lewis, Brianna L. (2014) 'Using diagrams to make meaning in grounded theory data collection and analysis', in Patrick Brindle (ed.), *SAGE Cases in Methodology*. http://srmo.sagepub.com/cases: SAGE. Reprinted with permission.
3 Kennedy, Brianna L., Murphy, Amy S., and Jordan, Adam (2017) 'Title I middle school administrators' beliefs and choices about using corporal punishment and exclusionary discipline', *American Journal of Education*, 123: 243–280. Reprinted with permission.

FURTHER READING

Charmaz, Kathy (2014) *Constructing Grounded Theory* (2nd edn). Los Angeles: Sage.
De Waal, Cornelius (2013) *Peirce: A Guide for the Perplexed*. London: Bloomsbury.
Swedberg, Richard (ed.) (2014) *Theorizing in Social Science: The Context of Discovery*. Stanford, CA: Stanford University Press.
Tavory, Iddo, and Timmermans, Stefan (2014) *Abductive Analysis: Theorizing Qualitative Research*. Chicago, IL: The University of Chicago Press.

REFERENCES

Alvesson, Mats, and Kärreman, Dan (2011) *Qualitative Research and Theory Development: Mystery as Method*. London: Sage.
Alvesson, Mats, and Sköldberg, Kaj (2008) *Tolkning och Reflektion: Vetenskapsteori och Kvalitativ Metod* [Interpretation and Reflection: Philosophy of Science and Qualitative Methods] (2nd edn). Lund: Studentlitteratur.
Anderson, Douglas R. (1986) 'The evolution of Peirce's concept of abduction', *Transactions of the Charles S. Peirce Society*, 22(2): 145–64.
Anderson, Douglas. R. (1987) *Creativity and the Philosophy of C.S. Pierce*. Dordrecht: Martinus Nijhoff.
Atkinson, Paul, and Delamont, Sara (2005) 'Analytic perspectives', in Norman K. Denzin and Yvonna. S. Lincoln (eds.), *The SAGE Handbook of Qualitative Research* (3rd edn). Thousand Oaks, CA: Sage, pp. 821–40.
Blumer, Herbert (1969) *Symbolic Interactionism*. Berkeley, CA: University of California Press.
Bryant, Antony (2009) 'Grounded theory and pragmatism: The curious case of Anselm Strauss', *Forum: Qualitative Social Research*, 10(3): Art. 2. Retrieved July 4, 2011, from http://www.qualitative-research.net/index.php/fqs/article/viewArticle/1358/2850.
Carson, David (2009) 'The abduction of Sherlock Holmes', *International Journal of Police Science and Management*, 11(2): 193–202.
Chalmers, Alan F. (1999) *What is This Thing Called Science?* (3rd edn). New York: Open University Press.
Charmaz, Kathy (2011) 'Grounded theory methods in social justice research', in Norman K. Denzin and Yvonna. S. Lincoln (eds.), *The SAGE Handbook of Qualitative Research* (4th edn). Thousand Oaks, CA: Sage, pp. 359–80.
Charmaz, Kathy (2014) *Constructing Grounded Theory* (2nd edn). Los Angeles, CA: Sage.
Charmaz, Kathy, Thornberg, Robert, and Keane, Elaine (2018) 'Evolving grounded theory and social justice inquiry', in Norman K. Denzin and Yvonna S. Lincoln (eds.), *The SAGE Handbook of Qualitative Research* (5th edn). Thousand Oaks, CA: Sage, pp. 411–43.
Corbin, Juliet, and Strauss, Anselm (2015) *Basics of Qualitative Research* (4th edn). Thousand Oaks, CA: Sage.
Delamont, Sara (2002) *Fieldwork in Educational Settings: Methods, Pitfalls and Perspectives* (2nd edn). London: Routledge.
Delamont, Sara, and Atkinson, Paul (1995) *Fighting Familiarity: Essays on Education and Ethnography*. Cresskill, NJ: Hampton Press.

Delamont, Sara, Atkinson, Paul, and Pugsley, Lesley (2010) 'The concept smacks of magic: Fighting familiarity today', *Teaching and Teacher Education*, 26(1): 3–10.

De Waal, Cornelius (2013) *Peirce: A Guide for the Perplexed*. London: Bloomsbury.

Douven, Igor (2011) 'Pierce on abduction', in Edward. N. Zalta (Principal ed.), *Stanford Encyclopedia of Philosophy*. Retrieved July 4, 2011, from http://plato.stanford.edu/entries/abduction/.

Dressman, Mark (2007) 'Theoretically framed: Argument and desire in the production of general knowledge about literacy', *Reading Research Quarterly*, 42(3): 332–63.

Dressman, Mark (2008) *Using Social Theory in Educational Research: A Practical Guide*. New York: Routledge.

Eco, Umberto (1981) 'Guessing: From Aristotle to Sherlock Holmes', *Versus*, 30: 3–19.

El Khachab, C. (2013) 'The logical goodness of abduction in C.S. Peirce's thought', *Transactions of the Charles S. Peirce Society*, 49(2): 157–77.

Glaser, Barney G. (1978) *Theoretical Sensitivity*. Mill Valley, CA: Sociology Press.

Glaser, Barney G. (1998) *Doing Grounded Theory: Issues and Discussions*. Mill Valley, CA: Sociology Press.

Glaser, Barney G. (2005) *The Grounded Theory Perspective III: Theoretical Coding*. Mill Valley, CA: Sociology Press.

Glaser, Barney, and Strauss, Anselm (1967) *The Discovery of Grounded Theory*. Chicago, IL: Aldine Transaction Press.

Hammersley, Martin, and Atkinson, Paul (2007) *Ethnography: Principles in Practice* (3rd edn). New York: Routledge.

Hanson, Norwood R. (1965) *Patterns of Discovery: An Inquiry into the Conceptual Foundations of Science*. Cambridge: Cambridge University Press.

Kelle, Udo (1995) 'Theories as heuristic tools in qualitative research', in Ilja Maso, Paul A. Atkinson, Sara Delamont and Jef C. Verhoeven (eds.), *Openness in Research: The Tension Between Self and Other*. Assen: van Gorcum, pp. 33–50.

Kelle, Udo (2014) 'Theorization from data', in Uwe Flick (ed.), *The SAGE Handbook of Qualitative Data Analysis*. London: Sage, pp. 554–68.

Kennedy, Brianna L., Murphy, Amy S., and Jordan, Adam (2017) 'Title I middle school administrators' beliefs and choices about using corporal punishment and exclusionary discipline', *American Journal of Education*, 123(2): 243–80.

Kennedy-Lewis, Brianna L. (2014) 'Using diagrams to make meaning in grounded theory data collection and analysis', in Patrick Brindle (ed.), *SAGE Cases in Methodology*, available at http://srmo.sagepub.com/cases

Lincoln, Yvonna S., Lynham, Susan A., and Guba, Egon G. (2011) 'Paradigmatic controversies, contradictions, and emerging confluences, revisited', in Norman K. Denzin and Yvonna S. Lincoln (eds.), *The SAGE Handbook of Qualitative Research* (4th edn). Thousand Oaks, CA: Sage, pp. 97–128.

Lipscomb, Martin (2012) 'Abductive reasoning and qualitative research', *Nursing Philosophy*, 13(4): 244–56.

Lorie, Sandra, and Lee, David (2007) 'Administrator beliefs about students referred for classroom disruption: A pilot investigation', *Learning Disabilities*, 14(4): 255–64.

Losen, Daniel, and Gillespie, Jonathan (2012) *Opportunities Suspended: The Disparate Impact of Disciplinary Exclusion from School*. Los Angeles, CA: The Center for Civil Rights Remedies.

McCallin, Antoniette (2006) 'Grappling with the literature in a grounded theory study', *Grounded Theory Review*, 5(2/3): 11–27.

McKaughan, Daniel J. (2008) 'From ugly duckling to Swan: C.S. Peirce, abduction, and the pursuit of scientific theories', *Transactions of the Charles S. Peirce Society*, 44(3): 446–68.

Mukuria, Gathogo (2002) 'Disciplinary challenges: How do principals address this dilemma?', *Urban Education*, 37(3): 432–52.

Paavola, Sami (2004) 'Abduction as a logic and methodology of discovery: The importance of strategies', *Foundation of Science*, 9(3): 267–83.

Peirce, Charles S. (1960/1979) *Collected Papers of Charles Sanders Pierce. Vol. I: Principle of Philosophy; Vol. II: Elements of Logic* (edited by A. W. Burks). Cambridge, MA: Harvard University Press.

Phillips, Denis C., and Burbules, Nicholas C. (2000) *Postpositivism and Educational Research*. London: Rowman & Littlefield.

Reichertz, Jo (2007) 'Abduction: The logic of discovery of grounded theory', in Antony Bryant and Kathy Charmaz (eds.), *The SAGE Handbook of Grounded Theory*. London: Sage, pp. 214–28.

Schurz, Gerhard (2008) 'Patterns of abduction', *Synthese*, 164(2): 201–34.

Schwandt, Thomas A. (1996) 'Farewell to criteriology', *Qualitative Inquiry*, 2(1): 58–72.

Stake, Robert E. (1995) *The Art of Case Study Research*. Thousand Oaks, CA: Sage.

Tavory, Iddo, and Timmermans, Stefan (2014) *Abductive Analysis: Theorizing Qualitative Research*. Chicago, IL: The University of Chicago Press.

Thayer-Bacon, Barbara J. (2003) 'Pragmatism and feminism as qualified relativism', *Studies in Philosophy and Education*, 22(6): 417–38.

Thornberg, Robert (2012) 'Informed grounded theory', *Scandinavian Journal of Educational Research*, 56(3): 243–59.

Thornberg, Robert and Charmaz, Kathy (2014) 'Grounded theory and theoretical coding', in Uwe Flick (ed.), *The SAGE Handbook of Qualitative Data Analysis*. London: Sage, pp. 153–69.

Truzzi, Marcello (1976) 'Selective attention: Sherlock Holmes: Applied social psychologist', in William B. Sanders (ed.), *The Sociologist as Detective* (2nd edn). New York: Praeger, pp. 50–86.

Upside Down – Reinventing Research Design[1]

Giampietro Gobo

INTRODUCTION

'Concept', 'hypothesis', 'indicator', 'variable', 'operationalization', 'cause', 'sampling', 'generalization', 'model', 'validation' seem old-fashioned terms – oddments of quantitative and positivistic approaches which are today already epistemologically outdated. There is some truth in this view.

However, they can acquire different meanings (as frequently happens in the history of ideas) compatible with a more constructivist perspective. These alternative meanings can be detected also in some of the most influential voices of qualitative methods, if we read them carefully:

> The freedom and flexibility that we claim for generating theory from quantitative data will lead to new strategies and styles of quantitative analysis, with their own rules yet to be discovered. And these new styles of analysis will bring out the richness of quantitative data that is seen only implicitly while the focus remains on verification.

For example, in verification studies cross-tabulations of quantitative variables continually and inadvertently lead to discoveries of new social patterns and new hypotheses, but are often ignored as *not* being the purpose of the research. In this chapter, we shall present *one* new strategy of quantitative analysis that facilitates the generation of theory from quantitative data. It is a variation of Lazarsfeld's elaboration analysis of survey data (Glaser and Strauss, 1967, p. 186, italics in the original text).

Purging these terms of positivist ideology[2] and the prejudices of qualitative researchers, and presenting them in a new framework, could make it possible to rejoin methods and approaches considered distant and irreconcilable. In other words, the coveted full integration in mixed methods research (see Morse et al., Chapter 36, this volume, and Hesse-Biber, Chapter 35, this volume) the long-awaited 'third paradigm' (Morgan, 2007), could be achieved if different tendencies could find a home in a single revisited and updated framework.

> **Box 5.1**
>
> In the waiting room, there are 12 people. Most are elderly and only two are young. The medical examinations last about half an hour each. Interviewed after the examination, nearly all patients were very pleased with the conversation with the doctor. Only one confided that she was very disappointed.

REVERSING CONVENTIONAL METHODOLOGICAL KNOWLEDGE

In this ethnographic note (Box 5.1; see Buscatto, Chapter 21, this volume), collected in a doctor's office, the researcher has 'counted' (12 people), 'measured' (around 30 minutes), 'classified' (elderly and young patients) and 'scaled' (very pleased, very disappointed). This episode shows that 'measuring', 'counting', 'scaling' and 'classifying' social instances and sequences are only different-but-complementary ways of collecting, assembling and analyzing data also in qualitative research. This is not tediously to repeat what many authors have been saying for decades (the list would be too long and the risk of excluding some too high): that the conventional distinction between quantitative and qualitative is based on highly problematic assumptions that have scant grounding, because these different 'mental models' (Maxwell et al., 2015) still exist and they have their own good reasons. However, they can be rejoined by revitalizing (not abandoning) this constellation of terms within an innovative agenda, a new epistemological framework, a novel methodological mindfulness. In other words, by changing their meanings.

Constructing the Research Topic

With the exception of those situations where research comes with specific goals or well-defined hypotheses, the research topic is initially nebulous, at best. There are several reasons for this. When the research is commissioned – contrary to what one might expect – the 'customers' often have only a vague idea of what they want to know, and their cognitive interest only becomes clear during further interactions with the researcher. In many other cases, the 'customers', especially if they are individuals, are more interested in solving a problem than in promoting analytical, theoretically informed work. Even in the case of research projects submitted to grant-awarding institutions, these projects are unlikely to entirely reflect what the research will be actually trying to do. Finally, in the case of self-sponsored research (such as theses, dissertations and some post-doctoral research), the research topic is defined in the course of the research, or results from negotiation with several stakeholders. I deliberately use the term research 'topic' (i.e. concepts) rather than the conventional 'object', because the world is populated more with concepts than objects (see the following two examples).

So, what we call 'objects' are, in fact, concepts, topics, or discourse accomplishments shaped by researchers' negotiations and theoretical assumptions which, in their turn, are a mixture of commonsense and scientific knowledge, because social phenomena are primarily ideas (Hayek, 1949, p. III; Jarvie, 1972). The former may *become* objects through research practices, but their nature is conceptual and discursive.

Outlining the Research Topic

In light of the previous discussion, it seems clear that – unless definitive hypotheses have already been formulated – a research topic is defined with greater precision *in the course*

> **Box 5.2 Two examples: researching family and poverty**
>
> The family is a much less palpable object than is commonly believed. When researchers try to define theoretically what constitutes a family (in order to later select a sample of families to interview), they realize that their own beliefs have a tremendous effect on its definition: is a group of monks or of students living under the same roof a family? Is a gay couple a family? Must there be a couple for a family to exist or can separated or divorced mothers (with children) also be defined as families? In the past, by 'family' was meant the union between two people of opposite sex (i.e. a heterosexual couple) formalized by a marriage ceremony. In the 1998 the US Bureau of the Census defined a family as 'a group of two persons or more (one of whom is a householder) related by birth, marriage or adoption and residing together'; a married couple as a 'husband and wife enumerated as members of the same household'; an unmarried couple as 'two unrelated adults of the opposite sex (one of whom is a householder) who share a housing unit with or without the presence of children under age 15'. These definitions, equating families with households, inevitably ignore increasingly common relationship constellations that extend across households. Similarly, they preclude the examination of increasingly common unmarried but cohabiting couples. In fact, today the *concept* of family, for some researchers (not for all!), is very different and extends to include many other types of relationship, and social research has adjusted accordingly. As can be seen, the social and political construction of the object 'family' is an important factor in how it is commonly understood and, even, how it is operationalized by researchers.
>
> It is (again) important to decide which criteria the researcher will adopt in order to define (theoretically) what constitutes a poor person in order to include her/him in a sample for interview. This may involve employing a cut-off afforded by the poverty line, but even this is problematic. Poverty, too, is something impalpable – even if this statement may seem ridiculous. But if we set aside the starving people on television or in refugee camps, and concentrate on the poor in Europe or America, researchers have difficulty in defining a poor person (i.e. specifying the concept). Is poverty only an economic phenomenon? If so, how can we account for elderly people who live in conditions (commonly defined) as poverty, but who are discovered, following their deaths, to have had a large sum of money in the bank or hidden under the mattress? Is not poverty a cultural phenomenon as well, therefore? And if we cannot clearly define poverty, how can we begin to study it?

of the research (Flick, 2018): the focus narrows, new aspects (ethical, social or political) of the problem emerge, and resources are totted up (funding obtained, time available before deadlines, number of collaborators). This is a strength of qualitative research, not a weakness; an element of its flexibility and adaptive ability diametrically opposed to the rigidity of much quantitative research, which 'bends' the research topic to the requirements of the method (rather than the reverse).

The decision to restrict the cognitive field is usually taken after *problematizing* at three levels, which recur and interweave in ethnographic research:

1 conceptualization of the phenomenon to investigate;
2 operational definition;
3 sampling strategy.

Several authors (among them Spradley, 1980, p. 34; Hammersley and Atkinson, 1983, p. 175; Silverman, 1993, p. 46) have written that the 'funnel' is the best metaphor to describe the course of ethnographic research.

When selecting a research topic, it is preferable to avoid overly ambitious projects, because they carry high risks of dispersion or may produce only superficial results. Aiming to obtain a complete picture of a phenomenon with just one research project is the best recipe for inquiry disaster (Silverman and Gubrium, 1994).

A research design should also be flexible enough so that it can be adapted to the irregular flow of decisions required to deal with unexpected events in the field, as exemplified, for instance, by the experience of the American organizational scholar, Alvin W. Gouldner. While he was studying the bureaucracy of a small American mining company, a wildcat strike unexpectedly forced him to modify his initial design, and he, therefore, shifted to studying – and, ultimately, to developing a general theory about – group conflicts. It is therefore important for the research design to be 'cognitively open': that is to say, configured so that 'the unexpected is expected'. Blumer's proposal that the concepts and categories of research should be treated as 'sensitizing concepts' (guiding concepts) rather than as 'definitive concepts' goes in the same direction. The former do not enable 'the user to move directly to the instance and its relevant content [in that they] give the user a general sense of reference and guidance in approaching empirical instances. Whereas definitive concepts provide prescriptions of what to see, sensitizing concepts merely suggest directions along which to look' (Blumer, 1969, p. 148).

Sensitizing concepts help researchers to approach the empirical reality by ensuring that they can always correct themselves and modify their ideas.

MANAGING RESEARCHERS' PRE-ASSUMPTIONS: THE ROLE OF REFLEXIVITY

Before describing the three main levels involved in research design, I would stress a danger ever-present in the researchers' work of interpretation: that of being excessively conditioned by their assumptions and prejudices.

Prejudices may be either positive or negative. We may be favorably disposed toward the socially excluded (as were some members of the Chicago School) or hold a negative attitude toward them (as did Talcott Parsons). Either way – positive or negative – this is a prejudice. This is unavoidable since we need such prejudices as heuristic, cognitive tools in order to explore the world and make decisions. Nevertheless, our overall reasoning capability may be more or less influenced by such prejudices and, as a result, we may be biased to a greater or lesser extent. This is what we are referring to when we speak of reflexivity. Widely acknowledged today, therefore, is the risk of attributing characteristics to the culture being studied that do not belong to that culture, but stem from the researcher's prejudices (Cicourel, 1964; Garfinkel, 1967; McHugh, 1968; Zimmerman and Pollner, 1970; Mehan and Wood, 1975, pp. 225–38). Social scientists are thus in danger of ingenuously constructing a sociological object into which they transfer the properties of the conceptual apparatus used for their research.

Is it possible to escape from this circular process of prejudice reinforcement? The short answer is 'no, from a theoretical point of view it is not'. In a more pragmatic sense, however, it should be kept in mind that this hermeneutic circle is tractable, at least to some extent. As the American cultural anthropologist Clifford Geertz wisely put it:

> I have never been impressed by the argument that, as complete objectivity is impossible in these matters (as, of course it is), one might as well let one's sentiments run loose. As Robert Solow has remarked, that is like saying that as a perfectly aseptic environment is impossible, one might as well conduct surgery in a sewer. (1973, p. 30)

It is therefore possible to invent strategies that can help the researcher reflexively to avoid gross errors, at least, and to partly remedy the irremediability of the hermeneutic circle. One of these strategies is *conceptualization*.

CONCEPTUALIZING THE TOPIC

Technically speaking, with research we aim mainly to determine *the status of cases with regard to an attribute relevant to a concept*. To the uninitiated, this expression may seem incomprehensible. Nevertheless, an example will help clarify its meaning: for instance, if we want to study the quality of the relationship between telephone companies and their customers. Quality is made up of many attributes: the speed with which calls are answered; efficiency in handling requests for information; the attention paid to dealing with complaints; and so on. Let us take the last attribute: our research might conclude that the five companies in the sample are largely inattentive to customer complaints. Using technical language, what we have surveyed is the status (inattentive) of the five cases observed on the attribute 'ability to deal with customer complaints' relative to the research topic (concept) 'quality of the relationship with customers'.

Why have I called 'ability to deal with customer complaints' an *attribute* rather than a characteristic or 'property' (Glaser and Strauss, 1967, pp. 23, 36–9, 55–8, 106–9, 193, 248–9) or aspect of a business organization? Because *characteristic* or *aspect* implies that the ability to deal with customer complaints is a *property of the object* 'organization'; that it is a (quite independent) component of this object; and that the researcher's task is only to observe and collect information about it. The term *attribute* more clearly conveys the idea that this is a *concept*, which the researcher *attributes* (constructively) to his or her research topic. What are improperly called the characteristics of an object are not independent 'things', rather, they are 'cognitive instruments' which always result from a discretionary operation performed by the researcher.

Dissecting the Topic

It is evident from the example that it is important to reflect carefully on the topic of one's research before going into the field and making observations (see Wästerfors, Chapter 20, this volume). Conceptualization helps clarify what information is necessary for the research and what data must be collected in the field (Strauss and Corbin, 1990, p. 63).

The first step in conceptualizing consists of reflecting about the relations between the research topic and its possible attributes. For this purpose, the research topic is broken down, deconstructed, into simpler elements or parts (see Figure 5.1).

This process suggests which aspects should be carefully observed and which can be omitted from observation as irrelevant or potentially liable to make the research too extensive – bearing in mind that here 'omit' does not mean eliminate but 'leave in the background'. Given that observing everything is cognitively impossible, it is advisable to focus on a few aspects and study only those in detail. It would also be extremely helpful

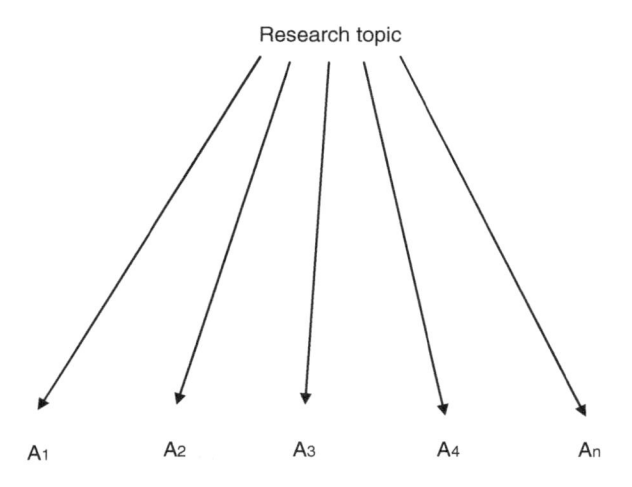

Figure 5.1 The research topic and its attributes (A)

> **Box 5.3   Research questions at work**
>
> To fully appreciate this process, consider the following imaginary conversation between two PhD students:
>
> Alex   I want to study the doctor/patient relationship......
> Ben   Why precisely that relationship and not something else, like health policies, hospital bureaucracy, the lobbies of doctors, and pharmaceutical companies?
> Alex   Because I'm interested in interactions.
> Ben   So you've got a specific theoretical approach in mind, have you?
> Alex   Yes, I'm interested in interactional approaches.
> Ben   What do you mean by interaction? What interactions do you want to observe? Those between the doctor and the patient or also those between the patient and the doctor's secretary, those between the doctor and his secretary, or the interactions among the patients in the waiting room?
> Alex   Er …… I don't know …… I'll have to think about it ……
> Ben   But what aspect of the doctor/patient interaction do you want to observe? What particular details interest you? Welcome rituals, presentation rituals, the doctor's rhetorical strategies, misunderstandings between the doctor and the patient, the patient's difficulties in describing his symptoms, the power relation and asymmetry between them?
> Alex   I don't know …… I don't know …… I've still got to think about all that ……

to try to identify dimensions in advance of addressing attributes. A dimension is a cluster of several attributes, a sub-concept, which can offer the researchers much more control on their inferential process when making important decisions such as omitting one attribute from the research. It must also be noted that, often, a single attribute can indicate more than one dimension. In order to achieve unidimensionality, so that an attribute is indicative of only one particular aspect of our topic, it is advisable to utilize dimensions as an intermediate step.

Research Questions

Actively reflecting on the concepts and breaking them down into attributes also helps the researcher define the units of analysis and, subsequently, to design the sampling strategy better. If these operations are neglected, information will be collected on cases so disparate that comparative analysis will be difficult – if not immediately impossible. As the researcher reflects on the relationship between the attributes and the research topic, a number of questions arise. These are what we call 'research questions'. It is, therefore, improper to ask researchers and students to elaborate on their research questions before moving on to conceptualize what really matters in their research (Flick, 2018).

Although Ben's attitude might seem rude, these questions are in fact extremely useful for Alex because they prompt him to reflect on his research topic and to specify and narrow it down to something feasible. It does not help Alex to have only a vague idea of what he is interested in. Moreover, as the reader will have probably noticed, this kind of exercise is much more fruitful if it is conducted with another person or in a group, rather than being engaged in by one researcher involved in a solitary exercise of meditation.

While it is not always necessary for researchers, especially the more experienced and skilled ones, to go over all these questions before entering the field, proper conceptualization is certainly a necessary prerequisite for good quality research, as it breaks a research topic down into empirically observable aspects. In addition, it helps to formulate 'clear and testable research questions' (Yin, 1984, pp. 29–35).

The Role of Theory in Conceptualization

The research questions asked in the above imaginary dialog (Box 5.3) privilege a particular approach which concentrates on the participants' actions rather than their inner states. It dwells on what people do as opposed to what they think, and it focuses on relations rather than individuals. As Sacks (1992) points out, this approach requires the researcher to tackle what is most directly observable (actions) while according only secondary importance to motives, attitudes, and mental frameworks. The latter are not eliminated out of court, but may, eventually, be reconsidered on the basis of actions and conversations:

> The question that ethnographers have traditionally asked – 'How do participants see things?' – has meant in practice the presumption that reality lies outside the words spoken in a particular time and space. The [alternative] question – 'How do participants do things?' – suggests that the microsocial order can be appreciated more fully by studying how speech and other face-to-face behaviours constitute reality within actual mundane situations. (Maynard, 1989, p. 144, quoted in Silverman, 1993, p. 54)

That leaves us facing a necessity. A researcher's account cannot coincide with the meanings of the observed people or with their thoughts, because the scientist's view of research participants' everyday life cannot, by definition, correspond to the actors' experience of it (Schwartz and Jacobs, 1979, p. 183). As Silverman critically remarks, 'if ethnography reduces social life to the definitions of the participants, it becomes a purely "subjectivist" sociology which loses sight of social phenomena' (1993, p. 54).

The same criticism could be applied to cognitive or psycho-sociological research on social representations aiming to reveal mental models or cognitive schemas that are considered to be stable or recurrent within a social group or an organization. These approaches maintain the idea that culture is located in the minds of social actors and, according to the famous expression of the American cognitive anthropologist, Ward Goodenough (1957), consists of 'whatever it is one has to know or believe in order to operate in a manner acceptable to its members' in all requisite social situations. According to this view, a culture can be described by reconstructing categories, taxonomies and systematic rules to produce something akin to an ethnographic algorithm, whereby the person applying it is mistaken for a competent member of the group. Unlike these theories, Geertz draws an apt analogy with a Beethoven quartet: 'no one would, I think, identify it with its score, with the skills and knowledge needed to play it, with the understanding of it possessed by its performers or auditors' (1973, p. 11). Just as the music does not consist merely of the score, so a society does not consist only of its rules.

OPERATIONAL DEFINITIONS: WHAT ARE THEY AND WHY DO WE NEED THEM?

'Operational definition' is another expression rejected by qualitative researchers because it is a vestigial holdover from logical positivism. They are right on this. However, by doing so, they 'throw the baby out with the bathwater', as they usually do with other terms (see below). Avoiding simply emotive reactions to these (considered) positivist terms, it is possible to attribute to them a different (more constructivist) meaning related to the formal properties of human reasoning (see Maxwell, Chapter 2, this volume).

The research work of social scientists consists mainly in making sense of events (that they observe) through classifying them. For example, on observing the way that nursing staff at many rest homes keep the elderly residents in bed for as long as possible, a social scientist may ask why they do so?

This behavior may be a 'sign of status' (Glaser and Strauss 1967, pp. 23, 83–5, 210) or a *clue* of:

a. the nursing staff's concern for the well-being of the elderly residents;
b. the existence of practices designed to achieve greater social control;
c. an organizational response to a shortage of staff.

The relation between the event and the three different concepts (explanations, therefore causes) proposed takes the form of a *relationship of indication*, where the event is *evidence* for the presence, or otherwise, of a particular concept. It is not a prerogative of scientific reasoning; rather, it is a formal property of common-sense reasoning. In other words, when social actors (researchers included) interpret behavior, they constantly – often unawares – connect together concepts and attributes, indicators and variables. Interpretation is nothing other than the rapid, tacit, and recurrent activation of relationships of indication. Garfinkel, explicitly borrowing an expression from the Hungarian sociologist and philosopher Karl Mannheim, has called this process the 'documentary method of interpretation':

> the method consists of treating an actual appearance as 'the document of', as 'pointing to', as 'standing on behalf of' a presupposed underlying pattern. Not only is the underlying pattern derived from its individual documentary evidences, but the individual documentary evidences, in their turn, are interpreted on the basis of 'what is known' about the underlying pattern. Each is used to elaborate the other. (Garfinkel, 1962, p. 691)

Operational Definition

An operational definition consists of the set of conventions that guide the researcher's interpretive activity. It is called *operational* (in order to distinguish it from the kind of *lexical* definition found in dictionaries) because it tells us what do: that is to say, it has a practical intent. Hence, through these conventions, the status of each case on the attribute X is determined, assigned to one of the categories established (coding), and recorded so that it can be analyzed using the techniques that the researcher intends to employ. Many of these conventions are customs, which guide the knowledge-gathering process. Among these customs are the procedures used to gain access to the field, the devices (guarantees, informal contracts) employed to overcome actors' potential diffidence, the way in which the ethnographic notes are collected, and the procedures followed in order to verify the truthfulness of the replies obtained.

The operational definition helps the ethnographer to discipline the observation, the information gathering, and the attributes that s/he deems to be connected to the topic studied, within a relationship of indication. In other words, the operational definition adds rigor to the researcher's interpretive activity. The expression 'operational definition of a concept' comes from the quantitative approach. However, also in qualitative approaches one can find a parallel (amended) conceptual framework. Particularly, Glaser and Strauss talked extensively about relating dimensions, concepts, categories and properties (1967, pp. 23, 36–9, 55–8, 106–9, 193, 248–9). Although they and Denzin (1969) recommended that the operational definition of the concept be developed only *after* the research has begun, when the researcher has obtained an initial understanding of the phenomenon and 'the situated meaning of concepts is discovered' (Denzin, 1969, p. 925), there is nothing to stop the researcher from developing it *before* the research starts if s/he already has specific hypotheses to control.

The operational definition is the cognitive activity that is unique to science and which distinguishes it from other knowledge-gathering endeavors. All the other cognitive activities to be found in science (like formulating hypotheses, sampling, generalizing, drawing comparisons, making forecasts, checking the veracity of statements, etc.) are

> **Box 5.4 Case study: what is difficult?**
>
> My dissertation was based on discourse analysis of tape-recorded standardized interviews. One focus was whether interviewees found it relatively easy to answer with closed-ended (or multiple choice) questions, or whether they had difficulties in choosing a response alternative. The first methodological problem that I encountered concerned the concept of 'difficulty'. By simply listening to the tapes, how could I decide when the interviewees were finding it difficult to answer? What for me seemed to be difficulty might not seem so for another researcher who listened to the tape after me. I wanted my interpretations to be well argued, in order to forestall the criticisms of carelessness or arbitrariness certain to be made of my work by survey researchers. To solve my methodological problem, I first established the meaning (therefore the definition) of 'difficulty in choosing a response alternative' and then considered what might be good indicators of this concept. In short, I invented an operational definition of 'difficulty'. For the record, I operationalized the concept by means of three indicators:
>
> 1   the time taken by respondents to select a response alternative;
> 2   the perplexities/hesitations that they expressed;
> 3   their comments disapproving or critical of the multiple-choice format.

also present in common-sense reasoning. But operational definition is not. It enables us to 'problematize the observation' (Cicourel, 1964, p. 128), *de-naturalize* the social world that we are investigating, in contrast to the behavior of the member who observes it as natural, obvious, taken-for-granted, normal.

Rescue the Variable!

Qualitative researchers have also been much opposed to the use of variables, believing that research should not be impeded by such restraints. Again, they forget that the use of variables and indicators is also part of common-sense reasoning. We saw previously that indicator-based reasoning is intrinsic to the 'documentary method of interpretation'; variables, too, are constantly present in our discourses and thoughts. Consider the following verbal exchange between Amanda and two of her friends who she sees eating slices of cake in the cafeteria:

Amanda: How's the cake?
Bernie: So so.
Carl: For me it's quite good.

What difference is there between this evaluation and the scale of 5 response alternatives (very good/fairly good/half and half/fairly bad/very bad) commonly used in questionnaires? None. So, there is space for a meaning of 'variable' alternative to the positivist strict sense.

Etymologically, 'variable' means something that varies. Age, satisfaction, feelings, and so on can vary.

Everything that varies could be a variable. Also a term/concept could be either a status or a variable: 'depression' could be a status on the variable disease; and it could be a variable itself with different statuses or levels (high, low, etc. degrees of depression). Likewise, 'rain' could be a status on the variable 'weather' or a variable itself (moderate, heavy etc. rain). Glaser and Strauss (1967, pp. 205–10, 211–20, 245–9) deal at length with variables in a new and a non-positivist way. Also Strauss and Corbin, when talking about their researches on chronic diseases, write: 'One can conceptualize this dimension as pertaining to the property of **degree of intensity**. Pain can vary along a continuum of degree from very bad (severe) to not so bad (mild)… Is it continuous, intermittent, or temporary?' (1990, p. 205, bold in original). Previously, on representing properties and dimensions graphically, they ended up with the following schema (Table 5.1), which closely recalls the Lazarsfeldian framework

Table 5.1 The link between category, properties, and dimensional range

Category	Properties		Dimensional range (applied to each incident)	
watching	frequency	often	---------------------------	never
	extent	more	---------------------------	less
	intensity	high	---------------------------	low
	duration	long	---------------------------	short

Source: Strauss and Corbin (1990, pp. 72 and 101–2)

Box 5.5 Indicators and variables in Balinese cockfights

Clifford Geertz studied the clandestine bets wagered on cockfights in Bali. It seems odd that Geertz should have chosen such an esoteric topic for research; yet he wrote that it was 'a revelation of what being Balinese "is really like" as these more celebrated phenomena' (1972, p. 417) like art, forms of law, educational models, and so on, provide valuable insights. Geertz watched a total of fifty-seven cockfights and constructed the meaning of the practice, the logic of betting, and other details. He then classified the clandestine bets (using a dichotomous variable, I would say): 'deep' and 'shallow'. In the former case, usually 'the amounts of money are great [as opposed to smaller amounts of money wagered in shallow games], much more is at stake than material gain: namely, esteem, honor, dignity, respect – in a word (…) status. It is at stake symbolically, for (a few cases of ruined addict gamblers aside) no one's status is actually altered by the outcome of a cockfight' (1972, p. 433).

But how could a deep game be distinguished from a shallow one? How could the observer know that one type of situation rather than the other was in progress? What was it that differentiated between the two types of game? Geertz listed 17 'facts' (1972, p. 473) – what we can straightforwardly call *indicators* – for the presence of a deep game. The first of these indicators was: 'A man virtually never bets against a cock owned by a member of his own kingroup. Usually he will feel obliged to bet for it, the more so the closer the kin tie and the deeper the fight. If he is certain in his mind that it will not win, he may just not bet at all, particularly if it is only a second cousin's bird or if the fight is a shallow one. But as a rule he will feel he must support it and, in deep games, nearly always does' (1972, p. 437).

(to whom even Glaser and Strauss, 1967, p. 23, note 3, pp. 190–3 refer).

It is in this sense that one can interpret (without misinterpreting) Blumer's criticism of 'variable analysis'. He criticized not the use of variables in itself, but rather the standardized usage. Indeed, he mentioned three kinds of 'generic variables' useful for social research and stated: 'obviously the study of human group life calls for a wide range of variables' (1956, p. 683). His criticism related to the automatic use of the same operational definition for any research: 'each of these variables, even though a class term, has substance only in a given historical context. The variables do not stand directly for items of abstract human group life' (p. 684).

The conventional distinction between thinking of the world in terms of variables and correlations and in terms of events and processes does not hold in both theory and practice. It is *just* a matter of ideological and identity contrapositions.

Indeed, if we analyze the work of ethnographers without too many ideological prejudices, we find that they use indicators (Glaser and Strauss, 1967, p. 23, chapters III and IV, p. 210) and variables to distinguish among statuses on attributes.

By the way, first cousin or second cousin, and so on, are just statuses on the variable kingroup! Had he so wished, Geertz could also have constructed a grid showing the frequency of each of the seventeen indicators. For example, he could have associated

Table 5.2 Some differences between qualitative and quantitative research

Terms	Concepts (meanings)	
	Quantitative research	*Qualitative research*
Operational definition	An activity that must be done before beginning research	Activity rarely done before beginning research. More frequently it is performed *during* research, when the researcher has gained an understanding of the phenomenon
Indicator	*Standardized* conceptual device to design the understanding of a phenomenon	*Situational* conceptual device to gain better understanding of the relationship between evidence and the underlying pattern
Variable	*Standardized* operative device for *measuring* a phenomenon	The possibility to measure meanings is rejected. Variables are *situational* operative devices for improving the rigor of the researcher's interpretation
Hhypotheses	Assertions to be *verified* or *tested*	Assertions to be *checked* or *documented* through rhetorical devices

the indicator 'kin loyalty' with the variable 'betting against a kinsman's cock', and then added the following alternative responses: 'never', 'sometimes', 'often'. The systematic observation might have shown that there was kin loyalty in 95 percent of cases, or in only 72 percent. The latter finding would have made a major difference to the assessment of the level of the community's compliance with the kin loyalty convention – which at first sight had seemed unwavering.

This is not new. As Maxwell writes:

> Becker (1970, pp. 39–62), Erickson (2007), Hammersley (1992, pp. 159–73), and Miles and Huberman (1984) have supported the inclusion of numerical data in qualitative research practices and reports. Becker (1970) argued that qualitative researchers frequently make quantitative claims in verbal form, using terms such as *many*, *often*, *typically*, *sometimes*, and so on. He argued that numbers have the value of making such claims more precise and coined the term *quasi statistics* for simple counts of things to support terms such as *some*, *usually*, and *most*. (Maxwell, 2010, p. 476)

Sandelowski et al. made a similar point about 'quantitizing' qualitative data, stating that this is done in qualitative research 'to facilitate pattern recognition or otherwise to extract meaning from qualitative data, account for all data, document analytic moves, and verify interpretations' (2009, p. 210, quoted in Maxwell, 2010, p. 476).

In summary, the operational definition transforms the indicators relative to the attributes of a concept into variables. A variable is, therefore, the outcome of the operational definition – its terminal; the device with which the researcher collects information or analyzes their ethnographic notes. Indicators and variables are, therefore, two sides of the same coin: the indicator is situated at the conceptual level; the variable pertains to the practical one. Variables serve to detect differences and to communicate them. The main difference from qualitative research is the standardized use of these devices (see Table 5.2). Unlike survey and experimental researchers, qualitative researchers do not reify, objectify or standardize their devices, using them always in the same way in all their research. Instead, they construct their devices situationally, finding *ad hoc* remedies for every research problem. However, they should pay more attention to variables and seek to become as competent as their qualitative colleagues in designing variables, paying particular attention to ensuring that they avoid conceptual overlaps among attributes while trying to be as thorough as possible.

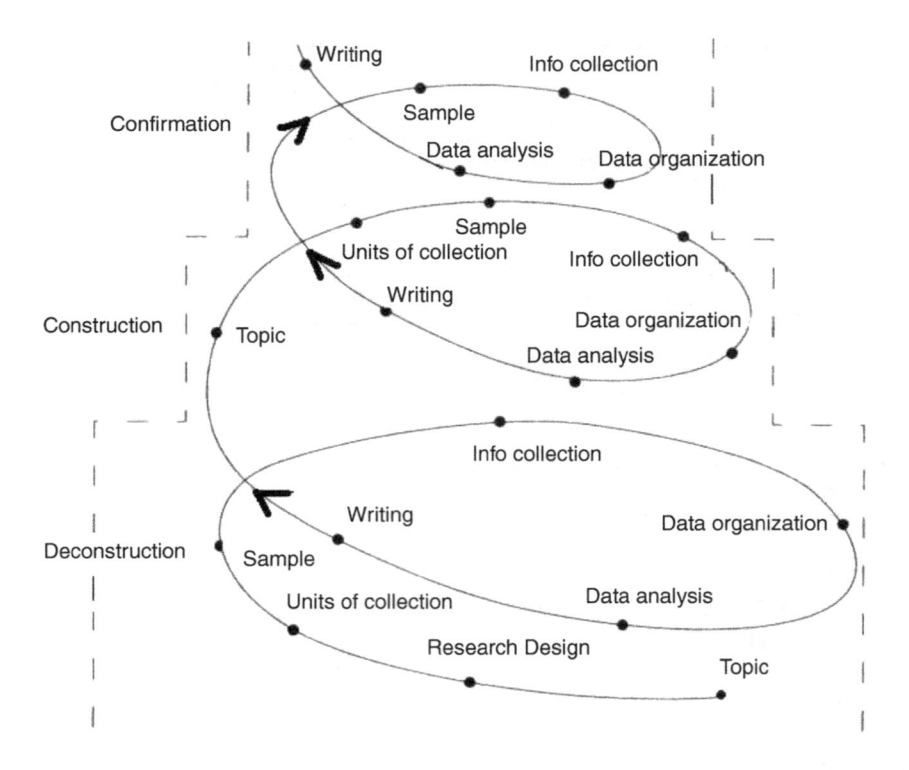

Figure 5.2 The (spiral-shaped) model of ethnographic research

Conceptualization and Operationalization: A Reflexive Process

In qualitative research the coding of an event is not the final act in the data-gathering process; rather, it is only an intermediate stage in the construction of the variables. Given the reflexive and spiraling nature of ethnographic research (see Figure 5.2), the operational definition is partly or wholly recast in successive phases of research: the concepts, hypotheses, and indicators change. Hence conceptualization and operationalization interweave in a constant reflexive process of reciprocal adjustments, by virtue of the possible re-specification of the original formulation of a concept, or the reconceptualization of the data: 'a series of empirical indicators relevant to each data base and hypothesis must be constructed, and, research must progress in a formative manner in which hypotheses and data continually interrelate' (Denzin, 1969, p. 926).

Documenting the operational definition process is of paramount importance in assuring the coherence of the researcher's interpretations and in corroborating them.

INVENTING HYPOTHESES

Another common misconception about qualitative research is that it approaches a research topic without any hypotheses and, instead, tries to understand and describe phenomena better (Agar, 1986, p. 12).

Apart from the fact that, as Silverman ironically points out, 'qualitative research would look a little odd, after a history of over 100 years, if it had no hypotheses to test!' (2000,

> **Box 5.6 Case study: hypothesis as a form of common-sense reasoning**
>
> Consider the following example: you are driving your car. At a certain point, there is a queue of vehicles in front of you. What do you think? That the queue has formed (a) because of an accident or (b) because of road works or (c) because of traffic lights ahead? In any case, you have unconsciously produced three different hypotheses, which may have practical consequences according to which of them seems most plausible. If it is the first, you will make a U-turn and look for another route to your destination. If you instead decide to wait until the traffic starts moving again, you may check your hypotheses and discover the cause of the tailback.

p. 8), hypotheses and understanding/describing are not conflicting issues, and having hypotheses can be helpful. While we advise readers to avoid oversimplifications such as that hypotheses are 'educated guesses', we must stress that such sophisticated research devices, rich in theory and designed to be documented, are grounded on the same logical reasoning that we routinely use, often unconsciously.

All our hypotheses are based on a previous theoretical knowledge of the phenomenon that allows us to make some inference based on what we are observing, or about to observe; and to be a proper hypothesis it must define some documentable expectations. Moving on to a more formal level, from a *methodological point of view*, a hypothesis is an assertion – conjectural in nature – about the relationships between certain attributes in a research topic. *From an operational point of view*, a hypothesis is an assertion about the relationships between two or more variables that produces an observable expected outcome.

Glaser and Strauss (1967, pp. 83, 194ff, 230, 241), Schatzman and Strauss (1973, pp. 12–13, 53, 57, 76), and Strauss and Corbin (1990, pp. 107, 108, 111–2, 148, 253) argue that hypotheses are indispensable for research; though these should be formulated and tested only *after* the ethnographic notes have been collected (inductive hypotheses) so that the researcher goes into the field without preconceived ideas. Unlike Hymes (1978), Silverman (1993, p. 44) and Yin (1994, pp. 29–35) maintain that ethnographers can perfectly well conduct a hypothesis-oriented ethnography, provided that they already have a good level of knowledge about the culture that they are studying.

Whether hypotheses are more or less specified and formalized also depends on the amount of knowledge that the researcher possesses. Based on our level of confidence in our expectations we may design *working* or *guiding* hypotheses.

DRAWING MODELS

Models are graphical representations of hypotheses, as we can see in some charts produced by textual analysis software (see Figure 5.3).

A hypothesis may be descriptive and neutral, in that it states the existence of a relationship between two attributes or variables without specifying its direction, or it may be directional and explanatory, suggesting a causal relationship (e.g. A → B). For example, Strauss et al. (1964) conducted an empirical study on the rules and informal agreements present in various psychiatric hospitals. They then constructed a causal model in which the differences among the rules applied at the hospitals were explained by the existence of different patient care practices. However, these practices were, in their turn, conditioned by the professional models learned at different schools by the hospital staff and which reflected different psychiatric ideologies. Other models can

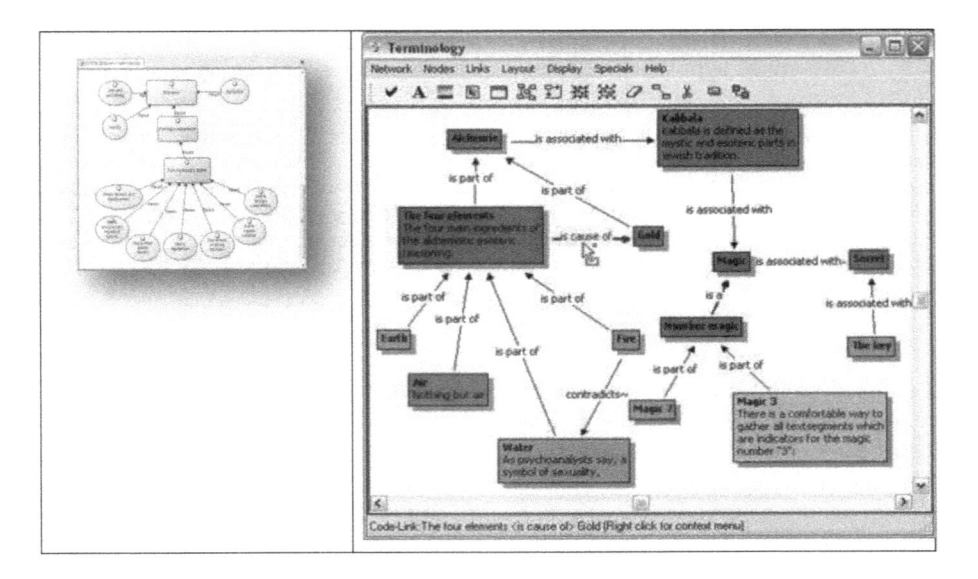

Figure 5.3 Models from Atlas.ti 7 (left) and NVivo 10 (right)

be found, Glaser and Strauss (1964) illustrating the 'social loss' phenomenon, or in Strauss and Corbin (1990, p. 222) about the relationship among body, biography, and trajectory.

Maxwell has persuasively shown, unlike many qualitative researchers who believe that causation is an inappropriate concept in qualitative research, that thinking in terms of causality (besides being part of everyday reasoning) is highly compatible with qualitative research; the latter, due to its capacity to focus actions and meanings, could enlighten causal *processes* much better than conventional qualitative research. In addition, he points out: 'if you want to work against injustice and oppression, you need to understand the *causes* of the particular forms of injustice and oppression you are dealing with, and how to counteract and overcome these causes' (2012, p. 658).

The relationship between variables may take various forms: a simple association or correlation, a symmetric relation, or an asymmetric relation such as causation. We must be careful, in the social sciences, with regard to making claims about causation. Causal relations require, in fact, more than the evidence of correlations because, at the very least, the researcher must be able to identify the cause and the effect, where the cause precedes the effect in time, and must be able to exclude the intervention of other factors. It is evident that it is very hard to have enough information to satisfy both these requirements simultaneously; and also because an effect, far from determinism and mechanicism, can retroact on the cause in an inter-dependence relationship.

Spurious Associations

Spurious associations are widely neglected in qualitative research methodology. However, they are very common in both commonsense reasoning and social theory; consequently, many research findings are trapped by them: we believe that A → B, but this is an illusion because both A and B are influenced by C, an intervening variable (or 'intervening condition' in Strauss and Corbin, 1990, pp. 86, 102–4, 151–2) which we have not considered.

> **Box 5.7 Closed-circuit television (CCTV) and crime**
>
> When action is taken by a politician or a decision-maker to deal with a problem, that action is expected to have effects (possibly positive ones): in other words, it is expected to solve the problem, or at least to improve the situation. Assessors are usually brought in to verify whether these benefits have really been produced. Unfortunately, most decision-makers and assessors have a positivist mentality that induces them to believe that there is a cause/effect relation between a given action and the subsequent social change. Not infrequently, however, a change (B) is not so much the effect of action (A) as it is of intervention by other social mechanisms (or intervening variables). This, therefore, is a classic example of spurious association.
>
> The methodologist Ray Pawson and the criminologist Nick Tilly describe the following case. Closed-circuit television (CCTV) is installed in a car park and a decrease in car thefts is noted. At first sight, one might think that the introduction of CCTV (A) produced the decrease in thefts (B). However, it is unlikely that television cameras in themselves possess this magical power: 'there is nothing about CCTV in car parks which intrinsically inhibits car crime' (1997, p.: 78). Instead, the concomitance of specific conditions is necessary for them to be really effective:
>
> 1. There should be someone (a police officer, security guard, etc.) who observes the images transmitted by the CCTV cameras in real time and is able to intervene immediately. Otherwise a thief wearing a balaclava or a hood concealing his face can act undisturbed and without the risk of being identified.
> 2. The CCTV cameras should be linked to a police station situated in the immediate vicinity so that the police can intervene immediately.
> 3. There should be no obstacles (pillars, guardrails, etc.) blocking the camera sightlines and behind which the thief is able to act unobserved: but this only happens in the case of open-air car parks.
> 4. The car park should be well lit, otherwise, the camera images will not be sharply defined and thieves will be more difficult to identify.
> 5. Car thieves from other towns (even a considerable distance away) may be unconcerned about the presence of CCTV. Their faces are often not in the local police force's files (which contain photographs of local criminals), so that there is little risk of their being recognized and arrested. In fact, this type of criminal is different from a terrorist or serial killer, whose photographs are displayed in all police stations.
>
> If these conditions (and many others – see Pawson and Tilly, 1997, p.: 78ff) are not in place, CCTV in itself may be ineffectual. Instead, the decline in car crime may (also) have been due to many factors. For instance, the presence of CCTV cameras may have:
>
> - induced car owners not to lock their vehicles: their carelessness might be recorded on film, and some insurance companies do not reimburse careless policy holders;
> - increased traffic in the car park, thus increasing social control: if it becomes widely known that CCTV has been installed in a car park, so that people consider it more secure, there may be more users, and therefore greater social control. Thieves will consequently be deterred.

The deception of spurious association is often lying in wait, and it is not always easy to avoid. However, if the reasoning is extended to include spurious associations, the research becomes more complex and difficult, but also interesting and counter-intuitive because it makes our explanations much less ingenuous, our theories more refined, and social research more credible.

Of course, we know (and have done so for a long time) that reality is more complex than a model can depict. In the 1930s, the Polish semanticist Alfred H. S. Korzybski stated this principle in a frequently abused quote: 'a map is not the territory' (1933, p. 58). Later the American mathematician Solomon W. Golomb, referring to mathematical modeling, put it nicely: 'interchanging a model with reality would be like going to a restaurant and eating the menu'. However, notwithstanding the greater complexity of reality, we should abandon modeling because it makes the complexity more understandable. The simplest theories are usually the ones most successful in communicating such complexity.

MAIN CURRENT TYPES OF RESEARCH DESIGNS

Creswell (2013) suggests that there are five approaches to qualitative research (and related research designs): narrative, phenomenological, grounded theory, ethnography, and case study. Flick (2014) proposes an alternative classification: case study, comparative study, retrospective study, snapshot, and longitudinal study. However, if we look at what a researcher concretely does and how s/he practically acts during the whole research process, we could envision the following classification (see Gobo, 2008, chapter 2, table 3), based on the *main* cognitive modes activated when gathering information: discursive interview (listening), ethnography (observing), documentary methodology (reading), transformative methodology (operationalizing) and speculative methodology (introspecting and reflecting). Related to these five methodologies are specific types of research, data collection, and data analysis techniques.

Each methodology has an actual inner force (like language in Austin's speech act theory), a specific performativity, a particular agency. It embodies a distinct capacity to construct data, a defined methodological world view (*Weltanschauung*). In other words, through their inner power, methodologies closely concur (with the researcher, the participants, the research setting, the organizational and institutional constraints and opportunities) to build the data. This is why data collected by discursive interviews and focus groups, ethnographies and so on, are often different, never overlap, and frequently conflict. There is a strong link (though not a deterministic one, of course) between the type of datum collected and the type of research methodology: what you get with one methodology, you do not get with another (see Becker and Geer, 1957, for an early comparison between participant observation and conversational interview). Methods are like fruit trees: each tree produces a specific fruit.

CONCLUSION

The main hindrance to a systemic, interactive, dynamic and integrated mixed methods design is represented by the still existing separate languages and mental models on how to design and conduct research. However, these oppositions could be rejoined by revitalizing (with new and different meanings) the constellation of terms, listed at the beginning of this chapter. From this point of view, 'it does not seem legitimate to use expressions like quantitative and qualitative in reference to method' (Campelli, 1991, pp. 45–6). Because, as the pragmatist philosopher John Dewey (1938) pointed out, the logic of social-scientific research (the method) is unique and always follows the same criteria of scientific validation and the same general procedural steps: formulation of the problem, conceptualization, construction of the empirical base, and analysis and interpretation of the data. Not by chance, Dewey and pragmatism are furthermore cited as the load-bearing epistemological core of mixed methods (Morgan, 2007).

It is probably time to reconcile the quantitative and qualitative divide by developing a single framework – not, however, from a potentially disastrous neo-positivist point of view, but from a phenomenological and constructivist one.

Table 5.3 Main methodologies and techniques in qualitative research

Methodologies	Pivotal cognitive modes	Research types	Gathering structure	Data collection techniques	Data management techniques	Data analysis techniques
Discursive interview	listening	biographic hermeneutic	little or partly structured	**individual interview** (in-depth, narrative, open-ended, semi-structured, topical, problem-centered, with the double, realistic, interview control question, ecocultural family interview, ethnographic interview) **collective interview** (group, *focus* and *delphi*)	transcription & coding	narrative analysis discourse analysis thematic analysis Grounded Theory
Ethnography	observing	hermeneutic ergonomic	non-structured structured	participant (e.g. cool hunting, mystery shopping, shadowing) non-participant	fieldnotes grid matrix	fieldnote analysis Grounded Theory factor analysis
Documentary	reading	textual archive	little or partly structured structured	letters, diaries, documents, images (photo, video), class projects, transcripts large textual dataset (newspapers, magazines) *ecological files* census and register office database	coding matrix matrix	thematic analysis, narrative analysis, discourse analysis, Foucauldian discourse analysis, Grounded Theory, conversation analysis, content analysis covariance
Transformative	Operationalizing	action-research intervention-res. *participatory res.* cooperative res. socio-analysis psychoanalysis systemics experimental computational evaluation	little or partly structured structured	individual interview collective interview sociodrama candid camera breaching studies individual colloquium couple colloquium family colloquium experiment simulation test	transcription/coding fieldnotes matrix grid vector matrix	thematic analysis fieldnote analysis covariance sociography causal analysis of symptoms causal analysis covariance sociography
Speculative	introspecting reflecting	phenomenological comparative	non-structured structured	individual experience (thought experiments, breaching studies, inverted lenses) database	personal notes truth tables (dichotomous variables)	category analysis autoethnography causal analysis (formal logic) rating

Note

1 I thank Rose Barbour, Joseph Maxwell and Uwe Flick for their useful comments and suggestions.

FURTHER READING

Creswell, John W. (2013) *Qualitative Inquiry & Research Design: Choosing Among Five Approaches* (3rd edn). Los Angeles: Sage.
Flick, Uwe (2018) *Designing Qualitative Research* (2nd edn). London: Sage.
Maxwell, Joseph A. (2013) *Qualitative Research Design: An Interactive Approach* (3rd edn). Los Angeles: Sage.

REFERENCES

Agar, Michael H. (1986) *Speaking of Ethnography*. London: Sage.
Becker, Howard S. (1970) *Sociological Work: Method and Substance*. New Brunswick, NJ: Transaction Books.
Becker, H. S., and Geer, B. (1957) 'Participant observation and interviewing: A comparison', *Human Organization*, 16(3): 28–32.
Blumer, H. (1956) 'Sociological analysis and the "variable"', *American Sociological Review*, 21(6): 633–60.
Blumer, Herbert (1969) *Symbolic Interactionism*. New York: Prentice-Hall.
Campelli, Enzo (1991) *Il metodo e il suo contrario. Sul recupero della problematica del metodo in sociologia*. Milano: Angeli.
Cicourel, Aaron V. (1964) *Method and Measurement in Sociology*. New York: Free Press.
Creswell, John W. (2013) *Qualitative Inquiry & Research Design: Choosing Among Five Approaches* (3rd edn). Los Angeles, CA: Sage.
Denzin, N. K. (1969) 'Symbolic interactionism and ethnomethodology: A proposed synthesis', *American Sociological Review*, 34(6): 922–34.
Dewey, John (1938) *Logic, the Theory of Inquiry*. New York: Henry Holt and Co.
Erickson, Frederick (2007) 'Specifying "usually" and "some": Using simple descriptive statistics in qualitative inquiry', *Paper presented at the Congress of Qualitative Inquiry*, Urbana, IL.
Flick, Uwe (2014) *An Introduction to Qualitative Research* (5th edn). London: Sage.
Flick, Uwe (2018) *Designing Qualitative Research* (2nd edn). London: Sage.
Garfinkel, Harold (1962) 'Common sense knowledge of social structures: The documentary method of interpretation in lay and professional fact finding', in Jordan M. Scher (ed.), *Theories of the Mind*. New York: The Free Press, pp. 76–103.
Garfinkel, Harold (1967) *Studies in Ethnomethodology*. Englewood Cliffs, NJ: Prentice-Hall.
Geertz, C. (1972) 'Deep play: Notes on the Balinese cockfight', *Dedalus*, 101(1): 1–37.
Geertz, Clifford (1973) *The Interpretation of Cultures*. New York: Basic Books.
Glaser, B. G., and Strauss, A. L. (1964) 'The social loss of dying patients', *American Journal of Nursing*, 64(6): 119–21.
Glaser, Barney G., and Strauss, Anselm L. (1967) *The Discovery of Grounded Theory*. Chicago, IL: Aldine.
Gobo, Giampietro (2008) *Doing Ethnography*. London: Sage.
Goodenough, Ward (1957) 'Oceana and the problem of controls in the study of cultural and human evolution', *Journal of the Polynesian Society*, 66(2): 146–55.
Hammersley, Martin (1992) *What's Wrong with Ethnography? Methodological Explorations*. London: Routledge.
Hammersley, Martin, and Atkinson, Paul (1983) *Ethnography: Principles in Practice*. London: Tavistock.
Hayek, Friedrich A. (1949) *Individualism and Economic Order*. London: Routledge & Kegan Paul.
Hymes, Dell H. (1978), What is Ethnography? Working paper in sociolinguistics, 45. Austin, TX: Southwest Educational Development Laboratory.
Jarvie, Ian C. (1972) *Concepts and Society*. London: Routledge & Kegan Paul.
Korzybski, Alfred H. S. (1933) *Science and Sanity: An Introduction to Non-Aristotelian Systems and General Semantics*. Chicago, IL: International Non-Aristotelian Library, Institute of General Semantics.
Maynard, Douglas (1989) 'On the ethnography and analysis of discourse in institutional settings', in James A. Holstein and Gale Miller

(eds.), *Perspective in Social Problems*, vol. 1. Greenwich, CT: JAI Press, pp. 127–46.

Maxwell, J. A. (2010) 'Using numbers in qualitative research', *Qualitative Inquiry*, 16(6): 475–82.

Maxwell, J. A. (2012) 'The importance of qualitative research for causal explanation in education', *Qualitative Inquiry*, 18(8): 649–55.

Maxwell, Joseph, Chmiel Margaret, and Rogers, Silvia E. (2015) 'Designing integration in multimethod and mixed methods research', in Sharlene Nagy Hesse-Biber, and Burke Johnson (eds.), *The Oxford Handbook of Multimethod and Mixed Methods Research Inquiry*, Oxford: Oxford University Press, pp. 223–39.

McHugh, Peter (1968) *Defining the Situation*. Indianapolis, IN: Bobbs-Merrill.

Mehan, Hugh, and Wood, H. Houston (1975) *The Reality of Ethnomethodology*. New York: Wiley.

Miles, Matthew B., and Huberman, Michael A. (1984) *Qualitative Data Analysis: A Sourcebook of New Methods*. Beverly Hills, CA: Sage.

Morgan, D. L. (2007) 'Combining qualitative and quantitative methods–paradigms lost and pragmatism regained: methodological implications of combining qualitative and quantitative methods', *Journal of Mixed Methods Research*, 1(1), 48–76.

Pawson, Ray, and Tilley, Nick (1997) *Realistic Evaluation*. London: Sage.

Sacks, Harvey (1992) *Lectures on Conversation* (vol. 1). Oxford: Blackwell.

Sandelowski, M., Voils, C. I., and Knafl, G. (2009) 'On quantitizing', *Journal of Mixed Method Research*, 3(3), 208–22.

Schatzman, Leonard, and Strauss, Anselm L. (1973) *Field Research*. Englewood Cliffs, NJ: Prentice-Hall.

Schwartz, Howard, and Jacobs, Jarry (1979) *Qualitative Sociology*. New York: The Free Press.

Silverman, David (1993) *Interpreting Qualitative Data*. London: Sage.

Silverman, David (2000) *Doing Qualitative Research*. London: Sage.

Silverman, D., and Gubrium, J. (1994) 'Competing strategies for analyzing the contexts of social interaction', *Sociological Inquiry*, 64(2): 179–88.

Spradley, James P. (1980) *Participant Observation*. Holt Rinehart and Winston: New York.

Strauss, Anselm L., and Corbin, Juliet (1990) *Basics of Qualitative Research*. Thousand Oaks, CA: Sage.

Strauss, Anselm L., Schatzman Leonard, Bucher Rue, Ehrlich Danuta, and Sabshin Melvin (1964) *Psychiatric Ideologies and Institutions*. New York: Free Press of Glencoe.

Yin, Robert K. (1984) *Case Study Research* (2nd edn). Thousand Oaks, CA: Sage.

Zimmerman, Don H., and Pollner, Melvin (1970) 'The everyday world as a phenomenon', in Harold B. Pepinsky (ed.), *People and Information*. Oxford: Pergamon Press, pp. 33–56.

Sampling and Generalization[1]

Margrit Schreier

INTRODUCTION

In their textbook about empirical research methodology in the social sciences, 6 and Bellamy write: 'Making warranted inferences is the whole point and the only point of doing social research' (2012, p. 14). Empirical research, in other words, does not limit itself to describing those instances included in a given study. It wants to go beyond those instances and arrive at conclusions of broader relevance.

This is true of qualitative just as much as of quantitative research (on the extent and type of generalizations in qualitative research see Onwuegbuzie and Leech, 2010).[2] When Lynd and Lynd (1929), for example, set about studying the community they called 'Middletown' in the early twentieth century, their goal was not to provide an in-depth description of this one community. Instead, they wanted to draw conclusions about contemporary life in the US in a Midwestern community on the threshold of industrialization in more general terms. And they selected the community in question very carefully to make sure that the community was indeed typical of Midwestern communities at that time. They looked at climate, population size, growth rate, presence and number of industries, presence of local artistic life, any local problems, and chose 'Middletown' on all of those grounds (see Gobo, Chapter 5, this volume). They were thus very much aware that the conclusions we can draw, that is, the kinds of generalizations we can make, are closely connected to the instances we study, that is, our sample. The instances, in 6 and Bellamy's (2012) terms, act as the 'warrants' for our conclusions.

Qualitative research, with its holistic and in-depth approach, typically limits itself to a few instances or units only, ranging from the single case study (as in the study of 'Middletown') to a sample size of around 20 to 40 (although sample sizes can, in rare cases, also be considerably larger). These units or instances can be very diverse in nature: not only people, but documents, events, interactions, behaviours, etc. can all be sampled. The numbers in qualitative are much smaller than sample sizes in quantitative research. If qualitative research wants to arrive at conclusions that go beyond the instances studied, but can only include comparatively few units, one would expect qualitative researchers to reflect all the more carefully about selection and generalization. But this is not the case. The topic of sampling has long been neglected (Higginbottom, 2004; Onwuegbuzie and Leech, 2007; Robinson, 2014), although there has been an increased interest in the topic in recent years (e.g. the monograph on the topic by Emmel, 2013, and the increasing attention to sampling in textbooks). What it means to generalize in qualitative research, what kinds of conclusions can be drawn based on the units we have studied, is a topic that is only occasionally touched upon (e.g. Gobo, 2008; Lincoln and Guba, 1979; Maxwell and Chmiel, 2014; Stake, 1978).

In the following, I will start out with some methodological considerations, focusing first on concepts of generalizing, next on sampling and criteria and considerations underlying sampling in qualitative research. This includes the question of sample size and the use of saturation as a criterion for deciding when to stop sampling. In the next section, selected sampling strategies in qualitative research will be described in more detail, followed by considerations of how generalization and selection strategies are related in some selected qualitative research traditions. The chapter closes with describing some recent developments in qualitative sampling methodology. Throughout the chapter, the terms 'sampling', 'selecting units', and 'selecting instances' will be used interchangeably.

GENERALIZING IN QUALITATIVE RESEARCH: METHODOLOGICAL CONSIDERATIONS

Generalizing in Quantitative Social Science

In quantitative research, the concept of generalization is closely linked to that of external validity, specifically to the concept of population generalization, namely the extent to which we can generalize from the sample to the population. This type of generalization has also been termed *empirical generalization* (Lewis et al., 2014; Maxwell and Chmiel, 2014) or *numerical generalization* (Flick, 2004). In quantitative research, empirical generalization is typically realized as *statistical* or *probabilistic generalization*: It is possible to generalize from the sample to the population to the extent that the sample is indeed representative of the population, and statistics is used to provide the level of confidence or conversely the margin of error that underlies this estimate of representativeness (Williams, 2002).

Statistical generalization in this sense has become the default understanding of generalization in the social sciences. But empirical generalization does not equal statistical generalization. Statistics is a tool that in quantitative research is used to warrant the conclusion from the sample to the population. But there may be other ways of justifying this conclusion. It is also worth keeping in mind another characteristic of both statistical and empirical generalization: They are essentially context-free. The conclusion from the sample to the population applies, regardless of the specific context and the specific circumstances (Williams, 2002).

When quantitative researchers argue that qualitative research does not allow for generalization, this criticism is typically based on an understanding of generalizability in the sense of statistical generalizability. Indeed, samples in qualitative research are mostly not representative of a population, and using statistics as a warrant underlying the conclusion from sample to population is then not an option (although Onwuegbuzie and Leech, 2010, report that 36 per cent of the qualitative studies they examined used statistical generalization). Some qualitative methodologists have been just as sceptical of achieving generalizability in qualitative research. This is expressed by the famous dictum of Lincoln and Guba (1979, p. 110): 'The only generalization is that there is no generalization.' For quantitative methodologists the supposed inability of qualitative research to arrive at empirical generalizations constitutes a criticism of qualitative research. Lincoln and Guba, on the other hand, as well as Denzin (1983), reject the notion of statistical and empirical generalizability precisely because they do not take context into account – because they are, one might say, too general:

> It is virtually impossible to imagine any kind of human behaviour that is not heavily mediated by the context in which it occurs. One can easily conclude that generalizations that are intended to be context-free will have little that is useful to say about human behaviour. (Guba and Lincoln, 1981, p. 62)

Reconceptualizing Generalization in Qualitative Research

Several suggestions have been made for reconceptualizing generalization so as to make it more compatible with the principles underlying qualitative research. These suggestions fall into three groups or types: modifying the notion of empirical generalization, transferability as an alternative conceptualization, and theoretical generalization as an alternative conceptualization (Lewis et al., 2014; Maxwell and Chmiel, 2014; Polit and Beck, 2010; for a more complex and extensive classification see Gobo, 2008; and Gobo, Chapter 5, this volume).

Modifying the notion of empirical generalization entails 'lowering the threshold' for what can be called a generalization. This applies, for example, to the notion of so-called *moderatum generalizations* proposed by Williams (2002) for interpretive social research. They are based on the assumption of 'cultural consistency', of a constant structural element in the area under research, and they involve an inductive inference from the particular instance(s) studied to this underlying structure. Moderatum generalizations constitute a 'weaker version' of the type of empirical generalization used elsewhere in the social and the natural sciences.

Another reconceptualization of generalization in qualitative research focuses on the concept of *transferability* (Maxwell and Chmiel, 2014; Schofield, 1990). This notion takes the highly contextualized nature of qualitative research as its starting point, that is, the very characteristic which, from the perspective of the quantitative social sciences, stands in the way of empirical generalization in qualitative research. With transferability, the core concern is not to generalize to an abstract and decontextualized population, but to determine whether the findings obtained for one instance or set of instances in one specific context also apply to other instances in a different context. The extent to which the findings can be transferred from one case to another depends on the similarity between the respective contexts. Assessing the similarity of a 'source' and a 'target' context in turn requires detailed information about the context in which the study was conducted. Lincoln and Guba (1979) speak of the degree of *fittingness* between the two contexts and refer to the need for *thick description*, according to Geertz (1973), of the context in which the first study was carried out. It is noteworthy that the notion of transferability entails, so to speak, a division of tasks between the authors and the readers of a study. It is the responsibility of the authors to provide a sufficiently 'thick description', but only the reader can assess the degree of fittingness between the context of the study and any other context to which the findings may or may not apply. The idea of transferability underlies several reconceptualizations of generalization that have been proposed in the literature, such as the concept of naturalistic generalization developed by Stake (1978) or the notion of generalization as a working hypothesis suggested by Cronbach (1975).

Both the notions of moderatum generalization and transferability are based on considerations of the relationship between a sample and a population (or the relationship between a sample and another sample), that is, what Yin (2014, pp. 57–62) calls a *sampling logic*. The third alternative conceptualization of generalization, that of *theoretical generalization* (Schwandt, 2001, pp. 2–3; also called analytic generalization), moves away from the idea of population and sample and is based on what Yin terms a *replication logic* (2014, pp. 57–62). With theoretical generalization, the purpose of the research is not to generalize to a population or to other instances, but to build a theory or to identify a causal mechanism. Instances are selected either so as to be similar to each other (*literal replication*) or different from each other in one key aspect (*theoretical replication*), the same way studies build upon each other, leading to a differentiation of theory. This notion of theoretical generalization is – in somewhat different versions – used in case study research, in grounded theory methodology, and in analytic induction.

External and Internal Generalization

As mentioned in the previous section, the concept of generalizability has, in the quantitative research tradition, been discussed as one aspect of external validity. This suggests a focus on the relationship between the sample and the population, on how representative the instances included in the sample are of the population. But in qualitative research, where typically few instances are examined in detail, another relationship gains in importance, namely the relationship between our observations and the case in its entirety: how well is the variability within a given instance represented in our observations? Hammersley and Atkinson (1995) point to the importance of adequately representing contexts as well as points in time or a time period. They refer to this as *within-case sampling*. Along similar lines, Onwuegbuzie and Leech (2005) refer to the 'truth space' of an interviewee and whether the data obtained in any given interview adequately represent that truth space (see also the concept of internal validity in Maxwell and Chmiel, 2014). The considerations underlying internal and external generalization are similar in structural terms. Generalizing within an instance is subject to the same restrictions and considerations as generalizing beyond that instance: in both situations, we have to ask ourselves what kind of generalization is appropriate – moderatum empirical, transferability, or theoretical generalization – and select our sampling strategy accordingly.

SAMPLING IN QUALITATIVE RESEARCH: METHODOLOGICAL CONSIDERATIONS

Sampling Strategies: An Overview

In the methodological literature, three types of sampling strategies are distinguished: random, convenience, and purposive sampling. In the following, key characteristics and underlying concepts of the three groups of sampling strategies are briefly described.

Random sampling

Random sampling is typically used in quantitative research, especially in survey-type research, in order to support empirical generalization, that is, generalizing from a sample to a population (on random sampling, see Daniel, 2012, chapter 3). This is possible to the extent that the sample is indeed *representative* of the population. The importance of random sampling in quantitative research derives from its role in generating such a representative sample. Based on a sampling frame, that is, a list of all members of the population, the sample is chosen such that every member of the population has an equal chance (above zero) of being included in the sample, and the members of the sample are selected using a truly random procedure (e.g. a random number generator).

If these steps are followed and if the population and the sample are sufficiently large, the procedure of random sampling results in a sample that is (sufficiently) representative. The margin of error in generalizing from the sample to the population can be specified using confidence intervals and inferential statistics. Various subtypes of random sampling have been developed beside the process of simple random sampling described above, such as systematic, cluster, or stratified random sampling.

But a random sample is not necessarily a representative sample (Gobo, 2004). In the first place, random sampling will result in a representative sample only if the above conditions are met. Also, representativeness of a sample with respect to a population constitutes a goal, whereas random sampling is a procedure, a means towards that goal. And random sampling is not the only way of obtaining a representative sample. Other strategies include, for instance, selecting typical cases or even – depending on the population – selecting any case at all (see the section on 'phenomenology' below).

Purposive sampling

The term *purposive sampling* (also called purposeful sampling) refers to a group of sampling strategies typically used in qualitative research. The key idea underlying purposive sampling is to select instances that are *information rich* with a view to answering the research question (for an overview see Emmel, 2013; Flick, 2014, chapter 13; Mason, 2002, chapter 7; Patton, 2015, module 30; Ritchie et al., 2014). A large variety of purposeful sampling strategies has been described in the literature, including, for example, homogeneous sampling, heterogeneous sampling, maximum variation sampling, theoretical sampling, sampling according to a qualitative sampling guide, snowball sampling, sampling typical, extreme, intense, critical, or outlier cases, and many others (Patton, 2015, module 30; Teddlie and Yu, 2007).

The precise meaning of 'information rich', however, and therefore the selection of a specific strategy, depends on the research question and on the goal of the study (Marshall, 1996; Palinkas et al., 2015). Describing a phenomenon in all its variations, for example, requires a type of maximum variation sampling (Higginbottom, 2004; Merkens, 2004). If the goal is to generate a theory, theoretical sampling in the tradition of grounded theory methodology will often be the strategy of choice (see the section on 'theoretical sampling' below). If a theory is to be tested, selecting an atypical or critical case would be a useful strategy (Mitchell, 1983). And transferability requires a detailed description of specific types of cases, for example, a typical or common case or an intense case (Yin, 2013, pp. 51–5).

Several criteria have been used to distinguish between different types of purposive sampling strategies and different ways of conducting purposive sampling. A first criterion concerns the point in time when a decision concerning the sample composition is made (Flick, 2014, pp. 168–9; Merkens, 2004): this can either be specified in advance, in analogy to the sampling procedure in quantitative research (examples would be stratified purposive sampling or selecting specific types of cases). Or else the composition of the sample can emerge over the course of the study, as in sequential sampling, snowball sampling, theoretical sampling, or analytic induction. This latter emergent procedure is generally considered to be more appropriate to the iterative, emergent nature of qualitative research (Palinkas et al., 2015). In actual research, advance decisions about sample composition are often combined with modifications as they emerge during the research process.

A second criterion relates to the relationship between the units in the sample (Boehnke et al., 2010; Palinkas et al., 2015; Robinson, 2014), distinguishing between homogeneous samples (as in criterion sampling, or in selecting typical cases) and heterogeneous samples (e.g. maximum variation sampling, or theoretical sampling). A third criterion for distinguishing between purposeful sampling strategies relates to the underlying goal (Onwuegbuzie and Leech, 2007; Patton, 2015, chapter 5), such as selecting specific types of cases (typical, intense, extreme, etc.), selecting with a view to representativeness or to contrast.

Convenience sampling

Convenience sampling (also called ad hoc sampling, opportunistic sampling) constitutes the third type of sampling strategy. Here cases are selected based on availability. Asking one's fellow students, for example, to participate in a study for this semester's research project, would constitute a case of convenience sampling. This sampling strategy has a 'bad reputation' with both quantitative and qualitative researchers: from the perspective of quantitative research, it fails to produce a representative sample (Daniel, 2012, chapter 3); from the perspective of qualitative research, it has been criticized for insufficiently taking the goal of the study and the criterion of information richness into account. Depending upon the goal of the research and the population under study, 'any case' can, however, be perfectly suitable (Gobo, 2008; see the section on 'phenomenology' below).

Is My Sample Large Enough?

The role of sample size in qualitative research

The question of sample size in qualitative research is discussed very controversially. Some authors argue that, other than in quantitative research where sample size in relation to the population is crucial for statistical generalization, sample size is irrelevant in qualitative research or at best of secondary concern. According to this position, selecting information-rich instances that are relevant to the research question and sample composition are considered more important than sample size (e.g. Crouch and McKenzie, 2006; Patton, 2015, chapter 5). Others argue that sample size plays a role in qualitative research as well (e.g. Onwuegbuzie and Leech, 2005; Sandelowski, 1995).

In purely practical terms, researchers are often required to specify an approximate sample size, for example, when submitting grant applications or presenting a PhD proposal. Not surprisingly, methodologists also differ when it comes to making recommendations for sample size in such cases. Some authors do make recommendations (for overviews, see Guest et al., 2006; Guetterman, 2015; Mason, 2010). Others argue that deciding on sample size before engaging in data collection contradicts the emergent nature of qualitative research, and call for a sampling process that is constantly adjusted as the research unfolds (e.g. Mason, 2010; Palinkas et al., 2015; Robinson, 2014; Trotter, 2012). A middle way between these two extremes is the suggestion to work with an advance specification of minimal sample size, which is then adjusted during the research process (Francis et al., 2010; Patton, 2015, module 40). Positions concerning recommendations for sample size in qualitative research thus range from specific numbers to 'it depends'.

Key factors to take into consideration when deciding on a suitable sample size include the extent of variation in the phenomenon under study (Bryman, 2016; Charmaz, 2014; Francis et al., 2010; Palinkas et al., 2015; Robinson, 2014), the research goal (Marshall, 1996; Patton, 2015, module 40), the scope of the theory or conclusions (Charmaz, 2014; Morse, 2000). The overall recommendation is that sample size should increase with the heterogeneity of the phenomenon and the breadth and generality of the conclusions aimed for. Depending on the research goal, however, a single instance may be perfectly sufficient (e.g. Patton, 2015, module 40; Yin, 2014, pp. 51–6). Some authors also draw attention to external constraints, such as the time and the resources available for the study or the requirements by external agencies such as review boards (Flick, 2014; Patton, 2015, module 40). Another factor concerns the research tradition in which the study is carried out (Guest et al., 2006; see the section on 'sampling in different traditions' below).

The advance specification of sample size runs the danger of oversampling, that is, including more instances than necessary (Francis et al., 2010). In his analysis of sample size of the 51 most frequently cited qualitative studies in five research traditions, Guetterman (2015) found a surprisingly high average sample size of 87 participants. Mason, in examining sample size in qualitative dissertations, found sample sizes of 20–30 participants to be most frequent, with a surprising number of sample sizes constituting multiples of 10. Guetterman concludes from this that such round numbers are most likely the result of an advance specification of sample size – which may well be higher than needed. Oversampling carries the methodological danger of allowing for only an insufficient analysis of each individual case (Guetterman, 2015), and it carries the ethical danger of unnecessarily drawing upon the resources of participants (Francis et al., 2010). Sampling in qualitative research should therefore include as many cases as are needed with a view to the research question, but it should not model itself on quantitative standards of 'the more, the better' or a preference for round numbers.

The criterion of saturation

But how exactly do we know that we have included as many cases as needed? The criterion that is most often used in qualitative research to conclude the sampling process is the criterion of *saturation*. Saturation was initially developed in the context of grounded theory methodology, and it specifies to stop sampling when including more cases does not contribute any new information about the concepts that have been developed and about their dimensions (Schwandt, 2001, p. 111). Today, however, the concept of saturation is often used in the more general sense of thematic saturation (Bowen, 2008; Guest et al., 2006).

But it often remains unclear what the exact criteria are for determining when saturation has been reached (Bowen, 2008; Francis et al., 2010; O'Reilly and Parker, 2012). Guest et al. (2006) examined their own interview analysis for evidence of saturation. They concluded that saturation was reached after 12 interviews, with key themes emerging from the analysis of only 6 interviews. Francis et al. (2010) arrive at similar conclusions. They suggest specifying an initial sample size of n = 10 at which to examine the degree of saturation reached. This initial sample size, they argue, should be combined with a set number of additional cases at which the degree of saturation is to be re-examined; for their own research, they set this number at n = 3. Both Guest et al. (2006) and Francis et al. (2010) emphasize, however, that their recommendation targets interview studies on comparatively homogeneous phenomena.

Saturation, despite its prevalence, has been criticized on methodological grounds. Dey (1999) argues that saturation is always a matter of degree. Also, saturation is not always the most appropriate criterion for deciding when to stop sampling (O'Reilly and Parker, 2012).

SELECTED PURPOSIVE SAMPLING STRATEGIES

In this section, some selected purposive sampling strategies that are frequently used in qualitative research are presented in more detail: theoretical sampling, stratified purposive sampling, criterion sampling, and selecting specific cases. It should be noted that the different strategies are not mutually exclusive and that several strategies can be combined in one study.

> **Case Study: 'Precarious Ordering'**
>
> In her study of the experiences of women providing care, Wuest (2001) develops a middle-range theory with a focus on what she calls *precarious ordering*, based on a total of 65 interviews with women facing a variety of demands for care (caring for children with otitis media with effusion, Alzheimer's disease, and leaving abusive relationships). Precarious ordering involves a two-stage iterative process of negotiating demands for care and own resources, moving from daily struggles to re-patterning care.
>
> She starts out her process of theoretical sampling by talking to childrearing middle-class women, both employed and unemployed. Her initial data analysis points her to the importance of increasing demands and types of demands and of the dissonance between demands and resources. To further explore the role of varying demands, she continues by interviewing women who face higher than average demands (mothers of physically and mentally disabled children) and women who face fewer demands (women with adult children and children away from home). Her interviews with mothers of disabled children lead her to the question of strengths and strategies developed by the women during the coping process and the role of the relationship with the partner. To explore these two factors, she talks to other women with heavy, but different demands for care (sick relatives) and women with diverse partners (e.g. a lesbian partner, a partner from a different culture). The role of resources and the distinction between helpful and unhelpful resources are further highlighted through interviews with women in economically difficult situations. Wuest thus moves through cycles of comparing and contrasting different types of caring demands, different kinds of settings, support systems, and resources, especially in terms of the relationship with a partner.

Theoretical Sampling

Theoretical sampling was developed in the context of grounded theory methodology and is very much a part of the overall iterative grounded theory methodology in combination with a process of constant comparison (Glaser, 1978; Strauss, 1987; for an overview see Draucker et al., 2007). Theoretical sampling takes place in constant interrelation with data collection and data analysis, and it is guided by the concepts and the theory emerging in the research process. More instances and more data are added so as to develop the emerging categories and their dimensions, and relate them to each other:

> Theoretical sampling means that the sampling of additional incidents, events, activities, populations, and so on is directed by the evolving theoretical constructs. Comparisons between the explanatory adequacy of the theoretical constructs and the empirical indicators go on continuously until theoretical saturation is reached (i.e. additional analysis no longer contributes to anything new about this concept). (Schwandt, 2001, p. 111)

In terms of sample composition, theoretical sampling yields a heterogeneous sample that allows for comparing different instantiations of a concept. The sampling process is emergent and flexible, and the goal of the sampling strategy, as the name says, is to develop a theory that is grounded in the data. While the strategy is well established in the methodological literature and is the default strategy in grounded theory studies, it is nevertheless difficult to find detailed descriptions of how sampling choices are revised and modified in response to emergent concepts (Draucker et al., 2007). The above case study by Wuest (2001) on the experiences of women providing care to others constitutes an exception. While Wuest acknowledges the difficulty of documenting what is essentially a process of following up on various conceptual dimensions simultaneously, she describes the theoretical sampling process and the choices she made at various stages of the research process in exemplary and enlightening detail.

Stratified Purposive Sampling

Like theoretical sampling, stratified purposive sampling results in a heterogeneous sample that represents different manifestations of the phenomenon under study (Ritchie et al., 2014;

Case Study: 'Stakeholder Opinions on Priority Setting in Health Care'

In the following study we used stratified purposive sampling to explore the range of opinions from different stakeholder groups and their reasons surrounding the setting of priorities in the German health care system (Schreier et al., 2008; Winkelhage et al., 2013). In a first step, we selected six stakeholder groups representing a variety of different positions and roles. We assumed that, because of these different positions, they would be likely to differ in their interests and opinions concerning priority setting in health care: healthy members of the general population, patients, physicians, nursing personnel, representatives of the public health insurance system, and politicians. In a second step, a literature search was carried out for each stakeholder group separately in order to identify factors likely to affect attitudes towards health care. Taking patients as an example, relevant factors included age (18–30, 31–62, above 62), the severity of a patient's disease (light versus severe; as judged by a physician), level of education (no training qualification, training qualification, university degree), and area of origin (former Federal Republic of Germany versus former German Democratic Republic). With four relevant factors, not all factor combinations could be realized, and some cells remain empty. The factors were combined into the following sampling guide, resulting in a sample of 12 participants (see Table 6.1). The study showed, for example, the different interests and attitudes of physicians compared to patients. Patients were more likely to place hope even in less effective treatments, and they emphasized the importance of obtaining the consent of the family when deciding about life-prolonging measures (Winkelhage et al., 2013).

Table 6.1 Sampling guide for stratified purposive sampling of patients

Age group	Severity of symptoms	Level of education			Total
		No training qualification	Training qualification	University degree	
18–30 yrs	Light	FDR	GDR		2
	Severe		GDR	FDR	2
31–62 yrs	Light		FDR	GDR	2
	Severe	FDR		GDR	2
Above 62	Light	GDR		FDR	2
	Severe	GDR	FDR		2
Total		4	4	4	12

termed 'quota sampling' in Patton, 2015, p. 268). In contrast to theoretical sampling, however, stratified purposive sampling entails a top-down approach, that is, decisions about the composition of the sample are made before data collection. In a first step, the researcher has to decide which factors are known or likely to cause variation in the phenomenon of interest. In a second step, two to a maximum of four such factors are selected for constructing a sampling guide. Step three involves combining the factors of choice in a cross-table. At this point the researcher has to decide whether all possible combinations of all factors are to be realized or else, if not, which factor combinations will be included. With more than two factors, it is usually not possible to conduct sampling for all possible factor combinations. The resulting sampling guide is displayed in a table, with each factor combination corresponding to a cell. In a final step, the researcher will decide how many units to sample for each cell or factor combination. Depending on how many cells there are in the sampling guide ('sample matrix' according to Ritchie et al., 2014), one or two units will typically be included. Stratified purposive sampling is useful for exploring the various manifestations of a phenomenon for similarities and differences.

As the term 'sampling *guide*' implies, a sampling guide is not cast in stone and can

> **Case Study: 'Meanings of House, Home, and Family among Vietnamese Refugees in Canada'**
>
> Huyen Dam and John Eyles (2012) used criterion sampling in their study exploring the meanings of house, home, and family among former Vietnamese refugees in the Canadian city of Hamilton. To be included in the study, participants had to be former Boat people who had lived in Hamilton for at least 15 years. Bounding the phenomenon in terms of origin, refugee history, and in terms of place ensured that the experiences of the participants were sufficiently comparable. Requiring the participants to have lived in Hamilton for a period of 15 years allowed the researchers to capture the experience of settling and how this changed over time. The study shows, for example, the importance of culture and family for the participants, and how these core values allow them to re-establish a sense of home after having been uprooted and relocated.

be modified as the selection process unfolds (Morse, 2000). In the above study, for example, it proved difficult to find participants without any training qualification, especially in the oldest age group, and participants from other age groups or with training qualification were substituted. A sampling guide can and should also be modified if it emerges during the study that factors other than the ones informing the sampling guide affect the phenomenon under study. In this case a combination of concept-driven and data-driven sampling is realized (for an example, see Johnson, 1991).

Another, more flexible variant of stratified purposive sampling is *maximum variation sampling* (Patton, 2015, p. 267). As in stratified purposive sampling, the researcher starts out by identifying factors that lead to variation in the phenomenon under study. But instead of systematically combining these factors, they serve as a broad framework orienting the sampling process, with a view to including as much variation in the sample as possible. In their interview study on how older persons experience living at home, for example, De Jonge et al. (2011) included participants who differed with respect to age, gender, living conditions, type of dwelling, tenure, and location in the city or in the countryside, without specifying which combinations were to be included. They used a matrix, however, to record the specific combination of characteristics represented by the participants in their sample, to ensure and document sufficient variation of their cases.

Criterion Sampling

In criterion sampling, the objective is to include instances in the sample that match a predefined profile (Coyne, 1997; Patton, 2015, p. 281). Usually this involves a combination of characteristics, which, together, specify a phenomenon under study or a restricted population in which this phenomenon is likely to occur. The resulting sample is homogeneous with respect to the selected criteria (but may be heterogeneous in other respects), and decisions about these criteria are made in advance. This sampling strategy is especially useful for exploring a phenomenon in depth.

SAMPLING IN DIFFERENT RESEARCH TRADITIONS

One of the factors influencing the type of generalization aimed for and the consequently optimal sample size is the methodological tradition in which a study is carried out (Bryman in Baker and Edwards, 2012; Higginbottom, 2004; Robinson, 2014). Empirical analysis of sample sizes in different qualitative research traditions shows that the number of cases differs quite substantially between approaches (Guetterman, 2015; Mason, 2010). In the following, a few selected approaches will be discussed with a view to sampling and generalization issues:

interview studies, the case study, and phenomenology (for grounded theory methodology see the sections on 'theoretical sampling' and 'theoretical saturation').

Interview Studies

Many recommendations concerning sample size in qualitative research relate to the use of interview data (see Roulston and Choi, Chapter 15, this volume) in particular (e.g. Crouch and McKenzie, 2006; Mason, 2010). Recommendations range from 10 to 13 units (Francis et al., 2010) up to between 60 and 150 (Gerson and Horowitz, 2002, p. 223). This large variety of recommendations is not surprising, considering that as a method for data collection, the interview can be used within a great variety of different research traditions and with a view towards different kinds of generalization. Instead of examining optimal sample size in interview studies, it seems more promising to look at sample sizes in different approaches where interviews, observation, and other methods for collecting qualitative data are used (cf. the analysis of interview-based dissertations from different traditions in Mason, 2010).

The Case Study

In the case study, different methods of data collection are combined to allow for an in-depth analysis of one or several cases and their subunits (Yin, 2014, chapter 1). Descriptive case studies are especially suitable for yielding 'thick descriptions' and therefore lend themselves well to generalization in the sense of transferability. Explanatory case studies are more suitable for analytic generalization, being used for generating and for building theory (Mitchell, 1983).

In terms of sampling, case studies require complex decisions on multiple levels. In a first step, the case or cases have to be selected. In single case studies, this often involves selecting a case with a view to a population, e.g. a typical case or an intense case (Yin, 2014, pp. 51–6). Single case studies allow for moderatum generalizations based on structural and cultural consistency (Williams, 2002). In multiple case studies, the key concern in sampling is the underlying logic of replication, that is, the question of how the cases relate to each other (Yin, 2014, pp. 56–63). Based on a literal replication logic, cases are selected so as to be similar to each other. If the study follows a theoretical replication logic, cases are selected so as to contrast with each other on relevant dimensions. In a second step, within-case sampling is necessary to ensure internal generalizability (Maxwell and Chmiel, 2014). In principle, any purposive sampling strategy can be used, but maximum variation sampling seems especially useful for representing different aspects of a case, such as persons, points in time, or contexts (Higginbottom, 2004).

In his analysis of sample size for case studies in the fields of health and education, Guetterman (2015) found that the number of cases ranged from 1 to 8, and the number of participants or observations ranging from 1 to 700. This suggests that researchers conducting case studies tend to limit themselves to a few cases only, thus allowing for a detailed analysis of each case. The wide range of number of participants and observations, however, indicates that the 'thickness' of the resulting descriptions varies considerably.

Phenomenology

Phenomenology has the aim of identifying the 'essence' of the human experience of a phenomenon (overview in Lewis and Staehler, 2010). By aiming to describe the common characteristics of that experience, phenomenology by definition also aims for (empirical) generalization. Because the respective experience is assumed to be universal, the experience of any human being qualified to have that experience is considered a case in point.

Consequently, no special sampling strategy is required, that is, convenience sampling would be sufficient: Any individual who meets the conditions for having the experience under study would be a suitable participant, and because of the relative homogeneity of the phenomenon, comparatively small samples would be acceptable. This is, indeed, reflected in smaller sample sizes found in Guetterman's (2015) analysis, ranging from 8 to 52 participants. Similar considerations concerning the assumed universal nature of a phenomenon or an underlying structure are found in studies on the organization of everyday talk (e.g. Schegloff and Sacks, 1974; see Jackson, Chapter 18, this volume) or in objective hermeneutics (overview in Wernet, 2014).

CONCLUSION

Recently there has been increasing attention to what qualitative researchers actually do during the sampling process. These articles have already been cited in the previous sections: Onwuegbuzie and Leech (2010) examined studies published in *Qualitative Report* for whether the authors generalized their findings and what type of generalization they drew upon. Guetterman (2015) and Mason (2010) conducted research on sample sizes in studies from different qualitative traditions, and Guest et al. (2006) examined their own data for evidence of saturation. More empirical studies of this kind are needed to better understand what qualitative researchers actually do in terms of sampling and generalization.

Another development is related to the increasing use of mixed methods designs in the social sciences (see Hesse-Biber, Chapter 35, this volume; Morse et al., Chapter 36, this volume). Discussions of sampling in mixed methods designs include descriptions of purposive sampling strategies, thereby contributing to making them more visible in the social science methods literature (e.g. Teddlie and Yu, 2007). Some strategies that are considered purposive in a qualitative research context, such as stratified purposive sampling or random purposive sampling, have in fact been classified as 'mixed' strategies within this mixed methods context.

The mixed methods research tradition is relevant to developments in purposive sampling in yet another respect. Many purposive sampling strategies, such as stratified purposive sampling or selecting certain types of cases, require prior knowledge about the phenomenon in question and its distribution. This is where mixing methods can be highly useful in informing the purposive sampling process. Within a sequential design, for example, the findings of a first quantitative phase can be used in order to purposefully select instances for a second qualitative phase of the research (for sequential designs see Creswell and Plano Clark, 2011, chapter 3).

While the topic of purposive sampling has been receiving increasing attention, this is not the case for the topic of generalizing in qualitative research, and even less so for the relationship between types of generalization and sampling strategies. This will be an important focus of future qualitative research methodology in this area.

Notes

1. I thank Uwe Flick, Giampietro Gobo, and an anonymous reviewer for their helpful comments.
2. The term 'qualitative research' encompasses so many different research traditions and approaches that it constitutes a gross oversimplification to lump them together under this one label. It would be more appropriate to examine each tradition separately. As this is beyond the scope of this chapter, I will continue to use the term throughout, but ask the reader to keep in mind the diversity of approaches. I will also look at a few approaches in more detail in section 5 below.

FURTHER READING

Gobo, Giampietro (2004) 'Sampling, representativeness, and generalizability', in Clive Seale, Giampietro Gobo, Jaber F. Gubrium, and

David Silverman (eds), *Qualitative Research Practice*. London: Sage, pp. 435–56.

Maxwell, Joseph A., and Chmiel, Margaret (2014) 'Generalization in and from qualitative analysis', in Uwe Flick (ed.), *SAGE Handbook of Qualitative Data Analysis*. London: Sage, pp. 540–53.

Patton, Michael Q. (2015) 'Designing qualitative studies', in Michael Q. Patton (ed.), *Qualitative Evaluation and Research Methods* (4th edn). Newbury Park: Sage, pp. 243–326.

REFERENCES

6, Perri, and Bellamy, Christine (2012) *Principles of Methodology. Research Design in Social Science*. London: Sage.

Baker, Sarah E., and Edwards, Rosalind (2012) 'How many qualitative interviews is enough? Expert voices and early career reflections on sampling and cases in qualitative research', National Centre for Research Methods Review Paper, available at http://eprints.ncrm.ac.uk/2273/4/how_many_interviews.pdf.

Boehnke, Klaus, Lietz, Petra, Schreier, Margrit, and Wilhelm, Adalbert (2010) 'Sampling: The selection of cases for culturally comparative psychological research', in Fons van de Vijver and David Matsumoto (eds), *Methods of Cross-cultural Research*. Cambridge: Cambridge University Press, pp. 101–29.

Bowen, G. A. (2008) 'Naturalistic enquiry and the saturation concept: A research note', *Qualitative Research*, 8(1): 137–52.

Bryman, Alan (2016) *Social Research Methods* (5th edn). Oxford: Oxford University Press.

Charmaz, Kathy (2014) *Constructing Grounded Theory: A Practical Guide Through Qualitative Analysis (2nd edn)*. London: Sage.

Coyne, I. T. (1997) 'Sampling in qualitative research. Purposeful and theoretical sampling: merging or clear boundaries?' *Journal of Advanced Nursing*, 26(3): 623–30.

Creswell, John W., and Plano Clark, Vicky L. (2011) *Designing and Conducting Mixed Methods Research* (2nd edn). Thousand Oaks, CA: Sage.

Cronbach, L. J. (1975) 'Beyond the two disciplines of scientific psychology', *American Psychologist*, 30(2): 116–27.

Crouch, M., and McKenzie, H. (2006) 'The logic of small samples in interview-based qualitative research', *Social Science Information*, 45(4): 483–99.

Dam, H., and Eyles, J. (2012) '"Home tonight? What? Where?" An exploratory study of the meanings of house, home and family among the former Vietnamese refugees in a Canadian city [49 paragraphs]', *Forum Qualitative Sozialforschung/Forum: Qualitative Social Research*, 13(2): Art. 19, available at http://nbn-resolving.de/urn:nbn:de:0114-fqs1202193.

Daniel, Johnny (2012) *Sampling Essentials*. London: Sage.

De Jonge, D., Jones, A., Philipps, R., and Chung, M. (2011) 'Understanding the essence of home: Older people's experience of home in Australia', *Journal of Occupational Therapy*, 18(1): 39–47.

Denzin, Norman K. (1983) 'Interpretive interactionism', in Gareth Morgan (ed.), *Beyond Method. Strategies for Social Research*. Beverly Hills, CA: Sage, pp. 129–48.

Dey, Ian (1999) *Grounding Grounded Theory: Guidelines for Qualitative Inquiry*. Bingley: Emerald Group.

Draucker, C. B., Martsolf, D. S., Ross, R., and Rusk, T. B. (2007) 'Theoretical sampling and category development in grounded theory', *Qualitative Health Research*, 17(8): 1137–48.

Emmel, Nick (2013) *Sampling and Choosing Cases in Qualitative Research. A Realist Approach*. London: Sage.

Flick, Uwe (2004) 'Design and process in qualitative research', in Uwe Flick, Ernst von Kardorff and Ines Steinke (eds), *A Companion to Qualitative Research*. London: Sage, pp. 146–53.

Flick, Uwe (2014) *Introduction to Qualitative Research* (5th edn). London: Sage.

Francis, J. J., Johnston, M., Robertson, C., Glidewell, L., Entwistle, V., Eccles, M. P., and Grimshaw, J. M. (2010) 'What is an adequate sample size? Operationalising data saturation for theory-based interview studies', *Psychology and Health*, 25(10): 1229–45.

Geertz, Clifford (1973) 'Thick description: Toward an interpretive theory of culture', in Clifford Geertz (ed.), *The Interpretation of Cultures*. New York: Basic Books, pp. 3–30.

Gerson, Kathleen, and Horowitz, Ruth (2002) 'Observation and interviewing: Options and choices', in Tim May (ed.), *Qualitative Research in Action*. London: Sage, pp. 199–224.

Glaser, Barney (1978) *Theoretical Sensitivity*. Mill Valley, CA: Sociology Press.

Gobo, Giampietro (2004) 'Sampling, representativeness, and generalizability', in Clive Seale, Giampietro Gobo, Jaber F. Gubrium and David Silverman (eds), *Qualitative Research Practice*. London: Sage, pp. 435–56.

Gobo, Giampietro (2008) 'Re-conceptualizing generalization. Old issues in a new frame', in Pertti Alasuutari, Leonard Bickman and Julia Brannen (eds), *The SAGE Handbook of Social Research Methods*. London: Sage, pp. 193–213.

Guba, Egon G., and Lincoln, Y.S. (1981) *Effective Evaluation*. San Francisco, CA: Jossey-Bass.

Guest, G., Bunce, A., and Johnson, L. (2006) 'How many interviews are enough? An experiment with data saturation and variability', *Field Methods*, 18(1): 59–82.

Guetterman, Timothy C. (2015) 'Descriptions of sampling practices within five approaches to qualitative research in education and the health sciences [48 paragraphs]', *Forum Qualitative Sozialforschung/Forum: Qualitative Social Research*, 16(2): Art. 25, available at http://nbn-resolving.de/urn:nbn:de:0114-fqs1502256.

Hammersley, Martyn, and Atkinson, Paul (1995) *Ethnography: Principles in Practice* (2nd edn). Milton Park: Routledge.

Higginbottom, G. (2004) 'Sampling issues in qualitative research', *Nurse Researcher*, 12(1): 7–19.

Johnson, Jeffrey C. (1991) *Selecting Ethnographic Informants*. London: Sage.

Lewis, Jane, Ritchie, Jane, Ormston, Rachel, and Morrell, Gareth (2014) 'Generalising from qualitative research', in Jane Ritchie, Jane Lewis, Carol M. Nicholls and Rachel Ormston (eds), *Qualitative Research Practice. A Guide for Social Science Students and Researchers*. London: Sage, pp. 347–63.

Lewis, Michael, and Staehler, Tanja (2010) *Phenomenology: An Introduction*. New York: Continuum.

Lincoln, Yvonne S., and Guba, Egon G. (1979) *Naturalistic Inquiry*. Newbury Park, CA: Sage.

Lynd, Robert S., and Lynd, Helen M. (1929) *Middletown. A Study in Modern American Culture*. New York: Harcourt Brace Jovanovich.

Marshall, M. N. (1996) 'Sampling for qualitative research', *Family Practice*, 13(6): 522–25.

Mason, Jennifer (2002) *Qualitative Researching* (2nd edn). London: Sage.

Mason, M. (2010) 'Sample size and saturation in PhD studies using qualitative interviews [63 paragraphs]', *Forum Qualitative Sozialforschung/Forum: Qualitative Social Research*, 11(3): Art. 8, available at http://nbn-resolving.de/urn:nbn:de:0114-fqs100387.

Maxwell, Joseph A., and Chmiel, Margaret (2014) 'Generalization in and from qualitative analysis', in Uwe Flick (ed.), *SAGE Handbook of Qualitative Data Analysis*. London: Sage, pp. 540–53.

Merkens, Hans (2004) 'Selection procedures, sampling, case construction', in Uwe Flick, Ernst von Kardorff and Ines Steinke (eds), *A Companion to Qualitative Research*. London: Sage, pp. 165–71.

Mitchell, C. (1983) 'Case and situation analysis', *The Sociological Review*, 31(2): 187–211.

Morse, J. (2000) 'Editorial: Determining sample size', *Qualitative Health Research*, 10(1): 3–5.

Onwuegbuzie, A. J., and Leech, N. (2005) 'Taking the "q" out of research: Teaching research methodology courses without the divide between quantitative and qualitative paradigms', *Quality & Quantity*, 39(3): 267–96.

Onwuegbuzie, Anthony J., and Leech, Nancy (2007) 'A call for qualitative power analyses', *Quality & Quantity*, 41(1): 105–21.

Onwuegbuzie, A. J., and Leech, N. (2010) 'Generalization practices in qualitative research: A mixed methods case study', *Quality & Quantity*, 44(5): 881–92.

O'Reilly, M., and Parker, N. (2012) '"Unsatisfactory saturation": A critical exploration of the notion of saturated sample sizes in qualitative research', *Qualitative Research*, 13(2): 190–7.

Palinkas, L. A., Horwitz, S. M., Green, C. A., Wisdom, J. P., Duan, N., and Hoagwood, K. (2015) 'Purposeful sampling for qualitative data collection and analysis in mixed method implementation research', *Administration and Policy in Mental Health and Mental Health Services Research*, 42(5): 533–44.

Patton, Michael Q. (2015) *Qualitative Evaluation and Research Methods* (4th edn). Newbury Park: Sage.

Polit, D. F., and Beck, C. (2010) 'Generalization in quantitative and qualitative research: Myths and strategies', *International Journal of Nursing Studies*, *47*(11): 1451–8.

Ritchie, Jane, Lewis, Jane, Elam, Gilliam, Tennant, Rosalind, and Rahim, Nilufer (2014) 'Designing and selecting samples', in Jane Ritchie, Jane Lewis, Carol M. Nicholls and Rachel Ormston (eds), *Qualitative Research Practice. A Guide for Social Science Students and Researchers*. London: Sage, pp. 111–45.

Robinson, O. C. (2014) 'Sampling in interview-based qualitative research: A theoretical and practical guide', *Qualitative Research in Psychology*, *11*(1): 25–41.

Sandelowski, M. (1995) 'Sample size in qualitative research', *Research in Nursing & Health*, *18*(2): 179–83.

Schegloff, E. A., and Sacks, H. (1974) 'A simplest systematics for the organization of turn-taking for conversation', *Language*, *50*(4): 696–735.

Schofield, Janet W. (1990) 'Increasing the generalizability of qualitative research', in Elliot W. Eisner and Alan Peshkin (eds), *Qualitative Inquiry in Education: The Continuing Debate*. New York: Teachers College Press, pp. 201–42.

Schreier, Margrit, Schmitz-Justen, Felix, Diederich, Adele, Lietz, Petra, Winkelhage, Jeanette, and Heil, Simone (2008) Sampling in qualitativen Untersuchungen: Entwicklung eines Stichprobenplanes zur Erfassung von Präferenzen unterschiedlicher Stakeholdergruppen zu Fragen der Priorisierung medizinischer Leistungen, FOR655, 12, available at http://www.priorisierung-in-der-medizin.de/documents/FOR655_Nr12_Schreier_et_al.pdf.

Schwandt, Thomas A. (2001) *Dictionary of Qualitative Inquiry* (2nd edn). Thousand Oaks, CA: Sage.

Stake, R. E. (1978) 'The case study method in social inquiry', *Educational Researcher*, *7*(2): 5–8.

Strauss, Anselm (1987) *Qualitative Analysis for Social Scientists*. Cambridge: Cambridge University Press.

Teddlie, C., and Yu, F. (2007) 'Mixed methods sampling: A typology with examples', *Journal of Mixed Methods Research*, *1*(1): 77–100.

Trotter, R. L. (2012) 'Qualitative research sample design and sample size: Resolving and unresolved issues and inferential imperatives', *Preventive Medicine*, *55*(5): 398–400.

Wernet, Andreas (2014) 'Hermeneutics and objective hermeneutics', in Uwe Flick (ed.), *SAGE Handbook of Qualitative Data Analysis*. London: Sage, pp. 125–43.

Williams, Malcolm (2002) 'Generalization in interpretive research', in Tim May (ed.), *Qualitative Research in Action*. London: Sage, pp. 125–43.

Winkelhage, J., Schreier, M., and Diederich, A. (2013) 'Priority setting in health care. Attitudes of physicians and patients', *Health 2013*, *5*(4): 712–19.

Wuest, J. (2001) 'Precarious ordering: Toward a formal theory of women's caring', *Health Care for Women International*, *22*(1–2): 167–93.

Yin, Robert K. (2014) *Case Study Research. Design and Methods* (5th edn). Thousand Oaks, CA: Sage.

Accessing the Research Field

Andrew Bengry

The process of gaining access to fieldwork settings and research participants is widely overlooked in social research methodological literature, and treated as a fairly unproblematic and 'check box' stage of the research process (Doykos et al., 2014). Much attention is given to the abstract processes involved in research design, such as formulating research questions and hypotheses, reviewing research and applying theory, methodology, sampling strategies, ethics, and identifying methods for collecting and analysing data (e.g. Bryman, 2015; Silverman, 2013). Far less attention is given to the practical process of implementing a research design (see Gobo, Chapter 5, this volume) and establishing access to a given field setting in order to collect data (Crowhurst, 2013; Turner and Almack, 2016). The transitional stage between research design and data collection is rarely acknowledged, let alone critically examined, which can leave researchers with little formal guidance on *how* to negotiate their way into field settings and establish and maintain the relations that facilitate the process of collecting data.

Field settings and sample populations (see Schreier, Chapter 6, this volume) may be systematically identified in the process of designing a study, but it does not then follow that accessing those settings and recruiting from particular sample populations will in practice be a systematic process (Turner and Almack, 2016). Researchers often find themselves unprepared for the situated practical challenges and ethical dilemmas they encounter in the field and the manoeuvres and tactics they sometimes need to employ in order to gain access to a fieldwork setting, implement a research design and collect data (Cunliffe and Alcadipani da Silveira, 2016; Calvey, 2008). Research is often represented as a linear procedure with a distinct beginning, middle and end, but in practice it is a more complex social process, which is shaped through the interactions between the researcher and researched (Doykos et al., 2014). This complex process can pose many challenges, but can be particularly exacting in fieldwork settings where groups and individuals who are identified as potential research participants are reluctant to engage with a research project (Groger et al., 1999; Doykos et al., 2014), or actively resist researchers' attempts to recruit them (Bengry-Howell and Griffin, 2011).

The concept of 'the field' is used extensively across the social sciences to denote a 'naturalistic' research setting, in contrast with more controlled laboratory or library settings where research might be conducted (McCall, 2006). As a methodological setting the field has been under-theorised, outside of literature concerned with ethnography (see Buscatto, Chapter 21, this volume) and the *Fieldwork Tradition*, wherein researchers are, to differing degrees, situated as participant observers within the fieldwork settings under study (McCall, 2006). The *Fieldwork Tradition* employs a very particular understanding of the field as a naturalistic geographical location wherein participants can be studied 'in situ', and a researcher's role is to capture and represent cultural life as it 'naturally' occurs within that location (McCall, 2006). Post-modern constructions of 'the field' have transcended its link to a geographical or spatial location (Clifford, 1997), and applied the term more broadly to cultural settings and sites of social interaction. This more fluid notion of 'the field' has more recently been utilised to theorise online sites of social interaction and Internet-based communities, which Kozinets (2002) has termed the 'field behind the screen' (see Markham and Gammelby, Chapter 29, this volume).

This chapter employs this broader and more fluid conceptualisation of 'the field' as referring to the sociocultural context or setting in which research is conducted and relations with research participants are established, either directly or through a gatekeeper. It draws on literature from across the social sciences to examine factors that can affect field access and accessibility, challenges that can be encountered in the field, and processes through which field access is negotiated and established. The chapter concludes with three case examples drawn from the author's experience of conducting research in 'naturalistic' field settings. The first example examines the process of negotiating field access through an institutional gatekeeper, the second the process of negotiating access to a private friendship group, and the third the process of negotiating offline access to participants through an online social media platform.

ACCESS AND ACCESSIBILITY

Field settings vary in terms of their accessibility for research purposes, and the opportunities they provide for researchers to conduct fieldwork or recruit participants for a study. Lofland et al. (1995) identify three dimensions of variability between research settings, which can affect their accessibility to researchers. First, where fieldwork settings are situated on the public/private continuum, where *public* denotes open spaces where freedom of access is largely unregulated, in contrast with *private* spaces where access is restricted to certain individuals or groups. Lofland et al. (1995). argue researchers tend to categorise fieldwork settings at either end of this continuum, and not consider variability in the extent to which settings are public or private. Settings classed as public may be viewed differently by those inhabiting them, or incorporate discrete spaces symbolically demarcated as 'private', although located within a public setting with open access. Examples of the latter would be the 'private' spaces marked by windbreaks, deck chairs, blankets and towels on public beaches (Ruane, 2007, p. 23). Occupied tables in bars, cafés and restaurants, and benches in public parks, may also be constituted as private spaces by those using them, despite being located within a public setting where access is open and largely unregulated.

The second dimension Lofland et al. (1995) identify concerns the behavioural constraints that may be associated with fieldwork settings, and how behaviour is regulated to differing degrees in different social contexts. In this respect, freedom to access a setting classed as *public* does not guarantee freedom of action, as behavioural expectations and constraints can vary between settings. Gaining access to and maintaining a presence within a given field setting may require a researcher to compose themselves in a certain way and perform certain practices that carry meaning and value within that context, and without this prior knowledge they can easily make mistakes that can jeopardise their capacity to remain in that setting (De Laine, 2000, p. 64). Spatial practices and behavioural expectations (see Kusenbach, Chapter 22, this volume), and the meanings attached to them, do not only vary between settings, but often between groups and individuals who occupy settings and claim the 'right to space' at any given point in time (Mitchell, 2003). This can pose a dilemma for researchers seeking to conduct fieldwork with marginalised groups whose claims to space and practices are deemed illegitimate. In such cases, researchers may need to meet certain behavioural expectations in order to gain acceptance and maintain a presence within the group they wish to study, whilst not directly associating themselves with practices that might jeopardise their position as a professional researcher. This is a particular concern for field researchers using ethnographic methods or participant observation to study individuals or groups whose behaviour is problematised, for example, research on football hooliganism (Giulianotti, 1995), and young men who modify and illegally race cars (Bengry-Howell and Griffin, 2008).

The third dimension Lofland et al. (1995) highlight concerns accessibility to field settings based on personal attributes, for example, gender, age, ethnicity, education and occupation. They distinguish between *inclusive* settings, where personal attributes have minimal impact on access, and *exclusive* settings, where access is limited to those possessing certain personal attributes. The distinction between inclusive and exclusive social settings, like open and closed settings, serves as a continuum with many degrees of variability. One's personal attributes may facilitate or hinder access to some situations, but not others (Pole and Lampard, 2002, p. 45). For example, a researcher's ethnic and religious background may help them to establish trust and access to a group with similar attributes, for example, a Bengali Muslim researcher studying a Bengali Muslim community (Ryan et al., 2011). Personal attributes can also serve as a barrier to obtaining access in contexts where they are viewed as problematic (Doykos et al., 2014; Scourfield and Coffey, 2004).

The focus on personal attributes has more recently been superseded by a more nuanced consideration of the complex and fluid processes whereby the researcher and the research subject construct and position each other within the field (Fawcett and Hearn, 2004; Kennedy-Macfoy, 2013; Doykos et al., 2014). Discussions of positionality often use the concepts of *insider* and *outsider* to consider how the researcher is constructed and positioned by field participants. Whether a researcher is positioned as an insider or outsider is contextual and a reflection of how they are perceived by field participants, which is 'contingent on time and space in the field' (Sanghera and Thapar-Björkert, 2008, p. 554). Insider and outsider positions are not predicated on fixed or absolute notions of identity and status (Merton, 1972), but rather the relative cultural proximity between researcher and researched within the field of study (Hodkinson, 2005). Researchers who are positioned as 'insiders' within a target group or community often find they can connect and develop rapport with participants more effectively than those who are positioned as 'outsiders' (Doykos et al., 2014), but 'insider' status can also result in participants self-censoring if they perceive they are being judged by a peer (Ryan et al., 2011). In some cases, how a researcher is positioned by field participants can be so problematic that they are constituted as a threat and treated with suspicion; for example, the case of a male researcher working on a project exploring constructions of gender in social work teams, who, when he contacted a social services manager requesting access to one of the teams, was viewed as a potential 'paedophile' (Scourfield and Coffey, 2004).

ONLINE FIELDS

The three dimensions of accessibility have become less distinct with the advent of the Internet and the emergence of online fields (see Lindgren, Chapter 28, this volume; Weller et al., Chapter 31, this volume). The capacity to access archived and live social interactions online has transformed many of the practices associated with the social sciences (Kozinets, 2015), and removed barriers to access that offline researchers need to negotiate. Online researchers often have open access to the field settings they are investigating and the capacity to position themselves as an invisible 'lurking observer', without needing to negotiate with participants or gatekeepers in order to establish and maintain a presence (Griffin and Bengry-Howell, 2017).

Online fields raise complex ethical issues regarding the nuanced nature of the public and private in online settings (Lange, 2008; see Tiidenberg, Chapter 30, this volume), and this complexity has increased with the advent of web 2.0 (Snee, 2008; Morey et al., 2012). Participants in online settings, which may be publicly accessible, often have similar expectations of privacy as they would in offline settings (Smith et al., 2011). 'Naturally occurring' conversations a researcher might encounter online should, Jacobson (1999) argues, be treated like conversation one might overhear in a public park and not as a public conversation, if those involved have reasonable expectations of privacy (see Ditchfield and Meredith, Chapter 32, this volume). As the range of online settings has extended and diversified, debates around what researchers can access on the Internet and legitimately utilise as data have become more complex (Roberts, 2015; Snee, 2013). The advent of practices such as blogging (see Weller et al., Chapter 31, this volume) have added to this complexity and raised questions about whether online postings should be viewed as a textual representation of a 'person' or as a text that a person has published online (Snee, 2013). If bloggers are constituted as human subjects, rather than authors and publishers, then accessing blogs for the purpose of gathering 'data' requires a researcher to inform the blogger that they are involved in a research project and allow them to decide whether or not they want to participate (Snee, 2013). If online bloggers are viewed as authors who are publishing online, then their output is deemed to be already in the public domain and, like other public texts, utilisable as 'data', provided it is referenced through citation to the source blog (Snee, 2013).

Field accessibility online is less of a methodological concern than an ethical one, with the nature of the setting, researcher visibility and whether or not consent is required to use the source material being primary considerations. Heath et al. (1999) argue that 'lurking' online without identifying oneself as a researcher encroaches on individual privacy and creates an unequal power relationship between an anonymous researcher and subjects who are studied covertly. However, ascertaining the status of online settings and how to constitute online participants and researchers is never straightforward, and becoming more complex as new technologies, types of community and online practices emerge (Roberts, 2015; see Tiidenberg, Chapter 30, this volume).

ETHICAL ACCESS

Most social research is underpinned by the key ethical principle that research should be conducted overtly and participants should be informed about a study and provide consent before they are engaged in the research process (see Mertens, Chapter 3, this volume). This places ethical constraints on the methods that researchers might employ to access a field setting and collect data. Although a researcher might in principle be able to access a variety of settings, including some that might be considered 'closed', surreptitiously (i.e. by not informing anyone of their agenda or obtaining permission to undertake research) to do so would be generally regarded as unethical. Covert research is mostly deemed to be unjustifiable and, moreover, potentially damaging not only to research participants, but also to the fields from which future research participants might be recruited (Homan, 1991).

The British Sociological Association (BSA) (2002) in their statement of ethical practice highlight 'serious ethical and legal issues' surrounding covert research, because it violates an individual's *right* to privacy and to be informed and provide consent if they are to be studied. The British Psychological Society (BPS) (2010) places similar emphasis on the importance of privacy in their code of human research ethics, and, in the case of studies conducted in 'natural' settings as opposed to lab settings, recommends that observational research should only be conducted without obtaining consent in contexts where people might expect to be observed by strangers. Both the BSA and BPS acknowledge that in exceptional circumstances covert research may be justifiable, if a strong argument can be presented that participants' behaviour would be affected if they knew they were being studied (BSA, 2002); or there is strong scientific merit in withholding information in order to achieve a particular research objective; and appropriate risk management and harm reduction strategies are in place to ensure participants' well-being (BPS, 2010). In practice, when conducting research in public settings, it may be impossible to obtain consent from everyone in situ and avoid some element of covert observation (see Wästerfors, Chapter 20, this volume). For a researcher to assume a totally overt role in such a setting, everyone they came into contact with would need to be aware they are conducting a research study. This is in contrast with a researcher assuming a totally covert role, where they are effectively 'under cover' and most or all of the people they encounter are unaware that they are being studied.

With the advent of online fields and research the ethical issues surrounding covert research have been compounded. The ethical requirement to obtain consent prior to access is undermined by the public nature of many online fields, and the practical difficulties surrounding the identification and contacting of participants (Morey et al., 2012). Official ethical guidelines for researchers have been relatively slow to respond to the challenges posed by the Internet. The BSA's statement of ethical practice vaguely advises that researchers 'should take special care when carrying out research via the Internet' and acknowledges that 'ethical standards for internet research are not well developed as yet' (BSA, 2002). Ethical guidelines for online research are constantly being developed and updated, but the constant and accelerating rate of change in computer-mediated communication makes it impossible to anticipate all of the ethical issues that might occur (BPS, 2010; see Tiidenberg, Chapter 30, this volume). Guidelines often fail to anticipate sea change in the practices of Internet users, and the very nature of communication on the Internet (Morey et al., 2012, p. 197).

The onus is placed on the individual researcher to 'ensure that they are familiar with ongoing debates on the ethics of Internet research', but the BSA do advise, again vaguely, 'erring on the side of caution in making judgements affecting the well-being of online research participants' (Morey et al., 2012, p. 197). The BPS more specifically identify a number of ethical issues primarily concerning levels of 'identifiability' and 'observation' of online research participants (BPS, 2007). The BPS guidelines recommend that consent should be obtained in all cases when a researcher intends to observe participants online or collect data based on their online activity. Drawing on the key ethical principle that research participants should not be deceived, they suggest that deception is most likely to occur in contexts where researchers join chat rooms or discussion groups in order to 'lurk' and collect qualitative data.

ESTABLISHING FIELD ACCESS

Field access is not simply an instrumental process of establishing a presence within a given setting to collect data, but rather a social process of initiating, negotiating and maintaining field relations, either directly with participants, or indirectly through a gatekeeper. Cassell (1988) draws a distinction between physical and social access to field settings, where physical access refers to one's capacity to enter a field and contact potential research subjects, groups and gatekeepers, whilst social access refers to the establishing of field relations that facilitate the process of collecting research data. Gaining physical access to a setting does not necessarily guarantee social access to the individuals or groups that occupy it (Clark, 2011). Establishing social access requires a researcher to gain social acceptance or legitimacy within a field setting, and with the key individuals and groups they hope to engage in their research (Cassell, 1988). Negotiating social access can be a challenging stage of the research process, particularly when physical access is obtained, but potential participants or gatekeepers don't engage, or resist attempts to engage, them. In such circumstance, researchers might resort to unethical practices and forms of 'methodological grooming', where they attempt to advance their research agenda by managing impressions of a study and relations in the field. For example, a researcher might: conceal or misrepresent a study's true aims and problematic aspects of its design; exaggerate possible positive, and minimise negative, outcomes for participants; use rapport strategically to assuage concerns and cajole individuals or groups to participate; employ other clandestine practices to manufacture consent, circumvent resistance and gain access (Bengry-Howell and Griffin, 2011). For additional reading on ethical dilemmas relating to deception and field access, see Alcadipani and Hodgson (2009); Calvey (2008); Cunliffe and Alcadipani da Silveira (2016); Duncombe and Jessop (2002).

When establishing and maintaining field relations, the position and identity of the researcher relative to those whom they wish to study is integral to the research process. Many researchers embark on fieldwork from a position where they are a social outsider with no prior contact with the individuals or groups they wish to study, and are attempting to establish what Jacobs (2006) refers to as 'cold access', either directly or indirectly through an intermediary or gatekeeper. Conversely, researchers may share a significant degree of cultural proximity and common attributes with the individuals and groups they wish to research, and are consequently able to establish access with minimal negotiation because they are positioned as an 'insider' when they enter the field (Hodkinson, 2005). The process of gaining field access, many have argued, needs to be carefully 'managed', particularly in the early stages of a study (Hobbs and May, 1993; Lofland et al., 1995). Researchers often attempt to manage impressions of a study to ensure it is perceived favourably, by regulating the information they share about its focus, scope or implications (Homan, 1991). In some cases, researchers have deliberately misled potential participants and gatekeepers, when they believed clearly stating their research goals could result in access being denied (Atkinson and Hammersley, 1994, p. 68).

Cunliffe and Alcadipani da Silveira (2016) suggest that researchers often use deception unintentionally in order to gain and maintain access, and this raises important questions about transparency in research. They reject an instrumental approach to obtaining access, which privileges the researcher's goals and agency, and the use of instrumental techniques to manage impressions. Instead they propose a transactional approach where the researcher–researched relationship is based on integrity, moral accountability, mutuality and reciprocity, and research provides something of value to participants in exchange for data collection. From this perspective, access is contingent on and negotiated around a 'research bargain' between researcher and research subject, which is of mutual benefit to both parties. Establishing this bargain requires transparency about research goals, design and methods, but also the nature of the research relationship. Trust plays a key role in this process, and Cunliffe and Alcadipani da Silveira (2016) argue that establishing trust may require a researcher to demonstrate their commitment to research participants through 'commitment acts' that serve to 'humanise' them within the field setting they are attempting to access. Harrison et al. (2001) suggest such 'actions of reciprocity' serve to not only demonstrate a researcher's trustworthiness, but also to facilitate the process of obtaining access by positioning the researcher as a subject within a field setting under study.

Social research is an 'embodied spatial practice' (Clifford, 1997, p. 186), which arguably requires some degree of identity management regarding how a researcher presents themselves, and is perceived within field settings (Doykos et al., 2014). Researchers have been known to modify aspects of their appearance in an attempt to position themselves, and by association their research, favourably within the cultural contexts they wish to study (Atkinson and Hammersley, 1994; Angrosino, 2007; see Buscatto, Chapter 21, this volume). Whilst such practices may raise ethical concerns regarding deception, there are limitations to the extent that researchers can manage perceptions, and prevent others from constructing an identity for them outside of their control (Jorgenson, 1991).

In most cases field relations are established through a discursive process of negotiation, which often involves some degree of 'rapport management' (Duncombe and Jessop, 2002). Feminist researchers have highlighted ethical issues associated with the process of 'doing rapport' in order to facilitate field access, and its use as a persuasive tool for 'agenda setting' and 'managing consent' in fieldwork settings (Duncombe and Jessop, 2002). Viewing rapport as a persuasive tool for managing impressions raises questions about informed consent and voluntary research participation, and how field access can be established ethically, rather than surreptitiously elicited through a systematic and more insidious process of 'methodological grooming' (Bengry-Howell and Griffin, 2011).

With the advent of the Internet and online fields, many of the practical challenges and dilemmas surrounding field access are effectively inverted. Establishing 'physical' access and some degree of social access may require little or, in some cases, no negotiation, as the data that a researcher might collect are often already in the public domain. Online researchers may have open access to the field they wish to study and the capacity to assume a covert position as a 'lurking observer' within communities, without having to communicate directly with field participants or gatekeepers. Not all online communities are open access, however, and in the case of closed-groups on social media platforms that are password protected and technologically private, establishing access for research purposes can be more challenging than in offline settings (Snee, 2013; see Markham, Chapter 33, this volume).

The processes through which field access and consent are obtained are rarely straightforward, and the terms surrounding data collection are rarely unconditional. Field access is conditionally bound by the terms upon which it is negotiated and granted (Cunliffe and Alcadipani da Silveira, 2016), whether that be directly with potential participants, or indirectly through a gatekeeper. In both cases, access is facilitated through 'relationships' that researchers develop in the field and their capacity to gain and maintain the acceptance and trust of those whom they encounter (Feldman et al., 2003).

To illustrate some of the challenges that researchers can encounter when attempting to establish field access and field relations, and how they can be circumvented, three case examples from the author's research experience will now be considered.

CASE ONE: ESTABLISHING FIELD ACCESS THROUGH INSTITUTIONAL GATEKEEPERS

The first case example is taken from the 'How should we tell the children?' study, which was conducted between 2011 and 2013 by the Centre for Sexual Health research at the University of Southampton (Stone et al., 2014; McGinn et al., 2016). The study was funded by the Leverhulme Trust and investigated parental perspectives on the sexual socialisation of young children (4–7 years), specifically, parents' experiences of talking to young children about sexual matters, their reactions and responses to their child's emerging sexual curiosity, and their desires and fears regarding sexual knowledge in the early childhood years. One hundred and ten parents and carers (82 males; 28 females) from a variety of socio-economic and ethnic backgrounds participated in the study, which comprised 27 focus group discussions (see Morgan and Hoffman, Chapter 16, this volume) and 49 follow-up individual telephone interviews (see Stone et al., 2014; see Roulston and Choi, Chapter 15, this volume).

Participants in the study were recruited using a recruitment flyer with a reply slip, which was distributed through selected primary schools in four local authority regions in the South East of England: two situated in a large urban metropolitan area, and two in a rural county. The local authority regions and primary schools were selected to provide an ethnic and socio-economically diverse sampling frame. All of the local authorities in the metropolitan area and rural county were ranked and stratified based on the proportion of ethnic minorities in the population, and one local authority was randomly selected from the upper and lower quintiles in each area. Primary schools in the four selected local authority areas were then ranked and stratified based on the proportion of pupils receiving free school meals, and schools that fell within the upper and lower quintiles in each local authority area were selected as sites in which to promote the study. This sampling strategy, whilst it was designed to maximise ethnic and socio-economic diversity, was contingent on establishing field access to each of the selected primary schools in order to recruit parents. Each school was an independent closed setting with an institutional gatekeeper, in this case the head teacher, who is formally responsible for making decisions about whether to grant or withhold access for activities, such as research (Heath et al., 2007), but in some instances school secretaries, who acted on the school's behalf.

The first stage of the research process involved contacting head teachers by email at each of the selected schools to inform them about the study and invite them to distribute the recruitment flyer to parents and carers with children at Foundation Stage 2 (key stage zero) and Key Stage One in the UK national curriculum. Prior to establishing this initial contact, the research team gave considerable thought to the design of the recruitment flyer for parents and the information sheets for head teachers and participants. The team were cognisant of the sensitive nature of the study and the importance of presenting it in a manner that would be deemed appropriate by head teachers, school staff and parents alike. Much attention was given to how the study was framed and the terminology that was used, with three draft versions of the flyer being produced before the team finally agreed on the design. Similar attention was paid to the wording of the information sheets for head teachers and participating parents, along with the email that was to be sent to head teachers inviting their schools to become involved in the project.

Head teachers at each of the 70 primary schools identified through the sampling procedure were contacted and 14 agreed to distribute the flyer, 48 declined and eight didn't respond, despite repeated attempts to contact them. Some 2,065 flyers were distributed to parents at the 14 schools where access was granted, but only 49 parents returned reply slips; 76 short of the target of 125 participants in the study. Only five of the 14 primary schools generated sufficient response from parents to run a school-based focus group as originally intended; at five other schools parents had to be aggregated to make up the numbers to run two focus groups, and at six of the schools no parents returned reply slips at all.

In an attempt to increase the number of participants, a decision was taken to extend the sampling frame to include primary schools in each local authority region from the second and fourth quintiles, based on the proportion of pupils receiving free school meals. A further 51 schools were selected and head teachers at each of these schools were contacted. Eight responded and agreed to provide access to distribute the flyer, 10 declined and 32 didn't respond despite repeated attempts to contact them. There were 1,564 recruitment flyers distributed to parents at the eight schools where access had been established, but this only resulted in 23 returned reply slips from parents at four schools, enough to run a small focus group at each school; at four schools no reply slips were returned despite distributing 634 flyers.

The total number of parents recruited had now increased to 72, still 53 short of the target of 125. To address this shortfall a second revision was made to the sampling frame to include schools within the remaining middle quintile, based on the proportion of pupils receiving free school meals, which amounted to 39 schools. Head teachers at all 39 schools were contacted, but only one agreed to provide access to distribute the flyer, seven declined, and 31 did not respond. There were 247 flyers distributed at the one participating school, but no parents returned reply slips.

A third adjustment was made to the sampling frame, and two additional local authority regions were randomly selected from the upper and lower quintiles, based on the initial ranking of local authorities based on the proportion of ethnic minorities in the population. Primary schools in the selected regions were ranked and stratified as previously, based on the proportion of children in receipt of free schools, and 92 schools were selected from the upper and lower quintiles. Head teachers were contacted at each of these schools and four agreed to provide access to distribute the flyer, nine declined and 79 did not respond. Some 673 flyers were distributed at the four participating schools, which resulted in five returned reply slips at one school, and no response from parents at the remaining three. These five participants increased the total number recruited to 77, still 48 short of the target of 125.

The research team made a final adaptation to the sampling frame (see Schreier, Chapter 6, this volume) and extended the field beyond primary schools, to also include children's centres, Sure Start centres and parenting groups (including some catering for fathers) situated within the local authority regions that had been previously selected. The people responsible for running the centres and groups were contacted and arrangements were made to visit groups and attempt to recruit parents and carers directly. This recruitment technique proved to be successful and the number of participants recruited increased to the final total of 110.

The time and effort that was required to recruit participants for this study far exceeded expectations, and a key hurdle was establishing field access, which was restricted by head teachers, or whoever read the email invitation and declined on the school's behalf. Before embarking on the study the research team had anticipated some degree of resistance from head teachers and parents, due to the sensitive nature of the study, but had been surprised by the high number of head teachers who declined to distribute the flyer or ignored emails regarding the study. It was decided to investigate this further by contacting head teachers who had refused access, and asking them to provide feedback on why they had felt unable to support the study. Seventy-three head teachers were emailed, 11 didn't respond, but 62 did provide some, albeit brief, explanation. Twenty suggested capacity issues precluded them from supporting the study, with 13 stating that their schools were particularly busy at the time of year when they had been contacted, two that they had no capacity for getting involved in activities like research, and three that their schools were already involved in university research projects and had no additional capacity.

Of greater interest were the head teachers who stated they had declined because of the sensitive nature of the topic under investigation. Twenty-nine stated that they (and their schools) were not interested in this study, with one explaining that 'the project is not something our school feels able to support'. Five head teachers claimed they had declined because of parental sensitivities, as one put it 'the sensitive nature of the topic and how our parents will respond'. Two of these head teachers claimed to be representing the views of parents at their schools who they suggested 'would not be interested in the study', presumably without consulting them to ascertain whether or not this was the case.

The decisions of institutional gatekeepers, such as head teachers, are often taken as a proxy for those in their charge (Heath et al., 2007). In the case of the example considered here, head teachers' decisions served to extend this proxy to include parents as well. This illustrates how institutional gatekeepers can regulate and restrict access to a field setting or population, and how their thoughts and actions (or inaction) can impact on the implementation of a study (Reeves, 2010). Whilst some head teachers actively denied access to distribute the flyer promoting the study, there were more who passively denied access by not responding to emails and attempts to contact them by telephone. Even in cases where head teachers granted physical access to the school to distribute the flyer, it provided no guarantee that social access to parents would be established, as so many did not return reply slips to indicate they were interested in participating in the study.

In a small number of instances, head teachers who granted physical access also actively assisted in facilitating social access to parents, by writing letters of support that were sent to parents along with the recruitment flyer. In these instances, parental interest in the study was much greater and resulted in a higher number returning reply slips and going on to participate in the study. In primary schools, where head teachers agreed to distribute the flyer, but did not include a supporting letter, response rates from parents were much lower and in some instances there was no response. This highlights the importance of establishing positive field relations with gatekeepers, and how these relations can help to facilitate the process of establishing a wider field access (Clark, 2011). Negotiating social access to schools and actively engaging head teachers in endorsing the study (Crowhurst, 2013), although time consuming, proved to be a far superior and more effective mechanism for recruiting participants than a more instrumental approach, where schools were asked purely to distribute a flyer to parents without personal contact.

The next two case examples also highlight the importance of field relations in the processes of establishing access and negotiating the conditions under which it is to be granted, particularly in contexts where a researcher is attempting to extend the level of access or negotiate access to another field setting.

CASE TWO: NEGOTIATING ACCESS TO PRIVATE FRIENDSHIP GROUPS

This case example examines the process of extending field access and negotiating a transition from a bounded research interview to a more intensive field-based encounter.

The Young People and Alcohol study (conducted between 2005 and 2008) investigated the drinking practices of young adults in the 18–25-year age range and the meanings they associate with alcohol consumption and drinking to the point of intoxication (see Griffin et al., 2008, 2009; Szmigin et al., 2008). The study was conducted in two geographical locations: 'Rowchester', a major metropolitan area in the English Midlands, and two towns in semi-rural locations in the English West Country. It involved 84 young people (52 females, 32 males); most self-identified their ethnic origin as White British, eight as British Asian and three as Black. Participants were mostly full-time college students from middle-class backgrounds, who were recruited through local further education colleges, and some young people from working-class backgrounds who attended FE colleges on a day-release basis.

The study employed a multi-modal qualitative methodology, which combined focus group discussions and semi-structured individual interviews, with participant observation conducted within the bars and clubs that form the night-time economies, which have been driving urban renewal strategies in cities across the UK since the 1990s (Chatterton and Hollands, 2003). The study was conducted in two stages. The first 'interview stage' comprised 15 focus group discussions (participants were recruited from existing friendship groups), and eight semi-structured individual interviews (see Roulston and Choi, Chapter 15, this volume and Morgan and Hoffman, Chapter 16, this volume). The second 'observation' stage of the project employed ethnographic methods to investigate drinking contexts and practices. Methodologically, the two stages of the project were linked, and at the end of focus group discussions participants were invited to provide their consent individually to two researchers (one male, one female) accompanying them on an evening out with their friends.

Recruiting participants who were willing to participate in the second stage of the project posed many challenges. The observation stage extended the level of social access and research involvement that participants had been asked to consent to prior to the focus group discussion, and, thus, required the terms of consent to be renegotiated (Miller and Bell, 2002). This involved more detailed explanation and clarification regarding the wider aims of the study, the purpose of the fieldwork and the intentions of the researchers. It also involved reassuring participants that the primary intention was to observe the social contexts in which they drank and practices related to the consumption of particular alcoholic drinks, rather than individual behaviour. Participants were also assured that access would be limited and only required for a couple of hours of their evening, after which they would be left to socialise with their friends as they would do ordinarily. When the observation stage of the study was introduced at the end of the focus group discussion it was often met with some surprise. Female participants generally expressed more reservations than males, but in most instances at least one participant from each focus group self-selected for the second stage of the study. However, when researchers attempted to contact them again to make specific arrangements almost all withdrew their interest, or repeatedly deflected attempts to recruit them.

One young man, 'Brian', however, greeted follow-up calls with apparent enthusiasm, although he was reluctant to make specific arrangements. Contact was maintained for some time until he identified an evening when he and his friends would be happy for researchers to accompany them. Arrangements were made to ring him on the day to finalise details, but when attempts were made to contact him he did not answer the call. Attempts to contact him after that date also proved unsuccessful and the access that had been discussed informally over a number of months failed to materialise.

Another young man, 'Marko', at the end of a focus group discussion expressed interest in participating in the fieldwork. However, it was discovered after the discussion that the mobile phone number he had provided appeared to be missing a digit. As Marko had appeared enthusiastic about the observation stage of the study this was taken to be an error, rather than a tactic to avoid being contacted. During the focus group discussion, he had made a number of references to the local band he played guitar in, which was becoming popular and receiving a high number of 'hits' on its Myspace page. Using the information he shared, his band's Myspace page was easily identified and a message was sent, via Myspace, explaining the problem with the telephone number and enquiring if he was still interested in participating in the fieldwork. Two weeks passed without a reply to this message, and when a further attempt was made to access the band's Myspace page it became apparent that it was no longer available. Whilst there is no evidence to suggest Marko deleted his band's Myspace page, or blocked access to the researchers, to avoid participating in the study, or being contacted again, it was an interpretation of events that was hard to ignore. The decision to contact Marko through a social media platform using information he had shared during the focus group discussion, rather than using the mobile number he had provided, raised ethical questions about the practices that researchers might employ, to establish field access, that transcend the limits of consent, which in Marko's case had been limited to providing a telephone number to establish future contact.

During another focus group discussion, a young woman called 'Rose', suggested, half-jokingly, that one of the researchers working on the study should 'come along' one night with her and her mates, to see 'what it was really like'. This provided a good opportunity to introduce the 'observation' stage of the study and following a short informal interaction a date for the fieldwork was provisionally agreed for the following month. However, once again, attempts to contact her by text and telephone in the week leading up to the arranged date proved unsuccessful, as did attempts to contact her on the day. On the following Monday a text was received from Rose, in which she apologised for her lack of contact and stated that she would have to withdraw from the project. She explained that she had accidentally left her mobile phone at her boyfriend's house, and he had seen the text messages regarding the proposed field encounter and 'got the wrong idea', assuming that she was arranging to meet someone for a date behind his back. This had caused an argument with her boyfriend and consequently she no longer felt able to participate in the study. This unforeseen incident illustrates how establishing informal contact with participants for the purpose of obtaining field access can impact on their lives, irrespective of the intentions of the researcher.

Future attempts to establish field access employed a more overt strategy of active negotiation with participants regarding the nature and conditions of access they were willing to consent to. Two female focus group participants 'Helen' and 'Sara' expressed an interest in the fieldwork, but also expressed reservations about the research and whether it could negatively impact on young drinkers like themselves. They readily acknowledged that when they went out with their mates they like to 'get a bit pissed', but also that documenting their practices could be potentially damaging in a discursive context where young people's drinking was being scrutinised and widely criticised.

After much discussion about how the research team might consider and represent young people's drinking practices without contributing to the moral panic about 'binge drinking', Helen and Sara agreed to participate in the fieldwork on the understanding that their consent was bounded by the conditions that the research team would not 'say anything nasty' about them or portray them in a manner that made young people 'look bad'. Access was to be granted on the basis of an informal contract and an assurance from the research team that they would not under any circumstances 'betray her trust'. During negotiations, Helen acted as an equal and empowered participant who defined and imposed research parameters, rather than being subject to a less ethical 'methodological grooming' process wherein a researcher managed the process of obtaining consent and access to meet their research agenda (Bengry-Howell and Griffin, 2011). Social access for the 'observational' stage of this study in this instance was finally established through an ethical process of establishing conditional access based on mutual trust and bounded consent, and maintained by honouring the terms upon which it had been granted.

CASE THREE: NEGOTIATING OFFLINE ACCESS TO ONLINE PARTICIPANTS

The final case example also addresses the process of attempting to extend access, but in this instance negotiating the transition from contact in an online field to an offline field encounter.

The music festivals and free parties (illegal raves) study (conducted between 2007 and 2010) investigated the impact of corporate involvement in young people's leisure spaces, and on how consumers negotiate these spaces and the meanings they associate with their consumption practices (see Bengry-Howell et al., 2011; Griffin et al., 2017). The study employed a multi-modal methodology, which combined a market mapping of corporate involvement across the sector and at key events, participant observation, semi-structured in-situ group and individual interviews, post-event focus group discussions, email interviews and online ethnography. This case example is drawn from the second stage of the study, which focused on unlicensed free parties, and examines the process of negotiating offline access to members of the 'Psyporeal' sound system following initial online contact.

Free party networks were investigated in this study using online and offline ethnographic methods which, in the case of the former, utilised a variety of social media platforms including a Facebook profile, which was set up to promote the study and establish contact with Free Party networks. The Psyporeal sound system was first identified among the Facebook 'friends' network of another sound system, which researchers were able to access when the sound system accepted a 'friend request' from the project. Members of Psyporeal were subsequently sent a friend request along with a message about the project. The request was accepted and Psyporeal responded to the message expressing interest in the study and almost immediately started contributing to discussions about free parties, which were taking place on the project's Facebook timeline. The anti-commercial values that members of Psyporeal expressed and the values they more broadly associated with the Free Party scene immediately caught the research team's attention, and the research assistant working on the project (Yvette Morey) messaged them through Facebook to invite them to participate in an offline interview. Psyporeal responded and reiterated their interest in the project, but declined the invitation to be interviewed, stating that they had nothing to gain from such an encounter, although they appreciated why the researchers might find it useful to talk to them. Their resistance was limited, however, to participating in an offline interview and they had no reservations about answering questions by email, or sharing the 'magic number' which would enable members of the research team to obtain details about, and attend, their next party.

As principal investigator on this project I was particularly interested in interviewing the people involved with this sound system, so decided to contact them myself through Facebook. Drawing on experience I had gained during the early 1990s through attending British free festivals and living temporarily as a 'new age traveller', I attempted to position myself as an 'insider' who understood Psyporeal's concerns and had a shared investment in documenting free party culture from the perspective of those involved in it. Assuming this position enabled me to facilitate a process of negotiation, in which I mobilised the cultural capital embodied in the person I 'used to be', rather than the person I would necessarily claim to 'be' now. During these negotiations, information regarding the study was not concealed or fabricated, but framed in a manner that constituted the study as documenting an important subculture that was often overlooked or represented unfairly. By being able to position myself as a cultural 'insider' it provided greater opportunity to engage with and address some of the concerns members of Psyporeal had about how the free party scene would be represented. It played an important role in establishing trust and communication and a two-way relationship, which enabled them to influence how the research was conducted, and how the findings from the project were represented. This reciprocal relationship culminated not only in a face-to-face interview, but their ongoing involvement in the project and co-organisation of a dissemination event called 'Bringing the party home': A multimedia celebration of music festival and free party scenes, which was held as part of the ESRC Festival of Social Science Week (13 March 2010, Trinity Centre, Bristol, UK).

CONCLUSION

Establishing and maintaining field access is a fundamental and critical stage of the research process, which is often overlooked in literature concerned with social research methods and methodology (Doykos et al., 2014; Cunliffe and Alcadipani da Silveira, 2016). Whilst not all social research requires the same level of field access as ethnography, a great deal is conducted within 'naturalistic' settings and requires some degree of access to be established before it can be implemented (Feldman et al., 2003). At the minimal level, this might consist of contacting and negotiating with a gatekeeper or partner in the field to gain their support and assistance in promoting the study or facilitating the research process (Crowhurst, 2013) by, for example, distributing a questionnaire. Even in settings where participants are to be recruited directly, rather than through an intermediary, establishing physical access for recruitment purposes often requires some negotiation in order to obtain permission to, for example, display a poster promoting a study, distribute a recruitment flyer or approach potential participants within a particular field setting.

The case examples that have been presented in this chapter are drawn from studies that have investigated sensitive topics, or attempted to gain access to what might be considered 'hard-to-reach' groups (see Chamberlain and Hodgetts, Chapter 42, this volume). However, the dilemmas and challenges that they highlight are more broadly relevant to the process of establishing field access for research more generally. The first case examines ways in which institutional gatekeepers can affect the implementation of research that requires access to closed and private settings, for example, schools, hospitals, occupational settings, prisons and closed-membership groups. Institutional gatekeepers stand at the metaphorical gate to the field under their control (Crowhurst, 2013), and can provide or deny access without explanation, deflect access by being evasive, or block access by ignoring attempts to contact them, leaving a researcher with very little they can do to influence their actions.

The point of gatekeepers in this context is to 'get around them' (McGivern, 2006) and if the challenges associated with achieving this are not anticipated, gatekeepers can seriously impact on the implementation of a study, and may require certain elements of its design to be amended, compromised or even abandoned in order for it to proceed (Crowhurst, 2013; Clark, 2011). Some of the challenges concerning gatekeepers may be purely practical, for example, them not having the time or capacity to engage with a study and facilitate access (Clark, 2011), or associated with how a study is perceived by gatekeepers, and whether it is deemed interesting, appropriate and relevant to their interests. When a study is perceived positively by a gatekeeper they can sometimes be called upon to 'bat for the researcher' (Crowhurst, 2013) and help to facilitate the research process by providing a physical and social bridge between the researcher and the field under investigation (Clark, 2011). This arrangement is most likely to occur when the aims of a study and the conditions of access are negotiated and deemed to be mutually beneficial to all parties.

The second case example also demonstrates the importance of reciprocity in establishing and maintaining field access and, in this instance, extending access from a bounded research encounter, such as a focus group or individual interview, to a more fluid field-based encounter with a deeper level of access. The challenges that were encountered when trying to implement the observation stage of the Young People and Alcohol study highlight ethical dilemmas researchers can face when they are attempting to negotiate access, albeit temporarily, to participants' private social lives. Relations between researchers and research participants are more fluid, and in some instances, can become problematic, when they are situated within the informal context of a field-based setting, rather than a more formal research encounter where boundaries and the terms of the interaction are more clearly defined (Knowles, 2006; Scourfield and Coffey, 2004; Grauerholz et al., 2012; Calvey, 2008). In field-based settings establishing informal contracts, or 'research bargains' (Cunliffe and Alcadipani da Silveira, 2016), predicated on a mutual understanding of the purpose of fieldwork and conditions of access are fundamental to establishing and maintaining access ethically, and ensuring that participants are able to actively define the terms upon which access is granted (Harrison et al., 2001), rather than their consent being managed through a more insidious process of methodological grooming (Bengry-Howell and Griffin, 2011).

The third case example is also concerned with the role that reciprocity plays in establishing field access, but in this instance when negotiating the transition from a more equitable online encounter to an offline encounter, wherein the research participant is potentially more exposed to the power differential that defines the researcher–researched relationship (Coffey, 1996). Establishing trust and a common agenda played an important role in negotiating this transition, which was facilitated by leveraging my identity and positioning myself as an 'insider' who understood and shared participants' concerns (Doykos et al., 2014), based on my historic association with free festival culture, and was to some extent 'matched' to the target community (Ryan et al., 2011). This common cultural capital was a resource that I could mobilise to circumvent concerns and establish positive field relations with members of the Psyporeal sound system, which not only facilitated their involvement in an offline interview, but also actively engaged them in the project more generally, where they played a key role in shaping how field observations were interpreted and the findings of the project were disseminated.

Gaining access to field settings and establishing field relations are complex and often challenging processes, which can raise practical and ethical dilemmas that researchers may not have anticipated before entering into the 'field' (Doykos et al., 2014; Turner and Almack, 2016; Crowhurst, 2013; Calvey, 2008). This chapter has provided some theoretical and methodological tools for constituting different types of field setting, along with case examples of field-based challenges and strategies that researchers employed to overcome them. Field settings are highly variable in their accessibility to researchers, and this partly reflects the extent to which settings might be considered public or private, or open or closed, generally (Lofland et al., 1995). Certain settings are defined by behavioural constraints, or reserved for groups that possess certain attributes or characteristics (Lofland et al., 1995). Establishing and maintaining field access requires a researcher to negotiate and address the specific situated challenges associated with the setting in question, and develop a reflexive strategy that is tailored, but flexible enough to be adapted when a researcher is immersed in the field (Doykos et al., 2014; Cunliffe and Alcadipani da Silveira, 2016). Personal attributes can play a role in how a researcher is constituted within different fieldwork settings, and the extent to which they are positioned as an insider or outsider (Doykos et al., 2014). How a researcher is positioned and their capacity to shape how others position them is integral to the process of negotiating and establishing field access (Fawcett and Hearn, 2004; Kennedy-Macfoy, 2013; Doykos et al., 2014), which many have argued should be a carefully managed process. The extent to which field access can and should be managed raises ethical questions concerning key research principles such as informed consent (Miller and Boulton, 2007; Miller and Bell, 2002) and whether or not research should be conducted overtly, rather than covertly (Calvey, 2008). These ethical challenges can be compounded in online settings where access to the field and data, in the sense that these concepts are understood in offline settings, may be 'open' and not contingent on a researcher gaining social acceptance, permission from a gatekeeper or consent from field participants, in order to establish and maintain a presence and study interactions (Snee, 2013; Roberts, 2015).

Professional standards and codes of ethical practice, and research ethics committees, can inform principles of research practice but they cannot regulate the activities of researchers once they are in the field (Bengry-Howell and Griffin, 2011; Cunliffe and Alcadipani da Silveira, 2016). In a field-based setting, ethics becomes a highly contingent, dynamic, temporal, occasioned and situated affair (Calvey, 2008), which is shaped by the values and principles that a researcher holds, and the everyday decisions and judgements they make in the field (Miller and Bell, 2002). Establishing field access poses both a practical and ethical challenge for researchers, in which they must balance their professional commitment to conduct research effectively with a commitment to ethical practice in how they establish and maintain a research presence in the field.

FURTHER READING

Alcadipani, R., and Hodgson, D. (2009) 'By any means necessary? Ethnographic access, ethics and the critical researcher', *Tamara Journal*, 7(4): 127–46.

Doykos, B., Brinkley-Rubinstein, L., Craven, K., McCormack, M., and Geller, J. (2014) 'Leveraging identity, gaining access: Explorations of self in diverse field-based research settings', *Journal of Community Practice*, 22(1–2): 130–49.

Miller, Tina, and Bell, Linda (2002) 'Consenting to what? Issues of access, gate-keepers and "informed" consent', in Melanie Mauthner, Maxine Birch, Julie Jessop and Tina Miller (eds.), *Ethics in Qualitative Research*. London: Sage, pp. 53–70.

REFERENCES

Alcadipani, R., and Hodgson, D. (2009) 'By any means necessary? Ethnographic access, ethics and the critical researcher', *Tamara Journal*, 7(4): 127–46.

Angrosino, Michael (2007) *Doing Ethnographic and Observational Research*. London: Sage.

Atkinson, Paul, and Hammersley, Martyn (1994) 'Ethnography and participant observation', in Norman K. Denzin and Yvonna S. Lincoln (eds.) *Handbook of Qualitative Research*. Thousand Oaks, CA: Sage, pp. 248–61.

Bengry-Howell, A., and Griffin, C. (2008) 'Self-made motormen: The material construction of working-class masculine identities through car modification', *Journal of Youth Studies*, 10(4): 439–58.

Bengry-Howell, A., and Griffin, C. (2011) 'Negotiating access in ethnographic research with "hard to reach" young people: establishing common ground or a process of methodological grooming?', *International Journal of Social Research Methodology*, 15(5): 406–15.

Bengry-Howell, A., Morey, Y.M., Griffin, C., Szmigin, I., and Riley, S., (2011) *Negotiating Managed Consumption: Young People, Branding and Social Identification Processes*. ESRC End of Award Report, RES-061-25-0129. Swindon: ESRC.

British Psychological Society (2007) Guidelines for ethical practice in Psychological research online. Retrieved 26 July 2017 from http://www.bps.org.uk/sites/default/files/documents/conducting_research_on_the_internet-guidelines_for_ethical_practice_in_psychological_research_online.pdf

British Psychological Society (2010) *Code of Human Research Ethics*. Retrieved 5 May 2016 from http://www.bps.org.uk/sites/default/files/documents/code_of_human_research_ethics.pdf

British Sociological Association (2002) *Statement of Ethical Practice*. Retrieved 5 May 2016 from http://www.britsoc.co.uk/media/27107/StatementofEthicalPractice.pdf?1462459241460

Bryman, Alan (2015) *Social Research Methods* (5th edn). Oxford: Oxford University Press.

Calvey, D. (2008) 'The art and politics of covert research: Doing "situated ethics" in the field', *Sociology*, 42(5), 905–18.

Cassell, Joan (1988) 'The relationship of observer to observed when studying up', in Robert G. Burgess (ed.), *Studies in Qualitative Methodology*. Greenwich, CT: JAI Press, pp. 89–108.

Chatterton, Paul, and Hollands, Robert (2003) *Urban Nightscapes: Youth Cultures, Pleasure Spaces and Corporate Power*. London: Routledge.

Clark, T. (2011) 'Gaining and maintaining access: Exploring the mechanisms that support and challenge the relationship between gatekeepers and researchers', *Qualitative Social Work*, 10(4): 485–502.

Clifford, James (1997) 'Spatial practices: fieldwork, travel and the disciplining of anthropology', in Akhil Gupta and James Ferguson (eds.), *Anthropological Locations: Boundaries and Grounds for a Field Science*. Berkeley, CA: University of California Press, pp. 185–221.

Coffey, A. (1996) 'The power of accounts: Authority and authorship in ethnography', *Qualitative Studies in Education*, 9(1): 61–74.

Crowhurst, I. (2013) 'The fallacy of the instrumental gate? Contextualising the process of gaining access through gatekeepers', *International Journal of Social Research Methodology*, 16(6): 463–75.

Cunliffe, A.L., and Alcadipani da Silveira, R. (2016) 'The politics of access in fieldwork: Immersion, backstage dramas and deception', *Organisational Research Methods*, 19(4): 535–61.

De Laine, Marlene (2000) *Fieldwork, Participation and Practice: Ethics and Dilemmas in Qualitative Research*. London: Sage.

Doykos, B., Brinkley-Rubinstein, L., Craven, K., McCormack, M., and Geller, J. (2014) 'Leveraging identity, gaining access: Explorations of self in diverse field-based research settings', *Journal of Community Practice*, 22(1–2): 130–49.

Duncombe, Jean, and Jessop, Julie (2002). '"Doing rapport" and ethics of "faking friendship"', in Melanie Mauthner, Maxine Birch, Julie Jessop and Tina Miller (eds.), *Ethics in Qualitative Research*. London: Sage, pp. 107–22.

Fawcett, B., and Hearn, J. (2004) 'Researching others: Epistemology, experience, standpoints and participation', *International Journal of Social Research Methodology*, 7(3): 201–18.

Feldman, Martha, Bell, Jeannine, and Berger, Michelle (eds.) (2003) *Gaining Access: A Practical and Theoretical Guide for Qualitative Research*. Walnut Creek, CA: Altamira Press.

Giulianotti, R. (1995) 'Participant observation and research into football hooliganism: Reflections on the problems of entrée and everyday risks', *Sociology of Sport Journal*, 12(1): 1–20.

Grauerholz, L., Barringer, M., Colyer, T., Guittar, N., Hecht, J., Rayburn, R.L., and Swart, E. (2012) 'Attraction in the field: What we need to acknowledge and implications for research and teaching', *Qualitative Inquiry*, 19(3): 167–78.

Griffin, Christine, and Bengry-Howell, Andrew (2017) 'Ethnography', in Carla Willig and Wendy Stainton-Rogers (eds.), *The SAGE Handbook of Qualitative Research in Psychology* (2nd edn). London: Sage, pp. 38–54.

Griffin, Christine, Bengry-Howell, Andrew, Hackley, Chris, Mistral, Wilm, and Szmigin, Isabelle (2008) *Branded Consumption and Social Identification: Young People and Alcohol*. Full Research Report ESRC End of Award Report, RES-148-25-0021. Swindon: ESRC.

Griffin, C., Bengry-Howell, A., Hackley, C., Mistral, W., and Szmigin, I. (2009) '"Every time I do it I absolutely annihilate myself": Loss of (self-)consciousness and loss of memory in young people's drinking narratives', *Sociology – The Journal of the British Sociological Association*, 43(3): 457–76.

Griffin, C., Bengry-Howell, A., Morey, Y.M., Szmigin, I., and Riley, S. (2017) '"We achieve the impossible": Discourses of freedom and escape at music festivals and free parties', *Journal of Consumer Culture*, DOI: 10.1177/1469540516684187.

Groger, L., Mayberry, P.S., and Straker, J.K. (1999) 'What we didn't learn because of who would not talk to us', *Qualitative Health Research*, 9(6): 829–35.

Harrison, J., MacGibbon, L., and Morton, M. (2001) 'Regimes of trustworthiness in qualitative research: The rigors of reciprocity', *Qualitative Inquiry*, 7(3), 323–45.

Heath, D., Kock, E., and Montoya, M. (1999) 'Nodes and queries: Linking locations in networked fields of inquiry', *American Behavioural Scientist*, 43(3): 450–63.

Heath, S., Charles, V., Crow, G., and Wiles, R. (2007) 'Informed consent, gatekeepers and go-betweens: Negotiating consent in child- and youth-orientated institutions', *British Educational Research Journal*, 33(3): 403–17.

Hobbs, Dick, and May, Tim (eds.) (1993) *Interpreting the Field*. Oxford: Clarendon Press.

Hodkinson, P. (2005). '"Insider research" in the study of youth cultures', *Journal of Youth Studies*, 8(2): 131–49.

Homan, Roger (1991) *The Ethics of Social Research*. London: Macmillan.

Jacobs, Bruce A. (2006) 'The case for dangerous fieldwork', in Dick Hobbs and Richard Wright (eds.), *The Sage Handbook of Fieldwork*. London: Sage, pp. 157–70.

Jacobson, D. (1999) 'Doing research in cyberspace', *Field Methods*, 11(2): 127–45.

Jorgenson, Jane (1991). 'Co-constructing the interviewer/co-constructing "family"', in F. Steier (ed.), *Research and Reflexivity*. London: Sage, pp. 210–26.

Kennedy-Macfoy, M. (2013). '"It's important for the students to meet someone like you": How perceptions of the researcher can affect gaining access, building rapport and security co-operation in school-based research', *International Journal of Social Research Methodology*, 16(6): 491–502.

Knowles, C. (2006) 'Handling your baggage in the field: Reflections on research relationships', *International Journal of Social Research Methodology*, 9(5): 393–404.

Kozinets, R. (2002) 'The field behind the screen: Using netnography for marketing research in online communities', *Journal of Marketing Research*, 39(1): 61–72.

Kozinets, Robert (2015) *Netnography: Redefined*. Los Angeles: Sage.

Lange, P. (2008) 'Publicly private and privately public: Social networking on YouTube', *Journal of Computer-Mediated Communication*, 13(1): 361–80.

Lofland, John, Snow, David, Anderson, Leon, and Lofland, Lyn H. (1995) *Analyzing Social Settings: A Guide to Qualitative Observation and Analysis* (4th edn). Belmont, CA: Wadsworth.

McCall, George J. (2006) 'The fieldwork tradition', in Dick Hobbs and Richard Wright (eds.), *The Sage Handbook of Fieldwork*. London: Sage, pp. 3–21.

McGinn, L., Ingham, R., Stone, N., and Bengry-Howell, A. (2016) 'Parental interpretations of "childhood innocence": implications for early sexuality education', *Health Education*, 116(6): 580–94.

McGivern, Yvonne (2006) *The Practice of Market and Social Research: An Introduction*. Harlow: Financial Times Prentice Hall.

Merton, Robert. K. (1972) 'Insiders and outsiders: A chapter in the sociology of knowledge', *American Journal of Sociology*, 78(1): 9–47.

Miller, Tina, and Bell, Linda (2002) 'Consenting to what? Issues of access, gate-keepers and "informed" consent', in Melanie Mauthner, Maxine Birch, Julie Jessop and Tina Miller (eds.), *Ethics in Qualitative Research*. London: Sage, pp. 53–70.

Miller, Tina, and Boulton, Mary (2007) 'Changing constructions of informed consent: Qualitative research and complex social worlds', *Social Science & Medicine*, 65(11): 2199–211.

Mitchell, Don (2003) *The Right to the City: Social Justice and the Fight for Public Space*. New York: Guilford.

Morey, Yvette, Bengry-Howell, Andrew, and Griffin, Christine (2012) 'Public profiles, private parties: Exploring the ethical dilemmas posed by digital ethnography in the context of Web 2.0', in Sue Heath and C. Walker (eds.), *Innovations in Youth Research*. London: Palgrave, pp. 195–209.

Pole, Christopher. J., and Lampard, Richard. (2002) *Practical Social Investigation: Qualitative and Quantitative Methods in Social Research*. London: Routledge.

Reeves, C.L. (2010) 'A difficult negotiation: Fieldwork relations with gatekeepers', *Qualitative Research*, 10: 315–31.

Roberts, L.D. (2015) 'Ethical issues in conducting qualitative research in online communities', *Qualitative Research in Psychology*, 12(3): 314–25.

Ruane, Janet (2007) *Essentials of Research Methods: A Guide to Social Science Research*. Oxford: Blackwell Publishing.

Ryan, L., Kofman, E., and Aaron, P. (2011) 'Insiders and outsiders: Working with peer researchers in researching Muslim communities', *International Journal of Social Research Methodology*, 14(1): 49–60.

Sanghera, G.S., and Thapar-Björkert, S. (2008) 'Methodological dilemmas: Gatekeepers and positionality in Bradford', *Ethnic and Racial Studies*, 31(3): 543–62.

Scourfield, J., and Coffey, A. (2004) 'Access, ethics and the (re)construction of gender: The case of researcher as suspected "paedophile"', *International Journal of Social Research Methodology*, 9(1): 29–40.

Silverman, David (2013) *Doing Qualitative Research: A Practical Handbook* (4th edn). London Sage.

Smith, H.J., Dinev, T., and Xu, H. (2011) 'Information privacy research: An interdisciplinary review', *MIS Quarterly*, 35(4), 989–1016.

Snee, H. (2008) Web 2.0 as a Social Science Research Tool, ESRC Government Placement Scheme, The British Library. Retrieved 25 May 2016 from http://www.bl.uk/reshelp/bldept/socsci/socint/web2/web2.pdf

Snee, H. (2013) 'Making ethical decisions in an online context: Reflections on using blogs to explore narratives of experience', *Methodological Innovations Online*, 8(2): 52–67.

Stone, Nicole, Bengry-Howell, Andrew, Ingham, Roger, and McGinn, Laura (2014) *How should we tell the children?' Early sexual socialisation and sexuality education: parental perspectives* (Technical Report, RPG-050). Retrieved 7 June 2016 from University of Southampton Research Repository. http://eprints.soton.ac.uk/364705/1.hasCoversheetVersion/Technical%20report.pdf

Szmigin, I., Griffin, C., Mistral, W., Bengry-Howell, A., Weale, L., and Hackley, C. (2008) 'Re-framing "binge drinking" as calculated hedonism: Empirical evidence from the UK', *International Journal of Drug Policy*, 19(5): 359–66.

Turner, N., and Almack, K. (2016) 'Recruiting young people to sensitive research: Turning the "wheels within wheels"', *International Journal of Social Research Methodology*, 20(5) pp. 1–13.

Recording and Transcribing Social Interaction

Christopher Joseph Jenks

Recording and transcribing social interaction are practical skills that require many years of experience to master, and both these research methods are underpinned by a number of theoretical and political issues. Despite the importance of transcript-based research in the humanities and social sciences, researchers have devoted very little time in publishing works that explore the complexities and challenges of recording and transcribing social interaction data. This contribution narrows this gap by engaging in the literature that addresses both the theories and practices related to recording and transcribing social interaction. In addition to discussing the theoretical issues involved in conducting transcript-based research, the chapter explores, among other things:

- the methodological challenges of representing the highly granular nature of social interaction in transcripts with finite space;
- the ways in which transcription practices both enhance and complicate the process of representing spoken words and embodied actions into static objects;
- the politics of recording and transcribing; and
- how researcher subjectivities are inextricable to representational decisions.

The aim in this chapter is to argue that the theories and practices that underpin and shape recording and transcription work are highly complex and inherently problematic. The chapter argues that, while there is no monolithic way of recording and transcribing talk and interaction, there are several universal theoretical, methodological, and political issues that must be taken into consideration while conducting transcript-based research.

INTRODUCTION

The contributions made to qualitative research by scholars conducting investigations with transcripts of social interaction have been, and continue to be, significant. Many seminal studies rely extensively on transcripts, including, but of course not limited to, Goffman (1981), Gumperz (1982), Schiffrin (1987), and Tannen (1994). Such research inspires, and is often the center of discussion in, books that review the theoretical issues and methodological principles of discourse analysis (e.g. Coulthard, 2014; Gee, 2014; Schegloff, 2007; Schiffrin et al., 2003; Wooffitt, 2005; see Rau et al., Chapter 19, this volume) and narrative research (e.g. Andrews, 2014; Bold, 2012; Maynes et al. 2012; Pagnucci 2004; see Murray, Chapter 17, this volume). Indeed, a search on most academic databases with the key words 'discourse analysis' or 'narrative analysis' reveals many introductory and state-of-the-art publications on the issues of analyzing social interaction. The number of publications on discourse and narrative analysis is remarkable given the relatively short history of the area of study. Despite this large and growing body of discourse and narrative analytic work, publications that deal exclusively with the methodological principles of recording and transcribing social interaction are more difficult to find (for books on transcription, see Edwards and Lampert, 1993; Jenks, 2011; Rapley, 2018; Tench, 2011; for articles on transcription, see Bucholtz, 2000; Jefferson, 1996; Meredith, 2015; Mondada, 2007). The disparity between analysis-oriented and transcript-focused publications, especially in book form, is peculiar given the inextricable connection between analyzing and transcribing. For instance, analytic observations of social interaction are limited to what has been captured by a recording device, which is further restricted when such data are later transcribed, yet little attention is given to how researchers reach the stage where their transcripts are 'ready' for analytic observations. Many introductory books on discourse and narrative analysis either consider transcription issues in passing or do not engage in such a discussion.

The omission of any serious discussion of transcription issues in such publications demonstrates the lack of importance placed on transcribing social interaction. For too long researchers have treated transcription as a job for research assistants, or worse, as a fixed, final, and completely accurate representation of data recordings. The assumption that transcripts require little or no attention after the transcription job is 'complete' demonstrates that many researchers handle transcribing and analyzing as disconnected tasks. Yet, recording and transcribing social interaction are both inextricably connected to the analytic process (Jenks, 2013; Tilley, 2003).

The lack of attention to, and appreciation of, recording and transcribing are not new issues in scholarship. Nearly three decades ago, for example, Cook (1990, p. 1) discussed the theoretical and methodological challenges facing transcript-based researchers.

> Indeed it would seem to be the central problem of such an approach: for it is hard to see how features can be analysed that cannot be in some measure transcribed. Yet this central and – considering the quantity and quality of potentially relevant extralinguistic factors – apparently insurmountable problem of devising such a system has not been fully confronted (there is a marked lack of studies specifically discussing the issue) and most transcription systems are presented without theoretical discussion. (1990, p. 1)

The importance of transcripts to the analysis of spoken communication data cannot be overstated. Advances in online media technology allow scholars to include raw data in their published empirical papers, and indeed such recordings are the closest representations of 'reality' that can be disseminated for later scrutiny. However, the transcript not only aids the reader in identifying utterances, gestures, embodied actions, and the like that may be difficult to scrutinize in raw data recordings, written representations of social interaction also allow researchers to select interactional features from an ostensibly infinite range of phenomena that reflect their empirical objectives and subjectivities. This latter issue can be viewed as an 'insurmountable problem' (Cook, 1990) or a necessary part of conducting transcript-based research (Mondada, 2007). That is to say, the ostensibly infinite range of phenomena that can be recorded and transcribed may be viewed as a problem that cannot be overcome or simply a limitation that exists in conducting such research. It is clear, given the number of discourse and narrative analytic publications over the past three or four decades, that researchers have rejected the former view. That is, discourse and narrative analysts do not view the issue of entextualization, a 'process of capturing the fluidity of social interaction on the printed page' (Bucholtz, 2007, p. 785), as a critical flaw in, or debilitating to, transcript-based research.

Accepting the inherent problems with conducting transcript-based research does not mean, however, that researchers are free from addressing the challenges and problems that come with transcription work, nor does it imply that discourse and narrative analysts should neglect the role technology can play in advancing transcript-based research.

These and other transcription issues are the focal point of discussion in this chapter. Specifically, the sections that follow explore the methodological challenges and empirical issues of conducting transcript-based research. Before doing so, it must be noted that while the term 'transcript-based research' may give some readers the impression that such work privileges transcripts in the analytic process, and indeed this may be the case when disseminating and publishing empirical papers, data recordings are central to analyzing social interaction. Transcripts, especially during the analytic stage, should always be read with data recordings.

RECORDING SOCIAL INTERACTION

Recording data is a form of social interaction. In this sense, social interaction is both the phenomenon under investigation and the means in which the phenomenon is investigated. Entering into a research site, setting up recording devices, taking observational notes in an inconspicuous location or participating with research participants, making adjustments to camera positions and angles, and seeking consent to produce records of life events, are all forms of social interaction. These and other recording acts and procedures contribute to, in both covert and overt ways, the establishment of a site of sociality. That is to say, recording devices and field researchers are never removed or detached from the phenomenon being observed, but are rather situated within, and a part of, what eventually gets stored as permanent records of social interaction.

Thus, recording social interaction is an inherently subjective endeavor. It lacks a great deal of objectivity, in part because researchers spend very little time sharing and discussing best approaches to data recording. Consequently, there are no established guidelines from which the research community can evaluate data collection tools and methods. Researchers, and especially doctoral students and early career researchers, are often only told to be inconspicuous with their audio/video recorders and to ensure that such devices pick up the social phenomena under investigation. This lack of discussion regarding recording social interaction does not mean, however, that transcript-based research is inherently problematic and should thus be avoided. The inherently subjective nature of transcript-based research simply means that researchers must confront and discuss their influence in the production and transcription of data recordings. This may entail discussing recording plans with colleagues, maintaining a journal that details best practices for particular contexts and research sites, and detailing in publications the approach used to collect data. The latter practice, while not commonly exercised, can resolve a lot of the confusion and ambiguity that exists within the literature regarding best data recording practices.

Despite the challenges in conducting transcript-based research, all scholarship, including quantitative studies, possess varying degrees of subjectivity. While this universal aspect of empiricism means that social interaction researchers must be mindful of how to collect and transcribe data, such scholars are not bound to the same set of methodological principles that are observed in approaches that give the impression of being more 'objective' (cf. quantitative studies). Researchers working with transcripts, in other words, understand that validity in data collection (see Barbour, Chapter 14, this volume) does not carry with it the same set of implications as designing, say, questionnaires. However, because data recordings and transcripts are often viewed as objective and accurate representations of reality, transcript-based researchers have a great deal of responsibility to confront this widely held misconception. Transcript-based researchers must confront, for example, the methodological issues that guide, and are guided by, the steps taken to capture phenomena for later inspection. Put differently, transcript-based research that does not address the theoretical and practical issues that have come to shape a particular investigation is inherently problematic and should be viewed with skepticism.

These methodological issues, which are unique to capturing social interaction, transcend Labov's (1972) observer's paradox: namely that research participants might talk or interact differently than when they are not observed with a recording device. Although scholars must be cognizant of, and address the problems associated with, the very real possibility of influencing how interactants speak and what they say, the notion that recording data is a form of social interaction encourages researchers to carefully consider how their presence in, and decisions that guide, the investigatory process shape how the research community interprets the reality that is presented in transcripts. For example, data recorders are artifacts of empirical objectives; they are placed in predetermined positions within a social encounter or scene. Data recorders reflect strategic foresight, and if such devices shape how interaction unfolds, the researcher will most likely never know. A slight shift in gaze as a result of the presence of a recording device, for instance, may have a significant role in how a social encounter is managed, but it is difficult, if not impossible, in most research sites for researchers to identify such subtle shifts, especially if the recorder was not strategically placed to capture the gaze in the first place. In this sense, recording devices capture only what the researcher believes to be socially and interactionally significant; and while recording and transcription decisions that stem from such biases may lead to capturing unforeseen (and useful) data, ultimately what appears in transcripts are detached from how speakers manage communication in real time.

Thus, recording social interaction involves balancing what a researcher believes to be important for the interactants, and in a social encounter with empirical objectives and theoretical beliefs, logistical considerations and constraints, and the resources and tools available for transcribing and disseminating research. These issues guide a number of recording decisions, including how many audio/video recorders are used at a research site, the placement of such devices, the quality of data records (e.g. high definition), the frequency with which data are collected, whether additional audio capturing tools will be used and where they will be located, and what software programs are utilized to process files. Again, these issues and decisions are inextricable to the analytic process, as they shape what ultimately ends up in a transcript for later scrutiny.

TRANSCRIBING SOCIAL INTERACTION

A transcript is a record of social interaction; it may be created and used to examine anything from dialectal features to ideological constructions. More importantly, a transcript is a theoretical construct. That is, a transcript reflects a scholar's unique research interests, empirical goals, and disciplinary traditions. Because of this, transcription variation is a common feature of transcript-based research. Transcription variation happens within and across disciplinary boundaries: even scholars that subscribe to heavily top-down approaches may have different interpretations regarding how a stretch of talk should appear on a transcript. For example, two conversation analysts transcribing the same data recording may produce different transcripts (cf. Roberts and Robinson, 2004; see Jackson, Chapter 18, this volume). Of course, transcription variation across disciplines will be even greater. These sorts of disparity represent important methodological challenges, and indeed some scholars have in recent years explored the sources of transcription variation and its effect on producing such work (e.g. Bucholtz, 2007), though the fact remains that the topic receives little attention in the literature.

The act of transcribing social interaction allows, and indeed requires in most publication venues, researchers to transform an ephemeral, and largely fluid, experience into a permanent record of textual, spatial, and visual representations that take on new meanings as the transcript moves from one stage and space of investigation to another. In this sense, a transcript is an evolving object, and no single analyst has control over how the social interaction represented 'on paper' is to be interpreted.

For some researchers, the inherently subjective nature of transcribing is highly problematic. This is especially true of scholars in the business of coding and quantifying linguistic features. The work of some psycholinguists, for instance, relies on transcribers (who are often not the ones doing the analysis) to identify linguistic features in transcripts so that statistical computations can be made to count or track a communicative phenomenon (see, for example, Kuiken and Vedder, 2007). Statistical results, which often give the appearance of being objective, are then used to establish a theoretical position. Because transcripts (and data recordings) are often not provided alongside numerical results, such researchers are encouraged to address the potential threat of transcription subjectivity (cf. inter-transcriber reliability measures).

Despite attempts to present transcription as an objective endeavor, most qualitative researchers embrace the rich, nuanced, and highly complex nature of social interaction. Indeed, it can be said that transcription variation is viewed by qualitative researchers as an inherently productive feature of transcript-based research. This is most demonstrable in the widespread practice of sharing (when possible and within ethical guidelines) not only transcripts, but also data recordings to the research community. Put differently, qualitative researchers address transcription variation in and through several investigatory practices. A qualitative researcher may, for example, share data recordings and transcripts in what is often referred to as a 'data session', which is a group-based analysis gathering where multiple analysts provide their own perspectives to the transcript and/or phenomena under investigation.

Although transcription variation is an important issue and one that will be open to discussion for as long as technology is unable to accurately and automatically transcribe data recordings, the more important and immediate issue is not whether transcription variation should be avoided. Variation in transcripts will exist as long as humans are involved in the act of entextualization. The issue of variation, rather, highlights that transcription practices are highly contextualized objects, and in order for the field to advance, scholars must continue to reveal, discuss, and explore how their disciplinary subjectivities and theoretical positions shape what is ultimately presented to the larger academic community.

The need to be more cognizant and vocal of transcription practices brings the discussion back to the observation that transcripts are theoretical constructs. It is important to remind the academic community that, while transcripts of social interaction are often the only or last thing that is disseminated for peer review, the act of transcribing is not merely something that researchers do in response to making data recordings. The same time, care, and attention given to the analyses of social interaction should be given to transcription practices. In other words, more publication space must be devoted to the discussion of transcription theories and practices. Of the large number of publications on the discourse and narrative analytic methods used for social interaction research, many spend very little, if any, time exploring the early stages of conducting such scholarship. For example, how does a researcher move from recording data to disseminating detailed transcript-based analytic observations? While the space that is needed to discuss transcription issues is open to debate, the theoretical and methodological facets of creating and disseminating transcripts deserve further attention. The representation of social interaction data is, after all and as mentioned previously, inextricable to the analytic process.

The discussion below represents an attempt at exploring some of the transcription issues that shape how researchers come to represent their data recordings (see also, for example, Duranti, 2006; Ochs, 1979). That is, the discussion that follows provides a concise, but certainly not comprehensive, overview of several important transcription issues. The remaining part of the chapter is organized into four overlapping sections: open and closed transcripts, entextualization, representational decisions, and political considerations.

Open and Closed Transcripts

Transcripts can be viewed as being either open or closed. An open transcript is based on the idea that data recordings, as well as transcripts, are tools to develop research questions. A researcher creating an open transcript will abandon most or all *a priori* assumptions pertaining to what aspects of spoken discourse will be analyzed. This entails transcribing, as much as possible, every seeable and hearable feature of talk and interaction that is captured (for a glossary of transcript symbols for conversation analytic research, see Jefferson, 2004; and see Jackson, Chapter 18, this volume). A scholar may wish to, for example, transcribe audible breathing, timed pauses, the onset of overlapping talk, turn-ending intonation, marked fluctuations in voice amplitude, and background noises. Simply put, an open transcript has more transcription detail than a closed transcript because the researcher does not know what she or he will investigate, and is theoretically motivated to treat all social interaction as potentially important (cf. conversation analysis and discursive psychology).

A closed transcript is based on the idea that data recordings, as well as transcripts, are products of predefined research questions and/or predetermined empirical objectives. In other words, research questions and empirical objectives shape what is included and omitted in data recordings and transcripts. A closed transcript entails a largely deductive process of shaping records of phenomena to fit a specific investigatory agenda. Because of this, closed transcripts often lack the transcription detail seen in open transcripts.

It is important to note that the notion of open and closed transcripts does not suggest that transcribing is a binary endeavor guided by clearly demarcated methodological boundaries. Open and closed transcripts must be conceptualized as a continuum. For example, a conversation analyst cannot possibly transcribe every feature of embodied action (or even spoken communication) in any given stretch of social interaction without creating an incomprehensible transcript. In the same vein, critical discourse analysts may wish to include some finer details of talk that reflect their analytic interests. Conceptualizing transcripts as either open or closed highlights the highly subjective nature of transcribing social interaction. What ultimately appears on a transcript is a reflection of research questions, theoretical positions, and the practical constraints of transforming the dynamic into the static. This observation can be better understood by exploring the issue of entextualization.

Entextualization

Transcribing social interaction is a form of entextualization in that it requires making a number of different representational decisions that transform an ephemeral experience into a somewhat static object. Among the many representational decisions that are made during the transcription process, an analyst must establish the layout of the transcript (e.g. margin size, font type, and line spacing), determine levels of prosodic and vocal detail (e.g. inhalations, laugh particles, and marked fluctuations in voice amplitude), decide where to place interactional pauses (e.g. intra-turn and inter-turn pauses), and select the best visual arrangements to depict embodied actions and body movements (e.g. hand gestures, gaze, and spatial positioning of speakers), to name a few.

The representational decisions that are made during the transcription process highlight one of the biggest challenges facing transcript-based researchers. Of the seemingly infinite array of social interaction detail present in data recordings, what specific features will be transcribed? Although the previous discussion on open and closed transcripts provides some guidance on this matter, the disciplinary and empirical justifications for making certain representational decisions during the transcription process do not negate the fact that data recordings contain highly complex patterns of communication involving spoken utterances, embodied actions, and interactional features, and that researchers must package such phenomena into a spatially deprived document. How is it then possible, theoretically speaking, to transcribe social interaction? The simple, yet somewhat convoluted, answer is that transcribing social interaction entails establishing and carrying out an investigatory plan that uses representational/transcription conventions to generate analytic observations. The social interaction features that are selected, transcribed, and used to generate analytic observations must, however, obey the spatial 'laws' or limitations of the document that is used to disseminate the findings.

The previous observations, and namely the notion that transcribing is restricted by the medium in which communication data are represented, highlights one of the most noteworthy methodological flaws in transcript-based research. That is, transcript-based research involves entextualization, which is, to put it bluntly, an act of reductionism. Put differently, transcripts are reductionist tools, as they are not only based solely on data recordings that represent the perspective of the camera operator, but the spatial limitations also mean that they are only capable of representing the fluidity of social interaction as a series of communication lines that, when read together as an unfolding event, are meant to depict a dynamic encounter. This situation, or process, is analogous to putting together a series of still photos of a sprinter running down a track in order to depict the movements made while running. A video recording (see knoblauch et al., Chapter 23, this volume) of this event would provide, despite being removed from the actual act of running, a much better representation of the phenomenon than a series of static acts.

Entextualization also means that transcripts are created outside of the immediate context in which social interaction occurs. Because transcribing social interaction involves transferring data recordings onto a storage device of some sort, running such records on a computer for closer inspection, representing the phenomena as a static object, and generating analytic observations as a result, the document that is ultimately created, and which represents the transcript, takes on new spatial and representational meanings throughout the research process (Silverstein and Urban, 1996). Therefore, it is important to understand how the representational decisions made throughout the research process both reflect research subjectivities and shape the visual appearance of transcripts.

Representational Decisions: Readability, Granularity, Accuracy, and Research Agenda

Because progressing through the many stages of social interaction research (e.g. moving from transcription to dissemination) entails moving further away from the phenomenon under investigation, transcripts are often best read alongside data recordings. Although there are no major logistical or practical challenges in reading transcripts with data recordings before disseminating research (e.g. sharing preliminary findings with colleagues), it is often the case, and for numerous practical reasons, that this is not possible during the publication stage. For some publishers, data recordings, and even smaller segments of talk taken from larger stretches of social interaction, take up an enormous amount of storage space and are thus a financial burden. For some empirical studies, ethical considerations (see Mertens, Chapter 3, this volume), including the protection of anonymity, may prevent a scholar from making data recordings available to the public. The challenges and obstacles of disseminating data recordings means that it is necessary to remind the academic community that published transcripts are often the only source of 'data' to which readers have access. This reminder can take several forms, including providing disclaimers about the limitations of representing social interaction in transcripts and noting in detail in published empirical papers how and why representational decisions were made. Despite its potential to transform how readers view and interpret transcripts, the latter approach is not employed in much of what gets published in social interaction scholarship.

Because transcripts can never fully depict social interaction, and are rarely published alongside data recordings, researchers must make representational decisions based on the understanding that their intended audience will have limited access to the actual communicative event. In practical terms, this means taking into consideration, and balancing, four overlapping transcription issues: readability, granularity, accuracy, and research agenda. All four issues are integral to what and how social interaction is represented in transcripts.

Readability relates to the comprehension of the intended audience. The issue of readability can be addressed by using standard writing conventions to enhance clarity. Granularity concerns the degree to which a researcher is faithful to the highly nuanced and complex nature of social interaction. The issue of granularity can be addressed by using non-standard writing conventions (i.e. symbols and punctuation marks) to depict the dynamic nature of social interaction. Accuracy, as the name implies, relates to the extent to which social and interactional features present in a data recording are transcribed for later inspection. A decision based on the issue of accuracy may be addressed by including most of the spoken (e.g. backchannels and speech perturbations), interactional (e.g. pauses), and embodied actions (e.g. hand gestures) visible and hearable in a data recording. While accuracy is closely related granularity, the two issues should not be used synonymously. For example, a transcript may be 'accurate' in that it includes most of the talk in a data recording, but omits several phonological features (granularity). Finally, research agenda concerns the top-down approach of making representational decisions based on predetermined empirical goals. For example, a researcher interested in grammatical errors in talk may omit interactional pauses.

One of the challenges in transcribing social interaction is that readability, granularity, accuracy, and research agenda can act as opposing forces in the representation of communication data. For example, although readability and granularity are both important transcription issues, they counteract each other while transcribing social interaction. A transcript faithful to the phonological features of talk is more difficult to read than one that represents communication using standard orthography. For many researchers, however, transcription detail outweighs the benefits in having a more readable and widely accessible transcript.

The example of readability and granularity demonstrates that transcribing social interaction requires being cognizant of how one representational decision may be bound to other transcription issues. Take, for example, the issue of the research agenda. A researcher interested in using content analysis may be theoretically motivated to disregard the issue of granularity. In so doing, however, the researcher may also create a less accurate transcript. In a similar vein, a researcher interested in understanding speech complexity may spend a significant amount of time detailing the highly granular nature of turn-ending intonation while omitting altogether gestures and embodied actions (cf. accuracy).

A highly granular transcript will, of course, be more difficult to read.

The table below (Table 8.1) summarizes the four aforementioned transcription issues and their representational implications.

Political Considerations

The theory-laden nature of transcribing social interaction (see Maxwell, Chapter 2, this volume) means that representational decisions are inherently political. Although theory, such as the empirical justification to omit or include a particular interactional feature in a transcript, gives the impression of being neutral and objective, belief systems (or theoretical principles) are not created in a vacuum. A theory is the product of historical struggles, changing societal belief systems, and decades of academic debate, to name a few. The theories that guide transcript-based research, though comparatively young, are no exception.

The representation of speech styles and dialectal varieties, such as marginalized forms of English, provides an excellent starting point to this discussion. Transcribing marginalized varieties of English requires a researcher to, among other things, weigh the benefits of granularity and accuracy. Should a researcher transcribe the speech of a particular community as it sounds, or are there motivations or justifications to 'standardize' or 'sanitize' the

Table 8.1 Representational decisions

Transcription Issue	Representational Implication
Readability	Transcripts often have a readership. As such, transcripts should, to some extent, reflect the needs of the intended audience.
Granularity	Social interaction is an exceptionally nuanced endeavor mediated by a number of different contextual affordances. Transcribing requires determining how certain features of social interaction will be represented and why they have been included in a transcript.
Accuracy	The highly complex nature of social interaction requires omitting a great deal of information. Researchers must decide how faithful they will be in the representation of communication data.
Research Agenda	Transcripts reflect researcher subjectivities, including disciplinary traditions and theoretical positions. In other words, transcripts are research constructs.

talk? The extent to which a marginalized variety of English is accurately, and in detail, represented in a transcript is not based entirely on disciplinary and/or empirical reasons.

To extend this example further, research dealing with the issue of how to transcribe speech styles and dialectal varieties states that there are two (non-binary) approaches to the representation of such social interaction features: standardization and vernacularization (see Jenks, 2011, p. 19). Standardization entails transcribing social interaction according to standard spelling conventions. Vernacularization uses non-standard spelling, symbols, and punctuation marks to represent talk as it is being spoken (e.g. transcribing a Northern British speaker using flat vowels). Standardization and vernacularization often shape how pronunciation and contractions are transcribed (e.g. 'I want to go out' versus 'I wanna go out'), but can also influence how grammatical features appear on transcripts (e.g. 'I don't have any' versus 'I ain't got none').

Vernacularization is guided by a number of theoretical principles. In conversation analysis, for example, vernacularization is partly shaped by the notion that all features of social interaction are potentially important to the analytic process. Transcribing accurately and producing highly granular transcripts represent other justifications for adopting vernacularization (cf. pronunciational particulars; see Jefferson, 1983). In the case of a marginalized variety of English, for instance, a researcher that is informed by conversation analytic principles may need to use non-standard spelling, symbols, and punctuation marks to accurately represent the pronunciational particulars of this community. This transcription practice is often referred to as eye dialect or orthographic metonymy (see Bucholtz, 2000). Eye dialect or orthographic metonymy would appear as 'wha'cha doin'' rather than 'what are you doing'. Vernacularization may also involve using the International Phonetic Alphabet.

Although vernacularization, including eye dialect or orthographic metonymy, is faithful to the unique speech patterns of communities, using non-standard spelling, symbols, and punctuation marks to transcribe certain speech communities may be read as defective speech, or worse, reinforce stereotypical depictions and negative belief systems (Jaffe and Walton, 2000). This is particularly true of studies examining language learners, low socioeconomic communities, immigrants, and refugees (see Resch and Enzenhofer, Chapter 9, this volume, and Sørensen et al., Chapter 10, this volume).

Standardization, on the other hand, shields the participants under investigation from stereotypical depictions. For example, 'what are you doing' provides less identifying information than 'wha'cha doin''. The standardization of speech does not lead to cartoon or stereotypical representations of speech styles and dialectal varieties, but this approach also has political consequences. First, the name standardization is, in and of itself, a political statement. The approach suggests that marginalized speech communities speak a 'non-standard' variety. Furthermore, standardization removes the unique ways individuals and speech communities interact and communicate. Put differently, standardization homogenizes speech communities, and potentially erases the idiosyncrasies between and within racial and ethnic groups. It can be said that standardization treats individuals and speech communities as 'generic social beings' (Jenks, 2011, p. 20). Despite the political implications of homogenizing speech communities to fit a 'standard' mold, many researchers adopt some form of standardization because conventional spellings make it easier to search for key words and phrases in large data sets. A corpus linguist, for example, relies on the ability to group features of talk and interaction into categories. Such researchers are thus less theoretically motivated to represent pronunciational particulars because doing so would create different categories of talk and interaction that are either the same or possess overlapping features.

CONCLUSION

The discussion has thus far depicted transcription work as inherently subjective, theoretical, and political. This does not mean, however, that transcript-based research is inferior to other forms of qualitative (and quantitative) research. All forms of research possess varying degrees of subjectivity and are the result of theoretical and political motivations. With regard to qualitative research, transcripts provide an exceptionally transparent, comparatively speaking, way of disseminating analytic observations and findings. For example, transcripts allow the academic community to scrutinize analytic observations and findings with the same data source used by the analyst. In other words, the data source (i.e. the transcript) used to generate analytic observations is not hidden away for only the analyst to see, but rather is made public so that the academic community can come to their own conclusions.

Furthermore, transcripts often possess some objectivity because transcription systems, which include symbols that are the result of years of consideration and evolving practice, are used to not only represent communication data, but such conventions are also crucial to how the research community determines the quality of transcript-based scholarship. The transcription conventions that make up the different systems or approaches to the representation of communication data transforms an incomprehensible transcript into a document that can be understood by many. Simply put, transcription conventions help maintain objectivity, as they offer a system of representing social interaction in a reasonably systematic way (for a comparison of three widely used transcription systems, see Jenks, 2011, p. 115).

While transcription conventions offer a systematic way of transcribing social interaction, transcripts are no more objective than any other qualitative method (e.g. observation tools) if the transcriber does not possess a certain set of competences. One such competency involves the proficiency to listen to data recordings while selecting the appropriate convention for each sound or movement being made. This competency requires other competences: a transcriber must possess a reasonably high level of linguistic proficiency in the language(s) of the data recording, a thorough knowledge of the contextual variables that shape the interaction and interactants under investigation, and an awareness of why the transcript is being produced in the first place (cf. research agenda). Put differently, transcribing social interaction involves using transcription conventions to transform data recordings into transcripts, but this process is also highly dependent on an analyst's ability to make sense of, and convey meaning from, the interaction and interactants that make up data recordings. This is especially true of multilingual data that require translations and/or the representation and presentation of multiple languages in one transcript.

The competences required to transcribe social interaction, and the transcription issues discussed in previous sections, demonstrate that transcript-based research is a highly complex task. The transcription issues discussed in this chapter should help dispel the common assumption that transcribing is detached from theory and removed from the analytic process. This chapter also argued that transcripts are never completely objective nor are they entirely accurate representations of social interaction. Transcripts are never completely objective because they are theoretical constructs: researchers create them because of a need to carry out research. Although this observation states the obvious, such statements help remind the academic community that transcripts reflect disciplinary and methodological interests. For example, this issue of granularity is not only about what and how much is transcribed, but also relates to what extent transcribing highly detailed features of social interaction helps fulfill an empirical objective.

The reflexive relationship between transcription and analysis also means that transcripts are inherently limited and skewed. All transcript-based research is bound to time, space, and resource limitations, and transcripts are therefore never complete representations of social interaction. Similarly, transcripts are never entirely accurate. Transcripts, on the one hand, possess varying degrees of inaccuracy, as data recordings possess an almost infinite number of nuances and layers of social interaction. On the other hand, transcripts possess finite space: a letter (or A4) size document does not have enough 'white space' to represent communication data in its true dynamic state. Despite advances in word recognition technology, this disparity in space and detail will exist for many years to come. Furthermore, transcripts are based on data recordings that have been created with recording devices placed in locations that primarily represent the interests and biases of the researcher. That is, transcripts are skewed representations of social interaction in that they do not reflect the ongoing and changing orientations of the participants under investigation. Yet, despite the inherently limited and skewed nature of transcripts, transcript-based research has made, and continues to make, a significant impact in language and social interaction scholarship.

To end this concise overview of recording and transcribing social interaction, it must be noted that scholarship must continue to devote more time and space to exploring the theoretical, methodological, and political issues and implications of transcript-based research. Transcribing social interaction, despite being an inherently subjective research endeavor, is a powerful way of uncovering and understanding the rich and complex ways language and social interaction are organized and unfold. In order to exploit the benefits of transcript-based research, however, scholars must reflexively engage in the ways their subjectivities influence how interactants and interaction are depicted to the larger academic community.

FURTHER READING

Bolden, G. B. (2015) 'Transcribing *as* research: "Manual" transcription and conversation analysis', *Research on Language and Social Interaction*, 48(3): 276–80.

Kowal, Sabine, and O'Connell, Daniel C. (2014) 'Transcription as a crucial step of data analysis', in Uwe Flick (ed.), *The SAGE Handbook of Qualitative Data Analysis*. London: Sage, pp. 64–77.

O'Connell, D. C., and Kowal, S. (2000) 'Transcription and the issue of standardization', *Journal of Psycholinguistic Research*, 28: 103–20.

REFERENCES

Andrews, Molly (2014) *Narrative Imagination and Everyday Life*. Oxford: Oxford University Press.

Bold, Christine (2012) *Using Narrative in Research*. London: Sage.

Bucholtz, M. (2000) 'The politics of transcription', *Journal of Pragmatics*, 32(10): 1439–65.

Bucholtz, M. (2007) 'Variation in transcription', *Discourse Studies*, 9(6): 784–808.

Cook, G. (1990) 'Transcribing infinity: Problems of context presentation', *Journal of Pragmatics*, 14(1): 1–24.

Coulthard, Margaret (2014) *An Introduction to Discourse Analysis*. London: Routledge.

Duranti, A. (2006) 'Transcripts, like shadows on a wall', *Mind, Culture, and Activity*, 13(4): 301–10.

Edwards, Jane A., and Lampert, Martin D. (eds.) (1993) *Talking Data: Transcription and Coding in Discourse Research*. Hillsdale: Lawrence Erlbaum.

Gee, James P. (2014) *An Introduction to Discourse Analysis: Theory and Method*. London: Routledge.

Goffman, Erving (1981) *Forms of Talk*. Philadelphia, PA: University of Pennsylvania Press.

Gumperz, John J. (1982) *Discourse Strategies*. Cambridge: Cambridge University Press.

Jaffe, A. and Walton, S. (2000) 'The voices people read: Orthography and the representation of non-standard speech', *Journal of Sociolinguistics*, 4(4): 561–87.

Jefferson, G. (1983) 'Issues in the transcription of naturally-occurring talk: Caricature vs. capturing pronunciational particulars', *Tilburg Papers in Language and Literature*, 34: 1–12.

Jefferson, G. (1996) 'A case of transcriptional stereotyping', *Journal of Pragmatics*, 26(2): 159–70.

Jefferson, Gail (2004) 'Glossary of transcript symbols with an introduction', in Gene H. Lerner (ed.), *Conversation Analysis: Studies from the First Generation*. Amsterdam: John Benjamins, pp. 13–31.

Jenks, Christopher J. (2011) *Transcribing Talk and Interaction: Issues in the Representation of Communication Data*. Amsterdam: John Benjamins.

Jenks, C. J. (2013) 'Working with transcripts: An abridged review of issues in transcription', *Language and Linguistic Compass*, 7(4): 251–61.

Kuiken, F. and Vedder, I. (2007) 'Task complexity and measures of linguistic performance in L2 Writing', *IRAL*, 45(3): 261–84.

Labov, William (1972) *Sociolinguistic Patterns*. Philadelphia, PA: University of Pennsylvania Press.

Maynes, Mary Jo, Pierce, Jennifer L., and Laslett, Barbara (2012) *Telling Stories*. New York: Cornell University Press.

Meredith, J. (2015) 'Transcribing screen-capture data: The process of developing a transcription system for multi-modal text-based data', *International Journal of Social Research Methodology*: 1–14.

Mondada, L. (2007) 'Commentary: Transcript variations and the indexicality of transcribing practices', *Discourse Studies*, 9(6): 809–21.

Ochs, Elinor (1979) 'Transcription as theory', in Elinor Ochs and Bambi Schieffelin (eds.), *Developmental Pragmatics*. New York, NY: Academic Press, pp. 43–72.

Pagnucci, Gian S. (2004) *Living the Narrative Life*. Portsmouth: Boynton/Cook Publishers.

Rapley, Tim (2018) *Doing Conversation, Discourse and Document Analysis* (2nd edn). London: Sage.

Roberts, F. and Robinson, J. D. (2004) 'Interobserver agreement on first-stage conversation analytic transcription', *Human Communication Research*, 30(3): 376–410.

Schegloff, Emanuel A. (2007) *Sequence Organization in Interaction*. Cambridge: Cambridge University Press.

Schiffrin, Deborah (1987) *Discourse Markers*. Cambridge: Cambridge University Press.

Schiffrin, Deborah, Tannen, Deborah, and Hamilton, Heidi E. (eds.) (2003) *The Handbook of Discourse Analysis*. Oxford: Blackwell.

Silverstein, Michael, and Urban, Greg (1996) *Natural Histories of Discourse*. Chicago, IL: University of Chicago Press.

Tannen, Deborah (1994) *Gender and Discourse*. Oxford: Oxford University Press.

Tench, Paul (2011) *Transcribing the Sound of English*. Cambridge: Cambridge University Press.

Tilley, S. A. (2003) '"Challenging" research practices: Turning a critical lens on the work of transcription', *Qualitative Inquiry*, 9(5): 750–73.

Wooffitt, Robin (2005) *Conversation Analysis and Discourse Analysis: A Comparative and Critical Introduction*. London: Sage.

9

Collecting Data in Other Languages – Strategies for Cross-Language Research in Multilingual Societies

Katharina Resch and Edith Enzenhofer

INTRODUCTION

There is increasing awareness for social research to include participants who are not fluent in the dominant research language, such as ethnic minority groups, refugees, migrants, or people with a bilingual or multilingual background. The presumptions, also, that societies are monolingual or that interview partners use only one language in their everyday communication have increasingly been questioned (Blommaert, 2010). Despite these shifts of paradigms, challenges of cross-language research are rarely mentioned in mainstream empirical handbooks or accounts for qualitative empirical research (Denzin and Lincoln, 2011; Creswell, 2014; Choi et al., 2012, p. 654). Research findings are often presented without any reference to the language of data collection or the language of the research participants (Temple and Young, 2004, p. 164) and the impact of language 'on research processes tends to be underestimated and underanalyzed' (Shklarov, 2007, p. 530).

'Language (in)visibility' (Temple and Young, 2004, p. 162) seems to be a blind spot in qualitative research, which otherwise is very aware of the interconnectedness of language and the creation of meaning. The majority of qualitative research accounts are presented in English, giving the impression that the language used bears no significance for interpretation. Other research accounts, however, give reference to language issues at various points of their research (Halai, 2007; Shklarov, 2007; Lauterbach, 2014; Temple and Young, 2004; Flick, 2014, Littig and Pöchhacker, 2014). We believe that qualitative research should elaborate solutions for the challenges related to cross-language research, such as the need for quality standards for translation (see also Sørensen et al., Chapter 10, this volume).

There are different strategies for dealing with language barriers in qualitative research: The researchers might speak the language(s) of their potential interviewees themselves, or they might involve lay researchers/translators/

interpreters (community researchers)[1] with specific language skills or professional translators/interpreters. Independent of the chosen strategy, social constructivist and interpretive approaches would agree that the very position of people involved in the research process has an influence on the way the data are collected, analyzed, and interpreted based on their understanding of the social world (Choi et al., 2012; Temple and Young, 2004, p. 164; Inhetveen, 2012). Involving translators, interpreters or community researchers in the research process does not pose a problem *per se*, but it can be seen as a 'presentation or transparency problem' if it is not made public how and under which cross-language circumstances research has taken place.

From a positivist view, translators or interpreters have been considered as threats to validity or methodological rigor. Fears are that they might change meanings, distort or modify what has been said or reduce the content (Lauterbach, 2014, p. 15; Shklarov, 2007, p. 530). Translators' actions are either expected to be neutral and invisible (Shklarov, 2007, p. 532) or they might be treated as suspicious, needing control of some sort (Berman and Tyyskä, 2011). We argue instead that translators should be appreciated as the first recipients of the material (Eco, 2003a) and as key players in any cross-language research, as they are co-producers of data and thus of meaning (Berman and Tyyskä, 2011; Choi et al., 2012, p. 653). Littig and Pöchhacker (2014, p. 1087) use the term 'translational interventions' for translation – a wording that acknowledges the significance of translation in the data collection process. Consequently, researchers should tackle quality issues by reflecting the whole process in a comprehensive way (see, below, the section on 'assuring quality' and Barbour, Chapter 14, this volume) rather than by monitoring one group of professionals.

In order to make good choices in the beginning of the data collection process, it is essential to make the role of the involved translators/interpreters or community researchers transparent, and to avoid the risk of translation processes and translators becoming 'invisible' (the disappearing translator – Temple and Young, 2004, p. 165; Enzenhofer and Resch, 2013, p. 205; Shklarov, 2007, p. 532).

Several publications in recent years have put cross-language issues into their focus of publication (Shklarov, 2007; Ross, 2010; Enzenhofer and Resch, 2011; Berman and Tyyskä, 2011; Littig and Pöchhacker, 2014). However, there are few publications, which really speak about the translation process as such, particularly not from the perspective of translation studies. Social sciences and translation studies have, in the last few years, made attempts to grow together (Wolf and Fukari, 2007; Littig and Pöchhacker, 2014; Enzenhofer and Resch, 2011), since qualitative research is mostly text-based research and translation scientists are text experts. We believe that the key issues in cross-language research require further interdisciplinary collaboration between translation studies and social sciences (Enzenhofer and Resch, 2011).

A comprehensive discussion of translation processes in qualitative social research also requires a consideration of the benefits of multilingual research approaches, a critical reflection on language preference and language dominance, bi- and multilingualism, cultural diversity in society (see Sørensen et al., Chapter 10, this volume), and the resulting methodological and practical implications for research.

This chapter is relevant for cross-language research in general and for various qualitative approaches in the data collection process. However, we will put a strong focus on qualitative interview techniques (such as semi-structured interviews, biographic and narrative interviews, group interviews, expert interviews, etc.; see Roulston and Choi, Chapter 15, this volume) and discuss recommendations for translation issues in the context of these interviews, and thus, spare other methods of qualitative data collection. We will suggest different cross-language data collection strategies in this book chapter, which researchers can wisely choose from, according to their research circumstances.

RATIONALE OF MULTILINGUAL DATA COLLECTION

Conducting multilingual qualitative research has three major rationales: ensuring inclusive social research, making diversity between and within groups and societies visible, and increasing cultural competence of the involved researchers.

Ensuring Inclusive Social Research

In the last decade, societies have been recognized as being diverse in many regards (Vertovec, 2007). Issues such as migration or refugee movements and the related changes of society have come into the focus of public debate. As a consequence, there has been increasing awareness for the need to develop suitable research strategies, which capture these developments and work as inclusively as possible. This requires a critical reflection of unilingual research strategies that might exclude minorities or perpetuate the myth of – ethnically or linguistically – homogeneous societies (Blommaert, 2010). Among other aspects, social researchers might wish to ensure that also people who are not in command of the respective country's majority language are given the chance to express themselves as research and interview partners. Thus, one benefit of multilingual research is to make diverse – and often vulnerable – groups and their perceptions, experiences and needs visible and to include their experiences into the discourse.

The need for multilingual research approaches is particularly obvious where either people with migration experience and/or communication issues are at the focus of the research project. There are many subgroups of migrants with a great variety of first languages, who do not (or not yet) speak the host country's language well enough to feel comfortable giving an interview. In such cases, it is necessary to offer multilingual interview settings in order to be able to reach the research aim at all.

However, one should not fall into the trap of putting multilingual research in the corner of migration studies and leaving it to a small segment of colleagues dedicated to this particular field. Language barriers are most likely to be present and important in all forms of societal fields and are a part of inherent power relations. Why should citizens who do not speak the country's official language fluently not have a say on urban planning, technological innovations, or emergency services? In consequence, in the scope of social sciences, there should be a general awareness about who might be given or denied a voice if research is conducted in the majority language only. Speaking and being heard, as well as dominance of languages, are part of power relations (Spivak, 1988; Berman and Tyyskä, 2011).

Language dominance is also an issue at the level of research institutions. Nurjannah et al. (2014) develop their recommendations for translation processes in the context of the need to publish in English in order to receive recognition of the international scientific community. If one wishes to bring research results obtained in a language other than English to a broader audience, he or she has to apply translation strategies, which should be reflected.

Acknowledging Diversity Within Groups and Individuals

Researchers can reflect diversity and multilingualism on the level of social groups, but also on the level of the individual (see Sørensen et al., Chapter 10, this volume). This idea adds rich insights to qualitative research, but it is disguised when all text material is 'translated' into standard language (Spivak, 1993/2001). In qualitative research, such a homogenization might happen at the stage when a transcription (see Jenks, Chapter 8, this volume) converts spoken language into written language while failing to make specific dialects, idioms or expressions of a social group visible. Maintaining language diversity in the material, challenges the myth of having *one* mother tongue and, subsequently, can help to revise perceptions of a homogeneous society (or of a homogeneous 'majority society').

From research on multilingualism we learn to understand the flexible use of language(s) as the expression of agency. Multilingual people use their language repertoire depending on the communication context and on their communication goal. Phenomena such as code-switching, code-mixing or style-shifting (practices of alternating between languages or varieties of language in conversation) can fulfill different communicative functions, such as dealing with semantic gaps, avoiding taboo words that seem inappropriate in the first language, expression of social belonging, exclusion of third partners, affection, rhetoric emphasis, demonstration of prestige and many others (Malik, 1994; Auer, 2002; Holmes, 2000; Abalhassan and Al Shalawi, 2000). Thus, the analysis of code-switching processes in an interview session can provide major insights for interpretation (Halai, 2007). However, this information gets lost if the transcription does not contain any information about the speaker's use of languages(s).

Increasing 'Cultural Competence'

Lead researchers select multilingual staff members, community researchers or translators mostly for one obvious reason: because they provide language competence otherwise not available (i.e. Pashtu). Another – often implicit – expectation when involving persons who speak a desired language is that they also provide 'cultural competence'. This expectation might include the assumption, for instance, that they know how to approach Afghan women and men in an appropriate way.

The length of this book chapter does not allow for a critical elaboration of the construct 'culture', however, a word of caution is necessary: Language competence alone cannot be equalized with 'cultural representation' or 'cultural competence'. A seemingly 'shared language' (see the remarks on multilingualism within groups and individuals in the section on the 'rationale of multilingual data collection' above) might facilitate communication, but it does by no means ensure homogeneity or even 'sameness' with respect to education, participation and privileges, life experiences, religious and ideological positions, or the expression of cultural habits. Many researchers experienced that a focus on the 'same mother tongue' bears the risk of overlooking profound differences or power relations in other regards (Gutierrez Rodriguez, 2006; Shklarov, 2007; Enzenhofer and Resch, 2011; Berman and Tyyskä, 2011). As a consequence, community researchers should not solely be employed on the basis of their language skills (Temple et al., 2006), and if so, it will influence the dynamics of the interview process and the material produced.

Having said this, the value of involving people with a specific social or ethnic background is for good reason recognized in practice and will also be elaborated in this book chapter. They are considered gatekeepers to their communities (Berman and Tyyskä, 2011) or otherwise inaccessible social groups and can be viewed as 'cultural brokers' (Temple et al., 2006, paragraph 20). This refers to their position in specific social networks or communities, to which the researchers have limited access, and means that they act as middlepersons between the research participants and the lead researchers and can moderate and negotiate meaning in case of differing or conflicting views or understandings (Shklarov, 2007).

THE DATA COLLECTION PROCESS AND THE ROLES OF THE MULTI-/BI-/UNILINGUAL RESEARCHERS

In cross-language research, there are different options for involving translators or community researchers in the process of data collection, and this choice has an impact on the quality of data. However, very few studies provide references on how translators were selected and on the researcher–translator relationship (Choi et al., 2012, p. 653). In this section, we will map the different roles and functions that are required in the process of data collection in cross-language research and the pros and cons of each of these strategies.

Distinguished Roles

When lead researchers begin planning their research, they will start by defining the aim of the project and the research question(s). Then they might proceed with laying out the process of data collection, analysis and interpretation. In this context, the different roles and functions should be clarified and distinguished, as they are at risk of becoming somewhat 'blurred'. These different roles might include:

- *gatekeepers* to a specific community and recruiters of interview partners;
- *key informants* as providers of community-specific information;
- *facilitators* of interviews or focus groups;
- (oral) *interpreters* of interviews or focus groups in participant's language;
- *transcribers* of audio material in participant's language;
- *translators* of transcripts into research language. (Berman and Tyyskä, 2011, p. 181).

Different tasks and sub-tasks in the research and translation process might overlap (i.e. recruiting interview partners and conducting interviews), as they are frequently not contractually separated. This makes the process of quality assurance difficult. It is revealing and astonishing at the same time that there is no consequent standard term for the professionals fulfilling these tasks (Berman and Tyyskä, 2011, p. 185). Consequently, their roles are not systematically reflected upon in the research process. In some cases, this might lead to unclear briefings.

When involved in cross-language research, community researchers or translators are most likely to be part of the process, but in a very limited sense: Most of them are employed only for a very specific task and are not meant to play more than this role in the research process (Temple and Young, 2004, p. 172). Their selective participation might end right after the transmission of the transcripts and payment – with the risk that little discussion about the interview takes place in the research team. Berman and Tyyskä (2011, p. 186) critically comment that their 'translators/interviewers were working "for" us rather than "with" us'. This can lead to marginalization, little appreciation, low status and lack of acknowledgment for their important work, but also to precarious working conditions, underestimation of the workload as well as little pay (Ross, 2010, p. 7; Enzenhofer and Resch, 2011, paragraph 88).

Two 'blind spots' seem to be worth mentioning: the amount of work required for providing an adequate access to the community and for the translation of transcripts.

As lead researchers mostly do not have direct access to minority groups – they are not 'community insiders' – translators often are asked to recruit interview partners as part of their work package, because it seems practicable (Temple et al., 2006, paragraph 25). Their responsibility is to access interview partners from their own personal networks, institutions, or associations or community centers (Temple et al., 2006). However, research teams often neglect that recruiting interview partners from minority groups requires labor-intensive strategies, which are not necessarily reflected in the pay. Also their function as 'key informant' (Berman and Tyyskä, 2011, p. 181) or research counselor, for example, regarding possible barriers to even attend an interview, often goes without saying.

The roles of the transcriber and the translator of the transcript are often combined, and fixed-rate payments might lead to a gross underestimation of the translation task, which differs between languages. From our experience with cross-language research, the translation of a transcript in German takes between four to six times as long as the interview duration, but up to twenty times as long if the transcript has to be translated as well. The time needed depends on the translator's experience as well as on the complexity and the structural differences of the languages involved (Enzenhofer and Resch, 2011, paragraph 88).

Strategies in Cross-Language Data Collection

The language of data collection is not only relevant during the interview session itself, but also during transcription, coding, advanced coding, reporting and team discussions (Nurjannah et al., 2014, p. 1). So how can the data collection process in cross-language research be organized? What are the advantages and disadvantages of the different strategies? There are different ways of realizing data collection, as Table 9.1 shows.

Bilingual researchers

Researchers who are fluent in minority languages are rare (Temple and Young, 2004, p. 168), and to our perception their availability differs in various national and educational contexts (i.e. in Austria, social exclusion of second generation migrants in higher education is a limiting factor). If studies target one community of interviewees only (i.e. Iranian immigrants in Canada) it seems feasible to find researchers with appropriate language skills, but if the study focuses on a number of communities (i.e. Syrian, Afghan, Chechen and Nigerian refugees arriving in Germany in 2015), then more than one interview language would be required.

Community researchers

The combination of language competence and their function as gatekeepers and key informants is certainly beneficial for many research projects. However, it is recommended that staff engaging in translation should also have competence and experience related with social research (Littig and Pöchhacker, 2014; Tarozzi, 2013). Knowing the aim of the research and being aware of one's own situational role in the data collection process are essential for conducting interviews (Lauterbach, 2014). Here the lead researchers should introduce the *Skopos* (aim, purpose; see the section on 'professional translations skills' below) of the translation as well (Nord, 2012a, 2012b). Furthermore, certain research topics (i.e. childbirth, bullying, terminal disease) might require specific skills related to sensitive and ethically responsible interviewing, an issue which cannot be elaborated here.

Against the background of these various competences, it is hard to imagine finding adequate community translators necessary for the qualitative research processes for all languages. Researchers often narrow the selection criteria for community translators down to language skills only. Often times a translator for a rare language ('rare' refers to a specific context, i.e. Urdu in Austria) cannot be found, and this is when we recommend choosing another data collection strategy, for example, to conduct qualitative interviews in tandem.

In general, a lack of preparation of community researchers or lay interpreters by the research team can negatively influence the quality of data (Lauterbach, 2014, p. 14). When people with a more narrow scope of skills conduct the interview, then the interviewer briefing becomes exceedingly more important. Especially in expert interviews, it should be an option to give community researchers a quasi-expert status in the data

Table 9.1 Strategies in cross-language data collection

	Data Collection Strategy	Advantages	Disadvantages
Bilingual researcher	Interviews are conducted in the language of the researcher Researchers themselves speak the target language and conduct the interviews themselves; they are bilingual See Lauterbach, 2014; Temple and Young, 2004; Choi et al., 2012; Shklarov, 2007	Researcher can work alone and needs no additional staff members Direct lingual access to the material Researchers do field work themselves	Limitation: Researchers do not speak all target languages Depends on structural factors whether minority members are available as researchers (social exclusion of minorities in the education system) The target language might not be the first or strongest language of the researcher, so he/she might miss nuances in the interview Researchers are academics and there could be a social gradient towards interview partners
Community researcher	Interviews are conducted in the participant's language(s) Lead researchers work with field researchers from a particular community who have the language skills needed Community researchers conduct interviews and the same person translates the transcript into the target language (lay translators) See Choi et al., 2012; Temple et al., 2006	Community researchers have lived experience in the community and know the conventions there Community researchers can also recruit participants Key informants – provide background information about the community Lay interpreters and translators are not as expensive as professionals	Generally not academics Particular need for briefing/training in both interviewing and translating techniques They might not be available for certain communities Lead researchers do not do field work themselves Lead researchers have no lingual access to primary data
Professional interpreter/translator	Researchers employ a professional interpreter/translator for conducting the interview itself and for translating the transcript into the target language(s) See Enzenhofer and Resch, 2011; Littig and Pöchhacker, 2014	Professionals provide comprehensive skills in text writing, editing, translating and many others Professional translation of the transcript Professional contracting phase (aim of the translation, important aspects)	Interpreters are not trained to conduct interviews and need briefing about qualitative research Professionals might speak the language but not live in the target community themselves Lead researchers do not do field work themselves Lead researchers have no lingual access to primary data Expensive strategy
Researcher–interpreter tandem	Tandem interviews are conducted with a researcher and an interpreter (twin/tandem process)	Each person can concentrate on their own task Works well for semi-structured or expert interviews Researchers do field work themselves	Not practicable for narrative interviews, biographic or problem-centered interviews The interpreting process will break the flow of the interview Double pay, double time
Researcher using relay language	Interviews are conducted by the researcher in a third language (relay language, lingua franca, i.e. English), which is neither the mother tongue of the interview partner (i.e. Somali) nor of the researcher (i.e. Swedish)	Could be the only strategy for rare languages Researchers do field work themselves Often used for expert interviews Material is produced in English which is mostly also the reporting language	The interview partner cannot express himself in her/his first language Own competences in English as lingua franca might be overestimated Particularities and nuances of the language could get lost

collection process (Littig and Pöchhacker, 2014) to narrow the gap between main and community researchers, but also toward the expert.

Another caveat should be stressed: The option to involve multilingual community translators who not only master the language barrier but also act as contact persons might be a practicable or even the only way to approach the persons of interest at all, while simultaneously keeping a comfortable and comforting distance from them. The researchers who outsource fieldwork and receive the neatly translated transcription of an interview are not – unlike the researchers in ethnographic research (see Buscatto, Chapter 21, this volume) – forced to interact physically and emotionally with a concrete other, they are not exposed to living conditions, deprivation, fascination, aversion, confusion, compassion, irritation and other 'side effects' of qualitative research.

Professional interpreters / translators

Most of the points mentioned above are equally valid for professional translators. The only exception is the question of the *Skopos* (aim, purpose of the translation – see below). Professional interpreters and translators are trained to recognize a professional contracting phase, which includes the context for which the translation is needed, the target audience, the form of the product (transcript), remarks or a de-briefing with the researcher etc.

Researcher–interpreter tandems

A researcher and an interpreter conducting an interview together are a good solution for semi-structured or expert interviews (see Bogner et al., Chapter 41, this volume), but are not recommendable for narrative or biographic interviews, in which the interviewee is supposed to engage in a long elaboration of a topic. If an interpreter is involved in narrative or biographic interviews, narrations are always paused, because the interpreter can only remember a certain amount of sentences or words. In this case, the interviewee has time to think about his/her next sentence but would have possibly – without interruption – said something else. In addition, interpreters can feel the urge to interrupt an interviewee if they have the feeling that the input will be too long to remember (Lauterbach, 2014, pp. 35, 42). If interviewees confront interpreters with a too long narration, the risk of reducing the content is high, and this might lead to an exclusion of the lead researcher in the tandem interview ('lost in translation'). When tandems work together for the first time, we recommend getting to know each other well in a briefing but also to conduct a test interview in order to have time to adapt to their specific role in the interview situation. The researchers, for instance, need to develop a feeling for how many sentences the interpreter can remember to assure a certain 'flow' in the interview.

Researchers using a relay language (lingua franca)

This translation strategy brings limitations both for the researcher and for the interview partner. The latter would probably enjoy the option of expressing herself/himself freely in her/his first language. The social scientist finds himself/herself in the role of a translator without formal training. Even if a researcher speaks fluent English, this does not mean that he/she can cope with different regional varieties of English, like Nigerian or Indian English, equally well. Following Przyborski and Wohlrab-Sahr (2008, p. 308), a self-critical assessment of the researcher's competence in English seems advisable.

Consequences for the timing of translation

Articles focusing on cross-language research also discuss the timing of translation in the research process (Nurjannah et al., 2014, p. 2). At what stage should the translation of the transcript take place, if the interview is not conducted in the research language?

Some argue that only final reports should be translated into the research language, but not all material produced until that point. Others recommend that the translation should take place as soon as possible, that is, after transcription, as not all members of the research team might speak all languages and would be excluded from analysis (Nurjannah et al., 2014, p. 2). Thus, main researchers must consider the composition of the research team when deciding upon the timing of translation. Some studies indicate that coding is easier when it is done in the language of the interviewee and thus with an original transcript (Nurjannah et al., 2014, p. 6). For instance, in a study with Indonesian women all codes were categorized when using Indonesian, but not when using English. So, it was possible to perform the initial coding in Indonesian, and then categories and subcategories were translated into English – used for team discussion and advanced coding.

PROFESSIONAL TRANSLATION SKILLS AND THEIR BENEFITS FOR TRANSLATING QUALITATIVE DATA

Requirements for translating transcripts for qualitative research are high and transcripts represent a very specific genre of texts – written representations of oral language. For this reason, a lot can be learned from the discipline of translation, a profession with high relevance and currency for a globalized world and its mobile culture. While translators are an occupational group who work with written texts which can be corrected, repeated and re-written multiple times, interpreting is a profession that works with oral texts, which cannot be corrected, repeated or re-designed after they have been said (simultaneous and consecutive interpreting). The profession of translation/interpreting is as multifold as its contexts: multilingual instruction manuals, technology, scientific texts, movies, medicine, literature etc.

The training of professional translators/interpreters mainly involves the production of equivalence, which is complex and difficult in itself (Ross, 2010). Text equivalence means producing a target text on four levels: equivalent syntax, lexis, style and meaning (Burbekova and Nurzhanova, 2014). Equivalence is needed if the source text and the target text have the same function. However, in some cases this is not the case and professional translators then decide whether equivalence makes sense or whether they should choose to produce an adequate translation ('equivalence versus adequacy'). If the source text in German is for instance a scientific journal article written for social scientists, but the target text in English has a different audience (i.e. students in their first year of studies), then the text needs an *adequate* translation, not an *equivalent* one (since the function of the text has changed).

Still, many translators are asked to translate 'as literally as possible', reacting to fearful employers who are afraid that the translated text will not be equivalent to the original one, but that is actually not the issue. About thirty years ago, a pragmatic turn in translation studies took place, leading to the *Skopos* theory (Snell-Hornby, 2006). Professional translators identify the *Skopos* (the aim and purpose) of the translation in the contracting phase and then integrate the communicative function of the text into their translation strategy (Nord, 2012a, 2012b).

According to the *Skopos* theory, originally developed by Reiss and Vermeer (1984; Vermeer, 1996), the entire communicative act is re-coded into another language, not just mere words (Vermeer, 2002; Renn, 2002; Snell-Hornby, 2002; Nord, 2012b; Martin de Leon, 2008; Littig and Pöchhacker, 2014). *Skopos* theory hereby corresponds to social constructivist and interpretive sociology, as they claim the position of a text or person in the social world. The *Skopos* theory is in line with the requirements of qualitative research approaches, as it demands a contextualization of the translation process. What is being said depends on who says it to whom for which purpose (Renn, 2002, p. 29). Equivalence does not make sense in all contexts, when, for example, a US advertising slogan is translated for a billboard in Saudi Arabia.

According to Eco (2003a, 2003b), translation does not enable us to say exactly the same thing in another language; however, it helps us to say 'almost' the same thing. The degree of freedom given in this process is based upon negotiation. This negotiation process involves various partners – the author, the text, the reader and the publisher – and their goals, and implies losing and winning. The choice about which losses to accept in return for which gains depends on the *Skopos*. So translating is not about an ordinary 1:1 coding of mere words. It is a communicative act, which needs a degree of professionalization.

Professional translators are mainly trained to negotiate the *Skopos* and have a range of skills one cannot easily find within lay translators or community researchers:

- language skills: i.e. active and passive language skills, text expertise, editing of texts;
- intercultural skills: i.e. knowing the social conventions of cultures, differing accents and dialects, knowing the history of cultures and countries;
- research skills: i.e. looking at parallel texts;
- technical skills: i.e. translation strategies, translation software, terminology databases, software for speech pattern recognition;
- professional skills: i.e. types of texts, expert knowledge for specific texts and text conventions (engine building, medical ingredients, poetry etc.).

Translators have to make different decisions in the translation process (Ross, 2010). According to Venuti's distinction (1995), translation requires a choice between domesticating and foreignizing strategies: Domestication makes a text conform to the conventions of the target audience, with the risk of 'eliminating every roughness and vanishing the translator' (Tarozzi, 2013, paragraph 18). Foreignization instead 'means purposely maintaining some "estranging" elements of the parlance of the culture of origin which, though they may undermine the overall fluency of the text, serve to remind the reader of its difference and distance from the host culture' (Tarozzi, 2013, paragraph 18). Tarozzi (2013, paragraph 45) not only considers this double movement between the 'foreigner in his text and the reader in his willingness to enter the text' desirable. He also argues that the tension between these poles forces the researchers to state their position toward the social groups and the social context in question.

Benjamin (1996, p. 260) advises the translator not only to represent the content (das Gemeinte – what is meant) but to respect the form of expression (die Art des Meinens – how it is expressed): 'A real translation is transparent; it does not cover the original, does not block its light, but allows the pure language, as though reinforced by its own medium, to shine upon the original all the more fully.' Spivak, from a postcolonial standpoint, expresses concerns about the ideological consequences if the specific quality of a language, particularly from non-European contexts, gets lost by translating to a globalized Standard English: 'This happens when all the literature of the world gets translated in a sort of with-it translatese, so that the literature by a woman in Palestine begins to resemble, in the feel of its prose, something by a man in Taiwan' (1993/2001, pp. 314–16).

Interview transcripts are unique text types. They contain elements of 'informative texts' (like legal texts, recipes, product descriptions) and 'expressive texts' (like poems, newspaper articles, letters) as they convey a subjective (emotional) view on a topic by an interview partner, but must also meet informative standards and convey information. All text types follow different text conventions and can be distinguished from one another by their structure, their form (layout, use of capital letters, bold letters etc.), their lexis, their grammar, their style, typical phrases ('Once upon a time…'), and their punctuation.

Furthermore, transcripts have the specific feature whereby oral language is transferred into written language (Ross, 2010). Our speech is full of repetition, stumbles, interruptions and revisions – so why should the transcript not be? While other text types should, as a basic principle, be easy to read and not confuse the reader due to its form, transcripts are allowed to unsettle the reader (or research team), as this might be useful for analysis. Sometimes it seems to be an implicit norm that the more detailed a transcript, the more precise and scientific the text (Ross, 2010, p. 10). However, very detailed transcriptions – for instance with extensive punctuation – run the risk of being simplified for reporting reasons. This might lower the threshold for editing the translation as well and 'polishing' distinct features of spoken language.

Professional translators are trained to view their translations as legally valid documents. If this rigour is applied to documents used in qualitative research, such as transcripts, then more attention has to be paid to their quality.

As the translation of research transcripts has a different *Skopos* than that of literature, for instance, nothing speaks against using footnotes in the transcript to display meta-information, for example, about dialects and idioms, context specific or unusual wording, code-switching, proverbs, etc.

For community researchers and lay translators it might be helpful to understand that the assessment criteria of their work is not the equivalence of the source and target text (if this is even possible from oral to written language) nor the elegance of the wording in the transcript, but the ability to find a way to express the specific qualities of the interview situation and the particular social context on a language level, taking into account the *Skopos*. Knowing this, translators might be less likely to shy away from maintaining characteristic features of spoken language like, for example, interrupted sentences, grammar errors, common spoken disfluencies, etc. They should also be invited to make ambiguous wording or translation difficulties transparent, that is, by indicating possible translation alternatives or writing memos about these difficulties. This allows the whole research team then to enter into a discussion about the underlying interpretive process in the analysis phase.

ASSURING QUALITY OF CROSS-LANGUAGE DATA

When considering quality assurance of translation processes, a researcher has to master the paradox of acknowledging the fundamental openness and creative potential of hermeneutic processes while defining standards to make eventual analytic steps transparent. There is without doubt a dynamic tension in this process.

If qualitative research is based on translated material, this translation is already the result of a reconstructive process by which the meaning – as it is understood by the translator – is transferred into another language. The interpretation process precedes the translation process, influencing the translation strategies made later (Eco, 2003a).

Now this double hermeneutic process can be seen as a risk or an opportunity. Tarozzi (2013, paragraph 35), quoting Calvino's essay title (1982) 'Translating is the True Way to Read a Text', encourages us to use the double interpretation process as an analytic resource: 'Because translation always presupposes a process of understanding – interpretation – analysis, it can represent a precious new instrument in the researcher's hand to deal with data.' In this sense, the translator receives acknowledgment as the first recipient of the material (Eco, 2003a), and his/her perception might be a valuable contribution to the interpretation process.

Berman and Tyyskä (2011, p. 180) argue against a positivist notion of 'treating the interpreter as merely a mechanical and potentially problematic part of the research process' and warn against the impetus of controlling these staff via monitoring. Instead, they suggest a participatory approach, incorporating the translators as active producers of knowledge (2011, p. 181f). Such a notion not only requires involving multilingual staff members in all stages of the research process, it also means conceptualizing the creation of meaning as a constructive process in which multilingual translators, who often provide a crucial understanding of the interview context, should be invited.

Temple and Young (2004, p. 163) point to the fact that under a positivist framework the focus is on the product – with the aim of obtaining a 'correct' translation. Interpretive paradigms instead would rather investigate the process of knowledge production. Already the World Health Organization (WHO, 1997, quoted by Regmi et al., 2010, p. 21) recommended validating translations by a review panel made up of experts and bilingual members of the involved social groups. Authors recently working in the field (Resch and Enzenhofer, 2012; Regmi et al., 2010) agree on encouraging an exchange about differing perceptions between researchers and translators. Such differing perceptions might manifest themselves as translation alternatives in the best case, pointing to a 'dual perception of meanings' (Shklarov, 2007, p. 532), but might also become visible in the form of 'mistakes' such as omissions, changing informal or slang expressions to standard language etc. Berman and Tyyskä (2011, p. 181) point out that such 'mistakes' might be done to please the employer (2011, p. 185), and Resch and Enzenhofer (2012) would see them as a lack of clear instruction. In both cases, a reflection of the differing perceptions might be a valuable source for understanding. Inhetveen (2012) developed a systematic approach by comparing interpreting during an interview with a subsequent translation of the transcribed material. Reflecting possible discrepancies of both written and oral translation serves a) a diagnostic function (when the research team reconstructs the translation strategy) and b) a heuristic function (when the research team receives additional insight into the content aspects, which allows for multiple interpretation and uses these insights for their analysis).

Research Budgets and its Consequences for Translation

When talking about recommendations, the institutional framework in which the research is conducted, has to be taken into account, as it has a profound effect on the quality of translation and of data (Enzenhofer and Resch, 2011; Berman and Tyyskä, 2011, p. 187). This means taking into consideration funding resources, calculating translation costs into project budgets from the onset, modes of payment for external translators or community researchers, forms of contracts, time constraints, etc. When calculating the budget for a cross-language research project, the project manager has to be sure about the strategy (see Table 9.1 above), as he/she might have to calculate a tandem, an external translator, community researchers or none of them if one participating researcher is bilingual.

Studies, in which the translation process is openly discussed, acknowledge that budgets are limited (Berman and Tyyskä, 2011; Ross, 2010, p. 8). Often there is no money for pre-testing of the translated interview guide or full debriefings after the interview with the translator. Their services are often paid for as an honorarium, but single services (e.g. translation, transcription, recruiting) are often not separated in the receipt but put together under one heading, so there is no transparency regarding which task costs which amount of money.

There are accounts from previous research projects that relate how translators and community researchers tend to be badly paid, the status of their work is considered to be low and it is not integrated well into the overall research process (Ross, 2010, p. 7). Added to this, their contracts of employment tend to be precarious. So, of course, quality of data might be limited by these framework conditions.

Taking Action for Quality Assurance

Ultimately, lead researchers all across the world are expected to produce readable English research reports and publications. However, the process of how language played a role in the data collection process has to be made transparent, not only in migration studies, but in all qualitative research. The final product of a qualitative interview study in cross-country research can and must show the origin of data and the production process of language. Practices of rewriting translated interview quotations in order to assimilate them to Standard English and to meet the expectations of funders, academia, publishing houses or readers (Temple et al., 2006) are strongly discouraged.

What seems to be crucial in terms of quality assurance is to consult the involved temporary staff – depending on which data collection strategy the research team chooses (see Table 9.1). Examples of good practice are, for instance, full briefing and de-briefing before and after the field research phase or in-depth reflection interviews with the involved translators (Temple et al., 2006) in order to find out about potential challenges related to translation. This especially applies if lead researchers choose not to work in the field themselves.

Following are recommendations from Enzenhofer and Resch (2013, p. 222) for the *process of data collection*:

- Clearly state the role of the community researchers/translators in the research process (co-producer of knowledge, key informant etc. – see the section on data collection above) – and the modes and dates of briefings, common analysis sessions, etc.
- Provide a clear overview of tasks, distinguished in sub-tasks as well as an estimation of workdays for each sub-task. The different roles and functions in the research process should be stated separately and it should be made clear to which degree the recruiting of interview partners in a certain community is also the task of the community researcher/translator.
- Give explicit administrative information: time of employment, budget for each task, which form of provided and expected material, degree of detail in transcripts, modes of payment.
- Separately pay for conducting interviews, writing transcripts, and translating transcripts.
- Distribute templates (for memos) or good practice transcripts, show how transcripts should look at the end of the fieldwork, especially if community researchers/translators are new to the task; also you can add rules of transcription (handbooks, handouts etc.)
- Ask your translating staff for feedback on the time required for translation of transcripts in order to ensure realistic project planning in the future (i.e. the duration of the interview 1:6 translation of the transcript).

Enzenhofer and Resch (2013, pp. 222, 223) also set out recommendations for the *quality of products*:

- Transcript:
  ○ Clarify the *Skopos* of the transcription; show the transcriber how and in which way the transcript will be analyzed and interpreted.
  ○ Give clear instructions about rules of transcription depending on your method of analysis (content analysis, hermeneutical analysis etc.); show an example of a transcript.
  ○ Give instructions about how to use footnotes, how to mark code-switching and code-mixing in the translated transcript, and how to deal with dialects etc. since transcription handbooks usually do not give instructions about how to manage these aspects.
- Translated transcript:
  ○ Clarify the *Skopos* of the translation: How will the transcript be used and by whom? Who will have to understand the transcript?
  ○ Give instructions about how to mark particularities of the source text in terms of regional, socio-cultural or sub-group characteristics.

○ Ask the translator to explain which translation strategy was chosen.
- Documentation: Make it clear that the comments and remarks of the translator are extremely useful for qualitative data analysis and should have room somewhere in the document (footnotes, endnotes etc.). They are needed to document challenges in the translation process (for instance if in a certain language there is no word for 'rape') and how this translation challenge was solved.

CONCLUSION

The data collection process in cross-language research can be organized with at least five different strategies, which all have advantages and disadvantages. There are different ways of achieving data collection and different ways of handling the challenges in cross-language research:

1. Bilingual researchers
2. Community researchers
3. Professional translators/interpreters
4. Tandem interviews
5. Interviewing in a relay language/lingua franca

It is of utmost importance to distinguish and clarify the roles of involved community researchers, translators or interpreters at an early stage in the research process to avoid role conflicts (Shklarov, 2007, p. 532) or loss in data quality. Tasks like recruiting interview partners, facilitating interviews, oral interpreting, transcription of audio material and translation of the transcript should be held apart.

Also, we argue for the improvement of structural conditions in which cross-language research takes place. Ethical considerations should also be developed to protect community researchers, translators or interpreters and their work. We see the risks as generally involving low wages for a highly difficult task, a workload mostly being underestimated even by experienced lead researchers, issues of confidentiality, and possible tensions in the community, which can make the life of the community researcher difficult post interview.

We see community researchers, translators or interpreters as co-researchers and active participants, who should be incorporated into the research process openly and in all stages (full integration). They are co-producers of data and of meaning, and this process has to be opened up to fully grasp the production process of qualitative data. González y González and Lincoln (2006, paragraph 22, 39) consequently claim equal collaboration in research teams, including even shared authorship and intellectual property rights. In general, we argue for invisible translation to be made visible in final reports or research publications if language did play a role in qualitative data collection. We conclude, along with Littig and Pöchhacker (2014, p. 1090) that it is important to apply a strategic approach to translation in qualitative research and to pay 'consistent attention to linguistic and cultural issues throughout the research process, from research design to data generation and analysis to reporting'. Social science and translation studies should consider close collaboration in the future to further improve related quality standards and mutual understanding between the disciplines.

Note

1. In the following text we will use the term 'community researchers' for community members who are involved in research projects without necessarily having academic training, but have undergone a specific briefing. In translation science, the analogous concept would be 'community interpreter'. Following our previous publications (Enzenhofer and Resch, 2011 and 2013; Resch and Enzenhofer, 2012), we use the term 'lay interpreters', following the same meaning.

FURTHER READING

Berman, R. C. and Tyyskä, V. (2011) 'A critical reflection on the use of translators/interpreters in a qualitative cross-language research project', *International Journal of Qualitative Methods*, 10(1): 178–89.

Littig, B. and Pöchhacker, F. (2014) 'Socio-translational collaboration: The case of expert interviews', *Qualitative Inquiry*, 20(9): 1085–95.

Shklarov, S. (2007) 'Double vision uncertainty: The bilingual researcher and the ethics of cross-language research', *Qualitative Health Research*, 17(4): 529–38.

REFERENCES

Abalhassan, Kh. M., and Al Shalawi, H. G. (2000) 'Code-switching behavior of Arab speakers of English as a second language in the United States', *Intercultural Communication Studies*, X(1): 179–88.

Auer, Peter (ed.) (2002) *Code-Switching in Conversation: Language, Interaction and Identity*. London: Routledge.

Benjamin, Walter (1996) 'The task of the translator', in Marcus Bullock and Michael W. Jennings (eds.), *Selected Writings, Volume 1, 1913–1926*. Cambridge, MA and London: The Belknap Press of Harvard University Press, pp. 253–63.

Berman, R. C., and Tyyskä, V. (2011) 'A critical reflection on the use of translators/interpreters in a qualitative cross-language research project', *International Journal of Qualitative Methods*, 10(1): 178–89.

Blommaert, Jan (2010) *The Sociolinguistics of Globalization. Cambridge Approaches to Language Contact*. Cambridge: Cambridge University Press.

Burbekova, S., and Nurzhanova, A. (2014) 'Problems of translation theory and practice: Original and translated text equivalence', *Procedia – Social and Behavioral Sciences*, 136(2014): 119–23.

Calvino, Italo (1995 [1982]). Tradurre è il vero modo di leggere un testo [Translating is the true way to read a text]. In Mario Barenghi (ed.), *Saggi 1945–85* (Vol. II, pp. 1825–31). Milan: Mondadori.

Choi, J., Kushner, K. E., Mill, J., and Lai, D. W. L. (2012) 'Understanding the language, the culture, the experience: Translation in cross-cultural research', *International Journal of Qualitative Methods*, 11(5): 652–65.

Creswell, John W. (2014) *Research Design: Qualitative, Quantitative, and Mixed Methods Approaches* (4th edn). Los Angeles, London, New Delhi, Singapore, Washington, DC: Sage.

Denzin, Norman K., and Lincoln, Yvonna (eds.) (2011) *The SAGE Handbook of Qualitative Research* (4th edn). Los Angeles, London, New Delhi, Singapore, Washington, DC: Sage.

Eco, Umberto (2003a) *Dire quasi la stessa cosa. Esperienze di traduzione*. Milano: Bompiani.

Eco, Umberto (2003b) *Mouse or Rat? Translation as Negotiation*. London: Weidenfeld & Nicolson.

Enzenhofer, E., and Resch, K. (2011) 'Übersetzungsprozesse und deren Qualitätssicherung in der qualitativen Sozialforschung', *Forum Qualitative Sozialforschung/Forum: Qualitative Social Research*, 12(2), retrieved via http://www.qualitative-research.net/index.php/fqs/rt/printerFriendly/1652/3176 [Accessed March 29, 2016].

Enzenhofer, Edith, and Resch, Katharina (2013) 'Unsichtbare Übersetzung? Die Bedeutung der Übersetzungsqualität für das Fremdverstehen in der qualitativen Sozialforschung', in Richard Bettmann and Michael Roslon (eds.), *Going the Distance. Impulse für die Interkulturelle Qualitative Sozialforschung*. Wiesbaden: Springer Fachmedien, pp. 203–30.

Flick, U. (2014) 'Challenges for qualitative inquiry as a global endeavor: Introduction to the special Issue', *Qualitative Inquiry*, 20(9): 1059–63.

González y González, E. M., and Lincoln, Y. S. (2006) 'Decolonizing qualitative research: Non-traditional reporting forms in the academy', *Forum Qualitative Sozialforschung/Forum: Qualitative Social Research*, 7(4), available at http://www.qualitative-research.net/index.php/fqs/article/view/162 [Accessed March 29, 2016].

Gutierrez Rodriguez, Encarnacion (2006) *Positionalität übersetzen. Über postkoloniale Verschränkungen und transversales Verstehen*. Linz: eipcp European Institute for Progressive Cultural Policies, available at http://eipcp.net/transversal/0606/gutierrezrodriguez/de [Accessed March 29, 2016].

Halai, Nelofer (2007) 'Making use of bilingual interview data: Some expressions from the field', *Qualitative Research Report*, 12(3): 344–55.

Holmes, Janet (2000) *An Introduction to Sociolinguistics* (2nd edn). Wellington: Longman.

Inhetveen, K. (2012) 'Translation challenges: Qualitative interviewing in a multi-lingual field', *Qualitative Sociology Review*, 8(2): 28–45.

Lauterbach, G. (2014) 'Dolmetscher/inneneinsatz in der qualitativen Sozialforschung. Zu Anforderungen und Auswirkungen in gedolmetschten Interviews', *Forum Qualitative Sozialforschung/Forum: Qualitative Social Research*, 15(2) available at http://www.ssoar.info/ssoar/handle/document/43298 [Accessed March 29, 2016].

Littig, B., and Pöchhacker, F. (2014) 'Socio-translational collaboration: The case of expert interviews', *Qualitative Inquiry*, 20(9): 1085–95.

Malik, Lalita (1994) *Socio-linguistics: A Study of Code-switching*. New Delhi: Anmol Publications.

Martin de Leon, C. (2008) 'Skopos and beyond: A critical study of functionalism', *Target – International Journal of Translation Studies*, 20(1): 1–28.

Nord, C. (2012a) 'Quo vadis, functional translatology?' *Target – International Journal of Translation Studies*, 24(1): 26–42.

Nord, C. (2012b) 'Quo paratranslation – a new paradigm or a re-invented wheel?' *Perspectives – Studies in Translatology*, 20(4): 399–409.

Nurjannah, Intansari, Mills, Jane, Park, Tanya, and Usher, Kim (2014) 'Conducting a grounded theory study in a language other than English: Procedures for ensuring the integrity of translation', *Sage Open*, (January–March): 1–10.

Przyborski, Aglaja, and Wohlrab-Sahr, Monika (2008) *Qualitative Sozialforschung: Ein Arbeitsbuch*. München: Oldenbourg.

Regmi, K., Naidoo, J., and Pilkington, P. (2010) 'Understanding the process of translation and transliteration in qualitative research', *International Journal of Qualitative Methods*, 9(1): 16–26.

Reiss, Katharina, and Vermeer, Hans (1984) *Grundlagen einer allgemeinen Translationstheorie*. Tübingen: Niedermeyer.

Renn, Joachim (2002) 'Einleitung: Übersetzen, Verstehen, Erklären. Soziales und sozialwissenschaftliches Übersetzen zwischen Erkennen und Anerkennen', in Joachim Renn, Jürgen Straub and Shingo Shimada (eds.), *Übersetzung als Medium des Kulturverstehens und sozialer Integration*. Frankfurt/Main: Campus, pp. 13–35.

Resch, Katharina, and Enzenhofer, Edith (2012) 'Muttersprachliche Interviewführung an der Schnittstelle zwischen Sozialwissenschaft und Translationswissenschaft: Relevanz, Grundlagen, Herausforderungen', in Jan Kruse, Stephanie Bethmann, Debora Niermann and Christian Schmieder (eds.), *Qualitative Interviewforschung in und mit fremden Sprachen*. Weinheim: Juventa, pp. 80–100.

Ross, J. (2010) 'Was that infinity of affinity? Applying insights from translation studies to qualitative research transcription', *Forum Qualitative Sozialforschung/Forum: Qualitative Social Research* 11(2), available at http://www.qualitative-research.net/index.php/fqs/article/view/1357 [Accessed March 29, 2016].

Shklarov, S. (2007) 'Double vision uncertainty: The bilingual researcher and the ethics of cross-language research', *Qualitative Health Research*, 17(4): 529–38.

Snell-Hornby, Mary (2002) 'Übersetzen als interdisziplinäres Handeln. Über neue Formen des kulturellen Transfers', in Joachim Renn, Jürgen Straub, and Shingo Shimada (eds.), *Übersetzung als Medium des Kulturverstehens und sozialer Integration*. Frankfurt am Main: Campus, pp. 144–60.

Snell-Hornby, M. (2006) *The Turns of Translation Studies. New Paradigms or Shifting Viewpoints?* Amsterdam and Philadelphia, PA: John Benjamins.

Spivak, Gayatri Chakravorty (1988) 'Can the subaltern speak?', in Cary Nelson and Lawrence Grossberg (eds.), *Marxism and the Interpretation of Culture*. Chicago, IL: University of Illinois Press, pp. 271–313.

Spivak, Gayatri Chakravorty (1993/2001) *Outside the Teaching Machine*. New York: Routledge.

Tarozzi, Massimiliano (2013) 'Translating and doing grounded theory methodology: Intercultural mediation as an analytic resource', *Forum Qualitative Sozialforschung/Forum: Qualitative Social Research*, 14(2), available at http://www.qualitative-research.net/index.php/fqs/article/view/1429 [Accessed March 29, 2016].

Temple, B., and Young, A. (2004) 'Qualitative research and translation dilemmas', *Qualitative Research*, 4(2): 161–78.

Temple, B., Edwards, R., and Alexander, C. (2006) 'Grasping at context: Cross language qualitative research as secondary qualitative data analysis', *Forum Qualitative Sozialforschung/Forum: Qualitative Social Research*, 7(4) available at http://www.qualitative-research.net/index.php/fqs/article/view/176 [Accessed: March 29, 2016].

Venuti, Lawrence (1995) *The Translator's Invisibility: A History of Translation*. London and New York: Routledge.

Vermeer, Hans J. (1996) *A Skopos Theory of Translation (Some Arguments For and Against)*. Heidelberg: TextContext.

Vermeer, Hans (2002) 'Erst die unmöglichkeit des übersetzens macht das übersetzen möglich', in Joachim Renn, Jürgen Straub, and Shingo Shimada (eds.), *Übersetzung als Medium des Kulturverstehens und sozialer Integration*. Frankfurt am Main: Campus, pp. 125–43.

Vertovec, S. (2007) 'Super-diversity and its implications', *Ethnic and Racial Studies*, 29(6): 1024–54.

Wolf, Michaela, and Fukari, Alexandra (eds.) (2007) *Constructing a Sociology of Translation*. Amsterdam, Philadelphia: John Benjamins Publishing Company.

From Scholastic to Emic Comparison: Generating Comparability and Handling Difference in Ethnographic Research

Estrid Sørensen, Alison Marlin and Jörg Niewöhner

INTRODUCTION

Comparison is central to the analytic and data collection practices of social science researchers, as well as to the everyday practices of people going about their daily lives. Comparison is, first and foremost, a way of making sense of things, organizing or describing them, and working with them. We might say that comparison is a way of working with differences and similarities between people, objects, concepts, feelings, and other sorts of things. When introducing his 'Ethnography in/of the World System', George Marcus (1995) noted that phenomena of and in contemporary worlds rarely rest immutably in one single site in which the ethnographer can stay for an extended period of time to learn about its cultural specificities (see also Buscatto, Chapter 21, this volume). More often, objects, concepts and people move across places, often disrespecting national, cultural, discursive or material boundaries. In our simultaneously global and local world, comparison is a crucial means for both researchers and participants to manage the mobility, the drift, the variations, and the differences that necessarily emerge. This is the case for researchers and observers, as well as for participants in a simultaneously global and local world on the move. Comparison may be used to manage differences arising when rules, standards and regulations are encountered in everyday life and discrepancies emerge between what is done in local practice and what is required by social or technical standards, or when new technologies are introduced that allow people to do what they are used to in new ways. In each of these and similar situations, differences emerge through socio-material practice, and often, comparison is used to deal with such differences. Social science data collection is also a socio-material practice in which differences emerge, differences that are often managed by means of comparison.

In this chapter we distinguish between different ways of understanding and doing comparison in ethnographic research, each of which have implications for data collection design, practice and subsequent data analysis. One way of conceptualizing difference and comparison, to which we have alluded above, is to see difference and comparison as emerging with and through practice. In contrast, much social science research takes differences between people, cultures and societies as intrinsic qualities belonging to these phenomena. In defining and (re)producing categories and differences (cf. Hacking, 2007), this latter approach relies on comparisons made by the researcher, such as between male and female, young and old, persons who live alone and those who live with others, and so on. We call comparisons that are conducted on the basis of dimensions defined prior to empirical research *scholastic comparisons*. In such comparisons, prior to beginning empirical work scholars define the *tertium comparationis*, i.e. the dimensions or grid according to which comparison is to be conducted. The *tertium comparationis* then guides the data collection, for instance, to determine the kind and number of data collection points.

In this chapter, we focus not on scholastic comparison and its application in social science research, which is well explored elsewhere (e.g. Somekh and Lewin, 2004), but rather on *emic comparison*. We suggest *emic comparison* as a method that investigates *how comparability is achieved and the role of social and material efforts invested in producing comparability* (cf. Niewöhner and Scheffer, 2010). We explain this method by imagining emic and scholastic comparison as the two extreme ends of a continuum. Any given piece of research is unlikely to be at one or the other extreme, but somewhere in between, having characteristics of both scholastic and emic comparison. We deliberately make this contrast between emic and scholastic comparison, comparing forms of comparison, in order to facilitate understanding; the comparison we make here is itself a way of handling differences. In introducing and exploring emic comparison, we turn to *ethnographic* research (see Buscatto, Chapter 21, this volume), and to work in anthropology and Science and Technology Studies. Emic comparison is most often done in ethnographic research, although we believe it has the potential to be used more widely in other forms of research. Ethnography also shares several core principles with emic comparison, and ethnographic work is thus an appropriate source for an introduction to emic comparison.

This chapter begins with an overview of comparison and data collection in the social sciences and of the form of comparison that has been most commonly found there, scholastic or *etic* comparison, and some of the critiques that have been leveled against it. The chapter then turns to *emic* comparison, looking for inspiration to anthropology and the innovative approaches to comparison that have arisen over the past decades in this discipline. It draws particularly on Science and Technology Studies and the works of social anthropologist Marilyn Strathern (1992, 2004, 2011), and discusses comparability and comparison as the result, rather than the starting point, of socio-material practices (cf. Sørensen, 2008). Through the presentation of six comparative ethnographic studies, different methodological practices are discussed along with their implications for data collection. The potential of examining comparison and comparability as a means of handling difference, as well as the importance of investigating the effects of comparison and comparability, are emphasized.

THE HISTORICAL DEVELOPMENT OF COMPARISON IN THE SOCIAL SCIENCES

Emile Durkheim (1895/1982) placed comparison at the heart of sociological proof, not least because of the early development of sociology with its cross-country and cross-cultural comparisons, as in the writings of

Tocqueville, Martineau, Comte, Marx and Weber. In subsequent disciplinary thought styles, different modes of comparison have been developed, ranging from those of structuralism (Lévi-Strauss, 1963) to ethnomethodology (Garfinkel, 1967). Such comparison has generally proceeded as scholastic comparison, in which the parameters on which to compare are determined by the researcher prior to data collection and analysis. Yet while its usefulness in sharpening analytical categories and better understanding their particularity/generality remains much appreciated, its limitations have also been a continuous matter of concern (Matthes, 1992; Sjoberg, 1955) as discussed further below. Interestingly, what we term scholastic comparison in this chapter has emerged largely unchanged from constructivist, postcolonial and feminist critique as well as the crisis of representation in the social and cultural sciences from the 1970s onwards (Clifford and Marcus, 1986; Said, 1979). Ethnographic comparison, in contrast, was deconstructed to reveal its reductionist and decontextualizing tendencies, and its claim to being fundamental to many forms of social inquiry was brought into question.

We briefly discuss the methodological and epistemological assumptions of comparing as a research practice in the social sciences, beginning with scholastic comparison and then moving to emic comparison, in order to explain (through a comparison) the nature and purpose of both modes of comparing. Methodologically and epistemologically, scholastic comparison relies on a number of assumptions, many of which emic comparison challenges, as will be discussed below. These assumptions can be summarized as follows (cf. Jupp, 2006):

- Research objects can be clearly and durably separated from contexts within which they may be situated.
- A *tertium comparationis* can be meaningfully defined prior to the act of comparing.
- The *tertium comparationis* can be translated into stable units that can be observed in research objects and measured against a meaningful scale.
- Research objects possess observable properties that are independent of the observing apparatus or the dependence is at least controlled by the observing apparatus alone.
- Research objects must be sufficiently similar so that (1) a *tertium comparationis* can be identified and (2) the analysis can focus on this *tertium comparationis* while holding 'everything else' constant, thus removing it from the analysis.

It is worth noting that these assumptions largely developed outside of the social sciences, namely in the natural sciences, psychology and medicine. These are quantifying disciplines, and hence these assumptions – even though also applied in qualitative research – are more amenable to the parts of the social sciences that operate with quantifying designs and methods, for example, surveys, large-scale data sets and variables therein, or quantitative text analyses. This kind of scholastic comparison is closely aligned with late modern architectures of knowledge production beyond the academy, as observed in rising audit cultures (Strathern, 2000) including benchmarking, scoring and ranking in domains as different as education, health or banking (cf. Porter and Ross, 2003). Comparison has become a preferred operation for producing this type of accountability (Niewöhner and Scheffer, 2008) and the instruments to gather data for such operations are omnipresent in everyday life across the globe (Rottenburg et al., 2015).

Within the qualitative registers of the social sciences, the assumptions underpinning scholastic comparison have been challenged by the major epistemological shift toward forms of constructivism and an increasingly interactive and performative understanding of method (Law, 2004). This critique has been articulated primarily in three forms as emphasized by Jörg Niewöhner and Thomas Scheffer (2010, p. 6):

- Those employing micro-level methods and focused on understanding a particular local setting emphasize the importance and emic character of their local settings and resist attempts

to isolate the studied phenomenon in order to generalize across fields or contexts (Star and Griesemer, 1989; Strathern, 2006). The duration of participant observation and the diverse types of collected data go along with calls for emic and incomparable accounts of each field. These claims, together with narrative strategies, contribute centrally to ethnographic authority (Clifford, 1988).
- Those interested in theory-driven analysis point out that analytical concepts are strongly bound to their 'native' contexts, and thus necessarily fail to capture meaning adequately in comparative settings. These scholars emphasize the contextual nature of language games and the 'impossibility of translation' (Lyotard, 1988).
- Those concerned with power relations in asymmetrical relationships criticize comparison for reinforcing existing hegemonies, thus reproducing and stabilizing highly problematic patterns of dominance and dependency (Collier, 1997; Nguyen, 2005).

Most generally, perhaps, the mechanistic nature of quantitative scholastic comparison has been questioned in anthropology. How much empirical impression and surprise can be generated by a method that brings scholastic concepts to bear on a field within a very rigid research design? The worry here has not primarily been about the validity of the comparative method, but as Strathern (2002a, p. xv) puts it, about the risk of comparison producing knowledge *like itself* rather than knowledge that others can '*invent around*', knowledge which lends itself to be 'added to, qualified, introduced into other contexts or travel'.

While it has long been agreed that social anthropology has only one method, the comparative method, and that comparison is impossible (Evans-Pritchard, 1963), the discipline has nevertheless experimented with ethnographic forms of comparison. Ethnography has undergone two important shifts that are relevant to this: first, it has problematized the relationship of research phenomenon/field or figure/ground as one that is dynamic and can be manipulated to great analytical effect. Second, ethnography has focused on the production of comparability as an analytically generative process. In the process of establishing comparability – or the failure to do so – analytical concepts, degrees of involvement (or 'modest withness' – Sørensen, 2009), boundaries of and connections between research fields, and perspectives are sharpened (see Buscatto, Chapter 21, this volume). It is to these ethnographic forms of producing comparability that we now turn.

ETHNOGRAPHIC EMIC COMPARISONS

One of the core principles of anthropological research is its objective to produce emic descriptions. 'You do two or two-and-a-half years in Java in which all you do is live with the people, write down everything, and try to figure out what the hell is going on …' explained Clifford Geertz in an interview (Olson 1991, p. 248). To some extent this quote resonates with a naïve anthropological attitude of the late nineteenth and early twentieth century, but Geertz expresses the crucial emic orientation of ethnographic methods that also applies to more theoretically informed versions. The ethnographer may have a research question in mind and she may focus on specific phenomena or processes, but she goes to the field site with an unsettled idea of how it may be configured, and of how her question is eventually to be posed and answered. She sets herself the task of learning to formulate her question and describe phenomena or processes in accordance with the specific ways in which they exist in the field site. This includes the situatedness or context-boundedness of phenomena in emic approaches. Emic means that the field has a say in drawing the boundary around it, and that local people and local practices contribute toward defining the interpretive categories researchers use. Emic approaches produce analytical categories, which retain traces of their practices of production. This understanding of *emic* as opposed to *etic* accounts is widespread throughout the social sciences. Etic refers to distant observers' analytical categories (justified on theoretical grounds) applied to a field also defined externally to the field (on methodological grounds). Accordingly, etic comparison is another term for scholastic comparison.

Often, emic is taken to refer to the perspectives people in the field express and accordingly emic accounts are sometimes seen as 'microphone holders' for the people they study. Following from this, emic comparison would be primarily about listening to and describing how people compare. This is indeed one focus of emic comparison, but there is more to it than that. More than a focus on what people do when they compare, emic comparison is about how phenomena are made comparable. Moving the research focus from the people who compare to the phenomena compared is not only a matter of extending the realm of data beyond a rather ethnocentric view. Central to the study of how phenomena are turned into comparable phenomena is that it draws attention to the continuous efforts – of social and material character – that are invested in achieving a comparison.

Comparing as a practice belongs to the practices we study and research practices alike. As is shown in the examples of emic comparisons below, the phenomena researchers compare are often comparable not due to intrinsically comparable qualities, but because comparability is established through the process of defining and engaging with the phenomena studied. This performative understanding follows insights from *Science and Technology Studies*, well expressed by Karen Barad's definition of a phenomenon as 'the ontological inseparability of agentially intra-acting "components"' (2007, pp. 308–9). Barad especially refers to two kinds of components: those that are being categorized, and the categories and categorization themselves. Not only comparability, but the phenomenon that is studied itself comes into being in the way it exists through its categorization. Categories contribute to the creation of comparability and thus it is important to understand how different categorizations create comparability in different ways. Following these performative lines of thought, the difference between scholastic and emic comparison lies in the question of whether the categorization achieved through the research process and the phenomenon studied are conceptualized and treated as mutually configured (the emic perspective) or not (the etic and scholastic perspective). Emic comparison is not about minimizing the categorization efforts of the researcher or research process. It is about the ongoing mutual configuration of categorization and the phenomena thus categorized; about the intra-action in shaping the phenomenon (cf. Barad, 2007).

Many of the recent developments in ethnographic comparison are inspired by the work of Strathern. Her research is permeated by a fascination for the workings of comparison and context. In her work on audit cultures, Strathern (2000, 2002b) points to how university rankings, indicators and comparisons between scientific achievements do not simply measure and make differences in scientific output visible. Comparisons and rankings become targets for scientists to aim for. In other words, producing comparability between scientists makes 'ranked-science' a different phenomenon – a different 'science' – from 'non-ranked-science', changing the whole pattern and goal of science (cf. Holbraad and Pedersen, 2009). Both the phenomenon (e.g. ranked-science) and the category (e.g. the ranking) according to which it might be compared, emerge in the same move. Such an approach urges analysts to consider category work *over time* as a matter of process, rather than as a static matter of assignment. For comparison, this means that the categories – or *tertia comparationis* – in relation to which phenomena might be compared are not considered distant to, separate from or preceding the phenomenon they categorize. Comparison here is not about defining two found phenomena against a previously determined category, but about creating comparable phenomena.

The suggestion that category and phenomenon emerge together rather than separately means a shift in the direction of analysis. In scholastic comparison, the categories or *tertia comparationis* in terms of which phenomena are compared are usually seen as the *context* for the phenomenon one wants to compare. Scholastic comparison is putting phenomena into context (cf. Strathern, 1987), moving 'outward' from the phenomenon to the context in which it is said to be placed. In contrast to this, Strathernian comparison can be said to move 'inwards', looking for how phenomena come to be comparable through the studied practices and the research practices alike (cf. Morita, 2013; Niewöhner and Scheffer, 2010).

Strathern's studies of Melanesian societies point to how comparisons and relations are created through exchange, as well as pointing to the internal relations within Western anthropological thinking, which are generated by the anthropological study of Melanesian society. The aim of such comparison is not in itself the identification of similarities or differences across cultures. Scholars seek to avoid depicting cultures as well-delimited homogeneous fields, and point to how comparisons emerge in practice as results of particular relations, connections or boundaries, and how cultures are thereby generated as comparable domains. Emic comparison applies comparison as an epistemic tool to learn about how cultures relate to each other, or how they define themselves in relation to, or by delimiting themselves from, the other. If, as with emic explorations of comparison, we examine the relations to other practices evoked by phenomena, not only do we learn about the differences between these practices, but also about their mutual internal relations, and thus their mutual comparative configurations. Accordingly, we learn that cross-cultural differences and similarities are not to be understood with reference to cultures themselves, to cultural logics or traditions, but to ways in which they relate practically to one another. Culture and comparison are not that which explains, but that which is to be explained.

In the following section we introduce six comparative ethnographic studies, each of which offers inspiration for developing methods that allow comparison without compromising the emic research principle. They are all, to some extent, inspired by or related to Strathernian comparison. The six studies do not provide an exhaustive overview of emic comparison, however they are collected from recent studies to provide a broad insight into different ways of doing ethnographic emic comparison. The first two studies reconstruct emic comparison, in the sense that they seek to describe how people in the field compare and create comparable phenomena (cf. Bohnsack, 2007). The four latter studies also do this, and in addition, they engage in cross-cultural comparison.

Reconstructing Different Forms of Emic Comparison Practices

Ethnographic work draws our attention to the ways comparison is enacted in practices of daily life. The first study to which we turn suggests a method for data collection that is appropriate when a researcher has already identified, and wishes to study, the emic comparison of phenomena; in this case, the researcher identified that comparisons were being made between DNA samples and populations and sought to study how this was being done. The focus of the data collection is then to identify how comparison is done in these practices, and particularly how comparability is achieved between the phenomena that are compared (see also Amelang and Beck, 2010). The comparative ethnographer must refrain from taking the phenomena compared for granted, and during data collection must carefully observe how, in practice, they come to be shaped in a specific way that makes them comparable. Often, different modes of comparison, different comparabilities and different comparable phenomena unfold next to each other. Identifying different modes of emic comparison may be the result of the data analysis, and hence may largely take place after the data collection process has been completed. However, beginning the search for different ways in which phenomena are shaped in order to be comparable during the data collection process helps the ethnographer to develop a sensitivity for describing the practical achievement of comparability.

Such were the data collection methods of Amade M'charek (2008), who investigated the ways in which forensic profilers compare individual DNA markers to larger DNA samples to identify the specificity of the former. Through participant observation she looked for different ways that comparability was achieved in practices of DNA profiling when seeking to identify suspects in serious crimes. The profilers' fundamental task was to identify a difference between a single person's DNA and all other persons' DNA, based on which it would be possible to point to the single person as the perpetrator. Put differently, a single person's DNA had to be made comparable to a whole population's DNA. The core challenge for the profilers was how to achieve this comparability. How to configure the individual DNA and the population's DNA in a way that would make it possible to establish a robust difference by making comparisons? M'charek identified different forms of comparing, two of which we will explain here.

The first form of comparing profiling practice M'charek describes is 'conventional DNA profiling', in which a DNA sample taken from the scene of a crime is compared to a sample taken from a suspect in order to identify that suspect as the perpetrator. Yet, it is not enough to compare the two samples, since many people carry the same DNA markers, and hence the DNA sample from the crime scene may correspond to the DNA sample of the suspect while also corresponding to DNA samples of many other people. Accordingly, achieving comparability like this is not useful for the profilers. In order to determine the guilt or innocence of a suspect, the two DNA samples must be compared to a reference population. In other words, profilers achieve the relevant comparability by defining the reference population in a way that makes it possible to exclude from that reference population one individual as the only person likely to display particular markers. In this form of comparison the population functions as what M'charek calls a 'technology of exclusion', something from which individuals may be excluded, thereby enabling comparability to be made and the difference between guilty and innocent to be managed.

A second form of profiling practice is applied when there is no suspect. The profilers' task is then to generate a profile as a basis for the police to search for a perpetrator. In this case the DNA sample from the crime scene is examined for markers that might indicate some visible characteristics of the suspect that will enable the police to identify that person, for example, a particular hair color or racial profile. By defining the population as consisting of colored-haired people, people of race, etc., the DNA markers make individuals comparable to this kind of population. M'charek argues that population here is figured as a 'technology of inclusion', as comparability is achieved through the mechanism of including a suspect into one of these populations, for example a population of red-haired persons. Similarly to the first profiling practice, this comparability works to manage significant differences: between DNA samples found at crime scenes and human beings with whom they may match up, and between individuals who are guilty of serious crimes and those who are innocent of them.

M'charek's study is an example of how we might investigate emically the efforts involved in creating comparability, rather than applying an etic comparison to what is found in the field. It presupposes that practices of comparison (DNA profiling) have been identified prior to the data collection process, but it leaves it to the empirical investigation to find out how the phenomena of interest are shaped in order to achieve comparability. M'charek found that comparability emerged in practices of comparison, and at the same time populations emerged as 'technologies of exclusion' and 'technologies of inclusion' respectively, phenomena that did not exist prior to the forensic practices of comparison.

Emerging Comparison

In the study presented in this section, the practices to compare were discovered during the course of the ethnographic study. The research started out with a design for data collection that did not involve comparison, but turned into a comparative study after the ethnographer realized that the phenomenon she studied was genuinely generated through comparison to make sense of their practices. The researcher turned the research into a comparative study in order to understand the phenomenon in question as it came into being as comparable. An important point for emic research to be learnt from this is that if it turns out during the course of the study that the research collection method applied resists retaining categorizations and traces of the practices of production of the phenomena studied, it is necessary to modify the design for data collection according to this insight. Refraining from such a redesign compromises the validity of the study. Thus, it is not to be considered a failure that the 'right' data collection design was not set up from the beginning. On the contrary, the need to change the design is an empirical discovery that most often reveals important insights about the phenomenon studied. For any research seeking to produce emic descriptions, it is important to be ready and able to follow the practical logics of how the field makes itself knowable, including making changes to data collection, where this is possible (administrative and/or ethics procedures at universities, and requirements attached to funding, may at times preclude such changes).

In her school ethnography, Estrid Sørensen (2009) was interested in how school children interacted in virtual worlds (see also Lindgren, Chapter 28, this volume). Together with teachers of a Danish fourth grade class she studied how the students built virtual settlements online and together with their Swedish peers. The virtual world was repeatedly compared to classroom practices. The virtual world seemed to work – and sometimes failed to work – in specific ways in this context due to the relationships it had to classroom practices. Together with its comparability the virtual world achieved a specific character as in diverse ways similar to and different from classroom practices. Originally the aim of the research project had been to study online interaction, yet this focus turned out not to allow the researcher to retain the traces in her study of how the virtual world was produced in the school context. Accordingly, Sørensen changed her study from being about the interactions in and around the virtual worlds to being a comparison between practices in the classroom and in the virtual world. The focus of the study thus came to be on how knowledge was produced differently through these different socio-material practices, and she learnt that the uneasiness she observed among students and teachers in the virtual world was based on its interference with the epistemic practices they were used to in the classroom. Knowledge production and technology were the *tertia comparationis* that established the virtual world as comparable to the classroom, that defined what it came to be in the school practice and that related the two places.

Sørensen's study is an example of the productivity of letting emic comparison and the search for comparability influence the data collection design. Discovering the comparability through which the phenomenon studied was produced also provided insight into the kinds of differences with which people were struggling.

CROSS-CULTURAL COMPARISONS

The remaining four comparative studies that we discuss in this chapter are all cross-cultural comparisons. As discussed above, comparison across cultures is particularly criticized in the social sciences and anthropology for its tendency to homogenize cultures and configure cultures through differences rather than through their mutual relations. The following four studies manage in different ways to avoid these potential problems of cross-cultural comparison. They all avoid starting out by defining different cultures and then describing one in light of the other, as is usually done in cross-cultural comparisons. They find ways to attend to cultural encounters, hybrid practices, objects and places through which cultures meet in emic practices. In all of them, the way comparison is done in the field site studied plays a crucial role for how data are collected.

Cross-Cultural Comparison: Encounter of Differences

In the first cross-cultural study we discuss, comparison is not the aim of the study. Rather, a comparative design is applied to make visible specificities of both of the compared practices. Because the relational specificities of phenomena emerge together with its comparability when confronted with other phenomena, this method is helpful for studying the relational order of practices, which can otherwise be difficult to observe, because they are taken as a matter of course. The same principle is applied in ethnomethodological breaching experiments (e.g. Garfinkel, 1967) in which researchers, by acting in unexpected ways, provoke people to perform differences between the ordinary and the deviant.

In the study by Salla Sariola and Bob Simpson (Sariola and Simpson, 2011; Simpson and Sariola, 2012) discussed here, comparison acts as a sort of lens, sensitizing the researchers to Sri Lankan doctors' everyday practices. Similar to M'charek (2008), Sariola and Simpson (2011) took a point of departure in a comparison that they had already identified. Yet rather than identifying different modes of comparing, they studied the specificities of medical practices that became visible through comparing two sets of practices. The research applied participant observation and interviews with doctors and researchers involved in one of the first randomized clinical trials conducted in Sri Lanka, a country with little history of medical research. The comparative phenomena were thus Western medical standards inscribed into the guidelines and procedures of the clinical trials, and the practices of the doctors in Sri Lanka who were called on to carry out the trials. An important point of the emic comparison involved in this research design was that the researchers used a comparison already occurring in the field ('natural data', cf. Silverman, 2006; see also Potter and Shaw, Chapter 12, this volume) as a tool to gain insights into the order of ordinary Sri Lankan medical practices.

Sariola, who collected the data, observed how the instruction of the clinical trial protocols to seek the patients' informed consent and randomly assign them to one or another treatment came to be generated as different and thus comparable to the Sri Lankan doctors' ordinary medical practice. Having to assign patients randomly to different treatments interfered with the usual relationship between Sri Lankan doctors and their patients, in which it is the doctor's duty to act in the best interest of the patient. The doctors were concerned that the patients' confidence in their ability to choose the best treatment would be eroded by giving them the detailed knowledge required for informed consent, as the patient might think the doctor incompetent to make the decision himself. Sariola and Simpson (Sariola and Simpson, 2011; Simpson and Sariola, 2012), by attending to how medical practices came to be in specific ways, when produced as a comparison between Western and Sri Lankan medical practices that was embodied in the clinical trial situation, were able to highlight the strategies adopted by people in the field to manage the differences thus enacted, and the different figures of the 'human subject' mobilized in and coordinating each set of practices.

Cross-Cultural Comparison: Differences Dissolving

Similar to Sariola and Simpson, Helen Verran's (1999, 2001) cross-cultural study took its point of departure in the introduction of Western standards in a non-Western part of the world. More specifically, her ethnographic study concerned the implementation of Western mathematics and science, and particularly the Western number system, in Nigerian schools in the 1970s. Verran attended carefully to the different practices of doing Western numbers and doing Yoruba numbers. The latter was the system widely used in the everyday practices of most Yoruba people at that time. The Yoruba number system differs most obviously from the base-10 Western system by being base-20. That the Western and Yoruba number systems were specific instances of the category 'numbers' and thus comparable, was already defined prior to Verran's study, not only by the researcher but also in the educational and political practices working to implement the Western number system in Nigerian schools.

However, during her research in Nigeria, Verran encountered practices that questioned this accepted division of Western and Yoruba number systems into two distinct systems, and hence, their comparability. Verran writes about a Yoruba math teacher, Mr Ojo, who had been taught the importance of teaching students the Western understanding of length as a continued extension, which could be measured using a ruler or tape measure. However, Mr Ojo modified this method. He gave each student a card of 10 centimeters and a string, asked them to measure the length of their body parts with the string, and by folding the string around the card find out how many times the length of the body part could be wound around the card. As she witnessed this, Verran was first shocked. Mr Ojo's card-and-string technology conveyed an understanding of length as dependent upon multiplication, which compromises the Western understanding of length as an extension (Verran, 1999). While the idea of length as a multiplication implied by the card-and-string method is integral to the Yoruba metric system, the method also made use of Western metrics, in terms of the scale applied.

Based on this observation Verran (1999, 2001) concluded that the categorization of the Western and the Yoruba number systems as separate, discrete and comparable entities does not hold in all practices. When she described how Mr Ojo very successfully merged the (only apparently) two systems into one operation, the number systems were not separable and thus not comparable. Apart from being an important finding about the practice of quantification, the finding questions the foundation for comparing what the educational reform introducing the Western number system had taken for granted as two different number systems, and thus for understanding Western and Yoruba cultures as homogeneous and distinct. Western and Yoruba number systems were comparable in practices of educational politics, but in Mr Ojo's classroom they were not. Seeking to produce an emic account of quantification practices, Verran (2001) concluded that while quantification practices tend to be hybrid, comparison tends to simplify them and render them singular and homogeneous.

Verran's study makes it clear that phenomena are not in themselves comparable and that comparability is achieved in and through specific practices, in this case the practices of politicians and scholars. It follows, therefore, that differences and comparability are absent in some practices. When this is the case, phenomena that originally or elsewhere are enacted as naturally distinct and comparable – such as Western and Yoruba culture – cease to be so. Only by attending to how differences and comparability are achieved in practice is it possible to discover when these become absent.

Multi-Sited Cross-Cultural Comparison

Other cross-cultural ethnographic studies start out by defining cultures as distinct and comparable independently of any identified emic comparison. This was the case in Sørensen's (2010) study of video game regulation practices in Germany and Denmark. However, she only defined this distinction as a point of departure, and in order to orient the data collection. She left it to the empirical study to determine how the phenomenon video-game-regulation-practices across Danish and German borders could be meaningfully categorized. Put differently, she turned the *tertium comparationis* itself into her research question: According to what parameters can the comparability of video game regulation practices be relevantly generated in Germany and Denmark? The answer to this question should at the same time provide insights into the specificities of each of the two countries' video game regulation practices.

Instead of letting the *tertium comparationis* guide the data collection, Sørensen let different field sites do so. Postponing a formulation of a final research question, she started out doing a multi-sited ethnography (Marcus, 1998). She identified the core sites in which video game regulation practices would be visible to her as a researcher: different institutions, conferences and documents. She visited and studied these in Denmark and in Germany, always seeking to answer the question, how video game regulation at this site could be made comparable to the practices of video game regulation at the other sites. This led to an understanding of the phenomenon video-game-regulation-practices as struggling to find ways of dealing with tensions between in principle supporting video game play while at the same time restricting it. The phenomenon also came to be described as investing great efforts in creating a friendly environment, that is, to gain acknowledgment from politicians and the general public for their activities. While the search for comparability revealed these characteristics in both countries it also defined video game regulation practices in the two countries as different in several ways. The study thereby defined general *tertia comparationis* that were relevant across all of the field sites, while at the same time letting the specificities of the regulation practices at each field site become visible. During the research process the study thus moved from being a multi-sited ethnography to being a multi-sited comparison.

Sørensen's study suggests a method for data collection that starts out by identifying field sites and then searching within these field-sites for ways to establish comparability between these sites. Contrary to the other studies discussed in this chapter, Sørensen did not seek to reconstruct the way in which participants themselves compared. Based on insight into the emic organization of practices, she herself pointed out their similarities and differences, thus combining emic and scholastic approaches.

Cross-Cultural Comparison Through Objects

The last study we present in this chapter suggests yet a different route for studying comparability. Atsuro Morita's ethnographic comparison very explicitly follows Strathern's ideas of comparison as a matter of recovering internal connections (Strathern, 2004). While Strathern's own studies are rather 'complex and sometimes perplexing' (Morita, 2013, p. 219), Morita proposes a rather simple model for how to conduct cross-cultural comparison whose focus is on internal connections. He does so by drawing attention to objects. Through the observation of objects it is possible to determine how differences and comparability are achieved.

In his studies among Thai engineers Morita (2013) followed the introduction of a rotary cultivator to regional farmers. After using the cultivator for a short time, farmers approached the engineers with the complaint that the plow frequently stopped working when weeds would twine around the rotary blades. Some engineers pointed to the Japanese fabrication of the cultivator as a relevant factor. Thai weeds are taller and stronger than Japanese ones, they emphasized. The narrow blades of the rotary cultivator might be able to cultivate Japanese paddy fields but they could not cut the stronger weeds one finds in the tropical environment of Thailand. They talked about the differences in temperature, soil and vegetation between Thai and Japanese farmlands. 'The mechanics' *comparative* knowledge is formed through an exploration of relations embodied in the machines they manipulate' (2013, p. 228, emphasis in original) Morita emphasizes. Or put differently: the comparability between Japanese and Thai environments arose through the difficulties with the cultivator. It was through the cultivator that the engineers came to categorize both Thai and Japanese weeds, and the working practices of Japanese and Thai farmers, as different, along with more fundamentally categorizing Japan and Thailand as different cultures. These categorizations and comparisons between Japan and Thailand were folded into their workings with the cultivator, Morita points out.

In this study Morita discovers a form of comparing in which the phenomena compared – Japan and Thailand – only emerged as comparable out of the practices around the cultivator. Morita points to the specificities of cultures as being evoked through practices in which the identification and emphasis on differences help in solving tasks at hand – in this case the modification of the rotary cultivator. As well as difference and comparability, the categories of Japan and Thailand as distinct but connected entities, and their cross-cultural relations, were created through cultivator practices. Objects travel across cultures and when they are integrated into a new practice they often generate comparable phenomena and cultural relations between the places through which they travel.

Morita's study is an example of how comparability can be identified by attending, in data collection, to objects and the relations they create between phenomena, which in the same process are shaped as different in specific ways.

DATA COLLECTION

A key characteristic of ethnographic methods, and particularly of performative methods such as those presented in this chapter, is that data collection is not clearly distinct from the formulation of the research question and data analysis (see Buscatto, Chapter 21, this volume). From the nexus of theory and empirical material that is typical of the ethnographic process (Knecht, 2012) arises a constant interaction between the construction of field, research question, analytical categories and empirical material. We saw this most clearly in Sørensen's (first) and Verran's studies. These researchers started data collection based on a non-comparative and a comparative research question respectively, but changed these after gaining insights into the categorizations applied in the practices they studied. Sørensen learnt that the phenomenon she studied – virtual environments – was emically defined through comparison, while Verran learnt that the categories she applied for comparison – Western and African – did not exist as such in the practices she studied. While Sørensen changed her research design (see Gobo, Chapter 5, this volume) following this insight, Verran applied this to analyze her data differently than she had originally intended.

From this follows the most general principle for data collection in emic comparison: researchers must continuously pay attention to how phenomena become comparable through the practices studied, how comparability is achieved through the research practice itself – and through reference to theory – and how these processes interrelate. Based on this, the researcher must decide whether changes should be made to the questions posed, the methods for research collection or the analysis of data. More specifically, the researcher has to attend to how the phenomena compared throughout these processes come to be categorized in order to be comparable, how the *tertium comparationis* comes to be established, and how participants and researchers alike engage with difference. Even though most of the studies above – and in anthropology in general – make use of participant observation (see Wästerfors, Chapter 20, this volume) and interviews (see Roulston and Choi, Chapter 15, this volume) to collect data, emic comparisons are not restricted to these methods. Rather, in line with a fundamental principle of ethnographic analysis, a multitude of different data are collected and co-produced with the field, using a wide set of methods, including quantitative or mapping approaches (see also Hesse-Biber, Chapter 35, this volume and Morse et al., Chapter 36, this volume).

A number of further observations can be made which point toward how best to employ emic comparison in data collection. All six studies attend to delimited situated practices: professional practices (M'charek, Morita, Sariola, Sørensen and Verran) and educational practices (Sørensen). Attending to delimited situated practices allows researchers to generate rich contextual data, in contrast to collecting data through methods such as surveys or laboratory experiments, that are more useful for isolating objects from their situated practices. Through M'charek's studies we learnt how attending to comparisons made by research participants can help to explain the phenomenon studied, as well as the analytic work done by participants.

The studies of Morita, Sariola and Verran show how following standards or new technologies as they are implemented in practice can be useful in cross-cultural emic comparisons, as they often challenge routines and require modifications to practices to align with those practices inscribed (Akrich, 1992) into the standards or technologies. Sørensen showed how focusing on different sites allows cross-cultural comparability to emerge through the researchers' movement between these.

Hence, comparing unsettles analytical categories and it unsettles the relationship between analysis and data collection. Grounded theory approaches stress the ongoing nature of data collection and its intermingling with the production of analytical categories and theory (Glaser and Strauss, 1999). Emic comparison extends this claim into the research design itself. It grants the 'native' forms of comparison in the field a greater role in shaping comparative processes – or making them fail. And it urges the researcher not only to think about the multiple fields within which data is embedded, but about how data and field are configured together through the practices of comparing.

CONCLUSION

Comparison has always been central to research in the social sciences, guiding research design, data collection and analysis. In this chapter, we have made a distinction between scholastic comparison, which relies on categories whose definition and/or importance have been established external to the field and prior to data collection, and emic comparison, where comparing and categorizing are 'native' to the field and developed throughout the research process. The social sciences have traditionally relied on scholastic comparison. Common *tertia comparationis* in the social sciences include age, gender, ethnicity or informants' perspectives. Such scholastic comparison relies on a number of assumptions, including that it is meaningful to define a *tertium comparationis* prior to the act of comparing, and prior to encountering the empirical material; that research objects possess observable properties that are independent of the observing apparatus or the dependence is at least controlled by the observing apparatus alone; and that research objects must be similar enough such that a *tertium comparationis* may be identified, and that the analysis may focus solely on this dimension while controlling for any other potentially confounding factors. Such assumptions, and scholarly comparison itself, are drawn from quantitative disciplines such as those in the natural sciences, and they have been heavily criticized by social scientists who take a qualitative approach.

Anthropologists have been particularly strong in their critique of scholastic comparison, as an approach that does not sit well with anthropology's ethnographic practice of staying in a field site for extended periods and seeking to understand what is happening there, on its inhabitants' own terms. Instead, anthropologists have developed forms of ethnographic comparison, in which there is a focus on the comparisons and categories used by those 'native' to the field site, on how people go about making comparisons, and how they achieve comparability in the phenomena that they seek to compare. In this chapter we have gone one step further and described 'emic comparison' as an approach in which the focus is on how comparability and comparable phenomena are co-produced in intra-action between comparing and the compared.

The six studies described in this chapter show, in different ways, how scholars have conducted emic comparison by attending to the situated processes through which comparability is achieved, and differences are handled, in the studied practices. They do this by focusing on the ways that phenomena are configured as comparable. Since the ethnographic research practices – through their specific attention to objects, sites, standards, technologies or other – in each of the studies contributed to configuring the phenomena in question as comparable, the focus on the compared phenomena also implied accounts of how the ethnographic research practices were involved in shaping the comparisons.

Revisiting the five assumptions underlying scholastic comparison – listed above – which emic comparison tends to challenge, we can now reformulate these assumptions to point to the central principles of emic comparison:

- The research phenomena compared are always configured and reconfigured together with the practices in and through which they are situated, including research practices. The term 'phenomenon' indicates this dependence of categorized and categorization.
- A *tertium comparationis* can be meaningfully achieved through a process of interaction between the field studied and the observing apparatus.
- The *tertium comparationis* can be translated into theoretical concepts that are dependent on, yet extensions of, the field studied.
- The phenomena compared achieve their observable properties in cooperation with the observing apparatus and in intra-action with the studied field, and can accordingly not be controlled by the observing apparatus alone.
- A *tertium comparationis* can be identified by describing how comparable phenomena relate in practice through their situated comparison. Comparability is achieved rather than being a pre-existing found object. Holding everything else constant would neglect the field's agency and compromise emic principles.

This chapter has presented examples of recent research, which mobilizes forms of emic comparison in order to demonstrate the opportunities and the role that such comparison might play in data collection. In doing so, we hope that this acts as a prompt to researchers to think about the forms of comparison that are mobilized in their research, before, during and after data collection, and by the people whose practices we study as well as in our own practices. Following in the footsteps of Strathern, we suggest the value in a 'hesitation', postponing the moment in which the relevant dimensions for comparison are settled on and comparisons are made.

FURTHER READING

Deville, Joe, Guggenheim, Michael and Hrdličková, Zuzana (eds) (2016) *Practicing Comparison: Logics, Relations, Collaborations*. Manchester: Mattering Press.

Fox, Richard G., and Gingrich, André (eds) (2002) *Anthropology, by Comparison*. London: Routledge.

Scheffer, Thomas, and Niewöhner, Jörg (eds) (2010) *Thick Comparison: Reviving the Ethnographic Aspiration*. Leiden: Brill.

REFERENCES

Akrich, Madeline (1992) 'The de-scription of technical objects', in Wiebe E. Bijker and John Law (eds), *Shaping Technology/Building Society: Studies in Sociotechnical Change*. Cambridge, MA: The MIT Press, pp. 205–24.

Amelang, Katrin, and Beck, Stefan (2010) 'Comparison in the wild and more disciplines' usages of an epistemic practice', in Thomas Scheffer and Jörg Niewöhner (eds), *Thick Comparison. Reviving the Ethnographic Aspiration*. Amsterdam: Brill, pp. 155–80.

Barad, Karen (2007) *Meeting the Universe Halfway: Quantum Physics and the Entanglement of Matter and Meaning*. Durham, NC: Duke University Press.

Bohnsack, Ralf (2007) *Rekonstruktive Sozialforschung: Einführung in qualitative Methoden*. Opladen/Framington Hills: Barbara Budrich.

Clifford, James (1988) *The Predicament of Culture: Twentieth-Century Ethnography, Literature, and Art*. Cambridge, MA: Harvard University Press, pp. 21–54.

Clifford, James, and Marcus, George (eds) (1986) *Writing Culture: The Poetics and Politics of Ethnography: A School of American Research Advanced Seminar*. Berkeley, CA: University of California Press.

Collier, Jane F. (1997) 'The waxing and waning of "subfields" in North American sociocultural anthropology', in Akhil Gupta and James Ferguson (eds), *Anthropological Locations: Boundaries and Grounds of a Field Science*. Berkeley, CA: University of California Press, pp. 117–30.

Durkheim, Emile, and Lukes, Steven (1982) *Rules of Sociological Method*. New York: Free Press.

Evans-Pritchard, Edward E. (1963) *The Comparative Method in Social Anthropology*. London: UL Athlone Press.

Garfinkel, Harold (1967) *Studies in Ethnomethodology*. Eaglewood Cliffs, NJ: Prentice-Hall.

Glaser, Barney G., and Strauss, Anselm L. (1999) *The Discovery of Grounded Theory: Strategies for Qualitative Research*. Piscataway, NJ: Transaction Publishers.

Hacking, I. (2007) 'Kinds of people: Moving targets', *Proceedings of the British Academy*, 151: 285–318.

Holbraad, M., and Pedersen, M. A. (2009) 'Planet M: The intense abstraction of Marilyn Strathern', *Anthropological Theory*, 9(4): 371–94.

Jupp, Victor (2006) *The Sage Dictionary of Social Research Methods*. New York: Sage.

Knecht, Michi (2012) 'Ethnographische praxis im feld der wissenschafts-, medizin- und technikanthropologie', in Stefan Beck, Estrid Sørensen and Jörg Niewöhner (eds), *Science and Technology Studies: Eine Sozialanthropologische Einführung*. Bielefeld, transcript, pp. 245–74 (in German).

Law, John (2004) *After Method: Mess in Social Science Research*. Abingdon: Routledge.

Lévi-Strauss, Claude (1963) *Structural Anthropology*. New York: Basic Books.

Lyotard, Jean-François (1988) *Le différend*. Minneapolis: University of Minnesota Press.

Marcus, G. E. (1995) 'Ethnography in/of the world system: The emergence of multi-sited ethnography', *Annual Review of Anthropology*, 24: 95–117.

Marcus, George E. (1998) *Ethnography Through Thick and Thin*. Princeton, NJ: Princeton University Press.

Matthes, Joachim (1992) 'The operation called "vergleichen"', in Joachim Matthes (ed.), *Zwischen den Kulturen*. Göttingen: Otto Schwartz, pp. 75–102.

M'charek, A. (2008) 'Contrasts and comparisons: Three practices of forensic investigation', *Comparative Sociology*, 7(3): 387–412.

Morita, A. (2013) 'The ethnographic machine: Experimenting with context and comparison in Strathernian ethnography', *Science, Technology & Human Values*, 39(2): 214–35.

Nguyen, Vinh-Kim (2005) 'Antiretroviral globalism, biopolitics, and therapeutic citizenship', in Aihwa Ong and Stephen J. Collier (eds), *Global Assemblages: Technology, Politics, and Ethics as Anthropological Problems*. Malden/Oxford: Blackwell, pp. 124–44.

Niewöhner, Jörg, and Scheffer, Thomas (2008) 'Introduction: Thick comparison', *Comparative Sociology*, 7(3): 273–85.

Niewöhner, Jörg, and Scheffer, Thomas (2010) 'Introduction. Thickening comparison: On the multiple facets of comparability', in Thomas Scheffer and Jörg Niewöhner (eds), *Thick Comparison: Reviving the Ethnographic Aspiration*. Leiden: Brill, pp. 1–16.

Olson, G. A. (1991) 'The social scientist as author: Clifford Geertz on ethnography and social construction', *Journal of Advanced Composition*, 11(2): 245–68.

Porter, Theodore M., and Ross, Dorothy (2003) *The Cambridge History of Science: Volume 7: The Modern Social Sciences*. Cambridge: Cambridge University Press.

Rottenburg, Richard, Merry, Sally E., Park, Sung-Joon, and Mugler, Johanna (eds) (2015) *The World of Indicators: The Making of Governmental Knowledge Through Quantification*. Cambridge: Cambridge University Press.

Said, Edward W. (1979) *Orientalism*. New York: Vintage Books.

Sariola, S., and Simpson, B. (2011) 'Theorising the "human subject" in biomedical research: International clinical trials and bioethics discourses in contemporary Sri Lanka', *Social Science & Medicine*, 73(4): 515–21.

Silverman, David (2006) *Interpreting Qualitative Data: Methods for Analysing Talk, Text and Interaction*. London: Sage.

Simpson, B., and Sariola, S. (2012) 'Blinding authority: Randomized clinical trials and the production of global scientific knowledge in contemporary Sri Lanka', *Science, Technology & Human Values*, 37(5): 555–75.

Sjoberg, Gideon (1955) 'The comparative method in the social sciences', *Philosophy of Science*, 22(2): 106–17.

Somekh, Bridget, and Lewin, Cathy (2004) *Research Methods in the Social Sciences*. London/Thousand Oaks: Sage.

Sørensen, E. (2008) 'Multi-sited comparison of "doing regulation"', *Comparative Sociology*, 7(3): 311–37.

Sørensen, Estrid (2009) *The Materiality of Learning: Technology and Knowledge in Educational Practice*. Cambridge, MA: Cambridge University Press.

Sørensen, Estrid (2010) 'Producing multi-sited comparability', in Thomas Scheffer and Jörg Niewöhner (eds), *Thick Comparisons: Reviving an Ethnographic Aspiration*. Leiden: Brill, pp. 43–78.

Star, S. L., and Griesemer, J. R. (1989) 'Institutional ecology, "translations" and boundary objects: Amateurs and professionals in Berkeley's Museum of Vertebrate Zoology, 1907–1939', *Social Studies of Science*, 19(4): 387–420.

Strathern, M. (1987) 'Out of context: The persuasive fictions of anthropology', *Current Anthropology*, 28(3): 251–81.

Strathern, Marilyn (1992) 'Parts and wholes: Refiguring relationships in a postplural world', in Adam Kuper (ed.) *Conceptualizing Society*. London/New York: Routledge, pp. 75–106.

Strathern, Marilyn (ed.) (2000) *Audit Cultures: Anthropological Studies in Accountability, Ethics and the Academy*. London/New York: Routledge.

Strathern, Marilyn (2002a) 'Not giving the game away', in André Gingrich and Richard G. Fox (eds), *Anthropology, by Comparison*. London: Routledge, pp. xiii–xvii.

Strathern, Marilyn (2002b) 'Abstraction and decontextualization: An anthropological comment', in Steve Woolgar (ed.), *Virtual Society? Technology, Hyperbole, Reality*. Oxford: Oxford University Press, pp. 302–14.

Strathern, Marilyn (2004) *Partial Connections*. Walnut Creek, CA: AltaMira Press.

Strathern, M. (2006) 'Knowledge on its travels: Dispersal and divergence in the makeup of communities', *Interdisciplinary Science Reviews*, 31(2): 149–62.

Strathern, Marilyn (2011) 'Binary license', *Common Knowledge*, 17(1): 87–103.

Verran, Helen (1999) 'Staying true to the laughter in Nigerian classrooms', in John Law and Annemarie Mol (eds), *Actor Network Theory and After*. Oxford: Blackwell Publishing, pp. 136–55.

Verran, Helen (2001) *Science and an African Logic*. Chicago: University of Chicago Press.

Data Collection in Secondary Analysis

Louise Corti

INTRODUCTION

This chapter examines prerequisites for enabling reuse or secondary analysis of qualitative data (informally known as SAQD) that has not been collected by the analyst. The first part of the chapter provides an overview of what people are doing with existing data, from new analysis to revisiting one's own data, and what challenges face them in their quest. The second part poses questions that a secondary analyst can ask of data, such as, are the data to hand a good fit for the proposed project? The role of detective comes to mind, appraising the materials and examining provenance to satisfy oneself that there is adequate context surrounding the data and that the limitations are understood and fully appreciated. In turn any characteristics or deficits highlighted can be set out as assumptions that help frame the secondary research tasks to be pursued. A discussion on the role that research context plays in secondary analysis ensues, highlighting practical examples of what materials can help recreate context, that both define and support the original data collection.

The third part looks at how those collecting primary data can best assemble, document and publish research data in anticipation of future access. Ethical and legal issues surrounding the status of participants' identities need to be part of this decision-making. A real example of how a challenging project has been prepared and shared for future secondary analysis is discussed. Finally the chapter briefly addresses new forms of publishing research that help both give 'voice' to data and greater transparency to research findings through data as evidence.

SECONDARY ANALYSIS – WHAT CAN BE DONE AND HOW?

Let us first consider the kinds of things people do with other people's qualitative data. It is worth pointing out that there are some notable distinctions between the aims of sociologists and historians and in their relationship with secondary data as sources for analysis. Baethge-Kinsky (2016) observes that

> historians are concerned with observing the present by looking at the past; their approach is thus defined by seeking to describe historical development. They prefer concrete observations such as: who were the actors; where did an event take place? Sociologists, on the other hand, tend to focus on aiming to predict the future or at least, make the future better through improving policy or social structure. Their focus might be on the roles of institutions, types of actors, and they might attempt to classify and compare groups of individuals or organisations by their characteristics and behaviour.

Further, the social scientist tends to have short-term needs for data, unless they are longitudinal in design. Once the data collector is finished with their wares they usually discard them to move on to new pursuits. However, for the historian, the value of data grows over time, so that in the distant future, secondary analysis becomes historical research.

Building on Corti and Thompson's original classification of types of reuse of qualitative data (and the counter arguments raised by researchers), the most popular kinds of reuses are summarised below (Corti and Thompson, 2004).

Providing Background Description and Historical Context

The opportunities for using data descriptively are extensive. Attitudes and behaviour of individuals, groups, organisations or societies can be gleaned from the contemporary or historical periods. Older social surveys undertaken in the 1960s, with handwritten open-ended questions and annotation notes added to the paper questionnaires, can illuminate survey methods of the period, for example Peter Townsend's (2014) archived national Survey of Poverty in the UK.

Towards the more qualitative end, fieldwork observation notes and in-depth interviews can complement more official sources from information reported by public bodies and the press. A UK example of this is the role of archived field notes and photographs that were compiled by Stanley Cohen for his work on mods and rockers gatherings in the 1960s, published as *Folk Devils and Moral Panics*, a core text for criminology teaching (Cohen, 1987). The press reports were damning, demonising and stigmatising the youth of the time as criminals with unruly behaviour. Cohen did not observe the level of criminality in his detailed observations, and coined the concept of 'moral panic' to describe escalation of that particular situation by official sources, a term we are all familiar with in modern sociology literature. Between the press reports and the sociologist's field notes the researcher can now build up a more balanced view of the history of youth culture during that time.

Researchers undertaking their own data collection can also make use of such existing resources that extend, enhance and complement their own data collection efforts.

Comparative Research, Restudy or Follow-Up

Existing data from a particular time or place or phenomenon studied can be used to compare with other sources to enhance a sample or to extend a study beyond its limitations, for example a particular geography or population. Having the methods archived can enable a restudy to be undertaken. Well-known early classic restudies undertaken by social observers include Rowntree's (1901) repeated surveys of poverty in the city of York in the UK. In the US, Glen Elder's archived study on *Children of the Great Depression* (1974) provides a qualitative longitudinal study, based on interviews and participant observation of

California cohorts interviewed since the 1920s. Follow-up studies of original participants require contact details of participants to be available, sometimes only available from the primary investigator.

Secondary Analysis

We use the term 'secondary analysis' here to define reuse of existing data from a different or new perspective, or to ask new questions of older data. A topic might be investigated that was not of interest to the original investigator, or data can be reinterpreted from a more contemporary perspective. Equally, secondary analysis can help make extended use of data collected on sensitive topics or collected from hard-to-reach populations; data that was initially difficult to negotiate access to and thus representing unique value (Fielding and Fielding, 2000).

Typically, the more detailed the original research material, the more potential there is for further exploitation. Two examples of rich data that have attracted multiple reuses by both scholars and students for new purposes are: the archived UK Edwardians life history interview study, comprising some 450 in-depth interviews (Thompson, 2009); and the Finnish collection of 850 autobiographical texts from a writing competition, *Everyday Experiences of Poverty, Self-Administered Writings* (Larivaar et al., 2011).

Replication or Validation of Published Work

Secondary analysis does not usually involve attempts to validate or undermine researchers' previous analyses. Enabling critical or supporting interpretations to be applied to the same data set can be valuable, for example, accumulating and contrasting researcher's individually applied coding schemes.

Seeking to replicate, verify or challenge published findings has become a more popular pursuit in the social sciences following instances of fraudulent research and bias in publishing results with positive outcomes. True scientific replication is troublesome for social science, as studies tend not to have equal social phenomena, and so identical research assumptions and conditions are unlikely to be fully met. Lawrence points out that the methods used to investigate and analyse the perceptions of the social class of the 'affluent' working classes in the late 1960s and 1970s in the UK may be contaminated by preconceptions of the fieldworkers (young university lecturers), of the time who held strong a priori ideas about 'bourgeois' aspirations, which would not be held nowadays (Lawrence, 2013). Coming at described fieldwork methods and data with an objective stance or a new angle of vision, can help to overcome the 'insight and oversight' from which an original investigator may suffer when fully immersed in their own study (Silva, 2007).

As we will see, well-documented data sets can help the new investigator reconstruct evidence by retracing original analytic steps used by the primary researcher, and assumptions made.

Research Design and Methodological Advancement

Consulting descriptions of the research design (see Gobo, Chapter 5, this volume), methods and instruments used in an original investigation can help in the design of a new study or the development of a research tool. Examples include: sampling methods, (see Schreier, Chapter 6, this volume), data collection and fieldwork strategies, and interview (see Roulston and Choi, Chapter 15, this volume), or observation (see Wästerfors, Chapter 20, this volume), guides. Research papers tend to have short and succinct methods sections, which may not reflect the complexity of the actual fieldwork that took place. Researchers' own fieldwork diaries or analytic notes can offer additional insight into the history and development of the research. A good example is Annette Lawson's fieldwork guide for her 1988 study of adultery, a comprehensive data collection that has been archived (Lawson, 2004). The mixed method (see Hesse-Biber, Chapter 35, this volume and Morse et al., Chapter 36, this volume) study data comprises questionnaires, audio recordings, interview and focus group transcripts (see Morgan and Hoffman, Chapter 16, this volume), and documentation such as letters, newspaper clippings, correspondence (see Rapley and Rees, Chapter 24, this volume), and the researcher's field notes. She compiled a comprehensive 56-page guide to her methods, with the sampling method being a specific focus. Haaker and Morgan-Brett (2017) discuss the challenges inherent in her particular sampling method, from reliability and ethical perspectives (see Mertens, Chapter 3, this volume). Lawson had wanted to find people to speak on a topic that, in the 1980s, was not only sensitive, but also one that people would go to great lengths to conceal.

Teaching and Learning

The use of real-life data in teaching in the social sciences adds substantive interest and relevance to courses and dissertations. Students can gain an understanding of many fundamental aspects of the research process by tracing back what another researcher did, providing adequate evidence is available: why was the study carried out and what questions did it seek to answer? It further helps students to be critical of approaches and methods, especially where the investigator is now famous (or infamous!). The Stanley Cohen example outlined above provides an appealing example of using data in teaching; so much so that the UK Data Service (2013) compiled a structured teaching resource based on it for use in introductory courses on crime and deviance.

THE CHALLENGES OF USING OTHERS' QUALITATIVE DATA

Reuse of research data collected by another can be a complex undertaking, but once the methods and caveats are appreciated, the reuser can fruitfully embrace exploiting the data collation efforts of others! There are different and perhaps more challenging epistemological and practical problems for the user to consider when reusing qualitative data compared to quantitative data. It is in the UK sociology literature where the most critical debate has been heard on the role of research fit and context, and the argument is slowly beginning to spread to other countries. Relevant literature that examines some of the real and perceived problems of reusing data is highlighted as we proceed.

Unfamiliarity with the Secondary Analysis Methods

In fields such as history, epidemiology and econometrics, secondary analysis is taken for granted as a valid research method. However, this is still not the case in other social science disciplines, and is even still relatively new for qualitative approaches. Reusing others' data requires time to get fully acquainted with materials and it can be time-consuming to locate suitable data sources and to check the content, but like any data collection or analysis task, adequate time always needs to be factored in.

It is useful to look at the historian's modus operandi for their research practices. A key part of their analytical task is to evaluate the evidence, examine its provenance, and assess the veracity of the sources. They may undertake related investigation about the event, period and place (Gunn and Faire, 2011). These scholars must embrace the slow and rigorous methods of documentary analysis.

Historians' research practices can teach us how to confront primary sources that we did not create. Indeed, scholars are beginning to incorporate social historical methods into mainstream sociology, as seen in work by Crow and Edwards (2012). As more researchers undertake and publish on reusing qualitative data, so it is incorporated into methods training courses, thus making reuse a more acceptable and accessible practice.

Discovery of Data and Fit of Data to One's Own Research Questions

The secondary analyst is almost always limited in access to 'ideal' data sources that would provide all the information they would like. While thousands of data collections exist, only very few see the light of day again, publicised via indexed online catalogues, through publications or by word of mouth.

Some countries offer greater visibility for research data. The UK is very well resourced with some 900 or more published qualitative data collections to choose from, whereas in other European countries finding data is much harder; infrastructure funding has not supported dedicated and sustained data acquisition and preservation. Figure 11.1 gives a brief snapshot of the volume of qualitative collections available in some of the national social science data archives in Europe (Bishop and Kuula-Luumi, 2017). In the US there is very little qualitative data publicly available.

Even if archived data that looks potentially useful can be located and easily accessed, it may be that data will not meet your exact needs. This may be due to the nature of the participants, for example, wrong age range, geographic region or ethnic group; or if particular questions of interest were not included in the topic guide for an interview. To properly assess the fit to new research questions, data sources must be evaluated, as described later.

Once located, navigating significant volumes of data can be difficult and time-consuming. Take the large-scale oral history collection of interviews from the *Family Life and Work Experience Before 1918* (or *The Edwardians*) study, undertaken in the early 1970s (Thompson, 2009). The author, as part of her role with the UK's Qualidata, has been responsible for curating this material, comprising some 450 interview recordings and transcriptions, since the mid-1990s, so brings some first-hand experience of its reuse.

Amounting to some 50,000 pages of interview transcription, the primary analysis of data, which pre-dated computer-assisted coding and analysis by some years, presented a logistical challenge. Working with the original paper format, research staff were employed to code the transcripts by a set of predetermined high-level thematic codes, such as family, food and so on. Copies of the transcripts were physically cut up by the themed extracts and these placed into labelled box files. As it turns out these boxes

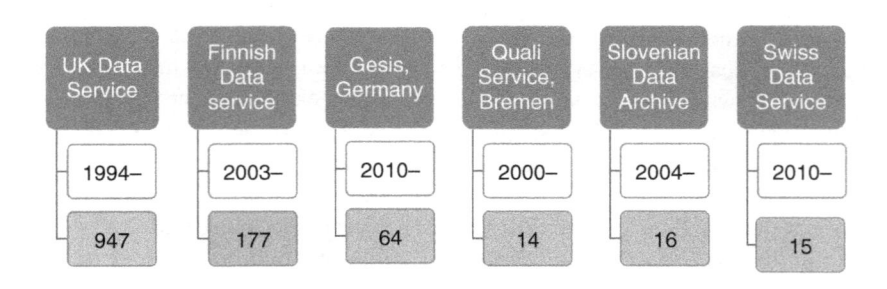

UK Data Service	Finnish Data service	Gesis, Germany	Quali Service, Bremen	Slovenian Data Archive	Swiss Data Service
1994–	2003–	2010–	2000–	2004–	2010–
947	177	64	14	16	15

Figure 11.1 European qualitative archives, date started collecting data and data volume

of themed extracts presented a gold mine for reusers, offering quick navigation and access to content that described the lives of working-class people in the Edwardian period. As a result, many users came to the Essex storeroom where they were housed to utilise the resource, resulting in many secondary publications.

Unsurprisingly, data presented digitally via user-friendly tools and interfaces, enables more efficient discovery and manipulations of data. In 2000, this collection was digitised and published via the web as a fully searchable open resource, in the UK Data Service's QualiBank (UK Data Service, 2014). Now the reusers game is upped, as they possess the power to search for key terms and explore the entirety of text. They can quickly locate relevant material, download the texts in bulk and upload these into a CAQDAS package of their choice. Audio extracts are also available to listen to, of benefit to those seeking to explore regional dialect and speech from the period.

Nothing Left to Analyse?

Many researchers invest heavily in a study and the resulting analysis and publications, but often quickly move on to the next project in the race to securing research funding. In some disciplines new fieldwork is almost viewed as *de rigueur*, like conducting new experiments, but we should also not forget the case of returning back to one's own data to reuse it.

Akerstrom et al. (2004) provide insight from their tale of revisiting their own data, where they applied new perspectives to the material. Akerstrom talks of her deep and satisfying reworking of a single interview that she had carried out 20 years previously, as a major narrative. Jacobbsen shows how she reused a whole set of materials to reconsider a position in the field. The authors point out the intimate and intricate relationship of data to analyst:

> If a researcher resembles a sculptor, this sculptor seems to be a peculiar one, using tools that are meshed with the material and materials that is meshed with the artist. (2004, p. 352)

Perhaps it is time to reconsider the status or value of 'that' older data of ours lurking in the bottom drawer of our locked filing cabinet (digital or otherwise).

'Enough' Contextual Information

Understanding the context of raw data can be troublesome and has created much debate. While there is always some ongoing, and usually healthy, disagreement on how to interpret 'data' from the field, Holstein and Gubrium feel that there is:

> no pressing need to decide, once and for all, the most appropriate framework for dealing with context ... (but that we) would benefit from viewing context as something that can be worked up, down, and across in the interest of comprehensive qualitative inquiry. (2004, p. 310)

Bearing this is mind when we approach data that we have not collated ourselves, we will certainly need to assemble some context. If there is no surviving documentation about the study and data, then this job is likely to be harder. Indeed, some critics of secondary analysis believe that the loss of original fieldwork experiences by a secondary analyst make interpretation of the raw data too difficult – while others claim that this privilege does not prevent reusers from drawing new interpretations from it – and see original supporting materials as an added bonus. The debates have helped to shed light on how researchers can best approach using existing data and the caveats that need to be considered when examining them (Hammersley, 2010; Irwin et al., 2012).

Returning to the disciplinary issue we highlighted earlier between the historian and the sociologist, an ethnographer may view loss of original context as a complete barrier to undertaking the reuse of anyone else's data. Yet the historian will likely happily roll up her sleeves and be grateful for any information that she can glean to help assess and augment any other data she has amassed. Consulting sometimes very old material, routinely they have to deal with a lack of immediate rich context for these information sources. Perhaps social scientists can learn from this approach.

What is of interest is recent evidence from users of the Finnish Data Service (FSD) as to how much context they say they require to press on with analysing third party data. FSD has fairly modest expectations for depositors of qualitative data with regards to extensive documentation of the primary project; hoping that this is an incentive to deposit data in a culture where data sharing is still relatively young (Bishop and Kuula, 2017). In practice, this means that while there is information available about fieldwork and data collection, there is often little detail about the primary project itself. This suffices for users who do not wish to replicate the original research but intend to use data to supplement their own data.

Selective Sampling in Secondary Analysis

When undertaking a social survey, sampling is a crucial part of research design to ensure representativeness of the universe under study, and so that generalisations can be made about behaviour, beliefs and attitudes and so on. In qualitative research, sampling is more difficult (see Schreier, Chapter 6, this volume). Emmell (2013) provides a good overview of sampling and case selection in qualitative research. While ideas drive choices in sampling, it is not the sample but the individual cases that are used to establish relationships between ideas and evidence. Thus it is the *cases* selected that are used to interpret and explain.

As choosing cases to drive conclusions and claims can be open to selection bias in primary research, the same goes for selection of cases in secondary analysis. There are challenges involved in sampling from very large quantities of qualitative data. Gillies and Edwards (2012) argue that a target data set sampled from secondary data must be pre-defined. They explain that, for a secondary analysis project they undertook:

> in drawing up our research plan, we specified that up to five 'accounts' would be taken from each classic study we selected as feasible sub-samples. (2012, p. 323)

Taking the Edwardians example discussed above, the secondary analysts who accessed the paper data were drawing their conclusions on extracts coded not by themselves but by others. The reanalyses suppose that the coders followed a consistent coding strategy. In a sense the reuser is now four steps away from the participant's original words in the research study (interview – transcription – coding – reanalysis), and this selective sampling of content and cases from extracts, likely has limitations.

Concerns about Ethical Reuse of Data

Worries about the status of informed consent or unintended use of personal information of the data can, justifiably, be seen as an obstacle to collating existing data for reuse (see Mertens, Chapter 3, this volume, and Tiidenberg, Chapter 30, this volume). It may seem that when data are shared there is a risk of eroding the trust initially established in the researcher–participant relationship. However, all research must conform to ethical and legal requirements especially with respect to data protection, and most available data have consented for further reuse or identifying information has been redacted, where necessary.

Most social scientists will strive to protect sources where this has been promised, whereas our historian will demand real names and places; anonymised data are a frustration for the historical researcher. Fortunately, time eradicates this problem and matured data sources do benefit from revealing as much information as possible. We will return to this matter in the final part of this chapter.

Summary

It is often enlightening to read other's experiences of reusing data, in the form of case studies or testimonies. Constructed resources for teaching are also helpful as they provide an already navigated journey through a data reuse scenario. The UK Data Service (2016a) offers case studies of reuse of qualitative data in research and teaching. Exemplars also come from established centres who themselves host archives of data. The Health Experiences Research Group at the University of Oxford in the UK provides examples of secondary analysis based on their 3,500+ interviews collection of personal experiences of illness and healthcare decision-making (Entwhistle et al., 2011).

GETTING STARTED WITH SECONDARY ANALYSIS: ASKING QUESTIONS OF THE DATA

Once potential data sources have been located and accessed, the next step is to embark on the role of detective seeking to investigate the nature and fit of the data. Review and assessment of provenance must be undertaken, thereby identifying any limitations or assumptions that will need to be borne in mind (and made explicit) for analysis. Where did it come from? How were data constructed? What was the relationship of the researcher to the participants? Are any of the key data missing? Is there an inventory or ledger? Issues like sample selection and the quality of transcription – or even whether these exist – are all critical in making decisions about the origins and processing of the original data. This process can be thought of as 'recontextualising' data, and it is useful to think about levels of context that can help us understand data.

While we discussed earlier the disagreement in the literature on the role of context in qualitative analysis, there is, nevertheless, often information available at various levels of context, which may be of practical use in assessing data (Bishop, 2006):

- Level of fieldwork interaction: interview transcripts with detailed annotation, such as indicating non-verbal cues.
- Level of the study: information about the fieldwork setting, interviewees and interviewers; detail about research planning and fieldwork implementation.
- Macro level: Information about the broader social, cultural or economic context within which the research takes place.

Thus, in addition to situational features, context can also include factors resulting from everyday interaction and interpretive processes.

Returning again to our disciplinary distinctions, the historian takes a huge interest in context, piecing together how what they observe in the data sources about the micro level relates to events at the macro level. Sociologists on the other hand rely less on historical context and focus more on comparing and contrasting the content of the materials to hand. The historian will take any relevant information they can find, whereas sociologists tend to want more context. The latter group may be fortunate enough to be able to interview the people who provided the original data. Approaches to evaluating data for its fit to a research question is thus partially driven by disciplinary needs.

In making a decision about the usefulness of a data source, there is no single test. A researcher must satisfy themselves that they can fully support their choice of source data as evidence. Table 11.1 sets out some questions to pose of secondary data, and suggests useful sources to look out for and consult as evidence. These sources may or may not be part of the collection, and may need to be gleaned from elsewhere.

As already noted, it is hard to find publications (as articles or chapters) that fully describe the method of a study in any detail, and often, in the short précis, the data collection appears as a linear, clinical, sanitised version of events, when often the pathway

Table 11.1 Key questions to ask of existing data and useful sources of evidence for appraisal

Assessment task	Questions to ask	Material source as evidence
Authenticity of the data	– Who carried out this study and for what reasons? – Was it motivated by any agenda e.g. political? – Who made it available? – What was the relationship of the investigator or researcher to those being studied?	– Documentation of project history, aims, objectives – Original research design material – Research proposal/funding application – Information on researchers and fieldwork approach – Substantive and methods outputs – Access via original investigator or archive – Resulting articles, presentations and outputs

Scope and nature of the data	– Is there an inventory or ledger?
	– How were the data collected and assembled?
	– How was the sampling carried out?
	– Are there any data missing?
	– Are there fieldwork protocols?
	– Is there a topic guide?
	– Are there transcriptions available for audio recordings?
	– Were data transcribed consistently, and what rules were used?
	– Are transcriptions in a language I can understand?
	– Are any secondary data sources used documented?
	– How were the data processed and validated?
	– Has any data been modified since collection?
		– Study-level information
		  ∘ Temporal coverage
		  ∘ Geographic coverage
		– Data-level information
		  ∘ Data list
		  ∘ Structure of data
		  ∘ Number of cases, files and relationships amongst items
		  ∘ Details of incomplete data
		  ∘ Information sheet
		  ∘ Consent procedures and consent form
		– Fieldwork and data collection protocols
		– Fieldwork documentation
		  ∘ Fieldworker recruitment
		  ∘ Sampling strategy and procedures/representation
		  ∘ Fieldwork location
		  ∘ Topic guide/questionnaires/observation grid
		  ∘ Scenarios & cues
		  ∘ Data collation/entry procedures and rules/templates
		  ∘ Interviewer instructions
		  ∘ Information on fieldworkers
		  ∘ Hardware and software used
		  ∘ Fieldnotes
		– Quality control
		  ∘ Digitisation and transcription procedures
		  ∘ Checking and quality assurance procedures
		  ∘ Details of proofing and editing carried out
		  ∘ Evidence of versioning of data
		– Information on secondary sources used
		– Methods description
		  ∘ Resulting articles, presentations and outputs

Ethics, consent and legal issues	– Was there permission gained to share this data beyond the research team? – Are there copies of the information sheet and consent forms? – Has the data been anonymised? – Is it ethically and legally ok to use?	– Data-sharing evidence present – Known restrictions on use of data – Original information sheet and consent forms

(Continued)

Table 11.1 Key questions to ask of existing data and useful sources of evidence for appraisal (Continued)

Assessment task	Questions to ask	Material source as evidence
Formats and accessibility of the data	– Has it been organised in a useful way? – How can I access the data? Can I take it away? – Is it born digital and will it need to be digitised? – Do I have the computing resources to host and analyse the data? – Can I open the files or do I need to access specialist analysis software, such as Atlas-ti or video software?	– Constructed finding aid or a data list – Analogue (paper, audio) or born digital files? – Check access conditions of data, e.g. used only on site? – Check file sizes and file extensions

has not been that smooth. These days, even the final published reports to funders are only four to six pages long, which does not leave much room for a thorough explanation of how the fieldwork went. An example of an excellent guide to an archived data set is from the 'Foot and Mouth' study below, which is quite unique in presenting an excellent orientation for the new user.

Once assessment has been made, with a positive outcome, the next challenge is to embark on a recontextualisation of data, complementing and comparing the raw data with other material, qualitative or otherwise. Analytic strategies will depend on what the user is familiar with – this could be coding and refining concepts, framework analysis or text mining, and might or might not involve computer analysis software. We should not forget that the analytic approach we choose to employ will also demonstrate how good our recontextualisation and reinterpretation of the original material has been.

PROVIDING CONTEXT WITH DATA: A NOTE ON THE DATA COLLECTOR'S ROLE

In seeking to help answer the data detective's questions, we have highlighted the critical role that the research context plays in enabling secondary analysis. In addition to supporting research design and fieldwork materials, there are practical ways in which raw data can be presented and published to help recreate context. In particular, digital user interfaces can help to present large amounts of data in an intuitive way, allowing the user to navigate around a collection.

Using Table 11.1 we showed the value of useful documentation to help support an understanding of raw data. How to 'package' this is a useful skill for a researcher wishing to share data for the future. There is a systematic and universal approach for this 'packaging', that was established by the UK's Qualidata in the early 1990s (UK Data Archive, 2015). Following these protocols, a more traditional collection of qualitative data, such as a combination of interview transcripts, and audio recordings, benefits from:

- using pseudonyms instead of real names, places and occupations where confidentiality promises have been made;
- clearly set out transcribed text, for example, clear speech demarcations/speaker tags;
- consistent file naming with each related item having a unique identifier (e.g. person number);
- a single at-a-glance finding aid, setting out item or file-level information in a single 'datalist' document (see Figure 11.2). This can list summary descriptive attributes or biographical characteristics of participants studied, such as: age, gender, occupation or location (but not enabling identification where promised); and details of the data items, such as file name, description, file format and size;

SN 2000 Family Life and Work Experience Before 1918, 1870-1973
Thompson, P.

Interview ID	Title	First Name(s)	Second Name	Occupation	Occupational class	Place of Interview	Date(s) of Interview	Name of interviewer	Interview Notes	No. of Pages	Text File Name
1	Mr	~	Keble	Postman	Semi-skilled manual	Colchester	~	~		55	2000int001
2	Mr	~	Stinchcombe	Farm labourer	Semi-skilled manual	~	~	~	Includes 29 page pilot interview	109	2000int002
3	Mrs	~	Duckers	Cleaner	Semi-skilled manual	London	19.02.1968	~	Includes 22 page pilot interview	78	2000int003
4	Mr	Gus	Knifton	General Omnibus Co.	Skilled manual	London	27.02.1968	~	Includes 14 page pilot interview	74	2000int004
5	Mr	John	Troy	Farm Worker	Semi-skilled manual	London	31.05.1968	~	Includes 21 page pilot interview	85	2000int005
6	Mrs	~	Craig	Tailoress	Skilled manual	London	08.03.1968	~	Includes 18 page pilot interview	61	2000int006
7	Mrs	Clara	Wilson	Head laundress	Semi-skilled manual	London	??.??.1968	Elizabeth Sloan	Includes 26 page pilot interview	73	2000int007
8	Mr	James	Rook	Porter	Unskilled manual	London	~	~	Includes 20 page pilot interview	82	2000int008
9	Mr	Edward William	Wiffen	Bottler - mineral water	Semi-skilled manual	Colchester	~	~		71	2000int009
10	Mr	Harry	Taylor	Wheelwright	Skilled manual	Kelvedon	~	~		96	2000int010
11	Mr	Norris	Thompson	Manager/owner of family shop	Employers and managers	Wilcot	~	~		116	2000int011

Figure 11.2 Datalist for an archived study at the UK Data Service

- file-level attributes added as a summary page or at the top of a text file;
- consistently labelled non-digital materials such as reports, photographs, transcriptions, handwritten fieldwork notes and analogue audio-visual recordings.

Qualitative software packages also have features for handling and managing data (Fielding and Lee, 2002). While these softwares can be invaluable, applications vary and each package has distinctive requirements for handling and exporting data and outputs. Each package tends to have a proprietary project format so that it is not always easy to exchange added-value information (such as coding, annotation or memos) between different softwares.

How Much Documentation is Enough?

A common question is *how much* documentation is needed to describe a research study and its resulting data, weighing up the burden of creating it versus its usefulness. There is no single answer, but if the project is well planned and well run there should already be a heap of useful information about every step. Post-hoc reconstruction of what was done is always that much harder. Researchers do benefit from thinking about data-sharing issues before they commence planning and fieldwork, that is, collecting data with future access and use in mind. A simple rule of thumb is, if in doubt – keep everything!

Preparing context might seem like an added administrative task for the data collector alongside the vast amount of work required for analysis and writing up. However, the benefits of sharing and future-proofing data are now recognised to extend the life of the research beyond its contemporary value.

Standards used by data publishers to review research data are a good indication of best practice and expectations. Some basic guiding principles for publishing well-documented and sustainable qualitative data are:

- proof and format any textual material;
- check each data file for disclosive information (where necessary);
- generate recommended file formats that users can open;
- give files meaningful and consistent names and organise into logical folders;
- create a datalist of all items in spreadsheet format;

- collate and prepare documentation for users that follows a narrative where possible, and avoiding too many separate documents;
- create a 'readme.txt' file that sets out what the user is to expect when they download the data;
- create a structured catalogue metadata for any online catalogue;
- gather all citations to related publications for inclusion in the catalogue record;
- publish the data via a suitable online repository system;
- ensure a Digital Object Identifier (DataCite DOI) is assigned to the data collection.

The Sage Handbook on *Managing and Sharing Research Data: A Guide to Good Practice* includes technical and legal advice, as well as examples and exercises developed from real data collections, and templates that researchers can use, such as: model consent forms that cover data sharing; transcription templates for transcribing interviews; and a datalist template for providing an inventory for qualitative data items (Corti et al., 2014; UK Data Service, 2011).

The evidence base of 900+ published qualitative data collections available from the UK Data Service Discover catalogue, which are largely derived from publicly funded research, set out many varied examples of documentation (UK Data Service, 2016b). The reader will benefit from browsing through the different kinds of study materials that the investigators have decided to present alongside their raw data. It is evident that some studies have provided more information about their research and methods than one can find in any of their standard academic publications.

Exposing and Publishing Qualitative Data

Presenting original data from a research study not only future-proofs the research but also helps support the transparency, accountability and integrity of the research process to the more critical eye. Digital media especially help analysts gain a more complete picture of the data supporting an analysis, particularly where results and data are presented in an environment that is open to exploration.

In the last five years or so, the 'transparency agenda' has re-emerged, this time in response to calls for scientific openness and a research audit in the wake of evidence of fraudulence, plagiarism and the lack of publishing negative or null findings in research (Unger et al., 2016). Journals are increasingly adding replication mandates, especially for quantitative research (DA-RT, 2015) and thus more research data sets are being published via this journal route. While this is a positive move in seeking to maintain high levels of scientific integrity, in some ways, any extreme approach to mandating the replication of findings would prove troublesome for qualitative research approaches. For example, replicating analysis of large volumes of data gathered from a long-running anthropological study would likely be impossible. Table 11.1 suggested what kinds of contextualising items might be useful for demonstrating context for data and integrity in the research process. A good compromise is likely to be where authors seek to share as much of the original data as possible in a digital format alongside a narrative that demonstrates the origin of their claims.

Even today, journals rarely offer dynamic reading interfaces, though some of the *Nature* journals are enabled with live interactive boxes, so that readers can watch videos while reading or run their own routines on data (see, for example, an article in *Nature* on data visualisation: http://www.nature.com/news/data-visualization-science-on-the-map-1.17024). Even by 2016, social science journals have been very slow on the uptake in embracing such data browsing interactivity, although some have enabled commenting by readers incorporated into the data browsing functionality.

Data to support published claims is best published in a stable repository that enables such interactive browsing and, therefore, greater exploratory power for the reader or reuser.

Corti et al. (2016), in a recently edited collection, invite readers to view data directly from an article, so that an excerpt quoted in an article can be viewed online in its original context.

The UK QualiBank hosts the underlying data and allows selected extracts of text, such as a paragraph from an interview transcript, to be highlighted and cited in an article with a persistent web address (URL); then reviewed by the reader in context as a highlighted paragraph, as shown in Figure 11.3 (UK Data Service, 2015).

Figure 11.4 shows the top of a transcript, which sets out some contextual characteristics of the interview and interviewee, for quick reference. A link back to the *Study Documentation* for the whole study can reveal more information such as study design, protocols and so on.

Finally, publishing research now embraces a wider portfolio of formats beyond the traditional peer-reviewed journal article. Blogs and vlogs, media embraced by journalists and citizen scientists, often point to recent reports and findings with creative visualisations, and offer timely exposure to their work and evidence base.

Challenges in Designing a Study for Future Use

In addition to providing sufficient documentation as context, there are four other areas that need to be taken into account when considering sharing 'human subject' data for future use: resources, consent, confidentiality and future data access mechanisms.

Resources

Planning for sharing may require some additional costs in terms of data preparation such as staff time, equipment, infrastructure and tools to document, organise, store and provide access to data. There is no single rule for allocating costs but they can be calculated by listing all activities required to make data shareable, and then costing each activity in terms of people's time or the physical

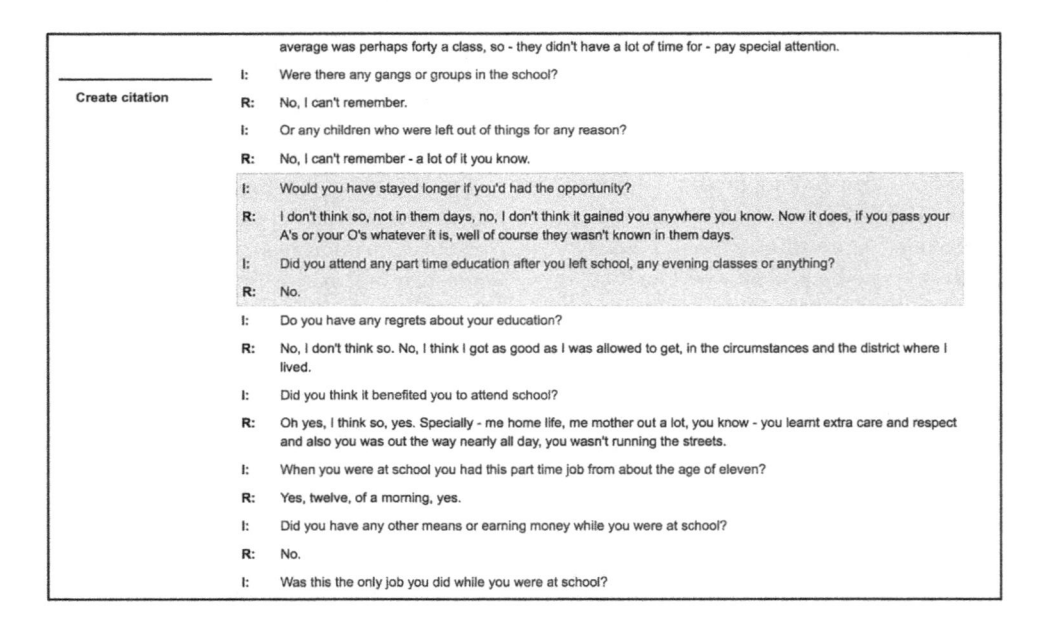

Figure 11.3   Cited extract from qualitative text in the UK QualiBank

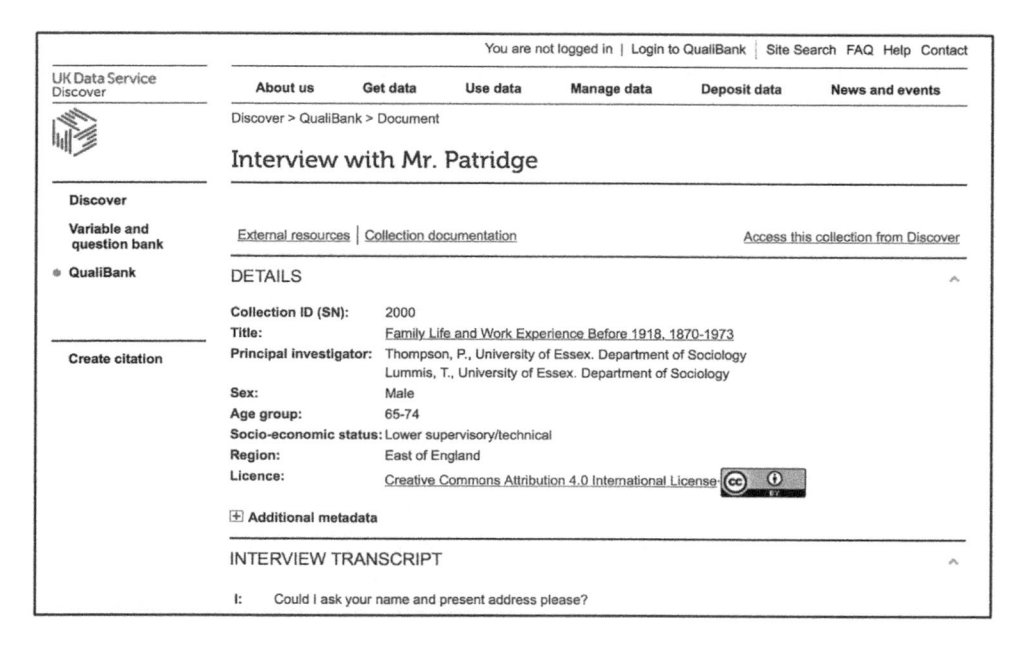

Figure 11.4 Header information for a qualitative interview text in the UK QualiBank

resources needed. Transcription (see Jenks, Chapter 8, this volume), and anonymisation are likely to bring additional costs for qualitative data.

Consent

Informed consent is required from participants to take part in research. In addition, participants should agree to the anticipated uses of the data collected as set out by the researcher (ESRC, 2015; Wiles et al., 2005). Where consent for future sharing can be gained at the time of fieldwork, this is extremely valuable – a gift for which future researchers will be grateful. Many researchers have been successful in adding clauses for future data sharing into their consent forms. Broad, enduring or open consent has produced high rates of participation (over 99 per cent) in some instances, such as at the Wales Cancer Bank (Wales Cancer Bank, 2007).

However, asking explicitly for consent to share data is often felt to be a threat to response rates or participation and candidness in the interview, though there is little concrete evidence to back this up. Kuula's (2011) study of retrospective consent highlights some interesting issues from the viewpoint of research participants in qualitative studies: one should not automatically assume that participants will not participate just because data sharing is discussed, and talking openly to them about it, independent of their wish to participate, may elicit less reluctance than anticipated. If permission to share data has not been sought during the research, then it may be possible to return back to gain retrospective permission.

Personal information, confidentiality and anonymisation

Most countries have legislation that covers the use of personal information, but a common misunderstanding is that 'Data protection' legislation applies to all research data in general that is gathered from participants. It does not. It applies only to personal or sensitive personal data, as defined by the Act and, further, does not apply to anonymised data or to information from deceased people (Information Commissioner's Office, 2013).

While some studies may have permission to use names, such as in life story testimonies or elite research, identifying data may need to be anonymised, for ethical, legal or commercial reasons. Pseudonyms or less precise descriptors can be used and, where possible, be consistent with names used in future publication. Planning in advance, and where possible agreeing with participants what can and cannot be recorded or transcribed can be a more effective way of creating data that accurately represents the contribution of participants. This is easier than spending time later removing information from a recording or transcript. Corti et al. (2014) in their Sage Handbook provide detailed guidance on how to anonymise qualitative data.

Access mechanisms

Assuming consent is given for future access, data may be openly available, restricted or embargoed for a period, depending on its level of sensitivity. Professionally run data archives use formal user agreements that require all users to agree to legally binding undertakings, such as not to pass data on to anyone else and not to disclose identities. Access to disclosive personal data, such as those held in secure labs (with data owner's permission), is conducted by vetting applications to use data and by sending users on training courses where they learn how to avoid accidental (or malicious) disclosure.

The digital multi-media UK Timescapes Archive of qualitative longitudinal data utilises a series of access gateways: for 'live' data still being collected, access is locked down to members of the research team; while collective decisions are made about which data can be shared more widely. The take-away message here is that being open and transparent about the longer-term value of data, and ensuring its safety, is key to gaining trust and enthusiasm for data sharing by researchers (Neale and Bishop, 2012).

EXAMPLE OF HOW DATA FROM A SENSITIVE TOPIC WAS SHARED

The 2001 foot and mouth animal disease outbreak had an enormous effect on the economic, social and political life of rural areas in the UK. A research project funded by the UK Department of Health, 'Health and social consequences of the foot and mouth disease epidemic in North Cumbria', produced evidence about the human health and social consequences of the epidemic (Mort, 2006). The study recruited a standing panel of 54 local people from the worst affected area in North Cumbria who wrote weekly diaries over a period of 18 months, describing how their lives had been affected by the crisis and the process of recovery they observed around them. The panel was recruited to reflect a broad range of occupations including farmers and their families, workers in related agricultural occupations, those in small businesses including tourism, hotel trades and rural business, health professionals, veterinary practitioners, voluntary organisations and residents living near disposal sites. The panel members produced 3,200 weekly diary entries of great intensity and diversity over an 18-month period. The data were supplemented by in-depth interviews with each respondent, focus group discussions and 16 other interviews with stakeholders.

On completion of the project the research team wanted to archive the valuable methods they had used and the data and testimony they had gathered. While they had gained standard consent from participants for initial participation in the project, they had not thought to include consent for sharing or archiving their data. They consulted with the panel of participants about retrospective consent procedures and sought expert advice from copyright law specialists to help draft terms of agreement that would give respondents a series of options about how their diaries, copies or portions of diaries, and/or their audio material would be archived.

The resulting qualitative data are now available to other researchers from the UK Data

Service with detailed and exemplary documentation, including an interview with the depositor about their own experiences. To give an idea of uptake for sharing data: 40 interview and diary transcripts were made available for reuse by registered users; three interviews and five diaries were embargoed until 2015; and seven panel members declined to archive their data; audio files are made available by permission from researchers. The methods and data have been reused in a new study 'Assessment of knowledge sources in animal disease control' that consolidates guidance on communication, designing of regulation and coordinated response for policymakers, and which combines economic and social as well as technical perspectives (Fish et al., 2011).

CONCLUSION

This chapter has set out best practice and challenges in collating and evaluating sources of data for conducting secondary analysis of qualitative data. Advice on how to get started has been presented, highlighting the different approaches used by social scientists and historians when confronting, evaluating and sampling existing data sources. It has tried to outline some of the practical and sometimes challenging issues for the data creator that face them in their desire to present their data for future visitation and exploitation. Finally the chapter discusses how data can be fruitfully published to engage with renewed emerging transparency requirements from academic journals and funders, helping to demonstrate trust in the findings while safeguarding the privacy of those who were involved in fieldwork.

FURTHER READING

Edwards, R. (ed.) (2012) 'Perspectives on working with archived textual and visual material in social research', *International Journal of Social Research Methodology* (Special Issue), 15(4): 259–262.

Corti, Louise, Van den Eynden, Veerle, Bishop, Libby, and Woollard, Matthew (2014) *Managing and Sharing Research Data: A Guide to Good Practice*. London: Sage. This handbook offers practical guidance for researchers, written by researchers, on all the issues involved in making research data sharable.

UK Data Service (2016) *Reusing Qualitative Data, Secondary Analysis*, University of Essex. Available at https://www.ukdataservice.ac.uk/use-data/secondary-analysis/reusing-qualitative-data. This web resource offers case studies, a detailed reading list, a short guide on reusing qualitative data, and links to teaching resources on the topic.

REFERENCES

Akerstrom, Malin, Jacobsson, Katarina, and Wästerfors, David (2004) 'Reanalysis of previously collected material', in Clive Seale, Giampietro Gobo, Jaber F. Gubrium and David Silverman (eds), *Qualitative Research Practice*. London: Sage, pp. 344–57.

Baethge-Kinsky, V. (2016) 'Soziologische und zeitgeschichtliche Perspektiven auf (arbeits-)soziologische Quellen: Konsequenzen für den Umgang mit Daten und ihrer Aufbereitung', Paper presented at SOFI workshop entitled *Decent work after the Boom*, Gottingen, 17–18 March 2016.

Bishop, L. (2006) 'A proposal for archiving context for secondary analysis', *Methodological Innovations Online* [Special Issue: Defining context for qualitative data], 1(2): 10–20.

Bishop, L., and Kuula-Luumi, A. (2017) 'Revisiting qualitative data reuse: A decade on', 7(1) *Sage Open*.

Cohen, Stanley (1987) *Folk Devils and Moral Panics: The Creation of the Mods and Rockers*. Oxford: Basil Blackwell.

Corti, L., Fielding, N., and Bishop, L. (2016) 'Editorial, Special issue – Digital representations: Opportunities for re-using and publishing digital qualitative data', 6(4) *Sage Open*.

Corti, Louise, and Thompson, Paul (2004) 'Secondary analysis of archive data', in Clive Seale, Giampietro Gobo, Jaber Gubrium and

David Silverman (eds), *Qualitative Research Practice*. London: Sage, pp. 327–43.

Corti, Louise, Van den Eynden, Veerle, Bishop, Libby, and Woollard, Matthew (2014) *Managing and Sharing Research Data: A Guide to Good Practice*. London: Sage.

Crow, G., and Edwards, R. (eds) (2012) 'Perspectives on working with archived textual and visual material in social research', Special Issue of *International Journal of Social Research Methods*, 15(4): 259–62.

DA-RT (2015) *Data Access and Research Transparency*, available at http://www.dartstatement.org/.

Elder, Glen (1974) *Children of the Great Depression*. Chicago, IL: University of Chicago Press.

Emmell, Nick (2013) *Sampling and Choosing Cases in Qualitative Research: A Realist Approach*. London: Sage.

Entwistle, V.A., France, E.F., Wyke, S., Jepson R., Hunt K., Ziebland S., and Thompson A. (2011) 'How information about other people's personal experiences can help with healthcare decision-making: A qualitative study', *Patient Education and Counseling*, 85(3): 291–e298.

ESRC (2015) Framework for Research Ethics, available at http://www.esrc.ac.uk/files/funding/guidance-for-applicants/esrc-framework-for-research-ethics-2015/.

Fielding, N., and Fielding, J. (2000) 'Resistance and adaptation to criminal identity: Using secondary analysis to evaluate classic studies of crime and deviance', *Sociology*, 34(4): 671–89.

Fielding, N.G., and Lee, R.M. (2002) 'New patterns in the adoption and use of qualitative software', *Field Methods*, 14(2): 197–216.

Fish, R., Austin, Z., Christley, R., Haygarth, P.M., Heathwaite, L.A., Latham, S., Medd, W., Mort, M., Oliver, D.M., Pickup, R., Wastling, J.M., and Wynne, B. (2011) 'Uncertainties in the governance of animal disease: an interdisciplinary framework for analysis', *Philosophical Transactions of the Royal Society B*, 366(1573): 2023–34.

Gillies, V., and Edwards, R. (2012) 'Working with archived classic family and community studies: Illuminating past and present conventions around acceptable research practice', *International Journal of Social Research Methodology*, 15(4): 321–30.

Gunn, Simon, and Faire, Lucy (2011) *Research Methods for History (Research Methods for the Arts and Humanities)*. Edinburgh: Edinburgh University Press.

Haaker, M., and Morgan-Brett, B. (2017) 'Developing research-led teaching: Two case studies of practical data re-use in the classroom', 7(2) *Sage Open*.

Hammersley, M. (2010) 'Can we re-use qualitative data via secondary analysis? Notes on some terminological and substantive issues', *Sociological Research Online*, 15(1): 5.

Holstein, James A., and Gubrium, Jaber F. (2004) 'Context: Working it up, down and across', in Clive Seale, Giampietro Gobo, Jaber F. Gubrium and David Silverman (eds), *Qualitative Research Practice*. London: Sage, Ch 17, pp. 267–81.

Information Commissioner's Office (2013) *Key Definitions of the Data Protection Act*, Information Commissioner's Office, available at https://ico.org.uk/for-organisations/guide-to-data-protection/key-definitions/.

Irwin, S., Bornat, J., and Winterton, M. (2012) 'Timescapes secondary analysis: Comparison, context and working across data sets', *Qualitative Research*, 12(1): 66–80.

Kuula, A. (2011) 'Methodological and ethical dilemmas of archiving qualitative data', *IASSIST Quarterly*, 34(3–4) and 35(1–2): 12–17.

Larivaara, Meri, Isola, Anna-Maria, and Mikkonen, Juka (2011) *Arkipäivän kokemuksia köyhyydestä*. Keuruu: Kustannusosakeyhtiö Avain. Available at http://www.koyhyyskirjoitukset.org/Everyday_Experiences_of_Povertybook.Pdf.

Lawrence, J. (2013) 'Class, "affluence" and the study of everyday life in Britain, c.1930–1964', *Cultural and Social History*, 10(2013): 273–99.

Lawson, A. (2004) *User Guide, Adultery: An Analysis of Love and Betrayal, 1920–1983*. [data collection]. UK Data Service. SN: 4858, available at http://dx.doi.org/10.5255/UKDA-SN-4858-2.

Mort, Maggie (2006) *Health and Social Consequences of the Foot and Mouth Disease Epidemic in North Cumbria, 2001–2003* [computer file]. Colchester, Essex: UK Data Archive [distributor], SN: 5407, available at http://dx.doi.org/10.5255/ UKDA-SN-5407-1.

Neale, B., and Bishop, E. (2012) 'The Timescapes archive: A stakeholder approach to archiving qualitative longitudinal data', *Qualitative Research,* 12(1): 53–65.

Rowntree, Seebohm (1901) *Poverty. A Study of Town Life.* London: Macmillan.

Silva, E. (2007) 'What's [yet] to be seen? Reusing qualitative data', *Sociological Research Online,* 12(3): 4.

Thompson, Paul (2009) *Family Life and Work Experience Before 1918, 1870–1973.* [data collection]. 7th Edition. UK Data Service. SN: 2000, available at http://dx.doi.org/10.5255/UKDA-SN-2000-1.

Townsend, Peter (2014) *Poverty in the United Kingdom: A Survey of Household Resources and Standards of Living, 1967–1969.* [data collection]. 2nd edn. UK Data Service. SN: 1671, available at http://dx.doi.org/10.5255/UKDA-SN-1671-1.

UK Data Archive (2015) Qualitative data collection ingest processing procedures, available at http://www.data-archive.ac.uk/media/54767/cd093-qualitativedatacollectioningestprocessingprocedures_08_00w.pdf.

UK Data Service (2011) Qualitative datalist, available at http://doc.ukdataservice.ac.uk/doc/2000/mrdoc/pdf/2000ulist.pdf.

UK Data Service (2013) Teaching resource: Folk devils and moral panics, available at http://ukdataservice.ac.uk/teaching-resources/folk-devils.aspx.

UK Data Service (2014) Introducing the UK Data Service QualiBank, available at https://www.ukdataservice.ac.uk/media/428412/qualibankguide.pdf.

UK Data Service (2015) Cited paragraph in QualiBank, available at https://discover.ukdataservice.ac.uk/QualiBank/Document/?cid=q-1dba72b1-d148-40e7-b3dc-a81ae230ca80.

UK Data Service (2016a) Case studies of reuse, available at https://www.ukdataservice.ac.uk/use-data/data-in-use/case-studies.

UK Data Service (2016b) Discover catalogue showing qualitative data collections, available at https://discover.ukdataservice.ac.uk/?sf=Data%20catalogue&df=DataTypeFacet_Qualitative%20and%20mixed%20methods%20data.

Unger, J.M., Barlow, W.E., Ramsey, S.D., LeBlanc M., Blanke C.D., and Hershman D.L. (2016) 'The scientific impact of positive and negative phase 3 cancer clinical trials', *JAMA Oncology* Jul 1; 2(7): 875–81.

Wales Cancer Bank (2007) Annual Report 2006–2007, available at http://www.walescancerbank.com/documents/WCBAnnualReport_2007.pdf.

Wiles, R., Heath, S., Crow, G., and Charles, V. (2005) 'Informed consent in social research: A literature review', *NCRM Methods Review Papers,* NCRM/001, available at http://eprints.ncrm.ac.uk/85/.

The Virtues of Naturalistic Data

Jonathan Potter and Chloe Shaw

INTRODUCTION

This chapter focuses on the reasons for working with naturalistic data. That is, it starts with an interest in *life as it happens* as far as possible independent of the researcher's constructions, practices, and interventions. Naturalistic data is in contrast to elicited data in qualitative social science; naturalistic rather than natural, to flag epistemic cautions that will be developed below. The chapter (a) suggests examples from the history of the use of naturalistic materials across the sciences and notes the limited presence of naturalistic materials in social sciences; (b) describes the test through which the two kinds of data can be distinguished and offers reasons for working with the more epistemically cautious notion of naturalistic data; (c) overviews objections to the idea that naturalistic data is in fact natural and lists responses to those objections. It goes on to consider a range of problems with the use of elicited data in techniques of qualitative data collection such as interviews, focus groups, and ethnographic work. It overviews some resources that will be important for those working with naturalistic material and provides some illustrative examples that highlight its distinctive strengths. It shows the value of using the naturalistic material in research that can lead to its application and shows how it can help build evidence-based training materials for professionals.

Overall, we will make the case that too much of social science has been developed using materials which are got up by researchers, flooded by their concepts, restricted by a huge range of structured scales and instruments, and stimulated by questions that are built out of an internally fixated history of social science. The use of naturalistic materials opens social science up to new questions, challenging its orthodoxies, and revealing orders of social life that have fallen into the gaps between the theories and instruments of mainstream approaches. Traditions such as conversation analysis (see

Jackson, Chapter 18, this volume), discursive psychology (see Rau et al., Chapter 19, this volume), video stimulated ethnography (see Knoblauch et al., Chapter 23, this volume) have exploited naturalistic materials most effectively; yet other approaches could benefit from engaging with the world as it happens, inspiring the development of new questions and new theory.

NATURAL DATA IN THE HISTORY OF SCIENCE AND SOCIAL SCIENCE

Observation and description are central features of scientific practices. The very notion of empirical research is based on that idea. Although many sciences have strong experimental and theoretical components, work on evolution, astronomy, and animal behavior is unimaginable without its basis in careful observational work. For example, Darwin's discovery of evolution was dependent on his development of careful, systematic, and extensive descriptive practices. Through his observations, Darwin was able to find evidence of variation within species, rather than of distinct species, as previously assumed by naturalists. And that in turn opened up the whole possibility that selection of those varied forms could be a motor for evolutionary change.

Observation is complicated, of course, as a range of philosophers, historians and sociologists of science have shown. Figures as diverse as Thomas Kuhn (1970), Paul Feyerabend (1975), and Norwood Hanson (1969) suggested that the nature of observation, what counts as empirical, varies by theoretical context or according to the broad research paradigm that the observations are collected within. Karl Popper (1959) pressed the case for treating observation as theory laden (see Maxwell, Chapter 2, this volume). Sociologists of science have themselves taken an empirical approach, looking, for example, at the separation of true phenomena from artifact in laboratory bench science (Lynch, 1985) or at observational practices (see Wästerfors, Chapter 20, this volume) in high-energy physics. In her study of the high-energy physics community at CERN, Karin Knorr Cetina (1999) documents the way that this community's work was dependent on the operation of their detector for identifying the traces of particular particles. The physicists spent more of their time running the particle detector with the aim of understanding its operation than using it to make new observations. In a sense, a major part of the work of these physicists involved explicating their own empirical capabilities.

The current chapter will focus on working with material that is naturalistic, that is, not got up by researchers using interviews, focus groups, and similar. Darwin recorded features of specimens found in the wild; high-energy physicists study the effect of high-speed collisions generated in particle accelerators. Loosely speaking, Darwin worked with natural data and the high-energy physics community and CERN elicited data. Let us not stay with these parallels from outside of social science. Our focus is on uses of naturalistic material in social science. We will consider three examples that illustrate increasingly more thorough engagement with naturalistic materials: (1) Barker's ecological psychology; (2) Bales' interaction process analysis and (3) ethnographic participant observation.

Barker and Ecological Psychology

As early as the 1940s Roger Barker was concerned that the study of human behavior had been overly dependent on experimentation and testing. Phil Schoggen (1991) notes that Barker (and his then colleague Wright) 'liked to think of themselves as naturalists of child behavior and habitat. They pointed out that, in its eagerness to win respect as a science, psychology early on became a predominantly experimental science and, as a consequence, has neglected the descriptive, natural history, ecological phase of science that has been prominent in the history of other fields' (1991, p. 238). Barker's team took up residence in the town of Oskaloosa in Kansas and made observations of people living ordinary lives. For example, *One Boy's Day* (Barker and Wright, 1951) is an entire book that describes a day in the life of Raymond, in the 13 hours from waking up until going to sleep. The nature of such description can be seen from the following, capturing the start of an evening meal:

> 20'30 [the time code]
> "C'mon," she calls in the same tone, "Anita, Winton, April, Greg."
> Immediately Winton walks, carrying the stick, to the little cubby area.
> He throws it in as before.
> It lands, supported somehow on top of the water heater, which means it sticks out about 2 feet in the passageway between the living room and the bathroom. He immediately walks to his place very purposefully as if he has been waiting to be called.
> He puts one hand on top of the back of the chair.
> With one hand underneath the seat of the chair he pulls it out very efficiently.
> The mother puts a plate of hot corn bread on the table as he is doing this.
> Winton slides into his chair from the left side.
> The other children also come to the table at about the same time from their own, independent places, except for Anita, who continues to sit on the floor working on the scrapbook.
> The mother looks over at her and says with strong annoyance, "C'mon now, you haven't been cleaning it up, you've just been playing with it."
> Greg tattles eagerly, "Yes, she's just been playing."
> 21'00
> "She has been playing. Okay!" the mother says. She sounds as if she must tone down her annoyance because of Greg's tattling.
> (Schoggen, 1991, pp. 239–40)

Barker's approach here is a significant attempt to capture natural data. The aim is precisely to capture what is happening irrespective of the actions and interests of the psychologist. Let us make a number of observations about what he has produced.

First, prior to easy, compact and cheap video technology, Barker is working with observers who are present with the participants and forced to make notes in real time. Given the complexity of what they are rendering – several people involved in different actions, specific items of talk, non-vocal and embodied actions – this is challenging to achieve. Modern recording technology provides different options and it is likely that, given Barker's interest in capturing the natural world of humanity as it happens, he would have at least supplemented the live observation with video.

Second, what we have through much of this kind of material is descriptive text, including a range of glosses. The challenge here is that our descriptive language is fundamentally bound up with action and evaluation. Potter's (1996) *Representing Reality* is an extended overview and argument showing the different traditions revealing different kinds of links between description and action. For example, 'Greg tattles eagerly' has a moral cast – it takes a censorious position on Greg: he is telling tales (rather than helping his parents out, say) and he is enthusiastically doing so (as opposed to reluctantly, say). It is not that there might not be practices in which a person revels in revealing another's wrongdoing – however, it is here wired into the description rather than putting the analyst and reader into a position where they can both come to such a conclusion (or not).

Third, although commentators have made much of the amount of detail that is captured in this material, it is actually lacking features that more recent interaction analysts (see Jackson, Chapter 18, this volume) have shown being used pervasively by humans as they coordinate actions and transact their business. For example, researchers have shown that timing is fundamental to interaction, with overlap, speed of delivery, and delay between speakers being an important part of understanding what actions are being done and how speakers' stances should be registered. A delay of less than 0.2 of a second can indicate to a speaker that an invitation is going to be turned down (Potter, 2006). Another dimension that is fundamental is intonation and prosody. Again, this is a live feature that helps define the specific action that is being done and how it should be understood by parties in the interaction and it is mostly missing from Barker's descriptions.

Finally, one of the features emphasized by interaction analysts is the importance of participants' interaction with one another to support an accurate understanding of what is going on. This is what the founder of conversation analyst, Harvey Sacks, referred to as the proof procedure (Sacks, 1992). People display their understanding of interaction as it unfolds and this display can be exploited by researchers (Sidnell, 2012). It is not possible to clearly recover the way the interaction is threaded together, and who is responding to who, in Barker's record.

Bales and Interaction Process Analysis

It is worth briefly considering Robert Bales' work on small group interaction processes (Bales, 1950). Although it was applied mostly to got-up interaction in laboratory settings, it has also been applied to more naturalistic materials. Interaction process analysis (IPA) was, at heart, a coding scheme that could be applied by an observer to unfolding interaction. For Bales, interaction in groups is a back and forth of acts such as 'agrees' (which he further categorized as 'social-emotional') or 'gives opinion' (further categorized as 'instrumental-adaptive'). As Anssi Peräkylä (2004) notes, Bales' work is the model for a lot of subsequent coding and counting-based social psychology. The key thing to highlight in our current overview is that even when applied to natural materials, the original interaction is transformed into categories, and instances within categories are counted. The analytic operations are on relationships between the counts of occurrences within categories.

There has been ample discussion of problems with Bales' categories and his way of understanding what an act is. However, the fundamental issue for us in relation to natural data is that there is no way of recovering the original interaction following coding. Whatever problems there are with Bales' coding, categories become inextricably baked into the data. While with Barker's work this is at least a partial possibility of recovering what Raymond, his most famous participant, for example, was doing from the data, that possibility is wiped out with Bales' coding. As researchers, we are faced with accepting Bales as accurate and appropriate and treating his inter-rater reliability measures as indicators that his observers could apply these categories rigorously. There is no independent way of auditing the conclusions of research that has been conducted using Bales' methods. This work does not offer a rich engagement with natural data, with life as it happens.

Ethnography and Participant Observation

There is no doubt that the ethnographic tradition of work in its different forms, whether in anthropology or sociology, provides rich researcher engagement with life as it happens (see Buscatto, Chapter 21, this volume). While Barker's non-participant observers stood back from the table and watched Raymond and his family eat, a participant ethnographer might sup with the family or accompany Raymond to school. While an observer using Bales' category scheme might study a decision-making group, or family therapy session, through a one-way mirror, the participant ethnographer would take part in some way. Moreover, their engagement would be extended, deep, and iterative. In classical anthropology the ethnographic expedition could take many months.

There are different ways of understanding what counts as data in ethnography (see, for example, Buscatto, Chapter 21, this volume, and Wästerfors, Chapter 20 this volume). There is a live attention to problems of representation and reactivity in some traditions of ethnography, particularly in the literature on the so-called crisis of representation (Atkinson, 1990; Clifford and Marcus, 1986). Some researchers, such as the noted sociologist of science Harry Collins (1983), have suggested that it is a mistake to think about ethnographic data as such; rather the ethnographic research process is dependent on the researcher's increasingly rich engagement through participation, observation, interviews, and reading documents. In effect ethnographers are using *themselves* as the research instrument and as they develop competence that parallels their participants they can then write about this with authority.

This is a thoughtful and internally coherent position. However, it leads us to ask a number of questions. First, how do we audit such research, if at all? Put another way, what do we have over and above a researcher telling us that this group (football ultras, gravity wave physicists) do this or believe that, to let us assess the adequacy of their claims? Second, the sort of issue that we noted with Barker is live – how can the participant researcher capture phenomena in the life work of her or his participants with a degree of granularity that can support analytic observations effectively. Put another way, there is a difference between being able as a participant to close a telephone call in an orderly manner on repeated occasions and being able to capture the precise ordering of turns, the overlap, the intonational contour, and so on, that take place, for example, in calls between a family member and a young adult staying in a home for people diagnosed with severe autism (Patterson and Potter, 2009).

Other ethnographers are more willing to talk about data, by which they typically suggest a mixture of open-ended interviews with cultural participants and observational notes (Hammersley and Atkinson, 2007). Open-ended interviews (see Roulston and Choi, Chapter 15, this volume), even when they are done as elements within extended periods of participation, are still got-up social events with the sorts of issues with them that Jonathan Potter and Alexa Hepburn (2005) have identified:

- They are flooded with social science categories, assumptions, and research agendas. These come in through the way participants are recruited, through the ordering and design of questions and through the different lexical items that the questions are built around.
- Interviewer and interviewee ask and answer questions on the basis of different footings – as disembodied expert, as member of a group, as someone directly accountable to an issue raised by an interviewer – and these different footings may lead to different kinds of response with the subsequent analytic complexity to tease them apart.
- Interviewer and interviewee are likely to orient to issues of stake and interest as the interview unfolds. People treat each other as having a stake in the claims that they make and are likely to manage the implications of that stake using a range of procedures (Edwards and Potter, 1992; Potter, 1996). Again, explicating this is a huge challenge for those analyzing open-ended interviews.

As David Silverman (2017) has argued, open-ended interviews have been over-used, and often poorly analyzed. However, this aspect of ethnography is not our topic here as such interviews are interactionally fabricated by the researcher rather than being naturally occurring events in the world of participants. We are more focused on the status of ethnographic descriptions.

The key issue with ethnographic description is how far cultural assumptions and theories are wired into them in the descriptive language, in what is selected for description, and in what is lost through the limitations of the observer. A description is importantly different from a record or transcript (see Jenks, Chapter 8, this volume). Harvey Sacks (1992, vol. 1, p. 436) puts this in the following way:

> It tends to be the case that even those anthropologists who consider themselves most radically oriented to an attempt to describe native systems of categorization – native thought systems – find themselves using their formulation of the real world as a way of getting a hold on what the natives are doing. (1992, vol. 1, p. 436)

Thus there is a difference between saying a participant 'starts to get upset' and recording changes in voice quality, timing, non-vocal movements, and the actual words used. This is the kind of issue we highlighted with respect to Greg 'tattling' and the mum 'toning down her annoyance' in Barker's data quoted above. The point is not that ethnography has not been used in a body of work that is often profound, striking, and insightful; rather, it is to highlight the limitations of ethnographic descriptions as natural data.

NATURALISTIC DATA – TWO KEY TESTS

In this section we will overview two tests that further refine what we mean by naturalistic data, and also indicate some epistemic cautions which are signaled by using natural*istic* rather than natural data.

The Unwell Social Scientist Test

The first test for naturalistic data is that it captures events, actions, phenomena in the social world that would have been produced whether the researcher had been present or not. If the researcher had become unwell, and was not available on the day of data collection those events, actions, and phenomena would have occurred regardless. This is the unwell social scientist test (Potter, 2002). Interviews, surveys, experiments, simulations, focus groups, and similar do not pass this test. What happens in them is dependent on the researcher asking the questions, booking the rooms, moderating the groups, managing the experimental protocols, and so on.

Thus, we could ask mothers and daughters about practices of advice giving, say, in interviews or focus groups. We could run an experiment where we exposed participants to different kinds of advice scenario and measured responses. Both of these got-up, researcher-initiated events would have to be cancelled without the presence of the researcher. In contrast, we could generate records of actual mother-daughter conversations, including those where advice came up, perhaps through recording phone calls or having a video placed in a home setting. These recordings do not depend on the presence of the researcher; if she is unwell they will happen anyway. They are designed to capture practices as far as possible that are independent of the actions and interests of the researcher. Which is not to say that they are free of issues of reactivity, as we discuss below.

The Recovery of Action Test

A second test captures the kinds of points made in the previous section about description and how far description embodies assumption and theory. The test is this: is it possible to get back to the actions, events, or phenomena from the descriptions provided by the researcher? Bales' categorization scheme is a clear failure in terms of this test. Once the observer has rendered events into codings using Bales' scheme there is no way of working back through them to recreate the flow of conversation in the group, the words and intonation used, and so on. Even Barker's extraordinarily detailed descriptive records are partial in what recovery of the original actions etc. is possible. We have descriptions of voice quality or glosses on actions, but we could not recover intonational contour from this, or the precise set of features that are glossed as tattling. We would struggle to study how tattling is recognizable, how it is built as a practice, or indeed, whether it makes sense as a practice, or whether it is a description grounded in the moral perspective of the older participants. So our second test for natural data is that it is collected in ways, and represented in forms that, as far as possible, work to avoid embedding theory and assumption within it.

In contrast, when collecting audio or video recordings of events in the world, such as a conversation between a doctor and patient, the data can be considered to be more natural*istic* in this regard; the data which comprises the recording of the conversation would have happened if the researcher had been there or not. The data captured is a record of the event as it actually happened, not removed to varying degrees by descriptions of the event from either the researcher or participants. Having an audio, or ideally a video recording in face-to-face interactions, provides for the possibility of repeated listening and watching as part of a rigorous analysis of real life events in the world (Heritage, 1984).

We will end our discussion of this second test with two qualifications. First, there is a seeming exception to the unwell psychologist test. There is a research tradition that takes social research itself as topic (Houtkoop-Steenstra, 2000; Puchta and Potter, 2004; Maynard et al, 2002). This is only an apparent exception, of course, as this research would have taken place irrespective of the health of the researcher who is studying the conduct of that research as opposed to the researchers involved in it. At this point it is worth reminding ourselves of Knorr Cetina's (1999) study where she notes how much time the high-energy physicists at CERN spent studying the operation of the particle detector rather than running experiments with it. We could argue that a mark of maturity in social sciences would be the devotion of serious analytic attention to the operation of social research methods. That would allow a more evidence-based evaluation of what they can achieve and of their limitations (an argument developed in Potter, 2012).

Second, a sophisticated appreciation of the philosophy and sociology of scientific knowledge noted above, combined with a recognition that there is a live potential for reactivity in most forms of even passive recording of interaction, means that the simple, pure empiricism implied by the notion of natural data should be treated with skepticism. And the idea that there is a hard and fast contrast between natural and contrived data is misleading. Following Potter (2002) we draw the distinction between contrived and natural*istic* data, marking our epistemic caution with the 'istic' qualifier to the 'natural'. However, the tests we have proposed above – 'the unwell social scientist test' and 'the recovery of action test' – do not require a purity of outcome. Naturalistic data is not free of possible reactivity, which is always something to manage. And as it is used in research studies, it is inevitably described, categorized, formulated, and so on. The point is that these descriptions, categorizations and formulations are, as far as practical, available for scrutiny by the research community. The two tests mark out a stance on data and an ambition to achieve better records of social life, where what is meant by 'better' is a topic for continual development.

NATURALISTIC DATA AND REACTIVITY: CRITIQUES AND RESPONSES

One of the issues that has come to the fore since the days of Barker and Bales is reactivity: the potential effect of being recorded (recruited to be in a study, working recorders, being recorded and filmed). It is worth considering its implications and management. In modern research the appropriate ethical safeguards ensure that participants consent to being recorded and understand that this is an important part of a research project. The concern is then that behavior becomes less natural as participants become self-conscious about their conduct (see Speer and Hutchby, 2003). Before going into the management of reactivity we would like to underline the comparison with experiments, questionnaires, participant observation, interviews, and surveys. Naturalistic data passes the two tests above. It is set against those other methods. If reactivity can be considered an issue for audio and video recording, then the problem is of a completely different order and much greater magnitude than other methods where the researcher has an active and ongoing part in soliciting reports, structuring responses, or by being present as the observed activity unfolds (Potter, 2012).

A number of practical approaches are typically used to minimize the extent to which the recording has an impact on participants' activity. First, technological advances enable compact and silent recording devices to be used to minimize moment-by-moment awareness of being recorded. These include video devices with small dimensions (a few centimeters and shrinking) and high quality internal microphones. Gone are the days where a documentary film crew needed a large camera, separate microphone and trailing cables. Now participants can be given easy-to-use large-storage cameras and asked to put them on a sideboard to make recordings of, say, family mealtimes.

Second, there can be periods of acclimatization to allow participants to get used to being recorded. This might involve recording a series of sessions and using only the later ones. It has been argued that, with mobile phones for video and audio recordings being an increasing part of culture, there is less to notice.

Third, the concerns that professionals may have about the adequacy of their conduct may need to be managed and assurances given (and followed) that the research process will be separate from their organizational processes of promotion and accountability. Professionals and clients can be reassured that their confidentiality and anonymity will be preserved and upheld for both audio and video data, through the use of modern technologies to anonymize the data (see page 191 for how this is done). They can also be reassured that, in the case of conversation analysis and discursive psychology, the focus is on interactional practices rather than categories of (or even individual) people or places (Psathas, 1995).

Fourth, data can be used where recording is a commonplace practice within a particular setting. There is no doubt that television news interviews are a tussle between interviewer and interviewee, but there is no extra reactive effect from the researcher building a corpus of, say, negative interrogatives and their operation (Clayman and Heritage, 2002). There are a range of data sources from legal, medical, therapeutic, and media settings where the recording was done for purposes intrinsic to the setting and bypassing issues of reactivity.

Fifth, and rather differently, reactivity can be managed through the researchers taking the phenomenon itself as a topic of study. Sue Speer and Ian Hutchby (2003) argue that participant orientations to the recorder should become a topic of study in its own right. In their article, they show the value of analyzing participants' explicit orientations to the recorder by analyzing how these orientations feature as part of the interaction itself; how such orientations contribute to the unfolding activities underway. There is more work to be done here, but there is no evidence of strong and systematic distorting effects resulting from audio and / or video recording in varied settings.

A second objection to the idea that naturalistic data is indeed natural, is the limitations to what information can be captured on the recording device. There are limits on the visual frame of the camera, although with technological advances wider angles are now available. Cameras are able to capture 180-degree shots so that all participants are captured, and multiple cameras enable facial expressions to be captured where they were otherwise obscured. However, in some very sensitive settings, such as therapy, it may sometimes only be possible to capture audio data, leaving visual information absent.

A third line of critique presses the claim that the pursuit of 'naturalistic' data has arisen from an impossible desire to seek more neutral and 'uncontaminated' data. Christine Griffin (2007) is an example of this, arguing for the virtues of more direct researcher involvement in the creation of data. It is worth quoting the response to Griffin in detail as it expresses the central contention of this chapter:

> This is critique by innuendo, and stands history on its head. In the 1980s the discourse analytic work that evolved into discursive psychology primarily worked with open-ended interviews. It criticized the idea that the interviewer should be passive and make minimal contributions and advocated 'a much more interventionalist and confrontative arena than is normal' and suggested interviews could be 'an active site where the respondent's interpretative resources are explored and engaged to the full' (Potter and Wetherell, 1987, p. 164). Our dissatisfaction with interviews, then, did not arise because interviews are insufficiently neutral. On the contrary, it arose because of the difficulty of achieving the desired activity. The excitement of working with naturalistic materials came from this dissatisfaction rather than a nostalgic positivistic wish for neutrality. Moreover, it is the pull of naturalistic material as an extraordinarily rich topic of study rather than the push of problems with interviews that has sustained the research. Given that naturalistic materials are both powerful and analytically tractable, the question becomes: why have interviews remained the default choice for qualitative researchers and why has there been so little justification of that use? (Potter and Hepburn, 2007, p. 278)

Ultimately, then, the aim is to minimize the impact of the researcher, primarily because of an interest in explicating the patterned and finessed way in which social life is organized (Potter, 2010), and because the more data are an internal and artifactual product of a specific research context, the less interesting they become (Potter, 2002).

Another version of this critique is to suggest that the common use of Jefferson-style transcription of talk gives (intentionally or not) the false impression of naturalism, of an independent objective reality existing independently of the researcher. David Bogen (1999) argues that the 'excessive detail' provided in CA transcripts is not there to support analysis but to provide an impression of solidity and actuality. Elliot Mischler (1991) developed an earlier but similar argument that such transcription conventions falsely give the impression of having achieved a more 'accurate' transcript, suggesting unattainable positivist orientations.

There are, no doubt, challenging issues here. Transcription is an exacting practice that takes time to learn to do well. The general answer to those who question why features of intonation, delay, stress and volume are included is that these features are live and consequential for the participants – something that the last decade of conversation analysis has shown in a now massive body of studies (see Jackson, Chapter 18, this volume, for a review). Transcription (see Jenks, Chapter 8, this volume) is an important area of development, particularly for challenging phenomena such as laughter, extreme upset, bodily movements, and cross-linguistic conversation (Hepburn and Bolden, 2012, 2017). Rather than arguing against the project of accurate transcription it is perhaps up to alternative approaches to demonstrate how different kinds of phenomena should be encoded. With conversation analysts and discursive psychologists, and increasingly researchers in other traditions, the transcript does not replace the audio or video recording – rather the process of research works with both, side by side (see Jackson, Chapter 18, this volume).

RESOURCES FOR SUPPORTING COLLECTING NATURALISTIC DATA

This section will briefly overview some resources for collecting and working with naturalistic materials.

Recording

Advances in technology and miniaturization now offer a wide array of options for capturing audio and video data. There are numerous publications that describe the practical issues involved in recording. A good starting place would be Lorenza Mondada, (2012a) and Paul Luff and Christian Heath (2012). Ruth Parry (2013) developed an online resource for researchers in considering the practicalities of audio and video recording. This includes information about the challenges of recording, equipment recommendations and considerations, as well as software options such as ELAN, Transana or CLAN to facilitate transcription.

Transcription

The standard method for transcription in conversation analytic studies is the Jefferson transcription system (Jefferson, 2004). Although the system has been most utilized in conversation analysis and discursive psychology, its rigor and focus on elements of talk that are interactionally consequential should make it a valuable resource for any social science approach that focuses on the world as it happens. Alexa Hepburn and Galina Bolden (2012, 2017) provide a detailed account and guide to using the Jefferson transcription system. This includes details about: transcript layout; the temporal and sequential relationship of talk; aspects of speech delivery; meta-communication and uncertain hearings; representing various other aspects of non-speech sounds such as sighing, laughing, and crying. They also provide a guide for representing non-English talk in a way that honors the original word order of the talk, while also capturing the interactional meaning of the utterance.

The use of video in conversation analytic work was pioneered by Charles Goodwin, in his significant work on gaze and gesture (1981). Since then, transcription has developed to capture gaze (see Goodwin, 1981; Rossano, 2012), gesture (Heath, 1986), and objects-in-interaction (Mondada, 2012b). A brief account of the transcription of video is given by Hepburn and Bolden (2012) where they overview the three main approaches to video transcription: transcriber commentary, specialized notational systems (see also Rossano, 2012), and visual representations including drawings and video grabs (see also Sidnell, 2006; Mondada 2007, 2012b; Laurier, 2014; see also Knoblauch et al., Chapter 23, this volume).

Practical Steps for Anonymization

Not all research participants either require or desire anonymity; they are often willing to take part in research because they support the project of finding out new knowledge or improving service delivery. Nevertheless, it is often important to protect the anonymity of participants. For example, health care professionals working in very challenging contexts may be appropriately concerned about their professional conduct being evaluated. Suspects in police interrogations, or clients undergoing psychotherapy should not expect that research will be a way for family members, say, to find out about crimes or crises. Beyond using pseudonyms to conceal identifiable details in transcripts, there are some important steps needed to preserve anonymity when presenting the audio or visual data.

Identifying names can be removed from the audio using most software programs – for example, Audacity, which has the function 'generate' – 'silence' for selected clips of sound. Pitch can also be distorted to a lower or higher pitch, so that the voice is unrecognizable by voice quality alone, although retaining many of its other features. We have found that a lower pitch can be more appropriate in sensitive contexts, with higher pitch sounding more humorous. Videos and stills of videos can be anonymized by pixilating the image or other forms of manipulation that turn the movie into a cartoon or sketch. This can be achieved easily using programs such as Windows Moviemaker. Further practical support on anonymizing audio and video can be found online (see Parry, 2013).

SOME VIRTUES OF WORKING WITH NATURALISTIC DATA

Conversation analysis and discursive psychology have both developed largely through working with naturalistic data. We will offer some illustrations to highlight virtues that have been delivered through the use of these materials. These research traditions highlight an interactional order in which timings of less than 0.2 of a second, and barely hearable prosodic contours, can be critical for how an action is responded to. This is work in which the analysis is unpacking broad vernacular categories such as 'laughter', 'upset', and 'advice', explicating a range of features and issues that are relevant to how these are produced and responded to.

Let us illustrate. The following comes from a series of studies on advice conducted by the second author and others. The aim was to explicate what the activity of giving advice is, including issues of delivery and receipt.

Extract 1: P2C8 – Sudocrem (Shaw and Hepburn, 2013)

```
1  Mum:  >Did you,< (0.2) did you
          think her ha:nd looked
2         any better.
3         (1.1)
4  Kat:  ↑>Yeah yeah,<↑=I hadn't
          really noticed to be
5         honest, So-rry,
6         (.)
7  Kat:  Why- <what did you put on it.
8  Mum:  S:udocream.
9         (0.5)
10 Kat:  Yeah that's what I've been
          putting on it.
11        (0.4)
12 Mum:  Yeah but I've been putting
          it on: sort of like (0.6)
13        every hour?
14        (0.6)
15 Kat:  Oh right.
16        (0.3)
17 Mum:  And she's ↑quite accepting,
18        (0.6)
19 Kat:  Yeah.=↑No I know I-↑ (0.3) I
          know.
20 Mum:  She walks round with her
          <hand out> sort of he he hah
21        hah hah
22        (.)
23 Kat:  Ye:ah
24 Mum:  hu .hhh Bless her.
```

Advice in this phone conversation is not delivered explicitly, but is nevertheless hearable as can be seen from the extract. Mum describes how she has been applying Sudocrem to Farah's hand to help alleviate her rash. In lines 12 to 13, she reports putting it on every hour. While Mum is providing information about what she has done, the implicit advice is that this is something that Katie herself could do, as Farah's mum. At first Katie treats this information as news worthy: 'Oh right', but without displaying a commitment to applying the cream. Part of the affordance of delivering advice as information is that the recipient can just treat it as information rather than accept or reject the advice (see Silverman, 1997). Mum continues her advice-implicative information-giving by discounting a possible obstacle – that Farah may not be accepting (line 17). By saying the problem doesn't lie with Farah, there is a potential for hearing that it lies with Katie, who is potentially negligent in not applying the cream regularly.

Katie's response orients to this potential critical dimension by explicitly resisting the advice. She negates the assumption that she didn't know (with 'no') and then makes two explicit claims of knowledge with 'I know'. Mum orients to this resistance by reflexively re-characterizing her previous turn, building on that turn to invoke Farah's animated behavior through which she demonstrates her over-willingness to have the cream applied. The unilateral laughter immediately after works to bring the sequence off in a non-problematic way (see Shaw, Hepburn and Potter 2013), moving the emphasis away from the problematic advice resistance and modulating the incipient blame. The laughter is finely coordinated to the action it follows; it is somewhat animated through the full and multiple laughter particles, picking up the animated nature of Farah's behavior.

Let us highlight some features of the extract and analysis that highlight the value of using natural data and the role of a precise transcript.

1. We see a diverse range of ways the action of advising can be designed. Without the careful study of this in situ it would be hard to identify these forms. Mostly we find advice is not delivered in simple, explicit, canonical constructions such as 'you should do X'.
2. Working in this way allows the identification of novel issues and dimensions to actions, such as the critical, negative dimension to advice that we see here.
3. The identification of the social nature of talk goes beyond a simple informational exchange; it is not simply the content of advice, that is, applying cream in this case, but the implications of accepting it that becomes relevant to the participant.
4. The identification of new ways in which activities such as laughter can be used goes beyond taken for granted assumptions. Here laughter was used to manage interactional trouble as opposed to being straightforwardly associated with humor. And we can understand this through using a transcript that captures the precise placement and delivery of that laughter.
5. Only by working with the original recording, combined with a high quality transcript, can we show certain features of the production of talk that are consequential. Here we see how laughter is delivered to support the action that is being conducted.

In the following section we illustrate the value of using naturalistic data when considering applied settings, and start to show the way this can have significant implications for practice guidelines and ultimately the well-being of patients.

THE VALUE OF USING NATURALISTIC MATERIALS TO SUPPORT APPLIED RESEARCH

The virtues of working with naturalistic data are exemplified in a research project investigating end-of-life decision-making in neonatal intensive care. In the case of neonatal decision-making, knowing how to effectively approach decision-making with the parents of extremely sick newborn babies is both challenging and important, as parents have to live with these decisions for the rest of their lives. Professional guidelines emphasize the 'best interest' of the baby, parental involvement, as well as shouldering the responsibility of the decision: 'to alleviate the burden of guilt that some parents feel' (Larcher et al., 2015, 18). However, little detail is provided on *how* doctors can achieve these ideals in the way they actually talk to parents. Furthermore, professional assessment and training of doctors in this area is locally decided (see Gallagher et al., 2015), and not based on an evidence base of what actually happens in these conversations.

In addition to the predominance of interview data, in this context, a number of studies have used an observational approach (Anspach, 1993; Orfali, 2004). Observational data enable closer exploration of the event itself and yet, as we have noted above, this kind of ethnographic observation is not effective for capturing the way these interactions unfold moment by moment in real time, and thus the implication of alternative decision-making approaches is left unexplored. Using audio and video recordings enables the researcher to get a version of events, which can then be viewed repeatedly, transcribed in detail and analyzed to support closer inspection.

The Parents and Neonatal Decisions Study (PND) set out to explore the decision-making process, collecting naturalistic data that could be used to develop an evidence base to inform communication training. It recorded conversations between doctors and parents, focusing on those specifically involved in end-of-life decision-making. This was not a simulation; these were real, testing, emotionally fraught, life-changing consequential conversations.

The study identified two different ways in which doctors initiated decision-making with the parents: making 'recommendations' and 'providing options'. Tracking the conversation in real time showed how choosing one design over the other could have important implications for parental involvement. The following extract shows the patterned way in which 'recommendations' were designed, as well as their implications for the unfolding talk.

Extract 2: F8R1 (Shaw et al., 2016)

```
 1 Dr:   =.hhh (0.3) we::, as a group
         of doctors, (0.4) an nurs↑es,
 2       (2.9) fee::l, (0.6) in his
         best interest, (1.3) we
         should*,
 3       (1.0) change his (0.2) active
         intensive care into (0.4)
 4       °palliative care.°
 5 M:    What does that mean.
(lines 6-47 deleted where the doctor
explains what palliative care is)
48 M:    [So 'cause he's not] making
         breathing effort [then-]=
49 Dr:                    [Ye:s]
50 M:    =you're basically saying
         that (0.3) you can't see him
51       making effort to breathe in
         °future.°=
52 Dr:   =>Yeah< that's because of
         his °ur° brain scan result
53       °ac[tually.°]
54 M:       [ Okay:, ]
55 Dr:   and >.hh you know combin-<
         it's ↑not just a brain scan.
56       (0.4)
57 Dr:   Taking [right from,]
58 M:    [(°I think we should°)] (0.5)
         doesn't [he,]
59 Dr:           [((Other Dr Name?))]
60 M:    (.) the doctor said that the
         swelling on his brain would
61       get bigger before it got
         better,
62 M:    So doesn't he nee- (.) like
         (0.3) it will
63       [have to get] (0.5) doesn't
         he need like (0.2)=
64 Dr:   [ It's, ]
65 M:    =time for it to see if it's
         gonna down at all, or (.)
66       like (0.3)
67 Dr:   tcha.hh (0.2) His brain
         sca:n, (0.9) is not going to:
68       (0.4) ch:ange anything.=What
         happens is the bon- amount
69       of bleeding is there:,=
```

Take the doctor's first turn in lines 1 to 4. Consider how it unfolds in real time to build an action. First, note how the morally laden 'we should' recommendation for a move out of treatment into palliative care (with its pessimism about outcome) is built. Instead of moving straight from 'we' to 'should' the speaker inserts 'as a group of doctors' showing an orientation to unpacking the 'we' as a group which can corroborate the advice (Potter, 1996). Note how, in line 1, the speaker then adds 'an nurs↑es', further building the corroboration. And in line 2 the, yet to be delivered, recommendation is characterized as in the baby's 'best interest', which treats resistance as going against those interests. Moreover, although the delivery is deliberate with lengthy pauses, the action is not complete until 'care' on line 4; this makes it hard for the mother to respond until that point, thus ensuring the proposal and its basis are delivered to the mother slowly and clearly.

Following the recommendation, there is then some initial problematic uptake as Mum enquires into what is actually being proposed (line 5). In lines not shown, the doctor explains what palliative care is, and the mother is left to formulate the negative upshot; that the baby would ultimately be allowed to die. We will return to the extract again when we see more problematic uptake from the mother. In lines 59 to 66, she begins to challenge the recommendation. She enquires about an alternative course of action, using a negatively framed question design 'doesn't he' (lines 58 and 63). This proposes that the answer is likely to be 'no' and therefore seeks agreement with an assertion (see Bolinger, 1957; Heritage, 2002). The mother's questioning provides evidence that she treats this recommendation as putting her in a position where it is difficult to press for an alternative course of action.

On the face of it, this extract embodies the official guidelines, which stress that recommendations should be collaborative. Yet it also illustrates how challenging it is for full parental involvement to be achieved. Furthermore, Shaw et al. argue that while:

references to 'best interest' by doctors when giving recommendations are understandable, given its emphasis in national guidelines (e.g. RCPCH, 2004), to conflate its 'philosophical' use into the language used to initiate such decisions as seen here has the potential to elicit less opportunity for parental involvement – through which babies' best interests could otherwise be more fully explored. (2016: 1239)

These are subtle and challenging issues. They are played out in carefully selected language in actual settings. It would be very hard to capture this in an interview or questionnaire. By researchers putting the effort into recruiting parents and medical practitioners willing to take part, and taking seriously the unfolding real-time specifics of their interaction when things go wrong, we are given a window on a delicate, and catastrophically fraught event for parents, that allows us to understand how support can be given and its problematics.

USING NATURALISTIC DATA TO INFORM TRAINING

Challenging material such as that discussed in the previous section has implications for developing training and formulating guidance for best practice. One of the features of working with actual materials collected from settings involving professional practice (medical, mediation, helplines, legal, and so on) is that the connection to training and applied implications is easier to map out than when extrapolating from an experimentally based theory or a regularity identified in survey research. Put simply, we are studying the raw complexity of professional practice and are able to make suggestions and recommendations for that very practice.

Naturalistic data facilitates immediate engagement with professionals as it provides the possibility of staying with the setting throughout, rather than having to translate the data back to the organization in the way that would be required for elicited data. Professionals get the unique opportunity to work with real data that provides authentic examples of how interaction unfolds. Indeed, Elizabeth Stokoe (2013) compared simulated and actual police investigative interviews and found there to be systematic differences in the way talk was produced. This raises important questions about the authenticity of simulated data; the default approach to communication training in medical settings (Stokoe, 2013).

The Conversation Analytic Role Play Method is an approach to communication training, developed by Stokoe and informed by conversation analytic research (Stokoe, 2014). Naturalistic data are played alongside scrolling transcript on the screen in workshops. The transcript is paused at key choice points and the professionals collaborate on what the appropriate next action should be and how it should be delivered. This environment maximizes the informed engagement of both professionals and analysts. The professionals have an extremely well-practiced procedural competence, developed through long periods of performing the practice and managing its contingencies; the analysts have a sophisticated take on actual records of this interaction. They are able to highlight moments of contingency where different options are available to the professional and, by stopping the recording at that point, engage the professionals in a high level discussion making explicit their aims, values and judgments. It has proven an enormously rich way for professionals to audit and improve their own practices; often it shows precisely how sophisticated they are at practices they may not have previously been able to fully articulate. For example, data from the neonatal study quoted above was used to develop a CARM workshop to support effective end-of-life decision-making with neonatal doctors (consultants and registrars) at University College London (see UCL, 2016, for more information).

Naturalistic data also have wider implications for practice. Indeed, in the neonatal context, training is designed to improve the experiences of both the doctors and parents in challenging contexts. Furthermore, because of the unique evidence base that is provided through the systematic exploration of what actually happens in these interactions, the results speak to the needs of health care professionals and agencies, where evidence-based practice is essential.

CONCLUSION

Some 15 years ago Jonathan Potter listed the following virtues for social researchers working with naturalistic data:

a. It does not flood the research setting with the researcher's own categories (embedded in questions, probes, stimuli, vignettes, and so on).
b. It does not put people in the position of disinterested experts on their own and others' practices, thoughts, and so on, encouraging them to provide normatively appropriate descriptions (as many interview and questionnaire studies do).
c. It does not leave the researcher to make a range of more or less problematic inferences from the data collection arena to topic (from interviews about counselling, say, to counselling itself) as the topic itself (counselling, perhaps) is directly studied.
d. It opens up a wide variety of novel issues and concerns that are outside the prior expectations embodied in questionnaires, experimental formats, interview questions, and so on.
e. It is a rich record of people living their lives, pursuing goals, managing institutional tasks, and so on (2002, p. 540).

In this chapter we have reviewed these issues, and they are still pertinent. What we have tried to do here is develop the applied and training virtues of working with naturalistic data. None of this is intended to say that social researchers should give up the practices that are the mainstay of modern qualitative social science: interviews, focus groups, various forms of ethnography. There can be virtues for researchers engaging directly, as Christine Griffin (2007) and Harry Collins (1983) have argued for different reasons. However, we are strongly of the view that across the wide expanse of social science the balance is wrong. Too much qualitative social science is based around a taken for granted assumption that the natural way to do research is to perform some qualitative interviews, a set of focus groups, or a period of ethnography. We would rather researchers thought more about the choices here, and developed clearer rationales for those choices. Given that records of actual action and events *can* be studied in a way that is systematic and rigorous, that *can* generate new questions and novel insights, and *can* be the basis for effective application and training, we would like the onus of justification to fall more on those adopting other kinds of data.

FURTHER READING

Hepburn, Alexa, and Bolden, Galina (2017) *Transcribing for Social Research*. London: Sage.
Potter, Jonathan, and Hepburn, Alexa (2012) 'Eight challenges for interview researchers', in Jaber F. Gubrium and James A. Holstein (eds.), *Handbook of Interview Research* (2nd edn). London: Sage, pp. 555–70.
Silverman, David (2007) *A Very Short, Fairly Interesting and Reasonably Cheap Book about Qualitative Research*. London: Sage.

REFERENCES

Anspach, Renee R. (1993) *Deciding Who Lives: Fateful Choices in the Intensive-Care Nursery*. Berkeley, CA: University of California Press.
Atkinson, Paul (1990) *The Ethnographic Imagination: The Textual Construction of Reality*. London: Routledge.
Bales, Robert F. (1950) *Interaction Process Analysis*. Cambridge, MA: Addison-Wesley.

Barker, Roger G., and Wright, Herbert Fletcher (1951) *One Boy's Day: A Specimen Record of Behavior*. New York: Harper.

Bogen, David (1999) *Order without Rules: Critical Theory and the Logic of Conversation*. New York: SUNY Press.

Bolinger, Dwight (1957) *Interrogative Structures of American English*. Tuscaloosa, AL: University of Alabama Press.

Clayman, Steven, and Heritage, John (2002) *The News Interview: Journalists and Public Figures on the Air*. Cambridge: Cambridge University Press.

Clifford, James, and Marcus, George E. (eds.) (1986) *Writing Culture: The Poetics and Politics of Ethnography*. Berkeley, CA: University of California Press.

Collins, Harry M. (1983) 'The meaning of lies: Accounts of action and participatory research', in G. Nigel Gilbert and P. Abell (eds.), *Accounts and Action*. Aldershot: Gower, pp. 69–78.

Edwards, Derek, and Potter, Jonathan (1992) *Discursive Psychology*. London: Sage.

Feyerabend, Paul (1975) *Against Method*. London: New Left Books.

Gallagher, Katie, Shaw, Chloe, and Marlow, Neil (2015) 'Experience of training in communication skills among trainee neonatologists', *Archives of Disease in Childhood. Fetal and Neonatal Edition*, 100(5): F468.

Goodwin, Charles (1981) *Conversational Organization: Interaction between Speakers and Hearers*. New York: Academic Press.

Griffin, Christine (2007) 'Being dead and being there: Research interviews, sharing hand cream and the preference for analysing "naturally occurring data"', *Discourse Studies*, 9(2): 246–69.

Hammersley, Martyn, and Atkinson, Paul (2007) *Ethnography: Principles in Practice* (3rd edn). London: Routledge.

Hanson, Norwood Russell (1969) *Perception and Discovery*. San Francisco, CA: Freeman, Cooper.

Heath, Christian (1986) *Body Movement and Speech in Medical Interaction*. New York: Cambridge University Press.

Hepburn, Alexa, and Bolden, Galina (2012) 'The conversation analytic approach to transcription', in Jack Sidnell and Tanya Stivers (eds.), *The Handbook of Conversation Analysis*. Oxford: Wiley-Blackwell, pp. 57–76.

Hepburn, Alexa, and Bolden, Galina (2017) *Transcribing for Social Research*. London: Sage.

Heritage, John (1984) *Garfinkel and Ethnomethodology*. Cambridge: Polity Press.

Heritage, John (2002) 'The limits of questioning: Negative interrogatives and hostile question content', *Journal of Pragmatics*, 34(10–11): 1427–46.

Houtkoop-Steenstra, Hanneke (2000) *Interaction and the Standardized Survey Interview: The Living Questionnaire*. Cambridge: Cambridge University Press.

Jefferson, Gail (2004) 'Glossary of transcript symbols with an introduction', in Gene Lerner (ed.) *Conversation Analysis: Studies from the First Generation*. Amsterdam: John Benjamins, pp. 13–32.

Knorr Cetina, Karin (1999) *Epistemic Cultures: How Scientists Make Knowledge*. Cambridge, MA: Harvard University Press.

Kuhn, Thomas S. (1970). *The Structure of Scientific Revolutions* (2nd edn). Chicago, IL: University of Chicago Press.

Larcher, Vic, Craig, Finella, Bhogal, Kiran, Wilkinson, Dominic and Brierley, Joe, on behalf of the Royal College of Paediatrics and Child Health (2015) 'Making decisions to limit treatment in life-limiting and life-threatening conditions in children: A framework for practice', *Archives of Disease in Childhood*, 100(Suppl 2): s1–s26.

Laurier, Eric (2014) 'The graphic transcript: Poaching comic book grammar for inscribing the visual, spatial and temporal aspects of action', *Geography Compass*, 8(4): 235–48.

Luff, Paul, and Heath, Christian (2012) 'Some "technical challenges" of video analysis: Social actions, objects, material realities and the problems of perspective', *Qualitative Research*, 12(3): 255–79.

Lynch, Michael (1985) *Art and Artifact in Laboratory Science*. London: Routledge and Kegan Paul.

Maynard, Douglas W., Houtkoop-Steenstra, Hanneke, Schaeffer, Nora Cate and van der Zouwen, Johannes (2002) *Standardization and Tacit Knowledge: Interaction and Practice in the Survey Interview*. New York: Wiley.

Mischler, Elliot G. (1991) 'Representing discourse: The rhetoric of transcription', *Journal of Narrative and Life History*, 1(4): 255–80.

Mondada, Lorenza (2007) 'Commentary: Transcript variations and the indexicality of transcribing practices', *Discourse Studies*, 9(6): 809–21.

Mondada, Lorenza (2012a) 'The conversation analytic approach to data collection', in Jack Sidnell and Tanya Stivers (eds.), *The Handbook of Conversation Analysis*. Oxford: Wiley-Blackwell, pp. 32–56.

Mondada, Lorenza (2012b) 'Video analysis and the temporality of inscriptions within social interaction: The case of architects at work', *Qualitative Research*, 12(3): 304–33.

Orfali, Kristina (2004) 'Parental role in medical decision-making: Fact or fiction? A comparative study of ethical dilemmas in French and American neonatal intensive care units', *Social Science & Medicine*, 58(10): 2009–22.

Parry, Ruth (2013) 'Report from a knowledge sharing workshop: Tools, techniques, tips, processes, software, hardware' [online]. Available at: http://emcawiki.net/Data_collection [accessed: 29 June 2016].

Patterson, Anne, and Potter, Jonathan (2009) 'Caring: Building a "psychological disposition" in pre-closing sequences in phone calls with a young adult with a learning disability', *British Journal of Social Psychology*, 48: 447–65.

Peräkylä, Anssi (2004) 'Two traditions of interaction research', *British Journal of Social Psychology*, 43(1): 1–20.

Popper, Karl R. (1959) *The Logic of Scientific Discovery*. London: Hutchinson.

Potter, Jonathan (1996a) *Representing Reality: Discourse, Rhetoric and Social Construction*. London: Sage.

Potter, Jonathan (1996b), Right and wrong footing. *Theory and Psychology*, 6, 31–39.

Potter, Jonathan (2002) 'Two kinds of natural', *Discourse Studies*, 4(4): 539–42.

Potter, J. (2006) 'Cognition and conversation', *Discourse Studies*, 8(1): 131–40.

Potter, Jonathan (2010) 'Contemporary discursive psychology: Issues, prospects, and Corcoran's awkward ontology', *The British Psychological Society*, 49(4): 657–78.

Potter, Jonathan (2012) 'Re-reading discourse and social psychology: Transforming social psychology', *British Journal of Social Psychology*, 51(3): 436–55.

Potter, Jonathan, and Hepburn, Alexa (2005) 'Qualitative interviews in psychology: Problems and possibilities', *Qualitative Research in Psychology*, 2(4): 281–307.

Potter, Jonathan, and Hepburn, Alexa (2007) 'Life is out there: A comment on Griffin', *Discourse Studies*, 9(2): 276–82.

Potter, Jonathan, and Wetherell, Margaret (1987) *Discourse and Social Psychology: Beyond Attitudes and Behaviour*. London: Sage.

Psathas, George (1995) *Conversation Analysis: The Study of Talk-in-Interaction*. Thousand Oaks, CA: Sage.

Puchta, Claudia, and Potter, Jonathan (2004) *Focus Group Practice*. London: Sage.

Rossano, Frederico (2012) 'Gaze in conversation', in Jack Sidnell and Tanya Stivers (eds.), *The Handbook of Conversation Analysis*. Oxford: Wiley-Blackwell, pp. 308–29.

Royal College of Paediatrics and Child Health (RCPCH) (2004) *Withholding or Withdrawing Life Sustaining Treatment in Children: A Framework for Practice* (2nd edn). London: RCPCH.

Sacks, Harvey (1992) *Lectures on Conversation* (2 vols.) Edited by Gail Jefferson with introductions by Emanuel A. Schegloff. Oxford: Basil Blackwell.

Schoggen, Phil (1991) 'Ecological psychology: One approach to development in context', in R. Cohen and A.W. Siegel (eds.), *Context and Development*. New York: Psychology Press, pp. 235–52.

Shaw, Chloe, and Hepburn, Alexa (2013) 'Managing the moral implications of advice in informal interaction', *Research on Language and Social Interaction*, 46(4): 344–62.

Shaw, Chloe, Hepburn, Alexa, Potter, Jonathan (2013) 'Having the last laugh: On post completion laughter particles', in Phillip Glenn and Elizabeth Holt (eds.), *Studies of Laughter in Interaction*. London: Bloomsbury Academic, pp. 91–106.

Shaw, Chloe, Stokoe, E., Gallagher, K., Aladangady, N., and Marlow, M. (2016) 'Parental involvement in neonatal critical care decision making', *Sociology of Health and Illness*, 38(8), 1217–42.

Sidnell, Jack (2006) 'Coordinating gesture, talk, and gaze in reenactments', *Research on Language & Social Interaction*, 39(4): 377–409.

Sidnell, Jack (2012) 'Basic conversation analytic methods', in Jack Sidnell and Tanya Stivers (eds.), *The Handbook of Conversation Analysis*. Oxford: Wiley-Blackwell, pp. 77–99.

Silverman, David (1997) *Discourses of Counseling: HIV Counseling as Social Interaction*. London: Sage.

Silverman, David (2017) 'How was it for you? The interview society and the irresistible rise of the [poorly analyzed] interview', *Qualitative Research*, 17(2), 144–58.

Speer, Susan A., and Hutchby, Ian (2003) 'From ethics to analytics: Aspects of participants' orientations to the presence and relevance of recording devices', *Sociology*, 37(2): 315–37.

Stokoe, Elizabeth (2013) 'The (in)authenticity of simulated talk: Comparing role-played and actual conversation and the implications for communication training', *Research on Language and Social Interaction*, 46(2): 1–21.

Stokoe, Elizabeth (2014) 'Conversation analytic role-play method (CARM): A method for training communication skills as an alternative to simulated role-play', *Research on Language and Social Interaction*, 47(3): 255–65.

UCL (2016). *Parents and Neonatal Decisions: News* [online] Available at: http://www.ucl.ac.uk/pnd/news [accessed: 20 May 2016].

Performance, Hermeneutics, Interpretation[1]

Norman K. Denzin

Ethnography, rhetoric, and performance join forces precisely on this front of resistance to totalizing thought. This is a performative cultural politics, which recuperates any lingering estrangement between rhetoric, ethnography, the poetic and the political. (Conquergood, 1992a, pp. 80, 96 paraphrase)

PROLOGUE

A Conundrum

How to write a chapter on qualitative data collection for a *Handbook of Data Collection* when the practices that produce data are under assault? Under such circumstances how can you address qualitative data collection as a major step in qualitative research. But address the topic we must. The skeptics and the advocates will not be silenced. Criticism and controversy come from all sides (Koro-Ljungberg, 2016). The argument is straightforward: things, words, 'become data only when theory acknowledges them as data' (St. Pierre, 2011, p. 621). In a single gesture, doubt replaces certainty, no theory, method, form of data analysis, discourse, genre or tradition has 'a universal and general claim as the "right" or privileged form of authoritative knowledge' (Richardson, 2000, p. 928; see also Denzin, 2013).

But even if data are dead we still need a word. What replaces data? After all, the advocates assert that we are an empirical, not a text-based humanities discipline. We connect our interpretive practices to events that go on in the social world. That is, we do more than read and interpret already published works. We write in ways that evoke experience in the world. We write stories that can be used, stories that can be trusted, stories that can change the world. Further, we are, after William James, radical empiricists (1912). That is, we only deal with materials that can be drawn from, and are based in, experience: performances, emotions, perceptions, feelings, actions. Experience cannot be quantified, counted or turned into a thing. Experience is an ongoing process. Experience, James reminds us, can never be reduced to a stream of data or to something called data. Experience is a process. It is messy, open-ended, inconclusive, tangled up in the writer's and reader's imagined interpretations. We need a bridge to the topic at hand.

AN ASIDE ON THE METHOD OF INSTANCES

Any given practice, event or performance that is studied is significant because it is an instance of a cultural practice that happened in a particular time and place. This practice cannot be generalized to other practices, its importance lies in the fact that it instantiates a cultural practice, a cultural performance (storytelling), and a set of shifting, conflicting cultural meanings (Fiske, 1994, p. 195). This is the logic of the method of instances. Every instance is unique and has its own logic.

An analogy may help. In discourse analysis 'no utterance is representative of other utterances, though of course it shares structural features with them; a discourse analyst studies utterances in order to understand how the potential of the linguistic system can be activated when it intersects at its moment of use with a social system' (Fiske, 1994, p. 195). This is the argument for the method of instances. The analyst's task is to understand how this instance works, to show what rules of interpretation are operating, to map and illuminate the structure of the interpretive event itself.

Whether the particular instance occurs again is irrelevant. Indeed this is an irrelevant question, because occurrence is unique and shaped by prior occurrences. The question of sampling (see Schreier, Chapter 6, this volume) from a population is also not an issue, for it is never possible to say in advance what an instance is an instance of (Psathas, 1995, p. 50). This means there is little concern for empirical generalization. Psathas is clear on this point. The goal is not an abstract, or empirical generalization, rather the aim is 'concerned with providing analyses that meet the criteria of unique adequacy' (1995, p. 50). Each analysis must be fitted to the case at hand, each 'must be studied to provide an analysis *uniquely adequate* for that particular phenomenon' (1995, p. 51, italics in original).

This approach to interpretation rejects a normative epistemology which presumes that what is normal is what is most representative in a larger population. A normative epistemology directs generalizations to this 'normal' population. This stance pays little attention to the processes that produce an instance in the first place. Furthermore, it ignores the 'non-representative' and marginal formations that can exist in any social structure (Fiske, 1994, p. 196). Finally, what is normal is reduced to what is most frequent. A normative epistemology requires a set of postpositivist, naturalistic criteria for evaluating methodological work. I reject normative epistemologies, even if data are dead.

SOMETHING MORE IS GOING ON

More is at play. There is a rupture that goes beyond instances, data and their meanings. The traditional concepts of narrative, meaning, voice, presence and representation are also put under erasure, regarded as pernicious leftovers from the twin ruins of post-positivism and humanistic qualitative inquiry (Jackson and Mazzei, 2012, p. vii). Materialist feminist ontologies inspire new analytics of data analysis, including defractive readings of data. Post-methodologists, posthumanist, post-empirical and post-qualitative frameworks call for new models of science, second empiricisms, reimagined social sciences, capacious sciences, sciences of difference, a science defined by becoming, a double(d) science (Lather, 2007; St. Pierre, 2011,

p. 613; MacLure, 2011). Where do data fit in these new spaces? Is there any longer even a need for the word? Why keep the word after you have deconstructed it?

New places are sought. For some this is a place where there are no data, where the search is for justice, moral arguments, a politics of representation, which seeks utopias of possibility, a politics of hope not a politics based on data (Madison, 2010). For others, data are reconfigured, re-read through new ontologies and new interpretive analytics (St. Pierre, 2011). For still others data are used for practical purposes, in framing claims for changes in social policy (Gómez et al., 2011).

These reconfigurations move in three directions at the same time. They interrogate the practices and politics of evidence that produce data. They support the call for new ways of making the mundane, taken-for-granted everyday world visible, whether through performance, or through disruptive post-empirical methodologies. These unruly methodologies read and interrupt traces of presence, whether from film, recordings or transcriptions. They do not privilege presence, voice, meaning or intentionality. Rather they seek performative interventions and representations that heighten critical reflective awareness leading to concrete forms of praxis.

Underneath it all it is assumed that we make the world visible through our interpretive practices. All texts have a material presence in the world. Nothing stands outside the text, even as it makes the material present. Neither the material nor the discursive are privileged. They fold into one another, get tangled up in one another. How a thing gets inside the text is shaped by a politics of representation. Language and speech do not mirror experience. They create experience and in the process transform and defer that which is being described. Meanings are always in motion, incomplete, partial, contradictory. There can never be a final, accurate, complete representation of a thing, an utterance or an action. There are only different representations of different representations. There is no longer any pure presence; – description becomes inscription erases collection becomes performance erases analysis becomes interpretation.

AIMS OF THIS CHAPTER

Embracing the performance turn, I connect the study of instances to interpretation, and to hermeneutics, and privilege performed experience as a way of knowing, as a method of critical inquiry and as a mode of understanding, as a way of making the meanings of instances visible. Hermeneutics does the work of interpretation with the potential of producing understanding. Knowing refers to those embodied, sensuous experiences, which create the conditions for understanding (Denzin, 1984, p. 282). Through performance I experience another's feelings, which are present in a remembering, a performance event (Pollock, 2005a). Performed experiences are the sites where felt emotion, memory, desire and understanding come together. I seek performative interpretations that are poetic, dramatic, critical and imaginative, interpretations that are interventions, interpretations that matter.

The self-as-subject-as-performer of another's text, enters into an ethical relationship with the other. I honor their presence. The other is no longer the other, there is no other, only a multitude of voices, movements, gestures, intersecting selves, performing for one another (Pollock, 2005a, p. 6, paraphrase). I bring my body, my flesh, my voice to your text. I circle around the hidden meanings in your narrative, I make these meanings visible with my voice and my body. This *archeology of unearthing*, Madison's phrase, is never neat or tidy. It is a continuous process of resurfacing, of digging, looking, feeling, moving, inspecting, tracing and re-tracing memories, new memories (Madison, 2005a, p. 150).

As an autoethnographer I embed myself in my own history, in my memories, in my stories from my past.

PERFORMANCE

Performance autoethnography is defined by a commitment to a politics of resistance, to a commitment to change, not just interpret, the world. Performance autoethnography addresses the structures and beliefs of neoliberalism as a public pedagogy, understanding that the cultural is always political (Giroux, 2014, p. 222). The political is always Missing reference performative. The performative is always pedagogical. To perform, to read, to analyze, to interpret, to write is to resist. Moral witnessing, civic courage and moral outrage are sustained forms of resistance (Giroux, 2014, p. 223). Interpretation is a performance.

Here is Anzaldua, on the politics of performance along the US–Mexico border. These words could have been written yesterday:

> The border Patrol hides behind the local McDonalds on the outskirts of Brownsville, Texas ... They set traps along the river beneath the bridge. Hunters in army-green uniforms stalk and track these economic refugees using the powerful nightvision of electronic sensing devices. Cornered by headlights, frisked, their arms stretched over their heads, *los mojados* are handcuffed, locked in jeeps, and then kicked back across the border, no home, just the thin edge of barbwire. (1987, pp. 12–13 paraphrase)

Refugees in a homeland that does not want them, wetbacks, no welcoming hand, only pain, suffering, humiliation, degradation, death (1987, p. 12). South of the Border, down Mexico way, North America's rubbish dump, no direction home (p. 11).

TOWARD A PERFORMATIVE CULTURAL POLITICS

Thinking the world as performance raises questions that can be clustered around six intersecting planes analyses (Conquergood, 2005, p. 361, paraphrase).[2] Each plane is predicated on the proposition that if we are all performers, and the world is a performance, not a text, then we need a model of inquiry, which is simultaneously political, reflexive, rhetorical and performative. This means it is necessary to rethink the relationship between politics, the performative-I and:

- performance, pedagogy and rhetorical reflexivity;
- performance and cultural process;
- performance and ethnographic praxis;
- performance and hermeneutics;
- performance and the act of scholarly representation;
- performance after the affective (new materialism) turn (MacLure, 2015).

Performance, Pedagogy and Rhetoric

The rhetorical/pedagogical turn in performance studies interrogates the ways in which the performance text functions as an ideological document. Key terms include:

- Pedagogy: To teach, to instruct, the pedagogical is ideological.
- Spectacle: A performative relationship between people, images and events (Garoian and Gaudelius, 2008, p. 24).
- Spectacle Pedagogy: The staging of media events using the visual codes of corporate, global capitalism (Garoian and Gaudelius, 2008, p. 24).
- Critical Spectacle Pedagogy: A pedagogical practice that reflexively critiques the apparatuses of global capital (Garoian and Gaudelius, 2008, pp. 24, 75; also Debord 1967/1994; Evans and Giroux, 2015).

This performance paradigm travels from theories of critical pedagogy to views of performance as intervention, interruption and resistance. Critical indigenous performance theater contributes to utopian discourses by staging doubly inverted minstrel performances. Using ventriloquized discourse, and the apparatuses of minstrel theater, white-and-blackface performers force spectators to confront themselves.

Native Canadian whiteface performers in Daniel David Moses's play, *Almighty Voice and His Wife* (1992) use these devices to turn the tables on whites. Just before the play's finale, the Interlocutor, dressed in top hat and tails, along with white gloves and studded white boots turns and taunts the audience.

> Interlocutor: You're the redskin! You're the wagon burner! That feather Head, Chief Bullshit. No Chief Shitting Bull! Oh, no, no. Bloodthirsty savage. Yes, you're the primitive. Uncivilized A cantankerous cannibal … You are the alcoholic, diseased, dirty … degenerate. (Quoted in Gilbert, 2003, p. 693)

Here critical spectacle pedagogy confronts the racist discourse defining First Nation and Native American persons. The language itself makes a spectacle of phrases like No Chief Shitting Bull. It brings the racism directly in front of the reader, it stages the racism in the here and now of the present.

Critical pedagogy understands performance as a form of inquiry. It views performance as a form of activism, as critique, as critical citizenship. It seeks a form of performative praxis that inspires and empowers persons to act on their utopian impulses. These moments are etched in history and popular memory. They are often addressed in testimonial and fact-based (and verbatim) theater, theater that bears witness to social injustice and encourages active ethical spectatorship.

Moises Kaufman, and his oral history play, *The Laramie Project* (2001)[3] is illustrative. He observes:

> There are moments in history when a particular event brings the various ideologies and beliefs prevailing in a culture into deep focus. At these junctures the event becomes a lightning rod of sorts, attracting and distilling the essence of these philosophies and convictions. By paying careful attention in moments like this to people's words, one is able to hear the way these prevailing ideas affect not only individual lives but also the culture at large. The trials of Oscar Wilde were such an event … The Brutal murder of Matthew Shephard was another event of this kind. (2014, p. ix)[4]

Spectacle pedagogy addresses these moments, those lightning rod occasions when power, ideology and politics come crashing down on ordinary people and their lives. It does so by staging and re-staging performances, which interrogate the cultural logics of the spectacle itself. Staged performances of culture are always appraisal of culture (Madison, 2010, p. 13). These re-stagings raise a series of questions asking always, 'How did this happen? What does it mean? How could it have been prevented? What are its consequences for the lives of ordinary people?' (Madison, 2010, pp. 12–13)

To answer these questions Kaufman's *Laramie Project* enlisted the help of Laramie citizens in the production of the play's script:

> Kaufman: We devoted two years of our lives to this Project. We returned to Laramie many times over the course of a year and a half and conducted more than two hundred interviews. (2001, p. vii)

When the project was completed, a member of the community reflected on the Shepard death and the play:

> Jonas Slonaker: Change is not an easy thing, and I don't think people were up to it here. They got what they wanted. Those two boys got what they deserve and we look good now. Justice has been served … You know it has been a year since Matthew Shepard died, and they haven't passed shit in Wyoming … at a state level, any town, nobody anywhere, has passed any kind of laws or hate crime legislation. … What's come out of it? (2001, p. 99)

A community member replies:

> Doc O'Connor: I been up to that site (where he was killed). I remembered to myself the night he and I drove around together, he said to me, … I can just picture what he was seeing. The last thing he saw in this earth was the sparkling lights. (2001, p. 99)

And as Kaufman's little theater group left Laramie, for the last time, a member commented:

Andy Paris: And in the distance I could see the sparkling lights of Laramie, Wyoming. (2001, p. 101)

Matthew's legacy, the pure, sparkling lights of Laramie, what a town could be.

Critics have argued that Kaufman's play smooths over the raw edges of homophobia in Laramie. Taken out of context, the play, as Pollock notes, reads a bit like a version of *Our Town*,[5] but this impression may be due, in part to the effect 'of repeated productions in communities across the United States in which the original actors/interviewers are re/displaced by actors playing interviewer/actors' (Pollock, 2005a, p. 6). This puts the representations of Laramie and the murder 'at one further remove from the reality of the audience members who might otherwise identify with the members of the Tectonic Theater as people-like-themselves' (p. 6).

Being further removed speaks directly to the relationship between representation, performance and reality, that is 'actual' events. Paraphrasing Pollock (2005, pp. 2–3), too many representations of living history try to collapse reality and representation. The goal is to give the impression that 'you were there'. But that is only an ideological construction, a modernist realist myth, which ignores the politics of representation.

The goal is to use critical pedagogy as the means to disrupt, expose and critique these structures of injustice. The stage becomes the site of resistance, the place where performative-I's confront and engage one another.

Paraphrasing Conquergood:

> The aim of performance is to bring self and other, the performative-I and the audience together so they can question, debate, and challenge one another. The performance resists conclusions. It is open-ended. It is committed to creating and keeping a dialogue ongoing. It is more like a hyphen, than a period. (2013, p. 75)

Madison (2005a, p. 146) elaborates:

> Performance involves seeing ourselves and showing ourselves to ourselves in a way that allows you to understand something new about who you are, it is a doubling, a kind of meta-narrative, performing performances of our inner and outer lives. For fieldwork performances there is another kind of performance going on as a result of invoking the nonfiction of other people's stories and vulnerabilities. (2005, p. 146, paraphrase)

A goal is to bring the audience into this space so they can co-experience this doubling, this meta-narrative and apply it to their own lives.

Critical Spectacle Pedagogy in Action

Picture the following scene. Bourbon Street, New Orleans, November 1985. A funeral and eulogy for the Free Southern Theater.[6]

> A black man, fringed, red, white and blue umbrella held high overhead leads Free Southern Theater members down Bourbon Street. They are carrying a casket and they are on their way to a funeral and an eulogy. African American musicians play brass and percussion. Theater members place old costumes, props, and scripts into the coffin which also contains a broken mirror. They are mourning the demise of the theater. The funeral party moves to Armstrong Park in front of Perseverance Hall II in Congo Square. The band plays 'Just a Closer Walk with Thee'. The casket is lowered into the grave. (Cohen-Cruz, 2005, p. 60, paraphrase)

Caron Atlas, who was present at the funeral, describes the event's impact:

> The funeral told me there was another way that art and politics connected with activism that went beyond artists as constituents. Here was theater tied to a social movement. Community-based theater companies[7] inspired by the Free Southern were challenged to ask, how do you do this with your own people, within your own context and culture? (Quoted in Cohen-Cruz, 2005, p. 61)

Performers, audiences, a stage, death, mourning, music, community, critical pedagogy, bodies acting together in the service of social change. Civil rights on the move.

Rhetorical reflexivity, as Conquergood notes, troubles the assumption that the world out there can be easily moved into a written text. There is always a gap between studying others where they are and representing them where they aren't (2006, p. 364). The flesh and blood subject cannot just be plunked down in a text through the use of quotations from field notes. We cannot speak for the other, and they have only a complicated, compromised presence outside our text. A critical performative reflexivity turns back on itself.

Ellis provides an example:

> As I reconstruct and revise a portion of my life-story, I seek to provide a framework that marks and holds the scenes in place, one that moves from beginning to end, and circles back to the beginning again. My goal is to model a way to reflectively make sense of experience ... As an autoethnographer I am both the author and focus of the story, the one who tells and the one who experiences, the observer and the observed ... an ethnographer and ... a storyteller. (2009, p. 13)

Multiple identities circulate in Ellis's text: ethnographer, autoethnographer, observer, subject, storyteller, narrator, the composer of a life story worth telling a life worth living (2009, p. 13).

Spry (2011, p. 35) extends the discussion, explicitly focusing on critical performances that interrupt, and challenge existing structures of power: 'In performative autoethnography the heart, body, mind, spirit *et al* are openly and critically reflective; as such, epistemologies of pain and of hope often emerge.'

Performance, Cultural Process, Politics

All pragmatists and performance ethnographers who have read John Dewey would agree with the second cluster: culture, like data, is a verb, a process, an ongoing performance, not a noun, or a product or a static thing. We cannot study cultural experience directly, just as we cannot study data directly. We study performances that produce those things we call data. We study experience in its performative representations, staged performances of culture. Experience has no existence apart from the storied acts of the performative-I (Pollock, 2007, p. 240). Performance becomes a tactic, a form of advocacy, of resistance, a cry for human rights and social justice,

Madison (2010, p. 9) provides an example, an imaginary scene in a death camp.[8]

> A death camp in Treblinka. A dancer stands naked in line waiting for her turn to enter the gas chamber. We see a human being with a natural power to command space reduced to a body taking up space, passively submitting to the prospect of death. A guard tells her to step in line and dance. She does, and carried away by her *authoritative action* and by her *repossession of self and a world* she dances up to the guard and – now within the compass of her space – takes his gun and shoots him. What a surprise, a zombie-like creature can spring back to life by means of a performance. The dancer is moved, carried away by the forces of performance and justice to enact the unimaginable. (Madison, 2010, p. 10)

Performance and Ethnographic Praxis

The third cluster brings the performative-I, performance and ethnographic praxis into play, highlighting the methodological implications of thinking about fieldwork as a collaborative process, or a co-performance (Conquergood, 1991, p. 190). The observer and the observed, the writer and the subject are co-performers or dueoethnographers in a performance event (Norris and Sawyer, 2012). Dueoethnographers enter a collaborative relationship with the other in order to learn about themselves. The writer and the other co-construct inquiry as a site of resistance (Norris and Sawyer, 2012, p. 10). This allows collaborative narratives of resistance to be constructed. Ethnographic praxis is a performance fashioned between 'mutually engaged collaborators in a fragile fiction' (Conquergood, 1986/2013, p. 21). Acts of activism are forged in such moments.

Performance autoethnographers struggle with the moral tensions and ethical ambiguities that surround this fiction. Geertz cautions, in fieldwork 'There is something very complicated and not altogether clear about the nature of sincerity and insincerity, genuineness and hypocrisy and self-deception'

(Geertz, 1968, p. 155). Autoethnographers-as-performers insert their experiences into the cultural process, as when Conquergood came to the assistance of his neighbors in Big Red, a Chicago Polyethnic tenement (Conquergood, 2013).

In the following scene Madison is caught in a dilemma involving praxis, politics and ethics. She is teaching in the English department at the University of Ghana at Legon in August 1999. A student strike protesting an increase in fees and tuition is going on. She supports the strike, but instructors have been encouraged to not cancel classes. In the midst of a class, young men wearing red bandanas and red T-shirts burst into the room, shouting:

Young Protesters: You know there is a strike. Why are you holding class? Do you know we are striking?
Madison: Yes, I know. I support you. Please look what is on the blackboard: read the words: Hegemony, alienation, neocolonialism, postcolonial theory. The students have listed your demands. See the lines they drew between empire and citizenship.
Young Protester: Why are you teaching at Legon?
Madison: So I can teach what is on the board to students here.
Young Protester (pointing to the blackboard): This is what you are teaching?
Second Protester: Okay, lets go. But Prof. no more classes today.
Madison: No more classes today.
Young Protesters (with great bravado): Onward! (Madison, 2010, p. 22).
Madison: Days after the rally, the campus was closed and students were required to leave the university grounds. Several weeks after the closing Queen Elizabeth II visited the campus. Students were allowed back. The streets and gutters were swept clean, Ghanaian and British flags adorned the streets, and the government reduced fees by 30 percent. There were celebrations. (Madison, 2010, p. 23, paraphrase)

In this complex performance, it is impossible to separate Ghanaian culture from the local acts of activism, and the politics of neoliberal political economy. The Ghanaian activists – student protesters – staged radical performances. These performances brought Madison, as a performance ethnographer, directly into the protesters' local story, a story which also included the Queen of England. Stories or scenes of activism cannot be told without invoking politics, economy and culture.

Performance, Hermeneutics, Interpretation

The fourth cluster connects performance to hermeneutics, and the interpretive process. I structure the interpretive process by using Conquergood's triad of triads. I seek performative interpretations that are poetic, dramatic, critical and imaginative, interpretations that are interventions.

Listening to the different voices in Kaufman's play or reading Madison's performance texts out loud allows me to hear my voice doing her voice, or the voices of the townspeople in Laramie. Through my version of their voice I connect to these performances. In these sounds and feelings I enter a co-constructed interpretive space. I become a storyteller, a performer.

The self-as-subject-as-performer of another's text, enters onto an ethical relationship with the other. I honor their presence. The other is no longer the other, there is no other, only a multitude of voices, movements, gestures, intersecting selves, performing for one another (Pollock, 2005a, p. 6, paraphrase). I bring my body, my flesh, my voice to your text. I circle around the hidden meanings in your narrative, I make these meanings visible with my voice and my body. This *archeology of unearthing*, Madison's phrase, is never neat or tidy. It is a continuous process of resurfacing, of digging, looking, feeling, moving, inspecting, tracing and re-tracing memories, new memories (Madison, 2005a, p. 150).

As an autoethnographer I embed myself in my own history, in my memories, in my stories from my past.

Performance and the Politics of Scholarly Representation

The fifth pairing questions the unbreakable link between hermeneutics, politics, pedagogy, ethics and scholarly representation. Writing in 1991 Conquergood (p. 190) remains firm on this point. We should treat performances as a complementary form of research publication, an alternative method, or way of interpreting and presenting one's ethnographic work. The performance text – a text meant to be performed – can take many forms, from ethnodrama to ethnotheater, poetry to a short story. It involves a movement from body (experiences) to paper (text) to stage (performance) (Spry, 2011, p. 26).

Performance texts, like an ethnodrama (Saldana, 2005, p. 2), are not intended to replace scholarly reports and articles ... it is just one of several forms that is available for representing ethnographic inquiry (Saldana, 2005, p. 2, paraphrase). Some work entirely within the field of performance – solo and collaborative performances, ethnodramas, ethnotheater, arts-based interventions. Some perform theory, where theory, writing and performing intersect (Madison, 1999, p. 107):

> **Soyini Madison:** This essay performatively expresses specific theoretical ruminations on class, language, and race. This writing is a performance, while it is or is not necessarily for the 'stage'. The performance seeks a felt-sensing meeting between theory, writing, and performing. The performer claims an uneasy possession of performance as a means of both subjectivity and freedom. Theory becomes another way to know performance better; and performance becomes the desired illuminator of theory. From the burlesque to the sublime, the performer conjures four different encounters with her theoretical fathers: Karl Marx, Ferdinand de Saussure, Jacques Derrida, and Frantz Fanon. Needing useful theory – from the 'high' ground of scholarship to the 'low' ground of ancient re/tellings – for useful purposes, the performer must first remember where theories begin.
>
> *Embodied Writing* (*The performer sits under a spotlight surrounded by books on performance. She touches, smells, and tastes some of the books. She holds one up to her ear. She notices you are there. She looks up to speak*)
>
> Performance has become too popular. Performance is everywhere. Today I want to perform a conversation with Karl Marx, Ferdinand de Saussure, Jacques Derrida, and Frantz Fanon, the only way I can make them meaningful is to talk with them. Bear with me. (p. 107, paraphrase)
>
> ***
>
> **Stage Right:** Spotlight shines on a diorama of Karl Marx, Ferdinand de Saussure, Jacques Derrida, and Frantz Fanon.
>
> ***
>
> **Soyini Madison:** These fathers are long on insight, but they have troubled me. They have come to occupy too much space, the inside, the outside and the in-between. This performance will help relocate them. I meet them as 'not-not-me'. I beg here for a space of imagination, for joy, purpose'. (Madison, 1999, p. 110, paraphrase)

Madison's performance of theory undoes the classic article format. She turns canonical sources (references) into speaking voices in a performance text where everybody is on the same level, the same stage. Now listen to Tami Spry. Picture her in your mind. She is seated in a wooden chair, on a small stage. A spotlight shines on her.

> For some time now my work has focused upon an ethnography of loss and healing. The body is tantamount as it is the presence and absence of bodies that constitute the experiential evidence of loss. Here is a passage from a work on the loss of our child: 'Paper and Skin: Bodies of Loss and Life':
>
> The words are enmeshed in the blood and bones of the mother and child. Arms ache and disarm themselves with the visceral absence of the other. Writing doesn't help me put my arms back on, but it does help me to remember that I had arms, and then, to show me that the arms are still usable in a way I can't yet understand. (2011, p. 21)

Loss, mourning, grief, pain. Performative autoethnography in motion. Words fail us and we fall back on our bodies, lurching, flailing, stumbling over shards of language (Spry, 2011, p. 27). Body as text. Karl Marx on stage with Soyini and Tami.

Performances deconstruct, or at least challenge the scholarly article as the preferred form of presentation (and representation). A performance authorizes itself, not through the citation of scholarly texts, but through its ability to critique, arouse, evoke and invoke emotional experience and understanding between performer and audience.

Performances become a critical site of power, and politics, in the fifth pair. A radical pedagogy underlies this notion of performative cultural politics. The performative becomes an act of doing, an act of resistance, a way of connecting the biographical, the pedagogical and the political (Conquergood, 2013, p. 41).

Performance, Affect and the New Materialisms

A rupture The traditional concepts of narrative, meaning, voice, presence and representation are put under erasure by the new material feminists (Jackson and Mazzei, 2012, p. vii; Koro-Ljungberg, 2016, p. 2); new (and familiar) names: Barad, Massumi, Braidotti, Pickering, Latour, Clough, Haraway, Lather.

Coole and Frost describe three themes that frame this discourse:

> First, is an ontological reorientation that is posthumanist in the sense that it conceives of matter itself as exhibiting agency. Second are biopolitical, and bioethical issues concerning the status of life and of the human. Third, the new scholarship reengages political economy emphasizing the relationship between the material details of everyday life and broader geopolitical and socio-economic structure. (2010, pp. 6–7, paraphrase)

New terms: mobile assemblages, infra-assemblage, intra-action, inter-assemblage, defraction, entangled, transversal, entangled agencies, eventful, immanent, transmutational, blockage, event, doings, plugging in, rhizomatic activity, BWOs, entanglement, agential realism – the materialist critique opens up multiple spaces, including a focus on cyborgs, and post-technological and post-human bodies, new ontologies of being and inquiry, a move away from epistemology, new views of voice, presence and performance. A concept of post-humanist performativity emerges. It embraces the mangle of post-human bodies, new body-machine-material entanglements (Jackson and Mazzei, 2012, p. 123).[9]

The Mangle of Body, Paper, Stage

Butler's concept of performativity is as central to the new discourse as it is for performance studies. Jackson and Mazzei (2012, pp. 117, 126, 127) elaborate on what they term posthumanist performativity:

> We re-think voice ... and the subject, not as a separation of the theoretical from the material, but as an enactment, as a performative practice, as posthumanist performativity, as performative practice, as the entanglement of material practices/doings/actions/understandings. (Paraphrase)

Butler explains this further:

> Performativity is both an agent, and a product of the social and the political. Gender and sexuality are performatives made visible through a process of making, doing and repetition. The performative 'I' is to a certain extent unknowable, threatened with becoming undone altogether (2004, p. 4, paraphrase).

Susan Hekman clarifies, using the language of the new materialism:

> The 'I' is a mangle composed of multiple elements. The social scripts defining subjecthood are a key aspect of that mangle. But the mangle also encompasses a body that is sexed and raced, a body that is located at a particular place in the social hierarchy, and a body/subject that has had a range of experiences. The result may be a subject that fits neatly into the definition of subject the social script circumscribe. Or, the results may be an 'I' that cannot find a script that fits, that resists scripts available to her/him. (2010, pp. 100–1, paraphrase)

This is Spry's performative-I, her textualized body:

> The performative-I is the feeling, thinking, moving, performing writer
> wanting to write in a way that seeps into the skin of the reader, melts into her bones. Moves through her blood, until the words become transformed

through her own body. I want to be personally and politically entangled by scholarship. Otherwise what is the point? (Spry, 2011, pp. 211–12, paraphrase)

Borrowing from the new materialist discourse, Spry's argument is framed by Barad's concept of agential realism which:

> situates knowledge claims in local experience where objectivity is literally embodied, privileging neither the material or the cultural, while interrogating the boundaries of reflexivity, and underlining the necessity of an ethic of knowing that has real, material consequences. (Barad, 2007, p. 23, paraphrase)

Back to square one: body, paper stage, the flesh and blood body intersects with the performative-I in a historical moment, writing its way forward, doing what's done, performativly seeking a discourse that moves the world (Spry, 2011, p. 23).

Consider Jackson and Mazzei's discussion of fashion and women's dress and the legacies of the 1980s:

> Suits with big shoulder pads, wide lapels, and 'ties' that said the more you can look like a man while still presenting a feminine image, the greater chance you will have for advancement. We could feel the effect, what it produced in us as women trying to assert ourselves and to be taken seriously … we were brought back to our own need to conform and fit in. (2012, p. 133)

The suit, the tie, shoulder pads, wide lapels, the entire material ensemble, being feminine, while looking like a man, Butler's 'I', performative acts, wearing the suit, the suit as a site of power (2012, p. 133) – thus does a materialist feminist discourse open a space for dialog between critical performance studies, the performative-I, critical pedagogy and the concept of posthumanist performativity.

A Reapprochment?

Feminist materialisms move in at least three directions at the same time. They interrogate the practices and politics of evidence that produce empirical material. They support the call for new ways of making the mundane, taken-for-granted everyday world visible through disruptive post-empirical methodologies. These unruly methodologies read and interrupt traces of presence, whether from film, recordings or transcriptions. They do not privilege presence, voice, meaning or intentionality. Rather they seek performative interventions and representations that heighten critical reflective awareness leading to concrete forms of praxis.

Underneath it all it is assumed that we still make the world visible through our interpretive practices. All texts have a material presence in the world. Nothing stands outside the text, even as it makes the material present. Neither the material nor the discursive are privileged. They fold into one another, get tangled up in one another. How a thing gets inside the text is shaped by a politics of representation. Language and speech do not mirror experience. They create experience and in the process transform and defer that which is being described. Meanings are always in motion, incomplete, partial, contradictory. There can never be a final, accurate, complete representation of a thing, an utterance or an action. There are only different representations of different representations. There is no longer any pure presence – description becomes inscription becomes performance.

A new paradigm is on the horizon, one that doubles back on itself and wanders in spaces that have not yet been named. It celebrates the implications for qualitative methodology of the recent (re)turn to materiality across the social sciences and humanities (MacLure, 2015, pp. 94–5). The 'new materialisms' promise to go beyond the old antagonisms of nature and culture, science and the social, discourse and matter. Performance studies scholars would agree. There is a reapprochment, threaded through the eye of the needle that passes from Conquergood to Butler to Barad to Madison to MacLure to Spry to Alexander.

THEATER AND A POLITICS OF RESISTANCE

The emphasis on the politics of resistance connects performance autoethnography to the global community-based performance movement, to Third World popular Theater, to applied theater, the International Popular Theatre Alliance, to performance art, performance studies and to critical participatory action theories (Schechner, 2015, pp. 158–9; Thompson and Schechner, 2004; Cohen-Cruz, 2005).

In this formation, performance autoethnography becomes a civic, participatory, collaborative project, an arts-based approach with parallels to Boal's Theatre of the Oppressed (1985), which draws on Freire's *Pedagogy of the Oppressed* (2000/1970, 1996; also Dennis, 2009, pp. 72–4).[10] For the dramatic, participatory model to be effective, the following elements need to be present. Scholars must have the energy, imagination, courage and commitment to create these texts (see Conquergood, 1985, p. 10). Audiences must be drawn to the sites where these performances take place, and they must be willing to suspend normal aesthetic frameworks, so that co-participatory performances can be produced.

Boal is clear on this: 'In the Theatre of the Oppressed we try to … make the dialogue between stage and audience totally transitive' (1995, p. 42; 1985, 2006). In these sites a shared field of emotional experience is created, and in these moments of sharing, critical cultural awareness is awakened. Performers enact scenes of oppression, and acknowledge the presence of the audience. Acting as a catalyst, the actor, or Joker, as Boal calls the person, introduces the scene and guides the audience in providing different endings, or solutions to a problem (Madison, 2012, p. 236; Boal, 1985, p. 186; 1995, p. 42).

In these performances the personal becomes political. This happens precisely at that moment when the conditions of identity construction are made problematic, and located in concrete history. Cohen-Cruz offers an example, his experience at a Broadway production of *Falsettoland* in the early 1990s:

> As the play's protagonist mourned the loss of his friend (lover?) to AIDS, I wept at the loss of my dear friend David and inadvertently leaned to the stranger to my left. He, weeping with an abandon that also seemed to transcend the death of the character, leaned in to me too, communicating great empathy. Everywhere I saw weeping spectators and felt that the theatrical event was a mass public funeral for our beloved friends lost to AIDS. (2005, p. 97)

The goal is to give back, to see performance as a form of activism, as critique, as critical citizenship. The goal is a performative praxis that inspires and empowers persons to act on their utopian impulses. These moments are etched in history and popular memory.

Back to Laramie, Wyoming, Ten Years Later

Kaufman and the members of the Tectonic Theater Project returned to Laramie, Wyoming on the 10th anniversary of Mr Shepard's death (Healy, 2008, p. A19). They re-interviewed town members, intending to use the new interviews in an epilogue to the play. They were disappointed to learn that nothing had been done to commemorate the anniversary of Matthew's death. Mr Kaufman was angry that there were as yet no hate-crimes law in Wyoming. But the city had changed.

> **Local Citizen:** Laramie has changed in some ways. The city council passed a bias crimes ordinance that tracks such crimes, but it does include penalties for them. There is an AIDS Walk now. Several residents have come out publicly as gay, in their churches or on campus, in part to honor Mr. Shepard's memory. The university hosts a four-day Shepard Symposium for Social Justice each spring, and there is talk of creating a degree minor in gay and lesbian studies. But there is no memorial to Mr. Shepard here in town. The log fence has been torn down where he lay dying for 18 hours on Oct. 7, 1998. There is no marker. Wild grass blows in the wind. You can see the lights of Laramie from the spot where he died.

Performance ethnography disguised as spectacle theater in the service of memory, social change and social justice.

Effects like these in Laramie represent, at some deep level, an emancipatory commitment to community action which performs social change, even if change is only an idea, whose time has yet to come. This form of performance inquiry helps people recover, and release themselves from the repressive constraints embedded in repressive racist and homophobic pedagogies.

A dramatic production like *Laramie* moves in three directions at the same time: it shapes subjects, audiences and performers. In honoring subjects who have been mistreated, such performances contribute to a more 'Enlightened and involved citizenship' (Madison, 1998, p. 281). These performances interrogate and evaluate specific social, educational, economic and political processes. This form of praxis can shape a cultural politics of change. It can help create a progressive and involved citizenship. The performance becomes the vehicle for moving persons, subjects, performers and audience members, into new, critical, political spaces. The performance gives the audience, and the performers, 'equipment for [this] journey: empathy and intellect, passion and critique' (Madison, 1998, p. 282).

Such performances enact a performance-centered evaluation pedagogy. Thus fusion of critical pedagogy and performance praxis, uses performance as a mode of inquiry, as a method of doing evaluation ethnography, as a path to understanding, as a tool for engaging collaboratively the meanings of experience, as a means to mobilize persons to take action in the world. This form of critical, collaborative, performance pedagogy privileges experience, the concept of voice and the importance of turning evaluation sites into democratic public spheres (see Worley, 1998). Critical performance pedagogy informs practice, which in turn supports the pedagogical conditions for an emancipatory politics (Worley, 1998, p. 139).

Extending Toni Morrison, the best art, the best performance autoethnographies are 'unquestionably political and irrevocably beautiful at the same time' (Morrison, 1994, p. 497). They help us extract meaning out of individual instances, the murder of Matthew Shepard.

IN CONCLUSION: BACK TO DATA AND ITS COLLECTION

The performance turn problematizes data, its collection and analysis. Of course data are not dead. Data are not passive objects waiting to be collected, coded, categorized, treated as evidence in a theoretical model. Data are verbs, processes made visible through the performative acts of the inquirer. Data are never passive. Data have agency. Data have presence. Data have presence in the individual instance. The method of instances allows data to have another day in court, but only when it is read back through the radical empiricism of William James.

Data, at one level, refer to the facts of experience, and we can never be without the facts of experience, but we cannot be controlled by them. Data are always fluid, transformative, unruly (MacLure, 2013a, 2013b; Koro-Ljungberg and MacLure, 2013). I have suggested that we need an emancipatory, performance-based approach to data. This discourse requires a re-reading of words like data, data collection and data analysis. A performance-based approach reads these words in terms of a critical theory of performance, ethnography culture, politics and pedagogy.

I've offered a bridge of sorts to the topic of this *Handbook*. We always need a away back, a way to move from theory and method and critique to the real world, to the world of human beings and human suffering. A performance-based approach is only one bridge that can be taken and it is not a bridge too far.

Notes

1. I thank Uwe Flick, Ping-Chun Hsiung and a third reviewer for their helpful comments on earlier drafts of this chapter which draws on Denzin (2017).
2. Conquergood has five intersecting planes. I add rhetoric and the new materialisms.
3. On October 7, 1998 a young gay man, Matthew Shepard, was discovered bound to a fence outside Laramie, Wyoming, savagely beaten, left to die. Matthew's death became a national symbol of intolerance. In the aftermath Kaufman and the members of the Tectonic Theater Project went to Laramie and conducted more than 200 interviews. From these transcripts the playwrights constructed the Laramie Project. Ten years later they returned to Laramie, producing a second play based on the ways the community was grappling with Matthew's legacy. The play has been performed over 2,000 times. The Tectonic Theater Project collaborated with Home Box Office (HBO) to make a film based on the play. It starred Peter Fonda, Laura Linney, Christina Ricci and Steve Buscemi. It opened the 2002 Sundance Film Festival, and was nominated for 4 Emmys.
4. Similar events include the murders of Michael Brown and Trayvon Martin, and the June 17, 2015, mass *shooting* of nine people, including a pastor, in the Emanuel African Methodist Episcopal Church in downtown *Charleston*, South Carolina.
5. *Our Town* is a 1938 three-act play by American playwright Thornton Wilder. It tells the story of the fictional American small town of Grover's Corners between 1901 and 1913 through the everyday lives of its citizens.
6. On the history of the theater see Cohen-Cruz, 2005, p. 37.
7. Cohen-Cruz (2005, pp. 7–8) distinguishes the amateur productions of community theater groups from the community-based performances of political activist groups, from the Harlem Renaissance to working class theater, the Little Theatre Movement, the Federal Theatre Project, the Free Southern Theater, El Treatro Campesino, and recently Act Up Theatre.
8. From Hallie (1969, p. 46).
9. See Maggie MacLure's Museum of Qualitative Data, http://museumofqualitativedata.info/; author/maggie/http://museumofqualitativedata.info/.
10. For histories of these movements in People's Theatre, Epic Theatre, Theatre of the Oppressed, participatory action research education and critical ethnography, see Conrad (2004) and Dennis (2009).

FURTHER READING

Cannella, Gaile S. (2015) 'Introduction: Engaging Critical Qualitative Science: Histories and Possibilities', in Gaile S. Canella, Michelle Slazar Perez and Penny A. Pasque (eds.), *Critical Qualitative Inquiry: Foundations and Futures*. Walnut Creek: Left Coast Press, pp. 7–30.

Spry, Tami (2016) *Autoethnography and the Other: Unsettling Power Through Utopian Performatives*. New York: Routledge.

Sughrua, William M. (2016) *Heightened Performative Autoethnography: Resisting Oppressive Spaces within Paradigms*. New York: Peter Lang.

REFERENCES

Anzaldua, Gloria (1987) *Borderlands/La Frontera: The New Mestiza*. San Francisco: Aunt Lute Books.

Barad, Karen (2007) *Meeting the Universe Halfway: Quantum Physics and the Entanglement of Matter and Meaning*. Durham: Duke University Press.

Boal, Augusto (1985) *The Theatre of the Oppressed*. New York: Theatre Communications Group (originally published, 1974).

Boal, Augusto (1995) *The Rainbow of Desire: The Boal Method of Theatre and Therapy*. London: Routledge.

Boal, Augusto (2006) *Aesthetics of the Oppressed*. London/New York: Routledge.

Butler, Judith (2004) *Undoing Gender*. New York: Routledge.

Cohen-Cruz, Jan (2005) *Local Acts: Community-Based Performance in the United States*. New Brunswick: Rutgers University Press.

Cohen-Cruz, Jan (2006) 'The Problem Democracy is Supposed to Solve', in D. Soyini Madison and Judith Hamera (eds.), *The Sage Handbook of Performance Studies*. Thousand Oaks, CA: Sage, pp. 427–45.

Conquergood, Dwight (1985) 'Performing as a Moral Act: Ethical Dimensions of the Ethnography of Performance', *Literature in Performance*, 5(1): 1–13 (reprinted as pp. 65–80 in Patrick Johnson (ed.) (2012) *Cultural*

Struggles: Performance, Ethnography, Praxis: Dwight Conquergood*, edited and an introduction by E. Patrick Johnson. Ann Arbor, MI: University of Michigan Press).

Conquergood, Dwight (1986) 'Performing Cultures: Ethnography, Epistemology and Ethics', in Edith Slembek (ed.), *Miteinander Sprechen und Handeln: Festschrift für Hellmut Geissmer*. Scriptor, pp. 55–147.

Conquergood, Dwight (1991) 'Rethinking Ethnography: Towards a Critical Cultural Politics', *Communication Monographs*, 58: 179–94.

Conquergood, Dwight (1992a) 'Ethnography, Rhetoric and Performance', *Quarterly Journal of Speech*, 78(1): 80–97.

Conquergood, Dwight (1992b) 'Life in Big Red: Struggles and Accommodations in a Chicago Polyethnic Tenement', in Louise Lamphere (ed.), *Structuring Diversity: Ethnographic Perspectives on the New Immigration*. Chicago: University of Chicago Press, pp. 95–144.

Conquergood, Dwight (1998) 'Beyond the Text: Toward a Performative Cultural Politics', in Sheron J. Dailey (ed.), *The Future of Performance Studies: Visions and Revisions*. Annadale, VA: National Communication Association, pp. 25–36.

Conquergood, Dwight (2002) 'Performance Studies: Interventions and Radical Research', *The Drama Review*, 46(2): 145–56.

Conquergood, Dwight (2005) 'Rethinking Ethnography: Towards a Critical Cultural Politics', in D. Soyini Madison and Judith Hamera (eds.), *The Sage Handbook of Performance Studies*. Thousand Oaks: Sage, pp. 351–65 (reprinted as pp. 81–103 in Patrick Johnson (ed.) (2012), *Cultural Struggles: Performance, Ethnography, Praxis: Dwight Conquergood*, edited and introduced by E. Patrick Johnson. Ann Arbor, MI: University of Michigan Press).

Conquergood, Dwight (2013) 'Performance Studies: Interventions and Radical Research', in Patrick Johnson (ed.), *Cultural Struggles: Performance, Ethnography, Praxis: Dwight Conquergood*. Ann Arbor, MI: University of Michigan Press, pp. 32–46 (originally published 2002).

Conrad, Diane (2004) 'Exploring Risky Youth: Popular Theatre as Participatory, Performative Research Method', *International Journal of Qualitative Methods*, 3(1): 12–25.

Coole, Diane and Samantha Frost (2010) 'Introducing the New Materialisms', in Diane Coole and Samantha Frost (eds.), *New Materialisms: Ontology, Agency, and Politics*. Durham: Duke University Press, pp. 1–46.

Debord, Guy (1994) *The Society of the Spectacle* (trans. Donald Nicholson-Smith). New York: Zone Books (originally 1967).

Dennis, B. (2009) 'Acting Up: Theater of the Oppressed as Critical Ethnography', *International Journal of Qualitative Methods*, 8(2): 61–96.

Denzin, Norman K. (1984) *On Understanding Emotion*. San Francisco, CA: Jossey-Bass.

Denzin, Norman K. (2009) *Qualitative Inquiry Under Fire*. Walnut Creek: Left Coast Press.

Denzin, Norman K. (2013) 'The Death of Data', *Cultural-Studies ⇔ Critical Methodologies*, 13(4): 353–6.

Denzin, Norman K. (2017) *Performance [Auto] Ethnography: Critical Pedagogy and the Politics of Culture* (2nd edn). Thousand Oaks, CA: Sage.

Dolan, Jill (2005) *Utopia in Performance: Finding Hope in the Theater*. Ann Arbor, MI: University of Michigan Press.

Du Bois, W. E. B. (1926) 'Krigwa Players Little Negro Theatre: The Story of a Little Theatre Movement', *Crisis*, 32(July): 134–6.

Ellis, Carolyn (2009) *Revision: Autoethnographic Reflections on Life and Work*. Walnut Creek, CA: Left Coast Press.

Evans, Brad and Giroux, Henry A. (2015) *Disposable Futures: The Seduction of Violence on the Age of Spectacle*. San Francisco, CA: City Lights Books.

Fiske, John (1994) 'Audiencing: Cultural Practice and Cultural Studies', in Norman K. Denzin and Yvonna S. Lincoln (eds.), *The Handbook of Qualitative Research*. Thousand Oaks, CA: Sage, pp. 189–98.

Freire, Paulo (1996) *Letters to Cristina: Reflections on My Life and Work* (translated by Donaldo Macedo with Quilda Macedo and Alexandre Oliveira). London: Routledge.

Freire, Paulo (2000) *Pedagogy of the Oppressed* (30th Anniversary edition, with an introduction by Donaldo Macedo). New York: Continuum (originally published 1970, 5th reprinting, 2015).

Garoian, Charles R. and Gaudelius, Y.M. (2008) *Spectacle Pedagogy: Art, Politics, and Visual Culture*. Albany: State University of New York.

Garoian, Charles R. (2013) *The Prosthetic Function of Art: Embodied Research and Practice*. Albany: State University of New York.

Geertz, C. (1968) 'Thinking as a Moral Act: Ethical Dimensions of Anthropological Fieldwork in the New States', *Antioch Review*, 28(2): 139–58.

Gilbert, H. (2003) 'Black and White and Re(a)d All Over Again: Indigenous Minstrelsy in Contemporary Canadian and Australian Theatre', *Theatre Journal*, 55: 679–98.

Giroux, Henry A. (2014) *The Violence of Organized Forgetting: Thinking Beyond America's Disimagination Machine*. San Francisco, CA: City Lights Bookstore.

Gómez, A., Puigvert, L., and Flecha, R. (2011) 'Critical Communicative Methodology: Informing Real Social Transformation Through Research', *Qualitative Inquiry*, 17(3): 235–45.

Healy, P. (2008) 'Laramie killing given epilogue a decade later', *The New York Times*, 17 September, A19.

Hekman, Susan (2010) *The Material of Knowledge: Feminist Disclosures*. Bloomington, IN: Indiana University Press.

Jackson, Alecia Y. and Mazzei, Lisa A. (2012) *Thinking with Theory in Qualitative Research: Viewing Data Across Multiple Perspectives*. London: Routledge.

James, William (1912) *Essays in Radical Empiricism*. New York: Longman, Green & Co.

Kaufman, Moises (2014) *The Laramie Project & the Laramie Project 10 Years Later*. New York: Vintage (originally published 2001).

Koro-Ljungberg, Mirka (2016) *Reconceptualizing Qualitative Research: Methodologies Without Methodology*. Thousand Oaks, CA: Sage.

Koro-Ljungberg, M. and MacLure, M. (2013) 'Provocations, Re-Un-Visions, Death and Other Possibilities of "Data"', *Cultural Studies ⇔ Critical Methodologies*, 13(4): 219–22.

Langellier, Kristin M. (1998) 'Voiceless Bodies, Bodiless Voices: The Future of Personal Narrative Performance', in Sheron J. Dailey (ed.), *The Future of Performance Studies: Visions and Revisions*. Annadale, VA: National Communication Association, pp. 207–13.

Lather P. (2007) *Getting Lost: Feminist Efforts Toward a Double(d) Science*. New York: State University of New York Press.

MacLure, Maggie (2011) 'Qualitative Inquiry: Where Are the Ruins?', *Qualitative Inquiry*, 17(10): 997–1005.

MacLure, Maggie (2013a) 'The Wonder of Data', *Cultural Studies ⇔ Critical Methodologies*, 13(4): 228–32.

MacLure, Maggie (2013b) 'Classification or Wonder? Coding as an Analytic Practice in Qualitative Research', in Rebecca Coleman and Jessica Ringrose (eds.), *Deleuze and Research Methodologies*. Edinburgh: University Press, pp. 164–83.

MacLure, Maggie (2015) 'The New Materialisms: A Thorn in the Flesh of Critical Qualitative Inquiry', in Gaile S. Canella, Michelle Slazar Perez and Penny A. Pasque (eds.), *Critical Qualitative Inquiry: Foundations and Futures*. Walnut Creek, CA: Left Coast Press, pp. 93–112.

Madison, D. Soyini (1998) 'Performances, Personal Narratives, and the Politics of Possibility', in Sheron J. Dailey (ed.), *The Future of Performance Studies: Visions and Revisions*. Annadale, VA: National Communication Association, pp. 276–86.

Madison, D.S. (1999) 'Performing Theory/Embodied Writing', *Text and Performance Quarterly*, 19(2): 107–24.

Madison, D. Soyini (2005a) 'My Desire is for the Poor to Speak Well of Me', in Della Pollock (ed.), *Remembering: Oral History Performance*. New York: Palgrave Macmillan, pp. 143–66.

Madison, D. Soyini (2005b) *Critical Ethnography*. Thousand Oaks, CA: Sage.

Madison, D.S. (2007) 'Co-performing Witnessing', *Cultural Studies*, 21(6): 826–31.

Madison, D. Soyini (2010) *Acts of Activism: Human Rights as Radical Performance*. Cambridge: Cambridge University Press.

Madison, D. Soyini (2012) *Critical Ethnography* (2nd edn). Thousand Oaks, CA: Sage.

Madison, D.S. (2013) 'That Was Then and This is Now', *Text and Performance Quarterly*, 33(3): 2017–211.

Madison, D. Soyini and Hamera, Judith (2006) 'Introduction: Performance Studies at the Intersections', in D. Soyini Madison and Judith Hamera (eds.), *The Sage Handbook of*

Performance Studies. Thousand Oaks: Sage, pp. xi–xxv.

Morrison, Toni (1994) 'Rootedness: The Ancestor as Foundation', in D. Soyini Madison, (ed.), *The Woman That I Am: The Literature and Culture of Contemporary Women of Color*. New York: St. Martin's Press.

Moses, Daniel David (1992) *Almighty Voice and His Wife*. Stratford, ON: Williams-Wallace.

Norris, Joe and Sawyer, Richard D. (2012) 'Toward a Dialogic Methodology', in Joe Norris, Richard S. Sawyer and Darren E. Lund (eds.), *Duoethnography: Dialogic Methods for Social Health and Educational Research*. Walnut Creek, CA: Left Coast Press, pp. 9–39.

Pollock, Della (2005a) 'Introduction: Remembering', in Della Pollock (ed.), *Remembering: Oral History Performance*. New York: Palgrave Macmillan, pp. 1–18.

Pollock, Della (2005b) *Introduction: Performances*. New York: Palgrave Macmillan.

Pollock, Della (2006) 'Memory, Remembering, and Histories of Change', in D. Soyini and Judith Hamera (eds.), *The Sage Handbook of Performance Studies*. Thousand Oaks, CA: Sage, pp. 87–105.

Psathas, George (1995) *Conversation Analysis*. Thousand Oaks, CA: Sage.

Richardson, Laurel (2000) 'Writing: A Method of Inquiry', in N.K. Denzin and Y.S. Lincoln (eds.), *Handbook of Qualitative Research* (2nd edn). Thousand Oaks: Sage, pp. 923–48.

Saldana, Johnny (2005) 'An Introduction to Ethnodrama', in J. Saldana (ed.), *Ethnodrama: An Anthology of Reality Theatre*. Walnut Creek, CA: Left Coast Press, pp. 1–36.

Saldana, Johnny (2011) *Ethnotheatre: Research from Page to Stage*. Walnut Creek, CA: Left Coast Press.

Schechner, Richard (2015) *Performed Imaginaries*. New York: Routledge.

Spry, Tamy (2011) *Body, Paper, Stage: Writing and Performing Autoethnography*. Walnut Creek, CA: Left Coast Press.

St. Pierre, Elizabeth Adams (2011) 'Post Qualitative Research: The Critique and the Coming After', in N.K. Denzin and Y.S. Lincoln (eds.), *Handbook of Qualitative Research* (4th edn). Thousand Oaks, CA: Sage, pp. 611–26.

Thompson, J. and Schechner, R. (2004) 'Why "Social Theatre"?', *The Drama Review*, 48(3): 11–16.

Weems, Mary E. (2013) 'One Love: Empathy and the Imagination-Intellect', in Mary E. Weems (ed.), *Writings of Healing and Resistance: Empathy and the Imagination-Intellect*. New York: Peter Lang, pp. 1–22.

Worley, D.W. (1998) 'Is Critical Performative Pedagogy Practical?', in Sheron J. Dailey (ed.), *The Future of Performance Studies: Visions and Revisions*. Washington, DC: National Communication Association, pp. 136–40.

14

Quality of Data Collection

Rosaline S. Barbour

INTRODUCTION

Although there have been protracted and lively debates about 'quality' in qualitative research (see Barbour, 2014a), these seldom focus on the quality of the *data* collected, but tend to relate to *outputs*, in the form of published papers or reports, and much of the discussion revolves around judging more accessible components, such as the adequacy of the research design employed and the rigour involved in the process of analysis. The picture is further muddied by the fact that the various qualitative traditions have different 'takes' on what constitutes data and, therefore, what makes for 'good' data. Quality, then, in relation to data collection, is a somewhat elusive concept and often it comes to our attention only after the event, through its absence: that is to say, when we seek to interpret our data and set about analysis. While many research proposals laud the benefits of qualitative research in terms of its capacity to produce rich data or 'thick description', researchers sometimes confess (at least to their peers) to their data being somewhat 'thin'. This can refer to several perceived shortcomings, including respondents who are not very forthcoming or expansive; 'missing data', where certain questions have not been addressed or information has not been gathered; a lack of data relating to key concerns of the research; or data that does not readily lend itself to linkages with theoretical concepts or frameworks.

This chapter asks, first, whether the collection of 'thin' data might be more accurately attributed to 'thin elicitation skills'. While acknowledging that providing researcher training can present a real challenge in the context of sometimes narrow research funding priorities and focus (including tight timetables and budgets) some practical advice is provided as to ways in which researchers can avoid collecting 'thin' data. It includes some hints as to how to probe for more considered or elaborate responses from interviewees or focus group participants.

In seeking to collect good quality data, it is essential to take account of the *purpose* of the research: funders' requirements inevitably shape judgements as to whether data is 'fit for purpose'. Whereas some research is commissioned with the policy, or professional practice context clearly in mind, other research overtly addresses disciplinary or theoretical concerns. For the former type of research, data may consist of collecting the views held by key stakeholders and/or identifying barriers and potential solutions. This is not to say that data collection is entirely mechanistic: taking a 'critical realist' (Maxwell, 2011; see Maxwell, Chapter 2, this volume) approach it is also possible to compare and contrast perspectives and to take account of the ways in which power dynamics and knowledge-making are intertwined (Henwood, 2008). Nor does this more practical focus preclude the use of theoretical frameworks and many qualitative researchers seek to simultaneously address both funders' and disciplinary concerns.

The discussion then moves on to focus on the need to anticipate analysis, facilitating this process by actively seeking to maximize the potential of the data generated, both with regard to ensuring the possibilities for comparison (see Sørensen et al., Chapter 10, this volume) and for interrogating theoretical frameworks. If the central questions of the research are borne in mind, it is argued that the researcher can actively encourage clarification, even while data are still being generated. This, obviously, demands considerable skill, as the researcher is required to multitask, dealing with the here-and-now of the research conversation or encounter, while relating this to the broader context for the research.

The next section of the chapter looks at setting the scene for collecting quality data, examining the role of both intellectual and practical work in seeking to engage with 'hard-to-reach' respondents and critically examining the assumptions of the various participants in the process – including gatekeepers.

It is also suggested that some of the problems attributed to the production of 'thin data' actually have their origins in what could be described as 'thin design skills'. Some of the decisions taken at an early stage in the research process have far-reaching implications for data collection. The analytic possibilities and limitations of different types of transcription (see Jenks, Chapter 8, this volume) or note-taking are considered, and it is argued that such considerations need to be taken into account at the outset of the research, rather than being left to be attended to once data collection is complete. Selection is also presented as key to producing quality data. Sampling strategies (see Schreier, Chapter 6, this volume) can work to either afford or suppress the potential to make meaningful comparisons, since this determines the diversity of participants selected or the composition of groups and ultimately impacts on the ability of both researcher and 'researched' to make such comparisons. Various other choices regarding the combination and sequencing of methods and the framing of the research also impact on the value of the data to be collected and crucially, its analytical potential. Eliciting 'good' data depends on a process of co-construction, with the researcher seeking clarification and encouraging participants to contextualize their responses – that is, engaging in comparison and (embryo) theorizing.

I then provide some suggestions as to how both researcher and research participants can 'go the extra distance' to produce 'rich' nuanced data. The possibilities and challenges afforded by a range of approaches, such as the use of diaries, focus group exercises, vignettes and visual materials are discussed. It is argued that interim findings and dissemination sessions can provide a useful opportunity to explore our initial hypotheses, and allow us to generate further fresh data. While careful questioning has its place, there is much to be gained by letting our participants take the lead, as their unsolicited observations can take our interpretations and theorizing in new directions. Rather than being viewed as an impediment to data collection, 'performativity' is presented as a resource to be harnessed for the purpose of sense-making – both on the part of research participants and researchers.

Finally, some thoughts are presented as to how to go about realizing theoretical potential in data collection. Consideration is given as to how researchers might set about attempting to translate disciplinary concerns and theoretical frameworks into words or images that are accessible to respondents, in order to allow relevant data to be elicited. The potential of 'in-vivo codes', different types of stimulus materials (including online sources) and the use of humour is discussed. I conclude by arguing that there are no easy solutions to ensuring quality in data collection, but that researchers are best served by taking a thorough, thoughtful, and imaginative approach, making their own decisions as to what is likely to work within the context of their specific research project and the demographic or phenomenon they are researching.

'THIN' DATA, 'THIN' ELICITATION OR 'THIN DESIGN' SKILLS?

'Thin' data may arise not simply as a result of the shortcomings of our respondents, but may, at times, reflect 'thin elicitation skills' and researchers need to learn how to make optimum use of interview schedules or focus group topic guides. Much of the guidance relating to the use of such 'tools' in qualitative research appears to suggest that these function in the same way in the hands of different researchers. Qualitative research encounters are, first and foremost, an exchange between researcher and participants, and personalities and predispositions of researchers play an important, if largely unsung, role (Barbour, 2014b). This is an issue that merits much more attention than it has traditionally been accorded. Although it is, undoubtedly, possible to enhance questioning capabilities through training, it is a somewhat uncomfortable observation that the skills involved in eliciting data come much more easily to some researchers than they do to others. Nevertheless, data elicitation skills can be improved with practice and, above all, when researchers have an opportunity to work alongside supervisors, mentors, and project managers who can help them to view, and engage fruitfully in, data collection as only one part of a bigger and more complex picture. Contract researchers are often required to 'hit the ground running' in terms of joining already established teams with a shared understanding of goals and theoretical assumptions about the project in hand, which may or may not be adequately transmitted to the new team member. This underlines the importance of researcher training and the crucial role played by team meetings, given that qualitative research so often involves a collaborative project.

As Bloor et al. (2001) observe, research participants can 'under-react' to our questions and it is, thus, essential to have some further approaches that we can pursue, in order to ensure that we make the most of our opportunity to elicit responses from our interviews/participants. Here, rather than being discouraged, perseverance and confidence are valuable assets that can be pressed into service. A simple 'No' from an interviewee can be further explored by commenting, for example, 'That was an emphatic "no" – would you always have said that/would you say that in all situations?' As many focus group (see Morgan and Hoffman, Chapter 16, this volume) commentators have pointed out, non-verbal cues can be extremely useful in terms of conveying meaning/intentions and the researcher can always draw attention to these and ask for an explanation, commenting, for example, 'You look surprised at that question…?' or 'You're pulling a face – do you disagree…?' While it can be helpful to have drawn up a set of prompts to be used if responses dry up, or further information is required, these should be employed with caution. One of the hardest skills to develop is that of tolerating silences (Barbour, 2014b), and novice researchers sometimes rush in, using prompts too early (when interviewees are still formulating their responses). Foreclosing participants' contributions in this way can result, unsurprisingly, in impoverished data.

Setting the Scene for Quality Data Collection: Access and Research Design Considerations

Some populations or subgroups – such as those already marginalized by dint of their sexuality, involvement in crime, or suspicion of those in authority – are generally viewed as 'hard-to-reach' (see Chamberlain and Hodgetts, Chapter 42, this volume) and extra efforts are often seen as being required in order to breach their defences and to engage them in our research. However, there may sometimes be simpler answers, and rethinking small details, or practicalities, such as settings or composition of groups can pay dividends. Such aspects can unwittingly compromise the willingness and capacity of respondents/participants to engage with our questions. The form of the encounter may also discourage certain potential participants from taking part: in some contexts, for example, where researchers are seeking to elicit the views of busy professionals, harassed family members, or elites, telephone interviews might be a better option than inevitably rushed face-to-face sessions.

Researchers may also encounter the opposite of the problem of 'hard-to-reach' respondents (see Bengry, Chapter 7, this volume), in the form of those who could be termed 'research-savvy' and, thus, likely to make a priori assumptions as to what we, as researchers, want from them by way of 'data'. Carrying out fieldwork in the West African country of Sierra Leone, which was recovering from a lengthy civil war, Berghs (2011) came across the phenomenon of stories of impairment, arising due to the widespread use during the war, of amputation as a weapon. She argued that this gave rise to what she described as 'dark' or 'voyeuristic' tourism, involving the creation of a new kind of 'capital' – that of accounts, images and bodily manifestations of violence – that is, the 'commodification' of the impaired body (2011, p. 256). A verbal explanation of the research was provided to elders in village, community and family settings and to educated elites. Nevertheless, 'community members still thought that "research" would be linked to having to repeat what happened to them in the war' (2011, p. 258).

Transcription

As Jenks (see Jenks, Chapter 8, this volume) underlines, transcription does not involve a monolithic approach. However, choices about transcription made early in the research process may shape possibilities. Verbatim transcripts can lend themselves to more detailed scrutiny, which can be illuminating. An example is provided by a detailed analysis of transcripts of focus groups with young people (aged 11–18 years), relating to the way in which alcohol and drinking were portrayed on television. In this case Atkinson et al. (2013), through examining the use of pronouns, identified what they term a 'third person' effect, which allowed participants to distance themselves, suggesting that television may influence others, but that they, themselves, were immune to such suggestions. If they stay alert and think ahead to analysis, researchers can perhaps identify and explore such usages with research participants while they are generating the data.

Jeffersonian transcription is required if a formal conversation analysis (CA), which pays close attention to the mechanics of speech and turn-taking, is to be carried out. However, even if full transcription is not carried out initially, taping interviews or discussions allows us to keep our options open with the possibility of carrying out more detailed transcription at a later stage (which might involve concentrating on key sections, notes, or accompanying field notes). While it is unlikely that researchers will identify significant linguistic or speech mechanisms during the actual process of data collection, presentation of interim findings might usefully further explore such hunches on the part of researchers.

Selection and Sampling

One of the principal – but frequently under-emphasized – merits of qualitative research is its capacity to afford comparison. This is the key to identifying and interrogating patterning in the data and to developing analytical arguments. Working backwards to the research design (see Gobo, Chapter 5, this volume) stage often explains shortcomings in data, such as insufficient attention having been paid to selection of research settings and sampling in order to ensure diversity – and, hence, potential for comparison. The *raison d'être* of purposive sampling (see Schreier, Chapter 6, this volume) is to furnish such possibilities and allow for identification and interrogation of patterning in data.

Selection is crucial, regardless of the variant of qualitative research involved, and regardless of whether the selection is intentional on the part of the researcher, or inadvertent (and here it is essential that the limitations of partial or partisan coverage are acknowledged). For example, in document analysis, it is important to have a reasonably well-defined question or set of questions to bring a focus to bear on interrogating documents – that is, with the researcher making 'analytic choices' (see Rapley and Rees, Chapter 24, this volume). Ravn et al. (2016), for example, explain that they restricted their analysis of Danish chronic care policy documents to six policies, spanning the period from 2005 to 2013, which were chosen because of their 'centrality' to debates and practice. This allowed for a detailed analysis of the vocabulary employed, the discourses appealed to, and the underlying value assumptions involved. Such applications provide an example of critical realism, involving the merging of a realist ontology (selecting documents on the basis of the frequency with which they are referenced and their influence) and a constructivist epistemology (acknowledging that documents are far from inert (Prior, 2008) but are actively constructed through, for example, the use of language, invoking of shared beliefs and goals) – as advocated by Maxwell (see Maxwell, Chapter 2, this volume).

Making Choices

Some proponents of qualitative research have argued that naturally-occurring data is inherently superior to data that is generated in situations engineered by the researchers (see Potter and Shaw, Chapter 12, this volume). However, this distinction may be over-stated, as data are always researcher-generated to a degree – since any fieldwork involves a choice (even if by default rather than design) of settings, times, or situations for observation. This overarching structure inevitably affords different views of the phenomenon under study.

Observational fieldwork might be employed as a precursor to developing interview schedules or focus group topic guides. Where this is also a major source of data, the most fruitful applications are, again, likely to revolve around clearly articulated research questions, which are developed and refined as fieldwork progresses. With regard to carrying out digital research, Markham (see Markham, Chapter 33, this volume and Markham and Gammelby, Chapter 29, this volume) points out that the goal of enquiry guides one's (analytic) gaze. There are no set guidelines; rather the researcher should explore the possibilities offered by the field of study and make choices accordingly. In identifying Australian breast cancer websites for their discourse analysis study, for example, Gibson et al. (2015) engaged in a process mirroring the way in which members of the public are likely to conduct online searches, starting with one site and using search engines and web links to identify a total of 18 relevant websites.

Morris and Anderson (2015) decided to focus for their study, concerned with representations of youth masculinity, on the four most successful male video-bloggers (vloggers) and restricted their analysis to posts on YouTube made over a 4-month period, but simultaneously sampled for the most-watched/most popular, and augmented their set of videos with newest and oldest posts and included collaborative videos. Such choices relate not to following specific procedures, but, rather, to the cultivation and application by the researcher of a general sensibility (see Lindgren, Chapter 28, this volume). Here, field notes (whether part of formal observational research practice, or merely a research diary) are likely to play a significant role and provide an invaluable resource for later consideration (see Wästerfors, Chapter 20, this volume).

Inductive analysis is usually viewed as involving reasoning after the event – that is, once all data are generated and the process of analysis begins in earnest. However, abductive logic – involving the invention and interrogation of hypotheses/explanations (see Kennedy and Thornberg, Chapter 4, this volume) can begin even while data are still being generated. This can lead to refinements in terms of what Knoblauch, Schnettler, and Tuma (see Knoblauch et al., Chapter 23, this volume) term 'field sampling', whereby the researcher is free to strategically select specific sub-settings, subgroups, or events, in order to follow up such hunches, with theorization evolving throughout the project (see Schreier, Chapter 6, this volume), with the researcher cultivating a 'flexible, adaptive and interpretive mindset' (see Markham and Gammelby, Chapter, 29, this volume).

Co-construction, Clarification and Contextualization

Interviews have frequently been described as 'conversations with a purpose'. Similarly, focus groups can usefully be viewed as 'discussions with a focus'. These definitions emphasize the active role of the researcher, both in planning the research and in eliciting the data. Semi-structured interview schedules or focus group topic guides are not to be drawn up lightly. Careful piloting can help to ensure that the resulting data is, indeed, likely to be 'fit for purpose' or 'congruent with the focus' of the research.

As with much that relates to the qualitative research endeavour, this involves striking a delicate balance and it is a wise researcher who leaves some room for participants to add their own observations or provide examples in the form of accounts or stories – even where the topic of research is relatively mundane. As Rapley (2001), amongst others, has pointed out, generating qualitative data involves a process of co-construction, and is not simply a case of drawing up a set of questions and posing them. Some qualitative researchers may view their role as 'bearing witness' for participants whose voices have previously been muted, and, although this is not a very widespread orientation, it has perhaps influenced the much more commonly encountered emphasis on the sanctity of respondents' words. Many qualitative researchers wrestle with ethical issues when selecting and presenting quotes to illustrate research findings papers. This reflects the tendency, in some quarters, to 'romanticize' respondents' views – something that Atkinson (1997) has warned against, urging us to subject these to a critical scrutiny equal to that with which we approach other discourses. Within a critical realist approach the researcher's mandate is generally to provide an overview and to tease out differences, variations and contradictions – that is, to produce an account that does not privilege an individual or section of respondents, but which seeks to critically explore the range of views and experiences elicited. This means that they are empowered to press for clarification, in terms of encouraging interviewees/focus group discussants/fieldwork participants to contextualize their comments, and to invite them to theorize alongside the researcher.

EXPLORING FURTHER OPTIONS

Some qualitative researchers have capitalized on their ability to 'flesh out' accounts, using diaries to afford a lens into how perceptions may shift on a daily basis. The diary method is, however, beset with challenges – not least the difficulty of keeping diarists motivated and the potential for intermittent entries or, even, strategic use of diaries. Diaries are likely to be most fruitful when combined with follow-up interviews, allowing diarists to explain how they contextualize their entries through ongoing interaction with the researcher. Diary formats vary enormously, ranging from free-form to those which are tightly structured, although the most successful appear to be those with a combination of closed and open questions (e.g. Broom et al., 2015). Again, however, it pays to consider the use to which this data is to be put, and it is vital to take time to think about providing clear instructions for 'solicited' diaries, if the data are to be 'fit for (your research) purpose'. Jones and Woolley (2015) were concerned with looking at the impact on commuters of London hosting the Olympic Games in 2012 and elected to use email diaries over a period of 10 days. This allowed the researchers to stay in regular contact with the diarists, since they were sent a daily email request, consisting of four questions, two of which were repeated each day, while the other two questions explored a variety of other issues.

Focus group (see Morgan and Hoffman, Chapter 16, this volume) researchers have employed – with varying degrees of success – a range of exercises designed to focus discussion on relevant issues. Some of these – particularly those ice-breaking exercises borrowed from marketing research – may fail to produce the desired nuanced data, because the exercises are utilized simply for the sake of following recommended procedures and may actually serve to estrange rather than engage participants. A very popular approach, which has come to be referred to, somewhat erroneously, as the 'nominal group technique' (Barbour, 2018), has enjoyed considerable popularity within fields such as health services research. This involves presenting focus group discussants with a list of issues/concerns with the request that they rank these in order of priority. While this may produce illuminating discussion as group members ponder the relative importance of items on the list, this is seldom mined as data, with research reports concentrating on the outcomes – or ranking – produced in these sessions. A notable exception is provided by Demant and Ravn (2010) who used a ranking exercise as stimulus material in order to explore the risk perceptions of Danish youths, as they weighed up the relative risks of different drugs. Subjecting their transcripts to detailed discourse analysis (see Rau et al., Chapter 19, this volume), the researchers found that the young people drew upon a number of logics, reflecting separate (but sometimes intersecting) discourses. These discourses were: naturalness (of the substances involved); route of (drug) administration (e.g. ingested or injected); addiction; morality and everyday life. The authors add that these discourses drew on general societal discourses and images of drug-taking and associated risks (2010, p. 540).

Although, until relatively recently, more popular amongst quantitative researchers, vignettes have been adopted by increasing numbers of qualitative researchers. These have usefully been defined as: '…sketches of fictional (or non-fictionalized) scenarios (where) the respondent is then invited to imagine, drawing on his or her own experience, how the central character in the scenario will behave' (Bloor and Wood, 2006, p. 183). Vignettes can go some way towards enticing those shy of sharing their personal experiences. As Jenkins et al. (2010) observe: 'By projecting situations onto hypothetical characters and asking the interviewee to put themselves in the protagonist's shoes, sensitive data ... can be obtained in an indirect, non-confrontational manner' (2010, p. 181).

Selection – or, more frequently, construction – of vignettes is not a straightforward matter and requires considerable skill and background knowledge on the part of the researcher, and trying out scenarios (or piloting) is essential in order to determine whether these are credible and, ultimately whether they are likely to generate the sort of data that is being sought (Barbour, 2014b, p. 119).

Above all, it is essential that the researcher focuses not simply on obtaining data, but on imagining the use to which this is to be put during the process of analysis, anticipating some of the challenges and seeking to 'problematize' the data generated, rather than merely posing the set questions. Vignettes can be further pressed into service in the form of unfolding scenarios (also discussed by Jenkins et al., 2010), which, while they involve a lot more work on the part of the researcher, allow for the exploration of choices and their consequences.

Rather than constructing elaborate scenarios, however, there is much to be gained from utilizing quotes, or, even, tweaking quotes (as Hussey et al., (2004) report having done in order to explore general practitioners'/family doctors' responses to extreme statements about issuing sickness certificates). Failing this, it is always possible to ask for reactions to real or hypothetical comments, by saying, for example, 'Some people I've spoken to have said XXXX – do you agree with that…?'

The potential of dissemination sessions for generating more data has gone largely untapped by qualitative researchers, and focus groups readily lend themselves to this (Barbour, 2018). Interestingly, Jenkins et al. (2016) report using research-generated composite vignettes (not associated with any one participant) in order to engage with members of the public with regard to the topic of early onset dementia, thus contributing to what they extol as a 'public sociology'. Clearly, such data chunks do not necessarily arise spontaneously in the course of carrying out research, but, with a little more work and thought from the researcher, these can be creatively re-formulated to form the basis for future research and debate.

In order to ensure that the resulting data are, indeed, 'fit for purpose', it is important that the researcher provides context, by explaining the purpose or focus of the research and giving clear instructions with regard to any exercises used, including those relating to taking photographs or selecting artefacts for sharing and discussion. A good example is provided by the work of Harman and Cappellini (2015) who carried out research with mothers of 11 children attending one primary school. Their research focus was on the insights into how 'good mothering' was constructed, enacted and made visible through assembling children's lunchboxes. They carried out an initial interview, after which they provided the mothers with disposable cameras and instructions to photograph lunchboxes prepared over a 10-day period. They then followed this up with a photo-elicitation interview (see Eberle, Chapter 25, this volume and Henwood et al., Chapter 38, this volume), during which they discussed the photos taken by the mothers. This illustrates the value of having a clearly defined and relatively tightly focused objective, providing clear instructions and using the artefacts produced (in this case photos) in order to generate further nuanced data. Unfortunately many photo-elicitation projects have less clearly specified goals and result in a mass of photos (some of which may be 'staged' – see Eberle, Chapter 25, this volume) and data that defy useful and analytically meaningful categorization.

In terms of providing instructions, however, sometimes 'less can be more'. Sheridan et al. (2011) encouraged their participants to carry out a graphic elicitation exercise – which they called 'timelining' – where women visualized their experiences with weight over time. Although a researcher was on hand to help with this exercise, crucially, the exercise allowed for women to decide for themselves the length of time period to depict. While some covered particular short periods, others covered whole lifetimes, allowing women scope to portray the relative importance of weight for them as individuals. Again these timelines were used as the focus for further discussion and women took them home and were free to further embellish their drawings. The research artefact, then, is not an end in itself, but, rather, the route to further data elicitation.

GOING THE EXTRA DISTANCE: (BOTH RESEARCHER AND PARTICIPANTS)

When the goal is to elicit 'rich' nuanced data it is essential to give research participants enough scope to theorize. This is the rationale behind the emphasis given in Grounded Theory to 'in-vivo' codes, which refer to the use by participants of their own words and concepts in order to explain their views and experiences. These are often similar to the 'soundbites' so beloved of journalists, in that they express complex ideas in a few colourful words (Barbour, 2014b). However, these do not automatically emerge as a result of our questioning, but rely, rather, on giving our respondents the space to explore and question their ideas, according them some choice in the matter. This is also compatible with a social constructionist approach, which recognizes that data can be valued not simply for what people are saying, but, rather, how it is being said and conceptualized.

Narrative researchers (see Murray, Chapter 17, this volume), following the lead of Riessman (1993), have been quick to capitalize on the analytical potential afforded by the ways in which people tell stories: where these start and finish, which components are accorded emphasis and which are minimized. As Hodgkin and Radstone (2003) remind us, 'memory is provisional, subjective, concerned with the present rather than fact and the past' (2003, p. 2).

I found that, when interviewing a range of professionals about their work with people with HIV/AIDS with the relatively small Scottish population affected at the time, I came across the same humorous story being recounted by different professionals, all claiming first-hand experience of the client involved (who had been providing sexual services in exchange for leniency from someone claiming to be reading her gas meter, despite her flat being all-electric). This story served as currency in a different way, however, and provided an insight into 'myth-making' amongst a group of workers who were attempting to deal with new professional and emotional demands (Barbour, 1998). What was important here, was not the veracity, or otherwise, of the story, but, rather, the functions that this telling and re-telling – served.

Several commentators have highlighted the 'performative' aspect of narratives (see Murray, Chapter 17, this volume) and, indeed, more generally, of what could be termed to be accounts. This, however, does not devalue such data, since, as qualitative researchers we are less concerned with establishing the 'truth' than we are to uncover how people make representations to themselves and significant or selected 'others'.

In the course of a project concerned with developing an appropriate and acceptable weight loss intervention for women postpartum, I was involved in eliciting focus group data with women who had recently had babies and who had identified as being keen to lose weight. This involved enticing participants to ponder or 'problematize' the issue of weight loss alongside researchers. Encouraged to relay their own experiences and explanations, the women engaged in various 'riffs' – about the role of the weather; their sheer enjoyment of food; and, knowingly, celebrated their ingenuity when 'cheating' while ostensibly following diets. While such data may be valuable in their own right, such exchanges – and providing such licence – are an important vector for the creative and potentially theoretically rich articulation of dilemmas, tensions, challenges and resourcefulness that are articulated and celebrated during the interaction. This provided a permissive stage for participants to share and co-construct responses:

> Penny – I think a lot of it's to do with the weather as well. When it's cold and miserable there's not much places or things you can go and do, whereas when it's a really nice, bright and a nice day you can go places and do things with the children as well, get exercise, and get fresh air and stuff. Whereas when its really freezing cold and raining nobody really wants to do much or go places unless you have a car or something.
> Tonia – I agree with that as well. I think a lot of people have SAD, but don't actually realize it – because I'm sure I do. I hate the winter. I do comfort eat in the winter, cause you hide in the big baggy jumpers and just go in the house, put your heating on, lounge on the couch and watch films and stuff like that, whereas in the Summer time you usually go out and do something.
> Shirley – Yes, definitely.
> Penny – Yes – your cup of tea keeps you cosy. And with a cup of tea comes a biscuit…
> Tonia – …and you can take sugar in your tea as well.
> (Focus Group 2)

Treats loomed large in women's accounts and were held to be necessary:

> Nan – I have a treat, once [voices overlap] is a treat night and I can have a pizza or I can have a Chinese, or I can have Thai, or we can go bucket of chicken at KFC, boneless. And that's once a week, and it's like that I've been good all week, that's [voices overlap]…
> Lorrie – I've just started on a diet, but I said that from the start, I'm not giving up a takeaway on a Friday night…
> Nan – No, because you've got to have something or else you're just like … but the end of the week you're slitting your wrists. So at least by Friday night you go, 'Yeah, I'm having the Chinese'.

> Eileen – (My diet)… it's green days and red days. One day you can eat all the meat you want with all your veggies and the next day you eat all the carbohydrates you want, all your baked tatties and beans and pastas and…
> Nan – Scones. Cake.
> Eileen – …Yeah, I don't think scones class as a carbohydrate.
> Nan – Yes, in my house it's carbs. Fruit scones are carbs [laughs]
> Eileen – Yeah, and there's fruit as well!
> Nan – Yup, one of my five a day!
> [Group laugh] …
> Eileen – Yeah, well I did get to the stage where I was starting to cheat with that as well. Because I knew the diet so well I could cheat.
> Rose – Is that right?
> Eileen – Yeah trick myself, …you know…carrot cake is healthy…see there's veg, carbohydrates, dairy, …yeah, your yoghurt. You know I started to cheat myself.
> (Focus Group 3)

One of the women in this group, Nan, later told a lengthy – and, very possibly, previously rehearsed – story about how she misleadingly labelled her preferred cheese as 'diet cheese', in order to discourage her husband from eating into her supplies. This was met with general approval and hilarity – probably because it celebrated the women's ability to transgress and reassert themselves in light of what they saw as unreasonable demands. The point is not whether this story was factually accurate; rather its value lies in its ability to sum up complex and contradictory feelings.

Stories allowed the women to weigh up the changes to their lives that having babies involved and they also talked about the difference that having had a baby had made to their lives and how their priorities might now have shifted:

> Jacqui – Being bigger doesn't bother me if I'm pushing a pram (demonstrates how the pram is in front of her stomach) or out with the kids. People can see I've had these kids (close together). But I went on a works night out. My sister was helping me get ready – 'We'll glam you up', but my confidence just wasn't there. I'm more (comfortable) with the mumsy stuff – that's my purpose in life. I'm not used to being in heels.
> (Focus Group 2)

Sharing, in a supportive environment, their discomfort and less than happy encounters with health care professionals and slimming coaches also encouraged the women to collaboratively mount challenges to health promotion advice – sometimes using particularly vivid language:

> Debbie – It was because the target weight they had ... that ... that was overweight and the target weight that I *am* is classified as 'obese'.
> Kim – That's like me when I got it done. It said that I was obese and I looked at myself and thought 'eh? – that can't be'.
> Laura – Yeah, I'd be quite happy to be 'overweight' in their categories. [laughs]
> Debbie – The target weight for my height was about nine and a half stone and I just thought, 'Do you know what? There's no way I'm going to get down to there, so they can stick it where the sun don't shine!'
> Laura – Mine was something like seven and a half stone and I was, like 'No way!' – I was maybe that when I was at school. Sorry...'
> Debbie – It's extremely unrealistic the actual BMI, it just was not achievable ... yeah, it just seemed so unachievable that it didn't matter ...
> [*Focus Group 1*]

Debbie's heartfelt comment – They can stick it where the sun don't shine!' – conveyed, simultaneously, defiance, hurt and exasperation. It is worthy of note that she did not articulate this view to the health care professional involved, but reported it as a personal response – one which she possibly had not previously shared with anyone. Importantly, the focus groups gave the women licence to explore and express their feelings in a researcher-created setting. However, given the lively exchanges that characterized these sessions, the interaction may not have been all that far-removed from snatches of everyday discussion between friends.

I have argued, elsewhere (Barbour, 2014c), that some of the tools of conversation and discourse analysis can usefully be brought to bear in analysing segments of focus group talk, using some of these excerpts to illustrate the application of this 'hybrid approach'. Whether or not one is engaged in doing a formal 'discourse analysis' it is useful to consider what discourses participants may be invoking, reproducing, reformulating, creating afresh, or challenging. They are not responding in a vacuum, but, rather, are producing a considered response to our questioning, drawing on all the social and cultural resources at their disposal.

REALIZING THEORETICAL POTENTIAL

All too often theoretical frameworks are brought into play rather late in the day, once all data have been collected and the process of analysis is well-advanced. If, in contrast, potential frameworks are pushed into service in order to frame questions for interview schedules or topic guides, the resulting data are likely to be much richer and 'fit for (theoretical) purpose'. Of course this is not always possible at the outset, but the iterative nature of qualitative research permits us to introduce relevant concepts as we become aware of their potential relevance. Many such theoretical frameworks are complex and rendering these accessible for consideration by our participants demands considerable effort on the part of the researcher (see Resch and Enzenhofer, Chapter 9, this volume) However, in seeking to marry the insights provided by our various disciplines and those from our research participants, we are also, inevitably, engaged in translation – from the academic to the lay register and vice versa. This is a major challenge when inviting explicit commentary from participants on researchers' framings (Henwood, 2008).

Sometimes, however, our respondents are much more skilled in this respect than are academic researchers. When analyzing data for two separate projects I became aware that my research participants were, in each case, actively producing a lay version of different established theoretical constructs. The first example comes from a study of the use of folic acid supplements by women immediately before and during the early stages of pregnancy (Barbour et al., 2012). As they sought to explain their behaviour, which frequently diverged from that recommended by health care providers. They produced afresh a version of what has become known as the 'prevention paradox' (Davison et al., 1991) whereby it is recognized that, while interventions may work at a population level, there is no guarantee that individuals will have good outcomes. With regard to another project, couples attending a fertility clinic invoked the construct of the 'neurotic infertile couple' – characterized by their obsession with conceiving, and unable to call a halt to treatment (Barbour et al., 2013). Crucially they sought to distance themselves from this stereotype. What they were appealing to constituted a lay version of the theory of biographical disruption (Bury, 1982), which has influenced much of the research in the field of chronic illness. While both of these observations arose out of the process of analysis, had I been alert enough to recognize these earlier, they could have been interrogated more systematically.

Dissemination sessions involving supplementary data collection might have afforded an opportunity to further explore the relevance of these theoretical frameworks for the topics in hand. Stimulus materials could play an important role here and may come into their own after initial analysis has been carried out, allowing for some of these more complex ideas to be interrogated.

It is worthy of note that research participants often draw our attention to the relevance of particular cartoons, storylines in TV soaps or comedy sketches, which may highlight conceptual tensions or paradoxes in a much more accessible way than we as academics are able to achieve. Some of the sources identified by research participants highlight the important function served by humour – a resource that is underused in research analysis. Paraphrasing Schopenhauer, Watson (2015) highlights the analytic as well as humorous potential of suddenly perceived 'incongruity'. She argues: 'While laughter is the interruption which brings about a change of outlook, humour ensures an attitude of play and an awareness of the comic potential of the human condition on the [on the part of the academic as both producer and consumer of research' (2015, p. 417).

This brings to mind C. Wright Mills' (1959) invitation to sociologists to engage in what he terms 'playfulness of mind' and Becker's (1998) advice regarding the potential of considering polarities, continua and the inverting of our research questions, in order to gain analytical purchase and enhance our theory-interrogating and theory-making. While it might seem sacrilegious to attempt to reduce to cartoon form the ideas of theorists such as Bourdieu, we should, perhaps, be a bit braver and take more risks in the pursuit of nuanced data. We may also need to introduce different materials for the various constituencies involved in our research projects. More recently, internet memes, at least for some demographics, may have largely taken over this function. Interestingly, they often rely for their effect on incongruity (as identified by Watson, 2015), frequently subverting expectations, allowing, variously, for self-mockery, status claims and expressions of political affiliation. The beauty of internet memes is that their use need not be restricted to online research, as they are likely to provide a shared point of reference for specific audiences that can be capitalized upon by the researcher (as stimulus materials), even if the research is being conducted offline. Thus, they can function as valuable windows to data, but it is essential that the researcher has a good grasp of the origins and appeal of the chosen materials, otherwise this may well backfire. Julien (2015) emphasizes the ways in which internet memes inherently involve inclusion or exclusion, rendering them, simultaneously, a potentially valuable source of nuanced data (for use with targeted groups), but also a potential minefield for the 'non-savvy' researcher – a case of *caveat investigator*?

CONCLUSION

The elicitation of good quality data is not a matter of chance: rather there is a vast amount of hidden effort involved. Rich and nuanced data depends on the exercise of consummate skills on the part of the researcher, who has to multitask, attending to the live exchange with interviewees or focus group participants, while simultaneously anticipating the process of analysis. Successful data collection involves ensuring both that the chosen research design affords opportunities for comparison and that these are constructively drawn upon while data are being generated, (as well as when they are being analyzed).

In addition to standard interview schedules or focus group topic guides, there is a wide range of options at our disposal (such as diaries, vignettes, stimulus materials, graphic elicitation or use of images), all of which can be used alongside more traditional questioning formats. However, the way in which we use these approaches shapes the resulting data and its capacity to engage participants in problematizing issues alongside researchers, which remains the best way to elicit rich data.

Even when contemplating new fields of research afforded by the burgeoning online environment and its ever-evolving formats, we would do well to revisit old, but frequently forgotten advice about cultivating a playful approach. This should not be reserved purely for the stage of analysis, but can also be rolled out to advantage when engaging with our research participants, who may well be better-equipped than ourselves to worry away at and make sense of complex theoretical constructs.

FURTHER READING

Barbour, Rosaline, S. (2014) *Introducing Qualitative Research: A Student's Guide*, London: Sage. (chapters 5–8).

Jenkins, N., Bloor, M., Fischer, J., Berney, L. and Neale, J. (2010) 'Putting it in context: The use of vignettes in qualitative interviewing', *Qualitative Research*, 10(2): 175–98.

Pauwels, L. (2010) 'Visual sociology reframed: An analytical synthesis and discussion of visual methods in social and cultural research', *Sociological Methods and Research*, 38(4): 545–81.

REFERENCES

Atkinson, Amanda, M., Bellis, Marks and Sumnall, Harry (2013) 'Young people's perspective on the portrayal of alcohol and drinking on television: Findings from a focus group study', *Addiction Research and Theory*, 21(2): 91–9.

Atkinson, Paul (1997) 'Narrative turn or blind alley?', *Qualitative Health Research*, 7(3): 325–44.

Barbour, Rosaline, S. (1998) 'Engagement, presentation and representation in research practice', in Rosaline S. Barbour and Guro Huby (eds.) *Meddling with Mythology: AIDS and The Social Construction of Knowledge*, London: Routledge, pp. 183–200.

Barbour, Rosaline, S. (2014a) 'Quality in data analysis', in Uwe Flick (ed.) *The SAGE Handbook of Qualitative Data Analysis*, London: Sage, pp. 496–509.

Barbour, Rosaline, S. (2014b) *Introducing Qualitative Research: A Student's Guide* (2nd edn), London: Sage.

Barbour, Rosaline, S. (2014c) 'Analyzing focus groups', in Uwe Flick (ed.) *The SAGE Handbook of Qualitative Data Analysis*, London: Sage, pp. 313–26.

Barbour, Rosaline, S. (2018) *Doing Focus Groups* (2nd edn), London: Sage.

Barbour, Rosaline, S. Macleod, M., Mires, G. and Anderson, A.S. (2012) 'Uptake of folic acid supplements before and during pregnancy: Focus group analysis of women's views and experiences', *Journal of Human Nutrition and Dietetics*, 25(2): 140–7.

Barbour, Rosaline, S. Porter, Maureen, A., Peddie, Valerie, L. and Bhattacharya, Siladitya (2013) 'Counselling in the context of cancer: Some sociological insights', *Human Fertility*, 16(1): 54–8.

Becker, Howard S. (1998) *The Tricks of the Trade*, Chicago: University of Chicago Press.

Berghs, Maria (2011) 'Paying for stories of impairment – parasitic or ethical? Reflections on undertaking anthropological research in post-conflict Sierra Leone', *Scandinavian Journal of Disability Studies*, 13(4): 255–70.

Bloor, Michael and Wood, Fiona (2006) *Keywords in Qualitative Methods: A Vocabulary of Research Concepts*, London: Sage.

Bloor, Michael, Frankland, Jane, Thomas, Michelle and Robson, Kate (2001) *Focus Groups in Social Research*, London: Sage.

Broom, Alex, F., Kirby, Emma, R., Adams, John and Refshauge, Kathryn, M. (2015) 'On illegitimacy, suffering and recognition: A diary study of women living with chronic pain', *Sociology*, 49(4): 937–54.

Bury, Michael (1982) 'Chronic illness as biographical disruption', *Sociology of Health and Illness*, 4(2): 167–82.

Davison, Charlie, Smith, George, D. and Frankel, Stephen (1991) 'Lay epidemiology and the prevention paradox: The implications of coronary candidacy for health education', *Sociology of Health and Illness*, 13(1): 1–19.

Demant, Jakob and Ravn, Signe (2010) 'Identifying drug risk perceptions in Danish youths: Ranking exercises in focus groups', *Drugs, Education, Prevention and Policy*, 17(5): 528–43.

Gibson, Alexandra, F., Lee, Christina and Crabb, Shona (2015) 'Reading between the lines: Applying multimodal critical discourse analysis to online constructions of breast cancer', *Qualitative Research in Psychology*, 12(3): 272–86.

Harman, Vicki and Cappellini, Benedetta (2015) 'Mothers on display: Lunchboxes, social class and moral accountability', *Sociology*, 49(4): 764–81.

Henwood, Karen (2008) 'Qualitative research, reflexivity and living with risk: Valuing and practising epistemic reflexivity and centring marginality', *Qualitative Research in Psychology*, 5(1): 45–55.

Hodgkin, Katherine and Radstone, Susannah (2003) *Contested Pasts: The Politics of Memory*, London/New York: Routledge.

Hussey, Susan, Hoddinott, Pat, Dowell, Jon, Wilson, Phil and Barbour, Rosaline, S. (2004) 'The sickness certification system in the UK: A qualitative study of the views of general practitioners in Scotland', *British Medical Journal*, 328: 88–92.

Jenkins, Nicholas, Bloor, Michael, Fischer, Jan, Berney, Lee and Neale, Joanne (2010) 'Putting it in context: The use of vignettes in qualitative interviewing', *Qualitative Research*, 10(20): 175–98.

Jenkins, Nicholas, Keyes, Sarah and Strange, Liz (2016) 'Creating vignettes of early onset dementia: An exercise in public sociology', *Sociology*, 50(1): 77–92.

Jones, Adam and Woolley, Janet (2015) 'The email diary: A promising research tool for the 21st century?', *Qualitative Research*, 15(6): 705–21.

Maxwell, Joseph, A. (2011) *A Realist Approach for Qualitative Research*, Thousand Oaks, CA: Sage.

Mills, C. Wright (1959) *The Sociological Imagination*, New York: Oxford University Press.

Morris, Max and Anderson, Eric (2015) 'Charlie is so cool like: Authenticity, popularity and inclusive masculinity on YouTube', *Sociology*, 49(6): 1200–17.

Prior, L. (2008) 'Repositioning documents in social research', *Sociology*, 42(5): 821–36.

Rapley, Timothy, J. (2001) 'The art(fulness) of open-ended interviewing: Some considerations on analyzing interviews', *Qualitative Research*, 1(3): 303–23.

Ravn, Iben, M., Frederiksen, Kirsten and Beedholm, Kirsten (2016) 'The chronic responsibility: A critical discourse analysis of Danish chronic care policies', *Qualitative Health Research*, 26(4): 545–54.

Riessman, Katherine (1993) *Narrative Analysis*, Newbury Park, CA: Sage.

Sheridan, Joanna, Chamberlain, Kerry and Dupuis, Ann (2011) '"Timelining": Visualizing experience', *Qualitative Research*, 11(5): 552–69.

Watson, Cate (2015) 'A sociologist walks into a bar (and other academic challenges): Towards a methodology of humour', *Sociology*, 49(3): 407–21.

PART III
Types of Data and How to Collect Them

Part III turns to issues of how to do the collection of qualitative data for specific types of data. In the thirteen chapters, specific *types of data* are the starting point for outlining the specific challenges they produce for data collection. Three types of data are focused here. As a first type, this part treats a range of *verbal data* in greater detail in five chapters. Data produced in interviews (see Roulston and Choi, Chapter 15, this volume) or focus groups (see Morgan and Hoffman, Chapter 16, this volume) and narrative data (see Murray, Chapter 17, this volume) are discussed. They are complemented by strategies such as conversation analysis (see Jackson, Chapter 18, this volume) and discourse analysis (see Rau et al., Chapter 19, this volume) and the issues of data collection in applying them.

As a second type of data, those produced in *ethnographic approaches* are in the focus of the next four chapters. Here we find observation as a general approach (see Wästerfors, Chapter 20, this volume) and ethnography (see Buscatto, Chapter 21, this volume) as the classical approaches in this area. These are complemented by more recent extensions such as mobile or go-along methods (see Kusenbach, Chapter 22, this volume) and focused ethnography based on videography (see Knoblauch et al., Chapter 23, this volume).

Finally we find a block of four chapters addressing the use of *material data*. Here, the use of documents is unfolded in detail (see Rapley and Rees, Chapter 24, this volume) as well as the use of images in qualitative research (see Eberle, Chapter 25, this volume) and media data such as television and film studies (see Mikos, Chapter 26, this volume). These visual approaches are complemented by using sounds as data (see Bull, Chapter 27, this volume).

Guideline questions as an orientation for writing chapters were the following: What characterizes the approach and what is intended to reach with it? What is the developmental background of the approach? Which is an outstanding example of using it? Which are the major theoretical background assumptions of the approach? How to proceed in applying the approach and what are its major practical procedures? What is a recent example of using it? Which are the main areas of using the approach? Which are the limits and outrange of the approach? Which are new developments and perspectives in this context?

Reading the chapters in Part III should help to answer questions like the following ones for a study and its method(s): What is the epistemological background of collecting qualitative data with this specific approach? What is the best way to plan data collection in qualitative research with this specific approach? What is the best way to document and elaborate data produced with this specific approach – e.g. transcribe interview data, elaborate field notes? What are steps in applying the selected approach for collecting the data? What characterizes good (and bad) example(s) of using the approach? What are the main stumbling blocks in using this approach? What are criteria of good practice with this approach of analyzing qualitative data? What are specific ethical issues in collecting qualitative data with this specific approach?

In answering questions like the ones just mentioned, the chapters in this part are meant to contribute to developing the methodological toolkit for qualitative data collection so that it becomes clearer how to use which method in sensitive ways of collecting empirical material in qualitative studies.

Qualitative Interviews

Kathryn Roulston and Myungweon Choi

INTRODUCTION

Interviews are omnipresent in contemporary society, and as a genre take in journalistic, media, clinical, job, parent–teacher, and research interviews among others. What these forms of interaction have in common is that they are driven by question–answer sequences. This chapter focuses on the research interview – which also exists in a wide range of forms. In terms of organization, interviews range from the tightly structured format of standardized survey interviews in which questions are asked in a specific order using the same format, to semi-structured interviews, in which the organization of topics is less tightly formatted. In the semi-structured interview, the same topics form the basis for questioning, yet interviewers' sequencing of questions is participant-led. At the other end of the spectrum from standardized or structured interviews are unstructured interviews, in which interviews are loosely formatted. Topics are participant-driven, and since the interviewer might not have a pre-formatted interview guide prior to the interview, talk is more likely to resemble everyday conversation. In this chapter, we focus on the semi-structured or 'open-ended' interview, in which researchers have identified topics about which they want to ask questions of individual participants. For group interviews, we refer readers to Morgan and Hoffman (see Morgan and Hoffman, Chapter 16, this volume).

In semi-structured interviews, follow-up questions – also referred to as probes – are formulated relative to what interviewees have already said. Researchers sequence questions to generate free-ranging conversations about research topics that are directed by what participants have to say. This kind of qualitative interview is widely used across disciplines as a primary research method. In this chapter we discuss the development of the interview method, theoretical perspectives, practical procedures involved in doing interview research, challenges and ethical issues, limitations of the method, and recent innovations.

BACKGROUND

Historical accounts of the development of interviewing are found in sociology (Platt, 2012; Lee, 2004, 2008, 2011), as well as methodological writing by sociologists such as Robert Merton (Merton et al., 1956/1990), David Riesman and Everett Hughes (Riesman and Benney, 1956; Benney and Hughes, 1956). According to Lee (2004, p. 870), both structured and unstructured interviews had become accepted forms of data collection in the field of sociology by the 1920s. Lee (2011) credits the work of psychotherapist Carl Rogers (1902–1987) as a significant influence in sociology through his training of interviewers in non-directive interviewing strategies in the 1940s.

Around the same time, others were contributing to interview methods. While Riesman, Hughes and Benney were refining survey interview methods, Robert Merton and his colleagues (1956/1990, p. 5) developed the 'focused interview' as a method to elicit information from individuals and groups concerning topics in communications research and propaganda. Initially this form of interview was used as an adjunct to the interpretation of statistical results. Thus, contemporary practice in the use of interviews for social research draws on two lineages: methodological examinations of interviewing used in opinion polling and standardized surveys, and research springing from ethnographic and life history traditions developed by the Chicago School (Lee, 2004). Ethnographers recognized the importance of field observations and interviews as complementary methods of data generation (Glaser and Strauss, 1967; Schatzman and Strauss, 1973). Yet the non-directive interview fell out of favor among sociologists in the post-World War II years, as scholars expressed reservations concerning its 'passivity, blandness, and drift' (Lee, 2011, p. 141), and turned either to participant observation as a way to bolster qualitative work, or standardized surveys and quantitative research to reinforce rigor.

Brenner (1981, p. 115), based on analyses of research published in the *American Sociological Review* and the *American Journal of Sociology*, asserted 35 years ago that data generated from interviewing and questionnaire methods accounted for around 90 percent of published research in these journals – with standardized survey interviews accounting for the bulk of these. Similarly, the promulgation of the interview method as a primary source for qualitative research studies has continued unabated in qualitative research methods texts. In practice, however, researchers use interview methods for different research purposes and do not necessarily mean the same thing when referring to qualitative interviews.

THEORIZING INTERVIEWS

Methodologically, interview data may be examined for referentialist content – reflections of the inner contents of peoples' minds and authentic selves – as well as interactional phenomena or 'speech events' (Koven, 2014) (i.e. how data are co-constructed). Researchers have also written about forms of interviewing, informed by different theoretical perspectives and used for a variety of research purposes (Roulston, 2010b). These include phenomenological interviews (deMarrais, 2004), ethnographic interviews (Spradley, 1979; Heyl, 2001), feminist interviews (DeVault and Gross, 2007), hermeneutic (Dinkins, 2005) and epistemic interviews (Brinkmann, 2007), the reflexive interview (Denzin, 2001), and intraviews (Kuntz and Presnall, 2012). Thus, researchers vary in how they refer to the qualitative interview and conceptualize their practice differently. As Koven (2014, p. 500) has argued, 'interviews are not one monolithic, predictable type of encounter that is equally familiar to everyone everywhere'.

APPROACHES TO INTERVIEWING

Phenomenological Interviews

Researchers interested in examining lived experience (van Manen, 1990) rely on *phenomenological interviews* that focus on the experiences of participants and the meanings they make of that experience (Seidman, 2012). Through phenomenological interviews, researchers generate detailed descriptions of participants' experiences about a phenomenon through asking open questions concerning the participants' feelings, perceptions, and understandings. These descriptions form the basis of the reconstructed interpretations or 'manifestations' of the phenomenon that is the focus of inquiry (Vagle, 2014).

Hermeneutic Interviews

Whereas in the phenomenological interview researchers are advised to take a neutral, non-directive stance, Dinkins writes about the *interpre-view* (2005) that draws on a hermeneutic process analogous to a Socratic approach to teaching. Here researchers and participants as co-inquirers engage in a shared dialog that evolves through questions and responses. The dialog focuses on reflections of both researchers *and* participants as they share ideas and reflect together. Interpretation is seen as an essential part of the interview process itself, rather than an isolated phase that occurs after the completion of the interview. Drawing on Dinkins' (2005) conceptualization of hermeneutic interviews, Brinkmann (2007) has forwarded the idea of *epistemic interviews* as a vehicle for developing knowledge rather than simply conveying experience. These conceptualizations of interviewing draw on a Socratic notion of dialog, in which researchers attempt to uncover participants' assumptions by openly challenging participants to account for and justify what they say. Thus, in interviews, a researcher's role is to ask challenging questions that seek justifications and rationales from participants. Brinkmann (2007, p. 1136) argues that when researchers and participants challenge one another – including participants disagreeing with or even objecting to researchers (Tanggaard, 2007) – the validity of analysis might be improved (see Barbour, Chapter 14, this volume).

Ethnographic Interviews

The purpose of *ethnographic interviewing* is to explore the meanings that people ascribe to actions and events in their cultural worlds, expressed in their own language (Roulston, 2010b, p. 19). To conduct ethnographic interviews, researchers need to conduct ongoing analyses of data generated via field notes of observations, participate in research settings, and conduct multiple interviews with informants over extended periods of time. It is critical for researchers to invest much time in making repeated contacts for extended observation and multiple interviews, thereby developing a genuine relationship involving mutual interest in the project. What differentiates ethnographic interviews from other qualitative interviews includes the duration and frequency of contact, the quality of the emerging relationship, and the focus on eliciting cultural meanings concerning the research topics and contexts (Heyl, 2001; see also Buscatto, Chapter 21, this volume).

Feminist Interviews

Feminist researchers use multiple forms of interviews, including semi-structured, unstructured, and oral and life history interviews with a view to producing knowledge about women's lives while promoting egalitarian relationships among women researchers and participants (Reinharz and Chase, 2002). What distinguishes feminist interviews from other qualitative interviews is not so much a particular approach to doing interviews, but that the application of the method authentically reflects feminist interests that promote equality for women. Since researchers conducting feminist interviews aim to work with participants in respectful and ethical ways to highlight women's voices, the use of language and discourse is critical. In particular, researchers attend to the productive powers of language; the subtle shades of meaning conveyed through nuance, gesture, and expression; the injuries and silences, and so on (DeVault and Gross, 2007, p. 173). DeVault (1990, p. 104) provides recommendations for feminist interviewers, including using the terms used by women in their daily lives, listening carefully for incompletely articulated issues, portraying participants respectfully, and representing research to be understood by audiences new to feminist work.

Postmodern Perspectives of Interviews

Researchers have used the interview as a means to develop performance texts about self and society (Denzin, 2001, p. 24). This is a postmodern conceptualization of interviewing that is fundamentally different from the traditional view of the interview as a method of data collection. This approach assumes that the interviewee has no essential self but provides various non-unitary performances of selves through his or her relationship with a particular interviewer. By questioning the possibility of generating truthful accounts and representation of interview data, talk generated in 'the reflective, dialogical, or performative interview' (Denzin, 2001, p. 24) may be represented in film, ethnodrama, plays, performance ethnographies, readers' theaters, and poetry and fiction (see Denzin, Chapter 13, this volume). By bringing people together in this new interpretive form of interview, researchers offer critique and suggestions about how the world could be different (Denzin, 2001).

Intraviews

Critiquing the simplistic use of the interview that abstracts humans as objects for analysis, Kuntz and Presnall (2012) draw on new materialist perspectives (Barad, 2007) to resituate the interview as a process-based, embodied, and emplaced 'intra-active event'. The interview is viewed as a co-creation among multiple bodies and forces, or *intraview*, where 'the prefix *intra* (meaning within) displaces *inter* (meaning between)' (Kuntz and Presnall, 2012, p. 733). This approach to interviewing engages with materialist theorizations that decenter 'the humanist subject and linguistic representation in favor of more diffractive ways of seeing and nomadic thinking' (2012, p. 734). Kuntz and Presnall (2012) illustrate what this might look like in practice in examining an interview conducted while walking with a participant. Through the act of walking, these authors argue, meaning is generated within the dynamic relations of moving bodies through physical space and time, as speakers negotiate 'paths and unforeseen interruptions' (2012, p. 733). Reconceptualizing interviews as intraviews calls on researchers to go beyond the focus on the words spoken to consideration of the relational becoming occurring within intra-actions (Barad, 2007)[1]. As another example of a new materialist conceptualization of interviewing as an 'entangled' encounter entailing 'material-discursive intra-activity', see Marn and Wolgemuth (2017).

GETTING PRACTICAL

Although there is a growing body of methodological literature that examines qualitative interviews as speech acts and unpacks the interactional features of interviews, research reports still largely take a referentialist orientation to interviews (Koven, 2014) that focuses on descriptions of people's inner thoughts, experiences and selves. This referentialist focus on getting in-depth or 'rich' descriptions is ubiquitous in methodological literature. Advice literature attends to what researchers should do during various phases of research, including preparation for, conducting, and analyzing and representing findings. We first provide a synopsis of this work.

PREPARING FOR INTERVIEWS

Ethical Review

Before conducting interviews with people, researchers must gain permission to conduct research with human subjects from the ethics review board/s with which they are affiliated (or institutional review boards (IRBs) in the US). Regulations concerning research with human subjects are subject to diverse interpretations across disciplinary traditions, cultural and institutional contexts, and countries – thus researchers must attend to what is required in their immediate setting. For example, oral history research is not subject to review by IRBs in the United States (Shopes and Ritchie, 2004), and the field of journalism is guided by different considerations (Sieber and Tolich, 2013). Specific ethical review boards may have different interpretations concerning what is required of researchers in conducting their studies (e.g. Janesick, 2015). Researchers must first learn what is required by the institutions with which they are affiliated, as well as what path must be taken in order to gain entry to a particular setting (e.g. research in some institutions may require review by another ethical review committee), and what is required in local contexts for gaining informed consent (see Mertens, Chapter 3, this volume).

Formulating Interview Guides

The point at which researchers formulate interview guides will depend on one's disciplinary and institutional affiliations, and specific research contexts. An interview guide is often required by an ethical review board in order to gain permission to conduct a study. In ethnographic research in fields such as anthropology and sociology in which participant observation is the primary method of data generation, researchers are likely to conduct significant fieldwork prior to developing protocols for formal interviews.

Formulating interview guides involves generating a list of questions and topics that are likely to elicit descriptions that speak to the research questions posed. Thought must also be given to the conceptual frames that will be used to analyze the data (Roulston, 2014), and the form of interview to be used. For example, although there is overlap in the kinds of interview questions that might be posed, the data generated in phenomenological, feminist, and ethnographic interviews will likely vary considerably. Similarly, how interviewers contribute to the talk will vary with each research project (Holstein and Gubrium, 1995) and how interviews are conceptualized.

Researchers consider the topics of talk about which questions might be asked, how to sequence the questions – usually beginning with broader questions before moving to more specific questions, and formulating open, rather than closed questions. For example, if one were to examine the research topic of online learning, a broad open question asked at the beginning of the interview might be:

- Tell me about your experiences with online delivery of course work prior to taking this course.

Potential follow-up topics might be suggested in the interview guide should participants not mention those. For example, a follow-up topic related to the question above might focus on tools used.

Reflecting on the Topic

Since interviewers rely on their own knowledge about the topic of research with which to ask questions and formulate follow-up prompts, how conversations unfold will be highly dependent on what researchers know. Thus the preparation phase for interview research for researchers conversant with a topic will vary considerably from those of researchers exploring topics about which they know little. For researchers who occupy 'insider' status relative to a topic, preparing for interviews may involve reflecting and thinking about one's preconceptions about a topic, what one already knows, or one's own experiences. Prior reflection, engaging in a 'bracketing' interview (Roulston, 2010b) or writing about what one knows about a topic, aids a researcher in articulating prior hypotheses about a topic that may interfere with being able to listen well to others.

The preparation phase for researchers engaged in learning about a new phenomenon may involve background research to understand jargon used in a particular culture (e.g. researchers might need to 'learn how to ask' about a new topic, Hoffmann, 2007, p. 336; Briggs, 1986). Without learning about participants' contexts, researchers may find it difficult to know what questions to ask, or even to understand what participants are trying to communicate. Thus, in ethnographic traditions, researchers may spend time observing a setting prior to conducting interviews.

Learning about participants prior to an interview is especially important for researchers examining experiences of elite participants (see Bogner et al., Chapter 41, this volume). For further strategies on working with elite populations, see Conti and O'Neil (2007), Harvey (2011), Bogner et al. (Chapter 41, this volume) and Mikecz (2012).

Technology

Researchers prepare for the technical requirements of interviewing by selecting and testing the equipment that they plan to use to record interviews. The early days of interviewing in which researchers hand-recorded notes of what was said have given way to successive waves of recording equipment (for a history of recording technologies in interview research, see Lee, 2004). Currently, researchers typically use some form of digital recording device to audio-record interviews, most recently smartphones (e.g. Goffman, 2014). Prior to conducting interviews, it is important to be familiar with the recording device, and have a back-up plan should equipment malfunction. Video-recording is frequently used in oral history projects in which recordings are being digitally archived for public dissemination (Hunt, 2012). In oral history research, researchers must prepare release forms in which participants provide consent for images and information collected in interviews to be made public.

Recruitment

Once permission has been gained for a study, the researcher can begin to recruit participants. This may involve the use of email notices, fliers or advertisements, or in some cases, face-to-face recruitment (e.g., research on sensitive topics). For further information on sampling and recruitment see Roulston and Martinez (2015) and Kristensen and Ravn (2015). Preparation also involves getting in touch with participants to arrange a suitable meeting place – preferably a quiet place, free from distractions, which will allow for good quality audio-recordings. Sometimes this will not be possible, so researchers must be flexible (see Bengry, Chapter 7, this volume).

The Conduct of the Interview

Informed consent

Prior to beginning an interview, researchers explain to participants what the research is about, and gain their informed consent for participation in the research. Again, there may be variation in how informed consent is gained (i.e. verbally, written) and how consent forms are structured, depending on the research design, research population, and the requirements for written consent. For example, if audio or video data are to be retained for other purposes (e.g. added to data repositories), the consent form might be tiered to allow participants to decide how data are used (see Mertens, Chapter 3, this volume).

Asking questions

Advice literature on qualitative interviewing has proliferated lengthy lists of recommendations for both what to do and what not to do. Rather than repeat such lists here, our recommendation is that interviewers come to interviews well-prepared with respect to the topic of the interview, with a good sense of what they hope to learn from the questions they anticipate asking, and with a willingness to listen carefully and learn from participants (Jacob and Furgerson, 2012; Roulston et al., 2003). Both novice and more experienced interviewers who talk more than they listen are likely to generate the kinds of data that they seek to find through asking leading questions and contributing their own viewpoints. These sorts of interviews jeopardize the scientific process, since they potentially provide more information about interviewers than interviewees, and inhibit participants from openly expressing their own views. Careful analysis of preliminary interviews can assist researchers in learning about the characteristics of their own talk, how conversations transpire with participants and whether or not the interviews conducted meet the needs of a specific project (Roulston, 2016). For example, for researchers conducting feminist inquiry, it may be appropriate to talk about one's own experiences and perspectives in an interview; for other kinds of research projects, this may be inappropriate. Thus, the quality of an interview must be judged relative to the researcher's purposes and theoretical assumptions about research (Roulston, 2010a; see Barbour, Chapter 14, this volume).

Cross-cultural interviewing and translation

Some researchers conduct interviews with participants of cultures to which they do not belong. Cross-cultural interviewing may involve further steps in preparation – this might include involvement of a translator within the interview, or collaboration with a researcher native to a participant's culture. For an example of how these strategies have worked in practice, see Court and Abbas (2013); for involvement of interpreters and translators, see Littig and Pöchhacker (2014). For a review of recommendations for cross-language research, see Squires (2009) and for generating data in foreign languages, see Resch and Enzenhofer (Chapter 9, this volume).

After the Interview

After interviews, researchers transcribe audio-recordings. We refer readers to other sources for more information on transcription (Poland, 2002; Skukauskaite, 2012; Jenks, 2011; see Jenks, Chapter 8, this volume). If interviews have been conducted in a language other than that of presentation, the researcher must make decisions about the point at which data will be translated (i.e. prior to or after analysis of data) (Temple and Young, 2004). Further, multiple approaches to presentation of translated data exist in the literature. For example, with reference to English-language publications, common approaches used include:

- Questions and answers during the interview are translated by an interpreter, and the translator's English interpretation is presented;
- Excerpts from interviews conducted in a language other than English are presented in English, with the original language included in block text beneath the translation; and
- Excerpts from interviews conducted in a language other than English are presented in English, interspersed with specific phrases in the native language (with translations) and a supportive glossary.

Since the detail of how talk is delivered is needed for analytic approaches such as conversation analysis (ten Have, 2007, pp. 109–110) or discursive psychology (Nikander, 2012), in this type of work translated data with the original language, side-by-side or underneath the original language, or full transcripts in the original language are more commonly seen.

Depending on how the research project has been designed, the study might involve multiple interviews over time. This allows time for the interviewer to begin the analysis process and present preliminary findings to participants in order to gain feedback as to whether their interpretations adequately reflect participants' viewpoints. This is a strong form of member validation (Seale, 1999; see Barbour, Chapter 14, this volume), and researchers who intend to do this must think about the consequences and plans of action for what they will do should participants disagree with how data have been interpreted and represented.

Data Analysis and Representation

The methods that researchers use to analyze and interpret interview data and represent participants are informed by the theoretical approaches and research design used for the study. Overviews of approaches to analyzing interview data include Miles et al. (2014), Saldaña (2013), and Wertz et al. (2011).

WHAT MAKES AN INTERVIEW *GOOD*?

From a researcher's perspective, 'good' interviewing practice is commonly seen to involve appropriate preparation, demonstration of respect for interviewees, intensive listening by the interviewer, development of thoughtful interview guides, interview guides that include fewer questions, formulation of short, open-ended questions, flexibility on the part of the interviewer to deviate from prior plans when necessary, effective use of follow-up questions to elicit extended descriptions, and the ability to help participants tell their stories. Ezzy (2010, p. 164) describes good interviews as 'not dominated by either the voice of the interviewer or the agendas of the interviewee. Rather, they feel like communion, where the tension between the research question and the experience of the interviewee is explored'. Perhaps overlooked is that interviewees who have a wealth of knowledge that they are willing to share and who are able to articulate their views and perspectives in ways that are rich and quotable make this kind of interview possible. The space to do this is facilitated when an interviewer is willing to learn through careful listening, and prompting when necessary. Yet this view of interviewing can potentially overlook opportunities for the analysis of interviews that seem to go 'wrong' and how these sorts of interviews can assist researchers in reflecting on research topics (e.g. Jacobsson and Åkerström, 2013; Prior, 2014). Wolgemuth et al. (2015) examined participants' experiences of participating in qualitative interview studies, and suggested that key issues that researchers need to consider in the design and conduct of interview research include how trusting relationships might be developed with participants, what questions allow participants to describe their experiences, and how opportunities for participants to talk about what is important to them might be provided (see Barbour, Chapter 14, this volume).

DEALING WITH CHALLENGES IN INTERVIEWS

Researchers have also reported challenges that occur in interviews, together with potential strategies that might be used (see Table 15.1 for an overview).

Table 15.1 shows that challenges in doing interview research are threaded throughout the process of planning, designing and conducting interviews, and analyzing and representing findings. Decision-making requires

Table 15.1 Challenges encountered in interviewing, and potential strategies that researchers use to address these

Challenges	Strategies to consider
Engaging in interviews	
Difficult topics and risky research	
• Conducting interviews about ethically sensitive topics (e.g. death and dying)	• Develop support mechanisms for researchers (e.g. counseling and debriefing, protocols for home visits)
• Management of safety and health of researcher and interviewees (e.g. conducting research in risky environments or interviewing participants for whom participation in research might have dangerous repercussions)	• Ensure safety of researchers (e.g. safety training) and participants (e.g. consider ethical implications for participants' engagement in research)
• Researching topics that might have a personal connection or significance	• Consider whether it is better not to pursue some research topics and/or questions
• Pursuing sensitive and/or challenging topics	• Reflect on and explore the researcher's emotional framing and engagement in interviews
• Dealing with difficult emotional issues that emerge in the interview (such as participants' personal hardships and problems)	• Consider the actions conveyed by interviewer's interactions in interviews (e.g. expressions of neutrality, empathy, alignment or disagreement with participants)
	• Seek participants' permission to intervene on their behalf if necessary; seek assistance if participant is in danger
	• Ensure that participants still consent to be part of the process; let them know their rights as participants
	• Consider the ethics of conducting the study; perhaps the participants need to represent themselves
Unexpected events and problematic locations	
• Overhearing audiences, and unexpected interruptions to interview	• Be flexible in dealing with unexpected events
• Contexts not conducive to the establishment of rapport (e.g. noisy environments)	• Prepare for interview to avoid problems (e.g. schedule interview for a place in which the interview will not be interrupted)
	• Adapt to cultural contexts in which private spaces for interviews may not be the social norm
Failures to generate the information anticipated from interviewees	• Conduct a pilot study to explore question formulation
	• Consider the fit of the research design and method used with research context
	• Examine interview data methodologically in order to gain greater understanding of how interviews unfold
	• Engage co-researchers to interview participants (e.g. adolescents)
	• Employ multiple methods to elicit data (e.g. video, participant observation, digital storytelling, photo elicitation)

(Continued)

Table 15.1 Challenges encountered in interviewing, and potential strategies that researchers use to address these (Continued)

Challenges	Strategies to consider
Interviewer (IR)–Interviewee (IE) relationships • Interviewing people who are different from the researcher (class, race & ethnicity, culture, age, gender, education, status) • Interviewing people who do not share the same language • Developing a shared understanding of language used with which to discuss topics	• Recognize limitations of who an interviewer can interview, and what the interviewer can elicit adequate data about; account for them in the design and conduct of the study • Use participatory research approaches to involve participants in the setting in generating data • Use a researcher journal to record methodological issues in interview encounters • Prepare for interviews by getting to know participants and establishing a shared language • Ensure the language in which interview is conducted allows interviewees to articulate their experiences; select an interpreting strategy as necessary • Find ways to establish commonality with participants to enhance rapport • Use gatekeepers to assist in establishing relationships with participants • Work with insiders to the group that you are working with; modify research design in order to generate other kinds of data or interview strategies
Reliability of interview data • Dealing with participants' recollections that appear to be contradictory, inaccurate, or not truthful	• Verify doubtful information via other sources • Check with participants about puzzling details • Examine the co-construction of interview data sequentially • Consider theorizations concerning the representation of 'truth' • Consider psychological research on the construction of memory, identity, and trauma in analytic approaches
Data analysis and representation Representation of the other • Negotiating conflicting interpretations and representations of data • Working with sensitive information that may be potentially harmful to participants, or could promote harmful stereotypes • Anonymizing data relative to sensitive topics	• Write in ways that the participants can recognize as truthful; represent others respectfully and value participants' stories • Avoid orienting to juicy leads or being unfair to participants in data representations • Recognize that representation is a political act • Undertake collaborative work or co-research with participants • Use alternative approaches to represent findings • Provide sufficient contextualization of data to portray participants' viewpoints accurately • Establish member checks with participants so that they can reply to the researcher's interpretations • Omit ethically sensitive data from representations that may be harmful to participants or was spoken off-record • Consider how representations might potentially contribute to stereotyping of participants

ethical reasoning related to particular contextual constraints. There are no rules to guide decision-making, and researchers take different courses of action based on varied reasoning (Tisdale, 2004; Whiteford and Trotter, 2008).

QUESTIONS ABOUT QUALITATIVE INTERVIEWS

Questions concerning the use of the interview method include whether or not use of interviews as a primary method threatens the rigor of research, how many interviews are appropriate, and the critiques and limitations of interview research. We address these next.

Interviews as the Primary Method

Many researchers use interviews as a sole method of data generation. This approach works well if the research purpose is to learn about people's beliefs, perspectives, and meaning-making. Narrative inquiry (see Murray, Chapter 17, this volume), for example, relies on interview data as the primary source. If research questions focus on generating facts about events or what people do, or examine how events occur in a setting, using interviews as a single method can be problematic, since it has long been known that people are subject to forgetfulness and may recall details inaccurately. Further, in interviews, people represent themselves differently depending on the social settings and audiences to whom they are speaking.

A key challenge with using qualitative interviews as the primary source of data stems from epistemological questions about how knowledge about the social world is constructed. If researchers are aiming for a neo-positivist account of the research phenomenon (i.e. what actually happens) (Roulston, 2010b), use of interview data as a sole data source is problematic. For researchers intent on representing how participants experience the social world and make meaning of their life experiences – that is not such a problem. This means that the way interviews are integrated in a study's design relates to epistemological concerns. What researchers do differs in practice (see Silverman, 2013, for cautions in the use of interviews).

Interviews as One of Multiple Methods

Qualitative researchers have used various forms of triangulation (see Flick, Chapter 34, this volume) to tackle the thorny issue of representing the 'truth' concerning research phenomena (Seale, 1999). *Data triangulation* refers to diverse data sources. In interview research, this could include multiple interviews with participants over time, or interviewing multiple members of a social setting in order to gain different perspectives of the phenomenon of research interest. *Methodological triangulation* refers to the use of multiple methods, such as participant observation, recording of naturally occurring data, examination of documents and artifacts and so forth. Next, we look at the integration of other forms of data in interview studies, including documents, visual methods, and participant observation.

Historians use documentary sources in order to verify accounts provided by participants of oral history interviews. In historical research, interviews may assume a secondary role to primary sources, such as archival data, in supporting interpretations. Oral history research can also be enriched by examination of documents and artifacts (Janesick, 2010).

Gillian Rose (2007) discusses photo-elicitation (see Eberle, Chapter 25, this volume) as an approach that is 'supportive' of researchers' interpretations. This approach uses photos – taken by participants or researchers – as a prompt within interviews to explore research topics. Interviewees are usually given guidelines concerning what to photograph, and in interviews, questions are posed to prompt reflection and meaning-making (Rose, 2007, pp. 240–2). For further information on the use of photos in longitudinal research, see Henwood et al. (Chapter 38, this volume).

Being there and recording one's observations of what is going on is primary data for ethnographers. Ethnographic interviewing involves asking questions in informal interviews as people go about their daily activities, as well as formal interviews in which researchers orient to particular topics that they want to pursue. Yet the lack of rigor attributed to studies in which the sole source of data is interviews is frequently attended to via qualitative studies with large sample sizes. For example, it is not uncommon to see published studies in which researchers have conducted a hundred or more interviews (e.g. Doucet, 2006; Barber, 2012).

HOW MANY INTERVIEWS?

Decision-making about sample size prompts many novice researches to ask: 'How many interviews are sufficient?' That depends. There are no rules for how many interviews are sufficient, since individual researchers must examine their fields of expertise, the design of their study, and consider if and when they believe they have sufficient data with which to answer their research questions. For a variety of views from senior and early career scholars, see Baker and Edwards (2012). Clearly, interview research that examines the life experiences of small numbers of participants over time yields different findings than studies in which hundreds of participants are involved. By focusing on depth, researchers sacrifice breadth, whereas focusing on breadth precludes depth. It is useful, then, to remember that all research is partial, and the aim of each study is to contribute understandings to a larger field of study.

LIMITATIONS AND CRITIQUES OF THE INTERVIEW METHOD

Atkinson and Silverman (1997) propose that the romantic impulse for self-narration in the 'Interview Society' has influenced social scientists to uncritically adopt the interview as a means of generating data. The reliance on interviewing by qualitative researchers has been critiqued by scholars who have argued for the value of using naturally occurring data (Potter and Hepburn, 2005; Silverman, 2005).

Further, the analysis and representation of interview data has been discussed repeatedly over several decades. Holstein and Gubrium (1995) advocated 20 years ago for integrating information about how interviews are conducted into reports from interview research. These calls for providing further information about the construction of interview data have continued (Silverman, 2017), and Potter and Hepburn (2012) have proposed a variety of strategies that might be used by interview researchers in analyzing and representing data to attend to the challenges of interview research. Yet, for the most part, researchers have done little to change the ways in which interview data are represented, perhaps due to the challenges of publication space to provide such detail in reports, and a lack of researcher understanding and preparation for doing such work (Roulston, 2016). It is our view that examining what goes on in interviews interactionally is enormously productive for thinking about the design and conduct of research, contributes to the social studies of interviewing (Rapley, 2012), and complements analyses that focus on the topics of talk (for an example, see Prior, 2015).

NEW DEVELOPMENTS AND PERSPECTIVES

In 2015, the online news source BuzzFeed claimed the first political interview conducted via emoji (images and smileys used in text-based messages). The interview subject, Australian foreign minister Julie Bishop, was subsequently questioned about her use of texts by the Australian Senate (Di Stefano, February 15, 2015; Ramzy, October 22, 2015). While this interview seemed to be more for amusement than for the generation of credible information, social researchers have always experimented with new technologies. Researchers conduct interviews via telephone (e.g. Lechuga, 2012), use online modes of communicating for recruiting interview subjects and conducting interviews, and develop tablet apps to facilitate conversational interviews with children (Ericsson, 2017). Review of methodological accounts of practice teaches us that any medium of communicating has both benefits and limitations. For example, Hirsch et al. (2014) describe benefits and limitations of using a social networking site (coachsurfing.org) for recruiting participants for face-to-face interviews in research conducted in India. Irvine et al. (2013) compare how interaction gets done in telephone interviews as compared to face-to-face interviews, finding in their data set that telephone interviews tended to generate shorter, less descriptive accounts.

Internet-mediated interview research includes the use of synchronous online interviews (Salmons, 2010), including various Voice over Internet Protocol (VoIP) platforms such as Skype™ (Deakin and Wakefield, 2014; Weller, 2015), asynchronous interviewing via email (Burns, 2010; Bampton and Cowton, 2002) and text messaging. Opdenakker (2006) compared face-to-face interviews with interviews conducted via email, MSN messenger and telephone, and discusses the advantages and disadvantages of different modes of communicating. Complications in using internet-based forms of communicating have been found to be exacerbated in cross-cultural research for both technical reasons and interpreting meaning in online communications (Frisoli, 2010).

CONCLUSION

Qualitative researchers from multiple disciplines use, adapt, and experiment with interviews. Researchers' interview practices are informed by the normative practices common to particular fields of study (e.g. history, sociology), or theoretical stance on research (e.g. feminist theory). For example, ethnographers are likely to value the importance of multiple data sources in ensuring the rigor of scholarly work, and are less likely to use interviews as a single source of data. To sum up, researchers vary considerably in the ways in which they discuss and use interviews. In this chapter, we have discussed some of the variations in the ways interviews have been used and conceptualized in social research. We hope to have conveyed some of the richness and diversity in how qualitative interview studies are conducted and what kinds of claims are warranted by qualitative data. Despite the differences, qualitative researchers continue to use interviews as a basic and, often times, primary part of their methodological toolkits.

ACKNOWLEDGMENTS

We thank the reviewers and editor for helpful comments which aided in revising earlier versions of the manuscript.

Note

1   Barad (2007, p. 179) writes: *'iterative intra-actions are the dynamics through which temporality and spatiality are produced and iteratively reconfigured in the materialization of phenomena and the (re) making of material-discursive boundaries and their constitutive exclusions'* (italics in original).

FURTHER READING

Gubrium, Jaber F., Holstein, James A., Marvasti, Amir B. and McKinney, Karyn D. (eds.) (2012) *The SAGE Handbook of Interview*

Research: The Complexity of the Craft (2nd edn). Los Angeles, CA: Sage.
Kvale, Steinar and Brinkmann, Svend (2009) *InterViews: Learning the Craft of Qualitative Research Interviewing* (2nd edn). Thousand Oaks, CA: Sage.
Talmy, Steven (2010) 'Qualitative interviews in applied linguistics: From research instrument to social practice', *Annual Review of Applied Linguistics*, 30, 128–48.

REFERENCES

Atkinson, Paul and Silverman, David (1997) 'Kundera's immortality: The interview society and the invention of the self', *Qualitative Inquiry*, 3(3): 304–25.
Baker, Sarah E. and Edwards, Rosalind (2012) 'How many qualitative interviews is enough? Expert voices and early career reflections on sampling and cases in qualitative research', *National Centre for Research Methods Review Paper*. Available at http://eprints.ncrm.ac.uk/2273/4/how_many_interviews.pdf [accessed July 25, 2016].
Bampton, Roberta and Cowton, Christopher J. (2002) 'The e-interview', *Forum: Qualitative Social Research* [Online Journal], 3(2). Available at http://www.qualitative-research.net/fqs/fqs-eng.htm [accessed July 25, 2016].
Barad, Karen (2007) *Meeting the Universe Halfway: Quantum Physics and the Entanglement of Matter and Meaning*. Durham and London: Duke University Press.
Barber, James P. (2012) 'Integration of learning: A grounded theory analysis of college students' learning', *American Educational Research Journal*, 49(3): 590–617.
Benney, Mark and Hughes, Everett C. (1956) 'Of sociology and the interview: Editorial preface', *American Journal of Sociology*, 62(2): 137–42.
Brenner, Michael (1981) 'Patterns of social structure in the research interview', in Michael Brenner (ed.), *Social Method and Social Life*. London and New York: Academic Press, pp. 115–58.
Briggs, Charles (1986) *Learning How to Ask: A Sociolinguistic Appraisal of the Role of the Interview in Social Science Research*. Cambridge: Cambridge University Press.
Brinkmann, Svend (2007) 'Could interviews be epistemic? An alternative to qualitative opinion polling', *Qualitative Inquiry*, 13(8): 1116–38.
Burns, Edgar (2010) 'Developing email interview practices in qualitative research', *Sociological Research Online* [Online Journal], 15(4). Available at: http://www.socresonline.org.uk/15/4/8.html [accessed July 25, 2016].
Conti, Joseph A. and O'Neil, Moira (2007) 'Studying power: Qualitative methods and the global elite', *Qualitative Research*, 7(1): 63–82.
Court, Deborah and Abbas, Randa (2013) 'Whose interview is it, anyway? Methodological and ethical challenges of insider–outsider research, multiple languages, and dual-researcher cooperation', *Qualitative Inquiry*, 19(6): 480–8.
Deakin, Hannah and Wakefield, Kelly (2014) 'Skype interviewing: Reflections of two PhD researchers', *Qualitative Research*, 14(5): 603–16.
deMarrais, Karen (2004) 'Qualitative interview studies: Learning through experience', in Karen deMarrais and Stephen D. Lapan (eds.), *Foundations for Research: Methods of Inquiry in Education and the Social Sciences*. Mahwah, NJ: Lawrence Erlbaum Associates, pp. 51–68.
Denzin, Norman K. (2001) 'The reflexive interview and a performative social science', *Qualitative Research*, 1(1): 23–46.
DeVault, Marjorie L. (1990) 'Talking and listening from women's standpoint: Feminist strategies for interviewing and analysis', *Social Problems*, 37(1): 96–116.
DeVault, Marjorie L. and Gross, Glenda (2007) 'Feminist interviewing: Experience, talk, and knowledge', in S. N. Hesse-Biber (ed.), *Handbook of Feminist Research: Theory and Praxis*. Thousand Oaks, CA: Sage, pp. 173–98.
Dinkins, Christine, S. (2005) 'Shared inquiry: Socratic-hermeneutic interpre-viewing', in Pamela M. Ironside (ed.), *Beyond Method: Philosophical Conversations in Healthcare Research and Scholarship*. Madison, WI: University of Wisconsin Press, pp. 111–47.
Di Stefano, M. (February 15, 2015) Julie Bishop describes serious diplomatic relationships with emoji. *Buzzfeed*. Available at: https://www.buzzfeed.com/markdistefano/emojiplomacy?utm_term=.il9x38eY0#.knPjezRK4 [accessed July 25, 2016].

Doucet, Andrea (2006) *Do Men Mother? Fathering, Care, and Domestic Responsibility.* Toronto, Canada: University of Toronto Press.

Ericsson, Stina (2017) *Ethics in norm-critical design for children.* Paper presented at the 18th Annual International Conference Dilemmas for Human Services 2015: Organizing, Designing and Managing, Växjö, Sweden September 9-11, 2015. http://dx.doi.org/10.15626/dirc.2015.08

Ezzy, Douglas (2010) 'Qualitative interviewing as an embodied emotional performance', *Qualitative Inquiry,* 16(3): 163–70.

Frisoli, P. St. John (2010) 'Assumptions, emotions, and interpretations as ethical moments: Navigating a small-scale cross-cultural online interviewing study', *International Journal of Qualitative Studies in Education,* 23(4): 393–405.

Glaser, Barney, G. and Strauss, Anselm, L. (1967) *The Discovery of Grounded Theory: Strategies for Qualitative Research.* New York: Aldine de Gruyter.

Goffman, Alicia, (2014) *On the Run: Fugitive Life in an American City.* Chicago, IL: Chicago University Press.

Harvey, William S. (2011) 'Strategies for conducting elite interviews', *Qualitative Research,* 11(4): 431–41.

Heyl, Barbara S. (2001) 'Ethnographic interviewing', in Paul Atkinson, Amanda Coffey, Sara Delamont, John Lofland and Lyn Lofland (eds.), *Handbook of Ethnography.* Thousand Oaks, CA: Sage, pp. 369–83.

Hirsch, Lily, Thompson, Kirrilly and Every, Danielle (2014) 'From computer to commuter: Considerations for the use of social networking sites for participant recruitment', *Qualitative Report,* 19(5): 1–13.

Hoffmann, Elizabeth A. (2007) 'Open-ended interviews, power, and emotional labor', *Journal of Contemporary Ethnography,* 36(3): 318–46.

Holstein, James A. and Gubrium, Jaber F. (1995) *The Active Interview.* Thousand Oaks, CA: Sage.

Hunt, Marjorie (2012) *Smithsonian Folklife and Oral History Interview Guide.* Available at http://www.museumonmainstreet.org/education/Oral_History_Guide_Final.pdf [accessed July 25, 2016].

Irvine, Annie, Drew, Paul and Sainsbury, Roy (2013) '"Am I not answering your questions properly?" Clarification, adequacy and responsiveness in semi-structured telephone and face-to-face interviews', *Qualitative Research,* 13(1): 87–106.

Jacob, Stacy A. and Furgerson, S. Paige (2012) 'Writing interview protocols and conducting interviews: Tips for students new to the field of qualitative research', *Qualitative Report,* 17(42): 1–10.

Jacobsson, Katarina and Åkerström, Malin (2013) 'Interviewees with an agenda: Learning from a "failed" interview', *Qualitative Research,* 13(6): 717–34.

Janesick, Valerie, J. (2010) *Oral History for the Qualitative Researcher: Choreographing the Story.* New York and London: The Guilford Press.

Janesick, Valerie, J. (2015) *Contemplative Qualitative Inquiry: Practicing the Zen of Research.* Walnut Creek, CA: Left Coast Press.

Jenks, Christopher, J. (2011) *Transcribing Talk and Interaction.* Amsterdam/Philadelphia: John Benjamins Publishing Company.

Koven, Michèle (2014) 'Interviewing: Practice, ideology, genre, and intertextuality', *Annual Review of Anthropology,* 43: 499–520.

Kristensen, Guro Korsnes and Ravn, Malin Noem (2015) 'The voices heard and the voices silenced: Recruitment processes in qualitative interview studies', *Qualitative Research,* 15(6): 722–37.

Kuntz, Aaron M. and Presnall, Marni M. (2012) 'Wandering the tactical: From interview to intraview', *Qualitative Inquiry,* 18(9): 732–44.

Lechuga, Vicente M. (2012) 'Exploring culture from a distance: The utility of telephone interviews in qualitative research', *International Journal of Qualitative Studies in Education,* 25(3): 251–68.

Lee, Raymond M. (2004) 'Recording technologies and the interview in sociology, 1920–2000', *Sociology,* 38(5): 869–89.

Lee, Raymond M. (2008) 'David Riesman and the sociology of the interview', *Sociological Quarterly,* 49(2): 285–307.

Lee, Raymond M. (2011) '"The most important technique ...": Carl Rogers, Hawthorne, and the rise and fall of nondirective interviewing in sociology', *Journal of the History of the Behavioral Sciences,* 47(2): 123–46.

Littig, Beate and Pöchhacker, Franz (2014) 'Socio-translational collaboration in qualitative inquiry: The case of expert interviews', *Qualitative Inquiry,* 20(9): 1085–95.

Marn, Travis M. and Wolgemuth, Jennifer R. (2017) 'Purposeful entanglements: A new materialist analysis of transformative interviews', *Qualitative Inquiry*, 23(5): 365–74.

Merton, Robert K., Fiske, Marjorie and Kendall, Patricia L. (1956/1990) *The Focused Interview: A Manual of Problems and Procedures*. New York: The Free Press.

Mikecz, Robert (2012) 'Interviewing elites: Addressing methodological issues', *Qualitative Inquiry*, 18(6): 482–93.

Miles, Matthew B., Huberman, A. Michael and Saldaña, Johnny (2014) *Qualitative Data Analysis: A Methods Sourcebook*. Los Angeles, CA: Sage.

Nikander, Pirjo (2012) 'Interviews as discourse data', in Jaber F. Gubrium, James A. Holstein, Amir Marvasti and Karyn D. McKinney (eds.), *The SAGE Handbook of Interview Research: The Complexity of the Craft*. Los Angeles, CA: Sage, pp. 397–414.

Opdenakker, Raymond (2006) 'Advantages and disadvantages of four interview techniques in qualitative research', *Forum: Qualitative Social Research* [Online Journal], 7(4). Available at http://www.qualitative-research.net/index.php/fqs/article/view/175/391 [Accessed July 25, 2016].

Platt, Jennifer (2012) 'The history of the interview', in Jaber F. Gubrium, James A. Holstein, Amir Marvasti and Karyn D. McKinney (eds.), *The SAGE Handbook of Interview Research: The Complexity of the Craft*. Los Angeles, CA: Sage, pp. 9–26.

Poland, Blake D. (2002) 'Transcription quality', in Jaber F. Gubrium, James A. Holstein (eds.), *Handbook of Interview Research: Context and Method*. Thousand Oaks, CA: Sage, pp. 629–50.

Potter, Jonathan and Hepburn, Alexa (2005) 'Qualitative interviews in psychology: Problems and possibilities', *Qualitative Research in Psychology*, 2(4): 281–307.

Potter, Jonathan and Hepburn, Alexa (2012) 'Eight challenges for interview researchers', in Jaber F. Gubrium, James A. Holstein, Amir Marvasti and Karyn D. McKinney (eds.), *The SAGE Handbook of Interview Research: The Complexity of the Craft*. Los Angeles, CA: Sage, pp. 555–70.

Prior, Matthew T. (2014) 'Re-examining alignment in a "failed" L2 autobiographical research interview', *Qualitative Inquiry*, 20(4): 495–508.

Prior, Matthew T. (2015) *Emotion and Discourse in L2 Narrative Research*. Bristol: Multilingual Matters.

Ramzy, Austin (October 22, 2015) 'Julie Bishop, foreign minister of Australia, raises eyebrows with emojis' *New York Times*. Available at: http://www.nytimes.com/2015/10/23/world/australia/australia-emoji-julie-bishop-diplomacy-vladimir-putin.html?_r=0 [accessed July 25, 2016].

Rapley, Tim (2012) 'The (extra)ordinary practices of qualitative interviewing', in Jaber F. Gubrium, James A. Holstein, Amir Marvasti and Karyn D. McKinney (eds.), *The SAGE Handbook of Interview Research: The Complexity of the Craft*. Los Angeles, CA: Sage, pp. 541–54.

Reinharz, Shulamit and Chase, Susan E. (2002) 'Interviewing women', in Jaber F. Gubrium, James A. Holstein (eds.), *Handbook of Interview Research: Context and Method*. Thousand Oaks, CA: Sage, pp. 221–38.

Riesman, David and Benney, Mark (1956) 'Asking and answering', *Journal of Business*, 29(4): 225–36.

Rose, Gillian (2007) *Visual Methodologies: An Introduction to the Interpretation of Visual Materials*. Thousand Oaks, CA: Sage.

Roulston, Kathryn (2010a) 'Considering quality in qualitative interviewing', *Qualitative Research*, 10(2): 199–228.

Roulston, Kathryn (2010b) *Reflective Interviewing: A Guide to Theory and Practice*. London and Thousand Oaks, CA: Sage.

Roulston, Kathryn (2014) 'Analyzing interview data', in U. Flick (ed.), *Handbook of Qualitative Data Analysis*. London: Sage, pp. 297–312.

Roulston, Kathryn (2016) 'Issues in methodological analyses of research interviews', *Qualitative Research Journal*, 16(1): 1–14.

Roulston, Kathryn and Martinez, B. (2015) 'Recruitment and sampling in consumer research', in Paul Hackett (ed.), *Consumer Ethnography: Qualitative and Cultural Approaches to Consumer Research*. New York and London: Routledge, pp. 33–52.

Roulston, Kathryn, deMarrais, Kathleen and Lewis, Jamie B. (2003) 'Learning to interview in the social sciences', *Qualitative Inquiry*, 9(4): 643–68.

Saldaña, Johnny (2013) *The Coding Manual for Qualitative Researchers*. Los Angeles, CA: Sage.

Salmons, Janet (2010) *Online Interviews in Real Time*. Los Angeles, CA: Sage.

Schatzman, Leonard and Strauss, Anselm (1973) *Field Research: Strategies for a Natural Sociology*. Englewood Cliffs, NJ: Prentice-Hall.

Seale, Clive (1999) *The Quality of Qualitative Research*. London: Sage.

Seidman, Irving (2012) *Interviewing as Qualitative Research: A Guide for Researchers in Education and the Social Sciences*. New York: Teachers College.

Shopes, Linda and Ritchie, Donald (2004) 'Exclusion of oral history from IRB reviews: An update', *Perspectives on History: The Newsmagazine of the American Historical Association*. Available at: https://www.historians.org/publications-and-directories/perspectives-on-history/march-2004/exclusion-of-oral-history-from-irb-reviews-an-update [accessed July 25, 2016].

Sieber, Joan E. and Tolich, Martin (2013) *Planning Ethically Responsible Research*. Los Angeles, CA: Sage.

Silverman, David (2005) *Doing Qualitative Research: A Practical Handbook*. London, Thousand Oaks, New Delhi: Sage.

Silverman, David (2013) 'What counts as qualitative research? Some cautionary comments', *Qualitative Sociology Review*, 9(2): 48–55.

Silverman, David (2017) 'How was it for you? The Interview Society and the irresistible rise of the (poorly analyzed) interview', *Qualitative Research*, 17(2): 144–58.

Skukauskaite, Audra (2012) 'Transparency in transcribing: Making visible theoretical bases impacting knowledge construction from open-ended interview records', *Forum: Qualitative Social Research* [Online Journal], 13(1), Art. 14 Available at: http://nbn-resolving.de/urn:nbn:de:0114-fqs1201146 [accessed July 25, 2016].

Spradley, James P. (1979) *The Ethnographic Interview*. Belmont, CA: Wadsworth.

Squires, Allison (2009) 'Methodological challenges in cross-language qualitative research: A research review', *International Journal of Nursing Studies*, 46(2): 277–87.

Tanggaard, Lene (2007) 'The research interview as discourses crossing swords: The researcher and apprentice on crossing roads', *Qualitative Inquiry*, 13(1): 160–76.

Temple, Bogusia and Young, Alys (2004) 'Qualitative research and translation dilemmas', *Qualitative Research*, 4(2): 161–78.

ten Have, P. (2007) *Doing Conversation Analysis: A Practical Guide*. London: Sage.

Tisdale, Kirsten (2004) 'Being vulnerable and being ethical with/in research', in Kathleen Bennett DeMarrais and Stephen D. Lapan (eds.), *Foundations of Research: Methods of Inquiry in Education and the Social Sciences*. Mahwah, NJ: Lawrence Erlbaum.

Vagle, Mark D. (2014) *Crafting Phenomenological Research*. Walnut Creek, CA: Left Coast Press.

van Manen, M. (1990) *Research Lived Experience: Human Science for an Action Sensitive Pedagogy*. Ontario, Canada: The Althouse Press.

Weller, Susie (2015) 'The potentials and pitfalls of using Skype for qualitative (longitudinal) interviews', *National Centre for Research Methods Working Paper*. Available at: http://eprints.ncrm.ac.uk/3757/1/Susie%20Weller.pdf [accessed July 25, 2016].

Wertz, Frederick J., Charmaz, Kathy, McMullen, Linda M., Josselson, Ruthellen, Anderson, Rosemarie and McSpadden, Emalinda (2011) *Five Ways of Doing Qualitative Analysis: Phenomenological Psychology, Grounded Theory, Discourse Analysis, Narrative Research, and Intuitive Inquiry*. New York and London: The Guilford Press.

Whiteford, Linda M. and Trotter, Robert T. (2008) *Ethics for Anthropological Research and Practice*. Long Grove, IL: Waveland Press.

Wolgemuth, Jennifer R., Erdil-Moody, Zeynep, Opsal, Tara, Cross, Jennifer E., Kaanta, Tanya, Dickmann, Ellyn M. and Colomer, Soria (2015) 'Participants' experiences of the qualitative interview: Considering the importance of research paradigms', *Qualitative Research*, 15(3): 351–72.

Focus Groups

David L. Morgan and Kim Hoffman

INTRODUCTION

The history of focus groups can be divided into three broad periods, beginning with their origin in the collaboration between Robert Merton and Paul Lazarsfeld in 1941 (for an account of this original session, see Merton, 1987). What Lazarsfeld brought to this partnership was an interest in using group discussions as data, while Merton contributed the kind of open-ended questioning that makes them recognizable as qualitative research. Merton and Lazarsfeld continued to work together on a number of war-related projects, which were reported first in an article (Merton and Kendall, 1946) and a decade later in a book (Merton et al., 1990). Yet, for reasons that are open to speculation, this introduction of the focus group did not take hold in the social sciences, where the method essentially disappeared from view for the next twenty-five years.

During this period of lack of interest from the social sciences, focus groups became firmly established in marketing research (Lee, 2010; Tadajewski, 2015). Interestingly, this use of focus groups was relatively close to the original purposes that Merton and Lazarsfeld pursued. In particular, the very first groups they did involved listener responses to radio programs, while much of their work in World War II concentrated on the production of propaganda. Hence, the use of focus groups to understand consumer behavior to produce advertising materials follows directly from their initial application.

From the point of view of social science research methods, it is the third period that is most interesting, marking the reintroduction of focus groups into the social sciences. The year 1988 is particularly noteworthy because it saw the publication of the first editions of what would become two of the most popular textbooks about focus groups (Krueger and Casey, 2015; Morgan, 1996). This production of 'how-to' books was quite different than the earlier tradition in marketing research, where it sometimes seemed as if the practical aspects of doing focus groups remained proprietary knowledge. For whatever reason, this second appearance of focus groups in the social sciences was much more successful than their original development, so that thousands of articles are now published every year that employ this method.

Regardless of when and where focus groups are used, their defining feature is the use of group interaction to produce qualitative data. One essential part of this interaction is the 'sharing and comparing' (Morgan, 2010, 2012) that goes on in group discussions. On the one hand, the process of sharing includes discussions of the ways that participants feel similar to each other; on the other hand, comparing gets at the differences between participants. For the researcher, these ongoing exchanges around similarities and differences provide insights into not just what participants think but also why they think the way they do.

This chapter begins by reviewing the uses for focus groups, as well as epistemological issues and the importance of interaction in focus groups. The core of the chapter then examines three basic aspects of research design for focus groups: selecting the participants, writing the questions, and moderating the groups. That is followed by a discussion of analysis strategies for focus groups data, along with current work in the area of online focus groups. In each case, we discuss the implications for collecting data using focus groups.

USES FOR FOCUS GROUPS

Over the years, social science researchers have found a wide range of potential uses for focus groups. In particular, studies that rely solely on focus groups (so-called 'standalone' focus groups) have become quite common, which contrasts with earlier uses that were primarily in combination with survey research (e.g. Folch-Lyon et al., 1981). Focus groups have thus become an all-purpose method that is widely used throughout qualitative research.

The most obvious comparison to other qualitative methods is between focus groups and individual interviews (see Roulston and Choi, Chapter 15, this volume). The strength of focus groups in this regard is the variety of different perspectives and experiences that participants reveal during their interactive discussion. This is especially important in the twin processes of sharing and comparing, which create dynamics that are not available in individual interviews. This means that focus groups are especially useful for investigating the extent of both consensus and diversity among the participants, as they engage in sharing and comparing among themselves with the moderator in a facilitating role.

By comparison, individual interviews provide a degree of depth and detail on each participant that is not available in focus groups. A 90-minute focus group with six participants will yield an average of 15 minutes per person, as opposed to the hour of more that would be heard in an individual interview. This points to at least one decision rule for using either focus groups or individual interviews: When the goal is to understand issues related to consensus and diversity across participants, focus groups are recommended, while individual interviews are preferred when the goal is to get in-depth information about each participant.

It is important not to overstate differences between focus groups and individual interviews, however. Often, they are best seen as complementary rather than competing methods. For example, individual key informant interviews can be a good starting point for planning a future set of focus groups. Alternatively, individual interviews can be a useful follow-up to focus groups, giving more opportunities to hear from participants whose thoughts and experiences are worth pursuing further. Finally, either individual interviews or focus groups can be used as 'member checks', where one method is used to get feedback after the researcher has done preliminary analyses on the data from another method (see Roulston and Choi, Chapter 15, this volume and Flick, Chapter 34, this volume).

Beyond combining individual interviews and focus groups in the same project, there are also a number of applications that combine focus groups with quantitative methods. In this regard, it is worth noting that Merton and his collaborators primarily developed focus groups for use with quantitative methods, which would now be known as mixed methods research (Creswell and Plano-Clark, 2010; Morgan, 2013; see Hesse-Biber, Chapter 35, this volume, and Morse et al., Chapter 36, this volume). One common role for focus groups in mixed methods is to provide preliminary inputs to the development of either survey instruments or program interventions. In this case, the success of the quantitative portion of the project depends on having materials that work well for the participants, and focus groups can provide participants' voices during this development phase. Focus groups can also be equally useful for following-up on surveys and experimental studies. In this case, the typical goal is to extend what was learned with the quantitative data by gaining a better sense of how and why those quantitative results came about.

Overall, this wide range of uses indicates a flexibility that means, for better or worse, there is no one right way to do focus groups. Instead, researchers need to be aware of the various options available, in order to make appropriate choices about how to do focus groups. Hence, the majority of this chapter will concentrate on the practical aspects of designing and conducting focus groups. Before that, however, we wish to address epistemological issues related to focus groups.

EPISTEMOLOGICAL ISSUES

Epistemology refers to 'what we regard as knowledge or evidence of things in the social world' (Mason, 1996, p. 13; see also Maxwell, Chapter 2, this volume). What epistemological stance should one take with regard to the knowledge generated in focus groups? Opinions vary as to whether the knowledge produced from focus groups can be seen as a natural phenomenon, one that resembles casually occurring 'real world' conversations, or if we should think about the production of knowledge as artificial, akin to an experimental intervention. Our view is that all interview settings are artificial to the extent they consist of researcher-produced environments established for the purpose of generating data. Of course, this interaction is 'naturalistic' rather than naturally occurring, because it is the researcher who provides the topics that will be the subject of that interaction. In addition, the researcher asks the questions, and beyond that may play either a more active or less active role in directing the discussions. But this does not mean that such interviews lack meaning to the participants – indeed these 'un-natural' settings often open up opportunities for self-expression that would not be possible otherwise, such as by providing opportunities to talk with peers about topics that might be more difficult to discuss in more routine settings.

One trap to avoid in this regard is the assumption that individual interviews represent a kind of 'gold standard' where the focus group introduces an element of bias due to the influences of the group on the individual (see Morrison, 1998 for an example of this argument). This assumes that each person has one 'true' set of attitudes that will be revealed only in the presence of a researcher in a one-to-one interview, rather than in a group setting with peers. Instead of arguing about whether one of these data collection formats is better than the other, it is more useful to treat them as different contexts – which may well produce different kinds of data.

A different issue relates to whether focus groups are specifically aligned with any particular set of epistemological assumptions; our argument that they are a general purpose qualitative method means they can be used with a variety of epistemological frameworks. Within the traditional social science approach to epistemology (Guba and Lincoln, 1994), this means that they could be used under either post-positivist or constructivist assumptions. This has led to a rather polarized treatment of the content expressed in focus groups. For example, Coule (2013) argues that a post-positivist approach would treat attitudes as pre-existing content, while a constructivist approach would treat the content as produced during the course of the conversation.

In contrast, our approach takes a pragmatist approach to the philosophy of knowledge (e.g. Morgan, 2007, 2013, 2014). From this perspective, focus groups serve as tools for producing knowledge, and the nature of such knowledge depends on both the prior beliefs that one brings to the research and the purposes that one hopes to serve through that research. For example, one's assumptions about the nature of attitudes would affect how one conducts one's research, as would the goals one hopes to meet through learning about those attitudes. Methods such as focus groups thus serve as a link between beliefs and action, where the meaning of those beliefs are found in the outcomes of the actions that follow from them.

From a pragmatist orientation, both the researcher and the participants bring a set of beliefs to the interview setting, which produces a cycle of acting on those beliefs, interpreting the outcomes of those actions, and updating one's beliefs based on those outcomes. For the participants, this can be a very active process, where each statement by the others in the group leads to a reassessment of one's own likely responses. Barbour states that participants can change their views in the middle of a focus group, especially when the topic is one not often discussed (Barbour, 2018). For the researcher, this cycling between actions and consequences can also have immediate implications, such as in the nature of the questions that we will be asked, within the context of the ongoing discussion. Alternatively, the experiences within any one focus group may also have longer-term consequences for the researcher, as either inputs to alter the analysis process or as insights about how to redesign the ongoing research project (see Maxwell, Chapter 2, this volume).

INTERACTION IN FOCUS GROUPS

As mentioned earlier, a significant distinction between one-on-one interviews and focus groups concerns the interaction that is the fundamental source of data in focus groups. Although it has been argued that researchers have not given enough emphasis to interaction in focus groups (Duggleby, 2005), this topic has recently received increasing attention (see review in Morgan, 2012). These considerations of interaction cover a wide range, from the micro-dynamics of pairwise exchanges to abstract consideration of the co-construction of meaning.

The micro-dynamics of focus groups have primarily been dealt with by analysts in the field of Conversation Analysis. Thus, Myers and Macnaghten (1999), after asking the question, 'Can focus groups be analyzed as talk?' were able to answer a resounding 'Yes' (see also Macnaghten and Myers, 2004). Following established procedures in Conversation Analysis (see Jackson, Chapter 18, this volume), much of this work has concentrated on relatively technical issues, such as turn-taking between pairs of participants. One notable feature of this work is that it seldom concentrates on the substantive topics that make up the group discussion. As such, it largely addresses questions of how interaction occurs, rather than what is contained in that conversation.

At a more abstract level, the interaction in focus groups has been treated as a co-construction of meaning among the participants (Wilkinson, 1998). Here, the issue is how participants create and give meaning to the content of their discussions. This approach thus largely reverses the emphasis in Conversation Analysis, by concentrating on questions about what is discussed in interaction, rather than how that interaction occurs. Unfortunately, work on the co-construction approach has remained relatively abstract, with a reliance on the detailed examination of quotations. As such, it remains mostly a conceptual orientation, rather than a method.

SELECTING PARTICIPANTS: GROUP COMPOSITION

An obvious factor that is critical to ensuring significant interaction between focus group members is group composition. When deciding who to invite to the focus groups, the researcher must keep two important considerations in mind: the relationship the participants have with the topic and the relationship the participants can have with each other. Rich interactions can occur when carefully considering group composition and maximizing the potential for 'common ground' to elicit sharing and comparing. An example might be a research project that explores the home-life effects of breast cancer in women with partners. While the focus groups could potentially group two or three couples together, an alternative scenario which capitalizes on the concept of homogeneous experiences would be to assign the women with breast cancer into their own groups and their partners into their own. This type of segmentation allows for comparison between the two homogeneous groups. In this example, the types of home-life effects reported by women experiencing the cancer can be compared against those reported by their partners.

Alternatively, heterogeneous focus groups present an opportunity for dialog of a different sort. Though homogeneous groups are traditionally favored in focus group composition to ensure respondents' comfort levels, there may be cases where heterogeneity to generate differing viewpoints is appropriate. For example, in an exploration of Americans' view on gun control, having heterogeneous groups may produce a 'preaching to the choir' effect among the participants on each side of the issue, which would be only mildly interesting to either the participants or the researchers. Heterogeneity in focus groups thus requires careful consideration by the research team, given that focus groups still need sufficient commonality between participants to maintain productive conversation and avoid undue conflict.

Unfortunately, there is virtually no empirical work on the impact of homogeneity or heterogeneity in focus groups. Instead, there has been a strong preference for homogeneity, because the success of bringing together similar participants is so well demonstrated. This means that there is correspondingly less experience in determining either the most effective situations for using heterogeneous groups or the procedures for working with such groups.

In individual interviews, confidentiality and safe spaces are more easily controlled, but in focus groups, the research team must be highly aware of asymmetry in the groups related to power dynamics, environments where some respondents might feel threatened, or topics which present discomfort for those with previous acquaintance. A different problem is grouping individuals whose security (emotional, physical, job, etc.) is at risk if they divulge certain kinds of information. For example, it would likely be unwise to group senior staff with their respective employees to explore communication and social dynamics in the workplace.

Sensitive topics in focus groups can be approached in terms of the self-disclosure of personal information. Under-disclosure occurs when someone in the conversation is concerned about how the other(s) will react. Under-disclosure is a concern for researchers given that they must elicit as much information as possible, often from strangers meeting each other for the first time. Participants are more likely to disclose sensitive information in homogeneous groups, where they are talking with peers who understand their shared circumstances. Alternatively, over-disclosure can also be a valid concern if one or more respondents in a focus group 'over share' on a sensitive topic and possibly exceed the limits promised in the ethical review process.

In addition, note that the issues listed above are moot if the researcher pays no attention to the recruitment of the participants. Recruitment is often treated as a clerical issue when the reality is that this initial engagement between the researchers and the respondents can influence the quality of the data acquired later in the focus group. Careful and professional communication with prospective respondents is key to making sure that the people not only show up, but walk in the door feeling informed, comfortable, and appreciated. Once again, however, recruitment is an issue where empirical research is non-existent, so whatever advice is available reflects researchers' accumulated experience, rather than comparative testing of different strategies (see Schreier, Chapter 6, this volume, and Bengry, Chapter 7, this volume).

Size is a crucial consideration in decisions about group composition. Typically, focus groups range in size from 5 to 10 people. Smaller sizes are particularly appropriate for sensitive topics and/or situations where the participants have a high level of engagement with the topic. More recently, there has also been considerable experimentation with dyadic interviews where there are only two participants (Morgan et al., 2013; Morgan, 2015). Dyadic interviews are similar to focus groups in that they seek to accomplish the 'sharing and comparing' dimension in interaction, but they limit the dynamic to a conversation between two people, rather than the complexity that can arise when multiple participants engage in a lively discussion. Similar to standard focus groups, the moderator is there primarily to help the respondents establish rapport and produce rich data. Dyadic interviews are especially well suited to interviewing spouses, and, are thus frequently used in the family studies literature (see review in Morgan, 2015).

Finally, there is the question of the number of groups. As with individual interviews, the most common recommendation is to seek 'saturation', so that further groups no longer provide any additional information. In practice, this means that the researcher has become so familiar with the content of the discussions that it is possible to predict how the participants will respond to almost any topic that gets raised during the discussion.

WRITING THE INTERVIEW QUESTIONS

When creating an interview guide, researchers can take several different approaches, each with their own level of influence over the interaction between participants and the data elicited from them. One alternative is to use less-structured interviews which create a 'bubbling up' of a wide range of potentially unanticipated responses. This approach necessarily uses fewer questions, with each lasting around 15 to 20 minutes. These interviews work best when the goal is to hear the participants' wide-ranging thoughts about the topic, with less emphasis on the specific types of questions that the researcher feels are important about a particular topic. A disadvantage is that the participants may take the interview in a direction that is not necessarily productive for the overall project. Alternatively, more structured interviews – with more targeted questions – reduce this problem, but at the cost of restricting the participants' frame of reference. In principle, semi-structured interviews would fall somewhere in the middle, but for focus groups, there is little guidance in the literature about what exactly this means. At a minimum, a semi-structured interview would mean that the moderator must be open to moving the interview toward more targeted questions and prompts if the group has a tendency to stray too far off-topic.

In other cases, however, the moderator may need to use more open-ended questions that prompt interaction and creativity to get the participants' 'juices flowing'. Thus, when doing semi-structured interviews, a skilled moderator must make the necessary adaptations, taking into consideration the constraints of the instrument approved during the ethics review.

Rather than selecting either a more or a less-structured approach, or splitting the difference between the two, a third option is a 'funnel' approach to interviewing, that includes both open-ended and highly targeted questions. Funnels work systematically from less-structured, open-ended questions to more structured, targeted questions. After introductions, the moderator begins the focus group with a broad question that is intended to engage the participants, by asking about the topic from their point of view. Subsequent questions successively narrow in on the research questions the researcher has in mind. For example, a funnel-oriented series of questions may begin with a question like 'What do you think are the most pressing issues around gun safety in the United States?' This could be followed by, 'Of those you have mentioned, which do you think should receive the highest priority from our policymakers?' and then more targeted questions such as 'If you were going to contact your legislators about your concerns, what kinds of things would you say?'

Another alternative is the 'inverted funnel approach', where the questions begin with narrower topics and then broaden to the more open-ended. This approach can be helpful in cases where the participants themselves may not have an immediately available set of thoughts about the topic. This approach often begins by asking about examples of concrete experiences, and then moves to more abstract issues. For example, if you were interested in how the culture of a particular neighborhood was affected by gentrification over a specific period of time, it might be helpful to begin with a very targeted question of the appropriate respondent group such as, 'When you were growing up in this neighborhood, did you have a favorite activity you enjoyed doing, or a favorite place you liked to go?', then expanding to things like, 'How have things changed since you were growing up in that neighborhood?', and eventually broadening to questions like 'How have things like gentrification made a difference, and why have they had the kinds of impacts that they have?'

Beyond considerations about the structure of the interview, it is also important to bear in mind, when creating the interview guide, how you imagine the participants might be feeling about the interview. This is particularly important for focus groups, given that the participants may be nervous about who else is in the room and how they will 'fit in' to the group or be thought of by the moderator in contrast to the other participants (Krueger, 1997a). In essence, there are two aspects of rapport in focus groups: between the moderator and the participants, and among the participants themselves. To foster both kinds of rapport, the initial introduction and first question(s) can help set a tone that is conducive to the goal of getting the participants to share and compare their thoughts and experiences. In focus groups, this often means a trade-off between asking questions that will get the participants talking with each other, versus concentrating on the things that are most directly important to the research. The key point is that the interaction among the participants is the source of the data, so the interview questions need to begin by generating discussions, which may mean delaying the most relevant questions until a good rapport has been established.

MODERATING THE GROUPS

Moderating focus groups is a learned skill but techniques exist that can improve the final outcome regardless of the moderator's level of experience. Effective moderators use their position to set a comfortable tone, elicit interaction between participants, and gently control the discussion such that rich data are produced. Ideally, all participants are made to feel comfortable expressing their opinion and having that opinion reacted to by the other participants (Krueger, 1997b; Wilkinson, 1998). Participants should feel they are empowered to participate freely and direct the flow of discourse. To accomplish this, there are various considerations and methods that can support the moderator in facilitating these interactions. Group composition is a major element in this regard, since sharing common ground will stimulate interaction among the participants. Another obvious but critical resource is asking questions that promote discussion among participants rather than clipped answers that bounce strictly between individual participants and the moderator. Additionally, the choice of moderator – an individual who is a relative match with the respondents in terms of age, gender, race, etc. – may influence the kind of data produced in a group setting, especially when discussing sensitive subjects.

Before considering the mechanics of moderation, we want to offer a note about logistics. Although a single individual can effectively facilitate a focus group, it is helpful to have two people involved. A common approach would be for the main moderator to manage the questions/discussion while an assistant observes, takes notes, and is available to help the moderator with any unanticipated needs. An especially important role for the assistant moderator is to ensure the recording equipment is functioning properly throughout the entire interview. This approach can also be advantageous to the research process if the two moderators debrief together afterward to co-create field notes as both moderators may have important – but different – observations. Additionally, a 'dual moderator' approach can be taken wherein both interviewers facilitate the group discussion. In the latter approach, it is important that the moderators each have a clear understanding of their respective roles so that the overall experience is enhanced. One common division of labor for this strategy involves one moderator who is more familiar with technical aspects of the topics and another who is more familiar with the group dynamics of facilitation. In addition, working as either an assistant moderator or half of a dual moderating team can be a useful technique for training new moderators.

Once again, the degree of structure can play a crucial role. If the research topic is relatively unexplored, the moderator may rely on a less-structured style that allows the participants to take the discussion where they may, while using interview questions only as a loose guide rather than a script. An example might be exploring the idea of addiction to technology in university students; given that relatively little is known about this phenomenon, important themes may need to emerge with a light touch on the part of the moderator to avoid imposing her or his own agenda. One noteworthy disadvantage to this approach is that generating data across groups in a less systematic format can pose challenges for analysis and reporting. Alternatively, if the researcher's agenda requires that the participants hit a relatively well-defined set of target topics, then a more measured and structured approach to the moderating can be taken. This more structured approach may also become necessary when there are one or more participants who are leading the group off-topic. When this occurs, the moderator can use prompts to re-orient the discussion back to the intended topic. These prompts can begin gently with non-verbal cues such as moving eye contact away from the respondent who is taking the discussion off target while giving non-verbal encouragement such as head-nodding to other participants. If this is unsuccessful, verbal prompts can then be employed to coax respondents back on track.

Overall, it is important not to assign moderating an overly central role in planning for focus groups. If the group composition brings together participants who are interested in discussing the questions in the interview guide, then the moderator needs little more than a respectful approach to hearing what participants have to say. In addition, when these conditions are met, it can be possible to rely on moderators who are familiar with the research topic and participants, even if they have little experience in conducting focus groups.

ANALYZING THE CONTENT OF FOCUS GROUPS

Generally speaking, the analysis of focus groups does not pose any issues that go beyond similar concerns in the analysis of individual interviews. In particular, most of the common analytic approaches in qualitative research are appropriate for focus groups, and this section summarizes some of them, along with their implications for data collection.

Summary-Based Reporting

The goal in Summary-Based Reporting is to determine which topics were most important to the participants through a descriptive account of the primary topics in the interviews. A simple standard for judging importance is whether a topic arose in nearly every focus group, as well as the extent to which it engaged the participants when it did arise. What matters is not just the frequency with which a topic is mentioned but also the level of interest and significance the participants attached to the topic. This requires a degree of judgment on the part of the analyst, but participants are usually clear about indicating which topics they find particularly important.

To examine these summaries, it is often helpful to create a group-by-question grid where each group is a row and each question is a column. The cells in this grid contain a summary of what a specific group said in response to a particular question. The most effective strategy for using this grid is to make comparisons across what each group said in response to each question. In essence, this moves from column to column, comparing what the different groups said in response to question number one, then question number two, and so on. The goal is to create an overall summary of what the full set of groups said about each question.

In terms of data collection, Summary-Based Reporting works best with relatively structured sets of questions. By asking similar questions in a similar order across the full set of groups, it is easier to make the kinds of comparisons that are typical of this analysis strategy. In contrast, less-structured interviews mean that a variety of topics can appear at a variety of locations in each group.

Content Analysis

Various forms of qualitative Content Analysis can be applied to focus groups (for example, Mayring, 2000; Vaismoradi et al., 2013) regardless of whether the analysis is driven by counting or by more qualitative approaches. The analytic system can be derived deductively, inductively, or alternatively through a combination of the two; the difference is how the codebook is created. In the deductive version, the codebook originates outside the data itself and is imposed in a top-down fashion. In the inductive version, the researcher creates the codebook by directly examining the data. This style of analysis is appropriate when working with exploratory- or discovery-oriented projects. The third alternative is a hybrid approach that begins with a few coding categories that are established deductively, before an inductive reading of the data that fills in the more detailed codes. For example, analysis would begin with the interview guide topics as the broad categories and then formulate more specific codes according to the actual content. Coded data can be analyzed numerically or studied from a more qualitative perspective. The former relies on the counting of codes whereas codes are treated as indicators of more latent content in the latter. Another alternative (Morgan, 1993; Morgan and Zhao, 1993) begins with counting codes to establish patterns in the data, followed by a qualitative reading of the relevant data to understand the process that produces those patterns.

Because Content Analysis can handle nearly anything that gets raised at any point in a focus group, it has relatively few implications for data collection. This means that most strategies for designing focus group research will be compatible with Content Analysis.

Thematic Analysis

Thematic Analysis is now the favored term for describing a general process of induction whereby the researcher reads and codes the data to understand what the participants have to say about the research topic. The most widely cited version of Thematic Analysis was developed by Braun and Clarke (2006, 2012), who proposed a six-step process: (1) immersion in the data through repeated reading of the transcripts; (2) systematic coding of the data; (3) development of preliminary themes; (4) revision of those themes; (5) selection of a final set of themes; (6) organization of the final written product around those themes. This approach can also be applied in both a more deductive format, where codes are based on pre-existing theory, or a more inductive fashion, where codes are derived from the interviews themselves.

Thematic Analysis is such a flexible strategy that it can be paired with almost any approach to data collection with focus groups. This makes it a good 'all-purpose' strategy for analyzing focus groups.

Grounded Theory

Grounded Theory advocates alternating data collection with analysis. Instead of collecting all the data in one stage of the research and then analyzing it in a separate stage, grounded theory calls for engaging in analysis throughout the research process and using the emerging results from that analysis to guide further data collection. For focus groups, this method might mean changing the questions asked, as some topics become well understood (i.e. 'saturated') and other unanticipated topics become increasingly relevant. An initial coding process, often known as 'open coding', generates a detailed line-by-line series of codes that is intended to fracture the data into small segments. Next, selective coding reorganizes the fractured data into conceptual categories. Finally, processes such as theoretical coding or axial coding arrive at a compact summary of the most meaningful aspects of the data.

In terms of data collection, Grounded Theory is undoubtedly the most prescriptive of the analysis approaches considered here. In particular, it requires that coding and analysis should be conducted right from the beginning of the data collection process, and that the research design should be flexible enough to accommodate insights that emerge from earlier data collection. In contrast, it is a poor fit to 'linear' data collection strategies that separate research design, data collection, and data analysis into separate and distinct steps.

ONLINE FOCUS GROUPS

Web-based focus groups offer an interesting and continually evolving opportunity to gather data. Online focus groups can take the shape of synchronous or asynchronous video and/or text (Morgan and Lobe, 2011). Synchronous methods allow participants to join together at a pre-specified time for 'real-time' interaction using text-based chat rooms, instant messenger protocols, and videoconferencing. Asynchronous methods allow participants to log in and contribute at different times in text form. Photos and images that add meaning to the discussion can be uploaded in certain applications such as iTracks.

Prospective respondents may not all have the same level of information technology (IT) literacy necessary to participate in an online focus group. It is helpful to provide participants with information prior to the focus group, including a 'how-to' guide and carrying out 'warm up' activities prior to data collection. Keeping groups relatively small is helpful; Sintjago and Link (2012) recommend around five participants so that bandwidth and troubleshooting are kept to a minimum. Participant recruitment for online focus groups can be similar to face-to-face interviews by accessing prospective respondents via email, social networking, snowballing, or face to face, with the added requirement that researchers must ensure respondents have the proper equipment and IT skills needed to participate. Also, it is important to consider the skills of the research team and their own comfort level with the technology to be used. Wilkerson et al. (2014) recommend that newcomers to the field perform several 'in-house' focus groups to ensure that the team is entirely comfortable and prepared to deal with technical glitches.

Of the online methods, synchronous videoconferencing is closest to the 'look and feel' of a face-to-face focus group. Within the limits of the Internet connection quality, participants are able to see facial expressions, add nuance and variability to their tone of voice, laugh, etc. in a way that they are unable to in text-based mediums. Various applications are available such as Skype, Go-to-meeting, Adobe Connect, and Zoom, among others. In a test of moderator and user experience, Sintjago and Link (2012) compared Skype and Adobe Connect for ease of use and data richness. They found that Adobe Connect provided a greater variety of controls for moderators to customize respondents' experiences such as customizable meeting rooms, breakout sessions, screen sharing, polling, notes, chat, and virtual whiteboards.

Synchronous, text-based focus groups are similar to synchronous videoconferencing in that they allow real-time responses to other participants' comments. A wide range of IM (instant message) and chat room technologies are available including MSN, AIM, Pidgin, and Windows Live. A problem unique to this method is that exchanges can create a situation where participants 'write over one another'. If a number of respondents are highly engaged and typing rapidly, it is not clear when an entry is either a new remark or a reply to a previous remark, also known as 'blurring'. In this case, the moderator should ask for the discussion to pause until the blurring ceases. Synchronous focus groups can be carried out in a short period of time and with few resources; however, if too few participants show up for the pre-scheduled day and time, additional groups and recruitment efforts must take place (Morgan, 2010).

The purpose of asynchronous focus groups is less about creating the feel of a face to-face-group and more about providing convenience to the respondent. There are a number of asynchronous platforms available online, including bulletin boards, forums, listservs, and free websites such as Google Groups. This environment, although not without problems such as attrition, can provide advantages in certain projects, especially for respondents who may be inhibited by a traditional focus group environment or prefer to have time to think about a particular question before providing their input. They can also meet the needs of those who would have difficulty coordinating their schedules for a synchronous group. Discussion threads are initiated by the moderator and can take place over days or even weeks. New questions and probes are provided daily, or every few days, by the moderator. Participants are asked to answer focal questions and also to provide feedback on other respondents' answers. Bandwidth requirements are negligible for text-only platforms and slightly higher for those that allow participants to record and upload video. A good example of the bulletin board method comes from Cook et al. (2014) who studied medically fragile young adults who would otherwise be unable to participate in a standard focus group. The method was a good match for their respondents as this provided them with the opportunity to respond on their own schedule if personal or medical situations came up, to have the opportunity to reflect on sensitive questions, provide fewer time constraints for participants who may have fatigued easily, have limited attention spans, or learning disabilities.

Online focus groups have tremendous potential with the growth of software and applications that can facilitate data collection across time and space. Each of the available tools involves varying costs, security, and privacy issues, hardware and user requirements, data capturing processes, and other considerations. Similar to face-to-face focus groups, the research team must develop an appropriate recruitment strategy, provide a highly skilled moderator who poses well-designed research questions, and of course ensure that the research objectives are achieved. All of the online methods share the ability to lower project costs and assemble a wide variety of participants across great distances. However, they also share the innate risks of producing data over the Internet with the associated lack of control and privacy. The issues surrounding maintaining confidentiality are particularly important for the future development on online focus groups, which makes this an important topic for future research (see the Chapters in Part VI of this volume).

CONCLUSION

Despite the 75-year history of focus groups, nearly all of the growth in the use of this method has occurred in the last 25 years. Using the Web of Science, we found fewer than 100 citations to focus groups in the years prior to 1990 and over 25,000 since then. We will thus conclude with a brief look backward and forward, to assess where focus groups have been and where they may be going.

Given the continuing interest in focus groups since their reintroduction to the social sciences, it is safe to say that they have become thoroughly institutionalized as a research method. In particular, there is now a set of relatively standardized practices that define the common wisdom about how to do focus groups. Many of these have been summarized here: homogeneous group composition, funnel-shaped interview guides, and less-structured approaches to moderating. The benefit of working within these practices is the high probability of a productive focus group.

The downside of this consensual set of best practices is that they tend to limit the further development of focus groups as a method. For example, social science researchers have largely carried over the practice of using homogeneous groups from marketing research, without reconsidering either why one might want to use more heterogeneous groups, or how one might do so. Similarly, there are any number of alternatives to funnels as a format for interviews, but there is only speculation about how those options would affect the nature of the interaction in focus groups. Finally, it is clear that marketing researchers typically rely on more structured moderating styles than social scientists, but again there is little information on how this affects the nature of the data.

Our recommendations for future directions thus emphasize investing in a program of methodological research on focus groups. In order to make choices about how to do focus groups, researchers need a better understanding of what difference it makes to use one option rather than another. Ultimately, we as focus group researchers need to improve the ability to link our procedures (how to do focus groups) and our purposes (why do focus groups one way rather than another), in order to avoid a one-size-fits-all approach.

FURTHER READING

Barbour, Rosaline (2018) *Doing Focus Groups* (2nd edn). Thousand Oaks, CA: Sage.

Krueger, Richard A. and Casey, Mary, A. (2015) *Focus Groups: A Practical Guide for Applied Research* (5th edn). Thousand Oaks, CA: Sage (1st edn, 1998).

Morgan, David L. (1996) *Focus Groups as Qualitative Research* (2nd edn). Thousand Oaks, CA: Sage (1st edn, 1989).

REFERENCES

Barbour, Rosaline (2018) *Doing Focus Groups* (2nd edn). Thousand Oaks, CA: Sage.

Braun, Virginia and Clarke, Victoria (2006) 'Using thematic analysis in psychology', *Qualitative Research in Psychology*, 3(2): 77–101.

Braun, Virginia and Clarke, Victoria (2012) 'Thematic analysis', in H. Cooper (ed.), *The Handbook of Research Methods in Psychology*. Washington, DC: American Psychological Association, pp. 51–71.

Cook, Karen, Jack, Susan, Siden, Hal, Thabane, Lehana and Browne, Gina (2014) 'Innovations in research with medically fragile populations: Using bulletin board focus groups', *The Qualitative Report*, 19(39): 1–12.

Coule, Tracey (2013) 'Theories of knowledge and focus groups in organization and management research', *Qualitative Research in Organizations and Management*, 8(2): 148–62.

Creswell, John W. and Plano-Clark, Vicky L. (2010) *Designing and Conducting Mixed Methods Research* (2nd edn). Thousand Oaks, CA: Sage.

Duggleby, Wendy (2005) 'What about interaction in focus group data?', *Qualitative Health Research*, 15(6): 832–40.

Folch-Lyon, E., de la Macorra, L. and Schearer, S. (1981) 'Focus group and survey research on family planning in Mexico', *Studies in Family Planning*, 12(12): 409–32.

Guba, Egon and Lincoln, Yvonna, S. (1994) 'Competing paradigms in qualitative research', in Norman, K. Denzin and Yvonna, S. Lincoln (eds.), *Handbook of Qualitative Research*. Thousand Oaks, CA: Sage, pp. 105–17.

Krueger, Richard, A. (1997a) *Developing Questions for Focus Groups*. Thousand Oaks, CA: Sage.

Krueger, Richard, A. (1997b) *Moderating Focus Groups*. Thousand Oaks, CA: Sage.

Krueger, Richard, A. and Casey, Mary, A. (2015) *Focus Groups: A Practical Guide for Applied Research* (5th edn). Thousand Oaks, CA: Sage (1st edn, 1998).

Lee, Raymond (2010) 'The secret life of focus group research: Robert Merton and the diffusion of a research method', *American Sociologist*, 41(2): 115–41.

Mason, Jennifer (1996) *Qualitative Researching*. Thousand Oaks, CA: Sage Publications.

Macnaghten, Phil and Myers, Greg (2004) 'Focus groups: The moderator's view and the analyst's view', in Clive Seale, Giampietro Gobo, Jaber F. Gubrium and David Silverman (eds.), *Qualitative Research Practice*. Thousand Oaks, CA: Sage, pp. 65–79.

Mayring, Phillip (2000) 'Qualitative content analysis', *Forum: Qualitative Social Research*, 1(2), Art. 20 available at http://nbn-resolving.de/urn:nbn:de:0114-fqs0002204

Merton, Robert K. (1987) 'The focused interview and focus groups: Continuities and discontinuities', *Public Opinion Quarterly*, 51(4): 550–66.

Merton, Robert K. and Kendall, Patricia L. (1946) 'The focused interview', *American Journal of Sociology*, 51(6): 541–57.

Merton, Robert K., Fiske, Marjorie and Kendall, Patricia (1990) *The Focused Interview*. New York: The Free Press (1st edn, 1956).

Morgan, David, L. (1993) *Successful Focus Groups: Advancing the State of the Art*. Thousand Oaks, CA: Sage.

Morgan, David, L. (1996) *Focus Groups as Qualitative Research* (2nd edn). Thousand Oaks, CA: Sage (1st edn, 1989).

Morgan, David, L. (2007) 'Paradigms lost and pragmatism regained: Methodological implications of combining qualitative and quantitative methods', *Journal of Mixed Methods Research*, 1(1): 48–76.

Morgan, David, L. (2010) 'Reconsidering the role of interaction in analyzing and reporting focus groups', *Qualitative Health Research*, 20(5): 718–22.

Morgan, David, L. (2012) 'Focus groups and social interaction', in Jaber F. Gubrium and James A. Holstein (eds.), *Handbook of Interview Research* (2nd edn). Thousand Oaks, CA: Sage, pp. 161–76.

Morgan, David, L. (2013) *Integrating Qualitative and Quantitative Methods: A Pragmatic Approach*. Thousand Oaks, CA: Sage.

Morgan, D. L. (2014) 'Pragmatism as a paradigm for social science research', *Qualitative Inquiry*, 20(8): 1045–53.

Morgan, David, L. (2015) *Essentials of Dyadic Interviewing*. Walnut Creek, CA: Left Coast Press.

Morgan, David, L. and Lobe, Bojana (2011) 'Online focus groups', in Sharlene Nagy Hesse-Biber (ed.), *The Handbook of Emergent Technologies in Social Research*. Oxford: Oxford University Press, pp. 199–230.

Morgan, David L. and Zhao, Ping Z. (1993) 'The doctor–caregiver relationship: Managing the care of family members with Alzheimer's disease', *Qualitative Health Research*, 3(2), 133–64.

Morgan, David L., Ataie, Jutta., Carder, Paula and Hoffman, Kim (2013) 'Introducing dyadic interviews as a method for collecting qualitative data', *Qualitative Health Research*, 23(9): 1276–84.

Morrison, David, E. (1998) *The Search for Method: Focus Groups and the Development of Mass Communication Research*. Luton: University of Luton Press.

Myers, Greg and Macnaghten, Phil (1999) 'Can focus groups be analysed as talk?', in Rosaline Barbour and Jenny Kitzinger (eds.), *Developing Focus Group Research: Politics, Theory and Practice*. Thousand Oaks, CA: Sage, pp. 173–85.

Sintjago, Alfonso and Link, Alison (2012) From Synchronous to Asynchronous: Researching Online Focus Groups Platforms. Retrieved from https://cultivatingchange.wp.d.umn.edu/from-synchronous-to-asynchronous/

Tadajewski, Mark (2015) 'Focus groups: History, epistemology and non-individualistic consumer research', *Consumption Markets & Culture*, 19(4): 319–345.

Vaismoradi, Mojtaba, Turunen, Hannele and Bondas, Terese (2013) 'Content analysis and thematic analysis: Implications for conducting a qualitative descriptive study', *Nursing and Health Sciences*, 15(3): 398–405.

Wilkerson, Michael J., Iantaffi, Alex, Grey, Jeremy, A., Bockting, Walter and Rosser, B. R. Simon (2014) 'Recommendations for Internet-based qualitative health research with hard-to-reach populations', *Qualitative Health Research*, 21(4): 561–74.

Wilkinson, Sue (1998) 'Focus groups in health research: Exploring the meanings of health and illness', *Journal of Health Psychology*, 3(3): 329–48.

Narrative Data

Michael Murray

INTRODUCTION

This chapter discusses a variety of forms of narrative data. It begins by reviewing the nature of narrative and the psychology of storytelling. It then proceeds to consider the most popular source of narrative data, which is the interview. This can vary substantially in form and can also be extended from face-to-face encounters to other sources such as diaries, letters and other written accounts of particular experiences. We will then consider various documentary forms of narrative ranging from dairies, autobiographies and various archival/historical sources. Narratives are not only written and spoken. Thus, we will also consider other forms such as visual narratives as presented in art and performative narratives as presented in drama.

FOUNDATIONS

Narrative inquiry is an interdisciplinary field, which is concerned with the stories we share in our everyday lives. It is premised upon the assumption that humans are storytelling creatures that make sense of their ever-changing world through those stories. Bruner (1999) argued that this urge to tell stories is particularly pronounced when there is a break or change in our lives. He distinguished between two forms of thinking: the paradigmatic and the narrative. While the former is based upon classification and categorisation, the latter is concerned with agency and transformation. Emphasising the centrality of narrative-making for making sense of change, Bruner noted: 'it is only when constituent beliefs in a folk psychology are violated that narratives are constructed [...] when things "are as they should be", the narratives of folk psychology are unnecessary' (1999, pp. 39–40).

Narratives are not only personal constructions but we can also consider collective narratives which are the stories shared by a particular community or culture (Smith, 2013). These different narratives interpenetrate such that in constructing a narrative about our own experiences we connect with these larger narratives. Hammack and Cohler (2009) introduced the concept narrative engagement to describe this process. Thus, rather than focusing upon a self-contained narrative, the concern is about how the personal narrative is actively constructed through this process of engagement with these larger (master) narratives.

Psychologists have been particularly concerned not just with the meaning-making character of narrative but also its role in identity formation. In telling stories, the person or collective is not only making sense of past events but also asserting to others and to themselves who they are. McAdams (1993) has argued: 'We are all tellers of tales. We seek to provide our scattered and often conflicting experiences with a sense of coherence by arranging the episodes of our lives into stories' (1993, p. 11).

In his subsequent work McAdams (2013) explored the narrative identity of what he described as highly generative people – those who were concerned with enriching the lives of future generations. These people he found were more likely to make sense of their lives through a redemption script. This is the story of the person who is giving back to others through their actions and, in doing so, redeeming themselves for their good fortune. In some ways it is drawing upon or engaging with the larger religious narrative of salvation through repentance.

Flowing from Bruner's idea that narrative thinking follows change, narrative therapists have emphasised that the inability to develop such a coherent narrative after a traumatic event can lead to ongoing distress. The aim of the therapist is to help the client develop a narrative account of past events with which they can live and which will enable them to develop a new life. White and Epston (1990) developed what has become known as narrative therapy which details strategies for encouraging the client to explore more life-affirming narrative accounts of their experiences and to challenge those master narratives that are disempowering.

Social and political scientists are also concerned with the character of the larger societal narratives that shape our sense of collective identity and also our everyday experiences. When people's life experiences do not chime with dominant narratives they experience distress. In the process of challenging these dominant narratives minority groups can promote counter-narratives, which help mobilise communities for change. For example, McKenzie-Mohr and Lafrance (2014) describe the dominant cultural narratives that oppress women and explore the process of developing alternative narratives of resistance.

Recently, psychologists (e.g. Bamberg, 2006; Georgakopoulou, 2006) have debated the distinction between big and small stories. While the former are more concerned with extensive narrative accounts of our lives, short stories are the, often incidental, details that pattern our everyday conversation. It is the exchange of these small stories that provides the means of maintaining our relationships with others. Their very openness provides an opportunity for the other to develop the conversation and affirm or challenge a shared identity.

With such a wide range of narrative forms it can be problematic attempting to restrict approaches to the study of narrative. This chapter is not designed to be comprehensive but to introduce the character of narrative data derived from interviews but also from other sources. It will illustrate the challenges in conducting this form of research through a series of examples.

INTERVIEWS

Since people share narratives in their everyday conversation it is not surprising that interviews are the most common source of narrative data. Indeed, Mishler (1986) has argued that storytelling is endemic in qualitative interviews but they have often been ignored by researchers. Traditionally, in the more structured interview the researcher has sought to obtain responses to very structured questions and to consider stories a distraction or deviation. The interviewee can either be discouraged from recounting such stories or their storied responses can be ignored in the data analysis. As Mishler commented:

> the apparent absence of narratives in reports of interview studies is an artefact of standard procedures for conducting, describing, and analysing interviews: interviewers interrupt respondents' answers and thereby suppress expression of their stories; when they appear, stories go unrecorded because they are viewed as irrelevant to the specific aims of specific questions; and stories that make it through these barriers are discarded at stages of coding and analysis. (1986, p. 106)

Alternatively, the interviewer can deliberately foster the telling of stories during an interview or deliberately explore the narrative structure of the interview subsequently. Adopting the former approach requires the researcher to adopt a semi-structured or unstructured format to the interview (see Roulston and Choi, Chapter 15, this volume).

The most extended format is the life-story interview in which the interviewee is encouraged to talk about their life. Admittedly, this can be problematic as there is so much to talk about and in the interview setting the interviewee is searching for some guidance from the researcher. For this reason the researcher can set some broad guidelines by being explicit about the purpose of the research. While the interviewer can provide some guidelines these are generous and the interviewee can deviate from them. As its name implies, the aim of the life-story interview is to encourage the participants to provide an extended account of their lives. The researcher will explain at the outset of the interview that the aim of the study is to learn about the person's life.

Several guides to the conduct of narrative interviews have evolved. Perhaps one of the most popular is McAdams' (1995) Life Story Protocol. This starts by deliberately inviting the participant to tell the story of their life. It provides a further guide by advising the participant that, in telling their story, they should focus on key experiences and structure their account almost in the form of chapters about their past, present and future. Throughout the interview the protocol provides suggestions for further questions to help direct the participant.

Such a guide is a useful starting point in designing a study and should be seen as a guide, not as a template. However, narratives are not just life stories in the most general sense but also stories about everyday experiences, especially disruptions of daily life. We can, in the interview setting, encourage participants to tell stories about particular experiences of change or turning points in their lives. Flick (2014) has termed this approach the *episodic* interview (see Flick, Chapter 34, this volume). In this format the aim is to promote narratives on situations within which certain experiences occurred (see Flick et al., 2015). Given the time and the opportunity,

---

Box 17.1   Sample interview guides

1 I would like you to tell me about yourself – where you were born, where you grew up, that sort of thing. You should not be in any way inhibited about what to say, but just tell me as much as possible about yourself.
2 I am interested in finding out what happened during the selection interview. You can begin at the time you left home for the meeting and just tell me as much as you can remember.

(Murray, 2015)

participants are often very willing to provide extended narrative accounts of different experiences. Some examples of interview guides are provided in Box 17.1. It is obvious from these that the researcher has a particular focus for the interview but provides lots of latitude for the participant to develop the narrative account.

Rosenthal (2004) has provided a detailed guide to conducting a biographical interview. She suggests beginning in a very open-ended format:

> Please tell me/us your family story and your personal life story; I/we am/are very interested in your whole life. Anything that occurs to you. You have as much time as you like. We/I won't ask you any questions for now. We/I will just make some notes on the things that we would like to ask you more about later, if we haven't got enough time today, perhaps in a second interview. (2004, p. 51)

This very broad question can be adjusted if the interest of the researcher is on a particular experience, for example, 'We are interested in your personal experience in this institution. Perhaps you might start by telling of your experience when you came to this institution, etc.' (2004, p. 51).

Rosenthal found that this open-ended format often led to a very extensive response from research participants often lasting for hours. The researcher's role was then to simply use a range of paralinguistics and short expressions to encourage the participant to continue with their story.

In the second phase of this interview guide the researcher introduces what Rosenthal (2004) has described as 'narrative-generating questions'. These are questions designed to encourage the participant to expand more on particular events or experiences of interest. She distinguished between 'internal narrative questions', which focus on material already discussed by the participant from 'external narrative questions', which take up issues not mentioned. In this way the researcher is able to work with the participant to develop an expanded life story.

Interview Setting

Whichever interview guide is used, the setting for the interview is important. The aim is that the interviewee feels comfortable such that they can recount details of their experiences. This requires the interviewer to clearly demonstrate both interest and also a degree of empathy with the interviewee. The participant may be wary and uncommunicative at the outset. It is for this reason that the interviewer may need to meet with some participants on a number of occasions to win their confidence and to encourage them to reflect on their life experiences. Throughout the interview, the role of the researcher is to provide supportive comments such that the interviewee is encouraged to further develop their narrative account. This can be a challenge as sometimes the interviewer may not be sympathetic with the views being expressed. For example, Billig (1978) discussed the challenge of conducting interviews with racists. Although, traditionally, researchers have limited themselves to one-off interviews, this will depend upon the participant and the topic. Sometimes, despite careful planning, the participant may be interrupted or their account may be quite lengthy. In these cases it is important to arrange a follow-up interview. Indeed, increasingly, narrative researchers have favoured extended interviews conducted over a series of occasions.

An alternative to the sit-down interview is the walk-along interview in which the researcher engages in a more free-flowing conversation with the participant about their lives or particular experiences. This method is part of the ethnographic tradition, which requires the researcher to spend considerable time with the research participant, getting to know their lives and collecting data in a much more extensive and informal manner. An example is the study of trailer communities by Margie Kusenbach (2003; see Kusenbach, Chapter 22, this volume) or Paul Atkinson (2006) attending opera rehearsals to try to understand the opera singer. This form of data collection can seem daunting to the researcher who is keen to collect the data and 'return to base'. However, it is through engaging in such unstructured conversations that the small stories about everyday lives can be exchanged and a more sophisticated understanding of human experience developed.

Squire (2007) in her study of the experience of living with HIV/AIDS in South Africa discussed the challenge of collecting detailed narrative accounts from her participants. Realising the weaknesses of single interviews, Squire developed a more extended process through which she attempted to get to know the participants. She described this as a form of participatory research in which she attempted to actively involve the participants in the project. It was not the classic participatory action research, which she felt required a much longer-term commitment and which involved the collaborative development of some form of action. Squire noted the problems involved in conducting this form of research:

> The research was participant directed, focused on the interviewee's own word; but it was guided by a list of areas for interview discussions. It was structured to include feedback and some followup interviews; but the realities of participants' complicated and resource-limited lives made these hard to implement fully. (2007, p. 61)

Role of the Interviewer

Increasingly in narrative research, the role of the interviewer is considered. This flows from awareness that the narrator is not simply telling their story in a vacuum but telling it to someone. The narrative is in many ways a co-construction in which the interviewer plays a role in shaping the narrative either deliberately or through who they are, or who they represent, in the eyes of the narrator.

It is for this reason that the researcher needs to reflect on who they are and how they contribute to the shaping of the narrative account. Squire, in discussing the role of the researcher in shaping the interview, admitted that this can be an ongoing challenge. As she says: 'I could be almost endlessly reflexive about this research. To ignore the power relations of interviews may implicitly reproduce them' (2007, p. 59).

An example that I have used elsewhere (Murray, 2015) is that of the older man with chronic pain being interviewed by a young female research worker. Throughout the interview the old man detailed a story of resilience and fortitude but after the tape recorder was switched off he burst into tears detailing how the pain had destroyed his life. This encounter can be interpreted at the interpersonal level (Murray, 2000) taking into consideration the role of the researcher. The old man was presenting a story of strength in relation to the young researcher but also to the wider research audience identified through the tape recorder. In his everyday life it was a narrative with which he identified but also one that he found difficult to reconcile with the actual pain experience. This is not to suggest that one narrative account is superior to another but it must be considered with reference to who s/he was talking to.

Impact of Interview

Another important feature of the narrative interview is its therapeutic quality. In providing the participant with the opportunity to articulate their story, which in other settings may have been ignored, can often be beneficial for the narrator. Mishler (1986) reflected on the impact of the interview on the participant. He argued that the nature of the semi-structured or unstructured interview is that it gives the participant the opportunity to take control, to express their view. Mishler went further to describe it as empowering and further argued that 'interviewing practices that empower respondents also produce narrative accounts' (1986, p. 119). However, not only does it produce narrative accounts but it can also lead to the potential for forms of action and change. As Mishler continued:

Through their narratives people may be moved beyond the text to the possibilities of action. That is, to be empowered is not only to speak in one's own voice and to tell one's own story, but to apply the understanding arrived at to action in accord with one's own wishes. (1986, p. 119)

Ewick and Silbey (1995) also take up this argument:

By allowing the silenced to speak, by refusing the flattening or distorting effects of traditional logico-scientific methods and dissertative modes of representation, narrative scholarship participates in rewriting social life in ways that are, or can be, liberatory. (1995, p. 199)

It was for these reasons that narrative research is often a method preferred by social activists. It becomes a means of celebrating the stories of those who have been marginalised. This was the original impetus behind the development of oral histories (Bornat, 2004). One of the founders of oral history in the UK, George Ewart Evans, was very aware of the therapeutic quality of the interview. He described one of its values as 'doing something for your informant as well as for your own purpose [...] we are taking part in a social therapy even if we do not realise it' (Evans, 1972, p. 70). This point was taken up by Bornat and Tetley (2010) in their discussion of the value of oral history for understanding the process of growing old.

Interview Context – Stories of Homeless Youth

Although interviews are a primary source of narrative data they can be supplemented with data, which can help locate the experiences described. Toolis and Hammack (2015) took up this challenge in their study of the narratives of homeless youth. They deliberately combined life-story interviews with ethnographic fieldwork (see Buscatto, Chapter 21, this volume). Before conducting the interviews Toolis had spent a year employed in a drop-in centre for homeless youth. This provided him with the opportunity to observe the users of the centre (the guests) and to become familiar with staff and the organisation. He then conducted detailed interviews with a sample of the guests using the Life Story Protocol developed by McAdams (1995). In conducting their analysis of the narrative accounts Toolis and Hammack selected those provided by four young people such that they could conduct a more detailed analysis informed by their understanding of the organisational setting coupled with a reflection on the interview process. They note that:

the purpose of presenting these case studies is not reduction or generalisability, but rather to interpret and expand upon the meaning that these participants have assigned to their experiences and identities. (Toolis and Hammack, 2015, p. 54)

In conducting their analysis they were able to connect the accounts of the participants with an understanding of the organisational structure of the drop-in centre and its everyday routines.

Another feature of their analysis was their use of the concept of narrative engagement. An example from the cases examined by Toolis and Hammack is that of Alejandro, whose personal narrative is illustrative of the process of narrative engagement with the master narrative of the American Dream. Within this master narrative, Alejandro presents a narrative of exclusion but not of personal failure. Toolis and Hammack summarised his narrative:

By attributing homelessness to undeserved poverty rather than a personal moral failing, Alejandro demonstrated resistance to the master narrative of homelessness in US society [...] He constructed a counternarrative that framed him and other homeless youth as 'good people' in a 'bad situation', thus subverting the potential contamination associated with stigma and exclusion. (2015, p. 56)

Alternatively, in his narrative account Alejandro could be said to be reflecting in his narrative account the more accepted explanation of poverty promoted by the organisation – so-called 'institution-speak'. Thus in interpreting the narrative account we can take into consideration the interpersonal context within which the narrative interview was conducted, the organisational setting and the broader socio-cultural narrative with which the narrator engages. This is what Murray (2000) meant by different levels of narrative analysis.

Untold Stories – Silences and Blank Spaces

Narrative accounts are not something that people can automatically provide when they are invited to do so. Rather, researchers have indicated that in the face of trauma individuals are often at a loss for words. An example of this is a study of the narrative accounts of refugees. The current period in our history is one of mass migration as millions of people flee from situations of war and oppression. This has promoted a turn to research designed to both understand the experience of migration and also to contribute to enhancing the lives of those who migrate. One such study is that by Puvimanasinghe et al. (2014), which aimed to further our understanding of the experiences of African refugees to Australia. This study focused on the individual life stories of a sample of refugees. These interviews adopted an unstructured life-story approach in which the participants were invited to tell the story of their lives. The guidance was open-ended:

> Now [Name], I would like you to tell me your life story in your own words and in a way most comfortable for you. I suggest that we begin from life in your home country and proceed to the time after leaving Sierra Leone until you came to Australia; the initial years in Australia, the later years and what life looks like to you in the future. (2014, p. 75)

The interviews lasted one to three hours and often took place over several sessions. The emphasis was on making the participant feel relaxed and accepted by the interviewer such that they could tell their stories in an extended fashion. One important aspect of this study was the concern not just with what the participants said but also their silences. Here they drew upon research on people who had experienced traumatic events. They referred to Spector-Mersel (2011) who argued that people use silence, omission and flattening as devices to maintain or reconstruct their identities. These processes were ways of not introducing, or minimising, certain experiences that contradicted their overall story.

For example, one of the cases Puvimanasinghe et al. examined was that of Edward who fled from the conflict in Burundi. He began by talking about life in Burundi but after two sentences moved on to life in the refugee camp and then to life in Australia. Puvimanasinghe et al. described these accounts as 'avoiding narratives' – ones where the narrator avoided discussion of the horrors of their earlier lives. This was frequent among refugees from Burundi but conversely among those from Sierra Leone there was more evidence of narratives that 'exceeded boundaries of disclosure'. These were narratives in which the participants initially drew a boundary around what they experienced but then returned in their narratives to expand upon the content. In this way, through the recounting they were attempting to 'integrate traumatic narratives, gain narrative fluidity, reconstruct more acceptable self-identities and make sense of their incomprehensible violence and loss' (p. 87). Puvimanasinghe et al. suggested various possible explanations for these different narrative accounts, ranging from cultural differences to the character of the relationship with the interviewer. This silence in the narrative account has been taken up by other researchers, including Langer (1991) who we will discuss later.

Group Interviews – Collective Stories

Interviews can also be conducted in groups (see Morgan and Hoffman, Chapter 16, this volume) with the aim of exploring the group narrative identity. An example of this is the study by Lohuis et al. (2016), which was designed to explore how health care teams make sense of their effectiveness through the telling of their team story. In this study, five teams of health employees participated in a narrative focus group in which they were guided by McAdams' (1995) life-story protocol, adopted for a group. At the outset the moderator asked the question: 'Imagine you are going to write a book about your team, what would the index of the book look like?' (Lohuis et al., 2016, p. 412). The responses to this question formed the starting point to encourage the team members to reflect upon how their team worked. Subsequently one of the authors spent time with each of the teams, building up an understanding of how they worked. This ethnographic information was then used to assist with the analysis of each of the group narratives.

A similar study was conducted by Prins et al. (2015), which was designed to explore the shared narrative of Moroccan-Dutch residents. This involved a series of focus group sessions with young Moroccan-Dutch residents. These focus groups were guided by a topic list, which encouraged the participants to share their experiences of school, work, neighbourhood, family and friends. The concern was not with the detailed life stories of individual participants but rather with the short stories of individuals' experiences. Following Riessman (1993) who argued that evaluation is the 'soul of the narrative' the researchers used an extensive definition of story, not just to refer to 'material that is neatly storied by way of episodes or events' but also to 'more fragmented references to identities claimed on the basis of experience' (1993, p. 170). The researchers were concerned with how the participants evaluated these short stories, in particular whether a certain story was considered illustrative of a positive or negative experience.

Prins et al. (2015) also went beyond the immediate focus group in conducting their research. They discussed the evaluations with participants in subsequent individual interviews and in informal conversations. This provided an opportunity for the participants 'to reflect on their contributions to the focus group and on the dynamics of the conversation' (2015, p. 171). The context of the storytelling was stressed such that 'Our participants thus recognised that their stories, like all stories, were constructed in relation to both their direct audience and to wider societal discourses in which their collective identity was cast in a negative way' (2015, p. 171).

Concern with exploring collective narratives has also frequently been the focus of community action initiatives. For example, in the study by Murray and Crummett (2010) the concern was to explore the potential of a community arts initiative in promoting social engagement among older people in a disadvantaged inner city area. In this study, the participants were invited in a focus group setting to describe their experience of living in the area. This group discussion was subsequently supplemented with a map-making exercise facilitated by a community artist in which the participants were invited to contribute photographs and other representations of the area to an extensive wall chart. In the making of this wall map, the participants had the opportunity in a more informal and extended format to talk about their neighbourhood. In this way, the map-making exercise was a technique that encouraged the discussion of shared narrative account of their neighbourhood.

Group interviews can also provide an opportunity to promote reflection on particular events and aid recall of certain, partly forgotten, episodes. It can even help give some order to confusing events and act as a check on more fanciful elaboration. Through the sharing of stories it can also be a means of building group solidarity.

Memory and Narrative

One recurring challenge to narrative researchers is the epistemological status of the narrative accounts collected through interviews and conversations. These accounts are shaped from the present, looking back. They are not contemporary accounts of events that are recorded alongside the events (see Freeman, 1993) or sterile accounts of events plucked from a memory chest. Rather, the narrator is shaping the account from the present and is telling the story to someone. It is for this reason that narrative researchers supplement their interviews with reference to other material. They may contrast the accounts given by different narrators about the same set of events. To some narrators an event may be tragic but to others it may open up new opportunities. The researcher explores these potential different interpretations, not to seek the ultimate truth behind the accounts but, rather, to understand the varied nature of human experience.

The extent to which that event is shared will also influence how the story is told. Coetzee and Rau (2009) take up this issue in their analysis of the narrative accounts of people who had endured traumatic experiences for sustained periods. In their exploration of the narratives of suffering told by former political prisoners in South Africa they discussed how the accounts were positioned within 'shared ideas and ideals' (p. 3). It was within this context of a shared political struggle that the former prisoners constructed their story. In this way 'memory goes beyond the definitive subjectivity of individual recall' (2009, p. 3). It is this political struggle that gives their story of suffering a sense of purpose.

DOCUMENTS

Both published and unpublished documents (see Rapley and Rees, Chapter 24, this volume) are an important means of accessing narrative accounts. Indeed, social scientists have historically drawn upon a wide range of documentary evidence. An early precursor of contemporary narrative research was the classic five-volume work *The Polish Peasant in Europe and America* published in 1918–1920 by William Thomas and Florian Znaniecki. This work made use of a variety of documentary sources, including letters and a full autobiography. The work provoked considerable discussion about methodology among social scientists at that time, leading to a series of reports including one by the social psychologist Gordon Allport (1942). In his report Allport enthusiastically acclaimed letters, diaries and other personal documents as an important source of information in exploring the human personality. He went on to spend a considerable portion of his career examining the so-called 'letters from Jenny' (Winter, 1993).

Diaries

Elliott (1997) has provided a review of the usage of diaries in social science research. She begins with reference to Allport's (1942) classic assessment in which she distinguishes between three forms of dairy: the intimate journal which includes records of private thoughts, the memoir which is a more 'impersonal' diary with potential for publication, and the log which is simply a listing of events. Diaries have a particular quality which distinguishes them from more considered autobiographies. This has been discussed by Plummer (2001) who described them as 'being sedimented into a particular moment in time; they do not emerge "all at once" as reflections on the past, but day by day strive to record an ever-changing present' (2001, p. 18). However, over time the diarist can be self-conscious of the process of diary writing such that s/he 'will eventually come to perceive the diary as a whole and to plan a selection of entries according to this plan' (2001, p. 18).

More recently there has been the formal development of research diaries that are designed to collect contemporaneous descriptions of particular experiences. Ida et al. (2012) in their review noted that use of research dairies has grown rapidly such that, at the time of their writing 250 journal articles per year reported their usage. Diaries can also vary in format from simple pencil-and-paper to telephone interviews, to electronic formats. Although diaries used in research have often followed a structured format they can also be unstructured and simply request the participants to regularly record their experiences over a certain period.

The use of research diaries can be supplemented with follow-up interviews, which give the research participants the opportunity to reflect upon certain incidents they reported and to place them within a larger narrative frame. An example of this approach was the study by Kenten (2010) of the experiences of lesbians and gay men. In this study a sample of participants were initially interviewed about their experience of being gay. After the interview, they were invited to keep a diary record of when they became aware of their sexuality. After their return, the content of the diaries was transcribed and loosely analysed, providing a guide to subsequent interviews that focused on the experience of keeping a diary and the participants' reflections on the various experiences described. The diary and the matched interviews were then analysed in tandem. In the analysis it was noted that 'most entries were written as short narratives about the day' (2010, section 5, line 5). But Kenten (2010) also noted that these episodic narratives were located within broader societal narratives, once again emphasising the connection between personal and larger narratives.

Autobiographies

One important documentary source of narrative data that has increasingly attracted the interest of social scientists is the published memoir or autobiography. Traditionally these have been written by great historical figures. However, this is changing with the proliferation of published accounts by the ordinary person. Frequently, these have centred on the experience of some traumatic event or series of events. Thus we have narrative accounts of living through various social conflicts such as war. We also have published accounts of more personal trauma such as abuse or the onset of serious illness.

Freeman (1993) in his study of a sample of published autobiographies has illustrated the potential value of such research. At the outset, Freeman compared the narrative data obtained from interviews with that in published accounts:

> Interviews, of the sort that social scientists often gather, are themselves texts, and while they may not have quite as much literary flourish as those we buy in bookstores, they are in their own right literary artefacts, taking the form of words, designed to give shape to some feature of experience. (1993, p. 7)

Freeman begins by considering the narrative character of the classic autobiography of St. Augustine. In writing down his narrative Augustine is publicly defining himself. In doing so he is not simply listing a series of events but constructing a story of himself. In starting his story with reference to God's magnanimousness, Augustine 'has in mind the "ending" he has become: a man who has seen the light of God and who, consequently, could look back on his life and see how it had been orchestrated by forces unseen and unknown at the time' (Freeman, 1993, p. 33). This is a recurrent theme in Freeman's book – the fact that in telling their story the person is looking back, selecting events and making connections, developing a narrative. Freeman (2013) also studied the narrative structure of Keith Richard's *Life*, providing further evidence that our sense of identity is negotiated between the stories told by oneself and others.

Contemporary autobiographies often centre on traumatic personal events such as sexual assault or serious illness. One frequent such topic is accounts of breast cancer. Murray (2009), in his analysis of a selection of published accounts of breast cancer, noted how the beginning of the accounts often emphasised how normal the women's lives had been. The women were just ordinary people. They had lived healthy lives until suddenly they were diagnosed with cancer. This was a dreadful experience for them and their families. The middle of the story concerned their dealings with the health system and the treatment they had received for the disease. Now that the treatment had been successful they looked back on the experience with relief but also with a certain amount of gratitude around the lessons that they had learned about life. A few of the women who were religious gave thanks to God for having given them this opportunity to suffer and to find redemption. However, this was unusual as most of the women placed their faith in medical science. Now that the treatment was over they could begin to close the story. However, the story was not fully ended since there was always the prospect of recurrence. Indeed, some of the autobiographies went through several editions that added new endings to accommodate the recurrence of the disease.

Today, the autobiography is one of the most popular genres of literature. It can be argued that one reason for this popularity is the decline of public faith in established religions and a search for new guides and role models. In this era, autobiographies provide a source for reaffirmation of our own, perhaps disorganised, belief systems but are also a source of moral guidance. Moreover, the autobiography not only helps make sense of the past but also offers a guide to the future. As Bruner (1995, p. 164) suggested: 'The publicness of autobiography constitutes something like an opportunity for an ever-renewable "conversation" about conceivable lives.'

An increasingly popular phenomenon is self-published stories of people who have experienced some traumatic episode in their lives. There are a large number of websites devoted to such stories, which provide a new source of narrative data. Often these are presented by the hosting agency as a means of providing hope and support for people who are unfortunately experiencing similar traumatic events. Overberg et al. (2006) conducted an analysis of cancer stories in Dutch on the Internet and found that most had provided a structure to aid the reader and some offered the opportunity for the reader to post their reactions to a particular story.

Another example is the work of Pederson (2013) who explored the content of stories posted on the Internet by unemployed youth (see Weller et al., Chapter 31, this volume). He conducted a narrative thematic analysis of a sample of these stories and classified them as presenting five identity types, which worked to engage in different ways with the master narrative of the American Dream.

Archives

There is increasing awareness of the wealth of narrative material contained in archives. Interest in these sources have largely been confined to historians or literary scholars but with the growth of such interdisciplinary fields as memory studies and holocaust studies, social scientists have become interested in this rich source of data (see Corti, Chapter 11, this volume). These archives contain extensive oral testimonies that have been collected for a range of purposes. They may have been collected by the state to provide a historical record of certain momentous events or they may be collected by the state as a means of fostering reconciliation between conflicting groups. This was the case with the establishment of the Truth and Reconciliation Commission in South Africa, which collected over 20,000 testimonies. In opening this commission, Desmond Tutu explicitly defined its purpose: 'We pray that all those people who have been injured in either body or spirit may receive healing through the work of this commission' (cited in Andrews, 2015, p. 41).

Some archives will contain not only written narrative accounts but also videoed accounts, sometimes supplemented with other material. One example is the Fortunoff Video Archive for Holocaust Testimonies, which was established in 1982 and now contains over 4,400 videotaped narrative accounts by individual survivors of the Holocaust. Although the researcher is required to go to Yale University library to access these accounts an expanding website is now making some of this material more widely available (http://web.library.yale.edu/testimonies). These testimonies range in length from half an hour to forty hours. The website details how they were compiled:

> Fortunoff Archive's interviewing methodology stresses the leadership role of the witness in structuring and telling his or her own story. Questions are primarily used to ascertain time and place, or elicit additional information about topics already mentioned, with an emphasis on open-ended questions that give the initiative to the witness. The witnesses are the experts in their own life story, and the interviewers are there to listen, to learn, and to clarify.

Extracts from some of the interviews have been published in various collections (e.g. Greene and Kumar, 2000). In addition, more detailed analysis of the testimonies has been produced by various researchers. Perhaps the most influential has been the work of Lawrence Langer, an English literature scholar. In his *Holocaust Testimonies*, Langer (1991) considered the process of personally constructing narrative recollections of these horrors. He emphasised that, rather than these narrative accounts being completed through emplotment, they remain unfinished, disrupted:

> Moral formulas about learning from experience and growing through suffering rapidly disintegrate into meaningless fragments of rhetorical consolation as the testimony of these interviews proceeds. (1991, p. xi)

In his detailed overview of hundreds of these narrative accounts, Langer searched for some commonalities and in doing so provided some insight into the process of both remembering and continuing to live with those horrific memories. As he said:

> Testimony is a form of remembering. The faculty of memory functions in the present to recall a personal history vexed by traumas that thwart smooth-flowing chronicles. Simultaneously, however, straining against what we might call disruptive memory is an effort to reconstruct a semblance of continuity in a life that began as, and now resumes what we would consider, a normal existence. (1991, p. 2)

It is this struggle to return to 'normality' that pervades the narratives and the lives of these survivors. Their's are stories of sadness and incomprehension of human evil against which they could do little.

Conversely, the narrative accounts stored in the Global Feminisms Project (GFP) are of feminist activists who recount lives of struggle for social justice. The GFP is an online repository of the oral histories of women who have devoted their lives to promoting social change. Those involved in the project from different countries around the world have selected a number of women in their country to be interviewed. The interviews followed a similar format:

> The interviews were semi-structured oral histories prompting women to speak about their familial background, career and academic experiences, and engagement with activism and movements. (Dutt and Grabe, 2014, p. 111)

The online account provides the transcripts and videos of the interviews (http://umich.edu/~glblfem/). They also contain, for some of the interviewees, a basic thematic analysis detailing the major experiences of the women. More recently, researchers have begun to explore in more detail the character of these narrative accounts. An example is the work of Dutt and Grabe (2014) who conducted a detailed analysis of the accounts of three of the women. Their analysis was informed by three social psychological concepts – positive marginality, conscientisation and social identity theory. Each of these concepts was used to interrogate a selection of narrative accounts. The authors also reflected upon how their own subjectivities influenced the process of analysis.

Narrative researchers can also explore other potential archival sources, not simply those from formal interviews. An example is the study by Inger Skjelsbaek (2015) who conducted an analysis of the sentencing judgements of sexual violence offenders stored in the court records of the International Criminal Tribunal for the Former Yugoslavia (ICTY). In this study the data consisted of the court proceedings of those who were convicted of having been the principal perpetrators of crimes of sexual violence. The records included the defence offered by the defendants as well as of the defendants and the cross-examinations. From this extensive detail Skjelsbaek constructed three primary perpetrator narratives. The first she termed 'narratives of chivalry' in which the perpetrator presented himself as being a good soldier who did not commit rape but rather in some distorted way acted as a protector of the victim. The second she termed narratives of opportunism in which the perpetrator was a repulsive individual who took advantage of the situation to satisfy his sexual urges. The third she termed narratives of remorse in which the perpetrators accepted their guilt and felt remorse for their actions.

Letters

Finally, another important source of narrative data is letters. A very large number of public and private archives contain thousands of letters detailing people's experiences of particular events. These can include letters to family members, friends or other individuals. Besides these personal letters, researchers can also explore the narrative content of public letters such as those sent to newspapers or public bodies. An example is the study reported by Tileaga (2011), which focused on a letter from what he describes as a 'Romanian public intellectual' to a major Romanian newspaper. In the letter the author details his experience of being an informer to the secret police. Tileaga describes the letter as 'a chronological/biographical journey – from the first encounters with the Securitate, through becoming an informer, to, ultimately, being put under surveillance' (2011, p. 205).

OTHER SOURCES

While the initial turn to narrative placed emphasis on verbal and written sources of data there is increasing interest in a wider range of sources. One such source is the visual medium, which can range from the use of video through photographs (see Eberle, Chapter 25, this volume) to graphic novels. Since these are often in the public domain the task of the researcher is to identify particular media that connect with the focus of the research. O'Donnell and Castello (2011) explored the narrative content of news broadcasts on Spanish and Catalan television channels. They were particularly interested in how the television channels presented news about social conflict from different national perspectives. Hoecker (2014) considered the organisation of visual narratives produced by national truth commissions in Peru and Guatemala. They considered how different media, including photographs and illustrations, were used to convey different perspectives.

One of the strengths of these visual approaches is that they can be used in a participatory action format to involve participants in the conduct of the research and also to promote certain forms of change. Earlier I referred to the study by Murray and Crummett (2010) in which we involved older residents of a disadvantaged community in developing a map of their neighbourhood. Through this process of collective map-making they were able to articulate a shared narrative of a community in decline.

The broader rapprochement between social science and the arts has also enabled narrative researchers to explore the potential of other art forms such as performance and drama. Peterson and Langelier (2006) talk about the 'turn to performance' (see Denzin, Chapter 13, this volume) in which the narrative is 'embodied in communication practices, constrained by situational and material conditions, embedded in fields of discourse, and strategically distributed to reproduce and critique existing relations of power and knowledge' (2010, p. 173). Langelier (1999) has detailed the particular qualities of performance, which adds to the individual oral narrative. These include the voice and body of the narrator and the fact that the performance is, in many ways, a conversation with the listening audiences both present and absent. In a study by Bernard et al. (2015), we explored the use of drama to represent the involvement of older people in the theatre. The study was thus a participatory and reflexive exercise in storytelling which was also designed to engage the audience in discussion and debate about the process of growing older.

CONCLUSION

The study of narrative continues to grow across the social sciences and connects increasingly with the arts and humanities. Historically, interest in narrative was located in those fields but the connection with them weakened with the rise of positivism. The study of narrative provides a bridge that will open up new ideas and methods. The rapid growth of the Internet and computer technology presents new possibilities for the development and exchange of stories. So, too, does the development of new forms of literature such as graphic novels and zines. These in turn provoke new ideas about retelling narratives through performance and art. Thus the narrative turn connects with the performative turn (e.g. Solinger et al., 2008) in moving from the collection of narrative accounts to their use in processes of social change. The narrative researcher is constantly involved in the process of the critique of stories exposing how they are constructed and the extent to which they contribute to personal or social suffering but also the extent to which they can contribute to enhancing human experience.

FURTHER READING

Goodwin, John (Ed.) (2012) *SAGE Biographical Research (4 Volumes)*. London: Sage.
Mishler, Elliot, G. (1986) *Research Interviewing. Context and Narrative*. Cambridge, MA: Harvard University Press.
Plummer, Ken (2001) *Documents of Life 2: An Invitation to a Critical Humanism*. London: Sage.

REFERENCES

Allport, Gordon (1942) *The Use of Personal Documents in Psychological Science*. New York: Social Science Research Council.
Andrews, Molly (2015) 'A very elementary transformation of one's existence: Narrating moments of political change', in Hazel Reid and Linden West (Eds.), *Constructing Narratives of Continuity and Change. A Transdisciplinary Approach to Researching Lives*. London: Routledge, pp. 37–48.
Atkinson, Paul (2006) *Everyday Arias: An Operatic Ethnography*. Lanham, MD: AltaMira Press.
Bamberg, Michael (2006) 'Stories: big or small: Why do we care?', *Narrative Inquiry*, 16(1), 139–47.
Bernard, Miriam, Rickett, Michelle, Amigoni, David, Munro, Lucy, Murray Michael and Rezzano, Jill (2015) 'Ages and stages: The place of theatre in the lives of older people', *Ageing & Society*, 35(6), 1119–45.
Billig, Michael (1978) *Fascists. Social Psychological View of the National Front*. London: Academic Press.
Bornat, Joanna (2004) 'Oral history', in Clive Seale, Giampetro Gobo, Jaber F. Gubrium and David Silverman (Eds.), *Qualitative Research Practice*. London: Sage, pp. 34–47.
Bornat, Joanna and Josie Tetley (2010) 'Introduction', in J. Bornat and J. Tetley (Eds.), *Oral History and Ageing*. London: Centre for Policy on Ageing.
Bruner, Jerome (1990) *Acts of Meaning*. Cambridge, MA: Harvard University Press.
Bruner, Jerome (1995) 'The autobiographical process', *Current Sociology*, 43(2), 161–78.
Coetzee, Jan K. and Rau, Asta (2009) 'Narrating trauma and suffering: Towards understanding

intersubjectively constituted memory', [49 paragraphs]. *Forum Qualitative Sozialforschung/ Forum: Qualitative Social Research,* 10(2), Art. 14. Available at http://nbn-resolving.de/urn:nbn:de:0114-fqs0902144.

Dutt, Anjali and Grabe Shelly (2014) 'Lifetime activism, marginality, and psychology: Narratives of lifelong feminist activists committed to social change', *Qualitative Psychology,* 1(2), 107–22.

Elliott, Heather (1997) 'The use of diaries in sociological research on health experience', *Sociological Research Online,* 2, (2). Available at http://www.socresonline.org.uk/2/2/7.html

Evans, George Ewart (1972) 'Approaches to interviewing', *Oral History,* 1(4), 56–71.

Ewick, Patricia and Susan S. Silbey (1995) 'Subversive stories and hegemonic tales: Towards a sociology of narrative', *Law & Society Review,* 29(2): 197–226.

Flick, Uwe (2014) *An Introduction to Qualitative Research* (5th edn). London/Thousand Oaks, CA/Delhi: Sage.

Flick, Uwe, Foster, Juliet and Caillaud, Sabine (2015) 'Researching social representations', in Gordon Sammut, Eleni Andreouli, Gaskell, George and Valsiner, Jaan (Eds.), *The Cambridge Handbook of Social Representations.* Cambridge: Cambridge University Press, pp. 64–82.

Freeman, Mark (1993) *Rewriting the Self: History, Memory, Narrative.* London: Routledge.

Freeman, Mark (2013) 'Axes of identity. Persona, perspective, and the meaning of (Keith Richards's) Life', in C. Holler and M. Klepper (Eds.), *Rethinking Narrative Identity. Persona and Perspective.* Amsterdam: John Benjamins.

Georgakopoulou, Alexandra (2006) 'Thinking big with small stories in narrative and identity analysis', *Narrative Inquiry,* 16(1): 122–30.

Greene, Joshua, M. and Kumar, Shiva (Eds.) (2000) *Witness. Voices from the Holocaust.* New York: Free Press.

Hammack, Phillip, L. and Bertram J. Cohler (2009) 'Narrative engagement and sexual identity: An interdisciplinary approach to the study of sexual lives', in P.L. Hammack and B.J. Cohler (Eds.), *The Study of Sexual Identity: Narrative Perspectives on the Gay and Lesbian Life Course.* New York: Oxford University Press, pp. 3–22.

Hoecker, Robin (2014) 'Visual narrative and trauma recovery', *Narrative Inquiry,* 24(2): 259–80.

Ida, Masumi, Shrout, Patrick E., Laurenceau, Jean-Philippe and Bolger, Niall (2012) 'Using diary methods in psychological research', in Harris Cooper (Ed.), *APA Handbook of Research Methods in Psychology, Vol. 1, Foundation, Planning and Measures.* Washington, DC: APA Books, pp. 277–305.

Kenten, Charlotte (2010) 'Narrating oneself: Reflections on the use of solicited diaries with diary interviews', *Forum Qualitative Sozialforschung/Forum: Qualitative Social Research,* [S.l.], 11(2): May 2010. ISSN 1438-5627. Available at http://www.qualitative-research.net/index.php/fqs/article/view/1314/2989

Kusenbach, Margarethe (2003) 'Street phenomenology: The go-along as ethnographic research tool', *Ethnography,* 4(3): 455–85.

Langelier, Kristin M. (1999) 'Personal narrative, performance, performativity: Two or three things I know for sure', *Text and Performance Quarterly,* 19(2): 125–44.

Langer, Lawrence, L. (1991). *Holocaust Testimonies. The Ruins of Memory.* New Haven, CT: Yale University Press.

Lohuis, Anne M., Sools A., Vuuren M. v. and Bohlmeijer, Ernst T. (2016) 'Narrative reflection as a means to explore team effectiveness', *Small Group Research,* 47(4): 406–37.

McAdams, Dan, P. (1993) *The Stories We Live By. Personal Myths and the Making of the Self.* New York: Guilford Press.

McAdams, Dan, P. (1995) *The Life Story Interview.* Evanston, IL: Northwestern University.

McAdams, Dan, P. (2013) *The Redemptive Self. Stories Americans Live By* (2nd edn). New York: Oxford University Press.

McKenzie-Mohr, Elizabeth and Michelle Lafrance (2014) *Women Voicing Resistance. Discursive and Narrative Explorations.* London: Routledge.

Mishler, Elliot, G. (1986) *Research Interviewing. Context and Narrative.* Cambridge, MA: Harvard University Press.

Murray, Michael (2000) 'Levels of narrative analysis in health psychology', *Journal of Health Psychology,* 5(3): 337–48.

Murray, Michael (2009) 'Telling stories and making sense of cancer', *International Journal of Narrative Practice*, 1(1): 25–36.

Murray, Michael (2015) 'Narrative psychology', in J.A. Smith (Ed.), *Qualitative Psychology. A Practical Guide to Research Methods*. London: Sage, pp. 85–107.

Murray, Michael and Crummett, Amanda (2010) '"I don't think they knew we could do these sorts of things": Social representations of community and participation in community arts by older people', *Journal of Health Psychology*, 15(5): 777–85.

O'Donnell, Hugh and Castello Enric (2011) 'Neighbourhood squabbles or claims of right? Narratives of conflict on Spanish and Catalan television', *Narrative Inquiry*, 21(2): 191–212.

Overberg, Regina, Toussaint, Pieter and Zwetsloot-Schonk, Bertie (2006) 'Illness stories on the internet: Features of websites disclosing breast cancer patients' stories in the Dutch language', *Patient Education and Counselling*, 61(3): 435–42.

Pederson, Joshua R. (2013) 'Disruptions of individual and cultural identities. How online stories of job loss and unemployment shift the American Dream', *Narrative Inquiry*, 23(2): 302–22.

Peterson, Eric E. and Langellier, K. M. (2006) 'The performance turn in narrative studies', *Narrative Inquiry*, 16(1): 173–80.

Plummer, Ken (2001) *Documents of Life 2. An Invitation to a Critical Humanism*. London/Thousand Oaks/New Delhi: Sage.

Prins, Jacomijne, Polletta, Francesca, Stekelenburg, Jacquelien van and Klandermans, Bert (2015) 'Exploring variation in the Moroccan-Dutch collective narrative: an intersectional approach', *Political Psychology*, 36(2): 165–80.

Puvimanasinghe, Teresa, Denson, Linley A., Augoustinos, Martha and Somasundaram, Daya (2014) 'Narrative and silence: How former refugees talk about loss and past trauma', *Journal of Refugee Studies*, 28(1): 69–92.

Riessman, Catherine Kohler (1993) *Narrative Analysis*. Newbury Park, London and New Delhi: Sage.

Rosenthal, Gabriele (2004) 'Biographical research', in Clive Seale, Giampietro Gobo, Jaber F. Gubrium and David Silverman (Eds.), *Qualitative Research Practice*. London: Sage, pp. 48–64.

Skjelsbaek, Inger (2015) 'The military perpetrator: A narrative analysis of sentencing judgments on sexual violence offenders at the International Criminal Tribunal for the Former Yugoslavia (ICTY)', *Journal of Social and Political Psychology*, 3(1): 46–70.

Smith, Deirdre (2013) 'The power of collective narratives to inform public policy: Reconceptualizing a principal's Qualification Program', *International Journal of Leadership in Education: Theory and Practice*, 16(3): 349–66.

Solinger, Rickie, Fox, Madeline, & Irani, Kayhan (2008) *Telling Stories to Change the World*. London: Routledge.

Spector-Mersel, G. (2011) 'Mechanisms of selection in claiming narrative identities: A model for interpreting narratives', *Qualitative Inquiry*, 17(2): 172–85.

Squire, Corinne (2007) *HIV in South Africa. Talking about the Big Thing*. London: Routledge.

Tileaga, C. (2011) '(Re)writing biography: Memory, identity, and textually mediated reality in coming to terms with the past', *Culture & Psychology*, 17(2): 197–215.

Toolis, E.E. and Hammack, P.L. (2015) 'The lived experience of homeless youth: A narrative approach', *Qualitative Psychology*, 2(1), 50–68.

White, Michael and David Epston (1990) *Narrative Means to Therapeutic Ends*. New York: W.W. Norton.

Winter, David, G. (1993) 'Gordon Allport and "Letters from Jenny"', in Kenneth Craik, Robert Hogan and Raymond Wolfe (Eds.), *Fifty Years of Personality Psychology*. New York: Plenum Press, pp. 147–63.

Data Collection in Conversation Analysis

Clare Jackson

INTRODUCTION

In speaking with others, we produce recognisable social activities that are fundamental for conducting our social lives (e.g. greetings, appreciations, complaints, apologies, invitations, requests, advice-giving, and so on). Conversation Analysis (CA) is essentially the study of how these activities are accomplished in conversations between people. At its core, CA is an approach to studying social action and its data are recordings of naturally occurring (or naturalistic) interactions. Consequently, data collection for conversation analytic purposes is, in some ways, straightforward because researchers are already immersed in, and surrounded by, data of interest: talk between friends, family, doctors and patients, lawyers and clients, journalists and politicians, teachers and students, and the like. Harvey Sacks, the originator of CA, worked somewhat opportunistically on any recorded interactions he was able to access; as he puts it, '*simply because I could get my hands on it and I could study it again and again*' (Sacks, 1984, p. 26). There is, however, a range of ethical and practical challenges in capturing talk for analytic purposes, not least due to the requirement that talk (data) is recorded (and increasingly videoed).

In this chapter, I begin with a description of Sacks' work on suicide prevention helplines to illustrate the particular insights into social life that can be gained through the close analysis of talk (second section). Following discussion of the status of 'natural' in naturally occurring data (third section), I introduce transcription as a central activity for conducting CA (fourth section) and then explore options for collecting data (fifth section) in ordinary and institutional contexts. I will end with recent applications of CA to studying computer-mediated communication.

THE BEGINNINGS OF CONVERSATION ANALYSIS

Conversation analysis is a relatively young discipline that originated in the work of Harvey Sacks, in collaboration with his colleagues, Emanuel Schegloff and Gail Jefferson. CA was inspired by Goffman's (1955, 1959, 1983) and Garfinkel's (1967) independent attempts to re-specify sociology's subject matter by opening it up to everyday life. Prior to this, everyday contexts tended to be dismissed as irrelevant and/or too chaotic for systematic analysis (Sacks, 1992). Sacks and colleagues took seriously both Goffman's account of the normative organisation of the interaction order (Drew and Wootton, 1988), and Garfinkel's ethnomethodological focus on people's practices for producing and recognising meaningful social actions (Heritage, 1984). As Goffman's former students and having extensive contact with Garfinkel (Heritage, 2008), Sacks and Schegloff were primarily concerned with discovering whether it was possible to produce a systematic sociological description of actual situated events (Drew, 2005). They did not set out to investigate conversations, but as a Fellow of the Center for the Scientific Study of Suicide, in Los Angeles (1963–1964), Sacks had access to recordings of telephone calls to a suicide prevention helpline, and could repeatedly examine their contents. It was in studying these calls that Sacks had the insight that conversation is a primary site of co-ordinated social action. Participants in these calls were (presumed) strangers to each other and had to co-ordinate their talk to introduce themselves, offer help, establish a relevant problem, express concern, and so on. Sacks realised that the required competencies to be able to produce meaningful social action and to progress through a range of locally produced activities (that are not somehow pre-ordained) relies on the fundamental organisation of talk as a domain in its own right. That is, talk is (exquisitely) orderly and therefore analytically tractable.

Recalling this period, Schegloff (1992) points to the inspiration of a puzzle contained in a single call:

Extract 1 [Sacks, 1992, pp. 7–8]

```
01 A: This is Mr Smith may I help you
02 B: I can't hear you
03 A: This is Mr Smith
04 B: Smith?
05 A: Yes. Can I help you?
06 B: I don't know hhh I hope you can
```

Sacks had noticed that typically, when a call-taker gave their name, callers would provide theirs in the next turn. His puzzle with this call was that the caller (B) avoided giving his name without either explicitly refusing to do so or remaining silent in the next turn; he did something else instead. This 'something else' made sense as a next action; it was not random. The action of B's turn at line 2 is to indicate a possible problem of hearing. In response, A provides his name again (line 3). This might make a relevant space for B to now provide his name but instead he asks for confirmation of A's name (line 4). Once again, this action has meaning and makes contextual sense but is not yet dealing with the activities made relevant by the opening turn. In response, the call-taker confirms his name and re-issues the offer of help (line 5). This sets up a new sequence of talk in which B can begin his reason for calling (line 6) but without the expectation of giving his name.

Schegloff (1992) reports Sacks' hesitant wonder with the orderliness of social action evident in this and other calls. It appeared to Sacks that turns at talk set up expectable next actions (e.g. giving a name in a first turn sets up the expectation of a name in the next turn) but that there are also acceptable and sensible ways for recipients to do something else instead (e.g. express a failure of hearing, which sets up its own expectation that a prior turn will be repeated). As Sacks puts it:

> Someone says, 'This is Mr Smith' and the other supplies his own name. Someone says, 'May I help you?' and the other states his business. Someone

says, 'Huh?' or 'What did you say?' or, 'I can't hear you' and then the thing said before gets repeated. What we want then to find out is, can we first of all construct the objects that get used to make up a range of activities, and then see how it is those objects do get used? (Sacks, 1992, pp. 10–11)

Showing the transcript of a call that Sacks puzzled over decades ago points to some advantages of collecting (and transcribing – see Jenks, Chapter 8, this volume) recordings of naturally occurring data (see Potter and Shaw, Chapter 12, this volume). The transcript captures the details of what was actually said, so is not subject to exigencies of recall.[1] I can also present what Sacks made of this data and you can decide whether or not you agree with him. Perhaps most crucially, the telephone call transcribed here originally took place because one person was reaching out for help and was not elicited by and for the researchers. That is, the work of the suicide prevention helpline was ongoing regardless of the presence of recording devices. We will discuss the implications of this in more detail below, but for now note that recordings of naturally occurring data have life beyond the particular research project for which they are collected. It is common for analysts to come back to a piece of data many times for different purposes. For example, in reading Extract 1 you might be struck by the formality of the call-taker's expression of his own name (Mr Smith) and wonder what alternatives there might be for self-identifying in a call-opening (e.g. 'Dave', or 'suicide helpline') and the different kinds of 'work' these alternatives accomplish (see Hopper, 1992). So, whilst Sacks analysed the sequencing of social actions in Extract 1, another analyst might use it as part of a project to analyse how and with what interactional consequences, speakers identify themselves.

Working inductively on a broad range of corpora of recordings of conversations, Sacks and colleagues repeatedly demonstrate that interaction is inherently orderly; indeed that there is 'order at all points' (Sacks, 1984, pp. 22). Their detailed work established the basic machinery of any meaningful interaction, the ways speakers: manage taking turns at talk (Sacks et al., 1974); fix (repair) problems of speaking, hearing or understanding (Schegloff et al., 1977); and progress conversations through organised sequences of action (Schegloff, 1968). These three domains – turn-taking, repair and sequence – remain analytically important, and new domains of inquiry have developed (for an overview, see Sidnell and Stivers, 2013). The analytic naming of activities ('turn-taking' and so on) might appear jargonistic (Parker, 2005) and disconnected from the everyday contexts in which activities occur (Billig, 1999). However, they refer to the fundamental organisation of our social world. Work on 'repair', for example, reveals how speakers manage mutual understanding as a thoroughly social, as opposed to psychological, matter. That is, whatever cognitive or neurological processes occur internally, (lack of) understanding is displayed and managed *between* people in talk. Work on 'sequence organisation' reveals interactional constraints that shape progression of conversation by the force of conditional relevance; questions require answers (or some account of why an answer is not possible), invitations and offers require acceptance or declination, and so on (Schegloff, 2007; see also Stivers and Rossano, 2010). As Drew and Heritage (2006, p. 4) suggest, 'These organizations form the technical bedrock on which people build their social lives, and construct their sense of sociality with one another'.

So far, we have seen that a basic (empirically grounded) conversation analytic assumption is that everyday conversations are an appropriate domain for analysis. The insistence that data comprises of recordings of naturally occurring interactions follows this basic assumption.

NATURALLY OCCURRING DATA

The conversation analytic insistence on naturally occurring data is premised on the attempt to explicate people's methods for producing recognisable social activities; how speakers do things with talk, and are recognised by their recipients as doing these things. CA is therefore not concerned with people's intuitions or remembered accounts of what they 'do' in talk, but rather analyses the actual moments of 'doing'. The reasons for doing so are covered in detail by Potter and Shaw (Chapter 12, this volume), so here I will summarise key arguments.

Conversation analytic data contrasts with conventional forms of data in social science. For example, the requirement for data to be naturally occurring means that formal experimentation in which investigators necessarily manipulate variables tend not to be conducted in CA (see Heritage et al., 2007, for an exception). Interviews, the mainstay of qualitative investigation, are treated in CA as a particular form of institutional talk (Schegloff, 1998) and are not seen as providing analytic traction on interactional activities that are actually conducted elsewhere (Potter and Hepburn, 2005, 2007). Hypothetical or invented examples, common for structural linguistics (e.g. following Chomsky, 1965), are never analysed in CA. Finally, the recording of data frees analysts from the limitations of selection and memory biases that influence observations and the construction of ethnographic field notes. These criticisms of traditional forms of data collection apply insofar as researchers are investigating situated social action and do not inevitably pertain generally. That is, CA's data fits its purpose, and the requirement for naturally occurring data is not meant, as has sometimes been claimed (e.g. Whelan, 2012) to be dogmatic in relation to other forms of research.

CA continues to use naturally occurring recordings because these are essential for recovering and analysing the organisation of situated interactional activities. For this purpose, other forms of data are impoverished. The conversation analytic aim for collecting data is to acquire recordings of interactional practices as they occur in their original settings and to cumulatively build corpora, which can be analysed and re-analysed in the context of existing and new knowledge over time (Goodwin and Heritage, 1990).

The focus on what people do in authentic interactional moments lends CA a naturalist character that has been variously critiqued (e.g. Billig, 1999; Parker, 2005; Whelan, 2012). One concern, based on the 'observer's paradox' (Labov, 1972), is that people might change their conduct when they know they are being recorded, and as a consequence, any knowingly recorded talk is less than 'natural' (Hammersley, 2003). This challenging possibility is ultimately inescapable due to legal and ethical requirements to gain consent for recording (Speer and Hutchby, 2003). However, the matter is open to empirical investigation through, for example, analysing participants' demonstrable orientations to being recorded (Heath et al., 2010; Speer and Hutchby, 2003). For example, my corpus of telephone calls made and received by pre-teen and teenaged girls, includes my daughters, and they would occasionally tease me as the (later) over-hearing analyst by saying something like 'transcribe this Mum' followed by a string of nonsensical sounds. Clearly, in these moments the presence of a recording device changed what they would otherwise have done, or at least the manner in which they did it (teasing me being a normative activity). Nevertheless, these moments are visible and occurred within what were overwhelmingly, so far as I can tell, moments of interaction-as-usual. Grounded in extensive video research (see Knoblauch et al., Chapter 23, this volume) Heath et al. conclude that the extent to which recording devices alter conduct is overstated. In their words:

> Throughout our studies of a diverse range of settings and activities we found that within a short time, the camera is 'made at home'. It rarely receives notice or attention and there is little empirical evidence that it has transformed the ways in which participants accomplish actions. (2010, p. 49)

Given even a small risk that people react to being recorded, conversation analysts tend to characterise their data as *naturalistic* as opposed to *natural*. The activities, content and direction of conversations should be unsolicited (Lynch, 2002) and pass the conceptual 'unwell scientist test' proposed by Potter (2002) to distinguish between researcher-generated data and 'data' that would have occurred whether or not a researcher was present. To the extent that conversations are unsolicited by and for researchers, the data for CA are naturally occurring.

In this section, we have discussed the implications of capturing situated 'real' life activities. In the next section, we will briefly consider transcription, which is a central activity in CA, before moving on to discuss options for collecting data in the section thereafter.

TRANSCRIBING DATA

To aid detailed analyses of the moment-by-moment realisation of social action, CA requires hours of repeated listening to data and production, and the ongoing refinement of highly detailed transcripts (Hepburn and Bolden, 2013). Transcription (see Jenks, Chapter 8, this volume) is a central activity in CA, and though recordings remain the primary data, analysis frequently begins with transcription. In CA, it is conventional to use the transcription system first developed by Jefferson (2004), which uses basic symbols on a keyboard to convey the sorts of details that appear (empirically) to be consequential for interaction (e.g. speed, intonation, emphasis). Hence, transcripts reproduce not only *what* was said but also, as far as possible, *how* it was said. CA transcripts therefore include the 'messier' details (e.g. silences, hitches and hesitancies) that are frequently 'cleaned up' in traditional forms of transcription.

CA uses a standard layout for transcription, making use of a fixed width font (e.g. courier or courier new), line numbers, speaker identification and a range of symbols. The result can look off-putting but once familiar with the system, a CA transcript skilfully conveys analytically crucial details. For example, consider the following transcript of a telephone conversation between Penny and Stan.

Extract 2 [CTS05]

```
01  Sta:  I've not- .hhh I don't use
          buses you know
02        (.)
03  Sta:  Because the Met is jus so much
          more convenient.
04  Pen:  What are you just like fucking
          mi:les away and the
05        bus stop's right at the end of
          your stree:t
06  Sta:  Er::: no
07        (.)
08  Sta:  No
09        (.)
10  Sta:  Technicality °tech(h)ni°ca huh
          [huh
11  Pen:                    [Huh huh
12        [well [you just said the wo[rd=
13  Sta:  [You have to wait [for a bus.
          [You have
14  Pen:  =[convenience so that's what
          came to my mi:[nd.
15  Sta:  =[to wait fo- y- y- y- [you
16        have to wait for a certain bus
          which is going to
17        like ten minutes anyway .hh
          and like
18  Pen:  An' the- .hh yeah as oppose to
          like waiting every
19        three minutes for a Met [( ) ]
          seven=
20  Sta:  [Yeah but but]
21  Pen:  =minutes
22  Sta:  But you don't have to wait for
          a certain one
23        though do you and you don't
          have like to make
24        sure you've got the right one
          and stuff and and
25        [ring the bell] when you have
          to get off and=
26  Pen:  [It's tr- ]
27  Sta:  = stuff like th(h)at yo(h)u
          kn(h)ow hehehe
28        I'm just a freak. I'm sorry man.
```

Penny and Stan's conversation is something of a jokey disagreement arising from Stan's expressed preference to use a tram ('the Met') rather than the bus because trams are 'just so much more convenient' (line 3). Penny challenges this on the basis that she (demonstrably) knows Stan lives nearer a bus stop than a tram stop (lines 4–5). Notice that the transcript captures more than what each of them say about buses and trams. The disagreement lies not just in Penny and Stan's locally occasioned expressed views but also in the ways they convey these views. For example:

- Following Stan's opening statement that he does not use buses (line 1) there is a silence indicated by the symbol (.). Silences are measured in tenths of a second and are shown as numbers in brackets. For example, (0.5) indicates a silence of five-tenths of a second. When a silence is less than 0.2, transcribers use (.) to indicate a micro silence. Analytically, what is important here is that Penny could be but isn't talking, hence already indicating some possible problem.
- Penny and Stan stress certain words through emphasis – indicated by underlining (e.g. 'fucking mi:les', line 4), or sound stretches – indicated by colons (e.g. 'Er:::', line 6).
- They speak competitively by talking simultaneously for an extended period, as indicated by the square brackets showing onset and offset of overlapping talk (lines 10–20).
- During part of the overlap, Stan's talk appears dysfluent as he repeatedly starts and cuts off the first sound of 'you' (line 15), indicated by the first sound, followed by a dash (y-). Far from being dysfluent, this is a competitive move to 'survive' the overlap so that he can say his turn 'in the clear' (Schegloff, 2000).
- There are laughter particles in several places conveying the non-serious nature of the disagreement. Laughter (and breathiness more generally) are either indicated by h's (e.g. 'th(h)at yo(h)u kn(h)ow', line 27) or by trying to capture the sound more lexically (e.g. 'huh huh' line 11).

There is so much more going on in this extract but, for now, notice that the details of how things are said matter for the ways that social action is produced, and that these details can be represented in a transcript.

The transcript above represents spoken interaction during a telephone call. The advantage of telephone data (at least from landlines) is that it removes necessity to consider embodied conduct because the speakers are accomplishing whatever they are doing without sight of each other. As soon as speakers are co-present, analysts ought to attend to various embodied actions (e.g. gaze and gesture) that contribute to action formation. In overviewing transcription of video data, Hepburn and Bolden (2013) suggest that, given the enormity of possibly relevant embodied conduct, transcription of visible behaviour tends to be selective, based on the parameters of a particular project. At the most basic level, transcribers can indicate embodied actions in 'transcriber's notes' included in the main body of a transcript. These are usually presented in double parentheses – for example ((Mum passes salt to Sophie)). Another possibility is to present a series of images or diagrams depicting a particular moment in interaction. This retains something of the complexity of original context and can show in a basic way something like, for instance, Mum reaching for the salt, picking it up and handing it to Sophie. For more detailed analysis of embodied action, there are specialised notational systems that work either alongside the verbal transcript or within its lines, using square brackets to align talk with gesture. For illustrations of transcriptional methods for tracking eye gaze, see Goodwin (1981) and Rossano et al. (2009); for gestures, see Heath (1986) and Streeck (1993).

This section has briefly covered transcription, which as noted, is an important activity in CA but remember that transcripts are only a partial representation of actual data – the recordings themselves. In the next section, we turn to data collection.

COLLECTING DATA FOR CA

There is a range of options for obtaining data for conversation analytic purposes, including an option to study existing data. One upshot of the orderliness of interaction for analysts is that the organisation of social action ought to be discoverable in any data and, therefore, analysis might properly begin with any single case. The capacity for conversation analytic data to function, as part of the many and various research projects, is a real advantage, not just intellectually but also practically because it means that a beginning analyst need not necessarily collect new data. It is common for CA researchers to analyse existing corpora, particularly of ordinary interactions (e.g. telephone calls between family and friends) and a first step in any CA project might be to request permission from authors to access particular recordings and transcripts (responses will depend largely on conditions of ethical consents). It is crucial, however, that the data obtained in this way are the *recordings* and not just the transcripts. Analysis should proceed from recordings because even very detailed transcripts are reduced representations of talk.

Most researchers prefer to collect their own data, partly to develop relevant academic credentials, but also because they might be interested in contexts that are currently understudied. This was my position as a PhD student. I began with an interest in analysing how people produce themselves and others as gendered beings (Stockill and Kitzinger, 2007; Jackson, 2011, 2016). I had a particular ambition to comment critically on Gilligan's claim that adolescent girls lose their 'voice' in the transition from childhood to adulthood (e.g. Brown and Gilligan, 1993). To fulfil this ambition, I needed to work with a relevant set of data – a corpus of ordinary interactions that included the talk of adolescent women. I soon discovered that such a corpus did not exist.

Existing corpora of ordinary data were based mostly on the talk of US or British adults and late-teenagers. The mundane interactions of young women (and men) were relatively absent from CA corpora and so I collected my own data.

Building the CTS Corpus of Telephone Calls

The data collected for my thesis comprised 75 recordings of the naturally occurring telephone conversations made and received by nine participants in the period 2005 to 2007. My central participants were an opportunity sample of nine girls and young women aged between 12 and 19 years. All were recruited to the project through personal contacts and connections. I did not advertise or otherwise seek to recruit participants unknown to me personally. This decision was taken purely on pragmatic grounds; as the mother of (then) three teenage daughters, I had particular access to this population (and this raises ethical issues in its own right, which I will deal with more fully below). Three of the participants were my own daughters and the remainder were either their friends, or the daughters of my own friends. Most of the recordings are of interactions between the participants, but there are also calls to other friends, partners, siblings, parents (including me) and grandparents.

The equipment required for recording telephone calls is widely available from online and technology hardware stores (though be prepared to answer the clerk's questions about reasons for purchasing such devices!). I provided participants with a connector that permitted (selective) recording calls on a particular landline (this plugged directly into the telephone socket) and a small digital recorder. Technology has moved on in the years since I collected my data, and no doubt many young people (and adults) now converse on mobile phones that have inbuilt recording capacity.

In setting up my project, I considered the work in relation to the British Sociological Association's Statement of Ethical Practice, and, since I am a psychology graduate, to the British Psychological Society's Code of Ethics and Conduct. A common prerequisite for participation in academic research is that participants are given informed consent (the possible exception being ethnography). I was keenly aware of the particular importance of this for the young people with whom I would be working. I suspected that I might be privy to intimate details of the participants' lives and, further, that I might overhear aspects of young people's lives not normally shared with adults.

Explaining the nature and purpose of the research in ways that were both meaningful and candid raised some challenges, especially for the younger participants. I briefed participants (and where participants were under sixteen, their parents) on the aims of the project, informing them, in much simpler terms, that my principal interest lay in describing where and how gender is played out in telephone calls; in how girls display and orient to being girls in ordinary conversation.

All participants signed a consent form giving permission to record calls and to use the data for research purposes. Following ethical requirements that participants be alerted to, and consent to, the sharing of data with others, and following the models of consent commonly used by conversation analysts (e.g. see ten Have, 2007, p. 81), I sought separate permissions for: use of data in contexts beyond my own research; use in publications; display on academic websites; use in public professional contexts (e.g. teaching and conferences); and for placing in archives for other researchers.

Additionally, all participants were aware that they had the right to withdraw from the study at any point without explanation. Participants also had the right to withhold any parts of the data they did not want to submit for research purposes. I undertook to edit audio material as requested, as far as possible without listening to the extracts being removed.

Ethical codes require that participants be afforded (realistic) rights to anonymity and confidentiality. Clearly, there is an inherent threat to both anonymity and confidentiality in audio recordings of personal telephone calls. I adopted the standard steps (e.g. anonymising transcripts, secure storage of data, use of codes to break connections between recordings and the people featuring in them). The data collection and storage were in line with existing ethical codes. However, in my case there were two complicating factors: working with my own children and my presence in the data. I will take each in turn.

Complicating Ethics

There is a minority but noteworthy tradition of social scientists working with their own children as research participants (e.g. Darwin, 1877; Piaget, 1952). Research of this kind has been, on occasion, a basis for major theoretical and methodological developments but has also generated controversy. One of the tensions for working with children is their capacity to consent to participate in research. When the researcher is also the parent, this issue is amplified (see Mertens, Chapter 3, this volume).

In CA, Wootton (1997) worked with his young daughter on a conversation analytic project. Despite the fact that he was recording his daughter and regularly appeared in the data himself, Wootton does not discuss at any length the ethical or methodological dilemmas that might have arisen. Instead, he focuses on the implications of a single-case study. This is entirely in keeping with practices for conducting and reporting research at the time. Historically, then, analysts working with their own families have tended not to consider in a public way the ethical matters that arose for them.

In my own case, three of my four daughters were either approaching or were already in their teens when I started to collect data. I provided them with the same consent forms provided for others and they signed the forms gladly. Nevertheless, I wonder about the extent to which they were actually free to withhold their consent. Living with me, they were hardly unaware of the significance the research held for me. I am also keenly aware that a number of the assurances in the consent forms were difficult to put into practice when applied to my children. For example, the assurance for anonymity has been problematic because the small community of conversation analytic researchers are mostly aware that my data includes my daughters' interactions. In part, the decision to disclose the fact that my daughters were included was to pre-empt the less professional comments about participants that I had occasionally witnessed in data sessions.

A second major complication in the ethical assurances given was the declaration that I would not discuss the content of calls with parents. Plainly, this was impossible to deliver for my own children. My daughters were aware of this and nevertheless consented. For the most part, this did not cause problems because, like all participants, they were free either to switch off the recording device or to request that I refrain from listening to – and so delete – particular sections from the calls. These requests were seldom made, but when they were, I honoured them.

So, my daughters had some control and gave me the data freely, having considered for themselves the content they were willing to share. However, this is only part of the story. I also have to acknowledge my own responses to listening to my daughters' calls; especially the few occasions on which, as a mother, I would have censured the children for what I perceived to be problematic or unsafe conduct. I am privileged to have literally listened in on aspects of my daughters' lives I otherwise would not have been privy to. There was joy in this, as I learned something new about each of them. However, I was also discovering something of how the girls were in the world, away from me, and witness to descriptions of a range of behaviours that I will gloss as variously unsettling. As a mother, these matters would be worthy of discussion. As a researcher, I was not warranted to discuss them.

I never resolved this dilemma with satisfaction. My principal role was as a mother and on the rare occasion that troubling matters arose, which I saw might compromise my daughters' safety or health, I did comment on them. I was given some licence to do so by the fact that my children had freely chosen that I overhear these aspects of their lives. However, I was aware that I was treating my children differently from my other participants whose parents might be similarly disturbed by the content of their daughters' interactions.

The duality of the interrelations between mother/researcher and daughters/participants required careful navigation. I remain uncertain about the success of these navigations, which were heavily personal and highly contextualised. Ethical dilemmas are an ongoing and integral part of the research process and extend beyond those considered by mainstream ethical codes. That my daughters consented and had some control over the data does not sufficiently obviate the ethical quandaries that arose in practice. In offering these reflections, I do not claim to have reached a satisfactory conclusion. I am more confident of reaching a conclusion on the next matter – my own involvement in the data.

Being in the Data

It is not, as Kitzinger (2008) observes, entirely unusual for conversation analysts to appear in data. However, there are reasons to be cautious. For example, Wowk (2007, p. 148) explicitly criticises collecting data in which the analyst is a participant, claiming that, '…there has always been a caveat in CA advising against' this practice '…precisely to avoid attributing motive to speakers/hearers which are not publicly and equally available to all the parties to a conversation'. Kitzinger (2008) responds that if analysts have always been cautioned in these terms, it is a caution that even senior analysts have not heeded. The second part of Wowk's claim is more challenging. Taken further, with heightened awareness of interaction, analysts might be open to the suspicion that particular phenomena had appeared in the interaction because the analyst deliberately set the 'right' context for their delivery.

One advantage of CA data is that it is available for scrutiny by others. The presence of an analyst/participant in the data is retained for other analysts to see. This contrasts with research practices in which those collecting data make themselves invisible when the data are presented, or where the role played by the researcher in generating the data might be reflected upon, but not made available for scrutiny. My own visibility means that I am open to scrutiny both in terms of the influence I had in the progressive realisation of the interactions in which I participated and in terms of my analyses. This fact goes some way to guarding against suspicions about manufacturing data and importing too much into the analysis. Like all speakers, I have no choice but to participate in talk in ways that are meaningful and understandable to recipients. I am, therefore, simply not free to manipulate interaction in ways that provide an environment for the appearance of verbal practices I am interested in, without this being visible in the data. As Moerman (1988, p. xi) observes, 'the conscious actor cannot be the author of his or her own talk'. In any event, even if had I been able to 'order-up' particular phenomena, at the time I was collecting the data, my interests were in young women's assertiveness (contra Gilligan) and not in the topic I eventually studied – person reference – so I would have undoubtedly ended up 'ordering' the 'wrong' activities.

Having reflected on the potential problems associated with participating in my own data, I want now to consider whether there is any possible advantage to being so involved intimately in the research, not only through recording my own calls but those of my daughters and their friends. Might having ethnographic insight, for example, be helpful?

All talk is contextualised. As Moerman (1988, p. 8) puts it:

> We all know that all talk is thoroughly and multifariously embedded in the historical, cultural, social, biographical ... context of its occurrence. We make use of this in constructing and interpreting the sense, import and meaning of every bit of talk we encounter.

In writing this, Moerman was pointing to a deficiency in CA; that although CA is useful for understanding the organisation of talk, it tends to bypass the context for that talk's production. Moerman therefore proposes a synthesis between CA and ethnography. Implicit in this proposed synthesis is Moerman's understanding that 'context' is external to the mechanics of talk and that analysis is enriched by consideration of these external factors. This does not fit well with a conversation analytic perspective (Mandelbaum, 1990) because of the analytical risks involved in jumping too quickly to extrinsic factors. Nevertheless, ethnography is included in a list of useful skills that Maynard and Heritage point to in their account of CA as method:

> CA inquiries often make use of intuition, theory, ethnography and coding, depending on the study, the phenomenon of interest, the requirements of analysis, and the disciplined ways in which CA can be related to these other resources. (2005, p. 432)

It should be noted, however, that they refer to the *disciplined* ways in which CA can draw on ethnography (amongst other things). I take it, then, that Heritage and Maynard are not arguing for a synthesis in the way that Moerman does, but rather that ethnography can be applied to CA within its own tenets. That is, on occasion, knowing who the participants are, and the kinds of worlds they inhabit, can add usefully to a conversation analytic project, as long as the analysis does not substantively rely on these ethnographic details.

In relating these arguments to my own work, it might (debatably) be an advantage that I knew the participants, and I understood the context of their lives. For the most part, as the analyst, I personally knew (about) the referents when my participants referred to people and places. I also had insight into why a particular utterance was treated as laughable, benign or offensive. This does not mean that these things would be unavailable to other analysts – after all, anyone trained in CA can spot a recognitional person reference (Sacks and Schegloff, 1979), even if they do not personally know the referent, and can see moments when particular utterances are treated by recipients as being of one kind or another. However, the additional ethnographic details were analytically useful. It is a matter of being disciplined by constantly checking that analysis is demonstrably based in the data and not in what is independently known about the participants.

Whatever the controversies of a relationship between CA and ethnography, as video of co-present interaction has become more practical (and desirable), some form of ethnography usually takes place, especially in institutional settings, where decisions have to be made about what to film and where to position cameras to capture it all (Maynard, 2003).

Collecting Data in Institutional Contexts

As noted above in the second section, CA has its origins in calls to a suicide helpline and although much of the basic discovery of the organisation of talk arises from studies of ordinary interaction, CA has always had a concern with conversations that occur in institutional settings and has been applied to a wide range of settings (see Heritage and Drew, 1992; Heritage and Clayman, 2011). A common theme is that, relative to ordinary talk, the character of institutional talk changes more quickly (e.g. news interviews of the 70s are different to those that take place today) and the range of interactional practices is narrowed to accomplish relevant, though more restricted, goals. Accepting these differences, it is now more usual for CA studies to examine institutional practices in their own right, without comparison with ordinary talk.

I am involved in preparing a bid[3] to study how decisions are reached in the interactions that take place between women, their birth partners and healthcare practitioners during labour and birth. In part, this proposal builds off the acknowledged difficulties of translating into practice healthcare policies that instantiate shared decision-making (SDM) as a goal of medical interaction (Elwyn et al., 2010; Elwyn et al., 2013). SDM is fundamentally a relational process and skilled communication is key to ensuring that patients can participate in health decisions. However, as Pilnick (2008, p. 512) argues:

> what the offering and exercising of choice actually looks like in practice… remains unclear. The potential implications of these interactional processes, though, are immense, since… 'good' practice is ultimately achieved through interaction rather than through policy or regulation.

Recognising a need for materials based on the details of what 'really happens' in medical interactions to more effectively translate policy into practice, CA studies have focused on how decisions are made in and through conversations between healthcare practitioners and patients. It is with this in mind that I am currently working with colleagues to seek funding to collect and analyse recordings of women giving birth in maternity hospitals in the UK. Readers might imagine the ethical sensitivities of such a proposal (see Harte et al., 2017).

Much of the work so far undertaken to prepare the bid has been ethnographic in nature (see also Mondada, 2013), including the following steps:

- *Contacting and involving midwives and service-users in the design and implementation of the project.* The research team now comprises four academics, three Consultant Midwives and one service-user. The project proposal has been considered more broadly by additional academics, healthcare practitioners, university and health trust finance departments and relevant charitable organisations that represent the interests of pregnant women and their families.
- *Securing access to two maternity units for the purposes of data collection.* Locating and conversing with gatekeepers has been crucial.

- *Setting up a project advisory team* that includes a conversation analyst, an obstetrician, a psychologist and a former TV cameraman.
- *Trial filming with different audio and video recorders* to ascertain their viability and capacity to produce secure recordings (our preferred option being for cameras that record to remotely positioned and encrypted external hard drives).
- *Visiting maternity wards to gauge the best options for positioning cameras* in ways that capture as much detail as possible whilst remaining sensitive to women's dignity. We have taken a decision to position single static cameras that film labour rooms from a broad angle without the need for someone to be present for the recording. Different decisions are available though, and it is up to researchers to consider the various contingencies.

There has been extensive discussion of the ethical implications at every stage of the proposed research, from recruitment to dissemination, and it has taken years as opposed to months to reach the stage of submitting for funding. The time-consuming nature of the preparatory work is undoubtedly a disadvantage of conducting this type of research (and I can see why it is simpler to ask women retrospectively about their birth experiences). However, once implemented, a dataset of authentic births will support a range of projects beyond the initial research on SDM (with due ethical permissions in place).

As part of preparing for a proposal, we also conducted a pilot study of decision-making in labour based on data from the British television programme, *One Born Every Minute* (OBEM).[2] Data obtained from television is not typical but nor is it entirely unusual in CA (e.g. Clayman and Heritage, 2002) and can provide useful analytic insights so long as it is remembered that the data were filmed and edited in ways not initially designed for CA research (Mondada, 2013). The OBEM data, for instance, are not ideal for CA purposes because they are heavily edited. Our pilot findings are, therefore, based on a less than optimum dataset, and cannot represent the range of decision-making practices used across either the specific births shown nor across the labour wards that were filmed. Nevertheless, using this data, we saw a range of interactional strategies used by healthcare practitioners to initiate decision-making and these varied in the 'optionality' afforded to the participant in the responding turn (Drew et al., 2001; Shaw, 2013).[4] Whilst our findings have to be offered cautiously, I believe that analysing OBEM was useful in two ways:

- It was part of the ethnographic work on the context of birth in UK maternity units.
- It helped to demonstrate that CA work in this context would produce useful and impactful findings. I encourage CA researchers considering ethically sensitive or understudied environments to make use of any existing relevant TV programmes when preparing the ground for a funding bid.

In this section we have considered various options for collecting data for conversation analytic purposes. The limitations of conversation analytic research are briefly considered in the next section before moving to discuss a newly developing interest in analysing textual conversational data obtained from new technologies and social media.

THE LIMITS OF CA

CA is a method for studying everyday practices for producing social action and studies conversations because these are the primordial site of social activities. Its aim is to study the practices as they occur in their original context, and so the core data are recordings of naturally occurring data. It is therefore not suitable for studying people's views on the social activities they experience. As a consequence, CA does not typically involve interviewing people or otherwise surveying opinions and attitudes. This said, on occasion these kinds of data are collected to supplement interactional data (e.g. Heritage et al., 2007) but never to replace them. The focus on social action as produced *between* people means that CA is not used to analyse inner motivations and psychological states; conversation is not interrogated for signs of privately experienced thoughts and feelings. It does not deny that people have private experiences but rather that CA is unsuitable for their discovery. Perhaps more controversially, CA does not study conversations to investigate categorical *differences* that might arise from membership of particular social identities. For example, it is not used to study sex/gender differences in linguistic competencies or performances (Kitzinger, 2000). The overall rejection of this kind of comparative work in CA is based on an understanding of individuals as belonging to many and varied social categories (e.g. I am a woman, mother, daughter, sister, British, middle-aged, lecturer, feminist, pet-owner, vegetarian, tenant, and so on) and if one of these identities (e.g. gender) is always relevant for interaction then we ought to be able to see its pervasive presence in interaction (Schegloff, 1997). Analyses of interaction without assuming that gender is always/already relevant to ongoing activities has shown that some of the standard understandings that, say, women use tag questions to produce themselves as submissive, or that women say 'no' in ambiguous ways, are not empirically supportable (see Hepburn and Potter, 2011; and Kitzinger and Frith, 1999). CA does not deny the importance of categorical memberships but attempts to analyse moments when participants orient to them in their ongoing interactions. The attempt, then, is not to impose analytic categories on data. The arguments for and against this basic attempt are set out most fully in the Schegloff–Wetherell–Billig debate in the pages of *Discourse & Society* in the 1990s (Billig, 1999; Schegloff, 1997, 1998, 1999; Wetherell, 1998) and have been rehearsed several times since (see Speer and Stokoe, 2011). Readers are advised that CA attracts controversy and authors are regularly in the midst of producing defences of the approach as well as collecting and analysing data.

NEW DEVELOPMENTS

Though the basic form of data used in CA has remained fairly constant, the specific type of data produced is varied. In part, this variety arises from different types of technology used to make recordings, from audio-taping of telephone calls to digital video recording of complex co-present data (see Knoblauch et al., Chapter 23, this volume). There is also an increasing diversity of contexts for recording both ordinary and institutional data. A new development has been the analysis of textual conversations that take place, often asynchronously in online environments, collectively known as computer-mediated communication (CMC). There are tensions in this application because the immediate temporal aspects of synchronous interaction are missing, impacting, for example, practices for turn-taking and the organisation of sequence. However, CMC is inherently interactional (Meredith and Potter, 2013) and users draw on and adapt ordinary practices to produce orderly communication. CMC offers a rich and vast source of potential data and has the advantage of already being textual, hence (variously) reducing (and complicating) the need for transcription (Meredith, 2015). Ethical issues are also rather different but remain relevant. For example, the British Psychological Society has introduced ethical guidelines for what they call internet-mediated research (BPS, 2013) and the Association of Internet Researchers' guidelines remind researchers that 'participants', even if not visible, are 'real' individuals with rights to protection and respect (Markham et al., 2012; see Tiidenberg, Chapter 30, this volume). The implications and challenges of applying CA to study CMC remain under discussion, but as Giles et al. (2015) suggest:

> The academic community active in the field of interaction seems ready to further explore and develop CA for digital spaces. In the coming years, we envision the need for ongoing methodological discussions wherein scholars can share insights for their ongoing microanalysis of online data, as we

all work to refine the application of CA to online talk. (2015, p. 50)

CONCLUSION

In CA, data collection and the overall methodology cohere in distinctive ways. CA's core data arise directly from its theoretical and sociological underpinnings. Obtaining naturally occurring data is effortful, requiring many skills and decisions about whom and how to record. However, once obtained the data can serve multiple and varied conversation analytic projects.

Notes

1. Unfortunately, the original recording was lost as Sacks and colleagues reused tapes to record new data. We are left with the transcripts of these early recordings but it is important to note that it is the recordings, not the transcripts that are the primary data for CA.
2. *One Born Every Minute* is an observational documentary series shown in the UK on Channel 4. The programme makers placed cameras in the ceilings of every room in participating maternity units and filmed for 24 hours a day. Each episode shows, in edited form, the events that occur in two births, from admission to the ward to the birth of the baby.
3. This project has now been funded: NIHR Project ID 14/70/73
4. For a more detailed account of these findings see Jackson et al. (2017).

FURTHER READING

Heritage, John and Clayman, Steven (2011) *Talk in Action: Interactions, Identities, and Institutions*. Chichester: John Wiley & Sons.

Sidnell, Jack (2011) *Conversation Analysis: An Introduction*. Chichester: John Wiley & Sons.

Sidnell, Jack and Stivers, Tanya (Eds.) (2013) *The Handbook of Conversation Analysis*. Chichester: Wiley-Blackwell.

REFERENCES

Billig, Michael (1999) 'Whose terms? Whose ordinariness? Rhetoric and ideology in conversation analysis', *Discourse & Society*, *10*(4): 543–58.

British Psychological Society (2013) *Ethics Guidelines for Internet-mediated Research*. Retrieved from http://www.bps.org.uk/publications/policy-and-guidelines/research-guidelines-policy-documents/research-guidelines-poli.

Brown, Lyn Mikel and Gilligan, Carol (1993) 'Meeting at the crossroads: Women's psychology and girls' development', *Feminism & Psychology*, *3*(1): 11–35.

Chomsky, Noam (1965) *Aspects of the Theory of Syntax*. Cambridge, MA: MIT Press.

Clayman, Steven and Heritage, John (2002) *The News Interview: Journalists and Public Figures on the Air*. Cambridge: Cambridge University Press.

Darwin, Charles (1877) 'A biographical sketch of an infant', *Mind*, *2*(7): 285–94.

Drew, Paul (2005) 'Conversation analysis', in Kristine Fitch and Robert Sanders (Eds.), *Handbook of Language and Social Interaction*. London: Lawrence Erlbaum Associates, pp. 71–102.

Drew, Paul and Heritage, John (2006) 'Introduction', in Paul Drew and John Heritage (Eds.), *Conversation Analysis (Volume 1)*. London: Sage, pp. xxi–xxxvi.

Drew, Paul and Wootton, Anthony J. (1988) *Erving Goffman. Exploring the Interaction Order*. Cambridge: Polity.

Drew, Paul, Chatwin, John and Collins, Sarah (2001) 'Conversation analysis: A method for research into interactions between patients and health-care professionals', *Health Expectations*, *4*(1): 58–70.

Elwyn, Glyn, Laitner, Steve, Coulter, Angela, Walker, Emma, Watson, Paul and Thomson, Richard (2010) 'Implementing shared decision making in the NHS', *British Medical Journal*, *341*: c5146.

Elwyn, G., Scholl, I., Tietbohl, C., Mann, M., Edwards, A. G., Clay, C., ... Wexler, R. M. (2013) '"Many miles to go...": A systematic review of the implementation of patient decision support interventions into routine clinical practice', *BMC Medical Informatics and Decision Making*, *13*(Suppl 2), S14.

Garfinkel, Harold (1967) *Studies in Ethnomethodology*. Englewood Cliffs: Prentice Hall.

Giles, David, Stommel, Wyke, Paulus, Trena, Lester, Jessica and Reed, Darren (2015) 'Microanalysis of online data: The methodological development of "digital CA"', *Discourse, Context & Media*, 7: 45–51.

Goffman, Erving (1955) 'On face-work: An analysis of ritual elements in social interaction', *Psychiatry*, 18(3): 213–31.

Goffman, Erving (1959) *The Presentation of Self in Everyday Society*. New York: Garden City.

Goffman, Erving (1983) 'The interaction order: American Sociological Association, 1982 presidential address', *American Sociological Review*, 48(1), 1–17.

Goodwin, Charles (1981) *Conversational Organization: Interaction Between Speakers and Hearers*. New York: Academic Press.

Goodwin, Charles and Heritage, John (1990) 'Conversation analysis', *Annual Review of Anthropology*, 19(1), 283–307.

Hammersley, Martyn (2003) 'Conversation analysis and discourse analysis: Methods or paradigms?' *Discourse & Society*, 14(6), 751–81.

Harte, J. Davis, Homer, Caroline S., Sheehan, Athena, Leap, Nicky and Foureur, Maralyn (2017) 'Using video in childbirth research: Ethical approval challenges', *Nursing Ethics*, 24(2), 177–189

Heath, Christian (1986) *Body Movement and Speech in Medical Interaction*. Cambridge: Cambridge University Press.

Heath, Christian, Hindmarsh, Jon and Luff, Paul (2010) *Video in Qualitative Research*. London: Sage.

Hepburn, Alexa and Bolden, Galina (2013) 'The conversation analytic approach to transcription', in Jack Sidnell and Tanya Stivers (Eds.) *The Handbook of Conversation Analysis*. Chichester: Wiley-Blackwell, pp. 57–76.

Hepburn, Alexa and Potter, Jonathan (2011) 'Recipients designed: Tag questions and gender', in Susan A. Speer and Elizabeth H. Stokoe (Eds.), *Gender and Conversation*. Cambridge: Cambridge University Press, pp. 135–52.

Heritage, John (1984) *Garfinkel and Ethnomethodology*. Cambridge: Polity.

Heritage, John (2008) 'Conversation analysis as social theory', in Bryan Turner (Ed.), *The New Blackwell Companion to Social Theory*. Oxford: Blackwell, pp. 300–20.

Heritage, John and Clayman, Steven (2011) *Talk in Action: Interactions, Identities, and Institutions*. John Wiley & Sons.

Heritage, John and Drew, Paul (Eds.) (1992) *Talk at Work: Interaction in Institutional Settings*. Cambridge: Cambridge University Press.

Heritage, John, Robinson, Jeffrey D., Elliott, Mark N., Beckett, Megan and Wilkes, Michael (2007) 'Reducing patients' unmet concerns in primary are: The difference one word can make', *Journal of General Internal Medicine*, 22(10): 1429–33.

Hopper, Robert (1992) *Telephone Conversation*. Bloomington: Indiana University Press.

Jackson, Clare (2011) 'The gendered "I"', in Susan A. Speer and Elizabeth H. Stokoe (Eds.), *Gender and Conversation*. Cambridge: Cambridge University Press, pp. 31–47.

Jackson, Clare (2016) '"I sort of did stuff to him": A case study of tellability and taboo in young people's talk about sex', *Narrative Inquiry*, 26(1): 150–70.

Jackson, Clare, Land, Victoria and Holmes, Edward J. B. (2017) 'Healthcare professionals' assertions and women's responses during labour: A pilot conversation analytic study of data from *one born every minute*', *Patient Education and Counseling*, 100(3): 465–472.

Jefferson, Gail (2004) 'Glossary of transcript symbols with an introduction', in Gene H. Lerner (Ed.), *Conversation Analysis: Studies from the First Generation*. Amsterdam: John Benjamins, pp. 13–31.

Kitzinger, Celia (2000) 'Doing feminist conversation analysis', *Feminism & Psychology*, 10(2): 163–93.

Kitzinger, Celia (2008) 'Developing feminist conversation analysis: A response to Wowk', *Human Studies*, 31(2): 179–208.

Kitzinger, Celia and Frith, Hannah (1999) 'Just say no? The use of conversation analysis in developing a feminist perspective on sexual refusal', *Discourse & Society*, 10(3): 293–316.

Labov, William (1972) *Sociolinguistic Patterns*. University of Pennsylvania Press.

Lynch, Michael (2002) 'From naturally occurring data to naturally organized ordinary activities: Comment on Speer', *Discourse Studies*, 4(4), 531–7.

Mandelbaum, Jenny (1990) 'Beyond mundane reason: Conversation analysis and context',

Research on Language & Social Interaction, 24(1–4): 333–50.

Markham, Annette, Buchanan, Elizabeth and AoIR Committee (2012) 'Ethical decision-making and Internet research: Version 2.0. Recommendations from the AoIR Ethics Working Committee', *Final Draft, Association of Internet Researchers*. Retrieved from http://www.aoir.org/reports/ethics2.pdf.

Maynard, Douglas W. (2003) *Bad News, Good News: Conversational Order in Everyday Talk and Clinical Settings*. Chicago: University of Chicago Press.

Maynard, Douglas W. and Heritage, John (2005) 'Conversation analysis, doctor–patient interaction and medical communication', *Medical Education*, 39(4): 428–35.

Meredith, Joanne (2015) 'Transcribing screen-capture data: The process of developing a transcription system for multi-modal text-based data', *International Journal of Social Research Methodology*, 1–14.

Meredith, Joanne and Potter, Jonathan (2013) 'Conversation analysis and electronic interactions: Methodological, analytic and technical considerations', in Hwee Lim and Fay Sudweeks (Eds.), *Innovative Methods and Technologies for Electronic Discourse Analysis*. Hershey: IGI Global, pp. 370–93.

Moerman, Michael (1988) *Talking Culture: Ethnography and Conversation Analysis*. Philadelphia: University of Pennsylvania Press.

Mondada, Lorenza (2013) 'The conversation analytic approach to data collection', in Jack Sidnell and Tanya Stivers (Eds.), *The Handbook of Conversation Analysis*. Chichester: Wiley-Blackwell, pp. 32–56.

Parker, Ian (2005) *Qualitative Psychology: Introducing Radical Research*. Buckingham: Open University Press.

Piaget, Jean (1952) *The Origins of Intelligence in Children*. New York: Routledge and Kegan Paul.

Pilnick, Alison (2008) '"It's something for you both to think about": Choice and decision making in nuchal translucency screening for Down's syndrome', *Sociology of Health and Illness*, 30(4): 511–30.

Potter, Jonathan (2002) 'Two kinds of natural', *Discourse Studies*, 4(4): 539–42.

Potter, Jonathan and Hepburn, Alexa (2005) 'Qualitative interviews in psychology: Problems and possibilities', *Qualitative Research in Psychology*, 2(4): 281–307.

Potter, Jonathan and Hepburn, Alexa (2007) 'Life is out there – a comment on Griffin', *Discourse Studies*, 9(2): 276–82.

Rossano, Frederico, Brown, Penny, and Levinson, Stephen C. (2009) 'Gaze, questioning and culture', in Jack Sidnell (Ed.), *Conversation Analysis: Comparative Perspectives*. Cambridge: Cambridge University Press, pp. 187–249.

Sacks, Harvey (1984) 'Notes on methdology', in John Heritage and J. Maxwell Atkinson, (Eds.), *Structures of Social Action: Studies in Conversation Analysis*. Cambridge: Cambridge University Press, pp. 2–27.

Sacks, H. (1992) *Lectures on Conversation, 2 Vols*. Edited by Gail Jefferson. Oxford: Blackwell.

Sacks, Harvey and Schegloff, Emanuel A. (1979) 'Two preferences in the organization of reference to persons in conversation and their interaction', in George Psathas (Ed.), *Everyday Language: Studies in Ethnomethodology*. New York: Irvington, pp. 15–21.

Sacks, Harvey, Schegloff, Emanuel A. and Jefferson, Gail (1974) 'A simplest systematics for the organization of turn-taking for conversation', *Language*, 50(4): 696–735.

Schegloff, Emanuel A. (1968) 'Sequencing in conversational openings', *American Anthropologist*, 70(6): 1075–95.

Schegloff, Emanuel A. (1992) 'Introduction', in Gail Jefferson (Ed.), *Harvey Sacks: Lectures on Conversation*, Vol. 2. Oxford: Basil Blackwell, pp. ix–lxii.

Schegloff, Emanuel A. (1997) 'Whose text? Whose context?', *Discourse & Society*, 8(2): 165–87.

Schegloff, Emanuel A. (1998) 'Reply to Wetherell', *Discourse & Society*, 9(3): 413–16.

Schegloff, Emanuel A. (1999) 'Naivete vs. sophistication or discipline vs. self-indulgence: A rejoinder to Billig', *Discourse & Society*, 10(4): 577–82.

Schegloff, Emanuel A. (2007) *Sequence Organization in Interaction: A Primer in Conversation Analysis*. Cambridge: Cambridge University Press.

Schegloff, E. A., Jefferson, G. and Sacks, H. (1977) 'The preference for self-correction in the organization of repair in conversation', *Language*, 53(2): 361–82.

Shaw, Chloe (2013) *Advice-giving in telephone interactions between mothers and their young adult daughters.* (Unpublished doctoral thesis). Loughborough University, Loughborough, England.

Sidnell, Jack (2011) *Conversation Analysis: An Introduction.* Chichester: John Wiley & Sons.

Sidnell, Jack and Stivers, Tanya (Eds.) (2013) *The Handbook of Conversation Analysis.* Chichester: Wiley-Blackwell.

Speer, Susan A. and Hutchby, Ian (2003) 'From ethics to analytics: Aspects of participants' orientations to the presence and relevance of recording devices', *Sociology, 37*(2), 315–37.

Speer, Susan A. and Stokoe, Elizabeth H. (Eds.) (2011) *Gender and Conversation.* Cambridge: Cambridge University Press.

Stivers, Tanya and Rossano, Frederico (2010) 'Mobilizing response', *Research on Language and Social Interaction, 43*(1), 3–31.

Stockill, Clare and Kitzinger, Celia (2007) 'Gendered "people": How linguistically non-gendered terms can have gendered interactional relevance', *Feminism and Psychology, 17*(2): 224–36.

Streeck, Jürgen (1993) 'Gesture as communication I: Its coordination with gaze and speech', *Communications Monographs*, 60(4): 275–99.

ten Have, Paul (2007) *Doing Conversation Analysis: A Practical Guide.* London: Sage.

Wetherell, M. (1998) 'Positioning and interpretative repertoires: Conversation analysis and poststructuralism in dialogue', *Discourse & Society,* 9(3): 387–412.

Whelan, Pauline (2012) '"Oxymoronic and sociologically monstrous?", Feminist conversation analysis', *Qualitative Research in Psychology, 9*(4): 279–91.

Wootton, Anthony J. (1997) *Interaction and the Development of Mind.* Cambridge: Cambridge University Press.

Wowk, Maria T. (2007) 'Kitzinger's feminist conversation analysis: Critical observations', *Human Studies, 30*(2): 131–55.

Collecting Data for Analyzing Discourses

Asta Rau, Florian Elliker, and Jan K. Coetzee

WHAT IS DISCOURSE? WHAT IS DISCOURSE ANALYSIS?

The term discourse is so prevalent nowadays that its meaning has become indistinct and 'in danger of becoming all things to all people' (Kendall and Wickham, 1999, p. 35). In its most commonsense everyday use, discourse is simply a synonym for 'talk about something'. At this level we cannot speak of analysis. A more finely tuned use of the term 'discourse' is to signal patterns of language use and meanings that belong to specific social or disciplinary domains – for instance, religious discourse, psychological discourse, political discourse, and medical discourse. At this level we can speak of analysis to some extent, given that we need to interpret and understand something of the terminologies as well as the norms and key ideas that underlie domain-specific language and communication. Then there are highly specialized notions of discourse around which multiple theories and approaches continue to be built. Accompanying this proliferation of theories is a whole range of analytical constructs and customized terminologies that support and distinguish each theory or approach, as well as its definition of what discourse is. In the process, discourse has become a complex and contested term.

To understand what discourse is, and what Discourse Analysis involves, we need to chart some main streams of thought that shaped the study of language. We do this very briefly and within two broad paradigms: Structuralism and post-Structuralism. Readers interested in more sophisticated and critical categorizations would need to seek these in other texts.

Early twentieth-century language scholar Ferdinand de Saussure (1857–1913) proposed a general science of semiotics, concerned with the role of signs as part of social life (Chandler, 2007). De Saussure was also one of the founders of linguistics. His model for linguistic analysis was in step with a dominant philosophical tradition at that time:

Structuralism, which investigates structures – also called deep structures – underlying the surface features of phenomena (Chandler, 2007). Studies focused on formal aspects of language and speech, on their internal structuring, on language acquisition, and semantics – the translation of language into meaning. At that stage scholars analyzed these factors as if language was a fixed and closed system, unsullied by the many influences of context.

A radical departure from Structuralism was brought about by early post-Structural thinkers who argued for a new perspective of reality beyond the rigidity and limitations of structure. They saw reality as being fluid, contextually embedded, and essentially relational. Social scientists were challenged to look beyond the ideal of unbiased objectivity revered by positivist science, which was dominant at the time – and recognize the inevitable place, and role, of subjectivity in research. Out of this grew the Interpretive/Phenomenological paradigm with its focus on the relevance of understanding and interpretation in everyday life (Phillips, 1990). As is still the case, scholars of language retained a strong interest in linguistic structures, for instance grammar, syntax, and phonetics, and saw structure as the bed upon which the river of language flows. But their analytical concerns and constructs extended and deepened to make space for post-Structuralist views of reality and by association, of reality as reflected in language. From this emerged the notion of discourse: how language is used, by whom, in what contexts, how it is interpreted, and how it functions to shape meaning. We refine this definition further on, but for now it serves to introduce what Discourse Analysis involves.

Box 19.1

Discourse Analysis is the analysis of patterns in the structure and functioning of language, and in the constitution and communication of meaning as it unfolds and becomes manifested in specific contexts.

The 'critical turn' in the philosophy of social science – heralding in the critical paradigm – built on ideas from the Interpretive tradition, but sought to prod social science from its predominantly intellectual seat into the realm of action, specifically emancipatory action. With this new focus, the spotlight turned to power and how social reality is fundamentally shaped 'by power relations that are social and historically constituted' (Kincheloe et al., 2011, p. 164). While there are traditions of Discourse Analysis (DA) that do not consider themselves as belonging to a critical paradigm, the main developments in DA have been based there.

Around the 1960s, scholars working at the nexus between language, power, and knowledge began to advance the idea that consensus reality is an unstable representation of the real world; this consensus reality they argued, is constructed by, and naturalized via, ideologies embedded in language (Phillips, 1990; cf. Schütz, 1932; Schütz and Luckmann, 1974, 1989). From this rose a new movement: Social Constructionism/Constructivism, drawing deeply from sources in early post-Structuralist thought, constructionist ideas rose in prominence and were carried to a wide audience by Peter Berger and Thomas Luckmann's book *The Social Construction of Reality*, published in 1966.

WHAT IS CRITICAL DISCOURSE ANALYSIS?

Critical Discourse Analysis (CDA) materialized out of the Critical-Constructionist turn when scholars studying formal aspects of language and speech began recognizing the role of language in structuring social power (Wodak and Meyer, 2001, p. 3). CDA emerged in the mid-1960s to early-1970s, and by the late-1980s had become a well-established social science. But it was only following the launch of Teun van Dijk's journal *Discourse and Society* in the early 1990s, and the formation of a network of CDA scholars in early 1991, that the momentum of CDA began accelerating (Wodak, 2014, p. 302). CDA is now a globally established field of scholarship in manifold disciplines and comprising many different approaches.

> **Box 19.2**
>
> *Critical Discourse Analysis* (CDA) consists of the exposure, interrogation, and analysis of '... opaque as well as transparent structural relationships of dominance, discrimination, power and control' (Wodak and Meyer, 2009, p. 10) that are manifested in language, and more intricately, in discourse.
> *Discourse* refers to the interrelationship between language, worldviews, values, and context – and concerns how these interact with one another to (re)produce social structures and to shape the actions of individual and social actors.

SOME KEY APPROACHES IN CRITICAL DISCOURSE ANALYSIS

The diversity in CDA approaches is partly due to the multiple streams of thought and scholars in which CDA found its origins. Teun van Dijk (1993, p. 279) notes that approaches differ along 'national' lines – for instance 'between "French", "German", "British" or "American" directions of research', and also differ in terms of their epistemologies, theories, and methods.

It is not within the scope of this chapter to outline these many approaches. We can only acknowledge a few key and emerging players, with the disclaimer that we have left out many who should feature.

Norman Fairclough concentrated on investigating change at micro, meso, and macro social and cultural levels. A key notion in his work is 'intertextuality': how texts draw on elements and discourses contained in other texts to reproduce discourses, but also to open out possibilities for discursive change (Jørgensen and Phillips, 2002, p. 4; Fairclough, 2003, pp. 39–61).

CDA features strongly in discursive psychology via the work of scholars such as Jonathan Potter and Margaret Wetherell. The focus is less on macro-scale discursive change and more on individuals as the products, as well as producers, of discourse in specific contexts of interaction (Jørgensen and Phillips, 2002, p. 7; Potter and Wetherell, 1987).

Feminist scholars include Sue Wilkinson, and Celia Kitzinger – both from discursive psychology (Wilkinson and Kitzinger, 1995), and linguist Deborah Cameron (Cameron, 2001, 2006). Their work pivots on the feminist project of intellectual, social, and political change.

Teun van Dijk (1993, 1996) founded six journals, several dedicated to CDA. He argues for a 'cognitive interface' to relate the micro- and macro-levels of knowledge, attitudes, ideologies, and other social representations of social structures.

A newer development from the German world is Reiner Keller's (2011, 2013) sociology of knowledge approach to discourse (SKAD) in the tradition of Berger and Luckmann (1966). Drawing on the work of Michel Foucault (and others), SKAD extends theoretical concerns of interpretive research beyond micro-settings with systematized, institutionalized, expert-based (re)production and differentiation of knowledge on a meso- and macro-level of analysis.

Irrespective of the variations in CDA approaches, fundamental ideas underlie them all: (1) The role of power in the social (re)construction of reality; (2) Interrupting social inequities; and (3) Reflexivity and critique. These core ideas motivate research design and thus influence which data are collected for analysis, how they are collected, from whom, and why.

CORE IDEAS UNDERPINNING CRITICAL DISCOURSE ANALYSIS (CDA)

The role of power in the social (re)construction of reality

'Most of us, most of the time, are no more conscious of most of our assumptions than we are of the movement of the Earth – we are at one with them, as with it' (Nias, 1993, p. 47). Such assumptions are inherent and hidden in discourse. Discourse refers to the interrelationship between language, world views, values, and context – and concerns how these interact with one another to (re)produce social structures and to shape the actions of individual and social actors. These (re)production and shaping processes pivot on relations and processes of power. To do CDA it is essential to grasp how these processes work; we clarify and explain them via Michel Foucault's (1982, 1996) insights. Although 'Foucault is one of the theoretical "godfathers" of CDA' (Wodak, 2009, p. 10), not all CDA approaches theorize power from his perspective.

According to Foucault, relations of power exist in all human interactions and operate through rules of discourse. So rules of discourse are normative: they sanction or prohibit ways of thinking and being-in-the-world and thereby establish and entrench social norms. In doing so, rules of discourse construct social reality.

This construction occurs via ever-perpetuating cycles in which people become the targets as well as the vehicles of what they know and learn (Kendall and Wickham, 1999; Rau, 2008, p. 5). In these cycles people are targeted and conditioned by the sanctioned norms of societal structures and dominant discourses – when people reproduce what they know or accept as true according to these discourses, the discourses as well as the power relations inherent in them will be strengthened and entrenched. This is how dominance emerges, becomes organized and institutionalized, and crystallized in ideology – which is a 'coherent and relatively stable set of beliefs' (Wodak, 2009, p. 7). The Gramscian term 'hegemony' applies when people become complicit in reproducing the value systems of dominant groups to the extent that people act – knowingly or unknowingly – in the interest of the powerful (Eagleton, 1991).

These cycles in the construction of social reality converge with contextual factors, and with unexpected contingencies of everyday life, to position individuals and groups (i.e. subjects) differentially in relation to one another and their contexts. This differential subject positioning lies at the root of social inequalities. It allows for the rise of a hierarchy of power in which dominant groups – or power elites (van Dijk, 1993, p. 255) – gain greater access to and control over physical and symbolic resources, as well as over the processes whereby power is enacted.

Interrupting social inequities

Cycles in the construction of social reality not only result in the reproduction of dominant discourses. Individual and collective agency can interrupt and resist rules of discourse to mediate the emergence of new or adapted social institutions, discourses, and subjectivities. Foucault concedes that individual agency can influence the construction of reality, but in his analyses, individual agency is eclipsed by macro social structures and dominant discourses (Rau, 2004, 2008). Likewise, critical discourse analysts '… pay more attention to "top-down" relations of dominance than to "bottom-up" relations of resistance, compliance and acceptance' (van Dijk, 1993, p. 249). So 'while focusing on social power, we ignore purely personal power, unless enacted as an individual realization of group power, that is, by individuals as group members' (van Dijk, 1993, p. 254).

Two key aims of CDA position it firmly in a critical paradigm. The first is to expose and understand the relationships between discourse and power by interrogating, describing and explaining '… how power abuse is enacted, reproduced or legitimized by the text and talk of dominant groups or institutions' (van Dijk, 1996, p. 84). As Wodak (1996, p. 18) notes, in critiquing power it is 'fruitful to look at both "power in discourse" and "power over discourse."' The second aim is to mobilize such understanding in service of emancipating humans from repression and inequitable situations, including those arising from political, cultural, class, ethnic, racial, and gender inequalities. To this end, discourse analysts are urged to adopt an explicit sociopolitical positioning and apply research findings to bring about change. The latter ethic has led to the criticism that CDA 'sits on the fence between social research and political argumentation' (Wodak and Meyer, 2009, p. 33). This prompts us to ask: how do critical discourse analysts balance constructing with being constructed, and the professional with the personal?

Reflexivity and critique

Critical thinkers and researchers must be vigilant of their subjectivity and manage it. One avenue is: '… to constantly question and methodically distrust' (Bourdieu, in Bourdieu and Wacquant, 1992, p. 248) the assumptions, values, and discourses that underpin the ways in which we think, act, and even feel in relation to our work. Such mindfulness helps to alert us to the links between knowledge and power – and to the mutually constitutive dynamic between ourselves, our contexts, and our studies. Thus an outcome of reflexivity – and an indispensable aspect of CDA – is to position ourselves as clearly and transparently as possible vis-à-vis our professional practices and proclivities. When Foucault (1988, p. 38) asks 'How is the reflexivity of the subject and the discourse of truth linked?' he reminds us that reflexivity itself is not neutral, but is also constructed in discourse. Thus reflexivity itself needs to be problematized in critical thinking.

'Critique' is differently understood and applied in the various CDA approaches. What they do share is an understanding that criticality in CDA entails 'having distance to the data, embedding the data in the social, taking a political stance explicitly, and a focus on self-reflection as scholars doing research … [In addition, the] application of the results is important' (Wodak and Meyer, 2001, p. 9).

THE DISCOURSE-HISTORICAL APPROACH (DHA)

Ruth Wodak, Emeritus Distinguished Professor and Chair in Discourse Studies at Lancaster University developed the Discourse-Historical Approach (DHA) with former colleagues and PhD students in Vienna – among others, Rudolf de Cillia, Gertraud Benke, Helmut Gruber, Florian Menz, Martin Reisigl, Usama Suleiman, and Christine Anthonissen.

We feature the DHA here for several reasons. Wodak's work is well established internationally with a large body of publications to guide experienced as well as novice CDA scholars. DHA includes a focus on linguistic features of discourse and this provides an additional, interesting, entry point for analyses.

DHA is rooted in the core ideas underpinning CDA presented above. There are also specific features that steer study design and, by association, data collection.

Features of DHA

Box 19.3

DHA is *problem-oriented*. This is key to the approach.

By putting the problem first, DHA attempts to transcend paradigmatic, theoretical, and methodological controversies in the service of addressing social ills (Weiss and Wodak, 2003). So DHA encourages the application of *multiple methods and theories,* and *interdisciplinary* work.

There is no canon of data collection in DHA (Wodak and Meyer, 2001, p. 30). Operationalizing concepts, and thus collecting data, are problem-oriented and crafted mainly to fit specific research questions, which should always seek to address real and pressing social issues.

An *abductive approach* is adopted, which entails constant oscillation back and forth between theory and empirical data. Theorizing between micro and macro also occurs in a dialectic manner,

> not a unidirectional way. This places DHA firmly in a *hermeneutic tradition*, rather than an analytical-deductive tradition (Wodak, 2009, p. 27; 2014, p. 25). This implies that data collection is not a distinct phase that occurs apart from analysis and theorizing.
>
> *Historical context* is always analyzed, theorized, and integrated into interpretations and findings.
>
> *Fieldwork and ethnography* are used to explore the objects of investigation from the inside and are a prerequisite to analyzing discourse.
>
> DHA *analyzes linguistic categories* and phenomena of grammar and language use.

Analytical Constructs and Concerns

The final set of conceptual and procedural vectors of data collection are the main analytical constructs of DHA. We list and define them here as backdrop to the case studies that follow:

- Utterances are the smallest unit of speech made up of a continuous piece of speech that begins and ends with a clear pause.
- Texts are concrete forms of language use – its visual, written, or oral manifestations. We create sense out of text when we 'read' its meanings through our knowledge of the world. It is in texts that 'linguistic actions' are objectified (Wodak and Meyer, 2009, p. 89) and via texts that discourses are realized.
- Genre refers to the socially endorsed ways in which language is used, during particular types of social activity, by different people or communities of practice (Reisigl and Wodak, 2009, p. 90; Wodak and Meyer, 2009).
- Discourse is conceptualized in the same way as outlined in the core ideas underpinning CDA, presented earlier: it is a form of contextually embedded 'social practice' inherent in language. It is both 'socially constituted and socially constitutive' (Reisigl and Wodak, 2009, p. 90). It relates to a macro-topic. Claims for validity and truth are argued for by social actors who hold differing viewpoints, so a discourse is not a 'closed' semiotic unit but dynamic and open to new interpretations. New and hybrid discourses also form when discourses cross-pollinate between different fields of action (2009, p. 89). Thus analyses should address: '(a) macro-topic-relatedness, (b) pluri-perspectivity and (c) argumentativity' (2009, p. 89).
- Intertextual and interdiscursive relationships between utterances, texts, genres, and discourses are uncovered via linguistic analyses, as well as analyses of an array of 'frames' such as social, political, economic, historical, and situational factors (Reisigl and Wodak, 2009, p. 90). The aim of exploring these relationships is to track how discourses, genres and texts change in relation to other socio-institutional changes (2009, p. 90).
- De-contextualization occurs when an element of discourse is taken out of its context. Re-contextualization occurs when the element is transferred to a new context and its meaning becomes (partly) transformed in the process. DHA's historical orientation 'permits the reconstruction of how re-contextualization functions as an important process linking texts and discourses intertextually and interdiscursively over time' (2009, p. 95).
- Triangulation (see Flick, Chapter 34, this volume) is essential to DHA (Reisigl and Wodak, 2009, pp. 89, 93). It involves viewing a topic and its objects of investigation from multiple angles, taking into account a whole range of factors including background information, contexts, theories, empirical observations, and methods.
- Context, which forms the basis for triangulation, comprises four levels:
    1. The immediate, language or text-internal co-text and co-discourse;
    2. The intertextual and interdiscursive relationships;
    3. The 'context of situation', comprising social variables and institutional frames (includes substantive and program theories); and
    4. The broader sociopolitical and historical context that discursive practices are embedded in and related to (includes grand and meta theories) (Reisigl and Wodak, 2009, p. 93; Wodak, 2000, p. 6).
- Critique comprises three interrelated dimensions; these allow for the four levels of context to be integrated in a recursive manner into analyses (Reisigl and Wodak, 2009, p. 88; Kendall, 2007, p. 33):
    1. Text-immanent critique seeks '… inconsistencies, self-contradictions, paradoxes and dilemmas in the text-internal or discourse-internal structures' (Reisigl and Wodak, 2009, p. 88);

2. Socio-diagnostic critique looks at the 'persuasive or "manipulative" character of discursive practices' (2009, p. 88); and
3. Prospective critique involves devising effective communication strategies for the future application of research findings.

CASE STUDIES: APPLYING CDA'S CORE IDEAS AND DHA'S ANALYTICAL CONSTRUCTS

In the following case studies we illustrate how research questions intersect with core ideas and analytical constructs of DHA to drive data collection.

Case Study 1: Power in the Postgraduate Supervision Relationship

Introduction and initial research questions/foci

This case study derives from PhD work in South Africa. It focused on empirical work, rather than DHA's more 'classic' emphasis on archival research. It also departed from DHA in that the initial concept and empirical work were at the micro level. But then macro-level discourses operating in the higher education domain began to surface, and the research began exploring those, so ultimately it met DHA's requirement for macro-topic relatedness. The macro-topic in this case is the Knowledge-Based Economy (KBE), which targets education institutions via global neo-liberal economics and quasi-corporate management. As Lemmer (1997, p. 25) observes: 'Lyotard predicted that education, at all levels, is being rapidly commodified, amidst a kind of cultural cynicism towards larger philosophical issues ... Universities are becoming fundamental tools of progress in a very different way from what used to be proposed by the humanistic approach to development'. This issue has been taken up by prominent CDA and DHA scholars (Wodak, 2009, p. 11; Jessop et al., 2008).

Phase 1: Activation and Consultation of Preceding Theoretical Knowledge: Review of the Literature and Explorative Fieldwork

The research began with an Interpretive/Phenomenological orientation and a simple aim – to explore how postgraduate supervisors and their students experience power in the supervision relationship. Underlying assumptions, indeed biases, were that supervision is a tricky relationship, supervisors have the upper hand in terms of power, and they do not always exercise that power in a fair manner.

The first data collection activities were informal conversations with postgraduate students, supervisors, and academic managers. These generated insider information that proved essential for steering the research into relevant channels of enquiry. As noted in the introduction to DHA, early ethnographic work is essential in order to 'ground' the research in real issues/problems and better understand the research context.

Initial fieldwork significantly influenced sampling – an important aspect of data collection. First, it shaped sampling criteria; second, it provided an entrée to potential participants. The informal conversations showed that supervision at the Master's level differs from the PhD level and that to produce rich, in-depth work it would be better to select one qualification level, and opt for single-supervisor relationships. Differences in student and supervisor perspectives revealed in the conversations indicated that the best way to pinpoint contradictions and inconsistencies in supervision would be to solicit matched student–supervisor pairs. This made sampling difficult, as both parties had to be willing to participate, agree to have a third party in the middle of a quite private relationship, and speak openly about any difficulties. Another sampling decision was to solicit participants from different disciplines; this allows for comparisons between different domains of praxis within the university and fits, to some extent, DHA's preference for interdisciplinary work (Reisigl and Wodak, 2009; Weiss and Wodak, 2003). Different disciplines favor different research discourses, so sampling and data collection also provided for interdiscursive analyses. To 'contain' this diversity to some extent, and work within the scope and resources of a PhD project, only one university was selected as the study site. Because the research set up conditions for validity and truth to be debated by diverse actors, at different levels, with differing viewpoints, and from different disciplinary domains that privilege different research and disciplinary discourses – the sampling design satisfies DHA's requisite for triangulation. It also set up data collection to meet DHA's preference for analyses that focus on 'pluri-perspectivity', 'argumentativity' and 'interdisciplinarity' (Reisigl and Wodak, 2009, p. 89).

Simultaneously to the fieldwork was the initial sourcing and reading of literature on academic supervision. Central issues were identified and added to a growing list of questions to guide data collection. The search for a theory of power also began (cf. Scott, 1994). Foucault's insights stood out as the best fit for studying supervision as a relationship, because he views power as a series of relational processes and interrogates how they function. Furthermore, a theory of power linking it to the production of knowledge, and linking knowledge to identity – fits an academic context. After considerable time spent unraveling his constructs and insights, it became obvious that the study would have to shift from an Interpretive/Phenomenological tradition, to Critical Constructivism.

All these early forays into the topic – informal conversations, reading about supervision, finding a theory, and clarifying theoretical constructs – served to sharpen research foci, refine sampling, devise questions for data collection, and identify some a priori analytical codes. In true hermeneutic style, what was read influenced what was heard, and both combined to influence design, which in turn converged with what was subsequently read and heard, as cycles in the project and the analytical thinking slowly unfurled.

Phase 2: Systematic Collection of Data and Context Information

In a critical-constructivist paradigm, power, the construction of reality, and the interruption of inequity or power abuse are all of central interest in terms of the research topic. To be congruent with the ethics of the paradigm it is also vital to be mindful of how power operates in research processes. Semi-structured interviews were planned as the primary data collection procedure, but to balance power between researcher and participants these needed to become much more unstructured, and more like conversations. Key questions and issues were communicated to participants well before appointments, so they were properly informed and had time to think; importantly, they were invited to contribute to the draft discussion agenda. Supervisors and students were met with separately, so that power relations in supervision were not reproduced in the data collection process – although this may have happened anyway, in how they edited their narratives. Some were cautious, some were very relaxed speaking about supervision, and others used the data-gathering process to let off steam, perhaps even say 'the unsayable' knowing they would not see each other's narratives until their supervision was over. These are all considerations of bias, an important aspect of data collection to take into account and report on.

Data collection was augmented with field notes, made as soon as possible after every data collection activity; these proved useful to transcription and analysis. Field notes included information such as the researchers' own experience of meetings, observations of participants' body language, notes about contextual factors that may have influenced the narrative flow (e.g. interruptions, hesitations, emotions), and intuitive 'gut feelings' about the participants' narratives (see Murray, Chapter 17, this volume) and their motivations for selecting them. Probing motivations can help to reveal sub-texts and discourses at play during data collection processes, and in participants' stories. Researchers working in DHA want to know something about how a particular depiction of reality is co-constructed and intersubjectively constituted in the research process itself. But the technique should only be used when data collection ends, because it can interrupt spontaneity.

Another way to balance researcher power is to ask participants regularly for criticisms and insights on the research processes. Two supervisors criticized one data collection strategy, requiring them to identify/formulate, and then explore, metaphors of the supervision relationship. They proclaimed that in speech '…metaphors happen, in context, almost at a sub-conscious level – they're not purposefully crafted'. Nonetheless, they generously entered the spirit of the activity, and interesting data ensued. Another supervisor enjoyed our exchanges but noted that a conversational approach potentially allows researchers even more control over content and trajectories. He also wondered if we strayed into unnecessary tangents. These are challenges to bear in mind when working in an unstructured way. Reflexivity, questioning one's personal positioning, constantly interrogating the research design and processes, and debriefing with colleagues/supervisors, all help in managing researcher subjectivity. A more concrete tactic to ensure that data are not 'edited' by personal filters is to audio-record all meetings.

Phase 3: Selecting, Downsizing, and Processing Data for Analysis

It is essential to transcribe audio-recordings verbatim (see Jenks, Chapter 8, this volume). In DHA this means also accurately capturing all speech effects (e.g. pauses, laughter, hesitation, tone, etc.). With data gathered via conversational approaches and focus group discussions, other important speech effects to transcribe would be turn-taking, politeness, argumentation, and so forth. Another important power and validity technique was to recirculate transcripts to participants for their inputs. Usually their inputs stimulated additional data collection conversations, which continued until saturation.

Selecting and downsizing processes are more relevant to research requiring a large volume of documents – like archival work, or analyses of documents of life – where it is appropriate to trim the corpus of data as research questions shift or become clearer. With elicited data, different standards apply. All data are kept and analysts engage with the whole dataset, as discussed in 'Phase 5'.

Phase 4: Fine-Tuning Research Questions

Central to DHA is that the problem leads the study – not methodology, not theory, nor disciplinary norms. Working with Foucault's theoretical constructs pointed to a weakness in the original conceptualization of the problem, a weakness confirmed in data from supervisors: there was not enough focus in the literature review on higher education policies and global influences on universities. Data suggested that discourses operating via these channels influenced academic and managerial practices, and positioned subjects (academics and students) in particular ways in relation to one another, to the university context, and to the crux of postgraduate studies: the thesis itself. The original formulation marginalized the role of sociopolitical and historical contextual factors essential in DHA analyses. Relevant policies were sourced, discourses in them identified, and then integrated into the final analysis. The research focus expanded to exploring institutional and interpersonal power relations between postgraduate supervisors, their students, and the university domain.

Phase 5: Qualitative Pilot Data Analysis

As noted earlier, researchers should not discard or ignore elicited data that appear marginal, extraneous or irrelevant – because the data could prove relevant as the research progresses. Researchers should reflect on whether 'marginal' data may be counterfactual, that is, evidence for viewpoints that are valid-in-the-world, but filtered out by the researcher's own aims, assumptions, or preferences. They must also avoid privileging single maverick views or statements because of their (often sensational) appeal. Such caution was needed in this case study: there were highly emotive statements and extreme stories of power being inequitably exercised.

We now offer a summary of key findings to show how the data collection processes interfaced with information from the literature to generate analyses that satisfy DHA's core ideas and analytical criteria. One aspect of critique involves analyzing 'power in discourse' (Wodak, 1996, p. 18), which surfaces in linguistic effects. A range of these in participants' narrations, including tone, body language, and metaphor, pointed to interpersonal and institutional power. We focus here on genre – the socially endorsed ways in which language is used, during particular types of social activity, by different people or communities of practice (Reisigl and Wodak, 2009, p. 90; Wodak and Meyer, 2009). Genre surfaced in supervisors' complaints about underprepared students who had not mastered academic discourse despite having undergraduate degrees. Some students concurred: the ideas and the language of critical thinking in relation to authoritative texts felt alien to them. Some also had difficulty with the next level of critical thought – reflexivity – in relation to their own work. Practices associated with critical thinking were also alien to some: diffident students could not find their own voice because they viewed supervisors as omnipotent and all-knowing.

Analyses also focused on 'power over discourse' (Wodak, 1996, p. 18). Supervisors who helped struggling students to access academic discourse were sensitive to the fact that they generally come from contexts that remain historically disadvantaged by Apartheid education. Undergraduate education had done little to fix this, which was partly due to the 'global neo-liberal economic' discourse of the Knowledge-Based Economy (KBE) – which demands 'efficient' throughput and values practical skills-building over critical aptitude. Injunctions for throughput and to 'publish or perish' are normative rules in KBE – rules filtering down into local university contexts via corporate-style management cycles of surveillance, assessment and feedback (reward/punishment). These cycles shape supervision, including supervisors' expectations, and impact on the balance of autonomy and dependence in power relations between supervisors and students. Some supervisors assisted students toward, and allowed time for, developing critical thinking – their practices were attuned to values that resist 'commercial' hegemony. Others directed students down 'easy' research paths that more easily met time constraints and throughput pressures. Besides contestations between educational discourses (i.e. anarchic educational leadership discourse and humanistic discourse), analyses uncovered different research discourses at work (structural vs. postmodern orientations), as well as disciplinary discourses (e.g. holism; various psychology theories) – all of which shaped power relations in supervision.

Importantly, the data challenged initial assumptions: students exercised power in unexpected and sometimes oblique ways; supervisors generally did their best to deliver quality and/or quantity; and both parties had less individual autonomy than anticipated in relation to overarching discourses operating in the university domain.

Viewing data through the core ideas underpinning DHA enabled analyses of institutional and interpersonal power relations within discourses and across discourses – meeting DHA's interest in interdiscursivity. Core ideas also enabled the identification of two products of power processes in supervision: the thesis as an extrinsic product of education processes (thesis-as-product) and the person as an intrinsic product of learning processes (person-as-product). Analyses show how, in turn, these products converge to impact on the mediation of knowledge in the educational domain.

Reiterations of Phases

Shifting to a critical-constructivist paradigm and extending the literature review to include higher education policy and global influences on universities required additional data-gathering. This reiteration of two research phases significantly enriched subsequent analyses. The additional data and information enhanced the capacity of analyses to provide for DHA's three interrelated dimensions of critique: text-immanent critique, socio-diagnostic critique, and prospective critique (Reisigl and Wodak, 2009, p. 88). The latter is discussed next.

Final Phase: Application of Findings (Prospective Critique)

Findings were published via various academic platforms. And insights continue to be shared in workshops and seminars on postgraduate supervision; they also shape our own supervision practices.

Case Study 2: Transformation of Interracial Relations in Student Residences: Using Interviews and Participant Observation as Data Collection Methods for Analyzing Discourses

Introduction and Initial Research Questions/Foci

This case study demonstrates how an ethnographic (see Buscatto, Chapter 21, this volume) and interview (see Roulston and Choi, Chapter 15, this volume) approach to data collection can be used to analyze discourses. The focus is on how typical DHA features and concepts – such as reflexivity, critique, discourse, and context – shape the data collection strategy. Based primarily on 'elicited data' (for the distinction between naturalistic and elicited data, see Potter and Shaw, Chapter 12, this volume), the research phases of this case study form part of a hermeneutic, circular process, and are more closely intertwined than in other DHA projects. Not only may the research questions shift and be fine-tuned (Phase 4) throughout the entire project, but the systematic data collection (2), selection (3) and analysis (5) take place continuously.

The case study – conducted by the second author, following a preceding study initiated by the third author (Elliker et al., 2013) – examined a transformation process on a South African university campus that concerns the integration of historically segregated student residences with regard to racial population categories, namely 'black', 'white', 'colored', and 'Asian'. Initiated by the university administration after the end of Apartheid, the integration process faced protests and resistance particularly from the students who used to run the residences almost autonomously. The initial research question was to study how discourses related to race and ethnicity shaped the viewpoints of and relations between the different actors in this process. Typical for DHA projects, the study is characterized by a problem-orientation, as it deals with what most of the involved actors consider to be societal problems – among others, the historical legacy of racial segregation and its continued relevance in reproducing inequalities – and it examines a process directed at interrupting social inequalities. While some of these are historically imposed 'top-down' inequalities (van Dijk, 1993), many were constituted 'bottom-up', such as factions of the students resisting the racial integration of the residences.

Phase 1: Activation and Consultation of Preceding Theoretical Knowledge: Review of the Literature and Explorative Fieldwork

Preliminary exploratory fieldwork may entail all types of data collection strategies: participant observation, interviews, and any kind of natural data. In terms of conceiving a data collection strategy, this preliminary fieldwork: (a) should provide (provisional) clarity in terms of data collection methods, how they serve to identify and analyze the discourses, and how these methods allow discourses to be distinguished from other relevant semiotic practices in the social context(s) in which they are used; and (b) should furthermore sensitize the researcher to relevant critical dimensions that may impact the data collection.

a A data collection strategy must be developed with regard to the empirical field under investigation. The exploratory ethnographic fieldwork demonstrated that the residences formed groups with their own 'idiocultures' (Fine, 2010) that provide a host of relevant local categories and semiotic practices. As 'discursive universes', they constituted a local context in which discourses were reproduced. This warranted the choice of an ethnographic data collection strategy, as the typical semiotic practices that belonged to the residence culture needed to be distinguished from the discourse-related viewpoints that actors employed in re-contextualizing these local practices. The preliminary fieldwork also demonstrated that in many of these situations, specific viewpoints would be marginalized or silenced. To explore these voices, participant observation was complemented with semi-structured interviews that were held outside the residences.

b Any data collection process needs to consider the sociopolitical and historical context. In South Africa, this concerns historically formalized, racial segregation whose legacy manifests itself in the present by perpetuating the historic inequalities through different processes (Seekings and Nattrass, 2002). While racial categories are important in the transformation process (e.g. as a basis for affirmative action), they may also transport problematic essentializing notions that reify inequalities (Brubaker, 2002). Data collection methods must allow to critically reflect such phenomena; in the case at hand, the data collection methods needed to demonstrate how and to what purposes racial categories were used in the daily life of the student residences, but at the same time critically investigate the seemingly omnipresent salience of these categories. While participant observation allowed identification of the use of these categories in the daily residence life, interviews provided a way to collect more differentiated and nuanced data on the meaning of these racial categories.

In addition, the categorization of the researcher as 'white' (among other categorizations) shaped his relationship with the research participants: While for white Afrikaans-speaking students, this categorization implied a 'liberal' stance, black students associated it with a more 'conservative' position; both assumed that the researcher had a personal and 'categorical' stake in the integration process. The re-positioning of the researcher as 'European' provided (partially) a way to renegotiate a position that was regarded as not immediately involved in local matters; it also stimulated fruitful descriptive narrations as the researcher was assumed not to be familiar with the South African situation. Any data collection process must reflect on how such self- and other-categorizations may impact the production of data in relation to the discourses of interest.

Phase 2: Systematic Collection of Data and Context Information

A data collection strategy must consider how the semiotic practices of interest can be analyzed through different types of data and how the epistemological assumptions of the methods fit together. This section exemplifies this by discussing two of the three primary data collection methods: interviews and participant observation (naturally occurring artifacts were also used). As DHA aims at analyzing socially constitutive semiotic practices, interview methods must allow interview partners to share what is relevant to them. There is, meanwhile, a broad range of open-ended, semi-structured interview methods directed at this aim (Gubrium et al., 2012). They differ, however, in their epistemological assumptions, for example, with regard to what extent interview data may be taken as representing a reality outside the interview situation or whether interview data reveal their meaning on an implicit or explicit level. For this case study, 'problem-centered interviews' (PCIs; Witzel and Reiter, 2012) were chosen. The PCI is based on an interpretive yet realist approach to research that also underpinned our ethnographic fieldwork (Adler and Adler, 2008). As 'discursive-dialogic reconstructions of a problem' (Witzel and Reiter, 2012, p. 18), PCIs are mainly guided by three processes: problem-centering (the exploration of specific issues that constitute a relevant everyday problem), process orientation, and object orientation. Interviews usually follow three phases: in a first step, the researcher opens the interview with a short input designed to stimulate a long narration of the interview partner. After this initial narration, the interviewer continues with questions along the themes of interest that were prepared in advance, but remains open for the interview to go into a direction that is relevant for the interview partner. Third, the interviewer asks questions that are directed at elaborating more on what was said previously in the interview. During this stage, the PCI also employs communicative strategies that may ask for the clarification of contradictions or even (cautiously) thematize issues that are experienced as contested or uncomfortable. It is in this sense that the PCI strategy also involves a form of narrative and socio-diagnostic critique. This not only warrants reflexivity from the researcher but also grants the interview partner a reflexive role. The triangulation of ethnographic and interview data (see Flick, Chapter 34, this volume) facilitated thematizing contradictions and asking critical questions during the interviews, as the researcher could refer to shared everyday experiences with the interview participant.

An ethnoscience approach to participant observation (Spradley, 1979, 1980) – sharing the realist as well as interpretive underpinning of PCI – was used for mainly four purposes: first, it served to observe the use and effects of discourses in everyday settings, particularly in light of the preliminary discussion that indicated that the very same processes might be conceived and framed differently by different actors; second, observations allowed to register actions relevant for the transformation process but taken for granted to such an extent that they would not explicitly be narrated in the interviews; third, stays in the residence were used for ethnographic interviews; and fourth, as mentioned above, the participant observation established a shared everyday experience with the interviewees which could be referred to in the interview setting.

Phase 3: Selecting, Downsizing, and Processing Data for Analysis

While many DHA studies are based on relatively large numbers of documents and hence face the challenge of downsizing data for analysis, projects primarily based on ethnographic and interview data may result in a comparatively small data corpus. The challenge of this type of data collection lies in applying a sampling strategy that initially covers a broad range of semiotic practices while over time being aligned with and focused on the refined research questions. Qualitative research projects usually employ some kind of purposeful sampling. The case study applied the strategy of 'theoretical sampling' (see Schreier, Chapter 6, this volume) as developed within the Grounded Theory approach (Corbin and Strauss, 2008). Based on the literature review, the theoretical concepts, preliminary data analyses, and hypotheses are developed with regard to what the relevant dimensions are, along which a maximally contrasting data sample will contribute new empirical phenomena and theoretical insights. Once the range of typical phenomena has been explored through collecting data based on maximal contrasts, the phenomena are differentiated and saturated by collecting data based on minimal contrasts. In the case study, interview participants were initially selected along ethnic and racial categories; in later stages, interview partners who differed in terms of seniority with regard to the internal residence hierarchy were also selected. In terms of ethnographic fieldwork, the initial observations were geared toward describing the residence life broadly. Over time, the range of situations was continually narrowed, and focused in the end on a few recurring situations that proved particularly fruitful for reconstructing the discourses that were central to negotiations pertaining to the integration process.

Phase 4: Fine-Tuning Research Questions

In the circular DHA research process, reiterating the research phases is directed at discovering, reconstructing, and analytically focusing on those semiotic practices that are socially constitutive for the actors in the social field under investigation. What is relevant for the actors in the field may deviate from what the researcher expects at the outset. As a consequence, the research questions may shift throughout the entire data collection process (and may warrant the use of different or additional theories). They are fine-tuned in conjunction with continued data analysis (Phase 5). The phases of data collection should be increasingly focused in such a way that the additionally produced data speak directly to the refined research questions. In the case study, initially aimed at analyzing how race- and ethnicity-related discourses shaped the viewpoints of and relations between the different actors, the focus was broadened to include the question of how relatively resilient local practices contribute to the formation of differential power relations (which warranted the use of additional theories, for example, on how micro-hierarchies shape the power structure of groups). As a consequence, the exclusive focus on discourses shifted to the question of how local practices were contextualized and re-contextualized by different race- and ethnicity-related discourses.

Phase 5: Qualitative Pilot Data Analysis

Data analysis serves two main purposes: while overall directed at reconstructing and analyzing discourses, it is continuously employed to guide the sampling process, the data collection, and to refine the research questions (Phases 2–4). While there is a broad range of suitable qualitative data analysis methods (Flick, 2014), the data analysis methods must be underpinned by a similar epistemology as the data collection methods. In the case at hand, both data collection methods shared a realist approach to studying social realities; the data collected through PCIs were thus analyzed with the same methodology developed for the ethnoscience approach to ethnography (Spradley, 1979, 1980). The overall analytic approach is abductive: the reconstruction and identification of typical elements and relations in the data go along with using theoretical notions as sensitizing concepts. While this ensures the adequacy of the theoretical concepts, it aims at discovering new phenomena in the data that go beyond existing explanations and understandings (see Kennedy and Thornberg, Chapter 4, this volume).

The case study could demonstrate that features of the residence cultures were re-contextualized differently depending on the discourses that the students employed. With an analytical focus on the semiotic practices related to racial categories – a macro-topic in South African society – two dominant discourses were identified: a discourse of 'racial equality' and a discourse of 'culture'. Through participant observation data, the interdiscursive relationships, not just between these two discourses, but also between the discourses and the residence cultures, were analyzed. These two discourses were reconstructed through continued data analysis that, in turn, informed and focused further data collection.

Reiterations of Phases

Reiterating the phases ensures a continued sharpening of the focus on socially relevant semiotic practices and the alignment of the research questions with this focus. Data collection is continued to the point of theoretical and empirical saturation, that is, when additionally produced data do not contribute to further analytical insights, do not contribute elements that substantially add to the already discovered discourses, and do not suggest the existence of discourses that have been neglected so far. In the case study, the data collection process continued to the point where the two main discourses and the relevant elements of residences culture could be described in an empirically saturated manner.

Final Phase: Application of Findings (Prospective Critique)

The study examined a transformation process that was itself directed at interrupting social inequalities. The findings of the study were shared with the heads of the student residences, allowing a partial consideration of the findings in the ongoing transformation process. Some of the findings were published in an academic context.

CONCLUSION

After briefly exploring what discourse is and what Discourse Analysis (DA) involves, we introduced Critical Discourse Analysis (CDA) and the core ideas underpinning it. The chapter showcased one of many different approaches to CDA – the Discourse-Historical Approach (DHA). Key features and analytical constructs of DHA were presented in preparation for their illustration in two case studies. The case studies do not slavishly follow DHA, but integrate key concepts with others from the discourse analytical field. As Jørgensen and Phillips (2002, p. 4) note: 'multiperspectival work is not only permissible but positively valued in most forms of discourse analysis'.

DHA studies undergo – as many other qualitative approaches do – a shift of attention from 'traditional' data forms and sources toward non-verbal (semiotic, multimodal, visual) interactions and communications such as gestures, images, film, and transmedia projects. Recent research investigates, inter alia, multimedia semiotics, multiple timescales and hypertexts (for a discussion of this in DHA, see Wodak and Meyer, 2009). Both shifts bring along theoretical and empirical challenges that warrant further conceptual work and methodological reflections to adapt, redefine, and even reinvent qualitative data collection methods and the ways they are employed to analyze discourses.

FURTHER READING

Jørgensen, Marianne and Phillips, Louise (2002) *Discourse Analysis as Theory and Method*. London: Sage.

Keller, Reiner (2013) *Doing Discourse Research*. Thousand Oaks: Sage.
Wodak, Ruth (2011) *The Discourse of Politics in Action: Politics as Usual*. Basingstoke: Palgrave.

REFERENCES

Adler, Patricia A. and Adler, Peter (2008) 'Of rhetoric and representation: The four faces of ethnography', *The Sociological Quarterly*, 49(1): 1–30.
Berger, Peter L. and Luckmann, Thomas (1966) *The Social Construction of Reality: A Treatise in the Sociology of Knowledge*. New York: Doubleday.
Bourdieu, Pierre and Wacquant, Loïc J. D. (1992) *An Invitation to Reflexive Sociology*. Cambridge: Polity Press and Blackwell.
Brubaker, Rogers (2002) 'Ethnicity without groups', *Archives Européennes de Sociologie/European Journal of Sociology*, 43(2): 163–89.
Cameron, Deborah (2001) *Working with Spoken Discourse*. Thousand Oaks: Sage.
Cameron, Deborah (2006) *On Language and Sexual Politics*. London: Routledge.
Chandler, Daniel (2007) *Semiotics: The Basics* (2nd edn). London: Routledge.
Corbin, Juliet and Strauss, Anselm (2008) *Basics of Qualitative Research. Techniques and Procedures for Developing Grounded Theory* (3rd edn). Thousand Oaks: Sage (1st edn, 1990).
Eagleton, Terry (1991) *Ideology: An Introduction*. London: Verso.
Elliker, Florian, Coetzee, Jan K. and Kotze, P. Conrad (2013) 'On the interpretive work of reconstructing discourses and their local contexts', *Forum Qualitative Sozialforschung/Forum: Qualitative Social Research*, 14(3): Art. 4 (http://nbn-resolving.de/urn:nbn:de:0114-fqs130342).
Fairclough, Norman (2003) *Analysing Discourse: Textual Analysis for Social Research*. London and New York: Routledge.
Fine, Gary A. (2010) 'The sociology of the local: action and its publics', *Sociological Theory*, 28(4): 355–76.
Flick, Uwe (ed.) (2014) *The Sage Handbook of Qualitative Data Analysis*. London: Sage.
Foucault, Michel (1982) 'The subject and power', in John Scott (ed.), *Power: Critical*

Concepts (1996). London: Routledge, pp. 218–33.

Foucault, Michel (1988) *Politics, Philosophy, Culture: Interviews and Other Writings 1977–1984* (edited by Lawrence D. Kritzman). New York: Routledge.

Foucault, Michel (1996) *Foucault Live: Collected Interviews, 1961–1984* (edited by Sylvère Lotringer). New York: Semiotext.

Gubrium, Jaber F., Holstein, James A., Marvasti, Amir B. and McKinney, Karyn D. (2012) *The Sage Handbook of Interview Research. The Complexity of the Craft* (2nd edn). Thousand Oaks, CA: Sage (1st edn, 2002).

Jessop, Bob, Fairclough, Norman and Wodak, Ruth (2008) *Education and the Knowledge-based Economy in Europe*. La Vergne, Tennessee: Lightning Source.

Jørgensen, Marianne and Phillips, Louise (2002). *Discourse Analysis as Theory and Method*. London: Sage.

Keller, Reiner (2011) 'The sociology of knowledge approach to discourse (SKAD)', *Human Studies*, 34: 34–65.

Keller, Reiner (2013) *Doing Discourse Research* (Tr. B. Jenner). London: Sage.

Kendall, Gavin (2007) 'What is critical discourse analysis?', *Forum Qualitative Sozialforschung/Forum: Qualitative Social Research*, 8(2): Art. 29 (http://nbn-resolving.de/urn:nbn:de:0114-fqs0702297).

Kendall, Gavin and Wickham, Gary (1999) *Using Foucault's Methods*. London: Sage.

Kincheloe, Joe L., McLaren, Peter and Steinberg, Shirley R. (2011) 'Critical pedagogy and qualitative research', in Norman K. Denzin and Yvonna S. Lincoln (eds.), *The SAGE Handbook of Qualitative Research* (4th edn). London: Sage, pp. 163–77.

Lemmer, Eleanor M. (1997) 'A new context for the University? Postmodern strands in international patterns of higher education policy and practice', Inaugural address: International Review of University Reform, September 18, 1997, *Progressia*, 20(1): 16–33.

Nias, Jennifer (ed.) (1993) *The Human Nature of Learning: Selections from the Work of M. L. J. 'Jane' Abercrombie*. Buckingham: Open University Press.

Phillips, Denis C. (1990) *Philosophy, Science and Social Inquiry: Contemporary Methodological Controversies in Social Science and Related Applied Fields of Research*. Oxford: Pergamon Press.

Potter, Jonathan and Wetherell, Margaret (1987) *Discourse and Social Psychology: Beyond Attitudes and Behaviour*. London and Newbury Park, CA: Sage.

Rau, Asta (2004) *Supervision: A Foucaultian exploration of institutional and interpersonal power relations between postgraduate supervisors, their students and the university domain*. Grahamstown: Rhodes University (http://hdl.handle.net/10962/d1003671).

Rau, Asta (2008) 'Anarchic educational leadership: An alternative approach to postgraduate supervision', *Indo-Pacific Journal of Phenomenology (IPJP)*, 8: 1–17. Special Edition: Phenomenology and Education (http://www.ipjp.org/index.php?option=com_jdownloads&task=download.send&id=21&catid=6&m=0&Itemid=318).

Reisigl, Martin and Wodak, Ruth (2009) 'The discourse-historical approach (DHA)', in Ruth Wodak and Michael Meyer (eds.), *Methods for Critical Discourse Analysis* (2nd rev. edn). London: Sage, pp. 87–119.

Schütz, Alfred (1932) *The Phenomenology of the Social World*. Evanston, IL: Northwestern University Press.

Schütz, Alfred and Luckmann, Thomas (1974) *The Structures of the Life-World. Vol. 1*. London: Heinemann.

Schütz, Alfred and Luckmann, Thomas (1989) *The Structures of the Life-World. Vol. 2*. London: Heinemann.

Scott, John (ed.) (1994) *Power: Critical Concepts, Three Volumes*. London: Routledge.

Seekings, Jeremy and Nattrass, Nicoli (2002) 'Class, distribution and redistribution in Post-Apartheid South Africa', *Transformation: Critical Perspectives on Southern Africa*, 50: 1–30.

Spradley, James P. (1979) *The Ethnographic Interview*. New York, Chicago, London: Holt, Rinehart & Winston.

Spradley, James P. (1980) *Participant Observation*. New York, Chicago, London: Holt, Rinehart & Winston.

Van Dijk, Teun A. (1993) 'Principles of critical discourse analysis', *Discourse & Society*, 4(2): 249–83.

Van Dijk, Teun A. (1996) 'Discourse, power and access', in Carmen-Rosa Caldas-Coulthard and Malcolm Coulthard (eds.), *Texts and*

Practices: Readings in Critical Discourse Analysis. London: Routledge, pp. 84–104.

Weiss, Gilbert and Wodak, Ruth (eds.) (2003) *Critical Discourse Analysis: Theory and Interdisciplinarity*. London: Palgrave Macmillan.

Wilkinson, Sue and Kitzinger, Celia (eds.) (1995) *Feminism and Discourse: Psychological Perspectives*. Thousand Oaks, CA: Sage.

Witzel, Andreas and Reiter, Herwig (2012) *The Problem-centred Interview. Principles and Practices*. London: Sage.

Wodak, Ruth (1996) *Disorders of Discourse*. Michigan: Longman.

Wodak, Ruth (2000) 'Does sociolinguistics need social theory? New perspectives in Critical Discourse Analysis', Keynote speech, Sociolinguistics Symposium 2000, The Interface between Linguistics and Social Theory, University of the West of England, Bristol, 27 April 2000.

Wodak, Ruth (2009) 'Critical discourse analysis: History, agenda, theory, and methodology', in Ruth Wodak and Michael Meyer (eds.), *Methods for Critical Discourse Analysis* (2nd rev. edn). London: Sage, pp. 1–33.

Wodak, Ruth (2014) 'Critical discourse analysis', in Constant Leung and Brian V. Street (eds.), *The Routledge Companion to English Studies*. Oxford: Routledge, pp. 302–16.

Wodak, Ruth and Meyer, Michael (eds.) (2001) *Methods of Critical Discourse Analysis* (1st edn). London: Sage.

Wodak, Ruth and Meyer, Michael (eds.) (2009) *Methods for Critical Discourse Analysis* (2nd edn). London: Sage.

Observations

David Wästerfors

Qualitative researchers often need observations of people, their actions and settings, but apart from that general direction it is hard to pinpoint a superior kind of observational data. What to observe, and how, depends on the project. In this chapter I will try to show how the preferable kind of observations is a highly varied category. Then I will argue that there are still particular and quite fundamental qualities to strive for, even though every project is distinctive in its character. But first, let me start with the general aims of observations, the theoretical assumptions of the approach and its historical background.

COLLECTING DATA BY OBSERVATIONS

What social scientists typically aim for when making observations is to gather data on groups and people in their everyday lives. An observer often participates in daily routines of a setting and produces written accounts of ongoing interactions.

The observer usually tries to develop relations with the people in the setting and get as close as possible to their activities and experiences. Physical and social proximity is essential (Emerson et al., 1995, pp. 1–2). An opposite approach is 'arm chair research', where the researcher stays in the office and relies on second-hand reports. To collect observational data is to generate first-hand reports: to see, hear, feel and 'be there' personally. Drawing on field presence the researcher writes field notes that capture slices of social practice.

Erving Goffman (2001, p. 154) emphasizes the personal and corporal character of observations. You get data, he argues, 'by subjecting yourself, your own body and your own personality, and your own social situation, to the set of contingencies that play upon a set of individuals'. The aim is to get into and sustain relations to others as they respond to 'what life does to them'. It is not just a matter of listening and writing down what people say, it is a matter of 'tuning up' your body in relation to the setting, and being able to note also 'minor grunts and groans', subtle gestures and bodily responses (Goffman, 2001, pp. 154–5). The observer is not acting like an interviewer or a listener but as a witness.

Now it might sound like observations are purely inductive but that is a simplification. Observers do underline the importance of being open to anything, writing inclusive field notes, not imposing exogenous meanings, and so on (Goffman, 2001; Emerson et al., 1995), but the general advice is not to pretend to be blank or unprejudiced. The advice is that it is possible and recommendable to learn from a field. Observers are convinced that there are things 'out there' that we do not know despite all the books and articles we have read. There are interactions and processes, performances and routines, riddles and ambiguities that we cannot figure out at the desk.

This does not suggest pure induction (see Kennedy and Thornberg, Chapter 4, this volume) but, rather, empirical research that communicates with theory and previous research. In the seminal work *Street Corner Society*, William Foote Whyte (1943/1993, p. 287) talks about 'to take the theory out in the field', that is to animate theory and challenge it with observations. To get this process going, the researcher's subject is put to use. So when a fieldworker interacts with those studied (thereby also having some impact on them) it should not be seen as 'contaminating' the data. The fieldworker needs to get sensitive to how she is seen and treated by field members, and to use this information as a clue to understanding what is going on (Emerson et al., 1995, p. 3).

To enter the worlds of other people, to encounter their activities and concerns first hand and close up – that is the fieldworker's 'first commitment' (Emerson, 2001, p. 1; see Bengry, Chapter 7, this volume). On top of that, one continually has to grapple with a range of issues that never will be completely settled – for instance the tension between being involved and being detached, and between attending to the field and attending to how one constructs and represents one's observations of the field (Atkinson, 2001; Emerson, 2001, pp. 22–4).

In any case, 'being there' and witnessing are the foundation. It can be traced back to an ethnographic turn in anthropology in the beginning of the twentieth century (Emerson, 2001, p. 5, also see Buscatto, Chapter 21, this volume). A fieldworker in anthropology was at that point increasingly being seen not as an 'inquirer', relying on interviews and questionnaires, but as an observer. Anthropologists had started to get uneasy with established theories about others' cultures across the world and wanted to obtain more original and accurate data, and they had started to distrust missionaries and other untrained fieldworkers. Longer stays in the field, distance to colonial interpreters and direct contact with field members became the method, as in Bronislaw Malinowski's somewhat idealized approach (Emerson, 2001, pp. 6–8).

This kind of observation was then imported into sociology during the first decade of the twentieth century. It came to flourish in the Chicago school and its ambitions to propel students out into various social worlds within a sprawling metropolis (Emerson, 2001, p. 10). Field research could very well include documents, statistics and interviews but firsthand observations came to be distinguishing, for instance in Nels Anderson's *The Hobo* (1923/1961) and Paul G. Cressey's *The Taxi Dance Hall* (1932). William Foote Whyte's *Street Corner Society* (1943) turned into the 'substantive exemplar' (Emerson, 2001, p. 13), a model for generations of observers. Whyte argued that staying in 'Cornerville' – the Italian slum he was investigating – and describing people's activities in detail was the only way to gain knowledge of local life.

Also Erving Goffman's *Asylums* (1961/1990) remains a strong example. By spending a year in the company of patients at St. Elizabeth's Hospital in Washington, DC, Goffman managed to collect observational data on the social situation of inmates in what he identified as 'total institutions'. He specified the moral career of the inmates, the institution's privilege system and mortifying powers, and the inmates' adjustments and manipulations. Not only the formal features of an institution could be observed but also the informal ones, the 'underlife' (Goffman, 1961/1990, p. 176). *Asylums* could hardly have been written if Goffman had not been present in the 'daily round of petty contingencies' to which institutional members are subject (Goffman, 1961/1990, p. x). His everyday observations played a crucial role.

Social scientists have employed observations to analyze countless things. Crimes and social problems, subcultures and organizations, elites and social movements, youth and the elderly, family life and childhood, professionals and businessmen, face-to-face behavior and Internet variants – observations can be used all over the place. There are no limits other than the practicalities of getting access and the ethics of not exposing people's identities or threatening their integrity. No fieldworker should force a study upon people, and nowadays hidden observations are more or less deemed unethical. Normally, researchers ask for consent. An observation study in disguise needs very good reasons to be done, even though a completely transparent account of any study can be hard to present to field members (for a more comprehensive ethical discussion, see Buscatto, Chapter 21, this volume).

Still we may ask ourselves: observing what? I will now dive into a more contemporary project to illustrate how a particular style of doing observations can be developed. It is not intended as The Example but as one example. From this we may outline some principles of how to think about observations more concretely, especially as a beginner.

IT DEPENDS ON THE PROJECT

Let's say a researcher is involved in a project on power and the elderly (see Stephens et al., Chapter 40, this volume), more precisely: residents' influence at nursing homes (Harnett, 2010). Now any observation on people, actions and settings at nursing homes will not do. The researcher might very well find it intriguing to do crossword puzzles together with residents, and listen to their winding life stories over family photos, but that will most likely not generate any direct picture of the residents' influence.

Similarly, time spent among staff members, listening to their storytelling about weekends, vacations and family life, for instance, would not necessarily advance the project. The researcher will have to 'zoom in' on interactions between residents and staff in which power somehow stands out as crucial. She will probably find it especially rewarding to zoom in on particular interactions in which residents try to do things that staff members find improper, irritating or different: asking for an extra shower, demanding another blouse instead of the one staff members offer, requesting more time outdoors, and so on.

In such interactions, the issue of power in nursing homes will most likely become reportable in a much clearer sense than in other interactions (Harnett, 2010, pp. 295–99). As Emerson and his colleagues recommend: select a site in which the pursued phenomenon is 'particularly salient', and where its various issues 'concern the members' (Emerson et al., 1995, p. 134).

Such was the case for Tove Harnett (2010). She had worked part-time as a nursing aide for seven years and knew very well the strongly routinized regime that seldom facilitated residents' influence; however, she had not tried to write it up ethnographically. Still, doing crossword puzzles and looking at photo albums of family members also came to be rewarding. As a former caregiver, Harnett (2010, p. 294) wanted to balance her role at the nursing home at issue by spending time with residents in non-caregiving situations. Harnett tried to immerse herself in the setting, as ethnographers recommend (Emerson et al., 1995), but from the start, she was more familiar with the staff members' situation than that of the residents, and therefore had to work to get closer to the latter to limit one-sided participation (Harnett, 2010, p. 294). To spend time with residents could teach the researcher something on their practicalities and tempo, their viewpoints and backgrounds, their concerns.

What would have happened if the researcher had skipped the crosswords and family photos, and went directly to observing staff–resident interactions when residents articulated requests? How would another researcher have done without the years-long experience of working as a nursing aide? The only thing we know for sure is that each project is special in its composition of (a) researcher, (b) setting and (c) observed phenomena, and that each project, therefore, needs careful consideration before even tentatively defining what kind of observations one should strive for. Such considerations are probably best accomplished in tight relation to the setting at issue, and as an ongoing process rather than a prefabricated scheme.

Harnett felt a bit closer to staff than to residents as she entered the nursing home and started to interact with its members. If somebody would have said to her then, 'Keep away from the crosswords and go directly for residents' requests', as an observational recommendation, the study might have been much more insensitive to precisely those requests. If, on the contrary, the ethnographer allows herself to feel the need to get closer to residents' 'non-caregiving situations' that may equip her with a sort of observational sensitivity toward the fact that (1) residents typically find themselves in situations that are constituted far from the formal logic of running a nursing home as a whole, and that (2) 'caregiving situations' may be given a considerably broader definition than staff members typically grant.

Getting help fetching a pen for one's crossword, or reaching a photo album at the top of a shelf – if 'care' is defined from the standpoint of a given resident's everyday habits, it might stretch far beyond routinized bed-and-body caregiving work (Gubrium, 1975/1997, p. 124).

'Immersion', as Emerson et al. (1995, p. 2) write, 'gives the fieldworker access to the fluidity of others' lives and enhances his sensitivity'.

Ideal observational data, then, is hard to define. It depends on the researcher's interest and previous experiences, on his or her 'gaze' or theoretical perspective, on how the project unfolds in terms of relations, emotions and networks. A fieldworker is a person whose biography not only precedes the project and therefore forms it, but also gets actualized and developed in and through it. So to, beforehand, recommend precisely 'what to look for' is not possible. It is a matter of local negotiations with – and theoretical constructions of – the field.

Even if we just say 'try to get close to the phenomenon', 'zoom in on what the project is about', we may find ourselves asking, 'Well, what are the limits of this phenomenon, really?', and 'Given what I now see and hear, shouldn't I modify my project, or change it radically?' No matter how neat a project proposal looks on paper, a fieldworker may still stand in a given setting and strongly sense the need for adjustments.

... BUT THERE ARE STILL RECOGNIZED QUALITIES TO AIM FOR

By now I hope it is clear that I argue that any advice about observations must be contextually and reflexively situated (also see Buscatto, Chapter 21, this volume). For readers of method books, this comes as no surprise. Consider these excerpts from acknowledged authors:

> The ethnographer cannot take in everything; rather, he will, in conjunction with those in the setting, develop certain perspectives by engaging in some activities and relationships rather than others. Moreover, it will often be the case that relationships with those under study follow political fault lines in the setting, exposing the ethnographer selectively to varying priorities and points of view. As a result, the task for the ethnographer is not to determine 'the truth' but to reveal the multiple truths apparent in others' lives. (Emerson et al., 1995, p. 3)

> [...] we cannot include every detail and every scrap of knowledge. Not only are time and space at a premium in the production of any written account, so too is the reader's attention. Descriptions and exemplifications that are too dense, too detailed or too protracted will not normally lead to a usable text. [...] the ethnographer needs to construct accounts through partial, selective reporting. (Hammersley and Atkinson, 1983/2007, p. 198)

Such formulations underline how impossible it is to 'just observe'. What I would like to stress, though, is that there are still some quite uncontroversial qualities to aim for, more or less regardless of field relations, personal or theoretical biases and academic expectations. Three of them can be called (1) details, (2) sequences and (3) atmosphere. This is my argument: If the observer attends to some reasonable amount of specific and fine facets of what people do and say (details), and if the observer captures how things are accomplished in strings or chains of actions or practices (sequences), then he or she will most likely generate interesting material to draw on. The observer will also be helped if he or she finds a way to articulate what others experience wordlessly (atmosphere): the mood, the 'air' or tone of a social environment. If, on the other hand, the observer does *not* take these qualities into account at all, there might be difficulties in conducting analyses with the observational data as a base.

I will now try to exemplify these qualities and illustrate how they are embedded into established ethnographic traditions. I am certainly not arguing that these qualities would be the only ones to strive for. Rather, my aim is to review them in order to continue to, as Emerson and his colleagues write, 'demystify' ethnographic practices (Emerson et al., 1995, p. xii).

Details

There is a recurrent ideal of specification in qualitative observations, that one must not stay at general levels, not go into abstract or normative reasoning, and not summarize or jump to conclusions or lose oneself in theoretical models. An observer strives for details.

Looking at two teachers at work, for instance, a trained ethnographer would hardly be pleased with a note saying 'They went into a boring room and started an argument'. In relation to such a note, he or she would probably ask a series of self-reflexive questions to produce details. What, more precisely, made the room appear 'boring'? Did others in the field also act as if they defined it so? What was this 'argument' about? What words and gestures were employed? What happened before and after?

Even if an observer finds a note like this in the notebook at the end of the day, there are probably some remembrances of the episode that could be exposed to fill out details. Jottings are, as Emerson and his colleagues state, later developed into 'full field notes' (Emerson et al., 1995, pp. 48–52). The gaps, the things between the lines, the impressions that we know we have but did not have time or energy to write up – such aspects are highly useful when developing more story-like and scenic notes.

Taken even as jottings, the sentence is far from the mark. 'They went into a boring room and started an argument' could – also in the very situation when the note was written – be substituted with similar short phrases that include more details. For instance: 'walls with cracks, one shouting "Why did you do that?!"' Simply by pinpointing a small amount of detail, fieldworkers find themselves better equipped to elaborate their notes later on, and remembering what captured their attention in the first place.

So the urge for details need not always be an urge for endless descriptions: page after page with seemingly pointless facts. Rather, it is a way to capture and remember social life aided by what 'stood out' for the observer, a way to avoid or at least soften clichés and preconceived ways of seeing things. Anderson writes:

For example, to write down simply that 'the men were shabbily dressed' obscures much detail about specifically how the men dressed, or exactly which details led to the generalization of 'shabbily dressed'. (2005, p. 51)

'Obscures much detail' is the key phrase. A strong ideal would be to, on the contrary, clarify details, illuminate and disclose them. To make observations is to challenge oneself with an urge for details – in the field, at the desk, in one's dialog with data. We should try to 'detail the social and interactional processes that make up people's everyday lives' (Emerson et al., 1995, p. 11). Since such processes often are verbal, people's dialogs turn especially important: 'As far as possible ... speech should be rendered in a manner that approximates to a verbatim report' (Hammersley and Atkinson, 1983/2007, p. 145).

There is no need for panic. A complete observation is not possible. The trick is not to despise oneself for being unable to capture details all the time, but praise those occasions when at least some details are captured – and train oneself to repeat it. A 'detail' is, in any case, relatively and contextually defined.

In my observations of everyday life at youth care institutions, I have happened to focus on playful interactions, more precisely playfights or fictive violence (Wästerfors, 2016). This could be seen as a detail in itself. Nothing indicates that playfulness or playfights would be constitutive for these settings or dominating in any sense. From the beginning, I found this phenomenon quite peripheral and even unnoticed by many field members, let alone the institutions' outsiders, but gradually I came to look at it as sociologically telling. They exemplified institutional members' – particularly the youths' – striving for re-personalizing themselves within a quite depersonalizing institution. With the help of playfulness, these youths could 'touch' the adults both physically and socially, getting closer to them as persons and experiencing their idiosyncratic responses. Details played a significant role in capturing this phenomenon. This is how I tried to retell one episode in an article (Wästerfors, 2016, pp. 177–8):

After two lessons in technics in a workshop at one institution, a case of playfighting occurred between Ted, a pupil, and Hugo, a teacher, just before we left the workshop for lunch. I was close to not taking notice of it because I had followed Ted and Micke, another pupil, and their schoolwork since early that morning and had the feeling of being 'done', waiting for lunch myself. Ted and Micke had been taught in quite defined steps how to cut and weld metal into 'cats', a cat figure in black metal, with attached head, ears, tail, etc. At the top of the shelves in the workshop, there were series of such cats from previous pupils; they were way too big to bring home after the treatment period. At this point, we have taken off our blue overalls and are waiting for the other ones to finish their work and join us for the outdoor walk to the dining hall. Standing there and waiting, Ted and Hugo exchange some teasing comments and then suddenly Ted aims a kick at Hugo, in a slightly slow and 'open' way (i.e. very noticeable).

Hugo grabs Ted's leg just when Ted's kick is about to hit its target (Hugo's hip), he gets a grip on this kicking leg and then pushes Ted towards a desk behind him, filled with tools and a vice. Ted resists by grabbing Hugo's shoulder, and they both measure their strengths against each other for a moment, with some moans and 'argh!' It all happens very quickly and produces some noise; Ted is 19 and not a small boy, and Hugo is in his 40s. Then Hugo manages to put Ted on the desk behind him; he almost lifts him up and puts him there. The tools are pressed towards the edges as Ted's body is pushed upon the desk, in a sitting position. (field notes)

I then start commenting on these notes in the article by adding more observations:

Eventually, Hugo and Ted set themselves free from each other. Hugo stands in front of Ted, who is still sitting on the desk, which one should not do at all, strictly speaking, if following the rules of the institution. They are both a little breathless, with red faces, but not irritated. 'Lucky you!' Hugo says, and Ted replies, 'Or you!' and smiles, both jokingly implying that the other one is the weaker and consequently got off gently. [...] Hugo then checks his trousers and shirt, as if trying to make sure they did not get spoiled somehow.

First, 'I was close to not taking notice...' – the episode as a whole is a detail, a seemingly trivial phenomenon (cf. Silverman, 2007,

p. 16). Brief and passing playfights in institutional settings are far from the official program. So simply by including the episode in my observations, I managed to say something quite unexpected about the field. Nobody else wrote about these things; the episode was not included in any journal or incident report, and the institutional system does not recognize 'play' as relevant.

Second, the notes depicting the episodes are full of details: 'how to cut and weld metal into cats', 'blue overalls', 'a slightly slow and open' kick, a desk 'filled with tools and a vice', the exclamation 'Argh!', and tools being 'pressed towards the edges', for example.

Such details provide the account with data that avoid simplifications. I could have summarized the interaction by saying things like 'they tumble around a while in the workshop', but that would not have helped me to understand how playfights are accomplished, let alone convince readers that I have seen them. Accounts from observations entail a 'persuasive force' (Atkinson, 2001, p. 89) by depicting a scene for those who were not there.

But we may also note an absence of details. 'Some teasing comments', for instance, exchanged by Ted and Hugo at the beginning of the playful episode – what comments? Apparently I did not remember or hear these. 'Some moans' is another escape from details – one may ask what 'moans' I am referring to, and one may even ask what a moan is. One may also ask what it means to 'measure... strength against each other for a moment'. It seems like a clumsy way to summarize a series of body movements that I was not able to distinguish.

So I do not try to show an ideal observation. Another observer would be able to sharpen her senses (and pen) much more, and transform this episode – from interaction in situ to words on paper – in a much cleverer way. Training, style and talent vary. My point is more general: details help. Sensitivity for fine features, words uttered and seemingly pointless objects, creates credibility and rigor for any project. An observer should especially not hesitate in front of odd things, like big metal cats on a shelf in a workshop. There is a peculiar potential that precisely such things make a scene realistic, not because they are expected in – as in my case here – an institution for youth with criminal experiences, but because they are not expected. All details need not be actively involved in the analysis being crafted out of them. They can just stand there, reminding us about a remarkable world.

I think there is a lot to learn from Sara Danius' (2013) essay on the historical development of the modern novel, *Den blå tvålen*, meaning 'The Blue Soap'. The title is taken from a story by Gustave Flaubert in 1877, in which a bar of blue soap is mentioned as placed on a table. Flaubert only mentions it once and never returns to it. Danius argues that this blue soap represents a novelty in modern literature at the time: to start 'seeing things' in themselves – from an author's gaze – and not necessarily aiming for a particular dramatic significance with all written details. The mundane concreteness that finds its way into modern novels during the nineteenth century and onwards – the vivid descriptions of bodies, faces, objects, conversations, rooms and cities – is accomplished by an abundance of details, and that constitutes a new way of writing.

Danius (2013, p. 19) is not arguing that Flaubert's style 'reproduces' the world (avbildar, in Swedish). Rather, it 'makes it visible' (försynligar). This, too, we recognize from the ethnographic enterprise from the Chicago school and on. We cannot argue that an observer mirrors a reality, but we can argue that he or she actively makes it visible.

Then, coupled with this emerging nineteenth-century literary ambition of seeing things, Danius writes that there was a suspicion that today's ethnographers similarly recognize – a suspicion about what we really gain by all these detailed descriptions. If we can see the world, can we then see through it? I will touch upon this issue again in the conclusion.

Sequences

Another attractive quality for observers is sequences. To be able to show how phenomena evolve or relate to each other over time is valuable in any project. One particular gesture promotes or provokes another; one actor responds to another; a particular event unfolds step by step. It might take place slowly and subtly or rapidly and dramatically – in any case, a wide range of observable occurrences are possible to portray in terms of 'first this happened, then that'.

Observers, worried whether they are keeping an eye on sequences or not, can always ask, 'Then what happened?' or 'What happened before?' Such questions tend to sharpen our senses for gradually accomplished or emerging phenomena.

An eye for sequences helps observers in several ways. First and foremost, a static and reified picture of society is avoided. Attention is given to unfolding or activated contexts. The elderly's attempts to exert influence in a nursing home and their institutional constraints – to return to Harnett's (2010) observations – do not take place as a box in an elegant model, or as a dot in a list of policies. Rather, they take place as situated interactions. A concrete elderly resident in a concrete nursing home tries to achieve something by asking, making gestures or obstructing and then a concrete staff member responds. Aspects of the nursing home as such, we may argue, are virtually 'done' or reproduced in these kinds of interactions, so that what we 'see' is not only one actor responding to another, but also an institutional context brought to life. An example from Harnett's (2010, pp. 296–7) study:

> It is morning and I'm walking with Tina, a staff member, along the corridor. We have just finished helping one resident and left their room when Tina says that we can 'take' Nancy, another resident, next. On our way to Nancy's room, Charlie presses the alarm button in his room. Tina and I go to Charlie's room, open the door, and are met by the rank smell of urine. Charlie is in bed with soaked sheets. He looks up and asks to get up. 'Can't you stay in bed a bit longer? We'll come and help you later', Tina says. 'Everything is wet', says Charlie. Tina tells Charlie that he has to stay in bed and that Erica, another staff member, will come and help him later. Tina and I turn around and leave Charlie in his bed as we walk to Nancy, who lives in the room two doors down.

Harnett used these field notes to capture how residents typically needed situationally 'routine-free' staff members to be successful in their influence attempts. Since Tina was on her way to 'take' Nancy, another resident, she saw herself as sort of locked into an ongoing routine, and attached to the 'locally taken-for-granted reasons for not complying with residents' requests' (Harnett, 2010, p. 296). So Charlie's request is postponed and passed on to a colleague.

None of these findings could have been observed without attending to sequences. At the heart of the field notes, there is just a short one: Charlie asks to get up and Tina responds. First this happened, then that. These two actions seem quite tightly connected, probably taking place just seconds after another, or less. Then, as a wider but also still quite sequentially organized context, we get information about Tina and the fieldworker's original mission this morning, Charlie's alarm, his complaints ('everything is wet'), Tina's postponement of help, and so on.

These activities and circumstances are depicted more impressionistically. We do not get exact words for every line or account, and the previously helped resident (before Tina and Harnett entered Charlie's room) is just mentioned, as is Nancy, the next resident in the row. Still, these things are ordered in the field notes in a way that makes sense for an outsider. We can imagine a situation like this and its chains of events with the help of Harnett's eye for morning proceedings at a nursing home, and we can understand it.

One of the most insistent advocates for collecting sequences is David Silverman. Inspired by Harvey Sacks, he draws on findings from conversation analysis to make sociologists attend more to the everyday sequential organization of society. 'Social order', Silverman (2007, p. 48) argues, 'is to be found in even the tiniest activity' (cf. Sacks, 1992, p. 484, formula 'order at all points'). If, for instance, you say "hello" to somebody, or present yourself with your name, you subtly raise anticipations about how others should respond. They tend to be somewhat compelled to say "hello" too, or respond with their names. 'The first turn constitutes a "slot" for the second, and sets up an expectation about what this slot may properly contain' (Silverman, 2007, p. 65).

This, however, does not mean that sequences are mechanical. People may, for instance, respond 'I can't hear you', requesting repetition, and then the original 'slot' or conversational place is sidestepped (Silverman, 2007, p. 65). Now, there seems to be less space for the other to say 'hello' or a name as a response, even though all involved actors delicately and simultaneously pay respect to how an everyday conversation normally 'should' be done. There is no determinism in actual talk (or other interaction), but its participants usually recognize its sequential orders, thereby also reproducing them.

Conversation analysis has the advantage of working with recorded data, which allows the kind of fine-grained sequential analysis that both Silverman and Sacks advocate. However, the spirit of sequentiality can undoubtedly be translated into more inexact sets of data, which, on the other hand, has other advantages. Harnett is 'there' in a nursing home, able to capture its routinized tempo in the morning, the alarm that goes off, and even the smell of urine in Charlie's room (cf. Gubrium's, 1975/1997, similar approach in his pioneering work in nursing home ethnography). So, even though she does not tape-record Charlie's request and Tina's response, her data have sensory and contextual qualities.

Could we talk about a 'slot' during which Tina's help to get Charlie out of bed was 'invited' to happen, a slot that was passed and then 'closed' when Tina asked him to wait? Residents at nursing homes seem to strive to make use of quite ordinary structured openings for receiving 'extra' help and improvised exemptions – the caring work's 'slots' – whereas staff make use of institutional routines to close them.

If we go back to my field notes on playfights in the youth care institution, there is a peculiar detail at the end of the sequence with Ted and Hugo in the workshop. Hugo, the teacher, 'checks his trousers and shirt, as if trying to make sure they did not get spoiled somehow'. When analyzing playfights sequentially, I also tried to attend to what could happen after a 'core' sequence. Youth and staff could enjoy the aftermath of a playfight – breathless, relaxed and happy – yet, there were also traces of seriousness here, as when Hugo checks his clothes. By attending to those things, I was trying to show how members restore their institutional membership after having suspended it. We may talk about a sort of coda; that is, the post-narrative stage at which storytellers return to the present day and its reality (Labov, 1972, pp. 362–73; Riessman, 2008, p. 84).

So, observing sequences may also mean observing their aftermath and how it retrospectively contextualizes the events. In the case of Ted and Hugo, we might say that even though institutional members bracket their formal roles during playful interaction, they also accomplish subtle linkages between play and seriousness.

The narrative term 'coda' also reminds us about another benefit of observing sequences: it tends to make field notes powerfully story-like. A minimal story, according to structuralists such as Labov (1972, pp. 360–1), is a sequence of at least two clauses: first this happened, then that. If storytellers lack any such succession of events, where one thing leads to another, there is not much of a story to begin with. If, on the other hand, storytellers get their bearings with various sequences, they also find the necessary ingredients for their stories.

Therefore, by observing sequences, researchers gather data that are often relatively fun to communicate. There is of course a risk that, as Emerson and his colleagues point out (Emerson et al., 1995, p. 16), a narrative form could 'push' open-ended or disjointed interactions into seemingly coherent sequences. There is certainly nothing inherently invaluable with episodic and fragmented observations. However, if we look upon 'sequence' in the spirit of Harvey Sacks and David Silverman, we know that the 'stories' they indicate are anything but necessarily neat or complete. People may talk in disrupted and quirky ways, and the same thing goes for all human interactions.

Atmosphere

Atmosphere is the final attractive quality for observers that I want to highlight. The mostly wordless or elusive qualities in settings and situations are also desirable to distinguish when collecting observational data: the mood, the 'air' or tone of a social context. To be present in a field, and situated among the people who populate one's research, gives the researcher a good opportunity to sense aspects of an emotional and cultural milieu that others may have great trouble in reaching.

This may sound cryptic. Sensing 'the atmosphere', how do observers do it? Without any ambition to be all encompassing, I suggest two ways: contrasts and synecdoche. By distinguishing contrasting atmospheres in a given field (or, if possible, between different fields), each atmosphere may turn surprisingly clear, even when they may still appear quite elusive individually. Then, by treating details in observations as synecdoches – a rhetorical form where a part stands for the whole – we may similarly get a handle on what anthropologists sometimes call the 'ether' of a setting.

In my studies at youth care institutions, I have gradually realized that I have gathered data on two contrasting atmospheres: on the one hand: wards, on the other hand: schoolrooms or school buildings. The institutions are often constructed as 'cottage systems' in the countryside (Platt, 1969/1977), which means that each ward consists of a house or cottage in which a group of teenagers sleep and spend most of their time. Each institution harbors a series of such houses or cottages, in addition to school buildings, workshops, garages and often a central building with administration, a central kitchen, a large dining hall, and so forth. Staff and youth wander between houses and in corridors according to schedules, especially between school and wards.

At some institutions, youth are placed in separate school buildings during their lessons; at others they just walk to separate rooms within their ward house. In any case, school is separate from wards, as are their respective atmospheres. Whereas a ward appears to be a mixture between a prison, a boarding school and a recreation center, school areas are more cognitively and pedagogically oriented.

At the center of a ward, there is a TV and a generous sofa or a couple of comfortable armchairs. At the center of a schoolroom, there is a work table and a series of computers. A ward harbors video games and DVDs, and the youth sort of lie on the sofa or slumber in front of endless TV shows, in otherwise quite stripped living rooms. In schoolrooms, they sit up straight in front of screens, whiteboards, bookshelves, maps, posters and paintings. When the youth walk from one area to another, from wards with their laid-back mood of 'we're just doing time here, despite the fact that staff calls it therapy' to the learning expectations among the teachers, they also shift atmosphere. They may very well engage in sabotage toward pedagogical ambitions (Wästerfors, 2014, pp. 236–65), but a single institution entails different moods in and of itself.

My point is that the contrast between wards and school helped me to identify atmospheres. As youth wander from one area to another, I do the same as a fieldworker. I feel the expectation to sit up straight myself as I enter schoolrooms, and I feel the expectation to relax and be more spontaneous in the wards. Yet I do not think I would have been able to distinguish these things without a contrast. Indeed, the contrast has helped me to communicate to outsiders the 'air' or tone of youth care institutions.

Also, synecdoches help observers to capture atmospheres, or more specifically: the ethnographer's openness to look upon his or her data in synecdochal ways (Hammersley and Atkinson, 1983/2007, p. 198). A range of details from my examples in this chapter can be reviewed from this perspective: the blue overalls in the workshop where Ted and Hugo's playfight takes place, the 'rank smell of urine' in Charlie's room in the nursing home, the sofa in a youth care ward, the alarm equipment that its staff members carry, and so on. Each of these things can be picked up from field notes or memories, and made to stand for something wider – and to communicate this 'something wider', the observer can drop them strategically into his or her texts.

The blue overalls, for instance, stand for 'workshop' and 'labor', as well as the corresponding mood; youth care institutions have a long tradition of celebrating supposedly educational physical labor for troubled youth. The sofa, on the other hand, stands for comfort, relaxation and coziness, as well as for therapeutic talks. A 'rank smell of urine' in Harnett's notes, seems to stand for an emotional state of physical emergency and vulnerability.

In one of my notes from the youth care institutions, I tried to document the occasional atmosphere of panic or turmoil when the alarm would ring out over all the buildings. I could see how one boy was standing in front of a closed door with a window, hitting the door repeatedly. People around me were asking 'What's happening?!', 'What's happening?!' I wrote that, and added 'I can feel the adrenaline hit me', and 'How the hell do I switch off this beeping device [the alarm telephone for staff] that I've borrowed?!'

In another ethnographic project in which I was studying a leisure activity for youth with disabilities (Wästerfors, 2008), I tried to communicate an atmosphere of 'doing normalcy'.

These teenagers all had various diagnoses (Asperger's, autism, ADHD, etc.), and were used to being treated according to them, but the leisure activity was characterized by a very down-to-earth and simultaneously upfront mood. The activity had the form of a motor club. It took place in and around a garage, and the boys slowly repaired an old American car.

In the beginning, I had difficulties capturing the mundane and seemingly uneventful atmosphere (definitely far away from cases of panic in youth care institutions). I started to attend to what I later called 'doing normalcy' with the help of the field members' ironic yet still warm jargon. Participants were not treated as clients or patients, or as objects to feel sorry for, and such features of the setting were deeply appreciated and continuously reproduced:

> Dennis's mom arrives during coffee at the end of the night and one of the leaders talks with her. 'We don't like Dennis anymore', he says, loudly so that everybody hears. 'Really, what's he done now?' the mom answers, picking up the leader's irony. 'He wins too much.' 'Well, what's he been winning?' The leader tells about the competitions [that took place earlier]; Dennis is listening with great interest, as if he wondered how far the irony could be taken. 'Well, it was fun as long as it lasted,' Dennis's mom says and pretends to finish his membership by reaching out her hand to Dennis, as if preparing to leave with him. 'Two times I won', Dennis says a little later, whereupon the leader sighs, 'Yes, we knooow!' evoking everybody's laughter.

Again, my point is not to present these notes as ideal. Rather, the point is that details and sequences (and many other observable aspects, like objects, architecture, geographical positions and rituals) can be treated as synecdoches, making them stand for something relatively elusive. Through concrete facets of talk and gestures, and through small dramas in story-like formats, we can get a glimpse of a setting's ether. The atmosphere of the motor club that I was observing did not resemble a formal program or clinic for young people with disabilities, and joking episodes could be used to show that.

Basically all ethnographic data is synecdochal, as Hammersley and Atkinson state

(1983/2007, p. 198). Observers routinely select particular features as characteristic of places, persons or events. Examples are used in ways similar to oral rhetoric, as 'shortened induction' (Wästerfors and Holsánová, 2005). Still, this rhetorical effect must be slowly and wisely carved out to really make it shine.

CONCLUSION

In this chapter, I started by presenting the general aims of observations, the theoretical assumptions of this approach and the historical background. I then discussed three qualities – details, sequences and atmosphere – that may be especially helpful for observers in basically any project. Qualifications and disclaimers introduced my discussion; what type of observation you need depends on the project. We cannot give general advice for all observers in all projects, as if providing a universal scheme to hold up in front of one's eyes as one enters any field. There is no shortcut, in this respect. Each observer has to use his or her personal experiences while seeking out the opportunities that characterize each setting. Each observer has to find a way to map the woods, as Silverman (2007, p. 63) terms it (after MacNaghten and Myers, 2004), and get some preliminary overview of the terrain, before he or she starts focusing, 'chopping up trees'.

If an observer did not look for details, sequences and atmosphere, how would the data appear? We would probably then find ourselves with notes like, 'They went into a boring room and started an argument'. Without ambition to specify or unfold what is taking place, and without ambition to somehow communicate a tone or 'air' of the moment, much data would appear as dumb, mute or inarticulate. It would be quite similar, I guess, to our prejudices about this or that.

What we normally observe in our everyday life are reproductions of what 'everybody knows'. We see 'types' of people, we hear predictable conversations, and we experience highly recognizable events. The trick of making observations for analytic and theoretical purposes is to employ ethnographers' trained gaze and refined rhetoric to transport oneself around simplifications, summaries and generalizations, and instead get at something different. That is why we need original details, surprising sequences and innovative paths to show atmospheres.

We also need these qualities, I would argue, to set greater entities in social science in motion. A common objection against ethnographic data concerns the tension between an 'experience-near' approach, and 'theories about the effects of broader social structures' (Emerson et al., 1995, p. 134). Power, gender, age, class, disability and ethnicity, for instance, may at first sight seem to evaporate in the richness of descriptions. We see all these social worlds, but do we see through them?

My argument to nuance this tension is twofold. First, to theorize starts by naming phenomena, and for that we need observations (Swedberg, 2012) – not necessarily 'given' names from others' theories. Our gaze must be theoretically informed, but not theoretically programmed. In that sense we may be richly rewarded if we do not take for granted prefabricated ways to 'see through' things. Second, wider structuring processes – such as power, gender, class, age, disability and ethnicity – can be dynamically described and better explained by observing them in every day life, especially their details, their sequences and atmospheres. And if we spend time in a field we may very well find out that these processes do not need to be as 'experience-distant' as others might have told us. Society is here and now – in front of our eyes – and observations may help us create new knowledge out of that.

FURTHER READING

Emerson, Robert M. (ed.) (2001) *Contemporary Field Research. Perspectives and Formulations.* Prospect Heights, IL: Waveland Press.

Emerson, Robert M., Fretz, Rachel I. and Shaw, Linda L. (1995) *Writing Ethnographic Fieldnotes*. Chicago and London: The University of Chicago Press.

Sanjek, Roger (ed.) (1990) *Fieldnotes. The Makings of Anthropology*. Ithaca: Cornell University Press.

REFERENCES

Anderson, Elijah (2005) 'Jelly's place: An ethnographic memoir', *International Journal of Politics, Culture, and Society*, 19(2005): 35–52. © Springer Science+Business Media, LLC 2007. Reprinted with kind permission from Springer Science+Business Media via Copyright Clearance Center's Rightslink service.

Anderson, Nels (1923/1961) *The Hobo. The Sociology of the Homeless Man*. Chicago: The University of Chicago Press.

Atkinson, Paul (2001) 'Ethnography and the representation of reality', in Robert M. Emerson (ed.), *Contemporary Field Research. Perspectives and Formulations*. Prospect Heights, IL: Waveland Press.

Cressey, Paul G. (1932) *The Taxi Dance Hall. A Sociological Study in Commercialized Recreation and City Life*. Chicago: The University of Chicago Press.

Danius, Sara (2013) *Den blå tvålen. Romanen och konsten att göra saker och ting synliga*. Stockholm: Albert Bonniers Förlag.

Emerson, Robert M. (2001) 'Introduction: The development of ethnographic field research', in Robert M. Emerson (ed.), *Contemporary Field Research. Perspectives and Formulations*. Prospect Heights, IL: Waveland Press, pp. 1–26.

Emerson, Robert M., Fretz, Rachel I. and Shaw, Linda L. (1995) *Writing Ethnographic Fieldnotes*. Chicago and London: The University of Chicago Press.

Goffman, Erving (1961/1990) *Asylums. Essays on the Social Situation of Mental Patients and Other Inmates*. New York: Anchor Books.

Goffman, Erving (2001) 'On fieldwork', in Emerson, Robert M. (ed.), *Contemporary Field Research. Perspectives and Formulations*. Prospect Heights, IL: Waveland Press.

Gubrium, Jaber F. (1975/1997) *Living and Dying at Murray Manor*. Charlottesville and London: University Press of Virginia.

Hammersley, Martyn and Atkinson, Paul (1983/2007) *Ethnography. Principles in Practice*. London and New York: Routledge.

Harnett, Tove (2010) 'Seeking exemptions from nursing home routines: Residents' everyday influence attempts and institutional order', *Journal of Aging Studies*, 24(4): 292–301.

Labov, William (1972) *Language in the Inner City. Studies in the Black English Vernacular*. Philadelphia, PA: University of Pennsylvania Press.

MacNaghten, Phil and Myers, Greg (2004) 'Focus groups', in Giampietro Gobo, Clive Seale, Jaber F. Gubrium and David Silverman (eds), *Qualitative Research Practice*. London: Sage, pp. 65–79.

Platt, Anthony (1969/1977). *The Child Savers. The Invention of Delinquency*. Chicago: The University of Chicago Press.

Riessman, Catherine Kohler (2008) *Narrative Methods for the Human Sciences*. Los Angeles, CA: Sage.

Sacks, Harvey (1992) *Lectures on Conversation*. Oxford: Blackwell.

Silverman, David (2007) *A Very Short, Fairly Interesting and Reasonably Cheap Book About Qualitative Research*. London: Sage.

Swedberg, Richard (2012) 'Theorizing in sociology and social science: Turning to the context of discovery', *Theoretical Sociology*, 41(1): 1–40.

Wästerfors, David (2008) 'Doing normalcy: Attractive interactions for teenage boys with disabilities', *International Journal of Sociological Research*, 1(1): 1–21.

Wästerfors, David (2014) *Lektioner i motvind. Om skola för unga på institution*. Malmö, Sweden: Égalité.

Wästerfors, David (2016) 'Playfights as trouble and respite', *Journal of Contemporary Ethnography*, 45(2): 168–97.

Wästerfors, David and Holsánová, Jana (2005) 'Examples as crucial arguments in discourse on "others"', *TEXT – An Interdisciplinary Journal for the Study of Discourse*, 25(4): 519–54.

Whyte, William Foote (1943/1993) *Street Corner Society. The Social Structure of an Italian Slum*. Chicago and London: The University of Chicago Press.

Doing Ethnography: Ways and Reasons

Marie Buscatto

INTRODUCTION

More than a century ago, anthropologists adopted ethnography as their main method (Taylor, 2002). Early on, they defined general scientific principles guiding the study of 'foreign' societies (Gobo, 2008). But ethnography has, also very early on, been adopted by other disciplines, such as sociology, opening new ways to study contemporary societies (Madge, 1963). For instance, at the end of the nineteenth century, Frederick W. Taylor founded his 'scientific method' based on his personal observation of workers (see Wästerfors, Chapter 20, this volume). In the 1920s Elton Mayo and his colleagues founded the 'Human Resources School' following the 'Hawthorne experiment', which was mainly based on observations led among workers in a plant.[1] After World War II, prominent researchers in Chicago, such as Erving Goffman, Howard S. Becker or Donald Roy based some of their most renowned works – respectively dealing with mental illness, marijuana smokers, or plant workers – on long-term systematic observations.

This method has now become quite legitimate in sociology. What, then, is defined as ethnography? How may the use of ethnography enrich one's scientific results? How is an ethnographic study to be conducted over time? What are the issues to be dealt with to avoid ethnography's potential limits? What are the new developments? These are some of the questions to be dealt with in this chapter, based on current and past literature and my reflexive experience as an ethnographer.

WHAT IS ETHNOGRAPHY?

Ethnography is mainly defined as long-term observation (see Wästerfors, Chapter 20, this volume) personally conducted *in situ* by the researcher and aimed at producing specific data:

In its most characteristic form it involves the ethnographer participating, overtly or covertly, in people's daily lives for an extended period of time, watching what happens, listening to what is said, asking questions – in fact, collecting whatever data are available to throw light on the issues that are the focus of the research. (Hammersley and Atkinson, 1995 [1983], p. 1)

Ethnography may take several forms – participant, semi-participant, or external. It may be conducted in various ways – for example, following the same people through different places (see Kusenbach, Chapter 22, this volume) or being focused on one or several specific settings. It may be implemented in foreign countries over long periods of time (as in most anthropological works) or in the researcher's own country over shorter periods of time (as in most sociological works). It may be done overtly – those being observed know about it – or covertly. Ethnography can also be used to study society, adopting quite differing approaches. While Gary Alan Fine promotes a 'peopled ethnography', to be distinguished from 'postulated' or 'personal ethnographies' (2003), Loïc Wacquant defends the need for 'carnal sociology' (2005). Whereas James Clifford and George Marcus argue for the development of 'postmodern ethnographies' (1986), Howard Garfinkel is in favour of an 'ethnomethodological approach' (1967). If Michael Burawoy develops the 'extended case method' (1998), Barney Glaser and Anselm Strauss earlier expose the virtues of 'grounded theory' (1968).

In other words, even if one tends to associate ethnographic sociology with the interactionist paradigm, due to the powerful influence of the interactionist 'School of Chicago' researchers – Hughes, Goffman, Becker most notably – ethnography can also be used to develop any theoretical framework, be it Marxism, postmodern theory, ethnomethodology, phenomenology, conversation analysis (see Jackson, Chapter 18, this volume), pragmatism, or social fields. Those different uses are not necessarily compatible with each other since ways to collect, to interpret, and to present data may vary strongly among those sociologists, as powerfully discussed in Katz's (2004) controversial article. But whatever researchers' 'ethnographic styles' (Wacquant, 2003) and main theoretical framework, the two central features of ethnography remain the effective presence of the ethnographer in the world she studies and its long-term systematic observation:

> 'We characterize ethnography as sustained, explicit, methodical observation and paraphrasing of social situations in relation to their naturally occurring contexts.' (Weick, 1985, p. 568) (...) It excludes when the fieldworker does not remain in the field (for months or for years) to become saturated with first-hand knowledge of the setting. (Glaser and Strauss, 1967) (in Morrill and Fine 1997, p. 425)

Ethnographic data are mainly constituted from the researcher's personal *in situ* systematic observations carried out over time. But they also include any other data collected in the field during the course of observation, such as informal conversations, formal interviews (see Roulston and Choi, Chapter 15, this volume), documents (see Rapley and Rees, Chapter 24, this volume) or objects which are part of those observations (Gobo, 2008).

WHAT ARE THE MAIN CONTRIBUTIONS OF ETHNOGRAPHY TO THE STUDY OF SOCIAL PHENOMENA?

One may summarize ethnographic main contributions to the study of social phenomena around three main ideas.

First of all, ethnography provides a privileged access to 'invisible' or difficult to access social phenomena. Observation, as opposed to questionnaires or interviews, gives access to people's practices, and not to their oral justifications or representations

(LaPiere, 1934), that is, to all those 'natural', hidden, taboos or difficult to express practices which people have difficulty in describing (or would not like to describe even if they were aware of them). While interviews or questionnaires enable people to express opinions or to describe practices as they remember them, direct observation gives access to practices while they are performed. This has been key in unveiling dance musicians' or marijuana smokers' practices (Becker, 1963), the ways mental illness is daily fabricated through ritual practices in mental institutions (Goffman, 1961) or plant workers' resisting practices (Roy, 1952; see next section).

Moreover, since ethnography is led over time, the researcher is also able to discover the ways that practices are socially produced through action and interaction, how they are legitimated, how they get transformed through negotiation, conflict, and confrontation between actors. One may then better grasp key social logics, even if sometimes contradictory, which underline people's practices through time. As stated by Michael Rosen about organizational ethnography, 'by definition, ethnography is a longitudinal method, geared towards a process-based understanding of organizational life' (Rosen, 1991, p. 12). Following this argument, specific organizations can then be thoroughly defined as collective worlds which get produced, legitimated and transformed through organizational members' actions and interactions such as the specific neighbourhood investigated by Whyte (1943). Thanks to long-term personal observations, the researcher is able to produce a complete understanding of how a specific observed world (such as a hospital, a school, a neighbourhood or a restaurant) or a specific group of people (such as artists, sick people, drug dealers or homeless people) collectively produce their lives over time.

One last, but not the least of the advantages of ethnography, is to get access to multiple perspectives and practices as developed by observed people over time. In all social activities, logics of action may vary depending on the time of the day, the week, or the year. Actors' rationalities may also vary depending on several factors, which may change And since the ethnographer is to observe people's activities in the long run, she will be in a good position to distinguish exceptional facts from recurring activities, general rules and norms from disrupting behaviours… and see how those recurring and exceptional events work together to produce, legitimate and transform the observed world, group of people, or actions.

MACHINE WORKERS' RESISTING STRATEGIES: A HISTORICAL ILLUSTRATION

Let's take a famous historical example presented by the Chicagoan interactionist Donald Roy (1911–1980), which has highly influenced the development of the sociology of work. Based on the analysis of covert participant observations made during eleven months of work as a radial-drill operator in the machine shop of a steel-processing plant in 1944 and 1945, he showed how workers were fighting a rational and collective war against management through what he called 'restriction' practices. In his 1952 article, he describes the active strategies collectively shaped by machine workers in order to defend their economic and personal interests against management rules and orders: his ethnographic work unveiled two specific workers' resisting strategies, 'quota restriction' and 'goldbricking', as will be shown now.

Based on his own productive output, he first found that his behaviours were quite simple to describe: either he was getting a $1.25 to $1.34 an hour pay, or he was getting a salary far below the 0.85 cents official basic salary per hour. And what he called 'this bimodal pattern of hourly earnings for the ten-month period' (Roy, 1952, p. 428) appeared to be very close to those of his main fellow workers. It 'was the rule of the shop' and, based on his daily observations, this rule was clearly produced by two specific resisting strategies: 'quota restriction' and 'goldbricking'.

On the one hand, the concentration of the $1.25 to $1.34 level was due to 'quota restriction' behaviours: the fixed quota being considered as feasible to earn at least 1 dollar, workers did produce more than expected, but avoided producing too much above a 1.25 dollars quota, so that the set quota would remain as such (and would not be downgraded by the Methods Department). On the other, the concentration of hourly payments far below the normal pay of 0.85 cents was due to 'goldbricking' behaviours: when the quota was considered as too demanding to earn at least 1 dollar an hour, workers preferred to 'hold back' and to earn much less, so that the Methods Department would have to improve the quota. In both cases, workers then had 'free time', sometimes hours to spend, in order to respect both strategies and ensure the quotas remain feasible and acceptable to them. As observed by Roy, 'I reached the peak in quota restriction on June 27, with but three and a half hours of productive work out of the eight' (Roy, 1952, p. 433).

If those strategies were economically sound for those machine workers, they were also collectively developed. As regularly detailed by Roy, workers were spending a lot of time assessing jobs collectively, making sure that new hires did not work too fast and did not threaten their resisting strategies, and explaining to them all the gains to be drawn from such strategies (protect feasible quotas, avoid working too hard, having 'free time' on the job). Workers led a collective, even if hidden, war against management and the Methods Department.

Ethnography has been key in unveiling those practices since workers tend to hide them. Long-term observations also enabled Roy to discover the bimodal pattern of restriction and the ways it was collectively built-up over time. He also showed that despite the multiple jobs to be dealt with in this plant, this pattern did not change over time and was driven by machine workers' economic and personal interest. Roy's results have been key, right from the 1950s, in developing a better understanding of how first-level workers are able to collectively fight to defend their working conditions – including their level of earning – using quite rational and well-organized strategies as is now regularly demonstrated in all organizations (for example, see Buscatto, 2008).

BETTER GRASP 'GENDER AT WORK': A CONTEMPORARY ILLUSTRATION

Following this first historical example, I will now show how contemporary ethnography has been quite instrumental in better grasping gendered differences in work settings or situations. Overall, ethnography does enrich the identification and analysis of gender in work settings or situations precisely by inducing the researcher to focus on 'doing gender' (West and Zimmerman, 1987).[2] It is in daily interaction that 'sex-class makes itself felt, here in the organization of face-to-face interaction, for here understanding about sex-based dominance can be employed as a means of deciding who decides, who leads, and who follows' (Goffman, 1997, p. 208). Ethnography enables the researcher to unveil how gender segregation is produced by actors in the work context. Gender segregation, a complex, dynamic phenomenon operative at different points in the social order, is actually enacted by actors in the work situation. To deepen this initial conclusion, I will now describe the three specific contributions that ethnography can make to the study of gender in work situations in enabling researchers to spot disparaging gendered stereotypes, occupational networks, and norms (for detailed explanations, see Buscatto, 2010).

First of all, direct observation proves extremely effective not only in identifying existing gender stereotypes but also to grasp how they are constructed, how they operate in work situations and help produce professional legitimacy. For example, in my study of French jazz singers (Buscatto, 2007a, 2007b), through observing singers at work – rehearsing, performing on stage, jamming, – and in leisure situations – drinking, partying, going out, joking in informal situations, I progressively came to not only unveil two key feminine pejorative stereotypes associated with seduction and lack of technicality, but also the ways those pejorative stereotypes favoured a strong devaluation of those female singers, and their marginalization in the French jazz world. Due to those two stereotypes, female singers tended to be considered as potential sexual objects while their voice was not viewed as a 'real instrument', which negatively affected their reputation as professional musicians. By focusing my attention on daily interactions between musicians, ethnography helped identify this tie between specific negative gender stereotypes and their effects on men's and women's professional reputations.

Second of all, ethnography is useful not only in identifying the difficulty women have in getting into and remaining a part of 'masculine' social networks, but also and above all, in spotting the social 'reasons' for this, as shown in my study of women jazz instrumentalists (Buscatto, 2007a). Social networks are crucial when it comes to keeping one's place in fluid art worlds and constructing a relatively good professional reputation in them (Becker, 1982). I was able to show that French women jazz instrumentalists over the age of 30, whatever their musical reputation, could not make a living primarily from jazz, partly because they had such a hard time getting into stable social networks; in this regard they were extremely dependent on their male jazz musician (programmer, agent, or producer) husbands or partners (when they had one). It was by comparing my observations with statements from these men and women, collected in interviews and informal situations, that I realized that, except for friendly moments spent with their husbands' or partners' musician friends, these women instrumentalists were not likely to have any prolonged friendships with male jazz musicians. One reason appeared to be that, when playing music and sharing moments outside of musical work, jazzmen felt more comfortable with other jazzmen. Masculine socializations had prepared them to share more topics of interest, to behave in more similar ways on a daily basis. A second reason explaining female marginalization was their high seductive power – as for female singers – which made them difficult to envision as regular colleagues. Interviews did enable us to unveil this phenomenon: when musicians were asked to describe their professional connections (groups and invitations), female musicians were not often mentioned by their male counterparts as regular colleagues and female musicians had fewer opportunities to work on a regular basis as compared to their male colleagues. But observations were key in analysing why female musicians tended not to be treated as regular colleagues. Male-only interactions appeared much more relaxed, 'natural' and easy to handle for male musicians than mixed interactions, both in work situations – including dealing with conflicts and fights over music, – and in leisure situations – when partying, drinking, travelling. Male norms made it easier for men to work with other men in this jazz world, partly explaining female instrumentalists' marginalization over the age of 30.

Third, women may become 'fed up' with working in male milieus that they consider unlikely to include them professionally or where they find it difficult to gain recognition for their professional abilities. This difficulty is explained in part by the maleness of work norms that make it harder for women to participate than men. Here again, ethnography helps in identifying these gender norms and their possible effect on the construction of occupational work positions, as shown in my study about unionists (Buscatto, 2009). The very way that union activity operated was strongly marked by norms that are socially constructed as 'masculine' – topics of conversations, valued public behaviours, flexibility outside of work. All this made it difficult for women to gain a foothold in union worlds. As this example clearly showed, it was by comparing data collected in interviews – concerning areas of interest, modes of acceding to union positions, ideas about union activity – with data collected through observation – union member gatherings, social behaviour, the mutual inviting that union members do – that I could spot which social norms were valued and/or activated by sex and what their gender-related effects were on unionists' trajectories. Unionism was a 'male' activity, and as such it was less likely to attract women than men. When it did attract them 'anyway', it afforded them a position that they were then hard-pressed to construct in a 'masculine' way.

REFLEXIVITY AS A SCIENTIFIC MODEL

But then, how does one conduct an ethnographic study scientifically? The anthropologists who invented field studies in the late nineteenth century, most notably Bronislaw Malinowski and Edward E. Evans Pritchard, defined their way of proceeding to be scientific (Gobo, 2008). The stated aim was to collect ethnographic data in an objective way. But anthropology was destabilizing the positivist scientific model and ethnography soon appeared as incomplete, lacking and imperfect (Buscatto, 2016).[3] It thus could not be practised with a blind respect for the positivist method based on the presumed superiority of the hypothetico-deductive model and the understanding that it would ensure objectivity for the collected 'data'.

In the positivist method, researchers construct hypotheses, indicators and questions in order to ensure that they will not be caught up in, or tripped up by, preconceptions, which may conflict with the objectivity of the experimental method. But very soon, ethnographic researchers could not be considered as being protected from their theoretical or personal biases. They were potentially considered as systematically falling victim to them. And being integrated into the community they were studying offered no external guarantee that they would be able to break free of their ideologies, assumptions, or preconceptions. It was considered, very early on, that researchers' past experience, personality, and cultural orientations necessarily influence what they see and how they interpret it. Realizing this, anthropologists were quick to construct a reflexive scientific approach.

Reflexivity implies reconciling the opposites of involvement and detachment (Elias, 1956; Hughes, 1971). The intention of constant and rigorous adherence to this principle is to provide a solid basis for research without eroding its primary quality: the researcher's ability to adapt to the experience and realities of the people she is observing. Though involvement does imply constant flexibility and adaptability on the part of ethnographic researchers, they must still be vigilant about maintaining distance, remaining detached. Involvement is a construction that the researcher needs to analyse and negotiate with actors in connection with the rules structuring the social system in which they operate. Detachment is a continuous activity and guides the researcher's choices in all phases of his involvement: determining how to behave, what strategies to implement, the limits to impose on her action and analysing collected observations in relation to the roles played. But in her involvement, the researcher may go through phases of intense identification. The processes underlying that kind of identification then have to be analysed, deciphered, and contextualized so as to apprehend, if only after the fact, the workings of the action structuring the negotiated relationship between the researcher and the observed actors and to assess their implications for the study. These last activities are what is meant by detachment. Detachment thus requires the researcher to describe and critically question her way of viewing the world and the social conditions in which 'data' are produced in the research act (for developments, see Gobo, Chapter 5, this volume).

HOW DOES ONE START AN ETHNOGRAPHIC RESEARCH?

Following reflexivity as a scientific model, ethnography is supposedly an inductive method, which implies that one is to start observations as openly as possible in order to let analyses emerge from observations (as opposed to a deductive method which entices the researcher to start by developing strong theoretical-driven hypotheses to be tested empirically (for a detailed discussion of induction, deduction, abduction, see Kennedy and Thornberg, Chapter 4, this volume). As nicely stated by Atkinson 'we create the fields we study, in collaboration with hosts and informants, through the research acts we enact' (Atkinson, 2015, p. 26). However, as also asserted by Atkinson, even if ethnography does suggest that the observer is to let the field 'speak' through time, she is also to guide those observations whenever necessary. Indeed, sheer induction never happens since researchers, as educated human beings, do hold preconceived ideas about the world. So, one is to follow two main principles when entering his or her 'field', in order not to get trapped in such a sheer inductive illusion.

Before starting his field, the ethnographer is to wonder what to observe and how. Since she is far from being a neutral and fully open-minded human being, what is best here is to build up and define specific 'theoretical orientations' and 'target-question' in order to avoid, as much as possible, being influenced by preconceptions without being aware of them. Whether he is aware of them or not, 'theoretical orientations' shape the way the ethnographer defines his discipline scope, society as a whole, the ways individuals are shaped and how they participate in shaping society collectively. Ethnography being an inductive method which implies that the ethnographer is guided by what she observes in order to progressively fabricate sociological results, she does start conducting her observations as openly as possible, so that theoretical orientations are not to be confused with a specific school of thought. But theoretical orientations do participate in shaping how the ethnographer starts observing and it is important that she is aware of them so as to be able, if needed, to transform them over time. They also enable the ethnographer to define a 'target-question' being as adequate as it can be, right from the beginning. Indeed, the 'target-question' is directly linked to the 'theoretical orientations', while specifying the topic to be investigated over time, even in quite general terms (the 'target-question' is to be enriched, transformed, confirmed throughout the research). Thanks to this 'target-question' – for instance social mobility, illness trajectories, organizational socialization, gender at work, or urban dynamics – the ethnographer will be able to decide what is to be observed and how. The ethnographer can then more easily define where to start observations and how to lead them over time. It will guide the ethnographer in deciding where to observe, how and in which conditions, and can also be transformed over time based on a first analysis of initial observations (for instance if the target-question appears too narrow-minded or misconstructed or biased, based on a first analysis of data as detailed below).

If right from the beginning the observer is as open, fluid and available as possible and tries to be as close to and familiar with the people she observes, 'theoretical orientations' and 'target-questions' do enable her to be as efficient as she can be in developing rigorous sociological findings. Glaser and Strauss, while defending in their 1968 seminal book, ethnography as an inductive method – the 'grounded theory' – did define such guiding principles when illustrating their use of ethnography empirically:

> The general problem to be investigated was whether different ideologies did exist among the various psychiatric professionals. [...] Field work was begun first at the private hospital and directed initially only by the frameworks of ideas known as the 'sociology of work' and 'symbolic interactionism'. (Glaser and Strauss, 1968, p. 157)

In this example, they not only identify clear 'theoretical orientations' – 'sociology of work' and 'symbolic interactionism' – but also a well-defined 'target-question' – 'whether different ideologies did exist among the various psychiatric professionals'. Those choices led them to define one specific field – a psychiatric hospital, people to be observed, that is, all the people involved in treating psychiatric patients – and a long-term observation strategy in order to identify ways psychiatric professionals were collectively defining psychiatric illnesses and negotiating their roles in treating them through time.

As clearly stated by Atkinson:

> We do not pull theories and hypotheses out of thin air. We derive them from a variety of sources: our own prior exposure to phenomena, the work of others (published or otherwise) and our first engagements with our research field. (Atkinson, 2015, p. 56)

Based on his initial clearly-stated theoretical orientations and target-question, the researcher will decide what to observe – focusing on one or a few specific settings or following people (on 'Go-alongs', see Kusenbach, Chapter 22, this volume); how to do it – as a participant or non-participant observer, covertly or not; and along which timings – on a regular basis, evenings only, at different moments throughout the year. Studying freelance musicians who work in several separated places from a gendered perspective (Buscatto, 2007a, 2007b) led me to observe as many different situations as possible – concerts, rehearsals, parties, training sessions, jam sessions, private moments – as a participant and non-participant observer, while studying organizational socializations affecting first-level and middle-manager insurance workers led me to focus on two specific departments over a full year at different moments of their organizational life (Buscatto, 2008).

So researchers need to be aware how they build up their theoretical orientations and target-questions, how relevant they are, how they influence them in the process of entering the field and decide what to observe and how. This will help them make the most relevant decisions throughout the full research process.

HOW DOES ONE BUILD UP GROUNDED ANALYSES?

If the researcher is to be as open as possible while leading his first observations, he also needs to analyse them as soon as possible in order to produce the most appropriate working hypotheses or categories to orient his observational strategies over time. As stated very early on by Glaser and Strauss:

> Whether the sociologist as he jointly collects and analyses qualitative data, starts out in a confused state of noting almost everything he sees because it all seems significant, or whether he starts out with a more defined purpose, his work quickly leads to the generation of hypotheses. (Glaser and Strauss, 1968, p. 39)

Those first analyses, which are of course enlightened by initial theoretical orientations and target-question (see above), will help the ethnographer decide which situations to focus on in the next days and which actors to include (or not) in her next observations (Charmaz and Bryant, 2016). If the topic is familiar to the ethnographer (because similar research has been done and published in the past), she may start with what Giampetro Gobo calls 'working hypotheses' (Gobo, 2008; see Gobo, Chapter 5, this volume). If the topic is new and has not been explored yet or if the researcher wants to renew the current approach to this topic, she will more probably develop general 'guiding hypotheses'. Those hypotheses do help the ethnographer to better define what is to be observed, when and how, but should never constrain the observer completely, so that alternative hypotheses may be defined if they seem to fit better with what comes out of the analysis of the first observations conducted in the field. If unexpected observations ask for new concepts or categories (not to be found in the current literature), one is to develop an abductive reasoning. Abduction is key when one observes situations which cannot be explained by current concepts, leading the researcher to create new ones along the way so as to make sense of his field (Agar, 2006; see Kennedy and Thornberg, Chapter 4, this volume).

But those analyses do not mean anything if they are not based on notes which are to be as detailed and factual as possible (for detailed explanations and examples, see Wästerfors, Chapter 20, this volume). Notes may be taken on the spot (visibly if they do not affect observed people since they are accepted behaviours, such as in concerts, rehearsals, meetings or administrative work) or may be done in hidden places (toilets for instance) or afterwards (at home, in a café, at school…) when they might affect people's behaviours or are impossible to do, as in mobile work, illegal settings, or places of leisure. In all cases, one is to take as detailed and precise notes as possible of observed activities, observed people's characteristics (age, clothes, status, sex, links with other observed people if any), and observed places (size, configuration, or objects). Who is interacting with whom? Who is doing what and how? What are the objects or documents involved? Those are some of the questions those notes try to document. Of course, what is to be observed and reported highly depends on the target-question and the working hypotheses, which will help the ethnographer fine-tune them over time (and transform them according to what is observed). The researcher will be able to compare what can be compared, to distinguish recurring facts from exceptional facts, major actors from minor ones, to explain similarities and differences in rigorous and documented ways. If the ethnographer is eager to mention a personal remark (emotions, feelings, working hypotheses, or intuitions, methodological questions, categorizations…), he would rather indicate it in a way that clearly distinguishes it from factual observed details (a different colour, a noticeable sign, a large interval).

While observations are piling up, working hypotheses are getting fine-tuned, sociological analyses are getting specified, the ethnographer may decide to focus on specific situations or moments or people in order to confirm, enrich, or transform her target-question, her theoretical orientations, or her final analyses. For instance, after a few weeks observing workers at Hermes, an insurance company, I noticed that middle managers were experiencing quite a difficult situation and were feeling both humiliated and threatened. I then decided to observe more middle managers than expected in order to both better understand Hermes organizational socialization at work (my main target-question), and better grasp the experience of middle managers in big companies (the literature devoted to this specific question did not seem convincing to me, which enticed me to add this secondary target-question to my main one). Later on, in opposition to the literature devoted to middle management at the time, I was able to identify a 'social psychologization' phenomenon which was both producing and legitimating middle managers' difficulties in such companies (Buscatto, 2008).

The ethnographic process then appears as a circular one, oscillating between initial questions, observations, hypotheses, and conceptual analyses. First, theoretical orientations and target-questions lead the researcher to pick specific observational conditions and working hypotheses. Initial observations, once analysed, help the ethnographer question those orientations, questions, and hypotheses and either confirm or transform them. They progressively lead to the formulation of first conceptual categories and sociological results. This iterative and systematic research process, aimed at developing sound sociological explanations, may be labelled as either an actual version of the grounded theory (Charmaz and Bryant, 2016) or 'analytic induction' (for a discussion of analytic induction as compared to grounded theory, see Hammersley, 2010).

HOW DOES ONE CONDUCT A SCIENTIFIC ETHNOGRAPHIC RESEARCH?

But what does one exactly do when conducting a scientific ethnographic research?

'A cookbook approach towards collecting data and writing up one's results is rejected here' (Rosen, 1991, p. 11). Indeed, there is no single set of formulas or practical guidelines that will suffice to attain the desired scientific quality or goal. While finely detailed techniques may be developed to help researchers achieve rigorous, controlled practice, in the reflexive approach those techniques cannot be seen as mere procedures to be followed, standards to evaluate or rules to follow and check off:

> What we need to do now is to show the ways in which quality research can be every bit as credible as the best quantitative work. Part of that will involve recognizing that good quality research depends upon craft skills that ultimately transcend the kind of lists of factors that we have been reviewing in this chapter. (Silverman, 2006, p. 311)

HOW IS ONE TO PROCEED THEN?

There are many techniques that are useful in adopting a reflexive approach in ethnography. They include, for instance, 'saturation' (see below), 'triangulation' (see Flick, Chapter 34, this volume), 'counting' and 'measuring' (see Buscatto, 2016; and Gobo, Chapter 5, this volume), analysis of the social conditions in which 'data' are produced and analysed (see below), collective research, combining comparable cases (see below, as well as Sørensen et al., Chapter 10, this volume about comparison), note-taking technique (see above and see Wästerfors, Chapter 20, this volume), or sharing and 'discussing' research findings with observed actors (see Buscatto, 2008). To convey how reflexive approaches are effectively practised, I will here discuss two specific major techniques in detail: the first, comparison and the second, the analysis of social conditions in which 'data' are produced and analysed.

Using comparison throughout the scientific process

Comparative analysis is an ancient scientific practice, considered as key in developing reliable scientific results. For instance, very early on, Emile Durkheim asserts that 'la méthode comparative est la seule qui convienne à la sociologie' (Durkheim, 1986 [1895], p. 15).[4] Indeed, comparative analysis does enable the researcher to step from a specific case study to a higher level of generalization (conceptualizing, theorizing, or categorizing) in controlled ways. For Everett Hughes, 'the essence of the comparative frame is that one seeks differences in terms of dimensions to all the cases' (Hughes, 1971, p. 420). By connecting several specific observed groups or settings with each other, the researcher is able to unveil more conceptual explanations in rigorous ways. For Glaser and Strauss 'the constant comparing of many groups draws the sociologist's attention to their many similarities and differences. Considering this leads him to generate abstract categories and their properties, which, since they emerge from the data, will clearly be important to a theory explaining the kind of behaviour under observation' (Glaser and Strauss, 1968, p. 36).

But the ways groups or settings are to be compared fully depend on the research question. When he attempts to grasp the influence of state policies on the production of specific 'Factory regimes', the ethnographer Michael Burawoy compares companies with similar activities and organizations evolving in different countries (Burawoy, 1985). When I attempted to understand how organizational socializations were shaped within companies, I chose to compare two French insurance companies whose size, activities, and formal rules were quite similar, so that specific organizational socializations built-up by workers, unions and employers could be unveiled (Buscatto, 2008).

The researcher will have to decide how different or similar the groups or settings being compared should be. 'Minimizing differences among comparison groups also helps establish a definite set of conditions under which a category exists' (Glaser and Strauss, 1968, p. 56). It is best when one is studying an exploratory topic and wants to focus on a limited set of interpretive possibilities. This idea guided my choice of two French insurance companies sharing several traits (size, turnover, business objectives, types of customers) and of two similar departments dealing with the same activity in both companies, so that my study would focus on organizational socialization only. On the other hand, 'when maximizing differences among comparative groups (thereby maximizing differences in data) he possesses a more powerful means for stimulating the generation of theoretical properties once his basic framework has emerged' (Glaser and Strauss, 1968, p. 57). In this same study, this idea led me to observe very different types of workers (by sex, age, work, or time spent in the company) and diverse working units within both departments, so that organizational socialization could be defined thoroughly despite all individual differences and work units.

Comparison is not a natural reality, it is constructed by the ethnographer, based on her research question and working hypotheses. But since ethnographic research is not a chemistry experiment, the analysis is to be as rigorous as possible to avoid over-interpretation or mis-interpretation since compared groups, settings, or traits, even if precisely defined, are never fully similar.

Analysing the social conditions under which a research study is conducted

Another key technique to ensure the quality of one's research is to analyse the social conditions under which 'data' and data analysis are produced. As stated by Sudhir Venkatesh, reflecting on his ethnographic study of a poor public housing development in Chicago in the 1990s:

> Reconstructing the informants' point of view – in this case their perceptions of the fieldworker as, variously, academic hustler, 'nigger just like us' and 'Arab' – can aid the researcher in determining patterns of structure and meaning among the individual, group, and/or community under study. (Venkatesh, 2002, p. 91)

For reflexive sociologists, the ethnographic study and its interpretation are founded on the relation between the researcher(s) and the observed actors. The ways in which an ethnographer is allowed to observe people through time (or not), as well as ways she may interpret those observations, are indeed widely dependent on reciprocal social positions or roles negotiated (or not) between the observer and observed.

In reflexive sociological practice, the social conditions for producing empirical material are thus a fundamental component of the analysis when it comes to checking which data you produce and constructing a findings-based analysis. Ethnographers have identified several stages in the process in which it is helpful to analyse the observed–observer relationship: constructing the observed population; opening doors in the field; maintaining oneself in the field; determining how the researcher–observed actors' relationship is produced; and choosing how to analyse the collected data. The process unfolds over time and, as explained, it cannot follow predefined rules.

The ethnographer is thus to try out social positions or roles in the field in order to open closed doors, elicit invitations, circumvent prefabricated discourse, gain access to the unsaid or *taboo*, and interpret rationally what she has observed once the study is over. Those social positions are both defined by the field's possibilities and by the researcher's specific characteristics and strategies. For instance, if an ethnographer is to observe an organization, one may try to develop different social positions in the field – as an expert, as an academic, as a friend, as a worker, as a trainee – depending on what the ethnographer is observing, when, and how (Buscatto, 2008).

But social positions are also defined by the ethnographer's social characteristics as perceived by the observed actors – age, professional status, physical appearance, sex, or prior relationships with observed actors. People will act differently with the ethnographer depending on his perceived age, sex, social position, or physical attributes, in relation to the way those characteristics are defined and interpreted by people in the field. It is key for the ethnographer to become aware of perceived positions throughout his study, day after day, and to assess how they affect what is observed and what it tells him about social relationships within the field. Moreover, those social positions and social characteristics may also influence the way one is to define his research question.

For instance, being a woman in a very masculine world may entice one to study gendered relations in this social world due to the repeated gendered experiences the researcher is going through (Buscatto, 2007b), while being a dance musician (Becker, 1963) or a plant worker (Roy, 1952, see above) may lead the researcher to study ways dance musicians or plant workers define work on a daily basis. It not only makes one aware of those questions, but also opens up opportunities to do so by allowing one to observe several situations that enrich the analysis. While social relationships that are developed with the actors are constantly being constructed and reconstructed in a chaotic, experimental way, the researcher is also analysing it in depth so as to discover the best way to observe what needs to be observed, and interpret the experienced situations, whatever they happen to be.

HOW IS ONE TO DECIDE WHEN TO STOP COLLECTING ETHNOGRAPHIC DATA?

While defining one's field, based on her theoretical orientations and target-question, the researcher is able to guide her observational strategies as appropriately as possible and may even transform them over time based on the analysis of ongoing observations. She is progressively building up categories, or even concepts, which enable her to present sound and rigorous scientific results. But how does one assess she is finished with observations? How does one decide that the analysis is well grounded and the observation period is over? One analysis technique to be used here is what Glaser and Strauss have called 'saturation' (see Charmaz and Bryant, 2016 as well as Schreier, Chapter 6, this volume).

While the researcher, based on his observations, has progressively shaped categories, or even concepts throughout the study, which enable him to answer the 'target-question' in adequate terms, he is experiencing at some point not learning anything 'new' regarding those preliminary analyses when observing new situations and people. One is then to implement a few more observations in order to repeatedly experience this feeling of 'saturation' thoroughly and make sure it is not linked to boredom or over-interpretation. The ethnographer may consider this final phase as a perfect phase to test all working hypotheses, categories, or concepts in quite confortable ways. Most of the time, those first sociological conclusions are not yet formally expressed in academic terms, but they are sufficiently well-defined in sociological terms to be tested in the field.

For instance, while I was studying jazz singers from a gendered perspective, I did experience the saturation phenomenon in the last stages of my field observation, before starting to write the first scientific article presenting my findings in academic terms. I had not yet defined their situation as a gendered marginalization and had also not clearly defined the three key processes that were producing and legitimating this situation in the jazz world. But, thanks to my ongoing analysis of field observations and formal interviews, I had already assessed the gendered construction of their professional reputation and of musical relations shaped by female singers and male instrumentalists through interaction. The last weeks of observation made me feel 'saturation' and I decided to stop observing the jazz world in order to focus on writing this first academic article. But I was ready to renew observations if a thorough analysis had showed contradictions or conflicting interpretations which could not be settled based on collected data, which did not happen, as is the case if the saturation phenomenon is based on a systematic and rigorous analysis of observations aimed at answering one's target-question. But I did start new lengthy observations of the jazz world a few years later when I developed a new target-question – why are there so few female instrumentalists? This new target-question could not be answered based on my former observations, which had mainly focused on jazz singers, even if some data did already help me in doing so. I could then not only confirm what had already been demonstrated in this first article on female jazz singers, but also describe and explain how the marginalization of female jazz instrumentalists was daily produced and legitimated in the French jazz world (Buscatto, 2007a, 2007b).

So saturation is to be understood in relation to a specific target-question and is possible only if one is analysing his observations on a daily basis, enlightened by his explicit theoretical orientations and working hypotheses. Of course, saturation may be impeded either by lack of time (results are expected before this phenomenon is experienced thoroughly), or because the field is not available anymore (at the end of a contract or if people refuse to be observed any longer for instance). The researcher may then have to redefine the target-question, or reduce the scope or express the limits of his analysis, in order to ensure that sociological results which are presented in a written form do answer scientific expectations.

ETHNOGRAPHY AND ITS POTENTIAL LIMITS

Ethnography is often denigrated for its limited access to social phenomena and its difficulty in assessing the quality of results with rigor due both to the ethnographer's strong involvement in the field and the limited scope of this field. But those potential limits have long been discussed by ethnographers to show that ethnography may not only produce high-quality results, but also open the road to strong generalizations. Indeed, due to her long-term involvement in the field, the researcher has many opportunities to test her conclusions over time (saturation being one of them as shown above). Moreover, he may use observed people's feedback to improve his conclusions over time (Buscatto, 2008). Regarding generalizations, several ethnographers have demonstrated how ethnographic studies have built-up new strong concepts such as 'total institutions' (Goffman, 1961), 'moral entrepreneurs' (Becker, 1963) or 'factory regimes' (Burawoy, 1985) which enabled researchers using questionnaires or interviews to better analyse social phenomena afterwards.

Ethnography is also often criticized for its potential ethical limits since observed people are often very close to the observer and give her access to the most personal parts of their lives. But, as stated by Atkinson (2015), ethnography appears as quite an ethical method in that it not only implies a strong commitment of the researcher towards her observed people, but also tends to give the most accurate account of what is going on in the observed field. However, it does not prevent the researcher from answering some tricky ethical questions: how does one get people to consent to the observations they are enduring? How does one ensure that observed people do not get hurt along the way? Regarding the issue of consent, the majority of the time the situation is quite difficult to deal with. If one may easily ask consent of people observed on a recurring basis (the chore of most observations such as nurses in a hospital, street-people or employees in an insurance company), he will most of the time observe people who cannot be informed of his position without disturbing the observed activity (such as customers, patients, passers-by, temporary workers, the audience, etc.). Therefore, one has to admit that, if informed consent should be definitely obtained from people who are regularly observed, it may not be required from occasional observed people who are just passing through.

This leads us to what we consider as the most important issue in ethnography: how to make sure people do not get hurt when results are published? Published results may affect people in two main ways. On the one side, if one is to be recognized by colleagues, friends, or family, his or her reputation may be denigrated, even if it was not intended (for such a case see Whyte, 1943). The solution here is to ensure each individual's anonymity, not only by erasing all real names, but also by making sure that the people who know those persons can trace neither example nor portrait back to one specific individual. In observed worlds where people know each other well – such as the jazz world, an organization or an orchestra – the ethnographer is to give few details or to present composed portraits – mixing elements drawn from different observed people – so that observed people cannot be recognized by their colleagues, their friends, their family. On the other hand, the unveiling of social dynamics may appear to be giving a bad image of specific environments (as sexist, racist, or corrupted for instance). Here, the researcher is to describe social dynamics as rigorously as possible, and to present precise and neutral examples, which may never be connected to one or the other person involved. This will not avoid some observed people being unhappy with the ways their social world is described from a sociological perspective, but it will cancel the negative consequences those published results may have on individuals (including their self-esteem). Our final advice here would be to present intermediary results to observed people as often as possible (see Buscatto, 2008 and 2016). It will not only help the researcher avoid misinterpretations and enrich his final scientific results, but it will also give observed people the opportunity to get accustomed to sociological reasoning, present their points of view (even if disagreeing) and get the researcher to write in the most distanced and neutral style to avoid as many negative consequences as possible.

CONCLUSION

As demonstrated throughout this chapter, if ethnography is a quite powerful and insightful method, which has historically proven its scientific efficiency, it also requires a strong personal involvement of the ethnographer in the field to be maintained over a long period of time. Ethnography appears as a quite time-consuming method, which one is to adopt if one is ready to involve oneself, both intellectually and personally. But the involvement is worth the effort, even if not always academically rewarded, since results are often quite powerful in unveiling how observed worlds function in the long run.

But ethnography is also evolving quite radically in relation to several changes affecting contemporary societies. On the one hand, since more and more people spend time playing, exchanging ideas, developing relationships or sourcing information through the Internet (see the chapters in Part VI, of this volume), ethnographers are developing new ways to study virtual life. The question is, then, to assess if virtual ethnography is about observing people interactions with each other or about reading documents produced by people whose identities are not known (see the section dedicated to this issue in this volume). On the other hand, new techniques such as video or sound data are more and more often used by ethnographers to enrich their analysis (for video data see Knoblauch et al., Chapter 23, this volume, and for sound data see Bull, Chapter 27, this volume). And how those different data are to be articulated is to be worked out thoroughly (see Hesse-Biber, Chapter 35, this volume).

The future of ethnography thus relies on its ability to answer those new empirical and epistemological challenges in reflexive and rigorous ways, as fully demonstrated by several chapters in this volume.

Notes

1. If Taylor or Mayo are hardly considered as ethnographers by contemporary sociologists, they did pave the way to the use of ethnography in sociology.
2. This discussion on how ethnography helps better grasp gendered phenomena is not to be confused with (otherwise insightful) discussions on either how women (as opposed to men) may develop specific ethnographies (for instance due to their privileged access to specific fields or phenomena, as thoroughly discussed below and in Buscatto, 2007b), or on the construction of a 'feminist ethnography' led by women only and dedicated to the study of women (due to the fact that, on the one hand, women tended to be underrepresented among sociologists, and still are at the highest academic levels, and, on the other, women have been understudied in sociology, up until at least the early 2000s).
3. All ideas briefly presented here are thoroughly developed and illustrated in a chapter about reflexivity in ethnography (Buscatto, 2016).
4. 'The comparative method is the only one which suits sociology' (our translation). Durkheim devotes a full chapter to this question in the mentioned book.

FURTHER READING

Atkinson, Paul (2015) *For Ethnography*. London: Sage.
Gobo, Giampietro (2008) *Doing Ethnography*. London: Sage.
Silverman, David (ed.) (2016) *Qualitative Research. Issues of Theory, Method and Practice* (4th Edition). London: Sage.

REFERENCES

Agar, M. (2006) 'An ethnography by any other name…', *Forum: Qualitative Social Research*, 7(4), Art. 36: http://www.qualitative-research.net/index.php/fqs/article/view/177/395.
Atkinson, Paul (2015) *For Ethnography*. London: Sage.
Becker, Howard S. (1963) *Outsiders: Studies in the Sociology of Deviance*. New York: The Free Press.
Becker, Howard S. (1982) *Art Worlds*. Berkeley, CA: University of California Press.
Burawoy, Michael B. (1985) *The Politics of Production. Factory Regimes Under Capitalism and Socialism*. London: Verso.
Burawoy, M. B. (1998) 'The extended case method', *Sociological Theory*, 16(1): 4–33.
Buscatto, Marie (2007a) *Femmes du jazz: musicalités, féminités, marginalisations*. Paris: CNRS Editions.

Buscatto, Marie (2007b) 'Contributions of ethnography to a gendered sociology: the French jazz world', *Qualitative Sociology Review*, III(3): 46–58.

Buscatto, Marie (2008) 'Who allowed you to observe? A reflexive overt organizational ethnography', *Qualitative Sociology Review*, IV(3): 29–48.

Buscatto, Marie (2009) 'Syndicaliste en entreprise: une activité si masculine…', in Patricia Roux and Olivier Filleule (eds.) *Le sexe du militantisme*. Paris: Presses de Science Po, pp. 75–91.

Buscatto, Marie (2010) 'Using ethnography to study gender', in David Silverman (ed.) *Qualitative Research. Issues of Theory, Method and Practice* (3rd Edition). London: Sage, pp. 35–52.

Buscatto, Marie (2016) 'Practising reflexivity in ethnography', in David Silverman (ed.), *Qualitative Research. Issues of Theory, Method and Practice* (4th Edition). London: Sage, pp. 137–51.

Charmaz, Kathy and Bryant, Antony (2016) 'Constructing grounded theory analyses', in David Silverman (ed.), *Qualitative Research. Issues of Theory, Method and Practice* (4th Edition). London: Sage, pp. 347–62.

Clifford, James and Marcus, George E. (eds.) (1986) *Writing Culture. The Poetics and Politics of Ethnography*. Berkeley, CA: University of California Press.

Durkheim, Emile (1986 [1895]) *Les règles de la méthode sociologique*. Paris: PUF.

Elias, N. (1956) 'Problems of involvement and detachment', *The British Journal of Sociology*, VII(3): 226–52.

Fine, G. A. (2003) 'Towards a peopled ethnography: developing theory from group life', *Ethnography*, 4(1): 41–60.

Garfinkel, Howard (1967) *Studies in Ethnomethodology*. Englewood Cliffs, NJ: Prentice Hall.

Glaser, Barney G. and Strauss, Anselm L. (1968) *The Discovery of Grounded Theory. Strategies for Qualitative Research*. London: Weidenfeld and Nicolson.

Gobo, Giampietro (2008) *Doing Ethnography*. London: Sage.

Goffman, Erving (1961) *Asylums: Essays on the Social Situation of Mental Patients and Other Inmates*. New York: Anchor Books.

Goffman, Erving (1997) 'Frame analysis of gender', in Charles Lemert and Ann Branaman (eds.), *The Goffman Reader*. Malden, MA: Blackwell Publishers, pp. 201–27.

Hammersley, M. (2010) 'A historical and comparative note on the relationship between analytic induction and grounded theorising', *Forum: Qualitative Social Research*, 11(2), Art. 4, http://www.qualitative-research.net/index.php/fqs/article/view/1400/2994.

Hammersley, Martyn and Atkinson, Paul (1995 [1983]) *Ethnography. Principles in Practice*. New York: Routledge.

Hughes, Everett C. (1971) *The Sociological Eye: Selected Papers on Work, Self and the Study of Society (Volume 2)*. Chicago, IL: Aldine.

Katz, J. (2004) 'On the rhetoric and politics of ethnographic methodology', *Annals of the American Academy of Political and Social Science*, 595(1): 280–308.

LaPiere, R. T. (1934) 'Attitudes versus actions', *Social Forces*, 13(2): 230–7.

Madge, John (1963) *The Origins of Scientific Sociology*. London: Tavistock.

Morrill, C. and Fine, G. A. (1997) 'Ethnographic contributions to organizational sociology', *Sociological Methods and Research*, 25(4): 424–51.

Rosen, M. (1991) 'Coming to terms with the field: understanding and doing organizational ethnography', *Journal of Management Studies*, 28(1): 1–24.

Roy, D. (1952) 'Quota restriction and goldbricking in a machine shop', *American Journal of Sociology*, 57(5): 427–42.

Silverman, David (2006) *Interpreting Qualitative Data: Methods for Analyzing Talk, Text and Interaction*. London: Sage.

Taylor, Stephanie (ed.) (2002) *Ethnographic Research. A Reader*. London: Sage.

Venkatesh, S. (2002) '"Doin" the hustle": constructing the ethnographer in the American ghetto', *Ethnography*, 3(1): 91–111.

Wacquant, L. (2003) 'Ethnografeast: a progress report on the practice and promise of ethnography', *Ethnography*, 4(1): 5–14.

Wacquant, L. (2005) 'Carnal connections: on embodiment, apprenticeship, and membership', *Qualitative Sociology*, 28(4): 445–74.

Weick, Karl A. (1985) 'Systematic observational methods', in G. Lindzey and E. Aronson (eds.)

The Handbook of Social Psychology. New York: Random House, pp. 567–634.

West, C. and Zimmerman, D. (1987) 'Doing gender', *Gender & Society*, 1(2): 125–51.

Whyte, William Foote (1993 [1943]) *Street Corner Society. The Social Structure of an Italian Slum*. Chicago, IL: Chicago University Press.

22
Go-Alongs

Margarethe Kusenbach

INTRODUCTION

Having emerged less than fifteen years ago, research based on mobile methods is a young and developing form of inquiry. While there are many examples of scholars using, in effect, mobile methods before the turn of the twenty-first century in anthropology, sociology and some other disciplines (e.g. Kozol, 1995; Lynch, 1960), systematic applications and methodological reflections of mobile methods are more recent, with the earliest articles published in the 2000s (Anderson, 2004; Ingold, 2004; Kusenbach, 2003; McDonald, 2005). From then on, and especially since around 2010, the literature on mobile methods has grown dramatically in both volume and coverage. Mobile methods are now explored in a wide variety of academic disciplines, from communication to geography to health studies, and on several continents. The dissemination of mobile methods to different regions of the academy and the world is, in itself, an interesting case of mobility that deserves close examination on another occasion. Overall, the rapidly increasing interest in the topic has led to a surprisingly broad understanding and adoption of mobile methods in a short time period.

As of 2016, well over a hundred individual articles have been published on mobile research methods, in addition to a few dozen monographs, edited collections and special issues of journals – too many to list here. Two journals (*Mobilities* and *Transfers*) and a recent handbook (Adey et al., 2014) are devoted entirely to mobility studies, signaling the ongoing institutionalization of this new area of research. Another trend toward canonization is marked by the inclusion of mobile methods-themed sections and vignettes in disciplinary handbooks (e.g. Delamont, 2012), methods texts (e.g. Warren and Karner, 2009), and other instructional literature (e.g. Chen et al., 2012). Notably, several scholars have published insightful overviews of the larger field of mobility studies as well as various mobile methods (e.g. Hein et al., 2008; Merriman, 2014; Quinlan, 2008; Sheller, 2014).

For the purpose of depth rather than breadth, I here focus on a narrower version of what is considered mobile methods, which could be defined broadly as a group of innovative research methods that capture the increasing mobilities of people, goods and objects, images, ideas, and communication (Sheller and Urry, 2006). Being among the earliest contributors to this literature (Kusenbach, 2003), I have a particular interest in what I then, for lack of a more formal term, called 'go-alongs' – a label that has since been picked up by many, along with other names referring to similar practices, as discussed in more detail below. In simple terms, go-alongs are techniques of data collection during which researchers participate in patterns of movements with their human subjects. Researchers 'go along' (meaning they walk, run, ride, drive and so on) with study participants as the latter engage in more or less 'natural' spatial-social activities. Because going along with people requires researchers to enter a 'field' of some sort and meet study participants where their lives take place (see Bengry, Chapter 7, this volume), I first and foremost consider go-alongs to be an ethnographic research method (see Buscatto, Chapter 21, this volume), despite some modifications to the fieldworker's ideal of 'being there' while observing (see Wästerfors, Chapter 20, this volume) and participating in other people's lives. As a type of mobile method, go-alongs afford researchers innovative access and insights to issues of agency, identity and interaction on the one hand, and power, institutions and social structures on the other. With many others, I maintain that this new technique of data collection is worthy of inclusion in contemporary methodological toolkits and debates in the social sciences.

In the following section, I briefly outline the scholarly origins and contexts of mobile methods in general and go-alongs in particular. Next, I discuss some key characteristics of go-along research and then illustrate the method's two major types. The last three sections of the chapter address important issues scholars must consider when using go-alongs in their research, discuss the method's limitations and strengths, and offer thoughts on future directions. This chapter is an adaptation of an earlier overview of mobile methods written for another handbook (Kusenbach, 2012). I thank Elgar Publishing for permission to reuse some of the writing and many of the ideas developed in the earlier publication.

ORIGINS AND CONTEXTS

In this section I briefly sketch the academic milieus that gave rise to mobile methods in general, and the method of the go-along in particular. Two settings are especially noteworthy in this respect: first, the so-called Mobilities Paradigm and second, qualitative researchers' interest in phenomenology and methodological innovation. Other contexts that have spurred examinations of mobility in research methods – such as visual studies, technology and media studies, theories of the body and social network theories (Büscher and Urry, 2009; Hein et al., 2008; Sheller, 2014) as well as historical, artistic, literary and cinematic inspirations (Edensor, 2010; Jenks and Neves, 2000; Pink et al., 2010) – cannot be touched upon here.

The Mobilities Paradigm

Since the early 2000s, throughout numerous publications, scholars John Urry, Monika Büscher and Mimi Sheller have sketched out the contours of a new Mobilities Paradigm which is rooted in a broadly hailed 'Spatial Turn' of the social sciences. Bridging research on migration, transnationalism, globalization, tourism, transportation, cities, communication and other topics, the Mobilities Paradigm highlights the ubiquitous forms of travel that characterize modern societies: movements of people, goods and objects, images, ideas, and communication (Sheller, 2014). The rapid increase in local and global mobility, whether forced or voluntary, is viewed to be the result of new technologies and other innovations, as well as the growing interdependence of human networks and social systems. As social life and societies, for better or for worse, have become increasingly mobile, social scientists have developed new forms of research and representation that reflect these changes, giving rise to what is broadly called mobile methods (Sheller and Urry, 2006).

According to its founders, the Mobilities Paradigm signifies an ideological trend away from long-standing 'sedentary' tendencies in academia, in theory as well as in research. Mobility researchers take a stance against static world views defined by territorialism, nationalism and immobile structures. They move toward developing perspectives that transcend disciplinary and geographical boundaries, and that prioritize dynamism and social change. Mobility researchers continue to be inspired by a range of theoretical perspectives, including the work of Foucault, phenomenology, and critical and postcolonial theory (Sheller, 2014). According to Sheller, what characterizes mobility research writ large is that it

> is not simply about a topic (e.g. things that move, or the governance of mobility regimes, or the idea of an increasingly mobile world) but is even more pointedly a new way of approaching social research, social theory, and social agency. (2014, p. 801)

Compared with the ambitious transformations of the scholarly landscape envisioned by proponents of the Mobilities Paradigm, the goals of go-along users are on a much smaller scale. Nonetheless, the increasing popularity of mobility studies provides a conceptual backdrop, and perhaps an institutional base, for go-along users' more modest efforts toward improving social science methods of data collection. There is no doubt that the Mobilities Paradigm will continue to amplify and help disseminate their work.

Phenomenology and Methodological Innovation

Without connecting explicitly to the Mobilities Paradigm, numerous scholars writing about mobile methods draw on phenomenology – more specifically, on the works of phenomenologically minded philosophers (Casey, 1993), geographers (Relph, 1976; Tuan, 1976), sociologists (Simmel, 1989–2015; de Certeau, 1984) and others who have highlighted the significance, and even primacy, of the embodied spatial environment in human experience and social life. For instance, the philosopher Casey speaks of a 'constitutive coingredience' of self and place and claims that 'each is essential to the being of the other' (2001, p. 684; also see Ross et al., 2009). The argument goes that, if environment and place are fundamental features of human identity and social life, they must play an integral part in scholarly investigations and representations of these topics as well. Phenomenologically informed scholars often critique more traditional qualitative and ethnographic methods, such as participant observation and interviewing, on this ground.

On the one hand, ethnographers have pondered shortcomings and limitations of stationary observational research – such as inadequate access to participants' hidden identities and emotions, their reflections, and other locations, especially in comparison with interviews (Kleinman et al., 1994). In response, many of today's best ethnographies are based on triangulated data (see Flick, Chapter 34, this volume). They include a mixture of research techniques that routinely go beyond simply 'hanging out'. Ethnography is increasingly understood as a multi-sited (Hannerz, 2003; Marcus, 1995; for recent examples see Brown-Saracino 2010; Desmond 2016; Jerolmack 2013) and even global enterprise (Burawoy et al., 2000), requiring researchers to move from one place to the next in order to follow the spatial flows and patterns of the field (see Buscatto, Chapter 21, this volume). Even though some ethnographers nostalgically cling to the early twentieth-century image of fieldwork as something involving 'dirty pant seats' from sitting on doorsteps (to invoke Robert Parks' famous call to action), Duneier's (2004) 'shoe leather' is arguably a better metaphor for contemporary ethnographic research. In today's academic climate of limited budgets and institutional oversight, studying multiple sites requires much advance planning and careful sampling (see Schreier, Chapter 6, this volume). Contemporary ethnographers continue to mobilize and choreograph their fieldwork, in part due to the realization that their fields have become more fluid and complex.

On the other hand, a number of qualitative researchers who predominantly favored interviews became dissatisfied with the lack of 'emplacement' of this particular method, leading them to include detailed observations on what Elswood and Martin (2000) called the 'micro-geographies' of interviews (also see Brown and Durrheim, 2009; Lamont and Swidler, 2014; Riley, 2010; Sin, 2003). The result was a trend toward more dynamic and place-sensitive interviewing techniques that continues today. Jones and co-authors note that mobilizing interviews provides

> a means to take the interviewing process out of the 'safe' confines of the interview room and allow the environment and the act of walking itself to move the collection of interview data in productive and sometimes entirely unexpected directions. (2008, p. 8)

In short, an interest in more complex and phenomenologically sensitive ways of collecting data was building up within various scholarly contexts. The described two lines of critique met in the development of hybrid techniques that combined elements of both observations and interviews, and facilitated other innovations.

This second cluster of thought, rather than the new Mobilities Paradigm, was what triggered the experimental use of 'go-alongs' in my dissertation research which I conducted between 1997 and 2000 in two neighborhoods in the Hollywood area of Los Angeles. Building on a long-standing interest in phenomenology, and inspired by my own experiences of walking, bicycling, riding the bus and driving around Los Angeles, one of my goals in the dissertation was to study the practical – as opposed to mental – maps and movements in the everyday lives of research participants. However, over time, I came to realize that neither sit-down interviewing nor any amount of hanging out, and not even living in the area as a neighbor and genuine community member, facilitated insights into practical mapping on a deeper level. To bridge this gap, I began asking participants for follow-up interviews that would take us out of the house together and allow for better access to their understandings and uses of local space. Many of these outings – e.g. commuting, walking the dog, exercising, running errands – led to unexpected and fascinating realizations. While providing inspiration and guidance, my dissertation advisor Jack Katz kindly encouraged me to write about the promising results of my methodological experiments, leading to the 2003 publication of my 'go-along' article in the journal *Ethnography* in a special issue on phenomenology and ethnography. Perhaps more interesting than my personal discovery of mobile methods is the fact that other qualitative researchers, inspired by various constellations of ideas which prominently included phenomenology (Spinney 2015), published articles on mobilizing field research and interviews around the same time (Anderson, 2004; Ingold, 2004; McDonald, 2005). It appeared that the time was ripe for a new methodological approach.

CHARACTERISTICS OF GO-ALONG RESEARCH

As already stated, go-alongs are but one data collection technique in the much larger catalog of mobile methods. Go-alongs refer to 'methods of participating in patterns of movement while conducting research' (Büscher et al., 2011, p. 8). According to Hein and colleagues, go-alongs describe those instances where 'research subject and researcher are in motion in the "field"' (2008, p. 1276). Spinney offers another suitable definition of go-alongs, describing them as 'any method that attempts to (re)place the researchers alongside the participant in the context of the "doing" of mobility' (2015, p. 232).

Researchers have used various names to describe this kind of research, the informal 'go-along' being only one of them. Other labels include 'bimbling' and 'talking whilst walking' (Anderson, 2004), 'walking probes' (DeLeon and Cohen, 2005), 'mobile narratives' (Hall, 2009), 'shadowing' (Czarniawska, 2007; Ferguson, 2016; McDonald, 2005; Quinlan, 2008; Trouille and Tavory, 2016), 'walking interviews' (Evans and Jones, 2011), 'guided walks' (Ross et al., 2009), 'walking & talking' (Stals et al., 2014), 'walk-along interviews' (Van Cauwenberg et al., 2012), and likely many others. Despite its informality, the concept of the 'go-along' still appears useful because it works well as a noun and a verb, and because it does not limit the mode of researcher–participant mobility to walking. Besides, it is fairly short and carries no previous baggage that may result in bias or misunderstandings.

At this point in time, owing to its roots in ethnography and interviewing, the go-along is overwhelmingly qualitative which means that this technique is used to produce in-depth, non-numerical data sets involving a relatively small number of participants. The go-along is a tool for describing and understanding, rather than explaining and predicting, patterns of social and spatial engagement. Material or electronic aids and technologies (such as maps, photographs, GIS, GPS) can certainly be used in supportive ways while researchers go along with people in the field, however their use alone does not constitute a method of data collection (Merriman, 2014). The concept of method is not tied to the use of a particular tool or technology yet, rather, refers to a particular kind of relationship between researchers and research participants, and it is linked to theoretical ideas on the ways and possibilities of knowing (epistemologies).

In this sense, go-alongs as a scholarly method of data collection display the following five characteristics: they are (a) place-based, (b) person-centered, (c) interactive, (d) systematic, and (e) symbolic.

Place-Based

The statement that go-alongs are place-based encompasses two related ideas. For one, go-along practitioners subscribe to the belief that 'place matters'. They consider places and spatial environments to be important, if not essential, components of human experience and social life. For this reason, in order to better understand these issues, scholars see a need to move their research to the locations where the lives of participants happen or, literally, 'take place'. In other words, the go-along is a field-driven, ethnographic method of research that is situated within everyday contexts.

On a second level, saying that go-alongs are place-based goes beyond their mere location, as situating research in 'natural' places accomplishes something else. Researchers and participants involved in go-alongs not only encounter each other but they also unite in facing a third dimension together, the surrounding environment. Or, to use Hall's poignant metaphor, go-alongs entangle researchers and participants in 'three way conversations' (2009, p. 582). The social geographer Seamon (1979) suggested that human engagement with the environment unfolds on an 'awareness continuum' consisting of complete separation on the one hand and complete mergence on the other. When research happens in 'natural' locations, this continuum can be included as part of the investigation. Go-alongs thus produce insights into the qualities of environmental engagement, of the 'coingredience' of selves and places contemplated by Casey. In sum, everyday places not only provide authentic locations and backdrops for go-along data collection but they allow researchers to consider place and place-based relationships as integral components and topics of their work.

Person-Centered

Many scholars agree with Gieryn (2000) that place, as opposed to space, has three core components: a specific location, a material form and an infusion with social meaning. The latter, arguably place's most significant feature, is facilitated and accomplished through persons. While the environment, as just argued, can take on an almost agentic role, it is not the focus of go-along research in its own right. The primary goal of using go-alongs is to understand and theorize aspects of human experience and practice, thus issues that begin and end with socialized individuals. Go-along researchers are interested in places only inasmuch as they are part of individual or collective social experiences, as they are bestowed with meaning. This is what is meant by saying that go-alongs are person-centered.

Interactive

By definition, go-along research is not a solitary activity or an introspective exercise. Even though ethnographic reflexivity and positionality are desirable qualities of go-along research, it is not an auto-ethnographic method. Go-along researchers must interact with other persons who are being researched. These interactions typically occur face to face, in real time and place, or in what Sheller and Urry have called 'co-present immersion' (2006, p. 218). The use of mediated or asynchronous interactions is not inconceivable, yet it is doubtful whether these can produce the same nuanced data and insights. Stated otherwise, the go-along is an ethnographic method in which social interaction and personal relationships are critical instruments of data collection (Coffey, 1999). Just as with all fieldwork and interviews, go-alongs depend on functional, if not positive, relationships between researchers and participants. Without the goodwill and participation of research subjects, this form of investigation would not be successful.

Systematic

Go-along researchers strive to assemble cohesive and systematic sets of data. Similar to interview studies, conducting go-along research requires a thoughtful sampling of participants (see Small, 2009), followed by the repetition of a relatively focused research activity with each person. This sampling-based, cyclic approach to go-along research, purposed to result in a collection of limited individual encounters, is fundamentally different from the more linear sequence of gaining entry, getting along and exiting settings, and a special focus on key informants that is typical for ethnographic fieldwork. The goal of assembling a predefined and complete data set in go-along research goes beyond routine episodes of 'hanging out' with one or several insiders. Like interview research, go-along research is defined by a more strategic and systematic approach.

Symbolic

Lastly, go-along research is not primarily concerned with the technical or physical aspects of locations and movements but focuses on what they actually mean to the individuals, groups or cultures that use them. This point is linked with the interests of go-alongs in persons and place meanings, as discussed above. As people go through their everyday routines, they do not just move their physical bodies, even though the material and embodied aspects of mobility are significant in many ways. Places and movements are centrally linked to 'metamorphoses' of the self (Katz, 1999; Trouille and Tavory, 2016). As people depart from private homes and pass through neighborhoods and public spaces toward work, school, errands or play, their various identities and personal sensitivities ebb and flow in dialectic rhythms that both shape places and are shaped by them. The concept of the 'social realm' (Lofland, 1998) as both defined by, and defining, dominant forms of social interaction and relationships, is a case in point. The primary themes of go-along research are the symbolic personal and cultural places and mobilities that transcend the mechanics of spatiality and movement.

In sum, go-along research is rooted in ethnography's commitment to 'natural' environments and members' meanings (Emerson, 2001), and it thus reflects principles of symbolic interactionism, or interpretive sociology, as a theoretical home base within sociology. Nonetheless, go-along research is open to influences and critiques that originate in other disciplines, domains of research and theoretical paradigms.

TRAILS AND TOURS

Based on the above characteristics, go-alongs are best understood as a certain approach to researching others rather than a specific technique that would require one to follow a predefined series of steps. Researchers have a great deal of flexibility and creativity in carrying out go-along research, which is needed to design data collection with specific research questions, populations and locations in mind. The range of this kind of work is best described as a continuum based on who orchestrates the observed mobility, participants or researchers. On the one end, go-alongs take the form of 'trails' where routes and times of outings are entirely determined by participants, while on the other end they resemble 'tours' where researchers take more control (Evans and Jones, 2011).

Trails

Trails take advantage of 'natural' occasions for go-along research (Kusenbach, 2003, p. 463), meaning researchers study movements that occur within the real contexts of their informants' lives. Trails are systematic explorations of participants' mobile activities that already existed before researchers entered the scene and will most likely continue after researchers depart. This kind of go-along has also been called 'shadowing' by a number of scholars (e.g. Czarniawska, 2007; Ferguson, 2016; Jirón, 2011; McDonald, 2005; Trouille and Tavory, 2016), a verb that captures the involved research activity quite well. One slight advantage of the 'trail' concept may be that it also works as a noun, however there is no significant difference between the two.

A large portion of human mobility is composed of regular local outings, such as commuting to work or school, walking the dog, shopping for food, running errands, visiting others, exercising, and so on. Another suitable area for trail-based research lies in work-related rounds. Many private and work-related outings can be trailed or shadowed quite easily by researchers while producing very interesting results. Let me offer a handful of examples, selected from the large and diverse body of trail-based research.

- An interesting use of trails can be found in the work of Jirón (2007, 2011), who conducted extensive observations of research participants in

Santiago, Chile, while following them from home to work and back home, over the course of an entire day. The goal of the study was to compare mobility patterns and experiences across different income groups.
- In a fascinating study, Hall (2009) followed social outreach workers in the city of Cardiff, United Kingdom, while they were working. He strived to understand how these workers find the needy people they are seeking to support and how they 'read clues' of their clients' presence in the environment.
- Riley (2010) used trails in his research with British farmers, accompanying them as they fed their animals and tended to other duties. Similarly, in Cheshire et al.'s (2013) study of Australian farmers, researchers followed farmers around while they were working and taking breaks. Even though the authors refer to their method as a 'farm tour', it is evident that naturally occurring farming activities were the focus.
- After spending almost two years studying the social life of a Los Angeles park, Trouille (Trouille and Tavory, 2016) significantly enhanced his understanding of the park as a public space, and of the men who spent time there, by following the men around in their daily lives and routines beyond the park, an activity he described as 'shadowing'.
- In their research of adult 'picky eaters', Thompson and colleagues (2015) accompanied nine American study participants on naturally occurring trips to supermarkets, fast food restaurants and cafes to examine their food-related identities and behaviors.

Overall, go-alongs of the trail type tend to be fairly intensive in terms of the time and personal investment required of the researcher. They can include multiple modes of transportation such as walking, driving, bicycling, riding the bus, traveling by train and others. It is not uncommon for researchers to spend many hours or even days with their subjects, and to repeat the same or similar outings with one person several times. Examples of multi-sited studies that follow participants over very long, and often non-routine, distances and stretches of time, taking trailing or shadowing to an extreme form, can be found in migration and transnationalism research (e.g. Shutika, 2011). Obviously, the more time researchers spend with one person, the less they can focus on other participants, thus trading depth for coverage. Studying a very small number of participants, typically in the single digits, requires very thoughtful sampling. And very long research periods, over many hours or even days, require careful choices and strategies regarding data collection and documentation. Trouille and Tavory (2016) wisely caution against the impossibility of conducting a 'perfect' ethnography in which someone else's life and field research become one.

Tours

On the other end of the continuum, go-alongs can be organized as 'tours' which are more controlled by researchers, often shorter and more limited regarding the geographical area that is covered. However, what makes tours go-alongs, as opposed to outdoor experiments, is a primary interest in how participants use and experience *familiar* environments, even though the tours' exact time, length, mode of transportation and route may have been chosen by the researcher.

At the time of writing my go-along article (Kusenbach, 2003), I was more skeptical regarding the promise of such 'contrived' go-alongs than I am today. As with any semi-structured research technique, tours need to be designed carefully in a way that leaves room for spontaneity and narrative expression. When this is done, tours have certain advantages over trails that can outweigh their weaknesses, for instance allowing for a more systematic comparison of results across a larger sample of participants. The most productive strategies in tour-based research are the selection of places that have significant personal meanings to participants, and allowing participants to be in control of large parts of the outing. As DeLeon and Cohen put it, the task is to 'simply [...] walk around and encourage the informant to talk about past and current associations with the physical surroundings' (2005, p. 203).

Interestingly, Stals and colleagues (2014) note that go-along tours, which they call 'walking & talking', could be considered less intrusive because they do not pry into people's personal routines. The authors argue that their urban walking tours allowed for a high degree of control and expression by participants because they were allowed to select and show personally meaningful locations, making them more engaged and excited, in contrast to the dullness of moving through daily spatial routines. The literature features many interesting cases of researchers using go-along tours of which I can only mention a few examples here.

- Carpiano (2009) skillfully describes his use of neighborhood walking tours, which he conducted with residents of two neighborhoods in Milwaukie, United States, in order to study the role of local areas in shaping health outcomes.
- Ross and colleagues (2009) used what they call 'guided walks' in which young British study participants in public care led researchers to significant places in their everyday geographies. Similarly, Hall (2009) describes accompanying young people in the United Kingdom to places that the youth considered important while examining their spatial and social identities.
- Pink (2009) depicts a series of city tours given to her by city employees and activists in the town of Flintshire, United Kingdom, which were undertaken to study the slow city movement.
- Another kind of tour was used in a health-related study by Garcia and colleagues (2012) where American student research subjects were asked to first name helpful campus resources on matters of sexual health and then lead researchers to these locations.
- My own 2008–2010 research of mobile home parks in Florida included neighborhood tours during which forty participants were asked to walk with researchers around the community, on their own terms, in order to better understand their neighborhood and other place identities.

Go-along tours described in the research literature range from minimally structured prompts to walk around, to participant-led visits to significant places, to predetermined (yet still familiar) routes fully designed by researchers. While there are many variations, all tours have in common, first, that the outing is undertaken as research rather than being part of an informant's 'natural' mobile routines, and second, that participants maintain some degree of control over the event while taking the role of a tour guide, rather than someone who is being guided. Nonetheless, Ross and colleagues thoughtfully remind us that even when researchers are guided by research subjects, tours are highly interactive encounters in which all participants (researchers and subjects) ultimately co-construct what is going on (2009, pp. 608–9).

One issue that may complicate the basic distinction is the fact that some tours can be first-order, 'natural' phenomena, which may be studied via go-along trails. Some people give tours all the time, most obviously those who are doing it as part of their job. In recent years, the work of professional tour guides has garnered some scholarly attention (Farias, 2010; Wynn, 2011) and it is often explored through trailing or shadowing. However, 'natural' tours are not limited to work settings but can occur in informal social situations as well. Almost everyone has given or received an informal tour of a house or apartment, a school campus, a neighborhood. The familiarity and typically friendly nature of informal tours can be drawn upon by researchers, generally making go-along tours an enjoyable and successful strategy of data collection.

Some researchers utilize tours that are, strictly speaking, no longer go-alongs but more experimental in design. I now mention a few examples of borderline go-along tours to illustrate the difference.

- Chin (2001) took African American children on shopping trips to stores of their choice where they were each allowed to spend twenty dollars. This was not a routine experience for the kids, and some had never been to the stores they visited. Nonetheless, this method provided unique

insights into the consumption patterns of African American children.
- Sherren and colleagues (2016) took three groups of rural Canadians on boat tours to understand how they 'perceive and value' the surrounding landscape which had been altered by a dam. These tours produced insightful data even though they were not based on typical activities or familiar locations.
- Cauwenberg and colleagues (2012) used 'walk-along interviews' to explore pedestrian behaviors of seniors. Senior participants' typical walking destinations were randomly chosen by the researchers and highly structured mobile interviews along familiar and unfamiliar routes were conducted.

While these three examples of tours demonstrate innovative and creative research strategies, their description highlights the fact that not all research tours can be considered go-alongs, just as not all go-alongs can be considered tours.

IMPORTANT CONSIDERATIONS

When using go-alongs as a research method, scholars are faced with a number of important issues to consider. Among other concerns, it is especially pertinent to think about, first, the involved mode of mobility, second, the kind of researcher–participant engagement, and third, researchers' strategies for data collection and documentation. While there are no categorically right or wrong choices to be made regarding these issues, researchers must carefully reflect on the consequences and implications of their particular decisions, and weigh advantages against disadvantages to maximize outcomes.

Mode of Mobility

One vital consideration when following people is the utilized mode of transportation. When using trails, it is entirely determined by participants whereas when using tours, researchers typically decide how destinations are reached, ideally based on their study's particular goals or interests. In go-along research to date, the most frequently utilized mode of mobility is walking (e.g. Ingold and Vergunst, 2008). This trend is evident in some of the labels used to describe go-along research, such as 'walking interview'. The reasons for this choice are obvious: walking is a fundamental form of human movement which has been thoroughly studied and reflected upon in scholarly and other contexts (Solnit, 2001); walking is a flexible and variable activity, it is easy to do for almost everyone, and it is slow enough to allow for an outside focus yet active enough to create a fluid, rhythmic sense of movement. Most important, in my view, are that walking together creates a shared experience and point of view, and that it fosters a sense of connection and collaboration between subjects and researchers. There may be other physiological and psychological advantages to walking, alone or together, compared with other, more passive modes of mobility.

Despite the importance and advantages of walking, proponents of the Mobilities Paradigm have repeatedly reminded scholars to also pay attention to other forms of travel and they have pioneered such work. I cannot offer a comprehensive list of studies that have investigated other mobilities but I can mention some forms of movement that have been examined in the past: running, bicycling, skateboarding, parkour, horseback riding, snowboarding, rockclimbing, various kinds of driving and passengering, traveling by bus, subway, train, boat, airplane or other vehicles (Vannini, 2009). As already mentioned, some trail-based studies involve multiple modes of mobility.

Researcher–Participant Engagement

Second, there is the question of how researchers engage subjects verbally and/or non-verbally while going around with them. Verbal approaches range from using fairly structured interview guides to completely open conversations with no or very few prompts by investigators. Depending on researchers' goals and preferences, go-alongs can resemble open field observations or semi-structured interviews. Non-conversational forms of engagement that researchers may use in go-alongs with participants include writing, drawing, taking photographs, or simply being silent and observant together while letting bodies and environments do the 'talking' for a while. Most go-along researchers prefer a flexible approach in which they provide some advance prompts or ask specific questions but leave plenty of room for participant-initiated talk and silences. Again, there are no right or wrong choices, and the best forms of engagements are those that provide the deepest insights into one's research questions. Nonetheless, it is important to think about the information and types of data being collected (as well as the blind spots and omissions) that result from decisions regarding the forms and depths of researchers' engagement with subjects.

Documentation Strategies

A third, and for now last, important issue which has not been given sufficient attention in past years is the question of how the collected information will be documented (despite reminders by Carpiano, 2009 and Jones et al., 2008). Practitioners of go-alongs must develop adequate systems of recording their collaborative movements, observations, conversations and engagements. Records of spatial activities should be synchronized with other collected data. In other words, observations and conversations must be spatially contextualized, or 'geo-coded', in order to allow for the maximum payoff of using a mobile, place-sensitive research method. Researchers have certainly made progress in combining go-alongs with new technologies (such as GIS and GPS)

that go beyond paper and pencil, voice recorder and camera (e.g. Pink, 2007). Hein and colleagues correctly note that 'mobile methods represent an almost unique opportunity to explore cutting edge theory and technology simultaneously' (2008, p. 1280). Much remains to be discovered and critically reflected upon in these respects (Merriman, 2014). I suggest consulting the chapters on other data collection, documentation and representation strategies that are discussed in this *Handbook*.

LIMITATIONS AND STRENGTHS

This section discusses some limitations and strengths of go-alongs (also see Carpiano, 2009; Ferguson, 2016). Like any method of data collection, go-alongs are limited by thematic, practical and interpersonal aspects.

Thematically, in order for go-alongs to be effective, research participants must display a certain degree of environmental engagement which routinely happens when people are on the move (Seamon, 1979). Environmental engagement may also happen during more stationary activities, such as waiting for the bus, cooking, playing music, perhaps even watching a movie. But go-alongs are not useful for a study of meditation. Bissell (2010) thoughtfully comments on the current 'action' bias in mobile methods research and suggests ways of including more passive modes of experience in such studies. However, there are many research topics that cannot be examined well, or at all, via go-alongs, such as those that do not involve individual embodied activities that can be followed or observed, as for instance cognitive, historical or collective processes (Merriman, 2014). On the other end of the spectrum, study participants' engagement with their environments must be accessible and leave some room for reflection and conversation. Some mobile activities, for instance car racing or drug smuggling, may be too engaging, too dangerous or too secretive to be studied via the go-along method described in this chapter.

Next, there are important practical circumstances that can limit research subjects, researchers or both in their ability to engage in go-along research. Practical barriers may include lighting conditions, weather conditions such as temperature or wind, physical and legal access, and bodily capabilities. Not all people are able and willing to talk while moving or move while talking, or willing to take researchers on trails or tours. The idea of using go-alongs to study pedestrian mobility of seniors in Chicago during the winter or in Miami during the summer is a bad one for obvious reasons. While some practical barriers to using go-alongs can be overcome because they are variable and seasonal, others are permanent and require creativity by researchers in developing alternative approaches, potentially including virtual or simulated go-alongs.

Lastly, there are social complexities that can reduce the utility of go-alongs. As mentioned, go-alongs rely on social interaction and are embedded within larger fieldwork relationships (Coffey, 1999). In order for these relationships to work, researchers and participants must have a positive connection, and they must be willing to cooperate in meaningful ways. Like all research methods, go-alongs require understanding and consent from participants as well as a commitment by researchers to avoid or minimize harm. Even though institutional approval and oversight of studies involving human subjects may be less formalized in other countries when compared with the United States or Canada, ethical issues arise universally and require thoughtful anticipation and response (see Mertens, Chapter 3, this volume). Generally speaking, the social conditions for a successful use of go-alongs do not differ much from the ones for either observations or interviews. However, because go-alongs combine elements of both these techniques, there may be more topics and situations that socially limit their application.

In this next part, I touch upon the most notable advantages and strengths of go-alongs. One positive aspect of go-alongs is their ability to build bridges with participants who may not be easy to engage or recruit in more traditional ways (Carpiano, 2009). Numerous scholars use go-alongs to study children and teens (e.g. Ferguson, 2016; Ross et al., 2009), or to investigate sensitive topics such as sexual health (Garcia et al., 2012) or issues around food (Thompson et al., 2015). For instance, Ross and colleagues note that

> for us, the use of mobile methods offered much value in generating rich accounts of the everyday lives of young people [...] and supported our participatory approach, connecting well with the young people's own cultures and communication. (2009, p. 619)

The social advantages of go-alongs are not limited to examining non-traditional subjects or sensitive topics. It seems that in all such studies, going along, and especially walking along, with others fosters a 'distinct sociability' (Lee and Ingold, 2006) – a special connection based on sharing space, time and experience – that assists researchers in forging positive and productive relationships with participants. While this is clearly an advantage of the method, Ferguson (2016) appropriately cautions that the heightened emotionality and intimacy of go-along encounters also increases the ethical responsibilities of researchers.

A second and related advantage is that go-alongs are more participatory and democratic in comparison with more formal qualitative methods because they allow study subjects to control some parameters of the research. In go-along trails and tours, participants are the experts who literally lead researchers to their discoveries. Because go-alongs engage participants in places in which they already operate and encourage reflection, they carry the potential for fostering personal growth and advancing social change (Carpiano, 2009). Go-alongs can be incorporated productively in applied research designs where program evaluation and institutional improvements are pursued. In short, go-alongs and mobile methods have characteristics that make them suitable tools in the hands of engaged social scientists.

A third and perhaps most important advantage of go-alongs over either solitary observations or stationary interviews is the unique access they facilitate to otherwise unnoticed or distorted aspects of social life. Go-alongs can facilitate deep insights into participants' environmental perceptions and life histories, as well as illuminate community culture and social structures (for detailed examples, see Kusenbach, 2003). The general argument is that, when used sensibly, go-alongs can generate scholarly knowledge that is 'truer to life' (Hall, 2009, p. 582). Anderson emphasizes their unique potential for discovery in explaining that go-alongs help 'excavate levels of meaning both the researcher and researched may theretofore have been unaware of' (2004, p. 258). Because in go-along conversations, there is less pressure to fill silences and there are more opportunities for outside engagement, they permit researchers to explore 'nonverbalized' knowledge and practices (Riley, 2010). At the minimum, go-alongs allow interviewers time to formulate better questions and follow-ups (Riley, 2010), and they give ethnographers access to situated perceptions and meanings that simply cannot be observed (Trell and van Hooven, 2010; Trouille and Tavory, 2016).

Evans and Jones (2011) have actually put the frequently made claims of the superiority of 'walking interviews' to the test and directly compared the results of mobile interviews with the ones of sedentary interviews. The authors observed that walking interviews did produce more place-specific data, 'a narrative that unfolds through place, organizing experiences spatially rather than temporally' (2011, p. 856). Yet they also found that walking interviews were less productive when autobiographical narratives were the focus of study. In sum, the point is not to declare that go-alongs should replace stationary interviews or unstructured ethnographic observations as research methods (Merriman, 2014). What is argued is that go-alongs can assist researchers who investigate specific questions on the meaning and significance of places and certain social practices, and that they can unlock new angles and topics in the study of social life.

CONCLUSION

Go-alongs, and mobile methods more generally, have come a very long way since their first systematic arrival less than fifteen years ago, however we are still far from reaching, or even understanding, their full potential in social research. This last section discusses some promising current and future directions for this kind of inquiry.

I see two opportunities for making go-along research more perceptive of larger social contexts. It would be a welcome and significant contribution to strengthen the go-along's potential for making micro-macro links without abandoning its grounding in situated meanings. Manderscheid (2014) offers insightful critiques of the typical focus of go-along and mobile research on individual experiences as separated from social relationships and network contexts. One innovation, already suggested by Carpiano in 2009, could be to make go-alongs more social by focusing on larger social units, such as neighborhoods, as I have attempted in my mobile home park research. Recently, scholars have experimented with group outings, for instance merging focus groups with go-along tours in a Canadian study of altered natural landscapes (Sherren et al., 2016). Pawlowski and colleagues (2016) offer another example. This research team conducted group go-alongs with American schoolchildren to better understand their activity patterns during school recess. There is no doubt that much more can be done to expand the collective aspects and insights of go-along research.

A second way of making go-alongs more sensitive to larger historical and biographical contexts can be seen in recent efforts to recognize different kinds of mobility as (sub) cultures and identities, going beyond individually and biographically isolated movements in place. For instance, the concepts and current investigations of 'lifestyle mobility' (e.g. Ley-Cervantes and Duyvendak, 2017; Rickly, 2014) or 'lifestyle migration' (e.g. Hoey, 2014) open up many new directions for mobility-based research. Innovations along these lines highlight the symbolic characteristic of go-alongs that was discussed in the third section of this chapter, that is, their potential for capturing the larger social meanings of movements that transcend spatial and body mechanics. However, it is still unclear which exact contributions go-alongs as a research method can make in this emerging area and topic of interest.

I consider the biggest future promise of go-alongs and mobile methods to lie in their potential for bridging some long-standing divides. For one, go-alongs and mobile methods have already fostered intensive exchanges between members of different disciplines within the social sciences, such as (human) geography, sociology and anthropology. Moreover, new spaces for conversation have opened between social scientists on the one hand and humanities scholars and natural scientists on the other. It is increasingly common for members of English and Health Sciences Departments to incorporate go-alongs into their work and to contribute results and ideas to the interdisciplinary discussion of this method. Further, go-along and mobile methods discourse welcomes the input of more applied fields such as transportation, education and social work. The potential of mobile methods research to transcend the traditional boundaries of academic departments is remarkable. This can also be seen in the rise of 'mobility studies' as a new and interdisciplinary field.

On a smaller scale, dialog has been initiated by go-along and mobile methods research among different factions within disciplines. As mentioned, within sociology, go-alongs have clear roots in the interpretive theoretical paradigm, often referred to as Symbolic Interactionism in the United States. However, proponents of other theoretical schools, including critical theory and postmodernism/poststructuralism, have also discovered the go-along method and developed its capabilities for innovative and socially engaged research. This kind of theoretical bridging through go-alongs and mobile methods may have occurred in other disciplines as well. It is my experience that intradisciplinary debates between theoretical paradigms become much less entrenched when spaces for dialog and collaboration with members of *other* disciplines are created and used.

Another significant dimension of interconnection and integration is geographical. In the case of mobile methods and go-along research, important contributions have been made by scholars working on several continents, including Europe, Australia, North and South America. It is expected that go-alongs and mobile methods will spread even more widely in the future, potentially moving beyond industrialized nations into the regions of the Global South.

One last schism that has come under scrutiny in go-along and mobile methods research is the one between qualitative and quantitative methods, and the bifurcated domains of knowledge this divide has created in many disciplines (see Manderscheid, 2014; Sui and DeLyser, 2012). The inclusion of quantitative data and knowledge in mobile methods research is primarily facilitated through new technologies – highlighting yet another frontier, the one between low-tech (pen and paper, voice recorders) and high-tech, electronic approaches to data collection today. True to their name, many go-along and mobile methods researchers have shown little reverence for traditional procedures and ways of thinking, and they experiment with whatever new tools and technologies they can find to move their work forward.

One key strategy that has characterized go-along and mobile methods researchers from the very beginning is triangulation, meaning the use of more than one method of data collection in their work (e.g. Carpiano, 2009; Jirón, 2011; see Flick, Chapter 34, this volume). In past years, this often meant combining mobile methods with traditional observations or interviewing, and including visual data such as maps, photographs or film (e.g. Pink, 2007; also see Eberle, Chapter 25, this volume; Mikos, Chapter 26, this volume). Today, it is not uncommon for researchers to combine approaches that result in both qualitative and quantitative data sets. For instance, Pawlowski and colleagues (2016) paired go-along interviews with (qualitative) observations, GPS tracking and accelerometer data; Stals and colleagues (2014) use go-alongs together with photography, GPS tracking, emotion mapping, and ERP (Emotional Route Planning); and Spinney (2015) has added bio-sensing technologies as one of his tools (however, see Merriman, 2014 for a critique of the use of technologies in mobile methods research).

Triangulation certainly poses many questions about the comparability, analysis and presentation of data, especially when diverse textual, visual and numeric data sets are involved. It is too early to report on which combinations of techniques are most productive in answering which kinds of research questions. But it is not too early to predict that go-alongs, which are already a key instrument in the toolkit of mobile methods researchers, will continue to advance how social scientists collect and think about data in the future.

FURTHER READINGS

Adey, Peter, Bissell, David, Hannam, Kevin, Merriman Peter and Sheller, Mimi (2014) *The Routledge Handbook of Mobilities*. London: Routledge.

Hall, T. (2009) 'Footwork: Moving and knowing in local space(s)', *Qualitative Research* 9(5): 571–85.

Kusenbach, M. (2003) 'Street phenomenology: The go-along as ethnographic research tool', *Ethnography* 4(3): 455–85.

REFERENCES

Adey, Peter, Bissell, David, Hannam, Kevin, Merriman Peter and Sheller, Mimi (2014) *The Routledge Handbook of Mobilities*. London: Routledge.

Anderson, Jon (2004) 'Talking whilst walking: A geographical archeology of knowledge', *Area* 36(3): 254–61.

Bissell, David (2010) 'Narrating mobile methodologies: Active and passive empiricisms', in B. Fincham, M. McGuiness and L. Murray (eds.), *Mobile Methodologies*. New York: Palgrave Macmillan, pp. 53–68.

Brown, Lyndsay and Durrheim, Kevin (2009) 'Different kinds of knowing: Generating qualitative data through mobile interviewing', *Qualitative Inquiry* 15(5): 911–30.

Brown-Saracino, Japonica (2010) *A Neighborhood That Never Changes: Gentrification, Social Preservation, and the Search for Authenticity*. Chicago, IL: University of Chicago Press.

Burawoy, Michael, Blum, Joseph, Al, George, Gille, Zsusa, Gowan, Teresa, Haney, Lynn, Klawiter, Maren, Lopez, Stephan H., Riain, Sean O., and Thayer, Millie (2000) *Global Ethnography*. Berkeley, CA: University of California Press.

Büscher, Monika, and Urry, John (2009) 'Mobile methods and the empirical', *European Journal of Social Theory*, 12(1): 99–116.

Büscher, Monika., Urry, John, and Witchger, Katian (2011) *Mobile Methods*. Abingdon: Routledge.

Carpiano, Richard M. (2009) 'Come take a walk with me: The "go-along" interview as a novel method for studying implications of place for health and well-being', *Health & Place* 15(1): 263–72.

Casey, Edward S. (1993) *Getting Back Into Place*. Bloomington, IN: Indiana University Press.

Casey, Edward S. (2001) 'Between geography and philosophy: What does it mean to be in the place-world?', *Annals of the Association of American Geographers* 91(4): 683–93.

Cauwenberg, Jelle Van, Holle, Veerle Van and Simons, Dorien (2012) 'Environmental factors influencing older adults' walking for transportation: A study using walk-along interviews', *The International Journal of Behavioral Nutrition and Physical Activity* 9: 85.

Chen, Xiangming, Orum, Anthony M. and Paulsen, Krista E. (2012) *Introduction to Cities: How Place and Space Shape Human Experience*. Hoboken, NJ: Wiley-Blackwell.

Cheshire, Lynda, Meurk, Carla and Woods, Michael (2013) 'Decoupling farm, farming and place: Recombinant attachments of globally engaged family farmers', *Journal of Rural Studies* 30(April): 64–74.

Chin, Elizabeth (2001) *Purchasing Power: Black Kids and American Consumer Culture*. Minneapolis, MN: University of Minnesota Press.

Coffey, Amanda (1999) *The Ethnographic Self: Fieldwork and the Representation of Identity*. London: Sage.

Czarniawska, Barbara (2007) *Shadowing and Other Techniques for Doing Fieldwork in Modern Societies*. Malmo, Sweden: Liber.

De Certeau, Michel (1984) *The Practice of Everyday Life*. Berkeley, CA: University of California Press.

Delamont, Sarah (ed.) (2012) *Handbook of Qualitative Research in Education*. Cheltenham: Edward Elgar.

DeLeon, Jason Patrick and Cohen, Jeffrey H. (2005) 'Object and walking probes in ethnographic interviewing', *Field Methods* 17(2): 200–4.

Desmond, Matthew (2016) *Evicted: Poverty and Profit in the American City*. New York: Crown.

Duneier, Mitchell (2004) 'Scrutinizing the heat: On ethnic myths and the importance of shoe leather', *Contemporary Sociology* 38(2): 139–50.

Edensor, Tim (2010) 'Walking in rhythms: Place, regulation, style and the flow of experience', *Visual Studies* 25(1): 69–79.

Elswood, Sarah A. and Martin, Deborah G. (2000) '"Placing" interviews: Location and scales of power in qualitative research', *Professional Geographer* 52(4): 649–57.

Emerson, Robert M. (2001) 'Introduction: The development of ethnographic fieldwork', in R. M. Emerson (ed.), *Contemporary Field Research: Perspectives and Formulations* (2nd edn). Prospect Heights, IL: Waveland Press, pp. 1–53.

Evans, James and Jones, Phil (2011) 'The walking interview: Methodology, mobility and place', *Applied Geography* 31(2): 849–58.

Farías, Ignacio (2010) 'Sightseeing buses: Cruising, timing and the montage of attractions', *Mobilities* 5(3): 387–407.

Ferguson, Kirsten (2016) 'Lessons learned from using shadowing as a qualitative research technique in education', *Reflective Practice* 17(1): 15–26.

Garcia, Carolyn M., Eisenberg, Marla E., Frerich, Ellen A., Lechner, Kate E. and Lust, Katherine (2012) 'Conducting go-along interviews to understand context and promote health', *Qualitative Health Research* 22(10): 1395–403.

Gieryn, Thomas F. (2000) 'A space for place in sociology', *Annual Review of Sociology* 26: 463–96.

Hall, Tom (2009) 'Footwork: Moving and knowing in local space(s)', *Qualitative Research* 9(5): 571–85.

Hannerz, Ulf (2003) 'Being there… and there… and there! Reflections on multi-site ethnography', *Ethnography* 4(2): 201–16.

Hein, J. Ricketts, Evans, James and Jones, Phil (2008) 'Mobile methodologies: Theory, technology, and practice', *Geography Compass* 2(5): 1266–85.

Hoey, Brian A. (2014) *Opting for Elsewhere: Lifestyle Migration in the American Middle Class*. Nashville, TN: Vanderbilt University Press.

Ingold, Tim (2004) 'Culture on the ground: The world perceived through the feet', *Journal of Material Culture* 9(3): 211–40.

Ingold, Tim and Vergunst, Jo L. (eds) (2008) *Ways of Walking: Ethnography and Practice on Foot*. Hampshire: Ashgate.

Jenks, Chris and Neves, Tiago (2000) 'A walk on the wild side: Urban ethnography meets the flaneur', *Cultural Values* 4(1): 1–17.

Jerolmack, Colin (2013) *The Global Pigeon*. Chicago, IL: University of Chicago Press.

Jirón, Paola (2007) 'Unravelling invisible inequalities in the city through urban daily mobility: The case of Santiago de Chile', *Swiss Journal of Sociology* 33(1): 45–68.

Jirón, Paola (2011) 'On becoming "la sombra/ the shadow"', in Monika Büscher, John Urry and Katian Witchger (eds.), *Mobile Methods*. New York: Routledge, pp. 36–53.

Jones, Phil, Bunce, Griff, Evans, James, Gibbs, Hannah and Hein, J. Ricketts (2008) 'Exploring space and place with walking interviews', *Journal of Research Practice* 4(2): 1–9.

Katz, Jack (1999) *How Emotions Work*. Chicago: University of Chicago Press.

Kleinman, Sherryl, Stenross, Barbara and McMahon, Martha (1994) 'Privileging fieldwork over interviews: Consequences for identity and practice', *Symbolic Interaction* 17(1): 37–50.

Kozol, Jonathan (1995) *Amazing Grace: The Lives of Children and the Conscience of a Nation*. New York: Perennial.

Kusenbach, Margarethe (2003) 'Street phenomenology: The go-along as ethnographic research tool', *Ethnography* 4(3): 455–85.

Kusenbach, Margarethe (2012) 'Mobile methods', in Sarah Delmont (ed.), *Handbook of Qualitative Research in Education*. Cheltenham: Elgar, pp. 252–64.

Lamont, Michèle and Swidler, Ann (2014) 'Methodological pluralism and the possibilities and limits of interviewing', *Qualitative Sociology*, 37(2): 153–71.

Lee, Jo, and Ingold, Tim (2006) 'Fieldwork on foot: Perceiving, routing, socializing', in S. Coleman and P. Collins (eds.), *Locating the Field: Space, Place and Context in Anthropology*. Oxford: Berg, pp. 67–87.

Ley-Cervantes, Melissa and Duyvendak, Jan Willem (2017) 'At home in generic places: Personalizing strategies of the mobile rich', *Journal of Housing and the Built Environment* 31(1): 63–76.

Lofland, Lyn (1998) *The Public Realm: Exploring the City's Quintessential Social Territory*. New York: Aldine de Gruyter.

Lynch, Kevin (1960) *Image of the City*. Cambridge, MA: MIT Press.

Manderscheid, Katharina (2014) 'Criticising the solitary mobile subject: Researching relational mobilities and reflecting on mobile methods', *Mobilities* 9(2): 188–219.

Marcus, George E. (1995) 'Ethnography in/of the world system: The emergence of multi-sited ethnography', *Annual Review of Anthropology* 24: 95–117.

McDonald, Seonaidh (2005) 'Studying action in context: A qualitative shadowing method for organizational research', *Qualitative Research* 5(2): 455–73.

Merriman, Peter (2014) 'Rethinking mobile methods', *Mobilities* 9(2): 167–87.

Pawlowski, Charlotte Skau, Andersen, Henriette Bondo, Troelsen, Jens and Schipperijn, Jasper (2016) 'Children's physical activity behavior during school recess: A pilot study using GPS, accelerometer, participant observation, and go-along interview', *PLoS ONE* 11(2): e0148786, doi:10.1371/journal.pone.0148786.

Pink, Sarah (2007) 'Walking with video', *Visual Studies* 22(3): 240–52.

Pink, Sarah (2009) 'An urban tour', *Ethnography* 9(2): 175–96.

Pink, Sarah, Hubbard, Phil, O'Neill, Maggie and Radley, Alan (2010) 'Walking across disciplines: From ethnography to arts practice', *Visual Studies* 25(1): 1–7.

Quinlan, Elizabeth (2008) 'Conspicuous invisibility: Shadowing as a data collection strategy', *Qualitative Inquiry* 14(8): 1480–99.

Relph, Edward C. (1976) *Place and Placelessness*. London: Pion Limited.

Rickly, Jillian M. (2014) 'Lifestyle mobilities: A politics of lifestyle rock climbing', *Mobilities* 11(2): 1–21.

Riley, Mark (2010) 'Emplacing the research encounter: Exploring farm life histories', *Qualitative Inquiry* 16(8): 651–62.

Ross, Nicola J., Renold, Emma, Holland, Sally and Hillman, Alexandra (2009) 'Moving stories: Using mobile methods to explore the everyday lives of young people in public care', *Qualitative Research* 9(5): 605–23.

Seamon, David (1979) *A Geography of the Life World*. New York: St. Martin's Press.

Sheller, Mimi (2014) 'The new mobilities paradigm for a live sociology', *Current Sociology Review* 62(6): 789–811.

Sheller, Mimi and Urry, John (2006) 'The new mobilities paradigm', *Environment and Planning A* 38(2): 207–26.

Sherren, Kate, Beckley, Thomas M., Parkins, John R., Stedman, Richard C., Keilty, Kristina and Morin, Isabelle (2016) 'Learning (or living) to love the landscapes of hydroelectricity in Canada: Eliciting local perspectives on the Mactaquac Dam via Headpond boat tours', *Energy Research & Social Science* 16(April): 102–10.

Shutika, Debra L. (2011) *Beyond the Borderlands: Migration and Belonging in the United States and Mexico*. Berkeley, CA: University of California Press.

Simmel, Georg (1989–2015) *Gesamtausgabe. 24 Vols*. Frankfurt am Main, Germany: Suhrkamp.

Sin, C. H. (2003) 'Interviewing in "place": The socio-spatial construction of interview data', *Area* 35(3): 305–12.

Small, M. L. (2009) 'How many cases do I need?' On science and the logic of case selection in field-based research', *Ethnography* 10(1): 5–38.

Solnit, Rebecca (2001) *Wanderlust: A History of Walking*. Westminster, London: Penguin.

Spinney, J. (2015) 'Close encounters? Mobile methods, (post) phenomenology and affect', *Cultural Geographies* 22(2): 231–46.

Stals, Shenando, Smyth, Michael and Ijsselsteijn, Wijnand (2014) 'Walking & talking: Probing the urban lived experience', in NordiCHI 2014 Proceedings of the 8th Nordic Conference on Human-Computer Interaction: Fun, Fast, Foundational, pp. 737–46. http://dl.acm.org/citation.cfm?id=2641215.

Sui, D. and DeLyser, D. (2012) 'Crossing the qualitative–quantitative chasm: Hybrid geographies, the spatial turn, and volunteered geographic information (VGI)', *Progress in Human Geography* 36(1): 111–24.

Thompson, C., Cummins, S., Brown, T. and Kyle, R. (2015) 'What does it mean to be a "picky eater"? A qualitative study of food related identities and practices', *Appetite* 84(1): 235–9.

Trell, E.-M. and Van Hooven, B. (2010) 'Making sense of place: Exploring creative and (inter) active research methods with young people', *Fennia-International Journal of Geography* 188(1): 91–104.

Trouille, D. and Tavory, I. (2016) 'Shadowing warrants for intersituational variation in ethnography', *Sociological Methods & Research*, doi:10.1177/0049124115626171.

Tuan, Yi-Fu (1976) *Space and Place*. Minneapolis, MI: University of Minnesota Press.

Van Cauwenberg, J., Van Holle, V., Simons, D., Deridder, R., Clarys, P., Goubert, L., Nasar, J., Salmon, J., De Bourdeaudhuij, I. and Deforche, B. (2012) 'Environmental factors influencing older adults' walking for transportation: A study using walk-along interviews', *International Journal of Behavioral Nutrition and Physical Activity* 9(1): 85.

Vannini, Philip (ed) (2009) *The Culture of Alternative Mobilities*. New York: Routledge.

Warren, Carol A.B. and Karner, Tracy X. (2009) *Discovering Qualitative Methods* (2nd edn). New York: Oxford University Press.

Wynn, Jonathan (2011) *The Tour Guide: Walking and Talking New York*. Chicago, IL: University of Chicago Press.

23

Videography

Hubert Knoblauch, Bernt Schnettler and René Tuma

INTRODUCTION

In this chapter we focus exclusively on the question of data collection in videography. Data collection, of course, forms part of a more encompassing research process we call videography. For questions concerning the problem of video analysis, which constitutes the second pillar of videography, the theoretical assumptions implied in the analysis of natural audiovisual data and the relation between empirical analysis and culture and society in general, we must refer the reader to other publications, particularly our book (Knoblauch et al., 2015). In focusing on data collection, we need to pay special attention to ways in which videographic data are collected: Video analysis is embedded in the methodological framework of 'focused ethnography'. For this reason, we will address legal and ethical implications as well; in addition, technical problems of recording with the camera are discussed and illustrated by using several examples. Before turning to the topic of transcription, we will present the necessary preliminary steps in sampling and data processing.

Videography is a method that we use as researchers to examine the reciprocal action, based on communication – the interaction – of actors in different situations. Here we look back on a broad tradition of analyses in behavioral science or even of analyses of rituals in cultures that are more or less strange to us. The central feature of videography, in contrast to other methods dealing with visual data, is its focus on interaction rather than, for example, on media products and their effects (which goes hand in hand with a completely different set of problems in data collection).

The major feature of videography is that it links ethnographic fieldwork with analyses of video recordings of 'natural' interactions. In the following, before taking a closer look at the evaluation of the data acquired in videography, we specify focused ethnography as a practice of sociological fieldwork. We will discuss which situations we actually record most appropriately, where the focus lies, and how we select the data and prepare them for fine-grained analysis.

FOCUSED ETHNOGRAPHY

Regardless of where we want to investigate interactions – in the world of physicists or in the domain of midwives, in meetings or at the construction site, while people are dancing or playing music – the interactions always take place in a context, which we must understand, just as we must understand what is happening in that context. There are certain architectonic features of the location, institutional rules, and possibly specific specialized knowledge that the actors contribute to the interaction. The prerequisite for every video analysis, therefore, is an intimate knowledge of the field in which the recording is to take place: Whether making video recordings in the line control center of a subway system, at a drug-counseling center, or in a kindergarten – invariably, one must have acquainted oneself with the nature of the facility being studied, as well as with the specific sites and chronological sequences of events. Part of this knowledge can be acquired by means of research, but observation (see Wästerfors, Chapter 20, this volume) of the field is imperative, so that the perspective of the participants can be taken into account. During this observation a field report should be written down, so that spontaneous impressions are noted. In addition, (at least informal) interviews are conducted and documents of the field are gathered. Such a process of describing and analyzing the field can be referred to, in a general sense, as 'ethnography' (see Buscatto, Chapter 21, this volume). As researchers who live in a society with which we have at least everyday familiarity, we can draw on the knowledge we have of our society – be it everyday knowledge, on which we expatiate and reflect; or knowledge about the field, which we can obtain from the body of literature or other sources. This situation differs considerably from that of the ethnologists, who set out to study completely different cultures. In our own society, too, of course, there may be a lack of knowledge when we go into unfamiliar fields. Nevertheless, presumably there are only a few things that are truly strange to us: What we may perhaps lack is a certain specialized knowledge of the social world to be investigated. We do not know the special language of the quantum physicists or neurobiologists; are not acquainted with the practices of midwives or social workers; and even the conversations of computer gamers or musicians may perhaps sound incomprehensible at first – but only when they talk about their subject. To acquire this specialized knowledge, we have to spend time in the field, possibly learn something new, and above all talk with the people, even perform their activity ourselves at some point to see how this or that functions and what the subjective experience of playing computer games, of the hard daily work of a subway train controller, or of 'jamming' looks like. But we need not spend the entire day with the actors or even accompany them over the course of weeks and months. It is important to note that this approach, too, can be quite extensive and time-consuming, if the field requires it. But that depends on how familiar the researchers are with the specific context under scrutiny. In some cases, it might be necessary to be or become a mathematician oneself, to understand how certain communicative projects are communicated (Kiesow, 2016). In other cases, our everyday knowledge is sufficient to understand what is going on. Still, the interest of videography is concentrated on certain forms of interaction. For that purpose, the breakfast cereal eaten by the quantum physicist is surely irrelevant. Unlike ethnologists, we need not spend the entire day (and night) with the actors. Instead, we meet them at designated places at prearranged times and in specific contexts that are of interest to us. These may be, for example, the workplace,

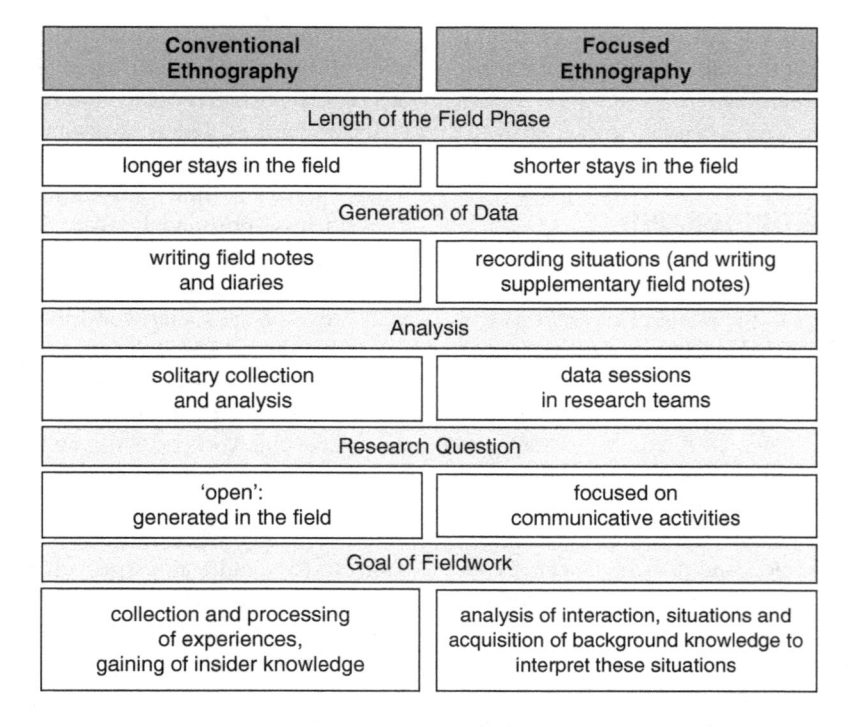

Conventional Ethnography	Focused Ethnography
Length of the Field Phase	
longer stays in the field	shorter stays in the field
Generation of Data	
writing field notes and diaries	recording situations (and writing supplementary field notes)
Analysis	
solitary collection and analysis	data sessions in research teams
Research Question	
'open': generated in the field	focused on communicative activities
Goal of Fieldwork	
collection and processing of experiences, gaining of insider knowledge	analysis of interaction, situations and acquisition of background knowledge to interpret these situations

Figure 23.1 Comparison of 'conventional' and 'focused' ethnography (based on Knoblauch, 2005)

school classes, an evening concert, or an LAN party.

This variant of fieldwork has its own tradition within sociology. Knoblauch (2005) has termed it 'focused ethnography'. Its characteristics can best be explained in contrast with 'conventional' ethnography (see Figure 23.1).

As distinguished from conventional field research with pen and paper, videography, as 'focused ethnography' using video, is based, with regard to its main data, on technical recording and thorough analysis of the recorded data in a research team. As Figure 23.1 shows, the knowledge gathered while in the field is then in forms of group analysis systematically brought up. Groups of researchers, unfamiliar with the field and researchers that have been there, create a productive contrast eliciting the important aspects. The most important part of the analysis then focuses on a detailed analysis of communicative actions. The ethnography delivers background knowledge to interpret the 'conserved' situations.

ACCESS TO THE FIELD

To obtain video data at all, we must first gain access to the field (see Bengry, Chapter 7, this volume). Most of the time, in our experience, 'getting in' has its pitfalls and problems, so that one has to proceed with caution. The people whom we want to film during their more or less everyday interactions may react with skepticism and justifiable disapproval to sociologists who come into the field in an imperious way, poke their noses into everything, give only vague information about their interests, and hold the camera right in front of everybody's nose. Therefore, a certain amount of tact is required. On the other hand, many people are glad to help, open, and even curious about what sociologists do and what they may find out. Thus it is necessary to render the field accessible by working hard to communicate in a sensitive manner. Finally, in a number of settings, there may indeed be a willingness to play a part in the study, yet formal regulations and legal provisions can potentially make video recordings difficult.

We can only give general guidelines for gaining access to the field, because the field always takes a different form. As a rule of thumb, however, let us point out the following: First it is necessary to decide who will be filmed, and where. Though public places and events in most cases are still relatively unproblematic (camera teams and tourists frequently film there, too), things become more difficult in closed areas and when the focus is on individual, identifiable persons. In most contexts, therefore, it is essential to explain the research activity to the participants and seek their consent ('informed consent'). In so doing, it is important to put your cards on the table, that is, to behave honestly and in a way that is commensurate with the field, and to inform the potential participants of your own objective. Not only do legal provisions and professional ethics require that of you, but your own wish for ongoing and promising work in the field also demands that you conduct yourself in such a way. To convince participants to become involved in videography, they need to be informed about what is planned and give their consent to it. This information should be framed in such a way that it tells the participants clearly and honestly about the use of the data for research purposes and dispels their reservations about the filming, on the one hand, and on the other hand, also avoids the use of professional jargon that is incomprehensible to outsiders. Heath et al. (2010), in their introduction, provide a number of very helpful pointers. For example, introducing one's research project in the form of a little presentation in the field has proved itself in practice. In the process, the points listed below can be explained and other data examples can be shown, in order to allay fears (in Knoblauch et al., 2015, chapter 8, we discuss ways to preserve anonymity). A cover letter should accompany or precede this public introduction of the research in the field.

In addition to the letter, reasons for contributing to this field should be made clear:

- Why this field?
- Why is the research question relevant?
- What benefit can the research results yield for the field?

Frequently, different participants have different misgivings and concerns. Some simply do not like being filmed, because they think they might 'make a fool of themselves' in front of the camera or be put in a bad light. This fear usually can be allayed if you explain that the point is not to analyze the individual persons, but their interactions and activities. This is especially tricky in work contexts as well, where employees frequently are leery of perceived control by outsiders: What helps here is the assurance that the pictures, as well as data and knowledge relating to individuals, will not be passed on to other parties, including company management.

Agreements of this kind should be made in writing to give both parties certitude. In organizations, a nondisclosure agreement is frequently concluded anyway, pledging not to pass on the videos as well as organization secrets. Such agreements create assurance on both sides. The people filmed should be granted the right to withdraw at any time and to have the data erased. During the signing, make sure to include agreements on utilization of the recordings for 'teaching and research purposes' and for data sessions on a small scale. Also useful are rules for subsequent publication of data excerpts, for which separate consultation and consent may be needed, if applicable. Companies in particular are frequently concerned at first that corporate secrets will become public knowledge and become known to competitors. Later, however, they often determine that the recorded data contain no secrets at all or that identifying particulars can easily be removed or altered. Here, access frequently can be secured by offering an external review and a concluding presentation. An additional fear is that the researcher might cause inconveniences, because no real 'field role' exists: Who will deal with the researcher? Does he have to be shown things all the time? Will he keep us from getting our work done? These questions are typical ones. The apprehensions underlying them should be cleared up in advance, for example, by taking a trainee role and assisting with the work, or, if that is not possible, by at least promising not to get in the way. In certain contexts, other problems arise: If, for example, children are involved, there is a need to obtain the consent of their parents and simultaneously to observe the rules already in existence in the setting (for example, at a school). Often, specific directives for other kinds of video recordings are already available. Sometimes these can be used. Unfortunately, however, it often is the case that they bear reference to something altogether different, such as TV broadcasts. Out of uncertainty, they are then used as a pretext for refusal. From Great Britain, another case is familiar. There, social science research in medical facilities became very complicated as a result of a rash decision to convene ethics commissions, which actually were intended for medical research. Even if access is granted, there is a need to proceed circumspectly in the field. Especially if the participants are skeptical, it is advisable to be present in the field without a camera or recording devices at first, and to talk with the participants (if you have time for it), watch them, and show interest in what they are doing. Here it can help to emphasize your interest in the specialized knowledge, the expertise, of the people being filmed. Issues of practical implementation, such as making changes in the space (for example, by setting up cameras in a museum) often must be resolved with the persons in charge inside the organization. Here one should proceed with tact. The ongoing negotiations, however, can be regarded as part of the ethnography and should be reflected as such.

RESEARCH ETHICS AND LEGAL REGULATIONS

In our research work we are obligated to abide by ethical standards (see Mertens, Chapter 3, this volume). The Code of Ethics of the various national associations for sociology and other disciplines lay down guidelines for empirical research. Regulations, however, vary from country to country and we strongly recommend checking the pertinent rules in your respective research area. In particular, it is the task of researchers to safeguard the personality rights of all individuals involved in the study as participants or subjects. In the process, the following points should be kept in mind:

- Participation in our investigations must be voluntary. Participation is based on informed consent, with as much detailed information as possible provided about the goals and methods of the research project in question ('informed consent'). If no information can be provided in advance, the researchers must look for other solutions.
- Attention must be paid to informing people in accordance with their educational level (for example, in the case of children, see MacDougall and Darbyshire, Chapter 39, this volume, appropriate informing and involvement of their parents is necessary).
- It is important to make sure that no disadvantages for the individuals observed arise from the analysis or from their participation in the research.
- For that purpose, it is necessary to properly preserve the anonymity of the individuals who are interviewed or studied.
- The research data must be securely stored and protected against unauthorized access by third parties. This applies especially to data in digital form and, of course, to video recordings as well.
- If other individuals (supporting staff, data sessions, transcribers) are involved in the research process, they too must adhere to the rules given above.

In addition to the voluntary ethical commitments of the specialist community, there also exist legal regulations that are applicable to research. The legal situation is not clear, however, and there exist no standard regulations. This is especially true with respect to international standards. We are referring to the legal framework in Germany. Here, the regulations applying to research are presently in a legal gray area – two rights are in opposition: on the one hand, the right of freedom of research and, on the other, personality rights, or the right to one's own image, which derives from personality rights (also known as the right to privacy). Generally speaking, the freedom of arts and sciences also applies, which allows science to do research, as long as it does not harm anyone. Both questions must be balanced also with respect to the question whether videos may be made accessible to a broader audience, or in what form; this is usually asked only when the research is concluded, and when publications are prepared. Here, the problem of depicting individuals can be solved by skillfully preserving anonymity and making adaptations. These rules apply, first of all, to public and semi-public spaces. It must be kept in mind, however, that in addition there exists a separately protected private sphere, which includes residences and other intimate situations. Private space is specifically protected, a violation (i.e. covert filming in the private sphere) is a criminal act. Because researchers are unlikely to be interested in conflicts, we advise you to secure the consent of the participants wherever possible, to avoid possible conflicts.

RECORDING, ETHNOGRAPHY, AND POSING OF QUESTIONS

Once you are in the field and can start the work, the first question asked is: What am I actually interested in here? The initial steps may be, for example, preparing a short description, making a short 'inventory' of the situation by asking questions like these: How does the place being studied look (little drawing), which actors are involved (short description), what things are they dealing with (list), and who is interacting with whom (observation record)? Using your own questions, you can now begin closer observation of what is going on. Frequently you think, 'But I already know what's going on here, after all, it's just everyday things.' Precisely at these moments, you must stop and ask yourself how this sense of familiarity is related to your own prior knowledge and what it is you actually want to find out; if applicable, you should note down such field experiences, because that produces a defamiliarization or 'bestrangement' effect that helps the researcher make this knowledge explicit (Amann, 1997). In the case of unfamiliar fields, intensive ethnography is called for, with the researchers acquiring the knowledge necessary for understanding the data.

Incidentally, this knowledge by no means has to be acquired in a linear fashion; once someone is sufficiently familiar with the local field, he or she can frequently reconstruct specific knowledge and contexts later, and with the support of the video footage. After the first analyses, new situations and focuses can be sought during subsequent periods spent in the field. The creation of recordings follows the process of theoretical sampling (see Schreier, Chapter 6, this volume), as the Grounded Theory method recommends (Strauss, 1987, p. 38ff.). This sampling is quite decisively supported by knowledge about the field: What kinds of facilities are there, how might these facilities modify the situations, from what are they distinguished – all these questions depend quite decisively on our knowledge about the field that is being investigated in the context of ethnographic research. At the same time, no unnecessary distinctions from quantitative research should be drawn, because after all, statistics and quantitative studies, too, frequently provide good indications of ethnographically relevant issues.

One should keep in mind, of course, that the objective of videography is by no means an ethnography. Rather, we are concerned with the analysis of interactions. It is for this reason, indeed, that we use the term 'video interaction analysis' for systematic engagement with audiovisual recordings. As we focus here on data collection, we cannot address the methods of analyzing interaction by means of video. Suffice it to say that it is based on the sequential analysis of multimodal communicative actions performed in time and the analysis of simultaneous visual elements. (For more detail see Knoblauch et al., 2015, chapter 6.) Accordingly, the researcher's camera focuses both on temporal and spatial respects of the interaction in social situations. Through prior observation, the researcher is to determine what is relevant in the social situation and what is not. And yet the interactions by no means have to take place only in one location; conversation analysis, even earlier, dealt with acoustic communication by telephone, and now, as we have seen, communication via computer screens, telephones, or other technological devices and media, is the subject of video analysis. Essentially, individual actors, too, can be studied, if we assume that their behavior represents a form of communication. Thus Streeck (1993) has visually examined the types of 'self-touch' used by actors. Here we follow Erving Goffman's idea that basically every behavior of individuals is performed as if it related to others – even when we are acting alone. Also originating with Goffman is the narrower notion of focusing that guides our recordings. He uses the term 'focused interaction' (Goffman, 1963) for the kind of interaction that occurs when people gather and apparently cooperate in such a way that their attention is quite consciously centered on a single common focal point. This is typical, for example, of a sequence of speaker turns in conversation.

No matter how we specifically make our recordings (on the technical aspects, see also Heath et al., 2010), the recordings of video interaction analyses, as a rule, have the same focus as the recorded interactions. This means that the camera operators must make an effort to capture the actors who are interacting with one another and by whom the partners in the interaction are guided. Thus it can be useful to set up several cameras if the parties are arranged facing each other, as at public events, for example. It can also mean that technical descriptions should also be included in the recording (or at least documented), as in the case of the work of one individual at a computer or joint work done by several persons on an interactive screen or on paper (Streeck and Kallmeyer, 2001; Heath and Luff, 2000; Büscher, 2005). It can also result in the use of a moving hand-held camera in case the focus changes quickly, as during work in operating rooms or in classrooms (Mohn, 2007; Schubert, 2007).

CAMERA POSITION AND SOUND

Using our own research examples, we outline below three typical recording situations and explain the methods with which video data are produced there in each case. Essentially, it is always important to prudently weigh various aspects against one another: preparation effort, costs for equipment, and possible interruption of the activity in the field are pitted against the objective of obtaining valuable data that can be analyzed well. Here, we primarily go into the essential technology. Advanced skills such as camera work or framing are secondary here, because it is 'sociological' pictures, not 'aesthetic' ones, which are important. Technical knowledge that can improve the shots, however, is not a bad thing either. With a 'hand-held camera' (see Mohn, 2007), somewhat more practice may even be required. At any rate, the recording of video data requires willingness in principle to come to grips with the recording technology, at least to some extent.

Figure 23.2 Sketch of experimental setup/positioning the camera for a long shot of the room

Following are some useful tips on preparations that should be made even before the recordings begin:

- It is advisable to test all the equipment thoroughly before going out to the field, and to make a packing list.
- You should take along enough spare batteries and memory cards or recording media. Additional batteries in microphones etc. should be tested before use.
- During shooting, it is important to check whether the sound is being correctly recorded by the camera by using headphones to make a test.
- If the camera has an appropriate feature, set it so that the autofocus does not keep adjusting itself, for example, when someone moves through the picture.
- Make sure to place cables so as to avoid creating tripping hazards.
- Set the time codes correctly, to make subsequent synchronization easier.
- Finally, make sure that the equipment and the (possibly privileged) recordings do not get lost.

Setting 1: Crisis Training – Room Shot with Fixed Camera

The first example deals with the recording of simulated crisis training, in which various disaster relief forces in a major city practice working together in an emergency. The research interest, however, did not focus on dealing with the crisis itself, but rather on the way people interact with one another in training situations.

In the course of the study, the various participating technicians, managers of the entities, and other experts from the police force and fire department were filmed while carrying out their tasks. As Figure 23.2. indicates, special attention was given to internal communication within the group and its use of various media and technologies, including computers, flip charts, and corkboards, in addition to direct conversation. The group's external communication was also examined, and for this purpose four cooperating teams, physically separated from each other, were filmed simultaneously.

This situation is well suited in principle for video recordings, because it took place in a self-contained work context. No uninvited passerby walked through the conference room. Satisfactory sound recordings were easily achievable because there was no significant background noise. To control the exercise on site, the actors themselves employed a monitoring camera. We decided to work in this room with a fixed camera in each room that stored images on memory cards. It was positioned so that in the long shot of the room, most of the interactions within the group could be easily seen and recorded. Even if one of the actors turned his back to the camera, his actions remained relatively easy to reconstruct. If the room is too small to be captured by the camera in a long

Figure 23.3 Street market interaction

shot, use of a wide-angle lens is a good idea. In the example shown, the camera was on a tripod in one corner of the room, protected by some small tables placed in front of it. It was fixed at eye level in a position roughly corresponding to that of a human observer. Thus all the transpiring events could be easily captured, on the whole. This advantage, however, was gained at the price of a disadvantage: low detail resolution. Therefore, at some moments, shots of the proceedings on the computer screens or detailed views of incoming fax messages would have helped to make the progress of the training more understandable. Unfortunately that was not possible. Owing to the high level of situation control, these data nonetheless could be subsequently used as incidental documents to supplement the video footage. These copies of emails and of the paperwork completed during the training, as well as photos of the corkboards that were utilized, were helpful secondary data that we were able to put to good use in analyzing the video material. The sound quality of the recording in the room was good. Nevertheless, we decided to attach to the camera an external microphone, which focused on the speaking actors and provided better understandability, even when comments were only mumbled. A second microphone placed on the table would have been even better for capturing all the conversations and noises relating to the interaction.

Setting 2: Street Market – Outdoor Shot with Elevated Fixed Camera

The second example comes from a street market in London, where the interaction between vendors and customers was to be looked at. This project of the WIT Workgroup at King's College in London was managed by Dirk vom Lehn. As Figure 23.3. indicates, the problems of execution were more substantial in this case. At first it was difficult to find vendors who would agree to be filmed. Many feared their business would fall off, or they wanted a high fee for their appearance in the video. An additional problem was caused by the busy foot traffic in the market. For such situations, it is a good idea to use so-called gorilla tripods, which can be attached to items such as lamps or fences – and in a slightly elevated position as well. In the case described, it was possible to fix the camera on a standard tripod, which was placed in front of a fence. Behind it, a café offered the researcher a convenient place from which he could have access to the camera. The market stand could easily be filmed from a distance of 3 to 4 meters, from the sidewalk just opposite. It was unavoidable, however, that people passing by crossed through the picture from time to time and blocked the view. The sound was the chief problem. The recordings are overlaid with such intense background noise that the

Figure 23.4 Shots from two camera angles (left: speaker, right: audience)

conversation of the vendor with his customers can scarcely be understood. There are two solutions for this: Either you use a good directional microphone and hope you have found a suitable orientation, or you use a wireless microphone set. The latter option was chosen in this case. For such purposes, special little transmitters and receivers are available. We were able to attach the transmitter and a lavalier microphone (lapel mic) directly to the vendor's clothing – with his consent, of course. With this method, the signal is stored directly on the video, by radio, which eliminates the need for time-consuming synchronization later. The use of a stationary Dictaphone would be an alternative solution, though it necessitates synchronization of the image and the sound afterwards and creates additional effort and expense. The conversations between the dealer and his customers can be understood with exceptional ease. Because no prior consent could be obtained from the passers-by, an info sign was put up next to the camera. It described the research and offered to delete the shots if there were any objections.

Setting 3: Shooting from Different Camera Angles

In some settings, one camera is insufficient to capture the ongoing interaction. Thus, in the research project on PowerPoint presentations (Schnettler and Knoblauch, 2007; Knoblauch, 2012), we were interested in the interaction between the audience and the speaker on the stage. Because the audience at most could be seen from behind on the speaker's camera, we decided to work with two cameras and edit the footage together synchronously, as Figure 23.4. shows. There are projects for which even more cameras can be useful, but you should not overdo it, because each additional camera means a substantial increase in the technical effort of preparation and post-processing. Besides, more recording devices result in great intrusiveness in the field. Finally, the slim resources available in social science research generally permit the evaluation of only one or two perspectives, so that additional shots at best can be brought in as a supplement. The quantities of data that accrue must not be underestimated.

Under the constraint of practical compromises, an increase in the volume of data can carry the risk of resulting in standardization or evaluating the data in a purely superficial way. The various camera angles must then be edited together with a variety of software. To simplify the synchronization, you should give a distinctive visual and audible signal (such as the clapperboard used in filmmaking) that is clearly identifiable for both cameras.

Figure 23.5 Navigation experiment recorded with eyetracking camera and follower

Setting 4: Moving Camera

Generally, static (fixed) cameras are preferable, because they provide steadier, smoother shots. One exception to this rule must be mentioned. In some situations, the focus of the interaction does not stay fixed on one spot, but varies as the participants move around in the area. In this case, it may make better sense to use a hand-held moving camera. However, there is a regularly recurring problem with this: one is usually a bit too slow in tracking with the camera, as a result of trying to pan to the shifting center of events after the fact. Actors point to an object, the filmmaker follows with the camera – and always gets there a moment too late to capture the very thing he was tracking with the camera. He too, with his camera work, is sequentially involved in the situation. Therefore, you should make sure to film in an anticipatory way, that is, to keep the possible objects of interest in view. Above all, avoid zooming and panning too much, because this greatly impedes the analysis of the recordings later on.

Other situations in which a hand-held camera can be useful are those in which coordination between the participants is being carried out in a highly focused way. For example, when very delicate work is being done, as in the case of the experienced nurse who, by a tiny movement of the tracheal tube, indicates 'on the patient' the angle at which the inexperienced doctor should insert the tube (Schubert, 2006, 2007); or a graphic designer who, with a slight tilt of his pen, hints at an idea before he draws it (Heath and Luff, 2000, p. 165ff.). Such details can be decisive for the interpretation. In the long shot, however, they go unseen. Usually they are detected only after a spell of fieldwork, as soon as it has also become clear where the focus of the analysis will lie and which sequences should be selected.

Once such situations are identified in ethnographic work, it is helpful to track them selectively with a moving camera and record them, as Figure 23.5. shows.

Recent Developments

Recent advances in camera development allow the researcher to experiment with new forms of video recordings. Already now eye tracking devices, 360° and 3D cameras, automatic long-term recording, and many more things are being used in specific settings. They offer new possibilities in offering new perspectives (for example, the viewer can change his vantage point, can take the perspective of the participant using VR-glasses) and allow for the collection and management of vast amounts of data (here quantitative and algorithmic approaches might support the research). However, the new forms usually cause new complexities, the planning and implementation in a specific context takes time and money and must be balanced with the effects of intrusiveness.

SAMPLING, LOGBOOK, AND RESEARCH PROCESS

The prerequisite for every video analysis is interest in a certain phenomenon of action and interaction. This interest generally is connected with the constructivist hypothesis that exact knowledge of forms of action and interaction sheds light on how the reality shaped by them comes into being. Moreover, it is also associated with the conjecture that the normative ideas prevailing outside of the situation and the actual action are by no means identical with what is going on in the situation. Once ethnographic knowledge has been acquired, recordings can be made. In the process, frequently more data are collected than is relevant for the specific research question. On the other hand, the recordings that have been produced may also turn out to be inappropriate for dealing with the question, because there was an inability to assess the situation well enough. In this case, more ethnographic research work and additional shooting are needed. Nevertheless, the video recordings should be kept – often new questions arise later, for which they can be important.

At any rate, for this reason the recorded video data – in addition to the ethnographic data – should be covered in an overview. This logbook is created by inspecting the entire recording, which, for the time being, is only coded roughly in an initial round of preliminary evaluation. Preliminary transcripts are prepared. Then the analyses and data sessions being initiated help to identify the corresponding units, so that it is worthwhile to do further coding. At the same time, it is crucial to make sure that these codings contain no predetermined categories. Rather, interpretive treatment of the data requires that the relevant categories be obtained from the observed interactions of the actors, that is, from the field itself. Then the logbook too can be treated as a kind of sample, in which similar, contrasting, or divergent cases are searched for. This search, which follows the principle of Grounded Theory (Strübing, 2004; Strauss, 1987; Strauss and Corbin, 1998), can be supplemented by additional ethnography and more recordings.

SELECTION OF SEQUENCES FOR DETAILED ANALYSIS

A major decision in the research process is defining the degree of detail with which you want to look at the material, in order to identify the appropriate sequences in the material and make it possible to find and compare them by coding the available footage; this is done first by using the question posed. Elsewhere (see Knoblauch et al., 2015, chapter 4) we made it clear that the video interaction analysis sequences and meaningful units of activity (such as an image, a minute, etc.) are not determined by the academics, but derived from the interrelated visual and vocal stretches of action of the actors. The actors indicate to each other what they are doing at the moment, when an activity begins, and when it ends. We can now use this determination of sequence as observers to define the boundaries of the units to be studied. It is necessary to establish when an activity is begun and ended again so that it can be located later in the available material and then compared. Thus we must constantly alternate between rough coding of the collected material and detailed, fine-grained analysis in order to iteratively determine our units of study.

ARCHIVING, DATA MANIPULATION, AND TRANSCRIPTION

After the collection of data in the field, the data usually are available to us in a camera or on a storage medium and must be prepared for subsequent analysis. The data must be added to a corpus and archived so that they are accessible in a suitable way (see Corti, Chapter 11, this volume). In this process, a few points must be kept in mind.

Archiving and Categorizing

After recording in the field, video data usually are available in a video format produced by the camera and in unedited data sets. The data usually are organized – and frequently provided with a time index – through selection of the filmed situations and of the moments when the camera was running. These markings, in combination with other field notes, can be good preliminary work for archiving. For selection of relevant sequences for analysis, it is necessary to categorize the data in terms of content as well – to put together a logbook, as described in the preceding chapter. This can be tackled in a number of different technical and organizational ways. For smaller projects, a well-thought-out file-folder structure, along with accompanying documentation using texts or tables, can be completely sufficient. Organization on the basis of a program for coding, such as MAXQDA or Atlas.ti, thanks to the advanced integration of video data, offers a number of advantages. In larger projects it may even be helpful to compile a database or store the files, indexed, on a server. In the process of selection for detailed analysis, short segments from the recordings are chosen, extracted, and observed in detail. Because incompatibilities often arise, it is helpful to convert these clips to a data format that is as compatible and system-independent as possible. This also must not become too large and thus 'unwieldy' (unfortunately, as video standards are in constant flux, we can give no reliable pointers here).

Backup of Data

Video data, like other research data, should be thoroughly protected. A special problem in comparison with data in text form is that video data can no longer be filed in the printed form, traditional for centuries, but are stored on sensitive and constantly changing data storage devices. Think of the problems that can arise even today in the use and conversion of film, Super 8, or even video data. Digital data media such as DVDs have only a limited lifetime, and it is not certain how long the reading devices will remain compatible. Hard drives can crash and are difficult to reconstruct. It makes sense to back up data regularly, store the backed up data in another location, and make sure that the data are always transferred to compatible media. Solutions that back up data to the cloud or the Internet are questionable, for reasons of data protection.

Preparation for Detailed Analyses

For joint data sessions, relevant sequences must be selected. For this purpose, the material is examined and interesting places are marked. This occurs, depending on the procedure preferred, by noting the time code or by tagging/coding with appropriate software. With reference to the research question, individual sequences are selected for detailed analysis. These sequences are extracted and pre-processed. Here it is helpful to retain the raw data in their original form. Clips that are used for the detailed analyses should be separated or copied. Frequently it can become necessary to later make additional clips from the original file, for example, to find out what happened before the sequence that was considered, to supplement these segments, or to observe them in context again at a later time. Preparation for the data session also includes a (rough) transcription (see Jenks, Chapter 8, this volume), at least of the verbal courses of interaction, which can serve during the session as an orientation guide and as a basis for an expanded transcription. As video analysis expands the analysis of spoken language (Conversation Analysis – see Jackson, Chapter 18, this volume) to all observable modalities, the final transcripts ought to include all turns necessary to explain the sequence at hand. As we do not know this in the beginning, the mere transcription of the spoken word, therefore, is a good start, but the analysis should then always focus on the video and the transcription adapted to the specific case.

Transcription System

The transcription conventions go back to the system developed by E.A. Schegloff. It was devised to provide practice in the transcription of talk interactions on the basis of the conventions of conversation analysis. Such transcription systems, also widely used in linguistic research, produce far more precise transcripts than those based purely on content analysis. The basic principle is verbatim transcription: Everything is written down as it was spoken, without any semantic approximations or adaptations to standard written language. All utterances are represented in written characters, exactly as acoustically recorded. It is especially important not to omit 'mistakes', pauses, overlaps, and paralinguistic elements; they must be transcribed as well. For video analysis, transcription is necessary to process the sequential arrangement of the events for analysis, and methodologically it is of fundamental significance. Consequently, mastering transcription is a basic prerequisite for the analytic work. It is a methodological skill, which can be acquired only in part through mediated instruction. Essentially, one learns the skill actually only by doing transcriptions oneself. In formal terms, transcribing is relatively simple, but it requires some practice to be mastered. One should not forget that transcription is already guiding the interpretation and analysis, for example, by fixing the degree of detailedness. Interpretation of video data and its analysis also feeds back on further data collection (for more detailed instructions about how to analyze video data and organize the research process cf. Knoblauch et al., 2015; Heath et al., 2010).

Transcription systems range from relatively simple, such as the GAT2 minimal transcript (Selting et al., 2011), to more sophisticated versions that also include specific details, such as prosodic dimensions, and allow more fine-grained analysis of the data. Very helpful guidelines for transcription are found in the work of Paul ten Have (2007), who offers a highly recommended website with numerous additional pointers for ethnomethodological conversation analysis: www.paultenhave.nl/resource.htm. Besides the transcription of the verbal interaction, a number of systems for the transcription of bodily movement and other modalities have been developed. Frequently, they follow a system that resembles a musical score, combining different simultaneous layers of communicative modes in order to inspect both its sequential and its synchronic features. From our practice we do not recommend to produce such work-intense score-transcripts of several modalities in an early phase of projects; they might be useful later on, however we recommend starting with a simple form and using transcripts as helpful tools rather than as outcomes on their own. In video analysis, it is important to follow the turn-by-turn sequence ranging across modalities and then, in a further step, develop suitable ways to represent the specific findings in a concise manner. For this reason simple software tools, such as a good player with slow motion and fine-grained control, often provides sufficiently useful help. More specific tools such as Transana (Schwab, 2006), Atlas.ti, or Feldpartitur (Moritz, 2011), Dartfish, Noldus Interact, or Folker might be beneficial for specific projects, but there is no all-in-one solution: Tools from linguistics are useful when the recorded situation is centered around verbal interaction, whereas a more motion-based tool from sports analysis is apt to capture the details of bodily working together.

CONCLUSION

Data collection is complemented by the analysis of video data in a way that is typically not linear but circular-iterative (see Figure 23.6).

Research Process

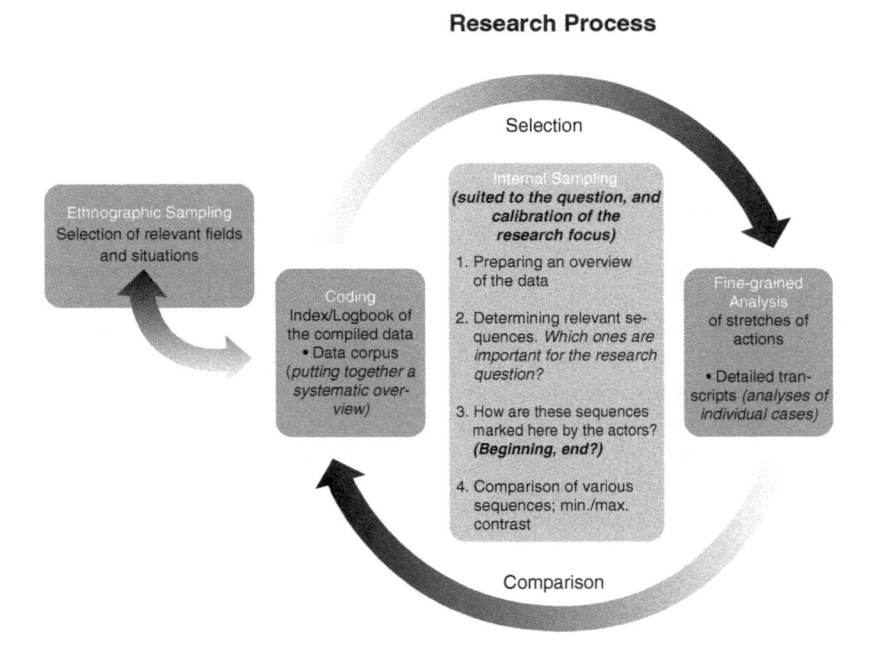

```
                          Selection
                    ┌─────────────────┐
                    │ Internal Sampling│
                    │ (suited to the question, and
                    │  calibration of the
                    │  research focus) │
┌──────────────┐    │ 1. Preparing an overview
│ Ethnographic │    │    of the data   │     ┌──────────────┐
│  Sampling    │    │                  │     │ Fine-grained │
│ Selection of │    │ 2. Determining relevant se-│ Analysis  │
│ relevant fields│  │    quences. Which ones are │ of stretches of
│ and situations│   │    important for the research│ actions │
└──────────────┘    │    question?     │     │              │
                    │                  │     │ • Detailed tran-
     ┌──────────┐   │ 3. How are these sequences│ scripts (analyses of
     │ Coding   │   │    marked here by the actors?│ individual cases)
     │Index/Logbook of│ (Beginning, end?)│     └──────────────┘
     │the compiled data│               │
     │ • Data corpus│  │ 4. Comparison of various
     │(putting together a│ sequences; min./max.
     │ systematic over-│  contrast       │
     │    view)   │    └─────────────────┘
     └──────────┘
                          Comparison
```

Figure 23.6 The research process (from Knoblauch et al., 2015)

The same holds true, of course, for the ethnographic process which is not only relevant to get a focus of video data but also poses the question how the field selected as well as the video data collected relate to larger contexts, such as social structure, culture, and society. How these relations are typically addressed, is a matter of theoretical framing and methodological considerations, which also reflect the very way data collection is done. (For the general methodological and theoretical issues concerning videography see Knoblauch et al., 2015, chapters 3 and 8.)

FURTHER READING

Heath, Christian, Jon Hindmarsh and Paul Luff (2010) *Video in Qualitative Research. Analysing Social Interaction in Everyday Life*. London: Sage.

Knoblauch, Hubert, Bernt Schnettler, Jürgen Raab and Hans-Georg Soeffner (eds.) (2006) *Video Analysis – Methodology and Methods. Qualitative Audiovisual Data Analysis in Sociology*. Frankfurt am Main, New York, Frankfurt, Basel: Peter Lang.

Knoblauch, Hubert, René Tuma and Bernt Schnettler (2015) *Videography. Introduction to Interpretive Video Analysis of Social Situations*. New York: Peter Lang.

REFERENCES

Amann, Klaus (1997) 'Die Befremdung der eigenen Kultur. Ein Programm', in Stefan Hirschauer and Klaus Amann (eds.), Die Befremdung der eigenen Kultur. Zur ethnographischen Herausforderung soziologischer Empirie. Frankfurt: Suhrkamp, pp. 7–52.

Büscher, M. (2005) 'Social life under the microscope?', *Sociological Research Online* No. 10.

Goffman, Erving (1963) *Behavior in Public Places. Notes on the Social Organization of Gatherings*. New York: The Free Press.

Heath, Christian and Paul Luff (2000) *Technology in Action*. Cambridge: Cambridge University Press.

Heath, Christian, Jon Hindmarsh and Paul Luff (2010) *Video in Qualitative Research. Analysing Social Interaction in Everyday Life*. London: Sage.

Kiesow, Christian (2016) *Die Mathematik als Denkwerk. Eine Studie zur kommunikativen und visuellen Performanz mathematischen Wissens*. Wiesbaden: VS.

Knoblauch, Hubert (2005) 'Focused ethnography', *Forum Qualitative Sozialforschung/Forum: Qualitative Social Research*, 6(3): Art 44, available at http://nbn-resolving.de/urn:nbn:de:0114-fqs0503440.

Knoblauch, Hubert (2012) *PowerPoint and the Communication Culture of Knowledge Society*. New York and Cambridge: Cambridge University Press.

Knoblauch, Hubert, René Tuma and Bernt Schnettler (2015) *Videography. Introduction to Interpretive Video Analysis of Social Situations*. New York: Peter Lang.

Mohn, Elisabeth (2007) 'Kamera-Ethnografie: Vom Blickentwurf zur Denkbewegung', in Gabriele Brandstetter and Gabriele Klein (eds.), *Methoden der Tanzwissenschaft. Modellanalysen zu Pina Bauschs 'Sacre du Printemps*. Bielefeld: transcript, pp. 173–94.

Moritz, Christine (2011) *Die Feldpartitur. Multikodale Traskription von Videodaten in der Qualitativen Sozialforschung*. Wiesbaden: VS.

Schnettler, Bernt and Hubert Knoblauch (2007) *PowerPoint-Präsentationen. Neue Formen der gesellschaftlichen Kommunikation von Wissen*. Konstanz: UVK.

Schubert, Cornelius (2006) 'Videographie im OP: Wie Videotechnik für technografische Studien im OP genutzt werden kann', in Werner Rammert and Cornelius Schubert (eds.), *Technografie. Zur Mikrosoziologie der Technik*. Frankfurt and New York: Campus, pp. 223–48.

Schubert, Cornelius (2007) 'Risk and safety in the operating theatre: An ethnographic study of socio-technical practices', in Regula Valérie Burri and Joseph Dumit (eds.), *Biomedicine as Culture. Instrumental Practices, Technoscientific Knowledge, and New Modes of Life*. London: Routledge, pp. 123–38.

Schwab, Götz (2006) 'Transana – ein Transkriptions – und Analyseprogramm zu Verarbeitungvon Videodaten am Computer', *Gesprächsforschung*, No. 7: 70–8.

Selting, Margret, Peter Auer, Dagmar Barth-Weingarten, Jörg Bergmann, Pia Bergmann, Karin Birkner, Elizabeth Couper-Kuhlen, Christian Meyer, Frank Oberzaucher and Susanne Uhmann (2011) 'A system for transcribing talk-in-interaction: GAT 2', translated and adapted for English by Elizabeth Couper-Kuhlen and Dagmar Barth, Gesprächsforschung No. 12: 121–51.

Strauss, Anselm L. (1987) *Qualitative Analysis for Social Scientists*. Cambridge/New York: Cambridge University Press.

Strauss, Anselm L. and Juliet M. Corbin (1998) *Basics of Qualitative Research: Techniques and Procedures for Developing Grounded Theory*. Thousand Oaks, CA: Sage.

Streeck, Jürgen (1993) '"Keep a Rope on Your Patience!" Über eine amerikanische Art des Umgangs mit sich selbst', in Peter Klein and Paul Ingwer (eds.), *Sprachliche Aufmerksamkeit. Festschrift für Walther Dieckmann*. Darmstadt: Winter Universitäts Verlag, pp. 195–201.

Streeck, Jürgen and Werner Kallmeyer (2001) 'Interaction by Inscription', *Journal of Pragmatics* No. 33: 465–90.

Strübing, Jörg (2004) *Grounded Theory. Zur sozialtheoretischen und epistemologischen Fundierung des Verfahrens der empirisch begründeten Theoriebildung*. Wiesbaden: VS.

ten Have, Paul (2007) *Doing Conversation Analysis. A Practical Guide* (2nd rev. edn). Los Angeles: Sage.

Collecting Documents as Data

Tim Rapley and Gethin Rees

INTRODUCTION

Documents, both paper-based and computer-mediated texts, are a ubiquitous aspect of the formation and enactment of contemporary life. Our interest in documents includes both the written elements of texts alongside the extra-textual elements – images, photographs, graphs, diagrams – that are routinely embedded in documents. The post-structural and post-modern turn in academia has led to an expansion of the meaning of the term 'text', to include buildings, bodies, clothing, alongside artefacts, devices and other aspects of material and technical culture. Simultaneously, interview transcripts, field notes and video-recordings are referred to and analysed as 'texts', but we will not focus on either of these genres of work here. Instead we are concentrating on three relatively distinct areas of work around documents:

- Docile documents to enable the analysis of documents as texts in their own right – ranging from the evolving explorations of the history of the present to the ordered, systemised, practices of the synthesis of qualitative research;
- Documents gathered alongside other forms of fieldwork to support a range of types of analytic work – covering the ad hoc ways that a range of theoretical and methodological traditions ask researchers to engage with aspects of documents to support and enhance claims;
- Documents in action to inform more naturalistic or ethnographic work on situated document use – focusing on the (small number of) studies that approach the in situ creation, development and use of documents as the core analytic focus.

Analytic work on and with documents can be loosely divided into two areas: work that focuses on the actual textual and extra-textual content of documents; and work that focuses on some aspect of the use, role and function of documents in everyday and organisational settings. The first focuses on the document as an object in its own right, the content of the document as static and immutable (Prior, 2008), as a 'docile' container of knowledge. Such work generally forgoes some form of empirical work on how people actually create, read, refer to or use the documents in question. Whereas the second area is primarily observational, seeking to understand some element of how documents are active agents in organisational and/or everyday life. Obviously, the same research topic can be approached in multiple ways within the same project. So, with a research project on, say, student evaluations of lecturers, you might focus on: the written comments students give (via discourse analysis – see Rau et al., Chapter 19, this volume); how results of these evaluations are fed-back on websites, internal memoranda or official reports (via discourse analysis); how lecturers introduce, distribute, collect and read such forms (via observation – see Wästerfors, Chapter 20, this volume); what students, lecturers and managerial staff think is the value of such documents (via interview – see Roulston and Choi, Chapter 15, this volume); the role of such evaluations in creating institutional change (via observation and interview), etcetera.

We should note that the collection and analysis of documents is also related to the research tradition of content analysis (Weber, 1990). In this, researchers gather specific documents, then establish a coding frame and apply that coding frame to the documents to count the number of times particular words, phrases or themes are used. Clearly, this enables descriptive and statistical findings to be established. However, this is often seen by some qualitative researchers as a relatively limited, albeit systematic approach, in that it predefines the key aspects of analysis alongside removing words and phrases from their immediate and broader context. There are also more qualitative approaches to content analysis that focus on manifest, latent and context-dependent meaning (see Schreier, 2014). Some researchers use content analysis alongside other more discursive methodologies, in part to gain a general overview of their data, although this is not discussed here.

So, to return to the substantive focus of this chapter, on the face of it you would think that collecting documents to undertake some kind of analytic work is quite a simple task. You have got a research question, or maybe an idea for a research question, and you have got a sense of the type of documents you want to work with. And in an electronic age, we generally have very good access to documents, as much of it is either digital in origin or becoming digitised. However, as soon as you start the process, you are faced with a range of practical and theoretical issues. Before we go any further, we want to explore aspects of these through a very mundane example.

SEARCHING, SEARCHING, SEARCHING

So, let us say we are interested in doing some work on 'parents' experiences of caring for children with Autism Spectrum Disorders' (ASD). And for an array of intellectual reasons, beyond practical issues of time, costs and access to study populations, we are interested in looking at how documents have engaged with this issue. We have a vast array of potential documents to focus on, including plays, diaries, government reports, charities' booklets, online support groups etc. However, we are going to use articles that academics have created. Clearly, focusing on academic texts already narrows down the possibilities of where to start to get access to this material. However, we are now faced with a very wide array of places to start, especially in terms of web-based sources. If we start with a basic web search, which we would routinely do, using the words 'parents' experiences of caring for children with ASD', we get over 43 million hits on Google. Briefly scanning the first few pages of results and then some random pages, we get a mixture of content from academic articles, charities and news agencies. The next phase would be a slightly more specialised database, say Google Scholar, a very useful site for a range of reasons – not least as you can see who has also cited the article. If searching for articles (and by that they include books and other academic outputs) using the same search term we get over 24,000. Again, scanning a few random pages shows a very broad range, from interview studies to randomised controlled trials (RCTs). Clearly, this is too much for us to manage – either there is a lot of academic work on parents' experiences of children with ASD or the search is too 'sensitive' but not 'specific' enough and so gives us access to too many possibilities.

We need some way to make this manageable. We have at least two options here:

- Refine the search in terms of the topical-focus – so we could focus on 'fathers' rather than parents;
- Refine the search in terms of methodological focus – so we could focus on 'qualitative' work rather than any method or methodology.

So, if we replace 'parent', and search with 'father', we still get over 21,000 results.

Now Google Scholar has some very limited functionality in terms of narrowing the search, for example, we could exclude certain keywords, like 'randomised', and so exclude RCTs, but that could also remove any articles which discuss RCTs and those might actually be useful. Even so, if we add '-randomised', so remove any with that word we are left with 20,900. Now, we also need to bear in mind we have two spellings here – UK and US English – so by using '-randomised' and '-randomized' we get down to 20,000 and adding '-survey' and '-questionnaire' we get to 17,900. Now, that might be a workable number in some contexts with very large teams, but for most it will still be unfeasible.

So, let's go to a more specialised electronic database, and as we are sociologists, we are going to look specifically at the database 'Sociological Abstracts'. We put ASD in the search box and we get 190 – including dissertations, journal articles, conference proceedings and books. We also have the option of using a range of search fields, one is the subject heading, where someone has already assigned or indexed a document with a specific, pre-defined term. In this case SU.exact ('AUTISM') now yields 584 results. Now clearly, using such a filter depends on people tagging the appropriate files, which does not always happen. We can then refine the search further, through adding 'AND parent' and we get to 240, and 'AND father' gets us 30. Clearly, that is very manageable, but we are far from happy – we know from the Google Scholar search, many potentially relevant articles are missing. In this context, when searching for academic work, one database is rarely enough.

So finally, let's try another track, let's turn to PubMED, a database for biological and health sciences, as much work on ASD is conducted in this area. This database has layers of technical ways to maximise access to the data they hold. With this database, we know content-specific search filters, amongst other things, have been developed by other researchers in order to get the maximum results. For example, one search filter for ASD for PubMED is:

- Autistic[tiab] OR autism[tiab] OR autistic disorder[mh] OR asperger syndrome[mh] OR child development disorders, pervasive[mh:noexp] OR asperger[tiab] OR asperger's[tiab] OR aspergers[tiab] OR pervasive development[tiab] OR pervasive develop-mental[tiab] OR pdd[tiab] (available at http://www.ncbi.nlm.nih.gov/pubmedhealth/PMH0066913/).

Note the range of terms used here – so far we have only searched the other databases using the acronym 'ASD' and the term 'Autism'. Yet clearly, in part due to historical changes in terminology, as well as the expansion of treatment, there is a range of ways it can be categorised. Note, this is only one ASD filter people have designed for PubMED, there are others on offer. Also, you should note that this search filter was designed for this specific database and so the search needs to be adapted for each database! Using the specific user-generated filters gives us very large results of over 36,000 documents on PubMED; for us, and for most researchers, we are again getting too much extraneous material, the search is not specific enough. So, we could try and focus on qualitative work only, again using methodological filters that others have developed, and we get around 800 in PubMED. Then we could refine, for 'parents' or 'fathers' – but what terms to use?

Well, that is three databases, there are other relevant ones we would need to search, download the references, then search for duplicates and then start some more in-depth reading to work out what is relevant and what to exclude, to refine our sample again. We could have also told a similar story, about searching for 'parents' experiences of caring for children with ASD' in blogs or newspaper articles. In terms of newspaper articles, refining the search to UK national newspapers only, via the Nexis database, we get over 3,000 articles via 'autism', which is reduced to over 500 with the term 'parent'. In terms of blogs, using the term 'autism' on searchblogspot.com, we get over 950,000 hits, and on blogsearchengine.com, over 9 million. With 'autism AND parent' we get 162,000 on searchblogspot.com and just under 8 million on blogsearchengine.com. As neither search engine offers many options to refine your search, this is clearly far from manageable.

Centrally, what our narrative of searching aims to demonstrate is three interrelated key issues: access, sampling and relevance. However, alongside those, we need to also consider another core issue, the issue of ethics.

Access

Textbook discussions often emphasise the difficult task of negotiating access to various forms of data (see Bengry, Chapter 7, this volume). Participants need to be recruited, organisations need to approve access and multiple gatekeepers must be approached in order to get hold of documents. This is a deficit model of access, where we are reliant on others to access the key documents we want to work with; and in part we highlight this above, albeit through discussion of access to specific databases. For instance, technical databases (e.g. PubMED), need some kind of organisational or individual subscription to access them. Moreover, you need to have the appropriate skills and knowledge to work with them in the most economical way. However, our discussion above highlights another issue, a surplus model of access where we are overwhelmed with potential options and sources. Clearly, this is tied to how porous your interface with the source of documents is – electronic documents are generally ready-to-hand.

Sampling

In an ideal world, we would all be working with a 'total population sample' of the documents we want to work with. With some research questions, in some contexts, with some methodologies, that might be a possibility. However, as we began to demonstrate above, generally you are overwhelmed with options, and need to develop a coherent sampling strategy (see Schreier, Chapter 6, this volume). Centrally, we need to know the archive of possible documents to sample from, in order to apply and subsequently justify, our purposive sampling decisions. We need to go through cycles of searching, scanning, reviewing, or even what Layder (1998) calls 'pre-coding', the output of the search and then refining the search, repeating that process, over and over. Outlined above, you saw a glimpse of some very mundane sampling decisions, with say, a focus on excluding articles that discuss randomised controlled trials. In this way, we seek to refine the material to produce something that is both practically manageable as well as analytically rich.

Relevance

Through the process of collecting documents you are also making a range of judgements:

judgements about the usefulness of a specific document for your research; judgements about fit with your (initial) research question and/or the other documents in the data set; and judgements about quality, for instance quality of access to the documents, as well as quality of the content. When working with documents, initially, you often have to make rapid appraisals around issues of relevance, so as to inform, enhance and refine your sampling. Over time, as you get to know the possibilities of your potential archive, the appraisals become more informed and analytic.

Ethics

In part, by focusing on working with academic texts, we silenced an explicit discussion of ethics. However, thinking about blogs raises a key issue: are blogs public or private spaces? (See Sugiura et al. 2016, and Weller et al., Chapter 31, this volume.) Do bloggers expect to be participants within studies? Do participants to academic studies or newspaper accounts expect to have some aspect of their 'data' or 'quotes' re-analysed, generally far outside the topic they gave consent to? Clearly, some documents are public documents, they are designed and tailored towards an active relationship and engagement with the public. Whereas others are clearly private documents, either password protected or found in locked rooms, where access needs to be mediated through a gatekeeper. As with the other decisions we discuss throughout this chapter, researchers are required to negotiate the difficult terrain of assessing whether a document has been ethically sourced and if its inclusion can be justified within a data set (see Mertens, Chapter 3, this volume, and Tiidenberg, Chapter 30, this volume).

In what follows, we are going to focus on these issues in a range of contexts. Centrally, we want to explore some of the practical and analytical issues faced by those working with documents.

WORKING WITH DOCILE DOCUMENTS

While there has been something of a shift in recent years, from analysing solely the content of a document, to having a greater appreciation of the ways documents are developed and used (Prior, 2003), the analysis of docile documents is still central. By far the most ubiquitous approach is some form of relatively close and detailed analysis of the language and meaning within the document, some form of, or relation to, discourse analysis. Such approaches are influenced by related theories and ideas emerging from such sources as linguistics, deconstructionism, phenomenology, post-structuralism, postmodernism, pragmatism, social constructionism and writers such as Austin, Foucault, Goffman, Garfinkel, Sacks, Schutz and Wittgenstein. A wide array of contemporary research traditions focus on, at some points, the analysis of language-in-use within documents, including Actor Network Theory, Critical Discourse Analysis, Critical Psychology, Discursive Psychology, Foucauldian Discourse Analysis and the Sociology of Scientific Knowledge. Each tradition has its own assumptions about how their analytic work should be done. However, whatever approach people take, and irrespective of the methodological traditions they follow, the practical work of collecting documents is the same.

As already outlined above, rather than struggling to access materials, the contemporary qualitative researcher is often in the position of having an embarrassment of riches when it comes to generating an archive of documents.

Organisational materials for public consumption, from governmental and non-governmental organisations, corporations, charities and learned societies and institutions, are available via web search engines. Past multimedia artefacts, including television programmes and films, are often available via institutional resources. Newspapers, magazines, diaries, biographies, literature and poetry are available, either electronically or physically, from libraries. While access to some of these resources is reliant upon the subscription policies of the libraries of which you are a member, services such as inter-library loans make documentary materials available easily and relatively cheaply.

Of course, missing from the above list are forms of documents not publicly available or physically bound to a specific location and which require alternative access arrangements. It is worth making the effort to track down more difficult to access documents, however, as they can be valuable sources of information.

- Currently, a huge volume of government and organisational documents is released and available for public scrutiny, however some files are closed. This is especially the case with sensitive material, often military and police reports, where documents may be closed and then only released into the public domain after a set number of years. Even when they are 'opened', some of the words may be obscured, some pages or whole files removed. Gidley (2003) used documents from The National Archives in London that had been publicly released many decades after the events they reported on. He used them to explore the experience of East London Jewish Radicals in the early twentieth century. As the individuals in these groups were closely monitored by the British police and other government departments, he found a wealth of material including: police-made transcriptions of anti-war meetings, reports of the various venues they congregated in and internal communications (memos) between civil servants. Engaging with this archive, Gidley not only discovered something about the radical groups themselves but also a history of the policing and governing of these communities.
- Some documents are restricted, especially those that have been produced for 'internal' consumption in an organisation or between individuals. Even some libraries' collections have restricted access, which may mean you need to get some form of special permission to visit them. Once you are aware that they actually exist, which is not always easy, to get access to such documents you will have to negotiate with the specific organisation or individuals you are working with.

For example, Moreira (2015) used internal documents of a patient organisation – the Alzheimer's Society – to explore their role in shaping health policy. Over a period of time, speaking to a range of people in the organisation and through a series of face-to-face meetings, he negotiated access to their internal archive. He was not allowed to take the original documents away from the building, and had to repeatedly visit their main office and take detailed notes from them. Through reading, sorting and exploring the range of documents within the archive, he could begin to describe the history of the organisation. He used this data, alongside other sources, to demonstrate the shifting forms of knowledge – from an initial focus on carers' knowledge to a hybrid of experiential, clinical and scientific knowledge – that this patient organisation deployed in their interactions with policy actors over time.

We should also note that some documents may be restricted in the terms that they employ, such as very technical or specialised language, abbreviations or conventions, or are written in a language you cannot read. However, during the course of your research, as you become more submerged in your archive, you should hopefully become more familiar with the language that those who are already members of the area take for granted. It is sometimes necessary to spend time interacting with members of the specific community that the documents come from. This enables you to begin to understand their practices. While these interactions may not become data for analysis, they can be integral to developing the 'vulgar competence' (Garfinkel and Wieder, 1992) or 'interactional expertise' (Collins and Evans, 2008) necessary to fully engage with the documents.

When you have access to documents, as noted above, a key decision that needs to be made is to assess the kinds of documents that, at least in the first instance, will be of value to the research question. Rees's recent study, a documentary analysis of discourses around a novel sleep disorder named Sexsomnia – that is, people who engage in sexual practices while asleep – meant a focus on a range of types of document. Given the nature of the condition, Sexsomnia is not something that is only discussed in medical literatures, as the symptoms of the condition often produced legal consequences: there could potentially be a legal paper-trail and the cases could also be reported in the media. As a result three databases were initially searched: potentially relevant academic literatures, using Google Scholar; legal discourses on the use of the defence and in particular trial descriptions via LexisNexis; and the third area, media reporting through the Nexis database.

When searching for documents, you often need to define the breadth of the search, and in so doing, define the sample frame. In Rees's case, this was bounded by the substantive topic – Sexsomnia as a distinct medical condition was first named in 2003 and the first criminal case in England and Wales to use Sexsomnia as a defence was in 2005. In this way, 2003 appeared as a suitable start date for the search and the end date was open-ended. However, through the process of working on the documents, it was discovered that men had been using sleep as a defence in sexual assault cases for a period far earlier than that date, it was just not labelled as Sexsomnia. In other contexts, more pragmatic decisions are made. For example, Seale's (2002) work on how cancer is portrayed in regional and national English-language newspapers across different cultures, focused on just one week's press output. By limiting the sample to a single week, he radically reduced the number of articles to work with. By focusing on articles written in English, he removed the cost of and potential problems with translation[1]. However, he still gained a comprehensive data set that allowed for comparison across countries.

Rees's initial search of the databases produced limited results for an array of pragmatic, technical and analytic reasons. For example, legal cases are only recorded when they impact a point of law and as none of the Sexsomnia cases had changed legislation or policy, they were not reported. For more information, the actual transcripts of trials would have been necessary, but this is often costly. In terms of media reporting, Rees was already aware of two criminal trials that had occurred, but they had not appeared as a result of the search. So, when generating the archive of documents, you routinely have to go through rounds of searching, reviewing the results, modifying ideas, and searching again, and reviewing, modifying and so on. In reviewing the small number of academic articles, Rees followed Layder (1998) in undertaking some preliminary coding (or 'pre-coding'), in order to get a sense of the types of academic discourses present around the condition. This first stage uncovered a range of articles, textbooks and discussions describing the condition, clinical cases and diagnostic signs as well as a group of documents related to the clinical tests that could be performed to assess whether a contested diagnosis of Sexsomnia was legitimate, particularly related to instances where a person was using the sleepwalking defence in a sexual assault case. This pre-coding stage had the effect of shifting the research question of the project. Rather than focusing upon discourses around Sexsomnia in particular, a more focused question developed around the expert debates surrounding diagnosis of Sexsomnia in criminal justice settings. Armed with this new focus, Rees proceeded to re-sample and re-review both the media and academic documents. Using the reference lists of the articles previously identified – a practice known as reference chaining or citation chaining – older articles were found, which extended the data set even further, but necessitated some clear judgements around whether the new material added novel information and/or what was relevant or not, that is, decisions about when to stop collecting documents.

Scott (1990) outlines four criteria to consider when assessing whether a document should become part of an archive: authenticity, credibility, meaning and representativeness:

- *Authenticity* relates to the legitimacy of the document. Is it actually what it claims to be? Clearly this has particular salience within work on historical documents and potentially even situations where there is the possibility for deception on the part of a gatekeeper who has supplied documents. Given the source, the Nexis database, this was not a consideration for Rees's study: he was getting access to articles that had appeared in newspapers.
- *Credibility* of a document relates to the content, and the extent to which the material can be trusted, whereas authenticity relates to the form of the document, that is, is the document actually what it claims to be? Credibility did become a concern for Rees, especially in relation to the news media reports. Greer (2012) notes that inexperienced journalists are often used as court reporters for crime stories, often resulting in inaccuracies or discrepancies in the reporting. Reading the media coverage of various trials, there were clearly differences amongst them with regards some of the details. While inconsistencies amongst newspaper articles did not necessarily result in the documents being removed from the archive, their credibility was often weakened and greater care was taken when using details from those documents throughout the analysis process.
- *Meaning* constituted the key determinant when establishing whether a document remained in Rees's archive. MacDonald and Tipton (1993) note that there are two levels of meaning: surface meaning (being able to understand the document) and a deeper meaning (the discourses within the text and that are understood through analytical techniques). Highlighting the discourses enables the analyst to determine if the document is relevant to the research questions as currently envisaged. As mentioned above, during the preliminary coding phases, Rees reformulated the research question, as he began to understand the potential analytic direction: the debate about the legitimacy of certain clinical tests in forensic contexts.
- *Representativeness* refers both to how well your sample of documents reflects the broader body of possible documents tied to this issue, alongside how typical a specific document is, given the broader context of documents within your archive. For Rees's newspaper articles, only some cases were reported in the national press, whereas more had been found from local newspapers. In order to ascertain that the omission of certain cases from national reporting was not an artefact of the sampling process, checks against issues from the particular timespans were made. In terms of the academic literature, Prior (2003) highlights that articles that are 'ambiguous or contradict prevailing assumptions' (2003, p. 157) are less likely to be published. This is particularly the case with novel science. This meant going in search of articles that might contradict the dominant discourse, what Patton (2002) refers to as deviant case sampling. Rees returned to the early literature found from reference lists and uncovered the ways that particular actors in the debate had amended their ideas over time and the impact of those changes. The documents collected provided a wealth of discourses, but eventually all appeared to be coalescing around particular trajectories – authors supported or were antagonistic to the use of the specific diagnostic tests, especially when used as evidence in court cases. Reflecting on the representativeness of the archive via returning to previously coded or omitted documents, and actively searching for contradictory cases, can result in a data set demonstrating something like saturation.[2]

In this section, we have explored the range of actions that are necessary: accessing documents from databases and pre-existing archives; rounds of searching, pre-coding, and analysis; and developing your archive in terms of the authenticity, credibility and meaning/relevance of the particular document, as well as the representativeness and data saturation of the entire archive. Working with documents is an emergent, iterative, process in which sampling is central. It is highly likely that accessing one document will actually draw your attention to more material you are likely to need to engage with. Those involved in such work are required to be explicit about the choices they make in relation to sampling; why for instance did they choose to include certain documents at the expense of others, why use blogs from between those dates and/or from those areas, be they geographical, disciplinary or organisational? An easy claim to make against document-based research is that the researcher had a particular argument in mind first and then found documents that helped present that argument. Recording your decisions as you go, as well as reporting your searches for negative cases, helps provide justifications for your choices. We will now turn to a relatively new approach that seeks to closely record, manage and evaluate the process of the collection of documents.

WORKING WITH DOCILE DOCUMENTS: SYSTEMATIC APPROACHES

The social, medical and political sciences have seen the rise of 'evidence-based' policy and practice. Central to this has been a move towards the aggregation and summary of published data through the method(ology) of systematic reviews and meta-analysis. They require people to collect, appraise, consolidate and re-analyse data from quantitative journal articles on a specific research topic in a systematic and transparent way (see Moreira, 2007). Over the last decade the diversity of approaches to a more systematic analysis of qualitative research articles has also grown steadily. Noblit and Hare's (1988) work on what they call 'meta-ethnography' has been influential. They sought to combine the findings of six ethnographic monographs on the impact of desegregation on urban schools in the US in the late 1970s. They translated the relatively diverse findings of the case studies into a general theory about the impact of desegregation. Following this inter-textual work, a range of approaches towards synthesising the findings of qualitative research has emerged. They have been referred to under various terms including: metasynthesis (Sandelowski and Barroso, 2007), critical interpretive synthesis (Dixon-Woods et al., 2006) and thematic synthesis (Thomas and Harden, 2008). They all rely on insights from Noblit and Hare's (1988) original work, and all seek to move beyond simply aggregating and summarising findings from qualitative research papers to actively create new conceptual models or theories and to provide evidence for future interventions.

As with quantitative systematic reviewing, this qualitative synthesis work involves pre-defined phases of searching, evaluation, data-extraction and (re)presentation. However, given the non-numerical nature of the findings they have adapted each stage in the process. Importantly the process echoes and draws on key ideas from how you conduct empirical, primary, qualitative research. However, a central difference to more traditional approaches is that researchers' practical actions and reasoning are recorded at each stage of the document-collection process and then reported in some detail.

Within this method, two approaches to searching and sampling prevail. One relies on very ordered, pre-defined, searches of electronic databases. The other is more ad hoc and emergent. Dixon-Woods et al. (2006) outline the processes they undertook when carrying out a review of access to healthcare by vulnerable groups:

> We piloted the use of a highly structured search strategy using protocol-driven searches across a range of electronic databases but ... found ... this unsatisfactory. In particular, it risked missing relevant materials by failing to pick up papers that, while not ostensibly about 'access', were nonetheless important to the aim of the review. We then developed a more organic process that fitted better with the emergent and exploratory nature of the review questions. This combined a number of strategies, including searching of electronic databases; searching websites; reference chaining; and contacts with experts. Crucially, we also used expertise within the team to identify relevant literature from adjacent fields not immediately or obviously relevant to the question of 'access'. (2006, p. 3)

Note here that this process of decision-making is recorded and then reported in detail with this approach. The idea is to be thorough and to enable other readers to be able to recover your searching practices, and so be able to reproduce the core aspects of that search.

Initially, Dixon-Woods et al. (2006) found over 100,000 documents and then used this to develop their sampling frame. This was informed by key papers identified prior to the formal review; they then used theoretical sampling to add, test and elaborate the emerging analysis. In other reviews, which are more narrowly focused studies, for example a review of experiences of medicine taking (see Pound et al., 2005), either a total population sample is used, or all papers within a specific time frame are worked on. However, what is specific to this approach is that they also engage in some kind of formal and explicit quality appraisal process of each paper. For example, some studies use structured checklists, like the Critical Appraisal Skills Programme (CASP) 2014 – Qualitative Research Checklist, in order to remove studies of 'insufficient quality' (see Hannes, 2011). There is, perhaps unsurprisingly, a great deal of debate about the usefulness or appropriateness of such checklists (see Barbour and Barbour, 2003; Dixon-Woods et al., 2004; see also Barbour, Chapter 14, this volume). Dixon-Woods et al. only excluded papers that they felt were 'fatally flawed' using the following prompts to inform their judgement:

- Are the aims and objectives of the research clearly stated?
- Is the research design clearly specified and appropriate for the aims and objectives of the research?
- Do the researchers provide a clear account of the process by which their findings were reproduced?
- Do the researchers display enough data to support their interpretations and conclusions?
- Is the method of analysis appropriate and adequately explicated? (2006, p. 4)

They excluded very few papers, as they were concerned to focus on both the relevance of the paper for the research questions alongside the quality. For them, conceptually weak papers could be potentially relevant in highlighting a specific aspect of the phenomena. What is interesting about this approach is how it seeks to formalise, and make public, aspects that those working on documents would often take for granted and see as relatively unremarkable. Its structured and formal processes are not for everyone.

DOCUMENTS ALONGSIDE FIELDWORK

With most types of qualitative fieldwork, almost irrespective of the topic, some aspects of the phenomena will be (re-)presented in and through paper or electronic documents. Whether the focus is on a specific set of practices, events, identities or contexts, documentary reality will play some part in that world. With fieldwork, the creation, use or engagement with documents is not the primary focus, but rather, at some points along the fieldwork journey, thinking about collecting documents might be useful. Clearly, this could be prior to fieldwork, where you look at the range of web-based and paper resources on your substantive topic, alongside emergent, ad hoc encounters, where a specific informant makes a comment about a document or you observe one of potential interest. In these contexts, we should, where possible, collect these and use them to inform, support and extend our analysis.

However, such ad hoc opportunistic sampling is not without issues. Clearly, some documents will be in the public domain, whereas others will be private to a specific person or group. Even when someone is willing for you to record some part or aspect of that private document – be it through field notes, a photocopy or a photograph – you clearly need to discuss the boundaries of use. Will they be willing for you to use direct quotes from it? Will they be willing for you to refer to it, or just to use it as additional knowledge to support background contextual work? Especially, in terms of work in organisational contexts, are they the right person to request permission from?

For example, Rapley was involved in some ethnographic fieldwork on the organisation of care for adolescents and young people in hospitals (Farre et al., 2016). Prior to entering the field, the research team were aware of the potential role documents could take. In the ethics application, it had already been outlined that:

> We will employ a combination of qualitative research techniques, including formal (audio-recorded) and informal (field notes) face-to-face interviews, non-participant observation of clinical and managerial work and meetings, and where appropriate the collection of relevant documents.

And during the fieldwork, at times, certain documents were collected. These included, amongst other things: externally focused and internally focused draft and finalised policy documents related to adolescents and young people; internal training materials; publicly available resources targeted at or about young people; and press releases. Clearly, the publicly available, external-facing documents were free for anyone to access and so specific permissions were not needed to collect them. However, in terms of the internal policy documents and training materials, explicit permission was gained from a range of actors, especially key senior gatekeepers in the organisations who had originally enabled access to the sites, in order to collect them. Analytically, these documentary resources were not central, but helped to understand the observations and interviews. The research team could map the ideals around enhancing adolescent and young people's care, embedded in both the policy documents and training, to the work on the ground. Clearly, in all cases, researchers need to be aware of the potential in collecting documents to support our fieldwork as well as the potential pragmatic, legal and ethical issues.

DOCUMENTS IN ACTION

We never just somehow neutrally or abstractly engage with documents, they are always engaged with in a specific context; as such, they are always read or used in a specific way, to do specific work. Work that focuses on documents in use, or rather documents in (inter)action, is a reasonably under-researched area. When it comes to researching other people's document use, you are only able to answer such questions with some depth of knowledge of that context – by observing and/or informally or formally interviewing the participants – as well as at times through video- or audio-based recordings. You may also need to follow the specific document as it moves from space to space or between people. You may need to ask questions about how it is central to different tasks in different situations. In general terms, such work seeks to combine a more micro-focus on moments of social interaction with and around documents in a range of settings, a meso-focus on the organisational ecology of a local context and a macro-focus on broader social and political factors.

Many facets of life are bureaucratically organised – and routinely involve coordinating a diverse array of professionals, administrators and technicians alongside others, including service users – over a range of activities, times and spaces. Documents often become integral, a 'glue' that binds these people and their work together. For example, Mehan et al.'s (1986) ethnographic study of the identification, classification and labelling of educationally disabled children shows us the important role that documents can play in the coordination of educational interactions, decision-making and organisational work. Their study draws on a range of methods including observation, interviews, video-recordings of meetings and lessons, alongside asking teachers to reflect on the videos of these lessons. They use the sequential 'paper-trail' that is created by a student (in class work, exams and educational testing sessions with the school psychologist) and created about a student (in their personal school records, School Appraisal Team Committee, Eligibility and Placement Committee meetings) to focus some of the fieldwork on the range of sites where bureaucratic assessment and classification work occurs in the special education referral process. Notably, Mehan et al. (1986) do not present us with the documents themselves, rather they focus on the distributed talk and actions of those people who create and use them.

So, when working in this way, the practical issues of access, sampling, relevance and ethics closely echo those you would expect in any ethnographic, interview or video-based study. Jenkings and Barber (2004, 2006) undertook a study of Hospital Drug and Therapeutic Committee's (DTC) meetings and focused on the role of documents in those meetings. DTCs control which of the new drugs will be available in a specific hospital. Document use is important in this process as the committee, in part, needs to base its decisions on published research evidence about the clinical and cost effectiveness of the drugs. Their data consisted of observing and audiotaping four consecutive meetings of two different DTCs. They negotiated access to the DTCs through key gatekeepers, in part through existing research contacts at each site. Sampling was driven by practical and conceptual issues: given the focused nature of such analytic work, they worked with two DTCs at different hospitals. Relevance was tied to fieldwork being focused on exploring the key aspects of the phenomena: shortly after entering the field, they also obtained all the documentation that was prepared for each meeting. This was important, as in some meetings one of the participants would often prepare a summary report of the research evidence on a specific drug, in others the participants would have been expected to have read pre-circulated research papers. Finally, ethical issues were driven by those common to qualitative work, those of informed consent and anonymity.

CONCLUSION

Given the ubiquity of paper and electronic documents in contemporary social and organisational life, the range of potential types of documents open to qualitative analysis is immense. However, the primary sources for much work are often policy documents (be they national, regional or local), organisational documents, newspapers and academic articles and textbooks. Documents in any broader sense – be they blogs, diaries, letters, magazines and the plethora of documents that make up web culture – are still relatively underused and under-analysed. On the one had this is quite surprising, given the centrality of documents to everyday experiences as well as the readiness-to-hand of document-based materials.

Nevertheless, we are slowly seeing the turn away from a focus solely on docile documents towards a focus on documents in action. We are also seeing, in the health sector at least, a turn towards a more systematised, and at times creative interpretive syntheses of academic work. New theoretical, methodological and analytic possibilities emerge; however, we are still left with a relatively limited corpus of work that focuses on the social and organisational lives of documents. Documents shape, and are reflexively shaped by, our perceptions, interactions, institutions, policies and society. They are central in the production, reproduction and transformation of our contemporary landscapes. As such, they deserve a more sustained and systematic analytic focus.

Notes

1 Translation is a potentially expensive and lengthy process, especially word-for-word, which ideally, should also be back-translated by someone else to assure that the meaning is not lost in the translation process. However, even this is not ideal in some contexts.

2 A long-standing but often over-looked area in the social sciences concerns the use of letters as a data source (Stanley, 2010). Researching with letters – or epistolary research – (see Moore et al.; 2016) draws attention to the decision-points identified here: for instance, which letters have been preserved and in what archives, and also aspects of efficiency in weighing-up visiting archives containing small numbers of letters compared with larger collections. Similarly the provenance of letters must be assessed to verify authenticity and understand the complex ways letters represent an external world of social relations, especially when some have been destroyed. We are grateful to Dr Andrea Salter for discussing this with us.

FURTHER READING

Moore, Niamh, Salter, Andrea, Stanley, Liz, and Tamboukou, Maria (2016) *The Archive Project: Archival Research in the Social Sciences*. Abingdon: Routledge.

Prior, Lindsay (2011) 'Introduction', in Lindsay Prior (ed.), *Using Documents and Records in Social Research Vol. 1*. London: Sage, pp. xxi–xxvii.

Scott, John (1990) *A Matter of Record: Documentary Sources in Social Research*. Cambridge: Polity Press.

Wetherell, Margaret, Taylor, Stephanie and Yates, Simenon J. (2001) *Discourse Theory and Practice: A Reader*. London: Sage, in association with The Open University.

REFERENCES

Barbour, Rosaline S. and Barbour, Michael (2003) 'Evaluating and synthesizing qualitative research: The need to develop a distinctive approach', *Journal of Evaluation in Clinical Practice*, 9(2): 179–86.

Collins, Harry M., and Evans, Robert (2008) *Rethinking Expertise*. Chicago: University of Chicago Press.

Critical Appraisal Skills Programme (CASP) (2014) *CASP Checklists* (http://www.casp-uk.net/#!casp-tools-checklists/c18f8).

Dixon-Woods, Mary, Cavers, Debbie, Agarwal, Shona, Annandale, Ellen, Arthur, Antony, Harvey, Janet, Hsu, Ron, Katbamna, Savita, Olsen, Richard, Smith, Lucy K., Riley, Richard and Sutton Alex J. (2006) 'Conducting a critical interpretive review of the literature on access to healthcare by vulnerable groups', *BMC Medical Research Methodology*, 6: 35.

Dixon-Woods, Mary, Shaw. Rachel Louise, Agarwal, Shona and Smith, Jonathan Alan (2004) 'The problem of appraising qualitative research', *Quality Safety and Health Care*, 13(3): 223–5.

Farre, Albert, Wood, Victoria, McDonagh, Janet E., Parr, Jeremy, Reape, Debbie and Rapley, Tim on behalf of the Transition Collaborative Group (2016) 'Health professionals' definitions of developmentally appropriate healthcare for young people: Conceptual dimensions and embedded controversies', *Archives of Disease in Childhood* 101 (7): 628–633.

Garfinkel, Harold, D. and Wieder, Lawrence (1992) 'Two incommensurable, asymmetrically alternate technologies of social analysis', in Graham Watson and Robert M. Seiler (eds.), *Text in Context: Studies in Ethnomethodology*. Newbury Park, California: Sage, pp. 175–206.

Gidley, Ben Peter (2003) 'Citizenship and belonging: East London Jewish Radicals 1903–1918', PhD dissertation, Goldsmiths' College. University of London.

Greer, Chris (2012) *Sex Crime and the Media: Sex Offending and the Press in a Divided Society*. London: Routledge.

Hannes, Karin (2011) 'Chapter 4: Critical appraisal of qualitative research', in Noyes, Jane, Booth, Andrew, Hannes, Karin, Harden, Angela, Harris, Janet, Lewin, Simon and Lockwood, Craig (eds.), *Supplementary Guidance for Inclusion of Qualitative Research in Cochrane Systematic Reviews of Interventions*. Cochrane Collaboration Qualitative Methods Group, 2011 (http://cqrmg.cochrane.org/supplemental-handbook-guidance).

Jenkings, K. Neil and Barber, Nick (2004) 'What constitutes evidence in hospital new drug decision making?', *Social Science and Medicine*, 58(9): 1757–66.

Jenkings, K. Neil and Barber, Nick (2006) 'Same evidence, different meanings: Transformation of textual evidence in hospital new drugs committees', *Text and Talk*, 26(2): 169–89.

Layder, Derek (1998) *Sociological Practice: Linking Theory and Social Research*. London: Sage.

Macdonald, Keith and Tipton, Colin (1993) 'Using documents', in Nigel Gilbert (ed.), *Researching Social Life*. London: Sage, pp. 187–200.

Mehan, Hugh, Hertweck, Alma and Meihls, J. Lee (1986) *Handicapping the Handicapped: Decision Making in Students' Educational Careers*. Stanford: Stanford University Press.

Moore, Niamh, Salter, Andrea, Stanley, Liz and Tamboukou, Maria (2016) *The Archive Project: Archival Research in the Social Sciences*. Abingdon: Routledge.

Moreira, Tiago (2007) 'Entangled evidence: Knowledge making in systematic reviews in health care', *Sociology of Health and Illness*, 29(2): 180–97.

Moreira, Tiago (2015) 'Understanding the role of patient organisations in health technology assessment', *Health Expectations*, 18(6): 3349–57.

Noblit, George W. and Hare, R. Dwight (1988) *Meta-ethnography: Synthesizing Qualitative Studies*. Newbury Park, CA: Sage.

Patton, Michael Q. (2002) *Qualitative Research & Evaluation Methods* (3rd edn). Thousand Oaks, CA: Sage.

Pound, Pandora, Britten, Nicky, Morgan, Myfanwy, Yardley, Lucy, Pope, Catherine, Daker-White, Gavin and Campbell, Rona (2005) 'Resisting medicines: A synthesis of qualitative studies of medicine taking', *Social Science & Medicine*, 61(1): 133–55.

Prior, Lindsay (2003) *Using Documents in Social Research*. London: Sage.

Prior, Lindsay (2008) 'Repositioning documents in social research', *Sociology*, 42(5): 821–36.

Sandelowski, Margarete and Barroso, Julie (2007) *Handbook for Synthesising Qualitative Research*. New York: Springer.

Schreier, Margrit (2014) 'Qualitative content analysis', in Uwe Flick (ed.), *The Sage Handbook of Qualitative Data Analysis*. London: Sage, pp. 170–83.

Scott John (1990) *A Matter of Record: Documentary Sources in Social Research*. Cambridge: Polity Press.

Seale, Clive (2002) 'Cancer heroics: A study of news reports with particular reference to gender', *Sociology*, 36(1): 107–26.

Stanley, Liz (2010) 'To the letter: Thomas & Znaniecki's The Polish Peasant ... and writing a life, sociologically speaking', *Life Writing*, 7(2): 137–51.

Sugiura, Lisa, Wiles, Rosemary and Pope, Catherine (2016) 'Ethical challenges in online research: public/private perceptions', *Research Ethics*, [Epub ahead of print] (http://dx.doi.org/10.1177/1747016116650720).

Thomas, James and Harden, Angela (2008) 'Methods for the thematic synthesis of qualitative research in systematic reviews', *BMC Medical Research Methodology*, 8: 45.

Weber, Robert P. (1990) *Basic Content Analysis* (2nd edn). Newbury Park, CA: Sage.

Collecting Images as Data

Thomas S. Eberle

Collecting images presupposes that we know what an image is. On a common-sense level, we have usually no problem in identifying an image as an image. Images are obviously human-made artifacts that are perceived by our visual sense, which implies that they are unamenable to visually impaired persons. A number of different genres is known to everybody, like sketches, drawings, paintings, graphic designs, logos, cartoons or photographs. The activity of collecting images is widespread in modern societies in a great variety – some collect cartoons, or postage stamps, others paintings of a certain artist, epoch or theme, and many collect photos on their smartphones, tablets and computers. Collecting images can be done professionally or as a hobby, systematically or casually (as, for instance, grandparents collecting the drawings of their grandchildren). As a common activity in society, collecting images is a worthwhile topic of sociological study in itself.

In this chapter, I focus exclusively on collecting images for the purpose of social scientific research. A classic tenet of qualitative social research says that the choice of methods depends on the research question. Which type of research question calls for collecting images? This obviously leads to the more fundamental question, that is, which kinds of information do images contain that cannot be provided by other types of data, like thick descriptions, interview data (see Roulston and Choi, Chapter 15, this volume), or documents (see Rapley and Rees, Chapter 24, this volume)? Without a clear answer to this question it does not make much sense to collect images. It is therefore not surprising that a great deal of the debates within visual sociology and visual studies are dedicated to this very issue. Some use photos as 'proofs of facts' and claim that a picture is more, and different, than a thousand words; others assert that images are specific reality constructions whose meaning remains ambivalent, subjective and diffuse and that their interpretation must be substantiated in words. Evidently, these debates are crucial. But they put above all the interpretation of images center-stage and leave the practical methods of collecting images in the shadow. I choose therefore a pragmatic approach here and set out to describe these methods – knowing that researchers who collect images are convinced of their value.

In the following, I begin with a brief historical overview about the use of photography in the social sciences and then discern three main methods of collecting images as data: first, collecting images that are produced by the researcher; second, collecting images that are produced by actors in the field for a research project; third, collecting images that were produced by actors for other purposes. I report subsequently on my own experiences with a project of a visual ethnography of an art fair. Then I discuss the question why we should collect images at all and conclude with some concrete guidelines as to how to proceed. I use the terms 'image' and 'picture' interchangeably and will not go into their different genres, but mainly concentrate on photography as photos are the most prevalent images in social research.

FROM DOCUMENTARY PHOTOGRAPHY TO VISUAL ANTHROPOLOGY AND SOCIOLOGY

From early on, cultural and social anthropologists made sketches and drawings in order to complement their verbal field notes. Visualizations allow for communicating certain phenomena more vividly and concretely than language can, as for instance, spatial arrangements, dwellings, the shape of all kinds of artifacts but also people working, dancing or practicing religious rituals. Later on, anthropologists increasingly used photo and film cameras as these devices proved to deliver more accurate, 'realistic' and trustworthy results. For a long time, however, photos were not considered as a sort of data in their own right, but rather as mere illustrations of scientific texts.

Photojournalism and Documentary Photography

The use of photography first boomed in different, non-scientific contexts: in photojournalism and documentary photography. The profession of a photojournalist emerged in the 1920s when print media increasingly published pictures. Those who worked for newspapers were eager 'to be in the right place at the right time' and deliver breaking-news stories. Magazines (like *Time*, *Life*, *National Geographic*, or *GEO*) developed a more attractive format for ambitious photographers, the photoessay or photoreportage, which allowed for longer reports and more complex storylines. In both contexts, photographic ambitions and aspirations were persistently confined by economic constraints.

Documentary photography emerged when social reform movements or government agencies intended to draw the public's attention to social issues such as poverty, injustice, homelessness, child labor, hazardous working conditions, etc. They commissioned photographers to produce a series of pictures to document the life conditions of a certain community. A famous example in the US is the photographic project of the Farm Security Administration (FSA). It was initiated in 1937 by Roy E. Stryker in order to document the life conditions of poor farmers during the Great Depression when much of the American Midwest farmland turned into a dustbowl. Stryker hired more than a dozen skilled photographers such as, for instance, Dorothea Lange, Walker Evans, Arthur Rothstein, Ben Shahn and John Collier Jr., instructed them carefully to photograph every detail of rural life and funded them. They produced about 250,000 photos, and about 77,000 made it to the press. Stryker wanted pictures that tell a story, and he made the selection himself. The FSA project helped establish documentary photography as a genre of its own. It was sociologically informed and used 'shooting scripts', that is, lists of objects, persons and practices to be photographed. The individual photographers developed their own style, and many of the pictures became legendary and were later presented in exhibitions at the MOMA and other prestigious institutions – photography became an art form (cf. Becker, 1974/1986, 1995; Harper, 2012).

Visual Anthropology and Sociology

Most social scientists abstained from a systematic use of photography in their research. Photos often illustrated anthropological texts showing artifacts and rituals in foreign indigenous tribes, often with a tourist's gaze focusing on the exotic. The beginning of visual anthropology is usually identified with the systematic study of the 'Balinese Character' by Margaret Mead and Gregory Bateson (1942). In more than 25,000 photos, plus some short movies, they documented the material culture (buildings, tools, etc.) and action patterns of the Balinese. Social rituals, routines and interactions were captured in sequences of photos that could be looked at like film clips and which made the temporal course of actions visible. With these images, the authors aimed at substantiating as well as enriching their textual ethnographic analyses. Mead and Bateson were social scientists using photography, but there were also photographers participating in anthropological projects. John Collier Jr. was such a photographer, who worked in the FSA project and later participated in a number of research projects where he photographed and filmed indigenous communities in North and South America. Based on these experiences, he published in 1967 his book *Visual Anthropology. Photography as a Research Method*, which has become a major reference for how to use photography in ethnographic research.

In sociology, the development was quite different: While sociology had an early liaison with photography, the two went increasingly separate ways: 'As sociology became more scientific and less openly political, photography became more personal, more artistic, and continued to be engaged politically' (Becker, 1974/1986, p. 230). 'More scientific' implied for a great deal of sociologists to construct 'grand theories' about complex societies, to equate empirical research with surveys which provide data that can be statistically analyzed, and to adhere to positivism which required objectivity of scientific statements and testable hypotheses (and not ambiguous images). Not even ethnographic sociologists in the tradition of the so-called Chicago School (see Buscatto, Chapter 21, this volume) used photographs. Only since the late 1960s, when the interpretive paradigm and qualitative methods swiftly gained ground, did visual sociology begin to emerge slowly. Howard Becker wrote a number of seminal contributions and inspiring reflections on how sociology and photography could get closer (1974, 1978, 1981, 1986, pp. 221–317), and in the mid-80s the interdisciplinary 'International Visual Sociology Association' (IVSA, http://visualsociology.org), with its journal *Visual Studies*, was founded. While the number of relevant publications steadily increased, it lasted 45 years after Collier's *Visual Anthropology* (1967) until a book *Visual Sociology* appeared (Harper, 2012).

From Photographs to Videos

A great deal of visual sociologists nowadays prefer to use moving videos (see Knoblauch et al., Chapter 23, this volume) instead of still photographs. Since the rise of ethnomethodology and conversation analysis (see Jackson, Chapter 18, this volume) sociologists increasingly became concerned with courses of action and their detailed sequential organization, and this is captured much more accurately by videos than by photographs. As a result, qualitative visual research is often associated with video-recordings rather than photographs (e.g. Knoblauch et al., 2006; Heath et al., 2010; see Knoblauch et al., Chapter 23, this volume).

Harper (2000, p. 144) states also that 'visual anthropology has largely evolved to film and video recording, at the exclusion of still photography'. A film or video contains much more visual information on bodily movements than a photograph, plus includes acoustic data; but interestingly enough, data analysis is then often done picture by picture, and for practical reasons publications often present single images from video sequences.

The Digital Revolution and the Exploding Number of Photographs

Looking back on the history of photography and its social uses in society, we can discern two major developments:

- The social uses of photography changed dramatically, interdependent with the enormous technological development. Photographing was for a long time either a profession or the hobby of the upper and middle class. Since the invention of the smartphone though it has become a pervasive activity around the globe. Nowadays, more than 20,000 photos are uploaded on the Internet per second, amounting to nearly two billion per day, with an upward trend.
- The use of photography in the social sciences varies in different disciplines as has been described comparing anthropology and sociology. Using photos in a research project in order to substantiate and enrich the findings is, however, only one possible way to go. The pervasiveness and the omnipresence of images in modern societies, the huge amount of pictures taken and disseminated in social networks or on other web platforms, makes the social uses of photography a topic in its own right – and one with many facets indeed.

COLLECTING IMAGES PRODUCED BY THE RESEARCHER

How to Photograph

If you choose to photograph yourself, you should be a skilled amateur photographer or have one in your research team. You should know how to use the camera and how to handle different lighting conditions (working with available light or using flashes, directly or indirectly). Although modern digital cameras produce reasonably good picture quality on automatic mode, you should master some key technical options of your camera. You should be aware that you get different results when you change the ISO settings or use different combinations of aperture and shutter speed. And you should know that the same scenery looks radically different when using a wide-angle, a normal or a tele-lens, and that this also affects the depth of field and the manner of optical distortion. All this basic knowledge can be acquired from a beginner's guide and photographic tutorials and, of course, by ample practice.

What to Photograph

When John Collier Jr. published his book *Visual Anthropology. Photography as a Research Method*, he wrote in the foreword ([1967] 1986, p. xi): 'The roots of this book lie in the Farm Security Administration and the photographic foresight of Roy E. Stryker.' Collier published the first edition in 1967 and a revised and expanded edition 1986 with his son (Collier and Collier, 1986). This book is still a very valuable guide for researchers who want to use a camera in their research and visually document what they observe. All the methodical reflections and every practical advice is substantiated with concrete examples from the research projects Collier Jr. worked on, and we find ample visual illustrations, too.

The book is full of tips on what to photograph in order to document an indigenous community and it presents many lists as 'shooting guides', for example:

- Mapping and surveying: Giving an overview of the relevant area and its infrastructure, like the community designs, the fields around the village with fences, gates and driveways, telephone and power lines, the buildings, the conditions of walls, roof, windows and yard, as well as decorative

painting, curtains in windows, visible order of things, flowers in gardens, etc. (1986, pp. 29–44).
- Cultural inventory: Indications of the economic level (furniture, rugs, poverty, etc.), home- and lifestyle, the aesthetic of the décor, the activities of the household, the character of order, signs of hospitality and relaxation (1986, pp. 48–50).
- Inventory of technology: Environmental location, raw materials in the shop, tools of the trade, how tools are used, how a craft proceeds, the products, the function of technology and the social structure in technology (1986, p. 67).
- Social interaction and relationships (no list, but illustrated by examples) (1986, pp. 77–97).

Some of the lists are very detailed with many different items under each subheading. Such shooting guides help to take stock of material objects and social behaviors and to not forget something, but they do not work as recipes: What is relevant to people in the field varies, therefore such shooting guides have always to get adapted to the local research field or sometimes developed nearly from scrap. In the later chapters of their book, Collier and Collier also discuss the use of films and videos in field research, as well as issues of data organization and methodical procedures of analysis (all of which are not of concern here). Most considerations on the technical equipment are outdated and can be skipped. Not, however, recommendations on what to consider when using a camera in a social community.

Establish Successful Field Rapport and Photo-elicited Interviews

The most important task is, as Collier and Collier (1986, pp. 19–28) emphasize, to establish a successful field rapport (see Bengry, Chapter 7, this volume). Participant observation (see Wästerfors, Chapter 20, this volume and Buscatto, Chapter 21, this volume) is crucial, photographers must develop social relationships with the people they want to photograph. This is a process that takes time. Photographers in the field should move slowly so people can get used to them as well as to being photographed. Photographers should be close to people, talk to them and avoid taking 'sneaking' pictures from a distance with a tele-lens, which they might perceive as being obtrusive. As a photographer you must be trustworthy and have an appreciative attitude toward the people you want to photograph, you must become so familiar to them that you eventually become an invisible observer. You must show respect for the local values, norms and social structure, and use diplomacy and tact. A safe approach to human organizations is to start with what local people are most proud of, and slowly move 'from the public to the most private, from the formal to the informal, in a reasonable fashion from the outside in' (1986, p. 27). The more a community feels your appreciation, the more it develops trust in you and displays a growing tolerance for what you choose to photograph. An effective means to build trust is further to show the photos to the photographed persons – people like to see the pictures you took of them, their home, their possessions, and so on, and appreciate the opportunity to view them and often spontaneously annotate them.

In this context, a most effective method of empirical research was developed: the photo-elicited interview; this involved showing people photos and asking them questions, such as: What is this? Who is this? What is happening here? What is this person doing? and so on. Which questions to ask depends on what can be seen in the photograph – and, of course, on your research interests. The interviewees often provide ample narrations that go far beyond what is shown in the photo; they tell the history of things and talk about relationships, the social structure and the further social, cultural and religious contexts. The narrations become the primary source of data, but elicited by photos. And the interviewer always learns how the natives interpret a photo, what the photographed objects, persons, behaviors and events mean to them. In a first phase of ethnographic research, this can greatly help orientation in a strange culture: Make photos, show them to the participants and ask them to explain the photos to you. Interactionally, photo-elicited interviews have the advantage in that the interview does not take place in the form of a face-to-face 'interrogation'; instead the attention is directed to the picture, which makes the interviewees spontaneously, and often in a much more lively fashion, talk about it (Collier and Collier, 1986, pp. 99–116; see also Harper, 2002, 2012, pp. 155–87; see also Henwood et al., Chapter 38, this volume).

Photography as a Research Tool

Photography as a research tool requires that the photos contribute toward answering a research question. In ethnographic research, the research question is often developed or elaborated in the course of the empirical study, much like the 'grounded theory approach' (Glaser and Strauss, 1967) suggests. Photos must be interpreted, and these interpretations should be provided by verbal accounts and linked to theoretical concepts. A research project must culminate in a theoretically informed conclusion. This is the most challenging step. Many amateur photographers produce huge collections of photos, but can neither relate them to a proper research question nor arrive at conclusive anthropological or sociological insights. To photograph everything you can observe, to just make an inventory of everything, does not suffice; the crucial question is 'for what?' What do these images tell us? How can they be interpreted and linked to theoretical concepts? What insights do they generate and substantiate?

Howard Becker (1974/1986) therefore demands that photographing must be guided by sociological research questions. He criticizes documentary photography of being 'intellectually and analytically thin' (1974, p. 9); 'photographers use theories that are overly simple. They do not acquire deep, differentiated and sophisticated knowledge of the people and activities they investigate' (1974, p. 10). Becker explores the ways in which photography can be guided by explicit sociological theories and how visual evidences can be linked to theoretical concepts. He recommends asking the same questions that Everett Hughes (1971) used to ask – what different kinds of people are there? What expectations in which recurring situations? Typical breaches of those expectations? Standard ways of settling these conflicts? – which link observations to theoretical concepts, such as status groups; norms, rules and common understandings; deviance and rule violations; and sanctions and conflict resolution (Becker, 1974/1986, pp. 248–9). He further suggests to proceed as ethnographic research does: Gather data (shoot pictures), then immediately begin with a preliminary analysis that leads to further questions and new ideas about what to look for the next day.

In spite of combining data-gathering and (preliminary) data analysis continuously, using photography as a research tool in ethnographic fieldwork comprises three main phases:

- In the exploration phase you seek orientation and comprehension of what is going on in the field; you establish rapport with the locals, attempt to get an overview and start with photos of public areas.
- In the second phase you elaborate the research focus and collect visual evidences of particular things that contribute to answering your research question.
- In the third phase you write a synthesis, interpreting the empirical findings with theoretical concepts that allow for conclusive insights.

How to proceed can be learned from researchers who have successfully gone through these phases. Much can be learned, for example, from another early pioneer who used photography as a research tool: Pierre Bourdieu (2012; Schultheis et al., 2009). In his fieldwork in Algeria, Bourdieu made thousands of photos to document the lifeworld of the Kabyles, people who were caught between traditional farming and modernity. In spite of the broad international reception of his work, Bourdieu's photographic research still is rather unknown and its systematic place in his work has been disregarded. His photos actually illustrate his texts about the habitus and ethos of pre-modern humans and their innate dignity. Bourdieu used the camera as a means to visually objectify social reality, and photography led to a 'conversion of his gaze' and made him a sociologist: He began to connect photography to sociological questions. He detected, for example, a social structure by kinship in the cemetery; then he would go to the marketplace wondering if he would find there the same kind of social organization. When he returned to France he used the same procedure in his homeland Béarn and also studied the social use of photography, 'A middle-brow art' (Bourdieu et al., 1990). Bourdieu's photographic archive is still unexploited, and his reflections on photography as a research method are still groundbreaking.

For a systematic overview of the current state of visual sociology, see Harper's book (2012). Doug Harper is an ethnographic sociologist and was a co-founder of the International Visual Sociology Association, in which he is still active (in 2013, elected its president). In his book he displays a broad knowledge of the relevant studies in the field and the pertinent literature. He also presents ample and detailed data from his own empirical work as a sociological photographer and photographing sociologist. *Visual Sociology* is thus a great resource book, full of hints and inspiration. For further resources on visual methodologies consult also the books of Banks (2018), Pink (2001, 2012), Rose (2011) and Margolis and Pauwels (2011). In spite of all this advice, using photography in social research still leaves much room for creative developments!

Archiving and Organizing Images

A final point to mention is archiving and organizing images. Many photographers produced tens of thousands of pictures but did not spend much time in organizing them. Bourdieu's photo archive is one such classic example: The photos were stored in boxes and remained there; some of them were screened and selected for publication and an exhibition ('Pierre Bourdieu. Images of Algeria. An elective affinity'), but most of them still await systematic analysis and organization (cf. Bourdieu, 2012). Digital photography has eased this task greatly: Modern software tools allow for automatic storage, easy selection and organization. You can rearrange pictures easily in different albums and create different storylines. Usually a research team produces thousands of pictures from the same field, and in the end only a few are selected for publication. Photography as a research method, therefore, not only implies a selection of what you are going to photograph at a specific site, but also a selection from the collected images. A rich collection permits the telling of quite different stories. An essential task in a research project, furthermore, is adding contextual information to the photographs. Modern cameras now automatically record date and time of a shot and, by GPS, the geographical location where the photo was taken. This helps much, but is not enough: In order to preserve an interpretation you also need verbal accounts, that is, audio-recordings and/or texts. Organizing an archive also means linking the different sorts of data.

COLLECTING IMAGES PRODUCED BY PARTICIPANTS FOR RESEARCH PURPOSES

Photos in ethnographic fieldwork were often taken by researchers who were amateur photographers. Ethnographers often also collaborated with professional photographers (to ensure the best possible quality). However, another procedure for collecting images is to invite the researched persons themselves to make the photos.

The basic conception is to capture the subject from the perspective of the participants, that is, the subjective perspective, more adequately, that means along their own relevancies – not only in respect of what they narrate about their lifeworld, but also how they see it. The idea is that it makes a difference if researchers take photos of what they consider to be important, or if the participants themselves make the choices of what to photograph. The practical problem of this approach is that each of the participants must be given a camera – which is costly – and get instruction on how to use it. Meanwhile, in the age of smartphones this has become less problematic as most people, even in the Third World, possess a smartphone with a built-in camera. Nevertheless, participants of a study have to be instructed as to what they should photograph, in order to meet the goals of a research project. Most of the time the task is to take pictures of what is relevant to them in their daily lives. This requires a reflection process and a change of perception, as most people usually photograph the remarkable, the extraordinary, the exceptional – and not the ordinary, everyday. So they are often instructed to take photos of what they encounter regularly, of what is meaningful and important to them, even though it may go unnoticed in everyday life, and of what represents the routine trajectory of their day.

This approach has not emerged in anthropological and sociological research, but rather in politically committed applied research, often combined with action research. Early attempts were made by Worth and Adair (1972) in their project 'Navajo Film Themselves' and by Wendy Ewald (1985) whose work and methodological considerations became very influential. Wang and Burris (1997) used this approach in their participatory action research project, with the intention to encourage women in a Chinese village to identify the desired changes of public health issues in their community. They called the procedure photovoice and defined it as a method that empowers people by turning passive research objects into reflecting and active participants. Photovoice research has spread widely over the past two decades, not so much center-stage of sociology and anthropology, but in the areas of education, social work, public health and community development and in specialized journals. Harper (2012, pp. 188–206) gives a conclusive overview of all the studies he found and classifies them in different categories.

The photovoice movement was generally critical of documentary photography, which was predominantly (but not only) done by white males of the Western middle class. Photovoice should give a voice to the oppressed, the underdogs, the poor, the women, the colonized, the marginalized – a voice not (only) by sound but by images, photos taken by themselves. To what extent these pictures really represent their subjective (and collective) views, is usually just asserted but methodologically difficult to prove. In any case, the photos do not speak for themselves; to capture the subjective perspective of the participants, they must comment upon and explain these photos. In other words, the images must be complemented by photo-elicited narrations – this time elicited by photos they have taken themselves.

There is an additional point: Many photovoice studies use photography not only as a research method, but also as a tool of empowerment (as is common in action research). Participants often reported that using a camera changed their perception, their attention and their awareness; that photographing made them reflect about many things they did not even notice before; and that it finally opened new vistas and new options for action.

COLLECTING IMAGES PRODUCED FOR OTHER PURPOSES

Many research projects do not necessitate the making of photographs, but rather, they analyze images that already exist – images that were produced for purposes other than social research. This requires a third procedure of collecting images: searching in photo archives, searching in newspapers and magazines or private collections, and searching on the Internet.

There are photo archives in many places, housing either collections of photos by renowned photographers (artists and photojournalists), or photos on certain subjects, or historical photos from the past. Increasingly, parts of such collections are published on the Internet for public access. The research questions that can be asked in regard to such collections is restricted by what has been collected. The first task is therefore to find out what is there, which collections exist, where they are and how you get access. The second task is to select those images that are relevant to the current research interest. Historical researchers have often made seminal use of historical images, and the existing collections are usually far from exploited.

Autobiographic researchers have often collected photo albums of families and then analyzed what they tell about the history of family lives. A common practice of researchers investigating mass media has also been collecting images from newspapers and magazines. A classic example is Goffman's (1979) study, Gender Advertisements, in which he examined how gender is displayed in commercials. His sampling strategy was not very systematic, he searched for gender commercials and collected whatever he found. His research interest was not a statistically adequate representation of gender displays, but rather a qualitative analysis of their properties. He identified the typical gender displays of women and men and their relationships in family, business and private lives, such as relative size, function ranking, ritualistic subordination, feminine touch, and others. Goffman's study of images is still an inspiring reading. As the print editions of newspapers and magazines are nowadays paired by electronic versions on the Internet, where many more images are published than in print, this collection strategy has meanwhile also turned into a search on the Internet.

The amount of images on the Internet is huge; as mentioned, about two billions of photos are uploaded globally every day. This allows for a broad spectrum of research questions. Communication and media studies, in particular, have specialized in investigating this area, such as the use of photos in social networks and messengers, in online newspaper reports and magazines, in online advertisements or on web galleries and photoblogs such as Instagram, Flickr, Google+, Slideshare, app.net, Tumblr, Linkedin, Xing, Tripadvisor, Myspace, Dropbox, and so on. This obviously confronts researchers with the problem of Big Data. While some collections in conventional photo archives can be quite extensive and challenging, the sheer amount of images on the Internet is excessively complex and therefore daunting (see Lindgren, Chapter 28, this volume, and Markham, Chapter 33, this volume). There are three basic options for collecting images on the Internet:

1. *You work with a search machine which is able to find images that fit certain topics.* Indeed, visual pattern recognition (such as, for example, face recognition) has greatly advanced and software companies are working hard to make further and significant progress in this area (which is very likely to be achieved). The pitfall for social researchers is usually that the algorithms are unknown, which makes the search process non-transparent.
2. *You define the research field in a manageable way.* For example, you restrict it to a group of students who volunteer to grant access to their Facebook accounts (see Ditchfield and Meredith, Chapter 32, this volume).
3. *You pick images that you encounter in your personal lifeworld.* This procedure is often practiced in qualitative research, but hardly accounted for explicitly.

OUR PROJECT OF DOING A VISUAL ETHNOGRAPHY OF THE ART BASEL

Project Goal and Field Access

Let me reflect on the practice of doing a visual ethnography based on a concrete example from my own research. My colleague and close friend Franz Schultheis launched a research project of the Art Basel. The Art Basel, founded in 1970 at Basel (Switzerland) has become the largest and most prestigious art fair in the world (with estimated sales of about one billion US dollars per year). Since the turn of the century, it has reached out to other regions with additional exhibitions in Miami (in 2002) and Hong Kong (in 2013). Each art fair takes place every year. The research entailed doing an ethnography of the Art Basel with the goal of exploring the art market 'where money meets art' (Schultheis et al., 2015). The art fair's directors agreed to the research project, which was funded by the Swiss National Foundation, they granted access and were very supportive. The study started in 2011 in Basel and was soon extended to Miami and later to Hong Kong (Schultheis et al., 2016). The primary method was participant observation, whereby the research team repeatedly visited all sites. From 2011 to 2015 there were also about 120 interviews conducted with all kinds of actors – artists, gallerists, curators, museum directors, art counselors and collectors – to gain an understanding of the workings of the art market at such a large and complex art fair. As an amateur photographer and phenomenological sociologist (Eberle, 2014a, 2014b, 2017), I was particularly interested in the visual aspects of the art fair, so we soon decided to also explore the potential of a visual ethnography. From 2011 to 2014 we visited the art fair in Basel several days every year, each time with a VIP card and a press card which gave us the right to take pictures (then prohibited to ordinary visitors). Over the years, we produced more than 6,000 photos of the art fair, mainly at the fair in Basel.

Visual Exploration of the Field

As is expected from ethnographers, we entered the new field with great openness, just 'nosing around'. With an ethnographer's gaze you want to find out 'what is going on here?' (Goffman, 1974); with a photographer's gaze you are looking for 'good' pictures. In this exploration phase we roamed around and photographed whatever caught our attention: artifacts, artwork, people, behaviors, interactions, situations, spatial arrangements. In Basel, the art fair takes place on two floors of the city's fairs and exhibition building and comprises about 300 galleries, and it is linked to a joint exhibition 'Art Unlimited' right next door. Each gallery has a booth of either 50 or 100 square meters, where artwork is presented for sale – paintings, drawings, photos, sculptures. The building is rectangular and has an atrium in the middle, and the booths are organized as cubes in rows. Wandering around, on our numerous visits, we got easily lost in the many corridors between the booths and at the many intersections; the fair is so large and complex that it is overwhelming. Due to this complexity and the limited timeframe of each fair, there was no chance to establish rapport with the people we photographed; we, rather, acted like photojournalists shooting pictures.

As usual, the extraordinary stood out: conspicuous artwork, colorful or fashionable dresses, beautiful people, cheerful encounters with hugs and kisses, special events of all sorts – all the things photojournalists consider attractive, newsworthy or 'telling'. As sociologists, however, we intended to focus more on the 'ordinary' and the 'typical'. What, for instance, is typical behavior of gallerists, of collectors, of visitors? In Garfinkel's (1967) formulation: What makes gallerists gallerists? What are their methods or accounting practices by which they make themselves recognizable as gallerists? While ethnomethodologists usually employ videos in order to record the temporal sequence of practices, a photographer attempts to capture typical practices within a fraction of a second, which requires catching the 'right' moment of a move. Such typical behaviors are: sitting at a table in their booth and starring at the screen either of their smartphone, their tablet or their laptop; standing in their booth, gazing at entering visitors and trying to make eye-contact, sometimes approaching someone and asking a question or starting a conversation; standing close to a 'potential customer' in front of a piece of art and talking about it, or showing him or her further pictures on a tablet or a laptop. We were able to identify gallerists (in the broad sense of the word, including employed salespersons) by such typical behaviors, but also by other insignia, like business suits and stylish dresses, sometimes casual or creatively elegant, women mostly with high heels and visible make-up. What is 'typical', however, cannot be seen on a single photograph; it can be demonstrated either by a series of photographs or be asserted by ethnographers verbally based upon their observations in the field.

Some Systematic Reflections

Nosing around in this unfamiliar territory was a very inspiring and rewarding experience: Going with the flow and observing what is going on. But as ethnographic photographers we soon engaged in some systematic reflections: What is visually perceivable and what is not? Which perceivable phenomena have been captured and which are still missing? Which phenomena are constitutive of this art fair and important for our goal of accomplishing an ethnography of the Art Basel, and which are not?

As the art fair was so complex, we had to proceed selectively. There were so many galleries and so many special events that we just could not photograph them all. We therefore chose a number of events from the program that we wanted to observe and photograph. And based on the visitor's map, which showed where each gallery was located, we selected a block of 60 booths (20 percent of the fair) that we documented systematically. As no aerial view of the building's floors was possible, we had to proceed booth by booth. The resulting photo collection was systematic, but we could not detect any visual evidence of that – we just 'knew' it. In other words, this procedure proved unyielding. We chose therefore a grounded theory approach, searching for 'sensitizing photos' (as an analog to 'sensitizing concepts'), pondering the saturation of visual representations and looking for contrasting instances.

Photographs of what happened in the booths and corridors were undoubtedly most crucial, but the fair also comprised other important areas: The security guards at the doors and next to expensive paintings; the crowd waiting in front of the main entrance; visitors standing at the cashier or at the cloakroom; people using elevators, stairs and lifts leading to the next floor, etc. Personal encounters for lunch or a drink in the atrium, at a bar or in a restaurant were obviously most essential and constitutive of the fair's ambiance. We photographed everything we could and strived for a most complete image collection of the fair, knowing that we would make a further selection from this collection later on.

Visual Evidences

The most crucial question was what insights our photos would generate or substantiate? We could perceive different ways of looking, of gestures, body postures, mimics, and interaction patterns; and different kinds of dresses, shoes, hairstyle, jewelry and other insignia. We generally could distinguish gallerists from visitors; and we could recognize that the visitors with VIP cards on the days with restricted access came (on average) from a different social class or strata than the visitors during the days of public access. Visual data can substantiate a number of claims. At the same time, it represents only the visual surface of the fair. The art world is a symbolic world constructed in communication, that is, by the institution's self-descriptions in marketing and public relations activities; by the narrations of artists, gallerists and collectors; and by the reports of art critics and journalists in newspapers and magazines as well as in radio and on TV. All these symbolic constructions genuinely evade visibility. It does not suffice to explore the visual aspects of these communications, it is absolutely essential to also understand their content. In the end, it therefore proved difficult to link our photos to the argumentation in our texts, which describe and analyze the art market. While the photos we used for the publication (Schultheis et al., 2015) make for vivid visual illustrations and representations of the fair's perceivable atmosphere, the potential of a visual ethnography is yet to be exploited (work in progress).

Legal Aspects

A further point worth mentioning is the fact that it may be legally problematic to publish pictures of persons. Many European countries acknowledge by law a person's right to his or her own picture. Taking photos of visitors at the art fair was our common practice, but for publication we had to select those pictures where photographed visitors were not identifiable. As we did not know any of them there was no way to ask for their consent to publish their photo, thus we chose predominantly images where we can only see their backs. In addition, we were obliged to identify each artwork on the photos we selected for publication in order to preserve the copyrights of the artists. This constitutes a basic drawback of visual ethnography: What may legally be shown and published in the end? (In this respect, social and cultural anthropologists often adopted a colonialist attitude.)

WHY COLLECT IMAGES?

Why should we collect images at all? What additional value do they provide for a research project? What can images tell us about a field that verbal accounts cannot? This inevitably leads us to some epistemological questions that I am now going to discuss briefly.

Visual Perception

Human perception is obviously multimodal and synaesthetic, and it does not just consist in sensations but is meaningful. Ontogenetically, perception precedes language. As John Berger (1972, p. 7) put it: 'Seeing comes before words. The child looks and recognizes before it can speak.' Phenomenology has provided a seminal epistemological framework for analyzing human 'experience' (Husserl, 2013) and 'perception' (Merleau-Ponty, 1996) in depth. Cognition and recognition are only possible with human consciousness, which is always a consciousness-of-something – we see something, we hear something, we feel something, we recognize something, etc. Phenomenology therefore investigates how 'phenomena' are constituted in subjective consciousness. Phenomena are perceived as a synthetic unity of 'noema' (properties of the perceived 'thing') and 'noesis' (subjective knowledge and attention of perceivers). Visual perception therefore consists of the light that the material world reflects, and likewise the interpretations humans make. The reflected light produces sensations of forms and colors, which are constituted as meaningful phenomena in subjective consciousness. The well-known figure-ground-relation implies that we see each phenomenon in a context (or 'outer horizon'), and when we change our gaze something else becomes the figure and the first figure turns to its horizon (ground). There is ample evidence that children can see figure-ground-relations and typify visual phenomena already at an early stage, even before learning a language. Opposite to semiotic approaches, phenomenologists emphasize the relevance of pre-predicative, pre-linguistic typifications (additional to and as a prerequisite for linguistic types) – and phenomenological sociologists also investigate asemiotic, not only semiotic communication.

Phenomena are interpreted on the basis of our social and cultural knowledge. Language plays, beyond doubt, a crucial role in the organization of meaning. However, knowledge comprises more than that – it includes embodied knowledge such as bodily skills, behavioral routines or cultural ways of seeing. Visual perception does not consist in sensations of forms and colors to which, subsequently, meanings get attached, but it is from the outset sensuous and meaningful: Depending on our knowledge and our relevance system in situ, our stream of consciousness constitutes continuously meaningful visual phenomena in synthetic acts. These include acts of appresentation by which 'we see more than we see', that is, we see more than our sensuous perception actually displays – for instance, we see a 'house' although we can only perceive its front. By appresentations, phenomena have therefore also an 'inner horizon'. Alfred Schutz (1962, p. 299) proposed to discern four different layers: With the apperceptual scheme, phenomena are constituted as meaningful, such as two wooden beams in a rectangular form on a roof; with the appresentational scheme we interpret it as a sign, namely a cross; with the referential scheme the cross refers to the suffering of Jesus Christ and Christianity; and with the contextual or interpretational scheme the personal attitude of interpreters to the Christian religion is reflected – are they Christians, Hindu or atheists? What are their attitudes to the cross and the Christian religion? All these meaning-layers of visual perception reside in the viewer's biographical stock of knowledge and are enacted in situ.

Interpretation of Images

These analyses apply to the visual perceptions of images as well. However, images constitute a different kind of reality, which calls for some additional considerations. First, we do not only see what is in the picture, we also recognize a picture as a 'picture'. Images are material artifacts and thus part of our lifeworld. We can touch them and examine their materiality. We perceive their size, their format and their frame. We can consider how the frame interacts with the picture and ponder how suitable the materials are to preserve the image, for how long and under which storage conditions.

Second, we also see what is in the picture, for instance a 'landscape' or a 'marketplace'. We are aware that some segment of a three-dimensional reality is represented in a two-dimensional image, and we have learned to 'see' the third dimension by perceiving things 'in perspective'. While in European painting the perspective was introduced not before the Renaissance, the global dissemination of photography has made it a universal 'viewing skill' to perceive smaller things as more distant and larger things as closer; this is, however, quite a complex process of synthetic acts in consciousness as our knowledge of the normal size of things and of their relation to each other must also be enacted: If the small thing next to a human is an elephant, it is evidently in the background, if it is a mouse, it could even be in the foreground.

If the image shows a 'real' scenery, the objects in the picture obviously represent something – something absent that is painted, drawn or photographed. It seems promising to apply a semiotic approach and 'read' visual objects as 'signs' (syntactics) that refer to something 'signified' and have a 'meaning' (semantics) that is 'decoded' by 'an interpreter' (pragmatics). As with linguistic signs, 'denotations' are discerned from 'connotations' to explore the meaning. Semiotic approaches have become prevalent in many disciplines (cultural studies, media studies) and more in Anglosaxon countries than in others (see, for instance, Stuart Hall, 1997). To some degree they have proved quite illuminating, but they also miss much of the visual. In a phenomenological perspective, images are more than just signs. When there are signs in an image they are also interpreted as signs. It is the same with symbols. But an image contains more than just codes and signs. Signs can be read, images are seen. While semiotic approaches reduce everything to a 'discursive logic', phenomenologists speak of a 'pictural logic'. In the German-speaking countries, phenomenological theories of images – as those, for example, by Rudolf Arnheim, Hans Belting, Gottfried Boehm or Bernhard Waldenfels – have become complex and prominent. The basic contention is that images have an 'intrinsic value', which is usually not accounted for by semiotic studies. The 'intrinsic value' of an image is all that can be seen in addition to signs, such as the formal composition of a picture, its layout, its planimetric composition, its perspectivity, its contrasts, its colors, light and shade or its scenic choreography (Max Imdahl). Cultural 'ways of seeing' (Berger, 1972) therefore cannot be adequately described in words only, they must be visually demonstrated (as Berger extensively did). Some phenomenological sociologists therefore propose to abstain from translating images into words, but rather study the cultural ways of seeing by comparative viewing: Images also relate to each other with similar kinds of motives and formal compositions (Soeffner, 2006). Masterpieces of painters as icons of photography have taught us specific ways of seeing.

The Additional Value of Images

Non-academic members of society usually do not demand intricate epistemological considerations as to what an image is – they intuitively grasp that pictures have a different quality than words (see Henwood et al., Chapter 38, this volume). They usually love to look at photos – in newspapers and magazines, on TV, on their smartphone and other electronic devices – and find it generally easy to make sense of them. Most will approve the saying 'a picture is worth a thousand words' without further thought, for attesting images an additional value is common sense. Why then has the use of images remained so scarce in the social sciences, while in the media and nowadays above all in the social media it has become global common practice?

In everyday life, images have a different function than in science; photographs are not scrutinized systematically, but they can affect us quite immediately and effectively. In his *Camera Lucida*, Roland Barthes (1981) analyzed a photo of his elderly mother and realized that it 'punched' him. He introduced the distinction between 'punctum' and 'studium': While the 'studium' refers to an emotionally detached analysis of photos, the 'punctum' breaks into the world of the spectator and hits him like an arrow, leaving a wound, as did the photo of his mother (that would not hit other viewers as it does not show their mother). In this late work Barthes developed a subject-centered theory of photography and created a link to phenomenology: He concluded that the 'noema' of a photograph is 'that's how it was'. A photograph creates a relation between the present and the past: It represents something in the present that was captured at a moment in the past. A photo often works as a memory device – it reminds us in great detail of personal experiences which have faded or are forgotten, and it also allows for a fresh look at a later stage in life. Interpretations are often easy as we were 'there' ourselves, we have perceived the 'real' event ourselves and 'know' what happened. Photos in mass media affect us differently, but their message is usually simple enough (for instance, in advertisements) or sufficiently explicated in the concomitant text.

Whether images contribute additional value to a research project depends on the research question. When analyzing visual perception as Berger (1972) did in *Ways of Seeing*, we evidently cannot do without pictures. But ethnographic research can, and does, as many examples show. What value can photos add to an ethnography (see Buscatto, Chapter 21, this volume)? It is obviously impossible to give a general answer that would be universally valid. The answer must be particular and depends on different factors: How important is the visually observable culture and material world for this project? Should it be presented in great detail or can the relevant aspects be sufficiently described by words? Is there a visual culture in our research field, do participants use images themselves? Once we decide to produce and use photos, we must carefully analyze them (Barthes' 'studium') and scrutinize which visual evidences the pictures actually display. We must reflect meticulously on how we interpret certain instances and how we link them to theoretical concepts. Many visual social scientists nowadays analyze pictures in the same way that art historians do, attempting to describe all the meaning-layers that can be detected – but it is often not clear what the goal of such an analysis is.

Images do not tell a story by themselves – they must be interpreted. Each interpretation necessarily involves cultural and biographical knowledge, different viewers may thus make different sense of what they perceive. Social scientists therefore must set out their own interpretation in writing. A photograph in itself cannot be 'true', only a particular interpretation of it can. That is why Becker (1978/1986, p. 276) suggests that sociologists ask which question a photo might answer? Which proposition is plausibly substantiated by a picture? As was mentioned above, Becker criticized much of documentary photography as intellectually and analytically thin. Many photographers reiterated simple statements and thought that their pictures speak for themselves; they did not reflect the epistemological assumptions, implicit theories and cultural ideologies involved in their ways of seeing. Likewise, Becker also named ethnographers who made untenable interpretations of photos, which they used in their research.

To conclude: The use of images in ethnographic research makes sense when the photographs display visual evidences that substantiate certain (social scientific) propositions. However, does this imply that the main message is formulated verbally and the picture is just attached to make the interpretation plausible (or 'testable')? How do we account for the pre-predicative meaning-layers, the 'pictural logics' and the 'intrinsic value' of pictures as described above? How can pictures be related to each other instead of reducing them to verbal accounts? In his essay on 'Visual Evidence' Becker (2002) explicates why he thinks that John Berger and Jean Mohr's book on migrant labor in Europe (Berger and Mohr, 1975) is a perfect example:

> It makes an analytic argument about the organization and functional significance of migrant labor for host countries, labor-exporting countries and for the migrants themselves. It provides solid textual and photographic evidence for that argument. The photographs seem unquestionably to contribute to the argument's credibility. (Becker, 2002, p. 4)

The book uses a narrative of an archetypical migrant laborer (a 'he'), told in great detail, but also uses statistics, theoretical arguments and photographs. Although the photos are not explained in words or directly linked to the text, they successfully 'deepen the argument'. The photos can be viewed in any sequence, but the idea is that the reader keeps all the images in mind, seeing the connections between them. In contrast to photojournalism these photos do not 'personalize' abstract things, giving them names, addresses and a concrete biography; instead they are notable for their impersonality and lack of sentimentality. Becker argues that these images represent 'specific generalizations ... they show us real instances of what the text talks about'. In sum, the pictures tell us that the abstract tale 'has a real, flesh and blood life' (2002, p. 11).

The Truth of Photos

On a common-sense level, photographs are usually trusted as representing a segment of reality as it existed when the picture was taken. When looking at a family photo album, we often experience the 'punctum' of a photo, the feeling 'that's how it was', and no one doubts that the images 'truthfully' represent how it was at the time: how I looked as a child, and how my parents looked when they were young, or our home and garden in the 1960s, and so on. We also experience how the photos that we took ourselves show in every detail, favorably or relentlessly, what the photographed persons and objects looked like. We also have a general trust in the checks and balances of our society's institutions: Juries disqualify photographers at award-winning competitions if they are caught for retouching their photos; mass media are publicly denounced if convicted of publishing faked pictures; and so on. But of course, in reality things are more complicated than that.

Photographs reflect the light of material objects most accurately, which makes them appear so 'realistic'. Yet, skilled photographers are quite aware that they exert a considerable influence on how pictures look. On the one hand, the technical equipment allows for a range of possible constructions, but also has its limitations. The diverse optical, physical, chemical and electronic processes all have their impact. On the other hand, photographers make specific uses of these processes to achieve aspired results. Furthermore, photographers choose their motifs, how they frame them and in what perspective; they also choose what is in the frame and at what time, and what is excluded. It is interesting which implicit theories photographers apply: How broad is the variety of pictures they take, and what do they consider uninteresting and not worth a photo? Which taboos do they consider and which legal constraints (e.g. in regard to censorship and possible sanctions)?

As Becker (1974/1986, 1978/1986) has pointed out repeatedly, a genuine threat to empirical truth is posed by photographers' artistic aspirations. Social scientists would oppose using photos of social sceneries that are staged and choreographed by the photographer; or photos that are retouched in the subsequently. Documentary photographers have, in opposition to their official ideology, done this time and again, and often not with bad intent but for aesthetic reasons. W. Eugene Smith (1918–78), to mention a famous example, hired trucks and cowherds and instructed local people as background actors to portray the visible life for his reportage 'The Spanish Village' (Mora and Hill, 1998). This was not cheating, as was done with propaganda war photos, but a suitable way to achieve 'thick' photographs, in which much happens at the same moment in an aesthetic composition – while in real life the same events would occur at different times of the day and never be aesthetically perfect. Subsequent work in the darkroom was always meant to optimize desired results, including retouching to eliminate unaesthetic (and 'unnecessary') detail or amplifying to achieve other effects.

In classic photography, manipulation required great skill, however with the present-day wide dissemination and development of digital photography with sophisticated image-processing software and the many apps for smartphones, picture editing has become common practice, in professional as well as in private contexts. Nowadays, the chance that images are either stage-managed or manipulated on the computer is higher than ever before; thus the trust that photos represent 'objective' reality has recently been deteriorating significantly. Meanwhile, digital image forensics, which examines the authenticity of photos, has become a demanding and challenging discipline; more and more, even serious news media become victims of faked pictures and unknowingly publish them. These days when there is so much talk about 'fake news' and 'alternative facts' the danger of 'faked images' and 'alternative pictures' is on the rise.

CONCLUSION

Collecting Images: Some Guidelines for How to Proceed

Images are a distinct sort of data and clearly different from verbal accounts. I attempt to sum up this chapter in the form of guidelines for how to proceed when collecting images.

I have identified three different collection strategies:

1 Collecting images produced by the researcher

Naturally, this first collection strategy where researchers make photographs themselves is the most detailed:

Field access:

i   Which field do you want to explore? Which visual evidences can be found in that field? Does it make sense to bring a camera and make pictures?
ii Is still photography the right medium or should you use video (in order to capture sequences of actions)?
iii How would you get access to the field? Who can give you which kind of permission (permission to enter, to stay for some time, to move around, to talk to people, to take pictures, to use audio-recordings, etc.)?
iv Which technical equipment suits this field best (type of camera, lenses, storage capacity, light, etc.)?

Research process:

i   How would you establish rapport with people? If suitable, try to interact with the locals who inhabit a place (an organization, a public place, a neighborhood, a home, etc.) and establish relationships in which mutual trust develops. (People in transit may stay anonymous.) Show respect for the local social structure (power, social status, rules of communication, etc.). Do not be obtrusive.
ii Photograph whatever you can in the exploration phase, but be sensitive to maintain the rapport: Begin taking pictures of what people are most proud of and then move slowly from the outside in, from the public to the private, from the formal to the informal, from the frontstage to the backstage. Stay close, abstain from 'sneaking' pictures.
iii Can you provide a visual overview (an aerial photograph or a Google map) of the relevant field and map it in more detail?
iv Make inventories of artifacts: of infrastructure, buildings, furniture, tools and technology, of order, style and décor, etc. (think about what is relevant).
v   Study social behaviors, activities (work and leisure) and interactions. Can you detect patterns, rituals, ceremonies? Signs of distinctions (dresses, behaviors, specific insignia)?
vi Do not separate the data-gathering phase from the data analysis phase. Rather, start anzalyzing the pictures as early as possible in the research process. Follow established methodological procedures of ethnographic research. Study the pictures very carefully and in great detail: What can you perceive and recognize? Which visual evidences can be found? What can you understand from the photos, and what is difficult to understand? Which new questions arise?
vii Show the photos to the members of your research team or to your students and find out what they see. Are different interpretations of the same photo plausible?
viii Use the photo-elicitation technique to find out what the actors in the field see on the pictures: How do they interpret what can be seen? How do they describe the photographed actors, activities, artifacts, spaces and so on? Record the verbal accounts and link them to the pictures.
ix Then continue with the process of data-gathering (taking pictures and talking to the inhabitants of the field) and with preliminary analyses and become more systematic. Observe if there are differences in daily rhythms of activities, differences of the use of spaces or in interactional patterns. Search for similarities and contrasts and document them, visually as well as verbally. Make pictures of the same place at different times and create series of photographs.

Scientific report:

i   Make early attempts to either generate ideas or link your visual evidences to existing theoretical concepts of your discipline – sociological, anthropological, psychological, political, educational. Which hypotheses could be formulated, which generalizations made? And how could they get tested, rejected or further substantiated?
ii Always keep in mind that in the end you will write a report that has a storyline, which must be sufficiently substantiated by the empirical evidences you have collected, both visual and verbal. Try to link visual evidences and theoretical arguments as closely as possible.
iii Consider the legal constraints to the publication of images (copyright; persons' right to their own picture).

2 Collecting images produced by participants for research purposes

Many of the previous points also apply to this second collection strategy. I avoid repetitions and just focus on the additional points which result from the fact that photographing is not done by the researchers but delegated to actors in the field. These actors are, however, guided by a research purpose.

i Involving field actors into a research project means turning them from research objects into research participants. Why would you decide to do that? Which are the advantages and disadvantages, compared to making the photos yourself (or by someone in your research team)?
ii Delegating photographing to lay actors in the field requires careful instruction, and trust that they follow your instruction. What is it that they should photograph? Should they take notes about time, date and place? And notes about why they chose this motif to photograph? And what it means to them? Or is such information collected in photo-elicited interviews later?
iii How are the photos used? Is it just to deliver information about what actors consider as relevant in their lifeworld? Information that is later 'translated' into a verbal account? Or are you considering using the photos in your research publication?
iv What type of research project do you aim at? An explorative-descriptive one where you use the participants to provide visual and verbal information? Or action research whereby you intend to empower the participants and motivate them for political action (like in the photovoice movement)?

Of course, this second collection strategy can be combined with the first: Researchers as well as actors take pictures.

3 Collecting images produced by actors for other purposes

This third collection strategy is quite different as research is done about photos that already exist. Most of them were not produced for research but for other purposes.

i Depending on your research interest you may either turn to photo archives or to the Internet or both.
ii In the Internet you are facing Big Data. You may use a search engine (like Google images) to find images of a certain type. The search is done by algorithms that remain non-transparent to most social researchers, and they work by pattern recognition and not on a semantic level. The search result is flawed, but search engines are nevertheless efficient in handling a large mass of images.
iii You can restrict the search by defining narrower limits of your research field (for instance, by investigating selfies of a limited number of teenagers on Facebook).
iv Or you can pick images that you encounter incidentally in your personal lifeworld and use them for research purposes. Such coincidental sampling is prevalent in qualitative research but hardly accounted for explicitly.

Guidelines are not recipes, they point to a direction where one could go. Guidelines must be applied by situating them in a concrete social field and by reflecting them carefully in the context of a research question and research project. I hope you will find them helpful.

FURTHER READING

Becker, Howard (1986) *Doing things together. Selected papers. Part 4: Photography*. Evanston, IL: Northwestern University Press, pp. 221–317.

Bourdieu, Pierre (2012) *Picturing Algeria*. Foreword by Craig Calhoun. Edited by Franz Schultheis and Christine Frisinghelli. New York: Columbia University Press.

Collier, John, Jr. and Collier, Malcolm (1986) *Visual Anthropology: Photography as a Research Method*. Albuquerque: University of New Mexico Press.

Harper, Douglas (2012) *Visual Sociology*. London and New York: Routledge.

REFERENCES

Banks, Marcus (2018) *Using Visual Data in Qualitative Research. Book 5 of The Sage Qualitative Research Kit*, edited by Uwe Flick (2nd edn). London: Sage.

Barthes, Roland (1981) *Camera Lucida. Reflections on Photography*. Tr. Richard Howard. New York: Hill and Wang.
Becker, Howard S. (1974) 'Photography and sociology', *Studies in the Anthropology of Visual Communication*, 1(1): 3–26. (Reprinted in Becker, 1986, pp. 223–71.)
Becker, Howard S. (1978) 'Do photographs tell the truth?', *Afterimage*, 5(8): 9–13. (Reprinted in Becker, 1986, pp. 273–92.)
Becker, Howard S. (1981) *Exploring Society Photographically*. Evanston: Mary and Leigh Block Gallery/Northwestern University.
Becker, Howard S. (1986) *Doing Things Together. Selected papers*. Evanston, IL: Northwestern University Press.
Becker, Howard S. (1995) 'Visual sociology, documentary photography, and photojournalism', *Visual Sociology*, 10(1–2): 5–14.
Becker, Howard S. (2002) 'Visual evidence: A Seventh Man, the specified generalization, and the work of the reader', *Visual Studies*, 17(1): 3–11.
Berger, John (1972) *Ways of Seeing*. London: BBC and Penguin.
Berger, John and Mohr, Jean (1975) *A Seventh Man: A Book of Images and Words about the Experience of Migrant Workers in Europe*. Harmondsworth: Penguin.
Bourdieu, Pierre (2012) *Picturing Algeria*. Foreword by Craig Calhoun. Edited by Franz Schultheis and Christine Frisinghelli. New York: Columbia University Press.
Bourdieu, Pierre, Boltanski, Luc, Castel, Robert, Chamboredon, Jean-Claude and Schnapper, Dominique (1990) *Photography: A Middle-Brow Art*. Tr. Shaun Whiteside. Cambridge: Polity.
Collier, John, Jr. and Collier, Malcolm (1986) *Visual Anthropology: Photography as a Research Method*. Albuquerque: University of New Mexico Press. (Original: Collier, John, Jr., 1967, *Photography as a Research Method*. New York: Holt, Rinehart and Winston.)
Eberle, Thomas S. (2014a) 'The art of making photos: Some phenomenological reflections', in Michael Barber and Jürgen Dreher (eds.), *Phenomenology, Social Sciences and the Arts*. Dordrecht: Springer, pp. 311–20.
Eberle, Thomas S. (2014b) 'Photographing as creative and communicative action', in Hubert Knoblauch, Mark Jacobs and René Tuma (eds.), *Communication, Culture, and Creativity*. Berlin u.a.: Peter Lang, pp. 137–53.
Eberle, Thomas S. (ed.) (2017) *Fotografie und Gesellschaft. Phänomenologische und wissenssoziologische Analysen*. Bielefeld: transcript.
Ewald, Wendy (1985) *Portrait and Dreams: Photographs and Stories by Children of the Appalachians*. New York: Writers and Readers Publishing.
Garfinkel, Harold (1967) *Studies in Ethnomethodology*. Englewood Cliffs, NJ: Prentice-Hall.
Glaser, Barney G. and Strauss, Anselm L. (1967) *The Discovery of Grounded Theory: Strategies for Qualitative Research*. Chicago: Aldine.
Goffman, Erving (1974) *Frame Analysis. An Essay on the Organization of Experience*. New York: Harper & Row.
Goffman, Erving (1979) *Gender Advertisements*. Cambridge, MA: Harvard University Press.
Hall, Stuart (1997) 'The work of representation', in Stuart Hall (ed.), *Representation. Cultural Representations and Signifying Practices*. London/Thousand Oaks/New Delhi: Sage, pp. 15–41.
Harper, Douglas (2000) 'The image in sociology: Histories and issues', *Journal des Anthropologues*, 80–81: 143–60.
Harper, Douglas (2002) 'Talking about pictures: A case of photo elicitation', *Visual Studies*, 17(1): 13–26.
Harper, Douglas (2012) *Visual Sociology*. London and New York: Routledge.
Heath, Christian, Hindmarsh, Jon and Luff, Paul (2010) *Video in Qualitative Research. Analyzing Social Interaction in Everyday Life*. London: Sage.
Hughes, Everett C. (1971) *The Sociological Eye*. Chicago: Aldine.
Husserl, Edmund (2013) *Cartesian Meditations: An Introduction to Phenomenology*. New York: Springer Science & Business Media.
Knoblauch, Hubert, Schnettler, Bernt, Raab, Jürgen and Soeffner, Hans-Georg (eds.) (2006) *Video Analysis. Methodology and Methods. Qualitative Audiovisual Data Analysis in Sociology*. Frankfurt am Main: Peter Lang.
Margolis, Eric and Pauwels, Luc (eds.) (2011) *The SAGE Handbook of Visual Research Methods*. London: Sage.

Mead, Margaret and Bateson, Gregory (1942) *Balinese Character: A Photographic Analysis*. New York: New York Academy of Sciences.

Merleau-Ponty, Maurice (1996) *Phenomenology of Perception*. Tr. Colin Smith. New Delhi: Motilal Banarsidass.

Mora, Gilles and Hill, John T. (eds.) (1998) *W. Eugene Smith. The Camera as Conscience*. London: Thames and Hudson.

Pink, Sarah (2001) *Doing Visual Ethnography*. London: Sage.

Pink, Sarah (2012) *Advances in Visual Methodology*. London: Sage.

Rose, Gillian (2011) *Visual Methodologies*. London: Sage.

Schultheis, Franz (2017) 'On the price of priceless goods. Sociological observations on and around Art Basel', *Journal for Art Market Studies*, 1(1): 1–15.

Schultheis, Franz, Holder, Patricia and Wagner, Constantin (2009) 'In Algeria: Pierre Bourdieu's photographic fieldwork', *The Sociological Review*, 57(3): 448–70.

Schultheis, Franz, Single, Erwin, Egger, Stephan and Mazzurana, Thomas (2015) *When Art Meets Money. Encounters at the Art Basel*. Tr. James Fearns (Kunstwissenschaftliche Bibliothek 44). Köln: Verlag der Buchhandlung Walter König.

Schultheis, Franz, Single, Erwin, Köfeler, Raphaela and Mazzurana, Thomas (2016) *Art Unlimited? Dynamics and Paradoxes of a Globalizing Art World. Cultures of Society 20*. Bielefeld: transcript.

Schutz, Alfred (1962) 'Symbol, reality, and society', in *Alfred Schutz, Collected Papers I: The Problem of Social Reality*. Edited by Maurice Natanson. The Hague: Martinus Nijhoff, pp. 287–356.

Soeffner, Hans-Georg (2006) 'Visual Sociology on the basis of "visual concentration"', in Hubert Knoblauch, Bernt Schnettler, Jürgen Raab, Hans-Georg Soeffner (eds.) *Video Analysis. Methodology and Methods. Qualitative Audiovisual Data Analysis in Sociology*. Frankfurt am Main: Peter Lang, pp. 205–17.

Wang, Caroline and Burris, Mary Ann (1997) 'Photovoice: Concept, methodology, and use for participatory needs assessment', *Health Education & Behavior*, 24(3): 369–87.

Worth, Sol and Adair, John (1972) *Through Navajo Film Eyes: An Exploration in Film Communication and Anthropology*. Bloomington, IN: Indiana University Press.

Collecting Media Data: TV and Film Studies

Lothar Mikos

INTRODUCTION

In this chapter I will focus on the collection of media data for textual analysis in film and television studies. While qualitative reception studies use the classic methods of qualitative social research (such as narrative interviews, see Murray, Chapter 17, this volume; group discussions, see Morgan and Hoffman, Chapter 16, this volume; and ethnographic observation, see Buscatto, Chapter 21, this volume), text-analytical studies follow the methods of film and television analysis (Mikos, 2014), qualitative content analysis (Schreier, 2014), discourse analysis (Willig, 2014; see Rau et al., Chapter 19, this volume), conversation analysis (Toerien, 2014; see Jackson, Chapter 18, this volume), the documentary method (Bohnsack, 2014) and the methods of cultural studies (Winter, 2014). These methods have in common the fact that they use two kinds of audiovisual data: (1) professionally produced films and television programs, and (2) films and videos produced by amateurs and, in the twenty-first century, uploaded to digital media platforms such as YouTube by the producers themselves as user-generated content (UGC). Such audiovisual data may be drawn from existing collections, or may be collected specifically for the purpose of a study. The digitalization of media technology has simplified both kinds of data collection, although limitations persist. The present chapter introduces the various kinds of audiovisual data associated with various kinds of studies, describes the technical means of obtaining and collecting data since digitalization, along with their limitations, and presents a critical view of the situation in regard to data in film and television studies.

The collection of media data is a precondition for textual analysis of film and television. However, the media data must also be collected. They must be physically available. Up to the 1960s, film copies could be archived, but their screening was only possible on an editing table. Textual analysis was possible only by direct watching.

Thus, before his emigration from Germany, Siegfried Kracauer had written numerous film critics for newspapers. The related experience was the basis for his work, *From Caligari to Hitler. A Psychological History of the German Film* (Kracauer, 1947), which he has written in the US. There was no way for him to see the films several times. It was true that, at the end of the 1920s and 1930s, the first departments had developed within existing institutions, which collected audiovisual data. The first film archives were also created at the time (Ballhausen, n.d.). It was only in 1956 that a videotape recorder was developed by Ampex, but it was used only in the television industry. But, in principle, it was also possible to archive TV broadcasts. However, this did not happen until the technology became cheaper and could be used extensively (Burns, 1998). In 1971, Sony developed the first VCR for the consumer market. Since then, the technology has evolved and archives that collected films and television broadcasts were digitalized (see the section on archives and the section on digitalization).

The collection of media data depends, among other things, on the subject matter of a project. For example, for a research on historical representations, it is necessary to rely on material from archives – unless the project is about the current representation of historical events in current productions. If, on the other hand, the project investigates current tendencies in the TV program, the research group has to create its own archive in order to document the programs to be analyzed. This was the case, for example, in the first studies on the reality show *Big Brother*, as the contributions from different countries show in the book *Big Brother International* (Mathijs and Jones, 2004). This method of documenting audiovisual data was also used in a comparison of historical representations in British and German television in 2005 and could show:

> While German docudramas about Nazism and the Second World War use a combination of documentary and fictional modes of representation to create a special kind of tension and magical aura in order to offer the German audience a sensual and emotional space to empathize with the perpetrators, British docudramas seem to be much more conventional in their distant documentary style and interested in the technical possibilities of visual and digital reconstruction of historical figures, locations and incidents. (Ebbrecht, 2007, p. 49)

Audiovisual data from archives, on the other hand, had to be used in investigations that examine historical material. One example is the study of the image of the Holocaust, which is produced by films (Ebbrecht-Hartmann, 2015). The theme of this project brings us to an important point why a textual analysis of films and television broadcasts is important: films and television programs represent social reality.

AUDIOVISUAL DATA AND SOCIAL REPRESENTATION

The present discussion is not concerned with audiovisual data produced in the context of the research project itself – for example, by using a camera to observe and document everyday life (see the chapter on videography – Knoblauch, et al., Chapter 23, this volume) – but with existing films and television programs that can be studied as data. Films and television programs, like photographs, can be seen as social facts (Loizos, 2000, p. 93), since they represent social reality and are a part of the social representation order (Mikos, 2014, p. 413 ff.). This is true of fictional as well as documentary films. They are cultural and social documents representing social realities. They correspond to social structures, this is their ideological component. For all representations are 'inseparable in power relations' (Orgad, 2012, p. 25). Thus, the texts themselves become a field of social conflict. They do not follow a uniform ideological line, for they are organized in a polysemic manner, that is, they contain several, structurally systematically different meanings. In the context of TV texts, Fiske (1987, p. 90ff.) even speaks of a semiotic excess or surplus. Film and TV texts cannot be controlled by a dominant ideology, because they are multi-tuned and can also be contradictory. They are part of an active process of production (Orgad, 2012, p. 17).

The reason for this lies in the textual structure of films and television shows, as well as in their communicative function. On the structural level, Francesco Casetti and Federico di Chio distinguish three levels of representation: the first level is about the content, which is represented in the pictures and shows itself in the scenery; on the second level, we are concerned with the modalities of representation, that is, with the represen-tation of something in the pictures; on the third level we are dealing with the concat-enation of the images with the aid of the montage, by means of which meanings arise which are not contained in the images them-selves (Casetti and di Chio, 1994, p. 115 ff.). Through the editing process some meanings can be favored and others cannot. When, for example, in a late night show during the argu-mentation of a guest, spectators are interbed-ded as intersections, who look bored or shake their heads; this commentary function is the result of the montage. In this way, a 'moral modalization of communication' can take place (see Keppler, 2001, p. 865). In films, this also depends on the established knowl-edge of people and situations.

At the level of the communicative function of film and television, the polysemy arises due to the fact that films and television shows are basically open to the knowledge, the emotions, the social communication and the practical sense of spectators (Mikos, 2014, 2015). Since the viewers are involved in life-world contexts and social discourses, they construct different meanings on the basis of the symbolic material of the film and televi-sion programs. At the level of content and representation, films and television shows become the occasion for the manifestation of life-world knowledge. As audiovisual sign systems they correspond to the representation system of the mental concepts of the specta-tors (see Hall, 2013, p. 14). In these mental concepts cognitions, emotions, social-com-municative situations and practical meaning are represented. They are based on the life experiences of the individuals who become spectators of a film or television show. Thus the mental perspectives also contain the spe-cific perspectives of social inequality from the subjective view of personal experience.

For the analysis of the meaning of the indi-vidual signs and of the cinematic or televisual code, it is important to distinguish between the denotative and the connotative meaning (see Hall, 2013, p. 23). 'Denotation' refers to the referential object, the meaning signi-fied is descriptive or 'obvious' (Casey et al., 2002, p. 222); 'connotation' means all pos-sible concepts that exist to a character or code. In this second dimension of signification, the signs and codes are connected with the 'fur-ther semantic field' of culture (Hall, 2013, p. 23). It must be borne in mind that denota-tion and connotation can refer to all levels of representation.

It is important to distinguish between con-tent and representation. For instance in the quiz show *Who wants to be a Millionaire?*, a quiz is given at the level of content, in which candidates have to answer questions in a multiple-choice procedure. The level of representation is about the legitimacy and importance of knowledge forms, as well as educational credentials for candidates and telephone jokers.

FORMS OF AUDIOVISUAL DATA

Since the invention of film at the close of the nineteenth century, and since the mass distri-bution of television in the mid-twentieth cen-tury, social communication is no longer conceivable without audiovisual moving pic-tures. Films and television programs can be examined in both historical and contemporary studies. Films of the 1930s may just as well be an object of study as current television news programs. Which films and television programs are relevant to a given research project depends on the research questions and the epistemological interest of the study.

In the history of film and television, aesthetic and narrative standardizations have been established, which not only structure the production and transmission processes, but also correspond to viewing habits and expectations of viewers. The different forms of these standards are based on structural constraints (technical, economic, political, juridical, etc.) of the respective medium, as well as on dramatic, narrative and creative means. Patterns and conventions have been formed which are referred to as the 'genre' (Altman, 1999; Bordwell and Thompson, 2013; Corrigan and White, 2012; Fiske, 1987; Mittell, 2004; Neale, 1987; Turner, 2009).

On a general level movies and television shows can be divided into two categories: fictional and non-fictional. If the narrated and illustrated story is invented, it belongs to the fictional realm. If it is based on events of the social reality represented in the medium, it is attributable to the non-fictional sphere. Film genres are classified according to different use and presentation forms. One can distinguish between feature film, documentary film, animation film, experimental film, educational film, advertising film and industrial film. Television categories can be distinguished according to use, journalism, presentation and transmission. There are news, documentaries, reports and magazines, as well as life style, talk, comedy, game and quiz shows in the non-fiction area, and TV films, TV movies, feature films, TV series and sitcoms in the fictional area. Distinguishable within these categories are different genres that summarize films or television shows according to common, typical characteristics. For example, the category of fiction film includes the genres of melodrama, western, comedy, crime, horror, science fiction film, etc., which in turn can form further sub-genres (Bordwell and Thompson, 2013; Corrigan and White, 2012; Turner, 2009). In the television genre, for example, in the category of documentaries, the genres of documentary films and television documentation, as well as theater, music and sport events etc. are included. And within that same television genre, are the various crime, physician and hospital, vampire and mystery series, etc.

Genres thus contribute to the routinization and ritualization of film and television communication through stereotyping (Schweinitz, 2011). Through their relation to social conditions, they are also subject to historical change. Genres are dynamic, because every new film or new TV show of a genre varies and changes it. They can, therefore, also be seen as a process (Altman, 1999).

For the purpose of this chapter different kinds of audiovisual data can be classified as follows: (1) documentary films, (2) narrative or fiction films, (3) advertising films, (4) video clips, 5) television entertainment shows, (6) television series, (7) news and reports, (8) sports broadcasts, and (9) amateur films and videos. Documentary films include sports films and all films of theater, opera and musical performances. Advertising films include corporate films. How the data material is accessible and usable is important for the research process. Films may be available in different formats (8mm, 16mm, 35mm or 70mm); or they may have been converted to other media; or they may be originally produced digitally and available only as digital data. Amateur films and videos were generally recorded on 8mm or 16mm film, later on video tape, and in the twenty-first century digitally, in a variety of video file formats. Television programs are generally available on videotape or in digital form. 'Data are what we see, hear or read: no more but certainly no less' (Melia, 1997, pp. 34–5.) It is important to be able to actually see the audiovisual data – and for that purpose, the appropriate technical equipment must be available to view the various formats. Digitalization has greatly simplified this issue for researchers.

How the audiovisual data are gathered depends on the kind of study that is being undertaken. For a study dealing with current events, the pertinent television programs must be documented. For this purpose, the researcher defines a period during which all news programs, for example, of all the major American networks and news broadcasters, such as CNN, are documented for the purpose of examining the presentation of, for example, the presidential candidates or the Middle East conflict and its importance in American foreign policy. Regardless of the technical equipment used for such documentation, the same equipment can be used to view the data collected. A research subject, such as gender representation in narrative films and family series in 1960s television, presents greater difficulties. Except for those films and television series from the 1960s that are still on the air today, the material will have to be obtained primarily from archives – and the study limited to what the archives contain. The research becomes significantly easier if the old films and television programs have been digitalized. If a film is available only in a 35mm copy, it may be difficult to view it unless a 35mm projector or flatbed editor is at hand. If an old television series is only extant on 2-inch tape, there will be little chance of viewing it today. It is very important when collecting audiovisual data to have access to the necessary technical equipment to view and analyze the material. Furthermore, the scope of a historical research project depends on what films and television programs are present in archives at all. Methodical sampling (see Schreier, Chapter 6, this volume) may be impossible if, for example, the study is limited to those archived 1960s films and television series that are available to the researcher. In such cases, the researcher must begin by constructing a corpus (Bauer and Aarts, 2000), which is limited to such material as is conserved in the archives and usable by the researcher. Archives are nonetheless a very important source, primarily for collecting historical audiovisual material.

ARCHIVES

A Google search for 'television archive' yields, in May 2016, 131 million results; 'TV archive' yields 211 million. The search term 'film archive' meanwhile yields 285 million results. There would seem to be an unbelievable number of archives that collect films and television programs. On a closer look, however, the numbers are significantly smaller, since many of the archives referenced have collected their material unsystematically, limiting themselves, for example, to specific topics or regions. At this point it must be noted that professional archives are curated: that is, the material they collect is selected, and the selection is determined by the purpose of the collection. There are very few state archives that collect everything. Generally, archives focus on certain media forms, specific kinds of productions or special topics. However, films and television programs can be obtained not only in such 'official' archives, but also on commercial digital platforms and from commercial businesses offering films and television programs as home entertainment products. In collecting audiovisual material, we must therefore resort to other sources in addition to classic archives. We can use the following kinds of sources: (1) conventional public archives operated by state agencies or foundations, or as departments of museums or educational institutions, (2) private archives, (3) the archives of television networks, (4) online platforms such as YouTube, (5) home entertainment distributors and dealers, and (6) commercial streaming services such as Netflix. Different sources will be used depending on the research topic; not every source is suitable for every project. Amateur films, for example, are more likely to be found in private archives and conventional archives devoted to films of this kind; in the digital world, amateur films are found on YouTube, where they are uploaded as user-generated content (UGC) or user-created content (UCC) (Burgess and Green, 2009,

p. 38 ff.). Silent films from the early days of cinema are more likely to be found in classic archives, or – in the case of important historic films – in home entertainment or in specialized YouTube channels. Television programs of the 1960s and 1970s are more commonly found in the archives of television networks and in classic archives.[1]

FILM ARCHIVES

A special characteristic of film and television is that these media are subject to national legislation, even though films and television programs are traded and distributed worldwide. The rights to commercialize individual films and television programs are generally acquired for a national territory, sometimes for a language area. Audiovisual products are therefore primarily found in the national archives of their respective country of production. However, they can also be archived in the countries in which they were shown in cinemas or on television. In the latter case, films are often archived not in the original version, but as modified for export. The original version of the film *Metropolis* by Fritz Lang (GER, 1927), for example, is considered lost. In 2001 it was reconstructed and restored from several different export versions (one American, one Russian and one Czech). In 2008, a 16mm copy of another export version of *Metropolis* was found in an archive in Buenos Aires: it had been brought from Germany to Argentina by a film distributor in 1927. The missing scenes it contained were then added to a restored version, which was published in 2010. The resulting version is still about 8 minutes shorter than the original, however. This example illustrates one of the major challenges of film research in archives. Because many films exist in several different versions, it is always necessary to verify which version is present in a given archive. The same is true of television programs, which are also adapted to national programming conventions when they are licensed internationally. Episodes of US television series, for example, that run 47 minutes in the original are shortened to 45 minutes for the German market, since programming timeslots for series are only 45 or 60 minutes long. Researchers who cite audiovisual material should therefore always indicate the version of a film or television program on which they base their analysis.

The International Federation of Film Archives (FIAF) was founded in 1938 and now has 150 member institutions in 74 countries. Its mission is

> to uphold a code of ethics for film preservation and practical standards for all areas of film archive work; to promote the creation of moving image archives in countries which lack them; to seek the improvement of the legal context within which film archives carry out their work; to promote film culture and facilitate historical research on both a national and international level; to foster training and expertise in preservation and other archive techniques; to ensure the permanent availability of material from the collections for study and research by the wider community; to encourage the collection and preservation of documents and materials relating to the cinema; to develop co-operation between members and to ensure the international availability of films and documents. (Available at http://www.fiafnet.org/pages/Community/Mission-FIAF.html)

FIAF also provides databases including a global index of film and television periodicals and 'Treasures from the Film Archives', a unique index of silent films in international film archives which 'provides filmographic and holdings information on over 53,000 silent shorts and features, fiction and non-fiction, from over 112 of the world's major film archives' (available at http://www.fiafnet.org/pages/Publications/About-FIAF-Databases.html). This database can be very helpful in searching for silent films.

Because films are generally still archived in the form of physical reels, however, researchers must travel to the archives to view them. A number of historic films have been digitalized and made available online, but they are still relatively few. In Germany, the Film Archives Department of the Federal Archives has been collecting all films produced using public funds in Germany since the 1950s, including German newsreels, documentaries and feature films (available at https://www.bundesarchiv.de/bundesarchiv/organisation/abteilung_fa/index.html.en). More than 70,000 reels of celluloid film are conserved in a special storage hall.

In France, the Cinémathèque Française collects films and makes them available to researchers and the public. The collection includes some 40,000 films. In the United Kingdom, the BFI National Archives, a department of the British Film Institute (BFI), collects mainly British films. The archives currently contain '60,000 fiction films, including features, on all gauges of film and formats of videotape; 120,000 non-fiction films, broadly tracing the history of the use of the moving image in non-fictional settings and for non-fiction purposes', (available at http://www.bfi.org.uk/archive-collections/about-bfi-national-archive/what-archive-contains). In the US, the Department of Film and Video of the Museum of Modern Art in New York contains some 14,000 films. The Film and Television Archives of the University of California at Los Angeles (UCLA) has a collection of some 220,000 films and television programs. The National Audio-Visual Conservation Center of the Library of Congress has some 6.3 million artifacts in its film, television and sound collections. The National Film Archive of India, under the auspices of the Ministry of Information and Broadcasting, has collected more than 10,000 films. The collection of the Cinemateca Brasileira in São Paulo includes some 200,000 reels of film. The Asian Film Archive in Singapore has collected about 1,500 films from the South and East Asian regions. In every country where films are made, there is a national film archive or a national film institute that collects films. Not all such archives are accessible to the public, but access is usually granted to researchers.

In addition to state and public archives, there are also private film and television archives. Private collectors tend to have highly specialized collections, however, which are open neither to the public nor to researchers. Another kind of private archive is that of the collections belonging to educational and research institutions or researchers. The Department of Theatre Studies at Freie Universität Berlin, for example, has a collection of AV material documenting theater performances from all over Germany. Other university departments have archived television programs as part of their research projects. Many of these collections are integrated in the given university's library.

TELEVISION ARCHIVES

The archiving of television programs began in the early 1960s with the invention of video tape recording. Earlier television programs were only conserved if they were recorded on film. In some countries, television programs are collected by state or public archives, such as the BFI National Archive in the UK and the National Audio-Visual Conservation Center of the Library of Congress and the UCLA Film and Television Archives in the US. Broadcasters and television networks also have their archives, which are generally not accessible to the public. Researchers are granted access only on special request, and must usually pay a fee for copies in a video cassette or DVD format. In Germany, the German Broadcasting Archives (Deutsches Rundfunkarchiv) contain all the recorded broadcasts of East German television. The public and private television networks also maintain archives in which they collect only audiovisual material for which the given network holds the licensing rights. The NBC Universal Archives in the US mainly provides news footage to producers and other broadcasters, charging a fee for user licenses. The BBC Archives in the

United Kingdom now cooperate with the agency Getty Images. BBC broadcasts are now collected and indexed by subject matter in the agency's BBC Motion Gallery. There are also archives that collect material on special topics, such as the London Television Archive, which only collects videos that relate to London. Other archives, such as the Vanderbilt Television News Archive, specialize in news broadcasts (Vianello and Einstein, 1984). Television archives generally contain journalistic shows produced by the broadcasting companies, such as news, documentaries and reports, as well as entertainment shows. They usually do not contain televised films and series, since these are most often produced and commercialized by external production companies.

DIGITALIZATION

Digitalization has changed both the nature of archives and the opportunities for researchers to access audiovisual material. Many archives have begun to digitalize some or all of their collections. The broadcasts collected in the BBC Motion Gallery, for example, are available in large part online, as are some of the materials of the BFI National Archive and the UCLA Film and Television Archives. In addition, there have been political initiatives to safeguard audiovisual heritage. European Union funds have been allocated to support two portals, the Europe Film Gateway (http://www.europeanfilmgateway.eu/) and EUscreen (http://www.euscreen.eu/). The Europe Film Gateway is connected with film archives in Europe and offers high-speed access to film material from those archives. EUscreen meanwhile concentrates its collection on television:

> The EUscreen portal offers free online access to thousands of items of audiovisual heritage. It brings together clips that provide an insight into the social, cultural, political and economic events that have shaped the 20th and 21st centuries. [...] EUscreen is also intended to be a resource for educators, researchers and media professionals searching for new audiovisual content from across Europe. The EUscreen portal was built by a consortium of European audiovisual archives, public broadcasters, academic and technical partners. It has been funded by the European Commission. The main objective of the project is to aggregate a comprehensive amount of professional audiovisual content. A large number of clips and programs have been selected by broadcasters and archives from all across Europe. (http://euscreen.eu/about.html)

The material available through these two portals depends on the cooperating archives and broadcasters. The EUscreen portal for example offers no material from German television because the German broadcasting agencies do not cooperate with the portal.

Thanks to digitalization, however, many television networks have their own online portals, which provide current television programs, in some (but not all) cases, free of charge. There are also portals such as the 'Archives of American Television', operated by the Television Academy Foundation. Rather than television programs, however, this portal offers hundreds of video interviews with television industry figures. These interviews are likely to be of interest only for projects concerned with the production cultures of American television.

YOUTUBE

Probably the world's largest digital audiovisual archive is the online video platform YouTube, founded in 2005 and acquired by Google in 2006. Videos are uploaded to YouTube not only by private users, but also by professionals and institutions. Users can view billions of videos online free of charge. 'User-generated content' makes up a large proportion of the uploaded videos, but videos uploaded by professional content providers are viewed more often (Burgess and Green, 2009). YouTube marked the beginning of a 'fundamental shift in the dynamics of the online distribution market' (Cunningham and Silver, 2013, p. 24). With time, the number of professional content providers placing their videos on YouTube steadily increased. 'In 2009, YouTube introduced high definition streaming with 16:9 aspect ratio and long-form content through a deal with MGM to introduce old movies for VOD[2]' (Cunningham and Silver, 2013, p. 25). YouTube also concluded license agreements with other film studios to permit access to their products. But often the audiovisual material on YouTube lacks meta-data.

The structure of YouTube allows users to create channels for their own content, to which other users can then subscribe. This makes the platform attractive to traditional archives. For example, the International Federation of Television Archives (FIAT/IFTA) provides online access to its videos only through YouTube. The organization's own website links directly to YouTube. The following archives – and this list is just a brief selection – also maintain YouTube channels: the Australian Television Archive, the Cartoon Network Archive, Film Archive Thailand, the Vintage Movie Archive, the East Anglian Film Archive, the BFI National Archive, the Texas Archive of the Moving Image, and the Chicago Film Archive. In addition, many online archives that provide films and television programs also maintain channels on YouTube, including the Charlie Chaplin Archive, the Travel Film Archive, the Newsreel Archive, the Vintage Movie Archive, and many more. Channels such as Cinenet, Inter-Pathé, Timeless Classic Movies, Timeless Western Movies and weloadtv offer full-length films, some of them in several languages. Searching YouTube channels in May 2016 yielded 7,497 channels under 'TV archive', 3,166 for 'film archive', and 3,302 for 'movie archive'. There is also a great deal of material to be found on YouTube outside of such specialized channels, however. Classic silent films can be viewed in full length, as can classic television entertainment shows of the 1960s and 1970s, historic sports broadcasts, and complete sports events, such as several of Muhammad Ali's boxing fights, for example. Such historic films and television programs are more likely to be available on YouTube than more recent content, which is usually found only in the form of brief excerpts uploaded by private users. Because academic studies generally refer to whole films and whole television programs, material found on YouTube must always be verified for completeness, as well as for specific film versions.

YouTube has not only changed the digital distribution of audiovisual content, but has also become a cultural archive, 'a massive, heterogeneous, but for the most part accidental and disordered, public archive' (Burgess and Green, 2009, p. 88). The platform's professionalization and the development of its channel structure gave more and more professional providers, including numerous archives, the opportunity to fill this giant collection with their content. 'YouTube implicitly recognized that archives were not the end of the media lifecycle, but rather a new beginning … YouTube gave new life to the moving image heritage and exposed archival material to a vast audience' (Prelinger, 2009, p. 274). This large audience includes media researchers, who may find material for qualitative media analysis methods on the portal. There is an important limitation, however, because licenses for audiovisual content are often limited to specific geographical areas, some videos found on YouTube are not available everywhere in the world.

COMMERCIAL MEDIA (DVD, BLU-RAY, STREAMING)

In addition to conventional film and television archives and YouTube, researchers can also draw on commercial providers for research material. When the VCR became a mass-market product, it created a home entertainment market in which films, television series and other television programs were offered for sale, first on video cassette, later on DVD and Blu-ray, and now online through streaming portals. Researchers planning a study of 1940s films or 1980s television series may find material for their analysis offered by DVD and Blu-ray dealers. The content on physical media is not free, of course. In the US, Amazon.com offers over 500,000 titles in the category Movies and TV. In Germany, Amazon.de offers more than 1.2 million films and more than 67,000 television series. Here again, regional licensing limits the films and television programs available in a given local market.

In addition to sales of physical media, audiovisual content is also available through online portals that offer streaming access to films, television series and documentaries, charging either a subscription rate or a pay-per-view fee. Providers such as Amazon Prime Instant Video, HBO Now, Hulu and Netflix primarily offer current television series and films, which are then licensed exclusively for streaming by the providers' national or transnational portals. Netflix Germany offers a different selection of content from Netflix in the US. HBO Now has a different selection in the US than HBO Nordic, which is accessible in the Scandinavian countries. Moreover, the streaming portals purchase time-limited licenses for films and television series. As sources for studies, they are therefore suitable mainly for projects dealing with very current phenomena.

LIMITATIONS

The licensing of films and television programs for national markets or geolinguistic areas limits the availability of audiovisual material such as films and television programs. Different materials are available in the different countries in which researchers work. The material available on an international online platform such as EUscreen, which is accessible throughout Europe, depends on which national broadcasters and institutions cooperate with the platform. Thus there are politically intentional legal limitations on the availability of audiovisual sources. The economic limitations, in turn, depend in part on the legal situation. While on-site access to many film archives is free, television archives often charge fees for their material, as do the commercial suppliers of films and television programs. The costs of acquiring materials therefore need to be determined and budgeted in planning research projects.

Finally, there are technical limitations. Those who want to study old films must have access to viewing equipment for 8mm, 16mm or 35mm film material. VCRs for older video cassette formats are also difficult to obtain. Researchers generally do not have access to players for many old video formats such as U-Matic and Beta. Digitalization has reduced such technical limitations since different digital formats generally only require appropriate software installed on a personal computer. In addition to the technical limitations, there are also media-specific limitations on archival material, particularly in regard to television. Many live broadcasts are not archived at all. The archives contain live broadcasts of major political, cultural and sports events, but not of live reality TV shows. At the time of the reality show *Big Brother*, there were not only evening summaries of the events of the past 24 hours, but full 24-hour broadcasts also ran live on pay TV channels and were streamed over the Internet (Bignell, 2013, pp. 287–8). These 24-hour broadcasts were not archived. They are no longer extant, hence no longer available for research. Similarly, some versions of old feature films and documentaries are no longer available.

Another challenge is the meta-data about films and TV broadcasts. If research is also about to investigate the development and production of a film or a TV show, archives, especially online archives, often lack the meta-data. For this, further searches in databases and possibly other archives are necessary. Metadata are important for historical research:

> Finally, investigators who are attempting to use a program, or aspects of a program, as a primary source must deal with one final contextual aspect of a program. They must be able to track and document the origins of that program information just as they would with any other type of primary source. This is not an easy task because, unlike print media where attribution and referencing are part and parcel of the writer's research process, broadcast producers typically do not maintain a detailed traceable record. (Godfrey, 2002, p. 496)

Researchers have to consult additional sources.

Finally, an important limitation of archives is the fact that the archived material is curated. There is someone (a person or an institution) who decides, what should be collected. There are huge collections of news programs and newsreels because they seem to be important as a historical resource. However, TV game and quiz shows, reality shows and television series were not seen as equally important (Scannell, 2010). There is no given standard for collecting audiovisual data.

CONCLUSION

Those who do textual analysis in media studies can avail themselves of several methods of gathering audiovisual material. The simplest, in the case of current studies of the medium of television and television programs, is to document the material personally. This allows the researcher to define a universe from which to select a sample (on data sampling, see Schreier, Chapter 6, this volume). For all other studies on historic television programs or historic and current films, investigators must research what films and television programs are available in the existing sources: conventional archives, online archives, YouTube and commercial home entertainment suppliers. In these cases, it may be a good idea to build a research corpus rather than a sample (see Bauer and Aarts, 2000). Since qualitative research analyzes exemplary cases rather than representative samples, this method can be very productive.

The limitations mentioned restrict the selection available for constructing a corpus, however. All the audiovisual material available in the sources must therefore be critically examined. In the case of films, it is necessary to determine which version of a given film is used. Individual films are often produced in different versions for showing in different countries (called export versions); newer films are sometimes available in a 'director's cut', a version containing scenes that were not included in the original cinema release. In the home entertainment market, films are also offered in 'enhanced DVD' versions, which are not identical to the films shown in cinemas. At the same time, films are often edited to make them releasable for young audiences, and then exist in 'cut' and 'uncut' versions. Boxed DVD sets of television series can also contain episodes that were not broadcast in certain countries for various reasons. Entertainment TV shows found on YouTube often turned out to be only excerpts lacking central elements. It is always recommended to refer to other material such as encyclopedias, production documents and other printed works to identify the version of a film or a television show. Accordingly, correct citations of audiovisual data are important in research practice. The British Universities Film and Video Council has developed suitable citation guidelines (BUFVC, 2013). The following format is recommended for feature films: 'Film Title [type, format]. Production credit, production company/sponsor/private, country of production, year of release, duration' (BUFVC, 2013, p. 8). An example: 'The Lord of the Rings: The Motion Picture Trilogy; Extended Edition [feature film, DVD]. Dir. Peter Jackson, New Line Cinema/ Wingnut Films, USA/New Zealand, 2003, 681 min. [New Line Home Entertainment, EDV 9254, 2004].' This information, and not least the running time, permits intersubjective verifiability of the analysis based on the same film or television program data.

Some researchers avoid the problem of searching for audiovisual data by accumulating their own collections over the course of their career, whether privately or in their institutions. The collected films and television programs may originate in various sources among those described. Such collections, however, are generally small and highly specialized. Nonetheless, they can be sufficient for qualitative analyses of exemplary cases.

Collecting data for film and television studies is an important component of the qualitative research process. In Gale Miller's words, 'Data-collection techniques matter because qualitative researchers' reports and analyses are built from, and limited by, their data' (Miller, 1997, p. 4). The audiovisual data collected must always be critically examined, first, to document the status of the data, and second, to make the study's data basis intersubjective and verifiable. The sources must be correctly cited in research reports, not only for that purpose but also to meet the requirements of 'fair use' of intellectual property. In written publications, screenshots of films and television programs are permitted; incorporating audiovisual material in online publications is a legal borderline area, however.

For qualitative media studies, the development of the research question is closely connected with the available audiovisual data, regardless of the sources used. A critical examination of the underlying data is indispensable. The quality of the audiovisual data is critical for the qualitative research process. Qualitative film and television analyses must be acutely aware of the data on which they are based and incorporate critical reflection on their sources. Only then can the qualitative research process succeed in ensuring intersubjective verifiability. A successful research project depends on the quality of the collection of audiovisual data.

Notes

1 A complete list of archives that collect audiovisual material would be too long to present here. Instead, the following discussion is intended to provide an overview and examples of the various kinds of archives.
2 Video on Demand

FURTHER READING

Bauer, Martin W. and Gaskell, George (eds.) (2000) *Qualitative Researching with Text, Image and Sound*. London: Sage.
Cunningham, Stuart and Silver, Jon (2013) *Screen Distribution and the New King Kongs of the Online World*. Basingstoke and New York: Palgrave Macmillan.
Turner, Graeme (2009) *Film as Social Practice* (4th edn). London and New York: Routledge.

REFERENCES

Altman, Rick (1999) *Film/Genre*. London: BFI.
Ballhausen, Thomas (n.d.) On the History and Function of Film Archives. Retrieved from http://www.efgproject.eu/downloads/Ballhausen - On the History and Function of Film Archives.pdf
Bauer, Martin W. and Aarts, Bas (2000) 'Corpus construction: A principle for qualitative data collection', in Martin W. Bauer and George Gaskell (eds.), *Qualitative Researching with Text, Image and Sound*. London: Sage, pp. 19–37.
Bignell, Jonathan (2013) *An Introduction to Television Studies* (3rd edn). London and New York: Routledge.
Bohnsack, Ralf (2014) 'Documentary method', in Uwe Flick (ed.), *The SAGE Handbook of Qualitative Data Analysis*. London: Sage, pp. 217–33.
Bordwell, David and Thompson, Kristin (2013) *Film Art. An Introduction* (10th edn). New York: McGrawHill.
BUFVC (2013) *Audiovisual Citation. BUFVC Guidelines for Referencing Moving Image and Sound*. London: British Universities Film & Video Council.

Burgess, Jean and Green, Joshua (2009) *YouTube. Online Video and Participatory Culture*. Cambridge and Malden, MA: Polity.

Burns, R. W. (1998) *Television: An International History of the Formative Years*. London: Institution of Electrical Engineers.

Casetti, Francesco and di Chio, Federico (1994) *Analisi del Film*. Milano: Bompiani.

Casey, Bernadette, Casey, Neil, Calvert, Ben, French, Liam and Lewis, Justin (2002) *Television Studies. The Key Concepts*. London and New York: Routledge.

Corrigan, Timothy and White, Patricia (2012) *The Film Experience. An Introduction* (3rd edn). Boston and New York: Bedford/St. Martin's.

Cunningham, Stuart and Silver, Jon (2013) *Screen Distribution and the New King Kongs of the Online World*. Basingstoke and New York: Palgrave Macmillan.

Ebbrecht, Tobias (2007) 'Docudramatizing history on TV. German and British docudrama and historical event television in the memorial year 2005', *European Journal of Cultural Studies*, 10, 1, 35–53.

Ebbrecht-Hartmann, Tobias (2015) 'Preserving memory or fabricating the past? How films constitute cinematic archives of the Holocaust', *Cinema & Cie*, 15, 24, 33–47.

Fiske, John (1987) *Television Culture*. London and New York: Methuen.

Godfrey, Donald G. (2002) 'Broadcast archives for historical research: Revisiting the Historical Method', in *Journal of Broadcasting & Electronic Media*, 46, 3, 493–503.

Hall, Stuart (2013) 'The work of representation', in Stuart Hall (ed.), *Representation. Cultural Representations and Signifying Practices* (2nd edn). London: Sage, pp. 1–59.

Keppler, Angela (2001) 'Formen der Moralisierung im Fernsehen', in Jutta Allmendinger (ed.), *Gute Gesellschaft? Verhandlungen des 30. Kongresses der Deutschen Gesellschaft für Soziologie in Köln 2000*. Opladen: Leske + Budrich, pp. 862–75.

Kracauer, Siegfried (1947) *From Caligari to Hitler. A Psychological History of the German Film*. Princeton, NJ: Princeton University Press.

Loizos, Peter (2000) 'Video, film and photographs as research documents', in Martin W. Bauer and George Gaskell (eds.), *Qualitative Researching with Text, Image and Sound*. London: Sage, pp. 93–107.

Mathijs, Ernest and Jones, Janet (eds.) (2004) *Big Brother International. Formats, Critics & Publics*. London: Wallflower Press.

Melia, Kath M. (1997) 'Producing "plausible stories": Interviewing student nurses', in Gale Miller and Robert Dingwall (eds.), *Context & Method in Qualitative Research*. London: Sage, pp. 26–36.

Mikos, Lothar (2014) 'Analysis of film', in Uwe Flick (ed.), *The SAGE Handbook of Qualitative Data Analysis*. London: Sage, pp. 409–23.

Mikos, Lothar (2015) *Film- und Fernsehanalyse* (3rd rev. edn). Konstanz & München: UVK.

Miller, Gale (1997) 'Introduction: Context and Method in Qualitative Research', in Gale Miller and Robert Dingwall (eds.), *Context & Method in Qualitative Research*. London: Sage, pp. 1–11.

Mittell, Jason (2004) *Genre and Television. From Cop Shows to Cartoons in American Culture*. New York & London: Routledge.

Neale, Stephen (1987) *Genre* (3rd edn). London: BFI.

Orgad, Shani (2012) *Media Representation and the Global Imagination*. Cambridge & Malden: Polity.

Prelinger, Rick (2009) 'The appearance of archives', in Pelle Snickars and Patrick Vonderau (eds.), *The YouTube Reader*. Stockholm: National Library of Sweden, pp. 268–74.

Scannell, Paddy (2010) 'Television and history: Questioning the archive', *The Communication Review*, 13, 1, 37–51.

Schreier, Margrit (2014) 'Qualitative content analysis', in Uwe Flick (ed.), *The SAGE Handbook of Qualitative Data Analysis*. London: Sage, pp. 170–83.

Schweinitz, Jörg (2011) *Film and Stereotype. A Challenge for Cinema and Theory*. New York: Columbia University Press.

Toerien, Merran (2014) 'Conversations and conversation analysis', in Uwe Flick (ed.), *The SAGE Handbook of Qualitative Data Analysis*. London: Sage, pp. 327–40.

Turner, Graeme (2009) *Film as Social Practice* (4th edn). London & New York: Routledge.

Vianello, Robert and Einstein, Daniel (1984) 'A guide to researching television programming', *Quarterly Review of Film Studies*, 9, 3, 252–5.

Willig, Carla (2014) 'Interpretation and analysis', in Uwe Flick (ed.), *The SAGE Handbook of Qualitative Data Analysis*. London: Sage, pp. 136–49.

Winter, Rainer (2014) 'Cultural studies', in Uwe Flick (ed.), *The SAGE Handbook of Qualitative Data Analysis*. London: Sage, pp. 247–61.

Sounds as Data

Michael Bull

We identify two broad methodological strands: sonic ethnographies, which rely on both conventionally written and more-than-textual representations of sonic qualities; and soundscape studies, which encompass a wide range of methods, including field recording, sound mapping and sound walks. (Gallagher and Prior, 2014, p. 272)

INTRODUCTION

Gallagher and Prior highlight two modes of researching the sonic, the first which has been dominent is the use of a variety of methods that, whilst focusing upon sound – use methods that other disciplines also use, such as qualitative interviewing, the use of historical documents and the like. The second research mode is one where sound is treated as 'sound' rather than being translated into another medium, such as text. This does not mean that 'text' is not used, merely that it is subordinated to 'sound' as in *soundwalks* and *sound mapping*. This chapter, written by a sociologist, will focus primarily upon research that appears to have significantly developed our understanding of the role of sound in society. There are differing arguments as to how we 'should' study sound from sociologists, anthropologists and historians who approach the subject from their own disciplinary interests and methodologies. Some researchers wish to understand or create an urban aesthetic of sound, for example, and these writers tend to favor distinct sonic methodologies that will be discussed toward the end of this chapter (LaBelle, 2006). In response to the development of sound studies as a discipline in its own right and as a subject that crosses over into many other disciplines it is pertinent to ask the following questions:

1. What, if any, are the special characteristics of sound?
2. Given the sensory nature of sound, what relationship exists between the sonic and the other senses – what is the role of sound in the more general development of what is referred to as 'sensory studies'?

3   Related to the above two points and in recognition that what counts as 'data' – sonic or otherwise – is inflected with a set of theoretical concerns. The Gallagher and Prior quote with which this chapter begins highlights what has become a pressing issue in Sound Studies – to what extent should our methods intrinsically involve sound as sound rather than the translation of the sonic into another medium, the medium with which you are reading this chapter at present – script?

BRIEF HISTORICAL CONTEXTUALIZATION OF THE RISE OF SOUND STUDIES

The last fifteen years has seen the rapid development of the field of Sound Studies. Sound is increasingly referred to in the works of historians, literary critics, sociologists, anthropologists, geographers, musicologists and media scholars. The study of sound is inherently interdisciplinary, undertaken both by those who specialize in sound and by others who wish to include a sonic element in their research. The focus upon sound is partly the result of a reevaluation of cultural sensory experience, coupled with a move away from an unreflectively visually based epistemology of experience that has dominated academic discourse in the social sciences, arts and humanities until recently (Howes, 2003). This 'sensory turn' in the arts, humanities and social sciences was itself a consequence of an increased concern with 'embodiment' as a focus for research in the 1980s, which had attempted to overcome the traditional mind–body dualism inherent in Western thought (Csordas, 1990). The sensory turn in research furthered this theoretical project by investigating 'the sensuous interrelationship of body-mind-environment' (Howes, 2005, p. 7). Throughout the following pages we will discover just how researchers have integrated this contextualization of sound in particular and the senses more generally into their understanding of cultural experience.

We have, over the previous few years, seen a series of books published retracing the complex and often divisive histories of sounds (Cockayne, 2007; Birdsall, 2012; Picker, 2003; Rath, 2003; Smith, 2001); historical and philosophical accounts of sound (Erlmann, 2011; Grimshaw and Garner, 2015; Schwartz, 2011); the changing character and nature of the voice (Connor, 2000; Rée, 1999); new analyses of the nature of architectural and urban sounds (Bijsterveld, 2016; Blesser and Salter, 2007; Thompson, 2002); the history of technological sound (Sterne, 2003; Suisman and Strasser, 2009) as well as a plethora of work on sonically based technologies (Bull, 2000, 2007; Goggin, 2006; Henriques, 2011). In addition to this there has been work highlighting the violence of sound (Johnson and Cloonan, 2009; Daughtry, 2015; Gilman, 2016; Pieslak, 2009) and religious sounds (Hirschkind, 2006; Pieslak, 2015).

THREE QUESTIONS

Question 1: What, if any, are the Special Characteristics of Sound?

> Sound is intrinsically and unignorably relational: it emanates, propagates, communicates, vibrates and agitates; it leaves a body and enters others; it binds and unbinds, harmonizes and traumatizes; it sends the body moving, the mind dreaming, the air oscillating. (LaBelle, 2010, p. 468)

> Studying cultures of sound implies an interest in the oft taken-for-granted ways in which people give meaning to the sounds they are surrounded with, in how they routinely act upon and use those sounds, and in how that has changed over time. But how can we get access to what is taken for granted in past and contemporary society? (Bijsterveld, 2016, p. 100)

The distinctiveness of sound tends to lie in its *temporal* and spatial nature. Historically, sound is defined by its specificity and immediacy – this siren that I now hear in the street outside – and by its transitoriness – the person shouting in the street outside my office has now walked away. The history of sonic experience has until the *age of mechanical reproduction* been one of the irretrievable disappearance of sounds. We can, for example, view a Michelangelo sculpture in Florence but we cannot hear the voice of Michelangelo although we can read his diaries.

With the advent of recording technologies such as the phonograph in the late nineteenth century up until the advent of digital technologies in the twenty-first century, sounds can now be increasingly captured for research purposes. Whilst we cannot hear the voice of Michelangelo we can now hear the voices of the famous and infamous; from the voices of the dead to the sounds of air-raid sirens in London in 1942. We can listen to the recorded music of Caruso and David Bowie as well as the voices of ordinary people embedded in radio programs from the 1920s onwards. The ability to store sonic data has expanded our ability to fix the sounds of the past and present within our research methodologies. However, this ability to abstract out the sonic from a broader sensory range of experience poses its own problems. These are problems of:

- Specificity
- Cultural contextualization
- Meaning

These three concerns will be highlighted throughout the following pages and are apparent in the following work by Brady (1999). The ability to fix, transpose and transport sound arose with the phonograph in the late nineteenth century, with its ability to document sound events. Erika Brady (1999) estimated that fourteen thousand cylinder recordings of North American Native Americans were made by ethnologists between 1890 and 1935 – these cylinders are now deposited in a wide range of museums and university departments, symbolizing the growing cultural value attached to collecting history. What could be better than archiving the dying sounds of a culture for future reference and a clearer understanding of lost sonic worlds? This desire to record had, she argues, positivist motivations – the recordings as such were interpreted as being objectively true – an accurate representation of that which was being recorded. Brady argues that these cylinders were seen, ironically given the present methodological concerns mentioned above, as mechanical tools enabling the researcher to transcribe sonic material into written text. It is for this reason, she argues, that many researchers failed to mention how indeed their material was gathered. The process of recording was frequently not mentioned by ethnographers of the time and as such assumed an air of invisibility. Early critics of the use of the phonograph by ethnographers mentioned the transformation and impoverishment of the ethnographic encounter in which the ethnographer relied upon the recoding machine to do all of the work. Importantly, in its *'fetishization'* of the sonic as representing what we would now refer to as a *'false objectivity'*, the recording was blind to all forms of nonverbal contextualization embedded in and acting beyond the recorded sound – the physicality of the culture in its ritualistic and material form. Hidden from view was the asymmetrical power relations embodied in the use of the ethnographic encounter between the researcher and the Native American. This example demonstrates the way in which theoretical concerns are bound to methodological ones and to the dangers of extracting the sonic from an understanding of embodiment more generally and the cultural specificities within which sonic practices are enacted and understood.

The twentieth century has seen a dramatic change in the sonic environment through the development of a range of acoustic technologies such as telephones, microphones, loudspeakers, phonographs, radios, tape recorders, compact discs, cellular phones, MP3 players, digital voice mail and talking computers that have transformed what it means to study and understand sonic experience.

Question 2: Sound and its Relation to the Other Senses

> The objects we perceive in our surroundings – cities, villages, fields and woods – bear the mark of having been worked upon by man. It is not only in clothing and appearance, in outward form and emotional make up that men are the products of history. Even the way they see and hear is inseparable from the social life process, as it has evolved over the millennia. The facts, which our senses present to us, are socially pre-formed in two ways: through the historical character of the object perceived and through the historical character of the perceiving organ. (Horkheimer, 1972, p. 200)

> Every sense delivers contributions characteristic of its individual nature to the construction of sociated existence; peculiarities of the social relationship correspond to the nuancing of its impressions; the prevalence of one or other of the senses in the contact of individuals often provides this contact with a sociological nuance that could otherwise not be produced. (Simmel, 1997, p. 78)

Sound Studies is part of a wider research perspective that has prioritized the importance of the senses in understanding the nature of the social world that we live in. Kathleen Geurts has articulated this concern as follows:

> How one becomes socialized toward the meaning of sights, sounds, smell, tastes and so forth, represents a critical aspect of how one acquires a mode of being-in the world, or an 'individual system of experiencing and organizing the world'. (Geurts, 2002, p. 235)

How this sensory system is organized becomes a function of cultural, social, political and technological change in society. Walter Benjamin noted the significance of the technological in its widest sense in the 1930s when he argued that technologies had 'subjected the human sensorium to a complex kind of training' (Benjamin, 2002, p. 104). This for Benjamin extended from the complex type of sensory training involved in traversing the city with its traffic lights, sirens and automobiles to the watching of films, which magnified, speeded up and slowed down the visual to produce what he called the 'optical unconscious'.

Within the sensory, sound now has become a central concern for scholars and researchers. Kelman argues that 'scholars of sound are interested in understanding how sound circulates and how it contributes to the ways in which we understand the world around us' (Kelman, 2010, p. 215).

Theodor Adorno in fleshing out the cultural nature of sensory experience that Max Horkheimer so eloquently described above, points to both the particularity of experience and its cultural grounding. Adorno is describing the seemingly 'natural' sounds of rain as it falls on the roof above him:

> We can tell whether we are happy by the sound of the wind. It warns the unhappy man of the fragility of his house, hounding him from shallow sleep and violent dreams. To the happy man it is the song of his protectedness: its furious howling concedes that it has power over him no longer. (Adorno, 1974, p. 49)

Adorno wrote these words whilst living in exile in Hollywood, having escaped from Nazi Germany before World War II. Adorno's response to the sounds of rain is a lament from one who experienced the fragility of his refugee home. The sound of the wind is the variable upon which Adorno's cultural specificity is written. Sensory experience is multi-faceted, rich and often contradictory. The Greek anthropologist Seremetakis (1994) describes in detail the tasting of a peach in her homeland, noting that the taste and smell of the peach differed from those peaches that she had eaten in her youth before the advent of commercial farming in Greece. The experience might well be an exercise in sensory nostalgia but also might represent a critique of the homogenization of taste in a fully commodified consumer culture. Sensory experience comes to us doubly filtered as Horkheimer argued – they are not raw data. Returning troops from Iraq often described staying away from firework displays both in America and the UK, frequently feeling sick with fear at hearing the explosions (Daughtry, 2015) just as sudden sounds would affect those troops who in World War I had suffered from shell-shock (Leese, 2014).

Equally, the sounds of police sirens in any industrial city might evoke feelings of security, salvation or fear, depending upon who you are, your social class, gender or ethnicity. Increasingly, our sensory environment is a mediated one as we stare and listen to our television, computer and smartphone screens. Our media emphasize the visual, the auditory and increasingly the tactile, whilst denying the senses of smell and taste.

Question 3: Sonic Methods – Sonic Data

> It is inadequate to rely solely on personal experience for understanding how people everywhere perceive the world. While humans share the same basic sensory capacities, these are developed and understood in different ways. (Howes and Classen, 2014, p. 9)

> We need to stress the preeminent importance of contextualizing the sounds that museum visitors hear. Rather than simply feeding sounds to ears, we need to help visitors understand the context in which those sounds were produced, and how their reproduction can tell us not only about the nature of the past, but also about our own intellectual preferences and prejudices. (Smith in Morat, 2014, p. 20)

The object of research and the questions that the researcher wishes to ask and explore determine the methods that they will choose. Beyond that, what counts, as 'data' to be used is partially a function of the disciplinary adherence of the researcher. Sounds, as we have noted, do not speak for themselves. Sounds 'have meanings that can only be fully understood within their particular cultural context' (Howes and Classen, 2014, p. 2). The relationship between the specificity of sonic experience and its more general patterns and cultural context remain central to research at least in the social sciences. Sound Studies is a broad church – a sociologist like myself prefers to study generalized patterns and meanings that may well be embedded in specific forms of experience. Later in this chapter I will discuss my ethnographic study of Walkman users to demonstrate the changing role of the social embedded in the sonic meanings constructed by Walkman users as they move through their everyday life. However, many sound artists prefer to give prominence to the way in which sound itself mediates cultural experience aesthetically and otherwise. These researchers might use sound walks, sonic exhibitions and personal recollection and experiments to discuss the way in which a variety of sounds are interpreted – whether that be experiencing and remembering the sounds of Hanoi (Osterjo and Thuy, 2016), exploring the sounds of aircraft as they fly over a farm on the edge of Tokyo airport and so on (Carlyle and Cox, 2012).

RESEARCH AND SONIC DATA

Historical Sonic Data

The historical exploration of sound is often referred to as a form of sonic archeology, yet this sonic history, as we will see, might equally span medieval European culture, nineteenth-century French culture, an investigation of the soundscapes of Nazi Germany between 1933 and 1945, to an understanding of the role of radio and the recording industry in the development of pop cultures in Western culture.

Given that the sounds of the distant past cannot literally be heard, then it might strike the reader as surprising that historians using traditional methodologies have undertaken some of the most impressive sonic research, which includes the use of a wide variety of written records both official and literary. Official historical documents are frequently written by the powerful and literate who define the world according to their own interests, prejudices and vision. For example, sensitivity to the supposedly oppressive nature of urban sounds is often class and culturally based. Cultures with strong notions of 'private space', understood as a form of entitlement, are more prone to dislike or discriminate against the noise of others. Historically, the production of 'noise' was frequently perceived as uncivilized within a bourgeois Western and, specifically, Northern European ethic in which silence was considered 'golden'. Creating an auditory space for oneself and one's family was increasingly a prerogative and strategy of elites who felt that noise was no respecter of private urban space. It might be argued that sonically based historical accounts might fall prey to this fundamental limitation in documentary evidence. Yet historians of sound have found ways to listen more deeply to those historical sources. Historians such as John Picker have used a variety of written records to demonstrate this class sensitivity toward 'noise'. From historical documentation we find that Charles Dickens, chronicler of the nineteenth-century industrial city, promoted government legislation to rid London of street musicians, for example.

> There is no protection, we say, for the ear is the most hapless faculty we have. It is at once the weakest and the most wonderful, the most ethereal and most persecuted of the senses ... A sense that, deliberately constituted, we subject day and night to torture which is very nearly the equivalent to cutting off a malefactor's eyelids and then crucifying him with his face to the sun. (*The Times* leader 1856, quoted in Picker, 2009, p. 66)

Social Class Sensitivity Toward Noise in Nineteenth-Century London

The use of historical documentation far preceded the industrial revolution, however. It is possible to listen in to much earlier forms of social life. The following account derives from official inquisitional records from the fourteenth century and represents a wonderful account of the sonic worlds of a distant past written by a scholar who would not consider himself to be a scholar of sound but nevertheless investigates the lives of a whole community in order to better understand their collective lifeworld.

Emmanuel Le Roy Ladurie, Montaillou. Cathars and the Catholics in a French Village 1294–1324

The historian La Roy Ladurie focused upon Montaillou, a fourteenth-century French village, which had been accused by the church of following the Cathar heresy whose principal belief was that the whole world was in a fallen state and hence evil, thus all was possible. The Cathar heresy was essentially an amoral belief system. The village was managed by village 'goodmen' who supplanted the traditional role of the Catholic clergy in the village and surrounding area. The Cathars were subject to a brutal inquisition by the Catholic Church in its effort to reassert its ecclesiastical authority in the area. La Roy Ladurie drew a vivid account of the everyday life of the village from the testimony of the villagers themselves – as if we, the reader, are eavesdropping on the accounts of village life in Montaillou. We hear the villagers give accounts of their marriages, loves, affairs; their children, their work and social and cultural relations as well as their notions of fate, magic and salvation – all verbatim:

> The basis for the story of Montaillou is the Inquisition Register of bishop Jacques Fournier ... What in the final analysis should we make of the resister's account of Montaillou ... I will limit myself to invoking the term 'tape recorder' – for such is the impression created by the extraordinary quality of the stenographers whom Fournier employed in his episcopal seat at Pamiers to write down the words of the villagers who appeared before him .... The register of Jacques Fournier, Bishop of Pamiers in Ariege in the Compte de Foix from 1318 to 1325, is of such exceptional interest ... he supervised a rigorous Inquisition in his diocese and, what is more important, saw to it that the depositions made to the Inquisition courts were meticulously recorded. In the process of revealing their position

on official Catholicism, the peasants examined by Fournier's inquisition, many from the village of Montaillou, have given an extraordinarily detailed and vivid picture of their everyday life. (La Roy Ladurie, 2005, p. xv)

Alain Corbin. Village Bells. Sound and Meaning in the Nineteenth-Century French Countryside

We see from the above account how text can illuminate the cultures of sound. Yet it is to the singular study of historical sound through the object of the 'village bell' that I now turn in order to discuss Alain Corbin's groundbreaking sonic text. Corbin based his account on a meticulously researched investigation of French local parish records from the nineteenth century. He used these accounts to construct an analysis of the cultural, and often contradictory, significance of the village bell.

> Bells provided a sort of auditory certification, transmitted information about the major events of private life, and solemnized rites of passage. When natural disaster threatened, when bandits or enemies loomed, when a fire took hold, only the tocsin could sound the alarm. Possessing a peal of bells was a prerequisite of modernity in a society increasingly subject to haste but as yet without any other means of transmitting information instantaneously ... this book is thus devoted to an element in the history of the auditory landscape. However, this history constitutes a vast field of research, the surface of which has barely been scratched. The time has come to tackle it and thus address a mass of primary materials that have scarcely been touched. These materials affect reality to a pronounced degree because they were very often constructed in haste, because they are instantaneous in their effects and because they reconstitute the flavor of territories. A history of representations of space and of the social imagination can no longer afford to neglect materials pertaining to auditory perception. (Corbin, 1998, pp. xi–xii)

Corbin charted the changing meaning of the village bell throughout the nineteenth century, focusing both on the integrative cultural moments and those that increasingly represented conflicting views of noise, time and regulation. As rural France became increasingly secularized, a traditional sonically unified system of management was replaced by a more urban, secular viewpoint that perceived bells as nuisance to be banned. The documentation that underpinned Corbin's work does not, however, furnish the reader with a total sonic account:

> We cannot be certain how frequently and how loudly the bells were rung, nor can we be sure about the number of peals, the complexity of codes, or the diversity of episcopal regulations ... the objective measurement of the frequency, form, and intensity of auditory messages does not allow us to reconstitute their impact upon the individual who heard them. The reception of such messages is determined at once by the texture of the sensory environment, the modes of attention brought to bear on the environment, and the procedures of decipherment. (Corbin, 1998, p. 4)

Carolyn Birdsall. Nazi Soundscapes. Sound, Technology and Urban Space in Germany, 1933–1945

We now move to a more recent historical analysis of sound in Nazi Germany that was able to gather sonic and documentary evidence from living participants and radio archives. Birdsall interviewed a small group of people who were either children or young adults during the period between 1933 and 1945 in Germany, in order to understand their sonic memories. She referred to these individuals as EARWITNESSES. Birdsall then followed up these personal testimonies with radio and archive material from the period. Her aim was to highlight the varied role of sound in the everyday life of German citizens at the time – both private and public:

> Despite their pervasiveness in many descriptions, these intense sound events remained ephemeral. The inability of these sounds to be captured by photography led to their absence in what has been termed the 'visual iconography' of warfare ... the overwhelming sensory experience of civilians has left few material traces, let alone recordings ...

My initial focus is thus primarily on how sound participated in expanding social practices of control during National Socialism. (Birdsall, 2012, p. 119)

CONTEMPORARY SONIC RESEARCH

Researching Walkman and iPod Use

My own work (Bull, 2000, 2007, 2013), as a sociologist, uses rather traditional research methodologies – qualitative interviews, diaries and questionnaires, although in the new edition of *The Auditory Culture Reader* (2016), which I have edited with Les Back (Bull and Back, 2016), we have included a supplementary website consisting of sonic material to be listened to whilst reading the text.

When I started out researching how 'Walkmans' were used in the 1990s there was a singular lack of empirical research into their use at that time. Given the difficulty of interviewing users whilst they are listening to music through headphones – which in effect signify 'leave me alone!' – I decided to employ a series of snowball samples of users. Each user was encouraged to bring along their Walkman and we would proceed with what they had listened to that day. For my subsequent iPod volume I wanted to look more closely at global meanings of use – so I employed a qualitative questionnaire to be filled out online. This resulted in over one thousand users globally filling out the questionnaire as against 80 interviews conducted for the Walkman book. I much preferred the qualitative interviews as I could respond directly to the interviewee's responses and whilst with the online questionnaires we could to and fro over the Internet, I found it more difficult to get a comprehensive sense of each user.

At the time of researching *Sounding Out the City* there was no comprehensive account of the auditory nature of everyday experience. Indeed, I had been brought up intellectually within this tradition. By focusing upon the auditory and the technologized nature of the everyday experience of personal stereo users, I attempted to explain their attempts at creating manageable sites of habitation and charted the multifaceted ways in which their experience was transformed and constructed through habitual use of a sonic technology – the Walkman. Through a close analysis of the interview material I demonstrated the ways in which personal stereos became a critical tool for users in their management of space and time, in their construction of boundaries around the self, and as a site of fantasy and memory… Sound, the audible, was thus put back onto the cognitive map of urban experience; sound as opposed to vision became the site for the critical investigation of urban life. The research proposed a reevaluation of the significance of the auditory in everyday experience, together with a re-assessment of the role and relation of the senses within urban experience. It also demonstrated how qualitative sonic empirical material (case studies/thick description) could be used to formulate new theoretical frameworks and explanations of urban behavior. Examples of the rich sonic descriptions given by users are given below:

> I think it creates a sense of kind of aura. Sort of like. Even though it's directly in your ears you feel like it's all around your head because you're coming. Because you're really aware it's just you. Only you can hear it. I'm really aware of my personal space. My own space anyway … I find it quite weird watching things that you normally associate certain sounds with. Like the sounds of walking up and down the stairs or tubes coming in and out. All those things that you hear, like when you've got a Walkman on you don't hear any of those. You've got your own soundtrack. You see them and it looks like they're moving differently because you've got a rhythm in your head. The way that they walk, they flow past you more. (Bull, 1999, p. 22)

> I use it on the beach. I feel that I'd be listening to my music. I have the sea, I have the sand. I have the warmth but I don't have all the crap around me. I can eliminate that and I can get much more out of what the ocean has to offer me. I can enjoy. I feel

that listening to my music, I can really pull those sun's rays. Not being disturbed by screaming kids and all that shouting which is not why I went there. I have my harmony with the sea and the sun ... The plane journey, flying out and back and you listen to different music, but it just helps me to still my mind and to center myself and I feel that by taking this tape with me I'm carrying that all day and I feel that I'm able to take more from the day and give more to the day. Whether that's right or wrong I don't know but that's how I feel. (Bull, 1999, pp. 36–7)

Most of the music I chose was very evocative of something and I associated it with a particular part of my journey. It became a way of describing that this part of the journey is bearable. You can get through this part. I remember there was a big escalator change at Green Park and I thought 'Right! If I don't have that particular music for that, then I'll fast forward it to get to that and then I can go up.' Like that it made it easier not to let work encroach onto non-work time. It was a way of not allowing thoughts like I've got that deadline and a meeting with so and so. Because the journey to work was so uniform and intrusive. (Bull, 1999, p. 63)

It's like looking through a one-way mirror. I'm looking at them but they can't see me. (Bull, 1999, p. 77)

These examples helped in the formulation and construction of an auditory epistemology of everyday urban life constructed around the concept of control: cognitively, interpersonally and aesthetically (control over one's moods, other people and the spaces of the city moved through). *Sound Moves, iPod Culture and Urban Experience* (Bull, 2007) followed this research agenda, updating it for the digital era – a world in which the user, through miniaturization, could hold their whole digital world in their hand as one user commented:

I now listen to music any time I can. Walking to and from work, at work, on vacation, on a train or airplane, even at home when I don't want to disturb my partner. I have any song I want to listen to at my fingertips at any particular moment. That amazes me. It truly is my own personal jukebox, and puts the soundtrack to my life in my pocket and at my fingertips. (Bull, 2007, p. 74)

More recently I have interviewed users of smartphones to investigate the use of mobile technologies that engage users audio-visually. The affordances created through smartphone use have complicated and extended the auditory and audio-visual strategies encompassed by traditional iPod use. Georgia, a twenty-two year old wakes up to her alarm on her smartphone; she often sleeps through the alarm, as she's grown accustomed to it. She wakes up and answers two text messages, gets up and goes for a shower, bringing her phone along to choose the same playlist as not only are the songs some of her favorites but also 'good morning songs like "Sunday Morning" by the Velvet Underground and Nico is very mellow and happy, and "People Have the Power" by Patti Smith is very energetic and inspiring leaving me ready for the day ahead' (Bull, 2013, p. 12). She takes her phone downstairs still listening to music and makes breakfast whilst reading the paper. She checks the train times on her phone app and goes out where she meets her friend Frankie on the train to work:

despite being sat next to my friend who I spent most of the morning arranging to meet, now I am with her I am once again on my phone, preferring to play a game than make conversation. She is also playing a game, which means that neither of us make any effort to communicate. (Bull, 2013, p. 14)

Georgia's response to the urban is similar to traditional mobile phone and iPod users. The technology merely allows her to engage in a wider range of mediating activities: 'Whenever I'm walking on my own, even for a short amount of time – like walking from my home to the bus stop – I have to either call someone on the phone or listen to my music. I hate being alone' (Georgia).

Equally, Michelle describes her three-hour train journey from London to Norwich to visit her boyfriend, 'I check my phone and make sure it is fully charged, it is necessary for me to have my phone fully charged so it will be able to handle the text messages, phone calls, the Internet and play music through my music playlist to last me the whole journey' (Bull, 2013, p. 16). Whilst waiting for the train Michelle waits at the station.

> I go on my phone to keep myself busy. When I'm bored and out in public I look to my phone in order to cope with the boredom. I text, call, go on Facebook and whatever. Time goes quicker when I am doing something, and not just waiting around doing nothing. (Bull, 2013, p. 16)

Urban users of these technologies are simultaneously transported to the global spaces of culture and yet are also embedded in the locations that they traverse – guided by their mobile multi-sensory technologies.

MIXING TRADITIONAL METHODS WITH INNOVATIVE METHODS

Waldock (2016) in this innovative study demonstrates how a researcher can capture the way in which an urban sonic environment changes over time. In order to do so Waldock studied an inner-city redevelopment scheme in Liverpool, called the 'Pathfinder Scheme', initiated by the then Labour government in the UK. The aim of the scheme was to demolish the old housing stock lived in primarily by working-class inhabitants and replace it with 'homes that meet the needs of modern living' (Waldock, 2016, p. 152). Many of the local residents were unwilling to move, especially as they were not to be rehoused in the same locale, but rather the area was meant to act as a magnate for the middle classes to return to the city center. The scheme saw more and more residents evicted and their homes boarded up. Waldock wished to study the sonic dimensions of this urban change, which involved a good deal of social conflict between the working-class residents who were being forcibly moved and council officials.

> My desire to understand these changes sonically and work with the residents rather than become another dominating power led me to create a community centric, Trinitarian methodology. The methodology aimed not only to capture the sounds of the area, but also people's connection to the sounds. I incorporated the roles of field recording/composer with that of anthropologist/ethnographer, as others have done before me, to utilize soundscape composition as a tool to encapsulate, analyze and represent change. The difference in my methodology is that I saw residents and myself in three roles, artist, activist and academic. (Waldock, 2016, p. 152)

Waldock correctly understood that people's experience of sounds, both domestic and public, differed from one person to the next. The residents were given crash courses in lisening and how to use their sound recording equipment:

> As artists, they recorded and controlled their own soundscape compositions over a period ranging from six to nine months. As academics they could produce a critical commentary on their work. In order to produce sound catalogues, sound montages or compositions, each resident had the opportunity to listen to their own recordings and edit their work. The editing process acted as a critical listening period, allowing them to reflect upon their connection to the sound, both emotional and aesthetic. (Waldock, 2016, p. 155)

One of the residents who recorded her sounds was moved by the council during the project:

> When we played the recording of her front door closing and locking, she commented on how familiar and safe the sound was, how the door of her new home didn't have the same latch and she was anxious because she couldn't always tell if it was locked. She also recorded the police helicopter circling over neighboring empty homes, and commented on the familiarity and reassurance of knowing that the police were there. (Waldock, 2016, p. 158)

METHODS THAT STRESS SOUND AND VOICE

Helen Wilson is a social geographer, so her take on the importance of soundwalks comes from a largely social science perspective, rather than an arts-based perspective. Wilson (2016) argues that it has become important for geographers to listen to the spaces and places that they study. We have seen this with the Waldock example given above.

A geographical interest in soundwalks has emerged out of collaborative relations between geographers and artists, where embodied and experimental accounts of space and landscape have been prioritized. A distinction might be made between a 'listening walk' – as a walk where there is a concentration on listening – and soundwalk, where there is some form of score. However, the distinction has been largely blurred by the growing practice of guided walks, whereby participants are guided around a pre-planned route that has been designed to encourage 'active listening', often through a combination of narration and sonic recomposition. An interest in promoting active listening can be seen in artistic explorations of urban space, which have encouraged walkers and participants to reflect anew on otherwise mundane spaces. (Wilson, 2016, pp. 165–6)

Researchers using soundwalks, for example, might encourage walkers to reflect on what they hear, or narrate their memories if they have any as they walk through a specific site. In this instance the sonic nature of the experience takes precedence over the textual – the writing of spaces. So minute sonic experiences, such as the everyday mundane sounds of the environment that might have special or personal meaning for the walker are articulated in their own right: 'When taken together, the recordings of soundscapes, people and oral narratives demonstrate what is to be gained from phonographic research' (Wilson, 2016, p. 168).

Karis Petty's (2016) work is based around an investigation as to how the visually impaired experience the countryside and is an excellent example as to how the use of a combination of traditional and innovative methods enables us to understand more fully how sound contributes to the make up of everyday experience. It also teaches us not to abstract the sonic from the other senses. Petty, a trained accompanist for the blind, looked at specific geographical locales and walks that her sample was both comfortable with and knowledgeable about. She accompanied them on all of their walks both individually and in groups:

My principal methodology was to walk one-to-one as their sites companion through changing weathers, seasons and environments of the park over two years. During these walks we collaboratively experimented with techniques to investigate and represent sensory experience, including writing descriptive walk diaries, filming, inclusive photography, auto-ethnography, conversational interviews and reflection. We used a field recorder to record the sound of these walks. When we listened back to these together in the interviews, it caught our attention that these recordings – this technological ear – did not capture the sounds, as we had perceived them in the woodlands. The recordings captured many sounds we had heard, such as the vibrant song of birds or playful cries of children, but did not capture other sounds, such as those heard in the practice of 'echolocation'. It was on a bright spring morning when Elen announced, 'blind people need to teach sighted people how to listen', that I started to consider: what can my companions hear? What are they listening to? But also, how are they listening? (Petty, 2016, p. 174)

Petty's acute observation leads her to explore the way in which the partially sighted feel sound through a process of 'echolocation'. She uses John Hull's observation that for him, 'perception is no longer specialized or located in a specific part of the body, but the whole body becomes an organ of perception. When I realized this, I no longer thought of myself as being blind, but a whole body seer…' (in Petty, 2016, p. 181).

CONCLUSION

Petty's work, as does the other examples referred to in this chapter, demonstrates that even for those interested in undertaking sonic research that it is nevertheless necessary for the researchers to 'learn how to listen' as one path toward understanding the complex nature of the sonic, and more importantly the nature of embodied knowledge itself. It also brings us back full circle to the contention mapped out at the beginning of this chapter, that sound studies represents an embodiment of the sensory turn in the academy – one which investigates the sensorial arrangement of the body situated historically, socially and spatially.

FURTHER READING

Bull, Michael and Black, Les (eds.) (2016) *The Auditory Culture Reader*. London: Bloomsbury Press.

Gilman, Lisa (2016) *My Music, My War. The Listening Habits of U.S. Troops in Iraq and Afghanistan*. Middletown: Wesleyan University Press.

Howes, David and Classen, Constance (2014) *Ways of Sensing. Understanding the Senses in Society*. London: Routledge.

Pinch, Trevor and Bisterveld, Karin (eds.) (2012) *The Oxford Handbook of Sound Studies*. Oxford: Oxford University Press.

Sterne, Jonathan (ed.) (2012) *The Sound Studies Reader*. Oxford: Routledge.

For those interested in the way in which soundwalks, sound mapping and field recording might be used in research, the following issue of the *Journal of Sonic Studies 12 (2016) – Encounters With Southeast Asia Through Sound* contains a range of articles that use these methods with great imagination. The first issue of *Sound Studies. An Interdisciplinary Journal* (2016) has a selection of articles that discuss the full range of interdisciplinary issues surrounding Sound Studies.

REFERENCES

Adorno, Theodor (1974) *Minima Moralia: Reflections on a Damaged Life*. London: New Left Books.

Benjamin, Walter (2002) *Selected Writings 1935–1938*. Cambridge: Harvard University Press.

Bijsterveld, Karin (2016) 'Ethnography and archival research', in Jens Pappenburg and Holger Schulze (eds.), *Sound as Popular Culture. A Research Companion*. Cambridge, MA: MIT Press, pp. 99–110.

Birdsall, Carolyn (2012) *Nazi Soundscapes. Sound, Technology and Urban Space in Germany, 1933–1945*. Amsterdam: Amsterdam University Press.

Blesser, Barry and Salter, Linda-Ruth (2007) *Spaces Speak, are you Listening? Experiencing Aural Architecture*. Cambridge, MA: MIT Press.

Brady, Erika (1999) *A Spiral Way. How the Phonograph Changed Ethnography*. Jackson, MS: University Press of Mississippi.

Bull, Michael (2000) *Sounding Out the City. Personal Stereos and the Management of Everyday Life*. Oxford: Berg.

Bull, Michael (2007) *Sound Moves, iPod Culture and Urban Experience*. London: Routledge.

Bull, Michael (2013) 'Sound mix: The framing of multi-sensory connections in urban culture', *Sound Effects*, 3(3): 26–45.

Bull, Michael and Back, Les (eds.) (2016) *The Auditory Culture Reader* (2nd edn). London: Bloomsbury Press.

Carlyle, Angus and Cox, Rupert (2012) *Air Pressure*. London: Wellcome Trust.

Cockayne, Emily (2007) *Hubbub. Filth, Noise and Stench in Britain*. New Haven, CT: Yale University Press.

Connor, Steven (2000) *Dumbstruck. A Cultural History of Ventriloquism*. Oxford: Oxford University Press.

Corbin, Alain (1998) *Village Bells. Sound and Meaning in the Nineteenth Century French Countryside*. New York: Columbia University Press.

Csordas, Thomas J. (1990) 'Embodiment as a paradigm for anthropology', *Ethos*, 18(1): 5–47.

Daughtry, Martin (2015) *Listening to War. Sound, Music, Trauma, and Survival in Wartime Iraq*. Oxford: Oxford University Press.

Erlmann, Veit (2011) *Reason and Resonance. A History of Modern Aurality*. Cambridge, MA: MIT Press.

Gallagher, Michael and Prior, Jonathan (2014) 'Sonic geographies: Exploring phonograph methods', *Human Geography*, 38(2): 267–84.

Geurts, Kathleen (2002) *Culture and the Senses: Bodily Ways of Knowing in an African Community*. Berkeley, CA: University of California Press.

Gilman, Lisa (2016) *My Music My War. The Listening Habits of U.S. Troops in Iraq and Afghanistan*. Connecticut: Wesleyan University Press.

Goggin, Gerard (2006) *Cellphone Culture. Mobile Technology in Everyday Life*. London: Routledge.

Grimshaw, Mark and Garner, Tom (2015) *Sonic Virtuality. Sound as Emergent Perception*. Oxford: Oxford University Press.

Henriques, Julian (2011) *Sonic Bodies. Reggae Sound Systems, Performance Techniques and Ways of Knowing*. New York: Continuum Press.

Hirschkind, Charles (2006) *The Ethical Soundscape. Cassette Sermons and Islamic Counterpublics*. New York: Columbia University Press.

Horkheimer, Max (1972) *Critical Theory, Collected Essays*. New York: Herder and Herder.

Howes, David (2003) *Sensual Relations. Engaging the Senses in Cultural and Social Theory*. Ann Arbor: University of Michigan Press.

Howes, David (ed.) (2005) *Empire of the Senses: The Sensual Culture Reader*. Oxford: Berg.

Howes, David and Classen, Constance (2014) *Ways of Sensing. Understanding the Senses in Society*. London: Routledge.

Johnson, Bruce and Cloonan, Martin (2009) *Dark Side of the Tune: Popular Music and Violence. Ashgate Popular and Folk Music Series*. Farnham: Ashgate.

Kelman, Ari Y. (2010) 'Rethinking the soundscape: A critical genealogy of a key term in sound studies', *The Senses and Society*, 5(2): 212–34.

LaBelle, Brandon (2006) *Background Noise. Perspectives on Sound Art*. New York: Continuum Press.

LaBelle, Brandon (2010) *Acoustic Territories. Sound Culture and Everyday Life*. New York: Continuum Press.

Ladurie, Le Roy (2005) *Montaillou. Cathars and Catholics in a French Village 1294–1324*. London: Folio Society.

Leese, Peter (2014) *Shell Shock. Traumatic Neurosis and the British Soldiers of the First World War*. Basingstoke: Palgrave Macmillan.

Morat, Daniel (2014) *Sounds of Modern History. Auditory Cultures in 19th and 20th Century Europe*. New York: Berghahn.

Osterjo, Stefan and Thuy, Nguyễn T. (2016) 'The sounds of Hanoi and the afterimage of the homeland', *Journal of Sonic Studies*, 12.

Petty, Karis (2016) 'Walking through the woodlands. Learning to listen with companions who have impaired vision', in Michael Bull and Les Back (eds.), *The Auditory Culture Reader*. London: Bloomsbury, pp. 173–83.

Picker, John (2003) *Victorian Soundscapes*. Oxford: Oxford University Press.

Pieslak, Jonathan (2009) *Sound Targets: American Soldiers and Music in the Iraq War*. Bloomington, IN: Indiana University Press.

Pieslak, Jonathan (2015) *Radicalism and Music. An Introduction to the Music Cultures of al-Qa'ida, Racist Skinheads, Christian Affiliated Radicals, and Eco-Animal Rights Militants*. Middletown: Wesleyan University Press.

Rath, Richard (2003) *How Early America Sounded*. New York: Cornell University Press.

Rée, Jonathan (1999) *I See A Voice: Language, Deafness and the Senses, A Philosophical Enquiry*. London: HarperCollins.

Schmidt, Leigh (2000) *Hearing Things. Religion, Illusion and the American Enlightenment*. Cambridge, MA: Harvard University Press.

Schwartz, Hillel (2011) *Making Noise. From Babel to the Big Bang and Beyond*. Cambridge, MA: MIT Press.

Seremetakis, Nadia (ed.) (1994) *The Senses Still. Perception and Memory as Material Culture in Modernity*. Chicago: University of Chicago Press.

Simmel, Georg (1997) *Simmel on Culture*. London: Sage.

Smith, Mark (2001) *Listening to Nineteenth-Century America*. Columbia: University of South Carolina Press.

Sterne, Jonathan (2003) *The Audible Past. Cultural Origins of Sound Reproduction*. Durham: Duke University Press.

Suisman, David and Strasser, Susan (eds.) (2009) *Sound in the Age of Mechanical Reproduction*. Philadelphia, PA: University of Pennsylvania Press.

Thompson, Emily (2002) *The Soundscape of Modernity. Architectural Acoustics and the Culture of Listening in America, 1900–1933*. Cambridge, MA: MIT Press.

Waldock, Jacqueline (2016) 'Hearing urban regeneration. Community composition as a tool for capturing change', in Michael Bull and Les Back (eds.), *The Auditory Culture Reader*. London: Bloomsbury Press, pp. 151–62.

Wilson, Helen (2016) 'Sonic geographies, sound walks and more-than-representational methods', in Michael Bull and Les Back (eds.), *The Auditory Culture Reader*. London: Bloomsbury Press, pp. 163–72.

PART IV

Digital and Internet Data

After more traditional approaches to data collection such as talking to and observing participants and their backgrounds, were the focus in the earlier part of the *Handbook* and complemented by approaches to material data (see Part III), Part IV turns to data collection from a different angle.

The six chapters in this part have the area of digital qualitative research and the study of internet forms of communication as the main focus. This area is maybe the most fascinating development not only for qualitative research, but here in particular. Fundamental questions of what data are in this context, and what they may be beyond, are raised as well as specific ethical concerns to be considered here. Therefore Part IV does not only comprise practical problems of how to do digital qualitative research, but also more general reflections. First, the idea of data in this realm is discussed in some detail (see Lindgren, Chapter 28, this volume), before epistemological questions connected to the concept of flow are unfolded (see Markham and Gammelby, Chapter 29, this volume). The particular challenges of ethics in digital research are taken up in the next chapter (see Tiidenberg, Chapter 30, this volume), before two areas of digital research practice are discussed as examples: Collecting data for analyzing blogs (see Weller et al., Chapter 31, this volume), and from Facebook (see Ditchfield and Meredith, Chapter 32, this volume). The final chapter in this Part provides a critical perspective on what data are in this realm of qualitative research (see Markham, Chapter 33, this volume).

Guideline questions as an orientation for writing chapters were the following: How did this kind of data become an issue for qualitative data collection? Which are theoretical and epistemological backgrounds of working with these data? What are specific challenges of working with these data? What is the best way to prepare and elaborate these data for analyzing them? What is the process – maybe step-by-step – in producing this kind of data? Which is a recent example of using this type of data in a qualitative study? Which are the limits and outrange of using this kind of data? What are new developments and perspectives in this context?

Reading the chapters in Part IV should help to answer questions like the following ones for a study and its method(s): What are the specific characteristics of this type of qualitative data? How does one plan data collection in qualitative research for this specific type of data? How should these data be prepared for analysis – what are the specific needs in transcribing or elaborating the data? What are the steps in applying the selected method for collecting this type of data? What characterizes good (and bad) example(s) of working with this type of data? What are the main stumbling blocks in collecting such data? What are criteria of good practice in working with this type of qualitative data? What are specific ethical issues in collecting this form of data?

In answering questions like the ones just mentioned, the chapters in this part are meant to contribute to developing sensitive ways of collecting empirical material in qualitative studies and thus to further develop the methodological toolkit for qualitative data collection.

The Concept of 'Data' in Digital Research

Simon Lindgren

The emergence and development of the Internet and social media has changed the parameters for social interaction. The transformation also changes how we think about research methods, and how we think about what constitutes data. Social and cultural research about the Internet and digital media is – due to its relative newness – a key area of methodological development. Our routine ways of going about research are rapidly transformed when one tries to capture the fast evolving patterns of sociality online and through digital tools. Research on digital media is – still some years into the 'information age' – giving rise to new methods, as well as new challenges and opportunities for analysing society and human behaviour (Sandvig and Hargittai, 2015).

Of course, with the Internet being such a big and ever-present part of today's societies, there is no one way of defining what 'digital research' is. It could be any type of study, using any kind of existing and established research method to say something about life in digital society. In the end, choosing a method for research comes down to the many choices that are made in relation to the aims of the study, the type of data to be analysed, personal preferences of the researcher, and so on. In this chapter, however, I will discuss a few important aspects and concepts that come to the fore when approaching the notion of data – and data collection – in relation to online settings. First, I will deal with the issue of so-called 'big data', and how the increased complexity of our social data environment more generally challenges the division between 'qualitative' and 'quantitative' altogether. The tensions between the availability of huge amounts of texts online, and the close reading ethos of qualitative research, is a topic that will be dealt with throughout the chapter. Furthermore, it is not an uncontroversial topic, in relation to a long-standing debate between 'interpretive' and 'positivist' methods (see Maxwell, Chapter 2, this volume). Some qualitative researchers will argue that no matter how 'big' data are available, close reading of smaller selections is always the way to go, while others will be more inspired by the opportunities and move in the direction of more mixed approaches.

In relation to that latter strategy I will, second, discuss what it means to conceive of one's approach as a methodological bricolage. Finally, I will underline the importance of maintaining a mindset of openness and experimentation when approaching the forms and potentials of digital data.

THE CHALLENGE OF BIG DATA

In recent years, following the breakthrough of social media, there has been extensive publicity and discussion around the idea and phenomenon of big data. This buzzword has been used to refer to not only the huge amounts of data about people's preferences and behaviours that are now generated and collected online, but also to an entire process of social transformation. The increased softwarisation of society, the prevalence of algorithms, as well as the rise of calculated publics, has made many hope that the gigantic datasets that are enabled will make the world a better place. In popular media, in data science, in relation to business and global development, in fields like policing and security, politics, healthcare, education and agriculture, big data has been seen as enabling completely new analyses and actions (Lupton, 2014). People from diverse fields – computer science, economics, mathematics, political science, bio-informatics, sociology – have been fascinated with the new possibilities and have started to hunt for data access, looking to get their hands on the huge masses of information generated in the digital society by and about people's interactions (boyd and Crawford, 2012).

Ever since the early days of computing, different forms of data have always been generated and stored. But the recent development towards so-called big data has been said to be revolutionary. Aside from the data that people generate on social platforms, more and more objects in our everyday lives – ranging from televisions and cars to refrigerators and lamps – have become digitised, 'smart', and attached to the Internet. This development is related to the advent of the so-called Internet of Things, a paradigm for research and development, drawing on 'the pervasive presence around us of a variety of things or objects – such as Radio-Frequency IDentification (RFID) tags, sensors, actuators, mobile phones, etc. – which, through unique addressing schemes, are able to interact with each other' (Atzori et al., 2010, p. 2787).

There are lots of opportunities today for monitoring people's social and natural environment. Anything, from phone call logs and web browsing history, to details on location and body movements through embedded GPS, compasses, gyroscopes and accelerometers, can be registered. Many apps, such as health trackers or apps for 'checking in' at different restaurants and cafés, can be downloaded for free. This is, in many cases, because the data generated by the users in turn is a product that can be sold by those who developed the app. This development is related to an entire debate about surveillance in digital society (Andrejevic, 2007), where some have argued that big data is big as in 'Big Brother'. Others have underlined how the new technologies also enable 'sousveillance' – citizen users 'watching from below'. Citizen technology researchers Steve Mann and Joseph Ferenbok write:

> New media has enabled a secondary gaze that moves along the power and veillance axis in different directions than surveillance practices. Sousveillance acts as a balancing force in a mediated society. Sousveillance does not exactly or necessarily counteract surveillance, but co-exists with surveillance within a social system that then provides a kind of feedback loop for different forms of looking – potentially creating a balancing force. (Mann and Ferenbok, 2013, p. 26)

So, there is a duality between threat and possibility here. Internet researchers Kate

Crawford and danah boyd note that with big data, 'as with all socio-technical phenomena, the currents of hope and fear often obscure the more nuanced and subtle shifts that are underway' (boyd and Crawford, 2012, p. 664).

Big data has been hailed as revolutionary, and as something that will make it possible not only to build more profitable business, but to make society better altogether. There is a growing industry for harvesting and selling social data for profit, and huge data storage centres are being built to deal with all of the data. Companies in the field of social media and digital information, such as Facebook, Microsoft, and Google, and online retailing companies like Amazon have been leading the way by developing ever new ways of harnessing user data for targeted and customised product development and advertising.

The big data collected in this manner has been argued to offer much greater precision and much more accurate predictive powers than previous forms of data. Merging data from multiple databases offers better precision and more predictive power. Furthermore, when combined with the current capacity of digital technology when it comes to harvesting, storage and analysis, this type of data is also said to offer opportunities, superior to anything ever seen before, to delve deeper into assessing human behaviours.

A COMPLEX DATA ENVIRONMENT

The emergence of big data is in fact just one out of many transformations within our general data environment, that affect opportunities as well as challenges when it comes to doing social research in digital society. For example, Kingsley Purdam, an expert in research methods, and his data scientist colleague Mark Elliot aptly point out that what is commonly talked about as 'big' data is in fact defined by several other things than just its large size: it registers things as they happen in real-time, it offers new possibilities to combine and compare datasets, and so on (Purdam and Elliot, 2015). However, even such characterisations are still not sufficient, say Purdam and Elliot. This is because those definitions still seem to assume that data is 'something we have', when in fact 'the reality and scale of the data transformation is that data is now something we are becoming immersed and embedded in'.

The notion of a 'data environment' underlines that people today are at the same time generators of, but also generated by, this new environment. 'Instead of people being researched', Purdam and Elliot say, 'they are the research' (Purdam and Elliot, 2015, p. 26). Their point, more concretely, is that new data types have emerged – and are constantly emerging – that demand new flexible approaches. Doing digital social research, therefore, often entails discovering and experimenting with challenges and possibilities of ever new types and combinations of information. In trying to describe the constantly changing data environment, Purdam and Elliot (2015, pp. 28–9), outline an eight-point typology of different data types based on how the data in question has been generated:

1 **Orthodox intentional data**: Data collected and used with the respondent's explicit agreement. All so-called orthodox social science data (e.g. survey, focus group or interview data, and data collected via observation) would come into this category. New orthodox methods continue to be developed.
2 **Participative intentional data**: In this category data are collected through some interactive process. This includes some new data forms, such as crowd-sourced data [...] and is a potential growth area.
3 **Consequential data**: Information that is collected as a necessary transaction that is secondary to some (other) interaction (e.g. administrative records, electronic health records, commercial transaction data and data from online game playing all come into this category).

4   **Self-published data**: Data deliberately self-recorded and published that can potentially be used for social science research either with or without explicit permission, given the information has been made public (e.g. long-form blogs, CVs and profiles).
5   **Social media data**: Data generated through some public, social process that can potentially be used for social science research, either with or without permission (e.g. micro-blogging platforms such as Twitter and Facebook, and, perhaps, online game data).
6   **Data traces**: Data that is 'left' (possibly unknowingly) through digital encounters, such as online search histories and purchasing, which can be used for social science research either by default use agreements or with explicit permission.
7   **Found data**: Data that is available in the public domain, such as observations of public spaces, which can include covert research methods.
8   **Synthetic data**: Where data has been simulated, imputed or synthesised. This can be derived from, or combined with, other data types.

The most important point here is that while social research traditionally relies on orthodox intentional data (1), such as surveys and interviews, digital society has enabled much more far reaching registration and collection of participative intentional data (2), consequential data (3), self-published data (4), and found data (7). These are types of data that indeed existed before digitally networked tools and platforms but which have been expanded and accentuated. The remaining types – social media data (5), data traces (6), and, at least chiefly, synthetic data (8) – are specific to digital society. Researchers that analyse this society therefore face dramatically altered conditions for the generation and gathering of data about social processes and interaction. As stated earlier, some researchers look for ways to apply the previously developed qualitative or quantitative perspectives in this new setting, while others – myself included – would argue that there is much to gain from trying to leave the 'qualitative' versus 'quantitative' paradigm behind.

TRANSGRESSING THE DIVISION BETWEEN QUALITATIVE AND QUANTITATIVE

The demarcation line, and sometimes open conflict, between qualitative and quantitative methodological approaches persists today as one of the Gordian knots of social science. In scholarly discourse, traces remain of a continuing *Methodenstreit* (method dispute) (Mennell, 1975). Scholars who prefer case-oriented methods will argue that in-depth understandings of a smaller set of observations is crucial for understanding the complexities of reality, and those who prefer variable-oriented approaches will argue that only the highly systematised analysis of larger numbers of cases will allow for making reliable statements about the true order of things.

But today it is becoming increasingly popular to employ combinations of qualitative and quantitative methods (see Hesse-Biber, Chapter 35, this volume, and Morse et al., Chapter 36, this volume), at the same time benefiting from their various strengths and balancing their respective weaknesses (Ragin, 2000; Brady and Collier, 2010). However, many mixed methods approaches rely on rigid definitions of the two respective paradigms to be combined, and suggest frameworks based on different forms of complementarity or 'triangulation' (Jick, 1979; Denzin, 2012; see Flick, Chapter 34, this volume).

Today, the massive amount of text content that is generated on social media and through other forms of computer-mediated communication has made some previously 'qualitative' scholars interested in how such data can be best used without succumbing to mere word-counting, and how the many technologies available for analysing it can be best harnessed. For example, when researching with digital data, we may find ourselves wanting to make sense of a corpus of blog posts, forum comments, YouTube video descriptions, Facebook postings, tweets, and so on.

In such cases, not only can automated methods for text mining complement qualitative approaches, but they can also be repurposed for more interpretive uses. Literary scholar Franco Moretti has coined the idea that text mining, as opposed to close reading of the text data, can be seen as distant reading. He goes so far as to say that there is an analytical point to not close reading texts, since this removes focus from the more general patterns that he thinks research should be focused on:

> The trouble with close reading ... is that it necessarily depends on an extremely small canon ... You invest so much in individual texts only if you think that very few of them really matter. Otherwise, it doesn't make sense ... What we really need is a little pact with the devil: we know how to read texts, now let's learn how not to read them. Distant reading: where distance ... is a condition of knowledge: it allows you to focus on units that are much smaller or much larger than the text: devices, themes, tropes – or genres and systems. And if, between the very small and the very large, the text itself disappears, well, it is one of those cases when one can justifiably say, Less is more. If we want to understand the system in its entirety, we must accept losing something. We always pay a price for theoretical knowledge: reality is infinitely rich; concepts are abstract, are poor. But it's precisely this 'poverty' that makes it possible to handle them, and therefore to know. (Moretti, 2013, pp. 48–9)

In relation to more interpretive approaches then, distant reading demands that the researcher is prepared to move away from conventional close reading in order to be able to grasp larger sets of data, and also to lose some degree of qualitative detail because of this. No matter if one would agree with Moretti's notion or not, we are now facing the challenge of large online texts that lay bare the fact that meaning-making happens in large numbers, as well as the fact that these large numbers in turn cannot be understood without in-depth interpretation. This inspires us to try to find entirely new approaches to qualitatively interpreting large masses of text. Texts are irrevocably embedded in arbitrary systems of language and culture from which their understanding must not be disconnected. While texts may be quantitatively deconstructed through approaches in content analysis (Krippendorff, 2004), physics (Bernhardsson et al., 2010) or computational linguistics, these methods will dissolve the data in ways that leave variable-oriented strategies as the only way to proceed with the analysis.

REVEALING THE MESSY DETAILS

In today's world, large amounts of social data are registered and aggregated independently of initiatives from researchers. This is illustrated by work such as that of computational sociologists Scott Golder and Michael Macy, whose research mapped people's affective states throughout the day, as expressed via Twitter posts in 84 countries, generating results of high interest to its subject-area, but using a research design that was by necessity dictated by the availability and character of the timestamped and text-based social media data (Golder and Macy, 2011). Examples of similar studies exist in several other fields where, while the issues dealt with are of high relevance, it is nonetheless the case that the researchers have confronted data that was largely already at hand and constituted in certain ways. This illustrates that the choices of the researcher, as regards designing the data may, at least in some respects, be increasingly backgrounded in digital society. While choosing between a qualitative or quantitative approach – as in opting for a survey or for in-depth interviews (see Roulston and Choi, Chapter 15, this volume) – will still have continued relevance in many contexts, scholars are now increasingly also facing the challenge of thinking up and constructing some of their 'methods' after the fact.

One of Purdam and Elliot's main points with presenting their typology, discussed in the previous section, is to argue that the complexity of today's data environment forces researchers to constantly think about the highly variable characteristics of data that they encounter or seek out. And one of the key challenges of entering this type of terrain is to constantly try out new ways of doing things. To know that the data we elicit or download, as well as the strategies we choose for making sense of it, are appropriate, we may test our strategy to see whether it produces good research results. The dilemma is, however, that in order to know that the results are good we must already have developed the appropriate method (Sandvig and Hargittai, 2015). Because of this constant – and potentially endless – need for experimentation and discovery, investigations drawing on new tools and approaches risk quickly getting stuck and intellectually unproductive.

Let's say that you are researching some aspect of social interaction on a platform like YouTube, and have decided that analysing user comments to videos seems to be the way to go. Now, if this had been survey responses, or interview transcriptions, you could rely on an entire canon of literature on methods and well established research practices for how to work with such data. Even though you might want to do things in new ways, or challenge the conventional ways of going about the research, you would at least have a sort of baseline, or common practice, to relate to and argue with. But in the case of YouTube comments, you would have to do a lot more groundwork. First, for example, you would have to find a way of collecting the comments. If the number of comments was large enough for it to be inconvenient to manually copy and paste them – which is often the case – you would have to find some tool or other for automatically capturing and downloading them. This risks putting you in a situation where you end up trialling and erroring yourself through a variety of browser plugins, scripts or applications that may or may not do what you want them to. This process can be very time-consuming, and it is not uncommon that the researcher becomes so engaged with this very quest for a tool, that he or she – instead of doing the social research that was initially intended – starts devoting aeons of time to scouring the net for ever 'better' tools, or to learning how to code. And this is only the first step out of several subsequent ones, where other challenges may throw you off track.

Once the comments are collected and ordered, there is a wide range of epistemological, ontological and ethical issues to deal with. What are the comments really? Are they individual utterances or conversations? How should you, if at all, take the likes and dislikes posted to the comments into consideration? Do all the comments relate to the YouTube video in question, or can the comment threads take on lives of their own, becoming forums for discussing other issues than those instigated by the video? How can you, ethically, use these data for research? Do you need the informed consent of all the people who have posted in the thread? And so on, basically, ad infinitum. In sum, because of such multidimensional complexity and undecidedness, research on digital society must embrace research methods as a creative act. Instead of relying on blueprints, copying and pasting run-of-the-mill methods sections into our papers, researchers must 'reveal the messy details of what they are actually doing, aiming toward mutual reflection, creativity, and learning that advances the state of the art' (Sandvig and Hargittai, 2015, p. 5).

METHODOLOGICAL BRICOLAGE

Nearly twenty years ago, Steve Jones wrote in the preface to a book about researching the Internet that 'we are still coming to grips with the changes that we feel are brought about by networked communication of the type so prominently made visible by the Internet' (Jones, 1999, p. x). And this is in fact still the case. Research on digital society has continued to be a sort of trading zone between conventional academic disciplines – it is truly transdisciplinary. In their book about Internet inquiry, Annette Markham and Nancy Baym explain that:

> While most disciplines have awakened to an understanding of the importance of the Internet in their fields, most do not have a richly developed core of scholars who agree on methodological approaches or standards. This absence of disciplinary boundaries keeps Internet studies both desirable and frustrating. (Markham and Baym, 2009, p. xiv)

This frustration, they argue, makes researchers of the digital society push the boundaries of 'disciplinary belonging' in ways that most academic research would benefit from doing more of. Furthermore, they write that as 'few people who study the Internet are trained by a person, let alone a program, that gave them specialized guidance on how to do it well', researchers of the digital society are by necessity forced to actively and critically navigate a landscape of old and new methods, seeking out ways of engaging with data that suit their particular projects (Markham and Baym, 2009, pp. xiii–xiv; see Markham, Chapter 33, this volume). As Jones explained already in 1999, it is seldom a workable solution to just straight ahead apply existing theories and methods when studying the digital society. Some such perspectives and approaches can most likely be, and have also to some extent been, repurposed for digital media research – for example, survey methods and interviews. But one must remember that the Internet, with its networked social tools and platforms, is 'a different sort of object', possessing an 'essential changeability' that demands a conscious shift of focus and method (Jones, 1999, p. xi).

Because of this, digital research often demands that the person carrying out the data collection and analysis is even more critical, and more reflecting, than what is already demanded by scholarship in general. The specific challenges of doing digital social research have, Markham and Baym (2009, pp. vii–viii) argue, 'prompted its researchers to confront, head-on, numerous questions that lurk less visibly in traditional research contexts'.

Against this background, and in relation to the discussion above regarding potentially transgressing the 'qualitative'/ 'quantitative' divide, the best strategy is methodological pragmatism: Focusing on the problem to be researched and on what type of knowledge is sought after. Instead of positioning oneself in one corner or another of the existing field of methods literature one can instead, methodologists Yvonna Lincoln and Norman Denzin say, conceive of one's research strategy as a form of bricolage (Denzin and Lincoln, 2000). Bricolage is a French term – popularised by cultural anthropologist Claude Lévi-Strauss in the 1960s – which refers to the process of improvising and putting pre-existing things together in new and adaptive ways (Lévi-Strauss, 1966). From that perspective, our research approach is not fully chosen beforehand, but rather emerges as a patchwork of solutions – old or new – to problems faced while carrying out the research. As put by critical pedagogy researcher Joe Kincheloe (2005, pp. 324–5): 'We actively construct our research methods from the tools at hand rather than passively receiving the "correct," universally applicable methodologies', and we 'steer clear of preexisting guidelines and checklists developed outside the specific demands of the inquiry at hand'. So, developing your method as a bricolage means putting your specific research task at the centre, letting your particular combination and application of methods take shape in relation to the needs that characterise the given task.

The previously discussed demand for reflexivity on behalf of the digital researcher operates on several different levels. Like the bricolage approach described above, Markham and Baym also argue that the research design is a constantly ongoing process and that it is to be expected that any study will be reframed continuously throughout the process of research. They write:

> Different questions occur at different stages of a research process, and the same questions reappear at different points. Second, the constitution of data is the result of a series of decisions at critical

junctures in the design and conduct of a study. The endless and jumbled network of links that comprise our research sites and subjects create endless sources of information that could be used as data in a project. We must constantly and thoroughly evaluate what will count as data and how we are distinguishing side issues from key sources of information. Reflexivity may enable us to minimize or at least acknowledge the ways in which our culturally embedded rationalities influence what is eventually labeled 'data'. (Markham and Baym, 2009, p. xviii)

As emphasised by Jones, it is important when researching the specificities of the Internet, to remember that its uses are always contextualised. Research subjects and data are part of physical space as much as they are part of 'cyberspace'. This means, Jones says, that:

> As a result the notion that our research should be 'grounded' takes on even greater significance when it comes to Internet research. That makes Internet research particularly interesting – and demanding. Not only is it important to be aware of and attuned to the diversity of online experience, it is important to recognize that online experience is at all times tethered in some fashion to offline experience. (Jones, 1999, p. xii)

So, while it is exciting to study the Internet and digital society, it is also especially challenging. New platforms, concepts, and social practices emerge fast enough for making the 'Internet' in itself, into a compelling area of inquiry. The field, Markham and Baym (2009, p. xiii) write, has a 'self-replenishing novelty [that] always holds out the promise for unique intellectual spaces'. But, as discussed above, new terrains of research bring with them new challenges and difficulties. First, there is a need for constant reflection about the role of the self in research. Processes of digital social research highlight that researchers are actually co-creators of the field of study. Our choices are often made in contexts where there are no standard agreed-upon rules for research design and practice, and this makes such choices more meaningful. Furthermore, the sometimes disembodied character of digital social settings makes it important to think extra hard about the relationship between researcher and researched.

CONCLUSION

Christian Sandvig and Eszter Hargittai discuss how digital media and the Internet can be seen as offering new tools for answering new, or old, questions in new ways. They give an example of how things that were not conceived as research instruments can still become used as such:

> In this view, online games like World of Warcraft were created by private companies to allow people to pretend to be night elves (or more accurately, for the company to make money from what people spend on subscriptions allowing them to pretend to be night elves). Yet these games might hold the potential to answer basic questions about the networked structure of human interaction. (Sandvig and Hargittai, 2015, p. 8)

Employing digital media as a research instrument offers 'a new kind of microscope' that we can use to shed light on both new issues that are specific to digital society, and on basic questions about human social life that are more long-standing (Sandvig and Hargittai, 2015, p. 6). Naturally, because of the multifaceted character of digitally networked tools and platforms, such uses can be of a wide variety. They can draw on new tools for collecting data via web scrapers, APIs or online repositories. And they can also include new devices and ways of analysing data, in the form of computerised language processing, the harnessing of geolocative hardware, new visualisation techniques, and so on. One example of when digital society as such metamorphose into research method is in the case of big data, as discussed earlier. But, Sandvig and Hargittai argue, the big data examples are not the most fascinating ones.

> We instead see that the actual revolution in digital research instrumentation is going on now, all around us, in smaller, 'ordinary' research projects.

We see it in the use of crowdsourcing to replace traditional pools of research participants; the use of hyperlink networks as a new source of data to study the relationships between organizations; or in the idea that writing your own Web-based application is now a viable data collection strategy. (Sandvig and Hargittai, 2015, p. 11)

The totality of all such innovations, experimentations, and renegotiations, are – as pointed out by Sandvig and Hargittai – today's examples of what historian of science Derek J. de Solla Price called instruments of revelation. When discussing the scientific revolution historically, he argued that its dominant driving force had been 'the use of a series of instruments of revelation that expanded the explicandum of science in many and almost fortuitous directions'. He also wrote of the importance of 'the social forces binding the amateurs together' (Price, 1986, p. 246). So, in the case of research on the Internet and digital media research then, we are now at that stage. A point where researchers often act like curiously experimenting enthusiasts – 'amateurs' – in testing and devising new 'instruments of revelation'.

FURTHER READING

Hargittai, Eszter and Sandvig, Christian (eds.) (2015) *Digital Research Confidential*. Cambridge, MA: MIT Press.
Kincheloe, J. L. (2005) 'On to the next level', *Qualitative Inquiry* 11(3): 323–50.
Markham, Annette and Baym, Nancy (eds.) (2009) *Internet Inquiry*. Los Angeles, CA: Sage.

REFERENCES

Andrejevic, Mark (2007) *iSpy: Surveillance and Power in the Interactive Era*. Lawrence: University Press of Kansas.
Atzori, L., Iera, A., and Morabito, G. (2010) 'The internet of things: A survey', *Computer Networks* 54(15): 2787–805.
Bernhardsson, S., da Rocha, Luis E. C., and Minnhagen, P. (2010) 'Size-dependent word frequencies and translational invariance of books', *Physica A: Statistical Mechanics and its Applications* 389(2): 330–41.
boyd, d. and Crawford, K. (2012) 'Critical questions for big data', *Information, Communication & Society* 15(5): 662–79.
Brady, Henry E. and Collier, David (2010) *Rethinking Social Inquiry*. Lanham, MD: Rowman & Littlefield Publishers.
Denzin, N. K. (2012) 'Triangulation 2.0', *Journal of Mixed Methods Research* 6(2): 80–8.
Denzin, Norman K. and Lincoln, Yvonna S. (eds.) (2000) *Handbook of Qualitative Research*. Thousand Oaks, CA: Sage.
Glaser, B. G. (1965) 'The constant comparative method of qualitative analysis', *Social Problems* 12(4): 436–45.
Glaser, Barney G. and Strauss, Anselm L. (1967) *The Discovery of Grounded Theory*. New York: Aldine de Gruyter.
Golder, S. A and Macy, M. W. (2011) 'Diurnal and seasonal mood vary with work, sleep, and day length across diverse cultures', *Science* 333(6051): 1878–1881.
Jick, T. D. (1979) 'Mixing qualitative and quantitative methods', *Administrative Science Quarterly* 24(4): 602–11.
Jones, Steve (1999) 'Preface', in Steve Jones (ed.), *Doing Internet Research: Critical Issues and Methods for Examining the Net*. Thousand Oaks, CA: Sage, ix–xiv.
Kincheloe, J. L. (2005) 'On to the next level', *Qualitative Inquiry* 11(3): 323–50.
Krippendorff, Klaus (2004) *Content Analysis*. London: Sage.
Lévi-Strauss, Claude (1966) *The Savage Mind*. Chicago: University of Chicago Press.
Lupton, Deborah (2014) *Digital Sociology*. Abingdon: Routledge.
Mann, S. and Ferenbok, J. (2013) 'New media and the power politics of sousveillance in a surveillance-dominated world', *Surveillance & Society* 11(1): n.p.
Markham, Annette and Baym, Nancy (eds.) (2009) *Internet Inquiry*. Los Angeles, CA: Sage.
Mennell, S. (1975) 'Ethnomethodology and the new "methodenstreit"', *Acta Sociologica* 18(4): 287–302.

Moretti, Franco. (2013) *Distant Reading*. London: Verso.
Price, Derek J. de Solla (1986) *Little Science, Big Science … And Beyond*. New York: Columbia University Press.
Purdam, Kingsley and Elliot, Mark (2015) 'The changing social science data landscape', in P. Halfpenny and R. Proctor (eds.), *Innovations in Digital Research Methods*. London: Sage, pp. 25–58.
Ragin, Charles C. (2000) *Fuzzy-Set Social Science*. Chicago: University of Chicago Press.
Sandvig, Christian and Hargittai, Eszter (2015) 'How to think about digital research', in Eszter Hargittai and Christian Sandvig (eds.), *Digital Research Confidential*. Cambridge, MA: MIT Press, pp. 1–28.

Moving Through Digital Flows: An Epistemological and Practical Approach

Annette N. Markham and Ane Kathrine Gammelby

INTRODUCTION

In this chapter, we centralize the concept of 'flow' as a primary way of making sense of digitally saturated social contexts. Although the concept is already a key element in qualitative inquiry, we discuss what this means both conceptually and practically in digital contexts where data seems concrete and readily accessible, or in contexts where the structures and boundaries seem plainly identifiable. The chapter (a) recommends flow logic as an epistemological stance toward the social world and its study, and (b) describes flow-mapping as one concrete method for studying digital culture.

We set the scene with our case study of Facebook (see also Ditchfield and Meredith, Chapter 32, this volume). As with most researchers in the field, we come up with novel approaches for looking at something because something goes wrong, or what we originally thought would work, doesn't. In this case, one of the authors, Ane Kathrine, was both overwhelmed by the sheer quantity of digital data available to her and stymied by the fact that no matter the quantity, it didn't have meaning. This is so common it might seem banal for anyone who has done research of Internet-mediated social experience. We can almost take for granted that we will take on sites and questions that are too big.

Our situation, like many, illustrates a very common problem for novice researchers. Even when *data is everywhere* and we have millions of units of information to choose from, *data will always be missing* (see Lindgren, Chapter 28, this volume).

> Ok, I admit it. It seemed like a straightforward project. The fact that there was a massive scope of archives, pages, and conversations made me feel it would be easy to find empirical material. In fact, it was. That's the problem. All the stakeholders on the project insisted it must be easy for me, since all the material to analyze would be already transcribed. Just go get it, they told me. – Ane Kathrine

Ane Kathrine (hereafter, AK), while doing research on Danish laypersons' practices of employing online peer communities when they struggle with long-term health issues, discovered not only the easiest of the problems – that most of what she wanted to actually study was not available, was missing, was embedded in lived experience, and was impossible to capture as data, but also a more complicated problem – that in the quest to solve the problem by reducing the size or scope of the field, one can miss the crux of the problem, which is not about size but movement. More specifically, how we move, and how the context moves.

> I've been involved in many online communities that deal with health issues. The terrain is familiar to me, like my back yard it seems. I decided to narrow my focus to Facebook groups, since in the Danish context, this is the most dominant social media[1] and the place where intense health-related discussions unfold. Even so, as I started looking at literally thousands of unfolding discussions about medical as well as everyday issues and insecurities related to life with illness, the topic, the scene, the importance of everything grew and grew. So what may have started out as a relatively contained project (Danish Facebook groups about migraines, e.g.) became an endless sea where I couldn't find any anchors. – AK

AK started using Clarke's (2005) situational analysis techniques for mapping to try to find her central concerns and lay these out in relation to other elements of the complex ecology she was studying. Working directly with Annette, she augmented Clarke's ideas with Markham's work on remix methods (2013), network sensibilities (2012), and ethnography in digital contexts.

AK's use of situational mapping embodies both a network sensibility and an iterative flow approach. Over time, it becomes clear to any qualitative researcher studying digitally saturated social contexts, whether online, offline, or as most social situations are now, seamless hybrids of both, that only a fraction of digitally saturated practices are represented in the empirical material that presents itself in the digital content.

> How should we measure the time members spend reading through posts and comments, making sense of these in relation to their own personal health? Someone might agree with the statement in a post but never transmit a response in a form that is captured, like a 'like' or a comment. Other times, someone might have a strong disagreement, but the strength of the emotion is not conveyed in the comment or 'angryface' emoji.
>
> To take this further, most of the emotional responses are not conveyed at all. This might be because it's a physical response (a shrug or a grin). Or the outcome of the emotional response might be a Google search to clarify a certain matter. – AK

Listening, interpreting, sitting with, being with, changing one's mind about the content of digital media: these turn out to be the most essential aspects of the experience. Yet this information remains invisible.

> There are so many reasons for the absence of communication. In any group, stigmatized or not, participants will feel a range of pressures, enact certain habits, and follow perceived or actual norms ... all of which might lead to an absence of traceable or archiveable communication.
>
> Basically, it's frustrating when you're trying to study something and the thing you're trying to study is not available to you. That's been my constant attitude about researching social media, which is why I had to find a different way through it. – AK

This example illustrates that situations are complicated. It also illustrates how we can sometimes get too focused on what we might call 'data' (see Flick, Chapter 1, this volume) since it seems so central to the situation. It can be everywhere, it can be missing, it manifests into what we might call digital data, objective bits of information with obdurate qualities. In the process of research, our analytical gaze is drawn to particular stuff, which leads to our inattention to other stuff.

It may seem unnecessary to mention these things since they are basic conditions of all research environments. However, digital contexts like Facebook present themselves as seemingly whole entities, rich with both content and meaning, ready for use as data in digital research. The ease with which social media data can be extracted and analyzed facilitates a distanced approach to social research; it can dull the researcher's sensibility that anything we label 'object' or 'culture' or 'data' exists only as a momentary capture of a continual flow of time/space.

> It's actually impossible to study 'Facebook' or another app. I realized quite soon in the study that it could never be 'just' a site, app, or technology, since it is only recognizable as it is used in cultural contexts. If we zoom in on Facebook's affordances, for example, these may seem like solid characteristics, but they're not experienced in this way.
> As I engaged in fieldwork, I realized that even the basic affordances change, depending on who's using the platform, and when. While the layout configurations may be finite at any given point in time, the main feature of the interface – for example, news feed – is unique to each user.
> It's not just that people see different advertisements or the content is unique. Their speed of clicking and scrolling varies, networks of friends vary, and the physical features of the interface also vary; Facebook is an app, nested within other apps or browsers, nested in operating systems, nested within physical devices that have been personalized.
> 'Facebook' is always someone's Facebook and not merely a digital artifact floating in time and space. – AK

These complications should not stop us from studying Facebook, or more appropriately, some aspect of Facebook. As many qualitative methodologists have reminded us over the past decades, methods are tools, and when we confront complexity, sometimes we need to find new ways of combining, adapting, or finding new tools.

What we emphasize in this chapter is that when the data is overwhelming, as it always will be in digital contexts, paying close and reflexive attention to how one's movements create a particular path through meaning is an important part of the methodology. Our choices and decisions about what to focus on create, not discover, what we eventually examine as data.

WORKING WITHIN A STRONG INTERPRETIVIST PERSPECTIVE

In a broad sense, we are working within the strength of many contemporary epistemologies whereby typical methods for data collection are only a fractional part of the overall lens through which we make sense of the world. A significant part of this sense-making tends to be blackboxed as 'interpretation'. This may work in qualitative methods textbooks to present a somewhat tidy and linear sequence for junior scholars to follow. But separating 'collection' from 'interpretation' is a misrepresentation of the actual process.

Finding close, local meaning in the contemporary world, where digital traces are a predominant form of evidence of action, relation, and materiality, requires one to make active and subjective choices about what to pay attention to. Doing it well requires no small measure of what Goodall discussed as 'interpretive authority' (2000), emphasizing that the choices are not driven by external empirical materials only, or perhaps not even primarily. Adopting a strong interpretive stance entails shifting our methodological focus away from 'data' we 'gather' with regard to 'stabilising' the empirical world we are curious to learn about while we do our research. Instead, our methods must acknowledge and reflect on movement and motion and then operate with such premises in mind.

This sort of stance aligns well with a long lineage of feminist and interpretive scholarship to insist on both identifying and taking an active, situated stance toward the research context. This stance, as Markham and Baym (2009) note, highlights and foregrounds how

> our research theories, methods, and interrelations are bounded by particular and situated rationalities. We live, conduct research, and find meaning from particular positions. As researchers our understandings of others is limited by unnoticed (as well as noticed) frames of reference. (p. 134)

The fact that we are situated, added to the principle that objects always only exist when they are momentarily lifted from context and arbitrarily frozen in time and place for examination, adds up to a challenging conundrum for anyone who wants to 'collect' something that can be called 'data' for use in a qualitative study (or any study, frankly).

By being proactive and reflexive, researchers can stimulate and trace their own actions to 'grab' (Senft, 2013) certain elements and make sense of them as they move. By carefully tracking our network sensibilities through such techniques as situational and concept mapping, we can help ourselves and others recognize what we're seeing and how we're grabbing. The maps then orient us (and later others) to what we have been up to.

In the remainder of this chapter, we discuss how and why a flow approach is a useful way of conceptualizing the practice of qualitative inquiry of digital social contexts as well as the characteristics of the situation from which data is drawn. We follow this by giving one possible set of instructions for such an approach.

WHAT IS FLOW?

We can conceptualize 'flow' as both what we study and how we move when we study. Culture is not comprehensively represented in the digital sediments, traces, or venues where these are found. Of course these sediments might represent useful markers or observation points. But a flow perspective deliberately questions whether this is true, acknowledging that in the digital Internet era, culturing (Rodriguez, 2002) is a much more apt term than culture when identifying the focus of study. This is because culture never stands still, and neither do we. The concept of flow can allow us to unhook from particular digital material, platforms, or cases, which enables us to consider more fully what counts for those involved in this ongoing culturing process. The concept also allows us to see that our sensemaking is always on the move, shifting from moment to moment as we try to stop time to make sense of what happened even as it is no longer happening. To distinguish between the produce and process of culturing, we define flow as something that describes what it is we study (product) and how we engage with it (process). Flow is an essential methodology grounding the interpretive movements of the late twentieth century, whether or not its adherents label their activities or objects with this label or not. We highlight it as a way of moving through, and understanding the entangled networks characteristic of, the digital era.

Flow as What We Study

Gareth Morgan (1986) used 'flux and transformation' as one metaphor to describe the continual, nonlinear, and elusive ways in which activity and culture exists. He was not the first or last to talk about cultures of, or as flow.[2] As noted previously (Markham, 2012), shifting from objects to flow can help loosen our grip on the myth that contexts have boundaries. As we give up the solidity of culture, context, situation, or case as a definable object, we must find different vocabularies to help us approach the study in a way that appreciates that they are not things. Whether we use Appadurai's 'scapes' (1990), Callon, Latour, and Law's actor networks (2005), or Donna Haraway's (2008) 'cats cradles', the idea is to find terminology that resonates with the context in ways that reduce our reliance on traditional positivist modes of social science. We find this task particularly important in the digital age, because flow is such an obvious mode of culturing through the mesh of electronic networks. To find a context, one must identify meaning in flow and transform it into something more concrete so that it can be analyzed. By first releasing control of what the object of analysis is, we can adopt a state of readiness so that relevant or salient patterns and questions arise. An inextricable part of identifying and reifying a product for inquiry is to also operationalize flow as the process by which we're doing this.

Flow as the Researcher's Activity

Finding meaning, in whatever we might call cultural flow, involves movement in and through meaning, materiality, time, space, and bodies. Anthropologist Sarah Pink (2007) discusses the importance of moving with and through situations to attend to the flows of meanings within material and digital culture. Markham's (1998) studies of digital culture, like many others', required shifting from place to placement, from location to locomotion.

Flow is immersive and directive. It necessarily includes decisions at critical junctures that will influence what eventually becomes the focus of analysis (Markham, 2003). As we move, we decide what to follow, what counts as data, and therefore what is discarded as non-data or non-relevant data. The movement is continual, as inevitable as breathing.

When we pay attention to how we are moving and what we are feeling and attending to as we move, we are doing nothing more than enacting our epistemologies, which might be situated in ethnography, grounded theory, actor network theory, ethnomethodology, etc. We could say that flow, in this sense, is simply a deliberate focus on the movements natural to all qualitative approaches. But within the huge density of entanglements in digitally saturated cultural phenomena, a key characteristic of flow as a process is that it becomes analytically selective,[3] not comprehensive. This characteristic is particularly important to foreground. Digital contexts can give the impression that the boundaries are quite clear, and in many cases, because of the quantity of data readily available and pre-archived, that the flow of activity has been completely captured. Such preformed boundaries or complete social contexts are illusionary (Markham, 1998; Hine, 2011). Focusing on the researcher's choices, made as a natural part of moving through rather than looking at, is a powerful lens. It forces responsibility for decisions on the researcher's shoulders. In this way, the study remains inductive and the researcher need not be locked into particular digital material or within a specific platform or case.

A FLOW-ORIENTED HEURISTIC

Adding to the idea of flow as both process and product, we can offer three basic heuristics that might usefully guide one's attitudes and practices when engaging in the natural processes of following the flows characteristic of any digital context. We have found these heuristics or reminders helpful for our own investigations. One will notice these heuristics are not exclusive to 'digital', which extends the usefulness of these points to other areas of research.

1   *Everything that is there is not all there is:* Digital media content only accounts for those aspects of digital culture that are visible and therefore traceable. This visual bias is seen most obviously when we focus on content – for example, texts and images sent. What we see is only a partial view of the outcome of our interactions, not the interactions themselves. Add to this the fact that through various affordances of platforms, certain aspects of our digital media use become visible, while others stay hidden. Take for example the practice of discussing one's health issues on Facebook. Certainly some issues are more inviting to discuss than others. While it might be productive to ask one's peers for a critical second opinion on one's doctor's advice, disclosing sensitive details about one's bodily dysfunctions is often far less inviting. This obviously frames what is being discussed and to what extent, but the contemplations – what we decide to *not* post, like, or comment on in such communities – are not traced. What might be a full-bodied engagement/lived experience of using digital media is not visible by default. This does not mean that these activities are uninteresting. Silence and listening are obviously analytically interesting, but difficult to capture in an object-oriented data collection – especially if the researcher is not immersed long-term in the field.

2 *What is there is not all there was:* Digital stuff disappears and changes. Digital media content that is available for retrospective retrieval constitutes a deeply flawed reflection of social interactions that unfolded in real-time. Digitally mediated interactions between human beings are *dynamically* created and *gradually* unfolding social events that are highly anchored in time. The temporality of social construction is only poorly preserved in historically retrievable digital media content. Even if one were to capture data in real-time to try to get at the unfolding dynamics of the situation, the next problem is that social media archives are incomplete by default and change over time. The idea of a 'full' data set is delusory. In digital contexts, what *is* there can seem quite complete, giving off[4] the impression of comprising a 'complete' representation of what was there, or resembles such a thing. Digital content is prone to constant changes as new stuff is potentially added while old stuff may be deleted (by users as well as by admins). Retrieving social media content is therefore not just a matter of finding the sweet spot where everything is there at the same time. Such moments don't actually exist because digital media content is not linearly produced. Alternatively, significant elements of interactions may be deliberately deleted, especially if the phenomenon is characterized by conflict, tension, or controversy.

3 *What is there is both too much and not enough:* Digital media content suffers a quantity/quality paradox. On the one hand, immense amounts of (big) data are automatically generated as our digital interactions are electronically logged. These electronic traces might provide us with valuable insights about our digital behaviors that are not easily observable otherwise and often not even conscious to us (see, for example, Hine, 2011, on 'unobtrusive data'). On the other hand, the vast quantity of automatically generated data is likely to cause data overload, and not all data points are equally interesting when doing qualitative research. Therefore, selection strategies are needed. However, setting up 'instrumental' sampling criteria with the main purpose of reducing the amount of data for analysis, such as sampling based on certain time spans, might not really help us capture what is interesting about our phenomenon of study. Retrieving data that has been generated during a randomly selected certain week, for example, is not the key to establishing a research interest or focus and can yield massive amounts of trivia with very little meaning. Taking everything as 'serious data' online is like an ethnographer spending five minutes in the field writing furiously all the details of what is happening. This is both impossible and somewhat meaningless in terms of understanding. Instead, reflexive, question-driven selection of data is needed.

These three points may seem fundamental. For seasoned qualitative researchers studying digitally-saturated social contexts, these have been long apparent (see Baym, 2013 or Dougherty, 2015 for longer discussions). For us, these heuristics don't just point out the flaws in contemporary trends around data conceptualizations and data collection practices. They can help qualitative researchers take a different approach, by refocusing attention to what might be considered data, given the context of the situation under study. This aligns with the heart of boyd and Crawford's (2012) critical provocations for big data and represented elsewhere in this *Handbook* (see Lindgren, Chapter 28, and Markham, Chapter 33, this volume): That data does not speak for itself. What appears as content is highly contextual and contingent on other aspects of life, both digital and analog. These contextualities frame, direct, and encourage certain media practices.

In what follows and concludes this chapter, we offer one of many possible sets of instructions for how to make sense of these flows. We draw on Adele Clarke's (2003, 2005) situational analysis and Markham's framework for using network sensibilities to explore complexity in Internet contexts (2012). Both authors build from larger and long-standing epistemologies undergirding feminist, symbolic interactionist, and postmodern understandings about how we grasp moments of meaning in the midst of cultural flows.

INSTRUCTION GUIDE FOR ENTERING AND MAPPING FLOWS

As mentioned previously, Ane Kathrine combined Markham's (2012) network sensibility with Clarke's situational mapping techniques, to transform her study from one that was primarily targeted to media content on Facebook to one that is more focused on her own movements through and with the flows of meaning, both within and outside Facebook; both online and offline; and both with participants and across multiple spaces and special interest communities. By doing so, she complicated the situation, went back and revised her research questions, complicated the situation again, revised the research questions again, and so on. While this certainly could describe how one might enact good ethnographic, grounded theory, or interpretive methods, it is guided by an overarching ideology that because one is operating in endless and massive networked flows, one must be more strongly aware of one's own motivations, curiosities, and instincts rather than relying on or continually trying to find an external rationale. As Ane Kathrine notes:

> This entails that we do not let ourselves be carried away by the existence of textual material (FB content) that presents itself as 'data' and study FB content mainly because it is so temptingly available. Rather, we should study selectively the parts of this material that is likely to help us expound our curiosities.
> My approach avoids reverence to discipline – suggested tools or techniques are used for elaborating this curiosity. As long as these methods are productive of pertinent insights and employed in a reflexive and ethical way, I trust the methodology to work. – AK

Drawing on Adele Clarke's core theories and techniques (2003, 2005) for situational mapping, as well as Markham's arguments about how (re)mixing methods can facilitate adaptive and ethical approaches to grappling with complexity in digitally saturated contexts (2013), we offer the following 'instructions' for moving into and through data flows to actively and reflexively generate data. It includes visually mapping various elements of the social situation of study, no matter if these are material objects (digital/non-digital) or analytical abstractions. Extending Markham and Lindgren's argument (2014) that such mapping has generative and ethical impact, we argue that making data more tangible and tinkerable sensitizes the researcher to the complexity and entanglements of digital phenomena, as well as the thought processes that go on in the researcher's mind throughout a study.[5] In a flow-oriented research process, the relevance of data emerges as a product of one's active analysis and reflexivity rather than as an a priori assumption.

1 *Phrase a Provisional Research Question*: Research questions are tools to think with. To enable a flow-oriented, rather than object-oriented approach, consider provisional, partial, even ridiculous questions. Consider a question that evokes something inside you and articulates your research curiosity. The question does not need to be fully comprehensive of your research interest, as long as it strikes a nerve. What makes you wonder? What seems problematic (to you, to somebody else, to society) in the situation of study? Does there seem to be any conflicting perspectives worth a closer look? Why did you consider researching a specific topic in the first place?

The research question is only intended to push you forward and direct your attention in a pertinent way. Here, a quick and dirty question that strikes a chord might be a more productive driver for the mapping you are about to begin than a carefully articulated, attemptingly precise or all-encompassing one.

> In my study of social media and health, what sparked my interest was that people discussing their health issues on Facebook often used online peer-networks as a backchannel for health information, and that this seemed to cause clashes with doctors. Initially I asked a broad question: 'How do patients use social media in relation to their health issues?'

I knew the question was just a tool to think with. So even though it made my social scientist self feel uncomfortable, I just made a random, not-exactly-false question to get going. In my head, I was not really meaning 'patients', because I knew they weren't really patients in terms of people receiving care. This developed into 'How do laypersons with health issues use social media?', as it empirically appeared that a lot of people did consult online peer-networks prior to or simply instead of consulting a doctor. I changed it a third time to people 'dealing' with health issues.

After more of the steps 2 to 6 below, I realized that the continual change of question was essential to building stronger 'provisions' for my inquiry adventure. – AK

We include 'phrase a provisional research question' as the first step even though it may seem obvious to seasoned researchers, because it is often a sticking point. Because the inquiry is driven by a question, it's logical the question should be a good one. But a key aspect of qualitative research is that there is a lot of messing about in the context before we end up with the actual research question. Asking a quick and dirty provisional question allows the researcher to use earlier stages of investigation and analysis as part of the actual study, not just the initial explorations to define the project.

Asking a provisional question was essential to dive into the empirical process early and then track this as part of the research project even if it was messy and untargeted.

If the research question turns out to be inexpedient for addressing what – during the research process – appears to be core to your research curiosity, you simply just change it. Therefore, don't waste too much energy trying to make this question 'the' research question with which you finally intend to frame your analysis. It is a catch-22; you cannot precisely articulate this before analyzing it. The idea is that this question is supposed to change during the research process as you gradually become more familiar with your topic of study. – AK

2   *Go with the Flow*: Play with the idea of being a spy[6] trying to unravel a mysterious and complex network. Let your demand to know (this should be somehow addressed in the research question) – rather than dogmatic ideas about specific methods – guide your attention and your actions. No matter if you study foreign service secrets, the implications of digitally saturated health, or creative networks, immersing yourself in your environment of study in order to get, if not an overview, then a 360-degree grounded perspective of the flow of things. Follow cues and hunches. Which agents and agencies should you pay attention to? Where are they located (physically, virtually, conceptually)? What are their habits, hurdles, workarounds, preferences, and resentments? Which technologies should you be aware of, and which activities do they facilitate, transform, or maybe render redundant?

Rich insights are often a matter of serendipity, which a researcher can lose if they plan too carefully.

Initially, I thought I was simply wasting time by letting go of a solid plan. But very soon, I realized I should not try to control the process with an iron grip. This goes against the grain of my training. I feel a lot of pressure to follow a strict plan as a researcher. I would feel differently if I was a spy, which is why I like this role better than scholar.

I moved more fluidly by simply moving. Once I let go of the fear of 'starting in the wrong place' or studying without a 'rigorous' sampling strategy or research design, I was able to freely engage with people, places, and activities. This pulled me in many directions and kept me moving forward. – AK

Rigor is not attained by sticking to an initial plan, at least not in non-positivist epistemologies. Being rigid, or sticking to the original plan, defeats the purpose of being grounded, exploring, or seeking meaning inductively. This reminder is useful at both the micro and macro level. By letting go of the necessity to use the tools we had planned to use from the beginning, we can adapt to the needs of the specific situation. By letting go of the need to figure out in advance all the strata of the 'big picture', one can be open to letting this emerge rather than being applied as an expected outcome.

I joined any and all online communities that exhibited interesting activities. There are so many, one could say it didn't matter where I went. Why privilege certain communities over others? I took advantage of opportunities that presented themselves. – AK

Ane Kathrine took advantage of her first-hand experience with her research topic, studying informally those communities to which she already had access. These were only starting points, so it was not necessary to be overly formal.

> I worried about whether or not I should ask for permission, get informed consent, or otherwise announce myself as a 'researcher'. This paralyzed me. Once I could embrace a mindset that it was 'just' poking around and 'going with the flow', I felt enormously free. This turned out to be productive in ways I never imagined. – AK

Typically, we might limit this messing around or going with the flow as an activity we do prior, or as a sideline, to the research project. Yet this is a critical stage in the research project. As we move about, we are already well underway, making sense of – and mentally mapping – 'what's going on here'. It is vital to track these unofficial field experiences and informal engagements by taking notes, or otherwise documenting them.

> Before I knew it, I found myself wanting to revisit (and render visible) these exploratory and seemingly random movements, because they helped demarcate not only where I had been and where I might go next, but where my attention was being drawn. – AK

If we presuppose that interpretive/qualitative research is about identifying analytical patterns pointing in somehow the same direction, it doesn't matter *where* exactly you start your research; you have to start *somewhere*. Patterns will emerge.

3 *Embrace Subjective Selectivity*: Generating flow-oriented data is an affective – not an instrumental – process. Here, we advocate following one's hunches and clues, regardless of whether or not these seem justified by some external logic, which is what any good spy would do, anyway.

> Why should I ignore my own knowledge and experience about the situation? I must have asked myself that a hundred times before I finally decided to stop ignoring it.
> The problem is that we're not trained to build a framework out of our own empirically informed experiences of a situation unless we're doing autoethnography, perhaps. Even as qualitative as my training was, I still looked for external design, waiting for the context to tell me how to formulate my questions. But I already knew this instinctively since I had been part of the context for years. – AK

A vital and natural part of qualitative research is not only selecting but also creating the field of inquiry by making active decisions about what to pay attention to. This is a process that begins early on as we develop provisional ideas about the possible connections between the different things we encounter in the field, and explore these empirically. No matter if the ideas appear to be dead ends, the researcher learns something, and this informs further research steps. This flow-oriented data collection might at times seem messy, even lacking rigor. However, it is key to remember that rigor lies in the stubbornly inductive, iterative *process* of constantly challenging[7] these developing ideas about the field while inquiring as to the eligibility and accuracy of the research question asked.[8]

> As the opportunities for next steps multiplied by each step I took, I needed to constantly critique my own moves and reflexively consider which of the many possible next steps might generate pertinent insights about the research question.
> My sampling changed over time, since what was pertinent at any given time changed. This was not a strategy. It was neither accidental nor deliberate. It just happened because I paid attention to my heart, my intuition, and my embodied sensibilities (or gut instincts). – AK

This emerges in relation to the field, as one receives feedback from the interactions one has with various elements of the situation. This interaction with the field is often overshadowed and obscured by paying too much heed to method, or what 'ought to' count as relevant or meaningful. For example, we often say that we should be iteratively guided by emerging research questions, and that we should 'follow' data, ideas, or people through the field to let meaning emerge. Enacting this is a matter of developing one's awareness of how the researcher's sensibilities are formed.

Understanding what 'iterative' means, in a lived experience sort of way, is a matter of paying attention to and also valuing one's own subjectivity in the relationship. This takes both self-awareness and confidence.

4   *Immerse and Engage, Preferably Over a Longer Period of Time*: Key when working 'flow-oriented' is to immerse oneself over a longer period of time in the social situation of study and embrace the complexity of the situation. Immersion (which relies on the researcher deliberately experiencing stuff) becomes more central than data collection (in terms of an action that seeks to extract empirical material from the natural setting and study it in another). The goal is not to describe the culture, as one might in an ethnography. Rather, it is to identify patterns and explore how these patterns repeat themselves or vary across a given field of interest.

Just as being a good spy presupposes proper training in a variety of investigative techniques, being a good qualitative researcher requires familiarity with different qualitative techniques.

> Oh, I ended up doing so many different things: I interviewed, of course, and did classic observation. But I also had people write me postcards, record video diaries, and send me screenshots. – AK

Immersion over time will inevitably help the researcher understand the situation at an adequately deep level to be able to critically evaluate the potentials and limitations of each method used.

> After I had been embedded for a long time, it became clear that it was not the number of interviewees that was important, but the quality of the insights I would get. So I shifted my strategy.
> I also decided to shift how I was interacting with interviewees. I was getting decent information in the typical interview but for some reason it didn't seem adequate. I first tried longer interviews. Then multiple interviews with the same people. I then shifted to walk-through interviewing, where I would watch them use social media while they talked about it. It was frustrating because I felt like I was just losing time and wasn't going to be able to use the materials I was getting.
> I finally realized that, all this time, I had been trying to extract meaning from the minds of interviewees, and that this would be available in the transcribed texts. But what was really valuable was to understand them, me, and the larger situation. I have to laugh, because that's the whole point, isn't it? – AK

The key to immersion is to let go of any prior expectations about what should count as 'data' in the field. This may seem obvious as a premise for qualitative research, but when we are locked into forms of immersion, we often don't really let ourselves simply be. Immersion helps us get through, over time, the tendency to transform whatever we encounter in the field as data for analysis or vice versa, to only interpret what it is possible to relate to or transform into data. Both can be counterproductive.

5   *Externalize Your Empirical Experiences and Impressions by Mapping Them*: As Markham and Lindgren (2014) describe, 'mapping is not just a cartographic activity of identifying where one is situated or one has been in order to direct or guide other travelers unfamiliar with the territory' (p. 11). When practiced with a *network sensibility* it becomes a strong method for transforming seeming solid, static, or isolated ideas, data, people, physical structures, and information infrastructures into interconnected, moving pieces, clusters, or nodes of heavy activity, lines of connection. It becomes a practical and nuanced way of stabilizing – for a moment of inspection or introspection – existence *in motion*.

> I couldn't stop drawing. I still can't. The first stage of mapping is to just get it out of my head and onto the page. In this way, I'm trying to visually extract the landscape of situational connections that develops over time inside my mind. Later, the goal is to compare maps, connect elements on certain maps to elements on other maps, broadening – and making much more complex – the entangled webs of connections. – AK

As a practical matter, this becomes a generative process of

> generating data, generating organizational strategies for one's data, generating multiple analytic coding schemes or categories, and generating links between levels such as local/global, relational/structural, and so forth. While the focus may be primarily directed toward the phenomenon, it is

equally beneficial to use network sensibilities as a reflexive tool to map one's own conceptual and epistemological standpoints. (Markham and Lindgren, 2014, p. 11)

Prior to mapping, the researcher will have some empirical experience with the situation of study, as mapping creates a relational overview of how multifaceted snippets of qualitative data seem to be connected. In other words, maps are about putting things in relation to each other, and it is necessary to have some kind of feel for these relations in order to render them visible in a visual format. In certain ways situational mapping resembles the act of mapping a crime scene as it is depicted in countless dramatic accounts. This involves compiling the evidence captured, connecting evidence to other evidence, developing hypotheses, locating critical gaps, and remarkable silencees in the situation of study.

There is no single or 'right' way of using mapping, as it is a highly intuitive process; what is meaningful varies from project to research project as well as researcher to researcher. However, for initiating a flow-oriented research process, it might often be productive to begin with *abstract situational maps/messy maps* (as suggested by Clarke, 2003).

> On paper, make a structured brainstorm, where you note down 'all the analytically pertinent human and non-human, material and symbolic/discursive elements of a particular situation as framed by those in it and by the analyst' (Clarke, 2003, p. 561). Write the date (!) and time (!) and then make hard copies (!) of the map. On different copies of the map, engage playfully by considering the internal relations between the various elements on the map. Code and categorize the elements on the map in order to identify resemblances and contradictions.
> Experiment with making different versions of the map, for example by connecting the elements on the map thematically, or simply by creating the map all over again. By doing so, you'll likely find yourself changing the appearance of the map, as you have already made sense of the connections between the elements of the map in new ways, simply by considering them. – AK

Mapping need not be performed in any particular way and maps don't have to be pretty.

> They're not for anyone besides me and they are meant to spark and generate ideas, not necessarily to find answers, depict the whole situation, or show my findings to others. Once you embrace this, you can play around with a range of different mapping techniques and styles. Maps are processual tools. – AK

Other generative ways of mapping are to map certain categories of elements, such as the human actors of the situation of study or the places/spaces of empirical interest (e.g. the digital universe and its internal connections).

Mapping of any form is a visual means of tracing the process of sensemaking, focusing on relevant clusters of meaning and connections between clusters, and engaging a different part of the cognitive process to generate data or explore ideas (Markham and Lindgren, 2014). So much meaning is embedded in the content and structure of the map. This is not necessarily a straightforward correspondence to what is going on in the situation or what has been said. It therefore is not intended to be an accurate rendering of the situation or a replication, in map form, of the data. It is, instead, an analytical rendering, whether this might be considered a condensation or a dispersion of elements, or something else.

> For me, there are immediate and longer-scale benefits: The immediate benefit from the process of mapping is that I can extract complex landscapes from my mind, and by this I don't mean extract some data from a larger set of data that comprise the situation, but an exploratory grab, in the way that Terri Senft[9] discusses. Over the longer project, the maps operate together. Thorough and iterative engagement with the generated maps allows me to explore the (density and character of the) connections between the various elements on the maps. – AK

6 *Repeat.* Key to a flow-oriented approach is that data collection and analysis are intertwined and simultaneous processes. When we do situational mapping, we both relate analytically to

our empirical experiences and also generate new data points. This might likely result in new insights as well as a need to revisit and modify the organizing research question. Preferably, the process of mapping should be repeated regularly throughout the study. Some maps might resemble others, some might look completely different, but over time (as analytic saturation is closer) the maps will stabilize into more tenable visual representations of the phenomenon of study.

CONCLUSION

In this chapter we argue for a flow-oriented rather than an object-oriented approach to qualitative digital research because making sense of culture (digital or otherwise) is not merely about analyzing tangible data points but also about making sense of the ephemeral connections and entanglements that exist between and beyond such data points. In contemporary digitally saturated culture the quantity of potential data generated is overwhelming, yet qualitatively 'what is there' is not necessarily comprehensive with regard to understanding the complexity of digital phenomena. This entails that we, as qualitative researchers, engage selectively with the vast amounts of material that can – but not necessarily should – be employed as data for analysis. It also insists that we remain open to the need for purposefully generating even more data.

Embracing a flow-oriented approach requires letting go of the end point in order to fully engage in an open-ended analytical mindset. There are obviously many ways that artists, spies, philosophers, and gardeners do this. In qualitative social research, the six-step process we discuss should be seen as only one of many techniques that could be used to enact and embody this mindset. Ours is a creative remix of long-standing principles of constructivist grounded theory, symbolic interaction, and postmodern ethnography, with a strong foundation of feminist epistemologies.

With this, we hope to contribute to ongoing conversations about how we might innovatively grapple with the complexities presented in our contemporary networked social worlds. As Markham has noted (2012), it is critical to consider the way that 'social media are changing the way we experience the world. What we consider self, structure, and 'the social' are far more temporal and ad hoc than fixed' (p. 52). In what might be called the postinternet era, considering one's role in constructing what counts – immediately or eventually – as data requires an ecological framework, a network sensibility, and methods that acknowledge that anything we find is one imaginary among many possible ones and thus is an outcome of one's choices to attend to certain elements of the situation rather than others. This doesn't invalidate one's study. Quite the opposite, it situates one's analysis and findings squarely within a perspective and in response or relation to the researcher's question. If the methods resonate with the phenomenon, and the choice of data sensibly fits the question and vice versa, it's more likely the goals of one's inquiry will be achieved and that the explanation of this process and the resulting arguments will be meritorious.

Any of us studying social or digital media will fully comprehend the power of working with large data sets. We also understand that there are epistemological and ontological dilemmas in using and embracing the term 'data' in qualitative inquiry, as this is a long-standing incommensurability with the strength of the qualitative approach. Working in the middle ground means simultaneously using and critically assessing whatever is eventually construed as data in our studies. Thus, we encourage qualitative researchers to not hide behind the rigor of traditional methods but be more present in their research. In this chapter, we hope we have provided a set of useful heuristics as well as a set of instructions. These can be considered, used, and adapted as needed to help build a reflexive mindset about what we're actually doing when we study complex situations where any new angle will yield a different set of data sets. We emphasize that the challenge for doing qualitative research in a datafication era is not as much about data as it is about reflexivity; the ability to discern what ought to count. The decisions we make as we move through these cultures of flow rely on our own interpretive authority rather than the temporary/temporal and arbitrarily objective or deceptively obdurate qualities of the stuff out there that we are attending to. This is true whether or not we recognize it. A flow-oriented approach is one way to make the interpretive more visible as a part of the process, and to provide an adaptive and flexible way to proceed within myriad choices of direction and outcome.

Notes

1. As noted by Danmarks Statistik, 2016: http://www.dst.dk/Site/Dst/Udgivelser/GetPubFile.aspx?id=20738&sid=itbef2016.
2. We could, for example, draw on the ideas that: anything we call a static object is a result of retrospective sensemaking (Weick, 1969); space is the crystallization of time (Castells, 2000); the 'individual', is not a universal concept (e.g. Strathern, 1992); that social reality is a continual negotiation of relations, through symbolic interactions (e.g. Blumer, 1969).
3. By 'selective' we mean to highlight the individual's decision, which is contextually situated, guided by the researcher's reflexive sensibilities, and yet likely based on a broader premise of selective or purposive sampling in qualitative inquiry (see Schreier, Chapter 6, this volume). Thus, it may be theoreticaly grounded and at the same time, a highly intuitive practice of 'follow the …' (Marcus, 1998); or even more precisely, Schiølin's (2012) injunction to 'Follow the verbs!', a reformulation of Latour's phrase, 'follow the actors' (e.g. 2005).
4. Again, here, we reference Goffman's (1959) distinctions between impressions given and given off. This might seem odd, since it lies outside Goffman's original use. We use it to emphasize that when we consider non-human agency, we can begin to see how data, like people, can 'give off' signals that are unintentional.
5. We are inspired by Adele Clarke's ideas about tinkering (2005), as well as how this idea connects to the work of a bricoleur (Levi-Strauss, 1966) as a strong epistemology for thinking about qualitative inquiry (Denzin and Lincoln, 2000; Kincheloe, 2001, 2005).
6. We prefer spy to detective, since we believe the detective is less open to study large-scale and complex networks over time without, perhaps, the immediate pressure to solve a case. Still, we're inspired by H. L. Goodall's (e.g. 1989, 2000) work on interpretive ethnography, who used the detective analogy quite often to describe a qualitative researcher's practices.
7. For a classic review of reflexivity, full of useful references to learn more about the specificities and subtlety with which reflexivity is enacted across a wide variety of disciplines, see Ashmore (1989).
8. For more on how quality and credibility are conceptualized in qualitative research, see Van Maanen (1988), Richardson (2000), Tracy (2010), Markham and Baym (2009); and Barbour, Chapter 14, this volume.
9. Terri Senft's (2013) notion of the grab is useful for understanding the temporal ways that we come to know situations and the temporary assemblages we use to produce such knowledge.

FURTHER READING

Clarke, Adele E. (2005) *Situational Analysis: Grounded Theory after the Postmodern Turn*. Thousand Oaks, CA: Sage.

Marcus, G. E. (1995) 'Ethnography in/of the world system: The emergence of multi-sited ethnography', *Annual Review of Anthropology*, 24: 95–117.

Markham, Annette N. (2013) 'Remix culture, remix methods: Reframing qualitative inquiry for social media contexts', in Norman K. Denzin and Michael D. Giardina (Eds.), *Global Dimensions of Qualitative Inquiry*. Walnut Creek, CA: Left Coast Press, Inc., pp. 63–81.

REFERENCES

Appadurai, Arjun (1990) 'Disjuncture and difference in the global cultural economy', *Theory, Culture & Society*, 7(2): 295–310. Available from: http://doi.org/10.1177/026327690007002017.

Ashmore, Malcolm (1989) *The Reflexive Thesis: Wrighting Sociology of Scientific Knowledge*. Chicago, IL: University of Chicago Press.

Baym, Nancy K. (2013) 'Data not seen: The uses and shortcomings of social media metrics', *First Monday*, 18(10). Available from: http://firstmonday.org/ojs/index.php/fm/article/view/4873. DOI:10.5210/fm.v18i10.4873.

Blumer, Herbert (1969) *Symbolic Interactionism: Perspective and Method*. Berkeley, CA: University of California Press.

boyd, danah, and Crawford, Kate (2012) 'Critical questions for big data: Provocations for a cultural, technological, and scholarly phenomenon', *Information, Communication & Society*, 15(5): 662–79.

Castells, Manuel (2000) *The Rise of the Network Society* (2nd edn). Oxford and Malden, MA: Blackwell Publishers.

Clarke, Adele E. (2003) 'Situational analyses: Grounded theory mapping after the postmodern turn', *Symbolic Interaction*, 26(4): 553–76.

Clarke, Adele E. (2005) *Situational Analysis: Grounded Theory After the Postmodern Turn*. Thousand Oaks, CA: Sage.

Denzin, Norman K. and Lincoln, Yvonna, S. (2000) 'The discipline and practice of qualitative research', in Norman K. Denzin, N. and Yvonna, S. Lincoln (Eds.), *Handbook of Qualitative Research*. Thousand Oaks, CA: Sage, pp. 1–28.

Dougherty, Meghan. (2015) *Virtual Digs: Excavating, Archiving, and Preserving the Web*. Unpublished manuscript.

Geertz, Clifford (1973) *The Interpretation of Cultures: Selected Essays*. New York: Basic Books.

Goffman, Erving (1959) *The Presentation of Self in Everyday Life*. London: Penguin.

Goodall, Harold L. (1989) *Casing a Promised Land: The Autobiography of an Organizational Detective as Cultural Ethnographer*. Carbondale, IL: Southern Illinois University Press.

Goodall, Harold L. (2000) *Writing the New Ethnography*. Walnut Creek, CA: Alta Mira.

Haraway, Donna (2008) *When Species Meet*. Minneapolis, MN: University of Minnesota Press.

Hine, Christine (2011) 'Internet research and unobtrusive methods', *Social Research Update*, (61): 1–4.

Kincheloe, Joe (2001) 'Describing the bricolage: Conceptualizing a new rigor in qualitative research', *Qualitative Inquiry*, 7(6): 679–92.

Kincheloe, Joe (2005) 'On to the next level: Continuing the conceptualization of the bricolage', *Qualitative Inquiry*, 11(3): 323–50. DOI:10.1177/1077800405275056.

Latour, Bruno (2005) *Reassembling the Social: An Introduction to Actor-Network-Theory*. Oxford: Oxford University Press.

Levi-Strauss, Claude (1966) *The Savage Mind (La Pensee Sauvage)*. Trans. George Weidenfeld. London: Weidenfeld and Nicolson, Ltd.

Marcus, George E. (1998) *Ethnography Through Thick and Thin*. Princeton, NJ: Princeton University Press.

Markham, Annette N. (1998) *Life Online: Researching Real Experience in Virtual Space*. Walnut Creek, CA: Altamira Press.

Markham, Annette N. (2003) 'Cultural junctures and ethical choices in Internet ethnography', in M. Thorset (Ed.), *Applied Ethics in Internet Research*. Trondheim, Norway: NTNU University Press, pp. 51–63.

Markham, Annette N. (2012) 'Moving into the flow: Using a network perspective to explore complexity in Internet contexts', in Stine Lomborg (Ed.), *Network Analysis: Methodological Challenges*. Aarhus, Denmark: University of Aarhus Center for Internet Research Monograph Series, pp. 47–58.

Markham, Annette N. (2013) 'Remix culture, remix methods: Reframing qualitative inquiry for social media contexts', in Norman K. Denzin and Michael D. Giardina (Eds.), *Global Dimensions of Qualitative Inquiry*. Walnut Creek, CA: Left Coast Press, Inc., pp. 63–81.

Markham, Annette N. and Baym, Nancy K. (Eds.) (2009) *Internet Inquiry: Conversations about Method*. London: Sage.

Markham, Annette N. and Lindgren, Simon (2014) 'From object to flow: Network sensibility, symbolic interactionism, and social media', in Mark D. Johns, Shing-Ling S. Chen, Laura A. Terlip (ed.) *Symbolic Interaction and New Social Media (Studies in Symbolic Interaction, Volume 43)* Emerald Group Publishing Limited, pp. 7–41.

Morgan, Gareth (1986) *Images of Organization*. Thousand Oaks, CA: Sage.

Pink, Sarah (2007) 'Walking with video', *Journal of Visual Studies*, 22(3): 240–52.

Richardson, Laurel (2000) 'Writing: A method of inquiry', in Norman K. Denzin and Yvonna, S. Lincoln (Eds.) *Handbook of Qualitative Research*. Thousand Oaks, CA: Sage, pp. 923–48.

Rodriguez, Amardo (2002) 'Culture to culturing. Re-imagining our understanding of intercultural relations', *Journal of Intercultural Communication*, 5. Available from: http://www.immi.se/intercultural/nr5/rodriguez.pdf.

Schiølin, Kasper (2012) 'Follow the verbs! A contribution to the study of the Heidegger–Latour connection', *Social Studies of Science*, 42(5): 775–86.

Senft, Theresa M. (2013) 'Hating Habermas: On exhibitionism, shame and life on the actually existing Internet', *Either/And*. Available from: http://eitherand.org/exhibitionism/hating-habermas-exhibitionismshame-life-actually-/.

Strathern, Marilyn (1992) *After Nature. English Kinship in the Late Twentieth Century*. Cambridge, UK: Cambridge University Press.

Tracy, Sarah J. (2010) 'Qualitative quality: Eight "big-tent" criteria for excellent qualitative research', *Qualitative Inquiry*, 16(10): 837–51.

Van Maanen, John (1988) *Tales of the Field: on Writing Ethnography*. Chicago, IL: University of Chicago Press.

Weick, Karl (1969) *The Social Psychology of Organizing*. New York: McGraw-Hill.

30

Ethics in Digital Research

Katrin Tiidenberg

INTRODUCTION

Research ethics as a topic of both public and scholarly debate tends to (re)surface when things go wrong. The history of research ethics could be told in our mistakes, and our collective attempts to learn from them. Ostensibly, we can start that history from the dehumanizing experiments of World War II, the Tuskegee syphilis study, and Stanley Milgram's groundbreaking yet disturbing research into human behavior. It can be said that (the reveal of) these mistakes led to the UN Declaration of Human Rights (1948), the Nuremberg Code (1949), the Declaration of Helsinki (1964), and the Belmont Report (1979); meant for protection of human subjects in biomedical and behavioral research; and continuously relevant in ethical management of most research happening with people today (see Mertens, Chapter 3, this volume).

Following the breadcrumb trail of research ethics failures through decades, we could tentatively add the uproar following the 2014 publication of the Facebook 'emotional contagion' study (Kramer et al., 2014) to the list. It meant researchers altering 689,000 Facebook users' news feeds to explore how exposure to emotional content influences what they posted. In May 2016 a student researcher leaked the data of 70,000 users of OKCupid (a dating platform), claiming he did so for the benefit of the scholarly community (Resnick, 2016). This indicates that while we may have learned from our past mistakes, and our newer ones may cause comparatively less harm, research ethics needs constant reflection. Neither the phenomena we study, the contexts we study them in, nor public perceptions of what is permissible are static.

The fact that an increasing amount of (social) research happens on, about, or with the help of the internet only complicates matters. While there is no consensus on the topic, compelling arguments have been made about the ethical specificity of digital context (Markham and Buchanan, 2015). Beaulieu and Estelalla (2012) even claim that internet research means a certain remediation of research practices, and thus a transformation of research objects, tools, and relations. Concurrently, digital research brings together a plethora of scholars with what can be diametrically opposing methodological, paradigmatic, epistemological, and ontological training and worldviews. Studies by scholars who consider themselves internet researchers coexist with experimental, correlational, and observational studies conducted online simply because it is convenient (Merriman, 2015; Tolich, 2014). This makes it quite difficult to agree on the need for, and content of, reasonable practices and sufficient standards for research.

In what follows, I outline some of the more persistent ethical issues that scholars involved in digital research face. Classic ethical concepts like informed consent, confidentiality, anonymity, privacy, publicity, and harm can be difficult to operationalize in a socio-technical context that is persistent, replicable, scalable, and searchable (boyd, 2010). In daily lives we often interact with software, interfaces and devices in ways that turn what we are used to considering an 'interactional context' into an 'active participant' (Markham, 2013). Scholars partaking in digital research, therefore, often find themselves faced with a lot of gray areas. Their individual sense of what is right and wrong; their discipline's conventions; the legal and institutional conditions of approval; and the competition for professional relevance in a world where a lot of research is undertaken by private companies like Facebook, may at times clash or collapse.

CHANGING DISCOURSES ABOUT THE INTERNET, SOCIABILITY, AND RESPONSIBILITY

Before moving on to ethics in digital qualitative data collection, I want to briefly address some of the current thinking on online interactions and sociability, particularly from the perspective of responsibility. Such discourses feed into and filter trending attitudes in research ethics.

Jose van Dijck (2013) offers a compelling theory of social media-driven changes in various social norms in her book *The Culture of Connectivity: A Critical History of Social Media*. For instance, the meaning and the norm of 'sharing' has, according to her, markedly shifted during the past decade. The coded structures of social media platforms like Facebook (see Ditchfield and Meredith, Chapter 32, this volume) impose buttons like 'Share' as social values. These 'have effects in cultural practices and legal disputes, far beyond platforms proper' (van Dijck, 2013, p. 21), but are alarmingly ambiguous in their meaning. In the example provided by van Dijck, sharing connotes both users distributing their own information to each other, as well as the sharing of that personal information by service providers with third parties (2013, p. 46). Similarly, Markham (2016, p. 192) points out that sharing has become the 'default relationship between the self and technological infrastructures', which discursively naturalizes the massive harvesting and storage of personal data by platforms. Markham (2016, p. 194) goes on to point out the dangers of the 'this is just how the internet works' discourse, which frames privacy as an individual burden, and removes 'agency from corporate interests, platform designs, and algorithmic activities that, in fact, quite powerfully and actively mediate how one's personal activities online become public and publicly available'.

These discursive and attitudinal shifts operate in a context where, despite Facebook CEO Mark Zuckerberg's attempts to convince us that our need for privacy indicates an unhealthy desire to hide something (Kirkpatrick, 2010a) or is perhaps a relic of the past (Kirkpatrick, 2010b), more than half of American social networking site users (58 percent) have changed their main site's privacy settings to only be accessible to friends (Madden, 2012). Practically, it does little to limit non-friends' access to much of our interactions on the site. Our comments on our friends' posts are governed by their privacy settings, not our own; and our friends get notifications of our comments on our other friends' posts, even if they are not themselves connected. It is not surprising then, that nearly half of social media users feel that managing their privacy controls is difficult (Madden, 2012), and they 'have limited control over how their data is used online' (Microsoft Trustworthy Computing, 2013). Yet, paradoxically, users also feel they are solely responsible for their privacy online (40 percent of all Europeans and 46 percent of all Americans, Kügler, 2014). Understandably this tension leads to the (American) public trusting Facebook even less than they trust the IRS or the post-Snowden NSA (boyd, 2016).

Additionally, the legally and morally dubious model of 'effective consent' (disclosure via terms of service agreement) has become a de facto standard in the industry (Flick, 2016, p. 17) and again operates by assigning responsibility to individual users instead of corporate players (2016, p. 20). Facebook's data policy (last revised January 30, 2015), for example, reveals that we have all agreed to them collecting information about what we do on the platform, what others do (sending us messages, uploading images of us), the constellations of people and groups around us, our device use (including geolocation), payments, third party websites and apps that we use that use Facebook services (e.g. when you log on to Slideshare using Facebook), information from companies we use that are owned by Facebook (i.e. Instagram, Whatsapp) and finally, and perhaps most eerily, about us and our activities 'on and off Facebook from third party partners', which might as well encompass one's entire web usage.

These troubling shifts in discourse of individual responsibility can be detected in the social research community itself (cf. Flick, 2016, or boyd, 2016, on lack of scholarly consensus regarding the ethical aspects of the aforementioned Facebook emotional contagion study, and Weller and Kinder-Kurlanda, 2015, for social media researchers' attitudes toward ethics in social media research). Researchers are having a hard time agreeing on what data is public and what data is private, and how publicly accessible data should be treated. Debates over boundaries and best practices of internet research ethics are ongoing (Flick, 2016; Markham and Buchanan, 2015; Mauthner et al., 2012). Various professional organizations – Association of Internet Researchers (Markham and Buchanan, 2012); the Norwegian National Committee for Research Ethics in the Social Sciences and the Humanities (NESH, 2014), The SATORI Ethics assessment in Internet Research Ethics (Shelley-Egan, 2015) – urge researchers to ask themselves those difficult questions, while increasingly realizing that the 'ethical guides of traditional disciplines are of limited usefulness' (Beaulieu and Estalella, 2012, p. 10).

DIGITAL QUALITATIVE DATA COLLECTION

Qualitative data collection on/in/through the internet is wide and varied, and as mentioned above, used by scholars from different disciplinary backgrounds. A brief look at the contents of this very *Handbook* reveals interviews (see Roulston and Choi, Chapter 15, this volume), focus group discussions (see Morgan and Hoffman, Chapter 16, this volume), observations (see Wästerfors, Chapter 20, this volume); and collection of textual, visual, audio and media data for narrative (see Murray, Chapter 17, this volume), conversation (see Jackson, Chapter 18, this volume), and discourse analyses (see Rau et al., Chapter 19, this volume) or performative ethnographies (see Denzin, Chapter 13, this volume). All of these can and are successfully conducted online and/or about internet-related phenomena. Our everyday lives weave through mediated and non-mediated contexts, thus delineating data collection by its digitality is problematic at best (for a persuasive complication of the online–offline divide in qualitative inquiry see Orgad (2009), and following responses by Bakardjieva (2009), and Gajjala (2009); see also Fielding, Chapter 37, this volume). Hence, it may be more sensible to focus on which internet-specific tensions arise in various methodological steps of qualitative data collection. After all, as Markham (2006) astutely points out, all of our methods decisions – from asking questions and defining field boundaries to interpreting data – are, in fact, ethics decisions (see also Mauthner et al., 2012, for a distilled discussion on what our methods 'do' ethically; see also Mertens, Chapter 3, this volume).

This approach shifts our focus from the collectables – from what we gather and create as data – to the process. We start thinking less about whether something was 'publicly' accessible and hence fair game to be grabbed and analyzed, and more about whether the fact that we can technically access it automatically means we should. Reviewing contributions from the early 2000s Eynon et al. (2008, p. 27) point out that, while digital research is not 'intrinsically more likely to be harmful than face-to-face methods', it can make it more difficult to evaluate risks of harm, and complicate judging participants' and wider publics' reactions to research. Analytically, this can be linked to the internet's affordances for human sociability – the fact that much of what used to be ephemeral in our everyday lives has become visible and traceable, often in 'forms divorced from both the source and the intended or actual audience' (Markham, 2011, p. 122; see also Markham, Chapter 33, this volume). Thus, while social media affordances of persistence, replicability, scalabilty and searchability (boyd, 2010) allow researchers unprecedented access to aspects of meaning-making or identity construction; they are also tinged with ambiguities of whether, what for, when, and for how long these processes should be observed, collected, and preserved for the sake of research.

CONTESTED CONCEPTS

Typically the focus of research ethics, as outlined in various declarations, acts, and guidelines, is on maintaining beneficence (minimization of harm and maximization of benefits), respect, and justice for people involved (Markham and Buchanan, 2012; see Mertens, Chapter 3, this volume). How these are translated into actual research practices (e.g. seeking informed consent or manipulating data for confidentiality, anonymity or privacy) in digitally saturated contexts continues to be an issue of significant debate. In the following I will describe some of the resurfacing complications surrounding these concepts.

Human Subjects Research

The 'human subjects model' can be considered a reaction to the harmful medical and experimental research conducted in the first half of the twentieth century, and is built on the concepts of confidentiality, anonymity, and informed consent; all derived from the basic human right to privacy (Eynon et al., 2008). While there are different approaches to what exactly counts as human subjects research, a typical definition focuses on interaction between the researcher and the participants, and the traceability of collected data to individuals (Walther, 2002). While in the earlier years of digital research there were some who advocated for considering online data text (White, 2002), it has become more common to be cautious, when estimating the 'humanness' of any data. This is more complicated in research where the unit of analysis is not a person, a group of people, or human behavior, but perhaps a malicious software attack, or density of a social network. Scholars may, in these cases, claim exemption from the human subjects model and the related ethics board review (Dittrich, 2015). However, as pointed out in the AoIR ethics guidelines:

> because all digital information at some point involves individual persons, consideration of principles related to research on human subjects may be necessary even if it is not immediately apparent how and where persons are involved in the research data. (Markham and Buchanan, 2012, p. 4)

Informed Consent

The idea of informed consent is grounded in principles of individual autonomy and beneficence. Broadly, it means that researchers commit to giving detailed information on the purpose, duration, methods, risks, and benefits of the study to participants, while participants have an absolute right to withdraw at any time (Marzano, 2012, p. 443).

The concept has a long history in medical and bioethics, where it is seen as an oversight mechanism to guarantee that research prioritizes participant welfare. Most ethics boards require that all research projects they deem human subjects research incorporate informed consent, or explicitly apply for an exception. Decisions over the need for, and type of informed consent procedures are based on the assumed steepness of risks. The more risk, the more formal (i.e. a signed form instead of an oral agreement) the informed consent process needs be. Risks are considered higher with research involving sensitive data or vulnerable participants, neither of which are as unproblematic as they may seem (cf. Egan et al., 2006, for a study where research participants with brain injuries found an ethics committee's ideas about their vulnerability patronizing and unhelpful). Exceptions tend to be given when risks of participating in the study are seen as minimal, for example, because of aggregation of data that is claimed to make it impossible to identify individual participants (cf. Zimmer, 2010, for how this as an assumption has backfired in the case of aggregated data collection from Facebook; see Ditchfield and Meredith, Chapter 32, this volume) and/or when research is not considered human subjects.

There are multiple tensions that arise when addressing the suitability of the informed consent model for digital research. On the one hand, there are worries that the mediated context makes it more difficult for the consent-seekers to 'determine autonomy, competence and understanding, and for consenters to understand the ramifications of the disclosure' (Flick, 2016, p. 17). On the other hand, it is quite common to claim that some spaces online can be considered public domain, and thus everything posted there can be considered 'naturally occurring data' (see Potter and Shaw, Chapter 12, this volume) and used without seeking any kind of explicit consent (cf. Rodham and Gavin, 2006, on informed consent and using data from message boards).

Additionally, the informed consent model is predicated on the expectation of research participants' autonomy, competence, and ability to understand risk; and assumptions of it being possible for researchers to imagine and predict future harm, including, for example, from storing data in a cloud, or sharing data in a data bank. Both of these assumptions are increasingly challenged as well (Mauthner, 2012; Markham, 2015; Markham and Buchanan, 2015).

Finally, voices from the ethnographic and feminist research traditions (Lomborg, 2012; Beaulieu and Estalella, 2012) point out the insufficiency and inappropriateness of rigid consent forms, and instead advocate for informed consent as a continuous negotiation (Lawson, 2004); a series of waivers of expected and behavioral social norms (Manson and O'Neill, 2007); or a situated decision that the researcher makes by focusing primarily on avoiding harm rather than consent per se (Markham and Buchanan, 2015). These approaches seem to be backed by studies about research participants' expectations toward the research process. Lewis and Graham (2007) found that participants reacted unfavorably to the idea of written consent, and were more interested in naturalistic, authentic approaches to information-giving.

Public or Private?

One of the more heated debates pertaining to digital research ethics is about what kinds of spaces, interactions, and data should be considered private, and which can be considered public. As Baym and boyd (2012, p. 322) point out, social media, thanks to its architecture and affordances, exponentially increases the potential for visibility and public engagement, thus requiring new skills and new mechanisms of control.

It is enticing to focus on the technical accessibility of information and define the internet as a vast public sphere. Categorizing it as such would seemingly release researchers from the difficult choices of making their presence known or seeking consent. This line of thinking is well illustrated in the following quote:

> it is important to recognize that any person who uses publicly available communication systems on the internet must be aware that these systems are, at their foundation and by definition, mechanisms for the storage, transmission, and retrieval of comments. While some participants have an expectation of privacy, it is extremely misplaced. (Walther, 2002, p. 207)

I would draw a parallel between the logic above and me saying that anyone traveling in the city must be aware that cars stop for pedestrians at lights and zebras. While it may be 'misplaced' for a person to cross randomly, I would not run them over based on my assumed right of way. Fortunately, an increasing number of social media researchers are less preoccupied with what people 'must' be aware of, and instead recognize that people and groups have particular expectations toward the privacy and publicity of their interactions no matter what their settings are (Bakardjieva and Feenberg, 2000; Ess and Jones, 2004; McKee and Porter, 2009; Sveningsson-Elm, 2009; Nissenbaum, 2010; Markham and Buchanan, 2012; Robards, 2013; Ess, 2014; Fileborn, 2015).

However, already a decade ago some authors (Barnes, 2006; Acquisti and Gross, 2006) noted a 'privacy paradox', where people claim they value privacy, yet their online practices seem to be counterproductive to maintaining it. A recent study from Hargittai and Marwick (2016) shows that while young adults may somewhat misunderstand risk or how effective particular privacy-protective behaviors are, these are not the sole reason for the privacy paradox. Rather, Hargittai and Marwick (2016, p. 3752) suggest that 'users have a sense of apathy or cynicism about online privacy, and specifically believe that privacy violations are inevitable and opting out is not an option'.

Defining something as private or public has implications for how we assume it should be treated in a research context. Can we look at it? Can we analyze it? Can we reproduce it? Should we alter it for the sake of confidentiality? How should we ask about using it? In a context, where terms of user agreements are entirely dictated by service providers, and produce accessible, user-generated content as a side effect, some claim that we should even assume that most publicity is unintended (Merriman, 2015). I find Donald Treadwell's (2014) thinking that differentiates intent of publication from publicity quite helpful here. According to him (2014, p. 51), most internet content – while public in the way billboards are – is much closer to informal discussions, or thinking aloud; than to stable opinions that have been published with intent.

The scope of this chapter does not allow us to fully delve into the complexity and the philosophical underpinnings of the concept of privacy, but Helen Nissenbaum's widely cited work (2004, 2010) is an excellent source. She suggests interpreting privacy through the lens of 'contextual integrity' (cf. also McKee and Porter, 2009, on 'perceived privacy', and Warrell and Jacobsen, 2014, on 'intended audiences'). In our everyday lives, we all move through a plurality of different realms, each of which involve a distinct set of norms, roles, and expectations (Nissenbaum, 2004, p. 137). These include norms of information flow. As long as the information is flowing appropriately (Nissenbaum, 2010, p. 2) we feel our privacy to be maintained. The difficulty for researchers lies in operationalizing this concept. Do we commit to always asking what people's expectations are? This is undoubtedly not possible in many research situations. Similarly it is naïve to assume that people's expectations are stable or informed.

Additionally, recent years' key texts (Markham and Buchanan, 2012; Lomborg, 2012; Markham and Buchanan, 2015) recommend 'the distance principle' as a mechanism of thinking about privacy. The distance principle examines the distance between the researcher and the participants, but more importantly between data collected and the persons who created whatever content the data consists of. Through that, the potential for causing harm, and the appropriate course of action in terms of informed consent is assessed (Lomborg, 2012, p. 22). The smaller the distance, the more careful we need to be. Distance is considered to be smaller between a small sample of identifiable status updates and the people who posted them, than it is, for example, between the people who have tweeted and a large sample of automatically scraped, aggregated tweets.

Finally, in some good advice from Markham and Buchanan (2015, p. 6) it might not be all that helpful to ask if something is private or public in contexts, where 'information flow is constant and public, where people are always connected, or where cutting, pasting, forwarding, reposting, and other mashup practices remix our personal information in globally distributed, complex networks'. Instead, they suggest (2015) that we focus on people's expectations; on the sensitivity and vulnerability of both people and data; and primarily, on the impetus to do no harm.

Anonymity and Confidentiality

Anonymity and confidentiality are classic promises made to research participants in social research, and concepts often contemplated together, although their focus is slightly different. Ethics review boards systematically require both for approval. While confidentiality means accessing and sharing personal information only as authorized by the person concerned (and typically includes assuring participants their data will not be accessed by anyone but the researchers), anonymity is about ensuring that the person cannot be identified from the research data (Felzmann, 2013, p. 20). Typically anonymity is deemed sufficiently established when 'personally identifiable information' like names and ID numbers are stripped (for a discussion on the differences between the US and European definitions of personally identifiable information and its implications for anonymity, see Zimmer, 2010, p. 319).

The plausibility of either of those promises is questionable in a context where data-mining technologies can link participants to the 'information they produce and consume via a range of mobile devices, game consoles and other internet based technologies' (Markham, 2012, p. 336), and potential risks to security and integrity of data are manifold (Buchanan et al., 2011). Incidentally, it has occasionally been implied that internet pseudonyms, which participants choose for themselves, are far enough removed from their legal identities, and are thus enough to ensure confidentiality. This assumption creates ample difficulties (see Sveningsson, 2004, for a discussion on the necessity of protecting participants' internet pseudonyms as well as their legal identities). Similarly some researchers (Kendall, 2002) have had experiences of their participants rejecting the anonymity researchers attempt to provide by changing names and details. This puts the scholar in a difficult position between respecting and empowering the participants, predicting possible harm, and institutional demands of their IRB approval.

Beaulieu and Estalella (2012, p. 11) point out that for mediated ethnographies, which use direct quotes from the web, removing identifying details and assigning new pseudonyms is not enough. They talk about 'traceability' instead of anonymity, and suggest it shifts our focus toward 'exposure, ownership and authorship' (2012, p. 5) of content published online. This may mean that ethnographers are simply no longer in a position to offer subject protection, as anonymization has become effectively impossible (2012, p. 12).

Alongside these discussions there are also questions regarding the security of data storage – the format it is stored in, its location, the duration of storage. Researchers are taking steps to increase security by using encryption, passwords, onscreen working methods, and tracking software (Aldridge et al., 2010), all of which, while helpful, are not guarantees of security.

Sharing and Storing Qualitative Data

It is more and more common for funding agencies and research governance institutions to require that researchers share their data in digital archives and depositories. This requirement can even be linked to withholding of final grant payments (Mauthner, 2012). Philosophically, it relies on an admirable expectation that information and research results are 'public goods', access to which is a basic right (Willinsky, 2006). However, it also implies normalization of standardized, automatized and regulated data collection and storage (Mauthner, 2012). This is particularly problematic for qualitative researchers, because it undermines the ontological, epistemological, and ethical implications of trust, rapport, and the dialogic co-construction of data – all long-standing traditions in qualitative inquiry. The emotional relationship that develops between a researcher and a participant during some qualitative research is seen as creating an additional layer of ethical responsibility, which is, arguably, not available when qualitative data is accessed from a data bank (Crossen-White, 2015, citing Richardson and Godfrey, 2003). Perhaps even more importantly, seeking informed consent to share qualitative interview data in an archive constitutes different 'moral and ontological conditions of possibility' for storytelling, which may alter the very stories we are told (Mauthner, 2012, p. 164). Yet, anonymizing qualitative data to the extent where it is shareable in good conscience, may lead to it losing so much of its contextual integrity that the scientific value of its future use becomes questionable (see Corti, Chapter 11, this volume).

Stolen and Hacked Data

Finally, a short note on using stolen or hacked data in research. Unfortunately, due to malicious privacy hacks and failures of technology, sets of data not intended to be publicly shared, viewed or researched, are regularly made available online. These data may offer interesting insights into various aspects of human co-existence. They may also be unproblematically taken advantage of by corporate or individual developers, researchers, or journalists, thus presenting temptation for scholars to 'make something good out of a bad thing'. Consequentialist claims that no further harm is coming to those whose data is reused, are sometimes employed to justify these desires. As a researcher interested in visual self-presentation, sexuality, and shame, I would have found analyzing the leaked images of the Snappening (thousands of Snapchat accounts were hacked and photos leaked in 2014) or the Fappening (a collection of almost 500 private pictures of celebrities were leaked in 2014) quite gratifying. Similarly, the leaked Ashley Madison data would have probably been of interest to scholars researching online sexual behavior, dating, interpersonal relations, or gender. What can be said about this?

While using hacked or stolen data is so far mostly absent from ethics guidelines, it is sometimes discussed among members of professional organizations (e.g. the AoIR mailing list) or at conferences. In line with the dilemmas described above, concepts of privacy and publicity are employed (the data are, after all, now 'public'), as well as conditions of aggregation and anonymization, for non-qualitative research. Because of the lack of published deliberations on the topic, I would here rely on Ben Zevenbergen's email (AoIR mailing list, ethics discussion, October 2015, cited with permission), which complements this chapter's contextual-ethics approach, and summarizes many of the opinions voiced in that discussion. Zevenbergen pointed out, and I agree, that using stolen, leaked, and hacked data for research adds more unintended audiences to it, and implicitly condones (perhaps even incentivizes) the act of hacking and publishing ill-sourced datasets, and should thus be avoided.

MAKING CHOICES

Considering the above-described complexity, it is unsurprising that experts are reluctant to recommend clear-cut one-size-fits-all guidelines. Instead a case-based, inductive approach is often recommended. Turning ethical decision-making into a deliberative process during all steps of inquiry enables 'a more proactive role in determining how best – on a case-by-case basis – to enact beneficence, justice, and respect for persons' (Markham and Buchanan, 2015, p. 8). To illustrate, I offer some examples of ethics-related decision-making in digital qualitative data collection from some of my own recent projects.

I will be drawing on examples from two research projects – first, an ethnography with a community of sexy-selfie enthusiasts on Tumblr.com, and then, a study of how pregnant women present themselves on Instagram. In both cases people post scantily clad (or unclad) pictures of their bodies on the internet, and the data is public in terms of the posts being accessible to everyone (one needs to have downloaded the Instagram app in the case of Instagram, but there is not even a need to have an account in the case of Tumblr).

The research questions of the Tumblr study (Figure 30.1) meant I was collecting data ethnographically (see Buscatto, Chapter 21, this volume), which included talking to people; and my data collection spanned years. In addition, the topic involved nudity and sexuality, and I was aware from my discussions with the participants that they perceived the space as somewhat private, despite it

RESEARCH QUESTIONS:

What do images MEAN FOR people who post them?

What do people DO when they post selfies?

Why are selfies experienced as affecting our bodies and selves?

→ DATA COLLECTION:

ETHNOGRAPHY (INTERVIEW, ANALYSIS OF BLOGS ETC.)

LONG TERM

↓

INFORMED CONSENT

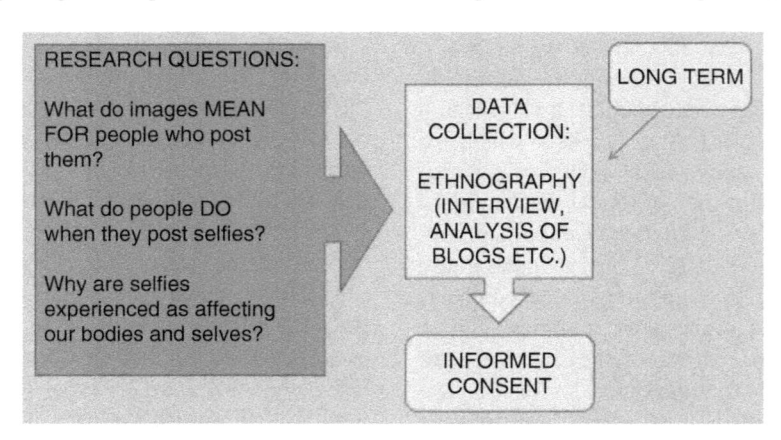

Figure 30.1 Tumblr study, research context

being technically publicly accessible. Thus I approached it as sensitive data. Taking all this into account, my choice to ask for informed consent is unsurprising.

During the Tumblr study, I found myself particularly drawn to the ideas of the ethics of care. Held (2006, p. 9) has defined care as both a value and a practice. The ethics of care ideally prescribes 'relations of trust and mutual respect' (Boellstorff et al., 2012, p. 129), and is seen as something that goes beyond avoiding harm. Based on recommendations in literature, I attempted to practice an ethics of care through dialogic consent, accurate portrayal, ethical fabrication, and doing good. These manifested as the following:

1   Despite having solicited 'blanket consent' at the beginning of my study, I double-checked with participants whenever entering a new stage of research ('I will now start looking at your images, is it still okay for me to do so?'), and when I wanted to include particular images in presentations or publications.
2   I kept interested participants in the loop of what I was doing to the data they helped me create via a research blog. It allowed me to do occasional member checks regarding some of my interpretations.
3   Markham (2012) has articulated the idea of ethical fabrication for protecting participants' privacy in contexts where public and private are shifting or difficult to interpret. She offers composite accounts, fictional narratives, and remix techniques as examples. I incorporated this idea, and devised some techniques particularly suitable for visual data. I edited all of the images I reproduced with an IOS application that made them look like pencil sketches, which retained visual and compositional detail, while reducing recognizability. I also somewhat altered the wording in the direct quotes from the web, doing reverse Google searches to make sure the altered text no longer (at least based on Google's data crawlers' current capabilities) led back to the blogs I studied.
4   While it is difficult to measure one's beneficial impact on the people studied without sounding hopelessly pretentious, it has been my understanding from five years' worth of conversations, that being a part of my research project has created enjoyable networks and carved out a space of self-reflection for my participants, which has had a therapeutic effect and assisted in them developing a certain sense of empowerment.

The second study I want to touch on had a markedly different context (Figure 30.2), both in terms of the questions and the practicalities. I was interested in people's self-presentations through the content they had chosen to publish on Instagram.

The practicalities of the project only allowed a month for data collection, but I had high-level technical assistance, which meant I could streamline it by experimenting with Instagram's API, which I had been curious about beforehand. Instagram doesn't have an internal messaging system[1] or reveal account holders' email addresses, thus my only option of reaching out to the approximately

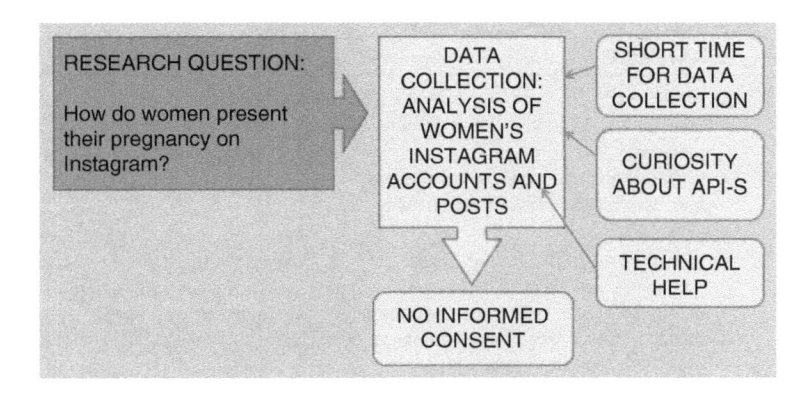

Figure 30.2   Instagram study, research context

250 accounts I included in the sample was by publicly commenting on their photos. I thought this was likely to be interpreted as 'creepy', and decided against it. This meant either forgoing informed consent or giving up on the project based on an assumption that the users would find my analysis of their images 'creepy' as well.

Table 30.1 shows my risk analysis to decide whether to continue without informed consent. Compared to my Tumblr study, people's practices indicated a markedly different perception of privacy. Where on Tumblr[2] people went to considerable length to protect their anonymity or, what has been called 'plausible deniability' by one of my participants, on Instagram real names and locations were regularly posted, and people systematically hashtagged their content to increase its searchability and visibility (e.g. concise informative hashtags and Instagram-specific attention-driven hashtags like #follow4follow or #like4like).

Based on the normative stances regulating pregnancy versus those policing sexually explicit conduct in Western capitalist societies, I decided the potential harm was much higher in the case of my research accidentally outing someone as a sex-blogger on Tumblr, than it was if I accidentally exposed someone as posting pregnancy- and family-related content from under their full name on Instagram. With significant unease, I thus decided to continue the study without informed consent, but tried to incorporate some of my practices of care developed during the Tumblr study.

a. I set up an Instagram account for purposes of accountability, described my study in the profile space, and offered an email address, where I could be reached (no one has emailed me, 18 people followed me back). I followed all of the accounts that had made it into my sample from this account. To turn accountability into a process, I used the researcher account to now and then go and 'like' some posts on the accounts in my sample.
b. I kept up my visual ethical fabrication techniques, and anonymized names and locations.
c. I 'outsourced' my member checks by engaging in regular dialog with trusted colleagues to make sure I portrayed these women accurately and fairly.

CONCLUSION

The purpose of this chapter has been to unsettle the approach to research ethics that equates it with a formalized list of rules, and can be seen as made dominant by the standardizing and streamlining attempts of ethics review boards, funding agencies, and research institutions today. Looking at widely used dictionary definitions of ethics we see that it may be interpreted as a consciousness of moral importance (Merriam Webster definition 2d) or a system of values (Merriam Webster definition 2a). In that case it becomes

Table 30.1 Comparing risk and privacy for the Tumblr study and the Instagram study

	NSFW TUMBLR	PREGNANCY ON INSTAGRAM
PERCEPTION OF PRIVACY	MORE PRIVATE • names, faces, locations, tattoos systematically removed • no hashtags, or personalized hashtags not intended for platform-wide searchability	MORE PUBLIC • names, faces, locations regularly included • hashtags suitable for searchability
POTENTIAL HARM FOR INDIVIDUAL	SEX = MORAL PANIC Accidental outing of participants' sexual preferences and lifestyles could cause harm to career, reputation, and personal relationships. People kept their blogs hidden from most of their other social networks.	PREGNANCY = SOCIALLY SUCCESSFUL STATE. Increase in social and moral capital for women, but are pregnant women vulnerable by default? What about the possible harm to unborn children?

> **Box 30.1**
>
> For other recent examples where qualitative researchers describe their ethics-related decision-making in great detail see Bianca Fileborn's and Stine Lomborg's work. Fileborn (2015) used Facebook to recruit study participants, and experienced a loss of control over where and with whom her recruitment advertisement was shared. She writes of the interesting conundrum of accountability, intended audiences, and her possible roles as a researcher, when friends of her friends comment on her study under these shared posts.
>
> Lomborg (2012, pp. 24–9) describes her decision-making regarding the necessity of informed consent in a Twitter- and blog-based research project. While all of her data were, supposedly, both public and non-sensitive, the perceived privacy of her informants led her to opting for informed consent.

impossible, if not absurd, to rely on an external checklist. After all, how does one practice consciousness through a list of mandatory steps? A checklist-driven mentality presumes that institutional boards and individual scientists are able to predict ethical issues. Yet, we know, even from the relatively short history of the internet that there may be issues '"downstream" and only rise to the surface due to a change in Internet architecture, Internet norms, or even legal changes' (Markham and Buchanan, 2015, p. 10).

Thus, to bring the chapter to a close, I would offer an anti-checklist checklist; a set of reminders for those planning digital qualitative data collection and open to the approach of research ethics as situated, responsible decision-making. These may serve as reminders at critical junctures in specific projects (Markham and Buchanan, 2012), and hopefully shift our orientation from the past to the future (Markham, 2015).

- Our discourses about both (research) ethics and the internet are a result of 'tangles of human and non-human elements, embedded in deep – often invisible – structures of software, politics and habits' (Markham, 2015, p. 247). It's important to interrogate our assumptions, talk to colleagues, read texts by scholars from different disciplines.
- Despite the dominant discourse of personal responsibility, the technological affordances of networked sociality seem to leave our privacy at other people's discretion much more than before. Just because something is technically accessible and collectable, doesn't mean it should be accessed and collected.
- Having previous experience with internet research, or being an avid internet user, does not guarantee our understanding of other people's internet use. Behavioral expectations and perceptions do not seamlessly translate from space to space and group to group.
- All methods questions are ethics questions – 'most basically, a method is nothing more or less than a means of getting something done. And every choice one makes about how to get something done is grounded in a set of moral principles' (Markham, 2006, p. 16). Thus, we need to consider the ethical implications in our methods of defining field boundaries; accessing participants; raising a sample; collecting, organizing, analyzing, and archiving information; representing ourselves and others in writing; framing knowledge; and maintaining professional autonomy (see Markham, 2006; and Mauthner et al., 2012).
- We should avoid being lulled into complacency by the seemingly increasing regulation of research ethics. We are still responsible for our own research, even after our ethical review forms have been approved (Mauthner, 2012). Neither the possibility nor sufficiency of informed consent, confidentiality, or anonymity; the definition and implications of vulnerability or beneficence; the delineation of something as private or public; or what publicity indicates for research are obvious or uniformly observable in digital settings. Instead, they almost always depend on the context. Having an ethics review board approval and following the steps outlined in it may be a good start, but it does not guarantee a problem-free research process, nor does it absolve the researcher from being constantly engaged.

Granted, approaching research ethics as a personal pledge to be critically situated in all of one's research-related decisions is not an overly comfortable stance. It is future oriented, carries an expectation of the unexpected, and demands a certain willingness to stomach uncertainty. Concurrently, we may claim that recurring ethics breaches indicate individual researchers' lack of ability to use self-reflection as outlined above. But lack of clarity and the need for ongoing dialogue and adjustments in how research practices are taught and honed is, not exactly new or unfamiliar for us as scholars. We know how to do this. It means extending the qualitative inquiry's epistemological and ontological sensitivity to context to study design and data collection. It means paying attention to what and how we teach.

Notes

1. Instagram Direct did not allow starting conversations with just text at that time, so I would have had to send an image to reach out, and since these accounts were not following me, they would have shown up as requests not as messages.
2. Both Tumblr and Instagram allow public and private accounts, the content posted to public accounts can be accessed without having a Tumblr account on Tumblr, but one has to have the Instagram app to be able to search the public content on Instagram. A viewer does not have to become a follower to view the public content of the posters neither on Instagram nor on Tumblr.

FURTHER READING

Markham, Annette N. and Buchanan, Elizabeth (2015) 'Ethical considerations in digital research contexts', in James D. Wright (ed.), *Encyclopedia for Social & Behavioral Sciences*. Oxford: Elsevier Science, pp. 606–13.

Nissenbaum, Helen (2010) *Privacy in Context: Technology, Policy, and the Integrity of Social Life*. Stanford, CA: Stanford University Press.

Zimmer, M. (2010) '"But the data is already public": On the ethics of research in Facebook', *Ethics and Information Technology*, 12(4): 313–25.

REFERENCES

Acquisti, A. and Gross, R. (2006) 'Imagined communities: Awareness, information sharing, and privacy on Facebook', *Lecture Notes in Computer Science*, 4258: 36–58.

Aldridge, J., Medina, J., and Ralphs, R. (2010) 'The problem of proliferation: Guidelines for improving the security of qualitative data in a digital age', *Research Ethics*, 6(1): 3–9.

Bakardjieva, Maria (2009) 'A response to Shani Orgad', in Annette N. Markham and Nancy K. Baym (eds.), *Internet Inquiry: Conversations about Method*, Los Angeles: Sage, pp. 54–60.

Bakardjieva, M. and Feenberg, A. (2000) 'Involving the virtual subject', *Ethics and Information Technology*, 2(4): 233–40.

Barnes, S. B. (2006) 'A privacy paradox: Social networking in the United States', *First Monday*, 11(9). Retrieved from http://firstmonday.org/article/view/1394/1312.

Baym, N. K. and boyd, d. (2012) 'Socially mediated publicness: An introduction', *Journal of Broadcasting & Electronic Media*, 56(3): 320–9.

Beaulieu, A. and Estalella, A. (2012) 'Rethinking research ethics for mediated settings', *Information, Communication & Society*, 15(1): 23–42.

Boellstorff, Tom, Nardi, Bonnie, Pearce, Celia, and Taylor, T. L. (2012) *Ethnography and Virtual Worlds: A Handbook of Method*. Princeton University Press, Kindle Edition.

boyd, danah (2010) 'Social network sites as networked publics: Affordances, dynamics, and implications', in Zizi Papacharissi (ed.), *Networked Self: Identity, Community, and Culture on Social Network Sites*. New York: Routledge, pp. 39–58.

boyd, d. (2016) 'Untangling research and practice: What Facebook's "emotional contagion" study teaches us', *Research Ethics*, 12(1): 4–13.

Buchanan, E., Aycock, J., Dexter, S., Dittrich, D., and Hvizdak, E. (2011) 'Computer science security research and human subjects: Emerging considerations for research ethics boards', *Journal of Empirical Research on Human Research Ethics*, 6(2): 71–83.

Crossen-White, Holly L. (2015) 'Using digital archives in historical research: What are the ethical concerns for a "forgotten" individual?', *Research Ethics*, 11(2): 108–19.

Dittrich, D. (2015) 'The ethics of social honeypots', *Research Ethics*, 11(4): 192–210.

Egan, J., Chenoweth, L. I., and McAuliffe, D. (2006) 'Email-facilitated qualitative interviews with traumatic brain injury survivors: A new accessible method', *Brain Injury*, 20(12): 1283–94.

Ess, Charles (2014) *Digital Media Ethics*. Cambridge, Malden: Polity Press.

Ess, Charles and Jones, Steve (2004) 'Ethical decision-making and internet research: Recommendations from the AoIR ethics working committee', in Elizabeth Buchanan (ed.), *Readings in Virtual Research Ethics: Issues and Controversies*. London: Information Science Publishing, pp. 27–44.

Eynon, Rebecca, Fry, Jenny, and Schroeder, Ralph (2008) 'The ethics of internet research', in Nigel Fielding, Raymond M. Lee and G. Blank (eds.), *The Handbook of Online Research Methods*, London: Sage, pp. 23–41.

Felzmann, Heike (2013) 'Ethical issues in internet research: International good practice and Irish research ethics documents', in Cathy Fowley, Claire English and Sylvie Thouseny (eds.), *Internet Research, Theory and Practice: Perspectives from Ireland*. Dublin: Research-publishing net, pp. 11–32.

Fileborn, B. (2015) 'Participant recruitment in an online era: A reflection on ethics and identity', *Research Ethics*, 12(2): 97–115.

Flick, C. (2016) 'Informed consent and the Facebook emotional manipulation study', *Research Ethics*, 12(1): 14–28.

Gajjala, Radhika (2009) 'Response to Shani Orgad', in Annette M. Markham and Nancy K. Baym (eds.), *Internet Inquiry: Conversations about Method*. Los Angeles: Sage, pp. 61–8.

Hargittai, E. and Marwick, A. (2016) '"What can I really do?" Explaining the privacy paradox with online apathy', *International Journal of Communication*, 10(2016): 3737–57.

Held, Virginia (2006) *The Ethics of Care: Personal, Political, Global*. Oxford: Oxford University Press.

Kendall, Lori (2002) *Hanging Out in the Virtual Pub: Masculinities and Relationships Online*. Berkeley, CA: University of California Press.

Kirkpatrick, Marshall (2010a) *The Facebook Effect: The Inside Story of the Company That Is Connecting the World*. New York: Simon & Schuster.

Kirkpatrick, Marshall (2010b) 'Facebook's Zuckerberg Says The Age of Privacy is Over, ReadWrite', Read Write. Retrieved from http://readwrite.com/2010/01/09/facebooks_zuckerberg_says_the_age_of_privacy_is_ov

Kramer, A. D. I., Guillory, J. E., and Hancock, J. T. (2014) 'Experimental evidence of massive-scale emotional contagion through social networks', *Proceedings of the National Academy of Sciences*, 111(24): 8788–90.

Kügler, Dennis (2014) 'Individuals should be responsible for their online privacy, not governments', says survey. Retrieved from https://www.ivpn.net/blog/individuals-responsible-online-privacy-governments-says-survey.

Lawson, Danielle (2004) 'Blurring the boundaries: Ethical considerations for online research using synchronous CMC forums', in Elizabeth A. Buchanan (ed.), *Readings in Virtual Research Ethics: Issues and Controversies*. Hershey, PA and London: Information Science Publishing, pp. 80–100.

Lewis, J. and Graham, J. (2007) 'Research participants' views on ethics in social research: Issues for research ethics committees', *Research Ethics*, 3(3): 73–9.

Lomborg, S. (2012) 'Personal internet archives and ethics', *Research Ethics*, 9(1): 20–31.

Madden, Mary (2012) 'Privacy management on social media sites', *Pew Research Center's Internet & American Life Project*. Retrieved from http://pewinternet.org/Reports/2012/Privacy-management-on-social-media.aspx.

Manson, Neil C. and O'Neill, Onora (2007) *Rethinking Informed Consent in Bioethics*. New York: Cambridge University Press.

Markham, A. N. (2006) 'Method as ethic, ethic as method', *Journal of Information Ethics*, 15(2): 37–55.

Markham, Annette N. (2011) 'Internet research', in David Silverman (ed.), *Qualitative Research: Theory, Method, and Practices* (3rd edn). London: Sage, pp. 111–27.

Markham, A. N. (2012) 'Fabrication as ethical practice: Qualitative inquiry in ambiguous internet contexts', *Information, Communication and Society*, 15(3): 334–53.

Markham, Annette N. (2013) 'Dramaturgy of digital experience', in Charles Edgley (ed.), *The Drama of Social Life: A Dramaturgical Handbook*. Burlington: Ashgate, pp. 279–94.

Markham, Annette N. (2015) 'Producing ethics [for the digital near future]', in R. A. Lind (ed.), *Producing Theory in a Digital World 2.0: The Intersection of Audiences and Production in Contemporary Theory, Volume 2*. New York: Peter Lang, pp. 247–56.

Markham, Annette N. (2016) 'From using to sharing: A story of shifting fault lines in privacy and data protection narratives', in Bastiaan Vanacker and Don Heider (eds.), *Digital Ethics*. London: Peter Lang, pp. 189–205.

Markham, Annette N., and Buchanan, Elizabeth (2012) 'Ethical Decision-Making and Internet Research, Recommendations from the AoIR Ethics Working Committee (Version 2.0)'. Retrieved from http://aoir.org/reports/ethics2.pdf.

Markham, Annette N., and Buchanan, Elizabeth (2015) 'Ethical considerations in digital research contexts', in James, D. Wright (ed.), *Encyclopedia for Social & Behavioral Sciences*. Waltham, MA: Elsevier, pp. 606–13.

Marzano, Marco (2012) 'Informed consent', in Jaber F. Gubrium, James A. Holstein, Amir B. Marvasti and Karyn D. McKinney (eds.), *The SAGE Handbook of Interview Research: The Complexity of the Craft*. London: Sage, pp. 443–56.

Mauthner, Melanie S. (2012) '"Accounting for our part of the entangled webs we weave": Ethical and moral issues in digital data sharing', in Tina Miller, Maxine Birch, Melanie Mauthner and Julie Jessop (eds.), *Ethics in Qualitative Research*. London: Sage, pp. 157–76.

Mauthner, Melanie, Birch, Maxine, Miller, Tina, and Jessop, Julie (2012) 'Conclusion: Navigating ethical dilemmas and new digital horizons', in Tina Miller, Maxine Birch, Melanie Mauthner and Julie Jessop (eds.), *Ethics in Qualitative Research* (2nd edn). London: Sage, pp. 176–87.

McKee, Heidi A. and Porter, James E. (2009) *The Ethics of Internet Research. A Rhetorical, Case-based Process*. New York: Peter Lang.

Merriman, B. (2015) 'Ethical issues in the employment of user-generated content as experimental stimulus: Defining the interests of creators', *Research Ethics*, 10(4): 196–207.

Microsoft Trustworthy Computing (2013) 2013 privacy survey results. Retrieved from http://download.microsoft.com/download/A/A/9/AA96E580-E0F6-4015-B5BB-ECF9A85368A3/Microsoft-Trustworthy-Computing-2013-Privacy-Survey-Results.pdf.

Nissenbaum, H. (2004) 'Privacy as contextual integrity', *Washington Law Review*, 79(119): 119–59.

Nissenbaum, Helen (2010) *Privacy in Context: Technology, Policy, and the Integrity of Social Life*. Stanford, CA: Stanford University Press.

Norwegian National Committee for Research Ethics in the Social Sciences and the Humanities (NESH) (2014) *Ethical Guidelines for Internet Research*.

Orgad, Shani (2009) 'Question two: How can researchers make sense of the issues involved in collecting and interpreting online and offline data?', in Annette N. Markham and Nancy K. Baym (eds.), *Internet Inquiry: Conversations about Method*, Los Angeles, CA: Sage, pp. 33–53.

Resnick, B. (2016) 'Researchers just released profile data on 70,000 OkCupid users without permission', Vox. Retrieved from: https://www.vox.com/2016/5/12/11666116/70000-okcupid-users-data-release

Richardson, J. C. and Godfrey, B. S. (2003) 'Towards ethical practice in the use of archived transcript interviews', *International Journal of Social Research Methodology*, 6(3): 347–55.

Robards, B. (2013) 'Friending participants: Managing the researcher–participant relationship on social network sites', *Young*, 21(3): 217–35.

Rodham, K. and Gavin, J. (2006) 'The ethics of using the internet to collect qualitative research data', *Research Ethics*, 2(3): 92–7.

Shelley-Egan, Clare (2015) *Ethics assessment in different fields: Internet Research Ethics*. Retrieved from http://satoriproject.eu/media/2.d.2-Internet-research-ethics.pdf.

Sveningsson, Malin (2004) 'Ethics in internet ethnography', in Elizabeth Buchanan (ed.), *Readings in Virtual Research Ethics: Issues and Controversies*. London: Information Science Publishing, pp. 45–61.

Sveningsson-Elm, Malin (2009) 'How do various notions of privacy influence decisions in qualitative internet research?', in Annette, N. Markham and Nancy K. Baym (eds.), *Internet Inquiry: Conversations about Method*. Los Angeles: Sage, pp. 69–87.

Tolich, M. (2014) 'What can Milgram and Zimbardo teach ethics committees and qualitative researchers about minimizing harm?', *Research Ethics*, 10(2): 86–96.

Treadwell, Donald (2014) *Introducing Communication Research: Paths of Inquiry* (2nd edn). Los Angeles: Sage.

Van Dijck, Jose (2013) *The Culture of Connectivity: A Critical History of Social Media*. Oxford University Press, Kindle Edition.

Walther, J.B. (2002) 'Research ethics in Internet enabled research: Human subjects issues and methodological myopia', *Ethics and Information Technology*, 4(3): 205–16.

Warrell, J. G. and Jacobsen, M. (2014) 'Internet research ethics and the policy gap for ethical practice in online research settings', *Canadian Journal of Higher Education Revue canadienne d'enseignement supérieur*, 44(1): 22–37.

Weller, Katrin and Kinder-Kurlanda, Katharina (2015) '"I love thinking about ethics!" Perspectives on ethics in social media research', Selected Papers of Internet Research, *Proceedings of ir15 – Boundaries and Intersections*. Retrieved from http://spir.aoir.org/index.php/spir/article/view/997.

White, M. (2002) 'Representations or people?', *Ethics and Information Technology*, 4(3): 249–66.

Willinsky, J. (2006) *The Access Principle: The Case for Open Access to Research and Scholarship*. Cambridge, MA: Massachusetts Institute of Technology.

Zevenbergen, Ben (2015) E-mail to the Association of Internet Researcher's mailing list, on the ethics of using hacked data, cited with permission.

Zimmer, M. (2010) '"But the data is already public": On the ethics of research in Facebook', *Ethics and Information Technology*, 12(4): pp. 313–25.

Collecting Data for Analyzing Blogs

Wivian Weller, Lucélia de Moraes Braga Bassalo and Nicolle Pfaff

INTRODUCTION

In the field of qualitative research, the last decades have seen a growing interest in collecting and analyzing data from the cyberspace, detected also by the number of new books and articles related to Internet research (see Fielding et al., 2017; Kozinets, 2015). This is due, in part, to a consensus that the impact of the Internet on social life is vast and unquestionable. This impact is noticed in every sphere of daily life, whether public or private, in personal, family, individual and institutional dimensions. Additionally, the Internet, as a worldwide web of interconnected computers, has led to the appearance of new forms of communication, affording new ways of interaction among an ever larger number of people.

Various authors have analyzed the importance of these transformations, leading to the creation of terms such as *cyberspace*, coined by William Gibson in 1984, to refer to the world that came into existence with the interconnection of the world wide web of computers. Lévy (1997) introduced the concept of *cyberculture* and pointed out that people's action in cyberspace – supplying, obtaining or making information circulate – has promoted different ways of seeing, being, thinking and feeling, which developed with the expansion of cyberspace. The author also advocates that virtual space is a real space, even if it is immaterial, as it has no territory.

In the 1990s, Manuel Castells (1996) introduced the concept of the *Network Society*, to refer to the exchange of information through digital networks which, themselves, connect with other networks, forming open structures that are constantly changing and adapting to the interests of individuals who use the network. However, although the Internet has brought significant changes in daily life, it does not exist in a self-managing way (at least to date). It is the desires, will and interests of people that drive its use, flow and dynamics. Behind software and hardware are individuals who devise, develop, use and discard different programs and applications. They are people who, in their processes of study and production, make obsolete or popular a particular type of a device, an application or a social network.

Internet access, in almost all regions of the world, has allowed for the exponential broadening of communication among people and access to information. The possibility of visiting websites of any country, sending emails or text messages to an individual or a group has deeply altered communication and entertainment processes, relations in the work environment and ways of accumulating knowledge. Connection with people, cultures and information has become possible for an unlimited number of individuals. In the perspective of Markham (2018), the fact that it has become more and more popular, to the point where it 'fits in one's pocket' (i.e. smartphones), has not diminished the importance of the Internet. The use of digital technologies in cultural experiences has increasingly been growing.

This chapter outlines practical and analytical procedures of data collection and analysis of blogs, using our own research as a case study. In the first section, we present a brief discussion about weblogs and their users. In the following sections, we will go on discussing topics such as the belonging of blogs to the field of qualitative research, the different types of qualitative data produced in blogs, and some practical steps in the construction of a sample and analysis of data from blogs.

A BRIEF CHARACTERIZATION OF BLOGS AND THEIR USERS

In the 1990s, a significant change took place in the way Internet users relate to the web. It became possible for the visitors of a particular website to leave comments, anticipating what later would be called Web 2.0 (Herring, 2011). This innovated communication via the web and significantly broadened forms of virtual interaction. Thus, instead of just visiting a page, people began to interact with it. It is in this context that the first weblogs or blogs appeared.

With the development of what is commonly called Web 2.0, creating websites became incredibly easy. Based on preconfigured models and simplified menus, content from different users could be combined and made available in a single place, in text, image and sound formats, definitively characterizing social interaction and active participation as elements of the Web 2.0 (Alexander and Levine, 2008; Herring, 2011). The central characteristic of the Web 2.0, according to O'Reilly (2007) is to create a network effect, developing a 'participation architecture' based on user contributions and appropriations. The world-scale proliferation of weblogs, or simply blogs, is directly related to the fact that any person can create and manage a blog, with no need for specific knowledge of computer programming to produce a website with a good look and regular updates. Blogs are interactive and flexible, and they allow visitors not only to read texts but also to leave their comments (Herring et al., 2004a, 2004b; Hookway, 2008). Thelwall and Wouters (2005) and Li (2007) also described other tools in blogs, such as permalinks (links to specific posts), trackbacks (which identify the creator of a link to a blog post) and blogrolls (lists of other recommended blogs), which enhance the possibilities for exchange.

Thousands of blogs on diverse subjects and with several goals comprise the *blogosphere*, which is in constant evolution (Agrawal and Li, 2008). Blogs are identified as a 'mode of computer-mediated communication (CMC)' and described as 'web-based journals' (Herring, 2004b). The 'Technorati Media 2013 Digital Influencer Report' indicates, moreover, that the form of posting most commonly used by bloggers is text (86 percent). Nevertheless blogs are multimodal, in that they integrate text, sound, symbols and visual data as well as links to further content. At the same time this integration refers to relations and interactions among different types of data and content (Jewitt, 2013). The topics in the blogs are placed in reverse chronological order through which individuals virtually socialize texts or postings and can receive feedback from other users (see also Blood, 2000; Bruns, 2005; Herring et al., 2005; Hookway, 2008). Blogs are also a platform 'of a continuously expanded collection of posts, each of which may express a micro-narrative, a comment that expresses an aspect of the writer or an image showing a version of themselves' (Rettberg, 2014, p. 35). In a blog, each post is preceded by a heading, indicating the date of the publication. In terms of content, blogs cover countless issues and areas, while the type of presentation reaches from a personal diary style to the professional presentation of news (see Tiidenberg, Chapter 30, this volume).

As for the bloggers' profiles, the 'Technorati Report State of the Blogosphere 2011' classifies them into five different types. The first type, the *hobbyist*, represents the majority of the blogosphere (60 percent), those who claim they keep a blog just for fun, for personal satisfaction, reporting their experiences, personal knowledge in certain areas of interest, opinions and reflections. The second and third types, *professional part-timer* or *professional full-timer*, are those types of users who obtain their total or partial income from this activity (18 percent). The fourth group, *corporate* (8 percent), represents corporative bloggers who are connected to a company or organization, whether because the blog is part of their work or because they were hired as bloggers. These blogs cover the fields of business and technology. The last group, *entrepreneurs* (13 percent), is formed by bloggers who keep blogs connected to an organization or company of their own.

With the rise of social networks, such as Facebook (see Ditchfield and Meredith, Chapter 32, this volume) and Instagram, blogs seem to be less popular, but they remain a relevant field of research, which deserves to be better explored and understood. In our chapter, particular attention will be given to blogs developed by young people with specific cultural, political or social interests. The study of social phenomena performed from data generated from blogs opens new perspectives for qualitative researchers but also demands new efforts in the process of collecting data and in the construction of analytical strategies.

RESEARCH ON BLOGS: INTERDISCIPLINARY AND MULTIMETHOD APPROACHES ON LIMITED OBJECTS

To give a short overview of the latitude of research opportunities based on blogs, in this chapter we will next outline the research interests and methods of analysis of current studies in selected fields.

Several studies have been carried out based on *travel blogs*. They include, for example, the work of Tseng and others (Tseng et al., 2015) using a computer-based analysis tool to describe the effect of the development of tourist interests on China, the application of netnography on narratives in blogs of travelers analyzing their travel experiences (Chandralal et al., 2015), content analysis of tourist perceptions on travel destinations (Sun et al., 2015) or studies dealing with the relation of authenticism and self-branding in blogs on travel issues (e.g. van Nuenen, 2016).

Other studies in the field of *social and political science* based on research of digital content were dedicated to political blogs. In this field, Garden (2016) used content analysis to understand the role of journalists in Australian polit-blogs; Jacky (2015) accompanied bloggers from different countries and investigated the relation between bloggers and deliberate democracy based on a hacking analytical perspective. Yang and Self (2015) analyzed effects of extremist blogs in the formation of opinions on Muslims in the US, based on a case study design applying hyperlink network analysis and resonance analysis.

Furthermore, in the field of *psychology*, there are a rising number of studies based on methods of online research with blogs. Elliott et al. (2017) carried out a study on low-income mothers wherein the authors analyzed personal narratives (see Murray, Chapter 17, this volume) from female mother bloggers concerning questions of family relations, motherhood and nutrition. Based on an interpretive phenomenological analysis, Smethurst and Kuss (2016) analyzed blogs to describe benefits and barriers forming part of anorexia nervosa recovery processes. Kotliar (2015) studied female depression in relation to the personal exhibition of feelings based on intimate narratives, published in blogs, from women with depression and Fawcett and Shrestha (2016) examined the role of blogging in facilitating healing for victims of sexual violence.

Last but not least, blogs are investigated as modes, spaces or products of *educational processes*. Bell (2016) highlights the formation of foreign students' experiences in writing blogs; Hagedorn and Piva (2014) analyze processes of self construction of youth as well as of identity formation based on the hermeneutic interpretation of online diaries. Furthermore, in the field of education, the use of weblogs as learning spaces in the framework of educational institutions gained popularity, mainly in higher education (see Tess, 2013) or in literacy and language learning (e.g. Hew and Cheung, 2013). Roth and Erstad (2013) use a learning ecology methodology, mapping 'funds of knowledge' of young people at school and beyond. The authors investigate interconnections between different spaces of learning in youth.

Current research on weblogs highlights their relevance for the expression, exchange and representations of individual and group experiences, their impact on media discourses, as well as coping and learning practices. Therefore, weblogs represent the developments of Web 2.0 and are discussed as interactive structures of digital communication.

BLOGS: A FIELD FOR QUALITATIVE RESEARCHERS

Different areas, such as education, social sciences and communication, perceive blogs as a netnographic environment (Kozinets et al., 2014) for research on varied topics. They can be seen as a field of virtual ethnographic research (see Buscatto, Chapter 21, this volume) that allows, for example, to monitor and to observe interaction practices among participants in a certain virtual address. The use of blogs for the analysis of social practices and in the reconstruction of individual or collective experiences is not a particular activity of a certain discipline but is circumscribed in the interdisciplinary field of qualitative research. The development of new forms of interaction, with the participation and collaboration of bloggers, indicates that these technological changes have broadened blog creation, to the point where they have begun to play an important role in the virtual world. They became an instrument to socialize, to share information, stances, interpretations, imports and meanings with other users. Blogs have been organized around the most diverse subjects and are kept by individuals or groups of people who make posts or publications (the bloggers) and by users who make comments. Gómez (2011) stated, based on a study with Spanish youngsters, that blogs, since it is usually a thematic and less rigid platform than other social networks, are more mature. The author concludes that, despite the explosion of social network users, blogs are still kept by young people as a valid form of communication, in particular by those who prefer to go beyond superficiality and to deepen in specific subjects and themes, which is possible in the dynamics of a blog. The blogosphere has become a significant space for investigation and data collection for qualitative researchers. Nicholas Hookway in *Entering the blogosphere* underlines this process:

> [b]logs offer substantial benefits for social scientific research providing similar, but far more extensive opportunities than their 'offline' parallel of qualitative diary research. First, they provide a publicly available, low-cost and instantaneous technique for collecting substantial amounts of data. Further, blogs are naturalistic data in textual form, allowing for the creation of immediate text without the resource intensiveness of tape recorders and transcription. (Hookway, 2008, p. 92)

The blog encompasses a type of language and a form of communication published in text form, which, for a qualitative researcher, becomes data (see Lindgren, Chapter 28, this volume and Markham, Chapter 33, this volume). Based on the data made available in the blogosphere, and among the many options offered, researchers can define a research object.

Markham (2004) underlines three aspects of web-based communication, which should be taken into account in qualitative research using the Internet, including research with blogs. First, there is the geographic dispersion, which means that distances are eliminated and lose their meaning, allowing for the participation of people from different parts of the world, which, previously, would have been logistically improbable; second, the temporal malleability which considers the use of time in an individualized and non-traditional manner; and finally, the multiple modalities, meaning that the user adds texts, images, and sounds in synchronous and asynchronous ways, preserving or not the anonymity of data producers. Such aspects used to be seen as advantages that optimize the work of researchers and persons interested in studies of blogs and other Internet environments.

Based on the massive spread of interactive spaces on the Internet, after the development of the so-called Web 2.0 from the 2000s onwards, one observes a growing adjustment of qualitative research in cyberspace. Since access to the sources is gained in just a few clicks, the large quantity of primary data enables qualitative researchers to develop complex data samples from blogs. Besides interests related to the specific type of interactive data, this can reduce costs and time in the process of data collection. At the same time there are several methodological assumptions that must be considered when collecting data from blogs. They will be discussed in the next section.

COLLECTING DATA FROM BLOGS: PRACTICAL AND ANALYTICAL PROCEDURES

The blog, as a space of interaction among users, is nurtured by the dynamics of making posts and comments. However, blogs can be removed from a website, a platform or a provider for various reasons, and can be altered at any time. Just one click is necessary to exclude or substitute a post, a text file or an image when desired. Hence, there are some limitations to research with blogs, and there is a risk of 'losing the field' completely or even being 'altered' as the administrator submits posts or comments, throughout the data collection process.

Deciding How to Choose Blogs for Qualitative Research

In discussing how to choose blogs from the blogosphere for qualitative analysis of social practices, we present some procedures based on our own research related to the analysis of a blog created and managed by an association of young Brazilian feminist women (see Bassalo, 2012). Our interest in a study of collective experiences of young feminists and their activities was motivated by the fact that the Brazilian youth generation, at the turn of the twentieth to the twenty-first century, achieved a unique place in the political and cultural scenarios, in the agenda of public policies, and as a research object (Sposito, 2009). This process was so significant that the Federal Constitution of Brazil was altered (Constitutional Amendment number 65, of July 13, 2010) with the inclusion of the term 'youth' in the articles of Constitution. This new political context and the role of internauts in the call for participation in activities and live events, especially in demonstrations in the streets, drew our attention to the use of the Internet and the development of blogs by young people. Some of our initial research questions were: If the Internet enables new forms of social interaction that lead to action and if it is a space in which to share collective experiences, how do the young people communicate their positions? Which issues are prominent? Which virtual spaces are designed specifically for young people? Which of them, despite the fact that they focus on young people and their interests, are characterized by being organized by young people themselves? Which of these addresses refer to the idea of collectiveness around feminist issues?

Based on interpretation being a fundamental element of reconstructive qualitative research (Pfaff et al., 2010), we began our ethnographic research with a preliminary analysis of websites and blogs. The survey, through virtual spaces and the selection of blogs for deeper analysis, was a laborious task as we also considered, at the time of research, the prerogative of being a virtual address in operation and independent of any institutional affiliation. Several steps were done at the beginning of the research. First, we searched for the various virtual addresses for young people such as websites and blogs. However, we found out that many virtual addresses were under the management of adults with their own views on being young and the subjects to be discussed. We also found many websites linked to particular institutions as a result of projects developed in universities, religious organizations, political parties and non-governmental organizations. In contrast, blogs emerged more often as virtual addresses kept by young people, whether managed personally or by groups. The preferences for creating blogs by young activists were probably related to the fact that very few or no resources were required to start and maintain a blog. Only blogs exclusively organized by youngsters were kept. After this first selection of blogs, we started, second, to organize the topics and subtopics identified in the discussions: This included the two main fields *homosexuality* – with posts about civil rights, violence against homosexuals and the right to visibility; and *women's rights* – considering legalizing abortion, the right to decide whether to have, not to have, or when to have children, the right to freedom and personal safety, and violence as an obstacle to the creation of gender equality.

Thus, after a preliminary analysis of various web addresses, a blog developed by a group of young women who called themselves 'young feminist activists' was selected for a deeper study. Among the blogs we searched, this was the only one which followed the characteristics we required: that it was proposed, created and maintained by young people; it was not a personal blog; it belonged to a collective organization of the youth; it was not linked to an institution, and it was active at the time of the investigation. In addition to these key features mentioned, it was created by young women whose aim was to get in contact with young feminist women in different states of Brazil, and it was designed to share information, interpretations and their own opinions on gender issues; and to have an extensive visual record of their activities. As a strategy to expand the communication with other young activists, it was created by young women in a public domain and with unrestricted access and requirements for browsing the blog.

To sum up our experiences, the sampling and selection process (see also Schreier, Chapter 6, this volume) consists of three main steps. In the first place we set certain criteria based on the research interest and question. This implies decisions about the context and the producers of a blog (i.e. institutional, professional or private; group vs. individual) as well as on the main issues and content (i.e. life, business, health, culture). As a second step, we draw maps or applied lists and tables in order to document the process and results of the investigation of blogs. Last but not least, the selection of a specific blog for deeper investigation was related to the study design and the sample size.

Types of Data and How to Collect Data from Blogs

The blog that we selected for a deeper analysis after the previous examination of websites and blogs, was composed of the pictorial and textual posts of the group, published between 2007 and 2011. Concomitant to almost weekly back-ups of the material posted on the blog, we started to organize them according to sorts of texts. We found that most posts were communications and invitations to seminars, debates, conferences, marches, walks and other feminist activities. We also identified documents as elaborated by the group of young feminists as well as official documents related to topics and themes of interests to the young women, such as laws and decrees. There were only a small number of posts with textual data that bore no relation to events or specific reports. However, the collection of photographs was extensive, and we were able to identify a pictorial discourse through the images.

This last aspect became relevant for the research and the images became the central data in our study. During the course of the research period, the girls produced and shared photos of their feminist practices and actions. Born in a technological era, they handle photographic equipment and techniques without effort (see Eberle, Chapter 25, this volume). As elements with visual content, the pictures appeared to communicate senses and symbolic meanings about being young, woman, feminist and Internet users. They also established information through the images about their performances in the feminist movement. During the time of data collection, the visual record in the blog, comprising 209 photographs, was opened to public viewing (with unrestricted access) in virtual albums located inside the blog and also in a photoblog and a photolog. In these photographs, the young women filtered out all biographical evidence of the pictures. These albums were created not for personal exhibitions, but to register the activities performed by a group of feminist youth. This singularity caught our interest in finding the group's motives for publishing these images. Was the purpose of posting the pictures to communicate their own view to a specific issue or merely to record the activities performed by their collectivity? What did the pictures reveal about their experiences, opinions and collective orientations?

Not all photographs published in the blog, however, could be considered 'adequate' to serve as a source of research. For example, we excluded pictures in which only produced materials such as posters and banners were identified. Due to the extent that photographs were considered visual narratives and, in the case of this study, as narratives of activities and shared experiences of young feminists, we only selected photographs of people for the analysis. A second criterion for the exclusion of pictures from the sample was related to technical elements of the picture such as plane, angle, form (or composition), frame, focus and sharpness, color and lighting. The intention was more about the classification of the pictures such as the subject, the technology employed, the photographer, what appears in the image, the place and disposition of the main components of the image (see Bohnsack, 2010b; Kossoy, 2001; Manini, 2001). Based on these aspects and guided by the documentary method (see the next section), the final criteria defined for the selection and constitution of our sample of pictures published in the blog were: photographs taken by the young women; pictures with narrative content, presentation of a related topic or subject; pictures containing people; and pictures published in high technical quality. At the end of the process, 203 photographs were selected as adequate data for the study.

All in all, for collecting data from blogs, it is important to take into account the multimodal, content diverse and dynamic character of blogs. Due to multimodality, it is necessary to define relevant types of data (i.e. textual or (audio-)visual) that best relate to the research interest and the selected study design. Despite thematic frames, blogs often include diverse types of content (i.e. information, documentation, opinion and discussion). Referring to this, the selection of relevant content is a second important selection process. Finally, as blogs are administrated content, posts or comments might change over time. So if data is supposed to be collected for more than a single time, it is important to regularly save the data.

Analysis of Qualitative Data from Blogs

Based on the pictures they shared through a blog with a broader community, the purpose of our research was the reconstruction of collective orientations of young feminists as well as issues related to being a young woman in Brazil. The methodological background was the reconstructive qualitative approach, specifically the documentary method (see Bohnsack, 2014; Bohnsack et al., 2010). The documentary method offers a deeper understanding of the *Weltanschauung* (worldviews) of a certain social group and access to the collective orientation of a group or individuals in unknown environments. Since the documentary method was developed for the interpretation of different types of images (Baltruschat, 2010; Bohnsack, 2010b), the photographs that comprise the blog's visual collection were taken as visual records of experiences that share and communicate opinions, ideas or, in Mannheimian language, worldviews (Mannheim, 1952, 1980).

After the final definition of the sample composed of images and texts published on the blog and of the theoretical and methodological frameworks, our analysis began with the following questions: How do young women use a blog to communicate their positions and interpretations of issues related to feminism? What understandings and meanings do they connect to gender? Which understandings and meanings do they share through the pictures? The main purpose of our study was the reconstruction of the collective orientations of young feminist women and the main issues related to being a young woman in Brazil based on the pictures they shared with a broader community. It must be noted that, due to the structure of the blog, posts are organized in chronological order,

---

Box 31.1

Brief summary about collecting data from blogs:

- Before starting to collect data from blogs, delineate first the purpose of your research and the problem question.
- Blogs contain different types of data such as written text, images, sounds and videos. Define what and how to collect the data.
- Blogs can be removed from a website, a platform or a provider for different reasons, and can be altered at any time. Save your data throughout the process of field research.

and the bloggers identified each picture per event. Also, they hid any type of personal name, in a clear process of depersonalization in the name of the group identity. The young women who appear in the photographs are identified as young feminists or feminist youth. They seem to have chosen the identity that motivated the creation of the blog: being young and feminist. Of the number of 203 photographs considered for the research, the main topic of 184 is their participation in feminist events and the claim for more visibility of young feminists in the adult feminist movement. In 19 photographs, one can identify themes that are at the center of the shared experiences of the young feminist bloggers, such as legalizing abortion, lesbianism, racial prejudice, women's health and violence against women. After applying the steps of the documentary method to the analysis of photographs (Bohnsack, 2010a, 2011), it was possible to identify, as a homologous pattern, the participation in the feminist movement as a central orientation for their practical activities. However, they also indicated, as a central theme of the visual narrative, the importance of gender justice that could be identified in the banners and posters that appeared in the analyzed pictures. A second homologous pattern identified in the interpretation of the pictures was related to the rejection of gender inequalities and gender relationships based on hierarchies (for more details see Bassalo, 2012). The identification of important topics, arguments, defenses and criticism identified through the interpretations of the images published in the blog revealed the importance of this type of data for qualitative research. Based on the documentary interpretation, it can be stated that the photographs represented a visual narrative of the activities and meanings these young feminist bloggers made use of while the blog remained active. That is, a narrative telling that images produce feelings, identifications, understandings of oneself and the environment.

Limits and Ethical Implications of Collecting Data from Blogs

Aware of the limits and the scope of research with subjects who interact in blogs, another aspect has been widely discussed: the ethical handling of virtual data (see Tiidenberg, Chapter 30, this volume). Just as in conventional or offline qualitative research, researchers who use the Internet in their investigations face ethical dilemmas, reinforced many times by the absence of a precise definition of the limits of the research in a certain digital environment. One of these dilemmas refers to the work with free access data, which leads us to questions such as: Does the flow of communication established online, in a public blog, belong to the public or private sphere? Should the posts and comments visible in the blog be treated as having specific authors, since they were made by someone? Or can they be considered independent of authorship? Should the personal information in public blogs be treated in an individual or a private manner? (Snee, 2013).

The principles of ethics in research for the online world are based on the same recommendations as those adopted for any qualitative research (see Mertens, Chapter 3, this volume). In order to guide researchers who use the Internet in considering the ethical dimension in every stage of their investigations the *Association of Internet Researchers* – AoIR – in December 2012 approved a document entitled *Ethical Decision-Making and Internet Research Recommendations from the AoIR Ethics Working Committee*. In principle, a blog is published in a public domain, but considering the AoIR (2012; see Markham and Buchanan, 2012) people may perceive their actions in this space as private or, rather, recognize the public character of their communication. They also may consider it limited to that space and restricted as to its use in other environments or for research.

Hence, since 2002, the AoIR finds that the research in virtual spaces implies a relationship of expectations and consensus between researcher and participants in an investigation. Also, the association calls attention to the need for establishing whether or not the research involves human beings. Information obtained by email, through virtual interviews or exchange of messages in real-time probably leads to a positive answer, that is, that the research involves people. On the other hand, if there is no direct connection between the investigation and the person who has produced the information or message, the answer may be negative, that is, it does not involve human beings. The document also points out that one must bear in mind that the authors of postings and comments may be directly or indirectly affected and harmed.

The *ESRC Framework for Research Ethics*, published in 2015 by the *Economic and Social Research Council* – ESRC, considers information publicly disseminated on the Internet as belonging to the public domain. However, the public nature of the information or the communication in social networks also requires a critical examination and protection of the identity of the persons involved (ESRC, 2015, p. 12). In this perspective, the AoIR (2012) does not prescribe practices, but indicates directions that can be used by researchers and guiding questions regarding the ethical performance of their research, such as:

- The establishment and conceptualization of the context of the research;
- Clearly defining who is involved in the study, where it takes place and what types of data will be gathered and analyzed;
- The participants' expectations;
- The establishment of the main object of study;
- The ethical association in the traditional collection of a certain type of information or data, the data storage and handling;
- The reduction of future risks with the publication of research reports;
- The assessment of harm, the risks and the benefits for the investigation, for participants and their communities, as well as for researchers;
- Autonomy guarantee;
- And the assessment of difficulties or possibilities to obtain authorization of participating minors or people in situations of vulnerability.

The online publication of texts, images, links and nicknames of users, allow for the tracking of information presented in research about blogs. In other words, the preservation of the participants' personal data anonymity should be a cause for concern of researchers and different mechanisms to protect the identities of the subjects should be considered, even if it is impossible to assure total anonymity (for more details see Tiidenberg, Chapter 30, this volume). The anonymity of authors or communities should be even greater in the contexts of vulnerability. A researcher should be aware of these aspects and clearly understand that subjects' rights must be considered above the benefits of the research since there is no way of foreseeing all possible ethical problems in the field (Markham and Buchanan, 2012, p. 4).

DATA COLLECTION FROM BLOGS: PERSPECTIVES AND RECOMMENDATIONS

Our research with young bloggers revealed how, with ease and agility, these young women assimilate the new forms of interaction via the web. In their adult life, they will belong to the generation educated in a digital society that will continue to interact in this way and with much more intimacy than the adults of today, who are only now beginning to comprehensively investigate them. In this sense, qualitative researchers need to clarify and create new procedures for digital research. For those who want to explore the plurality of topics existing in different types of blogs, we offer a set of recommendations that might be useful for new research projects:

- Virtual qualitative data has a fluid character. It can be removed or altered from a platform at any time. Hence, the routine of a blog researcher

- should include procedures to record and organize textual and audio-visual data. New software, such as screen recorders and secure cloud locations, offers the possibility not only of saving the data but also of working in collaboration with other investigators on the same material.
- Different types of virtual data presented in a blog also demand an adequate triangulation of its sources (see Flick, Chapter 34, this volume). Image, text and sound share the same web address and demand the appropriate handling of the sources. In the framework of the weblog they relate and interact with each other. Images are crucial in the construction of senses and meanings, and they take an important place in virtual environments, such as the blog. The reflection on proper methods for data collection and analysis of visual discourses presented in blogs is not secondary and demands the same attention and care, as attributed to text analysis methods.
- Posts and comments do not open access to specific experiences and to the respective milieu that gave meaning to or originated the collective orientations of the authors. This is another type of data that is constructed differently from that generated in face-to-face communications. Hence, comments from several participants in a post on a certain theme cannot be compared to a conversation in a focus group or group discussion.
- Analysing blogs and other online-based content requires new and adjusted strategies and tools in relation to the ethics of qualitative research. The discussion around the creation of new devices or strategies to hinder identification of participants will require further efforts. Other forms of codification and protection are necessary in the field of Internet research, which can hide the identity and avoid harmful effects on participants, such as cyber bullying.

CONCLUSION

We need to be aware that in the cybersphere, the ways of interaction and the nature of blogs are constantly changing. An example of such changes are micro-blogs, such as Twitter, in which texts posted with minimal amounts of characters or links leading to a text or image perform even faster processes of interaction, information and dissemination of world views. It must also be clear that technologies and devices for data collection and handling of virtual data cannot replace the 'manual work' of a qualitative researcher when it comes to a deeper interpretation and understanding of what data informs about the different realities of the virtual world, the question of how these realities are constituted, and the knowledge and experiences of human beings related to it. Thus, netnography (Kozinets, 2015; Kozinets et al., 2014) is not a substitute for face-to-face ethnography. They should be better seen as complementary to each other and as a result of new efforts in the improvement of qualitative research methods and their analytical strategies.

FURTHER READINGS

Hine, Christine (2015) *Ethnography for the Internet: Embedded, Embodied and Everyday*. London: Bloomsbury Academic.

Kozinets, Robert (2015) *Netnography: Redefined*. London: Sage.

Wakeford, Nina and Cohen, Kris (2008) 'Fieldnotes in public: Using blogs for research', in Nigel Fielding, Raymond M. Lee and Grant Blank (eds.), *The SAGE Handbook of Online Research Methods*. London: Sage, pp. 307–26.

REFERENCES

Agrawal, Nitin, and Li, Huan (2008) 'Blogosphere: Research issues, tools, and applications', *ACM SIGKDD Explorations Newsletter*, 10(1): 18–31.

Levine, Alan and Alexander, Bryan (2008) 'Web 2.0 storytelling: Emergence of a new genre', *EDUCAUSE Review*, 43(6): 40–56.

AoIR (2012) 'Ethical Decision-Making and Internet Research Recommendations from the AoIR Ethics Working Committee',

Association of Internet Researchers. Retrieved from: https://aoir.org/reports/ethics2.pdf.

Baltruschat, Astrid (2010) 'Film interpretation according to the documentary method', in R. Bohnsack, Ni. Pfaff, and W. Weller (eds.), *Qualitative Analysis and Documentary Method in International Educational Research*. Opladen & Farmington Hills: Barbara Budrich, pp. 311–42.

Bassalo, Lucélia de Moraes Braga (2012) *Entre sentidos e significados: um estudo sobre visões de mundo e discussões de gênero de jovens internautas*, Doctoral dissertation, Universidade de Brasília, Brasília, Brazil.

Bell, Robin (2016) 'Concerns and expectations of students participating in study abroad programmes: Blogging to reveal the dynamic student voice', *Journal of Research in International Education*, 15(3): 196–207.

Blood, Rebecca (2000) 'Weblogs: A history and perspective', Rebecca's pocket, September 7, 2000. Retrieved from: http://www.rebeccablood.net/essays/weblog_history.html

Bohnsack, Ralf (2010a) 'The interpretation of pictures and the documentary method', in R. Bohnsack, N. Pfaff, and W. Weller (eds.), *Qualitative Analysis and Documentary Method in International Educational Research*. Opladen & Farmington Hills: Barbara Budrich, pp. 267–92.

Bohnsack, Ralf (2011) *Qualitative Bild- und Videointerpretation. Einführung in die dokumentarische Methode. Opladen*, Farmington Hills: Barbara Budrich.

Bohnsack, Ralf (2014) 'Documentary method', in Uwe Flick (ed.), *The Sage Handbook of Qualitative Data Analysis*. London: Sage, pp. 217–33.

Bohnsack, Ralf, Pfaff, Nicolle, and Weller, Wivian (eds.) (2010) *Qualitative Analysis and Documentary Method in International Educational Research*. Opladen & Farmington Hills: Barbara Budrich.

Bruns, Axel (2005) *Gatewatching: Collaborative Online News Production*. New York: Peter Lang.

Castells, Mario (1996) *The Rise of the Network Society: The Information Age: Economy, Society and Culture, Volume I*. Malden, MA; Oxford: Blackwell.

Chandralal, Lalith, Rindfleish, Jennifer, and Valenzuela, Fredy (2015) 'An application of travel blog narratives to explore memorable tourism experiences', *Asia Pacific Journal of Tourism Research*, 20(6): 680–93.

Elliott, Heather, Squire, Corinne, and O'Connell, Rebecca (2017) 'Narratives of normativity and permissible transgression: Mothers' blogs about mothering, family and food in resource-constrained times', *Forum Qualitative Research*, 18(1). Retrieved from: http://www.qualitative-research.net/index.php/fqs/article/view/2775

ESRC (2015) *Framework for Research Ethics*. Retrieved from: http://www.esrc.ac.uk/files/funding/guidance-for-applicants/esrc-framework-for-research-ethics-2015/.

Fawcett, Hannah and Shrestha, Lalita (2016) 'Blogging about sexual assault: A thematic analysis', *Journal of Forensic Practice*, 18(1): 39–51.

Fielding, Nigel, Lee, Raymond M. and Blank, Grant (eds.) (2017) *The SAGE Handbook of Online Research Methods* (2nd edn). London: Sage.

Garden, Mary (2016) 'Australian journalist-blogs: A shift in audience relationships or mere window dressing?', *Journalism*, 17(3): 331–47.

Gómez, Raquel Pinilla (2011) 'La comunicacion de la juventud em lós blogs: nuevos diários para nuevos tiempos', *Revista de Estudios de Juventud: Jóvenes Em(red)ados*, (93): 117–26.

Hagedorn, Jörg and Piva, Franziska (2014) 'Jugend spricht. Schule als Material performativer Selbsterprobung und reflexiver Selbstvergewisserung', in Jörg H. (ed.), *Jugend, Schule und Identität. Selbstwerdung und Identitätskonstruktion im Kontext Schule*. Wiesbaden: SpringerVS, pp. 667–83.

Herring, Susan C. (2011) 'Discourse in Web 2.0: Familiar, reconfigured, and emergent', Georgetown University Round Table on Languages and Linguistics. Retrieved from: http://hdl.handle.net/11299/172825

Herring, Susan C., Kouper, Inna and Paolillo, John C. (2005) 'Conversations in the blogosphere: An analysis "from the bottom up"', Proceedings of the 38th Annual Hawaii International Conference on System Sciences.

Herring, Susan C., Kouper, Inna, Paolillo, John C., Scheidt, Lois Ann, Tyworth, Michael, Welsch, Peter, Wright, Elijah and Yu, Ning (2004b) *Women and Children Last: The*

Discursive Construction of Weblogs. Minneapolis and Saint Paul: University of Minnesota.

Herring, Susan C., Scheidt, Lois Ann, Bonus, Sabrina, and Wright, Elijah (2004a) 'Bridging the gap: A genre analysis of weblogs', *Proceedings of the 37th Annual Hawaii International Conference on System Sciences*.

Hew, Khe Foon, and Cheung, Wing Sum (2013) 'Use of Web 2.0 technologies in K-12 and higher education: The search for evidence-based practice', *Educational Research Review*, (9): 47–64.

Hine, Christine (2015) *Ethnography for the Internet: Embedded, Embodied and Everyday*. London: Bloomsbury Academic.

Hookway, Nicholas (2008) 'Entering the blogosphere: Some strategies for using blogs in social research', *Qualitative Research*, 8(1): 91–113.

Jacky, M. (2015) 'Bloggers and deliberative democracy in Indonesia's blogosphere', *Asian Social Science*, 11(28): 15.

Jewitt, Carey (2013) 'Multimodal methods for researching digital technologies', in Sarah Price, Carey Jewitt and Barry Brown (eds.), *The Sage Handbook of Digital Technology Research*. London/Thousand Oaks/New Delhi: Sage, pp. 250–65.

Kossoy, Boris (2001) *Fotografia & História*. São Paulo: Ateliê.

Kotliar, D. M. (2015) 'Depression narratives in blogs: A collaborative quest for coherence', *Qualitative Health Research*, 26(9): 1203–15.

Kozinets, Robert V. (2015) *Netnography: Redefined*. London: Sage.

Kozinets, Robert V., Dolbec, Piere-Yann and Earley, Amanda (2014) 'Netnographic analysis: Understanding culture through social media data', in Uwe Flick (ed.), *The Sage Handbook of Qualitative Data Analysis*. London: Sage, pp. 262–76.

Lévy, Pierre (1997) *Cyberculture: rapportauconseil de l'Europe*. Paris: Odile Jacob.

Li, Charlene (2007) *How Consumers Use Social Networks*. Cambridge, MA: Forrester Research.

Manini, Miriam Paula (2001) 'Análise Documentária de Imagens', *Informação & Sociedade: Estudos*, 11(1): 1–5.

Mannheim, Karl (1952) *Structures of Thinking*. London: Routledge and Kegan Paul.

Mannheim, Karl (1980) *Essays on the Sociology of Knowledge: Collected Works, Volume 5*. New York: Routledge.

Markham, Annette N. (2004) 'Internet communication as a tool for qualitative research', in David Silverman (ed.), *Qualitative Research: Theory, Method, and Practices* (2nd edn). London: Sage, pp. 95–124.

Markham, Annette N. (2018) 'Ethnography in the digital era: From fields to flow, descriptions to interventions', in N. K. Denzin, and Y. S. Lincoln (eds.), *The Sage Handbook of Qualitative Research* (5th edn). London: Sage, pp. 650–68.

Markham, Annette N. and Buchanan, Elizabeth (2012) 'Ethical Decision-Making and Internet Research, Recommendations from the AoIR Ethics Working Committee (Version 2.0)'. Retrieved from: http://www.aoir.org/reports/ethics2.pdf

O'Reilly, Tim (2007) 'What is Web 2.0?: Design Patterns and Business Models for the Next Generation of Software', *Communications & Strategies*. Retrieved from: http://hdl.handle.net/11299/172825

Pfaff, Nicolle, Bohnsack, Ralf, and Weller, Wivan (2010) 'Reconstructive research and the documentary method in Brazilian and German educational science: An introduction', in Ralf Bohnsack, Nicolle Pfaff, and Wivan Weller (eds.), *Qualitative Analysis and Documentary Method in International Educational Research*. Opladen & Farmington Hills: Barbara Budrich, pp. 7–38.

Rettberg, Jill Walker (2014) *Seeing Ourselves through Technology: How We use Selfies, Blogs and Wearable Devices to See and Shape Ourselves*. Basingstoke: Palgrave Macmillan.

Roth, Solveig and Erstad, Ola (2013) 'Networked lives for learning: Digital media and young people across formal and informal contexts', in Guglielmo Trentin and Manuela Repetto (eds.), *Using Network and Mobile Technology to Bridge Formal and Informal Learning*. Oxford/Cambridge/New Delhi: Chandos Publishing, pp. 119–52.

Smethurst, Laura and Kuss, Daria (2016) '"Learning to live your life again": An interpretative phenomenological analysis of weblogs documenting the inside experience of recovering from anorexia nervosa', *Journal* of Health Psychology. Retrieved from: https://doi.org/10.1177/1359105316651710

Snee, Helene (2013) 'Making ethical decisions in an online context: Reflections on using blogs to explore narratives of experience', *Methodological Innovations Online*, 8(2): 52–67.

Sposito, Marilia Pontes (2009) 'A pesquisa sobre jovens na Pós-Graduação: um balanço da produção discente em Educação, Serviço Social e Ciências Sociais (1999–2006)', in M. P. Sposito (ed.), *O Estado da Arte sobre juventude na pós-graduação brasileira, volume I*. Belo Horizonte: Argvmentvm, pp. 17–56.

Sun, Minghui, Ryan, Chris, and Pan, Steve (2015) 'Using Chinese travel blogs to examine perceived destination image: The case of New Zealand', *Journal of Travel Research*, 54(4): 543–55.

Technorati. State of the Blogosphere 2011 (2011). Retrieved from: http://technorati.com/state-of-the-blogosphere-2011/.

Technorati. *Technorati Media 2013 Digital Influencer Report (2013)*. Retrieved from: http://technorati.com/report/2013-dir/.

Tess, Paul A. (2013) 'The role of social media in higher education classes (real and virtual): A literature review', *Computers in Human Behavior*, 29(5): A60–A68.

Thelwall, Mike and Wouters, Paul (2005) 'What's the deal with the web/blogs/the Next big technology: A key role for information science in e-social science research?', in Fabio Crestani and Ian Ruthven (eds.), *Context: Nature, Impact, and Role*. Berlin: Springer, pp. 187–99.

Tseng, Chi, Wu, Bihu, Morrison, Alastair M., Zhang, Jingru, and Chen, Ying-Chen (2015) 'Travel blogs on China as a destination image formation agent: A qualitative analysis using Leximancer', *Tourism Management*, 46, 347–58.

Van Nuenen, Tom (2016) 'Here I am: Authenticity and self-branding on travel blogs Leximancer', *Tourist Studies*, 16(2): 192–212.

Wakeford, Nina and Cohen, Kris (2008) 'Fieldnotes in public: Using blogs for research', in Nigel Fielding, Raymond M. Lee and Grant Blank (eds.), *The SAGE Handbook of Online Research Methods*. London: Sage, pp. 307–26.

Yang, Aimei and Self, Charles (2015) 'Anti-Muslim prejudice in the virtual space: A case study of blog network structure and message features of the "Ground Zero mosque controversy"', *Media, War & Conflict*, 8(1): 46–69.

Collecting Qualitative Data from Facebook: Approaches and Methods

Hannah Ditchfield and Joanne Meredith

INTRODUCTION

There is a growing use of the Internet for social research, particularly for the collection of qualitative data. It is a fertile ground for such data, with textual material such as videos, blog posts, comments, social networking posts and so on, all becoming part of the expanse of qualitative material online. More recently, online content has become more multimodal with pictures, videos and audio being used in combination with the written, or typed, word (Herring, 2015). There are, then, numerous data types and, as a result, there appear to be no standardised procedures for collecting online qualitative data (Hewson, 2008).

There have been a number of books and articles published which address collecting Internet data across a number of different academic disciplines (see Coulson, 2015; Fielding et al., 2016). Three broad approaches to collecting data from and about online sources can be identified. The first is where researchers collect data *about* online platforms, uses and behaviours but do not collect such data using online methods. Examples of this include offline interviews as well as techniques such as user diaries (see Zhao et al., 2013), but also more experimental methods where participants are set specific tasks under controlled circumstances (see Walther et al., 2008). The second approach is where researchers use online tools to disseminate surveys or conduct interviews (see Roulston and Choi, Chapter 15, this volume) or focus groups (see Morgan and Hoffman, Chapter 16, this volume). This approach is utilised both by studies whose research questions *are* concerned with online issues (see Bowker and Tuffin, 2002; Turkle, 2011) but equally by those that *are not* (see Peel, 2010; Grov et al., 2011). The third, and most relevant approach to this chapter, is that of collecting data directly from online sites and platforms. In this approach, actual online artefacts such as Wikipedia articles, YouTube videos and comments, Tweets, or Facebook posts and pictures are collected from the sites of origin and these are the focus of the subsequent analysis. This third approach collects data that, arguably, is naturally occurring (Potter, 2004; see Potter and Shaw, Chapter 12, this volume); that is, it would exist in the online sphere whether or not the researcher had been there to collect the data.

The aim of this chapter is to explore in more detail the approach of collecting data directly from the Internet. However, due to the expanse of potential online research sites, it is impossible to cover all of these within the scope of this chapter. Therefore, we will focus our discussion on the social networking site *Facebook* (for a review of social networking sites see boyd and Ellison, 2007). Facebook is a fruitful site for research as it has been argued to be 'changing the way hundreds of millions of people relate to one another and share information' and as such, many social researchers have 'recognised the utility of Facebook as a novel tool to observe behaviour in a naturalistic setting, test hypotheses and recruit participants' (Wilson et al., 2012, p. 203). For researchers, Facebook provides an entirely preserved archive of data, with content made up of users' individual profiles usually featuring information 'about them' and pictures. In addition, they can post status updates on their own profiles, on wall posts on other people's profiles, and comment on both their own and other people's statuses. There is also the possibility of sending private messages to individuals or groups of Facebook friends. All such content is suitable data for qualitative analysis.

This chapter will discuss the practicalities of collecting qualitative data from Facebook using our own research as a case study. We used screen-capture software to collect status updates, comments and messenger interactions (HD: data collected 2015) and 'chats' (JM: data collected 2011–2012) from Facebook. Although we focus on Facebook and using screen-capture data, many of the processes we discuss, such as ethical considerations as well as sampling and access issues, will also apply to collecting data in other ways and from other online sites (for a broader discussion of capturing online data see Fielding et al., 2016).

In the next section, we will briefly outline the field of Facebook research. In subsequent sections, we will go on to discuss a number of issues related to data collection: 1) how to choose an appropriate method; 2) participant recruitment and sampling; 3) ethical considerations; 4) transcription and presentation of data. Finally, we will present some limitations and potential developments of online data collection.

DEVELOPMENT OF COLLECTING QUALITATIVE DATA FROM FACEBOOK

This section aims to outline the scope as well as the different ways that qualitative data has been collected from Facebook. Practical procedures related to data collection, such as sampling and ethical considerations, will be explored in the coming sections. In terms of scope, there is a predominance of work on who uses Facebook and the motivations for use, but also about relationships on Facebook and how these are managed through social interactions (Wilson et al., 2012). Our own research falls into this latter type (see Meredith, 2014). In terms of qualitative data that has been collected from Facebook, we see a wide range of examples, including written comments and wall posts (Lillqvist and Louhiala-Salminen, 2014), status updates (Carr et al., 2012), chat messages (Meredith, 2014; Meredith and Stokoe, 2014), pictures (Tifferet and Vilnai-Yauetz, 2014) and profile information (Zhao et al., 2008).

The ways in which these studies have collected data from Facebook vary. For example, Zhao et al. (2008) recruited participants who allowed their profile information to be downloaded from their accounts, focusing particularly on self-descriptions, networks and contact information. Lillqvist and Lauhaila-Salminen

(2014), however, did not recruit participants and instead copied and pasted posts directly from Facebook corporate pages. Data collection can also be participant-led, such as in Bazarova et al.'s (2012) study where they asked participants to submit their six latest status updates, chat messages and wall posts. Alternatively, researchers have also 'friended' participants on Facebook during the period of collection in order to collect interactions, such as status updates, directly from profile pages at certain intervals (Carr et al., 2012). Compared to these approaches of collecting data directly from Facebook, West and Trester (2013) adopted a more ethnographic approach (see Buscatto, Chapter 21, this volume), describing their work as a 'netnography' (see Hine, 2000; Kozinets, 2010). In this study, data was collected primarily through observational field notes on users' Facebook behaviours and activities. These field notes, though, were used in combination with collecting status updates and comments from participants' profiles. Data can, therefore, be collected from online sites through drawing on both online collection techniques (directly collecting posts) as well as offline collection techniques, such as field notes.

PRACTICAL PROCEDURES FOR COLLECTING DATA FROM FACEBOOK

In this section we firstly discuss how to decide on the most appropriate method of data collection; we will then explore how to recruit participants (if necessary), followed by a discussion on sampling. We will then discuss the ethical considerations of collecting data from Facebook, before a brief consideration of how to transcribe and present Facebook data. We use our own work as a case study to illustrate the process of collecting qualitative data from Facebook. In brief, for our research we recruited participants who collected either 'chat logs' or their public status updates and comment data.

They also video-recorded their computer screens, using screen-capture software called *liteCam* (for more about screen recording see Bhatt and de Roock, 2013). Participants downloaded this screen-capture software on to their own computer or laptop, collecting data whenever they would normally use Facebook, rather than having to go to a computer lab or use a specific computer (Garcia and Jacobs, 1999; Beisswenger, 2008). Participants simply had to start up liteCam and record their entire screen whilst they were interacting on Facebook, starting and stopping the recording whenever they wanted.

Deciding How to Collect Facebook Data: Theoretical and Methodological Assumptions

The decision of how to collect data is influenced by three interrelated elements: 1) the theoretical and epistemological stance; 2) the analytic approach to be taken; 3) the research question. Once these three elements have been explored, decisions on how to *ethically* collect data in the desired way can then be considered (see Tiidenberg, Chapter 30, this volume). It is well documented how different research approaches and methods reflect deeper theoretical assumptions 'concerning the kinds of objects we study and the kind of knowledge we can have of them' (Dolowitz et al., 2008, p. 26). For Facebook data, one approach is for researchers to treat it as a true reflection of participants' minds, uses and behaviours (see, for example, Zhao et al., 2008; Birnbaum, 2013). An alternative understanding is to view it as the participants 'doing' things with their postings (e.g. Carr et al., 2012; Lillqvist and Lauhaila-Salminen, 2014). In the latter approach, research moves away from treating *data-as-resource* and moves towards treating *data-as-topic* (Rapley, 2001). In other words, rather than seeing online data as 'a way to reach the people behind the screen'

(Flinkfeldt, 2011, p. 763), the content is analysed as a social practice in its own right (Lamerichs and te Molder, 2003). We both take a constructionist stance; that is, we understand Facebook data, as we would any type of data, as a social practice. We therefore focus on what people 'do' with their discourse and aim to understand concepts as *constructed* within the discourse itself (for data in digital research, see Lindgren, Chapter 28, this volume and Markham, Chapter 33, this volume).

The second element is the research question, which will be informed by the theoretical underpinnings of the author and project. Questions around why people use Facebook may not best be answered by collecting data directly from Facebook. However, questions around how people construct identity online are perhaps best answered by collecting posts directly from Facebook. Other questions, such as how people manage online interaction, are more likely to be answered by collecting data, not only from Facebook itself, but also using screen-capture data. As may be expected from our theoretical stance, our questions focused on how people talk and interact on Facebook, and on the similarities and differences between spoken and online interactional practices (Meredith, 2014).

The theoretical underpinnings of research will, inevitably, inform the method of analysis. The method of analysis also works to inform, but is also informed by, the research question. If postings on Facebook are seen as a reflection of participants' offline views and behaviours, then this might be more likely to lead to methods such as thematic analysis and grounded theory, with the aim of finding patterns and themes in terms of topics rather than discourses (Meredith, 2016). However, if the second theoretical stance is taken then the method of analysis is more likely to be discourse or conversation analytic (see Jackson, Chapter 18, this volume and Rau et al., Chapter 19, this volume), as these methods focus on how people 'do' things with their talk and how the interaction unfolds. We both had an interest in ordinary, everyday talk and were interested in analysing interactions in 'real-time'. This interest led us towards using discursive psychology (Edwards and Potter, 1992) and conversation analysis (Sacks, 1992; see Jackson, Chapter 18, this volume).

All of the considerations discussed above will feed into the decisions made about the method of data collection. For studies which focus more on the data as a reflection of participants' experiences, and use methods such as thematic analysis, collecting the data directly from the site, through simple copy–pasting, will most likely be sufficient (see, for example, Malik and Coulson, 2008, in relation to online forums). Even when the theoretical approach is more constructionist, using a similar method for collecting data may be appropriate (see Stommel, 2008; Giles 2014). We were interested not only in the messages sent via Facebook, both publicly and privately, but also in the process of constructing the eventual posted messages and chats. Collecting data using screen-capture software is a method that was able to address such an interest. From screen-capture we can gain access to live textual 'construction' and 'repair'; that is, how sentences are put together, corrected, tweaked and revised, as well as any pauses and interactional gaps. Details such as these would not be available if we simply asked for logs of interactions on Facebook, but they help us further to address our research questions that are concerned with interactional details. Collecting data in this way also links to our analytic preferences as researchers, as the 'real-time' form and nature of such data complements how real-time interaction has been a primary focus in relation to methods such as discursive psychology and conversation analysis (Edwards, 2005; Stokoe, 2009).

For decisions on how to collect data, then, the most important aspect is to be sure of the theoretical and epistemological position of the research. This position will inform both the research question and the analytic method, which will have subsequent implications for

Box 32.1 Summary box

- Deciding how to collect data from Facebook is influenced by three interrelated elements: 1) the theoretical and epistemological stance; 2) the analytic approach to be taken; 3) the research question.
- Depending on the theoretical underpinning, researchers can treat Facebook data as reflections or constructions of users' views, uses and behaviours.
- Theoretical underpinnings can affect the choice of analytical method.
- Research questions are informed by, but also inform, theoretical stances and analytical choices.
- Using screen-capture data may be appropriate for answering certain research questions.

the method of data collection. Our approach, research question and analytic method led to us using screen-capture methods for collecting our data. In the subsequent sections we will focus on the practicalities of using this particular method for collecting qualitative data from Facebook.

Accessing Qualitative Facebook Data

There are two main ways to access online qualitative data: 1) taking data directly from the site of interest with no involvement of participants or 2) recruiting participants to record or send data, or simply open barriers and allow access to their online worlds. Examples of studies that collect data directly from sites without communication with producers of such content include: Wikström (2014; Twitter data) and Lillqvist and Lauhaila-Salminen (2014; Facebook data). This approach is only possible when the data is not restricted by privacy settings as it can be accessed without users having to grant or allow access to the data. The main issue to consider here is to what extent this data is defined as public despite the possibility of access. More aspects of the ethics of such an approach are discussed later on in the chapter.

Facebook, for the most part, is a private space. Therefore, research on individual's Facebook pages often requires the recruitment of participants. This is the approach that we both took in our research, although we recruited our participants in different ways. For JM's study, she approached university classes to ask for volunteers to collect such data. Participants who volunteered via email were provided with a participant information sheet and asked to complete an online consent form. As such, data were collected from university students who were not necessarily known personally to her. Gaining consent online was suggested by the ethics committee of JM's institution. However, some committees may not accept online consent, meaning that recruitment of participants may be restricted by the necessity of gaining a physical signature. In HD's study, participants were recruited through her own Facebook network. A Facebook message explaining the topic area of the research was sent to all her Facebook friends. Anyone who came forward as interested in participating was then sent participant information sheets documenting all relevant information about the nature of data collection for the study. HD then met with participants face-to-face to download the software on to their personal computers. Note that this approach also restricted the sample to participants within travelling range.

A benefit of recruiting participants through the researcher's own Facebook network is that there is an established foundation of familiarity and trust between the participant and researcher. Despite the benefits of accessing participants through an inside network such as this, there are challenges to such an approach. For example, the researcher may be able to exert social pressure on potential participants. There is also the possibility of increased social awkwardness for both the researcher and participant due to collecting data from people with whom there is an existing connection (Ditchfield, 2014). To deal with these issues, the recruitment process was conducted through three steps (initial message, participant information sheet, face-to-face meeting) allowing the participant plenty of opportunity to fully understand the research. Participants were also in full control of when they recorded their interactions, meaning that if there were any interactions they did not want the researcher to see they could choose not to record at that time or to submit the file as part of the data corpus. Due to the more inside nature of this form of access, it was also essential to become reflexive about the role the researcher plays in the data collection process, continuously considering and evaluating our role in the research (Lee, 2015).

Two challenges that we both experienced in relation to participant recruitment were: 1) the recruitment of 'secondary participants' and 2) participant control. The first issue applies especially in relation to recording Facebook 'chats' and messages. Here, the co-participant (the person who the recruited participant was talking to) in that chat or message also needed to be 'recruited'. For this task, the participants themselves contacted their friends to ask if they would be willing for their chats to be recorded, although the secondary participants were not having their screen recorded. Thus, data collection required not only the agreement of a main participant, but also a number of 'secondary' participants. The second issue is related to the amount of control that participants had in the data collection process. Participants recorded, stopped and saved the screen-capture recordings at times to suit them, with no researcher present. They also were able to decide which video files were ultimately sent to the researcher as part of the data corpus. Compared to directly downloading material off Facebook, this leaves very little control in the hands of the researcher. There is, then, the requirement for mutual trust: the participant has to trust the researcher in terms of what they will do with the data and how they will maintain confidentiality and anonymity (see below), but the researcher also has to trust the participants to collect the required data. It is in this type of situation that offering participant incentives may be needed to encourage participation; however, stances on this can vary between institutions. JM chose to offer incentives for the time participants had to spend conducting the research. There are a number of issues around offering incentives to participate in research, but these are discussed in more depth elsewhere (e.g. Grant and Sugarman, 2004; Head, 2009).

There is another challenge that perhaps only non-typical Facebook users choose to participate in these kinds of research, potentially leading to issues around validity and

---

Box 32.2 Summary box

- There are two possible ways to collect data from Facebook: 1) directly, from public pages, without the knowledge of producers of content; 2) recruiting participants to collect private data.
- There are variations in how to approach recruitment, depending on what type of data is being collected and for what purposes.
- Reflexivity is essential, particularly if recruiting from insider networks.
- Often, with private data, consideration will need to be given to how to recruit 'secondary participants'.

reliability. However, one of the key features of CA/DA research is that the extracts and analysis are presented in full in any published material, so that readers can check whether the researcher is interpreting the data in the most appropriate way (Peräkylä, 2016). In terms of reliability, as qualitative researchers we acknowledge that there is no one single way in which people use Facebook, and what we are inevitably capturing are individuals' experiences (Braun and Clarke, 2013).

Deciding on Samples

Choosing or defining a research sample (see Schreier, Chapter 6, this volume) for a Facebook study is not dissimilar to the process in offline research in the sense that it is shaped by the research question. If the research does not involve recruiting participants, then the sample may be drawn from a particular time frame, such as a week or a month's worth of posts. It could also be that a sample comprises all relevant posts from a particular site, such as Burke and Goodman's (2012) analysis of anti-asylum seeker rhetoric in Facebook groups.

If the research involves recruiting participants, the sample may be a particular group or demographic, for instance, students, males, females or certain ages. However, a sample could also be the number of status updates, comment threads or Facebook users. It is difficult with online research to judge how large the sample of data will need to be. It can be tempting, if access to data is relatively simple, to collect as much data as possible. However, collecting too much data can be just as problematic as not collecting enough. It is often useful to first look at studies that have used similar data collection methods and set a 'bench mark'. However, it may be that as the data collection process starts, preliminary readings will suggest a modification of the sample or sample size if needed (Wood and Kroger, 2000).

It is useful here to give an example of our own sampling procedures. Neither of us were interested in any particular group, but rather in the talk and interaction itself. Thus, for our studies, the relevant sampling criteria simply consisted of being a Facebook user that actively used the functions under study ('chat', status updates, comments and posts). For both of us, we were limited to some extent by the fact that we had to recruit participants. Therefore, our sampling method was an opportunity sample in terms of who was willing to participate.

As our research focused on discursive practices, we both measured our sample size in terms of the number of chats, status updates and posts recorded rather than the number of participants. Counting our sample size in this way did not mean we were quantifying our data, but rather it was simply a method for managing data collection. We both had a small number of participants (4) but, in JM's work, for example, 75 chats were collected. One particular challenge to sampling data was, as noted above, the lack of control over what participants eventually returned to the sample. Although for JM's study, participants were asked to collect 50 chats each, in practice they often returned far

---

Box 32.3   Summary box

- Samples in Facebook research can be time frames, a particular page or group or, if recruiting participants, a particular type of user.
- Sample size can be measured in terms of number of profiles, number of posts, comments, chats or status updates or number of participants.
- How much data to collect needs to be assessed both before and during the data collection process.

fewer viable chats. Therefore, although it is important not to collect too much data, it is worthwhile 'over-recruiting' slightly, to take account of any issues when using these methods of data collection.

Ethical Considerations when Collecting Data from Facebook

The more general ethical considerations about online research are discussed in more depth elsewhere in this Handbook (see Tiidenberg, Chapter 30). Therefore, we will focus on the issues around collecting Facebook data, and more specifically on collecting screen-capture data. A key issue relating to ethics when collecting online data is whether a research site is public or private (see boyd, 2008; Whiteman, 2012). Facebook is, predominantly, a private space; however, if a profile or a page has limited privacy settings, there would be no obvious 'barriers' to go through to collect this. There are, though, arguments to suggest this is still ethically questionable due to content on sites such as Facebook being shared in a particular context without it being intended for use in research (D'Arcy and Young, 2012). This, therefore, raises distinct issues about people 'choosing to reveal information and having it used for a different purpose' regardless of whether the data is technically publicly available (D'Arcy and Young, 2012, p. 536). There are arguments to advocate that although being an 'eavesdropper' (recording or using conversations without the knowledge or consent of the author/speaker) is not ethically correct, being an 'overhearer' (recording or using interactions where users have not given informed consent but have been informed) is more ethically acceptable. This is because this position allows the analyst to sit outside the action but be a *known* intruder (D'Arcy and Young, 2012). With this approach, a researcher could collect data from a private Facebook page if they had informed participants that they were going to do so, but had not necessarily requested informed consent from all users. Often with this approach, participants are given a chance to 'opt out' of the research. However, if they do not explicitly state this, consent is assumed.

For our research, informed consent was obtained from the 'primary participants' (those participants who recorded their screens). This was due to the participants capturing the *construction* phase of their Facebook interactions, a private side of social media life only usually seen by the user themselves (Ditchfield, 2015). The bigger ethical challenge for us, though, arose from the 'secondary participants' (those whom the primary participants were talking to) (Meredith and Potter, 2013). In relation to Facebook chat interactions, secondary participants also provided informed consent due to this communication being the most private form on Facebook, going from inbox to inbox. For JM's study, this was achieved through participants asking their friends if they would agree to have their chats included in the corpus. The primary participants were provided with participant information sheets to send to their friends, which included the researcher's contact details as well as a link to the online consent form. If the secondary participants did not complete the consent form, then the chats could not be used as part of the study.

In HD's research, comments and status updates were also collected. This expansion added further complexity to the consent process by increasing the number of 'secondary participants' recruited for the study. With an individual's Facebook network commonly made up of hundreds of users, obtaining informed consent from every secondary participant on a participants' network is an unfeasible task. Considering these factors, it was decided that secondary participants, in terms of comments and status update interactions, would be informed of the research project and given the option to opt out. Primary participants sent a message to their network informing their Facebook friends

> **Box 32.4 JM and HD consent summary**
>
> - Facebook Chat Messages:
>   - Primary Participants: informed consent
>   - Secondary Participants: informed consent
> - Facebook Comments and status:
>   - Primary Participants: informed consent
>   - Secondary Participants: informed with opt-out option given

of the research they were involved in. This message featured HD's contact details and also made it clear that if they did not want to be involved they could opt out of the study. If secondary participants decided to opt out, the primary participant simply did not record their Facebook screen when interacting with an excluded party. If the excluded party was accidently recorded, the primary participant was asked to exclude that video file in the final selection sent to the researcher.

A further ethical consideration when collecting screen-capture data is the sensitivity of information. In terms of defining sensitive information, we left this in the hands of participants themselves. Our projects in no way required participants to talk about certain topics, therefore participants were free to make the decision on what they understood to be 'too sensitive' or 'too personal'. Participants remained in control of when and what data was recorded and sent to us as researchers. If anything 'too sensitive' was captured by the software, they were not obliged to send this as part of the research. Whilst using this software we also had to consider not just the information we would see on Facebook but also on other sites and platforms the participant may be using at the time. This poses a particular issue if, for example, the participant engages in online banking or Internet shopping whilst the software is recording. To deal with this, we requested that primary participants avoid going on other websites, particularly password protected sites, during the recording sessions. Although this could be a burden for participants and thus risk lowering the potential pool of recruits, it highlights how there is a balance to achieve between 'being ethical' and putting in place off-putting restrictions.

Other ethical issues, such as confidentiality and anonymity, were managed through changing names, locations, university courses and degrees, nationalities and so on (see Zimmer, 2010). The video data was also anonymised using Adobe Flash. For any piece of information that needed to be

> **Box 32.5 Summary box**
>
> - Even if data are being collected directly from Facebook, it is still important to consider ethical issues.
> - When collecting data from Facebook, it may be necessary to receive informed consent from both primary and secondary participants.
> - It is important to consider the sensitivity of what information may be seen through data collection processes and put suitable measures in place to protect both the participant and the researcher.
> - Assuring confidentiality and anonymity of participants is essential. For screen-capture data this involves anonymising video data, as well as transcripts.

anonymised, a new 'layer' was added to the video, which included blurs or solid shapes that covered this information. It was also possible, although very time-consuming, to move the blocks or blurs as the video played, to maintain anonymity. We also had to ensure that the data was kept secure, due to the risk of potential harm to participants. For our research, where the data included very large screen-capture videos, we kept data on an encrypted external hard drive with original copies of data being stored in a locked cabinet or box that only we had access to.

Presentation and Transcription

Most data collected from sites such as Facebook does not need to be transcribed as such, as the main part of the data is already text-based (for more on processes of transcription see Jenks, Chapter 8, this volume). However, it is worth considering, even with data collected directly from the site, how best to present this for analysis and publication. Often, screen-shots of data can be used (see Keating and Sunakawa, 2011), but this may not be the most accessible way to view the data. The majority of studies, particularly in the qualitative field, will re-format such data so that the separation between posts is obvious, and line numbers may be included (e.g. Antaki et al., 2005). However, when screen-capture data are collected it is necessary to transcribe the data so that it can be presented to others in journal articles, conferences, data sessions and so on (Meredith, 2015). There are a number of examples of different transcription systems for screen-capture data (see Garcia and Jacobs, 1999; Beisswenger, 2008), but some systems may be suitable for some types of data and not others. For the purposes of her research, JM developed a transcription system for the Facebook screen-capture data. This incorporated aspects such as when the participants were writing or deleting messages, when there was overlap between writing and posting messages, and how each individual chat intersected with one another (for more detail, see Meredith, 2015). Not all transcription systems will require as much detail, but it is important to consider, when using screen-capture data, how best to both transcribe and present it.

LIMITS TO COLLECTING DATA FROM FACEBOOK

As with any approach to collecting data, there are limitations. Crystal notes how it seems to be a standard convention for studies of online technology to 'begin or end by warning their readers that everything they contain is going to be soon out of date' (2001, p. 224). Our work is not an exception to this; indeed, social networking sites including Facebook regularly change their interfaces and introduce new features. For example, since JM's data was collected there have been changes to the functionality of Facebook chat, particularly the combining of the asynchronous and quasi-synchronous aspects of Facebook chat (Meredith, 2014). However, this does not necessarily mean our research, or any other like it, is 'out of date', but rather that our work can be seen as part of

---

Box 32.6 Summary box

- It is important to consider how to present online data in a way that is appropriate for publication.
- Data could be presented using screenshots, or in the form of a transcript.
- A transcription system may need to be developed for screen-capture data.

a cumulative collection of studies of online sites and spaces which can help us to understand the development of online communication.

Although using screen-capture data is a particularly innovative method in this field, there are a number of challenges when attempting to use screen-capture for collecting data from mobile/cell phones (for more discussion on collecting mobile data see Kusenbach, Chapter 22, this volume). More than half a billion people now access Facebook *solely* on their mobiles (Tech Crunch, 2015), which suggests that it is important to be able to collect such data from mobile platforms. With some data types, collecting data from Facebook via mobile is not essential as pictures and the content of written posts will look the same as on a computer screen, with no additional features being offered on mobile devices alone. However, if the analysis is focused on emoji use, for instance, the options available to participants and the way such graphics are displayed can alter, depending on the device used. Also, practically, if a large segment of Facebook users access the site solely from their mobiles, there is increased difficulty in finding participants to take part in research that requires the use of a laptop.

There are few screen-capture programs that can collect data from mobile phones, and these often require them to be plugged into a laptop. Whilst there are some applications (for example Display Recorder, Screen Recorder and Shou) that can record a mobile screen without being connected to a laptop, most operating systems do not allow such applications to run. This is because, if malicious, an app could theoretically continue recording even after the user thinks it is off. A further issue is that if participants are recording their mobile phone screens, there is more chance that sensitive information (such as passwords) could be compromised because of the visibility of the keyboard on-screen. However, Brown et al. (2014), developed a software application of their own to collect screen-capture data from mobile phones. Their application does not provide a continuous recording like liteCam but instead takes four images of a mobile screen per second. This limits the exact timing of some recorded actions which, for analytic methods such as conversation analysis, can pose challenges.

Collecting Facebook data can be more complex compared to other social media platforms such as Twitter, which tend to be more open and accessible (Wasin, 2015). As has been noted, for private data the researcher is most often limited by who will take part in the study and what data they choose to provide. For public data, there is a much broader potential sample of data. Although much online data, such as Tweets, seems to be rarely kept private (Pew Research Centre, 2013), a large amount of online data, which is suitable for qualitative research is private (e.g. WhatsApp, Tinder, emails, Facebook, Skype, Facetime). The private nature of these sites means that there are potentially more access and ethical hurdles to overcome. However, we would argue that these media platforms are rich sources of qualitative data, and therefore it is worth trying to gain access to such data.

FACEBOOK DATA COLLECTION: NEW DIRECTIONS

Due to the increased usage of Facebook on mobiles, more research in this area is needed on how to collect data from mobile and tablet devices. As well as the software applications being developed (Brown et al., 2014) more studies now are gaining access to private interactions (e.g. Sampietro, 2015; Licoppe et al., 2015). In terms of screen-capture, new software is gradually being introduced for businesses to, for example, allow consumers to record technical problems they may have with a company's application or website. These applications are available on some operating systems and models and may offer hope to researchers wishing to overcome the limitation of not being able to make continuous recordings of interactions on mobiles.

CONCLUSION

A lot of online content, including on Facebook, is multimodal in nature with images, written text, sound and video all working simultaneously on the same platforms. Similarly, participants will often be using multiple platforms at once. Androutsopoulous (2015) has recently argued that we are perhaps entering into a 'third wave' of digital research and we now need to extend our empirical arenas to 'go multi everything'. He called for data collection to develop multi-site (studying how users interact with different platforms simultaneously), multi-medium (studying users simultaneously engaging with different media) and multi-mode (studying users simultaneously using different forms of communication in one medium) approaches to research in order to capture the current digital climate. In turn, then, to research digital media in this 'multi everything' way perhaps also calls for multi-perspective and multi-method data collection when it comes to researching platforms such as Facebook.

FURTHER READINGS

Jowett, A. (2015) 'A case for using online discussion forums in critical psychological research', *Qualitative Research in Psychology*, 12(3): 287–97.

Mayr, Philipp and Weller, Katrin (2017) 'Think before you collect: Setting up a data collection approach for social media studies', In Luke Sloan and Anabel Quan-Haase (eds.), *Sage Handbook of Social Media Research Methods*, London: Sage, pp. 107–24

Miller, Daniel (2011) *Tales from Facebook*. Cambridge: Polity Press.

REFERENCES

Androutsopoulous, J. (2015) 'Towards a third wave of digital discourse studies', paper presented at the Approaches to Digital Discourse Analysis Conference, Valencia.

Antaki, C., Ardévol, E., Núñez, F., and Vayreda, A. (2005) 'For she who knows who she is: Managing accountability in online forum messages', *Journal of Computer-Mediated Communication*, 11(1). Retrieved from http://jcmc.indiana.edu/vol11/issue1/antaki.html.

Bazarova, N.N., Taft, J.G., Choi, Y.H., and Cosley, D. (2012) 'Managing impressions and relationships on Facebook: Self-presentational and relational concerns revealed through the analysis of language style', *Journal of Language and Social Psychology*, 32(2): 121–41.

Beisswenger, M. (2008) 'Situated chat analysis as a window to the user's perspective: Aspects of temporal and sequential organization', *Language@ internet*, 5(6): 1–19.

Bhatt, I. and de Roock, R. (2013) 'Capturing the sociomateriality of digital literacy events', *Research in Learning Technology*, 21. Retrieved from http://dx.doi.org/10.3402/rlt.v21.21281.

Birnbaum, M.G. (2013) 'The fronts students use: Facebook and the standardization of self-presentations', *Journal of College Student Development*, 54(2): 155–7.

Bowker, N. and Tuffin, K. (2002) 'Disability discourses for online identities', *Disability & Society*, 17(3): 327–44.

boyd, D. (2008) 'Facebook's privacy trainwreck', *Convergence: The International Journal of Research into New Media Technologies*, 14(1): 13–20.

boyd, D. and Ellison, N.B. (2007) 'Social network sites: Definition, history, and scholarship', *Journal of Computer-Mediated Communication*, 13(1): 210–30.

Braun, Virginia and Clarke, Victoria (2013) *Successful Qualitative Research: A Practical Guide for Beginners*. London: Sage.

Brown, B., McGregor, M., and McMillan, D. (2014) '100 days of iPhone use: Understanding the Details of Mobile Device Use', paper presented at MobileHCI, Toronto.

Burke, S. and Goodman, S. (2012) '"Bring back Hitler's gas chambers": Asylum seeking,

Nazis and Facebook – a discursive analysis', *Discourse & Society*, 23(1): 19–33.
Carr, C.T., Schrok, D.B., and Dauterman, P. (2012) 'Speech acts within Facebook status messages', *Journal of Language and Social Psychology*, 31(2): 176–96.
Coulson, Neil (2015) *Online Research Methods for Psychologists*. London: Palgrave Macmillan.
Crystal, David (2001) *Language and the Internet*. Cambridge: Cambridge University Press.
D'Arcy, A. and Young, T.M. (2012) 'Ethics and social media: Implications for sociolinguistics in the networked public', *Journal of Sociolinguistics*, 16(4): 532–46.
Ditchfield, H. (2014) 'Screen capture software: The benefits and challenges', paper presented at the PhD Seminar Series, Leicester.
Ditchfield, H. (2015) 'More private than a private message: Screen capture software and the hidden privacy layer', paper presented at The Micro Analysis of Online Data Conference, Zurich.
Dolowitz, David, Buckler, Steve, and Sweeney, Fionnghuala (2008) *Researching Online*. New York: Palgrave Macmillan.
Edwards, D. (2005) 'Moaning, whinging and laughing: The subjective side of complaints', *Discourse Studies*, 7(1): 5–29.
Edwards, Derek and Potter, Jonathan (1992) *Discursive Psychology*. London: Sage.
Fielding, Nigel G., Lee, Raymond M., and Blank, Grant (eds.) (2016) *The Sage Handbook of Online Research Methods* (2nd edn). London: Sage (1st edn, 2008).
Flinkfeldt, M. (2011) '"Filling one's days": Managing sick leave legitimacy in an online forum', *Sociology of Health & Illness*, 33(5): 761–76.
Garcia, A. and Jacobs, J. (1999) 'The eyes of the beholder: Understanding the turn-taking system in quasi-synchronous computer-mediated communication', *Research on Language and Social Interaction*, 32(4): 337–67.
Giles, D.C. (2014) '"DSM-V is taking away our identity": The reaction of the online community to the proposed changes in the diagnosis of Asperger's disorder', *Health*, 18(2): 179–95.
Grant, R.W. and Sugarman, J. (2004) 'Ethics in human subjects research: Do incentives matter?', *Journal of Medicine and Philosophy*, 29(6): 717–38.
Grov, C., Gillespie, B.J., Royce, T., and Lever, J. (2011) 'Perceived consequences of casual online sexual activities on heterosexual relationships: A US online survey', *Archives of Sexual Behavior*, 40(2): 429–39.
Head, E. (2009) 'The ethics and implications of paying participants in qualitative research', *International Journal of Social Research Methodology*, 12(4): 335–44.
Herring, S. (2015) 'The co-evolution of computer mediated discourse analysis and CMC', paper presented at the Approaches to Digital Discourse Analysis Conference, Valencia.
Hewson, Claire (2008) 'Internet-mediated research as an emergent method and its potential role in facilitating mixed methods research', in Sharlene N. Hesse-Biber and Patricia Leavy (eds.), *Handbook of Emergent Methods*. New York: Guilford Press, pp. 543–70.
Hine, Christine (2000) *Virtual Ethnography*. London: Sage.
Keating, Elizabeth, and Sunakawa, Chiho (2011) '"A full inspiration tray": Multimodality across real and virtual spaces', in Jürgen Streeck, Charles Goodwin and Curtis LeBaron (eds.), *Embodied Interaction: Language and Body in the Material World*. Cambridge: Cambridge University Press, pp. 194–204.
Kozinets, Robert (2010) *Netnography: Doing Ethnographic Research Online*. London: Sage.
Lamerichs, J. and te Molder, H. (2003) 'Computer-mediated communication: From cognitive to a discursive model', *New Media & Society*, 5(4): 451–73.
Lee, C. (2015) 'The researcher's role in digital discourse analysis', paper presented at the Approaches to Digital Discourse Analysis Conference, Valencia.
Licoppe, C., Rivière, C.A., and Morel, J. (2015) 'Grindr casual hook-ups as interactional achievements', *New Media & Society*, Online first. DOI: 10.1177/1461444815589702.
Lillqvist, E. and Louhiala-Salminen, L. (2014) 'Facing Facebook impression management strategies in company–consumer interactions', *Journal of Business and Technical Communication*, 28(1): 3–30.
Malik, S.H. and Coulson, N. (2008) 'The male experience of infertility: A thematic analysis of an online infertility support group bulletin

board', *Journal of Reproductive and Infant Psychology*, 26(1): 18–30.

Meredith, Joanne (2014) 'Chatting online: Comparing spoken and online written interaction between friends', PhD dissertation, Loughborough University.

Meredith, Joanne. (2015) 'Transcribing screen-capture data: The process of developing a transcription system for multi-modal text-based data', *International Journal of Social Research Methodology*. Online first. DOI: 10.1080/13645579.2015.1082291.

Meredith, Joanne (2016) 'Using discourse and conversation analysis to analyse online data', in David Silverman (ed.), *Qualitative Research* (4th edn). London: Sage, pp. 261–76.

Meredith, Joanne and Potter, Jonathan (2013) 'Conversation analysis and electronic interactions: Methodological, analytic and technical considerations', in Hwee Ling Lim and Fay Sudweeks (eds.), *Innovative Methods and Technologies for Electronic Discourse Analysis*. IGI Global, pp. 370–5.

Meredith, J. and Stokoe, E. (2014) 'Repair: Comparing Facebook "chat" with spoken interaction', *Discourse & Communication*, 8(2): 181–207.

Peel, E. (2010) 'Pregnancy loss in lesbian and bisexual women: An online survey of experiences', *Human Reproduction*, 25(3): 721–7.

Peräkylä, Anssi (2016) 'Validity in qualitative research', in David Silverman (ed.), *Qualitative Research* (4th edn). London: Sage, pp. 413–28.

Pew Research Centre (2013) *Teens, Social Media and Privacy*. Retrieved from http://www.pewinternet.org/2013/05/21/teens-social-media-and-privacy/.

Potter, Jonathan (2004) 'Discourse analysis as a way of analysing naturally occurring talk', in David Silverman (ed.), *Qualitative Research: Theory, Method and Practice*. London: Sage, pp. 200–1.

Rapley, T. (2001) 'The art(fullness) of open ended interviewing: Some considerations on analysing interviews', *Qualitative Research*, 1(3): 303–23.

Sacks, Harvey (1992) *Lectures on Conversation* (Volumes 1 and 2, edited by Gail Jefferson). Oxford: Blackwell.

Sampietro, A. (2015) 'Are emoji's the new punctuation marks? Insights from Whatsapp chat', paper presented at the Approaches to Digital Discourse Analysis Conference, Valencia.

Stokoe, E. (2009) 'Doing actions with identity categories: Complaints and denials in neighbour disputes', *Text & Talk – An Interdisciplinary Journal of Language, Discourse Communication Studies*, 29(1): 75–97.

Stommel, W. (2008) 'Conversation analysis and community of practice as approaches to studying online community', *Language@Internet*, 5, Article 5. Retrieved from http://www.languageatinternet.org/articles/2008/1537.

Tech Crunch (2015) *More Than Half a Billion People Access Facebook Solely from Mobile*. Retrieved from http://techcrunch.com/2015/01/28/facebook-mobile-only-2/.

Tifferet, S. and Vilnai-Yavetz, I. (2014) 'Gender differences in Facebook self-presentation: An international randomized study', *Computers in Human Behavior*, 35: 388–99.

Turkle, Sherry (2011) *Alone Together: Why we Expect More from Technology and Less from Ourselves*. New York: Basic Books.

Walther, J.B., Van Der Heide, B., Kim, S., Westerman, D., and Tong, S.T. (2008) 'The role of friends' appearance and behavior on evaluations of individuals on Facebook: Are we known by the company we keep?', *Human Communication Research*, 34(1): 28–49.

Wasin, A. (2015) *Using Twitter as a data source: An overview of current social media research tools*. Retrieved from http://blogs.lse.ac.uk/impactofsocialsciences/2015/07/10/social-media-research-tools-overview/.

West, Laura and Trester, Anne Marie (2013) 'Facework on Facebook: Conversations on social media', in Deborah Tannen and Anne Marie Trester (eds.), *Discourse 2.0: Language and New Media*. Washington, DC: Georgetown University Press, pp. 133–54.

Whiteman, Natasha (2012) *Undoing Ethics: Rethinking Practice in Online Research*. London: Springer.

Wikström, P. (2014) '#srynotfunny: Communicative functions of hashtags on Twitter', *SKY Journal of Linguistics*, 27: 127–52.

Wilson, R.E., Gosling, S.D., and Graham, L.T. (2012) 'A review of Facebook research in the social sciences', *Perspectives on Psychological Science*, 7(3): 203–20.

Wood, Linda and Kroger, Rolf (2000) *Doing Discourse Analysis: Methods for Studying Action in Talk and Text*. London: Sage.

Zhao, S., Grasmuck, S., and Martin, J. (2008) 'Identity construction on Facebook: Digital empowerment in anchored relationships', *Computers in Human Behavior*, 24(5): 1816–36.

Zhao, X., Salehi, N., Naranjit, S., Alwaalan, S., Voida, S., and Cosley, D. (2013) 'The many faces of Facebook: Experiencing social media as performance, exhibition, and personal archive', *Proceedings of the SIGCHI Conference on Human Factors in Computing Systems*, pp. 1–10.

Zimmer, M. (2010) '"But the data is already public": On the ethics of research in Facebook', *Ethics and Information Technology*, 12(4): 313–25.

Troubling the Concept of Data in Qualitative Digital Research

Annette N. Markham

INTRODUCTION

In late 2016, the unanticipated results of the US presidential election sent a shock wave through the world, including the digital data science community. All the election polls predicted that Hillary Clinton would win. All of them turned out to be wrong. Even the republican candidate did not expect to win, based on the data analytics. It seemed a failure of data.[1]

This chapter focuses on the concept of data to clarify how it operates on our research sensibilities. By deconstructing the concept, we can better situate it, consider whether or not we should use the term at all, or be more clear in our definitions of what we mean when we explain our research to others. Drawing on current critical academic responses[2] to the rise of data and big data, I posit that data operates on at least two levels; *as thing and as ideology*. Though inextricable in practice, we can separate these concepts momentarily to begin to identify how quite different meanings might be operating in our theoretical frameworks, research design, and everyday activities. Once these dual levels are recognized – a process that requires conscious and critical self-reflexivity – one can more strategically frame and use the interpretation of data in multiple and nuanced ways, to add layers of meaning or augment the analytical processes.

The term 'data' refers to many things (see Flick, Chapter 1, this volume, and Lindgren, Chapter 28, this volume). For example, we could think of data as the representation of *traces* of human and non-human behaviors and experiences, isolated and observed as discrete objects. While not the only way to describe data, this conceptualization has become prominent in the so-called digital age, information age, or internet age for good reason. Our social situations are increasingly embedded in, or saturated with, digital and global networks of information flows. We leave traces everywhere when we connect to the internet. Massive amounts of information can be collected. Any of us who use the internet know that we are continually producing data that will be archived – by us, by marketers, by the companies who provide our devices, platforms, apps, and so forth. The information itself is microscopic and detailed. Whether produced deliberately or not, it is possible to archive these traces, transforming them to units of information that can then be combined with data that has been produced, archived, and transformed elsewhere.

Computation of large datasets can reveal interesting patterns and yield novel insights about human behavior. Perhaps because data is so plentiful, miniscule, and detailed, we – and here I mean data scientists as well as politicians and citizens – can sometimes forget that it is not meaningful in itself. This mistake sometimes takes the form of assuming the parts add up to the whole. Or conflating data with knowledge. Whatever the specific form of faulty reasoning, overvaluing the immediate meaning and truth value of data is a problem amplified by the size and number of datasets involved in even the most basic of algorithmic calculations. We have reached an era when we no longer have the human computational power to calculate the math necessary to analyze massive datasets.[3] Algorithms take the place of human cognition and we must trust various self-learning mathematical models (or neural networks) to make the computations for us.

'Data' is not a bad term in itself, but because its value in this decade of big data is overstated, many faulty logics and premises about data, truth, and algorithmic computation can end up influencing how we make sense of the world around us. Returning to November 9, 2016, the night of the US elections, shock about this unforeseen turn of predicted outcomes shifted to anger; social media exploded into heated arguments about who or what was to blame for such miscalculations in the expected results. Was it Hillary Clinton's team that failed to analyze the data correctly? Were journalists biased against and therefore blind to the poor or uneducated whites who came out in droves to vote for Donald Trump? Did the polling companies collect data inadequately? Were the algorithms and formulas underlying the polls or forecasts wrong? One might ask: why was everyone so shocked? As boyd and Crawford (2012) remind us in their critique of exaggerations about the power of big data, data never speak for themselves, but are interpreted. But when we are continually confronted by 'facts' that are beyond our human cognitive ability to double check, common sense can fail. We simply believe what is seen, or more precisely, what the numbers tell us. At least in the immediate aftermath of the 2016 elections, frustration continued to grow.

As many realized and have discussed since, finding the best tools or metrics for collecting and analyzing data is not the answer. It is the failure of interpretation that always catches us in the end. This became an even more paramount truth as we faced a third shock wave in the weeks after the election – that fake news had been widely planted, believed, and spread through social networking sites like Facebook. Alongside 'post-truth' as OED's word of the year,[4] the public was continually reminded that any supposed fact or truth could be believed, despite the blatant absence of any evidence.

Let me underline the key point in relation to this chapter: Interpretation, not data, is where we should be focusing our attention. This should be a comfortable statement for those familiar with epistemologies and approaches that are labeled qualitative, for whom the term 'data' has been problematized for decades. 'Data' and 'Computation' are not favored terms to describe qualitative methods because they symbolically indicate an approach fundamentally opposed to the hallmark of qualitative inquiry, which is inductive, immersive, and interpretive. How should qualitative researchers respond to this new tidal shift toward datafication? How do we design studies when 'data' becomes the predominant concept for giving shape or meaning to cultural materiality? We could simply refuse to use the term, since it does not fit well with the qualitative enterprise. Or we could try to replace 'data' with other terms. Neither option confronts the more insidious problem, which is not data itself, or the growth of computation as a way of knowing, but the revival and creeping spread of positivist procedures and frameworks. Retaining the strength of the qualitative approach requires critical awareness of what guides our practical choices and everyday practices.

THE IMPORTANCE OF DISTURBING CONCEPTS

Concepts are multiplicitous and therefore ambiguous. They shape and target our sensibilities and thus function as powerful guides for action. But because concepts are comprised of multiple meanings, they shift in meaning and emphasis over time and use. They also allow for specification and transformation within context. Both the concept of 'data' and the concept of 'digital' are shifty creatures in this decade, since they are in high and varied use across multiple stages of discourse. It is important to continually re-examine our concepts, to keep them from stabilizing, at which point they take on more power than they deserve, to define and delimit what and how we make sense of the world.

Throughout what follows, I propose we continually disturb the concept of data, testing it against other viable terminologies that might frame and inform our inquiry practices. In such a way, we can better articulate what we mean when we use the term to describe what we're up to, whether this is related to 'the digital' or not. We'll also have better research results in the end, since this reflexive exercise can do nothing but improve our research designs.

Another concept, 'digital', is central to this chapter. As a concept, this term functions on multiple levels. Most directly, whatever we call 'the digital' is born from the transformation of tangible, visual, or audible analog material into a binary system of zeros and ones, which become 'on' or 'off' electrical impulses in a computer system. Networked, the digital travels through the Internet. Machine language systems help us transform these bits back into meaningful information. This definition functions at a literal level to help us comprehend what is meant by the term. It is at other levels where we find meaning for what we might label digital identity, digital media, digital culture, or digital data.

Digital never stands alone as a topic of inquiry. As a modifier for some other concept, digital operates metonymically to stand in for countless modes of interaction, types of information, platforms for interaction, and cultural formations. For the past two decades, we have been living on a planet where many social if not human processes are digitally saturated, Internet-mediated, and globally networked. It is high time to move beyond 'digital' as the default modifier, grammatically and conceptually speaking, especially because to be useful at all, the term must be defined each time it is used, to identify the specificity of meaning within context (for more on this injunction, see also Bakardjieva, 2012; Deuze, 2012; Hine, 2015; Horst and Miller, 2012; Markham, 2017; Turkle, 2011).

Below, I offer a framework for digital researchers to consider how data, first as *things*, can be conceptually specified as: a) background information, b) emergent materiality, c) fragment of artifact, and d) evidence. I then shift to the second frame: a discussion of data as an *ideology*, initially discussing the prevailing data science ideologies and later offering an alternative that is more aligned with interpretive ontologies. I conclude the chapter by returning to the basics of strong qualitative approaches as a reminder of the importance of – in this era of data-everything – troubling and reflexively tweaking research design concepts so that they work for us rather than the other way around.

DATA AS THING[5]

It's easy to conceptualize data as a thing since this is how it is presented to us in everyday advertisements, in statistical graphs, and poll percentages. Long before digital archives, geolocation tracking apps, self-tracking devices, and SurveyMonkey, humans transformed actions, behaviors, and objects into units of information that can be examined closely. In ancient times, we charted the position of stars, giving common shapes to the heavens and providing maps for humans to navigate without land-based reference points. Transforming motions into discrete units in the early 1900s, Frank and Lillian Gilbreth, along with Frederick Taylor, founded a still current practice of using time and motion studies to standardize movements of workers on factory assembly lines or behind the counter at any fast food restaurant, like McDonald's. Transforming beliefs into numeric values is standard practice in psychology and sociology, where we might measure everything from personality to voting preference.

In addition to dissecting and separating a whole into component parts, datafication is also the result of abstraction, whereby the complex is rendered sensible by means of simplification and categorization. The manner of abstraction depends on one's goal, of course, but in any case, the outcome of any abstraction will be largely if not entirely based on what is focused on and therefore what is seen.[6]

Whatever we call data, therefore, is the material result of a series of choices made at critical junctures. An important quality of a qualitative approach is to pay attention to and honor the complexity of lived experience. Generally, this means researchers transform practices, experience, conversations, and movements into standardized units with great care, only after long consideration about whether or not this 'theme' or 'code' adequately captures the essence or meaning. This is not about condensing meaning, but trying to grasp what is essentially complex. The idea of 'data' sits uncomfortably within this effort. As experience is categorized to make sense of a situation or phenomenon, or more colloquially what Marcus (1998) would call 'what is going on here', the process is, through and through, one of interpretation. The key to good qualitative inquiry is honing this interpretive strength. Thus, data can become a double-bind term in qualitative research because it focuses our attention on exactly the wrong part of the process, yet at the same time gives a common ground vocabulary to help others identify the focus of our gaze.

The basic starting point for working through and around this double bind is to more precisely define what we mean when we're using the term data. This will help us find distinctions and clarify what it is not. There are many useful textbook(ish) guides or typologies (see, for example, the typology described by Lindgren, Chapter 28, this volume) to help us conceptualize data in a broad sense. Here, I specify four ways in which we can think about data as a thing:

1 First, data as background information: what we use to search for good research questions. It is the stuff[7] that helps us engage in a process called pattern recognition.
2 Second, data as emergent: the stuff, material or otherwise, that emerges as you focus – on a phenomenon, on a situation, on a text, on a stream of tweets.
3 Third, data as a fragment of an artifact: whether we say it's emergent, found, or made, data is a partial, non-representative signal or indicator of something else.
4 Fourth, data as the word we use for evidence: the stuff we use to support a claim, focus readers' attention on something, or provide details in larger arguments.

1. Data as Background Information

Data helps us search for patterns. In this sense, we can use pre-existing or create data sets to wander around, searching for interesting occurrences or trends. In a playful way, one can experiment with different analytical tools to see how these occurrences, interactions, or trends might be visualized. In doing so, we might be hoping a research question will emerge. We might be looking for verification of a hunch, to locate a specific target for inquiry. Many tools allow us to access and mess around in massive data sets. Data scraping[8] is a common tool designed to gather lots of information. Scraping can be used to search for a bigger picture or to find multiple standpoints. Here, we might be seeking a broad view to counter our own seeing, which cannot help but be situated in what is one's own 'filter bubble' or 'echo chamber'. Scraping can be interesting and might identify some patterns, but we must calculate the payoff of such a cumbersome and multistage process.

Patterns are not the end point, but the beginning point. After the identification of patterns, the qualitative researcher begins to test whether the patterns articulate or point to valuable questions to ask. Here, then, data is used as background information to inform one's research inquiry. It informs the direction and type of interpretation that will follow.

Importantly, it is not necessary to use computation to identify patterns. Indeed, the hallmark of qualitative inquiry is that it is driven not by data but by our questions. These questions emerge because we've already noticed patterns in our own prior contact with, connection to, or immersion in the phenomenon. One's study of any digital media context is likely not coming out of the blue, but as a result of the informal inquiry we were engaged in before we called it research. The data for such background knowledge may therefore be different than any archived dataset one might access.

2. Data as Emergent

In qualitative inquiry, anything we consider to be an object for analysis is generated by our choice to focus on certain particularities versus others. When we choose an angle for our attention, whether we are an algorithm or a person, certain data will become more likely or possible than other options. So, data is not pre-formed, but is made, apparating[9] when we choose to focus on it.

Qualitative inquiry is an emergent process; informal interest or immersion in a particular context drives us to ask scholarly questions. At that point, we begin to define that which we study in more concrete terms and make official those things we've likely been doing a long time. We start to write down or track our observations, record our conversations with people, and archive images, texts, or other materials. Some aspects of the situation fed our interest long before we started collecting anything we might label as data. When we identify these activities as part of our research process, we can shift our notion from data as an all-encompassing or *a priori* object into a more nuanced notion that data emerges as 'object' or 'data' because we have decided to focus on a particular question, which highlights certain material and obscures the rest.

This conceptualization of data as an emergent rather than a priori aspect of inquiry foregrounds the importance of the questions we cannot help but ask when we focus our gaze in specific directions. Focusing on the questions allows the possibilities for what counts as data to blossom. We are no longer trapped by thinking that we only collect what is visible or archivable, or that we must collect all of whatever it is.

3. Digital Data as Fragments or Artifacts

Often, we collect data about people, places, or things when we don't have access to the original context. Alternatively, data are[10] continually produced or derived from lingering traces of presence or actions that are caught and stored automatically or for unrelated reasons (e.g. time and date stamps in the metatag information on photos, or location data that might be collected coincidentally by a car hire company and end up passing through many database aggregators to then end up in the hands of social media marketers). When we reflect on what data represent (browsing through this book as well as other ongoing critiques of data, big data, and datafication), it should be clear that data are always a partial representation of some specific aspect of a thing, not the entirety. As Baym (2013) and others have argued, even the most robust digital data metric yields a partial and unrepresentative sample. As she argues, this is not a technical glitch to be solved, but a characteristic of human interaction, which naturally occurs in ways that are not traceable because these interactions are not signals given or given off, in the Goffmanian sense, but meanings emerging from and happening throughout interactions. Her argument is one of many that problematizes the mistaken assumptions that everything that is digital qualifies as data and everything that happens through digital media is capturable as data.

Data are like pot shards to an archeologist, fragments of information that can be used, along with other sensibilities, to make sense of the situation. Put together, these shards might construct the likeness of the thing, but they can never be the thing itself, as Latour (1999) noted about soil in the Amazon. Because meaning occurs outside that which can be collected as data, these fragments might convey meaning to us, but only after they are pieced together, situated after the fact into a context that fundamentally no longer exists. As Geertz (1973) eloquently noted about our efforts to interpret culture, 'what we call our data are really our own constructions of other people's constructions of what they and their compatriots are up to' (1973, p. 10).

In a practical sense, as many authors in this *Handbook* discuss, collecting data is a deliberate sampling method that requires careful analysis about what is actually represented.

If we think of data as clues, presented in fragments and moments, it can help us determine what, among this and other stuff, are needed to fully address one's research question. Extending my repeated theme of the chapter, the key to good digital data collection is not bound to either the data or the methods, but rather to the good fit between what is available and what questions one can feasibly and sensibly address.

4. Data as Evidence

This last point highlights how we use data. Starting from the outset of a project, research design emerges from early immersion in a context, where one's questions (research questions or just everyday questions) prompt a direction for the analytical gaze. As these questions turn our heads, data emerges that helps us address these questions. The entire process may appear on the surface to be data-driven, because there is a tight rhythm between stimuli and sensemaking. Put more simply, we are in a dynamic relationship with the contexts we study. As we enter, move within, and move through this relationship, it might initially seem strange, but over time, we start to make sense. This iterative and reflexive dynamic – as a long string of scholars have articulated in better ways than I ever could – narrows our attention. Data might be used (or become) our focus (object) of analysis but in a larger sense, the process of analysis and interpretation yields an account, whereby we incorporate data as supporting evidence.

To finish this section, it's important to reiterate that the idea of data is highly ambiguous. While useful, these four definitions are not mutually exclusive or all inclusive. Many such typologies exist; this one focuses specifically on how research is designed if data is conceptualized as a thing. It should be considered a starting point for specifying the many meanings that data inherits throughout different stages of the research project.

DATA AS IDEOLOGY

The shift toward 'big data' in the first decade of the twenty-first century may have been a pragmatic adoption of a term to describe massive amounts of information and the exponential growth of computational power, but it has strengthened a steadily encroaching ideological shift that includes the growing operationalization of human experience into discrete data points, numeric units, or pre-determined categories of meaning, which can, because of their concrete qualities, be captured, recombined with data points from other humans, and analyzed to find large cultural patterns. This influences all forms of scientific inquiry, including qualitative inquiry.

Over the past 300 years, the concept of data shifted from something that could be taken for granted in argument, to that which is pre-semantic, pre-factual, and pre-analytical (Rosenberg, 2013). As a matter of rhetoric, Rosenberg continues, data has become understood as distinguishable from 'fact' in that it (data) is irreducible: 'When a fact is proven false, it ceases to be a fact. False data is data nonetheless' (2013, p. 18). The rhetorical power of such logic is potent. When events, people, behaviors, interactions, or other dynamic human processes are framed as data that can be collected, these complexities necessarily end up gaining objective, or even obdurate shapes and qualities, because the baseline conceptualization of data specifies that data can be held, measured, and aggregated with other things.

It is important to recognize and actively counter this ideology since it is both alluring and deeply flawed. In qualitative research, it can trap us into believing that we have access to complete records of what happened, or can capture every element of the social situation, when even in the most surveilled and archived situations, this is not possible. Baym (2013) reinforces this point in her analysis of the limitations of how social media is measured through various metrics, noting, 'it has never been more essential to remind ourselves what data are not seen, and what cannot be measured'. Social media metrics, she reminds us, are not only non-representative samples, they are also skewed by algorithms that foreground some content over other content. Most of all, she continues, 'their meanings – seemingly so obvious – are inherently ambiguous'. Ultimately, she concludes, 'it is not clear what visible social media metrics might mean or, more accurately, what range of meanings they collapse'.

Despite the good sense we might apply in situ during our qualitative studies, it is difficult to resist the ideology behind big data. As boyd and Crawford (2012) aptly note, 'Big Data not only refers to very large data sets and the tools and procedures used to manipulate and analyze them, but also to a computational turn in thought and research (2012, p. 3, drawing on Burkholder, 1992). This computational turn, they continue, functions as orthodoxy, radically shifting how we think about research (2012, p. 3–4). The undercurrent of the past five years of big data discourse is one 'where all other forms of analysis can be sidelined by production lines of numbers, privileged as having a direct line to raw knowledge' (2012, p. 4).

Even though we might know better when we give it careful consideration, this 'direct line' boyd and Crawford mention seems to work in our everyday experiences with our platforms, apps, and devices, where big data computation is almost magical in its eerie accuracy. Take personalized advertising, which now occurs almost instantaneously online. Predictive modeling has become a sophisticated tool for marketing, whereby snippets of code, algorithms in this case, are used to filter and process massive data sets from multiple sources. Just a few clicks are needed to activate thousands of processes that occur over distributed computer networks. There is a fuzzy relationship between what you click on and what you desire, but the result of this algorithmic processing can appear seamless. It is only recognized as magic when the algorithms fail and we see ads that are totally off target. Otherwise, the system just works. I see bargains and sales on items I pause on in my Instagram feed. News is targeted and fine-tuned depending on friend networks, organizational affiliation, and geolocation. This same sort of computation can work on billions of data points across the genome to locate the most precise genetic markers and, through DNA analysis services such as *23andMe*, find genealogical lines for us that we never knew existed.

Repeated exposure to such computational finesse can function powerfully to reinforce the premise that data itself gives us insight, that data simply speaks for itself. However, when we thingify everything, we set and spring multiple traps. We set a flawed premise in place when we separate, flatten, and equalize everything as a unit of information. More subtly, we can be snared by our own common premise that 'data analysis' is the underlying framework for our studies. Over time, as Rosenberg's careful rhetorical analysis of the term highlights, prioritizing data as the central element of a study can mislead readers of our research to believe that data is not simply one of many sources for analytical inspiration, but the *entirety* of what the researcher needs. This is not to say we should dismiss data as being unimportant in our research projects. Rather, the goal may be to shift the ideology back to the core of qualitative epistemologies, to refocus our attention.

Let me offer some provocation: For the qualitative researcher, data is a red herring of the brightest color. It directs our attention to objects, pieces of texts, and the outcomes of interactions rather than the interactions themselves, all the while distracting us from the point that this is not where meaning resides. Data, as an ideological concept, beguiles us to think that it *is* the reality, when in fact it is only a fragment or artifact, not even of the whole, but only of whatever we chose to focus on as we made decisions that led us to where we are situated. Focusing on data can easily distract us from the much larger and complex process and practice of qualitative inquiry. If we're going to use the term 'data', we must co-opt it through an interpretive ontology.

In 2004, I articulated questions that, for me, were crucial for the ethical and nuanced study of people embedded in digital contexts:

> As researchers and members of various communities and cultures, what do we use to construct a sense of who the Other really is?
>
> In what ways do our methods of comprehending [social life] either disavow or validate multiplicitous, polyvocal, ever-shifting constructions of identity?
>
> To what extent do we acknowledge our own participation in the construction of the subject of inquiry? (Markham, 2004, p. 372)

These are still vital questions, in that they cut to the heart of what many of us seek when we study people. These questions frame an ethically sensitive approach for digital research design, returning specifically to the relationship between the researcher and that which is researched and what happens when we extract certain elements of experience from its moment and transform it into something more abstract than what it was. Transformation and abstraction are necessary to sensemaking. These two activities are the outcomes of decisions we make at critical junctures throughout the process of inquiry, each of which impacts what is later understood to be known.

In this sense, we only ever *make* data. When we pick up various tools to collect, manage, sort, and analyze any phenomenon, we are choosing specific lenses through which we can better comprehend the subject. These tools, whether in the form of philosophical prose, theoretical premises, conceptual models, or methodological techniques, will help us focus our attention. Combined, they enable us to carve out meaning from the many overlapping contexts of the situation. Our unique set of tools also hides, obscures, minimizes, sets aside, and otherwise filters out other possibilities. Our senses are rarely, if ever, unhooked from these filters, many of which are so taken for granted as natural ways of knowing that we don't notice how with them we encapsulate, control, and otherwise trap the Other into boxes that fit them perfectly because their potential has been shaped to make the perfect fit.

Using Interpretive Ontologies as an Active Disturbance to Data Science

This century marks the age of distraction. Amazon's 'Alexa', my latest gadget, is an electronic sensor in my house that also conveniently functions as a speaker for my music. This IoT, or Internet of Things, listens to me while I move around the house. I talk with it and as I do, it learns my habits. We can connect this sensor to our lightbulbs, thermostats, and health care facilities. The value of this device is convenience. The amazement, contentment, and occasional irritation I feel is a distraction from the facts that I must pay for many additional services to get it to work seamlessly, it continually collects and shares data about me with multiple third parties, and it is changing how I make queries in my head.[11]

As qualitative researchers in this century, we need an ideology that provokes, raises questions, keeps us out of our comfort zone. I find an occasional shake-up necessary for myself, because the world around us is so deceptively 'figured out'. In this decade, we don't question as much why the interface of Facebook looks as it does. News is fed (through the feed). All friends are the same (unless we choose otherwise). In this decade, we don't remain disturbed long enough for us to shift our methods to fit a critical mindset in any sustained way. Consider how quickly we forget that the US, as Snowden revealed in 2014, collected massive data on its citizens without justification; or that various social media platforms like OKCupid or Facebook experiment with the emotional responses of citizens without letting us know we're part of a laboratory study in the guise of A/B testing.[12] These are only two of many critical turning points with actual and serious consequence for the shape of future societies.

We need to remain disturbed by the rising tide of datafication. Data analytics give us powerful tools to see, combine, compute, and understand phenomena like never before. This can have a remarkable and positive impact, so the data era is, in many ways, a wonderful and astonishing time to be a researcher. At the same time, these results coincide with a strong trend across all industries toward transforming 'humans (and their data) into data' (Grinter, 2013, p. 10). Qualitative researchers are uniquely equipped to resist deeply flawed but popular ideas that we should collect and archive everything because we have the technical ability to do so; that data is neutral and objective; that data can be stripped and cleaned adequately to protect individuals; or that given the right technologies, data collection can be complete.

An ideology of data for qualitative researchers necessarily includes competing elements, or even dialectics. On the one hand, if we maintain focus on the question, our position, and what is going on around us, as we study the phenomenon, we need not really worry about data at all. We're finding it all the time, generating it as we sense and pay attention to patterns in our own unique, human ways. As we continue to focus attention on the situation, data will continue to be created as we let certain stuff emerge from the larger flows of social life. Likewise, other data will be lost to us, not because we once had it and we lost it, but because it is not part of what we are attending to. For some other researcher, a different set will emerge, because of their particular way of seeing and attending to the details. And in the end, we'll select certain data and ignore others to tell the rest about what we think we know. This is a natural part of storytelling as well as science.

On the other hand, qualitative researchers should not ignore data, datafication, or the research designs that undergird data science. We need to comprehend the logics of computational research design to combat it when necessary. For example, the ability to aggregate and cross reference is used for anything from building location-based apps that label certain neighborhoods as 'sketchy', as in the case of SketchFactor, an app that eventually shut down from accusations that it was racist (Marantz, 2015), to conducting predictive policing of citizens (Brayne, 2015), a science and practice that gains more ground annually. In both cases, we should be disturbed that data is used in these ways because these sciences rely on algorithmic abstraction that is not infallible; but to adequately respond, we must understand the nuances of how the second case is the result of vastly different research efforts than the first.

This does not mean we should give ground regarding the fundamental principles or practices of qualitative inquiry. As I have written elsewhere:

> One type of response to the rise of data, datafication and big data has been to defend ethnographic research within the discursive frame of data, insisting that ethnography is about 'small data', 'all ethnography is big data', or 'big data needs thick data'. These responses help justify ethnography but yield epistemological ground, so that the entire baseline for appropriate ethnographic inquiry shifts to a new register. (Markham, 2017, p. 8)

When qualitative researchers use phrases like 'data collection', it should be with clarity that this terminology is more a convenience for separating and managing materials or a rhetorical tactic than an ontological claim. As a strategic choice, this terminology usefully situates one's research inside the sciences within research institutions. It helps social studies to be accepted as social sciences.

Meanwhile, we cannot forget that the impact of totalizing the 'stuff' of culture as data that can be collected, measured, and analyzed through scientific methods is devastating. The power of computation is undeniable. By continually collecting and archiving information, as well as transforming historical paper documents into digital form, we can use data science methods to see significant political, biological, climate, and social trends. As datafication is normalized, those qualities of inquiry that are not quantifiable become abnormal. How can we measure embodiment, emotion, and other complexities that function as material evidence as well as an interpretive process (Davies and Spencer, 2010)? We may insist that qualitative inquiry is fundamentally interpretive, but this is a difficult stance to maintain when the systems surrounding the methods for qualitative inquiry actively de-legitimize interpretation as an individual, subjective, and key role in the process.

The ongoing risk, which the interpretive movement has long sought to combat (see the many authors in the edited collections of Denzin and Lincoln, e.g. 2017), is that qualitative inquiry is subsumed within a larger paradigm of data science, whereby a qualitative perspective is seen to contribute merely a type of analysis, rather than a worldview. This is exacerbated by the division of methods into the faulty categories of qualitative and quantitative, which implies that the enterprise is essentially the same except that the method of handling and analyzing data differs.

To pre-empt and resist this trend, we must continue to highlight and explore what qualitative modes of inquiry are for and how these ways of knowing are performed. This means, at the very least, promoting interpretation as the more central consideration than data; defining data more precisely and variously as it is actually used in one's study; and finally, highlighting interpretive conceptual frameworks and ideologies.

CONCLUSION

Some of the authors in Part IV of this volume propose novel ways to deal with, or think about, data within qualitative analysis of complex digital situations. They all argue for the same thing: *qualitative research is driven by context and question, not data.* They all understand that *collecting* digital data is a misnomer. As we make choices along our pathways to meaning, we continually sample from the past and present material world, whether that is represented in atoms or bits. We speculate, using a what-if or other future-oriented focus. We play around with ideas, move them around on paper or in concept maps. The authors represented here each understand, sometimes through trial and error, that putting data at the forefront of qualitative inquiry is the worst sort of trap because it deludes us into thinking we have already collected the knowledge when, in actuality, what qualitative inquiry produces is a bricolage of multiple voices, actors, and perspectives filtered through our own unique gaze and interpretive lenses.

Notes

1. It's difficult to pinpoint only one example of the tsunami of Tweets and news stories about 'data failure', but it's representative in Republican strategist Mike Murphy's early statement on MSNBC and Twitter that 'data has died', Wired's later report, 'Trump's Win Isn't the Death of Data – It Was Flawed All Along' (Metz, 2016) and a November 10 story by the *New York Times*, 'How Data Failed Us in Calling an Election' (Lohr and Singer, 2016).
2. This ongoing and important discussion can be followed across the edited collection by Lisa Gitelman, 2013; a special issue of *First Monday* in 2013; the special issue of *Media, Culture, & Society* in 2015 that responded to the landmark article by boyd and Crawford in 2012; the blog series coming out of *Data & Society*, and the 'data ethnographies' series emerging from the Digital Ethnography Research Centre at RMIT, 2015.
3. For a short review of some key shifts in how we're thinking about data processing in the era of big data, see Ouelette (2013).
4. https://en.oxforddictionaries.com/word-of-the-year/word-of-the-year-2016.
5. I use singular versus plural grammar deliberately here, to reflect my argument that it is deceptively easy to treat data as if it has an incontrovertible 'itness'. While some may argue that the plural is grammatically correct, 'it seems preferable in modern English to allow context to determine whether the term should be treated as a plural or as a collective singular, since the connotations are different' (Rosenberg, 2013, p. 19).
6. For an excellent popular history and discussion of data, datafication, and big data, see Schonenberg and Crokier (2014).
7. Here, I really do mean 'stuff' rather than any other word. In this sense, I take inspiration from various sources that the *Stanford Encyclopedia of Philosophy* calls 'stuff ontology' (Steen, 2012). If we temporarily carve out information for inspection from the universe of matter/thought or, as Karen Barad (2007) might say, 'material discursives', an appropriate term for this selection is 'stuff'. It is not data, not object, not matter, and not thing, but an amalgam or combination that, if not countable, might be measurable, and if not measurable, at least analyzable.
8. The recent invention of 'scraping' allows one to gather information from a website, platform, account, or database and transform it into something that other programs can read, or that is easier to work with because it is standardized data. For purposes of this example, we can use the simple definition of web scrapers by developer Macwright: 'web scrapers do the task of a very industrious user – they navigate websites, parse pages, and save information in bulk' (2012, n.p.). Information is transformed from one state to another to create a standardized dataset that can be read or used by other programs. This is often used for large-scale qualitative analysis, aggregation and computation, or storage.
9. I mean apparate versus appear, because it conveys the sense of magically appearing. The term originates in the fictional series, Harry Potter. I suppose we could also use Schrödinger's cat as an illustrative example.
10. In this section I return to the plural form of data, since it makes more sense in this category.
11. This is not unique to Amazon's 'Alexa'. To note, my statement here is part of a larger set of arguments about how media influence us, starting with McLuhan's famous and still-important observations that the 'medium is the message' (1964).
12. To read more about these cases, see Greenwald (2013), Luca (2014), and McNeal (2014) respectively.

FURTHER READING

Gitelman, Lisa (ed.) (2013) *Raw Data is an Oxymoron*. Boston: MIT Press.

Markham, Annette and Baym, Nancy (eds.) (2009) *Internet Inquiry: Conversations about Method*. London: Sage.

Pink, Sarah, Ardevol, Elisenda, and Lanzeni, Débora (eds.) (2016) *Debora Digital Materialities: Design and Anthropology*. Huntingdon: Bloomsbury.

REFERENCES

Bakardjieval, M. (2012) 'Reconfiguring the mediapolis: New media and civic agency', *New Media Society*, 14(1): 63–79.

Barad, Karen (2007) *Meeting the Universe Halfway: Quantum Physics and the Entanglement of Matter and Meaning*. Durham, NC: Duke University Press.

Baym, N. (2013) 'Data not seen: The uses and shortcomings of social media metrics', *First Monday*, 18(10) available at http://www.ojphi.org/ojs/index.php/fm/article/view/4873/3752.

boyd, d. and Crawford, K. (2012) 'Critical questions for big data', *Information, Communication & Society*, 15(5): 662–79.

Brayne, S. (2015) Stratified Surveillance: Policing in the Age of Big Data. Unpublished dissertation.

Davies, James and Spencer, Dimitrina (eds.) (2010) *Emotions in the Field: The Psychology and Anthropology of Fieldwork Experience*. Stanford, CA: Stanford University Press.

Denzin, Norman K. and Lincoln, Yvonna S. (eds.) (2018) *The Sage Handbook of Qualitative Research*, 5th ed. Thousand Oaks, CA: Sage.

Deuze, Mark (2012) *Media Life*. Cambridge and Malden, MA: Polity Press.

Geertz, Clifford (1973) *The Interpretation of Cultures: Selected Essays*. New York: Basic Books.

Gitelman, Lisa (ed.) (2013) *Raw Data is an Oxymoron*. Boston: MIT Press.

Greenwald, G. (2013, June 6). NSA collecting phone records of millions of Verizon customers daily. Accessed January 1, 2017 from: https://www.theguardian.com/world/2013/jun/06/nsa-phone-records-verizon-court-order.

Grinter, B. (2013) 'A big data confession', *Interactions*, 20(4): 10–11.

Hine, Christine (2015) *Ethnography for the Internet: Embedded, Embodied and Everyday*. Huntingdon: Bloomsbury.

Horst, Heather and Miller, Daniel (2012) *Digital Anthropology*. London: Berg.

Latour, Bruno (1999). *Pandora's Hope: Essays on the Reality of Science Studies*. Cambridge, MA: Harvard University Press.

Lohr, S. and Singer, N. (2016, November 10) 'How data failed us in calling an election', *New York Times*. Accessed January 1, 2017 from: https://www.nytimes.com/2016/11/10/technology/the-data-said-clinton-would-win-why-you-shouldnt-have-believed-it.html.

Luca, M. (2014, June 29) 'Were OkCupid's and Facebook's experiments unethical?', *Harvard Business Review*. Accessed January 1, 2017 from: https://hbr.org/2014/07/were-okcupids-and-facebooks-experiments-unethical.

Macwright, T. (2012) 'On scrapers', Blog entry. Accessed January 1, 2017 from: http://www.macwright.org/2012/09/06/scrapers.html.

Marantz, A. (2015, July 29) 'When an app is called racist', *New Yorker Magazine*.

Marcus, George E. (1998) *Ethnography Through Thick and Thin*. Princeton, NJ: Princeton University Press.

Markham, Annette (2004) 'Internet as research context', in Clive Seale, Jaber Gubrium, David Silverman, and Giampietro Gobo (eds.), *Qualitative Research Practice*. London: Sage, pp. 358–74.

Markham, Annette (2013) 'Remix culture, remix methods: Reframing qualitative methods for social media contexts', in Norman K. Denzin and Michael Giardina (eds.), *Global Dimensions of Qualitative Inquiry*. Walnut Creek, CA: Left Coast Press, pp. 63–81.

Markham, Annette N. (2017) 'Ethnography in the digital era: From fields to flow, descriptions to interventions', in Norman K. Denzin, and Yvonna S. Lincoln (eds.), *The Sage Handbook of Qualitative Research*, 5th ed. Thousand Oaks, CA: Sage, pp. 650–68.

Markham, A. N. and Lindgren, S. (2014) 'From object to flow: Network sensibility, symbolic interactionism, and social media', *Studies in Symbolic Interaction*, 43: 7–41.

McLuhan, Marshall (1964) *Understanding Media: The Extensions of Man*. New York: McGraw Hill.

McNeal, G. (2014, June 28) 'Facebook manipulated user news feeds to create emotional responses', *Forbes Magazine*. Accessed January 1, 2017 from: http://www.forbes.com/sites/gregorymcneal/2014/06/28/facebook-manipulated-user-news-feeds-to-create-emotional-contagion/#4c9ef6cc5fd8.

Metz, C. (2016, 9 Nov) 'Trumps win isn't the death of data – It was flawed all along', *Wired*. Accessed January 1, 2017 from: https://www.wired.com/2016/11/trumps-win-isnt-death-data-flawed-along/.

Ouelette, J. (2013, June 9) 'The future fabric of data analysis', *Quanta Magazine*. Accessed December 9, 2017 from: https://www.quantamagazine.org/20131009-the-future-fabric-of-data-analysis/.

Rabinow, Paul, Marcus, George E., Faubion, James D., and Rees, Tobias (2008) *Designs for an Anthropology of the Contemporary*. Durham, NC: Duke University Press.

Rosenberg, Daniel (2013) 'Data before the act', in Lisa Gitelman (ed.), *'Raw data' is an Oxymoron*. Cambridge, MA: MIT Press, pp. 15–40.

Steen, M. (2016) 'The metaphysics of mass expressions', in *The Stanford Encyclopedia of Philosophy* (Winter 2016 Edition), Edward N. Zalta (ed.), URL = https://plato.stanford.edu/archives/win2016/entries/metaphysics-massexpress/.

Turkle, Sherry (2011) *Alone Together: Why We Expect More from Technology and Less from Each Other*. New York: Basic Books.

PART V

Triangulation and Mixed Methods

After illuminating qualitative data collection for two contexts – various kinds of verbal, ethnographic and material data (Part III) and for the specific questions linked to the use of digital data (Part IV) – we now turn to data collection with an extended approach. Part V treats *triangulation and mixed methods* as topics for qualitative data collection in five chapters.

First, ways of combining several forms of qualitative data in collecting them is discussed as triangulation (see Flick, Chapter 34, this volume), before two chapters address the use of qualitative methods and data in mixed methods research from two angles: (1) A theory-driven in-depth use of qualitative data (see Hesse-Biber, Chapter 35, this volume) is complemented by (2) a focus on sampling, pacing and reflexivity in using qualitative data in mixed methods contexts (see Morse et al., Chapter 36, this volume). Connecting to the previous part of the *Handbook*, the next chapter discusses more specifically the combination of digital and physical data in qualitative research (see Fielding, Chapter 37, this volume). The final chapter in this part addresses combinations of photos and interviews and connects to Part III of the *Handbook* in an exemplary way (see Henwood et al., Chapter 38, this volume).

Guideline questions as an orientation for writing chapters were the following: What characterizes this kind of combination in data collection and what is intended to reach with it? How did this kind of combination develop? What is an outstanding example of using it? Which are theoretical background assumptions of this kind of combination? How can this kind of combination and the practical procedures linked to it be described? What is a recent example of using it and in which areas is this kind of combination used? Which are the limits and outrange of this kind of combination and which are new developments and perspectives? Reading the chapters in Part V should help to answer questions like the following ones for a study and its method(s): What is the epistemological background of collecting qualitative data with this kind of combination? How does one plan data collection in qualitative research for this kind of combination? What is the best way to document and elaborate data produced with this kind of combination – for example, transcribing interview data, elaborating field notes? What are the steps in applying the selected combination for collecting the data? What characterizes good (and bad) example(s) of using this kind of combination? What are the main stumbling blocks in using it? What are the criteria of good practice with this kind of combination of producing qualitative data? What are the specific ethical issues in qualitative data collection with this kind of combination?

In answering questions like the ones just mentioned, the chapters in this part are meant to contribute to advancing the use of several types of qualitative data in and beyond the context of mixed methods and in linking digital and other realms of qualitative research.

Triangulation in Data Collection

Uwe Flick

INTRODUCTION

Triangulation as an Explicit and Implicit Principle

Triangulation has a long history in qualitative and social research as an implicit and explicit concept. The principle behind triangulation was used before the concept itself was introduced and formulated in the social sciences, thus it can be seen as an implicit concept in the history of qualitative research. The explicit concept was introduced in the 1970s by Norman Denzin (1970) who built on the earlier works of Campbell and Fiske (1959) and Webb et al. (1966). Over the years the concept 'triangulation' has not only been stimulating in the methodological discussion and research practice but also an issue for sometimes harsh debates about its adequacy. The concept and the critiques were also relevant for what became later the mixed methods discourse (see Hesse-Biber, Chapter 35, this volume, and Morse et al., Chapter 36, this volume). In this chapter, some historical remarks will be the starting point for outlining what triangulation is and what makes it relevant for qualitative research and for qualitative data collection in particular. In the second part, some examples will be discussed for illustrating potentials and limits of triangulation in qualitative data collection.

BACKGROUNDS OF TRIANGULATION

Various aims, and sometimes myths and reservations are linked to triangulation. It is also discussed when qualitative research is combined with quantitative approaches in order to give its results more grounding (see Kelle and Erzberger, 2004). In general, discussions of triangulation in qualitative research began in the 1970s when Norman Denzin (1970/1978) formulated a more systematic conceptualization of triangulation. In earlier examples of studying social problems in social research, such as the 'Polish Peasant' (Thomas and Znaniecki, 1918–1920) or the 'Marienthal' study (Jahoda et al., 1933/1971), the combination of several methodological approaches for unfolding problems such as unemployment or migration was used as a starting point with the aim of combining different perspectives on a social problem. Whyte (1955), in his classic ethnographic study of a street gang in a major city in the eastern USA in the 1940s, combined individual observations, personal notes, and other sources for presenting a comprehensive picture of a dynamic local culture. Whyte found access to a group of young second generation Italian migrants through the mediation of a key figure. After two years of participant observation he had obtained information about participants' motives, values and life-awareness and about the social organization, friendship relations, and loyalties of this local culture.

In the late 1920s, Jahoda et al. (1933/1971) studied how the inhabitants of a village psychologically coped with unemployment after the main employer in that area had gone bankrupt. Jahoda (1995, p. 121) later summarized the methodological procedures necessary for collecting the data leading for this issue in four rules: 1) Qualitative and quantitative methods should be combined for catching social reality; 2) Objective facts and subjective attitudes should be collected; 3) Current observations should be complemented by historical material; 4) Observation of spontaneous life and direct, planned interviews should be applied.

These rules refer to linking different methodological approaches – qualitative, quantitative, interviews, and observation – in the study of the individual and social perceptions of a critical turn in the life-situations of people and in a community. They also aim at collecting and triangulating data for a comprehensive understanding of a complex social situation. At the same time, we find several methodological perspectives in these principles, reaching from understanding subjective views and experiences and a structural, outside focus oriented on facts and measurement. In another early example of triangulation, Gregory Bateson and Margaret Mead (1942) combined verbal and visual data. A remarkable feature is the empirical approach of producing and analyzing more than 25,000 photographs, masses of filmed material, paintings and sculptures on the one hand, and using ethnographic conversations about this material on the other. Also, in *The Polish Peasant in Europe and America* by Thomas and Znaniecki (1918–1920), different sorts of data – 'undesigned records' and an exemplary life history produced by a participant for the study – were combined.

Put simply, the concept of triangulation means that an issue of research is considered – or in a constructivist formulation is constituted – from (at least) two points or perspectives. The process of turning this concept into a methodological principle in qualitative research was substantially advanced by Denzin in the 1970s with formulating the concept of triangulation as a more systematic approach for social and, in particular, qualitative research.

WHY TRIANGULATE?

For a long time, from the 1970s onward, in social research, in evaluation, and qualitative research in particular, triangulation as a methodological strategy was linked to the legitimization of studies:

> Good research practice obligates the researcher to triangulate, that is, to use multiple methods, data sources, and researchers to enhance the validity of research findings ... it is necessary to use multiple methods and sources of data in the execution of a study in order to withstand critique by colleagues. (Mathison, 1988, p. 13)

Triangulation then comes in at the end of a study when its validity is assessed. In this chapter, however, the focus will be not so much on such a retrospective legitimation of procedures and outcomes but on how triangulation can be used and made fruitful in an ongoing research and in particular in collecting qualitative data. The issue is, rather, how to use triangulation for making the cognitive process in an ongoing project more fertile by making use of several perspectives. In more recent versions of triangulation, the focus has shifted in this direction. The development of the discussion and concept over the years will be outlined in several steps and with versions of triangulation in the next step.

TRIANGULATION 1.0: DENZIN'S ORIGINAL CONCEPTUALIZATION

Denzin (1970/1978) spelled out triangulation in qualitative research as 'the combination of methodologies in the study of the same phenomenon' (1978, p. 291) and thus originally conceived triangulation as a strategy of validation. For this purpose, Denzin suggested four forms of triangulation: *Theoretical* triangulation refers to 'approaching the data with multiple perspectives and hypotheses in mind. Data that would refute central hypotheses could be collected, and various theoretical points of view could be placed side by side to assess their utility and power' (1970, p. 303). *Investigator* triangulation means that different observers or interviewers are employed to reveal and minimize biases coming from the individual researcher. Again, the scope of knowledge is to be extended and put on a more solid ground. *Data* triangulation refers to the 'use of different sources of data as distinct from using different methods in the production of data' (1970, p. 301). The strongest attention is paid to the fourth form Denzin suggested – *methodological* triangulation, for which two alternatives are suggested: within-method and between-methods triangulation.

Denzin's comprehensive proposal for designing and applying triangulation originally moved back and forth between the claim for validating results (by 'playing off methods against each other' – Denzin, 1978, p. 304), for increasing the reliability of procedures (several methods are more reliable than one method) and the grounding of theory development through the different forms of triangulation. At various points, the constitution of issues by methods is neglected in this proposal. Denzin repeatedly talked of applying methods to the 'same phenomenon'. A debate about the adequacy of using triangulation in qualitative research and of using this term for what it described began in the 1980s (see Flick, 1992, for details). Main critiques addressed the idea of validation of results through triangulation with other results, the idea of a master reality behind the use of several methods, and the idea of reducing bias. Fielding and Fielding (1986) conclude this discussion and see 'a case for triangulation, but not the one Denzin makes. We should combine theories and methods carefully and purposefully with the intention of adding breadth or depth to our analysis but not for the purpose of pursuing "objective" truth' (1986, p. 33).

TRIANGULATION 2.0: SOPHISTICATED RIGOR

Later, Denzin (e.g. 1989, p. 246) in responding to the critiques mentioned above sees triangulation in a more differentiated way using the concept of 'sophisticated rigor':

> Interpretive sociologists who employ the triangulated method are committed to sophisticated rigor, which means that they are committed to making their empirical, interpretive schemes as public as possible ... The phrase sophisticated rigor is intended to describe the work of any and

all sociologists who employ multiple methods, seek out diverse empirical sources, and attempt to develop interactionally grounded interpretations. (1989, p. 235–6)

Thus Denzin turns to seeing triangulation as a strategy toward a deeper understanding of an issue under study. The aim now is more to obtain knowledge and less to increase validity and objectivity in interpretations. Now, triangulation is neither understood as a strategy of confirming findings obtained with one methodological approach by those resulting from using a second approach. Rather, triangulation is aiming at broader, deeper, more comprehensive understandings of what is studied, often including or aiming at discrepancies and contradictions in the findings. Although referring to the original understanding of triangulation as the combination of several qualitative approaches, and despite using the term 'triangulation 2.0', Denzin (e.g. 2012) does not really present a strong position and argument for how to use and maintain the concept of triangulation in the context and in distinction to the discussions concerning mixed methods (see Hesse-Biber, Chapter 35, this volume, and Morse et al., Chapter 36, this volume). Despite the criticism the concept of triangulation has provoked and the attempts to push it aside in the context of mixed methods, there is still a place in the field for triangulation, which requires two aspects: To take into account what was the original context of inventing triangulation in the methodological field – to use several qualitative approaches (Denzin, 2012, p. 82) – and to take into account what has been critically discussed about the original aims (validation, confirmation of results) and how abandoning these aims has led to further developing the understanding of triangulation (see Flick, 1992 and 2012 for examples). In particular, during data collection in a qualitative study, triangulation can be an important asset on the route to a broader, more differentiated, and comprehensive understanding of what is studied.

TRIANGULATION 3.0: STRONG PROGRAM OF TRIANGULATION

Triangulation: A Weak and a Strong Program

The above discussions are a starting point for readdressing triangulation as a relevant concept for qualitative data collection, as distinct from the following usages: (1) Lincoln and Guba (1985) discuss triangulation as a *criterion* in qualitative research; (2) Bryman (1992) outlines an *assessment strategy* as a major task for using triangulation when other methods and the their results are employed for critically evaluating the results obtained with the first method; (3) The term 'triangulation' sometimes is also used for labeling a rather *pragmatic combination* of methods. Such uses of triangulation can be summarized as a *weak program* of triangulation and distinguished from a *strong program of triangulation*. In such a strong program of triangulation, it is first understood as a source of *extra knowledge* about the issue under study and not just as a way to confirm what is already known from a first approach (convergence of findings). Second, triangulation here is seen as *extending* a research program. This also includes the systematic selection of various methods and the combination of research perspectives (see Flick, 1992). Denzin (1970) has already suggested several levels of triangulation: In addition to methodological triangulation, which is differentiated into 'within-method' (e.g. the use of different subscales within a questionnaire) and 'between-method' triangulation, which will allow the triangulation of data, he suggested the triangulation of several investigators and of various theories. The triangulation of various methods can be applied by combining qualitative methods (e.g. interviews and participant observation), quantitative methods (e.g. questionnaires and tests), or qualitative, and quantitative methods. Within-method triangulation can be realized in methods like the episodic interview (see Flick, 2000a and below), which combines question–answer parts with invitations to recount relevant situations in a narrative. Both approaches have been developed against a background of theories about different forms of knowledge.

Systematic Triangulation of Perspectives

In a 'systematic triangulation of perspectives' (Flick, 1992) various research perspectives in qualitative research are triangulated in order to complement their strengths and to show their limits. This does not mean using a pragmatic combination of different methods, but taking into account their theoretical backgrounds as well. The starting points are classifications of the varieties of approaches in qualitative research, which are a basis for a theoretically grounded, systematic triangulation of qualitative approaches and perspectives. For example, we can triangulate subjective perspectives and knowledge with interactionist perspectives and practices on professional routines by combining interviews (see Roulston and Choi, Chapter 15, this volume) with conversation analysis (see Jackson, Chapter 18, this volume) of counseling practices (see below for an extended discussion of such a combination). This means that we apply triangulation on three levels in qualitative data collection: Triangulation of theoretical perspectives (subjective and interactionist), of methods (interviews and conversation analysis) and of data (statements and reports with process data).

Comprehensive Triangulation

After outlining the approach of a systematic triangulation of perspectives, we can take up the original suggestions by Denzin and his four alternative suggestions of applying triangulation. His suggestions can then be integrated in a more systematic model, which includes these alternatives as elements of a chain which the use of triangulation includes. (see Table 34.1).

Researchers interested in using the full potential of triangulation should include different researchers (investigator triangulation), either working in collaboration or independently. Ideally they would bring in different theoretical perspectives, which will lead to one of the versions of methodological triangulation (within or between methods). The result would be a triangulation of different kinds of data, which then allows a systematic triangulation of perspectives, if theoretical backgrounds and different aspects of the phenomenon under study are included in the approach. How far this whole chain can be pursued in the single research project should depend on the issue under study, the research question, and the resources in the project. Even if realized only in part, this strategy can contribute to managing and promoting the quality of qualitative research.

Table 34.1 Comprehensive triangulation

- Investigator triangulation ->
- Theory triangulation ->
- Methodological triangulation ->
  - within method
  - between methods
- Data triangulation ->
- Systematic triangulation of perspectives

WHAT IS TRIANGULATION AND WHAT IS NOT?

In further spelling out what triangulation means, in particular at times when it is threatened to be pushed aside by other forms of combinatory research designs, it might be helpful to summarize what triangulation is and what it is not.

Definition of Triangulation

We have worked with the following definition of triangulation for some time now (see Box 34.1).

For understanding the concept of triangulation better, it might be helpful to see what is *not* meant by it. In combining methods, it does not mean that one method is used for collecting data (e.g. an interview) and another one (e.g. coding) is used for analyzing those data. This is obvious and does not need an extra terminology. Neither does triangulation refer to the exploratory use of qualitative methods before the main study using a quantitative method. This is particularly the case if the exploratory study is not seen as a genuine and stand-alone part of the project, but is used only for developing a questionnaire, and the results of the first step do not become part of the final results of the whole study.

Triangulation can be applied at several phases of a qualitative research project. For example, several sub-projects can be pursued and their results can be linked, compared, used as complementary information etc. The sub-projects can both be based on qualitative methods (and data) or on qualitative and quantitative approaches. Setting up the combination at this stage is quite prominent in mixed methods or in what Kelle and Erzberger (2004) present as triangulation of qualitative and quantitative research. Triangulation can be applied in analyzing qualitative data by using several analytic approaches to the same data. Wertz et al. (2011) have done this by analyzing the same interview with, for example, grounded theory, discourse analysis, or a narrative approach.

TRIANGULATION IN COLLECTING QUALITATIVE DATA

Most often, however, triangulation is used in collecting data in a qualitative study. Here the two suggestions made by Denzin in the 1970s still provide an orientation for how to apply triangulation. They will be outlined as methodological principles next before several examples for both suggestions will be discussed.

Within-Method Triangulation: The Episodic Interview

If Denzin's idea of within-method triangulation is applied in qualitative data collection, it means that several methodological approaches are combined in one qualitative method. This

---

Box 34.1 Definition of triangulation

Triangulation includes researchers taking different perspectives on an issue under study or more generally in answering research questions. These perspectives can be substantiated by using several methods and/or in several theoretical approaches. Both are, or should be, linked. Furthermore, it refers to combining different sorts of data against the background of the theoretical perspectives that are applied to the data. As far as possible, these perspectives should be treated and applied on an equal footing and in an equally consequent way. At the same time, triangulation (of different methods or data sorts) should allow a principal surplus of knowledge. For example, triangulation should produce knowledge at different levels, which means they go beyond the knowledge made possible by one approach and thus contribute to promoting quality in research. (Flick 2018, p. 23)

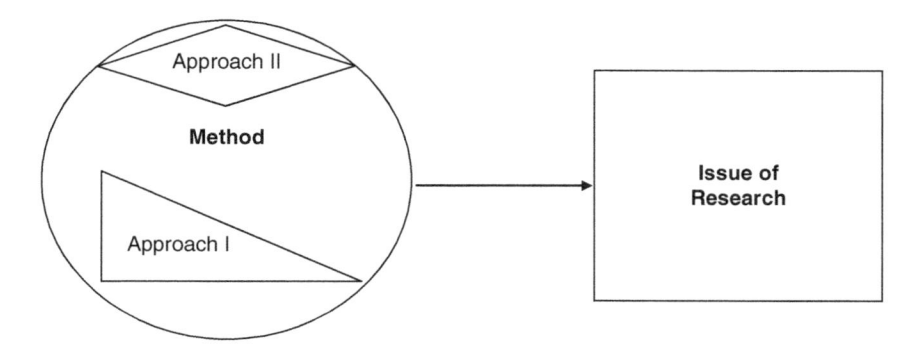

Figure 34.1 Within-method triangulation

includes the different aims and theoretical backgrounds of both approaches, but remains in the scope of one method (see Figure 34.1).

It depends on how method or methodological approach is understood but we could also apply this to ethnography as an example (see Buscatto, Chapter 21, this volume and below). But in our context here, we understand 'method' as a procedure combining several methodological approaches. An example of this form of triangulation is the episodic interview (see Flick, 2000a, 2018), which combines questions and narratives in approaching a specific issue. Examples of such combinations are addressing everyday knowledge about technological change (Flick, 1994, 1995), or laypeople's health concepts (Flick, 2000b) or those of professionals (see Flick et al., 2003).

TRIANGULATION OF THEORETICAL PERSPECTIVES IN ONE METHOD

This method is based on a specific theoretical background that refers to discussions and findings of the psychology of memory and knowledge, distinguishing between narrative-episodic and semantic-conceptual knowledge. Narrative-episodic knowledge is more oriented to situations, their context and progress, whereas semantic knowledge is more abstract, generalized and decontextualized from specific situations and events, and organized around concepts, definitions, and relations. Episodic knowledge can be accessed in narratives. Semantic knowledge is more easily accessed with (argumentative) statements. Narratives (see Murray, Chapter 17, this volume) are more sensitive to the context in which experiences are made, rather than other, more semantic models of knowledge. However, knowledge that abstracts more from such contexts is developed from a multitude of similar, generalizable experiences – for example, knowledge of concepts and rules. More so than in narratives, which are centered upon the particular (Bruner, 1990), semantic knowledge represents normal, rule-based, and generalized knowledge across a multitude of situations and experiences. This again is episodically concretized and fleshed out in narrative knowledge. Such abstract parts of knowledge, rather, are grouped around conceptual meanings and their (semantic) relations. This does not mean that narrative knowledge would not aim at meanings. The term 'semantic knowledge' (see also Maxwell, Chapter 2, this volume) has been used for some time following models of semantic memory and is based on a rather limited concept of meaning compared to narrative knowledge. Semantic models of knowledge were conceptualized following models of semantic memory, which have been studied in the cognitive psychology of memory for some time. Semantic knowledge consists of concepts linked by semantic relations. Akin to memory, semantic-conceptual knowledge is complemented by episodic parts. The starting point is Tulving's (1972) juxtaposition of semantic and episodic memory, which, in addition to concepts, includes memories of concrete situations. It is essential for a conception of episodic memory (or knowledge) that it is not built on concepts and their relations, but on memories of specific situations, events, or cases from one's own experience. Essential contents of such episodic knowledge and memory are concrete situations and what characterizes them such as location, time, what happened, who was involved, and so on. Episodic knowledge consists not only of autobiographical memory, but also of situation-related knowledge. This situational knowledge is the basis for 'generalising across concrete events, which produces general knowledge from episodic knowledge by decontextualisation and this general knowledge has lost the memory of time and localization' (Strube, 1989, p. 12). Semantic knowledge is based on the generalization of knowledge, which was first collected and stored as episodic knowledge referring to specific situations. Semantic knowledge has lost its situational specificity when it is transferred to other, similar situations and general concepts and rules of links between concepts or between situations have developed. Both episodic and semantic knowledge are complementary parts of our world knowledge. Such knowledge about the world then includes various components: Episodic knowledge refers to specific situations with their concrete (local-temporal, etc.) features; semantic knowledge refers concepts and relations abstracted from such concrete situations. Gradual forms of mixing and blending, like schemata of events and processes, complement this knowledge.

Because of this distinction between concrete-episodic and abstract-conceptual knowledge, a reflection of such models of storing knowledge and meaning-making with episodic knowledge becomes relevant '… as the primary form by which human experience is made meaningful. Narrative meaning is a cognitive process that organises human experiences into temporally meaningful episodes' (Polkinghorne, 1988, p. 1). The analysis of knowledge referring to situations and episodes becomes particularly relevant in this context.

Several Approaches in One Method

As an approach of within-method triangulation would suggest, the episodic interview explicitly approaches the parts of everyday knowledge just mentioned. Accordingly the episodic interview was designed as a method to collect the components of everyday knowledge as outlined in Figure 34.2.

The central element of the interview is that interviewees are repeatedly asked to present narratives of situations (e.g. 'If you look back, what was your first encounter with television? Could you please recount that situation for me?'). Also, chains of situations will be mentioned ('Please, could you recount how your day went yesterday, and where and when technology played a part in it?'). An interview guide will be prepared for orienting the interview to the topical domains for which such a narrative is required. To familiarize the interviewee with this form of interview, its basic principle is first explained (e.g. 'In this interview, I will ask you repeatedly to recount situations in which you have had certain experiences with technology in general or with specific technologies'). Such narrative incentives as the first large complex of questions are complemented by questions in which you ask for the interviewee's subjective definitions ('What do you link to the word "television" today?'). Also, you will ask for abstractive relations ('In your opinion, who should be responsible for change due to technology, who is able to or should

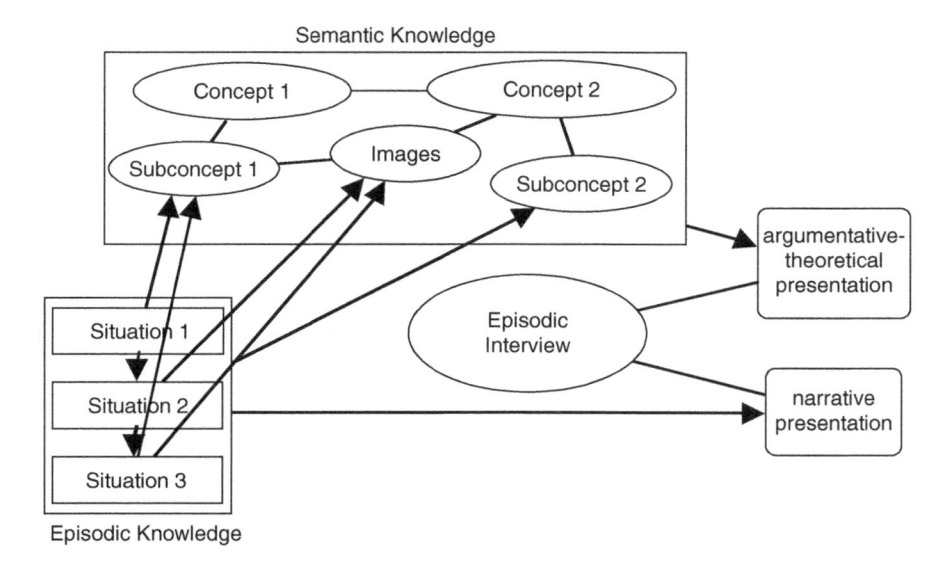

Figure 34.2 Areas of everyday knowledge in the episodic interview

take the responsibility?'). This is the second large complex of questions aimed at accessing semantic parts of everyday knowledge.

Between-Methods Triangulation

More often, the second form of methodological triangulation is applied, which refers to combining several qualitative methods or of qualitative and quantitative methods of data collection in a study (see Figure 34.3).

These methods are applied in their own rationale and logics. Triangulation then refers to the differing aspects or areas these methods allow to address. Sometimes triangulation refers to the different target groups that are studied with these methods. Examples for such a triangulation of target groups for instance include the use of interviews (such as the episodic interview) with a specific group of patients for analyzing their experiences with a specific treatment first. Then these data are triangulated with expert interviews done with service providers, for example, in order to analyze the experts' image of needs in treatment by this specific group of patients'. This form of triangulation should not only be limited to simply combining methods in a design, but also take the differing theoretical backgrounds of the methods into account – here theoretical assumptions about illness experiences on the one hand and about expert knowledge (see Bogner et al., Chapter 41, this volume) on the other hand. The theoretical differences are more obvious if the triangulation refers to subjective experiences, as mentioned in interviews and interactive practices, as becoming accessible in conversation analysis. Current examples of such combinations of methods will be discussed next.

Mobile Methods and Traditional, Systematic Research

One example for which methodological and data triangulation will become more important is the increasing use of mobile methods such as go-along methods (see Kusenbach, Chapter 22, this volume). In this context, a triangulation with more traditional qualitative approaches will be helpful. For

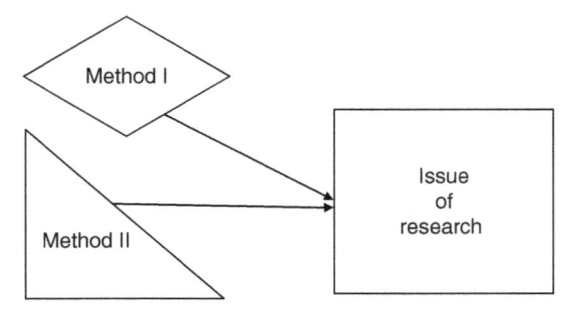

Figure 34.3 Between-methods triangulation

example, we first interview participants in a systematic way, and in a rather defined methodological setting, about their experiences with a specific topic such as being chronically ill. This will allow for establishing the dialog in the interview in great detail. If we do such an interview in an office for example we can run it without external disturbances. This will allow more and more to detail the interviewee's experiences with illness, treatment, support, and failure, for example. Then we go beyond such a defined social setting in an office in which the interview is applied and go more into the lifeworld of the participants. For this purpose we use go-along methods for exploring these lifeworlds by walking together through the social spaces that the participants use (or do not or no longer use) in their everyday lives. Go-along methods also include talking to participants but extend this talking to seeing what is talked about. However, talking with participants is not so much driven by the researchers' questions but by the spaces, objects, people, and the like who have 'met' in the go-along. This triangulation allows us to understand the ways in which chronic illness and treatment experiences shape the patients' access to social worlds and how they are excluded from certain areas. This triangulation is not only based on several methods but provides two distinct forms of data.

Virtual and Real Worlds

A major trend in qualitative research transfers methods of data collection to online research for studying virtual worlds and forms of communication in Internet research (see the Chapters in Part IV, this volume). In these contexts, you can see and use the Internet as a *tool* to study people you could not otherwise reach. But you can also see it as a *place* or as a *way of being* (for these three perspectives see Markham, Chapter 33, this volume). So there are several forms of studying people's experiences with using the Internet, social media (see Markham and Gammelby, Chapter 29, this volume), and other current forms of (online/virtual) communication (see Weller et al., Chapter 31, this volume). Marotzki (2003, pp. 151–2) outlines three basic research focuses in Internet research: when offline we study (in interviews, for example) how users deal with the Internet in their lifeworld; both online–offline, we analyze how the Internet has changed societal, institutional, or private areas of living (also by using interviews); and when online we study communication in virtual communities by using interaction analysis, which means advancing into the realms of qualitative online research. These forms of combining digital and non-digital/physical data can be triangulated in a more comprehensive approach (see Fielding, Chapter 37, this volume).

The Internet can be seen as a form of milieu or culture in which people develop specific forms of communication or, sometimes, specific identities. This requires a transfer of ethnographic methods to Internet research and to studying the ways of communication and self-presentation on the Internet: 'Reaching understandings of participants' sense of self and of the meanings they give to their online participation requires spending time with participants to observe what they do online as well as what they say they do' (Kendall, 1999, p. 62). These very brief allusions to online research open up a space for data triangulation and between-methods triangulation of two basic approaches to virtual worlds – for example, by studying Facebook users' communications in this type of social media (see Ditchfield and Meredith, Chapter 32, this volume), and to combine this with more traditional forms of interviewing for understanding the relevance and impacts that this form of communication has on daily lives offline. Combinations of methods could focus on interviews about how users experience threats to privacy and personal data coming from social media such as Facebook and the analysis of privacy-related practices being online.

Ethnography: Within- or Between-Methods Triangulation?

Triangulation has attracted great attention in ethnography. Much of the critical discussion of the concept originally suggested by Denzin (1970) came from ethnographers, but it has long continued to be used here. In this context, Hammersley and Atkinson have outlined several forms of triangulation: 'Data-source triangulation involves the comparison of data relating to the same phenomenon but deriving from different phases of fieldwork, different points of respondent validation, the accounts of different participants (including the ethnographer) involved in the setting' (1983, p. 198). Beyond triangulating data sources and different researchers, they mention 'technique triangulation' as a third form. In ethnographies, often several forms of data are collected through talking to people, observing practices, being a participant, analyzing documents, and the like.

As mentioned before, it depends on the understanding of ethnography, whether we find a within-method triangulation here, and these various approaches are used in an integrated design; or if we see collecting ethnographic data as a method, which can be triangulated with other methods fully applied in their systematics, such as specific interview forms. The first of these understandings can also be seen as *implicit* triangulation, which may play a role in every kind of ethnography (see Buscatto, Chapter 21, this volume). The second understanding can also be seen as *explicit* triangulation in ethnography (see Flick, 2018, for this distinction).

LEVELS OF TRIANGULATING DATA IN QUALITATIVE RESEARCH

In all of the combinations just mentioned, data collection can be based on triangulation on two levels. Combinations of interviews and observations, for example, can be applied to the single case. The same persons who are interviewed are also participants of the situations and practices that are observed. Their answers to questions and their activities are compared, brought together, and related to each other at the level of the single case as well. Sampling decisions can be taken in two steps. The same cases are selected for both parts of the study, but in a second step it is decided which of the participants are selected for an interview. The observations are analyzed, also referring to the single participants, so that the link between both forms of data can be established on the level of the single case. The link can be made in addition to – or only at – the level of data sets, which

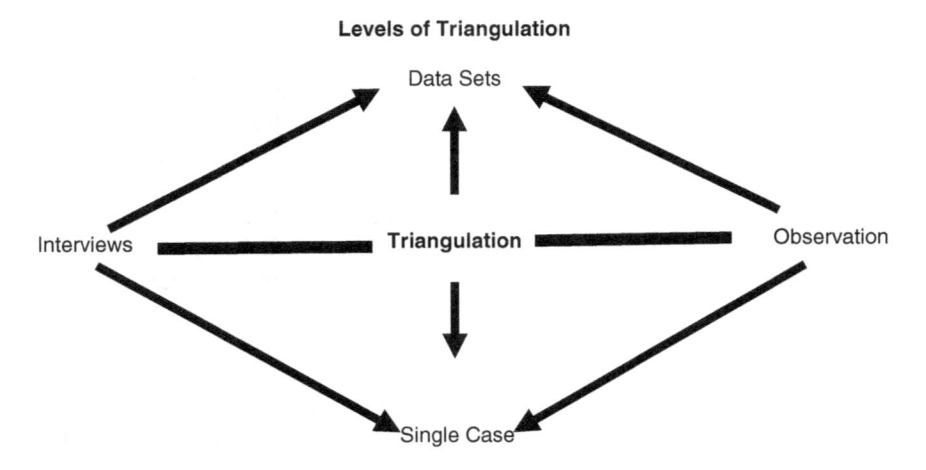

Figure 34.4 Levels of triangulation in data collection

means that the interviewees and the participants in the observations have not necessarily been the same people. The answers to the interview are analyzed and compared and a typology is developed. Then the patterns found in the observed practices are linked to the typology and compared with it (see Figure 34.4).

EXAMPLES OF USING TRIANGULATION IN DATA COLLECTION

In what follows, some examples of studies using triangulation in data collection in various ways will be briefly presented to make the application, strength, and limits of this strategy a bit more transparent.

Example I: Knowledge and Practices – Interviews and Conversation Analysis

In the first example, I reconstructed counselors' subjective theories of 'trust in counseling' and linked them to their counseling practices. I included 15 counselors in total – psychiatrists, psychologist and social workers – from sociopsychiatric services. The methodological overall strategy was oriented toward developing grounded theories in the field (according to Glaser and Strauss, 1967). A core aspect to be revealed in this strategy was the participants' knowledge of the phenomenon, for which the participants' subjective theories were reconstructed. The starting point is that people in everyday life – or in their professional practice – develop stocks of knowledge that are structured similarly to scientific theories. This knowledge is partly implicit, partly explicit. Research makes a subjective theory completely explicit by reconstructing it.

A second focus of the study in this example was how trust is produced and maintained in counseling practices. This can be studied in process analyses of consultations, which also show the functionality of the subjective theories as a form of expert knowledge for practice and routines. If we want to reach this goal, the methodological approaches should be located at different ends of the range of qualitative methods. According to Fielding and Fielding (1986), such a triangulation should, in the first way, focus on the meaning of the issue for the participants. This was the purpose of reconstructing counselors' subjective theories in interviews (see Flick

2014, Chapter 16, for the kind of interview that was applied). In the second way, the triangulation should analyze the structural aspects of the problem, which was pursued in (conversation) analyses of consultations. Accordingly, this study triangulated two perspectives: (1) a subjective intentional, reconstructive perspective, looking for the meaning of a phenomenon (like trust) for the individuals in their (professional) practices. (2) a structural-interactionist and interpretive perspective, which focuses on structural aspects of a phenomenon, like trust, as part of social practices. Therefore, activities and statements are contextualized in social interaction patterns. They describe the processes in the organization of conversations, and how they can be understood from the outside, with the perspective of the interactive process, and not from the inside with the perspective of the participant. Intentions and actions of the individual (counselor or client) are seen as accounts that can be analyzed in the context of the process and of the common production of what is going on. The triangulation of perspectives in this example refers to knowledge and interaction practices.

Example II: Migration, Addiction, and Illness Risks – Episodic and Expert Interviews

In the second example (see also Flick and Röhnsch, 2014), we wanted to understand how people with a migration background (here from the former Soviet Union – FSU – to Germany) experience problems of addiction, support offered by the health system in their target country, and how they deal with further health risks (such as Hepatitis C). We applied episodic interviews (see above) assuming that our interviewees have experienced two biographical disruptions (Bury, 1982): Migration experiences coming from an FSU-country to Germany and using drugs, becoming addicted, trying to quit the substances, looking for professional help, maybe failing with both and being drawn back into addiction again. Both experiences comprise processes over a longer period. They run parallel if the substance use began before the migration, or subsequently, if the addiction follows migration. They are fragmented in several periods and stages linked to specific situations, for example situations of deciding to migrate, of turning to drugs or alcohol, of trying to find (professional) help or deciding to discontinue a treatment etc. For taking such a disruption-oriented perspective on the relevant experiences, we applied the episodic interview as a method approaching small-scale narratives about specific situations rather than life-span narratives of individual life histories. Interviewees were invited to recount situations relevant for them in the context of the study's topic – for example, about how they started taking drugs, their decisions to quit them, seeking professional help or experiences with therapists, or how they learned that they were infected by diseases following addiction. Questions referred to the interviewees' representations of addiction or of hepatitis, for example. The main areas covered in the interviews were addiction and hepatitis-related illness experiences and practices; risk awareness; help-seeking behavior experiences with the health care system and expectations about help. Twenty-eight interviews were done in German, 18 were consecutively translated German–Russian/Russian–German or completely done and transcribed in Russian and then verbatim translated to German (see Resch and Enzenhofer, Chapter 9, this volume).

This second focus is on how service providers perceive the migrants in their day-to-day work – particularly in drug-related counseling or therapy – and which challenges they see for working with this target group. We interviewed 33 service providers from several areas of the health care system – social workers, psychologists, and physicians – with expert interviews (see Bogner et al., Chapter 41, this volume).

Our main focuses in the expert interviews were on the perception of the clients in therapy and counseling, on how the migrants dealt with hepatitis, on what was understood as good care, and on conditions of a good collaboration in working with the target group. The questions we pursued in this part of the study were: What are the requirements of health care for FSU-migrants in the view of service providers in the health care system? How are subjective needs of FSU-migrants represented? Which awareness of the FSU-migrants' use of alcohol and drugs and consecutive diseases related to this do service providers in the health and social system express? How relevant is the problem? How many people do service providers estimate to be affected? From the providers' point of view, what is lacking in the available services to fulfill the needs of FSU-migrants? What sort of cooperation with other services in and beyond the health care system exists? What are the demands for the coordination of services and what are the potentials and the limits? What consumption patterns and what protection and risk behavior do FSU-migrants have, from the point of view of the service providers? How do they estimate these coping needs and resources in the target group by taking the addiction as well as consequential diseases into account? The triangulation of perspectives here is on the level of the target groups – clients/addicted people and experts/therapists – and their views on the interplay of being migrant and having addiction problems. Methodologically, these perspectives were collected with two different forms of interviews and the kinds of data they provided.

Example III: Long-Term Unemployment and Migration – Interviews and Mobile Methods

In the third example the focus was on two groups of migrants to Germany (from Turkey and from the former Soviet Union) and their experiences with finding their way into regular work situations and with long-term unemployment and with the institutional support and pressure to find a job.

In order to meet the requirements imposed by our participants' diverse life-situations and corresponding research topic questions, we worked again with episodic interviews. They should provide sufficient room for participants to recount their experiences (of migrating, of being unemployed, of support and control by Jobcenters, and the like). Second, it should be possible to address different forms of knowledge for better covering the complexity of the issues at stake. The interviews addressed both episodic knowledge (referring to concrete situations and circumstances – e.g. when I first lost my job) and semantic knowledge (referring to concepts and connections between them – for example, what work means to them? What is the relevance of unemployment for the participants?). Interviewees were invited to recount situations relevant to them in the context of the study's topic – for example, about how they came to Germany, how they tried and found (or failed to find) access to regular work, to professional support or experiences with Jobcenters and service providers, or how they developed or maintained social networks in their 'new' environment. Questions beyond that invitation to recount situations and experiences, referred to the interviewees' representations of work or of unemployment, for example. The main areas covered in the interviews were experiences and practices related to work and/or unemployment; help-seeking behavior experiences with the social support system and expectations around help. Some interviews were conducted in German (12), the others were consecutively interpreted or completely done and transcribed in Russian (16) and then verbatim translated to German (see Resch and Enzenhofer, Chapter 9, this volume). For going beyond the data and limitations of interviewing as a first methodological approach for understanding lifeworlds and practices, we included the *go-alongs* (see Kusenbach, Chapter 22, this volume) as a second methodological approach. This method aims at gaining insights into the local lifeworlds of the study participants, getting closer to their own everyday relevancies and being able to analyze socio-spatial integration. We asked participants to choose the spatial center of their everyday life as a meeting point, from which places of major importance for them should be accessible and within walking distance. After meeting, participants were asked to describe spots of great importance to them – places they liked, disliked, or just used regularly – with the help of a street map, and then walked us to some of these places. The choice of the places shown and the route taken was left to the participants. While walking around they explained particular meanings and talked about activities associated with these places. This form of triangulating data from talking and walking allowed combining knowledge and experiences with practices and spatial approaches for a fuller picture of the issue under study (see Flick et al., 2017). The triangulation of perspectives here refers to knowledge and practices on the part of the participants. They were also complemented by expert interviews and focus groups in the further development of the study.

Example IV: Intercultural Concept of End-of-Life Care – Secondary Analysis, Expert Interviews, and Discourse Analysis

In the fourth example, we study issues of support in end-of-life care for people with a migration background. The growing and increasingly aging population in Germany makes issues of social justice concerning the distribution of available resources in the health care system, the acknowledgment of different values, as well as dealing with intercultural aspects from an ethical perspective, increasingly important. In view of the unequal opportunities for disadvantaged groups such as immigrants in nursing and hospice care and the lack of institutional structures in coping with these challenges, questions about possible causes of, and solutions to, these problems arise. This study aims at reconstructing the significance of the cultural diversity of the aging society in scientific and health policy discourses from a critical perspective on power relations. It intends to examine how these discourses inform the views of responsible actors in end-of-life care and whether and how the ideas of dying individuals and their relatives are represented in these discourses. From an organizational ethics perspective the study analyzes, if and how interculturality as a normative concept contributes to a good and equitable care at the end of life, considering the available resources.

To provide a comprehensive understanding of ethical aspects in intercultural care design, several qualitative methods are triangulated. A secondary analysis (see Corti, Chapter 11, this volume) of interview data with dying individuals and their relatives from a previous study aims at exploring their normative concepts and expectations of caregiving. A critical discourse analysis (see Rau et al., Chapter 19, this volume) of scientific publications and health policy documents aims at reconstructing the impact of normative concepts and discursive practices in previous discussions on health policy. This focuses especially on the legal and structural frameworks of nursing and hospice care at the end of life. Expert interviews (see Bogner et al., Chapter 41, this volume) are conducted with various actors in the health care system. They focus on their social representations of ethical responsibility and their role within the organization of care. The research process will be accompanied and complemented by round table discussions with external experts of ethics coming from philosophies and humanities. These approaches will allow for a comprehensive and well-grounded analysis of ethical issues linked to the question of social justice in the area of end-of-life care and migration. The triangulation of perspectives in data collection refers to secondary analysis and discourse analysis, to patients' and relatives' experiences compared to expert views.

TRIANGULATION 4.0: CHALLENGING DATA

So far the development of triangulation since the 1970s (and of precursors in the history of qualitative social sciences) has been outlined. This development went from a rather restricted confirmatory approach (which is still associated with triangulation in general, for example, in mixed methods discussions) to a more and more comprehensive and consolidating approach, unfolding research issues by triangulating research perspectives in a systematic way. At the end of this chapter we will take a different look at triangulation in qualitative data collection.

Data to Expect: Possible Outcomes of Triangulation

Applying triangulation in studies like the ones used here as examples can have three kinds of outcomes: 1) Data resulting from different methods converge, mutually confirm, and support the same conclusions. This was the aim in the beginning of using several methods. However, it is more interesting when 2) both sets of data focus on different aspects of an issue (e.g. subjective meanings of a specific illness and disease-related practices) but are complementary to each other and lead to a fuller picture. And of course data may 3) diverge or contradict, which means we should look for (theoretical and/or empirical) explanations for these contradictions. Seen from this perspective, triangulation becomes relevant and interesting if it goes beyond providing certainty and confirmation by using several approaches. In times when the concept of data is questioned and criticized from various angles (see Flick, Chapter 1, this volume, and in more detail Denzin, Chapter 13, this volume, and Markham, Chapter 33, this volume) triangulation in data collection can have another specific function. Instead of a naïve belief in 'all is data' (Glaser, 1992) or in the decisive superiority of specific forms of data (for the debate about naturally occurring data vs. elicited data – see Potter and Shaw, Chapter 12, this volume) triangulation of data can contribute toward challenging specific data, or specific forms of data, by providing a different perspective on a phenomenon under study. Different from the original use (Triangulation 1.0) this is not about confirming the reliability and validity of data by corroboration with other data, nor about adapting this idea to more interpretivist concepts (Triangulation 2.0) and not only about comprehensiveness and systematization of perspectives (Triangulation 3.0). Rather it is about discovering the limits and limitations of single types of data and thus about looking through a critical lens on specific forms of data, their pertinence, and reliability. In continuing the developmental lie of triangulation from 1.0 to 3.0, this will then be Triangulation 4.0. This version of triangulation aims at critically questioning the data produced with a specific method. But different from the early versions of triangulation, this questioning is not aiming at testing the validity or reliability of data and findings. Rather, it is scrutinizing the way that something in the social world is turned into data by a specific approach and thus this form of triangulation is challenging the data that are produced in specific methodological ways.

CONCLUSION

All in all, the versions of triangulation outlined in this chapter allow for extending insights coming from qualitative data collection in a systematic way. It should have become evident that triangulation is more than just combining several methods in a study. Rather the use of triangulation includes the combination of several theoretical perspectives (as backgrounds of methods) and of several target groups (those of the various methods). Triangulation can also mean the use of several methodological approaches for questioning methods and what is taken for granted for their use.

FURTHER READING

Denzin, Norman K. (1989) *The Research Act* (3rd edn). Englewood Cliffs, NJ: Prentice Hall.
Flick, Uwe (2014) *An Introduction to Qualitative Research* (5th edn). London, Thousand Oaks, CA: Sage.
Flick, Uwe (2018) *Doing Triangulation and Mixed Methods* (Book 9 of *The SAGE Qualitative Research Kit*, 2nd edn). London: Sage.

REFERENCES

Bateson, Gregory and Mead, Margaret (1942) *Balinese Character: A Photographic Analysis*, Vol. 2. New York: New York Academy of Sciences.
Bruner, Jerome (1990) *Acts of Meaning*. Cambridge, MA: Harvard University Press.
Bryman, Alan (1992) 'Quantitative and qualitative research: Further reflections on their integration', in Julia Brannen (ed.), *Mixing Methods: Quantitative and Qualitative Research*. Aldershot: Avebury, pp. 57–80.
Bury, M. (1982) 'Chronic illness as biographical disruption', *Sociology of Health and Illness*, 4 (2): 167–82.
Campbell, D. and Fiske, D. (1959) 'Convergent and discriminant validation by the multi-trait-multimethod-matrix', *Psychological Bulletin*, 56 (2): 81–105.
Denzin, Norman K. (1970/1978) *The Research Act*. Chicago, IL: Aldine.
Denzin, Norman K. (1989) *The Research Act* (3rd edn). Englewood Cliffs, NJ: Prentice Hall.
Denzin, N.K (2012) 'Triangulation 2.0', *Journal of Mixed Methods Research*, 6: 80–8.
Fielding, Nigel G. and Fielding, Jane L. (1986) *Linking Data*. Beverly Hills, CA: Sage.
Flick, U. (1992) 'Triangulation revisited. Strategy of or alternative to validation of qualitative data', *Journal for the Theory of Social Behavior*, 22 (2): 175–97.
Flick, U. (1994) 'Social representations and the social construction of everyday knowledge: theoretical and methodological queries', *Social Science Information*, 35(2): 179–97.
Flick, Uwe (1995) 'Social representations', in Rom Harré, Jonathan Smith and Luk van Langenhove (eds), *Rethinking Psychology*. London: Sage, pp. 70–96.
Flick, U. (2000a) 'Episodic interviewing', in M. Bauer and G. Gaskell (eds), *Qualitative Researching with Text, Image and Sound: A Handbook*. London: Sage, pp. 75–92.
Flick, U. (2000b) 'Qualitative inquiries into social representations of health', *Journal of Health Psychology*, 5 (3): 309–18.
Flick, Uwe (2012) 'Vulnerability and the politics of advocacy: Challenges for qualitative inquiry using multiple methods', in Norman K. Denzin and Michael Giardina (eds), *Qualitative Inquiry and the Politics of Advocacy*. Walnut Creek, CA: Left Coast Press, pp. 163–82.
Flick, Uwe (2014) *An Introduction to Qualitative Research* (5th edn). London, Thousand Oaks, CA: Sage.
Flick, Uwe (2018) *Doing Triangulation and Mixed Methods* (Book 9 of *The SAGE Qualitative Research Kit*, 2nd edn). London: Sage.
Flick, U. and Röhnsch, G. (2014) 'Migrating diseases – triangulating approaches: Challenges for qualitative inquiry as a global endeavor', *Qualitative Inquiry*, 20 (9): 1096–109.
Flick, U., Fischer, C., Neuber, A., Walter, U., and Schwartz, F. W. (2003) 'Health in the context of being old – representations held by health professionals', *Journal of Health Psychology*, 8(5): 539–56.
Flick, U., Hans, B., Hirseland, A., Rasche, S., and Röhnsch, G. (2017) 'Migration, unemployment, and lifeworld: Challenges for a new critical qualitative inquiry in Migration', *Qualitative Inquiry*, 23(1): 77–88. DOI:10.1177/1077800416655828.

Glaser, Barney G. (1992) *Basics of Grounded Theory Analysis*. Mill Valley, CA: The Sociology Press.

Glaser, Barney G. and Strauss, Anselm L. (1967) *The Discovery of Grounded Theory: Strategies for Qualitative Research*. New York: Aldine.

Hammersley, M. and Atkinson, P. (1983) *Ethnography: Principles in Practice*. London: Tavistock (2nd edn 1995, Routledge).

Jahoda, Marie (1995) 'Jahoda, M., Lazarsfeld, P. & Zeisel, H.: Die Arbeitslosen von Marienthal', in Uwe Flick, Ernst von Kardorff, Heiner Keupp, Lutz von Rosenstiel and Stephan Wolff (eds), *Handbuch Qualitative Sozialforschung* (2nd edn). Munich: Psychologie Verlags Union, pp. 119–22.

Jahoda, Marie, Lazarsfeld, Paul F., and Zeisel, Hans (1933/1971) *Marienthal: The Sociology of an Unemployed Community*. Chicago: Aldine-Atherton.

Kelle, Udo and Erzberger, Christian (2004) 'Quantitative and qualitative methods: No confrontation', in Uwe Flick, Ernst von Kardorff and Ines Steinke (eds), *A Companion to Qualitative Research*. London: Sage, pp. 172–7.

Kendall, L. (1999) 'Recontextualising cyberspace: Methodological considerations for on-line research', in S. Jones (ed.), *Doing Internet Research: Critical Issues and Methods for Examining the Net*. London: Sage, pp. 57–74.

Lincoln, Yvonna S. and Guba, Egon G. (1985) *Naturalistic Inquiry*. London: Sage.

Marotzki, W. (2003) 'Online-Ethnographie – Wege und Ergebnisse zur Forschung im Kulturraum Internet', in B. Bachmair, P. Diepold, and C. de Witt (eds), *Jahrbuch Medienpädagogik 3*. Opladen: Leske & Budrich, pp. 149–66.

Mathison, S. (1988) 'Why triangulate?', *Educational Researcher*, 17(2): 13–17.

Polkinghorne, Donald (1988) *Narrative Knowing and the Human Sciences*. Albany: State University of New York.

Strube, G. (1989) *Episodisches Wissen*. Arbeitspapiere der GMD (385), pp. 10–26.

Thomas, William and Znaniecki, Florian (1918–1920) *The Polish Peasant in Europe and America*, Vols 1–2. New York: Knopf.

Tulving, E. (1972) 'Episodic and semantic memory', in E. Tulving and W. Donaldson (eds), *Organization of Memory*. New York: Academic Press, pp. 381–403.

Webb, Eugene J., Campbell, Donald T., Schwartz, R. D., and Sechrest, L. (1966) *Unobtrusive Measures: Nonreactive Research in the Social Sciences*. Chicago: Rand McNally.

Wertz, Frederick J., Charmaz, Kathy, McMullen, Linda M., Josselson, Ruthellen, Anderson, Rosemarie, and McSpadden, Emalinda (2011) *Five Ways of Doing Qualitative Analysis*. New York: Guilford.

Whyte, William F. (1955) *Street Corner Society* (enlarged edn). Chicago, IL: University of Chicago Press.

35

Toward an Understanding of a Qualitatively Driven Mixed Methods Data Collection and Analysis: Moving Toward a Theoretically Centered Mixed Methods Praxis

Sharlene Hesse-Biber

INTRODUCTION: MIXED METHODS INQUIRY IN SEARCH OF A THEORY

The current history of mixed methods has witnessed the weak role that theory has played in research inquiry, leading some mixed methods researchers to make special note of the 'methods-centric approach' that often characterizes many mixed methods studies, whereby theoretical perspectives are often delinked from mixed methods research design phases, such that research design takes precedence over theoretical framing of the research issue. Hesse-Biber (2012) refers to this phenomenon as the 'thing-ness' problem in mixed methods inquiry whereby mixed methods often begins with the selection of a research design. By starting off with design, the research is drawn to the primacy of empirically-oriented aspects of the research project. This hyper focus on "method" promotes an overall favoring of "empirically-oriented" mixed methods projects focused on selection of a design, with little attention paid to the theoretical component of the research project itself. O'Cathain et al. (2007) content analyzed 75 mixed methods studies that were funded by Department of Health Research & Development programs between 1994 and 2004 with this concept in mind. The findings noted that journal publications, for the most part, did not mention a mixed methods theoretical approach, and rarely was the decision to use mixed methods driven by theoretical reasons, but more often driven by pragmatic issues that revolved around using a qualitative method to embellish the findings or complement the results of the quantitative component's findings.

Early on in the field of mixed methods, researchers primarily employed qualitative research methods and data in a 'handmaiden' or 'second best' role, subordinated to the more dominant positivist quantitative component. Part of the reason for doing so is that there was a lack of understanding for the critical role that the general 'Context of Discovery' plays in setting the course for how a mixed methods project proceeds. Thus, the current and most popular methodological default is that of a positivist quantitatively driven framework and mixed methods design. While this is beginning to lessen with the rising role that qualitative data collection approaches and methods play in a mixed methods project and the even, at times, privileging of qualitative methods, there remains within the mixed methods field an under-theorizing of just what role methodology plays across the research process. How do the findings of two different methods come together, if at all?

While there was an attempt early on to deal with paradigmatic differences in mixed methods projects, there emerged a view of practical pragmatism that often fostered an 'anything goes' stance. As Feilzer (2010) noted concerning pragmatism:

> [it] side steps the contentious issues of truth and reality, accepts, philosophically that there are singular and multiple realities that are open to inquiry and orients itself toward solving practical problems in the 'real world'. (Feilzer, 2010, p. 8)

This version of pragmatism boiled down to a 'what works' approach that was able to sidestep hard 'epistemological issues' as opposed to the 'philosophical pragmatic' approach Dewey (1925) and colleagues were engaged with early on (see Mutch, 2009). This *delinking of pragmatism from its philosophical roots*, whereby knowledge-building was no longer tied to a particular conceptual grounding, promoted, instead, a perspective of 'knowledge from nowhere', that, in turn, fostered a type of 'methodological eclecticism' (Mutch, 2009; see also Yanchar and Williams, 2006, p. 3). Making the decision to follow a practical pragmatism framework provided an opportunity for those researchers not versed in a range of theoretical perspectives to engage with a mixed methods praxis without worrying about the concerns of the arguments launched by those taking a purist approach. However, such a framing of pragmatism misrepresents its early foundational meaning. Clarke notes:

> In the United States, there has long been what I see as a misuse of the term pragmatic largely to equal expedience based in the logics of homo economicus, with some form of capitalism as the only reasonable path. In sharp contrast, pragmatists like Dewey and others referred to the pragmatic as what would work or be feasible to do, given the conditions of the situation. As such, it is more closely akin to Foucault's 'conditions of possibility' (Foucault, 1977), elucidating what needs to be taken into account to answer his question, 'What is to be done?' (Foucault, 1991, p. 84). (Clarke, 2012, p. 405)

This view of pragmatism continues to dominate understanding of how to bring theory into mixed methods inquiry – that is, this thinking side steps the role of theory and quickly moves toward a more empirical measurement of what makes a mixed methods study credible by focusing attention on the context of justification and outcomes. Such a perspective asks whether the mixed methods study works or does not work, leaving out any consideration of the role and process of understanding and conceptualizing how to bring theory into mixed methods inquiry across the research process.

BRINGING THEORY INTO MIXED METHODS INQUIRY

Central to the development of mixed methods research inquiry is the need for mixed methods researchers to demonstrate the link between their methodologies (theoretical perspectives) and research design (data collection, analytical, and interpretive methods/techniques).

There has been a growing movement urging mixed methods researchers to explicate and make visible the theoretical frameworks that underpin their research as well as provide some important guides for just how this might be done (see, for example, Cram and Mertens, 2015; Creswell and Plano Clark, 2011; Freshwater and Fisher, 2015; Fries, 2009; Hesse-Biber and Griffin, 2015; Harrits, 2011; Howes, 2015; Johnson, 2012; Jones, 2015; Mayoh and Onwuegbuzie, 2015; Popa and Guillermin, 2015; Shannon-Baker, 2015; Teddlie and Tashakkori, 2011). Howes's (2015) work also includes an in-depth example of just how the research can link the paradigm of dialectical pluralism as an organizing guide for carrying out the different phases of mixed methods research inquiry. This is particularly helpful, given that many mixed methods projects seek to tackle complex research questions that do not easily fit into a prior design template, which is especially the case with qualitative approaches to mixed methods inquiry. Evans et al. (2011) note that the conscious application of a theoretical framework onto mixed methods inquiry can also serve to navigate the research through the 'low swampy ground' of complex research goals.

This chapter provides mixed methods scholars with an explicit discussion of the role qualitatively driven perspectives play in mixed methods inquiry, with the goal of providing explicit applications of several qualitatively driven case study approaches to mixed methods inquiry with an emphasis on explicating the link between theoretical perspectives and the usage of mixed methods data collection and analytics.

WHAT IS A QUALITATIVELY DRIVEN THEORETICAL APPROACH TO MIXED METHODS RESEARCH?

A qualitative approach to research inquiry in general aims to privilege the exploration and understanding of how individuals make meaning within their social world. A qualitative approach encompasses several research traditions that hold the core assumption that reality is socially constructed and multiple. Denzin and Lincoln (1998) suggest that the theoretical variations among these approaches can be grouped into three categories: (1) *constructivist–interpretive*, (2) *critical* (Marxist, emancipatory), and (3) *feminist*.

A *constructivist or interpretive* approach assumes a subjective reality that consists of stories or meanings grounded in 'natural' settings. Constructivists in particular note that there is no 'objective' social reality 'out there'. A *critical paradigm* centers on examining issues of power, control, and ideology that are said to dominate our understanding of the social world. These perspectives look at how social life is reproduced and privileged by those who occupy positions of power, often in the name of liberating and exposing social injustice.[1] The search for 'truth' is not the goal of this perspective, instead seeking to reveal reality as 'representational' rather than 'real' or 'truthful'.

Feminist perspectives seek to understand the lived experiences of women and other oppressed groups. Their belief that knowledge does not exist outside of the social world leads feminist standpoint theorists (Smith, 1987; Harding, 1992; Collins, 1990) to be critical of many of the central tenets of positivism, especially the idea of researchers practicing 'objectivity' within the research process by placing aside their personal values. Feminist empiricists (Hundleby, 2012) seek to uncover the androcentric (male) bias in knowledge-building, which led early positivists to neglect or obscure 'subjugated' knowledge of women's lives. These male-biased researchers ignored the concerns and issues of women and failed to take into account the diversity of women's lives in terms of how their gender intersected with race, class, ethnicity, sexual preference, and so on (see Bhavnani, 2007).

It is important to note that positivist lines of thought are not always in conflict with qualitative approaches' search for subjective knowledge, at least not in a directly binary sense. Critical realism (see Maxwell, Chapter 2, this volume) is an exception to this overall dichotomous distinction in that, while it retains the positivistic idea that there is a reality 'out there', this reality, for the most part, remains unknown. Given this unknowable reality, critical realist scholarship places emphasis on subjective interpretations of reality, following the constructivism tradition. This theoretical standpoint is compatible with qualitative research and informs a great deal of mixed methods studies (Maxwell and Mittapalli, 2010).

QUALITATIVE METHODOLOGY

Methodology provides the theoretical perspective that links a research problem and approach with a particular method or methods of data collection and analysis. Methodologies are derived from a researcher's assumptions about the nature of existence (ontology) and the related nature of knowledge-building (epistemology).

Qualitative approaches offer a range of insights into the ongoing discussion of mixed methods research, especially concerning the mixing of research paradigms, power issues, and authority inside and outside the research process. Qualitative methodologies also offer a multifaceted view of the nuances of social reality, so as not to privilege the interests of any one person or group simply because they occupy a position of authority within a given society. In promoting a deep listening between the researcher and the researched, qualitatively driven praxis seeks to confront social justice and change by getting at 'deeper and more genuine expressions of beliefs and values that emerge through dialogue [and] foster a more accurate description of views held' (Howe, 2004, p. 54). Additionally, qualitative approaches tend to be open to new information – less confirmatory (hypothesis testing) than exploratory

and theory-generating. In fact, the process of qualitatively building knowledge is *iterative*, meaning that the researchers test out (in a much less formal manner) their analytical ideas as they continue to analyze, memo about, and collect more data. In grounded theory, this process is known as 'analytical induction' (see Charmaz, 2006).

THE NEGLECT OF QUALITATIVE APPROACHES TO MIXED METHODS RESEARCH INQUIRY

Mixed methods research is defined by its utilization of both a qualitative and quantitative approach within one research project or in a longitudinal design. Mixing can take many forms depending on the type of mixed methods research design – from incorporating findings from one component that builds onto a second component to integrating/weaving two components such that one informs the other. The bringing together of qualitative and quantitative components can also take place across the research process through mixing of methodologies, data collection methods, and mixing of analytical and interpretive techniques.

Some researchers fear that using mixed methods in the positivist orientation (using qualitative data to primarily illustrate or assist quantitative measure) can often lead to an 'adding and stirring' of qualitative methods. Using qualitative data to make a more robust survey question or sprinkling vignettes as narrative examples of the conclusions already quantitatively reached reduces the power of the qualitative research approaches. Methods that claim to employ a qualitative approach to a problem in this way are, in reality, reducing that research to a set of auxiliary techniques to supplement, humanize, or illustrate a primarily 'expert' quantitative research design (see, for example, Giddings, 2006).

Creswell et al. (2011) have noted that a common mixed methods design aims for triangulation (QUAN + QUAL; see, for this concept more generally, Flick, Chapter 34, this volume), whereby the motive may be either complementarity or divergence, but is often to simply validate quantitative statistical findings with qualitative data results. Yet, because this mixed methods design contains the assumption of a positivistic view that social reality is objective, the goal of such a validity-driven design remains, confirming the original QUAN findings with methodology that can sometimes obscure the original equal-footing intention. Bahl and Milne (2006, p. 198) also point out that within the field of marketing research, most studies employ a 'positivist orientation' whereby the qualitative component plays a 'supportive role', and Bryman's (2006) broader content analysis study of mixed methods research articles noted the same dominance of the QUAN component in most designs. He noted a lack of integration in researchers' findings, which led him to further interview mixed methods researchers on their motivation for using a mixed methods approach and the paucity of fully integrated mixed methods studies following a design of such intention. His research revealed that researchers frequently lean toward a specific methodology, often positivism, which makes it difficult to see the equal dialogue between findings to which their intial design choices may allude. In fact, some researchers noted their lack of training in qualitative approaches as a cause for their difficulty in figuring out how to properly integrate. Another important finding was that the structure of mixed methods studies, especially sequential studies, might have a built-in detrimental 'time lag', especially with the qualitative component.

A QUALITATIVELY DRIVEN MIXED METHODS: PROCESS-CENTERED NOT DESIGN-CENTRIC

This neglect of qualitative representation in traditional mixed methods has created a role of even greater importance for the qualitatively driven mixed methods approach in maintaining QUAL foundations. An important dimension of any qualitatively driven mixed methods project is *a commitment to privileging a qualitative approach over a quantitative approach* in that the quantitative component (quan) takes a secondary role by prioritizing qualitatively driven epistemology and methodology as the core of the overall mixed methods research project. The role of the secondary or auxiliary method is to ask a *set of sub-questions that enhance or clarify the core qualitatively driven research question/s* (Howe, 2004). There remains some disagreement as to whether or not the secondary component can, in fact, form a separate study by itself, as some researchers believe that to engage in a qualitatively driven design requires the secondary component being unable to stand on its own (see Morse and Niehaus, 2009). In this chapter, *we do not necessarily draw a sharp boundary around the ultimate contribution or distinction of a secondary method within a qualitatively driven approach*. While the core qualitative component drives the study, the secondary component's contribution may vary from significantly less dominant to taking, perhaps, an equal status role.

When working within a qualitatively driven set of methodologies, it is important to acknowledge that the iterative, ongoing process of the researcher being led by data to new questions means that *it may be difficult* to state upfront the exact mixed methods design – the type of data collection and analysis that will ultimately be utilized. Locking one's mixed methods project into a particular mixed methods design template a priori would be particularly challenging when doing research from a qualitatively driven standpoint.

Additionally, a qualitatively based mixed methods project may call on a *second qualitative method* as its auxiliary component in service of the primary QUAL method and in addition to a secondary quantitative method. The addition of a second qualitative method in such a *multimethod design* would serve a supplementary function by answering a different question, but primarily *supporting the core qualitatively driven approach and question.*

Figure 35.1 depicts the range of decisions faced by researchers when undertaking a mixed methods project. It is important to keep in mind that this is a somewhat simplified model, not accounting for the several

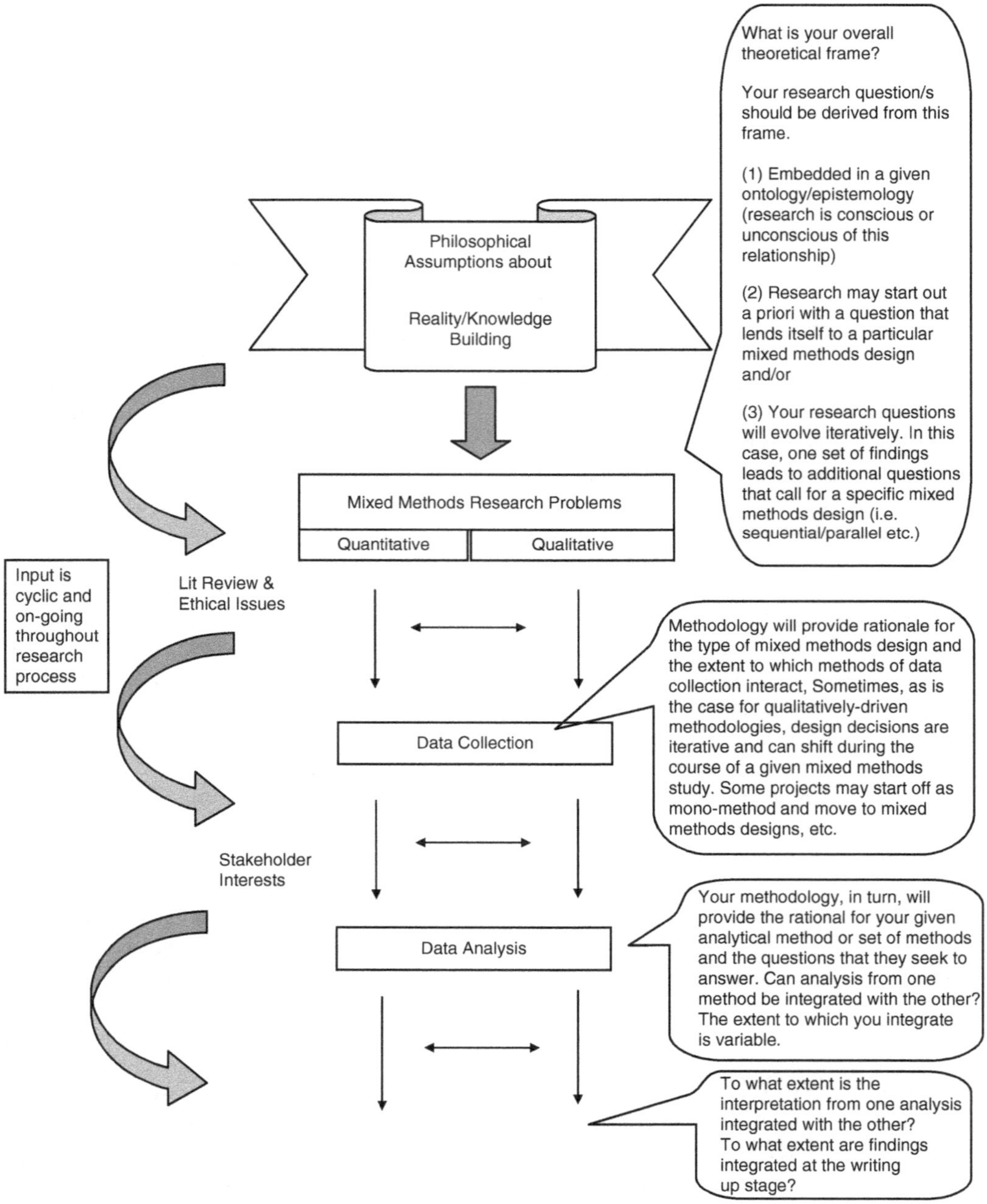
What is your overall theoretical frame?
Your research question/s should be derived from this frame.
(1) Embedded in a given ontology/epistemology (research is conscious or unconscious of this relationship)
(2) Research may start out a priori with a question that lends itself to a particular mixed methods design and/or
(3) Your research questions will evolve iteratively. In this case, one set of findings leads to additional questions that call for a specific mixed methods design (i.e. sequential/parallel etc.)
Philosophical Assumptions about
Reality/Knowledge Building
Mixed Methods Research Problems
Quantitative
Qualitative
Input is cyclic and on-going throughout research process
Lit Review & Ethical Issues
Methodology will provide rationale for the type of mixed methods design and the extent to which methods of data collection interact, Sometimes, as is the case for qualitatively-driven methodologies, design decisions are iterative and can shift during the course of a given mixed methods study. Some projects may start off as mono-method and move to mixed methods designs, etc.
Data Collection
Stakeholder Interests
Your methodology, in turn, will provide the rational for your given analytical method or set of methods and the questions that they seek to answer. Can analysis from one method be integrated with the other? The extent to which you integrate is variable.
Data Analysis
To what extent is the interpretation from one analysis integrated with the other?
To what extent are findings integrated at the writing up stage?

Figure 35.1 A theoretically-driven mixed methods process

potential iterations of the model that will arise as researchers gather, analyze, and interpret data, and in fact, may find that they need to collect additional data using yet another method of data collection, and so on.

The praxis of mixed methods research is *process-centered*. This means that first and foremost, *mixed methods research inquiry is theory- and question-driven*. It is imperative that researchers not allow their project to be a *design-driven* enterprise whereby a prior, particular prior mixed methods design template dictates in advance their data collection and analytical procedures. Of course, the division between design and process influences is more like a continuum than an exact dichotomy, and the integration of the two can and does offer an extra level of complexity to a variety of research studies that do not fit neatly into a full *process* or *design* box.

THEORY-DRIVEN APPROACHES TO THE MIXED METHODS RESEARCH PROCESS: CASE STUDIES OF QUALITATIVELY DRIVEN MIXED AND MULTIMETHODS RESEARCH INQUIRY

We will now take a look at several case studies that incorporate a qualitatively and theoretically driven mixed methods approach. Our aim in presenting three in-depth studies is to *uncover and explicate* in some detail, *the process of data collection, analysis and interpretation* that explores how theoretically derived mixed methods inquiry tackles data collection and analytical issues within a mixed methods project.

Once we move toward a *process-centered approach* that is theoretically driven and problem-centered with regard to data collection, analysis, and interpretation mixed methods inquiry, we open up the myriad innovative ways in which mixed methods analysis and interpretation can and does proceed. In this section, we seek to lay bare some data collection, analytical and interpretive challenges mixed methods researchers confront when mixing methods across a specific research project. We accomplish this by pinpointing those *barriers and facilitators* found at the point of conceptualizing the *research problem or collecting data* and the strategies, opportunities, and in some cases, missed opportunities researchers confront, especially with regard to their analysis and interpretation stages of their mixed methods research project.

Case Study 1: Using a Qualitatively Driven Mixed Methods Approach to Change the Status of Women in the Forestry Industry

Feminist geographer Maureen G. Reed is interested in women's lived experiences of working in male-dominated forestry work within nine rural communities of British Columbia. She notes that both research and government forestry policies in this area neglect women's work and community contributions, or consider them as peripheral to forestry work. Forestry work generally conjures up images of logging, including the hard physical labor, danger, and overall rough-and-tumble life that the occupation involves. These sentiments are echoed in government policy where, as she notes:

> women were considered part of forestry communities only when they were attached as partners to male workers who were considered the dominant breadwinners. In 1994, the Commission on Resources and Environment (CORE) reported that 'on Vancouver Island about 95% of resource workers are male, and about 80% of them are married ...' In this statement, CORE only considered women by their conjugal status and recognised only one possible status. Furthermore, CORE neglected that women themselves might be forestry workers with insights and experiences relevant to the changing employment conditions for forestry workers. (Reed, 2003a, p. 373)

The mid-1990s were an especially important time for the forestry industry in Canada as structural changes were tackled in terms of land management (moving from old growth to second growth of timber, debating controversial over-cutting and the lack of adequate tree-renewal policies, and moving toward new governmental forestry protection policies) as well as issues of land allocation, especially regarding Aboriginal First Nations' rights. The nature of forest work also began to change as government policy decreased logging and increased forest management jobs to accommodate the newly emerging demand for forest cultivation and planning. This transition from heavy labor to emphasized forestry management opened the door for women's employment in forestry. Reed started her research at this critical juncture of change from production to management in forestry work.

As a social activist geographer, Reed wants to unearth the subjugated experiences of women in forestry communities undergoing transition. She notes:

> I believe that the voices of women have been muted within the institutions that shape public policy making and that their stories are legitimate ones. My interest in activism is strategic. I deliberately go beyond the front lines of political protest and enter the communities, the homes, and the personal lives of forestry-town women whose stories have yet to be told. (Reed, 2003b, p. x)

Reed's specific research problem in this illustration focuses on women who are employed in the forestry industry, and forms the following research question: *How do women employed in the forestry industry experience living in forestry communities undergoing transition?*

Given her overall theoretical goal derived from *feminist standpoint epistemology* (Harding, 1991), Reed seeks to center women's lives with the goal of uncovering subjugated knowledge that will allow her to understand the extent of women's employed participation in forestry as well as their lived experiences, especially with regard to those women who have been actively involved in the transformation and restructuring of the forestry industry. This concentration on subjugated knowledge reveals the personal assumptions about the nature of reality that started Reed down her mixed methods path (see Figure 35.1). Reed thus seeks out a mixed methods approach to data collection and analysis.

Using a feminist standpoint perspective leads Reed and her research team to select several specific *qualitative research methods* that were also characterized by a feminist participatory approach (see Reinharz, 1992). She collects data from 37 *in-depth interviews* with women who work in forestry communities in rural British Columbia. She then follows up with three *focus groups* of women who had not been previously interviewed but who lived and worked in these same nine forestry communities. In addition, Reed selects and trains ten female 'community researchers' who gather additional in-depth interviews with local forestry women. We can note that her data collection incorporates an action research component by drawing on experts within the target population community. The data collected from these trained community researchers, as well as the subsequent data Reed collects from three focus groups consisting of participants who live in her target forestry community, serves to keep Reed focused on her research question, which consists of validating forestry women's lived experiences. Reed seeks out these additional data collection methods as important sources of women's voices in forestry and as a way of 'corroborating and refining emerging themes and social categories' from her intensive interviews (2003b, p. 21). She also sought out an additional layer of action research participation and feedback from women in forestry by holding a series of workshops *within these communities* as a way to find additional opportunities for data analysis that, again, seek input from women's voices in forestry work. Thus, Reed decides on a range of alternative qualitative methods of data collection *that allow her to continue to enhance her theoretical goals of understanding women's lived experiences, ones that refine and inform her overall research problem.*

Reed also gathers quantitative data by *content analyzing a sampling* of public policy documents and census track data on the forestry industry, the latter of which is used to unearth a demographic profile of women's overall employment in forestry occupations in the nine forestry communities of Vancouver, British Columbia. The decision and action to collect this quantitative data came at the beginning of the study as a way to contextualize her specific exploration of forestry women's world. The use of a quantitative census data collection method, while enhancing the *generalizability* of Reed's research by providing a regional point of comparison to her convenience sample of 50 women (37 of whom she interviewed about their lived experiences working in the forestry industry) and the focus group data that followed her in-depth interviews, allowed her to additionally examine the hidden bias of the census categories that measure those in forest work. More specifically she found that:

> These data are still derived from a narrow definition of forestry employment, and thereby underestimate the number of women who work in forestry occupations. For example, the Census counts include jobs in forest services such as inventory and measuration (measurement), while jobs in management, information or administrative services are omitted. (2003a, p. 377)

Reed's overall mixed methods data collection techniques proceeded in an *iterative* manner that defined her finished study (see Figure 35.1). In fact, she describes her research design as 'interactive applied research' (Reed, 2003b, p. 21). Her analysis of data collection and analysis phases do not fit neatly into any specific prior mixed methods template design, but unfold iteratively as she first collects data, then analyzes it, and then collects more data, and so on. While there is a sequencing of multiple qualitative methods followed by quantitative methods, how each of these data processes interacts with one another is driven by Reed's feminist epistemology that seeks to unearth women's marginalized experiences working in the male-dominated forestry industry – an industry that renders them invisible to policy makers, academics, and government agencies.

Reed's iterative deployment of mixed methods allows her to incorporate the findings from one method to inform the findings from another in a back-and-forth upward spiral motion of information flow and analysis, making it difficult to place her research into a specific mixed methods design box. Let's take a look at an example of this type of iteration process that places her qualitative findings in conversation with her quantitative data. This moment occurs when, in gathering her census track data, Reed notices that the census occupational categories reflect male-dominated cultures, leading to an undercount of women's actual contributions to forestry work. The occupational categories, she argues, are designed to reflect 'men in forestry occupations,' often excluding specific occupational categories, such as forestry-related office jobs, where women are in fact employed in forestry work (2003b, p. 103). Input from her *qualitative component data collection method* – in-depth interviews – allows her to question census definitions of occupational categories by suggesting the need for refinement of these categories in order to reflect women's occupational lives.

As Hesse-Biber and Yaiser (2004, p. 277) note, one aspect of feminist research scholars' work is to 'seek methods that empower their respondents and participants as well as their research'. By questioning census category data, Reed is aware of how categories of measurement can render invisible women's contributions to the forestry industry. Her use of findings from her qualitative data collection methods and analysis, then, provides her with new ways to unearth the marginalized perspectives of women, and to address their needs and concerns. At the same time, her work challenges the androcentrism of the official census occupational categories, opening up the possibility for a more equitable measurement of women's labor force contributions to the forestry industry as a whole.

Reed's further inclusion of an additional qualitative data collection component, *in-depth community-based focus groups and subsequent community-based workshops*, also allows for an integration of lived experience of forestry women into the analysis of the in-depth qualitative interview data. These subsequent qualitative methods components were informed by initial in-depth interviews and provided her with ways to refine and enrich women's voices in forestry while informing and enhancing her overall analysis and providing opportunities for her to ask new questions concerning her research problem as well as her interpretation of her overall research findings. For example, Reed notes that prior feminist literature painted an either/or view of forestry women; liberal interpretations saw them as victims and socialist interpretations saw their participation in the male-dominated work force as a victory over their disempowered social, economic, and political situation.

The ongoing findings gathered from her mixed methods data collection and analysis begin to have a dramatic impact on Reed's initial theoretical ideas regarding employed women's roles in male-dominated occupations. Instead of revealing a clear-cut answer to her original alternative theoretical model on women's employment in the forestry industry, she finds a dramatic *theoretical paradox* contained within the ongoing qualitative data she collects and analyzes iteratively (moving between the data collection and analysis steps of Figure 35.1); namely, that employed women in the forestry industry *both support and challenge patriarchal cultural practices* in their workplace and in their communities. In fact, what she demonstrates is the importance of taking into account women's social embeddedness within their communities in order to understand their contradictory behaviors. She states:

> Women's choices and perspectives about employment are located within systems of social relations and cultural norms that fix their work in particular social and geographic locations. In short, the discourses and practices of women in forestry were socially embedded within local and societal norms and values. Rather, contradictory ideas about inclusion and exclusion, and appropriate feminine and masculine behaviours ran simultaneously within individual interviews and across the discussions with women of differing employment, age, and life-stage status. Women's adoption of cultural norms and values associated with forestry reflected and reinforced their own marginality. Women are both social activists against patriarchal norms and at the same time compliant with some aspects of these norms. (Reed, 2003a, p. 387)

It is this *dual understanding* of how women are embedded socially and occupationally within their communities that allows Reed to understand first, how they simultaneously participate in their own subjugation while actively challenging their oppressed position, and second, how the interaction of these two forces continues to keep them at the margins of the forestry industry. She notes:

> The binary of victim/victor does not grant sufficient attention to the complexity and contradiction that characterize women's lives and perspectives. Rather, I suggest that through discourse and practice, women are co-creators of the forestry culture and communities that provide openings and closures for women in the paid work of forestry. Greater attention to women's participation in forestry – in practice and in discourse – provides more nuanced theoretical explanations and more accurate empirical descriptions to inform policy choices about forestry employment. (Reed, 2003a, p. 387)

Reed's overall study is *process-centered*. She is first and foremost guided by her initial theoretical ideas in her data collection methods, analysis, and interpretation, confronting the need to engage with the range of research questions before her. She is also engaged in refining her theoretical perspective and, in turn, her research questions, in light of the new information she gathers from the ongoing analysis and interpretation of the data she collects along the way. Her commitment to a feminist participatory praxis, especially the deployment of the 'participatory action' qualitative component (focus groups and community workshops) of her research, allows women's voices to become 'visible'.

Such visibility also, in turn, has profound policy implications. By making women's concerns and contributions visible through an ongoing theoretically driven iterative mixed methods model, forestry women now have an opportunity to be part of government policy initiatives and shape policy debates regarding rural forestry communities. Reed notes that previous government programs focused on retraining or sustaining men in forestry, providing them with resources and retirement packages. Perhaps now these resources can be made available to women workers in the forestry industry.

Reed's mixed methods research also demonstrates the need for *women to be more visible in theoretical models* with regard to understanding structural change in rural societies. Finally, she reminds researchers to practice 'reflexivity' with regard to how they deploy the very research concepts they use, and to be mindful of the particular biases that can often creep into our measurement tools. Even census categories are not immune to male bias and do reflect male-dominated cultures. Her data collection methods from in-depth interviews (see Roulston and Choi, Chapter 15, this volume) allow her to suggest refinement to quantitative data categories. Her in-depth focus groups and workshop feedback allow respondents to 'talk back' to the qualitative analytical component of her study, providing her with ways to refine her analysis and make space for re-evaluation of her initial theoretical lenses and research problem.

Case Study 2: Uncovering Subjugated Knowledge and Generating and Testing Theories of Inequality: Studying the Gender Gap in Public Opinion in Canada

Brenda O'Neill's (2009) research deals with the interface between feminism, religion, and women's political opinions. O'Neill turns a traditional feminist empiricist theoretical lens onto uncovering obscured knowledge regarding women's opinions in her field of political science, where female voices have largely been missing from academic social research. She notes, however, that her positivist leanings and feminist perspective were two paradigmatic characteristics, which elicited direct undermining of her work's validity at a research workshop attended early in the conception of the study. She explains:

> My approach to the discipline is solidly quantitative; the majority of my research employs quantitative methods of data collection and analysis but I am open to and recognize the benefit of employing more qualitative methods. In short, I believe that the research question ought to dictate the appropriate method to employ. The dominance of quantitative techniques in my work stems from my statistical training in the disciplines of economics and political science. I additionally identify as a feminist and my openness to qualitative methods stems from independent learning, research, and reading. My first academic invitation to contribute to an edited collection involved writing a chapter on the use of quantitative methods within feminist research (O'Neill, 1995). At the workshop where we were asked to deliver the papers, my presentation was interrupted by a researcher who turned to the editors and asked why my chapter was included in the volume given that feminists had largely discredited quantitative research methods. That experience galvanized my interest in methods, methodology and epistemology. (2009, p. 1)

O'Neill faced various roadblocks to carrying out this type of research in her field, including the difficulties of conducting secondary analysis from quantitative data sets that do not contain information by gender. She found that tapping into women's opinions on the variety of issues she wished to address, from feminism to religion to politics, required gathering her own data. This funding barrier is noted as an obstacle to mixed methods research projects, in that the enormous upfront costs of acquiring a quantitative data set are difficult to overcome in the early stages of a professional career.

O'Neill's research sought to answer the following question: What are the roles of religious beliefs and feminist identification in shaping women's political attitudes? Her theoretically driven research questions provided the rationale for the research design she started out with, thus bridging Figure 35.1's methodology gap between research problems and data collection by proposing an exploratory sequential mixed methods design. The first data collection component consisted of qualitative focus groups whose goal was to gather data on nine ethnically and age diverse focus groups of women (eight to ten women each) from a sample of Canadian cities that varied in size and region. Reed was not happy with the way religion had been measured in previous quantitative surveys, and so included a short quantitative survey nested into the focus group qualitative component in order to gather more grounded demographic data on the focus group participants (age, social class, religious affiliation). These new measures of women's religiosity, both in this nested quantitative (quan) component and the following, secondary quantitative survey, made clear that 'faith needed to be conceptualized beyond the narrow concepts of membership in a religious denomination and attendance at services. This is largely how more quantitative approaches to the study of political behavior have conceptualized religion: denomination (including a measure for evangelicalism), salience and attendance at services' (2009, p. 11).

This qualitative data collection component then informed a quantitative telephone survey of 1264 women aged 18 or older and drawn from ten Canadian provinces in a random sample (see Figure 35.2). The survey items were theoretically driven and were intended to gather data on a range of women's attitudes and beliefs regarding politics, feminism, and religion as well as standard demographics (SES, religious denomination, etc.). The goal of the survey was allowing O'Neill to draw a range of theoretical generalizations on women's political participation that were grounded in her qualitative research findings, effectively testing out her theory-driven qualitative findings on a random sample of Canadian provinces using survey items grounded in women's lived experiences around key factors she felt influenced their political participation.

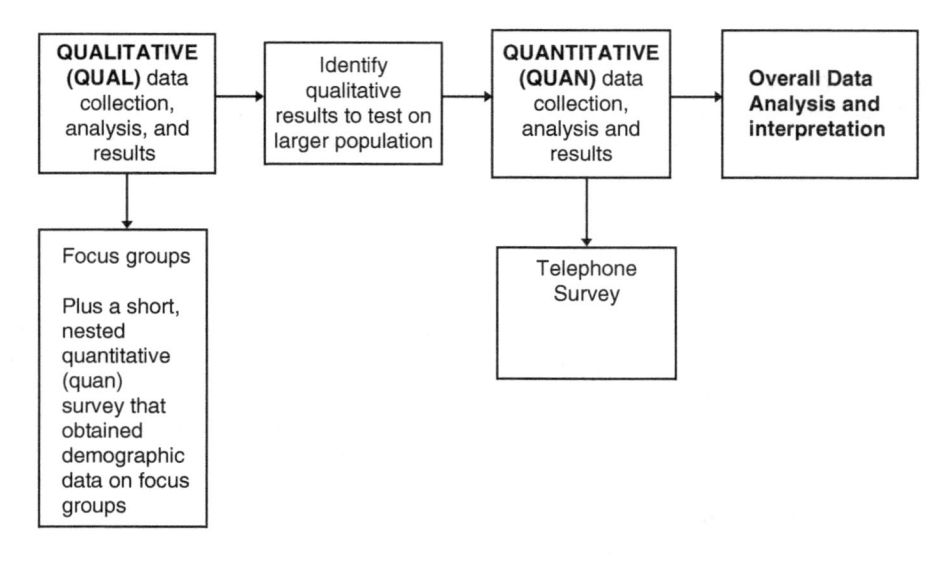

Figure 35.2 Sequential exploratory mixed methods design

This namely included their beliefs regarding politics, feminism, and religion and how these factors were also influenced by demographic and other additional factors gathered from research on political participation in general.

Let's take a look at O'Neill's *theoretical rationale* for conducting these two types of studies whose methodological aims differed, and how both data collection and analysis methods were in the service of her feminist theoretical framework onto understanding women's political participation, connecting the flow of Figure 35.1. Her overall goal was to 'set the record straight' regarding women's political attitudes and beliefs by unearthing women's subjugated knowledge. She additionally sought to inject research methods, measures, and concepts with women's voices, particularly in theoretically lacking areas such as the measurement of religion.

In addition, she sought to use her qualitative data about women's political participation, and its relation to religion and feminism, to generate theory to be 'test[ed] out' on the quantitative data. She sought to obtain measures well suited to capturing women's voices in order to get at subjugated knowledge, a feminist goal her qualitative component directly serviced. She wanted, in effect, to inform the questions of her quantitative survey through developing nonandrocentric measures of participation and unearthing a more robust understanding of religion and feminism. O'Neill's goal was to use these two methodological components as follows:

> By starting with a more qualitative method, I was able to incorporate the rich discussions into the construction of survey questions. And indeed, the ability to better capture the multi-dimensionality of concepts by using the Qual/Quant design has been identified by others (Leckenby and Hesse-Biber, 2007). More than this, however, the focus groups established the importance of a concept that I would have completely missed had I jumped immediately into the more quantitative method (e.g. the importance of spirituality). The focus groups also provided assistance with the choice of vocabulary and the phrasing of new questions that deviated from those employed in existing surveys. (2009, pp. 11–12)

Case Study 3: Uncovering Women's Subjugated Historical Labor Force Participation

Lotta Vikström is a *feminist historical demographer* who sought to explore nineteenth century occupational work performed by women outside of their prescribed domestic role as wives and mothers in Sweden (Vikström, 2003, 2010). The division of labor between men and women during this period was strict, with women's place defined as the 'home' sphere and men's as in the 'public/occupational' space. Vikström notes how historical data often mirror traditional gender ideologies about work and family roles. She states:

> Those who either asked for, or made these records, were often committed to dominant thoughts of their historical time and setting. Historical research has repeatedly presented a much more complicated picture than this when it comes to ordinary people. A gap between the ideal way of dealing with life and labor versus really applied strategies has often proven to be the case, in particular for women in the past. If we study women by looking into what they were supposed to do according to all the legal, religious, or ideological recommendations they had to consider, it would end into a rather sad history. (2003, p. 255)

Vikström's (2003, 2010) research project began with the desire to uncover knowledge about women's working lives, a goal which the researcher identified as a mixed methods research problem (see Figure 35.1) and thus sought to explore through *triangulation* within a concurrent mixed methods design. The quantitative demographic data she collected about women's family relationships (social class, marital status, number of children) and occupations during the period of 1860–1893 was obtained from the parish register (kyrkböcker) for the town of Sundsvall, Sweden. Local newspaper advertisements, police and patient records, and announcements placed by women seeking work make up her qualitative data, all from the town of Sundsvall during the same time period under study. These qualitative sources contained occupational information on how women historically described themselves and the type of work that they were seeking, thereby positioning their own work identities. It was during the studied time period that the town of Sundsvall, located on the Swedish coast about 400 kilometers from Stockholm, underwent industrialization as a result of the area's growing sawmill industry, and thereby upped the demand for women's labor, especially in the more 'traditional' sectors of the economy such as domestic services. As Vikström notes, her gathered informal sources of historical record 'reveal the voices of the otherwise silent women workers and tell us about their urban context' (2010, p. 259).

Vikström's feminist framework guided her selection of a concurrent data triangulated mixed methods design (Denzin, 1970). However, her goal in deploying such a design was not validation. Instead, her theoretical perspective sought to provide a mixed methods concurrent design that allowed her to explore in more analytic detail what she anticipated would be a large dissonant gap between her qualitative and quantitative component's findings, forming a strategy for unearthing subjugated knowledge of women's work histories whose information was held between the two data sets. In this sense, she used triangulation as a *heuristic analytical device* in order to unearth *new meanings* regarding women's labor force participation, which was subjugated and overshadowed, she theorized, by only looking at quantitative data findings (see data analysis, Figure 35.1). It is in this sense that her design was driven by a *feminist qualitative methodology* whose intent was 'to shed light on women's working lives' (2010, p. 221). Figure 35.3 depicts Vikström's mixed methods design.

More specifically, Vikström uses triangulation 'to identify the level and nature of dissonant data and thereby uncover the occupational gender biases frequently found in population registers' (2003, p. 212). A secondary goal to 'indicate complementarity between the sources' was also sought (2003, p. 212). She used the registers to mine quantitative population data identifying women by their name, age, and marital status in the hopes of cross-referencing 'comparable' data on the same specific women's further pursuits of work outside the home. This latter qualitative component of study consisted of scanning advertisements

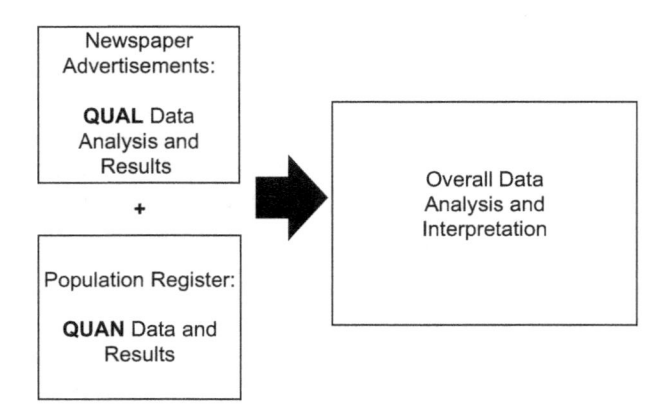

Figure 35.3 Vikström's (2003, 2010) Concurrent mixed methods design

and police or patient records that might yield additional information on the women listed in the register. She noted, 'Sundsvall's newspapers show that women frequently offered their various skills related to typical female sectors as the domestic service, fashion, and the catering trade' (2010, p. 254).

Vikström triangulated the data sets in order to find individuals that appeared in both segments during the same year, a pool which resulted in a sample of 204 women (Vikström, 2003, p. 214). In order to maximize the potential for analytical interaction between data sets, she coded her qualitative sources using the population register's coding standards. By analytically translating her qualitative codes into quantitative variables, thereby 'quantizing' her qualitative data as a heuristic feminist bridge (see Sandelowski et al., 2009), Vikström was able to further facilitate conversation between her mixed methods components. Analytically transforming information from both data sets revealed knowledge subjugated by exclusion from the parish register, particularly in the case of married women's work outside their homes. She notes,

> For many of them, forming a business or engaging in petty commerce was a strategy for survival, as being a servant was anathema for married women or females from the lower-middle strata and above ... Such commercial engagement proved invaluable to their subsistence especially where male relatives were incapable of supporting them. (Vikström, 2003, p. 216)

> Her transformation analysis of both data sets also reveals the power of dominant regimes in reinforcing women's dependent status as wives and mothers by subjugating their work outside the home to absence from public registers. (Vikström, 2003, p. 218)

Vikström's (2003, 2010) concurrent mixed methods design clearly seeks to uncover subjugated knowledge. Vikström placed the findings from her qualitative and quantitative components into analytic conversation with one another with the goal of triangulated complementarity whereby the findings from each method were distinctly different, yet added richness and complexity to understanding women's work and occupational roles. Vikström's study points to the importance of analytically going after *conflicting results* as a way to reveal *new* avenues of understanding and new research questions.

Vikström's research also revealed the importance of using triangulation as a *heuristic analytical tool* for looking at dissonant data and revealing new information that can further social change for women. Vikström argues in her final data interpretation (see Figure 35.1) that women's labor has historically played a vital role in both the public and private sphere and in 'setting the record straight'.

CONCLUSION

The Importance of a Theoretical Process-Centered Mixed Methods Inquiry

The case studies presented in this chapter focus on a qualitatively driven mixed methods approach and demonstrate in detail why it is important to privilege a mixed methods theoretically centered inquiry. The three case studies discussed happen to apply a theoretically driven, process-centered mixed methods framework that features a feminist theoretical lens, however, this is but one of many different types of theoretical perspectives as we pointed out earlier, that one might apply to a mixed methods inquiry, depending upon the particular goals of the research project.

Reed's mixed methods research design seeks to unearth knowledge that she feels is subjugated by traditional data collection measures of women's labor force participation in a primarily 'male-dominated' forestry industry. Reed starts off with the assumption that the employment of women in forestry renders them marginalized by academics, government agencies, and policymakers.

She further argues that women's representation in the forestry industry appears limited because of how women are under-counted as a result of the androcentric bias in the industry's collection of labor force participation data. According to Reed, this is largely due to the fact that certain types of employment are overlooked in those areas where women have been historically present. Here the goal of her analysis is one supported by a design that seeks not complementarity, but an interactive application of methods whereby the qualitative and quantitative findings are brought into an analytical relationship. The aim of this iterative design is to present findings in such a way that one informs the other in getting at a more complex understanding of women's labor force participation and lived experiences in the forestry industry.

Vikström's research project starts out with the goal of selecting a triangulated mixed methods design, not for the purposes of validation but instead to use the differing findings from each data collection method for asking a set of new questions that serves to add a more complex understanding of women's labor force participation. Each method provides her with different, parallel, but untethered, insights into understanding and uncovering hidden aspects of women's labor force participation. Her qualitative component's findings in particular offered new information not found in the quantitative measurements of women's contributions to the work force, opening up whole new layers of understandings of the extent of women's work contributions historically.

Vikström and Reed seek to understand the labor force participation of women, which has been subjugated by statistical measures. While both Vikström and Reed spend abundant amounts of time going back-and-forth by productively questioning findings from each method, their individual theoretical framings of the research problem and design leads them to analyze their quantitative and qualitative data differently in the hopes of yielding new information. In each case, the qualitative component's data collection, analysis and interpretation techniques suggest the need to revamp how women's labor force participation is measured by current quantitative measures, while the quantitative data, in turn, also reveals some unanticipated findings. For example, Reed had to temper her original assumptions regarding how women's participation is measured. Her qualitative data revealed that, when interviewed, forest women themselves found that they independently contribute to their own marginality through their everyday practices working in this industry.

Despite their differences in design adherence, both Reed's and Vikström's data collection, analysis and interpretation of findings reveal the tensions between a positivist versus an interpretive frame for understanding women's labor force participation – we observed, for example, that Reed struggled with adapting her design to explore how women's labor force participation in forestry was measured by formal census data (quantitative/positivist) versus the qualitative/interpretive data she personally gathered from more qualitatively driven labor force participation sources. Vikström, too, struggled with the data collection, analytical and interpretive process as she negotiated an interpretation of her findings based on disparate quantitative and qualitative analytical measures, ones that, when placed in conversation, allow her to get at a deeper understanding of how best to portray the depth of women's labor force participation historically.

Likewise, O'Neill (2009) started off her research project with a specific theoretical framing of feminist standpoint theory that seeks to understand lived experiences with regard to Canadian women's political participation and those factors which serve as barriers and facilitators to such action. She starts off her research with a qualitative data collection component whose goal was to inductively derive a set of measures of political participation grounded in women's lived experiences, which would then serve as input for her secondary component, a survey of women's political participation. Her exploratory qualitative component uncovered several important and hidden factors that shaped women's political perspectives, such as the role of spirituality in women's everyday lives. The insights she gained from in-depth interviews with women prior to her survey component provided O'Neill with a more valid set of survey research questions that were grounded in the lived experiences of her target population.

It is also important to note that when researchers embark on a mixed methods project, it is critical that they are trained in both qualitative and quantitative methodologies as well as diverse data collection, analytical, and interpretive techniques. When a researcher is unfamiliar with the range of methods and methodologies available, there may be a tendency for the less understood methodology and/or method to be subsumed to the other. When left unchecked, this can result in the unfamiliar method being given less weight than the more comfortable method, often leading to the favoring of one type of findings over another and a departure from more rigorous mixed methods design. Another common misstep occurs when the researcher reports each of the findings separately without discussing their relation, utilizing a parallel presentation of distinct, disconnected interpretations.

The exemplary case studies discussed in this chapter provide a *tracing* of the data collection and analytical process that mixed methods researchers engage in when they consciously link their theoretical perspectives to mixed methods research designs. This is an *interactional process* that contains within it the possibility for uncovering analytical meanings that can unearth subjugated knowledges that provide new insights.

Note

1 Some variations on this paradigm are said to include Marxist, feminist, ethnic, cultural, and queer studies. Denzin and Lincoln pose a separate paradigm for these variations, which they term 'materialist-realist ontology' (Denzin and Lincoln, 2000, p. 21)

FURTHER READING

Hesse-Biber, S. (2012). Weaving a multi methodology praxis to further the credibility of mixed methods randomized control trials, *Qualitative Inquiry*, *18*(10): 876–89.

Hesse-Biber, S. (2012). Feminist approaches to triangulation: Uncovering subjugated knowledge and fostering social change in Mixed Methods Research, *Journal of Mixed Methods Research*, 6(2): 137–46.

Hesse-Biber, Sharlene (2012). Feminist research: Exploring, interrogating, and transforming the interconnections of epistemology, methodology, and method, in Sharlene Hesse-Biber (ed.), *The Handbook of Feminist Research: Theory and Praxis* (2nd edn). Thousand Oaks, CA. Sage.

REFERENCES

Bahl, Shalini and Milne, George R. (2006). 'Mixed methods in interpretive research: An application to the study of the self-concept, in Russell W. Belk (ed.), *Handbook of Qualitative Research Methods in Marketing*. Cheltenham: Edward Elgar, pp. 198–218.

Bhavnani, Kum-Kum (2007). Interconnections and configurations: Toward a global feminist ethnography, in Sharlene Nagy Hesse-Biber (ed.), *Handbook of Feminist Research: Theory and Praxis*. Thousand Oaks, CA: Sage, pp. 639–49.

Bryman, A. (2006). Integrating quantitative and qualitative research: How is it done?, *Qualitative Research*, 6(1): 97–113.

Charmaz, Kathy (2006). *Constructing Grounded Theory: A Practical Guide Through Qualitative Analysis*. Thousand Oaks, CA: Sage.

Clarke, Adele E. (2012). Feminism, grounded theory, and situational analysis revisited, in Sharlene Nagy Hesse-Biber (ed.), *Handbook of Feminist Theory: Research and Practice*. Thousand Oaks, CA: Sage, pp. 388–412.

Collins, Patricia Hill (1990). *Black Feminist Thought: Knowledge, Consciousness, and the Politics of Empowerment*: Boston: Unwin Hyman.

Cram, Fiona and Mertens, Donna M. (2015). Transformative and indigenous frameworks for multimethod and mixed methods research, in Sharlene Nagy Hesse-Biber and R. Burke Johnson (eds.), *The Oxford Handbook of Multimethod and Mixed Methods Research Inquiry*. New York: Oxford University Press, pp. 91–109.

Creswell, John W. and Plano Clark, Vicky L. (2011). *Designing and Conducting Mixed Methods Research* (2nd edn). Thousand Oaks, CA: Sage.

Denzin, Norman K. (1970). Strategies of multiple triangulation, in Norman Denzin, *The Research Act in Sociology: A Theoretical Introduction to Sociological Method*. New York: McGraw-Hill, pp. 297–313.

Denzin, Norman K. and Lincoln, Yvonna S. (Eds.) (1998). *Strategies of Qualitative Inquiry*. Thousand Oaks, CA: Sage.

Denzin, Norman K, and Lincoln, Yvonna S. (eds.) (2000). *Handbook of Qualitative Research*. (2nd edn). Thousand Oaks, CA: Sage.

Dewey, John (1925). *Experience and Nature*. Whitefish, MT: Kessinger.

Evans, B. C., Coon, D. W., and Ume, E. (2011). Use of theoretical frameworks as a pragmatic guide for mixed methods studies: A methodological necessity, *Journal of Mixed Methods Research*, 5(4): 276–92.

Feilzer, M. Y. (2010). Doing Mixed Methods research pragmatically: Implications for the rediscovery of pragmatism as a research paradigm, *Journal of Mixed Methods Research*, 4(1): 6–16.

Foucault, Michel (1977). *Discipline and Punish: The Birth of the Prison* (1st American edn). New York: Pantheon Books.

Foucault, Michel (1991). Questions of method, in Graham Burchell, Colin Gordon and Peter Miller (eds.), *The Foucault Effect: Studies in Governmentality*. Hemel Hempstead: Harvester Wheatsheaf, pp. 73–86.

Freshwater, Dawn and Fisher, Pamela (2015). Mixed methods dissonance and values in research with marginalized groups, in Sharlene Nagy Hesse-Biber and R. Burke Johnson (eds.), *The Oxford Handbook of Multimethod and Mixed Methods Research Inquiry*. New York: Oxford University Press, pp. 665–76.

Fries, C. J. (2009). Bourdieu's reflexive sociology as a theoretical basis for mixed methods research: An application to complementary and alternative medicine, *Journal of Mixed Methods Research*, 3(4): 326–48.

Giddings, L. S. (2006). Mixed methods research: Positivism dressed in drag?, *Journal of Research in Nursing*, 11(3): 195–203.

Harding, Sandra G. (1991). *Whose Science? Whose Knowledge? Thinking from Women's Lives*. Ithaca: Cornell University Press.

Harding, Sandra G. (1992). Rethinking standpoint epistemology: What is "strong objectivity"? *Centennial Review*, 36(3): 437–70.

Harrits, G. S. (2011). More than method? A discussion of paradigm differences within mixed methods research, *Journal of Mixed Methods Research*, 5(2): 150–66.

Hesse-Biber, Sharlene (2015). Mixed Methods Research: The "Thing-ness" Problem. *Qualitative Health Research*, 6: 775–88.

Hesse-Biber, Sharlene Nagy and Griffin, Amy J. (2015). Feminist approaches to multimethod and mixed methods research: Theory and praxis, in Sharlene Nagy Hesse-Biber and R. Burke Johnson (eds.), *The Oxford Handbook of Multimethod and Mixed Methods Research Inquiry*. New York: Oxford University Press, pp. 72–90.

Hesse-Biber, Sharlene Nagy and Yaiser, Michelle L. (2004). *Feminist Perspectives on Social Research*. London: Oxford University Press.

Howe, K. R. (2004). A critique of experimentalism, *Qualitative Inquiry*, 10(4): 42–61.

Howes, L. M. (2015). Developing the methodology for an applied, interdisciplinary research project: Documenting the journey toward philosophical clarity, *Journal of Mixed Methods Research*, 1–19. DOI: 10.1177/1558689815622018.

Hundleby, Catherine (2012). Feminist empiricism, in Sharlene Nagy Hesse-Biber (ed.), *Handbook of Feminist Research: Theory and Praxis*. Thousand Oaks, CA: Sage, pp. 29–44.

Johnson, R. B. (2012). Dialectical pluralism and mixed research, *American Behavioral Scientist*, 56(6): 751–4. DOI:10.1177/0002764212442494.

Jones, K. (2015). Using a theory of practice to clarify epistemological challenges in mixed methods research: An example of theorizing, modeling and mapping changing West African seed systems, *Journal of Mixed Methods Research*, 1–19. DOI:10.1177/1558689815614960.

Leckenby, Denise and Hesse-Biber, Sharlene Nagy (2007). Feminist approaches to mixed-methods research, in Sharlene Nagy Hesse-Biber and Patricia L. Leavy (eds.), *Feminist Research Practice: A Primer*. Thousand Oaks, CA: Sage, pp. 249–91.

Maxwell, Joseph A. and Mittapalli, Kavita (2010). Realism as a stance for mixed method research, in Abbas M. Tashakkori and Charles B. Teddlie (eds.), *Handbook of Mixed Methods in Social and Behavioral Research* (2nd edn). Thousand Oaks, CA: Sage, pp. 145–67.

Mayoh, J. and Onwuegbuzie, A. J. (2015). Toward a conceptualization of mixed methods phenomenological research, *Journal of Mixed Methods Research*, 9(1): 91–107.

Morse, Janice and Niehaus, Linda (2009). *Mixed Method Design: Principles and Procedures*. Walnut Creek, CA: Left Coast Press.

Mutch, C. (2009). Mixed method research: Methodological eclecticism or muddled thinking?, *Journal of Educational Leadership, Policy and Practice*, 24(2): 18–30. Retrieved from http://search.informit.com.au/documentSummary;dn=942182859009376.

O'Cathain, A., Murphy, E., and Nicholl, J. (2007). Integration and publications as indicators of "yield" from mixed methods studies, *Journal of Mixed Methods Research*, 1(2): 147–63.

O'Neill, Brenda (1995). The gender gap: Reevaluating theory and method, in Sandra Burt and Lorraine Code (eds.), *Changing Methods: Feminists Reflect on Practice*. Peterborough, ON: Broadview Press, pp. 327–55.

O'Neill, Brenda (2009). A Mixed Methods Approach to Studying Women's Political Opinions, Prepared for Delivery at the First European Conference on Politics and Gender, Queen's University of Belfast, UK.

Popa, F. and Guillermin, M. (2015). Reflexive methodological pluralism: The case of environmental valuation, *Journal of Mixed Methods Research*, 1–17. DOI:10.1177/1558689815610250.

Reed, M. G. (2003a). Marginality and gender at work in forestry communities in British Columbia, Canada, *Journal of Rural Studies*, 19(3): 373–89.

Reed, Maureen Gail (2003b). *Taking Stands: Gender and the Sustainability of Rural Communities*. Vancouver: UBC Press.

Reinharz, Shulamit (1992). *Feminist Methods in Social Research*. New York: Open University Press.

Sandelowski, M., Volis, C. I., and Knafl, G. (2009). On quantizing, *Journal of Mixed Methods Research*, 3(3): 208–22.

Shannon-Baker, P. (2015). Making paradigms useful in mixed methods research, *Journal of Mixed Methods*. Online first, DOI:10.1177/1558689815575861.

Smith, Dorothy E. (1987). *The Everyday World as Problematic: A feminist Sociology*. Boston: Northeastern University Press.

Teddlie, Charles B. and Tashakkori, Abbas M. (2011). Mixed methods research: Contemporary issues in an emerging field, in Norman K. Denzin and Yvonna S. Lincoln (eds.), *The Sage Handbook of Qualitative Research* (4th edn). Thousand Oaks, CA: Sage, pp. 285–99.

Vikström, L. (2003). Different sources, different answers: Aspects of women's work in Sundvall, Sweden, 1860–1893, *Interchange*, 34(2/3): 241–59.

Vikström, L. (2010). Identifying dissonant and complementary data on women through the triangulation of historical sources, *International Journal of Social Research Methodology*, 13(3): 211–21.

Yanchar, S. and Williams, D. (2006). Reconsidering the compatibility thesis and eclecticism: Five proposed guidelines for method use, *Educational Researcher*, 35(9): 3–12.

Data-Related Issues in Qualitatively Driven Mixed-Method Designs: Sampling, Pacing, and Reflexivity

Janice M. Morse, Julianne Cheek, and Lauren Clark

INTRODUCTION

The overarching purpose of this chapter is to *make qualitative contributions to mixed methods accessible and powerful*. Our goal is to clarify methodological strategies that ensure qualitative components become as robust as possible when used in mixed methods. We begin our discussion by considering what is qualitatively driven mixed-method research. We then turn to consider the use of sampling, pacing, and reflexivity in this type of research. We conclude by recommending principles to assist researchers in clarifying and appreciating the contributions of qualitative inquiry to mixed-method research.[1]

The guiding principle of the chapter is that we must not detach qualitative forms of data used in mixed-method research from the wider field of qualitative inquiry, to which qualitative methods must relate. If the contribution of qualitative inquiry is minimized in quantitatively driven mixed-method design, then qualitative research cannot reach its full potential and the study loses explanatory power. On the other hand, robust qualitatively driven inquiry may make a substantial contribution to mixed-method design, elaborating, humanizing, and expanding understanding.

As noted over a decade ago, mixed-method designs have exploded in popularity (Mason, 2006), and that trend continues. Concurrently, terminology, structure, and even the principles – the rules – for what *is* good mixed-method research, have become complicated, contradictory, and contested (Johnson et al., 2007). As a community of mixed-method scholars we use various terminologies (Morse, 2016, 2017). We also harbor a range of views about how to collect and analyze mixed-method data (Teddlie and Tashakkori, 2003; Hesse-Biber and Johnson, 2015) we may even wonder what are 'data' in mixed-method studies, and we have not begun to debate the merits of alternative mixed-method designs (Dellinger and Leech, 2007; Johnson et al., 2007; Mertens, 2011) nor realized their full potential. Confusion also arises when we scrutinize the components of good mixed methods (Morse and Cheek, 2015) and how mixed-method designs differ from multiple method designs (Hesse-Biber et al., 2015).

When reflecting on the debates around these issues it became clear to us that these conversations stem from differences in terminology and assumptions about what exactly comprises the field known as mixed methods. Here we address only mixed-method designs, meaning one complete method plus one supplemental strategy, and we are primarily focused on qualitatively driven mixed-method designs. By qualitatively driven mixed-method design we refer to those designs in which the complete method is qualitative (specifically QUAL-*quan* or QUAL-*qual*).

INTRODUCING THE QUALITATIVE COMPONENT IN MIXED-METHOD DESIGN

There are five general reasons for including a qualitative component (either core or supplemental) in a mixed-method study. In each case listed below we provide guidance about how to manage qualitative data in a separate analytic process to maximize the contribution of qualitative results. The reasons are:

1 Sequentially increasing the understanding of a phenomenon
2 Obtaining different perspectives on the same phenomenon
3 The phenomenon demands different approaches
4 Increasing complexity
5 Increasing scope; determining boundaries.

1. Sequentially Increasing the Understanding of a Phenomenon

Depending on the researcher's stance toward the phenomenon being studied, the sequencing of qualitative methods may be sorted into two categories according to whether the inductive discovery (see Kennedy and Thornberg, Chapter 4, this volume) takes place as the study progresses; or if data are analyzed at a single point in time. Each category is now discussed.

Inductive discovery

This research is designed progressively. As data are simultaneously collected and analyzed, the researcher gains insight into 'what is going on'. The content of the interviews changes and becomes more specific, as the researcher develops understanding about the topic. Researchers may change their interview questions in response to what they discover they need to know more about. They also may need to confirm data about their emerging hunches, or move the focus of inquiry so they may learn (and gather data) about emergent aspects of the topic. With this increasing understanding, interviews become more specific. The same questions asked of the first participants are not necessarily those asked of later participants.

Analysis is conducted at the end of data collection

The second mode of conducting qualitative inquiry is to maintain similar data collection strategies for all participants, and conduct the analysis once all data are obtained. Analysis remains inductive, but investigator learning during the process of data collection (and researcher reflexivity) does not occur. Analysis is conducted all at once at the end of data collection (McIntosh and Morse, 2015).

Therefore, when using inductive discovery to sequentially increase understanding of the phenomenon, the researcher is learning as the study is being conducted, typical of many ethnographic (see Buscatto, Chapter 21, this volume) and grounded theory studies. It is commonplace to find something of interest that was unexpected, and something that would be better understood if an additional method beside the unstructured interview was used to examine this new aspect of the study. Therefore the researcher may decide to incorporate observations (DeWalt and DeWalt, 2011; see Wästerfors, Chapter 20, this volume), or a different type of interview strategy (see Roulston and Choi, Chapter 15, this volume) such as cognitive interviews (Willis, 2015), as a sequential component. These two data sets (the interview and the newly added observational, focus group, or cognitive interview data set) must be analyzed separately, and not immediately merged with the first set of unstructured interviews. When the researcher has an unexpected finding and needs to add a supplemental component to explore this finding, this component must be added sequentially, following the first project, with analysis conducted at the end of the study.

2. Obtaining different perspectives on the same phenomenon

Even at the proposal stage, some researchers will recognize that potential participants may have different perspectives on the phenomenon under study, and that blocking or stratifying the interview design to capture different segments of the prospective pool of participants would enrich the study (see Flick, Chapter 34, this volume). For instance, the researcher may realize that, when interviewing students, it would also be advantageous to learn what their teachers think about the topic; when interviewing wives, to also hear from the husbands; or if focused on a patient concern, to also interview the patient's family, physician, and nurse. These various perspectives may be about the same topic, but these data will vary greatly and should be analyzed separately until integrated at the point of interface.

If the researcher has a question and known ethnic or cultural variation provides different resources for answering that question, then the researcher must sample each group, and compare the results obtained from each group. Samples that include a few members from each group (but do not analyze these data as separate groups) lose the richness of comparative variation. Excluding minority experiences by presenting the majority view is inadequate. Presenting a homogenized experience meant to be inclusive of all ethnic or cultural variation is inadequate. Simply tagging a quote with a label indicating race or ethnicity of a speaker does not suffice. Without separate analysis of adequately sampled ethnic or cultural group experience, the richness, and differentiation of experience by culture or ethnicity is undeveloped and inadequately addressed.

3. The phenomenon demands different approaches

Keeping data sets separate occurs most rigidly with evaluation research. Often, in the

---

Box 36.1 Example: A qualitative component to recognize experience by ethnicity or culture

A mixed-method study (Nygaard et al. 2017) is currently underway to describe how women learn about, experience, manage, and then share with daughters, mothers, and friends the experience of pelvic organ prolapse. Presumed to be hereditary at least in part, the prolapse of bowel, bladder, or reproductive organs through the vaginal canal is seldom discussed, even among women in families with a strong history of prolapse. To understand the lived experience, and the cultural modes and mores of communicating about the experience, the research team designed a comparative ethnography of Mexican American and non-Hispanic Euro-American women. These data were complemented by quantitative medical data about the kind of prolapse and its staging. To merge the two sets of interview data and then analyze the data would homogenize the experience, producing an ethnography that was neither representative of the Mexican American nor the Euro-American women. More appropriately, we maintained two different but comparable datasets, inductively coding and analyzing women's experiences within their cultural group. In the research narrative, we compared the ethnographic results to the medical staging of prolapse over time.

evaluation of organizations, researchers assume that perspectives of the problem are different within different levels of the organizations, according to the role of the staff members. Data from various components of the organization are analyzed independently of others, and then compared and contrasted. These differences often demand that different methods of data collection be used, with questionnaires, semi-structured questionnaires, or focus groups used in areas with larger workforces, observational methods in areas such as factories with manual workflow, and unstructured interviews with management. These separate sets of data are analyzed using the appropriate methods for each data type.

4. Increasing complexity

Mixed-method designs are often, but not always, flexible enough to be responsive to the researcher's learning as the study proceeds. As ethnography, in particular, becomes more in depth, it may also become more complex in design as data analysis proceeds. The utility of methods used when the researcher was attempting to comprehend the scope of the problem and to determine the boundaries of the experience may be exhausted and necessitate additional methods. Informal interviews are not appropriate for exploring social networks microanalytically or exploring interpersonal relations (or whatever has become the focus of the research). In these situations, new research methods may be added to fully elicit data on an element uncovered in the ethnography.

5. Increasing scope, determining boundaries

When a study produces tantalizing results indicating the scope of the phenomenon may be larger, or the boundaries may be more expansive than first understood, an additional qualitative data set may supplement the study.

These five different reasons (see above) for including a qualitative component in a mixed-method study challenge researchers to diversify their mixed-method designs to accomplish different and important goals. From sequentially increasing the understanding to the phenomenon to responding to increasing complexity and different perspectives, an additional qualitative method can be developed to strengthen the study and provide more nuanced understanding of the phenomenon.

THE NATURE OF QUALITATIVE DATA IN MIXED-METHOD INQUIRY

Interviews are a prototypical qualitative data source. Interview types[2] (see Roulston and Choi, Chapter 15, this volume) differ by structure (as controlled or led by the

---

Box 36.2   Example: A qualitative component to fully elicit data on a specific sub-topic

A researcher may have deliberately conducted unstructured interviews of participants who have had a stroke. Increasing complexity may arise in the course of the study about how it feels to be dependent on others when learning to use a wheelchair. A set of focus groups specific to men and another set with women will generate more public data about the specific element of dependency and technology-use post-stroke. The interview and focus group data sets are both from different perspectives (although they may be from the same participants); one data set may be considered more private, more personal, and consist of feelings the sufferer may not have even disclosed to his wife; the other information about learning to use a wheelchair is shared more readily and more willingly spoken about in a public focus group. The important point is that these two data sets must be analyzed separately. Data sets cannot be mixed together or combined into themes or categories, without the loss of analytic integrity. Rather, data are mixed at the point of interface and integrated in the research narrative.

> **Box 36.3 Example: Increasing study scope with an additional qualitative component**
>
> In an ethnographic study Clark and Zimmer (2001) conducted on early childhood feeding in a Denver barrio, Mexican American and Mexican immigrant families told us about the ways feeding a baby was part of nourishing her body as well as embracing her within the Mexican family (Clark et al., 2013). Learning to eat Mexican food as part of the festivities around baptisms, weekend barbeques, and *quinceañeras* (a 'coming out' celebration for a girl's 15th birthday) was as much about enacting ethnic and family identity as about what and how much to eat. Although we understood this from interviews and participant observation, we also needed better insight into the day-to-day feeding decisions that mothers, fathers, siblings, and grandparents made with their toddlers, and recognized the scope of our study had to be increased. Life is lived on a daily basis, not just at times of festivity, and narrating the mundane food behaviors of daily life is hard to do in interviews. So we added a research component, called A Day in the Life, and we took over 3,000 photographs over a day-long period in three different households stratified by acculturation (Clark and Zimmer, 2001). In this case, increasing the scope of our understanding of toddler feeding was aided by a new photographic component to the study. And in keeping with our understanding of handling different kinds of qualitative data with the analytic tools most appropriate for the task at hand, we conducted content analysis of the photographic data set separately from the 36 interviews we had already collected with the three families. Later, the photographic results and the other ethnographic field notes and interviews were combined (Clark et al., 2013).

participant or by the researcher), function, and depth (from superficial to intimate); from eliciting the individual's reality to the community perspective, depth of knowledge they elicit (from public to private) and function or role they play in inquiry. Qualitative data are 'raw' data recorded directly as spoken by a participant; recorded observations of actual events; photographs or video recordings of events (see Knoblauch et al., Chapter 23, this volume) as they occur; and reported directly as verbatim text. Data may also be less direct: perceptions or experiences of participants' recorded during interviews; reports of the experiences of others, or records such as diaries (see Rapley and Rees, Chapter 24, this volume), or recalled narrative stories (see Murray, Chapter 17, this volume), videos, or interpretive poems, or songs. They may be provided by the person themselves, or reported by another. Data may take the form of informal conversations, brief or unplanned interviews, and participant observations that take place 'in the field'. Sometimes these informal data have been collected opportunistically as observations or conversations, and other times with the full knowledge and active participation of those being researched. Qualitative data also include the reflections of the researcher on the research process (Rea and Green, 2016; Shaw, 2010) and the collection of that data as part of the reflexivity[3] that is a hallmark of a qualitative approach.

Qualitative data are subjective, descriptive, and often non-equivalent as one interview may contain information, content, or description that the second may not (Morse, 2012, 2017). Interviews become more specific and focused on the question as the research process unfolds and the interviewer learns about the topic. Interviews may be immediate (i.e. recorded as they occur), or recalled and reported in an interview, a diary entry, or as a video-blog sometime after the experience occurred. Qualitative data are usually in a semi-permanent form, either as audio or video recording or as field notes (Emerson et al., 2011). Aside from obvious differences in form, each account may differ substantively in tone, content, and interpretation due to the attenuating effects of memory, reflection, audience, motivation, and purpose. Such is the nature of 'raw' qualitative data forwarded for qualitative analysis.

From verbal interviews or descriptions of observations (see Wästerfors, Chapter 20, this volume, and Buscatto, Chapter 21, this volume), data are compiled into multiple collections of text. Therefore, data are a *set*, a collection of stories, or themes or categories derived from interviews or observations, and it is the researchers who mold the form of these data to match the purpose and the method to be used. Exemplars presented in the final analysis are not single quotations; not single sentences or utterances that happen to be overheard; rather, the single quotations and exemplars illustrate and represent categories. This applies to the qualitative components (both QUAL and *qual*) of mixed-method studies (Morse and Cheek, 2014).

How Much Qual Makes a Qual Component?

The supplementary qualitative component (*qual*) in a mixed-method design poses particular challenges for qualitative research and qualitative researchers. This relates to how much adaptation of qualitative inquiry is possible for a supplemental component to still be considered qualitative inquiry. If there is no longer saturation of data, or no clear information given about how the questions were asked/areas probed in the *qual* component of the study, be it QUAL-*qual* or QUAN-*qual*, or if the participants were not purposively chosen, then is it still qualitative research? This is an important question to consider; recall a common definition of mixed-method research[4] is a design using quantitative and qualitative methods in the same study.[5] At what point does a supplemental qualitative component deviate sufficiently from principles of qualitative inquiry to be outside the realm of adequate qualitative methods?

As we have defined the supplemental strategy, data are not saturated, but data collection continues as long as the researcher is *certain* about the answer to the research question even if each of the categories have not reached saturation. *Certainty* applies to the supplemental component and is defined as existing when the researcher has a logical and defensible answer to a narrower question. In *saturation*, data are replicated and analytically the researcher understands the concept or category in all its depth and dimension. Recall that in qualitative research, a single participant may speak for other people (as shadowed data – Morse, 2001), and provides contextual explanations, so that common sense, logic, and the significance of the supplemental topic to the core component, also assist the researcher to gain certainty.

Best Practices for Mixed Methods Research in the Health Sciences (Creswell et al., 2011) is explicit in the definition of mixed-method research, with the third of five definitional attributes being 'employing rigorous quantitative research assessing magnitude *and* frequency of constructs and rigorous qualitative research exploring the meaning and understanding of constructs' (2011, p. 4 – our emphasis). Rigorous qualitative research involves much more than just using words or descriptive data rather than numbers. Yet, in many reports of the *qual* component there is little or no detail given as to the selection of either the participants or the questions asked or the observations made, and the way these data were analyzed. Put another way, there is no way of knowing if the qualitative data is rigorous or not or in keeping with accepted understandings of what rigorous qualitative research is. This is exacerbated when the *qual* data is simply blended with the QUAN or QUAL data in such a way that it is hard to tell what data actually came from the supplementary component of the study, and how exactly it was 'mixed' with data from the core component.

Just having data in some kind of qualitative form does not necessarily make the component qualitative research. Even if the supplementary component is not a complete study in its own right, then at the very least, details must be given about what was done to ensure that the data were collected in acceptable ways, according to accepted principles about rigor in qualitative inquiry. Details must also be given about what may not have been done or how a standard method is altered in the supplemental component (i.e. not sampled to saturation, or a limited number of variables used). The danger is that if deviations or truncations are not made explicit in the supplementary qualitative component report, then data remain unanalyzed – simply a set of words, and not a set of data (Cheek, 2015).

SAMPLING QUALITATIVE DATA

Sampling (see Schreier, Chapter 6, this volume) involves the most problematic part of mixed-method design, and not attending to the way your sample is obtained may pose a threat to validity (see Barbour, Chapter 14, this volume) for the entire study.[6] There are two ways to approach sampling (whether qualitative or quantitative) using individual and group samples, or of course other units (such as settings, events, documents, photographs, and so forth). Consider first the core component and whether it is comprised of individuals or groups. Useful questions include: Are you studying individuals, one by one across the two components, and then pooling the results? Or are you studying participants as a group in the core component? Second, consider the supplemental component and whether it is comprised of individuals or groups, and whether those sampled are the same participants or different from those in the core component. Useful questions include: Are you studying a group in the supplemental component? If so, do the two groups (core and supplemental component) consist of different participants? Whether using individuals or groups in core and supplemental samples, data will be analyzed within the core and the supplement, and then the results from each component will be compared and integrated to add to the understanding of the phenomenon (Morse and Niehaus, 2009).

Quantitative components require quantitatively justifiable samples, often large in size and randomized; qualitative components require samples that are small and purposeful. Each sample must be clearly delineated, and lack of partitioning of participant groups may further invalidate the study.[7] Further, because of the differences in modes of attaining quantitative and qualitative samples, participants, and data cannot be easily shared between the quantitative and qualitative components. Merging data from different samples in the analysis reduces the analytic integrity of the study.

PACING AND POOLING DATA

Here we focus on two key areas: *When* should data be collected in terms of the pacing of the study; and *who* do these data represent (the group? The individual?)? In other words, at *what stage* in the research design does the pooling of data occur?

When Should Data be Collected?

When is a pacing question. By pacing we mean where in the study design the data collection occurs. *Simultaneous* mixed-method design implies that data for both components – core and supplemental – are being collected and analyzed at the same time. *Sequential* mixed-method design implies that the supplemental component was collected after the core data were analyzed. But this may not always be the case. On occasion, data for one component may be collected before the other, but conceptually, in the analysis, both components may be analyzed at the same time, brought to the point of interface, and integrated in the narrative results.

> **Box 36.4 Example: Pacing data collection and analysis**
>
> In a hypothetical QUAL + *quan* study a researcher is exploring the strategies of enduring during treatment for breast cancer. The researcher conducts interviews with women who have been diagnosed with cancer and had one round of chemotherapy and radiation, obtaining longitudinal data – their stories of treatment. But some of these women have been given short courses of a tranquilizer to 'help them cope'. By obtaining permission to access their records, the researcher can now place drug administration data on a timeline for each participant. Or perhaps their hemoglobin level can be added to the timeline to see if that correlated with periods of reported fatigue. During analysis, the researcher will link the *quan* data with the QUAL interview data, and consider the study *simultaneously*, even though these data sets were not collected at the same moment.

Who Do These Data Represent?

In mixed-method designs there is a unique and varied relationship between sampling and data. Whereas the principles of sampling, adequacy (having enough data) and appropriateness (in topic – from the right informants), are issues to do with sampling, analytic *certainty*, and *saturation* are methodological concepts, as previously discussed. With certainty the sample size is narrower, and may be smaller, so that certainty may be reached more quickly than saturation. This introduces important questions: What is a *data set*? What is its composition? Who (or what) does it represent? How is its composition influenced by *data type*? And what is the *relationship* between data set and data type?

A *data set* consists of data that are cohesive and analyzed together. *Data type* refers to the composition of the data, as numerical or textual or visual images. There must be a logical and cohesive *relationship* between the data type, the data set, and the mode of sampling and the analytic style. *Relationship* includes recognizing if

- data are *linked across the core and supplemental components* for each individual prior to analysis (as in case-based analysis – Yin, 2015), or
- if data are pooled within each component and analyzed by group of *participants within each component* (as in variable-based analysis – Yin, 2015).

Thus, understanding the relationship of data set (sample) and data type (data) is the analytic key to mixed methods.

Researchers must always be clear about who their participants are representing during an interview. But the content of their interview often differs from their expected role or perspective: participants speak for themselves, but they also may report on others. During a single interview they may switch back and forth. In their analysis, researchers must attend to whom they are speaking for: Are they speaking as an individual, about their own experience? Are they reporting on others? Or are they speaking more generally, about the group?

The Consequences of Inappropriate Pooling

Implied comprehension is the homogenization of the analysis of the concepts or experiences of interest without segmenting the data according to subgroups, and ignoring those characteristics by not allowing for their emergence in the analysis. Despite the fact that the researcher has reported a demographic description of the sample in excruciating detail, the assumption within such studies is that cultures, ethnicity, genders, or ages, and so forth, are not significant enough in the analysis to create a separate sample of participants with that particular feature to compare with data from other groups. Alternatively, by ignoring these (cultural, or gender, or … and so forth) variables, implies that such variation is not important, or at most, is adequately addressed by simply identifying the data source at the end of each quotation. Or, perhaps the researcher who deliberately ignores variation, such as culture, gender, or other sociological variables, may be implicitly suggesting that such variation is not significant? If so, why do they bother reporting these categorical differences in the sample if they fail to use them in the analysis? The result is *implied comprehension* of the concepts or experiences across different groups, without actually testing if and how the groups differ. Diversity in the sample is reduced to tokenism, such as inserting an excerpt of an interview into the manuscript, and tagging the quotations by ethic group of the speaker. Attention to nuances in these data are critical for validity by preventing inappropriate pooling.

SAMPLING, PACING, AND REFLEXIVITY

Next, in this section we discuss a variety of qualitatively driven mixed-method designs, and the constraints and freedoms within mixed-method sampling and data collection, in the context of sampling pacing and reflexivity.

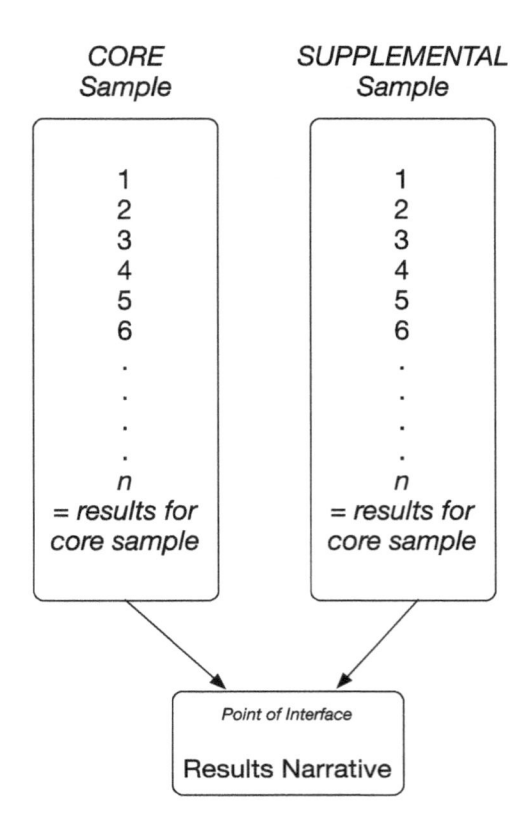

Figure 36.1 Sampling plan for two individual samples, pooled data for two data sets

The Interaction of the Sample and Data Collection Strategies

Two individual samples; two data sets; pooled data for each component

We may imagine a study with two samples, similar to the study of nurses and nurse administrators in a hospital described above. If this is a QUAL + qual design, data from the core sample is analyzed separately and combined at the point of interface with data analyzed for the supplemental component. In this case the researcher has two independent data sets, from two groups of participants, until the point of interface (see Figure 36.1).

Using the same analysis process for a QUAL+ *quan* design, perhaps involving the same hospital nurses in a study of medication errors. The *quan* could be a large quantitative data set all nurses ratings of structural supports for safe medication practices. The researcher would assure that samples for both components are adequate and appropriate. The QUAL sample would be selected according to principles of qualitative methods; the *quan* sample would be separate and selected from the population of nurses randomly and with an adequate sample size for quantitative analysis. This design is mixed-method because the supplemental *quan* is a single measure and cannot stand alone. If the measures used in the quantitative component were interesting enough to be published alone, then the design would be a multiple method (Morse and Niehaus, 2009; Morse, 2017).

Table 36.1 Mixed-method design: two samples, two data types, two data sets

Pacing	Representation of the Sample		Reflexivity
	Adequacy	Appropriateness	
QUAL + quan	Core QUAL with supplemental simultaneous, random quan sample	Core data + supplemental strategy data are selected according to needs of each component	Interim quan results may guide QUAL interviews; Final quan results adds description about the phenomenon or concept in general
QUAL → quan	Core QUAL with supplemental sequential quan sample	quan sample usually independent as the QUAL sample dissipated	May be conducted to confirm questions arising from the QUAL analysis
QUAN + qual	Core QUAN with supplemental simultaneous qual sample	Core data + supplemental strategy data are selected according to needs of each component	No reflexivity for simultaneous interaction of the two components because the QUAN is fixed
QUAN → qual	Core QUAN with supplemental sequential qual sample	qual sample usually independent as the QUAN sample dissipated	Usually conducted to answer questions arising reflexively from the QUAN analysis
QUAL + qual	May be one (or more) samples	One core and one (or more) supplemental qual strategies	Second data set expands the domain

The characteristics of the design are shown in Table 36.1. Note that these data are not *linked* by participant. The *quan* data does not inform about individual participants in the QUAL sample; only about the population from which the QUAL sample was selected.

The use of pooled data is the most common method of data management in mixed-method design. This perspective provides us with two different perspectives of the same phenomenon. Data from each component may be of different levels of description, illuminating the phenomenon further (as in same-paradigm QUAL+ *qual*, or QUAL→ *quan*), or supplemental *quan* measures that confirm or document concepts in the QUAL component.[8]

The general principles of qualitative and quantitative mixed methods are similarly applicable for same-paradigm qualitative mixed methods. The core QUAL (a complete qualitative study) may be enriched with a supplemental *qual* sample that cannot be accessed using the core method, resulting in a QUAL + *qual* design. The QUAL data are analyzed using a standard qualitative method. The supplemental *qual* data are also analyzed (separately) using thematic or categorical analysis. At the point of interface, these two data sets are integrated to build a richer description in the *results narrative*, with the supplemental *qual* used to expand the domain.

Alternatively, for QUAL + *quan* design the researcher may pull a separate adequate *quan* sample (large and randomly selected) from the population to obtain physical fitness scores, perhaps at the beginning of the

---

Box 36.5 Example: QUAL + *quan* two-sample, two data types

Consider a hypothetical study of an exercise program for overweight youths with disabilities. The researchers used grounded theory QUAL to analyze how youth managed their physical activity and weight during the 3-month program. A separate adequate *quan* sample of youths (large and randomly selected) from the population of youth with disabilities provides physical fitness data about baseline fitness, allowing for an evaluation of the group as a whole compared to national norms as well as change-over-time among those selected for the exercise intervention.

> **Box 36.6 Example: QUAL + *qual*, one sample, two data sets, two data types**
>
> In a grounded theory study of social support for exercise among people with disabilities, supplemental data generated through field notes taken during team debriefings provided observations of interactional difficulties among participants about which the participants were silent. Participants with intellectual disabilities found it difficult to negotiate turn-taking at the exercise machines, yet they were reluctant to share those 'squabbles' with researchers during the recorded weekly group exercise meetings. The interviews and observations were used reflexively by the research team. Observations in the gym during exercise sessions sensitized the team to the need for participant cues regarding turn-taking and the social norms of gym behavior. With the simultaneous nature of the interviews and observations in the QUAL + *qual* study, the two datasets enriched each other and sparked intervention refinement as we built in explicit lessons on taking turns and waiting one's turn in the gym (Clark et al., in review).

program, to evaluate the group as a whole compared to national norms. Note this design would answer a slightly different question: it would demonstrate the necessity for the program and illustrate that the subsample in the QUAL group were not atypical.

Sampling difficulties with pooled data, two-sample mixed methods

When data are pooled in each component, data are analyzed as group data within each component according to data type, and the results from each component are kept separate until the point of interface when they are integrated in the research narrative. Therefore, in the following designs, separate samples should be used for each component.

a. For QUAL + *quan*, the QUAL sample is too small for quantitative analysis, and the *quan* data are summed and compared *as pooled group* data with data from external norms. Alternatively, a second independent quantitative sample may be drawn from the population, and data are analyzed and combined at the point of interface.
b. For QUAN + *qual*, the QUAN sample is usually too large for qualitative purposes. The researcher has several sampling options for the *qual*:
Select the *qual* sample from the QUAN sample, using qualitative principles for selecting a purposeful sample; or
Select a separate *qual* purposeful sample from the population.

For studies using a sequential design (QUAL→*quan*, for example), sometimes the core sample is unavailable for continuing study because they have aged out or moved on. In these cases, the researcher has no option but to draw a new sample from the population, according to the needs of the qualitative or qualitative component, e.g. particular quan if QUAL-quan.

Linked data: one sample, two data types, one data set

In this case the researcher has one sample (one core group of participants), but using this sample develops two data sets (one for the core component and one as the supplemental component). These two data sets are two different types of data: one, for QUAL + *quan* studies will have the first data set qualitative, and numerical data *obtained from the same* participants, for the supplemental project. These two data sets, one that serves as the core and the one for the supplemental component, are linked to each participant *individually*, and add to the description of each participant. Once these two sets of data are individually linked with each participant, these data are then combined and presented at the *results narrative* (see, Table 36.2).

Design difficulties for quan

If you have supplemental quantitative data in a QUAL + *quan* design, because the qualitative sample is usually too small for quantitative analysis, the *quan* supplemental data must be interpreted using external norms (usually from published articles or obtained from the developer of the instrument). Each

Table 36.2 Mixed-method design: single core sample, two linked data sets, two data types

Pacing	Representation of the Sample		Reflexivity
	Adequacy	Appropriateness	
QUAL + *quan*	Core QUAL + *quan* supplemental measure using QUAL participants	Core QUAL, participant description 'embellished' by *quan* measures	*quan* conducted to add to description of each individual participant, by comparing individual scores with external normative scores, then linking to each participant in the QUAL sample
QUAN + *qual*	Core QUAN Sample too large for *qual* to access	*qual* – often short semi-structured questionnaires; or the QUAN sampled by some predetermined criteria	*qual* data adds description when no measure has been located for the QUAN variables

score obtained in your study is linked to the QUAL data for each individual, and incorporated into the textual description of each participant. Because you are working with a small purposefully selected sample in the *quan*, scores must be interpreted using external normative values. For example, if your qualitative question addresses the experience of social support, it is important to have some measure of social support, such as the Perceived Support Scale (PSS) (Krause, 1995). The scale would be administered to each participant and their scores used to supplement the description of social support generated through qualitative interviews for each participant (see Figure 36.2).

With designs using a quantitative (QUAN) core, the *qual* supplemental data may also be obtained from each participant (see Table 36.2). Because of the large QUAN sample, the researcher may purposefully select participants from the QUAN using some preset criteria from the QUAN, and then use these data, linked to the individual QUAN scores, to describe subsets of the core sample.

With QUAN-*qual* designs, if data are obtained from all of the QUAN sample, these *qual* data are by necessity often thin – perhaps even consisting of a short, targeted semi-structured questionnaire. These semi-structured results may then be transformed into quantitative data, remain linked to the respective QUAN score, and moved into the QUAN data set as a new variable (see

```
QUAL      SUPPLEMENTAL
Sample    quan Sample
1 ------1
2 ------2
3 ------3
4 ------4      Each quan score is compared
5 ------5      with external norms, and adds
6 ------6      separately to participant's
. ------.           description
. ------.
. ------.
n ------n      Results then combined
                        ↓
                  Point of Interface
                  Results Narrative
```

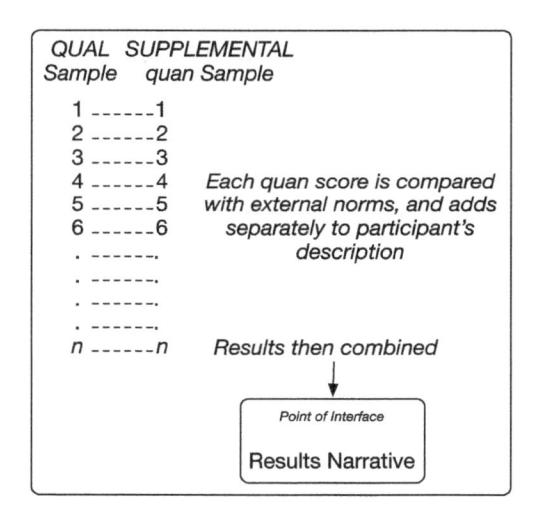

Figure 36.2 One sample, one data set, and two data types

Table 36.2). It is the parallel structure of both core and supplemental data sets that makes this conversion possible, and for this reason, Bryman (2008) noted that the most common method of data collection used for the *qual* component was semi-structured interviews.

Single Sample, Unlinked, Data Transformed

Are you using the supplemental *quan* strategy to add understanding of the group as a whole? In this case, the researcher has one

> **Box 36.7 Example: QUAL + *quan* using linked data within a single data set**
>
> An example of QUAL + *quan* using linked data within a single data set, extends from the previously mentioned study of an exercise program for youths who have disabilities. The researchers used grounded theory QUAL to analyze the experience of the program, but in this instance, using only the single QUAL sample, participants in the core grounded theory also participated in the supplemental *quan* data to provide measures of pre- and post-study physical endurance and flexibility. These *quan* data (with a smaller sample size) may be compared to national norms for people of the same age/gender/disability status. In this way, we would know the baseline fitness level of the exercisers and the effectiveness of the program.

qualitative (QUAL) sample, and has recognized a quantitative index to sort the qualitative sample into two (or more) groups of participants, according to the presence, or absence of the indicator. Then non-parametric statistics, such as chi square, may be used to explore further differences in the core QUAL data (see Table 36.3).

An example of using statistics to dichotomizing QUAL, qualitative interviews, is a study exploring health in the inner city. Morse (1987) recognized that the participants' definitions of health were either psychological (as in health-and-happiness) or physical (as in illness-and-pain). Segmenting the qualitative data set and transforming the definitions of health into a quantitative index, then further exploring the interviews to determine the self-rating of health, chi square analysis showed that those who defined health in psychological terms were healthy. On the other hand, those who defined health in physical terms rated themselves as ill, disabled, or physically compromised. In this way, quantitative sorting of qualitative data moved the analysis forward.

Instrument development

A second strategy may be to use the QUAL data for instrument development. This sequential design involves content analysis of qualitative data to form categories that become factors for instrument development (QUAL→ *quan*). From each factor and using the participants' own language, their experience is parsed into phrases indicative of the elements of the experience. Likert scale items are developed with a response format that allows participants to agree or disagree with the qualitatively derived item, scaling responses from 1 to 7 (strongly disagree to strongly agree). Researchers usually develop at least six items for each factor, then using standard psychometric methods, they administer the scale to a large sample (based on the number of items in the scale), factor analyze

Table 36.3 Mixed-method design: single sample, single set of data transformed

Pacing	Representation of the Sample		Reflexivity
	Adequacy and Number of participant samples	Appropriateness and Number of data sets	
QUAL→ *quan*	Core QUAL, usually semi-structured interview	1 data set	Data transformation 'Quantitize' – develop subsamples, e.g. dichotomize interviews
QUAL→ *quan*	Core QUAL, used for *quan* instrument development	1 data set	Instrument development: modified data; item identification using content analysis for quantitative instrument development

the results, refine the scale, and establish item–item correlations and overall subscale reliabilities (see Kieren and Morse, 1992; Morse and Kieren, 1993). The ultimate test of validity is the fit between the original content analysis categories and the factor analysis.

In QUAL→*quan* data transformations, are these data linked or not linked? Certainly they are linked for some of the procedure, and are traceable, but not linked by participant.

QUALITATIVELY DRIVEN MIXED-METHOD DESIGN FOR COMPLEX PHENOMENA

Complex mixed-method studies have various configurations according to their purpose. They qualify as complex because of the necessity of reflexivity in managing the number of components, and the malleability of the design supplements may be multiple data types with separate samples of subjects. Some components may use linked data, other pooled, depending on the purpose and the stage of the inquiry. These designs are shown on Table 36.4. In relation to this discussion of complex mixed-method studies, ethnography is a special case deserving discussion.

Ethnography as Mixed-Method Design?

The most important characteristic of an ethnography is that it is largely unplanned before the researcher enters the field, and consequently depends on reflexivity and the malleability of design. Apart from a general question of interest, details of the methods to be used are not known. Apart from the three strategies that comprise ethnography – interviews, participant observation, and field notes (see Buscatto, Chapter 21, this volume) – there exist a huge compendium of qualitative and quantitative strategies that may be used to explore various phenomena as the inquiry progresses (see Pelto, 2013). Simply, the ethnographic design, in reality, gives the researcher free range of a number of techniques – including quantitative strategies – according to inductive progress and what the researcher needs to find out.

The earliest mixed-method designs were used in anthropology (Fetters, 2016; Maxwell, 2015; Pelto, 2015, 2017). Pelto (2015) traced mixed methods used as early as 1938. The inductive nature of ethnography resembles an investigation – as is used by detectives solving a crime – wherein one component leads to increasing understanding and insight, that leads on to the next piece of the puzzle, research question(s), and design. Further, (sub)questions (arise as the study progresses, and the research design changes as understanding develops. Participants may or may not participate in more than one data set, but all participants are drawn from the same group or population. Data are usually pooled within each data set, but case studies may be used to illustrate particular points.

Occasionally one study (or part of a study), may be used as a *case study* to illustrate or to compare with another case study from another group or population. In this case, because the samples are drawn from different groups, the theoretical frame describing

Table 36.4 Mixed-method design: delineated group, multiple samples and data sets

Pacing	Representation of the Sample		Reflexivity
	Adequacy	Appropriateness	
QUAL + *quan* (or *qual*)	Usually sampled from one group; may be two or more	One method, different data sets (and different strategies) as inquiry progresses	As inductive inquiry progresses, new strategies are demanded e.g. ethnography

the rationale underlying the comparison is particularly significant in establishing, for example, why the two case studies may be compared.

EVALUATION RESEARCH DESIGNS AS COMPLEX MIXED-METHOD STUDIES

While ethnography may be used as evaluation research, traditional evaluation design (Caracelli and Greene, 1993; Greene, 2007; Ivankova, and Kawamura, 2010; Nastasi and Hitchcock, 2016) differs from ethnography, in that the evaluation components are usually identified at the proposal stage. The components or segments use pooled data within each component/sample. These segments often fit together laterally, rather like pieces in a jigsaw puzzle, with each segment supplementing the understanding of the others. Importantly, there is no cross-contamination of data types during analysis: they may consist of different types of interviews and observations, or even quantitative data or analysis of documents or records. Again, merging data from different segments may obscure differences between areas being evaluated. Rather, components are kept separate and merged at the point of interface, with the *results* from each segment fitting into the overall composition. This design is particularly important for evaluation studies testing implementations (Song et al., 2010).

Increasingly Complex Designs for Complex Phenomena

An example of a qualitatively driven mixed-method design with three quantitative supplemental components exploring and describing the suffering of patients with chronic pain and the alleviation of the suffering within a chronic pain management program was conducted by Dysvik et al. (2014). The QUAL component consisted of 34 written reports from Time 2 (t_2) and Time 3 (t_3). The three supplemental components consisted of items from the Brief Pain Inventory, Coping Strategies Questionnaire, and three subscales from the SF-36 Health Survey administered at t_1, t_2, and t_3 (see Dysvik et al., 2014; and Figure 36.3). In this study, each data set was obtained from the same sample of participants (at three different times), but each data set was *pooled*, and first analyzed *independently, as a set*: QUAL (t_2 and t_3) were compared, and the *quan* (t_1, t_2, and t_3) data sets were compared. *Then*, integration of the results of the QUAL and the three *quan* components occurred at the point of interface, and were reported in the *results narrative*.[9] Note that this study did not link participant's data within each data set, but analyzed them as pooled data. The investigators did not link the qualitative data with the quantitative scores, or look for individual participant changes across time.

This clear description provided by the authors is an excellent example of complex mixed-method design. They also presented clinically significant recommendations for programmatic change.

THE MALLEABILITY OF MIXED-METHOD RESEARCH

Mixed-method studies are proposed with various configurations according to their purpose, and to meet their aims. But qualitatively driven mixed methods, remain inductive, and the methods conducted during the course of the study often change, due to reflexivity, and the researchers' thinking matures. Thus, the methods actually used in the project may often have been unanticipated at the beginning of the study. What follows were multiple data types with separate samples of subjects, all within the inductive theoretical drive. Some components may use linked data, other pooled, depending on

> **Figure 1** Schematic overview of the QUAL–quan mixed-method design to reveal and compare changes. The left pathway illustrates the core component of the project (QUAL inductive drive). The right pathway illustrates the supplemental components of the project (quant deductive drive). The point of interface is the position at which the core and the supplemental components meet. The 'results narrative' refers to the write-up of the core component findings with the addition of the results of the supplemental components.

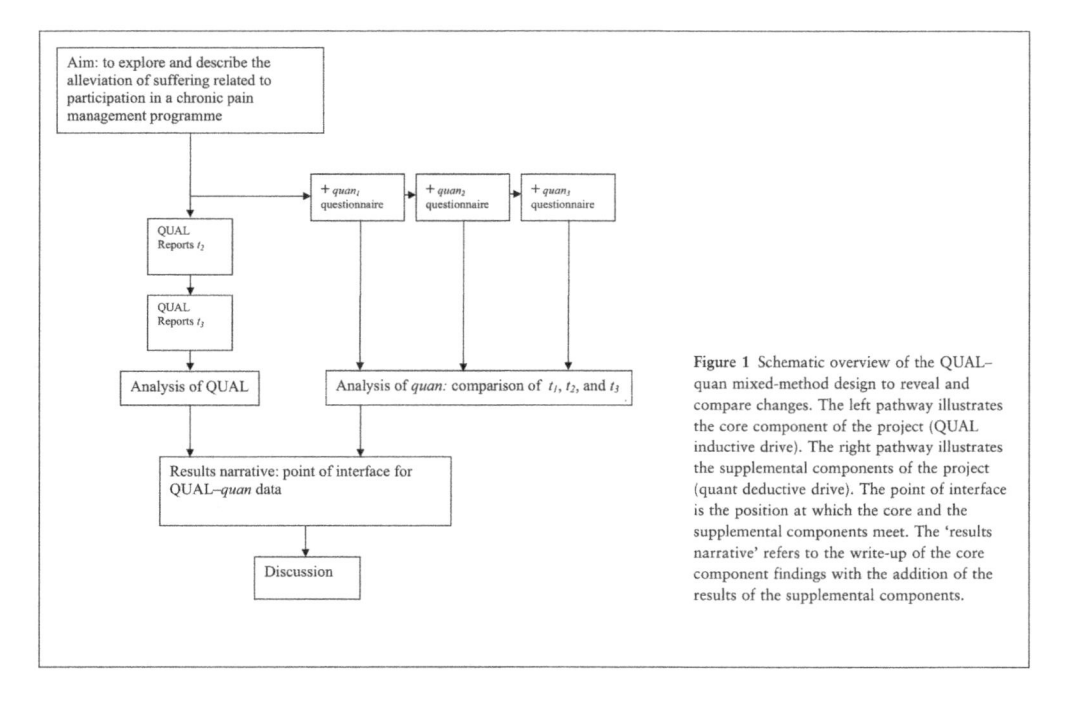

Figure 36.3 Schematic representation of a complex, qualitatively-driven mixed-method study featuring integration of a core qualitative and three supplemental quantitative components

Source: Dysvik, E., Kvaløy, J. T., and Furnes, B. (2014), *Journal of Clinical Nursing*, 23(5–6), p. 866; used with permission, John Wiley and Sons.

the purpose and the stage of the inquiry. Such is the malleability of mixed-method designs.

Are We Mixed Yet?

As noted, simply having two different types of data present in a study does not necessarily make the study a mixed-method study. Rather, a mixed-method study is derived from data, the pacing of study components, and the analytic reflexivity. These components are integrated in the research narrative. Mixed-method design must present what is done with that data, *why it is done*, and what makes the research stronger than if the two data sets that make it a mixed-method study were not present.

Data are not an entity that exist independently, to be picked up and dropped into new and different contexts without regard for the context from which they came or need to be developed. How that data were collected and the reason why are as much a part of the data set as, for example, the words in an interview or the numbers in a survey.

Similarly, decisions about data occur at all points of a research design, and those decisions must be surfaced as then, and only then, will it be clear what is being mixed, why and how in a study, and most important, what that mixing enables the study to do what it would not have been able to do if the 'mixing' had not occurred. It does not matter how good the techniques are if the overall design is not clearly understood and the purpose of the data is not clearly understood.

From the above we see that qualitative data must be respected within its own niche or data set. Exemplars that are used in any qualitative project (including qualitatively driven mixed-method designs) represent an analyzed *set* of data. Any quotations used to illustrate some particular part of the analysis, are representative of a coded category or theme, which in turn is representative of an individual, group or an experience. The quotation used illustrates or represents; it is not an entirety on its own. Again, it is formal data, not a random interesting comment. If, in the course of fieldwork, for instance, the researcher hears a comment of interest, that comment must be converted into data (consented, transcribed, and more data collected around the emerging category), according to principles of qualitative inquiry, and the category internally verified, in order for it to be included in the study.

CONCLUSION

Qualitative research, and qualitatively driven mixed-method design, is not a free-floating unstructured endeavor. It is systematic, solid, and rigorous. Data collection and resultant data sets are part of that but in themselves are not what makes something 'mixed'. It is the mixing of these data *sets* that expands the study beyond a single method. Clarity in reporting the research design makes the study comprehensible. Clinicians, teachers, evaluators, and other users of research will then benefit from the richness and applicability of qualitatively driven mixed-method research.

Notes

1. Some authors consider 'mixed methods' as a term referring to all combinations of methods. In this chapter, we refer to two complete methods as multiple method and one complete method plus a strategy from another method as a mixed-method design (Morse and Niehaus, 2009).
2. Formal qualitative interviews are primarily of four types: (1) formal unstructured interviews – the participants control the story, and the researcher assumes a listening role; (2) guided interviews – the researcher structures the participant's story, using 6 to 10 open-ended questions; (3) semi-structured interviews are partially controlled by the researcher, who plans the domain of the interview and questions to which the participant freely responds, and (4) conversational interviews used in focus groups (Morse, 2012).
3. Reflexivity extends from the reflection during analysis. In mixed methods, reflexivity enables questions and ideas arising from one component to be addressed in the other – or be addressed by adding an additional component to the study. Reflexivity increased validity by expanding the scope or depth of inquiry.
4. We disagree, of course, that mixed-method research requires both qualitative and quantitative methods. Same-paradigm mixed-method designs fit all of the principles of mixed-method research (e.g. QUAN-quan, QUAL-qual).
5. For a discussion of validity in mixed methods research, see Dellinger and Leech (2007).
6. In applying for funds for qualitative research, grant writers are often asked to provide an a priori count of anticipated research subjects, often by age, gender, and race/ethnicity. Sample size varies according to your methodological strategy, and the scope of the phenomenon under study. It is difficult to anticipate exact sample sizes prior to initiating a study.
7. Collins, Onwuegbuzie, and Jiao (2007) refer to this partitioning, or units within the sample, as the sampling scheme.
8. We use paradigm to refer to positivism (quantitative) and its alternative, qualitative (see Morgan, 2007).
9. Maxwell, Chmiel, and Rogers (2015) provide an interesting discussion of modes of integration in mixed and multiple method designs.

FURTHER READING

Cheek, J., Lipschitz, D. L., Abrams, E. M., Vago, D. R., and Nakamura, Y. (2015) 'Dynamic reflexivity in action – An armchair walk-through of a qualitatively driven mixed-method and multiple methods study of mindfulness training in schoolchildren', *Qualitative Health Research*, 25(6): 751–62, DOI: 1049732315582022.

Hesse-Biber, Sharlene, Rodriguez, Deborah, and Frost, Nogllaig A. (2015) 'A qualitatively driven approach to multimethod and mixed methods research', in Sharlene Hesse-Biber and Burke Johnson (eds.), *The Oxford Handbook of*

Multimethod and Mixed Methods Research Inquiry. New York: Oxford Press, pp. 3–20. DOI: 10.1093/oxfordhb/9780199933624.013.3.

Maxwell, J. A. (2016) 'Expanding the history and range of mixed methods research', Journal of Mixed Methods Research, 10(1): 12–17.

Maxwell, Joseph A., Chmiel, Margaret, and Rogers, Sylvia E. (2015) 'Designing integration in multimethod and mixed methods research', in Sharlene Hesse-Biber and Burke Johnson (eds.), The Oxford Handbook of Multimethod and Mixed Methods Research Inquiry. New York: Oxford University Press, pp. 223–39. DOI: 10.1093/oxfordhb/9780199933624.013.16.

Morse, Janice M. (2017) Developing Qualitative-Driven Mixed-Methods Design. New York: Routledge.

Pelto, Pertti (2017) Mixed Methods Research: A Personal History. New York: Routledge.

REFERENCES

Bryman, Alan (2008) 'Why do researchers integrate/combine/mesh/blend/ mix/merge/fuse quantitative and qualitative research', in Max Bergman (ed.), Advances in Mixed Methods Research. London: Sage, pp. 87–100.

Caracelli, V. J. and Greene, J. C. (1993) 'Designing integration in multimethod and mixed methods research', Educational Evaluation and Policy Analysis, 15(2): 195–207.

Cheek, Julianne (2015) 'It depends: Possible impacts of moving the field of mixed methods research toward best practice guidelines', in Sharlene Hesse-Biber and Burke Johnson (eds.), The Oxford Handbook of Multimethod and Mixed Methods Research Inquiry. New York: Oxford University Press, pp. 624–36. DOI: 10.1093/oxfordhb/9780199933624.013.3.

Clark, L. and Zimmer, L. (2001) 'What we learned from a photographic component in a study of Latino children's health', Field Methods, 13(4): 303–28.

Clark, L., Cardell, E., and Pett, M. A. (in review) 'Reducing overweight among young adults with intellectual disability by activating peer social networks', Global Qualitative Nursing Research.

Clark, Lauren, Johnson, S. L., O'Connor, M. E., and Lassetter, J. (2013) 'Cultural aspects of Latino early childhood obesity', in C. T. Beck (ed.), Routledge International Handbook of Qualitative Nursing Research. New York: Routledge, pp. 103–18.

Collins, K. M. T., Onwuegbuzie, A. J., and Jiao, Q. G. (2007) 'A mixed methods investigation of mixed methods sampling designs in social and health science research', Journal of Mixed Methods Research, 1(3): 267–94.

Creswell, John W., Klassen, Ann Carroll, Plano Clark, Vicki L., and Smith, Katharine Clegg (2011) Best Practices for Mixed Methods Research in the Health Sciences. Bethesda, MD: National Institutes of Health.

Dellinger, A. B., and Leech, N. L. (2007) 'Toward a unified validation framework in mixed methods research', Journal of Mixed Methods Research, 1(4): 309–32.

DeWalt, Kathleen M. and DeWalt, Billie R. (2011) Participant Observation: A Guide for Fieldworkers (2nd edn). Lanham (MD): Altamira Press.

Dysvik, E., Kvaløy, J. T., and Furnes, B. (2014) 'A mixed-method study exploring suffering and alleviation in participants attending a chronic pain management programme', Journal of Clinical Nursing, 23(5–6): 865–76.

Emerson, Robert M., Fretz, Rachael I., and Shaw, Linda, L. (2011) Writing Ethnographic Fieldnotes (2nd edn). Chicago, IL: University of Chicago Press.

Fetters, Michael D. (2016) '"Haven't we always been doing mixed methods research?": Lessons learned from the development of the horseless carriage', Journal of Mixed Methods Research, 10(1): 3–11. DOI: 10.1177/1558689815620883.

Greene, Jennifer C. (2007) Mixed Methods in Social Inquiry. San Francisco, CA: Jossey-Bass.

Hesse-Biber, Sharlene, and Johnson, R. Bourke (eds.) (2015) The Oxford Handbook of Multimethod and Mixed Methods Research Inquiry. New York: Oxford Press. DOI: 10.1093/oxfordhb/9780199933624.013.3.

Hesse-Biber, Sharlene, Rodriguez, Deborah and Frost, Nogllaig A. (2015) 'A qualitatively driven approach to multimethod and mixed methods research', in Sharlene Hesse-Biber and Burke Johnson (eds.), The Oxford Handbook of

Multimethod and Mixed Methods Research Inquiry. New York: Oxford Press, pp. 3–20. DOI: 10.1093/oxfordhb/9780199933624.013.3.

Ivankova, Nataliya V. and Kawamura, Yoko (2010) 'Emerging trends in the utilization of integrated designs in the social, behavioral and health sciences', in Charles Teddlie and Aabbas Tashakkori (eds.), *Handbook of Mixed Methods in Social and Behavioral Research* (2nd edn). Thousand Oaks, CA: Sage, pp. 581–612.

Johnson, R. B., Onwuegbuzie, A. J., and Turner, L. A. (2007) 'Toward a definition of mixed methods research', *Journal of Mixed Methods Research*, 1(2): 112–33. DOI: 10.1177/1558689806298224.

Kieren, D. and Morse, J. M. (1992) 'Preparation factors and menstrual attitudes of pre- and postmenarcheal girls', *Journal of Sex Education and Therapy*, 18(3): 155–74.

Krause, N. (1995) 'Negative interaction and satisfaction with social support among older adults', *Journal of Gerontology: Psychological Sciences*, 50B(2): P59–P73.

Mason, J. (2006) 'Mixing methods in a qualitatively driven way', *Qualitative Research*, 6(1): 9–25. DOI: 10.1177/1468794106058866.

Maxwell, Joseph A., Chmiel, Margaret, and Rogers, Sylvia E. (2015). 'Designing integration in multimethod and mixed methods research', in Sharlene Hesse-Biber and Burke Johnson (eds.), *The Oxford Handbook of Multimethod and Mixed Methods Research Inquiry.* New York: Oxford Press, pp. 223–39. DOI: 10.1093/oxfordhb/9780199933624.013.16.

McIntosh, M., and Morse, J. M. (2015) 'Situating and constructing diversity in semi-structured interviews', *Global Qualitative Nursing Research*, 2(Jan–Dec): 1–12, DOI: 10.1177/2333393615597674.

Mertens, D. M. (2011) 'Publishing mixed methods research', *Journal of Mixed Methods Research*, 5(1): 3–4. DOI: 10.1177/1558689810390217.

Morgan, D. L. (2007) 'Paradigms lost and pragmatism regained: Methodological implications of combining quantitative and qualitative methods', *Journal of Mixed Methods Research*, 1 (1): 48–76. DOI:10.1177/2345678906292462.

Morse, J. M. (1987) 'The meaning of health in an inner city community', *Nursing Papers/Perspectives in Nursing*, 19(2): 27–41.

Morse, J. M. (2001) 'Using shadowed data' (Editorial) *Qualitative Health Research*, 11(3): 291.

Morse, Janice M. (2012) 'The implications of interview type and structure in mixed-method designs', in Jaber F. Gubrium, James A. Holstein, Amir B. Marvasti, and Karyn D. McKinney (eds.), *The SAGE Handbook of Interview Research: The Complexity of the Craft.* Los Angeles, CA: Sage, pp. 193–204.

Morse, Janice M. (2017) *Developing Qualitative-Driven Mixed-Method Designs.* New York: Routledge.

Morse, J. M. and Cheek, J. (2014) 'Making room for qualitatively-driven mixed-method research', *Qualitative Health Research*, 24(1): 3–5. DOI:10.1177/1049732313513656.

Morse, J. M. and Cheek, J. (2015) 'Introducing qualitatively-driven mixed-method design', *Qualitative Health Research*, 25(6): 713–33. DOI: 10.1177/1049732315583299.

Morse, J. M. and Kieren, D. (1993) 'The adolescent menstrual attitude questionnaire, part II: Normative scores', *Health Care for Women International*, 14: 63–76.

Morse, Janice M. and Niehaus, Linda (2009) *Mixed-Method Design: Principles and Procedures.* Walnut Creek, CA: Left Coast.

Nastasi, Bonnie K. and Hitchcock, John H. (2016) *Mixed Methods Research and Culture-specific Interventions: Program Design and Evaluation.* Los Angeles, CA: Sage.

Nygaard. Ingrid , E., Clark, Erin, Clark, Lauren, Egger, Marlene, J., Hitchcock, Robert, Hsu, Yvonne, Norton, Peggy, SanchezBirkhead, Anna, Shaw, Janet, Sheng, Xiaoming, and Varner, Michael (2017). Physical and cultural determinants of postpartum pelvic floor support and symptoms following vaginal delivery: protocol for a mixed-methods prospective cohort study. *BMJ Open*, 7(1), e014252.

Pelto, Pertti J. (2013) *Applied Ethnography: Guidelines for Field Research.* New York: Routledge.

Pelto, P. J. (2015) 'What is so new about mixed methods?', *Qualitative Health Research*, 25(6): 734–45. DOI: 10.1177/1049732315573209.

Pelto, Pertti, J. (2017) *Mixed Methods Research: A Personal History.* New York: Routledge.

Rea, J. and Green, B. (2016) 'Portraying reflexivity in health services research', *Qualitative Health Research*, 26(11): 1543–49. DOI: 10.1177/1049732316634046.

Shaw, R. (2010) 'Embedding reflexivity within experiential qualitative psychology', *Qualitative Research in Psychology*, 7(3): 233–43.

Song, Mi-Lung, Sandelowski, Margarete, and Happ, Mary Beth (2010) 'Current practices and emerging trends in conducting mixed methods intervention studies in the health sciences', in Charles Teddlie and Abbas Tashakkori (eds.), *Handbook of Mixed Methods in Social and Behavioral Research* (2nd edn). Thousand Oaks, CA: Sage, pp. 725–47.

Teddlie, Charles, and Tashakkori, Abbas (2003) 'Major issues and controversies in the use of mixed methods in the social and behavioral sciences', in Charles Teddlie and Abbas Tashakkori (eds.), *Handbook of Mixed Methods in Social and Behavioral Research*. Thousand Oaks, CA: Sage, pp. 3–50.

Willis, Gordon B. (2015) *Analysis of the Cognitive Interview in Questionnaire Design*. Oxford: University of Oxford Press.

Yin, Robert Y. (2015) 'Causality, generalizability, and the future of mixed-methods research', in Sharlene Hesse-Biber and R. Burke Johnson (eds.), *The Oxford Handbook of Multimethod and Mixed Methods Research Inquiry.* New York: Oxford Press, pp. 652–63. DOI: 10.1093/oxfordhb/9780199933624.013.42.

Combining Digital and Physical Data

Nigel G. Fielding

INTRODUCTION

Despite over half a century during which digital technologies have made a growing impact on social research, it was not until the 1990s that the term 'research online' emerged as a new field of social research methods. The year 2008 saw publication of the first edition of the *Handbook of Online Research Methods* and, as its editors, Grant Blank, Ray Lee and I shared with our contributors the view that although 'online methods' were of considerable and growing significance, it remained appropriate to regard them as distinct from offline methods.

In 2017, and at least in the global North, it is fair to say that at least one part of the lifecycle of nearly any qualitative research project is likely to be carried out 'online'. While for some this may only be in the technical or practical sense of fieldwork data being held in computer files for word processing, it is increasingly the case that fieldwork data are initially collected online, and hence 'born digital', that various online platforms are used to access and exploit research data, that analysis is conducted using one or more of the proliferating kinds of software that support qualitative data analysis, and that researchers engaged in smaller projects as well as larger ones increasingly resort to online collaboration tools to facilitate joint work on a common dataset. Moreover, the content of online data materials is itself increasingly a central object of study in fields as diverse as politics and psychology. In the latter, some psychologists treat online communication as a distinct kind of communication whose direct analogy cannot be found in offline social behaviour.

These remarks have been directed to the conventional or established research community, but our view of who comprises the research community should not be myopic. Those with academic qualifications and holding a paid position in the research sphere no longer exert a monopoly over social research. The online world has encouraged the development of 'citizen social science', whose purposes range from personal research like finding the best school for one's children to lobbying on local causes such as saving playing fields from housing development and on through to efforts to transform or bring down governments. For many who have taken the role of 'citizen social scientists', or who simply carry out a piece of research for instrumental reasons, it is not only natural to conduct their project purely online, but to be blissfully unaware that the methods they are using have a long offline lineage.

This chapter will refer to offline research behaviour, and the data that represents it, as 'physical data', the contrast implicitly being with digital data that exists only in the online environment. Given its placing in a section on mixing methods, the chapter will consider what is important when Internet/digital data is used in combination with non-digital, non-Internet data, such as the data drawn from face-to-face interviews, field observation or documents and other artefacts that have not been digitized. An important point here is that, if methods are to be mixed, there needs to be a rationale for doing so. The answer to 'why combine?' should be based on better intellectual purchase, whether it is directed to traditional 'triangulation' for convergent validation (see Flick, Chapter 34, this volume), or to the more recent criterion of enhanced 'analytic density' (Fielding, 2009). Accordingly, the chapter will attempt to identify the principal kinds of differences, and similarities, between the two types of information against which we develop our analyses and conceptualizations as qualitative researchers and, where relevant, to say how mixing them can tell us more.

Observation (see Wästerfors, Chapter 20, this volume), interview (see Roulston and Choi, Chapter 15, this volume) and group discussion ('focus group' – see Morgan and Hoffman, Chapter 16, this volume) data are types of data with a lineage as long as social science itself. The array of qualitative data emergent from online/digital environments includes visual, virtual, textual, acoustic, digital and other kinds of data, some of which have an offline analogy and others of which do not. It is useful to think of these types of data (see Lindgren, Chapter 28, this volume) as representing an extension and diversification of ways that humans communicate and document their own, and others', lived social experience. The technical means by which these data are produced include technological innovations, some digital, some not. For instance, the shellac disc and audio cassette were radical innovations in their time, making it possible to create real-time recordings of respondents' voices at modest cost (see Lee, 2004).

There is little question that research increasingly, and sometimes entirely, involves engagement with the digital. However, it is the premise of this chapter that there remain some important differences between offline and online data; there are also a number of possible differences that remain subject to debate. This chapter is sympathetic to Orton-Johnson and Prior's (2013, p. 2) call to 'conceptually move beyond the binary oppositions of virtual/real and transformation/continuity' that have marked the early period of research commentaries on the online environment, such that we now seek to understand the relationship between technology, society and culture in more sophisticated, granular terms 'even as we reflect on the increasing normality and inclusion of the digital in everyday life'. This formula is good for methods as well as for conceptualization, although systematic explorations of the relationship between offline and online social research methods are sparse.

It does sometimes seem as if the world with which we are familiar as social researchers is increasingly out of joint with the digitally mediated world in which we live as private citizens. The research world is to some extent playing 'catch up' with what is really distinctive and what has stayed essentially the same. The key to exploring the relationship between the offline and the online in the sphere of research methods, particularly qualitative methods, is to understand the situated material practices involved. The point is made in more general terms by Orton-Johnson (2013, p. 186): 'If newer digital technologies and networks *do* mediate in qualitatively different ways to older media then the point is to demonstrate how this happens in ... everyday practices'. The chapter therefore considers what the distinction between the digital and non-digital is or means in several aspects of qualitative data collection and work with field data. These are covered in the chapter's main sections: Data Collection, Data Documentation, Theory, Ethics, Limits and Constraints.

DATA COLLECTION

One of the major issues in systematic research designs is the rationale for drawing the sample from which data will be obtained. In the case of qualitative research this runs into issues relating to generalizability (see Schreier, Chapter 6, this volume). Since qualitative research is customarily 'small N research', many methodologists regard qualitative methods as appropriate for discovery but not generalizable. However, online resources increasingly permit very large samples to be analysed qualitatively (while noting that in quantitative research, generalizability is not a simple function of sample size but of sample representativeness). The fact that the online environment 'permits' large samples does not imply that qualitative researchers are currently working with larger samples, but, where they do, it requires a degree of automation (based on machine coding and the use of expert systems; see Brent, 2016). For many qualitative researchers this represents a step too far, but the broader point is that, if generalizability is an issue, it may not remain one for qualitative researchers working in an online environment. An example of a field where this may be so is the use of 'sentiment analysis' in marketing and other work on attitudes

(see Thelwall, 2017). The case of sentiment analysis raises another point. Sentiment analysis is a hybrid method involving both quantitative and qualitative elements. In terms of data collection, for data integration to be possible using the tools of sentiment analysis, the qualitative data to be collected need to be designed from the outset such that they can be integrated with quantitative data.

Also, a relevant aspect of sampling is the distinction between 'natural' and 'elicited' data (see Potter and Shaw, Chapter 12, this volume). It is generally a good idea in terms of data quality (see Barbour, Chapter 14, this volume) for the researcher to mediate the data as little as possible when collecting it. For instance, interviewers are cautioned not to use leading questions or declare their own view on a topic to participants; we do fieldwork to find out what others think or do, not promulgate our own view. While naturally occurring data is sometimes used in qualitative research, such as in non-participant observation or unobtrusive methods (see Lee, 2000), it is a relatively modest enterprise. There is reason to argue that the picture is different in online research. We have all seen presentations illustrated by the stupendous numbers associated with online artefacts as they accumulate at an ever-greater rate. Blog content (see Weller et al., Chapter 31, this volume), tweets, advertisements on websites, Facebook posts (see Ditchfield and Meredith, Chapter 32, this volume) and 'likes', and so on, can all be treated as naturally occurring data. This is material that need not be mediated by researchers at all. However, we should be aware that it can be manipulated, and research has had a worrying role in that. In one case, researchers used social media data to find out the days of the week on which women felt least positive about their appearance. This information was then used by advertisers on Facebook (Kramer et al., 2014). Nevertheless, it is generally a positive thing that the online world provides a lot of data that only has to be 'captured' rather than elicited.

Before we examine the offline/online comparison in the standard canon of qualitative methods, we can identify the kinds of issues we should look for from a discussion of the transition undergone by researchers who are accustomed to the management and analysis of qualitative data using 'manual methods' but who then adopt qualitative software. Some of the difficulties that such researchers report include:

1. missing the ability to work directly on paper, resulting in a feeling of 'distance' from the data;
2. engaging in non-productive coding or analysis practices;
3. experiencing difficulties in managing analytic distance;
4. not recognizing when the software is not doing what you think it is doing; and
5. being tempted to turn qualitative data into quantitative data (Paulus and Lester, 2016, p. 406, following Gilbert et al., 2014).

From the time of Becker's *Sociological Work* (1970) onwards we have recognized that the distinction between data collection and data analysis is a somewhat artificial one in qualitative research. Accordingly, some of the issues that Paulus and Lester (2016) describe will also mark the online data collection stage of a study relative to the equivalent stage in an offline study. Alongside issues of 'trust', operating in an online environment when conducting qualitative fieldwork (see Tiidenberg, Chapter 30, this volume) can be marked by feelings of distance from research subjects, of missing the richness of face-to-face interaction. This is in itself an argument for combining the online and offline, for instance, by conducting at least some of a set of interviews offline before moving to the online medium to administer synchronous or asynchronous interviews (see Abrams, 2017). One might consider conducting pilot interviews in direct co-presence. One might also consider dividing samples in half, one for online and the other for offline, and including differences in response that may relate to the medium as an object of analytic inquiry themselves.

This is not to argue that either method has, or should have, primacy. Rather, it may be a question of the nature of the project or of its purposes whether the online or offline medium is preferable. Using again the example of CAQDAS, qualitative software enables the researcher '(1) to work efficiently with a large data-set; (2) work productively and transparently in teams; (3) manage data systematically, and (4) maintain portable and durable data' (Paulus and Lester 2016, p. 406). As may be obvious, these points are particularly advantageous for collaborative projects and projects that are working with large data volumes. The two characteristics are connected, and they speak directly to the online environment. We are increasingly working with large data volumes – 'big data' (see Lindgren, Chapter 28, this volume and Markham, Chapter 33, this volume) – and this may require work with others. Further, the practical exigencies of funding and the geographical dispersion of qualitative researchers means that software support will often be needed in order to work collaboratively. User studies tell us that many users of CAQDAS find the software particularly useful as an 'electronic filing cabinet', making it valuable at the data collection stage (Fielding, 2008).

Observation, Including Flow-Oriented Data

Direct observation of human behaviour is no doubt as old as humanity. Social psychology and interactionist sociology tell us that we construct our sense of who we are by paying attention to how others regard us, which conditions our own behaviour. We do this from such an early point in infancy that it is an unconscious process. We constantly monitor the behaviour of others in everyday social life. It is not a monopoly of the researcher. Even making detailed oral or written records of what we observe is not a monopoly of the researcher; village elders (oral), letter writers and diarists (written records) perform the same activity as the fieldworker. It cannot even be said that adopting a reflexive attitude towards our observations, and their recorded form, is the monopoly of the researcher. A dip into any novel by Charlotte Brontë tells us that. Perhaps the only sense in which the fieldworker differs from the everyday person is that the fieldworker will be aware that there is a canon of literature concerning observation as a research method.

The digital 'observer' does not, and cannot, directly witness the behaviour of others in the same unmediated way as being a participant in offline behaviour. If someone pulls your foot backward because you are swimming too slowly in the fast lane, and curses you as they pass, only the kind of person who has profound existential doubts would entertain the idea that what has just happened is an illusion. To you, the immediate experience of the physical is not a representation, it is your nervous system telling you your foot has been pulled and your ears reporting a curse. Moreover, if you get to the end of the lane and the other swimmer is there smiling and friendly, you have your direct experience of the physical event to draw on as a resource in attempting to interpret their contradictory behaviour. Where things get more complicated is when you write up your experience as data. As a sports scientist you are interested in 'pool rage' and the temptation will be strong to cite the experience as an example. That temptation may lead you to discount the fulsome apology and offer to buy you an energy drink made by your fellow swimmer. As you cogitate over your field note, you begin to suspect that the energy drink offer was a veiled insult – she is telling you that you need pepping up.

So what of the online observer? Perhaps someone filmed the pool incident and posted it online so others can watch the 'rage' remotely. Perhaps the pool's online newsletter carried an item about a nasty rage incident and appealing for better manners. The online observer can read the blog that you, furious about the incident, decided to write that very evening. But try as they may they cannot replicate the feeling of that hand on your heel or the exact sound received by your ears. Moreover, the online observer has to decide if the online footage is really a hoax – what kind of person stands at poolside with a smartphone trained on the pool waiting for incidents? And not only will the online observer have the dilemma of assessing 'skew' in the way you wrote your blog (analogous to the skew imposed on your field note by your lack of 'objectivity'), but they will have to appraise and control the 'genre' effect that makes blogs follow stylistic conventions and use tropes found in other blogs (see Weller et al., Chapter 31, this volume).

In the case of direct participant observation (see Buscatto, Chapter 21, this volume), then, the fieldworker working with physical data has a tough task, but that of the digital observer is considerably tougher. It may be a lot easier to collect 'field data' online, but its epistemological status makes interpreting it even harder.

If this comparative account of online/offline observation seems a little harsh on the online let us note that there are digital affordances that their offline equivalent cannot reproduce. Let us say that we are interested in social processes, the way that sequences of events build towards an event of analytic interest. In some quarters, like psychology, this is often called 'flow' (see Markham and Gammelby, Chapter 29, this volume). In sociology, process is of great importance in symbolic interactionism but also in causal theory, which revolves around the nature of the articulation between process and structure. The offline observer of flow, or process, must either use a time slice sampling approach (observing the same setting at different times), or ask participants to keep a time-use diary (both of which are subject to the effects of selectivity and subjectivity). Even the advance made by Carson and Csikszentmihalyi (1983), whose 'experiential sampling method' involved participants carrying a beeper that received a radio signal that was set off by researchers, at which point the participant had to write down what they were doing, is vulnerable to selectivity and subjectivity concerns, as well as relying on participant cooperation. The digital observer who wants to know what people are doing at a given time can draw on GPS technology on personal devices to determine their precise location, can analyse the 'digital traces' left by their online communications, and, with their cooperation, draw on remote sensor data reporting whether a room is occupied and by how many (via body heat sensing), whether a home entertainment device is on (via power consumption) and, if an appliance subscribes to 'Internet of things' technology, whether the fridge is full. These observations will be free of selectivity and subjectivity effects.

Unreconstructed lovers of 'physical data' may also say such information would also be free of interest, or require a lot of inferential work to make them say anything interesting. The point is that data collected by digital 'observation' provides a valuable supplement to, not a substitute for, physical observation. For some analytical purposes the other side of the coin applies, where our interest is in how people perform an activity online and we use physical observation to check or confirm an interpretation. Just as triangulation, which emerged before digital methods, argues that methods reliant on physical data are stronger in combination (for instance, checking an observed behaviour by asking people about it at interview), the online and offline sources of data are often stronger in combination.

Interviews and Group Discussions ('Focus Groups')

Like observation, the interview is as old as social science and conversational forms akin to it go back to the beginning of human society. Interviews have a plausible claim to be the most-used method of collecting physical data. If one wants to know something it seems the most natural thing in the world to ask a question. 'Natural', yes, but simple, no. The many tomes on the wording of interview questions, conduct of the interview, approach to transcription and the arguments for and against structured, semi-structured and unstructured formats suggest the complexities involved in collecting interview data. This leads some to prefer 'naturally occurring talk' collected by the professional equivalent of eavesdropping, such as conversation analysis, which compiles video recordings of various kinds of social interaction (Hindmarsh, 2017). Interviews are as subject to selectivity and subjectivity effects as is observation. Even conversation analysis has an equivalent concern with whether the presence of cameras affected the interaction, although it often addresses this problem by refraining from inferences about motives and meanings, instead concerning itself with analysing the intricacies of turn-taking, the effect of silences and so on.

The status of physical interview data is highly contested. While concerns about the epistemological status of such data go far back, they crystallized in the 1980s around the 'interviews as accounts' perspective introduced by Lyman and Scott (1989), where it is considered impossible to fully discount the possibility that interviewees render accounts of their motivations, actions and beliefs that are self-serving in various ways and that provide no reliable insight into what they actually do and what they actually believe. This approach has been writ large in recent years by the work of critics of interview methodology, such as Jaber Gubrium (2003), whose explorations of the discursive forms of the interview do nothing to reassure readers that interview data can be treated as factual or as affording insights into any kind of truth. Interviews are inescapably reflexive performances and the data are best treated as displaying rhetorical forms and popular tropes in contemporary discourse. Neo-positivists address such concerns by emphasizing various within-the-field controls, such as using vignettes to elicit data with less intervention from the interviewer, the need for detailed and accurate transcription, and after-the-field techniques, such as feeding transcripts and even interpretations back to participants for correction and/or comment. Between what one may regard as the extremes of conversation analysis and neo-positivism there are numerous other approaches to work with interview data, each with its own accommodation to the status of such data.

Online interviews can take a number of forms, the standard distinction being between synchronous and asynchronous interviewing. The former is undertaken in 'real time' and requires considerable cooperation by participants, including ways of handling interruptions and computer glitches. A contrasting point applies to asynchronous interviews. Since these involve participants making their responses when it suits them, the burden of responding is less, but there is a larger concern regarding the 'evenness' of response, since quite different contexts may apply to one occasion of responding compared to another. Unless the participant volunteers points that relate to context, the researcher cannot be certain whether variations in, say, depth and extent of response, relate to context effects, problems with the question, or waning (or waxing) interest in the topic. Regarding cooperation, it is absolutely the case that face-to-face, or telephone, interviews also require a considerable measure of cooperation, since, in nearly all cases, participants would be doing something other than an interview if the researcher had not asked them to participate. In the case of face-to-face interviews, though, it can be argued that the cognitive burden is little more than that sustained in any conversation between strangers, whereas the telephone does present some difficulties in responding to the interview format and, for many, is tiring after a few minutes.

Insofar as at least some participants – those who are comfortable with an online environment – may find participating in an online interview less inconvenient than an offline interview, the digital format has an advantage. There is also research evidence that some respondents are more comfortable in making disclosive responses and expressing sincere opinions in the relatively more anonymous setting of an online interview, at least in contrast to the face-to-face format. This point particularly applies to group discussions and focus groups (see Abrams, 2017). A further advantage relates to participants who, for various reasons, do not wish to be interviewed face to face, or who would find it physically difficult to do so. This may include people with aspects of physical appearance about which they are sensitive, people who are unable without difficulty to travel to an interview venue (noting that some ethics boards now discourage seeing participants in their own home or workplace), or people with extreme views that may be inhibited in expressing them directly to an interviewer but who are willing to share their views online. The other side of the latter coin is that extreme views expressed online may in fact be tongue-in-cheek or mischievous in some other way, this being much harder to assess when one only has an online artefact as opposed to having met the person.

Issues relating to question design (see Gobo, Chapter 5, this volume) are akin to the points above regarding problems interpreting online responses. If a question does not 'work' in a face-to-face interview it is often easy to see this from physical signs like the participant's facial expression. This may be harder with an online format unless one is using high quality video teleconferencing, which presumes that the participant has the necessary equipment and software on their device. This said, it is relatively straightforward to check if participants understand your questions both in synchronous formats or asynchronous formats, albeit that doing so in the latter slows things down and may lead to some impatience and/or awkwardness. It may be wise to pilot test your questions in the face-to-face format, perhaps with suitable colleagues or friends, even if the main body of interviews will be conducted online.

A final variant of interview format is of interest. In recent years a practice of 'mobile methods' (sometimes called 'go-along methods' – see Kusenbach, Chapter 22, this volume) has emerged. This seeks to gain insight by accompanying research participants as they go about their business, asking the participant to narrate their purposes, thoughts etc. as they proceed (Buscher et al., 2011). The author's research team used the technique in a study of policing and community safety, accompanying citizens who belonged to Neighbourhood Watch teams and who patrolled their residential locale, noting problems such as abandoned cars and reporting them to police. A GPS device was used to record the exact location during the walk, with the narrative recorded on a smartphone. This could then be linked to Streetview and a GIS record made of the exact point at which a particular comment was made. The GIS maps showed physical and social 'contours' of the area (e.g. where mixed use zoning applied as opposed to residential only, where there was a park, where an arrest had been made, etc.). The narrative was transcribed and coded and analysed in a CAQDAS package. Drawing on the combination of multiple and mobile methods we were able to evidence an interpretation as to why a series of unexplained window-breaking attacks had been made on a small set of houses in the neighbourhood (Fielding and Fielding, 2013), which led us to a new conceptualization of the perverse effects of housing and community safety policies. The mix of offline and digital technologies encountered no resistance, and some interest amongst participants, and the insight regarding the window-breaking attacks would literally not have been possible short of the ability to hold interview response in a way that exactly related it to locations on the GIS/Streetview part of the project.

Visual, Acoustic and Virtual Data

While there are important differences between online and offline formats when using observation and/or interview methods, and these may lead the researcher to prefer one or the other, when we come to visual, audio ('acoustic' – see Bull, Chapter 27, this volume) and virtual data there is little question that the online format is preferable. This is largely down to technical quality. It is true that old school cinema projectionists insist that digital formats do not exactly replicate the technical qualities of film, and it is also true that digital media struggle to emulate the richness of music recorded on vinyl. However, these are matters for the connoisseur. There are some corners of the social research world where technical standards need to be exacting – a prime instance is conversation analysis, where frame speeds and acoustic quality are important in deciding interpretations of recorded interaction. Those that work with still images may also have demanding requirements for picture quality; for instance, in marketing research and criminal forensics the variation in colour on a device's VDU and on the printed page may be crucial. But for the most part, qualitative researchers are content with a recording that is audible with clarity and with video that is well lit and has the right camera angle to capture the action of interest. Other researchers who are specifically interested in analysing online content do not even have to ponder format, although they may find it worthwhile to include an offline element, such as where reactions to a particular item of online content are sought from an offline focus group. This does not mean that online formats are entirely free of problems. A prominent one is the extent to which material from web pages can be captured for analysis in qualitative software.

Some CAQDAS packages have now developed components designed to capture online materials. NCapture is a web browser extension that supports users of NVivo software in capturing and analysing web pages, online PDFs and social media data such as YouTube, Facebook and Twitter. Users can opt for automatic transfer of metadata when classifying attributes, for including YouTube comments that have been posted, and for including Twitter retweets. There are also options for the format of the harvested material. With online content harvested as a PDF, the web page front-end structure, and the text in advertisements on the page, can be searched and coded. Embedded images can be coded, but presently the software allows only for the selection of rectangular areas, like other CAQDAS packages having similar functionality. Retrieval display is limited and can be distorted. Harvested material does retain its source active hyperlinks, so users can navigate from it back to the web to pursue interpretations and, if useful further material is found, re-harvest content that has been altered.

The cloud-based platform 'Texifter', is designed to enable users to process extensive online materials. It can harvest large-scale online archives and merge data from text files and email; it can survey open-ended questions, and sources including Facebook, Google+, Tumblr, Disqus and Twitter. Users can control the timespan for capturing web content and the frequency of sampling within the timeframe. Texifter can be set to capture material up to a year in advance. Automated classification is possible, as is redaction, and clustering of duplicated material for de-duplication. Metadata, for example, when and where a tweet was posted, or socio-demographic information, can be used to filter harvested material into sets.

Another point relating to work with visual data and qualitative software is the emergence of streamlined app versions of CAQDAS. App versions use icons to represent codes so you can work on a phone screen. MAXQDA's free app uses emoticons for quick coding 'on the fly'. The full version of the software mounted on a desktop or laptop converts these to word-based codes. Manual coding is laborious and if one changes one's mind about code assignment it involves marking up the data afresh. Also, most qualitative software allows users to compile code definitions in pop up boxes so as to keep coding on track. In these respects there is little to recommend manual methods. Software is beginning to appear that explicitly aims to make qualitative research more accessible for non-academics and students. For instance, Quirkos is a package that is designed to operate in a small-screen device environment, heavily employs touchscreen technology, and uses an intentionally limited range of icons to operate the program's main features.

Another occupant of the online-only, or at least online-best, category are those who are interested in capturing patterns representing human interaction. This is the domain of Social Network Analysis. It considers communication flows either in the abstract (e.g. the response dynamics between experts and naïve enquirers in an online forum dealing with the use of a particular consumer product) or with regard to the substantive content of the traffic, as in a study in which the author was involved, which built models to simulate the interaction over time of participants in criminal syndicates (specifically, extortion racket systems; see Fielding, 2016). The 'digital traces' left by various forms of online communication are not subject to first order trust issues of the kind discussed earlier, but remain subject to the possibility that some exchanges may be planted to throw off observers. The existence of the 'dark web' also means that they are subject to selectivity problems (in the organized crime study the information that determined the models was only as good as police intelligence).

DATA DOCUMENTATION

The online environment scores over the offline in some background practical considerations that are, nevertheless, important to robust and illuminating interpretive work. This particularly applies to capturing metadata, to which reference has already been made. Online artefacts often come either with metadata that is automatically assigned to content, or with metadata that can be used to classify and subset the harvested material, such as information about those Twitter users who are happy for their communications to be open to other users. There is no real offline equivalent. Such information has to be collected deliberately in offline work, and to be ethical in the awareness of the person who is its subject. It then has to be laboriously collated with the data. Thus the researcher has to collect 'facesheet'-type information like age, gender, occupation etc. and include it in each data artefact from that individual.

We have already considered several context effects. One way in which the online and the offline superficially coincide is in 'wide context' issues, such as a particular item of data having come into being at a time when a major event has the world's attention, such as the attack on the Twin Towers in 2001. Both the offline and the online may be affected, but participants cannot reliably be expected to make reference to the effect of such things on their response and the researcher may have to make note of it when collecting the data. One difference, though, is that the online environment can make it easier to recover secondary information, like a blog or a series of tweets that refer to the event, and the metadata can provide timing information that allows it to be aligned with response to, say, an asynchronous interview.

THEORY OF ONLINE/OFFLINE DATA COLLECTION

This being a handbook of data collection, the relevance of theory is primarily in respect of the logic and epistemology of method that underlies offline and online qualitative data collection. For decades the underlying epistemology of qualitative fieldwork was that the field offered a 'natural setting' that, provided the researcher did not intrude too much, afforded data that truly represented the nature of the social world. Data was like a butterfly that could simply be 'netted' by recording it in some way (field notes, transcripts, documents). Its meaning was available 'on the surface'. Gradually it came to be accepted that meaning did not lie on the surface but that much interpretive work was needed to discover 'meaning'. Alongside this, it came to be recognized that more than one interpretation was possible. There is no need to reproduce the long process by which relativism began to supplant, or at least jostle with, naturalistic understandings of data. Suffice it to say that the ontological status of qualitative data has increasingly become problematized.

We suspect that there is even greater ontological complexity to be negotiated in working with online data. Where the researcher's interest is in online artefacts of some kind, and they are readily captured, and the analysis does not use them to draw conclusions about offline behaviour or about the intentions or other characteristics of the creator of the online artefact, it is possible to discount ontological concerns about the status of the data. The issue there is whether there is anything particularly interesting in such work outside treatments of the online as genre. For those who do want to infer things about the social world from such material, things are not so easy. One cannot read Kitchin's famous characterization of 'big data' as anything other than declaring greater complexity:

> huge in volume, consisting of terabytes or petabytes of data; high in velocity, being created in or near real-time; diverse in variety, being structured and unstructured in nature; exhaustive in scope, striving to capture entire populations or systems (n=all); fine-grained in resolution ...; relational in nature, containing common fields that enable the conjoining of different data sets; flexible, holding the traits of extensionality (can add new fields easily) and scalability (can expand in size rapidly). (Kitchin, 2014, p. 262)

As well as scale, another principal issue about the nature of online data relates to the several dimensions of untrustworthiness of sources. Offline data can only appeal to direct witnessing through co-presence to claim that it is less subject to untrustworthiness. Whether the greater complexity that online data carry represents a distinct ontological status, or is simply a matter of degree or scale with which already known ontological issues must be negotiated, is not something we can settle here.

Ruppert et al. (2013, pp. 22–3) maintain that digital data, devices and platforms require us to re-think our assumptions about research methods. Amongst them are assumptions about 'transactional actors, heterogeneity, visualization, continuous time, whole populations, granularity, expertise, mobile and mobilizing, and non-coherence'. That is a large, if necessary, undertaking. Contemporary socio-technological understandings acknowledge that technologies like digital devices are shaped by social processes while also acting as agents that shape such processes. The field presently offers no definitive view of the implications this bears for qualitative work with online data. One of the principal tokens under debate relates to another dimension of trust. Like other fields of scholarship, recent years have seen social research take a hard 'knock' from the public. Whether it is the assistance that academics have given large corporations in exploiting sentiment analysis for marketing reasons or the failure of polls to correctly predict the outcome of elections and referenda, trust has fallen in research integrity, in the reliability and validity of data sources, in the persistence of online materials, in authors to narrate trustworthy stories, and in decision makers to weigh research evidence. Against this, the digital environment brings technical means to make the research transparency agenda a reality, for example, through open government websites and through journals increasingly hosting the data supporting the articles they publish. There are other ways in which the transparency afforded by digital media can serve as proxy for traditional criteria of trustworthiness. For instance, qualitative software and many other kinds of digital tools are 'self-documenting' in the sense that they make a record of program operations as they are performed, such that if queries are raised the process can be inspected.

This is not to foreshorten the debate flowing from Ruppert et al. (2013). It is not only worthwhile but also necessary to reassess the long-established assumptions that come to us from the legacy of offline methods. It is quite possible that such a reassessment would find that certain epistemological characteristics of the online research environment were in fact presaged by understandings that were put forward before the digital domain existed. An example can be taken from the field's engagement with the concept of the 'transactional actor'. Featuring in it are issues relating to perspectival subjectivity, standpoint and the slipperiness associated with the chronological fact that research interventions occur in real time and, since human agents can respond to research by altering their behaviour, no two interventions can study precisely the same configuration of the social world. Yet there are nevertheless ways in which such considerations play differently in the digital environment. We might take as an example the mundane experience where 'Fred' is responding to 'Ashley's' email to a discussion forum in the course of which a further email is received from 'Ashley', or an email arrives from 'Janice' commenting on 'Ashley's' email. We may be able to trace the revisions as Fred hurriedly rewrites his original response in light of the incoming emails, but we still cannot know what was in Fred's head as the emails came in, or, at least, can only infer Fred's thought process using the tools of the offline researcher (asking Fred what he was thinking). While the discourse in that scenario is mediated in ways that lack precise equivalents in the offline social world, that does not mean that pre-digital researchers did not realize that discourse can be mediated.

Ruppert et al. (2013) also highlight visualization, the digital tools designed to convey complex relationships via infographics. Infographics representing the body count in the Iraq war demonstrate not only communicative power but also the ability to distort reality in similar ways to earlier offline reportage. Compare, for example, the graphic 'Iraq's Bloody Toll', by Simon Scarr, published in the *South China Morning Post* (www.scmp.com/infographics/article/1284683/iraqs-bloody-toll) on 17 December 2011, with the very different impression given by a simple change in graphical rendering by Andy Cotgreave, published online as 'Iraq: Deaths on the Decline' (at http://gravyanecdote.com/uncategorized/should-you-trust-a-data-visualisation/) on 16 October 2014. Writing of the invention of the telegraph, Marx declared that it had conveyed more misinformation in a single day than had been disseminated by the Christian religion in the whole of its history. Perhaps the difference between offline/online visualization is just that a distorted understanding reaches more people more quickly. The safe conclusion to draw is that we need to systematically explore how the online and offline worlds display both semantically significant technical differences and thematic recurrence in understandings of the status of 'data'. That is an effort the field has only just begun.

However, one way in which the practical reality of online research is becoming differentiated from the offline environment is how digital resources enable the practice of team-based research. Team-based research is increasingly common both because of changes in the nature of data ('big data', real-time data etc.) and because digital tools make it possible for geographically dispersed researchers to collaborate around data. Team-based research often involves combining the offline and the online. If the meta-narrative of data collection involves data making themselves accountable to the researcher, and vice versa, a team-based practice of qualitative research amplifies the accountability because researchers must make their data, and their take on the data, trustworthy to other team members. Paulus (2016) describes the process involved in a collaboration of US-based and New Zealand-based researchers as a demanding but stimulating mix of the online and offline. As the team negotiated the shape of the project and how they would need to 'train' each other in their respective skills (specifically, varying expertise in the software to be used) it was realized that a face-to-face meeting was needed. The distance involved meant that the meeting would last several days to warrant the travel time invested. Work then proceeded digitally, but punctuated with further face-to-face meetings at key stages, held together by regular synchronous 'meetings' via Skype. Other accounts of dispersed collaborations found the qualitative software program 'Transana MU' adequate to support all the stages of data collection and analysis, the difference being that the collaboration involved only two researchers, one of whom was the developer of the program, and who already knew each other well. Also a factor was that the data were video clips of broadcast material relating to the UK banking crisis following the collapse of the US sub-prime mortgage market. Thus, it was not a matter of agreeing how to collect and manage the data but one where the UK partner needed to explain to the US partner who the people were in the data they collected.

Davidson (2016) identifies several stages in the transparency process – Triage, Showing and Reflecting. Taking the example of a study of 'sexting' by young people, the Triage step found a large middle ground where youths identified texts with sexual references as neither bad nor good but as contextual discussions, such as texts discussing how prevalent sexting was amongst their peers. The Showing stage involved the research team sharing codes, drilling down to the raw data and comparing their interpretations. The Reflecting stage applied interpretations drawn from the perspective of the different disciplines represented in the research team and culminating in a conceptualization based on the need to take a youth-centric perspective, working from the realization that young people themselves do not refer to 'sexting' either as a label or as a discrete kind of communication. Davidson also makes the valuable observation that the database representing the data collection component of a project can only be integrated with the data analysis stage if the two are developed in tandem throughout the full project, with the Triage, Showing and Reflecting stages being repeated regularly as a collective activity amongst team members. This is, of course, a team research version of Becker's 'sequential analysis' noted earlier.

ETHICS, LIMITS AND CONSTRAINTS

It is not the intention here to add to the reams of literature already existing on the ethics of social research (see Mertens, Chapter 3, this volume). What is worth noting is that new digital tools bring new instantiations of ethical dilemmas (see Tiidenberg, Chapter 30, this volume). We might take the case of 'Yik Yak', a social media tool facilitating communication in closed groups called 'herds' (Byrne, 2016). Herd members post opinion pieces to the program and members of their herd make upvotes and downvotes on the posts; five downvotes removes a message from the feed. The ethical issue is whether this is public or private communication. Herd members have anonymity, and the tool explicitly exists to debate sensitive matters. The terms of service say that anyone can use or re-post a message and the program itself sends 'hot yaks' to news organizations. The researcher can participate but cannot disclose their presence as a researcher because they would have to do so on every thread each time it appeared, and threads disappear after a time. There is no offline equivalent of the ethics issues here.

CONCLUSION: LIMITS AND CONSTRAINTS IN COMBINING ONLINE AND OFFLINE

Insofar as discussions of method are helpful in attending to fine-grained examination of the situated material practices of the researcher, it is important to include in those practices the intrusion of pragmatic constraints that include such mundane but impactful issues as deadline pressure and technological malfunctions. Moreover, rather than speak in the abstract of 'the researcher' we must also acknowledge the play of political economy on research, such that access to technologies necessary for research is not uniform but differently privileged both across and within societies. Writing of the practice of social network analysis – a field of research that has become increasingly heavily dependent on online resources and online content – Cavanagh (2013) makes the point that a distinct Internet version of the social network has come to stand for *all* network relations, including social and kinship networks. It only takes a moment's reflection to recognize that networks involving kin are different from networks of online interactants. There is a rich and multiplex character to the offline relations that, if pre-existing, can certainly be facilitated and deepened by making use of online resources, but there is a long way to go before online networks can approach in richness and complexity the relationships one has with one's parents, children and pets.

Cavanagh makes her point with respect to the 'flat ontology' that predominates in readings of networks based on Actor Network Theory and that is empirically demonstrated in analysis of data from the social media of online networks. She further argues that if we start from the 'fissured and relational' textures of the offline social world we are led to a fuller examination of social hierarchies and structural constraints than if we start with conceptualizations that reflect the formats of online interaction. In its effects on practical realities, the political economy of research demonstrates the 'durability of the offline in its physical and institutional forms' and the 'friction of existing institutional orders that constrain the potential freedoms and empowerment associated with the web' (Webster, 2013, p. 228). This is a fruitful agenda for future work as the field comes to terms with the new affordances of data collection in an online world.

FURTHER READING

Fielding, Nigel, Lee, Raymond, and Blank, Grant (eds.) (2017) *The Sage Handbook of Online Research Methods* (2nd edn). London: Sage.

Orton-Johnson, Kate and Prior, Nick (eds.) (2013) *Digital Sociology*. Basingstoke: Palgrave Macmillan.

Ruppert E., Law J., and Savage M. (2013) 'Reassembling social science methods', *Theory, Culture and Society*, 30 (4): 22–46.

REFERENCES

Abrams, Kate (2017) 'Online focus groups', in Nigel Fielding, Raymond M. Lee and Grant Blank (eds.) *The Sage Handbook of Online Research Methods* (2nd edn). London: Sage, pp. 435–50.

Becker, Howard S. (1970) *Sociological Work*. Chicago, IL: Aldine.

Brent, Ed (2017) 'Artificial intelligence/expert systems and online research', in Nigel Fielding, Raymond M. Lee and Grant Blank (eds.), *The Sage Handbook of Online Research Methods* (2nd edn). London: Sage, pp. 361–80.

Buscher, Monika, Urry, John and Witchger, Katian (eds.) (2011) *Mobile Methods*. London: Routledge.

Byrne, Caitlin (2016) 'Anonymous social media and qualitative inquiry', panel presentation, *International Congress of Qualitative Inquiry*, 20 May 2016, Urbana-Champaign, IL.

Carson, R. and Csikszentmihalyi, M. (1983) 'The experiential sampling method', *New Directions for Methodology of Social and Behavioural Science*, 15: 41–56.

Cavanagh, Allison (2013) 'Imagining networks: The sociology of connection in the digital age', in Kate Orton-Johnson and Nick Prior (eds.), *Digital Sociology*. Basingstoke: Palgrave Macmillan, pp. 169–85.

Davidson, Judith (2016) 'Negotiating digital tools in complex research teams', panel presentation, *International Congress of Qualitative Inquiry*, 20 May 2016, Urbana-Champaign, IL.

Fielding, Nigel (2008) 'The role of computer-assisted qualitative data analysis: Impact on emergent methods in qualitative research', in Sharlene Hesse-Biber and Patricia Leavy (eds), *Handbook of Emergent Methods*. New York: The Guilford Press, pp. 655–73.

Fielding, N. (2009) 'Going out on a limb: Postmodernism and multiple method research', *Current Sociology*, 57 (3): 427–47.

Fielding, N. (2016) 'The shaping of covert social networks: Isolating the effects of secrecy', *Trends in Organized Crime*. DOI: 10.1007/s12117-016-9277-0. Retrieved from http://link.springer.com/article/10.1007/s12117-016-9277-0.

Fielding, J. and Fielding, N. (2013) 'Integrating information from multiple methods into the analysis of perceived risk of crime: The role of georeferenced field data and mobile methods', *Journal of Criminology*, Volume 2013, DOI: 10.1155/2013/284259. Open Access.

Gilbert, Linda S., Jackson, Kristi, and di Gregorio, Sylvana (2014) 'Tools for analysing qualitative data: The history and relevance of qualitative data analysis software', in J. Michael Spector, M., Merrill, M.D., Elen, J., and Bishop, M.J. (eds.), *Handbook of Research on Educational Communications and Technology* (4th edn). New York: Springer, pp. 221–36.

Gubrium, Jaber (2003) *Postmodern Interviewing*. London: Sage.

Hindmarsh, Jon (2017) 'Tools for collaboration in video-based research', in Nigel Fielding, Raymond M. Lee and Grant Blank (eds.), *The Sage Handbook of Online Research Methods* (2nd edn). London: Sage, pp. 451–69.

Kitchin, I. (2014) 'Big data, new epistemologies and paradigm shifts', *Big Data & Society*, 1(1). Retrieved from http://doi.org/10.1177/2053951714528481.

Kramer, A., Guillory, J., and Hancock, J. (2014) 'Experimental evidence of massive-scale emotional contagion through social networks', *Proceedings of the National Academy of Sciences*, 111 (24): 8788–90.

Lee, Raymond (2000) *Unobtrusive Methods in Social Research*. Milton Keynes: Open University Press.

Lee, R. (2004) 'Recording technologies and the interview in sociology', *Sociology*, 38 (5): 869–89.

Lyman, Stanford and Scott, Marvin (1989) *A Sociology of the Absurd*. New York: Rowman & Littlefield.

Orton-Johnson, Kate (2013) 'Mediating the digital', in Kate Orton-Johnson and Nick Prior (eds.), *Digital Sociology*. Basingstoke: Palgrave Macmillan, pp. 186–93.

Orton-Johnson, Kate and Prior, Nick (2013) 'Introduction', in Kate Orton-Johnson and Nick Prior (eds.), *Digital Sociology*. Basingstoke: Palgrave Macmillan, pp. 1–9.

Paulus, Trena (2016) 'Teaching and Learning Qualitative Research at a Distance', panel presentation, *International Congress of Qualitative Inquiry*, 20 May 2016, Urbana-Champaign, IL.

Paulus, T. and. Lester, J. N. (2016) 'ATLAS.ti for conversation and discourse analysis studies', *International Journal of Social Research Methodology*, 19 (4): 405–28.

Ruppert, E., Law, J., and Savage, M. (2013) 'Reassembling social science methods', *Theory, Culture and Society*, 30 (4): 22–46.

Thelwall, Mike (2017), 'Sentiment Analysis for Small and Big Data', in Nigel Fielding, Raymond M. Lee and Grant Blank (eds.), *The SAGE Handbook of Online Research Methods,* London: Sage, pp. 344–360.

Webster, Andrew (2013) 'Digital technology and sociological windows', in Kate Orton-Johnson and Nick Prior (eds.), *Digital Sociology*. Basingstoke: Palgrave Macmillan, pp. 227–33.

Using Photographs in Interviews: When We Lack the Words to Say What Practice Means

Karen Henwood, Fiona Shirani and Christopher Groves

INTRODUCTION

Social scientific research is highly reliant on its awareness, and means, of addressing relevant methodological questions; and, increasingly, demonstrating methodological prowess is part of working as an accomplished social scientist. But knowing how to conduct research in methodologically rigorous, insightful and creative ways is not always well understood, nor the skilled practices involved easily acquired.

Assumptions can become so embedded in social research's mainstream that non-standard approaches have evolved to help question 'what everyone at first just considered, how they thought knowledge was validated, and what they thought reality was' (Hopf, 2008, p. 289). Various *turns* (qualitative, linguistic, discursive, narrative, interpretivist, practice-led, object-focused, material and psychosocial) – which have also been called periods or moments in the evolution of qualitative social science (Denzin and Lincoln, 2011) – have been depicted in accounts of how it is possible to approach the production of social scientific knowledge in a variety of different ways. This list of turns is not exhaustive, but it is lengthy enough to show just how many different, designated efforts have been made to find ways of furthering methodological exploration and diversity, and to make the adoption of each turn's particular way of staking or destabilising knowledge claims more convincing. Whilst it is not possible, or necessary here, to itemise or scrutinise such claims in and of themselves, it is important to acknowledge that developing interpretivist practices in empirical inquiry in ways that build on – rather than completely displace – the linguistic turn, continues to be at the heart of both our own research and that of other social researchers (see, for example, Taylor and McEvoy, 2015).

Linguistically aware research is very much part of the epistemological background to qualitative research in the social sciences, providing the means of using talk and text to generate understanding of processes involved in the social construction of versions of reality (Flick, 2006). Different styles or formats for generating interview data have proliferated and epistemic reflexivity about such matters is also part of qualitative ways of knowing, where the written word is no longer considered the central authority adjudicating on questions of rationality, truth and reason (Henwood, 2004). Although such linguistically attuned research gives priority to understanding the complexities of representational practices, the purpose of so doing is not simply to blur boundaries between more experimental and conventional reflexivity and writing genres (Seale, 1999). Rather, such understanding is a methodological requirement of research geared towards investigating the empirical world in ways that do not simply reduce it to a set of pre-given entities.

The linguistic sensibility of qualitative research rests, to some degree, on practitioners' acceptance of the potentials afforded by ideas for cultivating mediated forms of sensemaking (Wetherell et al., 2001) for example, through narrative (see Murray, Chapter 17, this volume) and images (see Eberle, Chapter 25, this volume). Interpretive researchers are then better equipped to grasp socially, culturally and historically embedded understandings of events, interactions, and processes making up the real world, and the contribution they make to social science investigations and understandings. Bringing resources that promote sensemaking centre stage is a means of contextualising accounts of how social activity is done. As a result, qualitative researchers become better able to study processes that are neither physical nor cultural, but are capable of producing understandings of a world that is simultaneously material and signified.

Whilst not all methodologically inspired qualitative research derives its ideas, arguments and methods of working directly from such linguistic frameworks, their more generic importance lies in how they have further bolstered a broad interest in studying the practicalities, situatedness, contextualisation and accountability of everyday life. Everyday life continues to fascinate as an object of study across diverse social science disciplines, prompting developments that link qualitative social science methodology with theoretical understanding of domains and systems of practice (social, environmental, domestic, mobile to name but a few) (see, for example, Maller and Strengers, 2013). Such knowledge of what passes as ordinary – because it is recursively part of everyday living – depends on asking questions about the character of tacit knowledge, mundane routines, embodied dispositions (as is particularly the case in writing about the legacy of Bourdieu). But, more importantly in our view, it has become a pivotal resource for finding ways to pose new empirical questions that are capable of directing investigations into some of the most intractable problems faced by both contemporary societies and individuals in their lives today. For us, along with many other researchers working at the social-environmental-technical interface, these are questions about environmental risk and resource depletion, sustainable transitions and the dynamics of social and technical change. Since 2011, we have been working on questions about everyday energy consumption, including from an environmental policy perspective where there is an explicit commitment to energy demand reduction as part of moving to a more sustainable future. We have made efforts to open up understanding of such problems through different methodological approaches. As such, methodological advance has been central to our intellectual project through combining more traditional skills in talk and text inquiry methods with an interest in visual data, visualisation practices and, more specifically, photo-elicitation methods (see Eberle, Chapter 25, this volume).

For our 'Energy Biographies' study (detailed below) we designed qualitative longitudinal interviews to bring out participants' perceptions, beliefs, values and intersubjective understandings of their everyday energy use in ways that were meaningful to them. The interviews generated data about various practical domains (such as home and family, leisure activities, travel to and from work) where everyday energy use contributed to maintaining what was, for our participants, a life worth living. But we also needed to embrace intellectual concerns about *how to study everyday practices in ways that interviewees could talk about*, given that elements of practices reside in the background of everyday life and so are not routinely available to conscious awareness. We sought means of studying mundane routines of everyday life as entangled practices (i.e. patterned activities comprising skills, technology and norms) embedded in wider socio-technical systems, but extended to encompass life-course, relational and sociocultural dynamics, and raising questions about identity formation and subjectivity (Groves et al., 2015, 2016a, 2016b; Henwood et al., 2015, 2016). We have also positioned our work as building on the strengths of qualitative research approaches so that practical assemblages of meaning-making are understood as involving *material and human* components. What matters to people when energy's perceptual status changes to include its materiality, since this no longer passes unnoticed or as inconsequential? Through our talk- and text-based, but visually enhanced methods, we have brought to the foreground the meaningful attachments people can make to everyday objects and devices that use energy, and how they perceive the wider energy-supplying infrastructure on which their lives routinely depend.

In what follows, we continue to explore the value we see in locating our own empirical studies in the ever-widening field of qualitative, interpretivist social science (Yanow and Schwartz-Shea, 2006). This utilises situated, everyday meaning-making, along with the dynamics and effects of discursive or wider cultural framings, as its sources of research data, and as a means of generating insight in ways that can contribute to bodies of substantive knowledge (Henwood and Pidgeon, 2015). The chapter engages critically with issues arising from our own methodologically innovative research, which has adopted a carefully crafted portfolio of qualitative longitudinal, multimodal and narrative interview methods in the rapidly developing research on sustainable energy transitions and everyday resource consumption. Drawing on multi-focus and multiple methods is a key research resource in contemporary approaches to social science research (Flick, 2006), but has to be approached as a complex, evolving methodological issue and address questions about the creative, yet rigorous, nature of study design. The chapter focuses in particular on the challenges and possibilities of bringing out the affordances of using participant-generated photographs with interview data. It makes reference to wider-ranging debates occurring in the UK and internationally about how to engage study participants so that they are able to comment on their own and others' everyday practices – in this case, ones with environmental significance. Our exemplar study discusses how to encompass multimodal data so that it is possible to approach the emergent possibilities such data afford, reflecting wider debates about what it means to approach mixed methods research in a qualitatively driven way (Mason, 2006).

MAKING THE INTANGIBLE VISIBLE IN STUDIES OF EVERYDAY ENERGY USE AND SUSTAINABLE PRACTICE

There is increasing interest in studies endeavouring to reach 'beyond' verbal language, seeking close-up knowledge of multiple meaning-making activities, and deploying multimodal methods (Reavey, 2011). Such approaches attend to a variety of modes that surround us (visual, verbal, bodily, audio, spatial) and the complex interplay between the meaning-making resources that are part of our experience (Dicks, 2014). To enhance understandings of important facets of everyday living (e.g. embodiment, environmental (dis)connectedness, conflicted identities), it has been suggested that approaches foregrounding multiple meanings meet the phenomenological aim of eliciting rich descriptions of lived experience (Bowes-Catton et al., 2011). Visual research methods form an important element of such experientially aligned, multimodal approaches, with photo-elicitation particularly well established and remaining an enduringly popular approach.

This chapter considers the merits of visual research methods in the context of our work on Energy Biographies – a large qualitative longitudinal research study that sought to explore everyday experiences and understandings of energy in the context of personal biographies. One of the key benefits emphasised by proponents of photo-elicitation is that images can help researchers to get at aspects of life that may otherwise remain invisible (Jewitt, 2012). How to make the invisible tangible is also an important concern for energy research, given conceptualisations of energy's invisibility (Burgess and Nye, 2008). Some highly significant efforts already exist in relation to energy and the sensory home (Pierce and Paulos, 2010; Pink, 2012). Visual methods have an unharnessed potential to make an important contribution in this field of research, engaging people in other potentially exciting, meaningful and productive ways (Bowden et al., 2015). Here we predominantly focus on one of the project's photo-elicitation activities, a second photograph and video task has been discussed in more detail elsewhere (Shirani et al., 2015b).

USING IMAGES IN RESEARCH

Visual methods have been described as the 'oldest new methods in qualitative research' (Travers, 2011, p. 5) but whilst photographs have been a central aspect of some sociologists' work for decades, visual research methods have experienced a sudden surge in popularity (Rose, 2014). Rose (2014) outlines three specific strengths of visual research methods that have been highlighted in the literature to date. First, they are argued to be effective in generating evidence that other methods cannot; second, they are particularly helpful in exploring the taken-for-granted things in participants' lives, and third; they are inherently collaborative. We consider each of these issues in turn.

Innovation is a significant feature of UK social science, particularly in the context of funders' expectations of methodological development (Taylor and Coffey, 2008). The increasing use of visual and multimodal methods – including those which utilise digital technologies – and the interweaving of social science with arts-based practices, mean qualitative research has been at the forefront of methodological creativity (Coffey, 2011). The use of photographs in particular has gained prominence in qualitative research, with studies forming a continuum from those that regard the image as data of itself, to those that use the image as a device to elicit talk. The latter appears to be a more popular approach, as Tinkler notes:

> For many researchers, the attraction of using participant-generated photography is that it is a means to get participants talking. People are often keen to talk about the photos they have taken and this facilitates discussion about aspects of their lives and experiences that might otherwise be difficult to explore. (2013, p. 151)

In this approach to photo-elicitation, visual methods are adopted because they are an activity, whilst visual properties are treated as incidental (Allan and Tinkler, 2015). Taking a 'traditionalist' approach then, showing an image is not in itself sociology, it only becomes so with a lot of explanatory text (Travers, 2011). Although some have been critical of this apparent disregard for the visual nature of the image, much has been made of the fruitful discussions that images can produce. For example, rather than describing the image, justifying the act of picturing (Radley, 2011) can encourage deep reflection about what it means to the participant, opening up discussion beyond the boundaries defined by the researcher. As Bolton et al. (2001) found, placing photography alongside other forms and sources of data and by contrasting the snapshot effect of photography with a longitudinal time-scale, they could include what lay 'beyond the frame'. Similarly, Croghan et al. (2008) contend that the photographic image allows participants to introduce new and possibly contentious topics in ways that are not possible in a purely verbal exchange. In this way, visual methods are advocated because of their ability to generate data that would not be possible to access with other approaches. Although, some have pointed to the paradox of advocating the unique ability of visual methods to convey information in ways not possible through words, written context is required to make the effects of the visual approaches evident (Rose, 2007).

One contended advantage of images is the ability to access the taken-for-granted aspects of everyday life. For example, Sweetman (2009) suggests that visual methods may be particularly well suited to investigating aspects of everyday lives that may be difficult to recognise or articulate. Thus, there is potential to make an original contribution through utilising visual methods to explore the implicit knowledges in everyday practices (Rose, 2014). This is particularly relevant in relation to investigating how energy is consumed in the home and workplace. How we use energy is dependent on practices that have material elements, including both devices and infrastructures. Whilst devices may fade into the background of everyday life somewhat, unless they malfunction, infrastructures are generally still less tangible. The need to render these material elements more visible and available for interpretation has thus been widely articulated by social scientists interested in energy (e.g. Shove, 1997; Strengers, 2011).

An important argument for visual methods has been their potential to shift the power balance of the research encounter, positioning the participant as 'expert' in explaining their images to the researcher (Liebenberg, 2009). Whilst this may be particularly beneficial when working with disempowered groups, the ability for participants to direct the research could have a wider appeal for making research participation a more engaging experience. For example, Richards (2011) suggests that visual methods are a particularly good way of increasing and sustaining participants' involvement in a research project because they are accessible to all and can also be fun. We suggest that visual approaches are therefore particularly useful in qualitative longitudinal research as they can help to sustain participant engagement over an extended time period (Weller, 2012; Shirani et al., 2015b).

MULTIMODALITY IN QUALITATIVE LONGITUDINAL RESEARCH

Many of the arguments surrounding visual methods take on a particular resonance in the context of qualitative longitudinal research (hereafter QLR). Alongside the surge in popularity of visual research methods there has been increasing interest from researchers and funders in QLR as part of a temporal turn within the social sciences (Thomson and McLeod, 2015). The current iteration of QLR coincides with new questions about how the 'empirical' is produced and understood within a digital landscape (Adkins and Lury, 2009; Thomson and McLeod, 2015), with digital technologies representing new possibilities for engaging participants. Arguments around methodological innovation are also pertinent within a QLR context, given that innovation and adaptation feature as trademarks of much

QLR (Weller, 2012). As Holland et al. (2006, p. 38) argue 'In order for a QLL study to remain creative and productive it is vital that new ideas, theories and methodologies are drawn into it.' Relatively little has been written about the use of visual or multimodal methods within longitudinal research, yet QLR provides more scope for methodological innovation and experimentation than other forms of qualitative research, given its extended timescales and inherent flexibility (Holland et al., 2006).[1] For example, whilst some multimodal activities may take up too much time to include in a one-off research design, there is greater opportunity to include them in a QLR design with multiple research encounters (Shirani et al., 2015b). The time and space for reflection and innovation is a key advantage of QLR, allowing researchers to adopt multiple methodological approaches, or hone in on and recognise the diversity and shifting nature of participants' interests and popular cultures of communication (Weller, 2012).

METHODS OF THE ENERGY BIOGRAPHIES PROJECT

This chapter presents data from Energy Biographies,[2] a qualitative longitudinal and multimodal study that aimed to explore everyday energy use in the context of past experiences and anticipated futures. Energy Biographies involved four diverse case sites across Wales and London: Ely and Caerau, a large inner-city ward of Cardiff; Peterston-Super-Ely, an affluent commuter village on the outskirts of Cardiff; Lammas Tir-y-Gafel, a low-impact, off-grid ecovillage in Pembrokeshire, west Wales; and the Royal Free Hospital, a large teaching hospital in North London. Between December 2011 and May 2012, 72 people were interviewed across the four case sites. A subsample of 36 people (again from across the four case sites) took part in two further qualitative longitudinal interviews, 6 and 12 months after the first. One of the project aims was to explore the utility of innovative (narrative, longitudinal and visual) methodological approaches for engaging people with their own energy practices. Therefore, in addition to the longitudinal narrative interviews, participants were also asked to participate in visual activities, the focus of this chapter.

The first activity was a photo-elicitation exercise. Participants were given camera phones and an instruction sheet, which asked them to take pictures relating to four themes: home and garden, out and about (including work), having fun and travel. Each theme related to a two-week calendar period and participants were sent a reminder of that fortnight's theme via text message. Researchers did not see the images until they returned for the second interview, when the pictures were loaded onto a laptop to be viewed and discussed simultaneously. This led to the second interviews being much more participant-directed as they took the role of 'expert' in explaining the images to the researcher (Rose, 2014), with this discussion forming the bulk of the second interviews. This task, therefore, was largely designed to elicit talk, rather than to produce images as objects of analysis.

Between the second and third interviews, participants undertook a text-prompted photo task. On ten occasions (the same dates and times across all case sites), participants were asked to take a picture of what they were doing and return this to the research team. Images and any accompanying captions were then put into photo timelines and taken back to participants for discussion during the third interview. Along with a video task, this photograph activity was particularly useful for prompting talk about anticipated futures (Shirani et al., 2015b).

Data Extracts from Energy Biographies

The photo-elicitation activity produced over 2,000 images, which presents a significant

Figure 38.1 Laura's bike seats

analytic challenge. As discussed above, the activity was designed to elicit talk rather than to produce images for stand-alone analysis, so here we present a selection of images and the accompanying extracts of interview discussion. We focus here on images that relate loosely to the theme of waste, which was an important issue to emerge from initial interviews (see Thomas et al., 2017) for discussion.

Laura

> I took it thinking oh yes I'm an eco person I have these on the back of our bikes but the ironic thing is I don't really use them anymore because when I was in the city it was really great to get around on bike everywhere and we used them a lot, it was great fun. But now we're living in the countryside we use the car all the time because the distances are just so much further apart ... It's a lie! That photo's a lie! [Laughs] ... But yeah so whereas we're more reliant on the car we don't, we use our own water, we deal with our own waste, we grow a lot of our own food, we have a lot of our own electricity so I think on balance, well I know for a fact because every year we have to do a carbon footprint analysis so yeah it is way down, way way down ... Ok oh and that little thing there that's a jam jar and it's got a cheque in for £12 and every week we get a £12 box of organic veg delivered from the local organic veg distribution but just recently I made the drastic measure of cancelling it because we're starting to, we've got so much ... so I just decided to cancel it so that's quite exciting actually! (Laura, Lammas; see Figure 38.1)

At first glance, the image of the bicycle seats would seem to signify Laura's identity as an 'eco person', yet her accompanying narrative highlights some of the challenges she has encountered in maintaining the environmentally friendly practices adopted when living in a city, now that she is living in an isolated ecovillage where all householders grow their own food as part of their land-based livelihood, but live in a rural location with different transport infrastructure. Whilst the increasing car use is potentially problematic, Laura counters this with a discussion of the many areas of life where she has become more sustainable, so 'on balance' the family's energy usage is well below average. The jam jar on the edge of the picture represents some of Laura's achievements in her efforts to live more sustainably – she has become so successful in growing her own food that she is able to take the 'drastic' measure of cancelling the family's vegetable order.

Making changes to energy practices is a recognisably important sustainable energy issue, which we have considered in our wider analysis by drawing out identity dynamics surrounding change in different temporal perspectives (Groves et al., 2015; Henwood et al., 2016). Laura's data is itself insightful in relation to these issues, indicating possibilities of change from within the perspective of her unusual, ordinary life.

In methodological terms, this image and accompanying text demonstrate how the photograph task made visible aspects of everyday life that appeared to conflict with the taker's sense of identity. Here, Laura 'took it thinking oh yes I'm an eco person' but discussion illuminates one way in which she feels her life has become less 'eco' since the move to the ecovillage. This extract represents the value of the image task for prompting reflections that go further than what is represented in the image itself. For example, Laura's comment that 'that photo's a lie!' indicates how her talk goes beyond what is depicted to discuss issues that are potentially challenging, suggesting that the accompanying talk is important for understanding what the participant is trying to convey with this image. This may be influenced by the design of the task to elicit talk, rather than to generate images to analyse independently.

Peter

Peter: that's the gas, that's the LPG ... that's the glaring, its bright red really isn't it? ... we use about 80 kilos a year which probably in the scheme of things isn't very much and particularly compared to the amount of diesel that the car burns its nothing but still you know it still is a part of it.

Interviewer: Do you think you're more conscious of ... your use of gas than say someone living in a sort of more conventional setting and being linked to mains gas?

Peter: Yeah definitely yeah but again that's to do with direct, you know, just direct contact with it, so if we had a gas pipe that came in here for example we'd be much less aware of the amount that we use, that we have to lug these 20 kilogram bottles round the back of the house every four months you know makes us really kind of aware of how much gas we use, its quite good in that way, yeah. (Peter, Lammas; see Figure 38.2)

The canister, and arrangements for its use, makes gas use particularly visible and measurable to Peter as it gives him 'direct contact' with the gas supply for his family's home, in contrast to those in more conventional housing where it is 'piped in' and therefore not something that has to be thought about in the same way. This visibility is increasingly important as a research topic as distinctions become less clear-cut between centralised energy production and storage and localised consumption.

The 'glaring' 'bright red' canister is highlighted in the image by it's contrast with the rural surroundings and natural materials of the house. Although the gas use is not ideal for Peter, he notes that 'in the scheme of things [it] isn't very much' given their other efforts, which shows similarities to Laura's account and justification of their overall efforts to live sustainably. By making visible this aspect of everyday energy use, Peter's photograph prompts discussion about the family's gas use and the way in which the work surrounding this, which would not need to be undertaken in conventional housing, piques his awareness of this aspect of energy use. In this case, his narrative relates relatively straightforwardly to what is depicted, suggesting that some images may have greater potential to be used independently of the accompanying text than others.

Figure 38.2   Peter's gas canister

Christine and Jeremy

These two images of greenhouses, whilst appearing quite similar, prompted different thoughts from their respective creators.

> That's the greenhouse, my husband's got an allotment so that's where he starts all his bits and pieces ... so that was just to show you know sort of being able to use the sun's source to start growing things really because before that they were in on the windowsills, the tomato plants and things like that, so for the sake of you know because they're quite reasonably priced and its plastic so it's safe and so I agreed to have the greenhouse because nobody could get injured ... But when we were caring for his father and everything got a bit too much and he couldn't spend any time over there I did spend a couple of hours trying to help him to clear it up ... the kids have offered, they

each gave him a voucher for his birthday and Father's day two hours of my time for the allotment which is more important than another bottle of beer! ... So and in fact it's got a double, it's a double-edged sword because he started his bits and pieces there, his seedlings there, he takes most to the allotment and grows them and then they come in this huge batch and then we have to freeze them, so we have a huge freezer in the shed with just his fruit and veg in there! [Laughs] (Christine, Ely; see Figure 38.3)

The greenhouse is primarily her husband's hobby, which Christine chose to photograph because it involves using natural resources to grow food, which is seen as a sustainable practice. Images of sun, water and soil were produced by participants across our case site areas, although predominantly at Lammas, to highlight the importance of natural resources. However, Christine's family differs from those at Lammas, as food growing is a hobby rather than a central aspect of food and income provision. Christine's narrative illustrates how this hobby is positioned in relation to family and caring responsibilities, which is a central theme of her account that we have discussed elsewhere (Groves et al., 2015). The greenhouse is accepted because it is a safe material (plastic rather than glass, which could potentially cause injury), but the hobby is neglected when an elderly family member requires care, and the children recognise that offering their time to help is regarded as more valuable than purchasing presents.

As with Laura, the image would initially appear to be a representation of a sustainable practice, yet the accompanying talk elicits a more complex dynamic. Christine describes how they run an additional freezer to store the food produced from the greenhouse and allotment, which has cost and energy implications. Among the issues we have considered in this regard are the ramifications of more-or-less supportive sociocultural narratives about changing energy use, and their negotiation within family relationships. We identify a particular role for care practices involving focused attention as breaking with unsustainable patterning of everyday energy use and consumption practices (Groves et al., 2016b).

In contrast, Jeremy's narrative about his greenhouse image centres on avoiding waste:

This is in our garden and it demonstrates a feature of my lifestyle par excellence in that I'm a fix-it, re-use it man and this actually was in the garden of our neighbours over the back ... they were talking quite a lot about getting rid of it and we said 'look if you're going to get rid of it we'll have it' ... it was able to be taken apart entirely, couldn't take the wooden structure apart because the screws and bolts were all rusted up, took all the glass out, unbolted it from the concrete base and at the suggestion of one of our friends got a couple of straight ladders and lashed it to the ladders ... then about eight people lifted it off the ground and passed it over the hedges of the gardens until it got into our garden. And then I re-did the base, fitted the concrete blocks, re-did bolts for that, we treated it and I got, I cut well quite a lot of the broken glass, the big bits to make little bits where it was broken and got some plastic sheets to put in it and they still make them in this model, firm is still there so I got some new kit for the rolling doors. So £2000 worth of greenhouse for £100 and quite a lot of weekends' effort but you know the satisfaction of there it is you know and its 45 years old, something like that but it's you know it's very good, it's hard wood very good quality. (Jeremy, Peterston; see Figure 38.4)

In this extract Jeremy gives a detailed description of his efforts to avoid waste by refurbishing an unwanted greenhouse.

Figure 38.3 Christine's greenhouse

Figure 38.4 Jeremy's greenhouse

Although the process was time-consuming and labour-intensive, it was considerably cheaper and more satisfying than purchasing new. Satisfactions of this kind are among the varied and textured meanings of waste, already elucidated in our own work on energy transitions (Thomas et al., in press), and of concern to ongoing research focusing on materials change and the circular economy (Goodwin et al., unpublished).

Undertaking these kinds of activities is part of Jeremy's identity as a 'fix it, re-use it man', which relates to his long-standing environmentalism (Shirani et al., 2015a). Again, the discussion here goes beyond what is depicted to encompass other aspects of identity, exemplifying something Jeremy sees as an important aspect of his lifestyle. Whilst these two images appear to be very similar, the accompanying text presents quite different accounts. Going beyond what is immediately depicted in the images; talk encompasses the issues of identity and relationships and interconnections with sustainability, which have been pivotal to the Energy Biographies project more widely. The images produced and their accompanying discussion therefore helped to corroborate these as important concerns.

Suzanna

I make the clothes ... [mum] washes them and does their hair and looks after them, fixes what needs fixing but they're all naked because I don't know why people give the dolls but don't give the clothes away so I was making, whenever I can I make the clothes and send the clothes back so I have the doll to use as a model. And they do this to raise money for charity but I find instead of sending a perfectly useable, playable doll to the landfill we can just recycle them, use them again, and this one she sent to me there's absolutely nothing wrong with the doll ... so why waste it? It's plastic, this is not going to disappear in the next week or two so instead of making new ones we can, or buying new clothes for the dolls I can just make with what I have at home ... the time that I put on it is very rewarding and I think a lot of people don't realise how rewarding it is ... So to me it's the reward of doing something, I put my time and once you get practice you can make the whole dress in an hour/an hour and a half so it's, but until you build enough practice to get there it might take a week to make a small dress and I think people are not ready to invest in the pleasure that you take from learning something and make something new ... So I think we're becoming detached from what we can give from ourselves because it's so easy to just, why am I going to buy a doll, a second hand doll if for £15 I buy a new one? And then we have vast amounts of very good stuff going to landfills just because people don't even care ... one of the things that they fund with the money not just from the dolls but from, it's a big charity, they have some work with children but they also do some courses for women that live in the slums and one of them is to teach them how to be cleaners ... So it's a, they are small changes but if you put them in the big picture each small change might have an effect on how the whole society is going ... and even if it's something that happens back in South America it might have an impact on us because we are all so dependent on each other and yeah we know that one thing that happens in Asia or in South America and North America can affect how much rain we get or we don't get. So it's a small programme but if we can help it to grow or to happen in many places you know it's better than nothing. (Suzanna, London; see Figure 38.5)

Suzanna's extract shows similarities to Jeremy's account in that she takes something that was going to be thrown away and makes it useable. Again, this requires time and

Figure 38.5 Suzanna's Barbie

effort, a recurring theme brought out by Energy Biographies research into waste, careful practices, and sustainable energy usage (Groves et al., 2016b; Thomas et al., in press). Along with the satisfaction of refurbishing an object, Suzanna finds it 'rewarding' that she can learn and develop a new skill, although recognises that this ethos seems to be at odds with mainstream Western society. In addition to these personal benefits, Suzanna's efforts are to create something that can generate income for a charity, the work of which she sees as having an impact for wider society. This indicates her ability to make a connection between the action she can take in her own life and the impacts for society more widely, which is something many people appear to struggle with (Shirani et al., 2015b). Without being asked to undertake the image task, Suzanna may not have related her account of refurbishing the dolls and, subsequently, her related discussion of various energy and environmental issues arising from this. Again, this image illustrates the importance of the accompanying text for understanding what the participant is trying to convey, but also shows how talk goes beyond what is represented to cover much wider issues, which may not otherwise have arisen.

CONCLUSION

Images can be a powerful tool in research. This chapter concerns using images to elicit talk, a popular approach, but one that has been criticised for sidelining visual aspects of the activity (Allan and Tinkler, 2015). However, this elicitation approach was fruitful in our own research for generating narratives that go beyond what is either represented in the image (what it reflects in the empirical world) or signified by it in a more abstract way (where visual effects require formal analysis of semiotic processes).

In taking images to capture everyday activities relating to energy use, what was made visible became a matter of discussion, creating a multimodal resource for sensemaking. In these ways, matters and concerns that otherwise might have gone unnoticed, or been over-looked because they are intangible in ordinary life, were opened up to inquiry. How to approach studying the nexus of complexities involved in making sustainable transitions, or changing energy practices, is far from obvious. Our visual plus talk (and text) methods enabled us to come to understand what was (potentially) important, and could be brought into view in multiple ways. We were able to explore, among other things, how people evaluated the way their life was going, invested in relationships with others, participated in energy-using practices, negotiated envisioned or unexpected changes, all of which were reflected upon from different perspectives embedded in time and place. All these were sources of 'data', presenting us with interpretive resources we could draw upon and use in analysis.

Working across visual and verbal modalities, attending both to what can be seen and then spoken about, is important in understanding how this methodological approach helped to engage people with their own energy practices. As we look forward, we can see some aspects of our work – on the emotional dimensions of energy attachments – aligning with efforts to investigate how talking about (energy use in) everyday life can be affective and affecting because it is materially part of the practical human activity of sense-making (Wetherell, 2015). Beyond our own research topic, working with images in this way offers opportunity to expand the scope of the interview interaction, allowing participants to have a greater role in directing the flow of talk and raise issues of potential importance that the researcher may not otherwise have considered.

Focusing on using images as an elicitation device for interview talk does not neglect working creatively with the images. Images inspired some of the exhibits for our project at a public exhibition to showcase the work of social science research projects concerned with energy and community.[3] In July 2013 we hosted a workshop to explore multimodal methods in energy research, where a range of presenters were asked to run a short session for colleagues to illustrate the approaches they had used in their own research. In our session we invited these academics to look at a selection of images produced by our participants, initially presented without the accompanying text, in order to explore how they would use and interpret the images alone. Suzanna's Barbie picture was one that people seemed to find particularly interesting, seemingly because it was unexpected in this context and difficult to know without the accompanying text how it related to issues of energy and environment. Feedback from this session suggested that because the images represent the everyday they are accessible, making it possible for people to impose their own interpretations and work creatively to create their own stories. Whilst there are clearly important ethical issues to consider in presenting images without the contextual information of their production and asking others to engage creatively with them, initial efforts suggest it would be possible to work with images in this way, despite the initial intention being to act as an elicitation device.

Multimodal activities may have a particularly useful place in qualitative longitudinal research. For example, the extended timeframes of the research provide greater scope for methodological innovation. Some participants may prefer the chance to direct the focus of the interview that comes with a photo-elicitation exercise, and in a longitudinal study there is opportunity to find out about these preferences and tailor later rounds of data collection accordingly. Longitudinal research requires a significant commitment from participants and maintaining the sample over time is an important concern. Incorporating multimodal activities in an effort to make the experience of participation more engaging may play an important role in keeping participants interested in the research. There was no sample attrition over the course of the Energy Biographies project, which may attest to the success of multimodal activities for sustaining engagement. Additional strategies such as sending reminders by text message of the themes about which we wanted them to take photographs were also described by participants as helping them to sustain interest in the activity. There is further potential in longitudinal research in asking participants to revisit the same image at different time points (e.g. Henwood et al., 2011).

We introduced our chapter by acknowledging various turns in qualitative research contributing to its methodological advance. Iterations in our use of the published literature on textual, visual and multimodal methods directed attention towards how to generate data, along with the benefits of using data in different modalities and formats. Presenting data from our Energy Biographies project showed how insights generated through interpretation of data have been at the heart of our ways of using empirical material (Flick, 2006, p. 294). Our project publications contain further insights about discoveries enabled by reflections on practice through our methodological work. We hope this chapter has piqued further interest in how, by evoking – or indeed inspiring – a creative and enhanced response to visual probes and photographic images, they can be an effective force for generating evidence in ways that talk and text methods alone cannot, by exploring the taken-for-granted things in participants' lives, and facilitating collaborative research.

Notes

1 See also http://bigqlr.ncrm.ac.uk/2016/04/25/guest-post-2/
2 See www.energybiographies.org for more detail
3 http://energybiographies.org/our-work/exhibition-2/

ACKNOWLEDGEMENTS

This chapter was prepared with support from the ESRC (RES-628-25-0028) and WEFO (511381-2). It is part of long-standing teamwork undertaken by the Cardiff University Understanding Risk Group (URG), Cardiff University. In addition to acknowledging the generous funding provided from the above sources, and that has assisted us in developing our methodological interests, we extend special thanks to Professor Nick Pidgeon (Director, URG) who has facilitated our work over a sustained period of time.

FURTHER READING

Henwood, Karen and Shirani, Fiona (2012) 'Researching the temporal', in Harris Cooper, Paul M. Camic, Debra L. Long, A. T. Panter, David Rindskopf, and Kenneth J. Sher (eds.), *APA Handbook of Research Methods in Psychology, Vol 2: Research Designs: Quantitative, Qualitative, Neuropsychological, and Biological.* Washington, DC: American Psychological Association, pp. 209–23.

Hitchings, R. (2012) 'People can talk about their practices', *Area.* 44(1): 61–7.

Reavey, Paula (ed.) (2011) *Visual Methods in Psychology: Using and Interpreting Images in Qualitative Research.* Hove: Psychology Press.

REFERENCES

Adkins, L. and Lury, C. (2009) 'What is the empirical?', *European Journal of Social Theory,* 12(1): 5–20.

Allan, A. and Tinkler, P. (2015) '"Seeing" into the past and "looking" forward to the future: Visual methods and gender and education research', *Gender and Education.* 27(7): 791–811.

Bolton, A., Pole, C., and Mizen, P. (2001) 'Picture this: Researching child workers'. *Sociology.* 35(2): 501–18.

Bowden, Flora, Lockton, Dan, Gheerawo, Rama and Brass, Clare (2015) *Drawing Energy: Exploring Perceptions of the Invisible.* London: Royal College of Art.

Bowes-Catton, Helen, Barker, Meg and Richards, Christina (2011) '"I didn't know that I could feel this relaxed in my body": Using visual methods to research bisexual people's embodied experiences of identity and space', in Patricia Reavey (ed.), *Visual Methods in Psychology: Using and Interpreting Images in Qualitative Research.* Hove: Psychology Press, pp. 255–70.

Burgess, J. and Nye, M. (2008) 'Re-materialising energy use through transparent monitoring systems', *Energy Policy,* 36(12): 4454–9.

Coffey, A. (2011) 'Revisiting innovation in qualitative research', *Qualitative Researcher,* 13: 1–2.

Croghan, R., Griffin, C., Hunter, J., and Phoenix, A. (2008) 'Young people's constructions of self: Notes on the use and analysis of the photo-elicitation methods', *International Journal of Social Research Methodology,* 11(4): 345–56.

Denzin, Norman and Lincoln, Yvonna S. (eds.) (2011) *Handbook of Qualitative Research* (4th edn). New York: Sage.

Dicks, B. (2014) 'Action, experience, communication: Three methodological paradigms for researching multimodal and multisensory settings', *Qualitative Research*, 14(6): 656–74.

Flick, Uwe (2006) *An Introduction to Qualitative Research* (3rd edn). London: Sage.

Goodwin, L., Evans, D., Cherry, C., Pidgeon, N., and Bates, M. (unpublished) 'Citizens', in M. Walport and I. Boyd (eds.), *From Waste to Resource Productivity: The Third Themed Annual Report of the Government Chief Scientific Adviser*. UK Government Office for Science and Defra.

Groves, C., Henwood, K., Shirani, F., Butler, C., Parkhill, K., and Pidgeon, N. (2015) 'Energy biographies: Narrative genres, lifecourse transitions, and practice change', *Science, Technology and Human Values*, 41(3): 483–508.

Groves, C., Henwood, K., Shirani, F., Butler, C., Parkhill, K., and Pidgeon, N. (2016a) 'Invested in unsustainability? On the psychosocial patterning of engagement in practices', *Environmental Values*, 25(3): 309–28. DOI: 10.3197/096327116X14598445991466.

Groves, C., Henwood, K., Shirani, F., Butler, C., Parkhill, K., and Pidgeon, N. (2016b) 'The grit in the oyster: Using energy biographies to question socio-technical imaginaries of "smartness"', *Journal of Responsible Innovation*, 3(1): 4–25.

Henwood, Karen L. (2004) 'Reinventing validity: A view from beyond the quality–quantity divide', in Zazie Todd, Brigitte Nerlich, Suzanne McKeown and David D. Clarke (eds.), *Mixing Methods In Psychology: The Integration of Qualitative and Quantitative Methods in Theory and Practice*. London: Routledge, pp. 37–58.

Henwood, Karen L. and Pidgeon, Nick F. (2015) 'Interpretive environmental risk research: Affect, discourses and change', in Jonathan Crighton, Christopher Candlin and Arthur Firkins (eds.), *Communicating Risk*. Basingstoke: Palgrave Macmillan, pp. 155–70.

Henwood, K., Groves, C., and Shirani, F. (2016) 'Relationality, entangled practices and psychosocial exploration of intergenerational dynamics in sustainable energy studies', *Families, Relationships and Societies*, 5(3): 393–410.

Henwood, Karen, Pidgeon, Nick, Groves, C., Shirani, F., Butler, C., and Parkhill, K. (2015) Energy Biographies Research Report.

Henwood, Karen, Shirani, Fiona and Finn, Mark (2011) '"So you think we've moved, changed, the representation got more what?" Methodological and analytical reflections on visual (photo-elicitation) methods used in the Men-as-Fathers study', in Paula Reavey (ed.), *Visual Methods in Psychology: Using and Interpreting Images in Qualitative Research*. Hove: Psychology Press, pp. 330–45.

Holland, J., Thomson, R., and Henderson, S. (2006) 'Qualitative longitudinal research: A discussion paper', *Families and Social Capital Research Group Working Paper No. 21*. London: London South Bank University.

Hopf, T. (2008) 'Interpretive methods: Empirical research and the interpretive turn', *The Journal of Politics*, 70(1): 289–90.

Jewitt, C. (2012) *An Introduction to Using Video for Research*. NCRM Working Paper 03/12.

Liebenberg, L. (2009) 'The visual image as discussion point: Increasing validity in boundary crossing research', *Qualitative Research*. 9(4): 441–67.

Maller, C. and Strengers, Y. (2013) 'The global migration of everyday life: Investigating the practice memories of Australian migrants', *Geoforum*, 44: 243–52.

Mason, J. (2006) 'Mixing methods in a qualitatively driven way', *Qualitative Research*, 6(1): 9–25.

Pierce, J. and Paulos, E. (2010) *Materialising Energy. DIS 10:* Proceedings of the 8th ACM Conference proceedings on Designing Interactive Systems. August 16–20, Aarhus, Denmark. DOI:10.1145/1858171.1858193.

Pink, S. (2012) 'Video and a sense of the invisible: Approaching domestic energy consumption through the sensory home', *Sociological Research Online*, 17(1): 3.

Radley, Alan (2011) 'Image and imagination', in Paula Reavey (ed.), *Visual Methods in Psychology: Using and Interpreting Images in Qualitative Research*. Hove: Psychology Press, pp. 17–28.

Reavey, Paula (2011) 'Introduction', in Paula Reavey (ed.), *Visual Methods in Psychology: Using and Interpreting Images in Qualitative Research*. Hove: Psychology Press, pp. 1–14.

Richards, N. (2011) Using Participatory Visual Methods. *Realities Toolkit #17*. Realities at the Morgan Centre, University of Manchester.

Rose, Gilliam (2007) *Visual Methodologies* (3rd edn). London: Sage.

Rose, G. (2014) 'On the relation between "visual research methods" and contemporary visual culture', *The Sociological Review*, 62(1): 24–46.

Seale, Clive (1999) *The Quality of Qualitative Research*. London: Sage.

Shirani, F., Butler, C., Henwood, K., Parkhill, K., and Pidgeon, N. (2015a) '"I'm not a tree hugger, I'm just like you": changing perceptions of sustainable lifestyles', *Environmental Politics*, 24(1): 57–74.

Shirani, F., Parkhill, K., Butler, C., Groves, C., Pidgeon, N., and Henwood, K. (2015b) 'Asking about the future: Insights from energy biographies', *International Journal of Social Research Methodology*, 19(4): 429–44.

Shove, Elizabeth (1997) 'Revealing the invisible: Sociology, energy and the environment', in Michael R. Redclift and Graham Woodgate (eds.), *The International Yearbook of Environmental and Resource Economics 2000/2001*. Cheltenham: Edward Elgar Publishing, pp. 261–73.

Strengers, Y. (2011) 'Negotiating everyday life: The role of energy and water consumption feedback', *Journal of Consumer Culture*. 11(3): 319–38.

Sweetman, P. (2009) 'Revealing habitus, illuminating practice: Bourdieu, photography and visual methods', *The Sociological Review*, 57(3): 491–511.

Taylor, C. and Coffey, Amanda (2008) 'Innovation in Qualitative Research Methods: Possibilities and Challenges', *Cardiff University School of Social Sciences Working Paper 121*.

Taylor, S. and McEvoy, J. (2015) 'Researching the psychosocial: An introduction', *Qualitative Research in Psychology*. 11(1): 1–90.

Thomas, G., Groves, C., Henwood, K., and Pidgeon, N. (2017) 'Texturing waste: Attachment and identity in everyday consumption and waste practices', *Environmental Values*, 26(6).

Thomson, R. and McLeod, J. (2015) 'New frontiers in qualitative longitudinal research: An agenda for research', *International Journal of Social Research Methodology*, 18(3): 243–50.

Tinkler, Penny (2013) *Using Photographs in Social and Historical Research*. London: Sage.

Travers, M. (2011) 'Visual methods: Innovation, decoration or distraction?', *Qualitative Researcher*, (13): 5–7.

Weller, S. (2012) 'Evolving creativity in qualitative longitudinal research with children and teenagers', *International Journal of Social Research Methodology*, 15(2): 119–33.

Wetherell, M. (2015) 'Trends in the turn to affect: A social psychologic al critique', *Body and Society*, 21(2): 139–66.

Wetherell, Margaret, Taylor, Stephanie and Yates, Simeon (eds.) (2001) *Discourse Theory and Practice*. London: Sage.

Yanow, Dvora and Schwartz-Shea, Peregrine (eds.) (2006) *Interpretation and Method: Empirical Research Methods and the Interpretive Turn*. London: Routledge.

PART VI

Collecting Data in Specific Populations

The previous parts of this *Handbook* had a methodological focus on specific types of data to be collected in qualitative research after some of the basics and concepts were unfolded in Part II. Part VI treats qualitative *data collection in specific populations* in four chapters. Of course we could use a much wider collection of fields, but the four chapters represent some exemplary populations. Children as research partners come with particular challenges (see MacDougall and Darbyshire, Chapter 39, this volume) as does research with old people (see Stephens et al., Chapter 40, this volume). Here we took the time and age dimension and two endpoints of this dimension as an orientation for selecting the examples. The second dimension reaches from experts and elites (see Bogner et al., Chapter 41, this volume) to hard-to-reach people (see Chamberlain and Hodgetts, Chapter 42, this volume).

Guideline questions as an orientation for writing chapters were the following: What are the challenges of planning qualitative data collection with this population? How is the history of researching this population and what is a good example from from this history which can be used for illustration? How has this population become relevant as a specific issue for the collection of qualitative data? What are basic assumptions in this context? Which are the theoretical backgrounds? Which are the different ways to deal with this population in collecting qualitative data and what is a recent example of doing so? Which are the new developments and perspectives in this field? What is the contribution of the discussion about this target group to the collection of qualitative data and critical reflection?

Reading the chapters in Part VI should help to answer questions like the following ones for a study and its method(s): What are the steps in planning how to collect the data with this population? What characterizes good (and bad) example(s) of collecting qualitative data in this target group? What characterizes good (and bad) example(s) of using the approach? What are the main stumbling blocks in collecting qualitative data with this population? What are criteria of good practice in producing qualitative data with this specific population? What are the specific ethical issues in qualitative data collection in this population?

In answering questions like the ones just mentioned, the chapters in this part are meant to contribute to connecting the methodological discussions in this *Handbook* to research practice in selected fields.

Collecting Qualitative Data with Children

Colin MacDougall and Philip Darbyshire

AIMS AND PLAN OF THE CHAPTER

The Hollywood film director W.C. Fields famously warned: 'Never work with animals or children' lest the actors be upset by children's unpredictability or upstaged by their performance. Vestiges of this sentiment linger in the folklore of qualitative research with children,[1] rendering data collection more daunting than necessary. Like actors, good qualitative researchers use tried and trusted skills to anticipate and manage the unpredictability of children, or the adult-designed structures surrounding them. Researchers also know when and how to step back, enabling children's experiences to take their rightful place on the qualitative stage.

This chapter helps qualitative researchers to pause data collection until sound epistemological thinking has devised a best methodology for their question. We start by explaining how contemporary representations of childhood challenge conventional ways of knowing the world.

We then illustrate key examples of good data collection practice across countries and research questions that help researchers value their backgrounds in qualitative methods and decide when and how to adapt and innovate for research with children. Drawing on exemplars, we illustrate how to navigate methodological options facing novice and experienced researchers alike. A central tenet of all research involving children is the need for adults to adapt, such as when, during a qualitative study examining children's accounts of exercise, sport, physical activity and play, the facilitators planned a 'show me' technique to ask children to demonstrate activities they had described. This morphed into something of a 'methodological first' – the 'jumping focus group' where the participant children showed the researchers the physicality of some of their play and games. Without this challenge to the focus group norms, we may not have discovered all of the varieties of 'chasey' that were played (Darbyshire et al., 2005).

This decision was straightforward because, as active chief investigators we (CM and PD) could use our authority to adjust methods on the spot. It is more difficult when the intent of collecting data in a participatory way clashes with a world of incompatible adult-centred paradigms. For example, during another study, one of us arrived at a school expecting, as arranged, to conduct a focus group in a multi-purpose space to minimise symbols of adult power. Instead the school principal ushered us to the formal staff room and announced they were staying for the focus group. The children were so quiet that we could not use the data, wasting the children's time and suppressing their voices. On reflection, we vowed in future to draw on the language of children's rights and act as duty bearers to challenge and question understandings, that powerful adults have of children and childhood, that shape methods (MacDougall et al., 2014).

HISTORY OF RESEARCH WITH CHILDREN

Looking from 2017 it is pleasing to note the rapid progress from predominantly positivist research on children to an acceptance of qualitative data collection with children. We well remember from our backgrounds in psychology, public health and children's nursing, when children were research subjects but never co-participants, studied but not heard, researched *on* but never *with* (Darbyshire, 2000).

Fields such as education, child psychology and child health, often framed children as objects of adult study whose alleged immaturity, unreliability, capriciousness and unformed mini-adult status rendered them incapable of providing useful data. While no research method is *good* or *bad* per se, a methodological orthodoxy limiting data collection to methods derived from adult-centred epistemologies does children a disservice. We also question attempts to 'understand children's worlds' within some ostensible qualitative approaches where parents, carers, teachers or other proxy adults speak for children or authoritatively interpret children's data, such as their drawings or photography.

Critical and progressive social, political, philosophical and epistemological movements have opened up new ways of understanding the broader phenomena of children and childhood. In the 1980s and 1990s many taken-for-granted concepts were radically challenged and revised. Feminism demanded more than simply benevolent involvement and vigorously criticised the economic, power, equity and emancipatory status quo. Similarly, the Disability Movement confronted the charity model whereby healthy society would kindly help the 'less fortunate'. These movements reflected alternative epistemologies to positivism such as a social constructionism and critical theory.

When 'childhood came of age, sociologically' (Jenks, 2000, p. 62), research could no longer uncritically adopt 'adultist' methodologies. The predominantly European *new sociology of childhood* was at the forefront of the sociological coming of age (James and Prout, 1997; James et al., 1998) and strongly influenced fields such as the new social studies of childhood, children's geographies, early childhood education, children and the media, environment and ecology, urban planning, disaster studies and more.

Change also arose from the growing mistrust of professional expertise and a reluctance to continue to allow experts to speak exclusively for people of all ages. Health services began to recognise and listen to 'the consumer perspective' or 'patient's voice': not only as complementary to professional expertise but also to make better health care decisions and reduce health care errors. As this movement advanced in adult health care, progress was also made in appreciating, seeking out and assessing 'the child's voice' in numerous aspects of children's health care.

Qualitative researchers were well placed to embrace the new sociology of childhood and drive fundamental change to all aspects of research involving children to ensure that data collection respectfully and ethically involves children as legitimate social actors with agency. They strive for genuine consultation, participation with children as valued partners or even being in charge, and oppose mere token gestures. These data collection and interpretive approaches were child friendly, engaged children and contributed to their emancipation by encouraging them to have their say in all matters of their lives.

Variations of a 'ladder of participation' were often used to conceptualise this sea change: climbing from manipulation or tokenism at the bottom to child initiated, directed and controlled (Shier, 2001). These new approaches to research with children went beyond theoretical concerns to contribute to practice and policy utility based on influential programmes of research, such as The United Kingdom's Economic and Social Research Council 'Children 5–16 Programme' and in the work of key non-government organisations such as Barnardo's and Save the Children. Such leadership from influential research and children's organisations provided a powerful justification for researchers to adopt these new research paradigms.

The Children's Rights movement added further impetus to the need for change in research with children, clearly articulating the need to involve children and to take seriously their views and perspectives, not as icing on a kindly research cake but as a fundamental human right. Article 12 of the UN Convention on the Rights of the Child became an article of faith for many childhood researchers.

THEORETICAL BACKGROUNDS

Our brief history has laid the foundations for what we term a *citizen-child theory* that takes a child-centred approach and argues for the rights of children to exercise agency in their own lives (MacDougall, 2009). The citizen-child inspired researcher problematises and reduces power relationships between adults and children during data collection and the wider structures and cultures of research and child engagement. The citizen-child approach upends the view of children as passive and compliant citizens and enhances opportunities for children to become participatory citizens. In keeping with the emancipatory and democratic aspirations of qualitative research, we use the word citizen with care because there are three different definitions. *Personally responsible citizens* obey the law, pay their taxes and are kind to others. *Participatory citizens* join organisations, vote in elections and volunteer to help others. *Socially critical citizens* will investigate why the situation is like it is and fight to achieve justice. The citizen-child approach draws on rights discourses to critique the representation of children as passive and compliant citizens, enhances opportunities for children to become participatory citizens and, through participation in research, invites them to consider their role in the world as advocates for social justice (adapted from Gibbs et al., 2013b, p. 130).

Researchers influenced by modern psychology have used biological, cognitive and behavioural studies to propose a series of developmental stages through which children progress on their way to adulthood. This *developmental child* theory is central to contemporary debates about the fundamental purpose of kindergarten, primary and tertiary education. As a dominant theory of childhood, it has been used to drive research – again including qualitative methods – to match policies, programmes and intervention to the most appropriate developmental stage, while also limiting participation in research until children are seen as developmentally capable (MacDougall, 2009).

Since the industrial revolution, attention has been focused on how best to identify and reduce risks to children, too often from adult institutions. The *child at risk* theory frames children as vulnerable and has made major contributions in child labour and slavery, physical abuse, sexual abuse and injury prevention. The downside of the at-risk or vulnerable child view for researchers, however, is that *all* children can be viewed as vulnerable and therefore in need of hyper-protection from everything. Thus, adults in their protector and gatekeeper roles can prevent children from participating in even the most benign of consultative research by claiming that they are 'safeguarding children' and protecting them from any level of unease, distress or harm, either during or following the research.

BASIC ASSUMPTIONS UNDERPINNING WHY CHILDREN ARE NOW RELEVANT IN THE COLLECTION OF QUALITATIVE DATA

The *citizen-child theory* combines two stories from the preceding discussion of history and theory. The first is a more reactive story that promotes child-centred research as a way of rejecting adultist and developmentally derived assumptions. The second is a more aspirational story that blends a children's rights approach with the participation and empowerment agenda to focus on the benefits of collecting data with children.

The more reactive story recounts how the *citizen-child* theory critiques data collection methods that frame children as *human becomings* rather than *human beings*, whereby adulthood is regarded as the goal of individual development (Qvortrup et al., 1994). According to Morrow (2002) it has adopted the following principles from the new sociology of childhood when collecting data with children:

- childhood is a social construction, not a biological fact, that varies over time as well as within and across societies;
- childhood is a variable of social analysis;
- children's social relationships and cultures are worthy of study in their own right, independent of the perspectives and concerns of adults;
- children are, and must be seen as, active in the construction and determination of their own lives, of the lives of those around them and of the societies in which they live.

The more aspirational story works from a rights-based approach that challenges how those of us steeped in needs-based or deficit approaches think. Children deserve resources by virtue of being human, not just because a deficit or need has been demonstrated by a scientific study. According to this story, qualitative research is one part of a broader movement towards conceptualising children as critical and socially responsible citizens.

Although in 2017 the reactive and aspirational stories converge and suggest similar strategies for data collection with children, we suggest on the basis of analyses of how paradigms change in science, that the *reaction against* story will inevitably be subsumed by the increasing sophistication and currency of the more *aspirational story*.

WORKING WITH CHILDREN IN COLLECTING QUALITATIVE DATA

Crotty (1998) described the qualitative researcher as a *bricoleur*; not a jack of all trades but an artisan, flexibly inventing new approaches from existing tools. We aim to assist *artisan bricoleurs* to blend a dash of creativity with some well-tried methods, after due consideration of epistemology and the research question. Box 39.1 is an extended quotation from an abstract from one study and is referred to throughout this section as we present a range of participatory data collection methods.

> **Box 39.1 Illustrate choices of methods to collect data *with* children**
>
> Children's interdependent mobility: compositions, collaborations and compromises
>
> 1. The *methodology* was based on a rights-based, child-centred participatory approach to understand how children negotiate and develop their everyday mobility in the contexts of parental rules, family routines, cultural influences, peer social connections, communication technologies and neighbourhood environments.
> 2. The *cohort was selected* because research shows the transition from primary to secondary school is an important stage in children's mobility development.
> 3. The *methods* began with site observation, moved to child focus group discussions and then accompanying children on their travel journeys.
> 4. This process was piloted with a class group of eight school children in their final year of primary school who acted as *research partners* to help shape the research design.
> 5. The methods were then repeated with different cohorts to compare across the transition from the last year of primary school to the first year of secondary school and although primarily oriented around children's perspectives, the methods were *contextualised with parent and teacher interviews*.
> 6. We began by *observing* a number of key sites and routes within the research area over a four-week period, initially touring the area by car and foot, and stationing ourselves outside schools, shopping centres and recreational facilities at busy times of the day (before and after school). The aim was to gather contextual data on the physical and social environments and to familiarise ourselves with local children's patterns and practices of mobility, informing subsequent methods.
> 7. We then undertook focus group discussions with children in groups of 5–8 (n = 48), which were conducted in schools with groups of mixed gender and diverse cultural background. The discussions were centred on two *visual photo-ordering exercises* that used images depicting places of, and then objects involved in, their neighbourhood travel. Visual aids have been shown to be an inclusive technique for stimulating children's responses, and we asked children to discuss and work together to order the importance of each image for their travel journeys.
> 8. We followed discussions with *mobile methods*. This involved travelling with ten children (six boys and four girls) drawn from the focus groups on an everyday travel journey. Again, the cultural background of these children was diverse. Children took researchers on routine travel journeys, predominantly to and from the school but also to places such as shops and parks, to show how they normally travelled, with questions generated by the environments and interactions that were observed during the journey (Nansen et al., 2015, p. 267).

A FIRST STAGE: ENTRY TO THE FIELD AND EXPLORING WHAT TO ASK

A crucial element of the study in Box 39.1 was the care taken in the first stage of research, as described in points 3, 4 and 6. Researchers should go into the field early to understand the context and develop relationships with relevant adults whose cooperation is often essential. The most pressing reasons for a carefully considered preliminary stage are to develop relevant questions and topic areas for children and to consider optimal approaches to engaging them that will evoke the best responses and the richest data. One multi-university study to develop a measure of child well-being started with interviews where children proposed *their* question ideas. These were triangulated (see Flick, Chapter 34, this volume) with existing scales to enable international comparisons of child well-being and then followed up with qualitative data collection to explain patterns of child well-being (Redmond et al., 2013).

Planning such a first stage of research brings practical and ethical benefits. When preparing grant applications for participatory research it can be problematic if reviewers critique the lack of detail about methods that can only be finalised during data collection. Similarly, institutional ethics committees (see Mertens, Chapter 3, this volume) require details about interview questions and other data collection methods. By providing a sound rationale for a rigorous first stage, reviewers and ethics committees can be assured that the research plan is theoretically sound and can be reviewed as the details of each stage emerge.

Data collection can be extended to multiple stages to enable children to give progressive consent as they get to know the researchers and the project. Multiple stages also open up the possibility for the children to choose or propose data collection methods they find suitable. While planning a children's component of a longitudinal study charting the recovery of victims of a disaster, researchers were concerned to avoid any harm from collecting in-depth interview data from children following such a harrowing event. As a result, they planned a multistage project, providing children with a series of opportunities to continue to the more in-depth stage, to stop at an early stage and to select data collection methods (Gibbs et al., 2013b).

OBSERVATION AND ETHNOGRAPHY

Observing (see Wästerfors, Chapter 20, this volume) children in the name of research was popularised by Piaget and others who launched developmental psychology by observing their own children. Observing children for research was popular partly because either in school or at play there was no need for close engagement with children. The non-participant observer could remain suitably detached while noting, recording and interpreting what they believed was happening across a range of childhood settings. Ethnographic observations tread a difficult path in avoiding the Scylla of over-exoticising the 'strange world of childhood' while also shunning the Charybdis of treating children simply as mini-adults with no unique characteristics and challenges.

Childhood ethnographers (see Buscatto, Chapter 21, this volume) face many of the data collection problems as their adult-focused counterparts, although access to children and childhood settings is becoming more difficult as children's gatekeepers face understandable demands to safeguard children from abuse.

Box 39.1 demonstrates two ways to conduct observations. Point 6 illustrates the contribution of observation to understanding the context in which data will be collected. Point 8 shows observations while children are moving through their environment. Known also as mobile methods, these are described later in the chapter. Observations on the move are important because of the critique that sociology focuses more on spaces and places than travel between them – an increasingly important part of life. Mobility for children is particularly important for data collection because how and when children gain independent mobility is a hotly contested topic.

It is now rare to conduct an entire study using observational data, more common to combine observations with other data and usual to collect such data in the first stage of a study.

FOCUS GROUPS AND INTERVIEWS

Individual and focus group interviews are widely accepted qualitative strategies in researching children's lives, as shown in Point 7 of Box 39.1. Focus groups (see Morgan and Hoffman, Chapter 16, this volume) with children may have advantages over individual interviews in that one participant's response may trigger others in the group, children may experience a sense of safety in numbers, particularly when discussing sensitive issues and they may feel less pressured to answer every question as others are also responding. Group or individual interviews (see Roulston and Choi, Chapter 15, this volume) should be akin to natural informal conversations that allow children to speak freely about the particular aspects of their lives under study. This latter point is important as focus groups should have a focus and researchers in their preparations will have planned how to ensure that discussions and conversations with the children remain 'focused but roomy', in staying related to the study questions but allowing potentially important or unexpected tangents to be opened and followed (Bugge et al., 2014).

The group dimension is also critical to this data collection approach with children. Children generally prefer to be in groups with peers and so a mixed focus group with 5-, 9- and 14-year-old boys and girls would be problematic. Depending on the numbers of children involved, groups of around three to six work well. In earlier work investigating the physical activity patterns of schoolchildren with chronic illness we used mixed focus groups for 4–6 and 7–9 year olds and separate boys' and girls' groups for 10–13 and 14–16 year olds (Fereday et al., 2009).

With tongue in cheek, we describe in Box 39.2 the value of the 'idiot adult' approach to data collection whereby the adult purposely redresses the existing power imbalances.

This approach is neither manipulative nor inauthentic if the researcher working within a new paradigm approach that values children's perspectives and accounts genuinely DOES want to discover children's perspectives firsthand, DOES want them to enjoy the process, DOES want to minimise power imbalances and DOES want to help them towards being able to provide their best accounts, stories, examples, thoughts, views and feelings.

Focus groups and interviews can stand alone to collect in-depth data. They can also include preparation for other methods such as visual sociology or mobile methods.

Box 39.2 The 'idiot adult'

Play

In trying to discover where young children play outdoors in the 2000s we may start by saying something like, 'Look, I really need your help, do you think you could help us? I'm a 60-year-old man and I haven't gone out to play for YEARS AND YEARS. I can't even remember what you do. Can you help me? Can you tell me some of the places you like to go to play/Some of the things that you like to do when you go out to play? That would be great.' A further useful prop was a notebook where researchers can say that what the children are going to tell you is SO important that you want to write everything down because they are so interesting and useful that you don't want to forget anything.

Serious Illness

In studies with seriously ill children, one of us (PD) had to consider understandable adult concerns that even mentioning such issues could be distressing or damaging. It was a revelation to discover how responsive children were when treated as equals in the interview/discussion process; when their views and experiences were genuinely valued. I explained that sometimes talking about your own health-type things can be hard but that children have SO much knowledge and experience that could help doctors and nurses to make things better for the children they are helping. I also said that I had not experienced cancer or renal failure and have no idea what it must be like, but that I have talked to lots of other children about their illnesses and lives and I DO have plenty of time and a notebook and I am really interested in what you might want to tell me. A good example of a 'can-opener' question – one that opens up a panoply of areas to explore came from a study about living with renal failure and dialysis, in which one child talked about himself and 'the kidney kids'. I responded by asking, 'Here's a good question, quite a hard one when you think about this one, if you were trying to tell other kids about what being a kidney kid was like or whatever, what important things would you want to tell them, what should people know about it?'

Focus groups or interviews can also follow other methods to ensure children's accounts of data, from their maps or photos, for example, are valued. Alternatively, a focus group or interview could be designed to incorporate other methods.

VISUAL SOCIOLOGY

Children's health and social care was changed irrevocably by the pioneering observational documentary film work of James and Joyce Robertson, which was as confronting as it was effective. 'A Two Year-Old Goes to Hospital' was a harrowing account of the near disintegration of a young girl who spent eight days in hospital for a minor operation (http://www.robertsonfilms.info). There, she was separated from her parents by archaic visiting restrictions and subjected to regimes of 'care' that would be utterly alien in any modern children's ward. Despite the health establishment subjecting the Robertsons and their filmic approach to extraordinary levels of vilification and resentment, their work was central to the landmark Platt Report in 1959, which shaped paediatric care until the present day.

Harper (1994, 2005) charts how visual sociology is moving from a focus on film (see Mikos, Chapter 26, this volume) and photography (see Eberle, Chapter 25, this volume) to incorporate digital technology. Visual data can illustrate a more positivist research article; draw on constructivism to explore how reality is constructed; or through a more critical theory lens, can rebalance power relationships between children and researchers. Visual methods are described in Point 7 of Box 39.1.

Photovoice, or the closely related Photo-elicitation, involves researchers providing children with a camera to take photographs relevant to the research, taking care to minimise directions about what adults think is important. Researchers can ask children to provide a caption or description. There is usually a follow-up interview or focus group encouraging children to discuss the photos either in a free discussion or in response to prompts. As a visual data production strategy, photovoice draws attention to people and places that children see as important at home, school, hospital or in their communities. Photography provides a direct (but of course also interpreted and selective) way to see the world and generate ideas very different from those from verbal or written interviews (Darbyshire et al., 2005).

Mapping is especially useful in ascertaining children's spatial and environmental perspectives and understandings: their neighbourhood, school, family and environment. Mapping can stand alone or complement other methods such as interviews and photography/photovoice. It can enable engagement, free responses and individual interpretations related to discussions within focus group topics. In our work on children's physical activity and place, mapping was invaluable (Darbyshire et al., 2005; MacDougall et al., 2004).

The heyday of children's drawings and artwork as research data in the age of psychoanalysis used adult projective techniques to bear on children's drawings to reveal the child's innermost mental states. In recent decades this approach has been largely superseded by more child-centred approaches where children are enabled to be more active participants, not only in their drawings but also in the explanation and interpretation of their own work. To avoid adultist interpretation the data from visual sociology focuses more on the child's account of the images than on the actual images.

We expect visual sociology to continue to move with the digital times, such as the use of *emoji* to stimulate focus group discussions about conceptions of well-being held by 3- to 5-year-old children (Fane et al., 2016), using social media as data, and using new possibilities from faster and smaller computing devices.

MOBILE METHODS

Points 3, 5 and 8 of Box 39.1 illustrate mobile methods (see Kusenbach, Chapter 22, this volume), which position children as experts in their lives by asking them to take the researcher on a tour of a salient area (Ross et al., 2009). Researchers and children plan a route, work out how to collect data (e.g. the route itself, interviews, photographs, observations) and balance independence with safety. Mobile methods inform areas such as urban planning, children in care and recovery from disasters. Theoretically, mobile methods are a form of visual sociology and also draw upon the *new mobilities paradigm*. All places are linked by at least some thin networks of connections that stretch beyond a single locale and the complex patterns of contemporary and changing activities require travel for social life and connections. It is extremely relevant for research about safety with children because mobile methods provide data about places, technologies and barriers that enhance the mobilities of some and reinforce the immobilities of others (Sheller and Urry, 2006).

The technical capacity now exists to extend from real world to virtual mobile methods by combining faster Wi-Fi with mapping and analysis software that enables children to demonstrate how they travel to and through spaces virtually. This is especially useful when it is difficult in reality to travel to places because of danger, expense, war or displacement.

DIGITAL TECHNOLOGIES AND SOCIAL MEDIA

It would be naïve to ignore how advances in digital and mobile technologies inform how researchers might engage with children now and in the future. It would be undisciplined to use new possibilities uncritically just because they are there. At the simplest level researchers may use new technologies and social networks to find particular groups of children, to invite them to take part in research and to collect data with them. Major social networking sites such as Facebook (see Ditchfield and Meredith, Chapter 32, this volume) and Twitter are already being used in adult and adolescent research and it is inevitable that even younger children will become engaged with research through these media, potentially bypassing what researchers may now understand as 'the usual channels'.

At a deeper level, the new age of mobile technologies and online social networks raise the possibility that the fundamental structures and power relationships within research will be challenged and disrupted. New platforms and peer-to-peer businesses will certainly spread and such disruptive innovation has the potential to transform possibilities for collecting data with children. See, for example, 'Patients Like Me' (https://www.patientslikeme.com). Social media approaches to engaging children in research will appear novel and exciting. However, the essential requirements to 'do no harm' and to safeguard and support any children who consent to helping adults with research will remain a bedrock principle, although the detail and practice of researchers' ethical comportment may have to adapt to these new data collection approaches.

THEATRE AND ARTS

Applied theatre is participatory and seeks to articulate explicit understandings about how we see and might want to change the world. Based on critical theory, it creates, analyses and represents research data; encouraging children to seize agency over how they express experiences. It reveals existing knowledge, produces new knowledge, recognises practical and embodied knowledge and values artistic forms of expression unconstrained by words and numbers. It represents one of many opportunities to expand the scope of data collection with children beyond numbers and words, challenging traditional research underpinnings and moving to more creative and expressive domains.

Following the earthquakes in Christchurch, New Zealand during 2010 and 2011, adult institutions constrained the role of victims – in theatre terms, spectators. Researchers used theatre to add to the lives of the children and to collect and tell the stories of hope children had for their city. One memorable moment of classroom drama became a partnership between the University of Auckland, UNESCO and the Mental Health Foundation. This partnership, known as the *Teaspoon of Light* project, has involved thousands of children across Christchurch. The project has used the arts to help reframe the children from victims to people with agency to repair dreams (Gibbs et al., 2013a).

NEW DEVELOPMENTS AND PERSPECTIVES

Including Children as Researchers or Co-Researchers

The rhetoric of the philosophical, epistemological or rights-based premises that children could or should be more actively involved as genuine partners in the research process is proving difficult to move to reality. We need answers to critical questions about projects that aim or claim to involve children as co-researchers, including:

To what extent were children involved in determining the research question(s) and foci of the study?

Earlier we described a Stage 1 of research that involves children in the research, once the study has been designed. The participatory element of Participatory Action Research and rights-based approaches requires the involvement of children before Stage 1: in the development of the study itself. This may be foundational to genuine co-researcher status for children as it disrupts the norm whereby most 'child-centred' adult researchers decide upon the research topic or questions alone and subsequently seek children's help with operational strategies.

How carefully were children supported and prepared to take on a meaningful co-researcher role in the project?

Time is a valuable research commodity. It demonstrates the commitment and genuine willingness of a research team in that they are prepared to spend considerable time and energy establishing and building the prior relationships with children that will be essential if they are to be able to work with adult *colleagues* in a more peer-to-peer research relationship.

What research training have the children been offered and how?

New adult researchers would expect appropriate research training or preparation as part of becoming a valued member of a research team. What efforts and approaches have the adult researchers used to provide the children with the knowledge, skills and confidence to understand more about the project, its goals and the role that they will play in the process?

Have the children had a genuine involvement and decision-making role in key aspects of data interpretation?

Again, such methodological decisions are usually taken by adults who readily accept that such considerations and their operation are not easy. Complexity and sophistication, however, cannot be played as trump cards to exclude children from contributing to analysis. In a study where children are deemed to be genuine co-researchers, it would be expected that they had contributed to data collection strategies and that their views and insights were incorporated as an integral part of data interpretation also.

Does the commitment to involving children as co-researchers extend throughout the study, to publication and dissemination/translation?

As the science of knowledge transfer and exchange advances, academic researchers no longer take sole carriage of developing recommendations. Instead, they are expected to involve potential users of research, who are often brought in to the research team as formal investigators. Similarly, research with and about children should involve children as bona fide co-researchers who play a role in publication and dissemination of the work. This can be done by involving the children as co-authors of papers and presentations and by working with them to develop child-friendly modes of dissemination and sharing of findings, such as the production of a 'parallel text' specifically designed for children. An excellent example of a 'parallel text' is in Bricher's (2001) PhD thesis involving children with disabilities.

What Questions to Ask?

Many studies collect data about the here and now of children's lives, especially education, play, physical activity and health. While this fits the *reaction against* aspect of the citizen-child approach, participatory and critical citizenship ideas discussed earlier propose that we encourage the trend towards asking the big questions about society and the planet: including economy, ecology, disasters, humanitarian settings and more (for example, MacLean et al., 2010).

Who to Ask?

In this new research area significant theoretical and methodological development has understandably occurred with populations who are easier to reach and respond to verbal and visual methods. Qualitative research's proud history of engagement and action with those who are marginalised and have difficulty with conventional communication channels will most likely extend to children. One example is research on social participation for children with disabilities involving communication difficulties, as opposed to focusing on services for their disabilities (Raghavendra et al., 2015).

Whither Age and Development?

The reaction against the *developmental child* approach can bring scepticism, silence or denial about how biological and cognitive development influence the interpretation of data from children. A 'citizen in the making' perspective invites us to match development to methods and codify a hierarchy of conceptual understandings expected from children as they assume more sophisticated citizenship roles.

Where Do Adults Fit?

Many studies only collect data from children to correct the historical imbalance in the social sciences. Just as feminism involves gender relations that render men the object of study, and cultural safety requires understanding of the dominant and marginalised cultures, childhood (and indeed the United Nations Convention on the Rights of the Child) inextricably involves adult–child relations requiring that adults be included where appropriate.

MIXING REPRESENTATIONS OF CHILDHOOD AND DATA COLLECTION METHODS

Today's researchers may work on data that are collected by multi-disciplinary teams, requiring negotiations about competing and complementary epistemologies. Qualitative data collection with children may comprise one strand of a broader project or occur in teams with broader remits than studying solely children. These forces combine to suggest careful consideration of how to introduce data collection with children into broader projects, negotiating the best mix of methods and epistemological compatibilities along the way.

Different epistemologies and their associated data collection methods do not, however, naturally fall into mutually exclusive categories dividing researchers into categories of good and bad. Theory, practice and policy are frequently best informed by combining the best representations and methods to answer the question. Citizen-child researchers now collect data with children about catastrophic disasters such as fire, tsunami and earthquake. Although there is increasing use of a citizen-child approach to such research this is neither the preferred nor the only perspective. Researchers in this field carefully consider how best to provide findings to guide the best mix of policies, reduce risks for children, protect children, provide post-disaster services relevant for their age and progressively enhance their citizenship.

We anticipate new representations of childhood to be debated, such as the *digital native* who at an early age is just as comfortable on line as in the sandpit. There could be a case for a *virtual child* interacting online throughout the world – often with people unknown to them and their parents. Representations could change to more of a *global child* as citizen-child approaches move from their primarily European roots. As political and social movements foreground the wisdom of Indigenous peoples rather than their disadvantage, we may see a new representation of the Indigenous childhood. There may be others, either on a local, regional or global level. Some might be new representations, others more cross-cutting or complementary representations. Whatever happens, we expect debates about the epistemology behind data collection with children will continue to reference variations of the classic positivist-subjective-constructionist-critical views while exploring representations and epistemologies more tailored to children.

European geographical and cultural contexts underpin dominant representations of childhood and their critiques. This matters because one Australian systematic review concluded that most child health studies did not mention whether Indigenous peoples in general (let alone children) were involved in design and implementation. As a result, studies were skewed to collect data about physical health in rural and remote locations – research that does not represent the demographics and lives of Indigenous peoples (Priest et al., 2009). Citizen-child researchers are well placed to create and work within these bridging spaces, exemplified by Australian work revealing the world views of Indigenous children (Priest et al., 2016) and research by Punch (2015, 2016) on cross-world dialogue with children.

CONTRIBUTION OF RESEARCH WITH CHILDREN TO THE COLLECTION OF QUALITATIVE DATA

Qualitative research is expanding and it may be tempting to subdivide towards ever-narrower specialisation. Researchers new to working with children may be overly guarded and over-anxious when first collecting data with children who are framed as almost frighteningly 'special'. We suggest in this chapter that the well-rounded *bricoleur* is ideally placed to draw upon those theories and principles of research design that have served qualitative research so well. Qualitative research as an emancipatory and democratic project seeks to change the world (Denzin and Lincoln, 2005). Similarly, contemporary qualitative research with and about childhood frames children as citizens in the making, with rights by virtue of being human, but who have been variously ignored by researchers; written about by adults; and valued not as *human beings*, but as human *becomings*. Bricoleur researchers reflect on day-to-day data collection to avoid unintended 'othering' of children that can so easily happen in a research milieu so imbued with adult-centric approaches. They bring a new dimension of political reflexivity considering political influences on the research process, researcher and participant.

The chapter started with a Hollywood-inspired metaphor and now closes with one from Australia concerning a bridging space between Western and Indigenous researchers. *Ganma* is an ancient metaphor derived from Australia's Northern Territory that has guided Indigenous people from this part of Australia and describes how a river of water from the sea (Western knowledge) and a river of water from the land (Indigenous knowledge) engulf each other, flowing together and becoming one. The forces of the streams combine to produce deeper understanding and truth and the foam produced when salt water mixes with fresh water represents a new kind of knowledge (O'Donnell, 2014, pp. 84–5). This metaphor serves as a general lesson for qualitative researchers as they reflect on their own culture and navigate the boundaries and spaces between various worlds and traditions.

ACKNOWLEDGEMENTS

We acknowledge the wonderful contribution to our research of Professor Wendy Schiller, formerly from the University of South Australia. Our research has been supported by competitive funding from a range of organisations, including the Australian Research Council. Our publications have been improved by many peer reviewers. We thank the schools and institutions who welcomed us as we collected data in ways that were often very different from their past experiences of research. We have learned from many leading qualitative researchers around the world who have collaborated and given us valuable advice about data collection with children and we thank them for being so collegial and generous with their time and knowledge. CM acknowledges research inspiration from the Southgate Institute for Health, Society and Equity at Flinders University in Adelaide, and past and present staff from the Jack Brockhoff Child Health and Wellbeing Program at the University of Melbourne, for their expertise, friendship and support. PD thanks all of the team who made the Nursing Research Department at Women's & Children's Hospital in South Australia such a beacon of child-centred research for 13 years. Finally, our thanks to the hundreds of children and young people who have taught us about their lives.

Note

1 Where we use 'children' this refers to children and young people.

FURTHER READING

James, Allison and Prout, Alan (eds.) (2015) *Constructing and Reconstructing Childhood: Contemporary Issues in the Sociological Study of Childhood.* Abingdon: Routledge (Routledge Education Classic Editions, 3rd edn).

Priest, N., Mackean, T., Davis, E., Briggs, L., and Waters, E. (2012) 'Aboriginal perspectives of child health and wellbeing in an urban setting: Developing a conceptual framework', *Health Sociology Review*, 21(2): 180–95.

Percy-Smith, Barry and Thomas, Nigel (eds.) (2009) *A Handbook of Children and Young People's Participation: Perspectives from Theory and Practice.* Abingdon: Routledge.

REFERENCES

Bricher, G. (2001) 'If you want to know anything just ask: Exploring disabled young people's experiences of health and healthcare',

PhD thesis, University of South Australia, Adelaide, Australia.
Bugge, K.E., Darbyshire, P., Røkholt, E.G., Haugstvedt, K.T.S., and Helseth, S. (2014) 'Young children's grief: Parents' understanding and coping', *Death Studies*, 38(1): 36–43.
Crotty, Michael (1998) *The Foundations of Social Research Meaning and Perspectives in the Research Process*. St. Leonards, NSW: Allen and Unwin.
Darbyshire, P. (2000) 'From research on children to research with children', *Neonatal, Paediatric and Child Health Nursing*, 3(1): 2–3.
Darbyshire, P., MacDougall, C., and Schiller, W. (2005) 'Multiple methods in qualitative research with children: More insight or just more?', *Qualitative Research*, 5(4): 417–36.
Denzin, Norman K. and Lincoln, Yvonna S. (eds) (2005) *The Sage Handbook of Qualitative Research*. Sage.
ESRC Children 5–16 Programme 'Introduction', http://www.hull.ac.uk/children5to16programme/intro.htm.
Fane, J., MacDougall, C., Redmond, G., Ivanovic, J., and Gibbs, L. (2016) 'Exploring the use of emojis as a visual research method for eliciting children's voices in childhood research', *Early Child Development and Care*, 1–16.
Fereday J., MacDougall, C., Spizzo, M., Darbyshire, P., and Schiller, W. (2009) '"There's nothing I can't do – I just put my mind to anything and I can do it"': a qualitative analysis of how children with chronic disease and their parents account for and manage physical activity', *BMC Pediatrics*, 9(1): 1–16.
Gibbs, L., MacDougall, C., and Harden, J. (2013a) 'Development of an ethical methodology for post-bushfire research with children', *Health Sociology Review*, 22(2): 114–23.
Gibbs, L., Mutch, C., O'Connor, P., and MacDougall, C. (2013b) 'Research with, by, for and about children: Lessons from disaster contexts', *Global Studies of Childhood*, 3(2): 129–41.
Harper, Douglas (1994) 'On the authority of the image: Visual sociology at the crossroads', in Norman K. Denzin and Yvonna S. Lincoln (eds.), *Handbook of Qualitative Research*. Thousand Oaks, CA: Sage, pp. 403–12.
Harper, Douglas (2005) 'What's new visually?', in Norman K. Denzin and Yvonna S. Lincoln (eds.), *Handbook of Qualitative Research*. Thousand Oaks, CA: Sage, pp. 747–62.
James, Allison and Prout Alan (1997) *Constructing and Reconstructing Childhood: Contemporary Issues in the Sociological Study of Childhood*. London: Routledge.
James Allison, Jenks, Chris, and Prout, Alan (1998) *Theorizing Childhood*. Cambridge: Polity Press.
Jenks, Chris (2000) 'Zeitgeist research on childhood', in Pia Christensen and Allison James (eds.), *Research With Children: Perspectives and Practices*. London: Routledge, pp. 62–76.
MacDougall, Colin (2009) 'Understanding twenty-first century childhood', in Helen Keleher and Colin MacDougall (eds.), *Understanding Health: A Determinants Approach*. Melbourne: Oxford University Press, pp. 287–307.
MacDougall., C., Gibbs, L., Block, K. and Priest, N. (2014) 'Can researchers using participatory methods with children overcome problems arising from adult power becoming inscribed in the research space?' Paper presented at the International Conference: Sharing space: an interdisciplinary approach to the spatial dimension of social relations. University of Rennes 2, Rennes, France.
MacDougall, C., Schiller, W., and Darbyshire, P. (2004) 'We have to live in the future', *Early Child Development and Care*, 174(4): 369–87.
MacLean, A., Harden, J., and Backett-Milburn, K. (2010) 'Financial trajectories: How parents and children discussed the impact of the recession', *Twenty-First Century Society*, 5(2): 159–70.
Morrow, Virginia (2002) 'Perspectives on children's agency within families', in Leon Kuczynski (ed.), *Handbook of Dynamics in Parent–Child Relations*. London: Sage, pp. 109–29.
Nansen, B., Gibbs, L., MacDougall, C., Vetere, F., Ross, N.J., and McKendrick, J. (2015) 'Children's interdependent mobility: Compositions, collaborations and compromises', *Children's Geographies*, 13(4): 467–81.

O'Donnell, K. (2014) *'Split three atoms and report tomorrow: The funding relationship between Aboriginal community controlled health organisations and government departments'*, Doctor of Public Health Dissertation, Flinders University, Adelaide, Australia.

Priest, N., Mackean, T., Waters, E., Davis, E., and Riggs, E. (2009) 'Indigenous child health research: A critical analysis of Australian studies', *Australian and New Zealand Journal of Public Health,* 33(1): 55–63.

Priest, Naomi, Thompson, Laura, Mackean, Tamara, Baker, Alice, and Waters, Elizabeth (2016) 'Yarning up with Koori kids – hearing the voices of Australian urban Indigenous children about their health and well-being', *Ethnicity and Health,* 22(6): 631–647

Punch, Samantha (2015) 'Possibilities for learning between childhoods and youth in the minority and majority worlds: Youth transitions as an example of cross-world dialogue', in Johanna Wyn and Helen Cahill (eds.), *Handbook of Children and Youth Studies.* Singapore: Springer, pp. 689–701.

Punch, Samantha (2016) 'Exploring children's agency across majority and minority world contexts', in Florian Esser, Meike S. Baader, Tanja Betz, Beatrice Hungerland (eds.), *Reconceptualising Agency and Childhood: New Perspectives in Childhood Studies. Routledge Research in Education.* London: Routledge, pp. 183–96.

Qvortrup, Jens, Bardy, Marjatta, Sgritta, Giovanni, and Wintersberger, Helmut (1994) *Childhood Matters: Social Theory, Practice and Politics* (Public Policy and Social Welfare). Aldershot: Avebury.

Raghavendra, P., Newman, L., Grace, E., and Wood, D. (2015) 'Enhancing social participation in young people with communication disabilities living in rural Australia: Outcomes of a home-based intervention for using social media', *Disability and Rehabilitation,* 37(17): 1576–90.

Redmond, G., Skattebol, J., and Saunders, P. (2013) 'The Australian Child Wellbeing Project: Overview', available at www.australianchildwellbeing.com.auhttp://www.sciencedirect.com/science/article/pii/S2214782914000104.

Ross, N.J., Renold, E., Holland, S., and Hillman, A. (2009) 'Moving stories: Using mobile methods to explore the everyday lives of children in public care', *Qualitative Research,* 9(5): 605–23.

Sheller, M. and Urry, J. (2006) 'The new mobilities paradigm', *Environment and Planning,* 38: 207–26.

Shier, H. (2001) 'Pathways to participation: Openings, opportunities and obligations', *Children and Society,* 15(2): 107–17.

Collecting Qualitative Data with Older People

Christine Stephens, Vanessa Burholt, and Norah Keating

INTRODUCTION

The world's population is now ageing at an unprecedented rate. Owing to declining fertility and improved longevity it is predicted that by 2020, older people will outnumber children for the first time in history (Kinsella and Wan, 2009). According to the World Health Organization (WHO, 2015) between 2000 and 2050, the proportion of the world's population aged over 60 years will double from about 11 per cent to 22 per cent. Essentially, this is an increase from 605 million people to 2 billion people aged over 60 years. This important demographic shift is positive for older people, but also presents challenges for policymakers. Many of the challenges to health and well-being associated with population ageing can be addressed by changes in behaviour and policy (Beard and Bloom, 2015). To support these changes we need to address the many gaps in our understandings of the needs of older people.

Older people have long been rendered invisible in medical and social research. Older people have been systematically excluded from clinical research on diseases that specifically affect older people, such as diabetes mellitus, cancer, or heart failure (Witham and McMurdo, 2007). Although alcohol is commonly used by older adults, the New Zealand Alcohol and Drug use Survey included only adults up to the age of 64 (Ministry of Health, 2010). This has not only excluded valuable information from the findings (such as high levels of alcohol use by some older people), but perpetuates assumptions around older people as a homogeneous group with low alcohol use. Calasanti and King (2005) describe how older people have been ignored completely in the study of masculinity and gender.

Population and longitudinal studies are presently being called upon to inform policy and health care changes. However, the research methods used to understand important questions about ageing and health also need to be reconsidered for the sake of 'meaningful progress' (Beard and Bloom, 2015). An important contribution in this regard is the development of good qualitative research. Qualitative studies are an important aspect of capturing the diversity of ageing experiences and issues. Small-scale, in-depth studies are appropriate when we need to answer questions about the ageing experience, to critique ageing assumptions of the broader population, or to reach smaller groups within populations. These sorts of enquiries apply to many different groups of older people such as older caregivers, older people living rurally or in other isolated situations, people who have immigrated (and may not have learned the dominant language), indigenous minority populations, older people with disabilities, and people whose lives have been ignored or criminalised (e.g. LGBT elders).

Because of the diversity of older people, a major challenge of planning qualitative data collection is to resist ageist and often untested assumptions regarding the homogeneity of older people. In talking about 'older people' as a population group to be studied, we tend to forget that 'age' is only about number of years lived. Based on a lifetime of transitions and experiences, people of older age are more diverse than any other group. Health and well-being levels are different, and these are related to differences in social class, race, ethnicity, gender, education level, and material wealth or deprivation (Victor, 2010). Minkler (1996) argued that these 'profound differences in life chances' were increasingly diverse towards the end of the twentieth century and this diversity continues to develop. Although ageist constructions tend to create assumptions about older people as homogeneous, people's different identities, health-related behaviours, and social situations are related to broad differences in health in older age. In this respect, although some older people may provide certain challenges to be overcome by qualitative researchers (such as difference in life experiences between younger and older co-researchers, prevalence of cognitive or physical disabilities, or decreased access to or familiarity with technology) these challenges do not apply to all older people, nor are they exclusively confined to research with older populations.

A primary consideration is that ageing after 60 years remains a developmental process so that 'ageing' is not the equivalent of being an aged person. All people above 60 years of age represented in the WHO statistics cited above represent a 40+ year age span which may be compared to the difference between 10 and 50 years of age in terms of development. Debates about the age at which people may be labelled 'old' will never be resolved, as the characteristics of certain age groups keep changing, especially as health improves, the age of eligibility for pensions shifts, and social constructions of 'elderly' or 'old' change. In the gerontological and health literature, although labels change, and new categories such as the 'young-old' or the 'fourth age' are created (see Gilleard and Higgs, 2013), there is no agreed age at which people change from being 'middle-aged' to 'old' and this can make studies in particular areas difficult to compare.

A second consideration is the tendency to equate ageing with disability. Again there is a wide range of abilities and the population of older people is generally far less disabled than stereotypes suggest (Reed and Clark, 1999). Disability is related to other factors, which if ameliorated would reduce disability among the older population further (Melzer et al., 2000). Such ageist constructions impact on the treatment of older people by policymakers, institutions, and professionals (Latimer, 1997; Reed and Clark, 1999). Researchers are in danger of making similar assumptions, particularly if guided by ethics committees which construct older people as universally vulnerable which is one reason for their exclusion from much research.

Gilleard and Higgs (2000) have suggested that the very multiple fragmentary cultures of ageing or different ways to be an older person in our societies means that ageing as a process must be highlighted as a social concern. As a researcher, the best way to confront issues of diversity is to focus on the specific characteristics and needs of the group engaged in your research as the basis for a well-defined research question. Just as the research approach and methodology will be integral aspects of that research question, so the definition of the population group, within the very broad category of 'older people', will also be an important consideration and one that requires some reflection.

All qualitative research methods can be used with older people, however different research questions call for different methodological approaches. The choice of methodology will in turn determine the choice of an appropriate data collection method. Here we provide some illustrations of the range of approaches to data collection that are useful in relation to particular research questions (the references here will provide more details about the methods used).

The data for questions around ageist attitudes may be collected in a variety of ways. Instances of natural conversations (see Potter and Shaw, Chapter 12, this volume) that can be recorded (e.g. care workers talking with older clients, nurses discussing older patients) are ideal data for studying ageism which is constructed in language and shared in everyday talk. These approaches to data collection can be found in medical settings in which opportunities to record data are available, and ageist attitudes and actions are an important issue. Coupland and Coupland (1994) provide a good example of this approach. Using exchanges between doctor and patient recorded in one geriatric outpatient clinic in a Welsh hospital, they showed how older people themselves draw on ageist discourses to disenfranchise themselves (but also to liberate themselves from the demands of a healthy lifestyle). Grainger (1993) analysed the recorded interactions between elderly patients and nursing staff during certain care routines on wards in two long-stay hospitals in Wales. They found that the nurses' talk prioritised physical tasks, such as bathing, which was often at odds with the patients' relational needs. These data are very valuable and may be interrogated in many ways. Wood and Kroger (1993) used secondary data from many sources, recorded in doctor/patient consultations in the UK and US, including Grainger's data, to specifically show the ways that forms of address (formal or intimate) are used to reproduce the powerlessness and dependence associated with ageing. Such data are also among the most difficult to collect because of many ethical and privacy issues, as well as practical issues of recording and participant agreement.

Other more publicly available sources of data have been used by researchers taking a discursive approach to studies of ageist attitudes (see Rau et al., Chapter 19, this volume). Examples include media accounts, collected across newspapers, to show publicly held attitudes (Fealy et al., 2012; Powell, 2014), or an examination of the television programme *The Golden Girls* for the way in which humorous devices were related to meanings of age (Harwood and Giles, 1992). Interviews (see Roulston and Choi, Chapter 15, this volume) with older people are also a good source of data, as in the interviews with 50-year-old women used to explore the morality of age-related norms by Nikander (2000).

When researchers turn to questions about older people's own experiences or preferences, asking older people directly in interviews or focus groups is the most straightforward method. Questions about the experience of ageing are often answered by taking a phenomenological approach which depends upon personal accounts. For example, Tulle (2008) conducted life history interviews with elite runners, aged 48 to 86, in Scotland to capture the details of bodily experience among a group of people whose physicality challenged the social norms of ageing bodies. Tulle used interviews and participant observation to capture the experience of running and to participate in social interactions among runners.

Interviews and focus groups (see Morgan and Hoffman, Chapter 16, this volume) have also been used to understand the aspects of housing that were important to community-dwelling older people. Peace et al. (2011) sought the views of people living in a wide range of different localities through nine group discussions. The results of the group work were then explored in depth in 54 interviews. These data were subjected to grounded theory analysis to develop a theory of person–environment interaction.

Collecting narratives (see Murray, Chapter 17, this volume) using audio recordings of interviews has been very useful in highlighting older people's housing preferences which have as much to do with functional, symbolic, and emotional attachments and meanings of home as with convenience and comfort (Wiles et al., 2012). Benbow and Kingston (2014) collected largely audio-taped spoken narratives from both people with dementia and their caregivers to identify themes of support, stress, and coping which highlighted the inter-relational and practical implications of these themes. Phoenix and Sparkes (2009) used one man's interview to show how people use stories to construct a positive ageing identity and resist negative narratives.

An observational approach (see Wästerfors, Chapter 20, this volume) to data collection is particularly appropriate for those who may be unable to speak for themselves, such as people with dementia. Kontos (2004) studied the maintenance of selfhood through embodied interactions with the world by residents of a care home using ethnographic methods (see Buscatto, Chapter 21, this volume). Field notes made by the researcher were based on observations of particular activities in the care home over eight months to explore the life world of individuals with Alzheimer's disease, including their appearance, social relationships, customs and communications, and bodily practices. Some ethnographic studies may draw on a variety of methods to capture people's perceptions. For example, Ponzetti (2003) explored housing preferences in rural areas by using photographs taken by participants, along with interview data.

Once the research question and methodological approach has been chosen, then the needs of a particular population group will also influence the methods to be used. For example, although focus groups are an excellent way to collect socially shared understandings, these groups are not suitable for hearing impaired people. Internet forums as a data collection method have been used to include those, such as employed people, or the caregivers of older people, who are physically isolated but have high levels of social media use (Horrell et al., 2015). Alternative methods have also been developed for interviewing participants in care homes with high proportions of cognitively impaired residents. These methods include the use of proxies (relatives or carers) to speak for the older person, or specialist communication tools such as 'talking mats' (Magee et al., 2008).

Given the breadth of this topic and importance of particular research questions, this chapter will focus on three areas for research: supportive environments for ageing, community inclusion and service provision for older people, and the sense of self maintained by older people with dementia. These examples have been chosen to show how researchers have approached specific issues in data collection with older people from the perspective of three different research questions.

WHAT MAKES COMMUNITIES GOOD PLACES TO GROW OLD?

Contemporary views of the well-being of older people place considerable emphasis on the environments in which they live. Environments encompass key elements of the extrinsic world including physical settings of home and neighbourhood, social networks of family and friends, neighbourhood and community, and the broader society representing attitudes and policies towards older persons (World Health Organization, 2015). The field of environmental gerontology is devoted to understanding these environments and older peoples' interactions with them. Rowles and Bernard (2013, p. 3) articulate an underlying premise of this perspective when they state: 'We are shaped by the physical and social environments of our life – where we were born, where we grew up, where we live today, and where we grow old.' Environments shape lifecourse trajectories and late life diversity (Dannefer, 2003).

Community environments have been of particular interest in recent years. They are positioned as important because it is in these bounded places that older people live their lives, connect with services and people, and construct their sense of belonging (Burholt et al., 2014; Means and Evans, 2012; Provencher et al., 2014). Community can provide stability across the life course. In countries such as the UK, the current cohort of older people is more likely than younger cohorts to have lived in the same community for most of their lives (Phillipson, 2007). 'Ageing in place' has become a metaphor for an ideal situation in which people grow older in familiar surroundings. There is evidence that older adults may prefer to remain in the same place despite their own functional limitations or environmental barriers that make it difficult to remain independent (Lien et al., 2015). Initiatives to promote ageing in place are growing in many countries (Greenfield, 2011). A global 'age-friendly communities' initiative has captured the imagination of governments, service providers and municipalities (Moulaert and Garon, 2016).

From the standpoint of researchers, determining the ways in which communities are good places to grow old requires further theoretical precision and empirical exploration. Supportive environments can foster well-being through bridging gaps between older persons' resources and their ability to live their lives as they wish. Equally, environments can be restrictive, excluding older people from strong family or friend relationships, community engagement or full citizenship (Scharf and Keating, 2012). Following Winterton et al. (2016) we believe that it is time to deconstruct the nature of communities in relation to how they interact with the lives of older rural adults.

Methods to Assess Diversity of Community Supportiveness to Older Adults

Methods presented here represent an approach to examining the supportiveness of community environments of older persons, informed by the assumptions presented in the previous section of the need to understand the interactions between community and older people; and assumptions related to diversity among older people themselves. Case study is the primary methodological approach, chosen because of its goal of investigating contemporary phenomena in their everyday context (Yin, 2014). Like older people, communities themselves are diverse and it is around these diversities in older people and in rural communities that methods were chosen.

Patton (2015) and Yin (2014) outline four main steps in case study methodology: identify a phenomenon of interest; define one or more cases where the phenomenon is manifest; describe each case in terms of its major characteristics and unique features; and present cross-case findings and insight into the phenomenon of interest. In this section we discuss issues that needed to be addressed in choosing methods in each of these areas. We illustrate these steps with methods used in a large Canadian programme of research on rural communities in Canada.

Identify a phenomenon of interest: Diversity in communities requires consideration of which types of communities are most relevant to the question at hand. Rural communities provide an excellent forum for the examination of discourses about community environments. There are relatively high proportions of older people in rural compared to urban areas (Rural and Small Town Canada Analysis Bulletin, 2008); concern about availability of formal services and support especially in remote areas (Skinner et al., 2008); and outmigration of young people seeking employment in larger areas (Chang et al., 2011). Importantly, there are conflicting discourses about growing old in rural communities. In countries such as Canada and Australia, with their low population density and vast geographies, rural communities are seen as poor places to grow old because they are distant from services and amenities and lacking in local capacity to provide them (Keane et al., 2012; Winterton et al., 2016). In contrast, beliefs in the supportiveness and generosity of rural communities lead to assumptions of rural places as good places to grow old (Keating et al., 2013). Challenging these assumptions requires active engagement with older rural residents in their community settings.

Stake (1995) argues that cases are always bounded, although sometimes the boundaries around cases are not easily defined. We chose a definition of 'rural' based on criteria from the national census of Canada that include population size, density, and distance from urban centres. Based on this definition, the average size of rural communities in Canada is approximately 1,700 (Keefe et al., 2004).

Identify one or more cases where the phenomenon is manifest: Case selection has been described as the primordial task of the case study researcher, requiring both a representative sample and variation on the dimensions of theoretical interest, all within a very small number of cases (Seawright and Gerring, 2008). Census community profiles were used to further select communities to understand rural community supportiveness (see http://www12.statcan.gc.ca/census-recensement/index-eng.cfm for examples of data available in these profiles). Four criteria were used. First, communities were chosen that had a population ranging from 1,000 to 3,000 people. Such communities are near the national average for rural community size and represent the small communities believed to be both socially supportive and bereft of services. From these, communities were chosen with a higher proportion of older adults than the provincial average. To best understand the diversity among rural older adults it was important to select communities in which many older adults live. Third, we used an available proxy for the level of community supportiveness provided to older adults which was the proportion of residents who reported that they had provided unpaid assistance to one or more older adults in the last year. Communities were categorised based on the level of supportiveness to older adults. This categorisation allowed us to understand how different contexts in which older adults live matter to their experiences of community supportiveness. Throughout the process of choosing communities, the focus on better understanding the interfaces between communities and their older residents was central. Final determination of the three rural communities was based on research access. The communities chosen were those in which the researchers had formed relationships with some community members which could facilitate data collection in the community.

Describe each case in terms of its major characteristics and unique features: Use of multiple data sources is a defining feature of case study research. Baxter and Jack (2008) stress the importance of making judicious choices about data sources, employing only those that will facilitate a holistic understanding of the phenomenon.

In our example, case community descriptions were developed from two sources. Archival materials including community histories and local newspapers were used for descriptions of changes in community characteristics and resources. Census of Canada community profiles provided information on population size, age distribution, gender distribution, education, and income across censuses from 1921. These descriptive community biographies were augmented with narratives that illustrated residents' views of the predominant characteristics of their communities. In combination they led to community labels including one called 'bypassed'. We relied heavily on narratives of older people who were long-time residents. For example, one corroborated the biography of that community of decline and privation in her comment: 'No bus, no train, no nothing ... one of these days the tide won't come in' (Keating et al., 2013).

'Embedded case study' is a term used for cases that have subunits. While the overall goal of a holistic understanding of the case remains, embedded cases require that questions be asked about both the case and its subunits (Rowley, 2002; Scholz and Tietje, 2002). Following this principle, a second set of methods was used to address community supportiveness from the perspective of key community stakeholders. The intent was to be inclusive and participatory. Standpoints of older people were privileged. Semi-structured interviews were developed to elicit their views of what makes a rural community a good place to grow old. Analyses of data from these stakeholder subunits resulted in the development of profiles of older persons (community active, stoic, marginalised, and frail) who had different experiences of community supportiveness. The profiles were based on personal resources, interactions with people, and level of and approach to community engagement (see Eales et al., 2008, and Keating and Eales, 2011, for a full description of the development of typologies of rural older adults).

To integrate these subunit findings into the overall understanding of community supportiveness, small invited consultation groups were held in each community to elicit feedback on preliminary findings. We were proactive in including older adults across ages and levels of community engagement. Others who were familiar with older adults and/or community issues locally were also invited: volunteers with seniors' organisations, and representatives of a range of community services such as health, church ministerial, retail grocery, and law enforcement services. The participants validated findings about different profiles of older adults and discussed the ways in which their community supported these different groups of older adults.

Present cross-case findings and insight into the phenomenon of interest: Studies in which multiple cases are used focus on the overall concept that cases have in common. Cross-case analysis requires what Stake (2006) describes as moving from the foreshadowed overall concept to the multi-case assertion. In our exemplar study, cross-case comparison was based on findings from both the cases communities and from the subunits of groups of people within them. Thus, cross-case analyses were based in examination of how community type (identified as farming, bucolic, or bypassed) might influence supportiveness to different groups of older adults (identified as community active, stoic, marginalised, and frail).

Theory-building can be an important outcome of case study research. Eisenhardt and Graebner (2007) assert that theory-building in case studies can be very sound given the rich real world context of the research and the groundedness of theory construction, which is based in close connection to the data. Theory about community supportiveness to older adults was a main focus of the cross-case analysis in the rural communities research described here. The findings allowed for a development of theoretical assumptions that went beyond a static question of whether rural communities are supportive to older adults, to dynamic, ecological assumptions. Communities are most supportive when the variety of needs and resources of older residents are a good fit with community resources. The perspectives of older residents were centrally important in understanding what makes for a 'good fit' and helped us articulate a belief that supportiveness is dynamic and reflects changes over time in both people and places (Keating et al., 2013).

HOW CAN CO-PRODUCED QUALITATIVE RESEARCH CONTRIBUTE TO COMMUNITY INCLUSION AND SERVICE DEVELOPMENT FOR OLDER PEOPLE IN THE COMMUNITY?

There are many reasons for involving older people in qualitative participatory research, for example personal, political, ethical, ontological, and epistemological motives. Ethically, and from a human rights perspective, research findings impact on the development of policy and practice, and therefore affect the lives of those 'being researched'. Accordingly, older people have a right to be involved in research that impacts upon their lives (Burholt et al., 2010). Participatory research can be used as a method of anti-oppression allowing older people control over the research process and the production of knowledge (Strier, 2007). It fits well with a critical gerontological perspective and can facilitate co-researchers (academics and lay seniors) to challenge and reshape ways in which societies construct ageing, and impact on the lives of older people (Ziegler and Scharf, 2013).

The theoretical foundations of participatory research can be traced to educational philosophers such as John Dewey and Paulo Freire. Freire (1970) describes politically engaged methods of teaching that provide participants with tools to understand and critically challenge 'realities' in society and equip them with knowledge that can be used to transform these (Freire, 1970). Similarly, Dewey saw education as the mechanism to develop social consciousness, which would provide the fuel for social transformation (Dewey, 1897). In this respect, participatory research can equip older people with the skills and knowledge to lobby for change (for example, in service delivery) and to positively impact on quality of life.

Participatory research is defined as that in which more than one older person contributes to and is meaningfully involved in any of the design, conduct, and dissemination of a study. By contributing to design, older people may help researchers circumnavigate any difficulties associated with particular groups (e.g. identifying preferred ways of working with people with dementia and/or their carers).

Methods of Participatory Research and Engagement with Older People

Various authors have developed 'principles of engagement' for participatory research (e.g. in community-based participatory research (Israel et al., 1998)); action research with older people (Blair and Minkler, 2009); and with disempowered groups (Whitmore and McGee, 2001). In particular, there are four main areas of this approach that a researcher should consider: (i) collaboration and equitable involvement in all phases of the research; (ii) solidarity and capacity-building; (iii) empowerment and action for social/systems change; and (iv) sustainability. To illustrate these principles of participatory research we draw on examples from the Rural North Wales Initiative for the Development of Support for Older People (RuralWIDe). RuralWIDe was a collaborative venture between university researchers, Age Concern Gwynedd a Môn and older volunteers. The project sought to empower older people by increasing the level and impact of their involvement in local communities through (a) the promotion of volunteering in isolated rural areas and (b) active participation in the planning and development of services to their own communities. It aimed to improve the knowledge and skills of older volunteers to enable them to be actively involved in the research process. The challenges of involving older people in participatory research should not be underestimated, and rigorous methods can ensure meaningful involvement. The lessons learned from RuralWIDe and other participatory projects are illustrated below under the principles of engagement.

Collaborative and equitable involvement in all phases of the research

In participatory research, issues of power relations and imbalances should be addressed by the researcher. For example, it is essential that older people's knowledge and lived experiences have parity with academic knowledge. Researchers should be prepared to reveal their own role and power in the research process, for example, entitlement to apply for funding when others are not. The researcher needs to be both critically reflective and transparent about their participation, social location, and identity with those with whom they work. In RuralWIDe the academics revealed their motives for involvement in the research, exposing personal backgrounds, and the monetary benefit of being involved in the project.

Simultaneously, it is essential to understand what older people wish to achieve from their involvement. In RuralWIDe, researchers spent time getting to know the volunteers, their interests, and experience. It is worth noting that older participants do not necessarily want to be involved in every stage of research. In RuralWIDe, some older people were happy to influence the study design while others were keen to be involved in interviews. Providing flexible methods of engagement can accommodate new people joining the project, while permitting others to drop out, or join at different stages.

Solidarity and capacity-building

To ensure equitable and meaningful involvement in all stages of the research it may be necessary to develop lay researcher skills through the provision of training. This can, for example, increase understanding of the inductive research cycle, ethical practices, and the variety of methods that are available for qualitative interviewing and analysis.

It is important to select the appropriate venue. In RuralWIDe we used private rooms in pubs and community centres close to or in the co-researchers' communities. Informal public settings provided comfortable training environments that did not have the trappings of more formal settings, such as the university. The researchers made the environments more hospitable by providing ample refreshments. This, along with the relaxed and informal attitude of the research team, helped to create a psychologically comfortable environment, which nurtured learning (Knowles, 1980).

Understanding the co-researchers' experiences is vital to developing support or training programmes. Any teaching strategy should capitalise upon the prior experiences of participants and acknowledge their motivations for taking part. It should build on people's skills using their knowledge when appropriate and providing support when required, building on the principles of andragogy: the 'art and science of teaching adults' (Knowles, 1980, p. 42; Rachal, 2002). In RuralWIDe, participants were volunteers and included an ex-postman and military photographer, a residential care home worker, a secretary, and a homemaker. They participated in the research for their own personal fulfilment or other personal motivation (e.g. to improve the situation of local older people).

Participatory research requires an element of skills exchange and co-learning so that all co-researchers can learn from each other. To achieve this, academic researchers must adopt anti-discriminatory practices. For example, sharing research documentation via email or online forums may not be appropriate for everyone (Evans et al., 2014) and issues associated with the use of specialist analytical software such as the cost of site or individual licenses, and help with writing and running complex analytical syntax may undermine inclusion.

There are many benefits for the research outcomes. For example, older people conducting research in their own communities may have 'insider status' and a greater ability to elicit data from potential interviewees than unfamiliar professional researchers who may be mistrusted (Richardson, 2014). In RuralWIDe the involvement of older people contributed to lower refusal rates. Furthermore, the ideational fluency and originality of older volunteers may be significantly different from that of academics (Burholt et al., 2010). RuralWIDe co-researchers formulated unusual research questions that were unconstrained by scientific or theoretical parameters within which the academics worked.

Throughout the cycle of participatory research, collaborators should aim to build mutual trust (Dickson and Green, 2001). Older researchers need to trust the academics to allow them authentic participation that can influence the research design and conduct, ultimately leading to action. Similarly, academic researchers need to trust that older co-researchers will carry out research in an ethical and scientifically robust way. A team on a participatory project moves towards becoming a collective with common goals for research, action and change (Averill, 2005).

Empowerment and action for social/systems change

One of the purposes of participatory research is to bring about social or systems change through increased community awareness, understanding, or attitudinal change which can lead to building public will and civic action. The generation of ownership of a participatory project is integral to its success. In RuralWIDe this was achieved by ensuring that the study addressed issues that the co-researchers felt were important.

Participatory projects commonly address issues for marginalised groups. In order to ensure fair representation, it may be necessary to permit others (beyond the core co-research team) to contribute to the research. In RuralWIDe, the first interpretations of the data were presented to Age Concern forums in Gwynedd. This gave other older people living in rural areas opportunities to reflect upon them. The amalgamation of the focus group comments with the initial analysis were developed into a report that described a project conducted by older people, for older people and included *their* recommendations on how support and services for older people in rural areas could be improved.

In order to achieve personal or group empowerment a targeted dissemination strategy is crucial. Co-researchers on RuralWIDe presented to a range of audiences including the British Society of Gerontology Annual Conference, the Annual Scientific meeting of the Gerontological Society of America and the European Commission in Brussels. A day conference was held within the county to disseminate the findings to local practitioners, service providers, councillors and politicians and the North Wales branch of the British Geriatric Society invited the older researchers to provide an account of difficulties encountered accessing specialist health services in remote areas. Ultimately the efforts of the participatory research team had a direct impact on local service provision and the recommendations from the study were included in the action plan for a Strategy for Good Ageing in Gwynedd.

Sustainability

Participatory research has the potential to increase the capacity of community organisations and individuals to conduct research. For academic researchers the end of funding (or publication) often marks the end of a project. However, for participatory projects, co-researchers may continue to exploit the data to influence change and use their skills to embark on new research ventures beyond the end of the funded period. Academics on RuralWIDe continued to respond to requests for help with research-related activities for several years after the project funding had terminated.

One way to ensure sustainability of participatory research is for older researchers to pass on their acquired skills and knowledge to others. In the case of RuralWIDE older researchers found ways to use new skills for the benefit of others: one became the Chair of a Welsh Government-funded network of people interested in health and social care research; two others joined an Expert Advisory Group influencing research priorities for older people in Wales. Thus, sustainability can be facilitated by an infrastructure that supports participatory research. Researchers should be aware that if a supportive infrastructure is not available, they may be requested to invest more human and financial resources to support older researchers long after the project funding has ceased.

HOW DO PEOPLE WITH DEMENTIA MAINTAIN THEIR SENSE OF SELF?

Qualitative research with people with dementia also focuses on inclusion. Assumptions of incompetence on the part of those diagnosed with dementia, and expectations that they are unable to provide reliable accounts, has meant that the people with dementia have often been ignored in favour of accounts from caregivers and professionals. This exclusion makes older persons with dementia more vulnerable to inappropriate treatment and care (Dewing, 2002). However, there is growing recognition of the rights of people with dementia and the value of understanding the person's perspective (Downs, 1997) and people with dementia are increasingly included in research as participants rather than objects of study (Dewing, 2002; Gillies, 2000; McKillop and Wilkinson, 2004).

An important shift has been towards recognition of a person's sense of self, despite memory loss and personality changes. The traditional view of the disappearance of the person has had profound implications for the treatment of dementia patients in research and care. Sabat and Harre (1992) and Ramanathan-Abbott (1994) provided influential accounts of the construction of self through the late stages of Alzheimer's disease. Based on linguistic analyses, they argued that the personal self remains intact, while the loss of self commonly attributed to dementia is the loss of the social self, based on other people's reactions. Several other authors have since concluded that the self is constructed within a social context (see Cohen-Mansfield et al., 2006) and have drawn on accounts by persons with dementia to explain how subjective experience is shaped through social and cultural location, personal identity, and interactions with family and carers (e.g. Gillies, 2000; Hulko, 2009). Caddell and Clare (2010) reviewed studies of identity and dementia to conclude that qualitative studies (including studies from social constructionist, narrative, and embodied self-perspectives) provide rich and detailed information regarding the subjective experience of self in dementia. They recommend ongoing enquiry to address unanswered questions about the nature of self in dementia, and how people with dementia are able to maintain their sense of self. Two main data collection methods have been used in this work: interviews between researcher and participant or observations of everyday interactions.

Interviews

The use of the interview is popular among researchers trying to include the views and perceptions of people with dementia (e.g. Gillies, 2000; Keady and Gilliard, 1999; Pearce et al., 2002; Pratt and Wilkinson, 2003). The numbers of participants are usually very small (sometimes single case studies; e.g. Hubbard et al., 2002), with a focus on gathering rich data.

Pratt (2002, pp. 165–81) describes the usefulness of interviews with people with dementia and some important issues from the researcher's perspective. These include the safety of the context, the methods used, and reflexive practice. To create a safe context for interviews, Pratt highlights the negotiation of relationships with gatekeepers and caregivers. It is also important to be aware of the possibility of distress on the part of the interviewee, particularly if the topic is related to the diagnosis of dementia. An interviewer must be prepared to cope with distress without excluding participants, and to provide appropriate responses to participants' questions (such as questions about the diagnosis and other participants' experiences) which are beyond the expertise or role of the interviewer. Methods that do not rely on accurate recall, but rather focus on participants' abilities (e.g. recognition of feelings and experiences) are recommended. Pratt also suggests using multiple interviews to develop rapport and to account for any changes in cognitive abilities over time. Finally, she stresses the importance of reflexive practice. Reflecting on the differences in perspective between researcher and interviewee, and on the interviewer's emotional reactions, is critical. Equally important is allowing the interviewee opportunities to reflect on the experience of the interview as it progresses, for example, some people may be distressed but want to share their experiences, whereas others choose to shift to a more comfortable topic.

McKillop and Wilkinson (2004) have provided guidance for interviewers from the perspective of an experienced participant in dementia research. These guidelines overlap with Pratt's advice but from the interviewee's perspective. These may be summarised as: Ask the participant directly for permission to be interviewed and to be audio recorded (with appropriate explanations); ask the carer for consent as a matter of courtesy and do not proceed if they will not agree; reschedule the interview if the participant tires; choose the time and place with care; choose the topics with care (possibly consulting with the carer about distressing topics); be personable and avoid signs of officialdom; assist with the practical details of repeat visits. Many of these principles could be applied to any interview situation; their application to people with dementia enables inclusion and respect for the interviewee.

Observational Studies

Observational studies have been used variously to record language in everyday interactions and non-verbal communications and actions. Numbers of participants may vary. For example, in a single case study, Sabat and Collins (1999) used recorded conversations and observations of one woman in a day care centre, along with interviews with her husband and the staff to show that Mrs F. maintained many social and emotional abilities, not recognised by staff or clinical records. In a larger study of constructions of self and identity, Tappen et al. (1999) recorded 45 conversations between 23 nursing home residents (in the later stages of probable Alzheimer's disease) and their nurses.

Hubbard et al. (2002) used ethnographic methods to observe the non-verbal communicative behaviours of ten participants in a day-care centre. Two researchers participated in the activities of the day-care centre and made notes during the observations and immediately after the observation session. They established that older people with dementia use, interpret, and define non-verbal communication with others. Kontos (2004) used the same methods, with 13 participants from a care home, to explore the notion that selfhood is embodied. Ethnographic participant observation was conducted eight hours a day, three days a week, for eight months. Detailed and descriptive field notes (elaborated afterwards) included descriptions of the setting, the actions and interactions of participants, their emotions, and non-verbal communication. Kontos showed how personal identity is expressed in preferences, customs, and social relationships.

These brief examples show that observational data-gathering is time intensive and requires attentive and reflexive relationships with participants. What is being observed in each situation depends on the research question, and the data-gathering depends on the relationships developed with the person with dementia, their caregivers, and family. Interview and observational methods are often combined. Hubbard et al. (2002) recommend that when working with institutionalised persons different methods should be chosen as appropriate to each person. Thus, gathering data requires a commitment of flexibility and time.

Ethical Issues

The earlier assumptions of persons' with dementia incompetence and vulnerability have raised ethical issues around data collection and particularly around consent to participate (see Mertens, Chapter 3, this volume). Although the opportunity to participate in a research interview may be empowering for people with dementia, the risk of harm such as invasion of privacy, is balanced against this good. Many voices currently support inclusion, noting that exclusion is unethical, people have a right to be heard (e.g. Swain et al., 1998) and people have the right to contribute to research that is about their own needs (Bartlett and Martin, 2002; Sherrat et al., 2007). Many of the ethical implications of involving older people with dementia in research are still being negotiated (Sherratt et al., 2007).

Bartlett and Martin (2002) outline three central and potentially problematic issues around informed consent: participants are fully informed, consent is given freely, and the person is competent to give consent. Providing information itself must be tailored to the individual's circumstances (McKillop and Wilkinson, 2004) and this is not always clear-cut. Gillies (2000) raises one central issue in her work with community-dwelling people with a diagnosis of dementia: most participants did not know about their diagnosis. Although a medical ethics committee, formal carers and services, informal carers, and ultimately the individual with dementia consented to the study, the participants themselves consented to interviews about their 'memory problem'. Gillies discusses the ethical dilemma of 'collusion with the non-sharing of such personal information' in terms of '…the medical nature of the diagnosis and the complex of relationships between person/physician, person/family, person/society, and person/researcher which has yet to be comprehensively addressed in research on dementia' (2000, p. 368). Bartlett and Martin (2002) addressed this same dilemma by deciding that the risk of deception was outweighed by the risk of doing harm through introducing a possibly distressing label (dementia) into the discussion.

Issues of consent and competence are raised when people are severely cognitively impaired. Lack of competence cannot be assumed, but, competence must be considered in terms of what people are consenting to (Downs, 1997). Because of the ongoing debates around what inclusion in research means to the person with dementia, each decision must be made in terms of the overarching ethical issues involved (Dewing, 2002). Sherratt et al. (2007) discuss the complexity of these issues with examples from research. For example, the value of including older people with dementia in an observational study without their overt consent may be deemed to outweigh any risks to themselves or their privacy. When competency is in doubt, consent is often sought through the caregivers or sometimes the physicians (see Bartlett and Martin, 2002). Sherratt et al. (2007) additionally provide a comprehensive account of the ethical guidelines available in different countries.

Researchers have noted that for persons with dementia in the community (e.g. Gillies, 2000) and living in care homes (e.g. Bartlett and Martin, 2002), there are several levels of gatekeepers that must be negotiated before the potential participant may be approached for consent. These include ethics committees, health organisations, care organisations, managers, health professionals or service providers, and family members or caregivers. Bartlett and Martin also describe the issues around caregivers or family who wish to be part of the interview situation.

There are several discussions of these issues now emerging in the literature. For example, Bartlett and Martin (2002) provide a helpful discussion from the researchers' perspective, including a case study as an example. Hubbard et al. (2002) discuss the details of consent for older people with different competencies, while Sherratt et al. (2007) provide an ethics board perspective on decisions about competency and rights including many examples from a wide range of research.

DISCUSSION

The three types of research questions and examples of data collection methods discussed above, involve quite different groups of older people in projects that ask applied questions about issues of community provision, health services, and engagement in community, as well as the important care implications of sense of self. To answer these questions, a variety of data collection methods has been employed as appropriate for community-dwelling participants or those in care. These methods include a comparative case study approach with the use of archival materials, focus groups, and interviews to study different communities; community participants as researchers of local issues, who develop their own research questions, conduct interviews, and participate in analysis and dissemination; and interviews and participant observation with people with dementia. Despite the differences in the research questions and the methods used, some clear principles that apply to the use of qualitative methods with older people may be identified. Researchers use qualitative methods to contribute to filling gaps in our knowledge about older people while:

1. being inclusive,
2. challenging assumptions of homogeneity, and
3. recognising that ageing occurs in a social context.

Qualitative methods are well suited to addressing these principles while building knowledge about older people. However, there is no single method. We need the whole qualitative repertoire to address questions and challenge assumptions. At the same time there are important methodological frontiers to be addressed, including those raised by our examples.

In regard to the first principle of inclusion, there are many issues that require continuous reflexive consideration of power relations and imbalances between the researcher and the researched. Community case study research exemplifies a participatory approach, which gives voice to many people in neglected areas. By allowing full expression of a variety of views, new understandings of the powerful effects of social and structural differences arise. Researchers using these approaches must be vigilant about the consideration of who gets included in such studies (and who may be excluded) and work towards recognising and avoiding any discriminatory practices. Research with people with dementia provides a good example of recent changes in understandings about the inclusion of those on the margins of society. A very positive shift to privilege the voices of those experiencing the phenomenon is welcomed by people with dementia themselves, and provides important lessons about challenging assumptions of incompetence and not objectifying people of interest. At the same time, this shift raises challenges regarding the time intensive and reflexive nature of the research and of the ethics of exclusion and the roles of gatekeepers. These are the same principles that apply to good research with any population, while highlighting the extra vigilance required with those who are vulnerable. There are important ethical issues around working with people with dementia that are still to be resolved. Co-produced participatory research potentially gives older people full rights to be involved in research about their own lives and needs, allowing them meaningful involvement and more control over the production of knowledge. However, participatory approaches are very difficult to implement, and the research that has been conducted spans a continuum from manipulation and tokenism to citizen control (Arnstein, 1969; Carter and Beresford, 2000; Tritter and McCallum, 2006). Despite its potential there is still relatively little 'good' participatory research with older people (Fudge et al., 2007; Burholt et al., 2010) while the approach has powerful potential in appropriate areas of work.

The second principle, challenging assumptions of homogeneity, means recognising the diversity of the ageing experience and this has similar implications as the principle of inclusion for qualitative data collection. The methods must be developed to suit the needs of the population, and designed to allow all voices to be heard, while paying careful attention to those on the margins. Researchers must also recognise the diversity of the contexts of ageing; like all people, older people live in different countries, in different social strata, in different types of communities and in different life circumstances.

The third principle recognises the social contexts of ageing. Growing older happens to us all but in a variety of social contexts that construct the ageing experience itself. Here the research question must be carefully considered to take into account issues of conceptualising and operationalising boundaries around contexts of interest. The data collection approach based on these sorts of questions can lead to challenging social assumptions about the 'right' way to age, the assumptions of policy discourses such as 'ageing in place', and the power of psychological and medical models of 'successful ageing'. Framing the research question and methods, in terms of the social context of older peoples' experiences and needs, has the ability to bring to the forefront popular discourses which construct assumptions about contexts such as 'rural communities are good/bad places to age'. Gerontological researchers can use qualitative methods to build theory about the interfaces between ageing experiences and contexts and how they change over time. There is much work to be done to understand the diversity of the social context and its effects on the process of ageing as well as on the aged. For example, being old may be secondary to the setting in regard to issues of welfare and inclusion. There remains much to be learned from understanding phenomena in different contexts, such as across different societies and nations.

CONCLUSION

Qualitative research with older people has the power to recognise ageism in all its forms and the use of appropriate data collection methods may reduce ageism, which is perpetuated by research methods themselves. For example, equating ageing with disability and incompetence will affect data collection methods by excluding those whose voices can contribute much relevant knowledge to the aims of improving the well-being of all older people. Recognising diversity, recognising the importance of the social context, and including all older people in research can be achieved through the use of appropriate qualitative data collection methods. At the same time, there is much to work towards. Being reflexive about the basis, the purpose, and the (wanted and unwanted) effects of all the methods we employ, is vitally important to the development of sound ethical approaches to research with older people.

FURTHER READING

HelpAge International. [available from *HelpAge Intl.*, PO Box 32832, London N1 9ZN, UK].

Heslop, Mandy (2002) *Participatory Research with Older People: A Sourcebook*. London: HelpAge International.

Keating, Norah (ed.) (2008) *Rural Ageing: A Good Place to Grow Old?* Bristol: The Policy Press.

Wilkinson, Heather (ed.) (2002) *The Perspectives of People with Dementia: Research Methods and Motivations*. London and Philadelphia: Jessica Kingsley Publishers.

REFERENCES

Arnstein, S. R. (1969) 'A ladder of citizen participation', *Journal of American Institute of Planners*, 35(4): 216–24.

Averill, J. B. (2005) 'Studies of rural elderly individuals: Merging critical ethnography with community-based action research', *Journal of Gerontological Nursing*, 31(12): 11–18.

Bartlett, Helen and Martin, Wendy (2002) 'Ethical issues in dementia care research', in Heather Wilkinson (ed.), *The Perspectives of People with Dementia: Research Methods and Motivations*. London and Philadelphia: Jessica Kinglsey Publishers, pp. 47–61.

Baxter, P. and Jack, S. (2008) 'Qualitative case study methodology: Study design and implementation for novice researchers', *The Qualitative Report*, 13(4): 544–59.

Beard, John R. and Bloom, David E. (2015) 'Towards a comprehensive public health response to population ageing', *Lancet* (London, England), 385(9968): 658–61.

Benbow, S. M. and Kingston, P. (2014) '"Talking about my experiences ... at times disturbing yet positive": Producing narratives with people living with dementia', *Dementia*. DOI: 10.1177/1471301214551845.

Blair, T. and Minkler, M. (2009) 'Participatory action research with older people: Key principles in practice', *The Gerontologist*, 49(5): 651–62.

Burholt, Vanessa, Curry, Nigel, Keating, Norah, and Eales, Jacquie (2014) 'Connecting with community: The nature of belonging among rural elders', in Catherine Hennessy, Robin Means, and Vanessa Burholt (eds.), *Countryside Connections: Older People, Community and Place in Rural Britain*. Bristol: The Policy Press, pp. 95–124.

Burholt, V., Nash, P., Naylor, D., and Windle, G. (2010) 'Training older volunteers in gerontological research in the United Kingdom: Moving towards an andragogical and emancipatory agenda', *Journal of Educational Gerontology*, 36: 753–80.

Caddell, L. S. and Clare, L. (2010) 'The impact of dementia on self and identity: A systematic review', *Clinical Psychology Review*, 30(1): 113–26.

Calasanti, T. and King, N. (2005) 'Firming the floppy penis: Age, class, and gender relations in the lives of old men', *Men and Masculinities*, 8(1): 3–23.

Carter, Tony and Beresford, Peter (2000) *Age and Change: Models of Involvement for Older People*. York: Joseph Rowntree Foundation.

Chang, H., Dong, X., and MacPhail, F. (2011) 'Labor migration and time use patterns of the left-behind children and elderly in rural China', *World Development*, 39(12): 2199–210.

Cohen-Mansfield, J., Parpura-Gill, A., and Golander, H. (2006) 'Utilization of self-identity roles for designing interventions for persons with dementia', *The Journals of Gerontology Series B: Psychological Sciences and Social Sciences*, 61(4): P202–P212.

Coupland, J. and Coupland, N. (1994) '"Old age doesn't come alone": Discursive representations of health-in-aging in geriatric medicine', *The International Journal of Aging and Human Development*, 39(1): 81–93.

Crichton, J. and Koch, T. (2007) 'Living with dementia: Curating self-identity', *Dementia*, 6(3): 365–81.

Dannefer, D. (2003) 'Cumulative advantage/disadvantage and the life course: Cross-fertilizing age and social science theory', *Journal of Gerontology: Social Sciences*, 58B(6): S327–S337.

Dewey, J. (1897) 'My pedagogic creed', *School Journal*, 54: 77–80.

Dewing, J. (2002) 'From ritual to relationship: A person-centred approach to consent in qualitative research with older people who have a dementia', *Dementia*, 1(2): 157–71.

Dickson, G. and Green, K. L. (2001). 'Participatory action research: Lessons learned with Aboriginal grandmothers', *Health Care for Women International*, 22: 471–82.

Downs, M. (1997) 'The emergence of the person in dementia research', *Ageing and Society*, 17(05): 597–607.

Eales, Jacquie, Keefe, Janice, and Keating, Norah (2008) 'Age-friendly rural communities', in Norah Keating (ed.), *Rural Ageing: A Good place to Grow Old?* Bristol: Policy Press, pp. 109–20.

Eisenhardt, K. and Graebner, M. (2007) 'Theory building from cases: Opportunities and challenges', *Academy of Management Journal*, 50(1): 25–32.

Evans, Simon, Jones, Ray, and Smithson, Janet (2014) 'Connecting with older people as project stakeholders: Lessons for public participation and engagement in rural research', in Catherine Hennessey, Robin Means and Vanessa Burholt (eds.), *Countryside Connections: Older People, Community and Place in Rural Britain*. Bristol: Policy Press, pp. 221–42.

Fealy, G., McNamara, M., Treacy, M. P., and Lyons, I. (2012) 'Constructing ageing and age identities: A case study of newspaper discourses', *Ageing and Society*, 32(1): 85–102. DOI:10.1017/S0144686X11000092.

Freire, P. (1970) *Pedagogy of the Oppressed*. New York: Continuum.

Fudge, N., Wolfe, C. D. A., and McKevitt, C. (2007) 'Involving older people in health research', *Age and Ageing*, 36(5): 492–500.

Gilleard, Chris and Higgs, Paul (2000) *Cultures of Ageing: Self, Citizen and the Body*. Harlow, England: Pearson Education Ltd.

Gilleard, C. and Higgs, P. (2013) 'The fourth age and the concept of a "social imaginary": A theoretical excursus', *Journal of Aging Studies*, 27(4): 368–76.

Gillies, B. A. (2000) 'A memory like clockwork: Accounts of living through dementia', *Ageing and Mental Health*, 4(4): 366–74.

Grainger, K. (1993) '"That's a lovely bath dear": Reality construction in the discourse of elderly care', *Journal of Aging Studies*, 7(3): 247–62.

Greenfield, E. (2011) 'Using ecological frameworks to advance a field of research, practice, and policy on aging-in-place initiatives', *The Gerontologist*, 52(1): 1–12.

Harwood, J. and Giles, H. (1992) '"Don't make me laugh": Age representations in a humorous context', *Discourse and Society*, 3(4): 403–36.

Horrell, B., Stephens, C., and Breheny, M. (2015) 'Online research with informal caregivers: Opportunities and challenges', *Qualitative Research in Psychology*, 12(3): 258–71.

Hubbard, G., Cook, A., Tester, S., and Downs, M. (2002a) 'Beyond words: Older people with dementia using and interpreting non-verbal behaviour', *Journal of Aging Studies*, 16: 155–67.

Hubbard, Gill, Downs, Murna, and Tester, Susan (2002b) 'Including the perspectives of older people in institutional care during the consent process', in Heather Wilkinson (ed.), *The Perspectives of People with Dementia: Research Methods and Motivations*. London and Philadelphia: Jessica Kingsley Publishers, pp. 63–82.

Hulko, W. (2009) 'From "not a big deal" to "hellish": Experiences of older people with dementia', *Journal of Aging Studies*, 23(3): 131–44.

Israel, B. A., Schulz, A. J., Parker, E. A., and Becker, A. B. (1998) 'Review of community-based research: Assessing partnership approaches to improve public health', *Annual Review of Public Health*, 19: 173–202.

Keady, John and Gilliard, Jane (1999) 'The early experience of Alzheimer's disease: Implications for partnership and practice', in Trevor Adams and Charlotte Clarke (eds.), *Dementia Care: Developing Partnerships in Practice*. London: Bailliere Tindall, pp. 227–56.

Keane, S., Lincoln, M., and Smith, T. (2012) 'Retention of allied health professionals in rural New South Wales: A thematic analysis of focus group discussions', *BMC Health Services Research*, 12(175). DOI:10.1186/1472-6963-12-175.

Keating, Norah, and Eales, Jacquie (2011) 'Diversity among older adults in rural Canada: Health in context', in Judith C. Kulig and Allison M. Williams (eds.), *Health in Rural Canada*. Vancouver, BC: UBC Press, pp. 427–46.

Keating, N., Eales, J., and Phillips, J. (2013) 'Age-friendly rural communities: Conceptualizing "best fit"', *Canadian Journal on Aging*, 2(4): 319–32.

Keefe, Janice, Fancey, Pamela, Keating, Norah, Frederick, Judith, Eales, Jacquie, and Dobbs, Bonnie (2004) 'Caring contexts of rural seniors: Phase I technical report'. (Submitted to Veterans Affairs Canada in partial fulfillment of PWGSC Contract #51019-017032/001/HAL). Edmonton: Authors.

Kinsella, Kevin and Wan, He (2009) 'An Aging World: 2008 (International Population Reports, P95/09-1)', US Washington, DC: US Census Bureau.

Knowles, Malcolm S. (1980) *The Modern Practice of Adult Education from Pedagogy to Andragogy*. Englewood Cliffs, NJ: Cambridge Adult Education.

Kontos, P. C. (2004) 'Ethnographic reflections on selfhood, embodiment and Alzheimer's disease', *Ageing and Society,* 24(6): 829–49.

Latimer, Joanna (1997) 'Figuring identities: Older people, medicine and time', in Anne Jamieson, Sarah Harper and Christina Victor (eds.), *Critical Approaches to Ageing and Later Life.* Buckingham: Open University Press, pp. 143–59.

Lien, L., Steggell, C., and Iwarsson, S. (2015) 'Adaptive strategies and person–environment fit among functionally limited older adults aging in place: A mixed methods approach', *International Journal of Environmental Research and Public Health,* 12: 11954–74.

Lyman, K. A. (1989) 'Bringing the social back in: A critique of the biomedicalization of dementia', *The Gerontologist,* 29(5): 597–605.

Magee, Helen, Parsons, Suzanne, and Askham, Janet (2008) *Measuring Dignity in Care for Older People.* London: Help the Aged.

McKillop, J. and Wilkinson, H. (2004) 'Make it easy on yourself! Advice to researchers from someone with dementia on being interviewed', *Dementia,* 3(2): 117–25.

Means, R. and Evans, S. (2012) 'Communities of place and communities of interest? An exploration of their changing role in later life', *Ageing and Society,* 32(08): 1300–18.

Melzer, D., McWilliams, B., Brayne, C., Johnson, T., and Bond, J. (2000) 'Socioeconomic status and the expectation of disability in old age: Estimates for England', *Journal of Epidemiology and Community Health,* 54(4): 286–92.

Ministry of Health (2010) *Drug Use in New Zealand: Key Results of the 2007/08 New Zealand Alcohol and Drug Use Survey.* Wellington: Ministry of Health.

Minkler, M. (1996) 'Critical perspectives on ageing: New challenges for gerontology', *Ageing and Society,* 16(04): 467–87.

Moulaert, Thibauld and Garon, Suzanne (eds.) (2016) *Age-friendly Cities and Communities in International Comparison. Political Lessons, Scientific Avenues and Democratic Issues.* New York: Springer.

Nikander, P. (2000) '"Old" versus "little girl" a discursive approach to age categorization and morality', *Journal of Aging Studies,* 14(4): 335–58.

O'Connor, D., Phinney, A., and Hulko, W. (2010) 'Dementia at the intersections: A unique case study exploring social location', *Journal of Aging Studies,* 24(1): 30–9.

Patton, Michael Q. (2015) *Qualitative Research and Evaluation Methods: Integrating Theory and Practice* (4th edn). Thousand Oaks, CA: Sage.

Peace, S., Holland, C., and Kellaher, L. (2011) '"Option recognition" in later life: Variations in ageing in place', *Ageing and Society,* 31(05): 734–57.

Pearce, A., Clare, L., and Pistrang, N. (2002) 'Managing sense of self coping in the early stages of Alzheimer's disease', *Dementia,* 1(2): 173–92.

Phillipson, C. (2007) 'The "elected" and the "excluded": Sociological perspectives on the experience of place and community in old age', *Ageing and Society,* 27(3): 321–42.

Phoenix, C. and Sparkes, A. C. (2009) 'Being Fred: Big stories, small stories and the accomplishment of a positive ageing identity', *Qualitative Research,* 9(2): 219–36.

Ponzetti, J. (2003) 'Growing old in rural communities: A visual methodology for studying place attachment', *Journal of Rural Community Psychology,* 6(1): 1–11.

Powell, J. L. (2014) 'Governmentality, social policy and the social construction of old age in England', *International Letters of Social and Humanistic Sciences,* 16: 108–21.

Pratt, Rebekah (2002) 'Nobody's ever asked how I felt', in Heather Wilkinson (ed.), *The Perspectives of People with Dementia: Research Methods and Motivations.* London and Philadelphia: Jessica Kingsley Publishers, pp. 165–82.

Pratt, R. and Wilkinson, H. (2003) 'A psychosocial model of understanding the experience of receiving a diagnosis of dementia', *Dementia,* 2(2): 181–99.

Provencher, C., Keating, N., Warburton, J., and Roos, V. (2014) 'Ageing and community', *Journal of Community and Applied Social Psychology,* 24(1): 1–11.

Rachal, J. R. (2002) 'Andragogy's detectives: A critique of the present and a proposal for the future', *Adult Education Quarterly,* 52(3): 210–27.

Ramanathan-Abbott, V. (1994) 'Interactional differences in Alzheimer's discourse: An examination of AD speech across two audiences', *Language in Society,* 23(01): 31–58.

Reed, J. and Clarke, C. L. (1999) 'Nursing older people: Constructing need and care', *Nursing Inquiry,* 6(3): 208–15.

Richardson, L. (2014) 'Engaging the public in policy research: Are community researchers the answer?', *Politics and Governance,* 2(1): 32–44.

Rowles, Graham and Bernard, Miriam (eds.) (2013) *Environmental Gerontology: Making Meaningful Places in Old Age.* New York: Springer.

Rowley, J. (2002) 'Using case studies in research', *Management Research News,* 25(1): 16–27.

Rural and Small Town Canada Analysis Bulletin (2008, 7(8)). Available from: http://www.uoguelph.ca/fare/FARE-talk/RST_Titles_Highlights_October2011.pdf.

Sabat, S. R. and Collins, M. (1999) 'Intact social, cognitive ability, and selfhood: A case study of Alzheimer's disease', *American Journal of Alzheimer's Disease,* 14(1): 11–19.

Sabat, S. and Harre, R. (1992) 'The construction and deconstruction of self in Alzheimer's disease', *Ageing and Society,* 12: 443–61.

Scharf, Thomas and Keating, Norah (2012) 'Social exclusion in later life: A global challenge', in Thomas Scharf and Norah Keating (eds.) *From Exclusion to Inclusion in Old Age: A Global Challenge.* Bristol: The Policy Press, pp. 1–16.

Scholz, Ronald and Tietje, Olaf (2002) *Embedded Case Study Methods: Integrating Quantitative and Qualitative Knowledge.* Thousand Oaks, CA: Sage.

Seawright, J. and Gerring, J. (2008) 'Case selection techniques in case study research: a menu of qualitative and quantitative options', *Political Research Quarterly,* 61(2): 294–308.

Sherratt, C., Soteriou, T., and Evans, S. (2007) 'Ethical issues in social research involving people with dementia', *Dementia,* 6(4): 463–79.

Skinner, M., Rosenberg, M., Lovell, S., Dunn, J., Everitt, J., Hanlon, N., and Rathwell, T. (2008) 'Services for seniors in small-town Canada: The paradox of community', *Canadian Journal of Nursing Research,* 40(1): 80–101.

Small, J. A., Geldart, K., Gutman, G., and Scott, M. A. C. (1998) 'The discourse of self in dementia', *Ageing and Society,* 18: 291–316.

Stake, Robert E. (1995) *The Art of Case Study Research.* Thousand Oaks, CA: Sage.

Stake, Robert E. (2006) *Multiple Case Study Analysis.* New York, NY: The Guilford Press.

Strier, R. (2007) 'Anti-oppressive research in social work', *British Journal of Social Work,* 37: 857–71.

Surr, C. A. (2006) 'Preservation of self in people with dementia living in residential care: A socio-biographical approach', *Social Science and Medicine,* 62: 1720–30.

Swain, J., Heyman, B., and Gillman, M. (1998) 'Public research, private concerns: Ethical issues in the use of open-ended interviews with people who have learning difficulties', *Disability and Society,* 13: 21–36.

Tappen, R. M., Williams, C., Fishman, S., and Touhy, T. (1999) 'Persistence of self in advanced Alzheimer's disease', *Journal of Nursing Scholarship,* 31(2): 121–5.

Tritter, J. and McCallum, A. (2006) 'The snakes and ladders of user involvement: Moving beyond Arnstein', *Health Policy,* 76(2): 156–68.

Tulle, Emmanuelle (2008) *Ageing, the Body and Social Change: Running in Later Life.* Basingstoke: Palgrave Macmillan.

Victor, Christina R. (2010) *Ageing, Health and Care.* Bristol: The Policy Press.

Whitmore, Elizabeth and McKee, Colette (2001) 'Six street youth who could …', in Peter Reason and Hilary Bradbury (eds.), *Handbook of Action Research.* London and Thousand Oaks, CA: Sage, pp. 396–402.

Wiles, J. L., Leibing, A., Guberman, N., Reeve, J., and Allen, R. E. S. (2012) 'The meaning of "Aging in Place" to older people', *The Gerontologist,* 52(3): 357–66.

Winterton, R., Warburton, J., Keating, N., Peterson, M., Berg, T., and Wilson, J. (2016) 'Understanding the influence of community characteristics on wellness for rural older adults: A meta-synthesis', *Journal of Rural Studies,* 45, 320–7.

Witham, M. D. and McMurdo, M. E. (2007) 'How to get older people included in clinical studies', *Drugs and Aging,* 24(3): 187–96.

Wood, L. A. and Kroger, R. O. (1993) 'Forms of address, discourse and aging', *Journal of Aging Studies,* 7(3): 263–77.

World Health Organization (2015) *World Report on Ageing and Health*. Available from http://www.who.int/ageing/publications/world-report-2015/en/.

Yin, Robert K. (2014) *Case Study Research: Design and Methods* (5th edn). Los Angeles, CA: Sage.

Ziegler, Friederike and Scharf, Thomas (2013). 'Community-based participatory action research: opportunities and challenges for critical gerontology', in Amanda Grenier, Jan Baars, Joseph Dohmen, and Chris Phillipson (eds.), *Ageing, Meaning and Social Structure: Connecting Critical and Humanistic Gerontology*. London: Policy Press, pp. 159–81.

Generating Qualitative Data with Experts and Elites

Alexander Bogner, Beate Littig and Wolfgang Menz

WHY INTERVIEW EXPERTS AND ELITES?

Unlike expert interviews, elite interviews have long been established as a basic form of qualitative interviewing. This may be due to the long-standing tradition and eminent importance of elite research in sociology, whereat this research was and still is coined by diverse and sometimes contradictory theoretical paradigms and political standpoints (Bottomore, 1993). In its early days, elite research was driven by the idea that, since the power elite controls society to a great extent, empirical insights into the worldviews and interests of the elite are necessary in order to understand societal order and change. From its beginning, empirical elite research was primarily based on generating qualitative data (see Dexter, 1970). Applying standardised methods and restrictive designs was viewed as inappropriate for investigating the elite empirically, since elites are used to developing their ideas in open communication and are trained to ad-lib. Therefore, conducting elite interviews, in other words, was (and still is) tantamount to carrying out qualitative interviews (see Roulston and Choi, Chapter 15, this volume).

In contrast, with respect to expert interviews, the widely held view is that even though expert interviews are frequently conducted in the many contexts and fields of social science, they are only rarely thought-through and to a lesser extent methodologically reflected (Meuser and Nagel, 2009). After all, in recent years the debate about expert interviews has gradually become more concrete (see Bogner et al., 2009). The focus of this debate lies primarily on issues of what constitutes an expert, the differences between the various forms of expert interviews and their role in research design, as well as the specifics of interviewing and interaction in comparison to other qualitative interview forms.

Regarding elite interviews, Littig (2009) has argued that qualitative data collection, with both elites and experts, faces similar methodological challenges: First of all, the access may be difficult in particular with regard to elites and high-level experts because they often tend to present themselves as unavailable (Conti and O'Neil, 2007; Pfadenhauer, 2009). Second, interviewee's statements may be influenced by various, subject-related variables such as gender, age or – and even more than in other interview settings – the professional status of the interviewer which he or she cannot control. Third, interviewers should apply different strategies of interviewing, dependent on their specific aims and the significance of the respective interview in the context of the research project (Mikecz, 2012). Short and clear-cut questions may result in a survey-style communication focusing on facts and information; in contrast, inviting interviewees to engage in detailed and extensive narratives may be helpful to gain insight into their worldviews and patterns of thought.

Expert interviews – again, similar to elite interviews – are now frequently considered a standard qualitative research method. With respect to the methodological debate (Flick, 2009), the expert interview is situated in the qualitative paradigm – even though, in principle, expert interviews can also follow standardised communication patterns as applied in quantitative research (survey). Today, qualitative expert interviews are carried out in different fields of the political sciences and social research, such as international relations, organisational research, policy research, gender studies, and so forth. Especially in the exploratory phase of a project, interviewing experts is regarded as a more efficient and concentrated method of generating data than, for instance, participatory observation (see Wästerfors, Chapter 20, this volume) or systematic quantitative surveys. Conducting expert interviews can serve to shorten time-consuming data-producing processes, particularly if the experts are the key to practical insider knowledge and are interviewed as surrogates for a wider circle of players. Expert interviews also lend themselves to those kinds of situations in which it might prove difficult or impossible to gain access to a particular social field (as is the case, for instance, with taboo subjects).

Beyond these efficiency aspects, the expert interview has attracted attention within the qualitative paradigm because experts have become a central object of empirical research in the social sciences during the last few decades. This resulted from a fundamental change: The role and the influence of experts in nearly all spheres of modern society have increasingly become problematised from science as well as from civil society actors. With an increase in counter-experts and laypeople challenging the knowledge claims of scientific experts, questions arose such as: Who is legitimately considered to be an expert? How concise, how certain or reflexive is expert knowledge? How is expertise produced in expert panels characterised by interdisciplinarity and a variety of worldviews and approaches? Obviously, the superiority of expert knowledge is no longer taken for granted even though (or because) its importance for individual everyday life decisions or political decision-making can hardly be denied. As a result, the expert increasingly becomes subject to empirical sociological research. In contrast, the elite interview was established as a standard qualitative research method long ago. This has to do with the fine tradition of elite theory in sociology.

SHORT HISTORY OF INTERVIEWING EXPERTS AND ELITES

A groundbreaking book on elite interviewing was first published in 1970 by the political scientist J.L. Dexter. In his understanding, elite interviews target particular social groups 'the influential, the prominent, the well-informed' (2006, p. 19), representatives of the political and economic elites, which might be reluctant to reveal their views or perspectives and therefore require special treatment:

> It is an interview with any interviewee – and stress should be placed on the word 'any' – who in terms of the current purposes of the interviewer is given special, non-standardized treatment. By special, non-standard treatment I mean: stressing the interviewee's definition of the situation, encouraging the interviewee to structure an account of the situation, letting the interviewee introduce to a considerable extent (an extent which will of course vary from project to project and interviewer to interviewer) his notion of what he regards as relevant, instead of relying upon the investigator's notions of relevance. (Dexter, 2006, p. 18)

What might sound like common knowledge for qualitative interviewing today was certainly innovative at a time dominated by quantitative standards. Following these standards Dexter drew attention to the fact that the purpose of interviewing the elite is not simply to gather objective facts and knowledge. He stressed that non-standardised interviews are always influenced by the social relationship between the interviewee and the interviewer, and thus guides the interaction. Dexter also gave many practical hints on how to conduct elite interviews like using open-ended questions, being flexible or listening carefully. Dexter's main characterisation of elite interviews is still shared by more recent literature. In fact, his vague definition of the elite has in essence remained constant in the methodological literature to date (e.g. Moyser and Wagstaffe, 1987; Seldon, 1996; Odendahl and Shaw, 2002; Harvey, 2011). Furthermore, interviews with the elite in Dexter's tradition are often not seen as a precise research tool. The sampling is not representative, the statements made by interviewees can be distorted by gaps in their memories, different interviewees can give different information on the same topic, etc. (e.g. Richards, 1996, p. 200f.).

In recent years, the term 'elite interview' has been used in the Anglo-American tradition to describe interviews with 'informants (usually male) who occupy a senior or middle management position' (Welch, et al. 2002, p. 613) or 'those who occupy senior management and Board level positions within organizations' (Harvey, 2011, p. 433). This functional definition of 'elites' comes close to the understanding of 'experts' as used in German-speaking countries to describe the counterpart to elite interviews, namely expert interviews. The latter have been regarded as a distinct interview form for some years (Bogner et al., 2002; Gläser and Laudel, 2004). The methodological debate on expert interviews started in 1991, when Meuser and Nagel published their article on a common research practice, expert interviews, which had not been methodologically reflected until then. In the following years a vivid debate led to the rise of a variety of approaches, which thus can no longer be referred to in singular (Bogner et al., 2009, 2014). Expert interviews differ in the notion of 'experts' (from a broad voluntarist to a narrow functionalist understanding), the purpose of the interviews (explorative, systematic, theory-generating) and the more interpretative-hermeneutic or positivist understanding of expert knowledge. However, with regard to methodology, the differences between the expert interview, which the German-language literature primarily refers to, and the elite interview the Anglophone world focuses on, are small.

EXPERTS AND ELITES AS SUBJECTS OF SOCIOLOGICAL RESEARCH

As far as elites and experts are concerned, recent social science research trends have proved relatively stable. Elite theory can be traced back to the early times of sociology including seminal studies such as Robert Michels' description of the 'iron law of oligarchy' (Michels, 1911), Thorstein Veblen's *Theory of the Leisure Class* (Veblen, 1899) or C. Wright Mill's critique of *The Power Elite* (Mills, 1956). In general, elite theory is guided by the assumption that a small minority, consisting of members of the economic elite and policy-planning networks, holds most power; pro-democratic theories consider this to be a fundamental threat to modern democracies. Regarding experts, the sociological debate sets in at a point in time when eminent scholars point to the ongoing specialisation and differentiation of modern society associated with the rise of technical experts and an 'intellectual', that is, science-based, technology (Ellul, 1964; Bell, 1973). Soon, these diagnoses of an increasing significance of expertise and expert systems fuelled a debate on whether modern societies are about to come under the experts' dominance ('technocracy').

In this context, the expert was considered an agent of truth and authority increasingly dominating political decision-making in modern societies ('truth speaks to power'). In contrast, more recent contributions point out that scientific self-criticism and the rise of counter-experts – often backed by protest movements – have long since contributed to terminating this golden age of expertise (Turner, 2002). Obviously, with regard to controversial issues such as global warming or genetically modified organisms (GMO) every kind of (scientific) expertise can be fundamentally challenged – with the help of alternative expertise. Theorists of a 'reflexive modernisation' consider this development to be a moment of societal self-enlightenment (Beck et al., 1994). Following Giddens (1991), expert knowledge is part of the 'institutional reflexivity' that supposes all premises of individual and organisational activity will be routinely examined in light of new information. However, at the same time, this growth in relevance of expert knowledge is paradoxically accompanied by a crisis of recognition on the part of the experts. Today, most people are experts in challenging expertise by taking 'alternative voices' into account. In regard to sociology, experts and elites have moved into the centre of interest both from modernisation theory as well as from the sociology of scientific knowledge (cf. Jasanoff et al., 1995; Maasen and Weingart, 2005).

These different strands of sociological theory were conducive to the development of a broader and more profound notion of what characterises an expert. In general, experts are considered to be people with special knowledge or skills, most often equated with professionals from the fields of science, engineering and technology. In this perspective experts are primarily defined in contrast to their counterpart, that is, laity. With the emergence of autonomous fields of professional action that are responsible for innovation, namely research and technology, the expert-lay division became increasingly established in modern societies. However, in the context of qualitative research, experts are not primarily interviewed because of an interesting 'solid' or canonical knowledge as one can find in handbooks and encyclopaedias. In fact, qualitative methodology does not believe in 'objective' knowledge or 'neutral' facts. Rather, it is primarily interested in expert knowledge because it determines social practices and institutions to a certain extent (Bogner and Menz, 2009). In other words: the social relevance of experts in modern life and their ability to affect people's practices to a significant degree – this is why social scientists interview them.

Accordingly, experts can be understood as people who possess specific knowledge that relates to a clearly demarcated range of problems and plays an authoritative role in decision-making of different kinds. Due to this knowledge, their interpretations provide guidelines for social action and structure a particular field of social action in a meaningful way.

Obviously, in the context of qualitative interviewing, expert knowledge is not only of interest because it is characterised by a high degree of reflexivity, of coherence or certainty. Rather, our interviews are – at least implicitly – based on the assumption that experts are able to exercise power in a particular social context by applying special knowledge. To put it simply: Following a sociology of knowledge perspective, experts represent or personify a complex interdependence of knowledge and power. This does not mean that the experts' power necessarily becomes manifest in political influence or economic wealth; rather, a good many times it may be limited. However, experts exert influence by determining the way people understand and interpret the world or particular problems; they exert influence by establishing a particular issue-framing, even if they are experts for the powerless or for neglected social problems. The particular significance of specific knowledge may be considered a major difference between experts and elites.

Elites are not primarily determined by special knowledge; rather, becoming a member of a certain elite group is mainly dependent on personal contacts and networks, family background, milieu, poise and habitus (Bottomore, 1993). Usually, elites – much more than experts – are characterised by an exceptionally high socio-economic status.

They rely on inherited social privileges and merits. Experts, in contrast, are considered to have outstanding cognitive abilities and the societal acceptance of their authority is highly dependent on their performance. Thus, the notion of expert implies a meritocratic semantics. Certainly, there may be interferences between elites and high-level experts as sometimes experts are appointed a leadership position in research institutions, corporations or even politics. Thereby, these outstanding experts holding a superior position become part of a certain segment of the elite; this expert-elite hybrid is characterised by a combination of highly relevant, reflexive knowledge and a remarkable degree of power.

Despite these and similar interferences, the focus on knowledge and power may serve as a good starting point to come to a methodologically sensible definition of experts and elites. The following diagram (see Figure 41.1) illustrates our (simplifying) attempt to differentiate

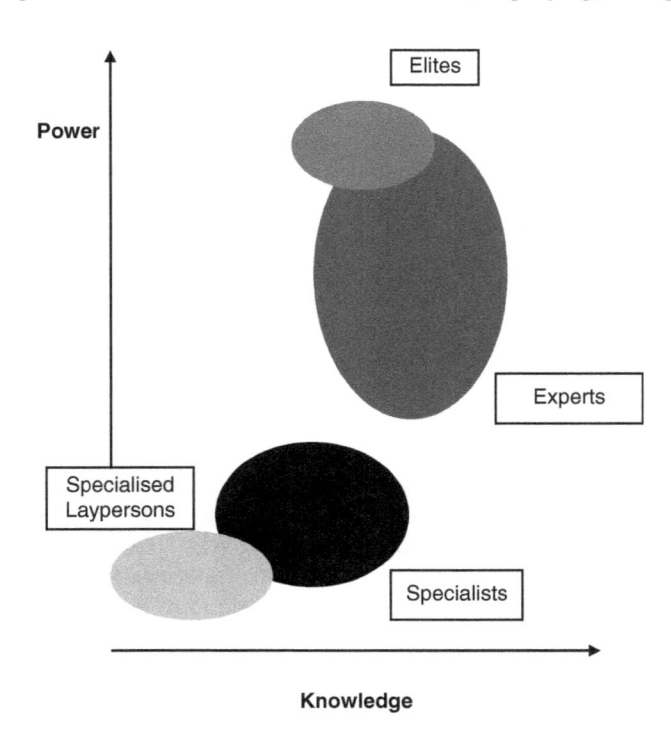

Figure 41.1 Experts and elites

between experts and elites along the two dimensions of knowledge and power.

In light of this diagram, it becomes obvious that interviews with the elite can, but do not necessarily have to, be expert interviews. This is because experts, defined by their special or professional knowledge and their influence on decision-making processes, can, but do not have to, be members of an elite group. In the end, this depends on their formal position, their influence on social practices and the extent to which they are able to determine what is considered to be relevant or not in a particular field of social action.

FORMS OF KNOWLEDGE AND INTERVIEWS WITH EXPERTS AND ELITES

Generally speaking, interviews (not only those with experts and elites) are aimed at uncovering some kind of knowledge the interviewees possess. If there were no differences in knowledge between the interviewer and the interviewee, interviewing would not make any sense. But what kind of knowledge is it the researchers are aiming at in interviews with experts and elites? At what kind of knowledge are expert and elite interviews aimed? As noted above it is not always 'correct' or 'better' knowledge the researcher wants to assemble. What form of knowledge the object of desire is, depends on the epistemological framework of the study that the interview is part of, as well as on its research design. At first we differentiate between three forms of knowledge relevant to the interview (cf. Bogner and Menz, 2009). After that we describe four types of interviews with experts and elites.

1 *Technical knowledge* comprises facts and information about operations and events governed by rules, application routines specific to a field, bureaucratic competences, and so on. This 'technical' knowledge remains most closely related to the understanding of expertise as a specific advantage, where an expert's knowledge can be distinguished from everyday knowledge because it is more systematic in its content, better thought-out and may be more reliable (for example, academic knowledge or specialised knowledge about a specific social area like an organisation, cf. Schütz, 1964). In this context, an expert's knowledge provides a specific kind of advantage because it is more systematic, better thought-through and likely more reliable than what can be learned from other sources. Similarly, its prominent position in society grants the elite privileged access to a certain kind of information that the researcher does not have.

 From a rigorous methodological point of view, the strength of the expert and elite interviews lies not primarily in this field of knowledge (even if interviews, especially expert interviews, are quite often used for this purpose). The expert or member of the elite could be mistaken or hold very subjective views – in other words: he or she is a potential cause of error. Consequently, if other sources for the facts and information need – for example, documents, statistics, textbooks – are available, they should be used instead. However, conducting interviews for the purpose of collecting 'objective' data and information is inevitable if these alternative sources of information are not accessible.

2 *Process knowledge* refers to the acquisition of information about sequences of actions, interaction routines, organisational constellations, and past or current events, in which the interviewee is directly involved or which at least are closely related to his or her field of action. Unlike technical knowledge, this is not specialised knowledge in a narrow sense (something one can acquire through educational qualifications), but more a matter of knowledge based on practical experience acquired through one's own context of action. It is therefore strongly connected to the expert or elite as a subject and not easily transferable. This form of knowledge is experience-based but unlike 'tacit knowledge' (Polanyi, 1966) it can be verbally expressed in an interview situation.

3 *Interpretative knowledge* (Bogner and Menz, 2009) entails subjective orientations, rules, points of view and interpretations, and thus renders expert end elite knowledge a heterogeneous

conglomeration. Interpretative knowledge does not only comprise (subjective) perceptions and descriptions of reality but also normative dispositions. As the researcher reconstructs this interpretative knowledge, he/she enters, to put it in old-fashioned terms, into the sphere of ideas and ideologies, of fragmentary, inconsistent configurations of meaning and patterns of explanation. It is not a homogeneous body of knowledge but a compilation of related but not necessarily logically structured interpretations. Interpretative knowledge does not presume that the expert or the elite has a 'better' access to reality (as is the case when the focus is on technical knowledge) than the interviewer. But he or she has a specific subjective perspective related to the research topic. This means the interviewee 'is always right', interpretative knowledge is always true; it is a social fact on its own.

It is almost impossible to tell, on the basis of something said in an interview, whether a statement should be considered 'technical knowledge' and as such in no need of further interpretation, or 'interpretative knowledge', that is the expression of a subjective construction of meaning on the part of the interviewee. The differentiation between the three kinds of knowledge is not based on any characteristics of the knowledge itself, but is primarily a construction of the social scientist interpreting it. It is always the result of an act of abstraction and systematisation performed by the researcher, an 'analytic construction'.

For example (Bogner et al., 2014, p. 17ff.), if a manager states that 'the activities of trade unions are harmful to the economic development of the firm' the researcher can classify this as correct 'objective' information or as the result of personal experience, for example, in a survey about the economic impact of trade unions' behaviour. In a more qualitative-oriented organisational case study the researcher would take this statement as 'interpretative knowledge' which is important not because of its truthfulness but because of the practical effects of it as an action orientation. If the manager's behaviour is guided by this 'knowledge' it will have an effect, for example, on patterns of industrial relations.

The analytic differentiation between the forms of knowledge in the interview makes it possible to describe the epistemological interest of different forms of the expert and elite interview more precisely. However, to distinguish between specific forms of expert and elite interviews, another differentiation is necessary: Interviews can take quite different positions within the research design. Especially expert interviews are quite often not the only method of data collection within a specific study. They are combined with other forms of interview techniques or with other qualitative methods, such as documentary analysis or observations. Furthermore, they are often part of a triangulation between qualitative and quantitative methods (Flick, 2011; Menz and Nies, 2017).

The expert interview owes its prominence in empirical social research partly to its use as an *exploratory* tool, which precedes the main methods of data collection. In both quantitative and qualitative research projects, expert interviews can serve to establish an initial orientation in a field that is either substantively new or poorly defined, as a way of helping the researcher to develop a clearer idea of the problem or as a preliminary move in the construction of a final interview guide. In this sense, exploratory interviews help to structure the area under investigation and to generate hypotheses. The experts interviewed may themselves be part of the group of interest to a study, but in many cases experts are deliberately used as a complementary source of information about the group of interest, the actual subject. In the latter case, the expert's role is that of someone who possesses 'contextual knowledge'.[1] Here, the main focus of the interview lies on the 'technical' and 'process knowledge'. Its function is to gather initial – not systematic, but nevertheless 'objective' – information about the context of the research topic, which is afterwards investigated in more detail with other methods.

Expert and elite interviews can also have an explorative function if they focus on 'interpretative knowledge'. Orientations, interpretations and evaluations are explored to get an impression of the field, for example, in order to formulate the first hypothesis, which can guide the further research. In this case the subsequent main study uses similar methods.

If the expert or elite interview is the (or one of the) main source(s) of data collection they can be called 'grounding interviews'. There are two forms of grounding interviews: The *systematising interview* is oriented towards gaining access to exclusive knowledge – both 'technical' and 'process knowledge' – possessed by the expert or the elite. This kind of interview is an attempt to obtain systematic and complete information. The interviewee enlightens the researcher on 'objective' matters. The main focus, though, is not on the interpretative character of knowledge but rather on its capacity to provide researchers with facts concerning the research question. Interviewees are a source of information with regard to the reconstruction of sequences of events and social situations: 'Experts are people who have special knowledge about social facts, and expert interviews are a way of gaining access to this knowledge' (Gläser and Laudel, 2004, p. 10). From this methodological perspective it is not the experts themselves that are the object of investigation; rather they function as informants, providing information about the actual object of investigation.

The second form of the grounding interview is the *theory-generating interview* (for more detail, see Bogner and Menz, 2009; Meuser and Nagel, 2009). In this case the interviewee no longer serves as the catalyst of the research process, or, put differently, as a means by which the researcher obtains useful information and elucidation of the issue under investigation. In essence, the goal of the theory-generating interview is to communicatively open up and analytically reconstruct the subjective dimension of knowledge. Here, the action orientations and implicit decision-making maxims of experts within a particular specialist field, or the elites, are the starting point for the formulation of theory. The researcher seeks to formulate a theoretically rich conceptualisation of (often implicit, yet reconstructible) knowledge, conceptions of the world and routines, which the experts and elites develop in their activities and which are constitutive for the functioning of social systems. In ideal terms, this procedure seeks to generate theory via the interpretative generalisation of a typology – in contrast to the representative statistical conclusions that result from standardised methods. Following Glaser and Strauss (1967), qualitative theory is here drawn up via theoretical sampling (see Schreier, Chapter 6, this volume) and comparative analysis (see Sørensen et al., Chapter 10, this volume). This constitutes a process of inductive theory formulation, at the conclusion of which the researcher will ideally have a 'formal' theory. It follows that the theory-generating interview must be classified as part of the methodological canon, oriented along the fundamental principles of interpretative sociology.

To sum up, we can distinguish between two main forms of interviews with regard to their function within the research design (see Gobo, Chapter 5, this volume):

- interviews with an exploratory function and
- interviews used for systematic data collection in order to ground comprehensive empirical descriptions and theoretical concepts.

Within each type we can differentiate between an informational and an interpretative focus of the interview. Informational interviews aim primarily at technical and process knowledge whereas interpretative interviews – situated in the 'interpretative paradigm' (Wilson, 1970) – focus on orientations and evaluations as subjective (but not necessarily individual) perspectives of experts and elites (see Table 41.1).

Table 41.1 Forms of expert and elite interviews in relation to their function in the research design and epistemological background

	Exploratory interviews	Grounding interviews
Informational Interviews	exploratory data collection	systematising interview
Interpretive Interviews	exploration of interpretations	theory-generating interview

INTERACTION IN EXPERT AND ELITE INTERVIEWS

Compared to ordinary, in-depth interviews the expert and elite interviews are characterised by a particular interaction structure. Usually, interviews are seen as having a certain kind of unbalanced power relations (there have been some efforts, for example from feminist research approaches, to reduce this asymmetry, e.g. Oakley, 1981). There often is a situation of 'studying down' (Plesner, 2011). The standard situation in interviews is an asymmetrical one in which the interviewer defines the setting and the topics. And it is seen as one of the main concerns of a good interviewing strategy 'to make somebody talk', to give the interviewee complete expression for unfolding his subjective position and attitudes.

Conversations with experts and elites are different. In this case, the researcher communicates with people who are usually well aware of their expertise and their social position and who are used to being 'in charge' and listened to by others. Expert and elite interviews which can be described as 'studying up' (Plesner, 2011) are at risk of the interviewee taking over the structuring of the course (Gillham, 2000, p. 82). In some cases he or she even displays a patronising attitude towards the interviewer, attempts to show how well disposed he or she is, and to dictate the content of the conversation to the (seemingly) inexperienced or inferior interviewer – often with a gender-specific bias if a young female researcher interviews an older male expert or member of the elite (Abels and Behrens, 2009).[2]

To avoid such adverse asymmetrical communication some authors suggest that the interviewer should deliberately demonstrate his or her own expertise in order to gain the recognition of the interviewee.[3] Trinczek, for example, argues that interviewers who want to conduct successful expert interviews with managers must, as an indispensable precondition, have expert status themselves or, as a minimum requirement, appear reasonably comparable to and an 'equal' of the interviewee in respect of age and qualifications.

> The interviewer is indeed required to be an expert himself: the more an interviewer demonstrates knowledgeability during the interview by giving competent assessments, stating reasons, and raising counterarguments, the more managers in turn will be willing to offer their own knowledge and take a stance on issues, thus disclosing their subjective structures of relevance and patterns of orientation in absence of strategic considerations. (Trinczek, 2009, p. 211)

There are many striking arguments for this position. If the expert interview is seen primarily as something that will produce 'useful information' and elucidation of 'facts' (as is the case with the informational interviews), the high level of specialist interaction between co-experts will have a productive effect and the interview will be of value for the detailed analysis of the issue at stake. If, on the other hand, the goal of the investigation is the reconstruction of interpretative knowledge (as is the case with theory-generating expert interviews), the 'technicist element' becomes problematic, since the implicit normative and practical premises of expert opinion will be presupposed as a shared basis of the conversation between expert and co-expert, and it will be difficult to gain access to them for the purposes of analysis.

That is why some authors (Abels and Behrens, 2009; Bogner and Menz, 2009) stress that an adverse asymmetrical interaction situation where the interviewer is seen as inferior or naïve is not generally problematic. Instead of reacting to these paternalistic behaviours by displaying resentment for not being perceived or taken seriously as an expert in the desired way, interviewers would be better advised to turn this discriminatory paternalism to their strategic advantage, as a way of making the collection of data more productive. Naïve questions stand a good chance of producing the most interesting and productive answers – especially in the framework of a research design that seeks to generate theory. The interviewers have the freedom to do whatever they want, and can ask questions that under other circumstances would have endangered the stabilised scheme of expectation. This can make it possible to gain access to information that might not otherwise be revealed, particularly because a naïve interviewer is seen as especially trustworthy (Abels and Behrens, 2009). On the other hand, the disadvantages of this interaction structure are obvious: interviewees sometimes bore researchers with interminable monologues about trivia or things they already know, they plod through the contents of textbooks, or retreat to common places. There is hardly any likelihood that difficult specialist issues can be clarified, since it is easier to ignore supplementary questions.

However, there is no 'best practice' concerning the interaction structure in interviews with experts and elites. Different forms of knowledge and different functions of the interview within the research design make different interaction situations more preferable than others. Furthermore, the interaction structures can only partly be influenced by the interviewer. However, choosing the adequate strategy of asking will have a positive influence on productive data collection in conversations with experts and elites. To give just some hints:

Interviews with experts and elites are usually semi-structured interviews, conducted with at least a rough topic guide,[4] which contains the central dimensions of the planned conversation. Exploratory interviews with experts and elites should be conducted as openly as possible, in order to make it possible to gather unexpected information and interpretations, which could have not been imagined when constructing the topic guide. The focus is on archiving initial breadth. Systematising interviews, in contrast, are based on a quite detailed topic guide, which entails a comprehensive catalogue of questions about facts. Characteristic for this interview is a permanent revision of the topic guide in the course of the research, according to the advancing state of information. Interviews aiming at interpretative knowledge, that is, theory-generating interviews, are using (thematically focused or problem-centred) narratives more extensively (see Witzel and Reiter, 2012), to give the interviewee space for presenting his or her orientations and beliefs.

The expert and elite interview has always had a certain thematic focus. The purpose of the interview is not to capture the interviewee as a 'whole person' (like some biographical interviews do) including as many facets as possible of the individual personality. Consequently, the topic guide usually includes topical or specialist questions and only some general question, for example, about the personal background. On the other hand, especially if the researchers are interested in substantively rich investigation of 'interpretative knowledge', they should not cut off statements of the interviewees, which on first sight seem to be private and of no immediate interest for our research topic. It is only in the phase of evaluating data that it becomes clear whether the relevance structures and patterns of orientations used by the expert can be reconstructed exclusively by using his or her explanations given from within the professional context, or whether it is also necessary to incorporate comments made from the personal sphere. It is frequently the case that the very interview passages in which common places and pithy sayings from everyday life are mobilised, or arguments relying on metaphors from the 'private sphere' are put forward, prove to be of particular interest. In practice, one can hardly distinguish between the interviewee as holder of a social role or position and the interviewee as a 'private person', and it makes no methodological sense to attempt to do so.

NEW DEVELOPMENTS AND PERSPECTIVES

Multilingualism and Translation

Multilingualism is a neglected problem in qualitative social research, including expert and elite interviews (see Resch and Enzenhofer, Chapter 9, this volume). This lack of attention is all the more surprising if we consider the accelerating pace of internationalisation in research, and comparative international research in particular, as well as the growing importance of international migration and multiculturalism in the social sciences. Researchers are thus increasingly likely to face methodological challenges arising from the use of different languages. The methodological consequences of multilingualism in social research affect all stages of the research process, from project design, to data collection and analysis to the presentation of results. This has major implications for quality assurance in the research process and for the quality of the findings. Conducting research in and with other languages ultimately confronts the researcher with fundamental hermeneutic and translatological questions, such as the possibility of understanding across languages, and the translatability of culture, that is, the possibility of understanding foreign cultures at all (Temple and Edwards, 2002; Inhetveen, 2012; Littig and Pöchhacker, 2014).

Beyond these fundamental methodological concerns, working with speakers of other languages also raises a number of practical questions like planning, budgeting, training etc. Consequently, if participants have different native languages, researchers often use English as a lingua franca. The use of international English is particularly common in political and business organisations. Accordingly both the respondent and the social scientist asking the questions are assumed to be proficient enough in English to conduct an interview. If this is not the case, the social researcher will usually make *ad hoc* arrangements for translation assistance, whether in the process of data collection or for transcription and analysis. Either option – 'English only' and *ad hoc* translation – is not without problems. Most crucially, there is a lack of established criteria by which one's own and other participants' linguistic and communicative competences might be assessed, especially when it comes to determining whether language skills are sufficient to grasp finer points of communication, such as irony, loaded words and connotations.

Considering the increasing internationalisation of expert interviews and their frequent use in comparative research designs, Littig and Pöchhacker (2014) draw attention to this blind spot in the methodological literature. They suggested 'socio-translational collaboration' as a way of coming to grips with linguistic challenges in expert interviewing. A collaborative approach bringing together social researchers and professionals with translational competence rests on two basic premises, that is, a substantial degree of mutual knowledge of the respective conceptual frameworks and working methods, and consistent consideration of linguistic and cultural issues in all stages of the research process. Conducting expert interviews in an international context means that both the social researcher and the translator (in the wider sense) need to have expertise in either domain: the translator must also understand the basics of qualitative interviewing in general, and the expert interview setting, in particular; the social researcher must also be familiar with cross-cultural language issues and ways of resolving them with various techniques of translation and interpreting. The awareness of language issues among social researchers is still very limited, and the topic of multilingualism rarely features in courses on qualitative methods. Whereas the methodological literature to date reflects a pragmatic attitude towards problems of language and translation which manifests itself in the *ad hoc* recruitment of 'native speakers' and a narrow focus on the interview itself, the socio-translational collaborative approach calls for a proactive engagement with translational and cross-cultural issues from the very start of the research process and throughout all of its stages (for strategies see Enzenhofer and Resch 2011; and Resch and Enzenhofer, Chapter 9, this volume).

Expert Interviews and Information Technologies

An important issue related to new technical means is interviewing via Skype or similar technical means. This has just become an option recently and thus not yet been reflected thoroughly in methodological terms (Deakin and Wakefield, 2014). However, reports on experiences with Skype are available (Salmons, 2010; Hanna, 2012; Weller, 2015). The gold standard of the interview situation certainly is the face-to-face interview. This has been stressed in the literature discussing telephone interviews with experts (Christmann, 2009). Compared to face-to-face interviews, telephone interviews allow for less control of the interview situation. The interviewer cannot know whether the interview partner is fully concentrated on the interview or distracted by other activities (answering emails or playing Internet games). The lack of non-verbal elements like eye contact is a disadvantage for the communicative situation: additional information, for example, about the engagement of the interviewee gets lost, the commitment to the interview might be reduced etc. To our experience interviews on the telephone tend to be shorter than face-to-face interviews. As a consequence this entails a loss of information. According to Christmann (2009) at least some of the disadvantages of telephone interviewing might be compensated by a clearly structured interview strategy (for detailed strategies, see Stephens, 2007). Especially for first informative or explorative interviews, the shortcomings of telephone interviews might be less severe. However, what might seem efficient (regarding time, travelling, budget) at first glance, could prove to be less effective with regard to the richness of information gained.

Interviews via Skype seem to be a better solution than telephone interviews if face-to-face interviews cannot be conducted due to time restrictions or budgetary reasons. As there is a virtual visual presence of the interview partners, the interview situation can be better controlled (on both sides). But side information about the interviewee's professional environment still gets lost. Given the target groups of expert and elite interviews it can be assumed that many of them are familiar with using recent technical devices; the younger generation more than the older. Thus Skype interviews will likely become more important in the future. For the time being, however, the most preferable interview situation is still face to face, though its advantages might be heightened (Weller, 2015).

In our times of the ongoing process of digitisation, it can be difficult to keep the identity of experts hidden. Consequently, the researcher should always clarify how much of the information obtained from the interviewee can be published in a non-anonymous form (e.g. as quotations). In some cases, it may be necessary to have the interviewee expressly authorise the use of the minutes or interview transcript for analysis or publication purposes. The expert should, in all cases, be given the assurance that all data will be treated in confidence. Issues of anonymity have become even more severe through the general use and availability of the Internet. This makes experts even more easily identifiable, ultimately worldwide. Consequently, expert interviews should not be used, or if so, very carefully, as demonstration material in courses or lectures. Quotes might unintentionally spread far and wide via the Internet or social media and could endanger the integrity of the interviewee.

Conclusion: Growing Diversity

It has been pointed out that expert and elite interviews have become diverse in the last few years. There is not just one way of doing expert or elite interviews. This holds also true for the analysis, be it with or without computer assistance. There is no standard procedure for analysing expert interviews. In principle, all qualitative social research analysis methods can be used, for example, the code-based procedures common in grounded theory or qualitative content analysis, or the sequential analyses applied in the hermeneutic sociology of knowledge or objective hermeneutics. A combination of different methods is also admissible.

The diversity of expert and elite interviewing provokes the question whether a methodological canonisation of these forms of interviewing is in sight. We would cautiously answer this question with no. The unfolding of the methodological debate has led to the refinement of the methodology, and thus to a greater variety of the overall aims and applications of the expert interview, the interview strategies and the consideration of general issues. This can be interpreted as beneficial for the plurality of methods and methodologies. The most suitable form of expert or elite interviews ultimately depends on the actual research project, its goals and the particular research questions at stake.

Notes

1 On the distinction in research logic between 'contextual knowledge' and 'operational knowledge', see Meuser and Nagel (2009).
2 Gender relations can play a twofold role in the interview. First, most of the experts are men, as there are relatively few women in management positions. Second, the probability of the participants 'doing gender' (i.e. assuming gender-specific roles, particularly in a mixed-gender setting) becomes highly likely. Doing gender can also become manifest in the content of the interview, for example, by using particular gendered metaphors ('the firm as the mother of its employees' etc.).
3 For ordinary in-depth interviews one basic rule is to avoid the ostentatious presentation of knowledge and expertise: 'Researchers need a degree of humility, the ability to be recipients of the participant's wisdom without needing to compete by demonstration of their own' (Legard et al., 2003, p. 143).
4 See for the design of a topic guide Arthur and Nazroo (2003); for topic guides in expert interviews see Gläser and Laudel (2004, p. 59ff).

FURTHER READING

Bogner, Alexander, Beate Littig and Wolfgang Menz (eds.) (2009) *Interviewing Experts*. Basingstoke: Palgrave Macmillan.

Dexter, Lewis A. (2006) *Elite and Specialized Interviewing*. With a New Introduction by Alan Ware and Martín Sánchez-Jankowski. University of Essex, Colchester: ECPR Press – ECPR classics.

Littig, B. and Pöchhacker, F. (2014) 'Socio-translational collaboration in qualitative inquiry: The case of expert interviews', *Qualitative Inquiry*. Special Issue: Flick, U. (ed): Challenges for Qualitative Inquiry as a Global Endeavor, 20(9): 1085–95.

REFERENCES

Abels, Gabriele and Maria Behrens (2009) 'Interviewing experts in political science: A reflection on gender and policy effects based on secondary analysis', in Alexander Bogner,

Beate Littig and Wolfgang Menz (eds.), *Interviewing Experts*. Basingstoke: Palgrave Macmillan, pp. 138–56.

Arthur, Su and James Nazroo (2003) 'Designing fieldwork strategies and materials', in Jane Ritchie and Jane Lewis (eds.), *Qualitative Research Practice. A Guide for Social Science Students and Researchers*. London: Sage, pp. 109–37.

Beck, Anthony Ulrich, Giddens, and Scott Lash (1994) *Reflexive Modernization – Politics, Tradition and Aesthetics in the Modern Social Order*. Stanford, CA: Stanford University Press.

Bell, Daniel (1973) *The Coming of Post-Industrial Society. A Venture in Social Forecasting*. New York: Harper Colophon Books.

Bogner, Alexander and Wolfgang Menz (2009) 'The theory-generating expert interview: Epistemological interest, forms of knowledge, interaction', in Alexander Bogner, Beate Littig and Wolfgang Menz (eds.), *Interviewing Experts*. Basingstoke: Palgrave Macmillan, pp. 43–80.

Bogner, Alexander, Beate Littig, and Wolfgang Menz (eds.) (2009) *Interviewing Experts*. Basingstoke: Palgrave Macmillan.

Bogner, Alexander, Beate Littig, and Wolfgang Menz (eds.) (2002) *Das Experteninterview – Theorie, Methode, Anwendung* (1st edn). Wiesbaden: Verlag für Sozialwissenschaften.

Bogner, Alexander, Wolfgang Menz and Beate Littig (2014) *Interviews mit Experten. Eine praxisorientierte Einführung*. Wiesbaden: SpringerVS.

Bottomore, Tom (1993) *Elites and Society*. London: Routledge.

Christmann, Gabriela C. (2009) 'Expert interviews on the telephone: A difficult undertaking', in Alexander Bogner, Beate Littig and Wolfgang Menz (eds.), *Interviewing Experts*. Basingstoke: Palgrave Macmillan, pp. 157–83.

Conti, Joseph A. and Moira O'Neil (2007) 'Studying power: Qualitative methods and the global elite', *Qualitative Research*, 7: 63–82.

Deakin, Hanna and Kelly Wakefield (2014) 'Skype interviewing: Reflections of two PhD researchers', *Qualitative Research*, 14(5): 603.

Dexter, Lewis A. (1970) *Elite and Specialized Interviewing*. Evanston: Northwestern University Press. Reprint: (2006) With a New Introduction by Alan Ware and Martín Sánchez-Jankowski. University of Essex, Colchester/UK: ECPR Press – ECPR classics.

Ellul, Jacques (1964) *The Technological Society*. New York: Vintage Books.

Enzenhofer, Edith and Katharina Resch (2011) 'Übersetzungsprozesse und deren Qualitätssicherung in der qualitativen Sozialforschung', *Forum Qualitative Sozialforschung/Forum: Qualitative Social Research*, 12(2). Retrieved from http://www.qualitative-research.net/index.php/fqs/rt/printerFriendly/1652/3176.

Flick, Uwe (2009) *An Introduction To Qualitative Research* (4th edn). London: Sage.

Flick, Uwe (2011) 'Mixing methods, triangulation, and integrated research', in Norman K. Denzin and Michael D. Giardina (eds.), *Qualitative Inquiry and Global Crises*. Walnut Creek: Left Coast Press, pp. 132–51.

Giddens, Anthony (1991) *Modernity and Self-Identity – Self and Society in the Late Modern Age*. Stanford, CA: Stanford University Press.

Gillham, Bill (2000) *The Research Interview*. London, New York: Continuum.

Glaser, Barney G. and Anselm L. Strauss (1967) *Discovery of Grounded Theory. Strategies for Qualitative Research*. Mill Valley: Sociology Press.

Gläser, Jochen and Grit Laudel (2004) *Experteninterviews und qualitative Inhaltsanalyse*. Wiesbaden: Verlag für Sozialwissenschaften.

Hanna P. (2012) 'Using internet technologies (such as Skype) as a research medium: A research note', *Qualitative Research*, 12: 239–42.

Harvey, William S. (2011) 'Strategies for conducting elite interviews', *Qualitative Research*, 11(4): 431–41.

Inhetveen, Katharina (2012) 'Translation challenges: Qualitative interviewing in a multilingual field', *Qualitative Sociology Review*, 8(2), 28–45. Retrieved from www.qualitativesociologyreview.org.

Jasanoff, Sheila, Gerald E. Markle James C. Petersen and Trevor Pinch (eds.) (1995) *Handbook of Science and Technology Studies*. Thousand Oaks, CA: Sage.

Kvale, Steinar (1996) *InterViews. An Introduction to Qualitative Research Interviewing*. Thousand Oaks CA and New Delhi: Sage.

Legard, Robin, Keegan Jiland and Ward Kit (2003) 'In-depth interviews', in Jane Ritchie and Jane Lewis (eds.), *Qualitative Research Practice. A Guide for Social Science Students and Researchers*. Thousand Oaks, CA and New Delhi: Sage, pp. 138–69.

Littig, Beate (2009) 'Interviewing the elite – interviewing experts: Is there a difference?', in Alexander Bogner, Beate Littig and Wolfgang Menz (eds.), *Interviewing Experts*. Basingstoke: Palgrave Macmillan, pp. 8–113.

Littig, Beate and Franz Pöchhacker (2014) 'Socio-translational collaboration in qualitative inquiry. The case of expert interviews', *Qualitative Inquiry*. Special Issue: Flick, U. (ed.): Challenges for Qualitative Inquiry as a Global Endeavor, 20(9): 1085–95.

Maasen, Sabine and Peter Weingart (eds.) (2005) *Democratization of Expertise? Exploring Novel Forms of Scientific Advice in Political Decision-Making*. Dordrecht: Springer.

Menz, Wolfgang and Sarah Nies, (2017) 'Methoden der Arbeitssoziologie', in Fritz Böhle, and G. Günter Voß (eds.), *Handbuch Arbeitssoziologie* (2nd edn). Wiesbaden: SpringerVS (forthcoming).

Meuser, Michael and Ulrike Nagel (1991) 'ExpertInneninterviews – vielfach erprobt, wenig bedacht. Ein Beitrag zur qualitativen Methodendiskussion', in Detlef Garz and Klaus Kraimer (eds.), *Qualitative empirische Sozialforschung: Konzepte, Methoden, Analysen*. Opaden: Westdeutscher Verlag, pp. 441–71.

Meuser, Michael and Ulrike Nagel (2009) 'The expert interview and changes in knowledge production', in Alexander Bogner, Beate Littig and Wolfgang Menz (eds.), *Interviewing Experts*. Basingstoke: Palgrave Macmillan, pp. 17–42.

Michels, Robert (1911) *Zur Soziologie des Parteiwesens in der modernen Demokratie. Untersuchungen über die oligarchischen Tendenzen des Gruppenlebens*. Leipzig: Klinkhardt.

Mikecz Robert (2012) 'Interviewing elites: Addressing methodological issues', *Qualitative Inquiry*, 18(6): 482–93.

Mills, C. Wright (1956) *The Power Elite*. New York: Oxford University Press.

Moyser, George and Margaret Wagstaffe (eds.) (1987) *Research Methods for Elite Studies*. London: Allen and Unwin.

Oakley, Ann (1981) 'Interviewing women: A contradiction in terms', in Helen Robert (ed.), *Doing Feminist Research*. New York: Routledge and Kegan Paul, pp. 30–60.

Odendahl, Teresa and Aileen M. Shaw (2002) 'Interviewing elites', in Jaber Gubrium and James Holstein (eds.), *Handbook of Interview Research: Context and Methodology*. Thousand Oaks, CA: Sage, pp. 299–316.

Pfadenhauer, Michaela (2009) 'At eye level. The expert interview – a talk between expert and quasi-expert', in Alexander Bogner, Beate Littig and Wolfgang Menz (eds.), *Interviewing Experts*. Basingstoke: Palgrave Macmillan, pp. 81–97.

Plesner, Ursula (2011) 'Studying sideways: Displacing the problem of power in research interviews with sociologists and journalists', *Qualitative Inquiry*, 17(6): 471–82.

Polanyi, Michael (1966) *The Tacit Dimension*. Garden City, NY: Doubleday.

Richards, David (1996) 'Elite interviewing: Approaches and pitfalls', *Politics*, 16(3): 199–204.

Salmons, Janet (2010): *Online Interviews in Real Time*. Los Angeles, CA: Sage.

Schütz, Alfred (1964) 'The well-informed citizen: An essay on the social distribution of knowledge', in Alfred Schütz (ed.), *Collected Papers*, Vol. 2. The Hague: Nijhoff, pp. 3–47.

Seldon, A. (1996) 'Elite interviews', in Brian Brivati, Julia Buxton and Anthony Seldon (eds.), *The Contemporary History Handbook*. Manchester: Manchester University Press, pp. 353–65.

Stephens, Neil (2007) 'Collecting data from elites and ultra elites: Telephone and face-to-face interviews with macroeconomists', *Qualitative Research*, 7(2): 203–16.

Temple, Bogusia and Rosalind Edwards (2002) 'Interpreters/translators and cross-language research: Reflexivity and border crossings', *International Journal of Qualitative Methods*, 1(2), Article 1. Retrieved from http://www.ualberta.ca/~ijqm/.

Trinczek, Rainer (2009) 'How to interview managers? Methodical and methodological aspects of expert interviews as a qualitative method in empirical social research', in Alexander Bogner, Beate Littig and Wolfgang Menz (eds.), *Interviewing Experts*. Basingstoke: Palgrave Macmillan, pp. 203–16.

Turner, Stephen (2002) 'What is the problem with experts?' *Social Studies of Science*, 31(1): 123–49.

Veblen, Thorstein (1899) *The Theory of the Leisure Class: An Economic Study of Institutions*. New York: Macmillan.

Welch, C., Marschan-Piekkari, R., Penttinen, H., and Tahvanainen, M. (2002) 'Corporate elites as informants in qualitative international business research', *International Business Research Review*, 11(5): 611–28.

Weller, Susie (2015) 'The potentials and pitfalls of using Skype for qualitative (longitudinal) interviews', National Centre for Research Methods. Retrieved from http://eprints.ncrm.ac.uk/3757.

Wilson, Thomas P. (1970) 'Normative and interpretive paradigms in sociology', in J. D. Douglas (ed.), *Understanding Everyday Life. Toward the Reconstruction of Sociological Knowledge*. Chicago, IL: Aldine, pp. 57–79.

Witzel, Andreas and Herwig Reiter (2012) *The Problem-centred Interview*. London: Sage.

Collecting Qualitative Data with Hard-to-Reach Groups

Kerry Chamberlain and Darrin Hodgetts

INTRODUCTION

The key concern of this chapter is 'hard-to-reach', what that means, and how we might generate qualitative research data working with the hard-to-reach. We first discuss what hard-to-reach might mean, and then consider pertinent issues for data collection with hard-to-reach groups – access (see Bengry, Chapter 7, this volume), gatekeeping, and sampling (see Schreier, Chapter 6, this volume), methods for qualitative research, and ethical concerns (see Mertens, Chapter 3, this volume), that can arise in working with such groups. We contend that most researchers tend to consider field research with the hard-to-reach as a difficult activity, requiring special care and attention, with strong possibilities of denied access, participant non-response, refusal, or incomplete participation. In contrast, we propose that researching with the hard-to-reach is no more difficult than other forms of field research, provided that initial work around consultancy and participation is undertaken, and the research is flexible and responsive to changing conditions as it progresses. We illustrate this with two case studies of research we have conducted with homeless people and impoverished families. Throughout the chapter we discuss the principles that underlie such research and produce effective solutions to working with hard-to-reach groups. In closing, we comment on the value of undertaking scholar-activist research in this domain.

In seeking to do research on a wide range of social issues, researchers often run up against problems of locating, accessing, and working with individuals or groups that can be considered as 'hard-to-reach' in some way. These individuals or groups can be hard-to-reach for a variety of reasons. Their lifestyle may make them highly mobile, such as transnational executives (e.g. Devadason, 2016), gypsy–travellers (e.g. Myers, 2016), or people who are homeless (e.g. Trussell and Mair, 2010), and therefore not easily accessible. Or they may be rare in the population, such as people with rare diseases and limited connections to others (e.g. Thompson and Phillips, 2007). They may be able to be identified and located but difficult to engage with, such as people with severe mental health problems (e.g. Lamb et al., 2015), people with dementia (e.g. Hoppitt et al., 2012), people close to death (e.g. Cowan, 2014), or recent migrants (e.g. Vahabi et al., 2015). They may be identifiable, but hidden from view, such as injecting drug users, drug dealers, burglars or others engaged in illegal activities (e.g. Curtis, 2011; Fleetwood, 2014; Hakansson et al., 2012). Or they may be unwilling because they are engaged in stigmatised or socially denigrated practices, such as sex workers (e.g. Benoit et al., 2005), young binge drinkers and 'boy racers' (e.g. Bengry-Howell and Griffin, 2012). They may be unwilling to engage because of the sensitive nature of the subject being investigated, such as victims of violence or sex workers (e.g. Allen et al., 2015). They may be unwilling to engage because of their activities and social locations. This may occur because of their membership of elite groups, such as wealthy people, politicians, or celebrities (see Bogner et al., Chapter 41, this volume). Such people can be hard-to-reach (see Mikecz, 2012) and actively resist participation in research because of their position and power (e.g. Featherstone, 2014), for the protection of knowledge, or because of political considerations (e.g. Lancaster, 2016). They may also be engaged in activities that they do not want to share, such as political activism (e.g. Dencik et al., 2016) or paramilitary activities (e.g. Feenan, 2002). They may be culturally different, and unwilling to engage with researchers that do not understand their cultural practices and beliefs (e.g. Brown and Scullion, 2010), or to hand over traditional or sacred knowledge to researchers (e.g. Battiste, 2016). So there are a wide variety of reasons why people, as potential research participants, may be hard-to-reach. And of course, these issues are not mutually exclusive, and may overlap, with several issues having relevance in particular cases or situations (Ellard-Gray et al., 2015).

Although there is a wide diversity of ways in which groups are rendered hard-to-reach groups, a good deal of the academic literature on hard-to-reach groups describes them as isolated from the mainstream in some way, often through being a minority, or of lower socio-economic standing, or less educated, and so on. However, describing hard-to-reach groups in this way is not only pejorative and potentially stigmatising, but it also tends to personalise and individualise the characteristics of group members, creating potential to blame them for their situations rather than see these as structurally caused. Friemuth and Mettger (1990) suggest that such labelling reveals the preconceptions about these groups that researchers may have, and bring into their research, through assuming such people lack problem-solving skills, literacy, social skills, and motivation, or are simply assumed to be 'uncooperative, ignorant, and dysfunctional' (Froonjian and Garnett, 2013, p. 835). This leads Friemuth and Mettger to argue that we should not use the term 'hard-to-reach'. However, we need to accept that some individuals and groups within our societies, because of their circumstances, activities, or as a result of their choice to restrict researcher access and contact, are more difficult to engage in our research than others. Hence, we will retain the use of the term here but recognise that it is both contested and open to interpretation.

ISSUES IN ENGAGING THE HARD-TO-REACH

One major concern in working with hard-to-reach groups is that the researcher is typically an 'outsider' – a person who does not belong to the group and therefore someone who does not understand its culture or ethos, is not perceived as sympathetic, or who does not 'belong'. The pros and cons of being an outsider or insider in conducting qualitative research have been widely debated in the literature (e.g. Berger, 2015; Corbin Dwyer and Buckle, 2009). As Berger (2015) argues, this can affect the research in three ways. First, insiders are likely to gain easier access to hard-to-reach groups because they are perceived as similar, and potentially as empathetic and understanding, in contrast to outsiders who may be distrusted on account of their differences. Second, this may affect the relationships that can be established, in that people may be more comfortable discussing their experiences with researchers who have a similar background, especially if sensitive topics are involved. This can consequently affect the quality and depth of data that might be collected. Third, the researcher's background and worldview can affect the ways in which he or she uses language, frames questions, and makes decisions about issues to probe and follow up. Consequently research engagements may be perturbed by a failure to understand questions or answers, or the loss of information by a failure to probe for or follow up on topics that may be raised tentatively. Further arguments raised about outsider research include that outsiders are potentially less likely to understand the experiences reported by participants (e.g. Hayfield and Huxley, 2015), that outsiders can benefit from a naïve questioning and interpretive stance (Savvides et al., 2014), and also be more trusted to retain information as confidential (Sixsmith et al., 2003). However, the simple classification of outsider/insider masks the complexities inherent in researcher–participant relationships (Gair, 2012) when researchers are operating in the 'space between' (Corbin Dwyer and Buckle, 2009), with such positionings bringing a complex mix of potential costs and benefits for the research (Eliason, 2016; Zempi, 2016).

Access, Gatekeeping, and Sampling

Determining who will be involved in the research processes raises a number of issues with hard-to-reach participants. Access to such participants (see Bengry, Chapter 7, this volume), can be difficult, especially when this is regulated by gatekeepers, such as organisational managers, gang leaders, carers, guardians, or whoever has the power to control access to the research participants. Obtaining access to children can be particularly difficult, as consenting may be required from parents or teachers, or both, who act as gatekeepers. Data collection with this group can be further complicated when guardians seek to be present during the data collection process (Pyer and Campbell, 2013). Gatekeepers can affect research in several ways beyond limiting access to participants, by imposing their own considerations of what constitutes 'proper research' and seeking to restrict or extend the focus of the project, by limiting what data can be collected, the scope of analysis that may be undertaken, and the content and availability of publications arising from the research. As with any other aspect of field research, or research more generally, working with, through, and around gatekeepers to access participants can be a complex, fluid, and somewhat unpredictable process, requiring tact, negotiation, compromise, and flexibility (Crowhurst and Kennedy-Macfoy, 2013; Turner and Almack, 2016). For hard-to-reach groups, even locating gatekeepers who might assist with access can be difficult (Crowhurst et al., 2013). Further, the relationship between gatekeepers and potential participants, particularly around issues of trust, is another important aspect determining participation in research (Emmel et al., 2007). Although much of the commentary on gatekeepers regards their involvement in research as potentially difficult and problematic, they can also be very helpful in gaining access to participants. Gatekeepers can facilitate access through acting as brokers, vouching for researchers, and building trust (Couch et al., 2015). In this case, it may be more appropriate to label such people as mediators of the research rather than as gatekeepers, as Kristensen and

Ravn (2015) propose. In general, the consensus from the commentaries on gatekeeping in the literature, dealing with access to a wide range of different hard-to-reach groups, is that it is important to establish trust between all parties, to build strong and robust relationships with gatekeepers, key stakeholders, and participant communities, to expect that negotiations for access will be continuing as the research progresses, and to expect change.

Once participant access is determined, the selection of participants for the research arises. Qualitative research sampling (see Schreier, Chapter 6, this volume) brings a number of considerations into play (Abrams, 2010). The usual approaches seek theoretical depth and insight, rather than representativeness and, consequently, researchers do not seek a defined number of cases or people to involve. Frequently the goal of sampling is to reach saturation, a point where no new ideas or new theoretical insights are apparent in the data (Fusch and Ness, 2015), although this can be a problematic process (see Nelson, 2016). The sampling process is not always standardised and fixed in advance of the research, but develops across the research process, changing in response to the researcher's reflexive considerations of practice, and in response to insights developed during data collection and analysis as the research progresses.

The apposite sampling of hard-to-reach participants is a concern raised by several researchers attempting to work with such people and groups (e.g. Abrams, 2010; Thompson and Phillips, 2007). In general, they argue for pragmatic approaches to sampling, using convenience samples located through agencies or street-based snowball sampling, noting that practical and institutional constraints function to preclude purposeful or theoretical sampling. However, these processes should not be abandoned outright as they have value for the research. Purposeful or purposive sampling, in one of its many variants (see Patton, 2015) is very commonly used in qualitative research, seeking to locate 'information-rich cases for in-depth study' (Patton, 2015, p. 264), and forms of this technique can be used for hard-to-reach participants and groups. Purposive sampling strategies that may have particular value for the hard-to-reach include the purposeful selection of: typical cases, which illustrate the phenomenon of interest, sampled either homogeneously or to maximise variation; extreme, deviant, or troublesome, cases, which illustrate the extremes of the phenomenon of interest; and critical cases, which can vividly illustrate the phenomenon or key aspects of it. Emmel (2013) argues also for theoretically driven purposive sampling, which develops and tests theoretical arguments through sampling processes that attempt to purposefully select cases that can illustrate the insights that researchers bring to the research, and which develop as the research engagements and analysis progresses. This theoretical sampling process will therefore be revised and varied as the research goes forward, in light of what is learned from previous cases. As Emmel (2013, p. 45) notes 'It is directed and re-cast by reflexive researchers towards the purpose of developing and testing theory into an intellectual puzzle about the social world'.

Some techniques that have been developed by quantitative researchers for sampling hard-to-reach groups, such as respondent-driven sampling and time-space sampling (e.g. Semaan, 2010), have potential to be adapted by qualitative researchers for sampling. For example, respondent-driven sampling is a formalised version of snowball sampling, where recruitment begins with a small number of researcher-identified participants from the target group, who then recruit another wave of participants, who in turn, recruit a further wave, and so on, until a suitable number of participants has been obtained. The value of this method lies in extending the network of people sampled beyond the researcher-driven one, for reaching beyond those participants who may have greater visibility in a community, and for reaching participants who may avoid public venues or who do not trust agencies (Semaan, 2010).

This technique does rely on some degree of association or connectedness within the group of interest so that viable networks for sampling are present. Thompson and Phillips (2007) provide a discussion of various ways in which less associated people may be sampled, including identifying and sampling networks, using media advertising and publicity, insider-based approaches, and outsider-based approaches, such as the 'anonymous stranger', where the researcher is identified as having skills to offer back in return for participation. In general, requests for participation are most successful when the proposed research engagement provides benefits for both the researcher and the participant (Kristensen and Ravn, 2015).

However, we should be aware that research in the field is always unpredictable to some degree, and researchers need to be flexible with their sampling strategies as the research progresses, adapting to failures to locate expected participants, non-response from participants in spite of follow-ups, responses from participants declining to participate for various reasons, and failures from gatekeepers or mediators to deliver participants as promised or expected (see Bengry, Chapter 7, this volume). Fortunately, qualitative research does not usually seek population representativeness, so these 'failures' of sampling can be adapted to successfully by participant substitution.

Also, we should note that our focus on hard-to-reach people could imply that the sampling focus will be on individuals, but this is not necessarily the case; we might just as easily be interested in sampling social processes that are hard to access (like burglary, doctor–patient interactions about sexually transmitted disease, life on the street, or parenting a dying child), or organisations (like policing, special schooling, or needle exchanges for users of illegal drugs), or documents (personal diaries and letters, or pornographic films) – all kinds of phenomena are open to investigation (Silverman, 2014).

Methods

There is a very wide range of methodologies and methods for undertaking qualitative research with groups and communities (Jason and Glenwick, 2016). Although almost any process of engagement with participants is potentially viable for research with people and groups considered hard-to-reach, there are some considerations here that can enhance data depth and quality. These are important given the difficulties that can be involved with access and recruitment in this context. These are important in light of the difficulties Given the need to establish trust in the researchers and the research processes, it can be functional to utilise some form of longitudinal engagement with participants (see Henwood et al., Chapter 38, this volume). This allows for enhanced rapport and increased trust as the research develops, and can lead to more depth and quality in the data gathered, which in turn can enhance analysis, interpretations, and possibilities for disseminations. Such approaches may draw on a particular methodology, such as action research or ethnography (see Buscatto, Chapter 21, this volume), which require in-depth engagement with participants over time (Couch et al., 2015), or involve the use of different methods across a number of data collection sessions with participants (Chamberlain et al., 2011). Such ongoing or multiple contacts with participants also allow for preliminary findings from earlier engagements to be revisited and reconsidered, both by researchers and participants. Other benefits include going beyond the standard interview to incorporate a range of participatory data collection processes, such as go-along interviews (Garcia et al., 2012; see Kusenbach, Chapter 22, this volume), photovoice (Sutton-Brown, 2014; see Henwood et al., Chapter 38, this volume), photo- and video-elicitation methods (Padgett et al., 2013; see Eberle, Chapter 25, this volume), diaries (Bernays et al., 2014), time-lining (Sheridan et al., 2011), mapping techniques (Green et al., 2016), life history (Hirsch and Philbin, 2016) and arts-based approaches (Coemans et al., 2015). These methods are considered to be participatory because they place data collection and direction in the hands of participants, effectively making them researchers of their own lives (Sheridan et al., 2011), increasing their involvement in the research and their motivation to contribute to it (Balbale et al., 2016). Accordingly, these 'beyond-text methods' force a rethink and rework of the ways in which researchers can and should engage with groups and communities (Beebeejaun et al., 2014), and promote collaborative approaches to data collection, and beyond. Further, when research is developed collaboratively with participants it promotes enhanced researcher reflexivity (e.g. Rooney, 2015), ensures that local knowledge and understandings are incorporated into data collection processes, that data will be correspondingly enriched, and can lead to knowledge that is an amalgam of local and academic understandings (Mayan and Daum, 2016a). Also, if the dynamics of experience or the change in social practices over time are of interest, then longitudinal data collection, either using the same methods repeated, different methods over time, or a combination of both, has other specific merits, allowing researchers (and participants) to follow a topic of interest through periods of transition and change (Henwood and Shirani, 2012; Koro-Ljungberg and Bussing, 2013).

Ethics

The growth of qualitative research in the social sciences and increasing regulatory frameworks for ethical approval of research have meant that ethical review and approval for social science research has become increasingly contested (Dingwall, 2006; Hammersley, 2009), especially around whether ethics committees are suitably knowledgeable when qualitative research methods are involved, or are suitably positioned to be the best judges of ethical practice for complex and potentially fluid field research (Birch et al., 2012; Burr and Reynolds, 2010). Beyond these concerns, ethical issues of consent, anonymity and confidentiality, and potential for harm can take on more acute edges when undertaking research with hard-to-reach participants and groups (see Mertens, Chapter 3, this volume).

Informed consent is itself a difficult issue, where the requirements for ethical practice in this area have changed substantially over the last four decades (Miller and Boulton, 2007), as ethical review committees have responded to such things as heightened perceptions of risk in society. This can impact on the hard-to-reach, as those engaged in illegal activities, those near death, those cognitively impaired, or those engaged with sensitive topics, may all be defined as at risk, rendering formal informed consent processes more complicated to complete. When gatekeepers are involved, then matters of consent become more problematic and issues of power and control can arise, raising concerns as to who is consenting to what, and for whom (Miller and Bell, 2011).

With the growth of qualitative research practice drawing on methodologies that engage participants longitudinally, such as participatory action research, ethnography, and time-oriented qualitative longitudinal research, issues of consent are confronted by the more fluid relationships between researchers and researched that such research demands. Informed consent processes for such research has been challenging for ethical review committees as they have moved from an essentially moral consideration of consent to a more regulatory perspective (Miller and Boulton, 2007; Neale, 2013). Qualitative research of that type frequently involves multiple engagements between researchers and participants, often using different methods and data collection processes, which problematises consent further (Rooney, 2015). In this situation Rooney (2015) advocates negotiating consent orally as the research progresses and then completing a formal consent process at the conclusion of the research. Further, participants who regard themselves as marginalised, socially excluded, or vulnerable because of their activities may be unwilling to give formalised consent in writing at the start of the research (Miller and Bell, 2011), yet quite agreeable to becoming involved if consent is provisional and ongoing as the research progresses. While these consenting practices are ethically reasonable, and would work well with hard-to-reach participants, they are unlikely to be well received by ethical review committees under their current bureaucratic and regulatory framing of ethical approval, with their demands for an anticipatory informed consent from participants (Murphy and Dingwall, 2007). Issues of consent become more complicated when our model of participant involvement moves from viewing them solely as sources of data to a more participatory perspective, engaging them as more involved research partners, as it does when we ask participants to read and comment on transcripts and initial analyses, approve the use of their own quotations, and so on. In these situations, anticipatory consent cannot be given, as we often have no initial idea of where the research analyses and findings will arrive, raising questions about what exactly was consented to when anticipatory consent is used (Miller and Bell, 2011). This reflects the tensions between procedural and practical ethics (Guillemin and Gillam, 2004) that become highlighted by research of this nature.

The issue of harm in research with hard-to-reach groups emerges in a number of ways. As noted earlier, such groups are often marginalised and vulnerable, and the presentation of research findings which focus on their shortcomings, limitations, illegal activities, or which situates them as personally responsible for their own situations (as often happens for impoverished people in contemporary neoliberal societies) does not serve their interests well (Thompson and Phillips, 2007). Approaching research involving such groups with this in mind has implications for what they might be asked to do, the responsibilities of the researchers, how consent is sought, and how trust is built between researchers and participants (Couch et al., 2015). Another major issue concerns confidentiality. Also, participants may not want to be identified because of their situations, and this can become a particular problem for longitudinal research, where a variety of in-depth material about specific participants is accumulated. For example, a publication providing a number of quotes from a particular injecting illegal drug taker to illustrate findings, although anonymised, may contain a limited range of incidental detail within each quote that retains anonymity, but if all these quotes are named to a participant and can be amalgamated, they may together provide sufficient information that could enable identification. A similar situation can arise when working with case studies, where a considerable amount of information about a single participant may be disclosed. Such situations require careful management of research materials as these move from a restricted access data set into publicly available research publications and other forms of dissemination. Finally, as we have emphasised throughout, engagements with hard-to-reach groups and communities are likely to be fluid and changing as the research progresses, and this can lead to changes in research practices and relationships. Involving groups and communities in research requires critical engagement with ethical principles and the underlying values guiding ethical review processes, as otherwise the research practices may themselves cause harm (Brunger and Wall, 2016). This requires the researcher to be continually alert to ongoing ethical concerns that might arise in the field and to be guided by ethical principles rather than rely on anticipatory ethical approvals and to 'go beyond the disciplining and normalizing institutional context within which our research practices and outcomes are shaped' (Gombert et al., 2016, p. 594).

ENSURING HARD-TO-REACH GROUPS BECOME LESS HARD-TO-REACH

From the outside, groups such as homeless people may seem hard-to-reach. However, we argue that relationships and research opportunities between these groups and researchers can be facilitated by utilising appropriate and responsive approaches to consultation, engagement and research activities. Hence, we argue for conducting research in partnership *with* such groups, rather then researching *on* them; this involves ensuring that the aims and objectives of the research is more about assisting rather than examining such people, and allowing them to retain control over what happens to them and how the research with them proceeds.

An essential component of this form of research engagement involves working in a consultative partnership, where research agendas and processes, and the basis for their choice, are communicated and consensually agreed (Kirwan et al., 2013). This requires the building of meaningful relationships in local settings and, quite often, long-term commitments to the communities involved (Mayan and Daum, 2016a). Notions of reciprocity, ethical engagement, immersion, researcher participation, and responsiveness are central for successful engagement. In these respects, we can be informed by the seminal work of scholars from the founding generation of community-based social science. For example, Marie Jahoda emphasised the importance of immersing ourselves as scholars within the lives and social problems faced by the groups with whom we seek to develop substantive knowledge that can form the basis of social action (Lazarfeld-Jahoda and Zeisel, 1933; see also Flick, Chapter 34, this volume).

Jahoda conducted research *with* rather than doing research *on* groups in order to ensure that actionable understandings with relevance for the experiences of local people could be developed (Jahoda, 1992). In a major project on unemployment, for example, Jahoda et al. (2002) involved the community in the focus and design of the research, and committed to not just documenting what was happening in the everyday lives of community members but also to activities that directly assisted the people around the research team. This extended to mending clothing and running a health service.

However, we do need to be aware that these relationships are complex, and need to be continually assessed and revised as the research develops, and particularly as the research ends. Differing relationships are likely to be formed with different players in the field; not only those experiencing the issues directly, but also their family members, people within their support networks, service providers, and agencies with which they are in contact, as well as community leaders and others, such as health care providers, may all be involved (Mayan and Daum, 2016a). The form of these relationships will depend on the nature of the issue under investigation and the connections established within the community engaged. These relationships also have potential to become muddled (Mayan and Daum, 2016b) as we negotiate differing forms of relationship with different community members across the time of the research. In undertaking such research, we are typically engaged in addressing issues of disparity, and are involved in seeking to promote different understandings and to achieve change. Working in such partnerships with such objectives requires taking risks and stepping beyond conventional academic roles. As Mayan and Daum (2016b) argue 'Taking risks engages us with society and with the explicit intent of confronting and changing the living conditions of people who are commonly underserved, hidden, and forgotten' (2016b, p. 74).

Mayan and Daum (2016b) suggest several strategies to enhance the building of successful relationships. These include learning about the community and community members, being visible and becoming known, participating in and contributing to community activities, and generally becoming involved in the life of the community. This builds acceptance and trust, and is facilitated by developing relationships that are informal, by participating in everyday activities such as conversations and sharing food. Importantly, embracing an ethics of reciprocity in relationships with community members can appreciably facilitate this. Reciprocity is a process based on exchange, aimed at creating equality between the different parties (Maiter et al., 2008), and diminishing the distance between academic and community members (Hodgetts et al., 2013). Basing relationships and engagements on reciprocity and exchange can illuminate and facilitate research processes; for example, considering data collection as an exchange of knowledge on one hand and capacity-building on the other (Maiter et al., 2008) forces consideration of how capacity-building can be incorporated in the research processes, and what participants receive in exchange for their participation.

Next we illustrate how we have responded to some of these fieldwork challenges by describing two case studies where we have been involved as researchers working with hard-to-reach groups. Both projects were built in partnership with a community agency, the Auckland City Mission, and were the outcome of a longer-term engagement with that agency for over a decade. Such long-term engagements with agencies bear fruit because they build and enable meaningful relations and trust, and lead to immersion in agency practices and fieldwork (Hodgetts et al., 2014b). Such involvement also produces reciprocal demands on the researchers, to sustain the relationships, give something back to the agency and the participants, and to produce knowledge that has practical benefit that is useful for the agency and beyond. Hence, such engagements often go far beyond the 'normal' activities of research. Central to both cases is the ethical principle of reciprocity in community research (Hodgetts et al., 2013). We acknowledge that working through an agency is not the only way that members of hard-to-reach groups can be engaged, and that other routes to engage appropriate participants more directly are available. However, we would also emphasise that engaging participants through an organisation or agency, around which they collect, does not avoid the processes of engagement with specific research participants, or the issues of ethical practice, trust, reciprocity, immersion, and responsiveness that are operative for successful field research.

Case 1: Homelessness

Several years ago we undertook a major research project into homelessness (Hodgetts et al., 2011). This was facilitated through a major charity, the Auckland City Mission, whose work included a drug and alcohol detoxification centre for impoverished people, a homeless support team, and a food bank. Agencies like this are important for researchers because they provide points of stability for people whose lives are characterised by transience, such as homeless people. The relationship with this agency was built up over a considerable time, before any research started. It was facilitated by several factors, including experience developed through prior research into homelessness by team members, a CEO who had listened to research presentations from team members and was supportive of further research into the topic, and a series of regular discussions with key staff at the agency about issues that arose as the research project and grant application were developed. These discussions ensured that the agency had a real stake in the research, and effectively became a research partner in the project. The agency also helped facilitate our access to other agencies that were then involved in the research. The relationships were cemented further by the creation of a Project Advisory Committee, consisting of key staff from these agencies and representatives of homeless people. This Committee met regularly with the research team, who reported on the progress of the research and sought advice on any issues emerging.

Our research grant application was successful, in part because we were clearly embedded in and supported by this key agency. Obtaining funding also meant that we could support a range of student research and develop emerging researchers within the project. This meant that students also needed to become embedded in the agency, which was facilitated by their volunteer work at the drop-in centre and the foodbank within the agency, alongside members of the research team, where they interacted with and gained the trust of the homeless support team members. It also meant that the research team members came into contact with a wide range of homeless people, many of whom became participants in the research. Research participation was strongly facilitated by these relationships and visible activities within the agency, as it meant that the researchers became familiar to many homeless people using the agency, and came to be accepted and trusted by them. Consequently, they committed to the research and this facilitated the longer-term engagements with them that were sought in the research, with initial interviews, follow-up interviews, and photo-elicitation projects and interviews. Ultimately, we worked with 58 homeless people who participated in the research; all completing one in-depth interview, most also completing photo-elicitation exercises, and some engaging in other research activities, such as go-along interviews (see Kusenbach, Chapter 22, this volume) and case studies, over a 2-year period of the research.

Although this research with this hard-to-reach group was substantially enhanced by the agency relationships, it did not always run smoothly. Homeless people are transient and the research needed to react to changes in circumstances, departures from the city, failures to show up, and so on. Not all participants completed all planned data collection processes, for a variety of reasons, so the data set was untidy. Field research of this nature requires both flexible researchers and flexibility in methods. It also requires the researchers to be responsive to opportunities. For example, we followed up an unexpected press report on homelessness, and incorporated the resultant material into the data set for analysis (see Hodgetts et al., 2008). We also sought data from domiciled people who were in proximity with homeless people in some way, using specific locations where homeless people gather rather than specific participant sampling, but we were only moderately successful in recruiting them (Hodgetts et al., 2011), largely because we did not have the same opportunities to build relationships with this group. We also intended to locate homeless people living in rural areas, but we could not find an ethical way to identify and contact them, so this component of the research could not be completed. This reinforced the value of using an agency as a key point of contact.

Reciprocal responsibilities between the researchers and agency staff were demonstrated across the research. The agency hosted class visits from community psychology students to learn about its activities, and supported student work placements at the site. The research team developed case studies from the research that were linked to practice, and workshopped with agency staff to inform and assist the agency in working with homeless people. We also ran a reading group with staff as part of a job enrichment programme, which enabled them to gain greater understandings of the issues faced by homeless clients, the social structures that drive homelessness, and how to enhance humane service responses. Other, more entertaining and enjoyable activities, involved such things as a debate between the research team and the homeless support team members. The moot was 'homelessness is a viable lifestyle option for everyone', with the research team taking the affirmative, and an audience composed of homeless people and friends, other researchers and friends, and various agency staff and friends. Reciprocity with participants was expressed in a wide range of ways, through such things as providing food as part of interviews, advising, and helping with problems such as approaching welfare agencies, connecting participants with relevant services, and following up on the actions taken. All of this reflects the way the relationship between the researchers and participants and the agency needed to be embedded and sustained across and beyond the research, and documents the range of planning, time, and commitment involved for all parties. It also reflects the fact that each party stood to gain benefits from the relationship, and that the research activity was not simply an academic exercise.

Case 2: Foodbank Users

This work was located in the same agency, the Auckland City Mission, and was a development arising from our homelessness research. We had found that the majority of homeless people had drifted into street life from precarious or impoverished backgrounds rather than dropping into homelessness from middle-class lifeworlds (Hodgetts et al., 2012). We became interested to look upstream at the experiences of precarious households that were populating street homelessness in Auckland. Having established strong relationships with this agency, the CEO invited us to work with agency staff to develop a research project from an initial idea they had formed around households that relied heavily on the agency foodbank. The project had two interrelated aims: to examine in depth the lives of impoverished people on a range of key issues; and to develop staff skills both in engaging in depth with agency clients and in staff understandings of research. The research team wrote a proposal that documented the research procedures and a budget, which were negotiated with the CEO, and approved by the CEO and the Board of the agency. The project was focused around high users of the foodbank, and we worked with a special team of social work staff who had volunteered to work on the project. The research, known as the Family100 Project, identified 100 families who were systematically sampled from the database of the food bank from the much larger pool of high users. These high users were contacted and their consent sought to participate in the research by the social workers in the team. This recruitment process continued until 100 families had agreed to participate. The research involved the social workers meeting with the participants every two weeks for a year, to discuss a range of topics that were pertinent to their daily lives. These topics or themes were determined by the research team during the development of the project in discussion with agency staff, who considered these to be the major issues for this group. The topics covered family background and relationships, housing, social services, income, and finances, debt, health, food, employment, education, and justice, with the topic for discussion with families changed monthly. Consequently each topic was discussed twice, at meetings which typically involved a structured interview focused on the key topic issues, and a mapping exercise related to the topic. These mapping exercises involved such activities as the researcher and participant working to diagram all the social service agencies a family had been in contact with for the last three months, with an indication of the quality of that relationship. The use of sustained, long-term repeat engagements also allowed us to gain insight into how these issues were working in concert for these people. Participants were compensated for their time with a foodbank parcel for their household each time they took part in an interview.

The research team met with the social workers every two weeks over 14 months, to plan out the data collection for the coming weeks, and were responsible for preparing the interview schedules and mapping procedures that were used for each interview, and training the social workers in their use. This also required several more general research-focused training sessions before interviews began, to cover issues such as using open questioning, creating conversational interviews, using mapping and drawing as graphic elicitation tools, and developing situational awareness of the structural causes of poverty. Day-to-day coordination of the project was handled by a Research Officer employed by the Auckland City Mission, who coordinated data collections and archiving, managed the interface between social workers and participants, and assisted with data analysis, dissemination, publications, and reports to the agency Board.

The Family100 Project produced a number of major challenges, given that it moved beyond a researcher-initiated model of research involving end-users, towards a more open, responsive, and immersive orientation involving ongoing dialogue and relationships between researchers, agency staff and agency clients (Hodgetts et al., 2014b). First, we needed to obtain ethical approval for the project from an international panel of experienced community researchers, as this was not available from our institutional ethics committee given the project was led by the Auckland City Mission. We also had to work with the social workers to ensure their understanding of appropriate ethical practice when involved as researchers with research participants and simultaneously as social workers with agency clients. Other major challenges centred on data collection and analysis, given that the research team members were not directly involved with the participants. We could not afford to record and transcribe all two-weekly interviews, and we therefore had the social workers complete four major recap interviews, between topics at three-month intervals, across the year with each participant, which were recorded and transcribed, and where they reviewed all issues discussed in the last four months (for the last two research themes). These, alongside the social workers' summary notes of each interview and the mappings from each interview, constituted the data sources for analysis and publications (e.g. Hodgetts et al., 2014a). Once again, the data set was messy, as some participants could not make particular meetings, some left the city and disengaged from the project, some were ill for periods and missed sessions, and some meetings were taken over by immediate problems that required the session to become more of an engagement between social worker and client.

Once again, this research required substantial investments of time from the research team, to build on established relationships, to develop the project collaboratively, and to work closely with Auckland City Mission staff in carrying it out. This involved the research team and agency in a number of reciprocal relationships beyond the family research. For instance, the project also had an internal agency objective, to develop social worker skills in research and client engagement. The research team followed this up by conducting individual interviews with the social workers covering reflection on their practice and relationship with client participants at the close of the research. As with the homelessness project, to meet researcher obligations for reciprocity by not limiting our outputs to scholarly publications, opportunities for other forms of dissemination of the findings were taken up. These included developing and presenting a workshop based on cases drawn from the Family100 dataset to the annual professional development event for Court judges (Hodgetts et al., 2013), preparing publications to disseminate the research findings to community audiences (Auckland City Mission, 2014; Garden, 2014), and by engaging with the Government Treasury, the Families Commission, and the local City Council. These aimed to present and engage these agencies with the practical implications of our findings about societal responses to people experiencing urban poverty and food insecurity. To reciprocate for participation in the project, considerable resources were also devoted to enhancing the jobs of the Mission staff involved, and to removing food insecurity from the participating families for the duration of the research.

Both of these research engagements required substantial investments of time on the part of the researchers, building relationships, establishing trust, delivering promised services and producing desired research products, and reciprocating contributions in a range of diverse ways. In return, the research activity was hugely facilitated in all aspects, but importantly, this work rendered the hard-to-reach as relatively easy to reach.

CONCLUSION

Central to facilitating successful research with hard-to-reach groups is an ethics of reciprocity and an associated way of conducting research that fosters inclusion, equality, collaboration, and dialogue (Hodgetts et al., 2013). Also, engaging with hard-to-reach groups requires critical reflexive work (Chamberlain, 2014), monitoring the project and altering research plans and directions in response to evolving situations in the field. Working in these ways signals the relevance and responsiveness of the research to the situations that such groups, and those working to support them, find themselves in. And, we argue, developing research projects involving these principles means that the 'hard-to-reach' effectively become easier to reach.

In research of this kind it is also important to consider the position of the scholar-activist (Murray, 2012; Routledge and Derickson, 2015), where research is conducted with a view to ensuring that it actually contributes to improving the circumstances of research participants. This involves generating practical knowledge from the research to improve lives, and taking it beyond the academy, in appropriate forms, in ways that can achieve change. This means conducting research that is not content only to produce formal academic knowledge, important though this is, and to undertake data collection designed to meet academic ends. Approaching research that involves communities, embedded in notions of reciprocity and equality, and working *with* rather than *on*, can require major revisions of our research approach. It is important that this is planned into the research from the beginning, as otherwise the potentiality of the research to achieve the desired ends may be constrained (Madeloni, 2014). Further, there is considerable benefit in doing so; not only do hard-to-reach participants benefit from researchers engaging with them in these ways, but researchers also benefit in that scholarship and activism are interdependent with each mutually informing and inspiring the other (Suzuki and Mayorga, 2014). The boundaries between scholarship and activism are malleable and to some degree artificial, and they can readily converge with appropriate planning and reflexive action (Routledge and Derickson, 2015).

Above all, approaching data collection with hard-to-reach groups involves actioning an ethics of reciprocity that facilitates a forging of closer human relationships with participants and others whose decisions impact on the lives of these groups, and brings benefits to all parties. In working this way, barriers to working with hard-to-reach groups tend to dissipate.

FURTHER READING

Bhopal, Kalwant and Deuchar, Ross (eds.) (2016) *Researching Marginalized Groups*. New York: Routledge.

Bonevski, B., Randell, M., Paul, C., Chapman, K., Twyman, L., Bryant, J., Brozek, I., and Hughes, C. (2014) 'Reaching the hard-to-reach: A systematic review of strategies for improving health and medical research with socially disadvantaged groups', *BMC Medical Research Methodology*, 14(1): 2. DOI: 10.1186/1471-2288-14-42.

Jason, Leonard A. and Glenwick, David S. (eds.) (2016) *Handbook of Methodological Approaches to Community-based Research: Qualitative, Quantitative, and Mixed Methods*. New York: Oxford.

REFERENCES

Abrams, L.S. (2010) 'Sampling "hard to reach" populations in qualitative research: The case of incarcerated youth', *Qualitative Social Work*, 9(4): 536–50.

Allen, C., Murphy, A., Kiselbach, S., VandenBerg, S. and Wiebe, E. (2015) 'Exploring the experience of chronic pain among female survival sex workers: A qualitative study', *BMC Family Practice*, 16: 182. DOI: 10.1186/s12875-015-0395-6.

Auckland City Mission (2014) *Demonstrating the Complexities of Being Poor: An Empathy Tool*. Auckland: Auckland City Mission. Available at http://www.aucklandcitymission.org.nz/latest-news/resources/.

Balbale, S., Locatelli, S., and LaVela, S. (2016) 'Through their eyes lessons learned using participatory methods in health care quality improvement projects', *Qualitative Health Research*, 26(10): 1382–92.

Battiste, Marie (2016) 'Research ethics for protecting indigenous knowledge and heritage', in Norman Denzin and Michael Giardina (eds.), *Ethical Futures in Qualitative Research: Decolonizing the Politics of Knowledge*. London: Routledge, pp. 111–33.

Beebeejaun, Y., Durose, C., Rees, J., Richardson, J., and Richardson, L. (2014) '"Beyond text": Exploring ethos and method in co-producing research with communities', *Community Development Journal*, 49(1): 37–53.

Bengry-Howell, A., and Griffin, C. (2012) 'Negotiating access in ethnographic research with "hard to reach" young people: Establishing common ground or a process of methodological grooming?', *International Journal of Social Research Methodology*, 15(5): 403–16.

Benoit, C., Jansson, M., Millar, A., and Phillips, R. (2005) 'Community-academic research on hard-to-reach populations: Benefits and challenges', *Qualitative Health Research*, 15(2): 263–82.

Berger, R. (2015) 'Now I see it, now I don't: Researcher's position and reflexivity in qualitative research', *Qualitative Research*, 15(2): 219–34.

Bernays, S., Rhodes, T., and Terzic, K.J. (2014) 'Embodied accounts of HIV and hope: Using audio diaries with interviews', *Qualitative Health Research*, 24(5): 629–40.

Birch, Maxine, Miller, Tina, Mauthner, Melanie, and Jessop, Julie (2012) 'Introduction to second edition', in Tina Miller, Maxine Birch, Melanie Mauthner and Julie Jessop (eds.), *Ethics in Qualitative Research* (2nd edn). London: Sage, pp. 1–13.

Brown, P. and Scullion, L. (2010) '"Doing research" with gypsy–travellers in England: Reflections on experience and practice', *Community Development Journal*, 45(2): 169–85.

Brunger, F. and Wall, D. (2016) '"What do they really mean by partnerships?" Questioning the unquestionable good in ethics guidelines promoting community engagement in indigenous health research', *Qualitative Health Research*, 26(13): 1862–77.

Burr, J. and Reynolds, P. (2010) 'The wrong paradigm? Social research and the predicates of ethical scrutiny', *Research Ethics*, 6(4): 128–33.

Chamberlain, Kerry (2014) 'Reflexivity: Fostering research quality, ethicality, criticality and creativity', in Michael Murray (ed.), *Critical Health Psychology* (2nd edn). Basingstoke: Palgrave Macmillan, pp. 165–81.

Chamberlain, K., Cain, T., Sheridan, J., and Dupuis, A. (2011) 'Pluralisms in qualitative research: From multiple methods to integrated methods', *Qualitative Research in Psychology*, 8(2): 151–69.

Coemans, S., Wang, Q., Leysen, J., and Hannes, K. (2015) 'The use of arts-based methods in community-based research with vulnerable populations: Protocol for a scoping review', *International Journal of Educational Research*, 71: 33–9.

Corbin Dwyer, S.C. and Buckle, J.L. (2009) 'The space between: On being an insider-outsider in qualitative research', *International Journal of Qualitative Methods*, 8(1): 54–63.

Couch, J., Durant, B., and Hill, J. (2015) 'Uncovering marginalised knowledges: Undertaking research with hard-to-reach young people', *International Journal of Multiple Research Approaches*, 8(1): 15–23.

Cowan, M.M. (2014) 'The lived experiences of the Sikh population of South East England when caring for a dying relative at home', *International Journal of Palliative Nursing*, 20(4): 179–86.

Crowhurst, I. and Kennedy-Macfoy, M. (2013) 'Troubling gatekeepers: Methodological considerations for social research', *International Journal of Social Research Methodology*, 16(6): 457–62.

Crowhurst, I., Roseneil, S., Hellesund, T., Santos, A.C., and Stoilova, M. (2013) 'Close encounters: Researching intimate lives in Europe', *International Journal of Social Research Methodology*, 16(6): 525–33.

Curtis, Ric (2011) 'Getting good data from people who do bad things: Effective methods and techniques for conducting research with hard-to-reach and hidden populations', in Wim Bernasco (ed.), *Offenders on Offending: Learning About Crime from Criminals*. London: Routledge, pp. 141–60.

Dencik, L., Hintz, A., and Cable, J. (2016) 'Towards data justice? The ambiguity of anti-surveillance resistance in political activism', *Big Data & Society*, 3(2): DOI: 2053951716679678.

Devadason, R. (2016) 'The golden handcuffs? Choice, compliance and relocation amongst transnational professionals and executives', *Journal of Ethnic and Migration Studies*, 1–18. DOI: 10.1080/1369183X.2016.1260444.

Dingwall, R. (2006) 'Confronting the anti-democrats: The unethical nature of ethical regulation in social science', *Medical Sociology Online*, 1(1): 51–8.

Eliason, M.J. (2016) 'Inside/out: Challenges of conducting research in lesbian communities', *Journal of Lesbian Studies*, 20(1): 136–56.

Ellard-Gray, A., Jeffrey, N.K., Choubak, M., and Crann, S.E. (2015) 'Finding the hidden participant: Solutions for recruiting hidden, hard-to-reach, and vulnerable populations', *International Journal of Qualitative Methods*, 14(5): DOI: 1609406915621420.

Emmel, Nick (2013) *Sampling and Choosing Cases in Qualitative Research: A Realist Approach*. London: Sage.

Emmel, N., Hughes, K., Greenhalgh, J., and Sales, A. (2007) 'Accessing socially excluded people – Trust and the gatekeeper in the researcher–participant relationship', *Sociological Research Online*, 12(2): 1–13. DOI: 10.5153/sro.1512.

Featherstone, Mike (2014) 'The rich and the super-rich: Mobility, consumption and luxury lifestyle', in Nita Mathur (ed.), *Consumer Culture, Modernity and Identity*. London: Sage, pp. 3–44.

Feenan, D. (2002) 'Researching paramilitary violence in Northern Ireland', *International Journal of Social Research Methodology*, 5(2): 147–63.

Fleetwood, J. (2014) 'Keeping out of trouble: Female crack cocaine dealers in England', *European Journal of Criminology*, 11(1): 91–109.

Friemuth, V.S. and Mettger, W. (1990) 'Is there a hard-to-reach audience?', *Public Health Reports*, 105(3): 223–33.

Froonjian, J. and Garnett, J.L. (2013) 'Reaching the hard to reach: Drawing lessons from research and practice', *International Journal of Public Administration*, 36(12): 831–39.

Fusch, P.I. and Ness, L.R. (2015) 'Are we there yet? Data saturation in qualitative research', *The Qualitative Report*, 20(9): 1408–16.

Gair, S. (2012) 'Feeling their stories: Contemplating empathy, insider/outsider positionings, and enriching qualitative research', *Qualitative Health Research*, 22(1): 134–43.

Garcia, C., Eisenberg, M., Frerich, E., Lechner, K., and Lust, K. (2012) 'Conducting go-along interviews to understand context and promote health', *Qualitative Health Research*, 22(10): 1395–403.

Garden, Emily (2014) *Speaking for Ourselves*. Auckland: Auckland City Mission. Available at http://www.aucklandcitymission.org.nz/latest-news/resources/.

Gombert, K., Douglas, F., McArdle, K., and Carlisle, S. (2016) 'Reflections on ethical dilemmas in working with so-called 'vulnerable' and 'hard-to-reach' groups: Experiences from the Foodways and Futures project', *Educational Action Research*, 24(4): 583–97.

Green, E.P., Warren, V.R., Broverman, S., Ogwang, B., and Puffer, E. (2016) 'Participatory mapping in low-resource settings: Three novel methods used to engage Kenyan youth and other community members in community-based HIV prevention research', *Global Public Health*, 11(5–6): 583–99.

Guillemin, M., and Gillam, L. (2004) 'Ethics, reflexivity, and "ethically important moments" in research', *Qualitative Inquiry*, 10(2): 261–80.

Hakansson, A., Isendahl, P., Wallin, C., and Berglund, M. (2012) 'Respondent-driven sampling in a syringe exchange setting', *Scandinavian Journal of Public Health*, 40(8): 725–29.

Hammersley, M. (2009) 'Against the ethicists: On the evils of ethical regulation', *International Journal of Social Research Methodology*, 12(3): 211–25.

Hayfield, N. and Huxley, C. (2015) 'Insider and outsider perspectives: Reflections on researcher identities in research with lesbian and bisexual women', *Qualitative Research in Psychology*, 12(2): 91–106.

Henwood, Karen, and Shirani, Fiona (2012) 'Researching the temporal', in Harris Cooper, Paul Camic, Debra Long, A. T. Panter, David Rindskopf, and Kenneth Sher (eds.), *Handbook of Research Methods in Psychology* (vol. 2). Washington, DC: American Psychological Association, pp. 209–23.

Hirsch, J. and Philbin, M. (2016) 'The heroines of their own stories: Insights from the use of life history drawings in research with a transnational migrant community', *Global Public Health*, 11(5–6): 762–82.

Hodgetts, D., Chamberlain, K., Groot, S., and Tankel, Y. (2014a) 'Urban poverty, structural violence and welfare provision for 100 families in Auckland', *Urban Studies*, 51(10): 2036–51.

Hodgetts, D., Chamberlain, K., Tankel, Y., and Groot, S. (2014b) 'Looking within and beyond the community: Lessons learned by researching, theorising and acting to address urban poverty and health', *Journal of Health Psychology*, 19(1): 97–102.

Hodgetts, D., Chamberlain, K., Tankel, Y. and Groot, S. (2013) 'Researching poverty to make a difference: The need for reciprocity and advocacy in community research,' *Australian Community Psychologist*, 25(1): 46–59.

Hodgetts, D., Stolte, O., Nikora, L., and Groot, S. (2012) 'Drifting along or dropping into homelessness: A class analysis of responses to homelessness', *Antipode*, 44(4): 1209–26.

Hodgetts, D., Stolte, O., Chamberlain, K., Radley, A., Nikora, L., Nabalarua, E., and Groot, S. (2008) 'A trip to the library: Homelessness and social inclusion', *Social & Cultural Geography*, 9(8): 933–53.

Hodgetts, D., Stolte, O., Radley, A., Leggatt-Cook, C., Groot, S., and Chamberlain, K. (2011) '"Near and Far": Social distancing in domiciled characterisations of homeless people', *Urban Studies*, 48(8): 1739–53.

Hoppitt, T., Shah, S., Bradburn, P., Gill, P., Calvert, M., Pall, H., Stewart, M., Fazil, Q., and Sackley, C. (2012) 'Reaching the "hard to reach": Strategies to recruit black and minority ethnic service users with rare long-term neurological conditions', *International Journal of Social Research Methodology*, 15(6): 485–95.

Jahoda, M. (1992) 'Reflections on Marienthal and after', *Journal of Occupational and Organizational Psychology*, 65(4): 355–8.

Jahoda, Marie, Lazarsfeld, Paul, and Zeisel, Hans (2002) *Marienthal: The Sociography of an Unemployed Community*. New Brunswick, NJ: Transaction.

Jason, Leonard A. and Glenwick David S. (eds.) (2016) *Handbook of Methodological Approaches to Community-based Research: Qualitative, Quantitative, and Mixed Methods*. New York: Oxford.

Kirwan, L., Lambe, B., and Carroll, P. (2013) 'An investigation into the partnership process of community-based health promotion for men', *International Journal of Health Promotion and Education*, 51(2): 108–20.

Koro-Ljungberg, M., and Bussing, R. (2013) 'Methodological modifications in a longitudinal qualitative research design', *Field Methods*, 25(4): 423–40.

Kristensen, G. and Ravn, M.N. (2015) 'The voices heard and the voices silenced: Recruitment processes in qualitative interview studies', *Qualitative Research*, 15(6): 722–37.

Lamb, J., Dowrick, C., Burroughs, H., Beatty, S., Edwards, S., Bristow, K., Clarke, P.,

Hammond, J., Waheed, W., Gabbay, M., and Gask, L. (2015) 'Community engagement in a complex intervention to improve access to primary mental health care for hard-to-reach groups', *Health Expectations*, 18(6): 2865–79.

Lancaster, K. (2016) 'Confidentiality, anonymity and power relations in elite interviewing: Conducting qualitative policy research in a politicised domain', *International Journal of Social Research Methodology*, 20(1): 93–103.

Lazarsfeld-Jahoda, Marie and Zeisel, Hans (1933) *Die Arbeitslosen von Marienthal. Ein soziographischer Versuch über die Wirkungen langdauernder Arbeitslosigkeit.* Leipzig: Verlag von S. Hirzel.

Madeloni, B. (2014) 'The movement we make is the community we become: On being an activist in the academy', *Multicultural Perspectives*, 16(1): 12–15.

Maiter, S., Simich, L., Jacobson, N., and Wise, J. (2008) 'Reciprocity: An ethic for community-based participatory action research', *Action Research*, 6(3): 305–25.

Mayan, Maria J. and Daum, Christine H. (2016a) 'Beyond dissemination: Generating and applying qualitative evidence through community-based participatory research', in Karin Olson, Richard A. Young, and Izabela Schultz (eds.), *Handbook of Qualitative Health Research for Evidence-Based Practice.* New York: Springer, pp. 441–52.

Mayan, M. and Daum, C. (2016b) 'Worth the risk? Muddled relationships in community-based participatory research', *Qualitative Health Research*, 26(1): 69–76.

Mikecz, R. (2012) 'Interviewing elites', *Qualitative Inquiry*, 18(6): 482–93.

Miller, Tina, and Bell, Linda. (2011) 'Consenting to what? Issues of access, gate-keeping and "informed" consent', in Melanie Mauthner, Maxine Birch, Julie Jessop and Tina Miller (eds.), *Ethics in Qualitative Research.* London: Sage, pp. 54–69.

Miller, T. and Boulton, M. (2007) 'Changing constructions of informed consent: Qualitative research and complex social worlds', *Social Science & Medicine*, 65(11): 2199–211.

Murphy, E. and Dingwall, R. (2007) 'Informed consent, anticipatory regulation and ethnographic practice', *Social Science & Medicine*, 65(11): 2223–34.

Murray, Michael (2012) 'Critical health psychology and the scholar-activist tradition', in Christine Horrocks and Sally Johnson (eds.), *Advances in Health Psychology: Critical Approaches.* Basingstoke: Palgrave Macmillan, pp. 29–43.

Myers, Martin (2016) 'Researching gypsies and their neighbours: The utility of the *stranger*', in Kalwant Bhopal and Ross Deuchar (eds.), *Researching Marginalized Groups.* New York: Routledge, pp. 211–24.

Neale, B. (2013) 'Adding time into the mix: Stakeholder ethics in qualitative longitudinal research', *Methodological Innovations Online*, 8(2): 6–20.

Nelson, J. (2016) 'Using conceptual depth criteria: Addressing the challenge of reaching saturation in qualitative research', *Qualitative Research*. DOI 10.1177/1468794116679873.

Padgett, D., Smith, B., Derejko, K.-S., Henwood, B., and Tiderington, E. (2013) 'A picture is worth…? Photo elicitation interviewing with formerly homeless adults', *Qualitative Health Research*, 23(11): 1435–44.

Patton, Michael Q. (2015). Qualitative Research and Evaluation Methods: Integrating Theory and Practice (4th edn). Thousand Oaks, CA: Sage.

Pyer, M. and Campbell, J. (2013) 'The "other participant" in the room: The effect of significant adults in research with children', *Research Ethics*, 9(4): 153–65.

Rooney, V.M. (2015) 'Consent in longitudinal intimacy research: Adjusting formal procedure as a means of enhancing reflexivity in ethically important decisions', *Qualitative Research*, 15(1): 71–84.

Routledge, P. and Derickson, K. (2015) 'Situated solidarities and the practice of scholar-activism', *Environment and Planning D: Society and Space*, 33(3): 391–407.

Savvides, N., Al-Youssef, J., Colin, M., and Garrido, C. (2014) 'Journeys into inner/outer space: Reflections on the methodological challenges of negotiating insider/outsider status in international educational research', *Research in Comparative and International Education*, 9(4): 412–25.

Semaan, S. (2010) 'Time-space sampling and respondent-driven sampling with hard-to-reach populations', *Methodological Innovations Online*, 5(2): 60–75.

Sheridan, J., Chamberlain, K., and Dupuis, A. (2011) 'Timelining: Visualizing experience', *Qualitative Research*, 11(5): 552–69.

Silverman, David (2014) *Interpreting Qualitative Data* (5th edn). London: Sage.

Sixsmith, J., Boneham, M., and Goldring, J.E. (2003) 'Accessing the community: Gaining insider perspectives from the outside', *Qualitative Health Research*, 13(4): 578–89.

Sutton-Brown, C.A. (2014) 'Photovoice: A methodological guide', *Photography & Culture*, 7(2): 169–86.

Suzuki, D. and Mayorga, E. (2014) 'Scholar-activism: A twice told tale', *Multicultural Perspectives*, 16(1): 16–20.

Thompson, S., and Phillips, D. (2007) 'Reaching and engaging hard-to-reach populations with a high proportion of nonassociative members', *Qualitative Health Research*, 17(9): 1292–303.

Trussell, D.E., and Mair, H. (2010) 'Seeking judgment free spaces: Poverty, leisure, and social inclusion', *Journal of Leisure Research*, 42(4): 513–33.

Turner, N. and Almack, K. (2016) 'Recruiting young people to sensitive research: Turning the "wheels within wheels"', *International Journal of Social Research Methodology*, 20(5): 485–97

Vahabi, M., Isaacs, S., Koc, M., and Damba, C. (2015) 'Challenges in recruiting hard-to-reach populations focusing on Latin American recent immigrants', *International Journal of Human Rights in Healthcare*, 8(1): 36–44.

Zempi, I. (2016) 'Negotiating constructions of insider and outsider status in research with veiled Muslim women victims of Islamophobic hate crime', *Sociological Research Online*, 21(4): 8. DOI: 10.5153/sro.4080.

Author Index

6, Perri 84

Aarts, Bas 416, 422
Abels, Gabriele 660, 661
Abrams, Kate 587, 590
Abrams, L.S. 671
Adair, John 399
Adorno, Theodor 429
Agrawal, N. 483
Åkerström, Malin 169, 240
Alcadipani da Silveira, R. 104–5
Allan, A. 602, 609
Almack, K. 99, 113, 670
Altman, Rick 415
Alvesson, Mats 52, 53
Anderson, A.S. 222
Anderson, Elijah 318–19
Anderson, J. 344, 347, 348, 356
Andrews, M. 119, 274
Androutsopoulous, J. 507
Anzaldua, Gloria 203
Atkinson, A.M. 220
Atkinson, Paul 24, 25, 51, 53, 60, 67, 87, 104, 105, 186, 222, 244, 267, 315, 318, 319, 320, 324, 325, 328, 333, 334, 340, 537

Baethge-Kinsky, V. 165
Bahl, Shalini 549
Bakardjieva, Maria 469, 471, 513
Baker, Sara 244
Bales, Robert 185, 187
Barad, Karen 152, 210, 236, 245n1, 521n7
Barber, N. 389
Barbour, Rosaline S. 217, 219, 220, 223, 224, 225, 227, 228, 253, 387
Barker, Roger G. 183–185, 186, 187, 188
Barroso, J. 386
Barthes, Roland 405–6
Bartlett, Helen 644–5
Bassalo, Lucélia de Moraes Braga 486–490
Bateson, Gregory 394, 528
Bauer, Martin W. 416, 422
Baxter, P. 637
Baym, Nancy K. 447–8, 453, 456, 471, 516, 517
Bazarova, N.N. 498
Beard, John R. 632, 633
Beaulieu, A. 466, 468, 470, 473
Becker, Howard S. 23, 75, 80, 228, 327, 328, 329, 331, 338, 339, 394, 397, 406, 407, 587, 596
Behrens, Maria 660, 661
Beißwenger, Michael 498, 505

Bellamy, Christine 84
Bell, Linda 109, 114, 673, 674
Bell, R. 485
Benbow, S.M 635
Bengry-Howel, Andrew 100, 101, 102, 104, 105, 111, 113, 114, 669
Benjamin, Walter 14, 140, 429
Benney, M. 234
Berger, John 403, 405, 406
Berger, Peter 298, 299
Berger, R. 670
Berghs, M. 220
Berman, R.C. 132, 133, 134, 135, 141–2
Bernard, Miriam 277, 636
Bhaskar, Roy 19–20, 22, 29n1
Bijsterveld, Karin 427
Billig, M. 267, 282, 283, 292
Birdsall, Carolyn 427, 432–3
Bishop, Libby 168, 170, 171, 178
Bissell, D. 354
Blair, T. 639
Blank, Grant 584
Blommaert, Jan 131, 133
Bloom, David E. 632, 633
Bloor, M. 219, 224
Blumer, Herbert 20–1, 68, 74
Boal, Augusto 211
Bogen, David 190
Bogner, Alexander 238, 652, 654, 655, 657–8, 659, 661
Bohnsack, Ralf 153, 412, 488, 489, 490
Bolden, Galina 190, 191, 284, 285
Bolton, A. 603
Bordwell, David 415
Bornat, J. 269
Bottomore, Tom 652, 656
Boulton, M. 673
Bourdieu, Pierre 228, 301, 397–8
Bowen, G.A. 90
boyd, danah 442, 443, 456, 467, 468, 469, 471, 497, 503, 512, 517, 521n2
Brady, Erika 428
Braun, Virginia 259, 502
Brenner, Michael 234
Bricher, G. 627
Brinkmann, S. 234, 235
Brown, B. 506
Brown, L.M. 286, 347
Brown, P. 669
Brubaker, Rogers 308
Bruner, J. 264, 265, 274, 533
Brydon-Miller, Mary 26, 35

Bryman, Alan 89, 93, 99, 530, 549, 575
Buchanan, Elizabeth 466, 468, 469, 470, 471, 472, 474, 477, 490, 491
Bucholtz, M. 120, 122, 127
Buckle, J.L 670
Bull, Michael 427, 433–5
Burawoy, Michael 328, 337, 339, 347
Burbules, Nicholas C. 54
Burgess, Jean 416, 419, 420
Burholt, Vanessa 636, 639, 641, 646
Burke, S. 502
Burris, Mary Ann 399
Bury, M. 228, 539
Buscatto, Marie 330–2, 334, 335, 336, 337, 338, 339, 340, 341n2
Büscher, Monika 345–6, 348, 368, 591
Butler, Judith 209–10
Byrne, Caitlin 596

Caddell, L.S. 642
Calasanti, T. 632
Calvey, D. 43
Cameron, Deborah 299
Campbell, Donald T. 19–20, 527
Cappellini, B. 224
Caracelli, V.J. 578
Carpiano, R.M. 352, 354, 355, 356, 358
Carr, C.T. 497, 498
Carson, R. 588–9
Casetti, Francesco 414
Casey, Bernadette 414
Casey, E.S. 346, 349
Cassell, Joan 104
Castells, Manuel 463n2, 482
Cavanagh, Allison 596
Chalmers, Alan F. 51
Chamberlain, Kerry 672, 680
Chandler, Daniel 297–8
Charmaz, Kathy 4, 52
Chase, S.E. 235
Cheek, Julianne 565, 569, 570
Cheshire, L. 351
Chilisa, Bagele 35
Chin, E. 352
Chmiel, Margaret 23, 85, 86, 87, 580n9
Choi, J. 131, 132, 135
Christians, Clifford G. 34, 35
Christmann, Gabriela C. 663
Cicourel, Aron 68, 73
Clare, L. 642
Clark, C.L. 633
Clarke, Adele E. 4, 452, 456, 457, 461, 463n5, 546
Clarke, Vicky L. 252, 259, 502, 547
Clark, Lauren 568, 574
Clark, T. 104, 108, 113
Classen, Constance 430
Clayman, Steven 189, 290, 291

Clifford, James 100, 105, 150, 151, 186, 328
Coetzee, Jan K. 272
Coffey, Amanda 101, 102, 113, 349, 355, 602
Cohen-Cruz, Jan 205, 211, 213n7
Cohen, J.H. 348, 351
Cohen, Stanley 165, 167
Cohler, B.J. 265
Collier, John Jr 393, 394, 395–7
Collins, Harold 186, 196, 384
Collins, K.M.T. 580
Collins, M. 643
Conquergood, Dwight 200, 203, 205, 206, 207, 208, 209, 210, 211, 213n2
Conti, Joseph A. 238, 653
Cook, G. 119
Cook, K. 260
Cook, T. 19
Coole, Diane 209
Corbin, Alain 432
Corbin, Juliet 26, 55, 59, 69, 73–4, 77, 78, 309, 373
Corrigan, Timothy 415
Corti, Louise 165, 175, 176, 178
Couch, J. 670, 672, 674
Coule, T. 253
Coulson, N. 496, 499
Coupland, J.& N. 634
Cram, Fiona 36, 37, 38, 39, 547
Crawford, Kate 442, 443, 456, 512, 517, 521n2
Crazy Bull, Cheryl 38, 39
Creswell, John W. 80, 159, 252, 547, 548–9, 569
Croghan, R. 603
Cronbach, L.J. 86
Cross, J.E. 39, 42
Crotty, Michael 620
Crowhurst, I. 108, 112–13, 670
Crummett, A. 271, 276
Crystal, David 505
Csikszentmihalyi, M. 588–9
Cunliffe, A.L. 104–5
Cunningham, Stuart 420
Czarniawska, B. 348, 350

Dam, Huyen 93
Damianakis, T. 44
Danius, Sara 320
Darbyshire, Philip 617, 618, 624
D'Arcy, A. 503
Darwin, Charles 431
Daughtry, Martin 427, 429
Daum, Christine H. 675–6
Davidson, Judith 595–6
Davies, James 520
Davison, C. 228
Deakin, Hanna 245, 663
De Jonge, D. 93
Delamont, Sara 53, 60, 344
DeLeon, J.P. 348, 351

Dellinger, A.B. 564
Demant, J. 223
Denzin, Norman K. 6, 35, 36, 38, 72, 76, 86, 131, 200, 202, 234, 236, 444, 447, 463n5, 520, 527–8, 529–30, 531–2, 537, 547, 558, 561n1, 599, 628
Derickson, K. 680
de Saussure, Ferdinand 208, 297
Devadason, R. 668
DeVault, M.L. 234, 236
Dewey, John 80, 206, 546, 639
Dewing, J. 642, 644
Dexter, Lewis A. 652, 653–654
Dey, Ian 90
di Chio, Federico 414
Dickens, Charles 183
Dingwall, R. 673, 674
Dinkins, C.S. 234, 235
Ditchfield, Hanna 501, 503
Dixon-Woods, M. 386–7
Downs, Murna 642, 644
Doykos, B.[etal] 99, 101, 105, 113, 114
Draucker, C.B. 91
Dressman, Mark 50
Drew, Paul 18, 281, 282, 290, 291
Duncombe, Jean 104, 105
Duneier, M. 347
Durkheim, Emile 149, 336, 341n4
Dwyer, Corbin 670
Dysvik, E. 578, 579

Eales, Jacquie 638
Ebbrecht-Hartmann, Tobias 413
Eberle, Thomas S. 401
Eco, Umberto 52, 132, 140, 141
Edwards, D. 499
Edwards, Rosalind 40, 93, 168, 170, 244, 662
Eisenhardt, K. 638
Elder, Glen 165
Elliker, Florian 307–11
Elliot, H. 272, 485
Elliot, Mark 443–4, 445
Ellis, Carolyn 42–3, 206
Ellison, N.B. 497
Elswood, S.A. 347
Elwyn, G. 290
Emerson, Robert M. 314, 315, 316, 317, 318, 319, 323, 325, 350, 568
Emmel, Nick 85, 88, 170, 670, 671
Entwistle, V.A. 171
Enzenhofer, Edith 132, 134, 135, 136, 142, 143–4, 144n1, 663
Epston, D. 265
Erstad, O. 485
Erzberger, Christian 527, 532
Estalella, A. 466, 468, 470, 473
Evans, Brad 203, 547
Evans, G.E. 269, 332

Evans, J. 348, 350, 356
Evans, R. 383
Evans, S. 636, 640
Evans, Walker 393
Ewald, Wendy 399
Eyles, John 93
Eynon, Rebecca 469
Ezzy, D. 240

Fairclough, Norman 299
Fane, J. 624
Fawcett, B. 101, 114
Fawcett, H. 485
Feilzer, M.Y. 546
Feldman, Martha 106, 112
Fereday, J. 623
Ferenbok, Joseph 442
Ferguson, K. 348, 350, 354, 355
Feyerabend, Paul 183
Fielding, Nigel G. 166, 174, 482, 496, 497, 529, 538, 585, 587, 591, 592
Fileborn, Bianca 471, 477
Fine, Gary A. 308, 328
Fiske, D. 527
Fiske, John 201, 414, 415, 527
Flick, Uwe 3, 4, 5, 7, 9, 10, 10–11, 28, 67, 70, 80, 85, 88, 90, 131, 266, 310, 468, 470, 529, 530–531, 532, 533, 537, 539, 541, 600, 601, 610, 653, 658
Folch-Lyon, E. 251
Francis, J.J. 89, 90, 94
Freeman, M. 272, 273
Freire, Paolo 211, 639
Friemuth, V.S. 669
Frith, H. 292
Frost, Samantha 209

Gallagher, Michael 426, 427
Gammelby, Anne Kathrine 452–3, 457–62
Garcia, A. 498, 505
Garcia, C.M. 352, 355
Garden, M. 484, 679
Garfinkel, Harold 68, 72, 150, 156, 281, 328, 382, 383, 401
Garoian, Charles R. 203
Gaudelius, Y.M. 203
Geertz, Clifford 68, 71, 74–5, 86, 151, 206, 516
Gerson, Kathleen 94
Geurts, Kathleen 429
Gibbs, L. 619, 622, 626
Gibson, A.F. 222
Gibson, William 482
Giddens, Anthony 655
Gidley, B. 383
Gieryn, T.F. 349
Gilbreth, Lillian 514
Giles, D. 292, 499
Giles, H. 634

Gilleard, Chris 633
Gillespie, Jonathan 55
Gillies, B.A. 642, 644
Gillies, V. 170
Gilligan, C. 286, 289
Giroux, Henry A. 203
Glaser, Barney G. 4, 50, 52, 54, 58, 65, 69, 72, 73, 74, 77, 78, 91, 234, 328, 333–4, 336–8, 397, 538, 542, 654, 659
Gobo, Giampietro 10, 80, 85, 86, 88, 89, 327, 328, 332, 334
Godfrey, Donald G. 422
Goffman, A. 238
Goffman, Erving 119, 281, 314–15, 315–16, 327, 328, 329, 330, 339, 368, 382, 400, 401, 463n4
Golder, Scott A. 445
Golomb, Solomon W. 79–80
Gombert, K. 675
Gómez, P.R. 485
Goodall, Harold L. 453, 463n6
Goodenough, Ward 71
Goodman, S. 502
Goodwin, Charles 191, 283, 285
Gouldner, Alvin W. 67
Graebner, M. 638
Graham, J. 471
Grainger, K. 634
Greene, Jennifer 28, 275, 578
Green, Joshua 416, 419, 420
Greer, C. 385
Griffin, Christine 100, 102, 104, 105, 109, 113, 190, 196, 669
Grinter, B. 519
Gross, G. 234, 236
Groves, Christopher 600, 601, 604–9
Guba, Egon 20, 22, 34, 35, 85, 86, 253, 530
Gubrium, Jaber F. 67, 169, 237, 244, 308, 317, 322, 589
Guest, G. 89, 90, 95
Guetterman, Timothy C. 89, 90, 94, 95

Haaker, M. 167
Hagedorn, J. 485
Hall, Stuart 404, 414
Hall, T. 348, 351, 352, 356
Hammack, P.L. 265, 269
Hammersley, Martyn 19, 24, 25, 36, 51, 67, 75, 87, 104, 105, 169, 186, 283, 318, 319, 324, 328, 336, 537, 673
Hanson, Norwood 51, 53, 183
Harding, Sandra G. 547, 552
Hare, R.D. 386
Hargittai, Eszter 441, 448–9, 471
Harman, V. 224
Harnett, Tove 316–17, 321, 322, 324
Harper, Douglas 394, 395, 397, 398, 399, 624
Harre, Rom 642

Harrison, J. 105, 113
Harvey, William S. 238, 654
Heath, Christian 191, 283, 285, 365, 368, 372, 374, 375, 394
Heath, D. 102
Heath, Sue 106, 108
Hein, J.R. 345, 348, 354
Hekman, Susan 209
Held, Virginia 475
Henwood, Karen 218, 227, 600, 601, 604–9, 610, 673
Hepburn, Alexa 186, 190, 191, 192, 244, 283, 284, 285, 292
Heritage, John 188, 189, 194, 281, 282, 283, 289, 290, 291
Herring, S.C. 483, 484, 496
Hesse-Biber, Sharlene N. 545, 547, 553, 557, 564, 565
Higginbottom, G. 85, 88, 94
Higgs, Paul 633
Hine, Christine 455, 456, 498, 513
Hirsch, J. 673
Hirsch, L. 245
Hodgetts, Darrin 676–80
Hodgkin, K. 225
Hodgson, D. 104
Hoffman Davis, Jessica 26
Holland, J. 604
Holstein, James A. 169, 237, 244
Hookway, Nicholas 483, 484, 486
Hopf, T. 599
Horkheimer, Max 429
Horowitz, Ruth 94
Horst, Heather 513
Howe, K.R. 548, 549
Howes, David 427, 430
Howes, L.M. 547
Hsiung, Ping-Chun 45
Hubbard, Gill 643, 644, 645
Huberman, A. Michael 20, 75
Hughes, Everett C. 234, 328, 332, 336, 397
Hussey, S. 224
Hutchby, I. 189, 283

Ingold, T. 344, 347, 353, 355
Inhetveen, Katharina 132, 142, 662
Irvine, A. 245

Jack, S. 637
Jackson, Alecia Y. 201, 209–10
Jackson, Clare 286–90, 293n3
Jacky, M. 484
Jacobbsen, A.F. 169
Jacobs, Bruce A. 104
Jacobs, J. 498, 505
Jacobson, D. 102
Jahoda, Marie 528, 675
James, Allison 618
James, William 200–1, 212

Janesick, V.J. 237, 243
Jefferson, Gail 119, 123, 127, 190, 191, 220, 281, 284
Jenkings, K.N. 389
Jenkins, N. 224
Jenks, Christopher J. 119, 127, 128, 220, 239, 345, 618
Jessop, Julie 104, 105
Jewitt, C. 484, 602
Jirón, P. 350, 358
Jørgensen, Marianne 299
Johnson, R. Burke 547, 564
Jones, A. 223
Jones, Janet 413
Jones, P. 347, 348, 350, 354, 356
Jones, Steve 446–7, 448, 471
Julien, C. 228

Kant, Immanuel 34
Kärreman, Dan 53
Katz, Jack 328, 347, 350
Keating, Norah 636, 637, 638
Keller, Reiner 299
Kelle, Udo 49–50, 51, 53, 54, 527, 532
Kelman, Ari Y. 429
Kendall, Gavin 297, 300, 302
Kendall, Lori 472, 537
Kendall, P. 250
Kennedy, Brianna 54–62
Kennedy-Macfoy, M. 101, 114, 670
Kieren, D. 577
Kincheloe, Joe L. 298, 447, 463
Kinder-Kurlanda, Katharina 468
King, J.R. 40, 44, 45
King, N. 632
Kingston, P. 635
Kirkpatrick, Marshall 467
Kitchener, Karen S. & Richard F. 34, 37
Kitchin, I. 593
Kitzinger, Celia 286, 288, 292, 299
Knoblauch, Hubert 9, 222, 363, 364, 365, 368, 371, 373, 375, 376, 394
Knorr Cetina, Karin 183, 188
Knowles, Malcolm S. 640
Kontos, P.C. 635, 643
Koro-Ljungberg, Mirka 200, 209, 212, 673
Korzybski, Alfred H.S. 79
Kotliar, D.M. 485
Koven, M. 234, 236
Kozinets, Robert 100, 102, 482, 485, 492, 498
Kracauer, Siegfried 413
Kramer, A. 466, 586
Kristensen, G.K. 238, 671, 672
Kroger, R.O. 502, 634
Krueger, R.A. 250, 256, 257
Kügler, Dennis 468
Kuhn, Thomas 20, 35, 183
Kuntz, A.M. 234, 236
Kusenbach, Margarethe 267, 344, 345, 350, 351, 352, 356

Kuss, D. 485
Kuula-Luumi, A. 168, 170, 177

LaBelle, Brandon 426, 427
Labov, William 121, 283, 322
Ladurie, Emmanuel Le Roy 431–2
LaFrance, Joan 38, 39
LaFrance, Michelle N. 265
Langer, L.L 270, 275
Lather, P. 201, 209
Latour, Bruno 454, 463n3, 516
Laudel, Grit 654, 659
Lauhaila-Salminen L. 497, 498, 500
Lauterbach, G. 131, 132, 136, 138
Lawrence, J. 166
Lawrence-Lightfoot, Sara 26
Lawson, Annette 167
Lazarsfeld, Paul 65, 250
Leech, Nancy L. 84, 85, 87, 89, 95, 564
Lee, Raymond M. 174, 234, 238, 250, 501, 584, 585, 586
Lemmer, Eleanor M. 303
Lester, J.N. 587
Lévi-Strauss, Claude 150, 447, 463n5
Lévy, P. 482
Lewis, J. 471
Li, C. 483
Lillqvist, E. 497, 498, 500
Lincoln, Yvonna S. 6, 20, 22, 34, 35–36, 37, 38, 40, 61, 85–6, 131, 144, 253, 447, 463n5, 520, 530, 547, 561n1, 599, 628
Lindgren, Simon 457, 460–1
Link, A. 260
Lipscomb, Martin 53
Littig, Beate 10, 131, 132, 136, 138, 139, 144, 239, 652–3, 662–3
Lobe, Bojana 259
Lofland, John 100–2, 104, 114
Lofland, Lyn 350
Lohuis, A.M. 271
Lomborg, Stine 470, 472, 477
Losen, Daniel 55
Luckman, Thomas 298, 299
Luff, Paul 191, 368, 372
Lyman, Standford 589
Lynch, Michael 183, 283
Lynd, Robert S. & Helen M. 84
Lyotard, Jean-François 151, 303

McAdams, D.P. 265, 266, 269, 271
McCall, George J. 100
MacDonald, K. 385
McDonald, S. 344, 347, 348, 350
MacDougall, Colin 618, 619, 624
McGinn, L. 106–8
McIntosh, M. 565
McKee, Heidi 471, 472

McKillop, J. 642, 643, 644
McLeod, J. 603
McLuhan, Marshall 521n11
MacLure, M. 202, 203, 210, 212, 213n9
Macnaghten, Phil 253, 325
Macwrighte, T. 521n8
Macy, Michael W. 445
Madden, Mary 468
Madill, Anna 20
Madison, D. Soyini 202, 204, 205, 206, 207, 208, 211, 212
Magee, Helen 635
Mair, H. 668
Maiter, S. 676
Malik, S.H. 499
Manderscheid, K. 356, 357
Mannheim, Karel 72, 489
Mann, Steve 442
Marcus, George E. 148, 150, 158, 186, 328, 347, 463, 514
Markham, Annette N. 221, 292, 447–8, 452, 453, 454, 455, 456, 457, 460–1, 462, 463n8, 466, 467, 468, 469, 470, 471, 472, 474, 475, 477, 483, 486, 490, 491, 513, 518, 520
Marn, T.M. 236
Marotzki, W. 536
Martin, D.G. 347
Martin, Wendy 644–5
Marwick, A. 471
Mason, Jennifer 89, 90, 93, 252, 564
Mason, M. 90, 94, 95, 564, 601
Mathijs, Ernest 413
Mathison, S. 528
Mauthner, Melanie S. 40, 468, 469, 470, 473, 477
Maxwell, Joseph A. 19, 20, 22, 23, 25, 26, 28, 66, 75, 78, 85, 86, 87, 94, 218, 548, 577, 580n9
Mayan, Maria J. 675–6
Maynard, Douglas W. 71, 188, 289, 290
Mayo, Elton 327, 341n1
Mazzei, Lisa A. 201, 209–10
M'charek, Amade 154–5, 160
Mead, Margaret 394, 528
Mehan, Hugh 68, 388
Melia, Kath 415
Menz, Wolfgang 655, 657, 658–9, 661
Meredith, Joanne 119, 292, 497, 499, 503, 505
Merkens, Hans 88
Merriman, B. 467, 471
Merriman, P. 345, 348, 354, 356, 358
Mertens, Donna M. 36, 37, 38, 39, 40, 41, 43, 44, 547, 564
Merton, Robert K. 11, 234, 250, 252
Mettger, W. 669
Meuser, Michael 652, 654, 659, 664n1
Meyer, Michael 298, 299, 301, 302, 306, 311
Michel, Robert 654
Mikecz, Robert 238, 653, 669

Mikos, Lothar 412, 413, 414
Miles, Matthew B. 75, 240
Miller, Daniel 513
Miller, Gale 423
Miller, Tina 109, 114, 673, 674
Mill, John Stuart 34
Mills, C. Wright 228, 654
Milne, George R. 549
Minkler, M. 633, 639
Mischler, Elliot G. 190
Mishler, E.G. 265, 266, 268
Mitchell, C. 88, 94
Mittapalli, Kavita 548
Moerman, M. 289
Mohn, Elisabeth 368
Mohr, Jean 406
Mondada, Lorenza 119, 120, 191, 290, 291
Moreira, T. 383, 386
Moretti, Franco 445
Morey, Yvette M. 103, 111
Morgan, David L. 65, 66, 80, 250–1, 252, 253, 255, 259, 260
Morgan, Gareth 454
Morgan-Brett, B. 167
Morita, Atsuro 153, 158–9, 160
Morris, M. 222
Morrison, D.E. 252
Morrison, Toni 212
Morrow, Virginia 620
Morse, Janice M. 89, 93, 549, 564–5, 568, 569, 570, 571, 572, 576, 577, 580n1, 580n2
Murphy, A. 674
Murray, Michael 266, 268, 270, 271, 273, 276, 680
Mutch, C. 546
Myers, Greg 253, 325
Myers, Martin 668

Nagel, Ulrike 652, 654, 659, 664n1
Nansen, B. 621
Nattrass, Nicoli 308
Neale, B. 40, 41, 178, 673
Neves, T. 345
Nias, Jennifer 300
Niehaus, Linda 549, 570, 572, 580n1
Nies, S. 658
Niewöhner, Jörg 149, 150, 153
Nikander, P. 239, 634
Nissenbaum, Helen 471–2
Noblit, G.W. 386
Nord, C. 136, 139
Norris, Joe 206
Novotny, Helga 10
Nurjannah, Intansari 133, 136, 138, 139
Nygaard, I.E. 566

O'Cathain, A. 545
O'Neill, Brenda 555–7, 560–1

O'Neil, Moira 238, 653
Onwuegbuzie, Anthony J. 84, 85, 87, 89, 95, 547, 580n7
O'Reilly, M. 90
O'Reilly, T. 483
Orgad, Shani 413–14, 469
Orton-Johnson, Kate 585, 586

Paavola, Sami 53
Palinkas, L.A. 88, 89
Parker, I. 282, 283
Parker, N. 90
Parry, Ruth 191
Patton, Michael Q. 385, 636–7, 671
Paulus, Trena 587, 595
Pawlowski C.S. 356, 358
Pawson, Ray 19, 22, 79
Peace, S. 635
Peirce, Charles S. 21, 50, 51
Pelto, Pertti 577
Peräkylä, Anssi 185, 502
Peshkin, Alan 25
Petty, Karis 436
Pfaff, Nicole 487–90
Philbin, M. 673
Phillips, Denis C. 23, 54, 669, 671, 672, 674
Phillips, Louise 298, 299, 311
Piaget, Jean 287, 622
Picker, John 427, 431
Pidgeon, N. 601
Pilnick, A. 290
Pink, Sarah 345, 352, 354, 358, 398, 455, 602
Piva, F. 485
Plano-Clark, V.L 252, 547
Platt, Anthony 323
Plesner, Ursula 660
Pöchhacker, Franz 10, 131, 132, 136, 138, 139, 144, 239, 662–3
Polkinghorne, Donald 534
Pollock, Della 202, 205, 206, 207
Popper, Karl R. 183
Porter, James E. 150, 471, 472
Potter, Jonathan 184, 185, 186, 187, 188, 189, 190, 194, 196, 244, 283, 284, 292, 299, 497, 499, 503
Pratt, Rebekah 642–3
Preissle, Judith 25
Prelinger, Rick 420
Presnall, M.M. 234, 236
Price, Derek J. de Solla 449
Priest, N. 628
Prins, J. 271
Prior, Jonathan 426, 427
Prior, Lindsay 221, 378, 382, 385
Prior, M.T. 240, 241
Prior, Nick 585
Prout, Alan 618
Psathas, George 189, 201
Punch, Samantha 628

Purdam, Kingsley 443–4, 445
Putnam, Hilary 21
Puvimanasinghe, T. 270

Quinlan, E. 345, 348

Radstone, S. 225
Ramanathan-Abbott, V. 642
Rapley, Tim 119, 222, 244, 387–8, 498
Rau, Asta 272, 300
Ravn, M.N. 238, 671, 672
Ravn, S. 221, 223
Rawls, John 34
Redmond, G. 621
Reed, J. 633
Reed, Maureen G. 551–5, 559–60
Rees, Tobias 383–5
Regmi, K. 142
Reichertz, Jo 50, 51, 54
Reinharz, Shulamit 235, 552
Reisigl, Martin 301, 302, 304, 306, 307
Reiss, Katharina 139
Reiter, Herwig 308, 661
Resch, Katharina 132, 134, 135, 136, 142, 143–4, 144n1, 663
Richards, N. 603
Richardson, Laurel 200, 463n8, 641
Riesman, David 234
Riessman, Catherine K. 225, 271, 322
Riley, M. 347, 351, 356
Ritchie, Jane 88, 91–2
Roberts, L.D. 102, 114
Robinson, O.C. 85, 88, 89
Röhnsch, Gundula 10, 11, 539
Rönsch, Gundula 10, 11, 539
Rooney, V.M. 673, 674
Rose, Gillian 243–4, 398, 602, 603, 604
Rosenberg, Daniel 517, 518, 521n5
Rosen, Michael 329, 336
Rosenthal, G. 267
Rossano, Frederico 191, 282, 285
Ross, J. 132, 135, 139, 140, 141, 142
Ross, N.J. 346, 348, 352, 355, 625
Roth, S. 485
Roulston, Kathryn 234, 235, 237, 238, 239, 243, 244
Routledge, P. 680
Rowles, Graham 636
Rowntree, Seebohm 165
Roy, Donald 327, 329–30, 338
Ruane, Janet 100
Ruppert, E. 594–5
Ryan, L. 101, 113

Sabat, S.R. 642, 643
Sacks, Harvey 71, 185, 186–7, 280, 281–2, 293n1, 321–3
Sadker, Myra & David 28

St. Pierre, Elizabeth A. 4, 5, 200, 201, 202
Saldana, Johnny 208, 240
Salmons, Janet 245, 663
Sandelowski, Margarete 75, 89, 386, 559
Sandvig, Christian 441, 446, 448–9
Sariola, Salla 156, 157, 160
Sawyer, Richard D. 206
Scharf, Thomas 636, 639
Schatzman, Leonard 77, 234
Schechner, Richard 211
Scheffer, Thomas 149, 150, 153
Schegloff, Emanuel A. 95, 119, 281, 282, 283, 285, 290, 292, 375
Schnettler, Bernt 222, 371, 376
Schoggen, Phil 183, 184
Schreier, Margrit 92, 379, 412, 463n3
Schubert, Cornelius 368, 372
Schultheis, Franz 397, 401, 403
Schütz, Alfred 298, 404, 657
Schwandt, Thomas 20, 21, 91
Scott, John 304, 384–5
Scott, Marvin 589
Scourfield, J. 101, 102
Scullion, L. 669
Seale, Clive 240, 243, 384, 600
Seamon, D. 348, 354
Seekings, Jeremy 308
Seidman, Irving E. 25, 235
Self, C. 484
Semaan, S. 671, 672
Senft, Theresa M. 454, 461, 463n9
Seremetakis, Nadia 429
Shadish, William R. 20
Shaw, Chloe 192, 194–5, 291
Sheller, Mimi 345–6, 349, 625
Sheridan, J. 225, 673
Sherratt, C. 644, 645
Sherren, K. 353, 356
Shirani, Fiona 602, 603, 604–9, 673
Shklarov, S. 131, 132, 134, 142, 144
Shrestha, L. 485
Sidnell, Jack 185, 191, 282
Silver, Jon 420
Silverman, David 67, 71, 76–7, 99, 156, 186, 192, 243, 244, 319, 321–3, 325, 336, 672
Simmel, Georg 346, 429
Simons, Helen 34
Simpson, Bob 156, 157
Sintjago, A. 260
Sköldberg, Kaj 52
Smethurst, L. 485
Smith, D.E. 547
Smith, H.J. 102
Smith, J.A. 264
Smith, John K. 20, 37
Smith, Mark 427, 430
Smith, W. Eugene 407

Snee, H. 102, 105, 114, 490
Snell-Hornby, Mary 139
Sørensen, Estrid 149, 151, 155, 158, 159, 160
Speer, Susan A. 189, 283, 292
Spencer, Dimitrina 520
Spinney, J. 347, 348, 358
Spivak, Gayartri Chakravorty 133, 134, 140
Spradley, James P. 67, 234, 309, 310
Spry, Tami 206, 208, 210
Stahl, N. 40, 44, 45, 637
Stake, Robert E. 61, 85, 86, 637, 638
Stals, S. 348, 352, 358
Stivers, T. 282
Stokoe, Elizabeth 195, 292, 497, 499
Stone, Nicole 106–8
Strathern, Marilyn 149, 150, 151, 152–3, 158, 161, 463n2
Strauss, Anselm L. 26, 54, 55, 59, 65, 69, 72, 73, 74, 77, 78, 91, 160, 234, 309, 328, 333–4, 336–7, 338, 367, 373, 397, 538, 659
Streeck, Jürgen 285, 368
Strengers, Y. 600, 603
Strube, G. 534
Stryker, Roy E. 393–4, 395
Sveningsson-Elm, Malin 471, 472
Sweetman, P. 603
Szmigin, I. 109

Tappan, Mark 25
Tarozzi, Massimiliano 136, 140, 141
Tashakkori, Aabbas 547, 564
Tavory, I. 348, 350, 351, 356
Taylor, C. 602
Taylor, Frederick W. 327, 341n1, 514
Teddlie, Charles 88, 95, 547, 564
Temple, Bogusia 131, 132, 134, 135, 136, 142, 143, 239, 662
ten Have, Paul 239, 287, 375
Tess, P.A. 485
Tetley, J. 269
Thelwall, M. 483, 586
Thomas, G. 605, 608, 609
Thomas, William 272, 528
Thompson, C. 351, 355
Thompson, J. 211, 386
Thompson, Kristin 415
Thompson, Paul 165, 166, 168
Thompson, S. 669, 671, 672, 674
Thomson, R. 603
Thornberg, Robert 52, 54, 61
Tilley, Nick 19, 22, 79
Timmermans, Stefan 51, 54
Tinkler, Penny 602
Tipton, C. 385
Tolich, M. 237, 467
Toolis, E.E. 269
Townsend, Peter 165

Travers, M. 602
Treadwell, Donald 471
Trester, Anne Marie 498
Trinczek, Rainer 660
Trouille, D. 348, 350, 351, 356
Trussell, D.E. 668
Tseng, C. 484
Tulle, Emmanuelle 634
Tulving, Endel 28, 534
Tuma, René 222, 376
Turkle, Sherry 496, 513
Turner, Graeme 415
Turner, N. 99, 113, 670
Tyyskä, V. 132, 133, 134, 135, 141–2

Urry, John 345–6, 349, 625

Van Cauwenberg, Jelle 348, 353
Van Dijck, Jose 467
Van Dijk, Teun 298, 299, 300, 307
Veblen, Thorstein 654
Venkatesh, Sudhir 337
Venuti, L. 140
Vermeer, Hans 139
Verran, Helen 157, 159, 160
Vikström, Lotta 557–9, 560
Vom Lehn, Dirk 370–1
Von Unger, H. 45–6

Wacquant, Loïc 301, 328
Wakefield, Kelly 245, 663
Waldock, Jacqueline 435
Walther, J.B. 469, 471, 496
Wang, Caroline 399
Wästerfors, David 319–20, 322, 323, 324, 325
Watson, C. 228
Webster, Andrew 597
Weiss, Robert S. 28–9
Weller, K. 468
Weller, S. 245, 603, 604, 663
Wertz, Frederick J. 240, 532
West, C. 330
West, Laura 498

Wetherell, Margaret 190, 299, 600, 610
White, M. 265, 469
White, Patricia 415
Whyte, William F. 315, 329, 340, 528
Wickham, Gary 297, 300
Wiles, J.L. 635
Wilkerson, J. 260
Wilkinson, Heather 642, 643, 644
Wilkinson, Sue 253, 257, 299
Williams, Malcolm 85, 86
Wilson, Helen 435–6
Wilson, R.E. 496
Wilson, Thomas 659
Winkelhage, Jeanette 92
Winter, D.G. 272
Winterton, R. 636, 637
Witzel, Andreas 308, 661
Wodak, Ruth 298–9, 300, 301, 302, 303, 304, 306, 307, 311
Wolgemuth, J.R. 236, 240
Wood, F. 224
Woodford, M.R. 44
Wood, L.A. 634
Woolley, J. 223
Wootton, A.J. 281, 287
Worth, Sol 399
Wouters, P. 483
Wuest, J. 91

Yaiser, Michelle 553
Yang, A. 484
Yin, Robert K. 87, 571, 636–7
Young, A. 131, 132, 135, 136, 142, 239
Young, T.M. 503

Zevenbergen, Ben 474
Zhao, P.Z. 259, 497, 498
Zhao, S. 497, 498
Zhao, X. 496
Zimmer, L. 568
Zimmer, M. 470, 472, 504
Zimmerman, D. 330
Znaniecki, Florian 272, 528

Subject Index

abduction 49–62
    case study: school administrators' perceptions of discipline 54–61
    deduction and induction 49–51
    defining 51–4, 222, 335
    in discourse historical analysis 301–2
access to research field 99–114
    case study: access to private friendship groups 109–11
    case study: access via institutional gatekeepers 106–8
    case study: offline access to online participants 111–12
    establishing 104–6
    ethics and 102–4
    factors influencing 100–2
    hard-to-reach groups 220, 670–1
    to existing data 178
    to Facebook data 500–2
    to video data 364–6
accuracy
    and big data 443
    ethical importance of 35, 36, 40–1, 42, 548
    impossibility of 202, 210
    in transcription 125–9, 135, 190
    use of technology 393, 394, 407, 428
    ways of promoting 28, 29, 178, 459, 476
activism
    as goal 34–7, 38, 39, 42–3, 44, 680
    in performance ethnography 200, 203, 205–7, 209, 211, 213n7
    in research 269, 275, 352, 552, 554, 639
addiction in Russian migrants to Germany (study) 539–40
African refugees (study) 270
agnosticism, theoretical 54
'Alexa' (Internet of Things) 519, 521n11
Algeria, Kabyles people (photographic study) 397–8
analysis and data collection
    abduction, deduction and induction 49–62, 81, 222
    issues in 11–12, 23–4, 587
    when to analyse 259, 565–6, 570–1
    see also mixed-method designs
analytic induction 548
anonymity
    and data recordings 125, 189, 191, 366–7
    and existing data 172, 177–8
    expert interviews 663–4
    hard-to-reach groups 673, 674
    and Internet research 472–3, 476, 501, 504–5, 590
    unwanted 46, 170

    when situation encourages identification 287, 340, 491, 492
    see also covert research
AoIR (Association of Internet Researchers) 292, 468, 470, 490, 491
applied research 193–5, 355–6, 399, 551–5
appropriateness, aim in qualitative research 7–8
archaeology of unearthing 202, 207
archives/archiving
    availability 274–6, 382–3
    context and provenance 11–12, 373–4, 384–5
    digital 456, 512
    ethical issues 41–2, 473–4
    film and television 413, 416–20, 421–2
    photographic 397–8, 400, 409
    qualitative data collections 168–9, 171, 176–7, 178
aretaic ethics (virtue theory) 34
Art Basel, visual ethnography of (study) 400–3
arts
    and qualitative research 276–7
    and research with children 624, 625–6
    see also performance/performed experiences
Asian Film Archive, Singapore 418
Association of Internet Researchers (AoIR) 292, 468, 470, 490, 491
Asylums. Essays on the social situation of mental patients and other inmates 315–6
asynchronous online methods 259–61
Atlas.ti (software program) 374, 375
A two-year old goes to hospital (film) 624
Auckland City Mission 676
audit cultures 152
authenticity, ethics principle 35–6
autobiographies 273–4
autoethnography 202, 203, 207

Balinese character: A photographic analysis 528
Balinese cockfights (study) 74
BBC Motion Gallery 419
Belmont Report 37, 38–40, 466
beneficence
    and digital research 466, 469–71, 472, 474, 477–8, 492
    ethics principle 34, 38–9, 367, 475
    and vulnerable groups 620, 625, 673, 674
between-methods triangulation 535–7
BFI (British Film Institute) National Archives 418
Big Brother (TV reality show) 413, 421
'big' data 3, 10–11, 400, 409, 442–3, 511–12, 517
'big research' 10–11

bilingual researchers 136, 137
biographical interviews 267
blogs, collecting data from 482–92
    characterizing blogs and bloggers 483–4
    perspectives and recommendations 491–2
    practical and analytical procedures 486–91
        analysing data 489–90
        choosing blogs 486–8
        limits and ethics 102, 490–1
        types of data and how to collect 488–9
    research on blogs 484–6
'blurring' in online focus groups 260
Boal, Augusto 211
BPS (British Psychological Society) 103, 292
Brazil, young feminists (blog study) 486–91
bricolage, methodological 446–8, 620
British Film Institute (BFI) National Archives 418
British Psychological Society (BPS) 103, 292
British Sociological Association (BSA) 103
British Universities Film and Video Council (BUFVC) 422
BSA (British Sociological Association) 103
budget considerations 142, 176, 347, 421, 663
    obtaining funding 290–1, 555, 580n6
BUFVC (British Universities Film and Video Council) 422
Burundi, refugees (study) 270

CA (Conversation Analysis) *see* conversation analysis (CA)
Camera lucida. Reflections on photography 405
cameras
    how to use 368–73, 395
    technology 398, 408
    use by participants 189, 224, 283, 399, 604, 624
    see also conversation analysis (CA)
Canada, rural communities supportive of elderly (study) 636–8
Canadian public opinion and gender (study) 555–7
CAQDAS, qualitative software 587, 591–2
case study method
    confidentiality 674
    main steps 636–8
    in qualitative research 6, 80, 84, 336, 577
    sampling 94
Cathars and Catholics in a 14[th]C French village (sound study) 431–2
causality/causation in qualitative research 22, 77–9, 81, 87, 588
CBPR (community-based participatory research) 42–3
CCTV (closed-circuit television) and crime (study) 79
CERN community (study) 183
childhood feeding among Mexican families (mixed-method study) 568
children and qualitative data collection 617–29
    basic assumptions/approaches 620
    case study: choosing methods 621
    data collection methods

digital technologies and social media 625
    focus groups and interviews 622–4
    mobile methods 625
    observation 622
    theatre and arts 625–6
    visual sociology 624
entering and exploring the field 621–2
history 618–19
links to broader concerns 627–9
new developments and perspectives 626–7
theoretical backgrounds 619–20
Children's Rights movement 619
chronic pain management program, patients in (mixed-method study) 578, 579
Cinemateca Brasileira, São Paolo 418
Cinémathèque Francaişe, France 418
citizen scientists
    children as 619, 620, 627, 628
    in social sciences 176, 442, 584–5
closed-circuit television (CCTV) and crime (study) 79
closed/open transcripts 123–4
CMC (computer-mediated communication) 292, 482
code-switching 134, 143
coding data
    in cross-language research 136, 139, 140
    in Interaction Process Analysis (IPA) 185–7
    open 55–61, 259
    pre-coding 381, 384, 385
    in research process 76, 81, 379, 461, 514
    software and technology 374–6, 517–8, 586, 592, 595
    using pre-determined codes 168, 373
collecting data *see* data collection, a realist approach
collective narratives 270–1, 276
combining digital and physical data *see* digital and physical data, combining
commercial media 420–1
community-based participatory research (CBPR) 42–3
community researchers
    considerations in using 42, 132, 142–3, 144, 144n1
    skills required 134, 136–8, 141
community safety and policing (go-along study) 591
comparison in social research 148–61
    case study: comparison through objects 158–9
    case study: differences dissolving 157–8
    case study: emerging comparison 155
    case study: encountering differences 156–7
    case study: multi-sited comparison 158
    case study: reconstructing different emic practices 153–5
    ethnographic emic comparison 151–9
    history - scholastic/etic comparison 149–51
    principles of emic comparison 159–61
comprehensive triangulation 531
computer-mediated communication (CMC) 292, 482

confidentiality
    in digital research 261, 467, 469–70, 472–3
    problematic situations 41, 254, 287–8, 663–4, 673, 674
    ways of ensuring 44, 173, 177–8, 189, 504–5
confirmability, ethics principle 35
consent *see* informed consent
consequential data 443
consequential (teleological) ethics 34
constructivist paradigm
    and critical realism 19–21, 24
    in qualitative research 35–7, 51, 54, 298, 547, 548
content analysis 81, 126, 258–9, 379, 576–7
contextual integrity 471–2, 473
contextualizing data
    participants' responses and actions 218, 222, 242, 354
    records and documents 11–12, 122, 169–70, 171–6
convenience sampling 89, 95, 671
conversation analysis (CA) 280–93
    case study: adolescent girls' production of gender 286–7
    collecting data 285–91
        analyst in the data 288–90
        ethics 286–8
        in institutional contexts 290–1
    and focus groups 253
    history 281–2
    limits 291–2
    naturally occurring data 192, 282–4
    new developments 292
    transcribing data 191, 220–1, 284–5
Conversation Analytic Role Play Method 195
counselling, trust in (study) 538–9
covert methodologies
    as collection strategy 42–3, 102–4, 328, 367
    machine operators' resistance strategies (study) 329–30
credibility, ethics principle 35
crime and CCTV (closed-circuit television), (study) 79
crisis training interaction, simulated (study) 369–70
criterion sampling 88, 93
critical constructivism 298, 304
critical discourse analysis *see* discourse analysis
critical paradigm 212, 298, 300–1, 547, 549, 625–6
critical realism *see* data collection, a realist approach
cross-cultural
    comparisons 149–51, 156–9, 160–1
    interviews 133, 239, 245
cross-language research 131–44
    assuring quality of data 141–4
        budget constraints 142–3, 389n1
        transparency and documentation 143–4
    data collection
        distinguish roles and functions 135–6
        strategies 136–9

dealing with language barriers 131–3
interviewing experts 662–3
professional translation 139–41
rationale 133–4
    acknowledging diversity 133–4
    ensuring inclusive social research 133
    increasing cultural competence 134
culturing 454
cyberculture 482

DA (Discourse Analysis) *see* discourse analysis (DA)
Danish/German video game regulation (comparative study) 158
Darwin, Charles 183
data
    defining 3–5, 200–2, 212, 511–13, 521n1
        data as ideology 517–20
        data as thing 514–6, 521n5, 521n7
    in digital research 441–9
        challenge of big data 442–3
        challenge of creating new tools 445–6, 448–9
        methodological bricolage 446–8
        transgressing qualitative-quantitative divide 444–5
        types of data 443–4
    role in research 12–13
data collection
    aims 7–8
    challenges 9–12
    definition 6–7
    methodological approaches 8–9
data collection, a realist approach 19–29
    collection methods 26–9, 218, 221, 222–3
    and research question 27
    using multiple methods 27–9
    defining realism 19–24, 29n1, 36, 548
    researcher relationships 25–6
    researcher subjectivity 24–5
datafication 463, 512, 514, 519–20
data quality, ensuring 217–29
    collecting good data 220–3
        access and research design 220
        co-construction, clarification and contextualization 222–3
        exploring further options 223–5
        going the extra distance 225–7
        making choices 221–2
        selection and sampling 221
        transcription 220–1
    determining what is good data 217–19
    realizing theoretical potential 227–9
data traces *see* 'traces' as data
decontextualization 12, 150, 169–70, 302, 533–4
deduction 50–51, 54–61, 258, 259, 333
    see also abduction
defamiliarization 53, 367

deontological ethics 34–5
dependability, ethics principle 35
description *see* 'thick' description
detachment/involvement of researcher 138, 315, 332–3, 405, 587, 622
DHA (Discourse-Historical Approach) 301–3
diaries
    participants' 81, 175, 178–9, 223, 272–3, 588
    researchers' 25, 166, 222
    see also blogs, collecting data from
Dickens, Charles 431
digital culture 451, 455–6, 462
digital flows, making sense of digital data 451–63
    challenges of digital saturation 451–3
    data collection and interpretation 453–4
    definitions 454–5, 588
        flow as researcher's activity 455
        flow as what is studied 454–5
    guide for entering and mapping flows 457–62
    three basic heuristics 455–6
digital and physical data, combining 584–97
    data collection 586–92
        interviews and group discussions 589–91
        observation and flow-oriented data 587–9
        visual, acoustic and virtual data 591–2
    data documentation 592–3
    digital/online and physical/offline data 584–6
    ethics, limits and constraints 596–7
    theory of online/offline data collection 593–6
disabled people and exercise (mixed-method study) 574, 576
discipline, school administrators' perceptions of (study) 55–61
discourse analysis (DA) 297–311
    case study: integrating racially segregated student residences 307–11
    case study: power in postgraduate-supervisor relationship 303–7
    core ideas 299–301
        interrupting social inequities 300–1
        power in constructing social reality 299–300
        reflexivity and critique 301
    critical discourse analysis (CDA) 298–301
    defining 201, 297–8
    discourse-historical approach (DHA) 301–3
    quality of data collection: case study 223
'distance principle' and privacy 472
distributive justice 39
DNA profiling (comparative study) 153–5
docile documents 378–87
documentary method of interpretation 72
documentary photography 393–4
documents as data, collecting 378–89
    docile documents 378–87
        access 381, 383
        assessment criteria 384–5
        case study: Sexsomnia 384
        ethics 382, 387–8
        practical and analytical issues 382–6
        relevance 381–2, 383–5
        sampling 381, 385, 387
        searching databases 379–81
        systematic approaches 386–7
    documents in action 388–9
        case study: hospital committees' use of documents 389
    and fieldwork 387–8
    types of 273–6
domestication in translation 140
drawings by children as research data 624
duoethnographers 206
dyadic interviews 255

Economic and Social Research Council (ESRC) Framework for Research Ethics 112, 177, 491
effective consent 468
elderly, community support in rural Canada (study) 636–8
elicited data 182, 183, 305, 306, 307
elites in research *see* experts and elites in research
emic comparison 148–61
empirical generalization 85–6, 87, 201
end-of-life care, intercultural concept of (study) 541–2
end-of-life decisionmaking in neonatal intensive care (study) 193–6
Energy Biographies project (study) 604–9
entextualization 120, 124–5
environmental gerontology 636
episodic interviews 266, 532–3, 535
ESRC (Economic and Social Research Council) Framework for Research Ethics 112, 177, 491
ethical committees *see* ethics review boards
ethics 33–46
    institutional perspective 37–40
        ethical principles 38–40
    methodological issues 40–4
        accurate representation 40–1
        purpose of research 42–3
        relationships in longitudinal studies 41–2
        small population size 43–4
    new developments 44–5
    philosophical perspectives 33–7
        constructivist paradigm 35–7
        Indigenous paradigm 37
        transformative paradigm 35–7
    questions to consider 45–6
    reusing data 170–1
    hard-to-reach groups 673–5
    see also anonymity; confidentiality; informed consent; private/public space
ethics in digital research 466–78
    changing discourses 467–9
    contested concepts 469–74
        anonymity and confidentiality 472–3

human subjects research 469–70
  informed consent 470–1
  public or private 471–2
  sharing and storing data 473
  stolen and hacked data 473–4
 making choices in data collection 474–6
 reminders during planning 476–8
 data from blogs 490–1
 Facebook research 503–5
 social media research 596–7
ethics review boards
 and CBPR 42
 compulsory review 33, 37, 114, 237
 digital research 468, 500
 Indigenous community committees 38
 and qualitative research 37–9, 621–2, 673–4
ethnographic research 327–41
 spiral-shaped model of 76
 defining 327–8
 contributions to social research 328–9
 reflexivity 332–3
 process
  analyses and hypotheses 334–6
  analysing conditions and relations 337–8
  comparison 336–7
  saturation 338–9
  theoretical framework and target question 333–4
 limits and ethics 339–40
 new technologies 341
 case study: machine operators' resistance strategies 329–30
 case study: dynamics of gender segregation 330–2
 autoethnography 202, 207
 conventional and focused ethnography 364
 and other methods 185–7, 206–7, 235, 244, 289–90
 see also comparison in social research
etic/scholastic comparison 149–51, 152, 153, 160–1
 see also comparison in social research
European qualitative data archives 168–9
Europe Film Gateway 419
EUscreen (European online audio-visual archive) 419, 421
evaluation research 212, 355, 528, 566–7, 578
exclusive/inclusive settings, field access in 101
exercise among people with disabilities (mixed-method study) 574, 576
experiential sampling 588
experts and elites in research 652–64
 forms of knowledge and interviews 657–60
  forms of interviews 658–60
  forms of knowledge 657–8
 history 653–4
 interaction in interviews with 660–2, 664n2, 664n3
 new developments and perspectives 662–4
  growing diversity 664
  information technologies 663–4
  multilingualism and translation 662–3
 reasons for interviewing 652–3
 as research subjects 654–7
external generalization 87
eye dialect 127

Facebook 3, 496–507
 case study: Free Party networks 111–12
 collecting data from 497–8
 ethics 466, 467–8, 477, 587
 new directions in data collection from 506–7
 practical procedures for collecting data 498–505
  access 500–2
  ethical considerations 503–5
  presentation and transcription 505
  sampling 502–3
  theoretical and methodological assumptions 498–500
 see also digital flows, making sense of digital data
fake news 407, 512
Falsettoland (Broadway show) 211
Family100 Project 678–80
Farm Security Administration (FSA) photographic project 393
feminism and qualitative research
 communitarian ethics 35
 ethnography 341n2
 interviews 235–6
 paradigm 201, 210, 548
 research projects 275, 486–91, 552–61
feminist women in Brazil (blog study) 486–91
FIAF (International Federation of Film Archives) 417
field access, gaining 99–114
field notes
 augmenting other data 167, 304–5, 568, 574
 and digital research 222, 498
 in ethnography 235, 335, 364, 367, 577
 in focus groups 257
 and observation 315, 318–20, 321
field sampling 222
film archives 417–8
Film Archives Department, Germany 418
film studies *see* media data, collecting
Film and Television Archives, UCLA 418
Finnish Data Service 168, 170
First Nations and Aboriginal Peoples (Canada) 38, 39
flows *see* digital flows, making sense of digital data
focused interviews 234
focus groups 250–61
 data analysis 258–9
 discussion questions 255–6
 eliciting quality data 222–3, 225–7
 epistemological issues 252–3
 history 250–1
 interaction in 253
 moderating 256–8

online 259–61
selecting participants 254–5
studies using 270–1
uses 251–2
working with children 622–4
foodbank users (study) 678–80
foot and mouth disease in UK (study) 178–9
foreignization in translation 127, 140
forestry industry, status of women in (study) 551–5
formal qualitative interviews 580n2
Fortunoff Video Archive of Holocaust Testimonies 274–5
Foucault, Michel 299–300, 301, 304, 546
found data 444
Framework for Research Ethics (ESRC) 112, 177, 491
France, Cinémathèque Française 418
Free Party networks (study) 111–12, 113
Free Southern Theater 205
French female jazz singers (ethnographic study) 330–2
From Caligari to Hitler. A psychological history of the German film 413
FSA (Farm Security Administration) photographic project 393
funding
    data infrastructure 11, 12, 168, 175, 418, 419
    demands on researchers 143, 155, 169, 218, 580n6
    and ethics 37, 473
funnels 67, 256

gatekeepers
    community researchers as 134, 135, 136–8
    digital research 102, 105
    and documents 381, 382, 385
    institutional 106–8, 112–13, 644–5
    and specific groups 620–2, 644–5, 670–2, 673
gay/lesbian experiences (study) 273
Gender Advertisements 400
gender gap in Canadian public opinion (study) 555–7
gender segregation in the work place (ethnographic studies) 330–2
generalization
    in different methods 93–5, 336, 339
    Internet research 586
    quantitative and qualitative research 23, 85–7
    and sampling 84–5, 87, 201
German/Danish video game regulation (comparative study) 158
Germany, culture and end-of-life-care (study) 541–2
Germany, Film Archives Department 418
Germany, health care priorities (study) 92
Germany, research funding 10–11
Global Feminisms Project (GFP) 275
globalization and qualitative data analysis 9–10
    see also cross-language research, rationale
go-alongs 344–58
    characteristics 348–50

    interactive 349
    person-centered 349
    place-based 348–9
    symbolic 349–50
    systematic 349
    current and future directions 356–8
    defined 267, 344–5, 348
    issues to consider 353–4
        documentation strategies 354
        mode of mobility 353
        researcher-participant engagement 353–4
        limitations, strengths, ethics 354–6
    origins and contexts 345–7
        phenomenology 346–7
        The Mobilities Paradigm 345–6
    policing and community safety (study) 591
    technology 348, 354, 357–8
    types 350–3
        tours 351–3
        trails 350–1
    working with children 625
    see also soundwalks
granularity in transcription 118, 125–7, 128
graphic elicitation *see* photographs in interviews
grounded theory
    and data 4, 26
    'in-vivo' codes 225
    research process in 49, 54, 61, 160, 259, 334–6, 548
    and sampling 90, 91
group interviews 270–1, 276

hacked data 473–4
hard-to-reach groups 668–80
    case study: foodbank users 678–80
    case study: homelessness 676–8
    defining 'hard-to-reach' 668–9
    issues for data collection 669–75
        access, gatekeeping and sampling 670–2
        ethics 673–5
        methods 672–3
        researcher as insider/outsider 669–70
    promoting accessibility 675–6
harm to participants, avoiding *see* beneficence
health care priorities in Germany (study) 92
Health Experiences Research Group, Oxford University 171
hermeneutics and qualitative research 68, 141, 202, 207, 208–9, 235
Holocaust Testimonies, Fortunoff Video Archive of 274–5
homelessness (study) 676–8
hospital committees' use of documents 389
'Human Resources School' 327
human subjects research model (ethics) 37, 102, 237, 355, 466, 469–70

hypotheses
    developing 76–8, 218, 222, 238
    in ethnography 332–3, 334–6, 339
    in quantitative and qualitative research 50, 52–4, 56–9, 61, 75, 548
    and theoretical triangulation 529

ICTY (International Criminal Tribunal for the Former Yugoslavia) 276
'idiot adult' in data collection with children 623
illegal raves/Free Party networks (study) 111–12
images as data, collecting 392–409
    case study: visual ethnography of Art Basel 400–3
        legal aspects 403
        project goal and field access 400–1
        some systematic reflections 402
        visual evidences 402–3
        visual exploration of field 401–2
    guidelines on process 407–9
    history of photos in social sciences 393–5
        digital revolution 395
        documentary photography 393–4
        from photographs to video 394–5
        visual anthropology and sociology 394
    images by participants 398–9
    images by researcher 395–8
        archiving and organizing images 398
        field rapport and photo-elicited interviews 396
        how to photograph 395
        photography as research tool 397–8
        what to photograph 395–6
    images produced for other purposes 399–400
    why collect images 403–7
        additional value of images 405–6
        interpretation of images 404–5
        truth of images 406–7
        visual perception 403–4
    working with children 624
    young Brazilian feminists (blog study) 488–9
inclusive/exclusive settings, field access in 101
inclusivity in qualitative research 34, 36, 133, 459, 566, 627
India, National Film Archive 418
Indian Health Service, US 38, 39
induction
    in ethnography 333–4
    in focus group data analysis 258, 259
    in mixed-method research 565–6
    use in qualitative research 51, 54–62, 222, 459, 577
inference 23, 26, 28, 84
    see also abduction
infographics 595
informed consent
    effective consent 468
    foregoing 476, 477
    how much information to give 105, 114, 156, 286–7, 366

Internet research 446, 469–71, 472, 473, 503–4
    in public settings 102, 103–4
    reusing data 11, 170, 177
    and specific groups 644, 673–4
    and specific methods 41, 43, 238, 340, 365, 475
    using online 500
insider/outsider, researcher as 101, 104, 112, 238, 669–70
Instagram, self-presentation on (ethnographic study) 474–6, 478n1, 478n2
instances, method of 201, 212
Institutional Review Boards (IRBs) *see* ethics review boards
Interaction Process Analysis (IPA) 185, 185–7
intercultural concept of end-of-life care (study) 541–2
internal generalization 87
International Criminal Tribunal for the Former Yugoslavia (ICTY) 276
International Federation of Film Archives (FIAF) 417
International Phonetic Alphabet 127
International Visual Sociology Association 394
Internet
    research
        ethics and access 102–6, 111–12, 114, 292
        triangulation in 536–7, 585
    social impact 277, 341, 395, 400, 441–443, 482–3
    see also blogs, collecting data from; Facebook
Internet of Things (IoT), 'Alexa' 442, 519, 521n11
interpretative knowledge 657–9, 662
interpreters *see* translators
interviews
    'good' practice 240
    group 270–271, 589–91
    interview guides 222–3, 237
    new developments 244–5
    sampling 94, 243, 244
    types 186, 233–4, 234–6, 265–7, 308–9, 580n2
    working with children 622–4
    see also experts and elites in research; qualitative interviews
intraviews 236
'in-vivo' codes 225
involvement/detachment of researcher 138, 315, 332–3, 405, 587, 622
IPA (interaction process analysis) 185–7
iPods in sound studies 433–5
IRBs (Institutional Review Boards) *see* ethics review boards
iterative approach
    and qualitative research 49, 52–3
    and research process 54–62, 227, 373, 375–6, 459–60, 549
    sampling and 88, 91

Japanese/Thai farming practices (comparative study) 158–9
jazz singers, French female (ethnographic study) 330–2

Jefferson transcription system 190, 191, 220–1
justice *see* social justice

Kabyles people, Algeria (photographic study) 397–398
Kant, Immanuel 34
Kaufman, Moises (playwright) 204–5, 211–12, 213n3
knowledge in expert interviews 657–8
Kracauer, Siegfried 413

labour force participation of women (study) 557–9
Lang, Fritz (filmmaker) 417
Laramie Project, The 204–5, 211–12, 213n3
lesbian/gay experiences (study) 273
letters as source of narrative data 276, 389n2
Library of Congress, National Audio-visual Conservation Center 418
Life Story Protocol 266, 269
linear-consequential approach 49, 259
lingua franca 137, 138, 144, 662
linguistics, standardization and vernacularization 126–7
literal replication 87
Liverpool inner-city redevelopment scheme (sound study) 435
logbook 373, 374
longitudinal studies 41–2, 603–4, 610, 672–3
'lurking', and online research 102, 104, 105

machine operators' resistance strategies (ethnographic study) 329–30
Maori, indigenous ethics guidelines 38, 39
mapping
    digital research and flow 451, 452, 454, 457–62
    research strategy 395, 426, 624, 625, 678, 679
marginalized communities
    dominant perspectives 34, 42
    ethics 36, 39–40, 44, 101, 674
    language issues 126–7, 135
    methods accommodating 220, 269, 399, 641
Marienthal. The Sociology of an unemployed community. 528
MAXQDA (software program) 374, 592
Mayo, Elton 327, 341n1
media data, collecting 412–23
    archives 416–17
    audiovisual data and social representation 413–14
    commercial media (DVD, Blu-ray, streaming) 420–1
    digitalization 419
    film archives 417–18
    forms of 414–16
    history 412–13
    limitations 421–2
    television archives 418–9
    Youtube 419–20
memes 228
meta-analysis 11–12, 386

meta-data 420, 421–2
    see also archives/archiving, context and provenance
meta-ethnography 386
method of instances 201, 212
'methodological grooming' 104, 105, 111, 113
methodological triangulation 243, 529, 530, 531, 535
Metropolis (film) 417
Mexican families, childhood feeding in (mixed-method study) 568
Middletown. A study in modern American culture. 84
Midwest dustbowl photographic project 393
migration and addiction (study) 539–40
migration and end-of-life care (study) 541–2
migration and long-term unemployment (study) 540–1
mixed-method designs 564–80
    and ethnography 577–8
    and evaluation research 578
    extent of qualitative component in 569–70
    interaction of sample and data collection strategies 572–7
    malleability of 578–80
    nature of qualitative data in 567–9
    pacing and pooling 570–2
        consequences of inappropriate pooling 571–2
        when should data be collected 570
        who do data represent 571
    reasons for including a qualitative component 565–7
        increasing complexity 567
        increasing scope, determining boundaries 567
        obtaining different perspectives on same phenomenon 566
        phenomenon demands different approaches 566–7
        sequentially increasing understanding of phenomenon 565–6
    sampling 95, 570, 580n6
mixed method research, definition 27–9, 569, 580n1, 580n4
mixed methods praxis, theoretically driven 545–61
    case study: gender gap in Canadian public opinion 555–7
    case study: women in forestry 551–5
    case study: women's labour force participation 557–9
    importance of theoretical, process-centered 559–61
    linking theory and mixed methods design 545–7
    neglect of qualitative approach in 548–9
    process-centered praxis 549–51
    what is a qualitative approach to 547–8
mobile methods *see* go-alongs
Mobilities Paradigm, The 345–6
mobility, children's interdependent (study) 621
mobilizing interviews 347
models/modelling 77–80
moderatum generalizations 86

MOMA (Museum of Modern Art), New York, Department of Film and Video 418
Montaillou, Cathars and Catholics in (sound study) 431–2
Moses, Daniel David (playwright) 204
moving cameras in recording data 373
multilingual research *see* cross-language research
multiple methods *see* mixed method praxis, theoretically driven; mixed-method designs
Museum of Modern Art, New York, Department of Film and Video 418
music festivals and free parties study 111–12, 113

narrative analysis 81, 119–20, 123
narrative data 264–77
    documents
        archives 274–6
        autobiographies 273–4
        diaries 272–3
        letters 272, 276
    interviews
        case study: homeless youth 269–70
        group 270–1
        interview guides 265–7
        memory 271–2
        role of interviewer 268
        setting 267–8
        silences 270
        therapeutic value 268–9
    nature of storytelling 264–5
    visual media and performance 276–7
narrative-episodic knowledge 533–4
National Audio-visual Conservation Center, Library of Congress 418
National Commission for the Protection of Human Subjects of Biomedical and Behavioral Research (1978) 37
National Film Archive of India 418
Native American sound recordings 428
naturalistic data 182–96
    history 183–8
        ecological psychology 183–5
        ethnography and participant observation 185–8
        interaction process analysis 185
    key tests for 187–8
        recovery of action test 187–8
        unwell social scientist test 187
    reactivity and critique 188–90
    resources for collecting 190–1
        anonymization 191
        recording 190–1
        transcription 191
    used to support applied research 193–5
    used in training 195–6
    virtues of 192–3, 196
naturally occurring data
    and conversation analysis 280, 282–4, 293, 589
    and Internet research 470, 496–7
    in qualitative research 156, 221, 586
'Navajo film themselves' project 399
Nazi soundscapes in urban Germany (sound study) 432–3
Neighbourhood Watch and policing (go-along study) 591
neonatal intensive care, end-of-life decisionmaking in (study) 193–6
neo-Nazis in Munich, trial against (study) 45
NESH (Norwegian National Committee for Research Ethics in the Social Sciences and Humanities) 468
netnography 485, 492, 498
network society 482
New Zealand Alcohol and Drug Use Survey 632
Nigerian schools, introduction of Western mathematics (comparative study) 157–8
no-harm principle *see* beneficence
normative epistemology 201
North American Native American sound recordings 428
North Cumbria, foot and mouth disease (study) 178–9
Norwegian National Committee for Research Ethics in the Social Sciences and Humanities (NESH) 468
numerical (empirical) generalization 85–6, 87, 201

observations 183, 314–25
    collecting data through 314–6
    project determines 316–7
    qualities for data collection via 317–25
        atmosphere 323–5
        details 318–20
        sequences 321–3
    and theory 325
    and ethnographic studies 327
    observer-observed relationship 337–8
    digital observation 587–9
    working with children 622
OKCupid (online dating platform) 466, 519
older people and qualitative data collection 632–46
    invisibility of elderly 632
    diversity among elderly 633
    studies using different methods 634–5
    case study: supportive communities 635–8
    case study: participatory research and community inclusion 639–42
    case study: sense of self among elderly with dementia 642–5
        ethics issues 644–5
        interviews 642–3
        observation 643–4
        principles 645–6
Olympic Games, impact on London commuters (study) 223
One Born Every Minute (OBEM), UK TV show 291, 293n2
online research *see* Internet, research

open/closed transcripts 123–4
open-ended interviews *see* qualitative interviews
operational definitions 71–6
oral history 269
organizational ethnography 329
orthodox intentional data 443
orthographic metronymy 127
outsiders/insiders and researcher 101, 104, 112, 238, 669–70

pain management program, patients in (mixed-method study) 578, 579
Parents and Neonatal Decisions Study (PND) 193–6
participant observation 185–7, 237, 588, 622
participants' perceptions and expectations 10, 101–2, 471–2, 491
participative intentional data 443
participatory research
    benefits 222, 225–8, 235, 603, 646, 672–3
    and communities 42–3
    constraints 268
    principles 639–42
'Pathfinder Scheme', Liverpool inner-city redevelopment scheme (sound study) 435
PCI (problem-centered interviews) 308–9
pelvic organ prolapse, women's experience of (mixed-method study) 566
performance/performed experiences 200–13
    affect and new materialisms 209–10
    and cultural process 206
    and data 212
    and ethnographic praxis 206–7
    and hermeneutics 207
    and interviews 236
    as narrative 276
    pedagogy and rhetoric 203–6
    and scholarly representation 208–9
    theater and a politics of resistance 211–12, 213n7
personal information sharing 3, 170, 177–8, 254–5, 467, 472–3, 490
phenomenology 94–5, 234–5, 298, 346–7, 403–5
photographs in interviews 243, 599–611
    with children 624
    the energy biographies project 604–9
    establishing rapport 396–7
    making the intangible visible 225, 599–602
    qualitative longitudinal research 603–4
    strengths of using 602–3, 609–11
    see also images as data, collecting
photojournalism 393–4
photovoice movement 399, 409, 624
physical and digital data, combining 584–97
pictures in qualitative research *see* images as data, collecting; photographs in interviews
'playfulness of mind' 228, 229

playfulness, theoretical 54
pluralism, theoretical 54
PND (Parents and Neonatal Decisions Study) 193–6
policing and community safety (go-along study) 591
Polish Peasant in Europe and America, The 272, 528
political considerations in transcription 126–7, 128
politics of resistance, and performance ethnography 203, 206–7, 211–12
positivist method 332, 513, 548, 618
postgraduate-supervisor relationships (study) 303–7
postpartum weight-loss study 225–7
post-Structuralism 298
PowerPoint presentations (study) 373
power in postgraduate-supervisor relationships (study) 303–7
pragmatism 21, 80, 447, 546
'precarious ordering' (study) 91
prejudices, researchers' 68, 186–7, 315
presidential election 2016, US 511, 512, 521n1
privacy paradox 471
private/public space
    blogs 382, 490–1
    in digital environment 467–78, 503, 506, 596
    gaining access 100-3, 105, 114
    in publishing results 367, 387
probabilistic (empirical) generalization 85–6, 87, 201
problem-centered interviews (PCI) 308–9
procedural justice 39–40
process knowledge 657
professional interpreters/translators 138, 139–41
pseudonyms, use of 173, 178, 472–3
Psyporeal sound system (study) 111–12, 113
public/private space *see* private/public space
purposive sampling 88–9, 90–3, 671

QLR (qualitative longitudinal research) 603–4
QUAL *see* mixed-method designs
QualiBank, UK 169, 176, 177
qualitative data archives 168–9, 171, 176–7, 178
qualitative interviews 233–45
    conducting 238–9
    dealing with challenges 240–3
    'good' interviews 240
    history 234
    limitations 244
    new developments 244–5
    preparing for 237–8
        ethical review 237
        formulating interview guides 237, 255–6
        recruitment 238
        reflecting on research topic 237–8
        technology 238
    processing after 239–40
    questions about use 243–4
    theory and approach 234–6
        ethnographic interviews 235

feminist interviews 235–6
hermeneutic interviews 235
intraviews 236
phenomenological interviews 234–5
postmodernism 236
see also photographs in interviews
qualitative longitudinal research 603–4
qualitative research
    aims 7–8
    challenges 9–12
    core assumptions 5–6
    definition 6–7
    methodological approaches 8–9, 80, 81
quality of qualitative research *see* data quality, ensuring
QUAN *see* mixed-method designs

racially segregated student residences, integration of (study) 307–11
random sampling 87–8
rapport
    in focus groups 255–6
    in researcher-participant relationship 25–6, 101, 104, 105, 396–7
    ways to establish 408, 643, 672
'raw' data 4
readability in transcription 125–7
realism, defined 19–24
reciprocity
    as ethics principle 26, 36, 41, 105, 113, 675
    and hard-to-reach groups 676, 678, 679, 680
recontextualization of existing data 171–6, 302
recording social interaction 118–29
    challenges 118–20
    as social interaction 120–1
    technology 190–1, 238
    transcription 121–7
        assuring quality 190–1, 220–1
        and conversation analysis 284–5
        cross-cultural interviews 140–1, 143–4
        entextualization 124–5
        open / closed transcripts 123–4
        political considerations 126–7
        representational decisions 125–6
        videography 375
    value and limitations 128–9
recovery of action test 187–8
reflexivity
    in digital research 446, 447–8, 457, 501
    in ethnographic research 332–3
    institutional 655
    and mixed methods designs 573, 575, 576, 577, 578–9
    in qualitative research 8, 24, 40, 68, 237–8, 580n3, 673
    rhetorical 205–6
refugees, African (study) 270
refugees, Vietnamese (study) 93

relay language in cross-language research 138
replication 87, 94, 166, 175, 569, 591
representativeness
    of data 514, 516, 517
    of documents 384–5
    in sampling 85, 87–9, 170, 586, 637, 671
research agenda, in transcription 125–6
research design, reinventing 65–82
    conceptualizing research topic 68–71
        dissecting the topic 69–70
        research questions 70
        theory and conceptualization 71
    inventing hypotheses 76–7
    drawing models 77–80
        spurious associations 78–80
    main types of design 80–1
    operational definitions 71–6
        conceptualization and operationalization 76
        operational definition 72–3
        variables 73–6
    reversing conventional knowledge 66–8
    role of reflexivity 68
researchers, influence of personal attributes 10, 24, 101–2, 104, 338, 669–70
research participants *see* participants; participatory research
research question
    in data collection process 7, 27, 70, 392, 457–62, 550
    participants help determine 42, 626
    and sampling 88–90
    and transcription 123–4
research relationships
    in focus groups 254–5
    researcher-gatekeeper 108, 620–2, 670–2
    researcher-participant 24–6, 41, 113, 348, 349, 396–7
        ethics in 43, 44–5, 104–5, 473
        marginalized and hard-to-reach groups 10, 669–71, 680
    researcher-translator 141–3
research topic 66–70
respect (ethical principle) 39
respondent-driven sampling 671
restricted documents 383
reusing qualitative data *see* secondary analysis
review boards, ethical *see* ethics review boards
Robertson, James & Joyce (filmmakers) 624
Rogers, Carl 234
RuralWIDe (Rural North Wales Initiative for the Development if Support for Older People) 639–42

St Augustine, autobiography 273
sampling and generalization 84–95
    in different research traditions 93–5
        case studies 94
        interview studies 94

phenomenology 94–5
generalizing in qualitative research 85–7
   external and internal generalization 87
   in quantitative research 85–6
   reconceptualised in qualitative research 86–7
purposive sampling 88-9, 90–3, 221
   criterion sampling 93
   stratified purposive sampling 91–3
   theoretical sampling 91
   random sampling 87–9
   sample size and saturation 89–90
SAQD (secondary analysis of qualitative data) 164–79
SATORI project 468
saturation
   principle of 85, 90, 91, 671
   in various methods 255, 305, 310, 338–9, 385, 569, 571
scholastic/etic comparison 149–51, 152, 153, 160–1
   see also comparison in social research
school administrators' perceptions of discipline (study) 55–61
'scraping' data 515, 521n8
screen-capture data 498, 499–500, 501, 504–5, 506
secondary analyses 164–79
   case study: foot and mouth disease 178–9
   challenges of using others' data 12, 167–71, 473
      'enough' context 169–70
      ethics 170–1
      fit with current research 168–9
      nothing left to analyse 169
      selective sampling 170
      unfamiliarity with methods 167–8
   providing context 173–8
      designing studies for future use 176–8
      'enough' documentation 174–5
      new forms of publishing data 175–6
      questions to ask of data 171–3
   types of data reuse 165–7
      advancing design and method 166–7
      answering new questions 166
      background description and context 165
      comparison, restudy and follow-up 165–6
      replication and validation 166
      teaching and learning 167
secondary participants 501, 503–4
selecting units/instances *see* sampling and generalization
self-published data 444
semantic-conceptual knowledge 533–4
semi-structured interviews *see* qualitative interviews
sensitizing concepts 68
sentiment analysis 586, 594
sequential analysis 596
serendipity 11, 458
Sexsomnia (document study) 384
sexual socialisation of children (study) 106–8
shadowing 350–1, 352

shared decision-making during labour (study) 290–1
sharing in social media 467
Sierra Leone, refugees (study) 270
silences
   in conversation analysis 284, 285
   in qualitative research 220, 270, 456, 589
simulated-crisis training interaction (study) 369–70
situated ethics 40, 43
situational mapping 451, 452, 454, 457–62
SKAD (sociology of knowledge approach to discourse) 299
Skopos theory in translation 139–40, 141
Skype, in interviews 245, 260, 663–4
Smith, W. Eugene 407
social access 104
social justice
   ethical principle 34–5, 36–7, 39–40, 42, 474
   and performance ethnography 202, 204–5
social media data 444
sociology of knowledge approach to discourse (SKAD) 299
sonic data *see* sounds as data
sounds as data 426–36
   combining traditional and innovative methods 435
   contemporary sonic research, Walkman and iPod 433–5
   historical context of sound studies 427
   historical sonic research 430–3
      Cathars and Catholics in a French village 431–2
      class sensitivity to noise, London 431
      Nazi soundscapes in urban Germany 432–3
      sound and meaning in 19[th]C rural France 432
   methods stressing sound and voice 435–6
   sound as data/sonic data 430
   sound and other senses 429–30
   special characteristics of sound 427–8
   see also videography, camera position and sound
soundwalks 427, 435–6
sousveillance in digital society 442
'Spanish Village', manipulated photo essay 407
spectacle and performance 203–6, 211–12
spurious associations 78–80
Sri Lankan medical practices (comparative study) 156–7
stakeholder opinions on priority setting in health care (study) 92
standardization in transcription 126–7, 133–4
statistical (empirical) generalization 85–6, 87, 201
street markets, filming 370–1
stolen data in digital research 473–4
storytelling *see* narrative data
stratified purposive sampling 91–3
Street Corner Society. The social structure of an Italian slum. 315, 528
structuralism 297–8
Stryker, Roy 393, 395
student residences, integration of racially segregated (study) 307–11

subjectivity
  participants' 71, 588–9
  in recording and transcribing data 118, 120, 121, 122, 128
  researchers' 24–5, 54, 68, 298, 459–60
summary-based reporting 258
surveillance in digital society 442
synchronous online methods 259–61
synthetic data 444
tandem interviews 138
target question in ethnography 333–4

Taylor, Frederick W. 327, 341n1, 514
team-based research 595–6
'Teaspoon of Light Project' (New Zealand) 626
technical knowledge 657
Technorati Media 2013 Digital Influencer Report 482
Technorati Report, State of the Blogosphere 2011 483
Tectonic Theater Project 205, 211, 213n3
teleological (consequential) ethics 34
television archives 418–19
television (TV) studies *see* media data, collecting
tertium comparationis 149, 150, 152–3, 158, 160–1
text mining 445
Thai/Japanese farming practices (comparative study) 158–9
Theatre of the Oppressed 211
The Laramie Project 204–5, 211–12, 213n3
thematic analysis 259
theoretical agnosticism 54
theoretical generalization 87
theoretical knowledge
  in qualitative research 49, 51, 52, 53, 77, 445
  use in discourse analysis 303–4, 307–8
theoretical replication 87
theoretical sampling 91
theory *see* research design, reinventing
'thick' description
  achieving 94, 235, 573–7, 602
  as aim 6, 28, 44, 86, 151, 183
  considerations 186–7, 187–8
  see also data quality, ensuring
Timescapes Knowledge Bank (UK) 41, 178
tours in go-along research 351–3
'traces' as data
  defining 3–4, 444, 511–12, 515–16
  issues in research 8, 453, 456, 589, 592
trails in go-along research 350–1
Transana MU (software program) 375, 595
transcription/transcribing social interaction *see* recording social interaction
transferability, ethics principle 35, 86
transformative paradigm 35–7
translation studies 132
translators
  competence 134, 138, 139–41, 389n1
  expert interviews 662–3
  influence 10, 132
  role 141–4
transparency
  in team-based research 595–6
  and technology 594
  towards other researchers 141, 143, 175, 178
  towards participants 105, 132, 316, 640
triangulation 527–43
  definition 243–4, 532
  reasons for 528–9
  development of concept 529–31, 542–3
    original conceptualization 529
    sophisticated rigor 529–30
    strong program of triangulation 530–1
  background/early examples 527–8
  contemporary examples of 538–42
    episodic and expert interviews 539–40
    interviews and conversation analysis 538–9
    interviews and mobile methods 540–1
    secondary analysis, expert interviews and discourse analysis 541–2
  between-methods 535–7
    mobile methods and traditional research 535–6
    virtual and real worlds 536–7
  within-method 532–5
    several approaches in one method 534–5
    several theoretical perspectives in one method 533–4
  levels of 537–8
  looking to the future 542
  ethnography - within-method or between-method 537
  in discourse-historical approach 302
  of data from blogs 492
  types 243
Tri-Council Policy Statement (Canada) 38
trust
  culture and researcher characteristics 10, 101, 670, 672
  and ethics 105, 475
  public opinion of research 594
  and research relationship 6, 26, 109–13, 501, 676
  and sharing data 170, 178
Truth and Reconciliation Commission (South Africa), narrative archive 274
'truth space' 87
Tumblr sexy-selfie enthusiasts (ethnographic study) 474–6, 478n2
TV (television) studies *see* media data, collecting
Twitter 445, 477, 492, 506, 625

UK Data Service 168, 169, 171
UK QualiBank 169, 176, 177
UK Timescapes Archive 178
unemployment and migration (study) 540–1
University of California, Los Angeles, Film and Television Archives 418

unwell social scientist test 187
US presidential election 2016 511, 512, 521n1

variables in qualitative research 65, 73–6
    see also mixed-method designs
vernacularization in transcription 127, 140
video conferencing 259–61, 590
videography 362–76
    research process 376
    camera position and sound 368–72
        different camera angles 371
        moving camera 372
        outdoor and elevated fixed camera 370–1
        preparation 369
        recent developments 372
        room and fixed camera 369–70
    dealing with collected data 373–5
        archiving and categorizing 374
        data backup 374
        preparation for detailed analyses 374–5
        transcription 191, 375
    ethics and legal regulations 366–7
    as focused ethnography 362–4
    gaining access 364–6
    logbook and preliminary evaluation 373
    recording, ethnography, questioning 367–8
    selecting sequences for analysis 373
video transcription 191, 375
Vietnamese refugees in Canada (study) 93
vignettes as data collection method 223–4
village bells, sound and meaning in rural France (sound study) 432
virtual worlds and classroom practices of fourth graders (study) 155
virtue theory (aretaic ethics) 34

visual anthropology/sociology 394, 395, 398, 624
visual ethnography of Art Basel (study) 400–3
visual perception 403–4
Vom Lehn, Dirk 370–1

walking interviews *see* go-alongs
Walkmans in sound studies 433–5
Web 2.0 102, 483, 485, 486
weblogs *see* blogs, collecting data from
weight-loss postpartum (study) 225–7
Western mathematics in Nigerian schools (comparative study) 157–8
within-case sampling 87
within-method triangulation 532–5
WIT (Work, Interaction and Technology) Workgroup, King's College (study) 370–1
women, demands for care on (study) 91
women in forestry (study) 551–5
women's experience of pelvic organ prolapse (mixed-method study) 566
women's labor force participation (study) 557–9
Work, Interaction and Technology (WIT) Workgroup, King's College (study) 370–1
World Health Organization (WHO) 142, 632, 633
writing, in qualitative research 6

Yik Yak (social media tool) 596
Yoruba number system and Western maths (comparative study) 157–8
young Brazilian feminist women (blog study) 486–91
Young People and Alcohol Study 109–11, 113
Youtube 412, 416–17, 419–20, 422, 446
Yugoslavia, International Criminal Tribunal for the Former 276